EUROPEAN SECURITIES LAW

EUROPEAN SECURITIES LAW

Edited by

RAJ PANASAR
PHILIP BOECKMAN

OXFORD
UNIVERSITY PRESS

OXFORD

UNIVERSITY PRESS

Great Clarendon Street, Oxford ox2 6DP

Oxford University Press is a department of the University of Oxford.
It furthers the University's objective of excellence in research, scholarship,
and education by publishing worldwide in

Oxford New York

Auckland Cape Town Dar es Salaam Hong Kong Karachi
Kuala Lumpur Madrid Melbourne Mexico City Nairobi
New Delhi Shanghai Taipei Toronto

With offices in

Argentina Austria Brazil Chile Czech Republic France Greece
Guatemala Hungary Italy Japan Poland Portugal Singapore
South Korea Switzerland Thailand Turkey Ukraine Vietnam

Oxford is a registered trade mark of Oxford University Press
in the UK and in certain other countries

Published in the United States
by Oxford University Press Inc., New York

British Library Cataloguing in Publication Data

Data available

Library of Congress Cataloging in Publication Data

Data available

Typeset by Glyph International Ltd, Bangalore, India
Printed in Great Britain
on acid-free paper by
Antony Rowe, Chippenham, Wiltshire

ISBN 978-0-19-957972-3

1 3 5 7 9 10 8 6 4 2

PREFACE

One of the principal objectives of the European Commission's Financial Services Action Plan (the 'FSAP') was to develop a large and efficient pan-European capital market to replace the mosaic of national retail markets, each subject to its own set of national laws and regulations.

In the ten years since its publication, the regulatory apparatus designed to give effect to the FSAP has grown into a staggering mass of materials, emanating from each of the levels envisioned by Alexandre Lamfalussy's Committee of Wise Men, as well as the multiple strata of national implementing measures.

Over the last decade, meanwhile, cross-border economic activity has accelerated, intensifying the need for market participants and practitioners to come to grips with the new set of harmonized rules governing European financial markets. For Europe's securities lawyers, the task of marshalling and mastering this material has represented a significant challenge.

The body of law gradually developing under the FSAP umbrella had only just started to progress from infancy to maturity, with key implementing measures becoming effective in most Member States, when it was put to an unexpected and challenging test by the recent global financial crisis.

One of the clearest examples of the current challenges is the relative difficulty faced by some distressed issuers in marking out the circumstances under which they should be allowed to delay public announcement of restructuring plans without either jeopardizing ongoing negotiations aimed at ensuring their financial recovery, on the one hand, or violating the obligation to promptly disclose inside information, on the other.

This book deals with the novelty and magnitude of European securities law by seeking to achieve an integrated treatment of the field in light of the unified purposes and architecture behind the FSAP. It is designed to do so primarily from the standpoint of those who are professionally engaged in the financial markets. Accordingly, it attempts to provide a readable guide to the structuring of securities transactions under the FSAP measures and to respond to a host of ambiguities that have emerged in connection with the practical implementation of such measures.

More specifically, the book is organized in three parts. The first part provides a critical overview of the European legislative process and regulatory framework, introducing the key EU directives and attempting to explain how those directives are intended to work as a single piece of legislation. The second part analyses a range of techniques for raising capital and undertaking business acquisitions in European markets, describing established market practices and interpreting some of the unresolved issues that attorneys, investment bankers and their clients are likely to encounter in the context of a deal. Finally, the third part looks separately at how some of the Member States of the EU have implemented the directives considered in part one, with a view to outlining the points of consistency as well as the most important persisting variations.

Of course, the law relating to the FSAP is in a constant state of flux. New measures are introduced to deal with perceived problems, which inevitably lead to new ambiguities and practical difficulties with which legal practitioners must grapple. Indeed, as we go to press, the European Commission has just released draft proposals, noted in Part One, for the amendment to the Prospectus Directive—one of the key pieces of legislation under the FSAP.

The editors wish to express their thanks to the distinguished practitioners who have participated in this collective project. Each of them has devoted significant time and energy to this publication, while continuing to meet the demands of their respective practices, and they have added to its informative value by contributing their own unique perspective on the subject matter covered. We would also like to acknowledge the thoughtful and thorough work of Stephen Glasper, Alexander Muller and other colleagues at our respective firms in reviewing drafts of the individual chapters and otherwise helping us finalize the publication. (The views expressed herein are those of the individual authors, and do not necessarily reflect the views of their or our firms or the editors.)

Raj S. Panasar
Philip J. Boeckman

London, November 2009

CONTENTS—SUMMARY

CONTENTS

2 DOING DEALS IN EUROPE

2. Equity

Raj Panasar, Cleary Gottlieb Steen & Hamilton LLP; Luis de Carlos, Uría Menéndez; Javier Redonet, Uría Menéndez

3. Debt Offerings and Programmes
Mark Trapnell, Freshfields Bruckhaus Deringer LLP

5. Liability for London Listing
Kathy Hughes, Slaughter and May

6. Takeovers and Stakebuilding

Tim Lewis, MacFarlanes LLP; Graham Gibb, Macfarlanes LLP

3 MEMBER STATE REGULATION

8. Austria
Florian Khol, Binder Grösswang

11. Finland

Petri Haussila, White & Case LLP; Petri Avikainen, White & Case LLP

13. Germany

Mark Strauch, Freshfields Bruckhaus Deringer LLP

17. The Netherlands
Derk Lemstra, Stibbe N.V.; Marius Josephus Jitta, Stibbe N.V.;
Rogier Raas, Stibbe N.V.

18. Portugal

Carlos Costa Andrade, Uría Menéndez; Ana Sá Couto, Uría Menéndez

19. Spain
Luis de Carlos, Uría Menéndez

Contents

LIST OF CONTRIBUTORS

Editors

Raj Panasar is a partner at Cleary Gottlieb Steen & Hamilton. He is a recognized expert on complex listings under the EU prospectus regime and is a member of the London Stock Exchange's Primary Markets Group. He has represented many issuers, including major emerging market companies, in their IPOs and international stock exchange listings. He has also represented many of the world's leading investment banks as underwriters of high profile capital markets transactions. After reading law at the London School of Economics, he qualified as a solicitor of the Supreme Court of England and Wales and gained admission to the Bar in New York.

Philip Boeckman is a partner in the Cravath, Swaine & Moore LLP Corporate Department. Philip's general corporate practice covers capital markets, including global public offerings, US listings and leveraged acquisition financings, as well as mergers and acquisitions. He is Co-Chairman of the International Bar Association's Securities Law Committee, and is a member of the Advisory Committee for the Practicing Law Institute's Eighth Annual Institute on Securities Regulation in Europe. Philip is also a member of the Editorial Board of *Capital Markets Law Journal*, and is the Vice Chair of the Board of Directors of the European High Yield Bond Association and Co-Chair of its Committee on Intercreditor Principles and Structuring.

Contributors

Chapter 1. The European Directives Relating to Issue and Trading of Securities

Lachlan Burn is a partner of Linklaters LLP. He joined Linklaters in 1974, becoming a partner in 1982. He spent five years on secondment to the firm's Paris office. His practice has focused on the international capital markets, covering all forms of securities, including equity, debt and structured derivatives. He was a member of the Legal Risk Review Committee, set up by the Bank of England in 1991and of the UK's Financial Markets Law Committee, between 2002 and 2006. He is currently a member of the Legal and Documentation Committee of the International Capital Market Association, the Primary Markets Group of the

London Stock Exchange and the Listing Authority Advisory Committee of the UK's Financial Services Authority. He is also a General Editor of the Capital Markets Law Journal, published by Oxford University Press.

Chapter 2. Equity

Raj Panasar: see Editors description above.

Luis de Carlos has been co-Managing Partner of Uría Menéndez since November 2005. He joined the firm in 1983 and became a partner in 1991. He has extensive experience in capital markets and also regularly advises on corporate governance, M&A, banking and corporate law matters. He is a lecturer on financial system regulation at the Universidad Pontificia de Comillas in Madrid and he is a regular speaker and commentator at seminars and conferences on subjects related to his field of expertise.

Javier Redonet is a partner with Uría Menéndez practising in the firm's capital markets and mergers and acquisitions groups. Having graduated from Universidad Pontificia de Comillas he was admitted to the Madrid Bar and joined the firm in 1997. He regularly advises issuers and underwriters on initial public offerings and issues and offers of equity, fixed-income and hybrid securities. He also deals with public merger and acquisition transactions and advises clients on corporate law and on securities regulatory issues, as well as listed companies on corporate governance matters.

Chapter 3. Debt Offerings and Programmes

Mark Trapnell was educated at Christ Church Oxford, and is a partner in Freshfields Bruckhaus Deringer LLP's London Office. He was previously based in Hong Kong from 1989 to 1993 and Germany from 1994 to 1997. He specializes in capital markets transactions including all types of debt capital markets issues (straight, equity-linked, hybrid and regulatory capital for banks and insurers), MTN programmes, debt liability management transactions as well as equity issues (including placings, rights issues and IPOs).

Chapter 4. Private Placements

Charles Howarth is a partner at Herbert Smith LLP and specializes in capital markets transactions and advises underwriters and issuers in relation to securities offerings by companies in the UK, the rest of Europe, and worldwide. Having graduated from Jesus College Cambridge, he trained in the City and was admitted as an English solicitor in 1992. He has worked in private practice, mainly in London and for three years in Frankfurt. He regularly advises all forms of capital markets transactions, including IPOs, rights issues, private placements, and debt and convertible issues.

Chapter 5. Liability for London Listing

Kathy Hughes is a corporate partner with Slaughter and May. She graduated from Brasenose College, Oxford in 1989 and joined the firm as a trainee in 1992. She has a broad corporate practice which has encompassed a wide range of transactions. Her work has included many initial and secondary public equity offerings, including a number of listed funds.

Chapter 6. Takeovers and Stakebuilding

Tim Lewis joined Macfarlanes LLP in 1985 and became a partner in 1994. He focuses on M&A and corporate finance, acting for bidders and targets in public takeovers and for acquirers and sellers in private company and business acquisitions. His practice extends to primary and secondary equity fund raisings, including flotations and rights and similar equity offerings.

Graham Gibb is a corporate partner with Macfarlanes LLP. Graham joined the firm in 2003 and became a partner in 2006. He advises on a broad range of corporate transactions, particularly in the public sector where he has significant experience of takeovers and equity capital markets work as well as in private M&A transactions.

Chapter 7. Special Considerations for Non-EU Issuers

Andrew R. Thompson is a corporate partner of Cravath, Swaine & Moore LLP. His practice focuses primarily on merger and acquisition transactions, including cross-border transactions. Andrew joined Cravath as an associate in 1999 and became a partner in 2007.

Chapter 8. Austria

Florian Khol is a partner in Binder Grösswang and specializes in capital markets, M&A and corporate. Florian deals with transactional matters and his areas of expertise focus specifically on all aspects of bond and equity listings for underwriters and issuers, corporate governance and compliance issues for banks as well as listed companies and mergers and acquisitions including public takeovers. Beside this, Florian has written numerous articles in international and Austrian law journals and books.

Chapter 9. Belgium

Jean-Pierre Blumberg is Regional Managing Partner for Europe and member of the Executive Committee of Linklaters LLP. He is a senior member of the Corporate and M&A practice group at Linklaters in Belgium. He is a graduate of the Universities of Antwerp (1977), Louvain (1980) and Cambridge (1981), a lecturer at the University of Antwerp (UA) in comparative law and a regular lecturer at the Antwerp University School of Management (UAMS) on M&A and public takeovers. He has published a series of articles on selected topics relating to company law, mergers and acquisitions as well as financial law. He is a member of various editorial boards and an independent director in listed companies. He is a member of the Board of Trustees of the Belgian Governance Institute and of other professional organisations.

Chapter 10. Denmark

Christian Lundgren is a partner with Kromann Reumert. Christian obtained his law degree from the University of Copenhagen in 1991. Christian previously worked for Cleary Gottlieb in Brussels. Christian specializes in M&A, company law and capital markets regulation. He represents Danish and foreign industrial clients, equity funds, etc. in connection with acquisition and sale of businesses, public tender offers and minority investments.

Pernille Høstrup Dalhoff has been with Kromann Reumert since 1999 and specializes in company law and capital markets regulation. Pernille Høstrup Dalhoff obtained her law degree from the University of Aarhus in 1999. She was admitted in 2002 and obtained right of audience before the Danish High Court in 2003.

Chapter 11. Finland

Petri Haussila is the executive partner of the Helsinki office of White & Case LLP and also acts as the head of the global securities practice group of White & Case. Prior to establishing the Helsinki office of White & Case in 1992, he practised law in Helsinki (1978-83) and New York and London (1984-92). He has both Finnish (Helsinki University, LL.M. 1978) and US (Columbia University, LL.M. 1984) law degrees and is a member of both the Finnish and the New York Bar Associations. In his 25 years as a securities lawyer, he has worked on numerous capital market and public M&A transactions in Finland and other Nordic countries as well as most other European countries and a number of other jurisdictions.

Petri Avikainen is a partner at the Helsinki office of White & Case LLP whose practice is mainly focused on capital market transactions and public M&A. He joined White & Case in 2000 after having completed a traineeship at the Finnish Financial Supervisory Authority and became a partner in 2010. He has a Finnish law degree (Turku University, LL.M 1999) and is a member of the Finnish Bar Association.

Chapter 12. France

Marie-Laurence Tibi is a partner in the Paris office of Cleary Gottlieb Steen & Hamilton LLP. Ms. Tibi's practice focuses on corporate finance and merger and acquisition transactions, including capital market transactions, structured financings and derivative products, joint ventures and public M&A transactions.

Ms. Tibi joined the firm in 1992 and became a partner in 2001. She received an LL.M degree from New York University in 1992 and a law degree from the University of Paris in 1991. She graduated from the Ecole des Hautes Etudes Commerciales (HEC) in 1988. Ms. Tibi is distinguished by *Chambers Global* for her experience in capital markets. Ms. Tibi is a member of the Bars in Paris and New York.

Chapter 13. Germany

Mark Strauch was born in the US in 1960. He received his legal education at the Vanderbilt University School of Law and is admitted to the New York bar. He began his career in New York working on capital markets and M&A transactions. He speaks German and English. Mark Strauch is a partner in the firm's Frankfurt office and specializes in capital markets and M&A transactions. His clients are mainly German, US and international companies as well as investment banks. He comes highly recommended by those with whom he has worked. He has extensive experience working with both large (e.g. Deutsche Bahn AG, Infineon AG, HeidelbergCement AG, Hamburger Hafen und Logistik AG, Gagfah S.A., Wacker Chemie AG) and smaller (e.g. Intercell, Addex Pharaceuticals, Jerini AG, Paion AG, Wilex AG) companies in connection with their IPOs and other capital markets transactions.

Chapter 14. Ireland

Jack O'Farrell is a consultant to, and was for more than 18 years a partner in, A&L Goodbody's Corporate Department. During his career he has specialized in public company takeovers and mergers, initial and secondary public offerings, venture capital transactions, corporate mergers and reorganizations and joint ventures. From 2004 to 2009, he was also partner in charge of knowledge development for the firm as a whole. Jack is also a member of the Business Law Committee of the Law Society of Ireland. He has been recommended by a number of leading publications including most recently IFLR 1000—2008 and 2009; Chambers Global 2008 and 2009; and PLC Which Lawyer?—2008 and 2009. Jack qualified as a solicitor in 1985 and holds a degree in Legal Science from Trinity College Dublin and a Masters Degree in law from Cambridge University in England.

Chapter 15. Italy

Pietro Fioruzzi is a partner of Cleary Gottlieb Steen & Hamilton LLP, Milan. He advises international and Italian corporate clients and investment banks on a wide range of corporate and financial matters, including capital markets transactions, corporate governance, securities regulatory issues, and public mergers and acquisitions. He also represents his clients before Italian courts with regard to capital markets matters. He acts as an expert to the Council of the Bars and Law Societies of the European Union (CCBE)'s Financial Services Committee. He has written and lectured extensively on corporate and financial matters in Italy, Europe and North Africa. He graduated from the State University of Milan law school and received an LL.M. degree from Harvard Law School. He is a member of the Bars in Milan and New York.

Chapter 16. Luxembourg

Philippe Hoss is a partner of Elvinger, Hoss & Prussen and holds a postgraduate degree (DEA) in business law from Paris I University (Panthéon Sorbonne). He is a member of the corporate, banking and finance group of Elvinger, Hoss & Prussen. His principal fields of activity are securities and capital markets, mergers and acquisitions, banking, finance, tax and investment funds.

He is a member of the 'Comité des Marchés de Valeurs Mobilières' (Securities' Markets Committee) and of various other committees at the Commission de Surveillance du Secteur Financier, the Luxembourg regulator of the financial sector.

He regularly lectures on various subjects relating to business and securities' legislation including in particular as part of the Luxembourg University LLM on European financial and banking law ('Master en droit européen, filière droit bancaire et financier (LLM)').

Chapter 17. Netherlands

Derk Lemstra studied at Leyden University and Columbia University in New York. He joined Stibbe in 1992 where he chairs the Capital Markets Group specializing in securities law and public M&A. He is an officer the Securities Law Committee of the International Bar Association and member of a number of financial sector advisory boards.

Marius Josephus Jitta studied at Leyden University and Paris University and joined Stibbe in 1973. He specializes in M&A, Restructuring, Corporate Litigation and Corporate Governance, and is Chairman of the Joint Committee on Corporate Law of the Dutch Bar Association and the Royal Organisation of Dutch Civil Law Notaries and a member of the Advisory Committee of the Autoriteit Financiële Markten (the Dutch Regulator of Financial Markets) on Financial Reporting.

Rogier Raas graduated from Leyden University in 1998 and obtained a Ph.D. degree in 2000. He joined Stibbe in 2000, and specializes in financial regulatory law. He is also a part-time professor in Dutch and European Banking and Securities Law at Leyden University.

Chapter 18. Portugal

Carlos Costa Andrade specializes in securities and commercial law. He is a graduate in Law (Universidade Católica Portuguesa, Lisboa, 1995) and postgraduate in EC law and securities (Faculdade de Direito da Universidade Clássica de Lisboa, 1997). He joined Uría Menéndez in 2001 and became a partner in 2005. He is also responsible for the Capital Markets practice of Uría Menéndez in Portugal. From 1995 to 1996 and from 1999 to 2001 he worked in Prof. Doutor Palma Carlos and Vasconcelos, F.Sá Carneiro, Fontes & Associado, respectively. Between 1996–1999 he was in-house counsel (Issuers and Market Division) at NYSE Euronext.

Ana Sá Couto specializes in securities and commercial law. She is a graduate in Law (Universidade Católica Portuguesa, Lisboa, 1997). She holds a postgraduate degree in securities (Faculdade de Direito da Universidade Clássica de Lisboa, 1998) and a post graduate degree in Banking law, Securities law and Insurance law (Faculdade de Direito da Universidade de Coimbra, 2001). She started her legal career in 1997, joined Uría Menéndez in 2002 and has been a senior associate of the firm since 2006. She was also deputy secretary of the MTS Portugal - Sociedade Gestora do Mercado Especial de Dívida Pública, SGMR, S.A.

Chapter 19. Spain
Luis de Carlos: see *Chapter 2. Equity* above.

Chapter 20. Sweden
Anders Lindblad is a partner in Mannheimer Swartling Advokatbyrå AB and specializes in capital market transactions for public companies such as for example takeovers, stock market listings, new share issues, mergers and demergers, as well as corporate governance issues. He is co-author of the 'Manual for Applying the Swedish Code of Corporate Governance' and author of 'Squeeze-out of minority shares – will the new Companies Act solve the problems?'.

Chapter 21. UK
Raj Panasar: see Editors description above.

Stephen Glasper is a lawyer at Cleary Gottlieb Steen & Hamilton. His practice focuses on international equity and debt capital markets transactions and UK corporate law matters, with a particular emphasis on advising clients in the emerging markets. He has represented both issuers and leading investment banks in the context of major IPOs and international stock exchange listings. He graduated with a first class degree in law from New College, Oxford before attending Harvard University as a graduate scholar. He is a solicitor of the Supreme Court of England and Wales.

TABLE OF CASES

EUROPEAN COMMISSION DECISIONS

NATIONAL COURTS

Ireland

United Kingdom

TABLE OF LEGISLATION

EUROPEAN LEGISLATION

Regulations

Regulation 44/2001/EC on jurisdiction
and the recognition and enforcement
of judgments in civil and commercial
matters [2001] OJ L21/1
('Brussels I') 1.112
Regulation 1606/2002/EC on the
application of international accounting
standards [2002] OJ L234
(IAS Regulation)....1.29, 1.145, 1.182,
3.166, 7.68, 13.138, 19.63
Art 4................... 1.183, 3.76
Regulation 2273/2003/EC implementing
Directive 2003/6 as regards exemptions
for buy-back programmes and stabiliza-
tion of financial instruments [2003] OJ
L336/33........1.193, 1.224, 7.275,
9.83, 9.192, 10.74, 10.83,
10.91, 20.212
Art 2(7) 10.74
Art 4(2) 7.272
Art 5(1)–(3) 7.269
Arts 7–11...................1.220
Art 8.......................7.163
Art 8(1)–(3) 10.93
Art 9(1) 1.222, 7.163
Art 9(1)(a)–(e) 10.94
Art 9(1)–(2) 7.164
Art 9(2) 10.96
Art 9(3) 9.84, 10.95
Art 9(5) 10.97

Arts 10–11 .... 1.223, 7.165
Art 10.......................9.84
Art 11......................10.99
Art 11(d) 9.82
Preamble, Art 2...............10.77
Preamble, s 19 ....10.83
Recital 2................ 7.267, 9.84
Regulation 139/2004/EC on the control
of concentrations between
undertakings [2004] OJ L24/1
(Merger Regulation)..........6.111
Regulation 809/2004/EC implementing
Directive 2003/71/EC as regards
information contained in prospectuses
[2004] OJ L149/1 (Prospectus Directive
Regulation) 1.25, 1.100, 2.77,
2.78, 2.93, 2.96, 3.06, 3.49,
3.52, 3.54, 3.59, 3.166, 3.175,
3.211, 7.45, 7.46, 7.56, 7.61,
7.64, 7.66, 7.68, 7.118, 8.76,
8.80, 8.82, 9.34, 9.36, 10.01,
11.03, 11.37, 11.50, 11.58,
12.101, 12.104, 12.118, 12.125,
13.39, 13.40, 13.41, 13.56, 13.71,
13.72, 13.74, 13.76, 13.125,
15.100, 15.106, 15.128,
15.155, 16.64, 17.29, 17.30,
18.59, 18.66, 18.71, 18.83, 19.66,
19.94, 19.95, 20.26, 20.69,
20.72, 20.73, 20.75, 20.82,
21.02, 21.55, 21.64
Art 2(9) 1.45, 7.103, 7.108
Art 2(10) 12.98, 17.70

NATIONAL LEGISLATION

AUSTRIA

FRANCE

GERMANY

Acts

UNITED STATES

ABBREVIATIONS

ABI   Association of British Insurers
AFM   Autoriteit Financiële Markten
AIM   Alternative Investment Market
AktG   Aktiengesetz
AMF   Autorité des Marchés Financiers
ASM   Authorized storage mechanism
ATX   Austrian Traded Index

BaFin   Bundesanstalt für Finanzdienstleistungsaufsicht
BME   Bolsas y Mercados Españoles
BO FWB   Börsenordnung für die Frankfurter Wertpapierbörse
BörsG   Börsengesetz

CARD   Combined Admissions and Reporting Directive
CBFA   Belgian Banking, Finance and Insurance Commission
CESR   Committee of European Securities Regulators
CFA   Consolidated Financial Act
CFD   Contract for difference
CGN   classic global note
CIS   Collective investment scheme
CJA 1993   Criminal Justice Act 1993
CMA   Capital Markets Act
CMC   capital market coach
CMVM   Securities Markets and Exchange Commission (Comissão do Mercado de Valores Mobiliários)
CNMV   Comisión Nacional del Mercado de Valores
CP   commercial paper
CSK   common safe keeper
CSSF   Commission de Surveillance du Secteur Financier
CVM   Portuguese centralized securities depositary system (Central de Valores Mobiliários)

DCC   Dutch Civil Code
DCGC   Dutch Corporate Governance Code
DIP   debt issuance programme
DNB   De Nederlandsche Bank
DTRs   Disclosure and Transparency Rules

EEA	European Economic Area
EC	European Commission
ECMR	EC Merger Regulation
EGM	Extraordinary general meeting
EMTN	Euro medium term note
ESCB	European System of Central Banks
ESME	European Securities Markets Expert Group
FFSA	Finnish Financial Supervisory Authority
FMA	[Austrian] Financial Market Authority
FRN	floating rate note
FSA	Financial Services Authority
FSAP	Financial Services Action Plan
FSE	Frankfurt Stock Exchange
FSMA 2000	Financial Services and Markets Act 2000
GAAP	generally accepted accounting principles
GDR	Global depositary receipt
GEM	Global Exchange Market
HGB	Handelsgesetzbuch
IAS	Internal Accounting Standards
IASB	International Accounting Standards Board
ICC	Italian Civil Code
ICSA	Institute of Chartered Secretaries and Administrators
IDS	information disclosure system
IEX	Irish Enterprise Exchange
IFRS	International Financial Reporting Standards
IM	information memorandum
IOSCO	International Organization of Securities Commissions
IPO	initial public offering
IR	Issuer Regulation
ISE	Irish Stock Exchange
ISEQ	Irish Stock Exchange Quotient
LMV	Ley del Mercado de Valores
LR	Listing Rules
LSE	London Stock Exchange/Luxembourg Stock Exchange
MAC	Mercato Alternativo del Capitale
MAD	Market Abuse Directive
MEFF	Mercado Español de Futuros Financieros
MFC	French Monetary and Financial Code
MiFID	Market in Financial Instruments Directive
MTF	multilateral trading facility

NGN	new global note
NIS	Network Information System
NOMAD	nominated adviser
OeKB	Oesterreichische Kontrollbank AG
PD	Prospectus Directive
PDMRs	persons discharging managerial responsibility
POD	Public Offers Directive
PPM	private placement memorandum
PSC	Portuguese Securities Code
PSM	Professional Securities Market
QIB	qualified institutional buyer
RIS	Regulatory Information Service
RNS	Regulatory News Service
SARs	Substantial Acquisition Rules
SDIR	system for the dissemination of regulated information
SEA	[Austrian] Stock Exchange Act
SEC	US Securities and Exchange Commission
SFM	Specialist fund market
SFSA	Swedish Financial Supervisory Authority
SIBE	Sistema de Interconexión Bursátil Español
SME	small- and medium-sized enterprise
SPAC	special purpose acquisition company
SPV	special purpose vehicle
SSA	Securities Supervision Act
SSF	Super-Sophisticated Investor Fund
TEFRA	Tax Equity and Fiscal Responsibility Act 1992
TOD	Transparency Directive
UKLA	United Kingdom Listing Authority
US SEC	US Securities and Exchange Commission
VSE	Vienna Stock Exchange
Wft	Wet op het financieel toezicht (Netherlands Financial Supervision Act)
WpPG	Wertpapierprospektgesetz

Part I

REGULATORY FRAMEWORK IN EUROPE

1

THE EUROPEAN DIRECTIVES
RELATING TO ISSUE AND TRADING
OF SECURITIES

1.1 Introduction

There is little purpose in laboriously trawling through the detailed provisions of **1.01** European Directives, article by article, in the order in which they appear on the legislative page. Anyone seeking such an approach should look elsewhere. Instead, this Section will attempt to review and, where necessary, interpret the various Directives that are most relevant to the securities markets, and to those who issue and invest in them, from the viewpoint of those who deal in those markets. The starting point, therefore, is the perceived requirements of the markets and their participants—for example, the need for pertinent and reliable information at the point of initial investment and a regular stream of updating information thereafter; and the need for investors to be protected against abusive practices and behaviour, so that they can invest confidently and without fear. This approach results, when dealing with the relevant Directives, in a certain amount of dashing from one part of a Directive to another or even between Directives because, although the Directives are not sequentially organized according to the logic adopted in this Section, they do have that logic as their foundation.

1.02   Section 1.2 attempts to set out an overview of the legislative purposes behind the Directives—an aerial view, taken from several thousand feet, to help the reader with orientation. The remaining Sections then consider each purpose in more detail, starting with the provision of information, both initial and during the life of the securities (Section 1.3); and then moving on to provisions designed to promote confidence in the markets among those using them, for example by requiring those who deal with investors to obtain authorization and to comply with detailed rules of conduct and by outlawing abusive practices (Section 1.4). The final Section then attempts some conclusions.

1.1.1 Background to the Directives

1.03   Before proceeding any further, however, it may be helpful to set the context by explaining the background to the various Directives that are discussed in this Section, which form part of a suite of 42 Directives introduced by the European Union under its Financial Services Action Plan ('FSAP').

1.1.1.1 Development of the FSAP

1.04   The process began in earnest at the Cardiff European Council in June 1998, at which member states concluded that 'to enable the single market to make its full contribution to competitiveness, growth and employment, still more needs to be done'. They therefore invited the Commission 'to table a framework for action by the time of the Vienna European Council to improve the single market in financial services, in particular examining the effectiveness of implementation of current legislation and identifying weaknesses which may require amending legislation'.[1] This prompted a Communication from the Commission[2] which highlighted the need to develop a legislative apparatus capable of responding to new regulatory challenges; to remove capital market fragmentation; to enable users and suppliers of financial services to exploit a single financial market, while maintaining a high level of consumer protection; to achieve closer coordination of supervisory authorities; and to create an integrated EU infrastructure to underpin retail and wholesale financial transactions.

---

[1]   Cardiff European Council, Presidency Conclusions paragraph 17 (http://ue.eu.int/ueDocs/cms_Data/docs/pressData/en/ec/54315.pdf).

[2]   COM (1998) 625 'Financial Services: building a framework for action' (http://ec.europa.eu/internal_market/finances/docs/actionplan/index/fs_en.pdf).

These somewhat generalized concepts received more concrete form in the **1.05** Commission's Financial Services Action Plan, published on 11 May 1999.[3] This important document starts by reminding the reader that a single market for financial services in the EU had been under construction since 1973. However, the document continues, the advent of the euro had led to a change in tempo. 'With the introduction of the euro', it says, 'there is a unique window of opportunity to equip the EU with a modern financial apparatus in which the cost of capital and financial intermediation are kept to a minimum. Corporate and household users of financial services will benefit significantly, and investment and employment across the Union will be stimulated'.

This concept was enthusiastically adopted at the Lisbon European Council in **1.06** March 2000, which set a tight timetable for the Financial Services Action Plan to be implemented by 2005.[4]

A 'Committee of Wise Men', under Alexandre Lamfalussy, was instructed by the EU's Economic and Finance Ministers to produce a report (the 'Lamfalussy Report'), setting out practical arrangements for EU rules to implement the FSAP. The final report was produced in February 2001.[5] It made important practical recommendations, including the need for a single prospectus for issuers, the modernization of the listing regime and the generalization of the mutual recognition principle.

These recommendations were incorporated into the FSAP, which sets out a **1.07** number of strategic objectives, including those related to the creation of a single EU wholesale market, for the development of open and secure retail markets and the development of state-of-the-art prudential rules and supervision. These objectives were in turn developed into a detailed list of some 42 measures, which are itemized in the Commission's FSAP evolution chart.[6]

In an attempt to underpin these concepts with reliable data, the Commission **1.08** asked London Economics, in conjunction with PricewaterhouseCoopers and Oxford Economic Forecasting, to produce a report, which appeared in November 2002.[7] This confirmed what had, until then, been intelligent guesswork. The empirical work described in the report indicated that 'trading costs in the equity

---

[3] COM (1999) 232 (http://ec.europa.eu/internal_market/finances/docs/actionplan/index/action_en.pdf).

[4] http://www.europarl.europa.eu/summits/lis1_en.htm, at paragraph 21.

[5] 'Final Report of The Committee of Wise Men on The Regulation of European Securities Markets', 15 February 2001.

[6] This can be found at http://ec.europa.eu/internal_market/finances/docs/actionplan/index/061003_measures_en.pdf.

[7] 'Quantification of the Macro-Economic Impact of Integration of EU Financial Markets', London Economics, November 2002.

markets could fall sharply as a result of full European financial integration'. This would have a knock-on effect on the cost of equity capital, which the report estimated would fall across Europe by about 40 basis points on average. Reduced clearance and settlement costs would produce a further saving of 10 basis points. In the bond markets, the report indicated that there would be a pronounced impact in the primary market, where financial market integration would produce a deeper and more liquid market and reduce credit spreads required by investors, resulting in a cost reduction of about 40 basis points. There would also be a shift from bank financing to cheaper bond financing.

1.09 At a macro-economic level, the report suggested that these cost savings would raise real EU GDP by 1.1% (or EUR 130 billion in 2002 prices); increase business investment by almost 6% and private consumption by 0.8%; and increase total employment by 0.5%.

These are tempting predictions; and the FSAP, which was already well under way, acquired an unstoppable head of steam.

1.1.1.2 Reasons for fragmentation of EEA financial markets

1.10 Perhaps the most important part of the FSAP publication is its identification of some of the elements of the previous regimes that had stood in the way of the development of a true pan-EEA capital market. Among these, the more important were:

- the need, when making a cross-border offering, to produce multiple sets of official documentation (such as the prospectus), meeting the different disclosure requirements of each member state in which an offer was to be made;
- the fragmentation of financial reporting regimes across the EEA, which stood in the way of the comparability that was fundamental for an efficient and integrated capital market; and
- different marketing rules for retail offers in each member state.

1.11 It is worth pausing for a moment to consider these barriers to cross-border markets, because they are fundamental to an understanding of the workings of the FSAP Directives, and to some of the continuing problems that still prevent pan-EEA offerings. Before 2005, the law governing the listing and public offering of securities in the EU was set out in two Directives—the Combined Admissions and Reporting Directive[8] ('CARD') and the Public Offers Directive ('POD').[9] CARD required that, as a condition for admission to listing, an issuer had to produce and publish a document (known as 'listing particulars') containing

---

[8] Directive 2001/34/EC.
[9] Directive 89/298/EEC.

specified information, which had to be approved by a competent authority before publication. CARD expressly provided that the approval of the competent authority in one state (the 'home state') had to be recognized for the purpose of admission to markets in another member state[10] (the 'host state')—in other words, the cost in time and money of obtaining multiple approvals for multiple listings was removed. However, crucially, CARD made this passport subject to any translation requirements that may be imposed by the authorities in the country where the second listing was sought. Listing particulars tended to be lengthy documents, so that the cost (and time) involved in making such translations formed an effective barrier to those who might otherwise wish to obtain multiple EU listings.

There was a further impediment. Listing particulars must be recognized by the **1.12** host state, said CARD, despite any exemptions or omissions from the content requirements allowed by the home state authority; but only if the exemption or derogation in question was of a type recognized in the rules of the host state. This gave the host state the ability to require additional disclosure in the passported listing particulars. Fear that such powers would be used by the host state (fuelled by instances of the actual exercise of such powers in a number of transactions) resulted in avoidance in some countries of secondary listings by issuers.

The public offering of unlisted securities was subject to the POD. This, too, **1.13** required the production and publication of an approved disclosure document (called a prospectus) when securities were offered to the public.[11] However, this requirement did not apply to public offers of listed securities[12] (which would fall instead under the CARD regime) or to any public offer after the first.[13] Again, there were arrangements for mutual recognition in a host state of a prospectus approved for a public offer in the home state.[14] Again, it was subject to translation requirements imposed by the host state. Again, the host state was given the ability to require the inclusion in the prospectus of additional information. While it is true that this was limited to certain areas, of which the most troublesome was the information that many host states required relating to their income tax system, the additional information could only be included on the basis of advice obtained from tax experts, which added significantly to the cost and time involved in carrying out a cross border public offer, thus acting as a deterrent to those considering making such an offering.

The FSAP Directives that were formulated to remove these obstacles form the **1.14** basis of the discussion that follows.

---

[10] CARD Article 38.
[11] POD Article 4.
[12] POD Articles 1 and 7.
[13] POD Article 1(1).
[14] POD Article 21(1).

1.1.1.3 Underlying purpose of the FSAP

1.15 Two of the FSAP Directives—the Prospectus Directive and the Transparency Directive—contain very important indications of the guiding principles behind the FSAP Directives. These are set out in recitals, which give guiding principles to the Commission as to how it should exercise the implementing powers given to it under those two Directives. This is a limited scope. But the principles are instructive of the overall purpose behind the Directives too—what is important to detailed implementation must also be important to the generality of the FSAP project. It is therefore worth setting out these principles at length. The Commission must respect:

— the need to ensure confidence in financial markets among small investors and small and medium-sized enterprises (SMEs) by promoting high standards of transparency in financial markets,
— the need to provide investors with a wide range of competing investment opportunities and a level of disclosure and protection tailored to their circumstances,
— the need to ensure that independent regulatory authorities enforce the rules consistently, especially as regards the fight against white-collar crime,
— the need for a high level of transparency and consultation with all market participants and with the European Parliament and the Council,
— the need to encourage innovation in financial markets if they are to be dynamic and efficient,
— the need to ensure systemic stability of the financial system by close and reactive monitoring of financial innovation,
— the importance of reducing the cost of, and increasing access to, capital,
— the need to balance, on a long-term basis, the costs and benefits to market participants (including SMEs and small investors) of any implementing measures,
— the need to foster the international competitiveness of the Community's financial markets without prejudice to a much-needed extension of international cooperation,
— the need to achieve a level playing field for all market participants by establishing Community legislation every time it is appropriate,
— the need to respect differences in national financial markets where these do not unduly impinge on the coherence of the single market,
— the need to ensure coherence with other Community legislation in this area, as imbalances in information and a lack of transparency may jeopardize the operation of the markets and above all harm consumers and small investors.[15]

1.1.2 European markets

1.16 Before discussing the Directives in detail, it is necessary to make a few introductory points. The first concerns the different types of European markets. The Directives discussed in the following pages mainly concern 'regulated' markets.

---

[15] Prospectus Directive Recital 41. The equivalent Recital in the TOD is Recital 36.

These are, essentially, markets that bring together buyers and sellers, in a way that enables them to enter into contracts for purchase and sale of financial instruments, which are authorized under the Market in Financial Instruments Directive ('MiFID').[16] In addition to regulated markets, a number of European states have other markets which are outside the scope of the Directives but are, instead, subject to national rules, usually imposed by the Stock Exchanges that run them. Examples of such markets include the London Stock Exchange's Professional Securities Market and the Luxembourg Stock Exchange's EuroMTF. These are colloquially known as 'Exchange regulated markets' (although for the purposes of the MiFID, they are technically multi-trading facilities or 'MTFs').

There is a further complication, in that some European markets have a dual aspect. **1.17** Securities that are admitted to them will also be admitted to the Official List (or 'listed'). In some respects, this is a product of history. The regulatory regime that preceded the FSAP Directives used the concept of admission to listing, rather than to regulated markets. This has been retained alongside the new regulated markets concept for two reasons—neither of which involves nostalgia or a penchant for history. The first reason has to do with the restrictions that are imposed on many investors in the EU and elsewhere (either through prudential legislation or regulation, or through self-imposed internal investment guidelines). Many of these restrictions still refer to securities that are listed rather than those that are admitted to regulated markets. Overnight abolition of the concept of listing would have produced, at best, confusion, with investors wondering whether they could continue to invest in and to hold securities that are no longer 'listed' and, at worst, market disruption as some decided to divest themselves of securities they considered they were no longer able to hold.

The second reason has to do with what are called 'super-equivalent' obligations **1.18** (such as rules on corporate governance) that are imposed in some regulated markets on issuers of shares. In the view of some, it would not have been possible to have imposed these obligations on issuers admitted purely to regulated markets because the Prospectus Directive, which deals with the requirements for such admission, is a 'maximum harmonisation' Directive. This means what it appears to say—a member state cannot through national legislation add to whatever is required by the Directive. Accordingly, states wishing to retain their super-equivalent requirements for share issuers created a market that was both regulated *and* listed. Admission to the regulated market required only compliance with the Prospectus Directive; but admission to listing required issuers of shares requiring a primary listing to sign up to the super-equivalent regime too. Those not willing

---

[16] MiFID Article 4(1)(14).

to do so were redirected to another part of the market, which required only compliance with the Directive.

1.1.3 Structure of European Legislation

1.19 The European legislative process, like many others, tends to be slow. There are two basic legislative tools—the Directive and the Regulation. The former is an instruction to member states requiring them to enact legislation that implements the provisions set out in the Directive. The latter is legislation that takes direct effect in the law of all member states, without the need for implementation through national legislation. But, prior to 2002, the introduction of both types of legislation required significant—some would say too much—time and effort.

1.20 Alexandre Lamfalussy's Committee of Wise Men was asked by the European Economic and Finance Ministers to examine the process and to devise ways of making it more efficient and expedient. The resulting proposal in the Lamfalussy Report, which was duly adopted, involved a new, four-stage process. Level 1 consists of a Directive which sets out the framework for the proposal. It is the bones, or outline, onto which the flesh, or detail, can be strapped. Level 2, which might consist either of another Directive or a Regulation, sets out much of the detail. Where interpretation is required (because little legislation is free from ambiguity or obscurity), this is given at Level 3 through guidance given, in the context of the Directives considered in this Section, by the Committee of European Securities Regulators ('CESR'). And, finally, Level 4 involves the Commission enforcing compliance of the whole regime across the EU.

1.21 A number of European legislative measures (including those discussed in this Section) apply not just to European Union members, but to states that are members of the European Economic Area (which adds to EU member states Liechtenstein, Iceland, and Norway).

1.2 Overview

1.22 As has been seen, one of the main objectives of the FSAP was to develop a large and efficient pan-European capital market, to replace the mosaic of national or domestic retail markets, subject to differing national laws and regulations, which then existed—despite previous efforts to harmonize them.

1.23 A market can only exist where there is a sufficient supply of sellers and buyers. Buyers will attend markets in greater numbers if they are confident that they will be treated fairly—that they will be given a sufficient explanation of what they are being offered, on which they can rely; that they can trust the seller; that they can be confident that the prices at which they buy are fair, and have not been manipulated to deceive them. The creation of a market that gives investors that confidence is, in a nutshell, the objective of the FSAP Directives that are the subject of this Section.

1.2.1 Disclosure

Securities markets are no different in many ways from any other form of market. **1.24** Before buying a security, an investor needs to know enough about the investment in order to make a sensible decision. With vegetables, sight, smell, touch and (if the stall-holder will allow) taste can provide most of the information needed for a decision to buy. None of these senses serves with securities, however, which are intangible things. So, something more is needed—a written description of terms of the security, of the business and prospects of the person issuing it (and on whom the performance of the promises made in the security depends) and of the risks involved in a decision to buy the security. A disclosure document, therefore, is required when an issuer offers securities to the market or obtains admission for its securities to the market, so that they can be traded.

The Prospectus Directive[17] provides that, before securities are offered to the pub- **1.25** lic or admitted to a regulated market, a prospectus must be prepared by the issuer or offeror, approved by a regulator and published. The prospectus must contain information about the issuer, its business, its financial position and its prospects, together with all information about the securities to which it relates, that is sufficient to enable investors to make an informed investment decision. Additional detailed requirements are added by the Regulation[18] under the Prospectus Directive (the 'PD Regulation'), at Level 2.

An investment decision will sometimes be a decision *not* to buy. An investor, **1.26** having a finite supply of money to invest, may decide to buy something else, rather than the issue that is described in the prospectus. However, most invest-ment decisions are not so much about whether or not to buy, but about whether or not to buy at a particular price—(there are few investments that investors will not touch at *any* price). So it is perhaps helpful to consider the prospectus as a document whose purpose is to enable investors to determine whether or not to invest at the offer or market price. In other words, it enables the market and those in it to determine the market price for the securities.

Once the securities have been launched on the regulated market,[19] and their initial **1.27** price has been determined, investors need to be kept informed by the issuer of

---

[17] Directive 2003/71/EC.
[18] Commission Regulation (EC) No 809/2004.
[19] It is important to note that the ongoing disclosure regime only applies, at the level of the FSAP Directives, to securities that are admitted to a regulated market and, even then, there are

changes in circumstances. The most important changes are those that have a significant effect on the market price of the securities. Such changes must be disclosed to the market promptly after their occurrence, under Article 6 of the Market Abuse Directive[20] ('MAD').

1.28 Investors also need regular updates from the issuer of the securities, giving a review, in the form of financial statements, of financial position and performance, and a review by the issuer's management of the issuer's recent activities and its immediate prospects and future plans. Such reports are required under the Transparency Directive[21] ('TOD').

1.29 The financial statements are of critical importance. They give a numerical view of matters that are critical to investors and to the pricing of the issuer's securities in the markets. It is therefore important that they should be as reliable and trustworthy as possible, and European legislation regulates both the accounting and auditing regime to which they are subject, through the TOD (which cross-refers to the Accounts Regulation[22] and the Statutory Audit Directive[23]).

1.30 Disclosure then, both at the point of initial admission to the market and on an ongoing basis thereafter, is crucial to a healthy market. It is important to understand, however, that disclosure is not, in itself, a good thing without limitation. Too much disclosure can have undesirable results—for example, excessive cost for little additional benefit; and, from the perspective of the investor, there is a point at which more disclosure makes the document difficult to understand, because important facts are buried under a mass of less important detail. The ideal is a disclosure document that is short, clear and comprehensive in its inclusion of all information an investor needs as the basis for his investment decision. There is a tension here, though. The requirement for 'comprehensive' disclosure, when coupled (as it is) with a stringent liability regime for failure to comply, will inevitably lead to length, and the inclusion of information on a 'just in case' basis. So there are competing interests in the disclosure world. On the one hand, investors want a document that is short, easy to read and includes all they need to know, with a right to claim compensation if it does not contain that information. On the other hand, the person charged with producing that document, faced with a very broad disclosure duty and tough liability rules to enforce it, must be given the ability to discharge

---

exemptions that apply—for example, where the only securities of the issuer that are admitted to the market are debt securities in denominations of EUR 50,000 or above (see TOD Article 8). However, some member states have elected to apply certain parts of the Directive regimes additionally to their exchange regulated markets, as well as to their regulated markets.

[20] Directive 2003/6/EC.
[21] Directive 2004/109/EC.
[22] Regulation (EC) No 1606/2002.
[23] Directive 2006/43/EC.

that duty, and reduce risks of liability, by including as much information as he believes necessary and in whatever format he thinks advisable. Such tensions are not easy to resolve, and tend in practice to result in longer disclosure documents, particularly when the liability regime is actively relied upon by investors or regulators.

1.2.2 Fair treatment

So much for disclosure. The market has the information it needs to decide whether to buy (or rather, at what price to buy). But price can also be influenced by other factors. For example, many purchasers are influenced by the blandishments of middlemen such as financial institutions that act as intermediaries between issuer and investor. Large, unfounded, promises by such people can induce a purchase, even when contradictory to information provided in the prospectus. Investors will not be attracted to markets if they cannot trust the middlemen with whom they have to deal. **1.31**

The Market in Financial Instruments Directive[24] ('MiFID') seeks to give investors confidence in this area, by requiring that anyone that acts as an intermediary in the market must be authorized to do so, and thereby subject itself to regulatory rules and oversight. **1.32**

The actions and behaviour of unscrupulous middlemen can also influence investment decisions. Just as the enthusiastic purchase by associates of the stall-holder can gull the innocent bystander into buying at the wrong price, so, in the securities markets, the deceptive actions of financial intermediaries and others can dupe the unwary investor. The spreading of false rumours or the buying and selling of securities between associates, to give an impression that the price is rising, will obtain a profit for such persons; but such practices will also have a deadening effect on the market, because honest investors will lose confidence in it and stay away. **1.33**

To avoid such consequences, the Market Abuse Directive seeks to outlaw such dishonest practices.

1.2.3 Protection against other, predatory, investors

Investors in shares have several additional concerns. As co-proprietors of the business, they do not want any other investor to acquire a significant proportion of the shares without being told about it; and, when that proportion is sufficiently large to give an element of control to that other shareholder, they want to be sure that, rather than having to continue with their investment, the other shareholder should make an offer for their shares, at a price that is linked to the recent market. **1.34**

---

[24] Directive 2004/39/EC.

1.35   The TOD gives some protection against the covert build-up of shareholding stakes, by requiring disclosure of acquisitions or disposals of shares that take a holding past specified percentage thresholds of the issuer's share capital. The Takeovers Directive[25] gives further protection, by requiring that when the stake is sufficiently large, the acquirer has to make a bid for the remaining shares in the issuer.

1.36   Shareholders with significant stakes in companies also have an interest in preserving their proportionate share of the capital—for example, to prevent their influence over management through their holding being eroded by an issue of new shares to others. Minor shareholders will also be concerned that, particularly where a new issue of shares is priced at a discount to the market price, they are included in any offer so that they can benefit from the advantageous terms. European company law typically provides protection to shareholders in this area, by requiring new issues of shares for cash consideration to be made to existing shareholders on a pre-emptive basis.

1.2.4 Summary

1.37   The logical map, therefore, that will be applied in the following description of the Directives, involves the following elements:

- initial disclosure, at the time of offer or admission, of all information the investor needs to decide whether to invest and, if so, at what price;
- ongoing disclosure by the issuer, of information that will significantly move the price, once formed;
- regular reporting to investors, in the form of audited and unaudited financial statements and management reviews of the issuer's recent activities and immediate prospects;
- keeping the markets (and its participants) honest, so that investors can deal confidently in them; and
- protecting the investor in shares against predatory stake-building and dilution.

1.3 Disclosure—Initial and Ongoing

1.38   Recitals to Directives are often instructive. Take the following, from the Prospectus Directive:

> The provision of full information concerning securities and issuers of those securities promotes, together with rules on the conduct of business, the protection of investors. Moreover, such information provides an effective means of increasing confidence in securities and thus of contributing to the proper functioning and development of securities markets. The appropriate way to make this information

---

[25] Directive 2004/25/EC.

available is to publish a prospectus. Investment in securities, like any other form of investment, involves risk. Safeguards for the protection of the interests of actual and potential investors are required in all member states in order to enable them to make an informed assessment of such risks and thus to take investment decisions in full knowledge of the facts.[26]

Or take the following, from the TOD: **1.39**

The disclosure of accurate, comprehensive and timely information about security issuers builds sustained investor confidence and allows an informed assessment of their business performance and assets. This enhances both investor protection and market efficiency.[27]

These recitals draw attention to a number of important regulatory concepts, namely that:

(a)   investor confidence is important to a successful market;

(b)   that confidence depends on the provision of information;

(c)   the information needs to be sufficient to enable the investor to make an informed assessment of the risks and to take an investment decision in full knowledge of the facts;

(d)   the information is so important that it needs to be policed, through conduct of business rules and the publication of a prospectus (which, as will be seen, requires official approval);

(e)   information at the point of the initial offer alone is insufficient—there needs to be a continuing flow of information to enable investors to continue to take investment decisions after the issue of the securities; and

(f)   information also has to do with market efficiency (which presumably means, among other things, achieving the correct price).

There is little to disagree with in this litany and much to support. It would be   **1.40**
a mean-minded individual who would quarrel with the idea of a well-informed and accurately priced market that attracts numerous confident investors who, by providing a healthy demand, supply the capital needs of the economy at a relatively cheap rate, creating wealth for shareholders and jobs for all. However, this utopian picture needs to be balanced by some consideration of the cost and administrative burden that is placed on the shoulders of those whose task it is to provide the information. There is a point at which more information ceases to be a good thing and becomes a disproportionate burden. A market that requires those managing businesses to spend too much time reporting what has happened will rue the consequences if management fails to have enough time to identify opportunities to develop the business. A similar balance needs to be struck in relation to liability

---

[26]   Prospectus Directive Recitals (18) and (19).
[27]   TOD Recital (1).

for errors or omissions from mandated disclosure. The stricter this is, the more conservative (and longer) the disclosure is likely to be, as those responsible for it seek to avoid litigation by including everything, whether material to investment decisions or not, and adopt over-cautious, mealy-mouthed language.

1.41 These recitals set out the intention. It is time to examine how the Directives execute that intention. The following discussion will track the sort of timeline that might be followed for a new issue of securities, rather than the sequence followed by the Prospectus Directive itself, in the hope that this approach will not only be more easily understood, because more logical, but also that it will be more useful to the practitioner.

1.3.1 Initial disclosure—the Prospectus Directive

1.3.1.1 Scope of the Directive

1.42 The Prospectus Directive is not all-embracing. It does not, for example, apply[28] to offers of non-transferrable securities[29] or certain short-term money market instruments.[30] Nor does it apply to all issuers, or all types of issue. Article 1(2) contains a long list of exempt issuers and types of issue, that fall entirely outside the scope of the Directive. For example, the Directive does not apply to:

- open-ended collective investment undertakings;
- non-equity securities issued by member states or their local or regional authorities;
- non-equity securities issued by a public international body (such as the World Bank or the European Bank for Reconstruction and Development), provided its membership includes an EU state;
- the European Central Bank or central banks of EU member states;
- securities that are unconditionally guaranteed by an EU member state or one of its regional or local authorities; and
- certain securitized deposits issued by European credit institutions.

1.43 The fact that these issuers or types of issue do not fall within the scope of the Directive does not, of course, mean that they are free from regulation. For example, various other Directives regulate the issue and offering of securities by open-ended collective investment undertakings.[31] It is perhaps difficult to imagine one EEA state applying a domestic disclosure regime to a fellow sovereign; but no doubt the

---

[28] See Prospectus Directive Article 2(1)(a).

[29] 'Transferrable securities' are defined in MiFID Article 4(1)(18) and include shares, bonds and a wide range of securitized derivatives.

[30] 'Money market instruments' are defined in MiFID Article 4(1)(19) as 'those classes of instruments which are normally dealt in on the money market, such as treasury bills, certificates of deposit and commercial papers and excluding instruments of payment'.

[31] For example, the UCITS Directive, 85/611/EEC.

possibility exists, because Article 1(3) of the Prospectus Directive permits sovereign issuers, and their regional and local authorities, to submit themselves voluntarily to the Prospectus Directive regime; and the only reason for their doing so would be to avail themselves of the passport that can be attached to the prospectus and, once obtained, makes the prospectus valid for offerings or admission to the regulated markets of every EEA state to which it applies, thus depriving the local authorities in the place of offering or admission of the ability to require additional disclosure.[32]

1.3.1.2 Pre-marketing

Many new issues of securities will be tested in the market before the decision to issue is taken. This is particularly so when the markets are depressed. Few issuers or underwriters are prepared to launch an issue without being reasonably certain that it will sell at an acceptable price. Sometimes, the pre-marketing will be carried out on a selective basis, with a few, but by no means all, investors being given information about the possible issue and asked for their views. Such pre-marketing raises market abuse issues, which are considered in Section 1.4.1.2.1. **1.44**

However, in some cases, the issue is advertised to the general public. This was a common approach, for example, in the United Kingdom during the 1980s, when a number of state-owned enterprises were offered to the public. Even more frequently, documents concerning the issue, such as an outline of the possible terms of the issue, will be circulated to a limited group of investors (usually institutions). Such communications will often be 'advertisements' for the purposes of the Prospectus Directive, thanks to a broad definition in Article 2(9) of the Prospectus Directive Regulation which defines advertisement as announcements: **1.45**

(a) relating to a specific offer to the public of securities or to an admission to trading on a regulated market; and

(b) aiming to specifically promote the potential subscription or acquisition of securities.[33]

Such advertisements are permitted,[34] provided they: **1.46**

(a) state that a prospectus has been or will be published and indicate where investors are or will be able to obtain it;

---

[32] See Prospectus Directive Article 17 and the discussion of the passport below.

[33] Prospectus Directive Regulation Article 2(9).

[34] This is made clear not only by the fact that there is no prohibition, but that Article 34 of the Prospectus Directive Regulation expressly provides that 'advertisements related to an offer to the public of securities or to an admission to trading on a regulated market may be disseminated to the public by interested parties, such as issuer, offeror or person asking for admission, the financial intermediaries that participate in the placing and/or underwriting of securities' before going on to list various permitted methods of publication.

(b) are clearly recognizable as advertisements;

(c) do not contain information that is inaccurate or misleading; and

(d) ensure that the information they contain is consistent with that which is (or will be) in the prospectus.[35]

1.47 The last of these requirements highlights an important practical concern. As will be seen, the prospectus, when it is produced, must contain all the information requirements of the investor.[36] It follows, therefore, that an advertisement cannot contain any material information that will *not* be included in the prospectus. The requirement also introduces a practical constraint, in that, to ensure compliance, it will normally be advisable to ensure that a fairly advanced draft of the prospectus is available before any meaningful advertisement is made.

1.48 In addition, an advertisement must not contain sufficient information on the terms of the offer and the securities to be offered, so as to enable an investor to decide to purchase or subscribe to these securities, otherwise it will amount to an offer to the public which, as will be seen, requires an approved prospectus to be published.

1.49 Article 34 of the Prospectus Directive Regulation specifies various non-exclusive methods of publishing advertisements, including the somewhat quaintly phrased 'telephone with or without human intervention'.

1.50 The list in Article 34 does also indicate that advertisements do not have to be published in the sense of being made available to the public in general. Selective advertising is expressly contemplated by the inclusion in the list of 'seminars and presentations'. This is a concept that is also implied in Article 15 of the Prospectus Directive itself, which requires that 'when according to this Directive no prospectus is required, material information provided by an issuer or an offeror and addressed to qualified investors or special categories of investors, including information disclosed in the context of meetings relating to offers of securities, shall be disclosed to all qualified investors or special categories of investors to whom the offer is exclusively addressed'.[37]

1.51 This provision is somewhat bizarre, in that it purports to deal with matters that are outside the scope of the Directive. It is difficult to quarrel with the concept that all investors in a similar position should be treated equally. Yet there is an assumption in the provision that all investors will always require the same information—an assumption that is often not borne out by the facts. A qualified (or 'professional') investor will, sometimes, focus on different aspects of a transaction and require

---

[35] See Prospectus Directive Article 15.
[36] See Prospectus Directive Article 5.
[37] Prospectus Directive Article 15(5).

information that is of interest to it alone. The requirement to distribute this information to others, who have no interest in it, therefore does little to protect investors, and merely adds to cost and creates an administrative burden.

1.3.1.3 The triggers for a prospectus

1.52 Two events trigger the requirement for the production of a prospectus—the making of an offer of transferable securities to the public; and the admission of transferable securities to an EEA regulated market.

1.53 **1.3.1.3.1 Public offers** The first of these triggers is perhaps the most interesting, in that it involves a definition of 'offer of securities to the public' that is worth quoting in full:

> 'offer of securities to the public' means a communication to persons in any form and by any means, presenting sufficient information on the terms of the offer and the securities to be offered, so as to enable an investor to decide to purchase or subscribe to these securities. This definition shall also be applicable to the placing of securities through financial intermediaries.[38]

This provides an excellent example of the danger of trying to understand a term by its label alone. To most people, making an offer will involve one person, who has (or can get hold of) securities, inviting another to buy those securities. Indeed, under the United Kingdom's implementation of the European regime that was replaced by the Prospectus Directive, this was precisely what was meant.[39] However, the definition in the Prospectus Directive is clearly much wider than a mere contractual offer. The reason for this is probably an inability among member states to agree on what should, and what should not, be caught. Certainly, the argument in favour of the United Kingdom's interpretation was put forward, but was rejected. Reasons for this were not made public, but it is to be assumed that certain states considered that certain communications that were not contractual offers, but were more in the nature of enticements, should be banned unless a prospectus had already been published.

1.54 There is some logic behind this view. Many in the market, particularly when it is going through one of its more exuberant phases, will take their investment decision early, without waiting for a prospectus—possibly even on the basis of a mere advertisement that cannot itself lead to the conclusion of a legal contract to buy.

---

[38] Prospectus Directive Article 2(1)(d).
[39] See the Public Offers of Securities Regulations 1995, Regulation 5 of which says that a person is offering securities if, as principal '(a) he makes an offer which, if accepted, would give rise to a contract for the issue or sale of the securities by him or another person with whom he has made arrangements for the issue or sale of the securities; or (b) he invites a person to make such an offer'.

1.55 The counter argument is that such non-contractual communications can, and should, be regulated by other means than the prior publication of a prospectus. Hot-headed investors who will buy on the basis of an advertisement alone probably will not read a prospectus even if one is available. But even more pertinent is the fact that communications that amount to inducements will be subject to the advertisement regime in the Prospectus Directive itself; and, in many countries, there will be specific regimes that require such inducements to be vetted by an authorized financial intermediary before they are issued.[40]

1.56 The definition of 'offer of securities to the public' is unhelpful thanks to its obscurity. The fact that there has to be 'sufficient information' on the terms of the offer to enable the investor to decide to invest assists to an extent, in two ways. First, there has to be an 'offer' about which the information is communicated. Presumably this is a real offer in the contractual sense, that is in contemplation, even if not yet made. If so, a communication made before anyone has offered to anyone, or decided to do so in the future, will not be an offer to the public and will not require a prospectus (although it may well be subject to the advertisement regime under the Prospectus Directive). Secondly, it may be possible to argue successfully, if challenged, that there cannot be sufficient information for the purposes of the definition unless the key terms of the offer (such as the price) are included in the communication.

1.57 It is interesting, however, that something as fundamental to the Prospectus Directive as this definition should have resulted in such disagreement between member states that the definition had to be given sufficient width to accommodate a variety of interpretations. Some would say that this did not augur well for the speedy creation of a pan-EEA retail securities market.

1.58 Not all public offers require a prospectus. Article 3(2) of the Prospectus Directive contains exemptions, the more important of which are:

- offers to 'qualified investors'[41] (which include legal entities authorized or regulated to operate in the financial markets, supranational institutions, sovereigns, central banks and legal entities which satisfy any two of the following criteria: (a) at least 250 employees; (b) a 'total balance sheet' of over EUR 43,000,000; and (c) an annual turnover exceeding EUR 50,000,000);

---

[40] See, for example, the United Kingdom's Financial Promotion regime under Financial Services and Markets Act 2000 section 21.

[41] Prospectus Directive Article 3(2)(a). Note that the Commission's proposed amendments to the Prospectus Directive (COM (2009) 491 final) would, if implemented, amend this definition, defining qualified investors instead as persons or entities that are considered to be or treated on request as professional clients or eligible counterparties for the purposes of MiFID.

- offers relating to securities with a denomination of at least EUR 50,000[42] or which can only be acquired for a consideration of at least EUR 50,000[43] (or, in each case, the equivalent in another currency);
- shares issued in substitution for shares of the same class already issued, if the issuing of such new shares does not involve any increase in the issued capital;[44]
- securities offered in connection with a takeover by means of an exchange offer or a merger, provided that a document is available containing information which is regarded by the competent authority as being equivalent to that of the prospectus taking into account the requirements of Community legislation;[45]
- shares offered, allotted or to be allotted free of charge to existing shareholders, and dividends paid out in the form of shares of the same class as the shares in respect of which such dividends are paid, provided that a document is made available containing information on the number and nature of the shares and the reasons for and details of the offer;[46]
- securities offered, allotted or to be allotted to existing or former directors or employees by their employer which has securities already admitted to trading on a regulated market or by an affiliated undertaking, provided that a document is made available containing information on the number and nature of the securities and the reasons for and details of the offer;[47]
- offers to fewer than 100 natural or legal persons per member state other than qualified investors.[48]

This last exemption created the possibility of avoidance of the Prospectus Directive's requirements. It would be possible for an offeror to make an offer to three qualified investors, each of whom would, in turn, make an offer to 99 natural or legal persons, thereby avoiding the need to produce a prospectus, even though ultimately more than 100 non-qualified investors received the offer.

To prevent this, some rather complex wording was introduced as a final paragraph to Article 3(2), which operates as an override to all of the exemptions and reads as follows:

1.59

> However, any subsequent resale of securities which were previously the subject of one or more of the types of offer mentioned in this paragraph shall be regarded as a separate offer and the definition set out in Article 2(1)(d) shall apply for the purpose

---

[42] Prospectus Directive Article 3(2)(d).
[43] Prospectus Directive Article 3(2)(c).
[44] Prospectus Directive Article 4(1)(a).
[45] Prospectus Directive Article 4(1)(b) and (c).
[46] Prospectus Directive Article 4(1)(d).
[47] Prospectus Directive Article 4(1)(e). Note that the Commission's proposed amendments to the Prospectus Directive (COM (2009) 491 final) would, if implemented, delete the requirement that the securities be already admitted to a regulated market.
[48] Prospectus Directive Article 3(2)(b).

of deciding whether that resale is an offer of securities to the public. The placement of securities through financial intermediaries shall be subject to publication of a prospectus if none of the conditions (a) to (e) [of Article 3(2)] are met for the final placement.

1.60 The first sentence of this proviso is relatively clear. What it is saying is, essentially, that each level of offering needs to be looked at separately. If A offers to B who offers to C, then it is necessary to look at A's offer and B's offer separately to determine whether or not an exemption applies. So, it would be possible for A's offer to be exempt (for example if B were a qualified investor) but for B's offer not to be, so that B would have to produce a prospectus. In other words, the fact that A's offer was exempt does not save B from the requirements of the Directive.

1.61 The second sentence, however, is more difficult and has led to much debate in the market. As has been seen, it is probably intended as an anti-avoidance device. The exemption from the prospectus regime of offers to fewer than 100 non-qualified investors in each member state creates an opportunity for unscrupulous offerors to split their offer into different parcels, each allocated to a different financial intermediary, with the intention that each financial intermediary would then on-sell to fewer than 100 non-qualified investors. The result would be that no prospectus would be required, the financial intermediaries being qualified investors and the on-sales being within the 100-person exemption.

1.62 What the final sentence of Article 3(2) appears to be saying is that, in such a case, the offers made by (or, to use the wording of the Article, 'through') the financial intermediaries must be aggregated and attributed to the original offeror, for the purpose of determining whether the 100-person exemption is available. If, on the facts, the original offeror has offered to, say, three financial intermediaries each of whom has then on-sold to 99 non-qualified investors, then that original offeror will have to produce a prospectus (because the total offers to non-qualified investors through the financial intermediaries amount to 297).

1.63 This provision is a sensible and necessary anti-avoidance device. It has, however, introduced considerable confusion in the financial markets, because the banks that arrange bond and other types of issues regularly include in their sales lists institutions that are themselves qualified investors, but that have non-exempt investors as customers. Where an issue is intended to be made on an exempt-only basis, without a prospectus under the Prospectus Directive, issuers and financial intermediaries are naturally concerned to ensure that such institutions do not, by using the 100-person exemption to offer to some of their customers, inadvertently put them in breach of the prospectus regime.

1.64 To avoid this possible risk, it is common practice in the international securities markets for issuers to impose contractual restrictions on the financial intermediaries who distribute the issue for them which require, among other things, that the financial intermediaries must not do anything that would result in the issuer having to produce a prospectus. This means, in practice, that the financial intermediaries must take care when offering the securities to others. It would, for example, be wrong for a financial intermediary, having entered into that contractual arrangement, to offer to several private banks without notifying them that there is no prospectus for the issue and that, therefore, they should not themselves offer to non-exempt persons. Indeed, if the private bank's customer base is largely non-exempt persons, it would be unwise for the financial intermediary to make any offer to it without further enquiry (for example as to discretionary management powers).

In a few cases, issuers have sought to impose a much stricter restriction on the   **1.65** financial intermediaries, or underwriters, who are appointed to distribute their issues. One version of this requires the underwriters to indemnify the issuer against the consequences of breach of the prospectus regime because of the actions of any person to whom they offer. Another requires the underwriters to pass on the contractual restriction imposed on them by the issuer, by making it a term of the offers made by them.

Each of these approaches is probably excessive. The last sentence of Article 3(2)   **1.66** only applies to 'the placement of securities through a financial intermediary'. 'Placement' and 'through' both necessarily imply an intention or active participation on the part of the original offeror. So, for example, if the issuer tells the underwriters to on-sell to private banks, so that non-exempt investors can receive an offer, or if it is reckless as to whether this happens, then the issuer may be said to have 'placed through'. However, it is difficult to see how an issuer can be accused of 'placing through' if it has imposed a contractual restriction on the underwriters requiring them not to do anything that would require the production of a prospectus. Such a restriction clearly negates any intention to 'place through'.

1.3.1.3.2 Admission to a regulated market   The second trigger for the produc-   **1.67** tion of a prospectus is the admission of securities to an EEA regulated market.[49] Again, there are exemptions, the more important of which are:

- shares representing, over a period of 12 months, less than 10 per cent of the number of shares of the same class already admitted to trading on the same regulated market;[50]
- shares issued in substitution for shares of the same class already admitted to trading on the same regulated market, if the issuing of such shares does not involve any increase in the issued capital;[51]

---

[49] Prospectus Directive Article 3(3).
[50] Prospectus Directive Article 4(2)(a).
[51] Prospectus Directive Article 4(2)(b).

- securities offered in connection with a takeover by means of an exchange offer or a merger, provided that a document is available containing information which is regarded by the competent authority as being equivalent to that of the prospectus, taking into account the requirements of Community legislation;[52]
- shares offered, allotted or to be allotted free of charge to existing shareholders, and dividends paid out in the form of shares of the same class as the shares in respect of which such dividends are paid, provided that the said shares are of the same class as the shares already admitted to trading on the same regulated market and that a document is made available containing information on the number and nature of the shares and the reasons for and details of the offer;[53]
- securities offered, allotted or to be allotted to existing or former directors or employees by their employer or an affiliated undertaking, provided that the said securities are of the same class as the securities already admitted to trading on the same regulated market and that a document is made available containing information on the number and nature of the securities and the reasons for and detail of the offer;[54]
- shares resulting from the conversion or exchange of other securities or from the exercise of the rights conferred by other securities, provided that the said shares are of the same class as the shares already admitted to trading on the same regulated market;[55]
- securities already admitted to trading on another regulated market, provided certain conditions are satisfied (as to length of admission, the original admission having been made on the basis of a document complying with Community legislation and the production of a summary).[56]

1.68 Most of these exemptions are self-explanatory and sensible. For example, there is no point in going to the expense of producing a prospectus for the admission of a limited number of shares, or for the swapping of one share for a similar share—particularly given the information that will have been supplied to the market under disclosure requirements of the Market Abuse Directive and TOD. It is equally pointless to require the production of a prospectus when there is another document that gives essentially the same information—such as a takeover or merger offer document. Free shares, or dividends in the form of shares, should also logically avoid the prospectus requirement, because the purpose of the disclosure is to protect through the provision of information—and someone who gets something for nothing has nothing to lose by it, and therefore needs no protection.

---

[52] Prospectus Directive Article 4(2)(c) and (d).
[53] Prospectus Directive Article 4(2)(e).
[54] Prospectus Directive Article 4(2)(f).
[55] Prospectus Directive Article 4(2)(g).
[56] Prospectus Directive Article 4(2)(h).

Convertible bonds can be an important source of funding for some companies—   **1.69**
not least for financial institutions that require regulatory capital. It would be
impractical to require the production of a prospectus for admission of the shares
issued on conversion, because conversion takes place over a period of time, and at
different times during that period. A requirement for a prospectus on admission
of the shares would therefore actually require multiple prospectuses and would
make such issues too costly to be feasible. Where the shares into which the bond
converts are of the same class as those already admitted to the market, there will
have been a prospectus for the original admission of those shares; and regular
updating of that information will have been provided under the disclosure regimes
imposed by the Market Abuse Directive and TOD. It therefore makes good sense
to allow admission of the shares resulting from conversion of the bond without
production of any further prospectus.

1.3.1.4 The content and format of a prospectus

1.3.1.4.1 Basic content requirement   Once the requirement to produce a pro-   **1.70**
spectus has been established, the next logical question to ask is what should go
into it. This question is answered at several levels. The Prospectus Directive itself
establishes a very broad, generic disclosure standard, by saying that:

> the prospectus shall contain all information which, according to the particular
> nature of the issuer and of the securities offered to the public or admitted to trading
> on a regulated market, is necessary to enable investors to make an informed assess-
> ment of the assets and liabilities, financial position, profit and losses, and prospects
> of the issuer and of any guarantor, and of the rights attaching to such securities.
> This information shall be presented in an easily analysable and comprehensible
> form.[57]

1.3.1.4.2 Detailed content requirements   This generic disclosure standard is   **1.71**
supplemented by detailed disclosure lists, which are contained in the Prospectus
Directive Regulation. The lists fall into three broad categories.

The first relates to the type of issue. The most stringent are those relating to equity   **1.72**
issues, with varying degrees of reduced disclosure for non-equity depending on
whether it is retail or wholesale. For this purpose, the Prospectus Directive makes
a distinction between equity and non-equity[58] and between retail and wholesale,[59]
based in the latter case on the denomination or minimum consideration payable,
setting the threshold at EUR 50,000 (or the equivalent in another currency).
The rationale for reduced detailed disclosure requirements for debt, as opposed

---

[57] Prospectus Directive Article 5(1).
[58] Prospectus Directive Article 7(2)(a).
[59] Prospectus Directive Article 7(2)(b), which makes the important point that 'the information
required in a prospectus shall be appropriate from the point of view of the investors concerned'.

to equity, is presumably that the former carries fewer risks than the latter and requires a different approach from the potential investor—the main question when investing in debt is whether the issuer will be able to pay; whereas an investment in shares will require a deeper evaluation, involving an assessment of the issuer's growth potential and ability to produce profits and pay dividends. As for the distinction between wholesale and retail, Recital 16 of the Prospectus Directive provides an eloquent explanation for differential disclosure requirements, saying:

> One of the objectives of this Directive is to protect investors. It is therefore appropriate to take account of the different requirements for protection of the various categories of investors and their level of expertise.

1.73   The second category of detailed disclosure lists relates to particular types of issuer. So, for example, there are disclosure requirements for banks (which, being regulated entities, do not have to make as much disclosure as non-regulated issuers) and for closed-ended collective investment schemes. Had time permitted, there would also have been disclosure lists for property, mineral, investment, scientific research-based companies, and shipping companies.[60]

1.74   The third category of disclosure lists comprises additional 'building blocks' to be added to the other lists, as appropriate. Examples include lists for pro-forma financial information (for example, where two companies have merged and it is desired to show their individual historic financial results on a combined basis);[61] for information on a guarantor;[62] and for additional information where the security subject to the prospectus is linked to a share of an entity in the same group as the issuer.[63]

1.75   The detailed disclosure requirements are wide ranging. They are, however, to be read as being subject to the generic disclosure requirement in Article 5 of the Prospectus Directive (the Prospectus Directive Regulation being, naturally, subordinate to the Directive itself). Accordingly, the disclosure duty is not discharged simply by copying out the items in the relevant Annex to the Prospectus Directive Regulation and filling in the relevant detail. If, in the circumstances of the particular issuer or securities being issued, there are facts that are not in the Prospectus Directive Regulation lists but are necessary to enable an investor to make an informed investment decision, those facts must be included in the prospectus.

1.76   The detailed requirements are also expressly acknowledged not to be exhaustive. Article 23(3) recognizes the dynamism of the capital markets by saying that,

---

[60] Prospectus Directive Regulation Article 23 and Annex XIX.
[61] Prospectus Directive Regulation Annex II.
[62] Prospectus Directive Regulation Annex VI.
[63] Prospectus Directive Regulation Annex XIV.

where a prospectus relates to a new type of security that is not provided for by the Annexes in the Regulation, the home state competent authority is to decide, in consultation with the issuer, what information concerning the securities is to be included in the prospectus. The competent authority has to notify the EU Commission when these circumstances occur.

1.3.1.4.3 Omission of information and derogations   Article 8(1) of the Prospectus Directive contains a useful provision that permits the omission of the final offer price and amount of securities to be offered. This facilitates the making of a public offer, using an approved prospectus, where the intention is to determine the level of market interest and the price at which the market will be willing to buy the issue. Without this permissive Article, such offers would be impossible (because they could not be made without a prospectus, and the prospectus would have to include the price and amount of the issue, these being information 'necessary to enable investors to make an informed assessment' of the issue within the scope of Article 5 of the Prospectus Directive). However, omission of price and amount is only permitted if the prospectus specifies either (a) the criteria and conditions in accordance with which these elements will be determined (or, for the price, a maximum price); or (b) that acceptances of the offer of securities may be withdrawn within not less than two working days after the final offer price and amount have been filed with the home state competent authority.

1.77

Once determined, the final offer price and amount of the issue must be filed with the home state competent authority.

Both the Prospectus Directive and its Regulation give the home state competent authority the power to grant derogations from the disclosure requirements. Article 8(2) of the Prospectus Directive gives this power where the competent authority considers that disclosure would be contrary to public interest or that disclosure would be seriously detrimental to the issuer (provided the omission would not be likely to mislead the public in their investment decision) or that the information is of minor importance only. Article 8(3) gives further derogation powers, but only for exceptional use, where certain information is inappropriate to the issuer's sphere of activity or its legal form or to the securities to which the prospectus relates.

1.78

The Prospectus Directive Regulation permits omission of information otherwise required by its detailed Annexes where that information is not pertinent to the issuer or to the offer of securities to which the prospectus relates.[64] While this is a helpful provision, it is perhaps an obvious qualification, given the requirement in Article 5 of the Prospectus Directive that a prospectus should be easily analysable

1.79

---

[64] Prospectus Directive Regulation Article 23(4).

and comprehensible (which it will not be if it includes information that is not pertinent).

1.80 **1.3.1.4.4 Limitations on competent authorities** Competent authorities do not have an entirely free hand in requiring the inclusion of information in a prospectus. Article 3 of the Prospectus Directive Regulation says that 'a competent authority shall not request that a prospectus contain information items which are not included in Annexes I to XVII'. At first sight, this appears to be a significant constraint. However, it needs to be reconciled with the role of the competent authority in giving its approval of a prospectus, which must include some kind of supervisory element designed to ensure compliance with the generic disclosure requirement under Article 5 of the Prospectus Directive. Article 3 of the Prospectus Directive Regulation needs to be read in the light of this and therefore probably has a more restricted meaning, to the effect that the competent authority cannot require any information that is not included in the Annexes to the Regulation where that additional information would not be necessary to enable investors to take an informed investment decision. So, for example, Article 3 of the Prospectus Directive Regulation would prevent a competent authority from asking for the information required by the Regulation's Annexes to be given in a different form; but it would not prevent it from requiring disclosure of something that is material to the investor's decision, but is not referred to in the Annexes.

1.81 **1.3.1.4.5 Incorporation by reference** The Prospectus Directive helpfully recognizes that replication within a prospectus of the full text of information that has already been provided elsewhere only wastes paper and time. Article 11 of the Prospectus Directive permits certain documents (or parts of documents) to be incorporated into a prospectus simply by inclusion of a cross-reference to them. The documents that may be incorporated by reference include documents that have been approved or filed under the Prospectus Directive itself (so that it is possible to incorporate one prospectus within another). It is also possible to incorporate documents that have been published in the preceding 12 months in a member state or in third countries in compliance with laws or rules dealing with the regulation of securities, issuers of securities and securities markets. This means that, for example, filings made with the US Securities and Exchange Commission can be incorporated into an EEA prospectus, provided they have been included in a list that has been filed with the home state competent authority and the document itself has been filed with that competent authority.

1.82 Article 11 also cross-refers to Directive 2001/34/EC which has been largely replaced by the TOD. It is to be hoped that, in due course, these references will be amended to refer instead to regulated information under the TOD.[65]

---

[65] This will be achieved if the Commission's proposals (COM (2009) 491 final) are adopted.

1.3.1.4.6 Different formats

1.3.1.4.6.1 (a) The multi-part prospectus   The Prospectus Directive permits **1.83**
several alternative formats for a prospectus. The first consists of a multi-part document. There are a number of separate elements to this—information relating to
the issuer; and information relating to the securities being admitted or offered.
This is an important point to grasp, because it helps to make sense of the different
detailed disclosure requirements that amplify Article 5 of the Prospectus Directive
under the Prospectus Directive Regulation, which are structured in a way that
corresponds to these separate sections of the multi-part prospectus.

A multi-part prospectus will consist of a number of separate documents,[66] namely   **1.84**
a registration document, a securities note and (save where the securities are high
denomination non-equity[67]) a summary. The registration document may only
contain the information required concerning the issuer.[68] The securities note,
as its name suggests, may only contain information concerning the securities
that are being admitted or offered,[69] although it may contain information on
the issuer where that information has changed since the registration document
was produced.[70] The idea here is that the information relating to the issuer in
the registration document can be produced and kept up to date 'on the shelf' and
then completed as a prospectus by the addition of a securities note when market
conditions make an issue desirable. This is, in theory, a fast track procedure
because, clearly, the production of a securities note alone at the time of issue is
much less time consuming than the production of a full description of the issuer
as well.

The summary is an interesting concept. Article 5(2) of the Prospectus Directive   **1.85**
says that:

> The summary shall, in a brief manner and in non-technical language, convey the
> essential characteristics and risks associated with the issuer, any guarantor and the
> securities, in the language in which the prospectus was originally drawn up.

This needs to be read in conjunction with recital 21 to the Prospectus Directive,
which says that:

> Information is a key factor in investor protection; a summary conveying the essential
> characteristics of, and risks associated with, the issuer, any guarantor and the securi-
> ties should be included in the prospectus. To ensure easy access to this information,
> the summary should be written in non-technical language and normally should

---

[66] Prospectus Directive Article 5(3).
[67] See final sentence of Prospectus Directive Article 5(2).
[68] Prospectus Directive Article 5(3).
[69] Prospectus Directive Article 5(3).
[70] Prospectus Directive Article 12 (2).

not exceed 2,500 words in the language in which the prospectus was originally drawn up.

1.86　But, the intelligent reader will ask, why have a summary at all? Shouldn't the investor (however simple-minded) read the whole prospectus rather than a summary which, by definition, will not contain all the information 'necessary to enable investors to make an informed assessment', particularly where that information is presented (as it must be) in a form that is easy to analyse and comprehensible (to repeat the words of Article 5)? And if the investor cannot (or will not) read the whole prospectus, will he not be protected by the interposition of a financial intermediary (who can and should read and understand it), which is required for non-professional investors under the MiFID?

1.87　Many of these questions are difficult to answer. There is a view that, despite all the logical arguments advanced against the summary requirement above, investors still need something short—a 'speed read'—to point them in the right direction. But perhaps the real explanation for the existence of the summary is to be found in the language regime introduced by the Prospectus Directive. One of the main impediments to the development of a pan-EEA retail securities market under the previous EU Directives[71] was the fact that, to be valid for use outside the state in which it had originally been approved, the prospectus had to be translated. So, if a public offer was to be made in five EEA states, five translations of a document tens (or even hundreds) of pages long would have to be produced, at great expense of time and money. The Prospectus Directive removes this barrier, by saying that a prospectus is valid in every member state provided it is in a language that is 'customary in sphere of international finance'.[72] However, it was considered to be unacceptable to have a prospectus for a retail offer in a country that is, in its entirety, in a language that is not spoken in that country; and the summary was therefore introduced—and each state in which a public offer is to be made is permitted to require that the summary (and the summary alone) be translated into its national language.[73]

1.88　Summaries, when viewed from the perspective of potential liability, are dangerous things. A summary of 2,500 words cannot, however skilfully constructed, convey the same thing as a document of several hundred pages; and (particularly with hindsight) the person producing the summary will be exposed to litigation at the suit of an investor who alleges he has lost money because the summary omitted some information that was important to his investment decision. To avoid this result, the Prospectus Directive provides in Article 6(2) that there is to be no

---

[71] POD and CARD—see 1.1 above.
[72] Prospectus Directive Article 19(2).
[73] Prospectus Directive Article 19(2) final sentence.

civil liability[74] for the person responsible for the prospectus unless the summary is misleading, inaccurate or inconsistent when read together with the other parts of the prospectus. The summary has to contain various notices, warning the reader about the nature of the summary, the possible costs of having it translated for use in legal proceedings and the limitation of liability referred to above.[75]

The Commission has proposed various amendments to the summary,[76] notably that it should include 'key information in order to enable investors to take informed investment decisions and to compare securities with other investment products'. The original proposals also reversed the liability regime that applies to this part of the summary, so that the person responsible for the summary was liable if it did not contain these new elements, even if they are included in the rest of the prospectus. This proposal presented significant difficulties. For example:

- The amendment requires the summary to meet the same standard as the pro-spectus itself (that is, the communication of information needed to enable an investment decision to be taken). Unless the prospectus becomes the summary, therefore, it is not clear how disclosure that is some hundreds of pages can be reduced to anything much shorter and still meet the same standard.
- It seems unreasonable to impose a very broad disclosure standard, with liability if the standard is not met within the summary itself, but at the same time to curtail the ability of the person preparing the summary to discharge his duty, by imposing a limit on the number of words and pages that can be used (by requiring that the summary be 'brief');
- The amendment removes the 2,500 word limit for the summary (while retain-ing the requirement that it should be 'brief'). This, coupled with the new extensive disclosure standard and the stand-alone liability regime, will result in much longer summaries. Summaries can be required by a host member state to be translated into its local language. Translation takes time and costs money. The result of the prosposal therefore may well be that issuers avoid pan-EEA non-exempt offerings, just as they did (for the same reason) under the previous public offer regime, referred to in the Introduction.
- The increased liability may well lead to an increase in advisory fees, thus increas-ing the cost of capital.
- The introduction of a stand-alone, brief summary giving all the key information necessary for an investment decision, to which liability attaches independently of the full prospectus, may actually undermine investor protection. Under the

---

[74] But note that this does not affect criminal liability—for example, where it can be proved beyond reasonable doubt that the information was deliberately omitted, because the investor would not buy if it were included.

[75] Prospectus Directive Article 5(2).

[76] See COM (2009) 491 final.

current regime, anyone offering securities to the retail investor (and sometimes to professional investors too) will have to comply with the MiFID regime, which is discussed in more detail later in this Section. Such offerors should understand the circumstances, experience and level of understanding of their clients and should have a full understanding of the products that they offer to them, so that they can determine whether they are suitable for the investor and, if they are, so that they can explain the products and the risks attached to them to the client. This understanding should be developed from a careful reading of the whole prospectus, not just the summary. But what financial intermediary will read a longer document when a shorter one is required to give the same information—particularly when they may have legal recourse to the person who prepared the summary if it does not contain all the key information?

• Competent authorities may also find the proposal problematic. Although it is not clear what they must do before they approve a prospectus, it is difficult to see how they can avoid involvement in making sure that the summary does, indeed, contain the key information.

• Finally, the requirement to provide key information 'to enable investors to compare the securities with other investment products' is too vague to be practical. Does it require comparison of a bond with a share? Or a derivative-linked security with a mortgage-backed security? Or a bond issued by Company A with one issued by Company B?

For these, and other, reasons it is greatly to be hoped that these proposals will be reconsidered and either dropped or further amended to avoid the problems outlined above.

1.89 *1.3.1.4.6.2 (b) The single document prospectus*   The second permitted format is a single document[77] containing all of the required elements—information on the issuer and the securities plus (if required) the summary. This is self-explanatory.

1.90 *1.3.1.4.6.3 (c) The base prospectus*   The third and final format for a prospectus, which is only available for non-equity securities, is another multi-document structure, consisting of a base prospectus (containing the required information concerning the issuer together with a description of the various different securities that may be issued from time to time—plus, if required, the summary) and final terms, which are produced at the time of an issue made under the base prospectus.[78] The final terms provide, essentially, the commercial terms of the particular securities being issued, together with an indication of which provisions relating to the securities contained in the base prospectus apply to the issue. In essence, therefore, the detailed contractual terms of all possible securities that might be issued under

---

[77] Prospectus Directive Article 5(2).
[78] Prospectus Directive Article 5(4).

the base prospectus are set out in the base prospectus; and the final terms fill in information, such as the interest rate or issue price, and act as a 'menu picker', telling the reader which detailed terms from the base prospectus apply.

The base prospectus format is extremely important in the debt and structured **1.91** products markets, because it provides frequent issuers with a very fast mechanism for accessing the markets. All the issuer needs to produce at the time of issue (unless there are material changes in the circumstances of the issuer) is the final terms, which are short and do not require approval by any competent authority.[79] Indeed, the Prospectus Directive is clear that the prospectus is the base prospectus alone[80] and that final terms merely complete this prospectus, without forming part of it.

Final terms may only contain information that is required for a securities note, in **1.92** the first, multi-part format.[81] To facilitate the reader's understanding, final terms must contain a clear and prominent statement 'indicating that the full information on the issuer and on the offer is only available on the basis of the combination of base prospectus and final terms and where the base prospectus is available'.[82] Where final terms are to be produced separately from the base prospectus (that is, on issuance under the offering programme) the base prospectus must indicate what information will be included in the final terms and their method of publication.[83] This is achieved in practice by the inclusion of proforma final terms in the base prospectus.[84]

The base prospectus format has produced much discussion, and a certain amount **1.93** of confusion, in the markets, for several reasons.

The first difficulty arises from the fact that, as will be seen, an issuer must issue and **1.94** publish a supplement containing significant new factors that arise between the publication of the prospectus and the admission to trading or the closing of the offer.[85] This provision is expressly applied in the context of the base prospectus format.[86] The problem is that, in the context of an offering programme, there is

---

[79] Prospectus Directive Recital 21.
[80] Prospectus Directive Article 2(1)(r).
[81] PD Regulation Article 22(4).
[82] Prospectus Directive Regulation Article 26(4).
[83] Prospectus Directive Regulation Article 22(5).
[84] The International Capital Market Association has produced a standard form for final terms that is used in most international Programmes —see http://www.icma-group.org.
[85] Prospectus Directive Article 16(1).
[86] Prospectus Directive Article 5(4) says in its penultimate paragraph that 'the information given in the base prospectus shall be supplemented, if necessary, in accordance with Article 16, with updated information on the issuer and on the securities to be offered to the public or to be admitted to trading on a regulated market'. A similar provision is to be found in Prospectus Directive Regulation Article 22(7).

already a document that updates the information in the base prospectus—the final terms—and it appears that this document may contain significant information. For example, Article 22(2) of the Prospectus Directive Regulation allows the omission from the base prospectus of information which is not known when the base prospectus is approved and which can only be determined at the time of the individual issues under the programme. What can be omitted from the base prospectus, the argument goes, can be included in the final terms. Clearly, at the time the base prospectus is approved, there is a great deal about possible future issues under the programme that is unknown—including the currency and other commercial terms, such as the interest and redemption amounts. This has led some to believe that the Prospectus Directive allows the inclusion in final terms of *any* commercial information about issues under a programme—including lengthy algebraic calculations for the determination of income or principal payments—however 'significant' those terms may be for the purposes of Article 16(1) of the Prospectus Directive.

1.95   It is difficult (and dangerous) to be too absolute about whether final terms can be used or whether a supplement is required. Much will depend on circumstances, which will vary greatly from issue to issue. However, the question is important given that the two types of updating document—supplements and final terms— are different in one very important respect; namely that supplements require prior approval by the home member state competent authority but final terms do not. So, an incorrect decision leading to the use of final terms where a supplement should have been produced will result in a breach of the prospectus requirement (which is, in some countries, a criminal offence).

1.96   Accordingly, some form of sensible generic test to determine when final terms can be used, and when they cannot, is needed. There is little overt assistance given by the Prospectus Directive or its Regulation; but it seems logical to focus on the trigger in Article 16(1) of the Prospectus Directive, which uses the term 'significant new factor'. What then is a 'significant new factor'? One practical approach would be to link this question to the risk factors and (where the programme contemplates issues in denominations below EUR 50,000 or its equivalent in another currency) the summary contained in the base prospectus. Risk factors must be included in a prospectus[87] and may, so far as they relate to the securities, be included in final terms. They are factors that are material to the securities admitted to trading in order to assess the market risk associated with those securities. The summary must convey 'the essential characteristics and risks associated with ... the securities'.[88] It may be sensible to interpret 'significant'

---

[87]   See Prospectus Directive Regulation Annex XII paragraph 2 and Annex IV paragraph 2.
[88]   Prospectus Directive Article 5(2).

under Article 16 of the Prospectus Directive in the light of these elements. A new element in the terms of the securities being issued is 'significant' if it is material to assess the market risk of those securities or is an essential characteristic or risk associated with those securities. In other words, if the new element would require an amendment to the risk factors or summary in the base prospectus, then a supplement should be produced; if not, then final terms may be used.

It must be acknowledged, however, that there are varying practices and interpretations in the various markets. **1.97**

Another problem with the Prospectus Directive's base prospectus format is that **1.98** it does not permit more than a single summary.[89] However, most offering programmes will contemplate the issue of a considerable range of different securities, some of them having a relatively complex, derivative or index-linked nature. Some programmes also include, within the same base prospectus, a number of possible issuers from the same group, each of which may use the single programme to make issues from time to time. Each of these factors make the requirement for a single summary irksome. A summary should be short and meaningful (conveying the 'essential characteristics and risks associated with the issuer, any guarantor and the securities'). They cannot normally exceed 2,500 words. Inevitably, if a programme includes a large number of different types of securities and a handful of issuers, not much can be said about any of them given the constraint on the number of words that can be used. The logical conclusion is that such programmes should be separated into a number of different programmes—so that meaningful summaries and risk factors can be included where, for example, each programme has only one issuer and provides only for three or four products. But this is not an efficient or cost effective approach—and it seems odd that long established market practices should be altered purely to comply with a somewhat artificial word limit. Much better, perhaps, to amend the summary requirement for programmes to permit separate summaries—perhaps one per issuer under the programme and, for complex securities, one per type of security. Such an approach would also achieve better investor protection, because the investor would receive a set of risk factors and a summary that are tailored specifically to what he is buying, rather than a composite document including risks and summaries of something that does not apply to his investment.

---

[89] Prospectus Directive Article 5(2) requires the inclusion of 'a' summary and both the Prospectus Directive and the Prospectus Directive Regulation refer throughout to the summary in the singular. Finally, Prospectus Directive Regulation Article 26(6) makes it clear that, where a programme provides for the issue of several different types of security the person drawing up the prospectus 'shall include a single summary in the base prospectus for all securities'.

1.3.1.5 *Approval of the prospectus*

1.99 **1.3.1.5.1 Approval**   Once produced, several further things have to happen to a prospectus before it is valid for admission of securities or a public offer. The first of these involves approval of the prospectus by a competent authority.[90] Interestingly, the Directive does not say what the competent authority has to do before it gives this approval, nor indeed what the purpose of the approval is. However, much can be inferred from the powers given to the competent authority to question the contents of the prospectus and to carry out various activities. So, for example, the competent authority is given time limits within which it must grant or refuse approval,[91] ranging from 20 working days for a first time issuer to 10 working days for existing issuers. However, the Prospectus Directive provides that if

> the competent authority finds, on reasonable grounds, that the documents submitted to it are incomplete or that supplementary information is needed, the time limits referred to in paragraphs 2 and 3 [of Article 13] shall apply only from the date on which such information is provided.[92]

1.100 Given that Article 5 of the Prospectus Directive requires that the prospectus should contain all information about the issuer that an investor needs to take its investment decision, any competent authority making such a finding must, presumably, have concluded that the prospectus did not contain such information. This raises interesting questions about how far a competent authority is required to go in checking the information in the draft prospectus that it has before it. Is it simply checking that the various detailed disclosure items required by the Prospectus Directive Regulation are addressed? Or is it applying, in its review of the prospectus, knowledge of the issuer it may be able to obtain from public sources (such as press reports and public documents)? If so, how far does it have to go in tracking down these public sources? Is it enough just to read press reports and public filings with stock exchanges? If so, how far back in time should this review go? Where the issuer is a regulated entity, such as a bank, and the competent authority is its regulator, must the competent authority apply the very considerable information it may have been given by the issuer, on a confidential basis, in its review? Or does the competent authority have to carry out due diligence—to visit and question the issuer—before approving the prospectus? (This last possibility, however outlandish it may seem, may have been contemplated by some, because competent authorities are empowered to carry out on-site inspections.)[93]

---

[90] Prospectus Directive Article 13(1).
[91] Prospectus Directive Article 13(2) and (3).
[92] Prospectus Directive Article 13(4).
[93] Prospectus Directive Article 21(4)(d).

Other powers given to the competent authority—including the power to require the inclusion of supplementary information in a prospectus and to require issuers, auditors and offerors to provide information[94]—indicate that the review by the competent authority prior to giving its approval is more than a bureaucratic 'box-ticking' exercise. It is probably intended that the competent authority should act as a gatekeeper to the market, using such knowledge as it may have or may be able reasonably to obtain about the issuer to ensure that the issuer or offeror meet their disclosure obligations and that it should apply such knowledge in assessing whether the prospectus does indeed contain that information, if it is important to the investment decision. There may also be a role for the competent authority in checking that the summary (if there is one) and the risk factors meet the requirements of the Directive. If there is such a duty in relation to risk factors, though, it may cause problems when applied to the terms of the securities, rather than simply the disclosure on the issuer. It is doubtful whether many competent authorities will wish (or even be able) to analyse the sometimes complex algebra that is often included in redemption and interest calculations for such securities, in order to be able to assess whether the risks inherent in the calculations are adequately disclosed in the risk factors. **1.101**

1.3.1.5.2 Which competent authority?   It is clearly impractical to have a prospectus approved more than once, even where the prospectus is to be used for admission to trading or a public offer in several member states—the time and cost implications would prevent the development of a cross border market. To resolve this difficulty, the Prospectus Directive contains provisions that identify the appropriate, single, competent authority whose approval is required; and that make that approval valid, once obtained, in every other member state without further approval. **1.102**

The mechanism for choosing the appropriate competent authority for approval of the prospectus proved to be one of the more politically sensitive elements in the negotiation of the Prospectus Directive. In theory, it should not matter which member state's competent authority gives the approval, because they all operate under the same, maximum harmonization, regime. However, some member states were anxious not to lose control over issuers domiciled in their jurisdictions, so the provisions for determining the appropriate competent authority are somewhat complex. **1.103**

Issuers from within the EEA have a choice, for certain types of issue, between the member state where they have their registered office and those member states where the securities to which the prospectus relates are to be admitted to a regulated market or offered to the public. This choice is limited, however, to prospectuses **1.104**

---

[94] Prospectus Directive Article 21(3).

relating to non-equity securities having a denomination of at least EUR 1,000 (or its equivalent in another currency), cash settled warrants and exchangeable securities (including physically settled warrants), where the securities for which they can be exchanged are not those of the issuer or any member of the issuer's group.[95] For all other securities (broadly equity and convertible securities), EEA issuers have no choice of competent authority for prospectus approval, but must use the authority of the state in which they have their registered office.[96]

1.105 Issuers from outside the EEA (referred to in the Prospectus Directive as 'third country issuers') have the same choice as EEA issuers for non-equity securities having a denomination of at least EUR 1,000 (or its equivalent in another currency) and exchangeable securities. For everything else, the home member state for prospectus approval purposes will be the state in which they intended to make their first public offer or their first admission to trading on a regulated market after 31 December 2005.[97]

1.106 **1.3.1.5.3 Community scope of approval** One of the main purposes behind the Prospectus Directive, it should be remembered, was the creation of an efficient, cross-border, securities market within the EEA. One of the main impediments to the development of such a market under previous legislative regimes had been the fact that, when a prospectus that had been approved in one jurisdiction (the 'home state') was taken to another country (the 'host state') to be used for admission to the markets or for a public offer in that host state, the authorities in the host state had the power to require additional disclosure (for example, concerning the host country's tax regime). This added very considerably to cost and to the time required to finalize the capital raising, and therefore acted as an impediment to cross-border listings and public offers.

1.107 The Prospectus Directive has made great improvements by removing such barriers,[98] by providing that a prospectus approved by the home state competent authority shall be valid for a public offer or admission of securities in any host

---

[95] Prospectus Directive Article 2(1)(m)(ii).

[96] Prospectus Directive Article 2(1)(m)(i). Note that the Commission's proposal to amend the Prospectus Directive (COM (2009) 491 final) would, if implemented, remove the distinction based on denomination, so that all non-equity issues have a choice between the competent authorities in the country of admission and the country of the public offer.

[97] Prospectus Directive Article 2(1)(m)(iii). There is a saving provision allowing third country issuers to elect a different state where the public offer that triggered the original choice was made by an offeror that was not the issuer.

[98] Although significant barriers still remain in a number of member states, ranging from requirements for inclusion in official bulletins of notices stating where the prospectus can be obtained, to rules requiring the translation of the constitutional documents of the issuer. There are also consumer protection laws, which lie outside the scope of the Prospectus Directive, that may require translation of parts of the prospectus—for example, the terms of the securities—because, without such translation, the contract for sale of the securities to retail investors may not be enforceable.

state, provided the host state competent authority is notified of the approval.[99] Indeed, the Prospectus Directive goes further and actually *forbids* the host state competent authority from undertaking any approval or administrative procedures relating to a prospectus.[100] The most that a host state competent authority is able to do, if it believes that significant factors have been omitted from the prospectus or that the prospectus contains material mistakes or inaccuracies, is to draw them to the attention of the home state competent authority.[101]

1.108 The Prospectus Directive contains detailed provisions for the notification of a prospectus to a host state competent authority.[102] Notification can only be made at the request of the issuer or the person responsible for the prospectus (such as an offeror). It has to be made by the home state competent authority within three working days of that request.[103] The notification takes the form of a certificate of approval, confirming that the prospectus has been drawn up in accordance with the Prospectus Directive and attaching a copy of the prospectus.

1.3.1.6 *Responsibility*

1.109 As the purpose of a prospectus is 'to ensure investor protection and market efficiency',[104] it is very important that it should be reliable. The Prospectus Directive therefore requires member states to identify those who are responsible for the information in the prospectus, that they be clearly identified in the prospectus by names and functions and that they declare within the prospectus that, to the best of their knowledge, the information is in accordance with the facts and the prospectus contains no omission likely to affect its import.[105]

1.110 Identification of responsible persons is, however, of little benefit unless sanctions are imposed on them should they fail to discharge their duties. The Prospectus Directive does not attempt to impose a harmonized liability regime in this area. Instead, it requires that member states should 'ensure that their laws, regulation and administrative provisions on civil liability apply to those persons responsible for the information given in a prospectus'.[106] This appears to be an extremely wide-ranging requirement, although it is probably sufficient if a member state applies some, though not all, of its civil liability regime by way of enforcing the prospectus regime (most states will, of course, have an extensive civil liability

---

[99] Prospectus Directive Article 17(1).
[100] Prospectus Directive Article 17(1) last sentence.
[101] Prospectus Directive Article 17(2).
[102] Prospectus Directive Article 18(1).
[103] This is reduced to one working day, if the original request was accompanied by a draft of the prospectus—see Prospectus Directive Article 18(1).
[104] Prospectus Directive Recital (10).
[105] Prospectus Directive Article 6(1).
[106] Prospectus Directive Article 6(2).

regime covering numerous areas of human activity, not all of which will be appropriate in the context of the Prospectus Directive).

1.111　The result is that Europe continues to suffer from a mosaic of differing liability regimes. This is probably inevitable at this stage in the development of the European Union; but it does present an impediment to the development of a true pan-EEA securities market. Issuers and financial intermediaries offering securities on a cross-border basis face the possibility of multi-jurisdictional litigation if the prospectus contains errors (or is alleged to do so). Worse, the result of that litigation may well differ according to where the action is brought. Investors in one country may succeed in their claims while investors in others may not. The costs involved in defending such multiple claims will often be considerable and will deplete the issuer's financial resources, while diverting large amounts of management time away from running the business.

1.112　The answer to this problem lies, it is suggested, in the development of a sensible conflicts of laws regime relating to prospectus liability. Two areas need to be addressed— the determination of a single system of law and the choice of a single jurisdiction to hear the claim. It would be logical that the law and jurisdiction should fix on the same member state. The question is, which one should that be. A sensible choice might be the home member state for the purpose of the approval of the prospectus (not least because the competent authority in that home member state might itself be taking administrative proceedings against the issuer of the allegedly false prospectus).[107]

1.3.1.7 Publication of the prospectus

1.113　By this stage in the proceedings, the issuer or offeror will have a prospectus that makes the required disclosure and has been properly approved by the appropriate competent authority. But it is important to remember the purpose of the Prospectus Directive, which is to provide investor protection by ensuring that investors take investment decisions in full knowledge of the facts.[108] Well-informed investors will have confidence in the markets, according to Recital 18 to the Directive; and the appropriate way to make this information available is by publishing the prospectus.

1.114　The publication requirements are set out in Article 14 of the Prospectus Directive. Publication must take place before the beginning of the public offer or the admission of the securities to the regulated market. In the case of an initial public offer of shares, the prospectus must be made available at least six working days before

---

[107]　See Council Regulation EC No 864/2007 ('Rome II') which deals with applicable law relating to non-contractual claims and Council Regulation EC No 44/2001 ('Brussels I') which deals with applicable jurisdiction.

[108]　See, for example Prospectus Directive Recital 19.

the end of the offer, to give investors sufficient time to read and understand its contents.[109]

Various different methods of publication are offered, including insertion in news-papers with wide circulation; by making physical copies freely available at certain locations; by electronic publication on the websites of issuers and others; and by electronic publication through the regulated market where the admission of the issue is sought.[110]

1.115

Choice is, more often than not, a virtue. However, from the perspective of those who need to be able to find and read the prospectus (including, apart from investors, those who service the payments once the securities are issued) a single, centralized, electronic repository that gives free access to all throughout the EEA would be a welcome improvement.

1.116

1.3.1.8 *Updating the prospectus*

There is often a gap, of some days (or even weeks), between the production and approval of a prospectus and the completion of the offer or admission to which it relates. During that period, circumstances can change. In addition, despite the best efforts of diligent issuers and their advisers, people can (and do) make mistakes. The Prospectus Directive recognizes these frailties of humans and the environment they live in by requiring that:

1.117

> Every significant new factor, material mistake or inaccuracy relating to the informa-tion included in the prospectus which is capable of affecting the assessment of the securities and which arises or is noted between the time when the prospectus is approved and the final closing of the offer to the public or, as the case may be, the time when trading on a regulated market begins, shall be mentioned in a supplement to the prospectus.[111]

Supplements require approval and publication in the same way as the prospectus to which they relate.[112]

---

[109] Prospectus Directive Article 14(1).

[110] Prospectus Directive Article 14(2).

[111] Prospectus Directive Article 16(1).

[112] The Commission's proposal for amendments to the Prospectus Directive (COM (2009) 491 final) includes a proposal to amend Article 16(1) so that the requirement to produce a supplement ceases on the *earlier* of commencement of trading on the regulated market and the final closing of the offer. This would produce a curious result if the offer ended after commencement of trading and a significant event occurred before the end of the offer. The offeror would have to amend the prospectus, to avoid misleading investors and incurring possible legal liability (say, in negligence). However, the amending document would not have to be approved by the competent authority, so that the change would result in a reduction of investor protection. Equally, although a prospectus would still be needed for non-exempt offers, the amending document would not have the benefit of the passport under the Prospectus Directive and therefore it may be difficult to use it in host member states.

1.3.1.9 *Withdrawal rights*

1.118   There would be little point in a regime that ensured that an investor had the information on which to base its investment decision before it received an offer if, once that offer had been made and accepted, the information could change in such a way as to make the investor regret its decision—unless, that is, the investor is given the ability to reconsider that decision and (if it does not like the changed circumstances) to withdraw from the contract.

1.119   The Prospectus Directive provides such a right, in Article 16(2), which in broad terms says that investors who have already agreed to purchase or subscribe securities before a supplement is published have the right, exercisable within not less than two working days[113] after the supplement's publication, to withdraw their acceptances.

1.120   This provision, while unobjectionable (or even desirable) in broad concept, has caused some considerable difficulties in practice. Different countries impose different periods during which the withdrawal right must be made available, with the result that offers in a number of different member states have to adopt whichever withdrawal period is the longest—the hares have to slow down to the pace of the tortoise.

1.121   But perhaps more serious than this is the fact that the trigger for the withdrawal right is the publication of a supplement, whatever the supplement may contain. It is doubtful whether those drafting the Prospectus Directive were aware that supplements are produced in the market for both substantive and technical reasons. So, for example, a supplement will be produced if the issuer becomes aware, after the prospectus is published, of major new litigation against it; but the issuer may also produce a supplement to amend the terms of the securities (which may be of a very minor nature or entirely to the benefit of the investor;[114] or which may not affect in any way the basis of the contract entered into with the investor[115]). It is difficult to see why the publication of supplements that do not (or should not) affect the investor's decision to buy should give the investor a withdrawal right. Indeed, the fact that the current regime does give a withdrawal right on publication of a supplement, whatever its content, acts as a disincentive

---

[113] The Commission's proposed amendments to the Prospectus Directive (COM (2009) 491 final) would change this to two working days, extendible by the issuer, offeror or the person asking for admission to the regulated market—but not, by implication, by anyone else. This should achieve a degree of harmonization of offer periods in a multi-jurisdictional offering, although the withdrawal periods in different states may be slightly different if different definitions of working day are applied in the relevant legislation.

[114] For example the inclusion of a simple put option.

[115] For example, where the supplement simply records the publication of interim results that are entirely in line with market expectations and have therefore been taken into account by those who have accepted offers to buy the securities.

to issuers, who may avoid publishing 'technical' supplements for fear of giving investors a free put option.

It is odd (and undesirable) that a regime that is designed to promote *more* useful **1.122** disclosure to the market should contain a provision that can operate to dissuade the publication of material that is useful, although of minor importance. Most developed systems of contract law deal with similar circumstances, giving contracting parties the right to withdraw if circumstances change; but they are limited to changed circumstances that affect the bargain between the parties in some fundamental way. Article 16(2) should, it is submitted, follow this lead, by limiting the withdrawal right to the publication of a supplement that contains information that has a significant effect on the price of the securities to which the prospectus relates. That price will have been based, in large part, on the information in the prospectus and reflects the market's view of the information bundle, expressed in monetary terms. It seems entirely reasonable, therefore, that it should only be information that changes the price that should allow withdrawal. Some may argue that this introduces a subjective test to the withdrawal right—whether something affects the price or not. However, subjectivity is already inextricably linked with the withdrawal right, in that the issuer or offeror only has to publish a supplement where the new factor is 'significant' or the mistake or inaccuracy is 'material'. Significance and materiality are judgments, exercised by the person who has to decide whether or not to publish the supplement. If he decides not to, then there will be no withdrawal right.

1.3.1.10 *Validity of a prospectus*

A prospectus (whatever its format) is valid for 12 months after its publication,[116] **1.123** provided it is properly updated in accordance with Article 16 of the Prospectus Directive.[117] This provision has given rise to several different interpretations in practice. In some markets, a connection has been drawn between this provision and Article 3(1) of the Prospectus Directive. The argument is made that, as a prospectus is valid for a year, the requirement in Article 3(1) for there to be a prospectus for non-exempt offers made during that year is already satisfied by the initial prospectus. So, if an issuer produces a prospectus (say, for a public offer of securities) on 20 January, then anyone can offer those securities on a non-exempt

---

[116] If the Commission's proposed amendment to the Prospectus Directive (COM (2009) 491 final) is adopted, this would be extended to 24 months. However, it is likely that the accretion of supplements over a two-year period will result in a prospectus failing to satisfy the requirement that the prospectus should be 'easily analysable and comprehensible' under Article 5(1), so that more frequent updates would probably be required. In addition, the production each year of an annual report, containing audited financial statements, will normally require a number of significant amendments to the prospectus, which can best be made by updating the prospectus itself rather than through a supplement.

[117] Prospectus Directive Articles 9(1) and 9(2).

basis at any time until the following 20 January without having to produce a further prospectus. The issuer's prospectus *is* the prospectus under Article 3(1) for the purpose of those non-exempt offers.

1.124 This interpretation is certainly plausible on the current wording of the Directive,[118] although it raises interesting questions concerning liability. It is a little difficult to see how, if the issuer knows that the prospectus it is publishing can be used in this way throughout the year, it can avoid having to update it on a continuous basis throughout the year. It is unlikely, given the investor protection focus of the Directive, which intends that the investor should have up-to-date information available to him at the point of sale, that the Prospectus Directive allows use of an out-of-date prospectus for the purpose of non-exempt offers during the year. This means that someone will have to update the prospectus—either the person making the non-exempt offer; or the person who produced the prospectus in the first place. Much will depend on the liability regime of the relevant member state; but it is entirely possible that the person who originally produced the prospectus, knowing that it is valid for a year and can be used by third parties for non-exempt offers during that period, will be liable if it is so used and is misleading because it has not been updated. The duty to update a prospectus continuously throughout the year following its publication is very onerous and costly—both in money and time—and it is difficult to see how that burden can be justified when the person on whom it is placed has not benefited from the non-exempt offers made by the third parties.

1.125 Another view of Article 9 (which is, in the author's view, more attractive) is that it is purely a limiting provision. What it is saying is that a prospectus must be renewed at least once a year (even if nothing has changed). In a way, this provision is a reinforcement of the supplementary prospectus regime under Article 16(1) of the Prospectus Directive. It is saying that issuers and offerors must update as circumstances change; but, because a prospectus becomes confusing when it has to be read with numerous updates, at least once a year, the prospectus has to be renewed, with all of the updates being written into the single document.

1.3.2 Timely ongoing disclosure—the Market Abuse Directive

1.126 Markets depend on disclosure. If the circumstances surrounding the issuer, its business, and its prospects change, but the market is unaware of the changes, then risk will be mispriced and those buying or selling the issuer's securities will be paying or receiving either too much or too little. If investors cannot trust a market's

---

[118] It will no longer be plausible, however, if the Commission's proposal to amend the Prospectus Directive (COM (2009) 491 final) is adopted, because the new text will make it clear that anyone making a non-exempt offer must produce a new prospectus for that offer, unless the issuer has actually consented to the use of its prospectus for the offer.

prices, they will be reluctant to trade in the market. Issuers will find that, with demand for funding outstripping supply, the cost of funding in the market will increase and they will seek funding elsewhere. In time, the market will die.

In the context of the regulated markets, therefore, disclosure is not a single event **1.127** at a fixed point in time, but a continuous process. It begins, as has been seen, with initial disclosure made through the prospectus prepared for the initial offering or admission to trading. This is extensive disclosure, because new money is being raised and, in some cases, the issuer itself will be new to the market. It is the fullest possible disclosure—'warts and all'—containing not just the major, price-affecting, information relating to the issuer, but also many elements that, in themselves are of much less interest but, combined with other equally unimportant elements, build up a mix of information that is important to the investment decision of those supplying new money to the issuer.

Because of the need to include copious information in a prospectus, such docu- **1.128** ments are very expensive to produce and keep up to date. The costs involved prohibit their production, except when new capital or funding is being raised or a new listing is being obtained.

It is important to note the fundamental difference between the raising of new **1.129** capital or funding by the issuer of securities and secondary market activity—that is normal trading between willing buyers and sellers either through a regulated market or through a multilateral trading facility[119] or off-market. In a secondary market, transaction money certainly passes from hand to hand; but none of it passes to the issuer. The issuer gets no direct monetary benefit from the transactions.[120] It is not, therefore, reasonable to expect the issuer to maintain the same level of disclosure to support secondary market transactions as when it is, itself, raising finance. And it is arguably not necessary that it should do so. Its initial prospectus has helped to form the initial market price for the securities; and all that the market should require thereafter, apart from regular annual and other financial reports (as to which see below), is information on changes that have a significant effect on that price. This information is provided under the *ad hoc* disclosure regime set out in the Market Abuse Directive.[121]

---

[119] A multilateral trading facility is a computerized facility which brings together multiple third-party buying and selling interests in financial instruments. They are typically operated by financial intermediaries.

[120] Although, clearly, an issuer is concerned that its share price should remain at a proper level, so that investors are attracted to invest when it brings new issues to the market; and the officers of the issuer will have an interest in the issuer's share price performance, where (as is often the case) their remuneration includes share options or the like.

[121] The motive behind Market Abuse Directive Article 6 was not, in fact, directly concerned with keeping the market informed; but was rather designed to prevent the misuse of inside information—for example, through those who had access to it dealing in the market ahead of its publication—and thereby undermining confidence in the market. However, as Market Abuse

1.130   Article 6 of the Market Abuse Directive provides that:

> member states shall ensure that issuers of financial instruments inform the public as
> soon as possible of inside information which directly concerns the said issuers.

'Inside information' is information of a precise nature which has not been made public, relating, directly or indirectly, to one or more issuers of financial instruments or to one or more financial instruments and which, if it were made public, would be likely to have a significant effect on the prices of those financial instruments or on the price of related derivative financial instruments.[122]

1.131   In relation to those who execute orders on behalf of others, the definition also includes knowledge of pending orders by those clients which is of a precise nature, which relates directly or indirectly to one or more issuers of financial instruments or to one or more financial instruments, and which, if it were made public, would be likely to have a significant effect on the prices of those financial instruments or on the price of related derivative financial instruments.

1.132   Helpfully, Recital 18 of the Market Abuse Directive makes it clear that the mere fact that market-makers or bodies authorized to act as counterparties pursue their legitimate business of buying or selling financial instruments is not, in itself, deemed to constitute the use of inside information. Nor is the dutiful carrying out of an order by persons authorized to execute orders on behalf of third parties (who may be insiders).

1.133   The definition in the Market Abuse Directive itself is amplified by a further Directive[123] by way (according to Recital 4 of that Directive) of creating legal certainty. The first amplification is somewhat mystifying, and therefore worth quoting in full. It says that:

> information shall be deemed to be of a precise nature if it indicates a set of circum-
> stances which exists or may reasonably be expected to come into existence or an event
> which has occurred or may reasonably be expected to do so and if it is specific enough
> to enable a conclusion to be drawn as to the possible effect of that set of circum-
> stances or event on the prices of financial instruments or related derivative financial
> instruments.[124]

1.134   This is a sophisticated linguistic (and intellectual) puzzle, but it does contain a couple of potentially useful notions. The first is to be found in the concept of

---

Directive Recital 12 makes clear, the purpose of the Directive is 'to ensure the integrity of Community financial markets and to enhance investor confidence in those markets'. That fair pricing of securities is one element necessary for that confidence is clear from the fact that the Market Abuse Directive outlaws actions that create a misleading impression as to price. It therefore seems logical to interpret Market Abuse Directive Article 6 as having a secondary purpose, namely to provide information to the market that will enable correct price formation in the market.

[122] Market Abuse Directive Article 1(1).
[123] Commission Directive 2003/124/EC, a Level 2 implementing measure.
[124] Ibid Article 1(1).

'reasonable expectation' in relation to events that have not yet occurred but may occur in the future. Article 6 of the Market Abuse Directive merely refers to 'information' which, to the unwary, might appear to mean an existing set of facts, not a possible future occurrence. The implementing Directive makes it clear that a future event (such as, for example, the strong possibility that the issuer's banks might not renew an important loan) can be inside information, if it might reasonably be expected to occur.

The second potentially helpful element is the clarification that information is only **1.135** inside information if it is specific enough to enable a conclusion to be drawn as to its possible effect on the price of the financial instruments. This is a gloss on the phrase 'would be likely to have a significant effect' on prices, in Article 6 of the Market Abuse Directive. Some would argue that drawing a conclusion is a more definite concept than 'being likely to'.

CESR has given additional guidance on the meaning of inside information,[125] **1.136** including the helpful observation that, in determining whether an event has occurred or circumstances exist, a key issue will be whether there is 'firm and objective evidence for this as opposed to rumours or speculation i.e. if it can be proved to have happened or to exist'. Also, when considering what may reasonably be expected to come into existence, the key issue, according to CESR, is whether it is reasonable to draw this conclusion based on the *ex ante* information available at the time—in other words, there is to be no second-guessing with the benefit of hindsight. Finally, CESR makes it clear that, save in exceptional circumstances, issuers have no obligation to respond to speculation or market rumour.

The implementing Directive also clarifies the meaning of 'information which, if **1.137** it were made public, would be likely to have a significant effect on the prices of financial instruments' in Article 6 of the Market Abuse Directive. It says that information will only have this effect if a reasonable investor would be likely to use it as part of the basis for his investment decisions.[126] Thus failure to disclose information may not result in a breach of the Market Abuse Directive, even though the market price of the securities does in fact move significantly once the information is made public, if only irrational investors would base their investment decisions on the information.

Article 6(2) of the Market Abuse Directive gives issuers a limited power to delay **1.138** disclosure of inside information[127] where such a delay is necessary so as not to prejudice its legitimate interests. But there are significant limitations to this power, in that the failure to disclose must not be likely to mislead the public. In addition,

---

[125] CESR/06-562b.
[126] Commission Directive 2003/124/EC Article 1(2).
[127] CESR has given guidance on when it might be legitimate to delay publication of inside information in CESR/06-562b.

the issuer must be able to ensure that the information remains confidential and it must inform its competent authority of the decision to delay disclosure.

1.139   The implementing Directive sets out various non-exhaustive instances of where delay in disclosure may be within the legitimate interests of the issuer, including where negotiations (for example, in relation to a major acquisition) are in course and the outcome would be likely to be affected by public disclosure. Equally, disclosure may be delayed where the financial viability of the issuer is in grave and imminent danger, although not within the scope of applicable insolvency law, if the disclosure would seriously jeopardize the interest of existing and potential shareholders by undermining the conclusion of specific negotiations designed to ensure the long-term financial recovery of the issuer.[128]

1.3.3   Regular ongoing disclosure—the Transparency Directive

1.140   The Prospectus Directive, as has been seen, provides investor protection by ensuring that investors are given information on which to base their investment decisions. The Market Abuse Directive supplements this by requiring that price-moving information is given to the market promptly after the issuer becomes aware of it. These disclosures are, however, incomplete, according to the methodology adopted by the FSAP Directives.

1.141   Markets also need regular reports, including financial statements giving a view of the issuer's financial position on a given date and performance of the issuer over the given period; but also bringing together into one place, in a coherent narrative, the various important events that have occurred during the period and their effect on the financial position and prospects of the issuer. Without such reports to consolidate the information flow, the mass of disparate information about issuers in the market would very quickly become incomprehensible to most investors.[129]

1.142   The TOD contains an extensive reporting regime for most issuers that are admitted to an EEA regulated market.

1.3.3.1   The reports

1.143   Issuers that are subject to the TOD reporting regime must produce annual,[130] semi-annual,[131] and (if they have shares admitted to an EEA regulated market)

---

[128]   Commission Directive 2003/124/EC Article 3(1).

[129]   TOD Recital 10 acknowledges the information continuum, saying 'an annual financial report should ensure information over the years once the issuer's securities have been admitted to a regulated market'.

[130]   TOD Article 4.

[131]   TOD Article 5.

interim reports,[132] between the annual and semi-annual reports. Their purpose is made abundantly clear—it is to give investors more protection by allowing them to form 'a more informed assessment of the issuer's situation'.[133] In the words of Recital 1 to the TOD:

> Efficient, transparent and integrated securities markets contribute to a genuine single market in the Community and foster growth and job creation by better allocation of capital and by reducing costs. The disclosure of accurate, comprehensive and timely information about security issuers builds sustained investor confidence and allows an informed assessment of their business performance and assets. This enhances both investor protection and market efficiency.

1.3.3.1.1 The annual report The annual report is, inevitably, the most comprehensive of the three TOD reports. It comprises three main elements, namely the financial statements (including the audit report); a narrative report; and a responsibility statement. **1.144**

Taking these in turn, the financial statements must be prepared in accordance with international financial reporting standards,[134] where the issuer is required to prepare consolidated accounts under the Seventh Council Directive.[135] Otherwise, the accounts may be drawn up according to the national law of the member state within which the issuer is incorporated. The financial statements must be audited in accordance with EU Directives and the audit report, signed by the auditor, has to be disclosed in full to the public together with the financial report.[136] **1.145**

The second element, the management report, is a narrative that requires both a backward-looking review of events during the period covered by the report and a degree of peering into the future. If the issuer is required to produce consolidated accounts, the contents of the report are extensive and are worth setting out in full:[137] **1.146**

1. The consolidated annual report shall include at least a fair review of the development and performance of the business and of the position of the undertakings included in the consolidation taken as a whole, together with a description of the principal risks and uncertainties that they face.
     The review shall be a balanced and comprehensive analysis of the development and performance of the business and of the position of the undertakings included in the consolidation taken as a whole, consistent with the size and complexity of the business. To the extent necessary for an understanding of such development, performance or position, the analysis shall include both financial and,

---

[132] TOD Article 6.

[133] TOD Recital 11, in relation to the semi-annual statements.

[134] TOD Article 4.3. This actually cross-refers to Regulation (EC) No 1606/2002.

[135] Council Directive 83/349/EEC of 13 June 1983 on consolidated accounts.

[136] The Fourth Council Directive 78/660/EC of 25 July 1978 and, if the issuer is required to prepare consolidated accounts, in accordance with Article 37 of Directive 83/349/EEC.

[137] Article 37 of Directive 83/349/EEC.

where appropriate, non-financial key performance indicators relevant to the particular business, including information relating to environmental and employee matters.

In providing its analysis, the consolidated annual report shall, where appropriate, provide references to and additional explanations of amounts reported in the consolidated accounts.

2. In respect of those undertakings, the report shall also give an indication of:

    (a) any important events that have occurred since the end of the financial year;

    (b) the likely future development of those undertakings taken as a whole;

    (c) the activities of those undertakings taken as whole in the field of research and development;

    (d) the number and nominal value or, in the absence of a nominal value, the accounting par value of all of the parent undertaking's shares held by that undertaking itself, by subsidiary undertakings of that undertaking or by a person acting in his own name but on behalf of those undertakings. A member state may require or permit the disclosure of these particulars in the notes on the accounts;

    (e) in relation to the use by the undertakings of financial instruments and, where material for the assessment of assets, liabilities, financial position and profit or loss,

      — the financial risk management objectives and policies of the undertakings, including their policies for hedging each major type of forecasted transaction for which hedge accounting is used, and

      — the exposure to price risk, credit risk, liquidity risk and cash flow risk;

    (f) a description of the main features of the group's internal control and risk management systems in relation to the process for preparing consolidated accounts, where an undertaking has its securities admitted to trading on a regulated market within the meaning of Article 4(1), point (14) of Directive 2004/39/EC of the European Parliament and of the Council of 21 April 2004 on markets in financial instruments.[138]

These are significant disclosure requirements which raise important questions, when considered in the light of the liability regime that applies to them (see 1.3.3.2 below).

1.147   The third element is the responsibility statement, which is a statement:

made by the persons responsible within the issuer, whose names and functions shall be clearly indicated, to the effect that, to the best of their knowledge, the financial statements prepared in accordance with the applicable set of accounting standards give a true and fair view of the assets, liabilities, financial position and profit or loss of the issuer and the undertakings included in the consolidation taken as a whole and that the management report includes a fair review of the development and performance of the business and the position of the issuer and the undertakings included

---

[138] Issuers that are not required to produce consolidated accounts must prepare their management report in accordance with Article 46 of Directive 78/660/EEC, which requires broadly similar disclosure, with the removal of references to subsidiaries.

in the consolidation taken as a whole, together with a description of the principal risks and uncertainties that they face.[139]

The annual report must be published, at the latest, four months after the end of each financial year and must remain publicly available for at least five years.[140]

1.3.3.1.2 The semi-annual report The semi-annual report has a similar struc-   **1.148**
ture to the annual report. However, instead of full audited financial statements, it only requires a 'condensed set of financial statements'.[141] These must be prepared on the basis of the international accounting standard applicable to interim financial reporting adopted by the Commission's Accounting Regulatory Committee,[142] but only where the issuer is required to prepare consolidated accounts. Where it is not required to do so, the half-yearly statement must include at least a condensed balance sheet, a condensed profit and loss account and explanatory notes on these accounts. It is important to note that the same principles for recognizing and measuring must be used as for the annual financial reports.[143]

If the financial statements have been audited or reviewed, the relevant report must   **1.149**
be included in full. If not, the report must state that fact.[144]

The half-yearly management report must include 'at least an indication of   **1.150**
important events that have occurred during the first six months of the financial year, and their impact on the condensed set of financial statements, together with a description of the principal risks and uncertainties of the remaining six months of the financial year'. Share issuers also have to include related party transactions.[145]

The responsibility statement must confirm that 'to the best of the [responsible   **1.151**
person's] knowledge, the condensed set of financial statements ... gives a true and fair view of the assets, liabilities, financial position and profit or loss' of the issuer and its subsidiaries (if any) and that 'the interim management report includes a fair review of the information' that is required to be in it.[146]

Again, this is a tough disclosure standard, coupled with a wide-ranging responsi-   **1.152**
bility. It is difficult to understand how both the annual report and the semi-annual report (which, by its own admission, contains much less information) can present a 'true and fair' view. 'True and fair' is a standard that has typically only been

---

[139] TOD Article 4(2)(c).
[140] TOD Article 4(1).
[141] TOD Article 5(2(a).
[142] TOD Article 5(3).
[143] TOD Article 5(3) second paragraph.
[144] TOD Article 5(5).
[145] TOD Article 5(4).
[146] TOD Article 5(2)(c).

applied to full, annual, financial statements. Having established such a view with the annual financial statements, it is not easy to see how, six months later, an issuer can give the same view, but by giving significantly less information. In many countries, there is jurisprudence and even statute law on what is (and is not) a 'true and fair' view. Accounting and auditing rules and procedures have also been established on the basis of the concept. But in all cases, the 'true and fair' standard is based on full disclosure, in the annual financial statements, not a much reduced subset of that disclosure.

1.153 The TOD makes an attempt to remove this inconvenience by saying that 'a condensed set of financial statements, as part of a half-yearly financial report, also represents a sufficient basis for giving such a true and fair view of the first six months of an issuer's financial year'.[147] It is, however, difficult to see how such a statement can operate to change laws and rules relating to accounting; and, even if it did, it is not helpful to have the same term applied to two very different disclosure levels.

1.154 The half-yearly report must be published as soon as possible after the end of the relevant period, but not later than two months after its end, and must remain available to the public for at least five years.[148]

1.155 **1.3.3.1.3 Interim reports**   Interim reports must be made by issuers whose shares are admitted to a regulated market, during the first and second halves of the financial year.[149] Two alternative methods of reporting are available:

(a) A narrative containing:
 — an explanation of material events and transactions that have taken place during the relevant period and their impact on the financial position of the issuer and its controlled undertakings, and
 — a general description of the financial position and performance of the issuer and its controlled undertakings during the relevant period.[150]

(b) A quarterly financial report published either under national legislation or the rules of the regulated market or on the issuer's own initiative.

1.156 The interim statements need not be accompanied by a responsibility statement. They must be published not earlier than ten weeks after the beginning and not later than six weeks before the end of the relevant six-month period.[151] Although these time constraints only refer to the making of the report, it is likely that the period referred to in the report must relate to the same time period (rather than,

---

147 TOD Recital 9.
148 TOD Article 5(1).
149 TOD Article 6(1).
150 TOD Article 6(1).
151 TOD Article 6(1).

for example, the first interim report being produced 75 days after the beginning of the financial year, but only relating to the first month of the year).

1.3.3.2 Liability[152]

Legislation often neglects to consider the impact of liability and potential litigation when it imposes disclosure duties. The TOD is no exception. To be fair, it does not itself impose any liability regime; but it does require member states to ensure that responsibility for the reports described above 'lies at least with the issuer or its administrative, management or supervisory bodies' and it goes on to require member states to 'ensure that their laws, regulations and administrative provisions on liability' apply to those persons.[153] This last requirement is not, of course, to be taken literally. Any legal system will have a multitude of provisions dealing with liability. Some of these will be inappropriate (for example, liability for inflicting personal injury). Others may be appropriate (for example, liability for misleading statements under statute, fraud, or in tort); but it is not likely that the TOD was intended to require *all* appropriate liability regimes to be applied to these reports. It will be enough if some are applied, sufficient to impose a suitable enforcement mechanism for the regime.

1.157

One problem with the TOD disclosure regime, however, is the fact that, while purporting to leave matters to member states, the Directive may well itself trigger liability regimes in each member state without their doing anything at all. This (probably inadvertent) result is due to the interaction between the provisions of the TOD that set out its purpose and laws that give rise to negligence liability.

1.158

For example, under English law, a person may be liable if he possesses particular skill and uses it to provide advice to another in circumstances where it is reasonable for that other person to rely upon it.

Applying this in the context of the TOD, the purpose of the reports is to assist investors in forming their investment decisions.[154] The issuer knows this (because the Directive says so) and knows that the reports will be communicated to investors (because it has to publish them) to be used for that purpose. And, finally, the issuer knows that the reports will be relied upon by investors for that purpose without independent enquiry (because they are documents required by statute).

1.159

---

[152] Parts of this section consist of shortened extracts from two much longer articles by the author in the Capital Markets Law Journal (OUP) entitled 'Only connect—the importance of considering disclosure requirements in the light of their legal consequences' (Volume 2 No 1 at page 41) and 'Disclosure in the EEA securities markets—making sense of the puzzle' (Volume 3 No 2 at page 139).

[153] TOD Article 7.

[154] See for example, Recitals 2, 5 and 7 and Article 6.

1.160   What, it may be asked, is wrong with that? The answer is, at least two things. First, if a Directive is to impose liability, it should do so directly, rather than through a back door. Those who are to be liable are entitled to know that they are liable and should be told so clearly.

1.161   Secondly, there are strong arguments that negligence liability is an inappropriate standard in this context. Disclosure is good; but only if it is done in the right way. If liability for disclosure is set with a hair trigger, there is a risk that those charged with writing the disclosure will become risk-averse and be inclined to play safe by making too much disclosure. Some may say that you can never have too much of a good thing, but in this context they would be wrong. There is a point at which disclosure becomes top heavy, with lesser or unimportant details obscuring or diverting attention from key information, so that the reader misses the point. Too much disclosure wastes the investor's time or (worse) obscures an important fact by burying it among a plethora of unimportant detail.

Considerations such as these led to changes in the English liability regime for annual and other reports.[155]

1.3.3.3 Regulated information

1.162   Besides requiring the production of regular annual, semi-annual and (for share issuers) interim reports, member states must ensure that issuers that are admitted to EEA regulated markets disclose regulated information.[156] This is defined as all information which the issuer is required to disclose under the TOD, Article 6 of the Market Abuse Directive or under the laws, regulations or administrative provisions of the home member state.[157] The concept is made wider, in the context of third country issuers, by the requirement to ensure that information disclosed in a third country 'which may be of importance for the public in the Community'[158] is disclosed, even if it is not regulated information within the definition. This last phrase is somewhat confusing (not least because such information, having been disclosed in a third country, will not, by definition, be regulated information, the meaning of which is restricted to information disclosed under a limited set of European legislation). It is, however, consistent with Recital 27, which says that 'it should be ensured that any additional relevant information about Community issuers or third country issuers, disclosure of which is required in a third country but not in a member state, is made available to the public in the Community'.

1.163   This Recital, it will be noted, refers not just to third country issuers but to Community issuers as well so that, for example, an EEA issuer that files information

---

[155] Financial Services and Markets Act 2000 section 90A.
[156] TOD Article 21.
[157] TOD Article 2(1)(k).
[158] TOD Article 23(3).

with the United States Securities Exchange Commission will have also to file that information under the TOD. Article 21 limits the disclosure obligation to information required by certain European legislation. Rather curiously, information that is *not* required by Community legislation but is, instead, required by foreign legislation, must be disclosed—but only thanks to Recital 27 (there being no equivalent Article requiring such disclosure of a Community issuer).

The requirement for third country issuers to file in the EEA disclosures made in third countries is unnervingly wide, referring as it does to information 'which may be of importance for the public in the Community'. This contrasts with the much more limited (and more sensible) language in Article 10 of the Prospectus Directive (which limits the information required for inclusion in the annual list, filed with the home state competent authority, to documents published in compliance with obligations under laws 'dealing with the regulation of securities, issuers of securities and securities markets'). The Commission has the power to adopt implementing measures defining the type of information disclosed in a third country that is of importance to the public in the Community and it could helpfully use this to align the TOD disclosure requirement with that in Article 10 of the Prospectus Directive.[159] **1.164**

1.3.3.4 Third country issuers

Most of the disclosure obligations in the TOD are formulated with only EEA issuers in mind. Issuers from third countries are, however, also subject to the obligations when they are admitted to the EEA regulated markets. However, rather than laboriously interweaving them into the detail of the disclosure requirements, the TOD attempts to deal with them in one blow, through Article 23. Article 23(1) gives the competent authority of the home member state the power to exempt a third country issuer from the requirements of Articles 4 to 7 (the annual, semi-annual, and interim reporting provisions) 'provided the law of the third country in question lays down equivalent requirements or such an issuer complies with requirements of the law of a third country that the competent authority of the home member state considers as equivalent'. The second of these alternatives allows issuers from one third country to adopt the requirements of another—for example, a Russian company using US accounting principles. **1.165**

The Commission also has the power to determine equivalence, in order to 'ensure the uniform application' of the power given to competent authorities. However, this power interestingly requires a determination based on equivalence with 'the international standards set by international organisations'. The Commission has **1.166**

---

[159] TOD Article 23(5). Although the reference in this Article is to paragraph 2 of Article 23, this is almost certainly a mistaken cross-reference, because paragraph 2 contains no reference to information of importance to the public in the Community, whereas paragraph 3 does.

until 20 January 2012 to determine equivalence of accounting standards used by third country issuers.[160]

1.3.3.5 Exemptions

1.167   Issuers that only have debt securities[161] in denominations at the date of issue of at least EUR 50,000 (or its equivalent in another currency) admitted to an EEA regulated market are exempt from the TOD reporting requirements of Articles 4 to 6 (the annual, semi-annual, and interim reporting provisions).[162] States, regional and local authorities, public international bodies of which at least one EEA state is a member, the European Central Bank and EEA national central banks are also exempt.[163]

1.168   Where the registered office of an issuer is in a third country, the competent authority of the home member state may exempt that issuer from reporting requirements, provided that the law of the third country in question lays down equivalent requirements or such an issuer complies with requirements of the law of a third country that the competent authority of the home member state considers as equivalent. Such equivalence has been granted in relation to the United States and Japan,[164] while work is continuing in order to determine equivalence in relation to Canadian, Korean, Chinese and Indian accounting principles.

1.3.3.6 Ongoing disclosure under the Prospectus Directive

1.169   The Prospectus Directive also contains a rudimentary ongoing disclosure provision, in Article 10,[165] which requires issuers whose securities are admitted to trading on a regulated market to file with their home state competent authority at least annually a document that contains or refers to all information that they have published or made available to the public over the preceding 12 months in one or more member states and in third countries in compliance with their obligations under Community and national laws and rules dealing with the regulation of securities, issuers of securities and securities markets. However, this obligation does not apply to issuers of non-equity securities whose denomination per unit amounts to at least EUR 50,000 (or its equivalent in another currency).

---

[160]   TOD Article 23(4) last paragraph.

[161]   Defined in TOD Article 2(1)(b) as 'bonds or other forms of transferable securitised debts, with the exception of securities which are equivalent to shares in companies or which, if converted or if the rights conferred by them are exercised, give rise to a right to acquire shares or securities equivalent to shares'.

[162]   TOD Article 8(1)(b).

[163]   TOD Article 8(1)(a).

[164]   Commission Decision 2008/961/EC.

[165]   The Commission's proposals for amendments to the Prospectus Directive (COM (2009) 491 final) would, if implemented, delete this provision and replace it by amending Article 11 so that regulated information under the TOD can be incorporated by reference.

This provision duplicates the requirements of the TOD (which, as has been **1.170** seen, requires issuers that are admitted to an EEA regulated market to provide to their home state competent authority copies of regulated information, including the documents identified by Article 10 of the Prospectus Directive). It is to be hoped that Article 10 of the Prospectus Directive will in due course be repealed.

1.3.3.7 Home/host state

The TOD, like the Prospectus Directive, establishes a home state competent **1.171** authority for each issuer that is admitted to the regulated market.[166] For an issuer that has its registered office in the Community and has shares or non-equity securities in denominations of less than EUR 1,000 admitted to a regulated market, the home competent authority is that in the member state in which it has its registered office. Third country issuers in the same situation are cross-referred to the Prospectus Directive. Their home state competent authority is that with which they file their annual list under Article 10 of the Prospectus Directive. This is not an entirely satisfactory means of identification, because issuers can, under the Prospectus Directive, have more than one home member state (for example, if they make an offer or obtain admission for non-equity securities with denominations of EUR 1,000 or more). However, it is likely that the home state that is intended by the definition in the TOD is that which is the home state under the Prospectus Directive for the sub-EUR 1,000 issue.

An issuer that does not have shares or sub-EUR 1,000 non-equity securities **1.172** admitted to a regulated market has a choice between the state in which it has its registered office and those states that have admitted its securities to a regulated market. Moreover, such issuers can change their home state competent authority every three years.

The home state competent authority is given very extensive powers. For example, **1.173** it is able to require auditors, issuers, holders of shares (or other financial instruments) to provide information and documents (without limitation). It may also require the issuer to disclose that information to the public or, alternatively, may publish it itself if the issuer fails to do so. It can suspend (or require the regulated market to suspend) or prohibit trading in securities for up to ten days if it has reasonable grounds for suspecting that the provisions of the laws implementing the Directive have been infringed. And it can name and shame persons who fail to comply with their obligations under the TOD.[167]

---

[166] TOD Article 2(1)(i).
[167] TOD Article 24(4).

1.3.3.8 Publication

1.174   All regulated information must be published using 'such media as may reasonably be relied upon for the effective dissemination of information to the public throughout the Community'.[168] The home member state is required to ensure that there is at least one officially appointed mechanism for the central storage of regulated information, complying with minimum standards of security, certainty as to the information source, time recording and easy access by end users.[169] Recital 25 to the TOD is interesting in this context, in that it refers to the importance of getting information about issuers to investors across the EEA in order to promote integration of European capital markets. Investors outside the issuer's home member state, it argues, should be on an equal footing with those within that member state. It then goes on to suggest that information should be available in the home member state 'in a centralized way allowing a European network to be built up, accessible at affordable prices for retail investors, while not leading to unnecessary duplication of filing requirements for issuers'. From a market perspective, a central repository would be ideal, if prices could be controlled in the absence of competition. If this cannot be done, then competitor systems following guidelines to ensure compatibility and inter-linking, would provide an adequate substitute. It is the latter solution that is contemplated by the TOD.

1.3.4 General comments on the disclosure regimes[170]

1.175   The three Directives described above form a disclosure continuum, starting with the initial disclosure when an issuer is first brought to the market (made through the prospectus) and continuing throughout the life of the issuer in the markets, through the disclosure of price-moving information (under Article 6 of the Market Abuse Directive) and the production of regular reports under the TOD. However, although all three Directives form part of the same continuum (at least, from the perspective of the market and the issuers that have to comply with them), their requirements are disconcertingly inconsistent.

1.176   For example, although all three regimes require disclosure of past events, they are not all triggered by the same types of event. So, for example, Article 5 of the Prospectus Directive, which is quoted at length earlier, sets out a very broad test— all information that is necessary to enable an investor to make an informed investment decision. The Market Abuse Directive requires disclosure of information which would be likely to have a significant effect on the price of the securities.

---

[168] TOD Article 20(1).
[169] TOD Article 21(2).
[170] The points made in this section are elaborated in an article by the author in the Capital Markets Law Journal entitled 'Disclosure in the EEA securities markets—making sense of the puzzle' (OUP, Volume 3 No 2 page 139).

The two tests are very different.[171] The question under the Prospectus Directive is 'would this information affect the investor's decision to buy?', whereas, under the Market Abuse Directive, the question is 'would this information affect the price?'. The interim report under the TOD sets an essay question, in which material events and transactions during the period must be described. Does 'material' mean 'would have a significant effect on the price', as in the Market Abuse Directive test? Or could it be argued that, as price-moving events will already have been disclosed under the Market Abuse Directive regime, 'material' must have a different (and wider) meaning under the TOD?

A further problem arises from the fact that each of the three disclosure regimes has **1.177** a forward-looking element. Sometimes this is express—as for example in the requirement to describe the 'prospects' of the issuer under the Prospectus Directive;[172] and the issuer's 'likely future development' and 'the principal risks and uncertainties facing the issuer' in the annual report under TOD.[173] Sometimes it is implicit, as in the requirement under the Market Abuse Directive to determine whether something 'would be likely' to have a significant effect on the share price, which not only requires one to guess the market's reaction to a future event (publication of the information) but also will normally involve the inclusion in the announcement of an assessment of the impact of the event described in the announcement on the future prospects of the company.

These inconsistencies are, at best, confusing and, at worst, dangerous, in that they **1.178** could result in complex litigation and additional costs for the raising of capital.

The disclosure regimes may also inadvertently create an increased risk of pan-EEA **1.179** litigation. Essentially, liability in tort for disclosure in any jurisdiction will be likely to be triggered by the publication of the disclosure in that jurisdiction. If an investor receives a misleading disclosure document in his own jurisdiction and relies on it to his detriment, he is likely to be able to sue the person who sent it to him, with the intention that he should use it for investment decisions, in that jurisdiction. This will almost certainly be the case in the EEA if the liability arises in tort, because under the Rome II Regulation[174] the proper law for determining a tortious claim is the place where the damage was suffered. In the context of disclosure made for the purpose of informing an investment decision, this is most likely to be the place where the investor reads and relies on the information.

---

[171] This is, perhaps, the product of the different primary purpose of the MAD, which is to prevent the misuse of inside information by requiring its prompt disclosure to the public.

[172] Prospectus Directive Article 5(1).

[173] Article 37 of Directive 83/349/EEC.

[174] Regulation (EC) No 864/2007 of the European Parliament and of the Council on the Law Applicable to Non-contractual Obligations ('Rome II'), Article 4.1.

1.180   This creates problems in relation to reports published under the TOD because Article 21(1) of the TOD requires the home member state of the issuer to 'require the issuer to use such media [for publication of regulated information] as may reasonably be relied upon for the effective dissemination of information to the public throughout the Community'. In other words, the issuer has no choice but to publish TOD disclosures in every country within the EEA, thereby incurring potential liability in tort under multiple regimes. It is difficult to see who would benefit from such multi-jurisdictional litigation, apart from lawyers.

1.3.5 Accounting and audit—the Accounting Regulations and Statutory Audit Directive

1.181   Financial statements are of paramount importance to those making investment decisions. They show, in numerical form, the financial position of the issuer at a given date, its profitability over a given period and (if there is a cash flow statement) its ability to generate cash from its operations. It follows with inevitability that such statements are subject to regulation, both as to the accounting conventions employed and the independent oversight of the auditors, when issuers seek and obtain admission to the EEA's regulated markets.

1.3.5.1 Accounts

1.182   The financial reporting regimes under the EU Accounts Regulation[175] (the 'Accounts Regulation'), the Prospectus Directive and the TOD are complex. In outline, though, the intention appears to be that the Prospectus Directive and TOD should follow the Accounts Regulation, rather than changing it.

This subsection summarizes the provisions of the Accounts Regulation and the two Directives and their impact on financial reporting by issuers admitted to EU regulated markets.

1.183   **1.3.5.1.1 Accounts in a prospectus**   A prospectus must include IFRS accounts for two years[176] or (for equity issuers) three years[177] if the issuer prepares accounts on a *consolidated* basis.[178] Issuers that have not been in operation for the full two- or three-year period must provide IFRS accounts for the period they have been in operation. If an EU issuer produces non-consolidated accounts, it must do so to

---

[175] Regulation (EC) No 1606/2002.

[176] For debt or derivative securities with denominations below EUR 50,000 (PD Regulation Annex IV paragraph 13.1 and for asset backed securities Annex VII paragraph 8.2).

[177] For equity (PD Regulation Annex I paragraph 20.1) and depositary receipts over shares (PD Regulation Annex X paragraph 20.1 and 20.1a).

[178] Accounts Regulation Article 4.

national accounting standards. Non-EU issuers must use IFRS, as adopted within the EU, or their own accounting standards if equivalent to IFRS.[179]

A company that is admitted to an EU regulated market *for the first time* only has to include IFRS accounts for the last year[180] or last two years[181] in the prospectus for that first admission. This is because such issuers are required under the Prospectus Directive Regulation to produce their financial statements for those years in a form consistent with that which will be adopted in their *next* annual financial statements (which, under the TOD, will have to be IFRS or equivalent).

1.184

1.3.5.1.1.1 Exemptions A prospectus for debt and derivative securities with denominations of EUR 50,000 or above can use the issuer's national accounting standards, with an explanation of major differences to IFRS.[182]

1.185

States and their regional and local authorities are not required to use IFRS.[183]

Public international bodies and issuers of debt securities guaranteed by an OECD state are also permitted to use their own accounting standards.[184]

1.3.5.1.2 Annual and semi-annual reports The annual financial statements must be prepared under IFRS if the issuer prepares accounts on a *consolidated* basis.[185] The parent company accounts must also be included, in the case of an EU issuer, and prepared in accordance with the laws of its member state.[186] If an EU issuer produces only non-consolidated accounts, it must do so to national accounting standards of its member state.[187]

1.186

The semi-annual financial statements must be prepared under IFRS if the issuer prepares accounts on a *consolidated* basis.[188] If it does not, the financial statements must contain at least a condensed balance sheet, a condensed profit and loss account and explanatory notes on these accounts, all of which must be prepared following the same principles for recognition and measuring as used for the annual financial statements.[189] If the semi-annual financial statements have been audited

1.187

---

[179] PD Regulation Annex I paragraph 20.1, Annex IV paragraph 13.1, Annex VII paragraph 8.2 and Annex X paragraph 20.1 and 20.1a.

[180] For debt or derivative securities with denominations below EUR 50,000 (PD Regulation Annex IV paragraph 13.1) and asset backed securities (PD Regulation Annex VII paragraph 8.2).

[181] For equity (PD Regulation Annex 1 paragraph 20.1) and depositary receipts over shares (PD Regulation Annex X paragraph 20.1 and 20.1a).

[182] Prospectus Directive Regulation Annex IX paragraph 11.1.

[183] Prospectus Directive Regulation Annex XVI.

[184] Prospectus Directive Regulation Annex XVII paragraph 4.1.

[185] TOD Article 4.3.

[186] TOD Article 4.3.

[187] TOD Article 4.3.

[188] TOD Article 5.3.

[189] TOD Article 5.3.

or reviewed by the auditors, the audit or review report must be included in the half-yearly report.[190] If not, a negative statement must be included.

1.3.5.2 *Audit*

1.188 Numbers are no good unless they can be relied upon. Because they are so important, the preparation of financial statements is not normally left entirely in the hands of the management of the company. In most countries, the law requires that the accounts must be reported on by duly qualified accountants. The report will essentially confirm two things—first, that relevant accounting principles have been applied (that is, the numbers have been correctly set out and computed); and secondly, that the accountants have carried out appropriate procedures designed to obtain sufficient appropriate audit evidence in accordance with the relevant auditing standards to determine with reasonable confidence whether the financial statements are free of material misstatement. In doing so they should comply with ethical guidelines issued by their relevant professional bodies.

The ethical guidelines which must be followed in this process typically include requirements as to integrity, objectivity, independence,[191] professional competence and due care.[192]

1.189 Issuers whose securities are admitted to the regulated market must ensure that their annual accounts or consolidated accounts are audited by someone who is approved by the member state requiring the audit, in accordance with the Statutory Audit Directive[193] ('SAD'). Individual auditors and firms may only be approved if they satisfy certain conditions, of which the more important are:

- Control—in the case of a firm, the majority of the voting rights must be held by audit firms or persons who are approved in a member state;[194]
- Management—in the case of a firm, a majority of the members of its management must be audit firms or persons who are approved in a member state;[195]
- Repute—the person or firm must be of good repute;[196]
- Education—an individual must have a university degree or equivalent and have passed an examination of professional competence sufficient to guarantee the

---

[190] TOD Article 5.5.

[191] SAD Article 22. The EU Commission published a detailed Recommendation on auditor independence on 16 May 2002—see Commission Recommendation 2002/590/EC.

[192] Note that member states are required to ensure that all statutory auditors and audit firms are subject to principles of professional ethics, covering at least their public interest function, their integrity and objectivity and their professional competence and due care—see SAD Article 21(1).

[193] Directive 2006/43/EC, Article 3(1).

[194] SAD Article 3(4)(b).

[195] SAD Article 3(4)(c).

[196] SAD Article 4.

necessary level of theoretical knowledge of subjects relevant to statutory audit[197] and the ability to apply such knowledge in practice;[198]

• Practical training—the individual must have completed a minimum of three years' practical training in the auditing of annual accounts, consolidated accounts or similar financial statements with persons competent to give such training.[199]

All statutory auditors and audit firms that are approved must be entered in a public register by the approving member state.[200]

1.190 An auditor from third countries may be approved by a member state as a statutory auditor, if that person has furnished proof that he or she complies with the requirements for an EU auditor, summarized above.[201] All auditors and audit firms from a third country that audit the annual or consolidated accounts of a company from a third country whose transferable securities are admitted to trading on an EEA regulated market must be registered with the competent authority in the country of that regulated market.[202] All registered third country auditors must be subject to the systems of oversight, quality assurance[203] and investigation and penalties operated by the relevant member state.[204] Crucially, if a third country auditor is not registered as required, the audit reports concerning annual accounts or consolidated accounts issued by it have no legal effect in that member state.[205] This means, for example, that the requirements of the Prospectus Directive or the TOD for audited accounts would not be met by such an audit report.

1.191 Approved auditors must carry out statutory audits in accordance with international auditing standards that are adopted by the Commission.[206] In addition, where the accounts are prepared on a consolidated basis, the group auditor must bear full responsibility for the audit report in relation to the entire consolidated accounts and, to enable it to do this, it must carry out a review of the audit work

---

[197] Including general accounting theory and principles, legal requirements and standards relating to the preparation of annual and consolidated accounts, international accounting and auditing standards, financial analysis, cost and management accounting, risk management and internal control; relevant legal and professional standards and professional ethics and independence standards—see SAD Article 8.

[198] SAD Articles 6 and 7.

[199] SAD Article 10.

[200] SAD Article 15.

[201] SAD Article 44.

[202] SAD Article 45(1). However, member states have a power to modify or disapply this requirement if they consider that equivalent third country requirements are met—see SAD Article 46(1).

[203] Unless the third country's system of quality assurance has been assessed as equivalent.

[204] SAD Article 45(3). However, member states have a power to modify or disapply this requirement if they consider that equivalent third country requirements are met—see SAD Article 46(1).

[205] SAD Article 45(4).

[206] SAD Article 26. In the absence of such adoption, member state auditors may follow their national auditing standards.

performed by third country auditors for the purposes of the group audit, retaining appropriate documentation of that review[207]. The Directive provides for a system of independent quality assurance[208] and public oversight[209] of statutory auditors and audit firms and provides for cooperation and mutual recognition between member states[210] and cooperation with competent authorities from third countries.[211]

1.4 Investor Protection

1.4.1 Keeping the market clean—the Market Abuse Directive

1.192 Markets depend on investors; and investors will only use markets that they trust. If an investor believes that prices are manipulated or that the market is populated by those who will cheat, the chances are that he will avoid the market. It is for this reason that the Market Abuse Directive seeks to outlaw abusive behaviour in the financial markets of the EEA. In the words of Recital 12 to the Directive:

> The objective of legislation against insider dealing is the same as that of legislation against market manipulation: to ensure the integrity of Community financial markets and to enhance investor confidence in those markets. It is therefore advisable to adopt combined rules to combat both insider dealing and market manipulation. A single Directive will ensure throughout the Community the same framework for allocation of responsibilities, enforcement and cooperation.

1.193 The market abuse regime under the Market Abuse Directive involves legislation at several different levels—the Market Abuse Directive itself; and several implementing measures, at Level 2, of which two are relevant in this context, namely Directive 2003/124/EC (the 'Market Manipulation Directive') and Commission Regulation (EC) No 2273/2003 (the 'MAD Regulation').

1.4.1.1 Scope

1.194 The Directive prohibits insider dealing and market manipulation in relation to *financial instruments* that are admitted (or subject to an application for admission) to an EEA regulated market.[212] 'Financial instrument' is broadly defined[213] and will catch most forms of security, including shares, bonds, warrants and GDRs. 'Regulated market' is defined by reference to Article 47 of the MiFID, under

---

[207] SAD Article 27.
[208] SAD Article 29 and Commission Recommendation 2008/362/EC.
[209] SAD Article 32.
[210] SAD Articles 33 and 34.
[211] SAD Article 47.
[212] MAD Article 9.
[213] MAD Article 1(3).

which each member state is required to identify which of its markets is to be within the definition and to notify its decision to the Commission.

Article 9 of the Market Abuse Directive goes on to say that the insider dealing **1.195** provisions also apply to financial instruments that are *not* admitted to an EEA regulated market, but whose value depends on a financial instrument that is so admitted. This is to prevent insiders profiting by manipulating the price of a bond admitted, say, in Tokyo that is convertible into shares admitted, say, to the French regulated market.

The Market Abuse Directive also deals with cross-border jurisdiction, requiring **1.196** each member state to apply the prohibitions and requirements provided for in the Directive to:

(a) actions carried out on its territory or abroad concerning financial instruments that are admitted to trading on a regulated market situated or operating within its territory or for which a request for admission to trading on such market has been made; and

(b) actions carried out on its territory concerning financial instruments that are admitted to trading on a regulated market in a member state or for which a request for admission to trading on such market has been made.[214]

So, if a security is admitted to a regulated market in state X, the authorities of state **1.197** X have the power to apply the market abuse regime to abuse carried out in relation to that security by person A, even though the abusive action took place in state Y; and the authorities in state Y can also take action against A.

1.4.1.2 Abusive behaviour

Abusive behaviour (the 'market abuse' that the Market Abuse Directive attempts **1.198** to eradicate) comprises a number of elements. The first group relates to insider dealing.

1.4.1.2.1 Insider dealing   Article 2 prohibits certain people who possess inside **1.199** information ('insiders') from using that information by acquiring or disposing of, or by trying to acquire or dispose of, for their own or another's account, either directly or indirectly, financial instruments to which that information relates. Article 3 of the Market Abuse Directive requires member states to prohibit any person who is an insider from disclosing inside information to another otherwise than in the normal course of the exercise of his employment, profession or duties. Such persons are also prohibited, by the same provision, from recommending or inducing another person, on the basis of inside information, to acquire or dispose of financial instruments to which that information relates. Article 4 extends these

---

[214] Market Abuse Directive Article 10.

prohibitions to anyone else who possesses inside information, who knows (or ought to know) that it is inside information.

1.200   The meaning of 'inside information' has already been discussed at some length (see Section 1.3.2) but (to refresh the memory) broadly comprises information that has not been made public relating, directly or indirectly, to one or more issuers of financial instruments or to one or more financial instruments and which, if it were made public, would be likely to have a significant effect on the prices of those financial instruments or on the price of related derivative financial instruments.

1.201   'Insiders' are defined in the second paragraph of Article 2 of the Market Abuse Directive, and include members of the management of the issuer;[215] shareholders of the issuer; those who have the inside information by virtue of their employment, profession, or duties (such as those responsible for the issuer's computer systems, secretaries who type confidential documents, and lawyers who are brought in to advise on the matter that is the subject of the inside information); and those who obtain the information by virtue of their criminal activities.

1.202   All insiders are subject to the prohibition on dealing in Article 2 of the Market Abuse Directive. Anyone else who has possession of information, without being an insider, but who ought reasonably to know that the information is inside information (for example, because he was given it by someone who was obviously an insider, such as the issuer's finance director) is also precluded from dealing or procuring others to deal, under Article 4. Article 3 completes the protective circle, by prohibiting disclosure of inside information by insiders, unless such disclosure is made in the normal course of the exercise of the employment, profession, or duties of the person making the disclosure; or the procuring by insiders of others to deal.

1.203   Where inside information is disclosed (without being made public), whether intentionally or unintentionally, then the issuer must make the inside information public, unless the person to whom the disclosure was made owes a duty of confidentiality.[216]

1.204   The Market Abuse Directive also contains provisions to facilitate the policing of the insider dealing regime by the relevant authorities. The most notable of these is the requirement for issuers, or persons acting on their behalf, to draw up a list of those

---

[215] 'Persons discharging managerial responsibilities within an issuer' are defined in Article 1(1) of Directive 2004/72/EC as those who are members of the administrative, management or supervisory bodies of the issuer; and senior executives who are not such members but who have access to inside information relating, directly or indirectly, to the issuer and have the power to make managerial decisions affecting the future developments and business prospects of the issuer.

[216] Market Abuse Directive Article 6(3).

persons who have access to inside information.[217] Such lists clearly facilitate any investigation or enforcement that may be needed, should insider dealing be suspected. This much is made clear by one of the implementing Directives,[218] which says that these lists may constitute 'a useful tool for competent authorities when monitoring the application of market abuse legislation'. The relevant authority has a ready-made list of potential suspects that it can use for the purposes of its investigations.

The same implementing Directive also suggests that the lists may provide issuers and their officers with a tool to control the flow of inside information and thereby manage their confidentiality duties.[219] The theory here is good—it is easier for an insider to control the distribution of inside information if it knows who the insiders are. However, the compilation and maintenance of these lists has proved very difficult in practice, given the detail that has to be included,[220] the obligation to update that detail promptly on an ongoing basis,[221] and the often very large number of people who necessarily have access to inside information in any large, confidential, transaction or situation. For example, where draft documentation is voluminous (as it often is), access to inside information will necessarily be given to many advisers and secretarial staff, who will be involved in its preparation, and often to many support staff, such as those responsible for maintaining computer systems, both within the issuer and the other party to the transaction and within their respective advisers (who may consist of lawyers, investment bankers, accountants and others). As people leave employment, or go on holiday, or fall sick, others will be brought in to perform their role, thus requiring the updating of the list. This is a considerable burden to set against the convenience of the resulting list to the investigating authorities. As a protective measure, however, the insider list adds little or nothing to the requirement to keep information confidential. **1.205**

The person who is responsible for drawing up the list must ensure that anyone added to it acknowledges the legal and regulatory duties entailed and is aware of the sanctions attaching to the misuse or improper circulation of the inside information.[222] **1.206**

Another policing provision is the requirement for persons discharging managerial responsibilities within an issuer, and persons closely associated with them, to notify to the relevant competent authority the existence of transactions conducted **1.207**

---

[217] Market Abuse Directive Article 6(3).

[218] Directive 2004/72/EC, Recital 6.

[219] Ibid.

[220] It is not just names of the insiders that must be included but reasons why the person is on the list. See Directive 2004/72/EC Article 5(2)(b).

[221] It is not just the addition or removal of a name that requires an update, but also a change to the reason why someone already on the list should be on the list—see Directive 2004/72/EC Article 5(3)(a).

[222] Directive 2004/72/EC Article 5(5).

on their own account relating to shares of the issuer, or to derivatives or other instruments linked to them. Such disclosures must be made public.[223] The intention is, presumably, to deter insider dealing by such persons by ensuring that their dealings are made public (and that, therefore, any proximity of such dealings to the publication of price-moving information can be duly investigated).[224]

1.208   The insider dealing provisions of the Market Abuse Directive are relevant in the context of pre-marketing of new issues of securities. As mentioned earlier (see Section 1.3.1.2), many new issues are tested out with investors before they are publicly announced, to assess whether there is sufficient market demand at suitable prices for the issue to be viable. Such pre-marketing can be (and often is) carried out on a wholly anonymous basis, so that, for example, the potential investor is given generalized information about the type of issue and issuer, which is insufficiently precise to amount to inside information.

1.209   However, sometimes (particularly when markets are difficult), precise information has to be given and care needs to be taken to ensure compliance with the provisions of the Market Abuse Directive. For example, the person making the disclosure needs to be confident that the recipient can keep the information confidential. The investor should be notified before being given the information that he is about to be made an insider (or 'brought over the wall'). This amounts to common sense, as much as anything else, as once over the wall the investor will be unable to deal in the issuer's securities until the inside information is made public (and one should never put someone out of the market without their prior consent). Careful consideration also needs to be given to:

- the content of the information package that the investor will be given;
- whether the information can, in fact be disclosed under Article 3 of Market Abuse Directive (which permits disclosure only where it is made in the normal course of the exercise of the employment, profession or duties of the person making the disclosure); and
- how the insider can be 'cleansed', by publication of the information (not least, so that he can reenter the market and get on with his job as an investor).

1.210   This last element can be difficult. Of course, if the only 'inside information' is the fact that the issuer may be about to issue securities, the public announcement of the issue will cleanse the insiders, without more. However, if the issue does not proceed, or if the inside information package includes more detailed information— for example about the financial state of the issuer—then it will be important to

---

[223] Market Abuse Directive Article 6(4).

[224] Note that, in the United Kingdom, disclosable transactions include grants of security over shares (by the creation of a security interest such as a pledge, mortgage or charge)—see the FSA's confirmation of 9 January 2009 at http://www.fsa.gov.uk/pages/Doing/UKLA/company/disclosure/index.shtml.

have agreed with the issuer, before the pre-marketing takes place, how the package will be made public. Failure to do so may result in investors being shut out of the market for prolonged periods.

1.4.1.2.2 Market manipulation Article 5 of the Market Abuse Directive requires member states to prohibit any person from engaging in market manipulation. Given the ingenuity of those who behave badly, and the unfortunate disposition of some market participants to do so, abusive behaviour (or 'market manipulation', as the Market Abuse Directive calls it) is deliberately defined in somewhat broad and generic (though lengthy) terms. Article 1(2) of the Market Abuse Directive sets out three main categories of market manipulation, as follows: **1.211**

(a) *Misleading as to supply, demand or price*: Transactions or orders to trade which give (or are likely to give) false or misleading signals as to the supply of, demand for or price of financial instruments, or which secure, for a person or collaborative group, the price of a financial instrument at an abnormal or artificial level;[225]

(b) *Fictitious devices and deception*: Transactions or orders to trade which employ fictitious devices or any other form of deception or contrivance;[226] and

(c) *Dissemination of false information*: Dissemination of information which gives (or is likely to give) false or misleading signals as to financial instruments.[227]

The first of these categories has a saving provision that recognizes that a person who enters into transactions or gives orders to trade is not manipulating the market if his reasons for doing so are legitimate and the transactions or orders conform to accepted market practices on the regulated market concerned. 'Accepted market practices' are defined as practices that are 'reasonably expected in one or more financial markets and are accepted by the competent authority in accordance with guidelines adopted by the Commission'. These are set out in Article 2(1) of Directive 2004/72/EC as a set of non-exhaustive factors to be taken into account in determining what is (or is not) an accepted market practice, including the transparency of the practice to the market, the effect on supply and demand and the impact of the practice on market liquidity. That Directive also requires competent authorities to consult with the market and each other before accepting a market practice and to disclose publicly any decisions they may take as to acceptability.[228] CESR has published guidelines to assist in this process.[229] **1.212**

---

[225] Market Abuse Directive Article 1(2)(a).
[226] Market Abuse Directive Article 1(2)(b).
[227] Market Abuse Directive Article 1(2)(c).
[228] Commission Directive 2003/124/EC Article 3.
[229] CESR/04-505b.

1.213   The last of the market manipulation categories expressly includes the dissemination of rumours and false or misleading news, where the person spreading the information knew, or ought to have known, that the information was false or misleading. For journalists, their professional rules are to be taken into account, unless they derive an advantage or profit from the dissemination of information.

1.214   These concepts are much easier to grasp through examples, particularly those at the extreme end of the spectrum where the behaviour is clearly wrong, so that is perhaps the place to start.

1.215   'Wash trades' are, unless for a legitimate reason, outlawed by the Market Abuse Directive regime. These are trades involving the buying or selling of securities where the beneficial ownership or market risk does not change, or where it is transferred only between parties acting in collusion, other than for a legitimate reason.[230]

1.216   'Abusive squeezes' are also illegal. These arise where a person agrees to buy securities for future delivery and, before delivery, buys up the supply of securities in the market, so that, to settle the trade, his seller has to buy from him, at whatever elevated price he decides to charge, to avoid default.

1.217   Also banished are the colourfully named practices of 'pumping and dumping' and 'trashing and cashing', which involve (in the first case) taking a position in an issuer's securities and then talking the issuer up, by spreading misleading or false news in the market, with a view (when the price of the securities has risen to a satisfactory level) to off-loading the holding in the market. Trashing and cashing involves the opposite—selling the issuer's securities short and then spreading bad news about the issuer, so the market price of the securities falls, enabling the investor to buy cheap to settle his short sale.

1.218   The position is less clear, however, further to the middle of the spectrum. Take, for examples, stabilization and buy-backs. First, stabilization. A new issue of securities increases supply in the marketplace. For example, the same issuer may already have $100 million of Floating Rate Notes in the market. When it issues a further $100 million, the supply in the market is doubled. Equally, an issue of $100 million by another issuer may be treated by the market as increasing supply, if the market treats both issuers as being equivalent borrowers.

1.219   Because price is dependent, in large part, on supply and demand, a new issue can have a disruptive effect on the price of existing issues. It can also take the market a

---

[230] Such trades will often involve a number of washes, from one person to another, at ever increasing prices, so that the market believes that the price is going up for legitimate reasons and will start to trade generally at those higher prices.

while to adjust to the new issue and to value it properly. During this time, the price of the issue can fluctuate, going through unusually high peaks and troughs, before the market adjusts and the price 'normalizes'. These peaks and troughs represent dangers (and opportunities) for investors. Some will buy when the price is at a peak and will lose money when the price drops; others will buy in the troughs and make money when the price rises.

Many investors are put off by such uncertainties as to price and this can lead **1.220** to their being reluctant to buy new issues—which is clearly undesirable. To avoid such investor reaction, the Market Abuse Directive Regulation permits[231] a practice known as stabilization, which is designed to even out the peaks and troughs.

Stabilization involves someone (the stabilizing manager) influencing the market **1.221** perception of the price of the securities by offering to buy them at a price which is higher than that prevailing in the market. However, because the stabilizing manager does not really want the securities, and its only motivation is to move the price upwards, stabilization may constitute market abuse under the Market Abuse Directive, because it is creating misleading impression as to the price, market or value of securities for the purpose of inducing people to buy or sell them.

In establishing a safe harbour for stabilization, however, the Market Abuse **1.222** Directive sets certain (somewhat complex) limitations on stabilizing activity. For example, Article 9(1) of the Market Abuse Directive Regulation requires disclosure before the opening of the offer period of the fact that there may be stabilization, that it may be discontinued at any time and that it is aimed at supporting the market price. The notice must also give details of the start and end of the stabilizing period, of the identity of the person carrying out the stabilization and certain other details. The idea of such disclosure is to alert the market to the fact that the price may be (legitimately) manipulated for a time so that those who prefer to avoid markets where such things happen can stay away.

The safe harbour also contains restrictions limiting the price at which stabiliz- **1.223** ation offers can be made, where the issue relates to shares or equity-linked securities;[232] and conditions for activities that are ancillary to stabilization, such as over-allotment.[233]

Buy-backs are also considered to be potentially abusive to the market—if they **1.224** were not thought to be so, there would be no need for the safe harbour provided for them by the Market Abuse Directive Regulation. The safe harbour is limited

---

[231] MAD Regulation Articles 7 to 11.
[232] Market Abuse Directive Regulation Article 10.
[233] Market Abuse Directive Regulation Article 11.

to buy-back programmes under which a company trades in its own shares in accordance with Articles 19 to 24 of Council Directive 77/91/EEC.[234] It is important to note that the harbour is limited to shares; and that this necessarily creates a degree of uncertainty in relation to buy-backs of other forms of security, such as bonds. This is unfortunate, because issuers regularly buy back their own debt securities in the market. However, as Recital 2 to the Market Abuse Directive Regulations says, the fact that something is not within the safe harbour does not automatically indicate that it is abusive.

1.225   The main question is whether a buy-back is itself manipulative of the market. Clearly, it might be—for example, if the issuer goes into a liquid market for its debt securities, buys a significant proportion of the issue which it then cancels, leaving an illiquid rump in the hands of investors, there may be an argument that the market has been abused. A misleading impression may have been created as to demand (because the market thought that the trades were with a normal market participant, rather than for cancellation of the securities) and supply (because the market may have thought that the securities would remain live, for eventual resale in the market). However, much will depend upon the facts of each individual case and buy-backs of debt securities can safely be carried out, in the right circumstances, even though outside the safe harbour.

1.226   The safe harbour for share buy-backs prescribes various conditions. Their purpose must be to reduce capital or to provide shares for satisfaction of a conversion right under a convertible bond or under employee share or other schemes.[235] The existence of the programme must be publicly disclosed before it starts to operate and transactions under it must be disclosed publicly no later than the end of the seventh market trading day after the transaction is executed.[236] There are also limits as to price and volume[237] and prohibitions on trading (at least, if the safe harbour is to be relied upon) during certain periods, such as when the issuer has decided to delay disclosure of inside information.[238]

1.227   **1.4.1.2.3 Market distortion in bids**   It is also worth noting that the Takeovers Directive[239] contains provisions that are designed to keep the market clean and avoid distortion or false pricing. So, Article 3(1)(d) provides that, in the context of a takeover bid:

---

[234] These provisions provide protections to investors by, for example, requiring the buy-back programme to be authorized by a resolution passed in a general meeting, which will set the duration of the programme, the maximum number of shares to be acquired, and the maximum and minimum consideration for any purchases under the programme.

[235] Market Abuse Directive Regulation Article 3.

[236] Market Abuse Directive Regulation Article 4(2) and (4).

[237] Market Abuse Directive Regulation Article 5.

[238] Market Abuse Directive Regulation Article 6.

[239] Directive 2004/25/EC.

false markets must not be created in the securities of the offeree company, of the offeror company or of any other company concerned by the bid in such a way that the rise or fall of the prices of the securities becomes artificial and the normal functioning of the markets is distorted.

Further, Article 6(1) requires that a decision to make a bid must be made public without delay. The purpose of this is made clear by Recital 12, which says that: **1.228**

> To reduce the scope for insider dealing, an offeror should be required to announce his/her decision to launch a bid as soon as possible and to inform the supervisory authority of the bid.

This recital presents an interesting example of how, sometimes, the FSAP Directives not only interlink, but overlap.

1.4.1.3 *Conflicts and research*

Another important aspect of a 'clean' market in which investors are willing to participate concerns the reliability of the research and advice that is available to them about the products in the market. Accordingly the Market Abuse Directive contains provisions that are designed to protect investors against conflicts of interest. These are considered together with the conflicts regime under MiFID, in Section 1.4.2.5 below. **1.229**

1.4.1.3.1 Competent authority The competent authority is given sweeping supervisory and investigative powers,[240] including the right to see any document, to demand information from any person and to summon any person to give evidence to it, carry out site visits, and to require telephone and data traffic records to be produced to it. It can require abusive practices to be discontinued, require a suspension of trading in any financial instruments that are affected by abusive behaviour and freeze and/or sequester assets. These powers can be exercised by the competent authority directly or in collaboration with other bodies or through delegation to another person (provided responsibility remains with the competent authority) or by application to the courts—or in any combination of these alternatives, as the implementing legislation provides.[241] **1.230**

1.4.1.3.2 Sanctions Each member state must ensure, in conformity with its national law, that the appropriate administrative measures can be taken or administrative sanctions be imposed against those who breach the requirements of the MAD, as implemented in that member state. Member states must ensure that these measures are effective, proportionate and dissuasive.[242] **1.231**

---

[240] Market Abuse Directive Article 12(2).
[241] Market Abuse Directive Article 12(1).
[242] Market Abuse Directive Article 14.

1.4.2 Intermediation—MiFID

1.232 The markets may be clean, thanks to the market abuse regime; but will they be properly run? What about the people in them? Are they the sort of people who will deal with investors honestly? Are they financially sound? How can investors know that they are getting a good service and reasonable prices? These are matters (among others) that are dealt with under legislation contained in the Markets in Financial Instruments Directive[243] ('MiFID') and implementing measures at Level 2, through Directive 2006/73/EC (the 'Level 2 Directive'), and Commission Regulation No 1287/2006 (the 'Regulation').

1.4.2.1 Authorization of firms

1.233 Perhaps the most fundamental provision of the MiFID is the authorization requirement, which is contained in Article 5(1) and reads as follows:

> Each member state shall require that the performance of investment services or activities as a regular occupation or business on a professional basis be subject to prior authorisation in accordance with the provisions of this Chapter. Such authorisation shall be granted by the home member state competent authority designated in accordance with Article 48.

1.234 'Investment services and activities' are broadly defined[244] to include dealing (that is, buying and selling) on own account, giving investment advice and underwriting financial instruments and or placing them with others. 'Financial instruments' for this purpose include all transferable securities, money-market instruments, options, futures, swaps and other derivatives relating to securities, currencies, financial indicies, commodities and various other things.[245] A number of other activities are also defined as 'ancillary services'.[246] These include the provision of custody or safekeeping services for financial instruments, lending money to enable an investor to buy the financial instruments being sold by the lender in the course of providing an investment service and the provision of foreign exchange facilities in connection with the provision of an investment service or activity.

1.235 It is perhaps sufficient to note, for the purposes of this work, that investment firms[247] who arrange issues of securities, such as shares and bonds, and sell those securities to investors in the market will be carrying out investment services and activities within the meaning set out above.

---

[243] Directive 2004/39/EC.
[244] MiFID Article 4(2) and Annex I Sections A and C.
[245] MiFID Annex I Section C.
[246] MiFID Article 4(1)(3) and Annex 1 Section B.
[247] Any legal person whose regular occupation or business is the provision of one or more investment services to third parties and/or the performance of one or more investment activities on a professional basis—MiFID Article 4(1).

Authorization is obtained from the home member state competent authority. **1.236**
The relevant 'home' is determined by reference to the location of the registered
office of the person requiring authorization (or its head office, if it has none).[248]
When authorization is granted, it must specify the investment services or activities which the investment firm is authorized to provide[249] (and may include any
relevant ancillary services). Once granted, the authorization is valid for the entire
Community[250]—in other words, multiple authorizations are avoided for investment firms doing business across the EEA.

The cross-border validity of MiFID authorization is developed in Articles 31 **1.237**
and 32 of MiFID. Member states are required to ensure that an authorized
firm 'may freely perform investment services and/or activities as well as ancillary
services within their territories, provided that such services and activities are covered by its authorization'.[251] It is important to note here that the passport only
works for the services and activities that are covered by the authorization and that
(as is to be expected) ancillary services may only be provided together with an
authorized investment service and/or activity. The host member state is prohibited from imposing additional requirements in respect of the matters covered by
MiFID.[252]

Where a firm intends to operate in a member state other than its home state, it **1.238**
must notify its intention to its home state authority, identifying that other state
and specifying what it intends to do there. The home state authority must then
forward that information to the other state within one month, after which the
firm may commence its operations in the other state.[253] Of course, business plans
change over time, and this is provided for in the Directive.[254]

Perhaps more controversially, MiFID also allows firms to operate outside their **1.239**
home member state through branches.[255] In other words, rather than constructing a network of subsidiaries in each member state, an authorized firm can simply
set up an office that is not an independent entity. Because they have no independent existence—and thus, for example, have no share capital of their own—it can
be much more difficult to monitor their activities. Crucially, should the firm
become insolvent, depositors will have access only to the deposit compensation
scheme that operates in the home state, rather than (as would often be the case for

---

[248] MiFID Article 4(20).
[249] MiFID Article 6(1).
[250] MiFID Article 6(3).
[251] MiFID Article 31(1).
[252] MiFID Article 31(1).
[253] MiFID Article 31(2) and (3).
[254] MiFID Article 31(4).
[255] MiFID Article 32.

a subsidiary) in the host state. For this reason, where it is intended that a firm will operate in several member states using a branch network, the home state authority must notify to the relevant host state authorities which compensation scheme applies.[256] As recent events have shown, the problems that arise when a financial group encounters liquidity or solvency problems can be more difficult to deal with when the group operates through branches and this may therefore be one aspect of MiFID which is closely scrutinized in the future.

1.240 The authorization regime does not merely look at the firm that is being authorized, but goes further by requiring that the persons who effectively direct its business must be 'of sufficiently good repute and sufficiently experienced as to ensure the sound and prudent management of the investment firm'.[257] Any changes to the management of the firm must be notified to the competent authority and the newcomers must satisfy the same test.[258]

1.241 Shareholders with qualifying holdings must also be notified to the competent authority,[259] which can refuse authorization if it is not satisfied with the suitability of such persons. Changes to qualifying holdings are subject to similar requirements.

1.242 Authorized persons are required to have sufficient initial[260] and continuing[261] capital to support their business.

1.243 Investment firms must comply with certain organizational requirements[262] including the establishment of policies and procedures sufficient to ensure compliance with the Directive, to prevent conflicts of interests from adversely affecting the interests of their clients and to maintain adequate records of services and transactions undertaken, so that the competent authority can monitor compliance with the Directive's obligations. Complementary to this last requirement is an obligation, placed on the shoulders of the home member state competent authority, to monitor the activities of investment firms to assess compliance with the Directive.[263]

---

[256] MiFID Article 32(4).
[257] MiFID Article 9(1).
[258] MiFID Article 9(2).
[259] MiFID Article 10(1). 'Qualifying holding' means a direct or indirect holding which represents 10% or more of the capital or voting rights of the firm or which makes it possible to exercise a significant influence over the management of the investment firm—MiFID Article 4(27).
[260] MiFID Article 12.
[261] See Directive 2006/48/EC and Directive 2006/49/EC.
[262] MiFID Article 13.
[263] MiFID Article 17.

1.4.2.2 *Conduct of business rules*

Perhaps the most important day to day protection for those dealing with invest-   **1.244**
ment firms in the market, however, is the imposition on firms of a detailed
and rigorous set of conduct of business rules.[264] These rules impose a general
requirement—that the investment firm must act honestly, fairly and professionally in accordance with the best interests of its clients.[265] There are also detailed
rules, including:

- requirements to ensure that client communications are fair, clear and not
  misleading;[266]
- requirements to ensure that clients are properly informed about what the firm
  will do for them and the risks associated with investments and investment strategies, and about the fees they will be charged;[267]
- requirements[268] for the firm to determine the client's knowledge and experience
  in investing so that it can assess the appropriateness of the investment for the
  client (the 'appropriateness requirement'), unless the investment services are
  provided to the client on an execution-only basis;[269] and for the firm to obtain
  sufficient information from the client to enable it to determine that the transactions recommended to, or entered into for, the client meets the client's investment objectives and the risks can be understood by, and possible financial losses
  can be borne by, the client (the 'suitability requirement');
- a requirement to maintain records of the terms of business entered into with
  clients;[270]
- a requirement to make regular reports to clients on the service provided to
  them;[271]
- a requirement to take all reasonable steps to obtain, when executing orders, the
  best possible result for the client taking into account price, costs, speed and

---

[264] MiFID Article 19.
[265] MiFID Article 19(1).
[266] MiFID Article 19(2).
[267] MiFID Article 19(3).
[268] The Level 2 MiFID Directive sets out detailed provisions for the assessment of suitability and
appropriateness in Articles 35 to 38.
[269] MiFID Article 19(6). This exception only applies where (a) the services relate to share trades
on a regulated market (or its equivalent outside the EEA), money market instruments and debt
securities (provided they do not have an embedded derivative element); (b) the service is provided at
the initiative of the client; (c) the client has been clearly told that the appropriateness and suitability
requirements do not apply to him; and (d) the investment firm complies with the conflict of interest
rules applicable to it (see Section 1.4.2.2.5).
[270] MiFID Article 19(7).
[271] MiFID Article 19(8).

other considerations relevant to the execution of the order for the client (known as the 'best execution' requirement);[272] and

- a requirement to execute client orders promptly, fairly and expeditiously, relative to other orders for other clients or the firm itself.[273]

1.245 The first of these requirements (to ensure that all information to clients is fair, clear and not misleading) is particularly relevant in the context of investment research.[274] Where a firm produces investment research, it must implement arrangements designed to ensure the independence of the persons producing the research.[275]

1.246 The Level 2 Directive sets out detailed conditions that have to be complied with to ensure that information is fair, clear and not misleading, where the information is sent to, or likely to be received by, retail clients or potential retail clients. This is a high level principle that sits above, and is intended to inform the policy behind, the more detailed conduct of business rules. These include the requirement that:

- it should not emphasize any potential benefits without giving a fair and prominent indication of any relevant risks;
- it must be sufficient for, and likely to be understood by, the average member of the group to whom it is directed, or by whom it is likely to be received;
- it must not disguise, diminish or obscure important items, statements or warnings;
- where it contains comparisons of one investment or service against another, the comparison must be meaningful, fair and balanced and the sources on which it is based must be specified, as must the key facts and assumptions on which it is based;
- past performance indicators must not be the most prominent feature and must cover the immediately preceding five years (or such shorter period as they have been in existence) and be based on complete 12-month periods. There must also be a warning that the past does not indicate the future; and

---

[272] MiFID Article 21. Article 44 of the Level 2 MiFID Directive sets out detailed criteria to be taken into account for determining best execution.

[273] MiFID Article 22.

[274] 'Investment research' is defined in Article 24(1) of the Level 2 MiFID Directive as research recommending or suggesting an investment strategy, expressly or implicitly, concerning financial instruments or their issuers, including any opinion as to present or future value or price of such instruments and intended for distribution to investors which (a) is labelled or described as investment research or otherwise presented as an objective or independent explanation of the matters contained in it; and (b), if the recommendation was made by an investment firm to a client, it would not constitute investment advice for the purposes of MiFID.

[275] Level 2 Directive Article 25.

- future performance indicators must not be based on or refer to simulated past performance, but must be based on reasonable assumptions supported by objective data. There must also be a prominent warning that forecasts are not a reliable indicator of future performance.[276]

1.4.2.3 *Application of conduct of business rules*

MiFID recognizes, helpfully, that some types of investor are better able to look after themselves when dealing with investment firms than others. It therefore introduces three categories of investor—eligible counterparties, professional clients and retail clients.

1.247

'Eligible counterparties' include entities such as investment firms, credit institutions, insurance companies, UCITS and their management companies, pension funds and other financial institutions authorized or regulated under Community law or the laws of a member state, national governments and their authorities, central banks and supranational organizations.[277]

1.248

A 'professional client' is someone who possesses the experience, knowledge and expertise to make his own investment decisions and properly assess the risks that he incurs.[278] To be a professional client, an investor must also fall within a specified list,[279] which includes many of those within the eligible counterparty list (such as credit institutions, investment firms, insurance companies and pension funds) together with large undertakings satisfying certain financial tests and other institutional investors whose main activity is investment in financial instruments.

1.249

The definition of retail client is (mercifully) short—this category includes everyone who is not a professional investor.[280]

1.250

These categories are not fixed for the purposes of all the business that may be done between an investment firm and its client (as will be clear from the fact that many institutions are both professional clients and eligible counterparties). So, for example, an investment firm may only treat someone as an eligible counterparty if it obtains an express confirmation from the client that it agrees to be so treated. This agreement can be generally applicable to all business done for the client, or on a transaction-by-transaction basis.[281] Equally, a professional client must be allowed to request to be treated as a retail client.[282]

1.251

---

[276] Level 2 Directive Article 27.
[277] MiFID Article 24(2).
[278] MiFID Article 4(11) and Annex II.
[279] MiFID Annex II.
[280] MiFID Article 4(12).
[281] MiFID Article 24(3). Even where a client has agreed to be treated as an eligible counterparty, it has the right to request, either generally or on a trade-by-trade basis, to be treated as a client who is entitled to the conduct of business protections—see MiFID Article 24(2) final paragraph.
[282] MiFID Annex II.

1.252 It is also possible for a retail client to 'opt up' to professional client status, if certain conditions are met, including that the firm has undertaken an adequate assessment of the expertise, experience and knowledge of the client in relation to the service provided.

1.253 The reason for the different categorizations, and for the ability given to clients to move from one category to another, is to be found in the fact that most of the protections in the conduct of business rules described above are disapplied where the client is an eligible counterparty.[283]

1.4.2.4 Ongoing supervision

1.254 Member states also have to ensure that appropriate measures are in place to enable the competent authority to monitor the activities of investment firms to ensure that they act honestly, fairly and professionally and in a manner which promotes the integrity of the markets.[284] There is an overlap here, acknowledged by the Directive, with the Market Abuse Directive regime. To assist competent authorities with this oversight, investment firms must keep data relating to all transactions in financial instruments they have carried out for at least five years[285] and must promptly report to the competent authority details of transactions in any financial instruments that are admitted to a regulated market.[286]

1.255 The MiFID also requires investment firms to put in place adequate measures and procedures designed to detect and minimize risks of failure to comply with the MiFID and to establish and maintain an internal compliance function, which operates independently, to monitor the adequacy and effectiveness of those measures and procedures and to assist those carrying out investment services and activities to comply with the firm's obligations under the Directive.[287] The compliance function must have the necessary authority, resources, expertise and access to all relevant information, must be headed by a compliance officer, and must be staffed with people who are not involved in the performance of the services or activities which they monitor.[288] In addition, and crucially, the remuneration of the compliance team must not compromise their objectivity or be likely to do so.[289]

1.256 Market risk also needs to be monitored and controlled. The MiFID requires investment firms to establish and maintain policies, procedures, arrangements

---

[283] MiFID Article 24(1).
[284] MiFID Article 25(1).
[285] MiFID Article 25(2).
[286] MiFID Article 25(3). The detail includes identification of the relevant instruments, quantity, dates and times of execution, and prices—MiFID Article 25(4).
[287] Level 2 Directive Article 6(1) and (2).
[288] Ibid Article 6(3)(a) to (c).
[289] Ibid Article 6(3)(d).

and mechanisms which identify risks relating to the firm's activities, processes and systems and to set these risks at the level tolerated by the firm.[290] Where the firm's business is of a size and complexity to justify it, there must be a risk function which operates independently and implements the risk policy and procedures and provides reports to senior management.[291]

The MiFID also imposes duties on senior managers, who are made responsible for ensuring that the firm complies with the Directive and for assessing and reviewing the effectiveness of the firm's arrangements and procedures for compliance and rectifying any deficiencies.[292] Investment firms must ensure that senior management receive frequent reports from the compliance, risk and audit functions.[293] Such reports are also copied to the firm's board or supervisory function (that is, those responsible for supervising the senior management).[294]   **1.257**

1.4.2.5 Conflicts—inducements and investment research

One of the things that will destroy confidence in a market more quickly than any other is the notion that the investment firm is motivated, in its dealings with its client, by interests other than those of the client. It is hardly surprising, therefore, that MiFID requires member states to ensure that investment firms take all reasonable steps to identify conflicts of interest between themselves (and their managers, employees and tied agents, or persons linked to them by control) and their clients, or between one client and another, that arise in the course of providing any investment and ancillary services.[295] Such conflicts must either be managed (for example, through the use of Chinese Walls), so that the risks of damage to the client will be prevented; or they must be clearly disclosed to the client before business is undertaken on its behalf.[296]   **1.258**

The concept is developed further in the Level 2 Directive, which sets out specific conflict situations that must, as a minimum, be addressed. These include situations where: **1.259**

- the firm or person is likely to make a financial gain, or avoid a financial loss, at the expense of the client;
- the firm or person has an interest in the outcome of a service provided to the client or of a transaction carried out on behalf of the client, which is distinct from the client's interest in that outcome;

---

[290] Ibid Article 7(1).
[291] Ibid Article 7(2).
[292] Ibid Article 9(1).
[293] Ibid Article 9(2).
[294] Ibid Article 9(3).
[295] MiFID Article 18(1).
[296] MiFID Article 18(2).

- the firm or that person has a financial or other incentive to favour the interest of another client or group of clients over the interests of the client;
- the firm or that person carries on the same business as the client;
- the firm or that person receives or will receive from a person other than the client an inducement in relation to a service provided to the client, in the form of monies, goods or services, other than the standard commission or fee for that service.[297]

1.260 Firms must establish, implement and maintain an effective conflicts of interest policy, set out in writing and appropriate to the size and complexity of the firm and its business.[298] This must also take account of conflicts arising out of the structure and business activities of other members of the firm's group—a difficult concept for many investment firms that operate on a global scale through many different subsidiaries and affiliates.

1.261 **1.4.2.5.1 Inducements** The last of the specific examples of conflict situations listed above is perhaps the most difficult to interpret in practice. Inducements are not only dealt with as part of the conflicts rule,[299] but also as part of the requirement under the MiFID to act honestly, fairly and professionally in accordance with the best interests of the client when carrying out investment services for it.[300] The Level 2 Directive sets out further detailed provisions relating to inducements under this second limb. Article 26 of that Directive starts with the presumption that investment firms are *not* regarded as acting honestly, fairly and professionally in accordance with the best interests of a client if, in relation to the provision of an investment or ancillary service to the client, they pay or are paid any fee or commission or provide or are provided with any non-monetary benefit.[301] Such a provision, without more, would clearly make the provision of many financial services an unremunerative exercise. Accordingly, limited exceptions are provided, including:

- where the fee or benefit is paid by the client or a person on behalf of the client;
- a fee provided by a third party where the existence, amount[302] and nature of the fee or benefit are clearly disclosed to the client, in a manner that is comprehensive, accurate and understandable, prior to the provision of the service, provided the fee or commission or benefit is designed to enhance the quality of the relevant service to the client and not impair compliance with the firm's duty to act in the best interests of the client; and

---

[297] Level 2 Directive Article 21.
[298] Level 2 Directive Article 22(1).
[299] MiFID Article 18.
[300] MiFID Article 19.
[301] Level 2 Directive Article 26.
[302] Or, where this cannot be ascertained, the method of calculating the amount.

- proper fees which enable or are necessary for the provision of investment services, such as custody costs, settlement or exchange fees, regulatory levies or legal fees, and which, by their nature, cannot give rise to conflicts with a firm's duties to act honestly, fairly and professionally in the client's best interests.[303]

There is already a great deal of complexity here (which causes considerable confusion in the market). But the matter is not left to the Directives alone. CESR has added its voice, at Level 3.[304] This makes the perhaps surprising statement[305] that the provisions described above 'should not be treated as applying only to payments or receipts that are made with the purpose or intent to influence the actions of a firm'. It then goes on to say that standard market commission or fees are within the inducements regime; that the regime applies to payments and benefits paid to or by an entity in the same group as the investment firm; and sets out a variety of detailed circumstances that should be considered in determining whether an arrangement is designed to enhance the quality of the service to the client. **1.262**

The complex mesh of Levels 1, 2 and 3 in this area is a prime example of how words can, indeed, be used in such a way as to obscure meaning. It might indeed have been clearer simply to say that every fee or benefit received by the service provider must be disclosed and be necessary to the provision of the service. **1.263**

1.4.2.5.2 Investment research   Another area where conflicts often arise involves the production of investment research. The Level 2 Directive defines investment research as 'research or other information recommending or suggesting an investment strategy, explicitly or implicitly, concerning one or several financial instruments or the issuers of financial instruments, including any opinion as to the present or future value or price of such instruments, intended for distribution channels or for the public', where, first, it is labelled as investment research or the equivalent or is presented as an objective or independent view of the matters contained in it; and, secondly, if the recommendation were made as a recommendation to a client, it would not constitute investment advice under the MiFID.[306] **1.264**

The Level 2 Directive requires that firms producing investment research must put in place organizational arrangements to ensure the objectivity and independence **1.265**

---

[303] Ibid Article 26 (a) and (b).

[304] See 'Inducements under MiFID', The Committee of European Securities Regulators CESR/07-228b.

[305] At least to those who look at the heading of a Directive provision for an indication of the meaning of the provision, to whom the word 'inducement' clearly conjures up the notion of a purpose or intent to influence another.

[306] Level 2 Directive Article 24.

of the analyst who writes the report and to prevent the analyst from trading in the securities to which the report relates.[307]

1.266 In addition to the MiFID conflicts regime, Article 6(5) of the Market Abuse Directive requires that:

> member states shall ensure that there is appropriate regulation in place to ensure that persons who produce or disseminate research concerning financial instruments or issuers of financial instruments and persons who produce or disseminate other information recommending or suggesting investment strategy, intended for distribution channels or for the public, take reasonable care to ensure that such information is fairly presented and disclose their interests or indicate conflicts of interest concerning the financial instruments to which that information relates.

1.267 Commission Directive 2003/125/EC sets out detailed measures designed to achieve this objective, including requirements for the disclosure of the identity of the person making any recommendation relating to investment;[308] and to ensure that recommendations are derived from reliable sources (or, if not, that fact is clearly stated), that facts are clearly distinguished from opinions or interpretations and that estimates or forecasts are clearly labelled and their assumptions are stated.[309] Additional, more onerous, obligations are imposed on professional analysts and regulated institutions.[310]

1.268 It is important for those dealing in the markets to know, when they receive an investment recommendation or advice, whether the person giving it has their interests wholly in mind, or is influenced by other considerations. Accordingly, the person giving the recommendation or advice must disclose:

> all relationships and circumstances that may reasonably be expected to impair the objectivity of the recommendation, in particular where relevant persons have a significant financial interest in one or more of the financial instruments which are the subject of the recommendation, or a significant conflict of interest with respect to an issuer to which the recommendation relates.[311]

1.269 Such relationships may include major shareholdings (either by the person making the recommendation in the issuer, or by the issuer in that person's share capital), or a business relationship, such as the person making the recommendation acting as market maker or liquidity provider in the issuer, and whether that person or an affiliate has, in the previous 12 months, acted as lead manager or co-lead manager of any issue by the issuer being recommended.[312]

---

[307] Level 2 Directive Article 25.
[308] Commission Directive 2003/125/EC Article 2.
[309] Ibid Article 3.
[310] Ibid Article 4.
[311] Ibid Article 5.
[312] Ibid Article 6.

Disclosure must also be made if the remuneration of the person making a **1.270** recommendation is tied to investment banking transactions performed by the investment firm for whom that person works or credit institution or any related legal person.[313] On the basis that markets need to attract investors, and investors will only attend markets where they can trust the advice and recommendations they will receive, these measures appear to be not only sensible, but necessary.

1.4.2.6 *Authorization of regulated markets*

Regulated markets, also, require authorization.[314] Authorization may only be **1.271** granted where the competent authority is satisfied that the operator of the market and the systems of the market comply with detailed requirements. The operator must be of good repute and sufficiently experienced as to ensure the sound and prudent management and operation of the market.[315] Persons in a position to exercise direct or indirect significant influence over the management of the market must be suitable, and the operator must identify such people to the competent authority.[316] The market must satisfy certain organizational requirements, to manage risks and conflicts between itself and its operator and those using the markets, and to ensure the efficient and timely operation of the market.[317] The market must have clear and transparent rules regarding admission of financial instruments to trading, that ensure fair, orderly and efficient trading.[318] The rules for admission of participants to the market must be non-discriminatory and based on objective criteria,[319] but must take account of the suitability and expertise of those participants.[320]

There are also detailed rules for public disclosure, both of prices at which offers to **1.272** transact are made and of prices at which transactions on regulated markets have been executed.[321]

1.4.3 **Controlling predators**

Because shares give ownership rights to companies, shareholders benefit from a **1.273** variety of different protective measures under EU Directives. These comprise the right to have public disclosure made to them when any one shareholder, or group

---

313 Ibid Article 6(3).
314 MiFID Article 36(1).
315 MiFID Article 37(1).
316 MiFID Article 38(1) and (2).
317 MiFID Article 39.
318 MiFID Article 40.
319 MiFID Article 42.
320 MiFID Article 42(3).
321 MiFID Articles 44 and 45.

of shareholders, is building up a stake (either to exert influence over the management of the company or to launch a takeover bid); the right to have any takeover bid mounted in a manner that is fair; and the right not to have proportionate shareholdings diluted through the issue of new shares without compensation.

1.4.3.1 Major shareholding disclosure

1.274 The first of these protections is provided under the TOD, which requires the home member state to ensure that, where a shareholder acquires or disposes of voting shares of an issuer whose shares are admitted to trading on a regulated market, it must notify the issuer of the proportion of voting rights held by it as a result of that acquisition or disposal where it exceeds or falls below certain thresholds.[322] Voting rights are calculated on the basis of all the voting shares, even if some voting rights have been suspended. Additional information must be given in relation to the specific class of shares that have been acquired or sold (which will only be relevant where there are several classes of shares carrying voting rights).

1.275 The TOD contains anti-avoidance provisions, capturing not just single shareholdings, but voting rights held by several persons where there is an agreement between them to vote in concert, or where the voting rights are attached to shares lodged as collateral and the person with whom they are lodged controls the voting rights and declares its intention to exercise them; and voting rights held by an entity controlled by another entity.[323]

1.276 Not all shares count for the purpose of these calculations. For example, there are exemptions for shares acquired for the sole purpose of clearing and settling within the usual short settlement cycle; for shares held by custodians (provided they can only exercise the voting rights under instructions given by their client); and for market-makers.[324]

1.277 The TOD sets out procedures for the notification and disclosure of major shareholdings, including the details that are to be notified and the timing for the notification.[325]

1.278 It is important to note that the regime catches not just direct holding of voting rights, but also the holding, directly or indirectly, of financial instruments that result in an entitlement to acquire, on the holder's initiative alone, shares to which

---

[322] TOD Article 9(1). The thresholds are 5%, 10%, 15%, 20%, 25%, 30%, 50% and 75%. The 30% and 75% thresholds may be replaced by one-third and two-thirds respectively (TOD Article 9(3)).

[323] TOD Article 10.

[324] TOD Article 9(3) and (4).

[325] TOD Article 12.

voting rights are attached and that are already issued.[326] The inclusion of equity derivatives in the disclosure regime in this way, while understandable, somewhat clouds the overall clarity of the disclosure, because it will necessarily bring with it an element of double counting. The shares to which the derivatives relate will exist, and have already potentially been disclosed by another person. The disclosure of the voting rights attached to the same shares in the context of an equity derivative raises the interesting notion that overall disclosure may amount to many multiples of the issued share capital of the issuer.

1.4.3.2 *Takeovers*

An investor in shares that are admitted to public markets is always subject to the risk that another investor, or group of investors, will acquire control of the issuer. Of course, such control can be used in many different ways, some of which may be beneficial to the minority investor and some of which may be harmful. It is fear of the latter that undermines confidence in markets and, when unchecked, can cause investors to hold back from buying shares in the public markets.   **1.279**

The Directive on Takeover Bids[327] (the 'Takeovers Directive') introduces important protections to investors in this area. It applies to takeover bids for the securities[328] of companies governed by the laws of member states, where all or some of those securities are admitted to trading on a regulated market.[329] 'Takeover bid' means, for this purpose, a public offer made to the holders of the securities of a company to acquire all or some of those securities, whether mandatory or voluntary, which follows or has as its objective the acquisition of control of the offeree company in accordance with national law.[330]   **1.280**

Where a takeover bid is mounted, certain principles must be observed: **1.281**

- equivalent treatment must be given to all holders of the same class of security;
- protection must be given to a resulting minority;
- those receiving the offer must be given sufficient information to enable them to reach an informed decision and sufficient time to absorb that information;

---

[326] TOD Article 13. This last phrase brings comfort to holders of convertible bonds (because the shares into which they convert are rarely issued until conversion. Indeed, it is difficult to know how convertible bonds could be sensibly brought within the disclosure regime, because the number of shares into which they might convert will fluctuate from day to day, being dependent on the share price.)

[327] Directive 2004/25/EC.

[328] This means transferable securities carrying voting rights in a company—see Takeovers Directive Article 2(1)(e).

[329] Takeovers Directive Article 1(1). The Directive does not apply to certain collective investment scheme companies.

[330] Takeovers Directive Article 2(1)(a).

- the offeror must ensure he has sufficient cash and other resources to fulfil his obligations under the offer;
- the board of the offeree company must act in the best interests of the company as a whole and must not deny its members the right to decide for themselves on the merits of the bid; and
- an offeree company must not be hindered in the conduct of its affairs for longer than is reasonable by a bid for its securities.[331]

1.282   Member states have to set up an authority to supervise compliance with the requirements of the Directive.[332] Jurisdiction rules give supervisory power to the authority in the country of the registered office of the offeree company or, if the company is only admitted to a regulated market in another member state, the authority in that other member state.[333]

1.283   The Directive contains specific provisions that add detail to the general principles set out above. So, for example, a person who, alone or with others, acquires a certain controlling percentage of the voting rights is required to make an offer, at a fair price,[334] for the remaining shares.[335] It is left to the relevant competent authority to determine what the controlling percentage is.[336] The consideration for the offer may be cash, or securities, or both—but if it includes securities, they must be liquid securities that are admitted to an EEA regulated market.[337] A cash alternative must be offered where the offeror, or those with whom he is acting, has acquired 5% or more of its holding for cash within the period leading up to the bid.[338]

1.284   A decision to make a bid must be promptly announced to the public[339] and an offer document, containing the information necessary to enable the holders of the offeree company's securities to reach a properly informed decision on the bid, must be produced and published, having been previously sent to the supervisory authority.[340] The offer document, once approved by the relevant supervisory authority, is valid in all other member states, whose authorities have only very limited powers to require the inclusion in it of additional information.[341] The offer document must contain details of the offer and, importantly,

---

[331] Takeovers Directive Article 3(1).
[332] Ibid Article 4(1).
[333] Ibid Article 4(2). There are also rules for determining jurisdiction where the issuer's securities are admitted to several EEA regulated markets.
[334] Determined by reference to recent market prices, under Article 5(4).
[335] Ibid Article 5(1).
[336] Ibid Article 5(3).
[337] Ibid Article 5(5).
[338] Ibid Article 5(5).
[339] Ibid Article 6(1).
[340] Ibid Article 6(2).
[341] Ibid Article 6(2) final paragraph.

a statement of the offeror's intentions with regard to the future business of the offeree company and, in so far as it is affected by the bid, the offeror company and with regard to the safeguarding of the jobs of their employees and management, including any material change in the conditions of employment, and in particular the offeror's strategic plans for the two companies and the likely repercussions on employment and the locations of the companies' places of business.[342]

The period allowed for acceptance of the bid must be not less than two, and not more than ten, weeks.[343]   **1.285**

Once a bid has been announced to the public, certain protective devices become ineffective against the bidder. So, for example, any restrictions on transfers of shares in the articles of association of the offeree company, or in a contract between the offeree company and its shareholders, are disapplied, as are any restrictions on voting rights at meetings to decide upon defensive measures.[344]   **1.286**

The board of the offeree company may not take action, other than seeking alternative bids, to frustrate the bid without authorization from the shareholders in general meeting.[345] It must also prepare a document giving its reasoned views on the bid and its impact on the issuer and its employees.[346]   **1.287**

Finally, the Directive contains important provisions allowing the successful bidder to buy out a residual minority[347] and allowing that minority to require the bidder to buy out their minority holding.[348]   **1.288**

1.4.3.3 Protection against dilution—rights issues

Investors who make substantial investments in shares are understandably concerned to ensure that their holding is not diluted. An investor who acquires, say, 10% of the share capital of a company, with a view to ensuring that his voice will, as a result, be listened to by management would be taking a risk if the company could, by issuing a substantial number of new shares to someone else, dilute his holding to a much lower proportion of the increased share capital. Equally, if (as is normally the case) the shares to be offered are priced at a discount to the current market price, all shareholders, big or small, stand to gain if they are included in the offering and risk a dilution in the value of their holding if they   **1.289**

---

[342] Ibid Article 6(3)(i).
[343] Ibid Article 7(1).
[344] Ibid Article 11. There are provisions requiring compensation for the holders of these abrogated rights.
[345] Ibid Article 9(2). Member states may opt out of this provision—see Article 12(1).
[346] Ibid Article 9(5).
[347] Ibid Article 15.
[348] Ibid Article 16.

are excluded. European law has, for some while, provided protection against such risks by requiring that when shares are issued for cash, they must be first offered to existing shareholders in proportion to their holding of the company's share capital.[349]

1.4.4 Changes to share rights and other information

1.290 Investors in securities that are traded on a regulated market need to know what they are buying. Accordingly, when changes are made to the rights attached to those securities, the issuer must make them public without delay.[350] This seems unobjectionable, and even perhaps obvious. Less obvious, though, is a requirement for issuers to make public without delay any new 'loan issues and in particular any guarantee or security in respect thereof'.[351] 'Loan issue' is not defined. If it refers to bank facilities as well as issues of debt instruments, then it gives rise to difficulties (not least the fact that many issuers borrow, sometimes on overdraft, on a regular basis, so that very frequent disclosures would be required). Indeed, even if (as is more likely) only issues of debt securities are intended, some issuers will be put to considerable inconvenience and cost, because they are frequent issuers. It is difficult to know what the purpose of this provision is, or how it accords with the Prospectus Directive, particularly where the bond issue in question is made under the qualified investor exemption and therefore expressly intended *not* to be brought to the attention of the general public.

1.291 Perhaps more sensibly, the TOD requires issuers to ensure that all facilities and information necessary to enable shareholders to exercise their rights are available in the home member state and that integrity of data is preserved.[352] Electronic communications are expressly permitted for these purposes, provided their use has been approved in general meeting and meets certain conditions.[353] Similar provisions are made for holders of non-equity securities.[354]

1.292 Finally, shareholders and other security holders of the issuer must be treated equally—in the case of shareholders, with those who are in the same position;[355]

---

[349] For example Article 29(1) of Council Directive 77/91/EEC requires that, whenever a company increases its share capital by offering shares for cash, the shares must be offered on a pre-emptive basis to existing shareholders in proportion to their current holding in the company's share capital.

[350] TOD Article 16(1) and (2).

[351] TOD Article 16(3).

[352] TOD Article 17(2). The provision goes into laborious detail about providing information on the place, time and agenda for the meeting, the making available of proxy forms and so on—matters that, in most countries, will already be adequately dealt with in the relevant company law.

[353] TOD Article 17(3).

[354] TOD Article 18.

[355] TOD Article 17(1).

and, in the case of debt securities, in respect of the rights attaching to the securities.[356] This last phrase causes confusion in the market from time to time, with some arguing that (for example) an offer to buy back debt securities cannot be made to only some of the existing bondholders. However, the wording is perfectly clear. For it to apply, the right in question must attach to the securities. These are the rights established in the contract itself. They do not typically include a right to receive an offer from the issuer to purchase the bond, so that buy-backs are not within the ambit of the provision.

1.5 Some Conclusions

'With the introduction of the euro', says the Commission's Financial Services Action Plan, 'there is a unique window of opportunity to equip the EU with a modern financial apparatus in which the cost of capital and financial intermediation are kept to a minimum. Corporate and household users of financial services will benefit significantly, and investment and employment across the Union will be stimulated.'[357] Great benefits were identified from the integration of the EEA's financial markets, even to the extent of providing numerical estimates for the potential growth in GDP and employment.[358] When objectives are set and promises are made, it is important to look back after a while to assess whether they have been achieved; and, if not, to ask why and to identify what more can be done.

1.293

There is no doubt that much progress has been made. Cross-border offerings of securities in the wholesale markets, which worked well for many decades prior to the FSAP Directives, work a little better after their arrival—not least thanks to the harmonization of the exemptions from the public offer prospectus requirement. It is also easier to make simultaneous retail offers in a number of different jurisdictions, thanks to the introduction of rules requiring acceptance of a single prospectus in a single language, subject to the approval of a single competent authority, for the purposes of any public offer in any member state. Financial intermediaries are helped in arranging and carrying out such offers by the harmonization of authorization requirements. And investors are, perhaps, more confident in the fairness of the markets, and the trustworthiness of those they deal with in the markets, thanks to the introduction of detailed conduct of business rules and the prohibitions on market abuse.

1.294

---

[356] TOD Article 18(1).

[357] COM (1999) 232 (http://ec.europa.eu/internal_market/finances/docs/actionplan/index/action_en.pdf).

[358] See the Introduction.

1.295   However, a true pan-EEA public offering of transferable securities remains a rare thing. Why? Part of the answer lies in the existence of barriers to such offers that none of the FSAP Directives has addressed; and part lies in the fact that the additional costs that are thrown up by these barriers are not outweighed by the potential reduction in the cost of capital that might be available to issuers through making a public offer.

1.296   These barriers include, for example, the lack of harmonization of the liability regimes of member states that apply to the disclosure regimes under the various FSAP Directives. One of the concerns of anyone charged with making disclosure will be to ensure that they discharge that duty diligently—and that they manage any liability risks they may run if they fail to do so. In the context of cross-border security offerings, liability is likely to be triggered in the jurisdiction in which the securities are sold. Questions such as whether the person owing the disclosure duty was negligent in carrying out that duty will be judged according to the laws of the member state in which the damage was suffered; and this is likely to be, in this context, the country in which the investor read and relied upon the disclosure. Faced with a kaleidoscope of different liability regimes, under many of which it is somewhat unclear as to who is liable and in what circumstances, it is perhaps only natural that many issuers will need a very hard push before venturing on a cross-border public offer—particularly when (as has typically been the case in the Euromarkets) institutional investors can supply most of the funding that issuers require, and can have offers made to them without the need for a prospectus.

1.297   Consumer protection laws provide another intractable example. As has been seen, one of the impediments to the development of a pan-EEA market that was identified by the Lamfalussy Report was the requirement, under the pre-FSAP regime, for the whole prospectus to be translated into the language of the host state. The Prospectus Directive removed this impediment, by stipulating that the prospectus would be valid if it was in a language that was customary in international finance and that the host state could only require translation of the 2,500-word summary. This was good; but it only applied to the prospectus. Many EEA states have consumer protection laws that are designed to ensure that consumers understand whatever they are buying and the terms of the sale contract. They do this, often, by saying that the contract is not enforceable against the consumer/purchaser unless it complies with certain requirements. In the context of public offers of securities, this sometimes means that the terms of the securities (which, after all, is the substance of the thing that the investor is buying) have to be translated into the language of the host state. If they are not, then the sale contract may not be enforceable. Translation is expensive; and costs have to be outweighed by benefits to make a cross-border offering viable.

Most issuers of securities have found, so far, that the fragmentation of Community law in these areas and the cost—and in some cases, the difficulty of knowing what the local laws mean in terms of liability and risk—act as powerful deterrents to pan-EEA offerings. **1.298**

This prompts a further question—does this matter? This sounds like an odd question, given that the objective of the FSAP is the development of the European cross-border securities market. For those who believe that a pan-EEA market must necessarily involve millions of retail investors investing directly in shares and bonds, of course it matters very much. A huge opportunity is being lost, as those investors find themselves restricted in the geographic scope of their investment activities. And the problem will become increasingly serious, as more and more people are required to save for their own retirement (with state-funded pensions coming under increasing pressure due to demographic shifts), so that demand for investment will increase at a much greater rate than the supply of investment opportunities. **1.299**

This model needs to be questioned, however—particularly in the light of the somewhat extreme difficulties that would be encountered in attempting to remove some of the remaining barriers to the pan-EEA market, by harmonizing consumer protection laws and liability regimes. If a thing cannot be done, or can only be done with extreme inconvenience and difficulty, a wise person will seek an alternative approach. **1.300**

One alternative approach lies in the increased use of intermediated investment—through pension funds and collective investment vehicles. Such institutional investors tend to remain outside the scope of the more invasive consumer protection regimes. They are staffed by people who are experts in investment matters and, in many cases, are themselves regulated entities. When they deal with retail investors as clients, they are subject to detailed rules on how they conduct their business, under the MiFID regime described above. True, the interposition of such institutions between the retail investor and the market introduces extra cost; yet such costs need to be set against the additional costs that are inevitably incurred in any direct offer to retail investors. **1.301**

Another approach would be to develop the concept of layered offerings, allowing direct investment by the public, but interposing a layer of private banks between the issuer of the securities and the retail investor. This is a model that is actively used in a number of European countries, and it has much to recommend it. The logical construct depends on the private banks having an understanding of the issuer and the risks and opportunities inherent in its securities, and also of the individual circumstances of their customers. The former understanding is derived from a combination of the market disclosures made by the issuer **1.302** (including, often, the initial prospectus produced for admission of the securities to the regulated market and ongoing disclosures under the Market Abuse Directive and the TOD) and the private banks' own research, based on publicly available information, into the issuer and the macro- (and micro-) economic environment in which it operates. The latter understanding is derived from the information that the private banks are required to obtain from the individual investor pursuant to the MiFID. This all sounds pretty similar to the arrangements under the FSAP Directives, which of course, it is—apart from one important difference. The FSAP Directives contemplate that the individual investor needs protection by being given a mass of information; the layered approach does not. When a private bank offers to its individual customer under the layered approach, there is no notion that the investor should be provided with a prospectus—either by the issuer or the private bank. Instead, the investor is relying solely on the advice of the private bank which, before giving that advice, will have diligently applied its knowledge and expertise to understanding the disclosure on the issuer and the securities being offered and to relating the assessment of the risks of the offering to the financial circumstances of the investor.

1.303   Perhaps the best answer is a combination of these approaches. Limited general offers to the public in, say, two or three countries can be combined with private placements through private banks in a couple of other countries, rounded off with wholesale-only offerings in every other member state. Indeed, a combination of private placements through private banks and wholesale offerings elsewhere is very much the model that has been developing since the introduction of the FSAP Directives. All that is lacking is the generalized offer by the issuer to all comers in selected jurisdictions. This is not the utopia envisioned, perhaps, when the FSAP was first mooted, where the same offer of securities could be made at the same time to everyone, everywhere in the EEA. But pragmatism sometimes has to prevail over theory, however desirable and attractive that theory may seem to be. To adapt slightly the words of a former French Prime Minister, we have a Europe which loves ideology; and we need pragmatism.[359]

---

[359] Jean-Pierre Raffarin in *The Independent* 11 May 2002.

PART 2

DOING DEALS IN EUROPE

2

EQUITY*

2.1 Preparing to Go Public

2.1.1 Introduction

Companies may turn to the public equity markets for all manner of reasons, **2.01**
although invariably it comes down to the fact that equity offerings can facilitate
development and growth and can help companies become more profitable in the
future. Key drivers include:

- Helping to fund further growth by raising equity capital for investment.
- Raising the company's profile and obtaining a 'badge of approval' as a result
  of the regulatory oversight that accompanies admission to the public equity
  markets. This can help obtain better terms from suppliers and customers,

---

* The contribution of Alfonso Ventoso of Uría Menéndez and Stephen Glasper of Cleary
Gottlieb Steen & Hamilton LLP to the drafting of this Chapter is acknowledged with thanks.

as well as reduce the cost of further capital that the company might want to raise, in both the debt and equity markets.

- Creating an acquisition currency in the form of publicly-traded equity, which can then be used as an attractive form of consideration for forays into the M&A market.
- Helping recruitment efforts—companies are more likely to attract and hold on to talent as public companies with a high profile. Being able to offer publicly-traded securities, or options over them, can also be a cheaper way of remunerating staff.
- Providing an exit for existing shareholders. This is often an important driver for private equity houses that have invested in companies and helped them develop into a ready-made prospect for other investors.

2.02   A classic IPO involves creating an immediate public market for a company's securities by listing on a stock exchange and offering its securities to widen its shareholder base. While IPOs tend to be reported as being *en vogue* among younger companies in the market eager to expand, they can also represent a good option for larger and more mature privately-owned companies seeking to further their development.

2.1.2 Advisers

2.03   An IPO is likely to represent a critical moment in a company's life, for which hard work and careful preparation will be required. It is customary for a company contemplating an IPO to engage specialist advisers to assist it in the preparation and execution of the deal from a commercial, marketing, accounting, and legal perspective.

2.1.2.1 *Investment banks*

2.04   The company will need to engage one or more investment banks, whose key roles will be to advise the issuer in connection with the transaction, to market the transaction to potential investors and, ultimately, to underwrite the deal in the event that they fail to shift the company's stock in the market. The underwriters will typically arrange themselves according to an inter-bank hierarchy of importance, discernable by various desirable titles such as 'book runner', 'global coordinator' and 'lead manager'.

2.05   The company is likely to rely on its chosen investment banks to undertake the following specific duties as underwriters of an IPO:

- provide commercial advice on the structure and timing of the transaction;
- assist with the preparation of the all-important equity story—the reason why a potential investor should put his hand in his pocket;

- assist with the deal documentation, including legal documents (most importantly, the prospectus) and marketing materials, in which the company will lay out its equity story;
- liaise with the regulators—particularly where the company is unfamiliar with the application processes for an IPO, an investment bank can use its experience, as well as its relationships with the authorities, to facilitate the transaction;
- arrange the syndication of the IPO among the banks taking on an underwriting commitment;
- market the IPO, including running the book during the book-building period;
- conduct stabilization activities, i.e. deal in the company's securities in the market once the deal has closed in order to massage peaks and troughs in the company's share price; and
- coordinate the company's other advisers.

The company will often enter into an engagement letter with its underwriters for the provision of the services listed above, or at least for those services that fall to be provided before the signing of an underwriting agreement, which is the key contract between the company and the underwriters (see Section 2.6 below). The underwriters' engagement letter, therefore, governs the relationship between the underwriters, the company and any selling shareholders during the preparatory period of the IPO until a definitive underwriting agreement is entered into. It sets out, *inter alia*, the underwriters' fees and reimbursable expenses during this period and, crucially, it details the terms on which the company will indemnify the underwriters in the event that the underwriters take a hit before the company goes to market (albeit unlikely, since it is the act of going to market that gives rise to possible losses for investors that they would seek to recover). **2.06**

The terms of the engagement letter are especially important to the extent that they hold persuasive value when the parties come to negotiate the underwriting agreement. In particular, the style of indemnity and the relevant carve-outs, and the lock-up undertakings of the company and any selling shareholders agreed in the engagement letter can come into play down the line. **2.07**

2.1.2.2 *Legal advisers*

Legal advisers assist the company and the underwriters in complying with the complex legal requirements involved in an IPO. If the proposed deal has an international component, the company will need both domestic and international advice. **2.08**

In a standard IPO transaction, the role of the company's lawyers will typically include the following:

- helping to assess the company's suitability for listing (for example, the adequacy of its corporate governance systems and controls and the composition of its board of directors, if, as a result of the IPO, the company will become subject to an exacting corporate governance regime) and to advise on steps to prepare for status as a public company;

- reviewing the company's corporate documents and preparing any corporate resolutions required to authorize the IPO and listing;
- helping to draft the prospectus/offering memorandum;
- participating in the due diligence effort;
- dealing with the relevant regulator, stock exchange and other authorities, including preparing the company's applications for listing/admission to trading and the approval of its prospectus;
- advising the company in its negotiations with the underwriters, including in relation to the underwriters' engagement letter and the underwriting agreement; and
- providing legal opinions to the underwriters on certain aspects of the transactions.

2.09 On the other side, the role of the underwriters' lawyers will typically involve the following:

- reviewing the prospectus;
- participating in the due diligence effort;
- drafting the underwriting agreement and assisting the underwriters in negotiating the underwriting agreement and other related contracts with the company's and selling shareholders' counsel;
- negotiating other relevant documents on behalf of the underwriters, including the auditors' comfort letters and the company counsel's legal opinion; and
- providing legal opinions to the underwriters on certain aspects of the transactions.

2.1.2.3 Auditors

2.10 The company's auditors will play a key role in a company's preparation for an IPO, typically delivering the following types of services:

- auditing the company's historical consolidated financial statements, including any adjustments required to ensure compliance with appropriate accounting standards;
- auditing or performing a limited review of any interim financial statements of the company required to be prepared in connection with the transaction;
- reviewing the financial information the company proposes to present in the prospectus/offering memorandum to confirm it has been properly extracted from the company's financial statements;
- depending on the company's financial history, preparing special reports on pro-forma historical financial statements and/or on projected financial information;

- providing a comfort letter to the underwriters (see Section 2.1.3.3 below);
- participating in the due diligence process.

2.1.2.4 *Other specialists*

In addition to investment banks, lawyers and auditors, the company may also **2.11** need to engage a range of additional specialists, depending on the deal. If, for example, the company is seduced by the *cache* of a primary listing in London, it will need to appoint a sponsor (although typically a member of the underwriting syndicate will perform this role). Broadly, the sponsor will assist the company in understanding and meeting its obligations under the United Kingdom listing rules, help ensure that the prospectus contains the appropriate disclosure, and deal with the United Kingdom Listing Authority (the 'UKLA')[1] and the London Stock Exchange (the 'LSE') throughout the process.

Other advisers and service providers that tend to crop up on IPOs include an **2.12** agent bank (to deal with the settlement of the offer), a public relations agency (to assist with communications with the press), a financial printer (to print and distribute the offering memorandum) and a roadshow consultant (to take care of roadshow arrangements).

2.1.3 Due diligence

2.1.3.1 *Purpose of the due diligence review*

The underwriters of a securities offering are typically rewarded handsomely for **2.13** their services, particularly if they are successful in building a book of investors ready to buy into the deal. But what they do is not without its risks, not least that of liability to aggrieved investors who, after participating in the offering, suffer loss on the company's securities—if such interests can form a case for liability against the underwriters, one should worry that they will. This is one of the reasons why the underwriters want to seek out all material facts about the issuer and its securities. One of the primary purposes of the underwriters' due diligence, therefore, is to establish a 'due diligence defence' to any possible investor claims, which is described in more detail in Chapter 4 of Part 2.

Companies and their directors also face a significant risk of liability to investors. **2.14** The due diligence process also helps to protect them, *inter alia*, by helping to uncover material information, which can then be properly disclosed in the prospectus.

---

[1] The UKLA is the branch of the UK regulator—the Financial Services Authority (the 'FSA')— that oversees applications for admission to the Official List (including the prospectus approval process), as well as listed companies' compliance with post-admission continuing obligations.

2.1.3.2 *Scope of the due diligence*

2.15 The due diligence review involves a combined effort on the part of the underwriters and their advisers, broadly focusing on the following issues:

- Business: the underwriters and the legal teams typically lead an analysis of the company's business, financial condition and performance, strategy, projections and business plan, material contracts, risks, strengths and weaknesses. It is often accompanied by site visits and meetings with the company, during which its senior management present the business and respond to rigorous questioning. Drafting sessions on the prospectus are also a key part of the due diligence process—they are often the setting for a thorough 'kicking of the tyres' as regards disclosures in the draft prospectus.
- Legal: the legal teams typically review the company's key legal documents (covering matters such as corporate, assets, financing, material contracts, regulatory, tax, human resources, litigation). It is common to set materiality thresholds to avoid populating a data room with unnecessary documents and to limit the documentary review to a manageable scope.
- Accounting: accountants are the source of a substantial level of comfort about the company's financial condition and the financial information the company proposes to present in the prospectus.
- Specialist areas: sometimes the underwriters will need to engage an independent expert or consultant, depending on the nature of the company's business and the sector in which it operates. If, say, the company operates in the real estate sector, the underwriters might want to bring in a real estate consultant to assess the value of the company's real estate portfolio. Or, if the company is in the business of oil and gas, the underwriters might call on an oil and gas consultant to deliver a report on the company's stated reserves and resources. In some cases, these reports are mandated by the regulators.

2.1.3.3 *Documenting the due diligence*

2.16 The various advisers engaged in the due diligence process will deliver to the underwriters a number of customary documents evidencing the review performed and the conclusions reached. These would typically include the following:

- Legal opinions: lawyers to both the company and the underwriters will be expected to deliver to the underwriters certain opinions relating to the issuer and the transaction.
- Disclosure letters: in addition to legal opinions, legal counsel will sometimes be expected to provide a disclosure letter containing a so-called '10b-5 negative assurance'[2] confirming in broad terms that, based on the review conducted,

---

[2] The 10b-5 letter takes its name from Rule 10b-5 under Section 10(b) of the US Exchange Act of 1934, which prohibits manipulative and deceptive practices in connection with securities trading.

nothing has come to the law firm's attention that causes it to believe that the prospectus suffers from a material misstatement or omission.

- Comfort letters: the company's auditors will be requested to deliver SAS72-style[3] or similar comfort letters that (i) confirm that the financial information contained in the prospectus has being properly extracted from the company's audited financial statements; and (ii) provide negative assurance opinions to the effect that nothing has come to the auditors' attention that causes them to believe that (a) any material modification would be required in the latest interim financial information for it to be in accordance with the applicable accounting standards; and (b) any material change in the company's key balance sheet items or profit and loss account has occurred from the date of the latest year-end or interim financial statements they have audited or reviewed. Comfort letters have increasingly become an area of battle in securities transactions, as accountants try to use these letters to chip away at their potential liability.

2.1.4 Eligibility for listing

A detailed, coordinated due diligence effort of the sort described above presupposes that the company in question stands at least a chance of overcoming the eligibility hurdles that stand between it and a successful IPO. In the case of a London-listed IPO, a company must satisfy the UKLA's eligibility requirements for admission to its official list, as well as the LSE's admission and disclosure standards that apply to applicants for admission to trading on its main market.

2.17

Eligibility requirements for listing and admission to trading cover a fair amount of common ground throughout the member states. They deal with matters concerning (i) the company (due incorporation, appropriate corporate authorizations, compliance with law, sufficient financial history); (ii) the securities (free transferability, whole class to be listed); and (iii) the market (sufficient free float and total market cap). The possibility for local nuances, however—peculiarities of national interpretation and application, the likes of which are elucidated in the jurisdictional expositions in Part 3—should not be overlooked.

2.18

It provides as follows: 'It shall be unlawful for any person, directly or indirectly, by the use of any means or instrumentality of interstate commerce, or of the mails or of any facility of any national securities exchange, [...] (b) To make any untrue statement of a material fact or to omit to state a material fact necessary in order to make the statements made, in the light of the circumstances under which they were made, not misleading, [...] in connection with the purchase or sale of any security.'

[3] 'SAS' stands for Statement on Auditing Standard promulgated by the Auditing Standards Board of the American Institute of Certified Public Accountants. 'SAS72' relates to 'Letters for Underwriters and Certain Other Requesting Parties'. While SAS72-style comfort letters are not required in relation to European securities deals, it has become more common for the underwriters to request them, particularly on transactions with a US component.

2.19   The company might have a lot of work to do to meet these eligibility requirements. While for some companies a few tweaks to the articles of association and
the make-up of the board of directors might be enough, for others, a sweeping
corporate restructuring might well be in order (see Section 2.1.5 below). Moreover,
meeting the eligibility pre-requisites is only half the battle. A company will have
to be more than ready for its new responsibilities as a listed company: getting the
periodic reports and accounts out on time (while making sure they are accurate),
making announcements whenever a shareholder does anything with its shares,
essentially having to shout out from the rooftops whenever anything material
happens that is likely to impact the price of the company's shares. This might
require a radical overhaul of the company's procedures, systems and controls—
indeed of its entire corporate culture.

2.1.5 Corporate restructuring and related-party transactions

2.1.5.1 *Pre-IPO corporate restructuring transactions*

2.20   A company planning to go to the market needs to ensure that it is in the right
shape to meet all applicable eligibility criteria, as well as the challenging scheme of
ongoing obligations that will apply once its listing is complete. Sometimes, getting ready to go to market will require a certain amount of internal re-jigging—
spin offs, hive-downs, acquisitions, disposals—to ensure that the right parts of
the company's business are offered up to investors. This might be necessary, for
example, if the company operates a number of independent business lines, some
of which are likely to be more attractive to investors than others. Here, the
company might want to put the less marketable business lines to one side so that
the public offering consists of only the good stuff.

2.21   In a smaller, family- or closely-owned company, the scenario might be that the
company holds its key operating assets (for example, factories, heavy machinery,
a fleet of trucks), but also a number of other assets and investments that belong to
the controlling shareholders and are completely alien to the company's core
business (say, a speedboat, a ski chalet and a minority stake in a tapas restaurant).
An underwriter may well advise that these should be kept out of the deal.[4] A thorough legal, tax and commercial analysis is required in these cases to design a
suitable, tax-efficient pre-offering restructuring transaction.

2.22   The following are important points to consider when planning a pre-offering
corporate restructuring:

---

[4] Another situation that is common with smaller family-owned businesses is where the controlling family owns the company's key assets and leases them to the company, which is unlikely to be
an arrangement that would appeal to prospective investors in an IPO.

- proper scheduling of the proposed transaction and the impact of this on the overall deal timetable;
- potential impact on the IPO from a valuation and marketing perspective;
- possible need for waivers or consents from creditors, partners in joint ventures and commercial counterparties, in advance of the proposed restructuring;
- possible need for pro-forma and separate financial statements to accompany the latest annual and interim financial statements that the company intends to present to investors in the prospectus —the preparation of pro-forma and separate financial statements can be costly and time-consuming (see Section 2.4.1.4 below).

2.1.5.2 Related-party transactions

Another fertile ground for attention in the build up to a public offering—particularly an IPO—is related-party transactions. It is not uncommon, particularly in family-owned outfits, for the company to have entered into (whether in the past or on a continuing basis) related-party transactions—financing, credit support arrangements, real estate asset leases and the like—with its controlling shareholders. It is possible that not all of these transactions were supported by appropriate documentation. And some or all of them might not have been conducted on arm's-length terms—it may be unclear whether the terms and conditions of the relevant transactions were on an arm's-length basis or perhaps the company paid no consideration at all. **2.23**

In these cases, the company and its financial advisers should: **2.24**

- consider whether the relevant transactions should be terminated or whether investors would accept such arrangements in a public company without it having an adverse impact on its valuation;
- arrange for appropriate agreements to be entered into to document the relevant transactions;
- establish a fair price and other terms for the relevant transactions;
- advise the company on the appropriate disclosure of those transactions in the financial statements and in the prospectus.

In the case of an integrated group of companies that decides to float one of its business units, the entity going public will usually have entered into related-party transactions with its parent or other group entities in the ordinary course of business. These transactions, which might involve the provision of centralized corporate services, financing, supplies, patent licences and all manner of other commercial arrangements, are likely to be indispensable to the company's business. Indeed, the synergies derived from such related-party arrangements might well be critical to the company's valuation and its marketability to investors. In these cases, terminating the relevant related-party transactions is unlikely to be **2.25** optimal. Instead, the company might consider entering into a framework agreement or protocol with the relevant related entities prior to the IPO, setting out transparent rules for the supervision of the existing transactions and the approval of any new ones. Such an agreement would offer comfort to potential investors if, for example, it assured them that the company's related-party transactions would be conducted on market terms, offered solutions to deal with conflicts of interest and provided safeguards for minority shareholders.

2.1.6 Shareholder agreements

2.26 A company preparing to offer securities to the market needs to consider whether the existing shareholders have any agreement in place that could stand in the way of an IPO. Shareholders in private companies often enter into shareholders' agreements to regulate their relationships, the exercise of their rights and the governance of the company. Such agreements are particularly common among private equity and other institutional investors. They might contain restrictions on the transfer of shares (such as pre-emption rights or tag-along and drag-along rights); provisions relating to shareholders' and directors' meetings (such as a list of reserved matters subject to increased quorum and/or majority requirements, veto rights and rights to nominate directors); and other provisions bestowing preferential voting or economic rights (which are structured by way of special classes of shares). Such provisions might also be incorporated into the company's articles of association.

2.27 The company's counsel must review these shareholders' agreements and the company's articles of association to ensure that they are suitable for a listed company and that they do not preclude the proposed IPO. For instance, provisions impeding the free transferability of the company's shares (for example, certain types of pre-emption rights or tag-along and drag-along rights) would have to be removed before any offering could take place, as would certain unorthodox provisions relating to the conduct of shareholders' and directors' meetings.

2.1.6.1 The case for a shareholders' agreement

2.28 Sometimes private companies operate not on the basis of documented shareholders' agreements, but rather on the basis of mutual understandings or undocumented 'gentlemen's agreements'. In such cases, if the company is considering an offering, a formal shareholders' agreement could be useful, particularly for shareholders that plan to retain control of the company after the IPO. Such an agreement can provide a clear framework for relationships between the company's main shareholders that can be presented to potential investors in the IPO (who, in turn, can factor the relevant information into their investment decision). It can also help to prevent certain problems down the line once the company has gone public and brought new investors on board. For example, any attempt on the part of a company's controlling shareholders to formalize their relationship *after* the company has gone public could be deemed to constitute a concerted shareholders' action, thereby triggering the obligation to make a mandatory offer for the company's entire share capital, pursuant to the Takeover Directive. This obligation would not apply, however, if the relevant concerted actions had been documented in a shareholders' agreement prior to the offering.

2.1.6.2 *IPO shareholders' agreements*

Irrespective of whether a shareholders' agreement is already in place, it might be helpful for the company's shareholders to enter into an agreement specifically to facilitate the proposed IPO. Such an agreement will usually contain a binding commitment on the part of the selling shareholders to sell all or part of their shares through the IPO (with or without a floor price) and an undertaking not to dispose of the shares in other circumstances. The agreement will also establish the structure of the offer, the number of shares to be sold by each selling shareholder and the mechanisms for the allocation of the fees and expenses incurred in the process. In addition, the agreement might contain an undertaking on the part of the shareholders to support the IPO process, for example, by agreeing to support any required shareholders' approvals and any necessary amendments to the company's articles of association in connection with the IPO.

2.29

2.1.6.3 *Relationship agreements*

In the UK market, the potential for abuses by controlling shareholders is often mitigated using an agreement known as a relationship agreement. It was previously used as a specific means of showing the FSA, as part of the eligibility process, that there were measures in place to allow the company to run its business independently of any controlling shareholder. Although the underlying eligibility rules were changed in July 2005, the establishment of a relationship agreement has remained market practice in primary listings with controlling shareholders.[5]

2.30

The types of terms provided for in a relationship agreement often include obligations that:

2.31

- the controlling shareholder will exercise its voting powers in relation to the company to ensure that the company is capable of carrying on its business for the benefit of the shareholders of the company as a whole and independently of the controlling shareholder or its associates;

---

[5] For this purpose, controlling shareholders are considered to be those with control of 30% or more of the voting rights at a general meeting or the ability to appoint directors with majority control of a board.

- all transactions and relationships between the controlling shareholder and the company will be conducted on arm's-length terms, on a normal commercial basis and in accordance with the FSA's related-party rules;
- the controlling shareholder will not exercise its voting rights in favour of any amendment to the constitutional documents of the company that would be contrary to the principle of independence of the company or would otherwise be inconsistent with the relationship agreement;
- in the event of a conflict of interest, any directors appointed by the controlling shareholder will not vote;
- the controlling shareholder will exercise its powers so that the company is managed in accordance with the principles of good corporate governance set out in the UK Combined Code on Corporate Governance (see Part 3, Chapter 21, Section 21.4.4);
- the controlling shareholder will not compete with the company or poach any of the company's senior employees.

Relationship agreements are also sometimes seen in listings of depositary receipts in London.

2.1.7 Designing the offer

2.1.7.1 Primary or secondary?

2.32   While for one company an IPO might represent a chance to raise new capital, for another it might signify the exit of an existing investor. Here we see the distinction between primary offers (offers of newly-issued shares of the company) and secondary offers (sales of existing shares of the company by one or more selling shareholders): in a primary offer the company takes the proceeds, while in a secondary offer the selling shareholders receive it all. It is common to see combined primary and secondary offers, which allow both company and shareholder to enjoy the spoils.

2.33   Primary offerings must cater for the fact that new shares are being created and issued. Corporate authorizations and approvals will be required, and the company might also face complications such as shareholders' pre-emption rights (pursuant to which new shares must be offered to existing shareholders in proportion to their current holdings before they can be offered to other parties). In addition, a company conducting a primary offering will be required to explain to investors how it intends to use the proceeds of the offer. In a secondary offer, it will merely declare that it will not receive any of the proceeds.

2.1.7.2 Retail or institutional offering?

2.34   When designing a securities offering, a company (and, where the offer contains a secondary component, any selling shareholder) needs to decide which type of investor to target. Typically, the choice is between an offering to the general public (retail offering), an offering to qualified investors only (institutional offering), or an offering to both.[6] The 'general public' consists of anyone deciding what to do with their hard-earned life savings. Qualified investors[7] include legal entities authorized or regulated to operate in the financial markets (for example, credit institutions, investment firms, insurance companies, collective investment schemes and pension funds) and unregulated entities whose sole activity consists of investing in securities.

The choice of target market is significant and the company is likely to take advice **2.35** on the matter from its underwriters. While retail offerings tend to be less flexible than institutional offerings, not to mention more expensive (they can entail a larger disclosure burden, and the underwriting fees and marketing expenses are often higher), the upside is that they enable the company to target a much deeper pool of potential investors. This generally means the company can generate more capital, which is of course what it wants to do.

2.1.7.3 US law considerations

The extraterritorial reach of US securities law, principally the US Securities Act of **2.36** 1933 (the 'US Securities Act'), is not to be underestimated. Even if on the face of it, a transaction has no connection at all with the United States, the US regulator— the US Securities and Exchange Commission ('SEC')—requires a registration in respect of any offering of securities, unless a registration exemption is available. The reason the SEC cares about offerings in Europe is the potential for such offerings to have a knock-on effect in the United States, particularly if a company makes 'direct selling efforts'[8] in the United States, as described in detail in Section 2.2.1.2 below.

For such a transaction—where securities are offered and sold outside the United **2.37** States—the US Securities Act provides an exemption from the registration require- ment under Regulation S (hence, such a transaction would be referred to as a 'Reg S' deal). The main requirements that must be satisfied for the company,

---

[6] Other groups of investors may be targeted as well, such as employees of the company and its affiliated entities.

[7] As defined in Prospectus Directive Article 2.1(a).

[8] 'Directed Selling Efforts' are defined as any activity undertaken for the purpose of, or that could reasonably be expected to have the effect of, conditioning the market in the US for any of the securi- ties being offered in reliance on Regulation S. This provision is intended to preclude marketing efforts in the US for securities purportedly being distributed outside the US. Sending materials to persons in the US or conducting telephonic or in-person roadshow meetings with persons in the US are not permitted.

any shareholders and the underwriters (and their respective affiliates) to be able to rely on Regulation S are the following:

- the offer or sale must be made in an 'off-shore transaction';[9] and
- there must be no directed selling efforts in the United States by the issuer, any shareholders, the underwriters, or their respective affiliates.[10]

2.38 Not that all companies planning an offering will want to work within the confines of Regulation S: the United States market is one of the main sources of institutional investor demand for equity securities and a great number of IPOs of European issuers involve the placing of securities to institutional investors in the United States. In these cases, one typically makes use of Rule 144A under the US Securities Act, which exempts resales of securities to qualified institutional buyers ('QIBs') from registration. Broadly, QIBs are institutions that own and invest on a discretionary basis and have a portfolio of securities of non-affiliated issuers totalling at least $100 million.

2.39 While Regulation S and Rule 144A provide exemptions from the registration requirements of the US Securities Act, they do not exempt the transaction from the general US anti-fraud rules.[11] This is why US due diligence standards have infiltrated European market practice—as described in Section 2.1.3.3 above, auditors' SAS72-style comfort letters and lawyers' 10b-5 disclosure letters are now standard fare in the context of what is largely a European deal.

2.2 Organizing the Transaction and Laying the Ground Rules

2.2.1 Publicity

2.40 Publicity in the context of a European securities offering, put simply, refers to any act on the part of the relevant company, any selling shareholder and their

---

[9] In an IPO, for an offer or sale to be considered an 'off-shore transaction' (i) the offer must not be made to a person in the US; and (ii) at the time the buy order for the security is originated, the buyer must be outside the US (or reasonably believed to be so by the seller). Offers and sales to off-shore affiliates of US mutual funds or of other US investors are permitted if the requirements of off-shore transaction and no directed selling efforts are complied with.

[10] There are some exceptions to the off-shore transaction and directed selling efforts definitions, such as offers and sales to the International Monetary Fund, the United Nations and other similar international organizations and their affiliates and pension plans and, also, offers and sales to discretionary accounts or similar accounts (other than an estate or trust) held for the benefit or account of a non-US person (as defined in Regulation S) even if the account holder is organized or located in the US (such accounts are deemed to be off-shore transactions, and contacts with the holders of such exempted accounts in their capacities as holders of such accounts do not constitute directed selling efforts).

[11] In particular, Section 10(b) of the US Exchange Act of 1934 and the related Rule 10b-5 promulgated by the SEC thereunder, which make unlawful the failure to disclose material facts or the use of false or misleading statements or any other manipulative or deceptive practices in connection with the purchase or sale of any security.

respective advisers, which may publicize the offering to potential investors. The key principles to which publicity must adhere are not altogether difficult and can be summarized in two words: truth and consistency.

2.2.1.1 Application of key principles

A company preparing to go to market must ensure that anything it (or its affiliates or advisers) communicates to the market (whether orally, in writing or otherwise) is true and accurate. This is perhaps easier said than done—it would take a considerable effort to scrutinize and verify every proposed statement to be made in the transaction marketing materials, not to mention all statements made in person. While a company should endeavour to do this wherever possible, in practice there is typically a reliable short cut, in the form of a central source document that has already undergone that process of scrutiny. Such document is the prospectus—or offering document, listing particulars, offering circular, offering memorandum, or any other name the deal team decides to call it. The prospectus is a document typically prepared with great care, whose contents have undergone thorough due diligence and sometimes an independent verification process as well. Here is where the principle of consistency comes into play: by making sure that things communicated within and without the prospectus are consistent, using the prospectus as a central source for information and the ultimate reference point, one is helping to ensure the accuracy of any publicity and ultimately to safeguard the fairness of the information package as a whole on which an investor can claim to have made its investment decision.

2.41

Using the prospectus as a control device in this manner certainly makes sense so far as the publicity in question overlaps with information set out in the prospectus. But what if the company wants to communicate information that the prospectus does not cover? The key question in this scenario is the following: 'why does one feel the need to say these things?' If it is because the information is material, then the information should in fact be included in the prospectus. And once the relevant information is included in the prospectus, as described above, one simply has to make sure that what is said is consistent. If, on the other hand, the information is not material, then why say it? The risk, of course, in making statements that are not included in the prospectus is that it leaves it open for an investor to argue that it made its investment decision on the basis of that separate statement, or at least took it into account, and because the statement was untrue and the investor lost money, it should be compensated. Equally, the investor might say that it made its investment decision on the basis of the prospectus, which failed to include something— the information contained in that separate statement—that would have been part of its investment decision and, therefore, it should be compensated for the money it has lost. Neither of these scenarios is pretty, and an investor will be tempted to say many things if it is sitting on a large loss that it wants to pass on to someone else.

2.42

2.43 Accordingly, by ensuring that all communications connected with the offering align with the information in the prospectus, the company will be able to manage the risk of liability in this context and, furthermore, will ensure that all investors have access to consistent information. These sentiments—consistency and equality of information—are clearly in play when one considers the terms of Article 15(5) of the Prospectus Directive. It is an interesting provision that applies whether or not the Prospectus Directive requires the company to publish a prospectus. It states that when material information is provided by an issuer to qualified investors or a special category of investors, including information disclosed in the context of meetings relating to offers of securities, that information must be disclosed to all of those people to whom the offer is made. And if a prospectus is required to be published, that information must be included in that prospectus.

2.2.1.2 *United States and United Kingdom publicity laws*

2.44 There are a number of reasons why companies preparing to offer securities need to be careful whom they communicate with. One very important reason is that there are heavy-hitting laws that control it, not least those imposed by the long arm of US federal securities laws, as discussed in Section 2.1.8.3 above. The SEC will pay extremely close attention to any company that it suspects of making 'direct selling efforts' into the United States.

2.45 For example, if a company makes an offering outside the United States, but puts up billboards in Idaho with pictures of happy senior citizens who have seemingly just cashed in on hefty profits from sales of the shares in that company, with a strap line that reads 'Do you want to be this happy? Buy HappyCo stock!', it is entirely likely that interest will be generated in Idaho for those securities (and worse still, that interest would be generated among the type of unsophisticated investor that regulators around the world vigorously protect). Such directed selling efforts may well result in flow-back of the securities from outside the United States into the United States. In the same way, talking to the press in the United States, holding conferences in the United States and, indeed, placing material on a website accessible from the United States may generate interest among investors in the United States and therefore encourage flow-back.

2.46 Accordingly, any publicity activity that can hit the United States needs to be given very careful consideration. Legal advisers should be consulted to advise on safely restricting the reach of publicity, the appropriate addition of certain legends to written publicity materials and other measures to reduce the risk of crossing the SEC.

2.47 The United Kingdom similarly has a strict set of publicity rules. Outside of the public offer rules, which are themselves tough and attract criminal sanctions, the

United Kingdom has rules on a lighter type of publicity called 'financial promotions' (see Part 3, Chapter 21, Section 21.3). Even if a communication does not qualify as an offer of securities to the public (because it does not give enough information to enable investors to make an investment decision), it may well still constitute a financial promotion. Financial promotions are generally prohibited: they cannot be made or directed to persons in the United Kingdom unless an exemption applies or it is approved by an authorized person, for example, a UK authorized bank. If an exemption is not available, and the financial promotion has not been so approved, the company and its officers could be in trouble.

The financial promotion regime also attracts criminal sanctions and in some circumstances could allow the investor to put the securities back to the company, which it may well want to do if the securities have fallen in value. In practice in European capital markets transactions, there are so many exemptions from the general prohibition, however, that it is very rare for a financial promotion to need approval by an authorized person. Indeed, one could argue, perhaps rather persuasively, that the regime has been diluted out of real relevance for these types of transactions, as it has largely become a case of including the right legend in any written communication. **2.48**

Market participants generally focus on these two key jurisdictions (and they do so at least partly because of the United States' history of aggressive enforcement in this area, and because it is difficult to imagine a European deal that does not include some nexus with the United Kingdom). In addition, companies should also take advice on the relevant rules in any other jurisdictions into which the securities are being offered (whether or not any sales are actually made), as well as the company's jurisdiction of incorporation. **2.49**

2.2.2 Research

Research, notwithstanding the mystique with which it is often cloaked by lawyers, and indeed bankers, is a rather simple concept, and most of the rules around it are well grounded in common sense. Ordinary course research reports (research reports that are written without regard to a particular securities offering) are commonly written about companies that are already public and aim to give an independent opinion on their value and the value of their securities. When a research report is written alongside a securities offering (referred to as 'deal research') the idea is no different, but the liability concerns for anyone associated with it are likely to be somewhat greater. **2.50**

2.2.2.1 Key principles

The principles that apply to research are not dissimilar to those that are relevant to publicity. But the central, and unique, principle relevant to research is independence. **2.51**

Although an investment bank (or its affiliate) writes deal research alongside a deal being led by that investment bank, there are rules requiring that research be independent, and if it is not independent, that the research clearly disclose that it is not. The FSA rules on research reports, including rules relating to independence, are contained in the FSA's Conduct of Business Sourcebook. Gone are the days, one would hope, when the managing director at the lead investment bank can bark at his research analyst colleague: 'make it say what we want, or else!'

2.52 Alongside the principle of independence runs that of truth: research must always be true and accurate. The investment banking team running the deal, without undermining the independence of the research, should check the draft research report for statements they think are factually inaccurate. They are likely to be in a position to do so as a result of their due diligence in relation to the deal. They will also have access (unlike the research analyst) to the prospectus, which, as discussed above, is a rather useful reference point. Beyond the facts, the draft research report will contain statements of opinion. These statements are the business of the research analyst, and should not be meddled with by the investment banking deal team. If, however, they are based on a factual misapprehension, and the internal policies of the bank allow the deal team to see them, they should bring that to the attention of the research analyst. Indeed, it is in everyone's interests for the opinions expressed in the research report to be based on reasonable grounds.

2.2.2.2 *Presentation of the research*

2.53 Prior to the publication of deal research, the company will typically stage a presentation to analysts about the company and its plans. One question is whether the company should review the draft research at this stage. Views vary on this, and are rather case dependent. In an IPO context, where there is often very little information about the company in the public domain, there is even greater pressure to ensure that the research report does not contain incorrect or misleading statements—given the scarcity of information on the company, investors are more likely to rely on the contents of the research report. It makes more sense in that context, therefore, for the company to review and comment on the factual statements.

2.54 In doing so, however, there is a potentially serious risk of which the company should be mindful. It is known as the risk of 'entanglement'. The more a company does to associate itself with the research, the greater the risk that the company is seen to adopt the research and the views contained in it. To help mitigate this risk, it is generally advisable for any draft research that is sent to the company for review to be redacted to strip out, in particular, financial projections, but also other information about the company that does not constitute historical fact. The temptation for the company to meddle with the research analysts' projections might be too great, and even if the company does not meddle with them, silence might itself be considered an expression of a view on the projections.

2.2.2.3 *Research and the advertisement regime*

Sometimes a question arises as to whether a research report falls within the defini- **2.55**
tion of an 'advertisement'. The significance of this question is that if a research
report is an advertisement, it must comply with the advertisement regime (see
Part 3, Chapter 21, Section 21.3), which, *inter alia*, requires the report to be
(i) consistent with the prospectus, accurate and not misleading (without reference
to any materiality qualifier); and (ii) clearly recognizable as an advertisement, with
the appropriate legend.

The UKLA has written on the subject[12] but unfortunately has done little other **2.56**
than confirm that it depends on 'the particular facts and circumstances' of the
case. It refers to a CESR feedback statement published in December 2003,[13]
which states that if the research is not related to a specific securities offering, it will
fall outside the scope of the advertisement regime. The unhelpful potential implication of this is that deal research would constitute an advertisement, but the
UKLA has neither said that it would, nor that it would not.

The UKLA alludes to the possibility that the presence of Chinese Walls and the **2.57**
use of blackout periods (discussed in Section 2.2.2.4 below) lessen the likelihood
that deal research would constitute an advertisement but then states that 'firms
will need to make the ultimate judgement on this matter in the light of the definition and the particular facts and circumstances'. In practice, market participants
generally do not treat research reports as advertisements, but some greater
certainty on this point would not go amiss.

2.2.2.4 *Blackout periods*

The existence of a customary blackout period—a period close to the offering **2.58**
during which research must not be published—predates the publication of
the Prospectus Directive and the establishment of the advertisement regime.
The practice, for the part of the blackout period that starts prior to publication of
an offering document, developed in the UK market to help dissociate research
reports from the prospectus, lest an investor became confused and thought
that the research report was in essence a prospectus. Whether or not there was any
real merit in this belief, the UKLA's reference to blackout periods in its List!
publication gives at least some substantive basis for retaining them. In practice,

---

[12] See List! Issue 12.
[13] CESR/03-400.

investment banks tend to start the blackout period around the one- or two-week mark prior to the publication of the preliminary prospectus, although it is not uncommon for the blackout to begin even closer than a week before the offering. The blackout period will commonly extend to 40 days following the commencement of the offering or in some deals 40 days after closing of the offering.

2.3 Dealing with the Regulator

2.3.1 The basic rules

2.59 There are three basic rules that market participants should follow when dealing with the regulator: (i) be nice to them; (ii) do not upset them; and (iii) do not be unpleasant to them. In addition, there is one overarching principle: tell the truth. There are no specific legal rules that deal with basic rules one to three, but it is hard to conclude that they do not make sense. Furthermore, in the United Kingdom at least, there is at least one legal provision that could result in jail-time if one were to flout the overarching principle. It is contained in section 398 of the Financial Services and Markets Act 2000, which makes it a criminal offence to knowingly or recklessly give the FSA information that is false or misleading in a material document.

2.60 Rules one to three should be considered in their broadest sense—they include, for example, giving the regulator notice of a deal and, where possible, its timetable, rather than notifying them of a deal for the first time by stuffing them with a draft prospectus. The rules also serve as a basic guide on how to deal with the regulator when you disagree with them, which will inevitably happen from time to time.

2.3.2 National variances

2.61 The important corollary to the above thoughts on dealing with the authorities is that different regulators (and even different departments within regulators) have different approaches to the way they will deal with market participants. For example, some European regulators—such as those in Ireland and Luxembourg— avoid direct contact with companies and their counsel by requiring a listing agent, through which communications are typically made. The UKLA, although it does not require a listing agent, requires the appointment of a sponsor for primary listings on the LSE and expects most communications for these types of deals to be undertaken by such sponsor. However, each of these regulators has in the past shown helpful flexibility.

2.62 Notwithstanding the requirement for a sponsor in the context of primary listings, the fact that the UKLA does not require a listing agent or other intermediary for most deals sometimes gives it an edge. It is in practice much easier to deal with issues when they arise if one can speak to the regulator directly rather than risk a Chinese whisper through a listing agent, however good the listing agent is (and there are some very good ones).

The UKLA is an example of one EEA regulator that operates a useful 'helpdesk' type facility, where experts are on hand to answer sensible queries regarding, *inter alia*, the likely practical application of its listing rules. Such helpdesks can sometimes deliver a crucial quick fix to a problem, but it really should go without saying that regulators do not like it if these helpdesks are used before market participants have exhausted their own internal resources, as well as available guidance and other literature issued by the particular regulator or by CESR. Regulators have been known to complain about the level of questions they are sometimes asked, and there seems little sense in upsetting them on this count (see above, rules one, two and three). **2.63**

2.3.3 Prospectus approval procedure

The first stage of dealing with a regulator often involves ticking off preliminary questions, typically on a no-names basis, that go to structure, disclosure requirements and financial statement issues (see Section 2.4.1.3 below). The UKLA's general policy is that no-names basis questions will not be binding on it when the actual deal is put to them on a named basis. Other regulators may have the same policy. When the deal is ripe to be disclosed to the regulator, one should refer to the earlier discussions and confirm the relevant matters on a named basis to avoid a disaster further down the track. If time allows, or if required by the regulator (the UKLA requires an eligibility letter for listings of shares and global depositary receipts) this might be in written form. **2.64**

The next stage typically involves submission of a draft prospectus. Some European regulators require a checklist to accompany the draft prospectus indicating which specific disclosure requirements are dealt with and where in the draft prospectus. Although this list takes time to prepare, it is a useful mechanism to make sure that all of the required disclosure requirements are satisfied in the first draft, and are not deleted as part of the ongoing drafting process. **2.65**

The Prospectus Directive states that the review period for a draft prospectus is a maximum of 10 business days or, if the company does not yet have any securities admitted to trading on a regulated market, 20 business days. But there is a sting in the tail—the regulator can restart this review period if it finds on reasonable grounds that supplementary information needs to be provided. So, in practice, these Prospectus Directive timelines are rather artificial and of little use in highlighting to a regulator if its review period risks breaching the proposed timetable. **2.66**

2.67 The reality is that one has to negotiate the timetable with the regulator as best one can. Part of that discussion should include informing the regulator in advance of the likely state of the first draft of the prospectus. For example, if the document will be missing the operating and financial review in relation to the latest full financial year because the related financials will not be available in time for the first submission, this is material to the discussion one has with the regulator. Importantly, different regulators have different attitudes to incomplete first submissions.

2.68 The third stage typically involves reviewing the regulator's comments on the first draft and dealing with them. The aim should be for this not to involve much more than one further submission. This stage also involves submission of all the ancillary forms in draft form, if this has not been done already, in readiness for actual admission to listing and trading. In some jurisdictions, this also requires liaising with the relevant stock exchange, if the exchange is not also the regulator. Once comments are cleared on the draft prospectus, it can be published in pre-liminary form prior to formal approval and distributed to professional investors. If 'when-issued' trading is to be sought (when-issued trading allows on-exchange trading of shares after they have been allocated to investors but before they have been issued at closing), the lead underwriters should by this point be in contact with the exchange and submitting the when-issued application forms to ensure trading can start once the securities have been priced and allocated to investors.

2.69 The fourth stage typically involves obtaining approval of the final prospectus and publishing it in accordance with the Prospectus Directive (see Section 2.4 below). This may also involve submission of the final application for listing or trading forms, as well as any declarations that might be required from sponsors and the like to the effect that the applicant is suitable for listing and that its prospectus satisfies the requirements of the Prospectus Directive.

2.70 The fifth and final stage typically involves providing the regulator, and if applicable, the exchange, with board resolutions and other ancillary documents to obtain admission at closing.

2.4 Drafting the Prospectus

2.4.1 The prospectus

2.71 From the lawyer's perspective, the prospectus is widely regarded as the single most important document. A banker might disagree and say it is the roadshow presentation or the analyst's presentation. But one can refer them to the section on publicity above, which discusses the use of the prospectus as the key reference point for all other marketing materials, including these other presentations.

2.4.1.1 *Prospectus format*

As discussed in Part 1, Article 5 of the Prospectus Directive permits a prospectus to be drafted according to a number of formats: (i) tripartite structure; (ii) base prospectus; or (iii) single document. **2.72**

An issuer's choice of structure depends largely on the frequency with which it intends to access the capital markets and the type of securities it issues. Applicants planning to make multiple issuances of securities over the course of a year are likely to opt for the tripartite structure unless they are planning a specific programme of issuances of debt securities, in which case they will likely produce a base prospectus. Applicants offering securities on a one-off basis are likely to go down the single document route. **2.73**

Whichever option is chosen, the prospectus must contain three discernable parts: (a) a registration document, containing information relating to the issuer; (b) a securities note, containing information relating to the securities to be offered to the public or to be admitted to trading on a regulated market; and (c) a summary (see Section 2.4.1.3.4 below). **2.74**

2.4.1.2 *Prospectus content*

Irrespective of the form or structure of a prospectus, it must contain the requisite information to satisfy (i) the overarching general disclosure obligation to provide 'the information necessary to enable investors to make an informed assessment of (a) the assets and liabilities, financial position, profits and losses, and prospects of the issuer of the transferable securities and any guarantor; and (b) the rights attaching to the transferable securities';[14] and (ii) the specific disclosure requirements set out under the Prospectus Regulation. For equity deals in Europe, the issuer will either be looking at the disclosure requirements for share issuers and shares—Annexes I, II and III—or the disclosure requirements for depositary receipt deals—Annex X. **2.75**

Although it might appear from the reference to three annexes for share deals, versus one annex for depositary receipt deals, that the disclosure requirements for share deals must be considerably more onerous, the requirements are actually very similar, and in practice, the actual disclosures are typically even less different. As a technical matter, share deals require inclusion of pro-forma financial statements if the company has experienced a 'significant gross change' in its business and the **2.76**

---

[14] Prospectus Directive Article 5.1.

inclusion of a working capital statement (a statement that the company and its group has sufficient working capital available for the group's requirements for the next 12 months from the publication of the prospectus), whereas non-share deals do not. However, if the company has made a significant acquisition or disposal, pro-forma financial statements will often be included in a non-share deal, even if not strictly required by the Prospectus Regulation, particularly if the offering includes a US component. Indeed, in Rule 144A deals in particular, the disclosure is likely to be prepared with a keen eye on the disclosure requirements for fully-fledged SEC registered offerings in the United States.

2.4.1.3 Key sections in the prospectus

2.77   The prospectus must be drawn up in accordance with the building block approach prescribed under the Prospectus Regulation. This involves identifying the annexes to the Prospectus Regulation that apply to the particular offering (depending on the nature of the offering and, in particular, the securities involved), and satisfying the content requirements prescribed by each applicable annex. While doing this, the company and its advisers, of course, must never lose sight of that all-important rule that the prospectus must contain all information that could be relevant to an investment decision. Otherwise they might find themselves in the lamentable position of diligently satisfying all Prospectus Regulation requirements and yet nonetheless failing to meet the overarching disclosure requirement under Article 5(1) of the Prospectus Directive.

2.78   The Prospectus Regulation requires the prospectus to contain a wide range of information relating to the company and its securities. However, certain sections of the prospectus are likely to be particularly interesting to investors and will consume the bulk of the drafting timetable. Aside from financial information, which is of course crucial and is dealt with separately from Section 2.4.1.4 below, the business description, the risk factors and the operating financial review are generally the sections of the prospectus that attract the most interest. In addition, each prospectus must contain a summary, which generally contains information lifted out of these key sections.

2.79   **2.4.1.3.1 Business description**   The business section is where the company describes itself to potential investors. It typically covers the following grounds:

- history and development;
- strengths and strategy;
- corporate and management structure;
- key assets;
- current operations: this will take up the bulk of the section and will cover matters such as products, pricing policy (see also 2.4.1.3.2 below), customers and suppliers, marketing and advertising activities, intellectual property, competition, information technology, insurance, employees and litigation.

The strengths and strategy part of the business section is something the invest- **2.80**
ment banks advising on the offering will be particularly interested in. The banks
are likely to be keen to ensure that the company's description of its key strengths
and current/future business strategy in the prospectus tallies with the company's
overall equity story.

2.4.1.3.2 Operating and financial review The operating and financial review **2.81**
section provides an analysis of the company's key financial data and current financial condition, together with a description of the principal risks and uncertainties
that it faces.

The section is likely to include: **2.82**

- a discussion of the presentation of the financial information and any segmentation
  of the company's business;
- a description of the significant factors that have had an impact on the company's
  development and latest results of operations;
- a description of each of the key line items included in the company's income
  statement, including a discussion of the key costs and expenses;
- an analysis of period on period changes in key income statement line items;
- an analysis of the company's liquidity and capital resources, including a discussion of the company's debt position, its historic cash flow performance and its
  plans for capital expenditures;
- a discussion of market risk, for example, exchange and interest rate risk;
- a discussion about the company's critical accounting policies, where the assumptions and judgments made may significantly affect the financial results of the
  company.

2.4.1.3.3 Risk factors The risk factors section should state the factors that **2.83**
could have a material adverse effect on the company and the value of the securities
being offered. This section might not always be pretty in the eyes of the company,
but it is extremely helpful in discharging the overarching disclosure obligation to
provide investors with all material information relating to the offering.
Furthermore, if something goes wrong with the company or its securities down
the line, the risks factors section is likely to be the first place any disgruntled investors will check. If the thing that went wrong was not disclosed as a risk, then the
company could be in trouble.

Above all, therefore, the risk factors section should aim to be comprehensive and **2.84**
should cover all material risks. If a mining company loses its principal licence to
mine six months after its IPO and the risk factors did not refer to the possibility
that this could happen, investors might well have a claim.

Advisers should pay more attention to the most material risks in particular, **2.85**
describing them with appropriate specificity, such that an investor can properly

appreciate what could go wrong—boilerplate language should be avoided. For example, if the company prepares a risk factor that refers to the possibility that it could be the subject of an antitrust investigation, such risk factor should also refer to any ongoing antitrust investigations against the company (either by describing such investigation, or by cross-referring to another part of the prospectus where it is described).

2.86   The risk factors are typically divided into sections, for example:

- *risks relating to the company and its group*: this might be sub-divided, for example, into risks relating to a proposed business strategy, risks relating to real estate, risks relating to the company's corporate structure, etc.
- *risks relating to the company's industry*: this might be sub-divided, for example, into risks relating to competition and demand, risks relating to prices, etc.
- *risks relating to the company's country of operation*: this is something one would expect to see for emerging markets and it might be sub-divided, for example, into economic risks, social and political risks, risks relating to the legal system, etc.
- *risks relating to the securities and the offering*: this might include risks relating to the liquidity of the market for the securities, the price of the securities and potential tax liabilities in connection with the offering.

2.87   **2.4.1.3.4 Summary**   The prospectus must contain a summary. The idea behind the summary is that an investor who is not in a position to digest the entire document can quickly identify the key information relating to the company, its securities and the offering. Indeed, in a situation where a prospectus is passported to another member state, it is often just the summary that must be translated into the language of the host member state (see Section 2.5 below). The summary is exactly that, however, and it seems rather unfair for the rules to put so much pressure on it having to include 'all the essential characteristics and risks associated with the issuer, and the securities' and at the same time to impose a word limit of 2,500 words on that section. The Prospectus Directive[15] also requires the summary to be drafted in plain language 'to ensure easy access to the information'. The summary typically covers the following matters: (i) basic information concerning the issuer; (ii) key information concerning the offering; and (iii) a list of the main risk factors.

2.88   In practice, as one might expect, the summary is often put together by lifting out key information from other key sections of the prospectus. For example, the summary might replicate the first several pages of the business description section, as well as the company's latest income statement and profit and loss account

---

[15] Article 5(2).

(thus providing 'basic information concerning the issuer'). Similarly, the summary description of risks might consist simply of the headings of each of the risks (which, despite being headings, can be rather long and detailed) set out in the risk factors section.

The summary must also contain a warning notice, advising investors that: (i) it **2.89** should be read as an introduction to the prospectus; (ii) any decision to invest in the securities should be based on consideration of the prospectus as a whole by the investor; (iii) where a claim relating to the information contained in a prospectus is brought before a court, the plaintiff investor might, under the national legislation of the member states, have to bear the costs of translating the prospectus before the legal proceedings are initiated; and (iv) civil liability attaches to those persons who have produced the summary, including any translation of the summary, and applied for its notification, but only if the summary is misleading, inaccurate or inconsistent when read together with the other parts of the prospectus.

2.4.1.4 *Financial disclosure in the prospectus*

The area of disclosure that often receives the most attention in the early stages **2.90** leading up to an IPO is the financial disclosure. What can the company produce in terms of financial statements? The reason this issue merits so much attention is that IPO candidates have often grown quickly, and on many occasions have done so by bolting on numerous businesses, each of which may or may not have its own track record. At the same time, financial disclosure is a key feature of good disclosure, so it is no surprise that the prospectus rules in Europe have a specific provision that, subject to certain limited exceptions, prospectuses for equity deals must include audited annual financial statements for the last three years, as well as interim financial statements if the last audited annual financial statements are older than nine months from the date of the prospectus. Notwithstanding this specific provision (and its shortcomings—see table below at 2.4.1.5), one must keep at least one eyelash of one eye on the page of the Prospectus Directive that requires prospectuses to include all material information. In addition, there are certain types of deals, for example primary listings on the LSE, in relation to which more onerous financial statement requirements apply.

2.4.1.5 *EEA rules on financial statement requirements and some of the issues*

The basic rule regarding the presentation of financial statements for share deals is **2.91** set out in Annex I of the Prospectus Regulation, which, to paraphrase, requires issuers to present audited historical financial information covering the latest three financial years (or such shorter period that the issuer has been in operation) and the audit report in respect of each year. The rule for depositary receipt deals is similar.

2.92 A detailed examination of this requirement helps to reveal some of its shortcomings and provides an opportunity to explain how these shortcomings are typically addressed. Below is a table setting out what the rule states, some of the questions raised by the rule as stated and the answers to those questions.

What the rule states	(Some of the) questions the rule raises	Answers
The rule requires audited historical financial information covering the latest three financial years (or such shorter period that the issuer has been in operation) and the audit report in respect of each year.	1. If we put a new holding company on top of the group, we don't need to include any financial statements at all?	1. For shares, and for convertible bonds that require disclosure to be prepared in accordance with Annex I of the UK Prospectus Rules, this scenario constitutes a 'complex financial history' (see Section 2.4.1.6 below) and the subsequent Complex Financial Histories Regulation will not let the issuer circumvent the requirement in this manner. In addition, one must remember the overarching obligation to include all material information in the prospectus. The Complex Financial History Regulation does not apply to depositary receipts and bonds, so one should apply the overarching rule to include all material information in the prospectus, and it would be sensible to look at the Complex Financial History Regulation by analogy.
	2. If the issuer has been in operation for six months prior to the date of the prospectus, and we have to include six months' financials, how can we do this given it takes time to produce audited financial statements, and every day we spend doing it means we have to add an extra day of financial information?	2. We would expect the regulator to take a sensible approach to this problem and allow inclusion of financial statements that are reasonably capable of being prepared and are also meaningful in the context of the transaction. The regulator might well grant a derogation from the requirement to include any financial statements, or might simply allow an opening balance sheet or a narrative explanation, if, for example, the operations are not significant.

(Continued)

What the rule states	(Some of the) questions the rule raises	Answers
The rule states that if the issuer has changed its accounting reference date during the period for which historical financial information is required, the audited historical information must cover at least 36 months, or the entire period for which the issuer has been in operation, whichever is the shorter.	1. The *entire* period for which the issuer has been in operation?	1. See the answer to question 2 above.
The financial information must be prepared in accordance with the IFRS Regulation that requires groups with an EEA holding company to prepare consolidated IFRS financial statements, or if that regulation is not applicable, a member state national GAAP.	1. Do all three years' financial statements for EEA issuers have to be prepared in accordance with IFRS? 2. If the issuer is not incorporated in the EEA, it can use a member state national GAAP? 3. I thought companies could also use US GAAP?	1. Actually, no. This language must be read with the language in the next column. The applied interpretation is that only the latest two years' financial statements need to be prepared in accordance with IFRS, assuming the next published financials will be prepared in accordance with IFRS under the Transparency Directive. If the next published financial statements will be published in accordance with national GAAP—and they can be if the prospectus was published before its last year's annual financial statements were published because under the IFRS Regulation the requirement to prepare IFRS financial statements depends on whether the company was admitted to trading on a regulated market as of its balance sheet date— then the prospectus can include three years of national GAAP accounts. 2. No. This is not what was intended. See below for the part of the rule that refers to third country issuers. This language essentially means that EEA issuers that fall outside the scope of the IFRS Regulation can use national GAAP instead. 3. They can if they are a non-EEA issuer—see the language below regarding third country issuers. One also needs to refer to the Equivalence Regulation.

(Continued)

What the rule states	(Some of the) questions the rule raises	Answers
The last two years' audited historical financial information must be presented and prepared in a form consistent with that which will be adopted in the issuer's next published annual financial statements having regard to accounting standards and policies and legislation applicable to such annual financial statements.	1. Oh dear, this is terribly onerous. (a) So the company has to restate the latest financials to match the policies and presentation for the next financials it publishes? (b) The first note in the company's financial statements sets out all the policy changes that will take place in the company's next financial statements—the company needs to deal with all of those *now*? (c) What about the changes the company doesn't even know about yet?	1. It would be, but … (a) Not necessarily. If the body of GAAP will differ as between the financial statements proposed to be included in the prospectus and the next published financial statements (for example, IFRS v. US GAAP) then yes, one cannot have such a mismatch. But see (b) below. (b) CESR Level Three Recommendations are very useful in this regard. The company does not have to deal with all of those changes within GAAP for the prospectus—the guidance is to follow the requirements of the applicable set of accounting standards (so if they do not require early restatement, there is no need to do so). (c) The regulators should not expect companies to worry about changes they cannot know about.
If the issuer has been operating in its current sphere of economic activity for less than one year, the audited historical financial information covering that period must be prepared in accordance with the standards applicable to annual financial statements under the IFRS Regulation.	The entire period?	See above.
For third country issuers, the historical financial information must be prepared according to the international accounting standards adopted pursuant to the IFRS Regulation or to	But what is equivalent to these standards?	See the Accounting Equivalence Regulation. Equivalent GAAPs at the moment include US GAAP, Canadian GAAP, Japanese GAAP, Chinese GAAP, Indian GAAP and South Korean GAAP (see the Equivalent GAAP Regulation).

(Continued)

What the rule states	(Some of the) questions the rule raises	Answers
a third country's national accounting standards equivalent to these standards. This historical financial information must be audited.		

2.4.1.6 *Track record requirements and complex financial histories*

The first row in the table above refers to a situation in which slavish adherence to   **2.93**
the letter of the Prospectus Regulation disclosure requirement and including
financial statements of the issuer only, regardless of its circumstances, would not
provide a fair or complete package of disclosure. In recognition of this, there are
rules—some attributable to European legislation, others born of measures devised
at the national level—that cater specifically for issuers with so-called complex
financial histories.

In short, separate financial statements for an acquired entity (i.e. an entity other   **2.94**
than the applicant company) are required if:

- the applicant is undertaking a primary listing of shares on the LSE and would
  not otherwise satisfy the three-year revenue-earning track record requirement;
- the applicant company is preparing a prospectus for shares, it has a complex
  financial history and the regulator requires such financial statements;
- the applicant company is preparing a prospectus for shares and it is required to
  include pro-forma financial statements;
- such financial statements are otherwise required to satisfy the requirement to
  include all material information;
- other rules, for example SEC rules, are relevant and would require it.

In short, pro-forma financial statements are required if: **2.95**

- the applicant company is preparing a prospectus for shares, it has a complex
  financial history and the regulator requires such financial statements;
- the applicant company is preparing a prospectus for shares and it has undergone a significant gross change;
- other rules, for example SEC rules, are relevant and would require it.

2.4.1.6.1 Requirements for London primary listings   In the context of pri-   **2.96**
mary listings on the LSE, the UK regulator takes a reasonably sensible (albeit
tough) approach to financial disclosure, which includes the application of rules
that are super-equivalent to the standards set out in the Prospectus Directive and
other relevant EEA legislation. Aside from a special rule that requires the latest

audited financial statements to be no older than six months from the date of the prospectus, the UK regulator applies another rather important rule that states that at least 75% of the applicant's business must be supported by a historic revenue-earning record that covers the period for which accounts are required. The reference to 'applicant' should be read as referring to the group as a whole at the time of the listing (or, if the group is on the verge of making a significant acquisition, the group with that target as part of the family). The three-year revenue-earning track record could require three years' financial statements (and those for an interim period, if applicable) for acquired entities.

2.97   The idea of the 75% historic revenue-earning track record rule is that it enables investors to examine the historic results of the business and make a reasonable assessment of its possible future prospects, in light of its particular circumstances and the general outlook for the relevant sector. In determining what amounts to 75% of the applicant's business for this purpose, the UKLA will take into account factors such as the assets, profitability and market capitalization of the group's business (see below for a more detailed discussion of how these tests are typically approached).

2.98   It is not unusual for the applicant to demonstrate the group's revenue-earning track record for 75% of the business by including separate financial statements for discrete parts of the group. For example, if IPOCo acquired BigCo (together with BigCo's subsidiaries) at some point in the middle of the three-year track record period, and BigCo (and its subsidiaries) is likely to represent more than 25% of the enlarged business of IPOCo at the time of the listing, the prospectus might contain three years' financial statements for IPOCo, and also separate financial statements for BigCo for the first two (or one-and-a-half) of those three years, with all of the financial statements prepared on a consistent basis to ensure comparability.

2.99   There is often some confusion about how to apply the 75% test. The answer is to consider what the best available data is to measure the significance of each relevant piece of the business not covered by the three years' consolidated financial statements of the holding company. To take the IPOCo/BigCo example: if recent data is available for the contribution of BigCo results to the consolidated results of IPOCo, that might be the best data to consider. It may not be so straightforward, particularly for profit data if, for example, there are substantial intra-group and centralized expenses that relate to the BigCo business but are difficult to strip out or apportion. In these situations, the company should consider what other meaningful data is available. It might, for example, be worthwhile to compare the annual or interim results of BigCo before it was acquired to the results of IPOCo on a consolidated basis for the latest year or interim period. It could well be that profitability is not the most compelling metric at all, because, for example, one would be comparing a nascent loss-making business to a seasoned profit-earning business or because intra-group transactions have not been undertaken at market (or current market) terms. The short answer is that this needs to be a case-by-case consideration of what measure makes most sense in determining whether a revenue-earning track record can be demonstrated for 75% of the business.

2.4.1.6.2 EEA-based requirements for complex financial histories The EEA-based requirements for complex financial histories could require three years' financial statements (and those for an interim period, if applicable) for acquired entities. These requirements relating to complex financial histories only apply to offerings of shares and certain types of convertible bonds. In such cases, if a company does indeed have a complex financial history, even if the revenue-earning track record requirement described above does not apply (because the regulator of the jurisdiction in question does not impose such super-equivalent provisions), the company wishing to undertake an equity offering may well be specifically required to include separate financial statements for an acquired business, and, in addition, to include pro-forma financial statements demonstrating the impact of a particular transaction on the company. **2.100**

According to the Prospectus Regulation, an issuer has a complex financial history if '(a) its entire business undertaking at the time that the prospectus is drawn up is not accurately represented in the historical financial information which it is required to provide under item 20.1 of Annex I; (b) that inaccuracy will affect the ability of an investor to make an informed assessment as mentioned in Article 5(1) of the Prospectus Directive; and (c) information relating to its business undertaking that is necessary for an investor to make such an assessment is included in financial information relating to another entity'. **2.101**

These problems are tortuous. In practice, they require consideration of the part of the group's business not covered by the issuer's financial statements (the missing part) to see if that missing part is material to an investment decision. If it is, the regulator has the discretion to require additional information for the missing part, or enough of it to cure the material omission.[16] They are generally used as proxies to determine materiality in this context—see Section 2.4.1.6.4 below. The additional information might include separate financial statements for the missing part and also pro-forma financial information that demonstrates the impact of the missing part on the issuer's financial statements (see Section 2.4.1.6.3 below). **2.102**

A straightforward and common example is where a brand new entity is incorporated specifically to serve as a holding company for a group to be taken to market. **2.103**

---

[16] The regulator has the same discretion if the company has made a 'significant financial commitment' at the date of the prospectus. A 'significant financial commitment' is defined as entering into a binding agreement to undertake a transaction which, on completion, is likely to give rise to a significant gross change. See discussion of significant gross change below.

The new holding company has no financial history of its own and is merely in place to hold the underlying business, which, in substance, forms the basis of the 'equity story' being bought by investors. In such circumstances, investors would reasonably expect to see the financial history of the underlying business in order to make an informed investment decision. Another common example is where the entity to be listed has existed for more than three years but has changed markedly during the year prior to the proposed offering, for instance, as a result of acquiring other businesses.

2.104 As noted above, the rules relating to complex financial histories only apply to prospectuses for shares and certain types of convertible bonds. This does not mean, however, that prospectuses for other types of securities will not need to include additional information. The overarching disclosure obligation to include all material information in the prospectus aims to keep issuers on the straight and narrow.[17] But there should be greater flexibility for these other prospectuses, and it may be that the expensive work of producing financial statements, and commissioning the audit can be replaced with qualitative information and key operating and performance indicators.

2.105 Companies will also need to consider non-EEA-based rules. In particular, if the transaction involves an offering of securities into the United States, US practice for financial disclosures will also need to be considered. Even for non-SEC registered offerings in the United States, the practice is to keep a focused eye on SEC rules by analogy, which could well lead to the conclusion that both separate and pro-forma financial statements should be included.

2.106 **2.4.1.6.3 Significant gross change and the requirement to include pro-forma financial statements** As explained above, if there have been a lot of changes in an applicant company's business because of significant acquisitions, or because a new holding company has been put in place, separate financial statements might be required for the acquired business, or for the 'real' underlying business to demonstrate a meaningful three-year revenue earning track record (if applicable), to respond to a complex financial history, or, more generally, to address the overarching requirement to ensure the prospectus discloses all material information. In addition to separate financial statements, it might also be necessary to include pro-forma financial information, depending on the nature of the proposed transaction. While the company (and indeed the regulator) has a degree of flexibility in deciding whether or not to include pro-forma financial information in a prospectus relating to a non-share deal, if it proposes to offer shares or certain types of

---

[17] Materiality in this context is customarily considered by reference to the 'significant gross change' tests outlined below.

convertible bonds and it has experienced a 'significant gross change' during the applicable track record period, pro-formas are likely to be required.

'Significant gross change' means 'a variation of more than 25%, relative to one or more indicators of the size of the issuer's business, in the situation of an issuer'.[18] Although technically the significant gross change analysis is discrete from the analysis as to whether a company has a three-year revenue earning track record, or a complex financial history, in practice, it is not altogether different. Indeed, the tests typically used to determine whether a company has a three-year revenue earning track record, or a complex financial history, or whether there has been a significant gross change (discussed at Section 2.4.1.6.4 below), are rather similar.

2.107

If a company has experienced a significant gross change, paragraph 20.2 of Annex I to the Prospectus Regulation requires the prospectus to include a description of how the relevant transaction (that caused the change in question) might have affected the issuer's assets, liabilities and earnings, had the transaction been undertaken at the commencement of the period being reported on or at the date reported. The paragraph goes on to state that this disclosure requirement will normally be satisfied by the inclusion of pro-forma financial information presented in the manner set out in Annex II to the Prospectus Regulation and reported on by independent accountants or auditors.

2.108

Given that Annex II only permits pro-forma financial statements to be included for the last full year and any subsequent interim period, it is clear that the 'significant gross change' analysis, unlike the three-year revenue earning track record and the complex financial history analysis, only needs to consider transactions that have taken place since the beginning of the last full year for which financial statements are included in the prospectus.

2.109

If pro-forma financial statements are included, paragraph 3 of Annex II of the UK Prospectus Rules requires that the sources of the pro-forma financial information must be stated and, if applicable, the financial statements of the acquired entities must be included in the prospectus.

2.110

2.4.1.6.4 Calculating a significant gross change The typical tests used to determine if an acquisition undertaken by the company constitutes a significant gross change are summarized below. If the tests produce a level of significance of 25% or more, it indicates that there has been a significant gross change and therefore pro-forma financial statements are required to show what the impact of the acquisition would have been if the acquisition had taken place at the beginning of the last full year for which historical financial statements are included.

2.111

---

[18] Prospectus Regulation Article 4a.6.

2.112 Regulators in Europe are not entirely consistent in their approach to and application of the tests, so practices from country to country will differ. However, the following tests will generally apply:

- if the acquisition results in the consolidation of the acquired business, the gross assets[19] of the acquired business as compared to the company's gross assets, in each case as of the date of the latest published balance sheet. If the acquisition does not result in the consolidation of the acquired business, the consideration for the acquired business together with liabilities assumed (if any) compared to the company's gross assets as of such date;

- if the acquisition results in the consolidation of the acquired business, the profits (after deducting all charges other than taxation) attributable to the acquired business, as compared to such profits of the company, in each case for the most recently completed fiscal year prior to the acquisition.[20] If the acquisition does not result in the consolidation of the acquired business, the means of calculation should be discussed with the regulator, but the regulator is likely to require the equity in the profits of the acquired business to be used as the basis for the calculation;

- the consideration (including the maximum amount of any deferred consideration) for the acquired business compared to the aggregate market value of all the ordinary shares (excluding treasury shares) of the company;[21]

- revenues of the acquired business as compared to the revenues of the company, calculated on an analogous basis with the profits test above;

- the aggregate, with respect to the acquired business, of:
  - the consideration as calculated above,
  - the market value of any of its shares and principal amount of debt securities which have not been acquired (or, if the market value of shares is not available, their nominal value),
  - all other liabilities (other than current liabilities) including for this purpose minority interests and deferred taxation, and
  - any excess of current liabilities over current assets,

- compared to the aggregate, with respect to the company, of:
  - the market value of its shares (excluding treasury shares) and the principal amount of its debt securities;
  - all other liabilities (other than current liabilities) including, for this purpose, minority interests and deferred taxation; and

---

[19] Gross assets means total non-current assets plus the total current assets.

[20] If either company or both companies had a loss in the relevant period, the absolute value of the loss should be used for purposes of the comparison.

[21] The date for the market capitalization is not specified for this purpose, but if the FSA does require this calculation to be made, it will likely have to be the market capitalization as at the close of business prior to the date the information is provided to the FSA.

- any excess of current liabilities over current assets;
- in the case of mineral extraction companies, one might also consider the volume or amount of proven and probable reserves attributable to the acquired business as compared to the volume or amount of proven and probable reserves of the company.

The regulator would typically expect these tests to be applied using the most com-   **2.113**
parable information available. If the applicant is in doubt over the comparability of the information, its advisers should discuss the matter with the regulator at the earliest possible stage.

There are no specific requirements for pro-forma financial statements for prospec-   **2.114**
tuses for securities other than shares or certain types of convertible bonds. However, pro-forma financial statements are often included regardless of the technical rules, because they can help investors to understand the relevant transaction, which, in turn, assists with the marketing effort, and/or because the offering is also being made into the United States, where one customarily looks to US disclosure standards by analogy.

2.5 Passporting a Prospectus

2.5.1 The passporting principle

One of the key principles laid down in the Prospectus Directive is the mutual   **2.115**
recognition or 'passporting' of prospectuses approved by the competent authority of a member state. The idea that a prospectus that is fit to document a deal in Sweden is also fit for one in Germany or France or the United Kingdom is intrinsically linked to the notion of a single European market.

It is in the context of a multi-jurisdictional offering or listing that the concept   **2.116**
of passporting really demonstrates its value: if a company were required to go to the trouble of preparing a separate prospectus for each jurisdiction in which it wants to offer or list its securities, such deals would be much less likely to happen.[22]

Passporting played a key role in some of the major European flotations and capi-   **2.117**
tal-raising transactions of the late 1990s and early 2000, such as Deutsche Telecom AG, which conducted a public offering in Germany, the United Kingdom, France, Belgium, The Netherlands, Luxembourg, Austria, Finland, Denmark, Norway, Ireland, Spain and Portugal. Similarly, Deutsche Post sought capital in Germany,

---

[22] It might also be necessary to passport a prospectus when a company, in conjunction with an IPO, offers shares to employees who are located in multiple member states.

the United Kingdom, Austria, Italy, the Netherlands and Spain, while Koninklijke KPN NV tapped the market in the Netherlands, Germany, Italy and Spain. In each case, one single approved prospectus covered the entire offering.

2.5.2 Passporting procedure

2.118   Any prospectus (including any supplements) approved by a company's home member state in connection with a public offer of securities or the admission of securities to trading on a regulated market (regardless of whether the relevant company is incorporated and domiciled in the EEA or in a third country) is valid for a public offer/admission to trading of the same securities in any other member state, provided that the competent authority of the home member state delivers to the competent authority of the host member state a certificate of approval (to confirm that the prospectus has been drawn up in accordance with the Prospectus Directive) and a copy of the relevant prospectus.[23] In some cases, it might be necessary to submit a translation of the prospectus (or just its summary), as discussed in Section 2.5.3 below.

2.119   In terms of timing, if the company submits a passporting request before or at the time it submits the draft prospectus for approval, the home member state authorities must deliver the certificate of approval to the host member state authorities no later than the working day after it has approved the prospectus. If the passporting request is submitted at a later point, the home member state authorities must provide the certificate within three working days of the request.

2.120   When the competent authority of a host member state receives a passporting notification, it is not permitted to subject the document to any administrative procedures or approval processes. In practice, it will normally acknowledge receipt of the passporting request and related documentation to the home member state and, in some cases, will publish the prospectus summary on its website.

2.5.3 Language

2.121   If a company prepares a prospectus for passporting into other member states, it must be drafted either in a language accepted by the competent authorities of each host member state or in a 'language customary in the sphere of international finance',[24] which at the moment, is English. Accordingly, if the prospectus is prepared in English, the company will not be required to translate it into another language. However, the company might be required to translate the summary if it intends to passport the prospectus into a non-English speaking member state and the relevant competent authority requires it.

---

[23] Prospectus Directive Articles 17 and 18.
[24] Prospectus Directive Article 19.

Where a company prepares a prospectus in a language that is not customary in the **2.122** sphere of international finance (for example, Finnish) and it intends to passport the prospectus to a non-Finnish-speaking member state, it will be required to translate the prospectus either into a language that is customary in the sphere of international finance (i.e. English), or into a language accepted by the competent authority in the host member state. It is worth noting, however, that it is the competent authority in the home member state that must insist on such a translation, and not (as is commonly but mistakenly believed) the competent authority in the host member state. Indeed, Article 19 of the Prospectus Directive makes it clear that in such circumstances, the competent authority in the host member state can only request a translation of the prospectus summary.

2.5.4 Jurisdictional overview

The following table summarizes key information regarding the requirements for **2.123** passporting a prospectus into the member states that are described in the jurisdictional chapters of Part 3.[25]

Member state	Competent authority	Languages accepted for the review of the prospectus[26]	Requirements in relation to the translation of prospectus summary for passporting[27]
Austria	Finanzmarktaufsicht	English and German.	The Financial Market Authority does not require a translation of the summary into German if the prospectus is published in English.
Belgium	Commission Bancaire et Financière et des Assurances	French, Dutch and English.	The Commission Bancaire, Financière et des Assurances requires the translation of the summary in French and Dutch if there is a public offer in Belgium (no translation in French and Dutch is required if there is only an admission on a regulated market in Belgium).

[25] The information in the table is based on the February 2009 CESR report 'Languages accepted for the purpose of the scrutiny of the Prospectus and requirements of translation of the Summary' (Ref. 09-133).

[26] This column includes the languages that each member state accepts when acting as home member state for the purpose of the scrutiny of the prospectus.

[27] This column provides information on whether or not a translation of the summary of a prospectus passported is required by the competent authority in each member state. In addition, it clarifies which are the language(s) acceptable for the translation of the summary when requested.

(Continued)

Member state	Competent authority	Languages accepted for the review of the prospectus	Requirements in relation to the translation of prospectus summary for passporting
			The issuer or offeror can choose to translate the summary in only one of those languages, but in that case it is not allowed to make any advertisement in the other language.
Denmark	Finanstilsynet	Finanstilsynet accepts Danish. As to Article 19.2, for the purpose of the scrutiny, Finanstilsynet accepts Danish, Norwegian, Swedish or English.	Finanstilsynet requires a translation of the summary into Danish with the exception of an issue of non-equity securities with a denomination of at least EUR 50,000.
Finland	Finanssivalvonta	Finnish and Swedish. However, English can also be accepted on special grounds.	Rahoitustarkastus requires a translation of the summary in Finnish or Swedish with the exception of an issue of non-equity securities with a denomination of at least EUR 50,000.
France	Autorité des marchés financiers	English and French.	When the prospectus has not been established in French, a translation of the summary in French is required except for admission to trading of non-equity securities having at least a denomination of EUR 50,000.
Germany	Bundesanstalt für Finanz-dienstleistungs-aufsicht	German and English.	For English prospectuses a translation of the summary into German is required, unless exclusively non-equity securities with a denomination of at least EUR 50,000 are admitted to trading on a regulated market.
Ireland	Irish Financial Services Regulatory Authority	Irish and English.	The summary must be translated into Irish or English. It is not necessary for an issuer of non-equity securities with a denomination of at least EUR 50,000 to translate the summary.

(Continued)

Member state	Competent authority	Languages accepted for the review of the prospectus	Requirements in relation to the translation of prospectus summary for passporting
Italy	Commissione Nazionale per le Società e la Borsa ('Consob')	—Where an offer to the public is made or admission to trading on a regulated market is sought only in Italy as the home member state, the prospectus shall be drawn up in Italian. —Where an offer to the public is made or admission to trading on a regulated market is sought in Italy as the host member state, the prospectus may be drawn up, at the choice of the issuer, offeror or person asking for admission to trading, either in Italian or in English.	If the prospectus is drawn up in English, Consob requires the translation of the summary in Italian, also for admission to trading on a regulated market of non-equity securities with denomination of at least EUR 50,000.
Luxembourg	Commission de surveillance du secteur financier ('CSSF')	English, French, German and Luxembourgish.	When the prospectus is not drafted in English, French, German or Luxembourgish, the CSSF requires the translation of the whole prospectus (included the summary if required) into one of these languages.
Netherlands	Autoriteit Financiële Markten	Dutch and English.	The Netherlands Authority for the Financial Markets does not require an additional translation of the summary in Dutch language if the prospectus is drawn up in English.
Portugal	Comissâo do Mercado de Valores Mobiliários ('CNMV')	Portuguese and English.	CMVM requires that the summary is translated into Portuguese. Such translation is not required for prospectuses relating to non-equity securities with a denomination of at least EUR 50,000 or for prospectus of non-equity securities intended to be listed on a market or market segment, which, by its characteristics, is only accessible to institutional investors.
Spain	Comisión Nacional del Mercado de Valores	Spanish and English.	The CNMV requires the translation of the summary into Spanish with the exception of prospectuses relating to non-equity securities with a denomination of at least EUR 50,000.

(Continued)

Member state	Competent authority	Languages accepted for the review of the prospectus	Requirements in relation to the translation of prospectus summary for passporting
Sweden	Finansinspektionen	Finansinspektionen accepts Swedish. It may accept other languages, for example, Danish, Norwegian or English, in special circumstances.	Finansinspektionen requires a Swedish translation of the summary in prospectuses passported into Sweden, with the exemption of prospectuses relating to non-equity securities with a denomination of at least EUR 50,000.
United Kingdom	Financial Services Authority	English.	The FSA requires a translation of the summary where the prospectus is drawn up in a language other than English that is customary in the sphere of international finance. Guidance as to what is customary in the sphere of international finance may be found in PR4.1.5A of the UKLA's Prospectus Rules.

2.6 Underwriting Agreements and Distribution Issues

2.6.1 Underwriting agreements in a nutshell

2.124 As explained in Section 2.1.2.1 above, the underwriting agreement is the key contractual document governing the relationship between the company, any selling shareholders and the underwriting syndicate. To sum it up, the document essentially says six things:

(1) I, the underwriter, promise to buy the securities if no one else does, as long as you make me comfortable that your business is in good order and the market has not gone belly up since I made this promise and, in light of the risk I am taking, you promise to pay me a handsome sum;

(2) You, the company, promise to issue the securities that I will shortly be promising to investors (as soon as an underwriting agreement is signed, an underwriter will try to mitigate its underwriting risk by allocating securities to investors and entering into a contract with them for them to buy the securities at the specified price);

(3) You promise that the prospectus, which investors are relying on to make their investment decision, is accurate, not misleading and contains all things material to an investor's investment decision;

(4) You promise that you are otherwise in good shape;

(5) You promise that you will not do anything that could jeopardize the offering efforts;

(6) You promise that if I suffer a loss (or if my affiliates or directors or employees suffer a loss) because of your (wrongful, or allegedly wrongful) actions, you will make me whole by indemnifying me (or them).

One might reasonably think that such a straightforward agreement could be dealt with in a few pages, and in the old days, underwriting agreements may well have been very short. But lawyers are additive creatures. Over the years, the underwriting agreement has grown to something much more voluminous. Indeed, the typical underwriting agreement for a London listed IPO has become a monstrous animal of more than 100 pages. **2.125**

2.6.2 Key areas of battle

The key areas of battle in the negotiation of an underwriting agreement are often the following: **2.126**

Underwriting commitment:
Will the underwriters stand side by side to each other and take the securities another underwriter failed to take when it was supposed to (a joint and several underwriting) or is each underwriter only responsible for its own promise to underwrite (a several underwriting)? If the offering involves a Rule 144A aspect (that is, there will be an offering to qualified institutional buyers in the United States), a several and not joint underwriting is standard. Several and not joint underwritings have become quite common, and some might say even standard practice, for modern European equity deals, even if they are 'Reg S only' (an offering outside the United States only). If, however, it is a 'Reg S only' offering of debt, the company can reasonably expect to have the benefit of a joint and several underwriting commitment. **2.127**

It is worth noting that even several underwritings are often not completely several. Typically, the relevant provision will contain a clause to the effect that an underwriter will promise to take up the slack created by a defaulting underwriter as long as it does not increase its underwriting commitment by more than 10% for example. **2.128**

Fees:
What handsome sum will the company pay each underwriter for taking the underwriting risk and putting its reputation on the line? **2.129**

Lock ups:
Under a lock-up provision, the locked-up party (usually the company and any selling shareholder, but possibly also other key shareholders and directors) agrees not to sell on the market similar securities to those being offered for a specified period following the offering. If new securities were dumped on the market, the increased supply would create downward pressure on the price of the securities, **2.130**

which, needless to say, would not sit well with the investors who participated in the offering. Nevertheless, the company may need the flexibility to raise money after the offering, so the scope of securities that the company is prohibited from issuing is likely to be a point of contention. The company also needs to be able to honour any incentive scheme commitments it has agreed with employees and directors, so specific exceptions may be in order.

2.131 The extent to which key shareholders, some of whom may have no involvement in the offering, will agree to be locked up can be a hot topic. Underwriters will naturally want them to commit to a lock-up, but will be mindful of the practicalities of this request. One trade is often that the shareholder is permitted to join the offering as a seller of some of its shares if it agrees to be locked up. The prospect of a decent return on its shareholding may tempt it to participate. A selling shareholder will typically be subject to a fairly tight lock-up, though specific exceptions can be up for negotiation.

2.132 The length of the lock-up is often an area of heavy negotiation. In the IPO context, a lock-up period of 180 days is common, although issuers with significant negotiating leverage occasionally are able to negotiate a shorter lock-up period. For follow-on equity offerings, shorter lock-up periods are more common than in the IPO context. In both contexts, issuers sometimes are able to negotiate an agreement that the underwriters will not unreasonably withhold their consent to a transaction that is governed by the lock-up clause.

2.133 Whatever the terms of the lock-up, it is reasonable to expect investors to care about the issue. If the lock-up is too loose or for too short a time, the effect may be reflected in the price they are willing to pay for the securities.

The interrelationship between the company and the selling shareholder:

2.134 In any underwriting agreement this needs substantial thought and often takes up precious negotiation time. How much potential liability is reasonable for a selling shareholder to take on will depend on multiple factors, the key ones of which are:

(i)   how large will the proceeds to the selling shareholder be, in absolute terms and also by comparison with the company itself?

(ii) how much liability is the company prepared to accept?

(iii) to what extent has the selling shareholder been involved in the management of the company in the past?

(iv) what future role, if any, will the selling shareholder play in the business of the company?

2.135 Generally, the larger the prospective proceeds and the greater its past and future involvement, the more a selling shareholder will be asked to give. Furthermore, if the company is in a position to negotiate a cap on its own liability (which is most likely the case in offerings that are largely or exclusively secondary[28]), the underwriters will almost certainly be looking to the selling shareholders to cover the risk of liabilities above the company's cap.

A selling shareholder might consider agreeing to one of the following options: **2.136**

(i) Very limited representations, warranties and undertakings, going to title to the shares and compliance with securities laws, with a cap on liability set at the total proceeds received by it, a higher cap or no cap. It is very unlikely that a selling shareholder could get away with no representations, warranties and undertakings at all—the underwriters would at least want to know that the selling shareholder owns the shares it is selling and that it has not been putting up billboards in Idaho encouraging senior citizens to think about investing in the company (see Section 2.2.1.2 above).

(ii) Same as paragraph (i) above, but with the addition of an indemnity from the selling shareholder in favour of the underwriters for breach of its representations and warranties with a cap of liability set at the total proceeds received by it, a higher cap or no cap.

(iii) Full representations, warranties and undertakings with a cap on liability to proceeds received by it, a higher cap or no cap.

(iv) Same as paragraph (iii) above, but with the addition of an indemnity from the selling shareholder in favour of the underwriters for breach of its representations and warranties with a cap on liability set at the total proceeds received by it, a higher cap or no cap.

(v) In addition to any of the above, security over some or all of its shares in the company for a limited period of time.

As a general matter, the selling shareholder needs to consider how much of the **2.137** disclosure it is willing to be contractually liable for, which might be (i) none of it; (ii) the information about it and its shares only; or (iii) all of it. The extent to which the selling shareholder is liable for the disclosure will of course be a key negotiation point, the outcome of which is likely to be reflected in the options (i) to (v) set out above.

Who counts as the 'selling shareholder' in this context is also important. Often, **2.138** although the shares are sold by a company, behind that company stand one or a few individuals. In that instance, careful consideration needs to be given as to whether the individuals will also enter into the underwriting agreement and make the same promises and agreements as the entity (which is the legal owner and therefore seller of the shares). It is conceivable that if the individuals do become

---

[28] Unless the offering in questions happens to constitute an IPO, in which case the company is likely to be on the hook for the full whack, regardless of the extent of its participation.

party to the underwriting agreement, it is in a substantially more limited manner than in the case of a selling shareholder. Having said that, underwriters often have great difficulty in persuading individuals to sign an underwriting agreement, unless those individuals are also directors and the offering involves a primary listing of shares in London. In the case of primary listings in London, it is fairly customary for directors to sign up to various promises and undertakings in the underwriting agreement, and this will be of significant comfort to underwriters if any of those directors are also selling shareholders.

The indemnity:

2.139 Indemnities in Europe are quite different in style to indemnities in the United States. Although one might expect indemnities to be heavier on companies in US underwriting agreements, the opposite is actually the case. A US-style indemnity can be described as 'disclosure indemnity', under which the company promises that if the underwriters suffer a loss as a result of an actual or alleged misstatement or omission of a material fact in the preliminary or final prospectus (or any amendment or supplement thereto), it will pay.

2.140 A typical European-style indemnity includes the US-style disclosure indemnity, but it also imposes an obligation on the company to pay the underwriters if there is an actual or alleged breach of any of the company's representations, warranties or undertakings. On its face, this is much wider than the disclosure indemnity. Arguably, however, the gap is narrowed somewhat if the company's representations, warranties and undertakings are appropriately qualified by materiality.[29] This is the case because if there has been a breach of a representation or warranty, and it is material, the underlying fact should have been disclosed in the offering document (hence, the breach of representation or warranty would also constitute a breach of the disclosure indemnity). However, one can conceive of a number of potential liabilities that would be caught by a breach of representations and warranties but not by a disclosure indemnity. For example, the company typically makes numerous securities law representations, warranties and undertakings (which are not typically qualified by materiality). If these provisions were to be breached by the company, it could lead to regulatory liability for underwriters. Investors might not be affected, so the prospectus might well have been fine as it was. In such a case, a disclosure indemnity would not enable the underwriters to recover the relevant regulatory liability. In contrast, the underwriters should be able to recover under a European-style indemnity, i.e. an indemnity formulated as one for breaches of representations and warranties by the company.

---

[29] Some representation and warranties—and certainly those that relate to the manner of sale of the relevant securities—are very unlikely to be subject to a materiality qualifier.

The broadest type of indemnity is a 'transaction indemnity', which requires the **2.141** issuer to indemnify the underwriter against all losses arising out of the services performed by the underwriter in connection with the offering (unless the loss arose from the relevant underwriter's (gross) negligence, bad faith or wilful misconduct —the 'negligence carve out'). If the company can be persuaded to agree to a transaction indemnity, there is sometimes a long debate as to whether the negligence carve out should be for 'negligence' or 'gross negligence' or some variation between the two.

Transaction indemnities are fairly common in sponsored primary listings of secu- **2.142** rities on the LSE but are less common in other types of listings and securities offerings.

Materiality carve-outs:

Many hours will be spent negotiating materiality qualifiers in the representations, **2.143** warranties and undertakings of the company. These are qualifiers that say, for example, there is no breach of representation or warranty unless the failure would reasonably be expected to result in a material adverse effect on the company. The definition of material adverse effect will be subject to hours of negotiation, often to determine if it will include material adverse effect in the prospects of the company as well as in its financial condition. This discussion can go either way.

Underwriters will often grant materiality carve-outs, provided they do not result **2.144** in 'double materiality'. Take, for example, the following representation:

> the company represents that it has not breached any agreement in any material respect, save for any such breach that would not reasonably be expected to have a material adverse effect.

Such a representation is not likely to pass muster with underwriters. In addition, **2.145** underwriters will often refuse to grant materiality carve-outs for matters that go to the fundamental integrity of the deal—for example, a representation that says that the company has done all it needs to do to issue the shares, provided that failure to do so would not reasonably be expected to have a material adverse effect, is also not likely to cut it with underwriters.

2.6.3 Timing and process

In equity deals, the underwriting agreement is typically signed at the time the **2.146** price of the securities is determined. It is, however, customary to try and have all significant points agreed prior to the deal being publicly announced. Underwriters are likely to feel that their bargaining power weakens once market expectations for a deal are high, and underwriters' reputations are already publicly on the line.

2.147 It is customary for underwriters' counsel to draft the underwriting agreement. When underwriting syndicates were small and led by a single bank, the starting point was commonly the particular standard form of that lead bank. Times have changed, however, and a horde of lead banks is not uncommon. Counsel will therefore often start with a neutral form. Consequently, underwriters' counsel must make sure that each of the lead banks is happy with the first draft of the underwriting agreement by ensuring the agreement covers all of the matters it needs to satisfy each bank's internal compliance policies. These policies on the one hand, and the issuer's view on what is fair on the other, often makes the negotiation of an underwriting agreement a tough yet enjoyable affair.

3

DEBT OFFERINGS AND PROGRAMMES

3.1 Overview

3.01 This Chapter considers how debt securities are typically issued into the Euromarkets. It is quite difficult to define what 'Euromarkets' means for this purpose. However, the market has typically operated in the past on the assumption that investors who acquire debt securities are primarily institutional investors or are otherwise sophisticated. Disclosure in relation to the issuer in the formal documentation supporting debt issuances has therefore tended to be relatively concise, at least in comparison to more recent documentation relating to equity issuances.

3.02 To some degree, these distinctions have become less apparent for a number of reasons. These include a general tendency towards including more (rather than less) disclosure for risk and liability reasons, the impact of the Prospectus Directive[1] which sets out a benchmark for disclosure standards based on the denomination of the debt security (see below) and possibly a trend towards issuers adopting common levels of disclosure in relation to all the different types of securities being issued, whether debt or equity.

3.03 This Chapter will look at the different types of debt securities that are typically issued into the Euromarkets and the documentation and steps involved in constituting, issuing and distributing the debt securities as well as the procedures for listing them on a European stock exchange.

3.04 Some European jurisdictions, for example Germany but, interestingly, not the United Kingdom, have well-developed domestic retail markets where the underlying investors in the securities are true retail investors (who might invest through facilities offered by branches of their local retail or savings banks), rather than financial institutions or other sophisticated investors. A discussion of how debt securities are issued into these markets is beyond the scope of this Chapter, save

---

[1] Directive 2003/71/EC.

where multi-jurisdictional retail offerings are carried out taking advantage of the simplified 'passporting' procedures of the Prospectus Directive.[2]

True retail offerings of the kind described in the previous paragraph should not **3.05** be confused with what might otherwise be described as a 'retail offering' for the purposes of the Prospectus Directive. In the context of the Prospectus Directive, a retail offering is any offering where the denomination of the debt securities concerned is less than EUR 50,000 (or its equivalent in other currencies) and is to be contrasted with a 'wholesale offering' of debt securities where the denomination of the debt securities is EUR 50,000 (or its equivalent in other currencies) or more.

The Prospectus Directive Regulation[3] has attached to it Annexes which set out the **3.06** detailed content requirements for Prospectus Directive compliant prospectuses. The denomination of the debt securities being issued is one factor that determines which Annexes of the Prospectus Directive Regulation apply to any prospectus or base prospectus prepared in respect of such offering, and will also dictate the level of disclosure contained in such prospectus. Broadly, in the case of a retail offering, there is a higher, more detailed level of disclosure in the relevant prospectus or base prospectus compared to a wholesale offering.

A retail offering, in the sense that the denomination of the debt securities is less **3.07** than EUR 50,000 (or its equivalent in other currencies), may be conducted on the basis that no Prospectus Directive compliant prospectus is needed (or, if it is, that it is solely for admission of the relevant securities for listing on an EEA regulated market). This would be achieved by conducting marketing and sales activities within the various exemptions provided in Article 4 of the Prospectus Directive and such an offering is referred to as an 'exempt offering', for obvious reasons. In contrast, a true retail offering of the kind described above is commonly described as a 'non-exempt offering' and would require preparation, approval and publication of a Prospectus Directive compliant prospectus.[4]

Finally, European and other issuers sometimes issue their debt securities into **3.08** investor markets within the United States in a way which does not involve the full ceremony of a US registered offering. This includes an offering under 'Rule 144A'[5] to US institutional investors known as 'qualified institutional buyers' or 'QIBs'.[6] Such offerings into the US capital markets involve navigation around complex

---

[2] See Chapter 1 on passporting.
[3] Commission Regulation (EC) No 809/2004.
[4] See further Section 3.9 below.
[5] Rule 144A adopted pursuant to the United States Securities Act of 1933, as amended.
[6] In general, a QIB is a sophisticated institutional investor such as an insurance company, a bank or an investment company that owns or invests on a discretionary basis at least $100 million of securities.

and far-reaching securities laws as well as a general fear (whether or not justified) of a consequent increased risk of disclosure liability. Such is the territorial scope of United States securities laws, that securities offerings made wholly outside of the United States and the United States securities markets and involving no directed selling efforts in the United States are nevertheless commonly described by reference to regulations made under those laws. These are 'Regulation S' or 'Reg S'[7] offerings. Offerings of debt and other securities made into the Euromarkets (and not into the United States) are made under Regulation S and are described as such so as to make it clear that those involved in the offering should be focusing their attentions mainly on the Prospectus Directive and other applicable non-US securities laws, assuming, among other things, that the appropriate Reg S legends and contractual selling and other restrictions appear in the documentation for the offering.[8] This Chapter assumes that any offering of debt securities is conducted wholly under Regulation S.

3.2 Types of Commonly Issued Debt Securities

3.2.1 Bonds or notes?

3.09 Bonds and notes are really the same thing and the expressions can be and are generally used interchangeably. There are a few apparent conventions: debt securities issued from a Euro Medium Term Note (EMTN) programme will generally be notes. Notes are thought to be of short- to medium-term maturity, whereas bonds might be of longer maturity. On the other hand, convertible or exchangeable debt securities are normally referred to as convertible or exchangeable bonds rather than notes. However, it really makes no difference and no doubt each market participant will have his or her own view on the distinction, and debt securities have the same basic legal form and constitution however they are described.

3.2.2 Senior notes

3.10 Senior notes, whether fixed rate or floating rate, are the most common types of notes issued into the Euromarkets. The word 'senior' is something of a misnomer. In fact, in a winding-up or liquidation of an issuer, its unsecured senior notes rank at the same level as other creditors of the issuer who are not subordinated or

---

[7] Regulation S adopted pursuant to the United States Securities Act of 1933, as amended.

[8] Compliance with Reg S also requires that certain restrictions be observed during the course of an offering—including with respect to publicity, websites, research reports and similar matters. In addition, it should be emphasized that offerings under Reg S or Rule 144A (and other unregistered offerings of securities) are not exempt from the application of the anti-fraud rules under the United States Federal Securities Laws: see, for example, Section 10(b) and Rule 10b-5 of the United States Exchange Act of 1934, as amended.

secured or statutorily preferred. Unsecured senior notes will therefore rank at the same level as an issuer's general creditors. Secured notes will rank above unsecured senior notes and subordinated notes[9] will rank junior to unsecured senior notes.

Senior notes are generally unsecured, though in some cases issuers might sell secured notes into the Euromarkets. Senior notes are therefore to be contrasted primarily with secured notes and subordinated notes. **3.11**

3.2.3 Fixed or floating rate?

The interest rate or 'coupon' on senior notes (and indeed, other forms of debt securities) are typically calculated by reference to either a fixed or floating rate of interest. This is not necessarily the case for structured notes[10] or zero coupon notes (which are normally issued at a discount to the amount to be repaid at maturity). In the case of fixed rate notes, the coupon is calculated on the basis of a fixed annual percentage of the principal amount of the notes and is payable at the intervals (i.e. on the interest payment dates) specified in the terms and conditions of the notes. These intervals may be monthly, quarterly, half-yearly or annual or at other specified intervals. **3.12**

In contrast, interest on floating rate notes (or 'FRNs') is calculated on the basis of an annual percentage rate calculated as the sum of a fixed margin above an annual interest rate determined by reference to a rate of interest specified by a third party market provider. For example, Euro denominated notes might be described as having a coupon of 1.5 per cent (or 150 bps) above the Euro Interbank Offered Rate (EURIBOR) for three-month deposits as specified on the relevant screen page by a third party service provider such as Reuters. **3.13**

3.2.4 Subordinated notes

Subordinated notes are issued by financial institutions (banks, insurance companies and others) for regulatory capital purposes since, depending upon their exact terms, they are capable of constituting tier 1 or tier 2 capital.[11] They are also issued by non-financial institution companies for various purposes, including supporting or enhancing the company's balance sheet and credit rating. Subordination is typically achieved by providing that in a winding-up or liquidation of the issuing company, recovery under the notes for holders is subject to the prior repayment in full of senior and general creditors as well as of any other creditors who, according to the terms and conditions of the subordinated notes, are expressed to rank in priority to the subordinated notes. **3.14**

---

[9] See 'Subordinated notes' in Section 3.2.4 below.
[10] See 'Structured notes' in Section 3.2.7 below.
[11] See 'Hybrid debt securities' in Section 3.2.8 below.

3.2.5 Equity linked notes

3.15 Equity linked notes are debt securities that are convertible or exchangeable (conventionally at the option of the holder, but occasionally at the option of the issuer or on a mandatory basis at a specified time) into share capital on the basis of a defined conversion or exchange ratio. A convertible bond issue is a debt instrument which is convertible into the ordinary shares (or common stock) of the issuer or into the ordinary shares (or common stock) of the issuer's ultimate parent. Such ordinary shares (or common stock) are typically of a class that is already admitted to trading on a stock exchange. If the conversion rights in the bonds are exercised, the terms and conditions of the bonds will typically provide for the obligation of the issuer to deliver the shares to be fulfilled by the issue of new (or possibly treasury) shares to the converting bondholder.

3.16 In contrast, an exchangeable bond is exchangeable by the holder (or occasionally on a mandatory basis by the issuer) into existing shares of a third party which are already listed on a stock exchange. A company might issue an exchangeable bond as a way, for example, of realizing value in relation to its holding of shares in a third party without, at the time of issuance, actually disposing of that economic interest. If the exchange rights in the bonds are exercised, the terms and conditions of the exchangeable bonds will typically provide for the obligation of the issuer to deliver the underlying shares to be fulfilled by physical delivery of the shares it holds (or shares it purchases in the market at the time) or sometimes (at the issuer's option) by payment of an equivalent cash amount.

3.17 The terms and conditions of both convertible and exchangeable bonds contain detailed provisions addressing conversion and exchange mechanics as well as possible adjustments to the conversion or exchange ratio as a consequence of various corporate actions by the company into whose shares the bonds can be converted or exchanged. The main philosophical difference (which may or may not be matched by reality in a given situation) between a convertible bond and an exchangeable bond is that in the case of a convertible bond the issuer of the bond is also (actually or economically) the issuer of the shares and so has control over corporate actions to the extent that they impact the value of the convertible bonds. As a consequence, the adjustment provisions in the terms and conditions of a convertible bond are primarily aimed at preserving the value of the underlying conversion right through adjustment to the conversion ratio.

3.18 In contrast, the issuer of an exchangeable bond often (but not always) has no control over the corporate actions of the issuer of the shares into which the exchangeable bonds exchange, and so the exchange ratio adjustment provisions address a notional 'basket' of rights initially represented by the shares into which the bonds exchange. That basket is tracked through the life of the bonds and the exchange right applies to a proportionate entitlement to that basket and whatever happens to it, but without requiring the issuer of the bond to contribute further value to the basket. So in the case of some corporate actions by the issuer of shares (such as a consolidation or share split), the consequences to a convertible bond and exchangeable bond conversion/exchange rights will be just the same—the exchange ratio will be adjusted mathematically to reflect the split or consolidation. However, in other cases, the result will be different. For example, in the case of a rights issue the conversion ratio will be adjusted to increase the number of shares received on conversion if the rights issue is carried out below the previous market price of the shares (or by more than a specified percentage, for example 5 per cent, below market price) since pricing is within the control of the issuer. On the other hand, the exchange ratio of an exchangeable bond will only be adjusted to the extent that the holder of the shares can preserve the value of the 'basket' without itself incurring cost or expense, for example by selling some of the rights to new shares in the market so as to fund taking up the remaining rights.

3.2.6 Commercial paper

Commercial paper (or 'CP') takes the form of debt securities having a maturity of less than one year. They are issued by issuers with high credit ratings. They are typically issued from dedicated CP programmes and are outside the scope of the Prospectus Directive. They are not considered further in this Chapter. **3.19**

3.2.7 Structured notes

There are a wide variety of debt securities that can be issued into the market which have some kind of additional structuring feature. Broadly, categories of such debt securities are divided into the following types: **3.20**

- *Derivatives*: a derivative is a debt security whose yield (or coupon) or amount repayable at maturity depends upon some other variable such as movements in an index (such as a stock market index), or the performance of another security or basket of securities or other investments.
- *Asset-backed securities*: an asset-backed instrument is a debt security which depends for payment of its coupon or yield upon an income stream from some other asset (for example, on a pool of mortgages or other securities) and in respect of which the principal amount payable upon maturity also depends upon the performance of those assets stocked.
- *Covered bonds*: these are debt instruments that are typically secured over and recourse in respect of which is limited to an identified pool of other assets, for example mortgages.

The variety of structured notes that can be issued is limited only by the imagination of issuers and their advisors. A detailed discussion of structured products is beyond the scope of this Chapter. **3.21**

3.2.8 Hybrid debt securities

3.22   Banks and insurers (and other regulated businesses) are required to maintain a specified level of capital. That capital is categorized, in the United Kingdom at least, into three levels or 'Tiers'. Tier 1 is the strongest form of capital and is mostly comprised of ordinary share capital, reserves and non-cumulative preference share capital. Tier 1 capital can also include a limited amount of 'hybrid' debt capital, that is, debt that has many of the economic features of equity (including coupons that are non-cumulative from the issuer's perspective, deep subordination and perpetual (or very long dated) maturity). Tier 2 capital includes undated (perpetual) subordinated debt as Upper Tier 2 capital and dated unsubordinated debt as Lower Tier 2 capital. Both hybrid Tier 1 capital and Tier 2 capital has been issued regularly into the debt capital markets, and the volume of hybrid Tier 1 debt issuance has increased significantly over the last ten years as financial institutions have sought efficient ways to finance their regulatory capital requirements. The detailed rules relating to the definition of Tier 1 capital and limits on the types and amounts of capital that can be included by banks within Tier 1 are set to change following the implementation of proposed changes to the Capital Requirements Directive and initiatives led by governments and the G20.[12] Corresponding changes are also likely to be made in relation to regulatory capital for insurers.

3.23   Some non-financial institution issuers have also issued a variety of hybrid debt instruments designed to support balance sheets and credit ratings, possibly in the context of substantial acquisitions. Issuance of 'corporate hybrids' has been fairly active in continental Europe (for instance, Germany) but less so in the United Kingdom, possibly because of some uncertainty surrounding the tax treatment of corporate hybrids.

3.3   Types of Offering of Debt Securities

3.3.1   Programme or stand-alone?

3.24   There are two main methods of issuing debt securities. By far the most common, particularly in recent years, is issuance under a debt programme, for example under a Euro Medium Term Note ('EMTN') Programme or Debt Issuance Programme ('DIP'), the two being largely the same. Alternatively, if an issuer does not have an EMTN Programme or DIP, or if the type of securities being issued are not suitable for a programme, debt securities can be issued on a 'stand-alone' basis. Examples of stand-alone debt issuances (even where the issuer concerned

---

[12]   2006/48/EU and 2006/49/EU.

has a programme) would include, for example, convertible and exchangeable bonds as well as hybrid debt securities,[13] though the debt programmes of many financial institutions have over the last few years begun to include the structural features necessary to enable the issuance of, for example, Tier 1 hybrid capital instruments.

The choice of whether to issue debt securities on the basis of a stand-alone **3.25** prospectus or under the base prospectus of a debt issuance programme is largely a practical one. If the debt issuance programme allows for the issue of the type of security being contemplated and is up to date, then clearly there is no reason not to use that programme for the proposed issue. If the programme does not contemplate the type of securities concerned, then the choice is whether to update the base prospectus for the programme to build in any necessary further terms and conditions and other consequential changes to allow for the issuance, or whether to prepare a prospectus on a stand-alone basis. An alternative would be to carry out an issue by means of a 'drawdown prospectus'. A drawdown prospectus is a form of stand-alone prospectus which includes the provisions and/or disclosure necessary to enable the particular securities to be issued, but which incorporates by reference the existing programme base prospectus. This speeds up the approval process for the prospectus compared to a stand-alone prospectus.[14]

If the proposed issuer does not have a debt issuance programme, the question is **3.26** whether it should establish one? The following are matters to consider:

3.3.1.1 Cost

The costs of putting together a debt issuance programme rather than issuing **3.27** securities on the basis of a stand-alone prospectus are greater, but perhaps not substantially so. The documentation for a debt issuance programme is relatively standard form, other than items such as the business description and issuer risk factors sections of the base prospectus. These will have to be prepared in any case for a stand-alone prospectus. On the other hand, once a debt issuance programme is established, the cost of carrying out subsequent issues under the programme will be much less.

3.3.1.2 Timing

Since debt issuance programme documentation is relatively standard form, it **3.28** can be prepared fairly quickly. Nevertheless, since it contemplates many different kinds of debt instruments and is written to allow regular issuance using no more than a set of final terms[15] and a prescribed form of syndication agreement,

---

[13] See Section 3.2.8.
[14] See further generally Section 3.7, 'Prospectus Supplements'.
[15] See Section 3.5.11.

programme documentation is necessarily more complex and voluminous than would be the case for a stand-alone issuance. This therefore means that the documentation for a programme will take slightly longer to prepare and finalize than that for a stand-alone issue. However, once a debt issuance programme is established, each subsequent issue under the programme will be significantly quicker to document and execute than a stand-alone issue. An outline timetable that indicates the different timescales that apply when executing a stand-alone bond issue compared to those applicable to an issue under a debt programme, is set out in Appendix 1 to this Chapter.

3.3.1.3 Updating

3.29 If the full benefits of a programme are to be achieved, it needs to be kept up to date. There is little purpose in having invested time and expense to establish a debt issuance programme if, at the time it is needed for a swift issue to take advantage of fleetingly favourable market conditions, it is discovered that it cannot be used because the base prospectus is not fully up to date and a supplement has first to be prepared, filed with the regulatory authorities, approved and published.[16]

3.30 For an issuer, the choice whether or not to establish a debt issuance programme is not necessarily an easy one. Based on the points set out above, the choice will ultimately depend on whether that issuer is likely to be a regular issuer in the market. In times of financial instability, when the ability of issuers to access financial markets or the cost of so doing is uncertain, it may well be worth issuers who are contemplating entering the market at some point in the future, considering establishing a debt issuance programme, even when in the past the decision might have been not to do so. In such times, the ability to move quickly to access a volatile market may more than justify the slightly greater time, expense and effort of establishing a programme.

3.3.2 Listed or unlisted?

3.31 Whether a particular issuance of debt securities is to be listed on a stock exchange or not, will depend upon a number of considerations, in particular:

- *Investor preferences*: would the target investors prefer or require the instruments to be listed on a stock exchange? For example, some investment funds may have a listing requirement included in their investment rules. Other investors may simply prefer listed securities for policy reasons.
- *Withholding tax*: United Kingdom issuers may well want the debt instruments listed on a 'recognized stock exchange'[17] so as to be able to pay the coupon on

---

[16] See Section 3.7, 'Prospectus Supplements'.

[17] Within the meaning of Section 1005 of the Income Tax Act 2007. As at 31 July 2009, recognized stock exchanges include the London Main Market, London Professional Securities Market,

the instruments free of withholding tax under the so-called 'quoted Eurobond exemption'.[18] In such a case the debt instruments would ideally be listed on a recognized stock exchange at closing, or at the latest, before the time of payment of the first coupon on the instrument so that coupon payments can be made free of withholding tax.

- *Costs*: whether the listing is to be on an EEA regulated market or some other stock exchange, there will be initial fees payable as well ongoing annual listing fees through the life of the debt security. There will also need to be a prospectus or listing particulars for the purpose of obtaining the listing, which will involve preparation costs.

- *Ongoing obligations*: listing debt securities on an EEA regulated market will result in a requirement for the issuer of those securities to comply with the relevant provisions of the Market Abuse Directive[19] in relation to the disclosure of 'inside information'.[20] It may also be subject to the provisions of the Transparency Directive[21] in relation to preparation and filing of periodic information such as annual reports and accounts or half-yearly financial information, depending upon the denomination of the debt securities concerned. Even if the debt securities are not listed on an EEA regulated market, the relevant stock exchange on which they are listed will nevertheless have its own rules relating to ongoing disclosure and periodic filing obligations. If an issuer already has its equity listed on the same market as its debt, the additional compliance burden resulting from the listing of debt securities is unlikely to be significant. It will be more significant, relatively, if the issuer does not already have securities listed on that market.

3.3.3 Listing on an EEA regulated market or a non-EEA regulated market?

EMTN programme documentation will invariably provide for the possibility of **3.32** listing the debt securities issued under that programme on a stock exchange. Provided the base prospectus for the programme has been approved as a Prospectus Directive compliant prospectus, that listing could be on an EEA regulated market. Alternatively, the listing document for the programme may be approved by the stock exchange (or by the relevant regulatory authority) for the purposes of listing on a market which is not an EEA regulated market: the London Stock Exchange's Professional Securities Market (PSM), the Luxembourg Stock Exchange's Euro MTF market and the Irish Stock Exchange's Global Exchange

---

Luxembourg Main Market, Luxembourg Euro MTF Market, the Channel Islands Stock Exchange, the New York Stock Exchange and others.

[18] See Section 882 of the Income Tax Act 2007.
[19] Directive 2003/6/EC.
[20] Market Abuse Directive Article 6.
[21] Directive 2004/109/EC.

Market (GEM) being common choices. Programme documentation will also typically permit debt securities to be issued that are not listed on any stock exchange, an approach sometimes adopted for private placings of debt securities.

3.33　Many issuers of debt securities and their investors will want the securities to be listed on an EEA regulated market, possibly for the investment criteria reasons mentioned above, or possibly for no reason other than such a listing being what is expected by and of high profile issuers. Listing on a non-EEA regulated market however, brings with it the possibility of lower costs as well as avoiding the need to have to comply with the Prospectus Directive in the preparation of the prospectus or base prospectus and avoiding compliance with the Transparency Directive's periodic reporting requirements once the debt securities have been listed. As noted above, non-EEA regulated markets will nevertheless have their own disclosure requirements both in relation to the original listing document and which apply on an ongoing basis. However, the requirements of the Prospectus Directive Regulation to include in the prospectus or base prospectus accounts prepared in accordance with IFRS (or 'equivalent') and the corresponding requirements in the Transparency Directive to publish annual and half-yearly financial statements (which in each case apply unless only debt securities having a denomination of at least EUR 50,000 (or its equivalent in other currencies) are listed) do not apply and are generally replaced by a less prescriptive approach.

3.34　EMTN programmes that provide for listing on an EEA regulated market will normally envisage listing on the regulated market of a stock exchange located in the jurisdiction of the 'home' member state [22] that approved the base prospectus. Such programmes may also provide for the possibility of listing debt securities issued under that programme on stock exchanges in other 'host' member states. [23] If the market of the stock exchange in another host member state on which the debt securities are to be listed is an EEA regulated market, that listing process will involve passporting the base prospectus as approved by the home member state into the host member state of the stock exchange concerned. This can be done at the request of the issuer either at the time of original approval of the base prospectus by the home member state or subsequently.

3.35　In brief, passporting[24] involves the issue by the home member state's regulatory authority to the regulatory authority of the relevant host member state of a certificate stating that the base prospectus has been prepared in accordance with the Prospectus Directive. Passporting an English language base prospectus has recently become a relatively straightforward process. Shortly after implementation of the

---

[22]　Defined in Prospectus Directive Article 2(1)(m).
[23]　Defined in Prospectus Directive Article 2(1)(n).
[24]　See Prospectus Directive Article 18 and Chapter 1.

Prospectus Directive, a number of member states required formalities (such as newspaper advertising) as part of the passporting process, in addition to the procedures set out in the Prospectus Directive. However, following representations to and by CESR, these additional requirements have gradually (but not entirely) dropped away and, for the most part, the most demanding additional requirement of passporting in the case of base prospectus in the English language (or in another language 'customary in the sphere of international finance'[25]), as envisaged in the Prospectus Directive,[26] is the preparation of a translation of the summary[27] contained in the prospectus or base prospectus into the official language of the host member state.

Stand-alone debt issues can be listed or unlisted and the same criteria as those referred to above will apply. **3.36**

3.3.4 Which stock exchange and/or home member state?

An important point to bear in mind is that in the context of the issue of debt **3.37** securities that have a denomination of EUR 1,000 (or its equivalent in other currencies) or more, the issuer is entitled to choose which member state is to be its home member state, in principle, on an issue-by-issue basis. If the denomination of the debt securities is less than EUR 1,000 (or its equivalent in other currencies) then the home member state for an EEA issuer will be the state where that issuer has its registered office, whilst the home member state for a non-EEA issuer will be the member state where the securities are intended to be offered to the public for the first time after 31 December 2003 or where the first application for admission to trading on an EEA regulated market is made.[28] There are a number of considerations in making and consequences arising from the choice of home member state:

• The regulatory authority of the chosen home member state will be the authority that will approve the prospectus or base prospectus. Whilst the Prospectus Directive, the Prospectus Directive Regulation, CESR Recommendations[29] and CESR FAQs[30] aim to provide a level playing field so far as the content requirements of prospectuses are concerned, nevertheless there is still scope for variation in the finer points of interpretation (within the terms of those rules and guidelines) and flexibility (or inflexibility) in their application. Differences of

---

[25] Prospectus Directive Article 19(2).
[26] See Prospectus Directive Article 19.
[27] See Section 3.5.3 below.
[28] See Prospectus Directive Article 2.1(m).
[29] CESR's recommendations for the consistent implementation of the European Commission's Regulation on Prospectuses No 809/2004CESR/05-054b. See also Section 3.4.1.
[30] See Section 3.4.1.

interpretation and application of the rules and guidelines are becoming fewer as regulatory authorities become more familiar with them and also as they become more familiar with how other authorities interpret and apply them. It may even be that the regulatory authorities consult each other with a view to achieving consistency between themselves, though this is only speculation! In this sense, forum shopping among regulatory authorities is probably now of limited (if any) purpose, and in making their choice, issuers are likely to focus instead more on: (i) costs, (ii) expected timing of the prospectus submission through to approval process (and how consistent the regulatory authority is in meeting an issuer's timing expectations) and (iii) predictability in its required submission and approval formalities as well as in its interpretation and application of the rules and guidelines referred to earlier. The last thing an issuer or its advisers want to happen is that part way through a prospectus review and approval process, the regulatory authority concerned announces that it will not meet a previously indicated or expected timetable, or it surprises an applicant issuer with a regulatory or formal requirement not previously encountered. Different regulatory authorities have varying reputations for all of these points and a prospective issuer that otherwise has a free choice will doubtless wish to obtain the views of its advisers. It is probably fair to say that, for the most part, the leading regulatory authorities for the approval of prospectuses for debt securities are well aware of the needs and expectations of issuers and have recently been working hard to address these issues.

- The choice of stock exchange (or market) for listing the issuer's debt securities will generally dictate the applicable home member state and accordingly the regulatory authority which is to approve the prospectus or base prospectus. So, for example, if the issuer's choice is to list its debt securities on the London Stock Exchange's regulated market, then the natural consequence will be that the United Kingdom will be the home member state for that issue and that the FSA (through the UKLA) will be the relevant regulatory authority to review and (hopefully) approve the prospectus or base prospectus. This isn't necessarily the case and under the Prospectus Directive the issuer technically has a choice of home member state and so in theory at least could, for example, choose Luxembourg as its home member state even if its debt securities were to be admitted to trading on the London Stock Exchange's regulated market. In practice, there would be little purpose in adopting this route if the debt securities were to be listed solely on the London Stock Exchange, as the passporting and admission process would result in some additional administrative burden and uncertainty as to the approval and listing process. However, if listing is to be on two or more stock exchanges, for example, London and Luxembourg, the issuer is free to choose which of the United Kingdom or Luxembourg is to be its home member state.

If an issuer already has debt securities listed on a particular stock exchange, then   **3.38**
the starting point in making a choice for a subsequent issue, absent other considerations, may well be to continue with that exchange for listing, on grounds of
familiarity and precedent, if no other. If an issuer has its registered office in a
member state, then a natural (but not invariable) tendency will be to list all its
publicly-traded securities, including its debt securities, on the member state's
domestic stock exchange.

3.3.5 Trustee or fiscal agent?

Stand-alone issues of debt securities or debt issuance programmes written under   **3.39**
English law are constituted either through the use of a trustee or without a trustee,
in which case administrative functions are typically carried out by a fiscal agent.

Where a trustee is appointed, the obligations under the terms and conditions of   **3.40**
the debt securities are of course owed to their holders, but the issuer (and any
guarantor) will also make payment and other performance covenants in favour of
the trustee. The terms and conditions of the debt securities will therefore reserve
a number of matters to the trustee. These include:

- the right to call an event of default in respect of (or to accelerate) the debt securities, which can only be done by the trustee (unless having become bound to
  accelerate the debt securities it fails to do so);
- enforcement of the debt securities (again, unless the trustee having become
  bound to enforce fails to do so);
- agreeing to modifications to the terms and conditions to correct a manifest
  error or otherwise where there is no material prejudice to holders;
- agreeing to waive potential breaches or to a substitution of the issuer, in each
  case again where there is no material prejudice to holders.

In contrast, where there is no trustee, the obligations of the issuer are owed solely   **3.41**
to each individual holder of debt securities who must accordingly fend for itself.
So, each holder is responsible for monitoring whether an event of default has
occurred and, if so, accelerating the debt securities and enforcing its rights.
Changes to terms and conditions or waivers of defaults can only really be achieved
through the convening and holding of meetings of holders and the passing of an
appropriate resolution.

Each structure therefore has its own advantages and disadvantages, for both hold-   **3.42**
ers and the issuer.

For an issuer, the main benefit of a trustee arrangement is that when necessary, it   **3.43**
can by and large deal with the trustee rather than individual holders and there is
flexibility and discretion built into the structure. As against this, trustees charge
fees. It may also sometimes seem to an issuer that, presumably for fear of actions

by holders, trustees are reluctant to exercise any of those conferred discretions other than in the most obvious of cases.

3.44 For holders, the main benefit of a trustee arrangement is likely to be the mechanism around the trustee calling an event of default and enforcement of the debt securities. Where the securities are held on an anonymous basis through accounts within clearance systems, this is likely to be an attractive advantage. Set against this, some holders may regret their loss of independent action to the collective actions of the trustee.

3.45 There are no hard and fast rules as to when a particular issue of debt securities written under English law should be constituted by a trust deed or otherwise. The more complex the debt security or programme (for example if there are extensive covenants or if the obligations of the issuer are secured), the more useful a trust structure is likely to be. Conversely, in the case of a plain vanilla obligation for an issuer with a high credit rating, a trust structure may be viewed as unnecessary and bringing only cost and little apparent benefit.

3.4 Preparation of the Prospectus or Base Prospectus—Applicable Regulations

3.4.1 Introduction

3.46 This Section describes the regulations that prescribe the format, contents and preparation procedures of a prospectus for an issue of debt securities that are to be offered to the public in the EEA (other than pursuant to an applicable exemption)[31] or that are to be admitted to trading on an EEA regulated market.

3.47 If the denomination of the debt securities is EUR 50,000 (or its equivalent in other currencies) or more, or if the denomination of the debt securities is to be less than EUR 50,000 (or its equivalent in other currencies) but any offer to the public will be carried out in compliance with one or more of the exemptions provided in the Prospectus Directive,[32] and in each case, provided the debt securities are not to be listed on an EEA regulated market, then there is no requirement to prepare a Prospectus Directive compliant prospectus or to have a prospectus approved by a regulatory authority pursuant to the Prospectus Directive.[33] However, other regulatory requirements might apply in the member states or other jurisdictions where such debt securities are to be offered or listed.

---

[31] See Chapter 1.
[32] See Prospectus Directive Article 3(2).
[33] See Prospectus Directive Article 3(2)(d).

This Section therefore applies to the format and contents of a prospectus or **3.48** base prospectus that contemplates either or both of (i) the admission of the debt securities to trading on an EEA regulated market and/or (ii) an offer to the public of debt securities which have a denomination of less than EUR 50,000 (or its equivalent in other currencies) and which are not being offered in reliance upon any of the exemptions provided for in the Prospectus Directive. Certain items of disclosure are not required under the Prospectus Directive in a prospectus or base prospectus which only contemplates the admission to trading on an EEA regu-lated market of debt securities with a minimum denomination of at least EUR 50,000 (or its equivalent in other currencies). For the purposes of this Section, a prospectus or base prospectus prepared on this basis is described as contemplating a 'wholesale offering' whilst a prospectus or base prospectus prepared for a public offering of debt securities with a denomination of EUR 50,000 or less (or its equivalent in other currencies) is described as contemplating a 'retail offering'.

The table set out in Appendix 2 of this Chapter highlights the main differences **3.49** (on a summary basis) between the required contents of a prospectus or base pro-spectus under the Prospectus Directive and Prospectus Directive Regulation for a prospectus or base prospectus that contemplates a retail offering compared to those for a wholesale offering.

For the purposes of the Prospectus Directive and Prospectus Directive Regulation, **3.50** a prospectus can be drawn up as a single document or as a registration document (which contains information relating to the issuer), securities note (which contains information relating to the securities being issued) and (if relevant) a summary.[34] Whilst the split document format is commonly used (outside the United Kingdom at least) as a kind of shelf registration facility for shares, its use for debt securities will be very limited given the specific provision in the Prospectus Directive and Prospectus Directive Regulation allowing for base prospectuses and final terms as a more convenient way of issuing debt securities on a repeat basis under a debt issuance programme.[35] This Section therefore assumes that a prospectus for debt securities will be drawn up either as a single stand-alone document or as a base prospectus.

The basic overarching disclosure standard for any Prospectus Directive compliant **3.51** prospectus (whether debt or equity, stand-alone or a base prospectus) is set out in Article 5(1) of the Prospectus Directive:

> Without prejudice to Article 8(2), the prospectus shall contain all information which, according to the particular nature of the issuer and of the securities offered to the public or admitted to trading on a regulated market, is necessary to enable

---

[34] See Prospectus Directive Regulation Article 5(3).
[35] See Prospectus Directive Article 5(4).

investors to make an informed assessment of the assets and liabilities, financial position, profit and losses, and prospects of the issuer and of any guarantor, and of the rights attaching to such securities. This information shall be presented in an easily analysable and comprehensible form.

3.52 Consistent with the so-called Lamfalussy Process of adopting EU regulations at several levels, the general provisions of the Prospectus Directive provide for implementing measures to be made addressing the format of prospectuses[36] as well as their detailed contents.[37] These second level implementing measures are in fact found in one place, the Prospectus Directive Regulation[38] and it is in this Regulation that the detailed contents requirements for prospectuses and base prospectuses are to be found, mostly in the form of specific Annexes addressing different types or denomination of securities. For the purposes of this Section, the relevant Annexes of the Prospectus Directive Regulation are:

- *Annex IV* Minimum disclosure requirements for the debt and derivative securities registration document (debt and derivative securities with a denomination per unit of less than EUR 50,000). This Annex is combined with Annex V (as well as any other applicable Annexes) to establish the contents requirement of a single prospectus (or a base prospectus) where the denomination of the debt securities is less than EUR 50,000 (or its equivalent in other currencies).
- *Annex V* Minimum disclosure requirements for the securities note related to debt securities (debt securities with a denomination per unit of less than EUR 50,000). This Annex is combined with Annex IV as noted above.
- *Annex VI* Minimum disclosure requirements for guarantees (where there is a guarantor of the debt securities).
- *Annex IX* Minimum disclosure requirements for the debt and derivative securities registration document (debt and derivative securities with a denomination per unit of at least EUR 50,000). This Annex is combined with Annex XIII (as well as any other applicable Annexes) to establish the contents requirement of a single prospectus (or a base prospectus) where the denomination of the debt securities is at least EUR 50,000 (or its equivalent in other currencies).
- *Annex XII* Minimum disclosure requirements for the securities note for derivative securities. This Annex is combined with Annex IV or Annex IX where a structured or derivative element is included in the terms of the debt securities or is contemplated in the base prospectus.[39]
- *Annex XIII* Minimum disclosure requirements for the securities note for debt securities with a denomination of at least EUR 50,000. This Annex is combined with Annex IX as noted above.

---

[36] See Prospectus Directive Article 6(5).
[37] See Prospectus Directive Article 7(1).
[38] Commission Regulation (EC) No 809/2004.
[39] See Section 3.2.7.

There are other Annexes to the Prospectus Directive Regulation that are poten-   **3.53**
tially applicable to a prospectus or base prospectus for debt securities, however
these relate to asset-backed securities (Annexes VII and VIII) and are not considered further in this Chapter. An overview of the contents requirements of the
above Annexes is set out in Appendix 3.

As well as the Prospectus Directive and the Prospectus Directive Regulation, in   **3.54**
keeping with the Lamfalussy Process there is a third level of guidance in relation
to the Prospectus Directive. This takes the form of:

- CESR's[40] recommendations for the consistent implementation of the European
  Commission's Regulation on Prospectuses No 809/2004.[41]
- 'Frequently Asked Questions' ('FAQs') published and updated from time to
  time by CESR.

The CESR FAQs,[42] whether or not asked, and the CESR recommendations
amount to very persuasive guidance that most regulatory authorities will be reluctant to ignore and so, in effect, amount to a further layer of regulation to be
observed in the preparation of a prospectus or base prospectus.

As well as CESR's recommendations and FAQs, a number of EEA regulatory   **3.55**
authorities publish their own views on matters. For example, the UKLA publishes
List![43] and has its own set of FAQs[44] and the Luxembourg Stock Exchange also
maintains its own set of FAQs.[45] All these different sources of rules, guidance or
discussion need to be consulted and reflected in any prospectus or base prospectus
which is to be approved for the purposes of the Prospectus Directive.

3.4.2 Format of a prospectus or base prospectus

Article 25 of the Prospectus Directive Regulation specifies the basic format of a   **3.56**
prospectus (in the form of a single document) or base prospectus.[46] It states what
order the key sections should appear in as follows:

- A clear and detailed table of contents;
- A summary (if one is needed);[47]

---

[40] Committee of European Securities Regulators.
[41] CESR/05-054b.
[42] See note 30.
[43] http://www.fsa.gov.uk/Pages/Library/Communication/NewsLetters/newsletters/index.
shtml.
[44] http://www.fsa.gov.uk/Pages/Doing/UKLA/global/faq/index.shtml.
[45] http://www.cssf.lu/fileadmin/files/MAF/FAQmod_211205eng.pdf;http://www.cssf.lu/
fileadmin/files/MAF/FAQII_151205_eng.pdf; http://www.cssf.lu/fileadmin/files/MAF/FAQIII_
141107_eng.pdf.
[46] See Prospectus Directive Regulation Article 25(1).
[47] See Section 3.5.3.

- Risk factors linked to the issuer and the type of securities;
- The other information required by the Annexes.

3.57 Many regulatory authorities are very strict about applying the above requirements. Whilst it is generally acknowledged that a prospectus is entitled to have a cover page before its table of contents, some regulatory authorities insist that any 'boilerplate' (disclaimers, US legends and other general statements) must appear later in the document. Others allow a short boilerplate section, no more than a couple of pages, before the table of contents. In reality, the great majority of the prospectus or base prospectus constitutes 'other information' and so can be ordered pretty much however the issuer wishes. In some cases, issuers follow precisely the order of other information requirements as set out in the Prospectus Directive Regulation Annexes, as this avoids the need to submit checklists to the regulatory authority reviewing the prospectus or base prospectus.[48]

3.5 The Principal Components of a Prospectus or Base Prospectus

3.58 This Section describes the main components typically found in a Prospectus Directive compliant prospectus or base prospectus and provides some commentary (which is hopefully helpful) on their contents, explaining why they are included and what they address, and setting out some practical suggestions when drafting these sections.

3.59 Appendix 3 of this Chapter sets out a table which summarizes the requirements of each applicable Annex[49] of the Prospectus Directive Regulation.

3.5.1 Front cover

3.60 The front cover of a prospectus or (in the case of a programme) the base prospectus packs in a surprising amount of information. It:

- in the case of a stand-alone prospectus, names the issuer and any guarantor(s);
- in the case of a base prospectus, names all of the possible issuers[50] under the programme and any guarantor(s);
- identifies itself as a 'base prospectus' or as a prospectus for the purposes of the Prospectus Directive;

---

[48] See Prospectus Directive Regulation Article 25(3) and (4).

[49] See Section 3.4.1.

[50] A programme can allow for more than one issuer, for example if issues are to be made by group SPVs or by subsidiaries located in various jurisdictions, as well as for more than one guarantor.

- specifies the amount of notes that are the subject of the offering or (in the case of a base prospectus) the maximum amount of notes that can be issued and be outstanding under the programme;
- in the case of a stand-alone prospectus, provides a summary description of the debt securities being offered including their general characteristics, coupon rate, redemption date and interest payment dates;
- in the case of a base prospectus, sets out the names of the arranger(s) of the programme (which will be one of the dealers) as well as of the dealers (in alphabetical order) under the programme or, in the case of a stand-alone prospectus, sets out the name of the bookrunner(s), the lead manager(s), any co-lead managers and any other managers (in each category, in alphabetical order);
- includes the date of the prospectus or base prospectus (which in the case of a base prospectus will, provided it has been kept up to date,[51] be valid for issues for up to 12 months from the stated date);
- contains a block of text that states the name of the regulatory authority that has approved the prospectus or base prospectus and the name of the regulated market to which the debt securities are being admitted to trading and, if relevant, the official list of the home member state regulatory authority to which they are being admitted. So, for example, the base prospectus for a Luxembourg-listed programme will state that the base prospectus has been approved by the Luxembourg Commission de Surveillance du Secteur Financier (CSSF) and that application has been made to admit debt securities issued under the programme to the official list and to trading on the regulated market of the Luxembourg Stock Exchange. Similarly, a London-listed programme will state that the base prospectus has been approved by the Financial Services Authority (FSA) and that application has been made for the debt securities to be admitted to the Official List of the UK Listing Authority (UKLA) and to the London Stock Exchange for them to be admitted to trading on its (main) regulated market. This section of text will also indicate to which other EEA member states, if any, the base prospectus has been passported.

3.5.2 Inside cover

The one or two permitted[52] pages between the front cover and the table of contents set out an issuer responsibility statement as well as other legends and disclaimers as follows:

3.61

- The Prospectus Directive Regulation requires, in Paragraph 1 of Annex IV (in relation to a retail offering) and Paragraph 1 of Annex IX (in relation to a wholesale offering), that a declaration be included by those responsible for the

---

[51] See Section 3.7, 'Prospectus Supplements'.
[52] See Section 3.4.2.

prospectus or base prospectus that 'having taken all reasonable care to ensure that such is the case, the information contained in the ... [prospectus] ... is, to the best of their knowledge, in accordance with the facts and contains no omission likely to affect its import'. The persons stated to be responsible for the prospectus or base prospectus are usually the issuer (or each issuer, assuming there is more than one) and any guarantor. The responsibility statement can be included on a 'split responsibility' basis, with named persons taking responsibility for only specified parts of the prospectus or base prospectus, provided at least one person (typically the issuer) takes responsibility for the entire prospectus.[53] Split responsibility statements in the context of a prospectus or base prospectus for debt securities are relatively uncommon, though in a group context it is possible that an issuer may, for example, wish only to accept responsibility for information about itself. Split responsibility statements are probably more common in prospectuses that contain a third party expert's report, where the expert concerned will only wish to take responsibility for its report and not for other parts of the prospectus. The responsibility statement may also sometimes be qualified, for example, in relation to the inclusion of third party information that has been obtained from public sources, where the statement may be confined to accepting responsibility for accurate reproduction of that public information, rather than for the accuracy and completeness of the information itself. Split responsibility statements or qualified responsibility statements are likely to be the subject of discussion with the relevant regulatory authority that is reviewing and approving the prospectus or base prospectus.

- Other notices and disclaimers are limited only by the motivation and energy of the draftsperson. Practice varies and there are no specific 'requirements', but the boilerplate might include some or all of the following:
  - a denial of the authority of any person to give information over and above that contained in the prospectus or base prospectus;
  - a disclaimer of responsibility for the contents of the prospectus or base prospectus by the lead manager, other managers, arranger(s) and dealers;
  - a statement to the effect that information in the prospectus or base prospectus may go stale after the date of its publication or after the date of publication of any supplement.[54] Whilst a prospectus or base prospectus should be updated in accordance with Article 16 of the Prospectus Directive to reflect any 'significant new factor, material mistake or inaccuracy relating to the information included in the [base] prospectus', this obligation only strictly applies between the date of approval of the prospectus and the date of the final closing of any offer to the publication or admission to trading of

---

[53] See CESR FAQ 48.
[54] See Section 3.7, 'Prospectus Supplements'.

relevant debt securities on an EEA regulated market. This means that base prospectuses are not required to be kept continually up to date, though they will need to be up to date before any further offering can be made under the programme.

• Language that specifies the regulatory regime applicable to the preparation of the prospectus or base prospectus in the context of the manner in which debt securities will be offered, in other words, whether the offering is wholesale or retail and, if retail, the manner in which any offering of debt securities with a denomination of less than EUR 50,000 (or its equivalent in other currencies) may actually be offered. This wording may include so-called 'retail cascades' language.[55]

3.5.3 Summary

A summary of the prospectus or base prospectus is only required where the issuance of debt securities with a denomination of less than EUR 50,000 (or its equivalent in other currencies) is contemplated. There is nothing to stop a summary being included in the case of a wholesale programme or offering. However, if one is included, it must comply with the requirements of Article 5(2) of the Prospectus Directive. Article 5(2) describes in broad terms the required content of the summary but also prescribes in rather more detail the warnings that need to be included in the summary.

3.62

This warning language is typically set out at the start of the summary and warns readers (fairly obviously) that it is only a summary and should be read in conjunction with the rest of the prospectus or base prospectus and (more importantly) also warns the reader that no civil liability attaches to making an investment decision based on the contents of the summary alone, unless the summary is misleading (whether in its original language or in any translation) when read together with any other part of the prospectus or base prospectus. This is an important principle since the summary is generally confined by regulatory authorities to a maximum of 2,500 words,[56] presenting a significant challenge to even the most concise draftsperson given the potentially wide scope that the summary is supposed to cover. This is particularly the case for a base prospectus for a debt issuance programme, since a programme will have its own complex mechanics to describe quite apart from the normal disclosure relating to the issuer(s), any guarantor(s), their respective businesses, risk factors, financial information, prospects and so on.[57]

---

[55] See Section 3.9.6.
[56] See Prospectus Directive Recital 21.
[57] The European Commission is consulting (2009/0132) on various changes to the Prospectus Directive including one proposal which would result in a longer summary section to which liability would attach other than on the limited basis stated above.

As a result of the 2,500 word limit, a practice has arisen in some cases of including a further 'Overview' (or similarly described) section addressing the detailed mechanics of the programme itself. The approach taken by the regulatory authorities in approving a base prospectus is not to object to a further 'Overview' section of this kind, provided it is not described as a summary of the base prospectus. One consequence of this approach is that the liability limitation wording described above will not apply to any 'Overview'. Nor can the language envisaged by the Prospectus Directive be included within any 'Overview' section resulting, at least in theory, in potentially greater scope for liability. Set against this, the 'Overview' section will normally be confined to the fairly technical mechanical contents of the prospectus or base prospectus, rather than any qualitative disclosure in relation to the issuer, guarantor(s) or their business or financial position.

3.63 So what is to be included in the summary section within the confines of the permitted 2,500 words?

- The Prospectus Directive Regulation[58] states that 'the issuer, the offeror or the person asking for admission to trading on a regulated market shall determine on its own the detailed content of the summary to the prospectus or base prospectus'.
- Paragraph I of Annex I to the Prospectus Directive appears to set out a list of the contents requirements of the summary which are to be covered. It is a rather confused list and in practice it is probably better to follow common sense and Article 24 of the Prospectus Directive Regulation. The key items of the summary contained in a prospectus or base prospectus for debt securities may therefore include:
  - a brief description of the issuer(s) and any guarantor(s). The language in any such description should be consistent for any given subject matter with that elsewhere in the prospectus, albeit, of course, briefer;
  - the names of other parties to the offering or programme (arranger(s), dealers, underwriters, agents and auditors);
  - risk factors—it can be quite challenging to reduce a complex risk factor to a line or two. It is quite a helpful discipline when drafting the risk factors themselves to include a line or so either as the title of the risk factor, or at the beginning of the text of each risk factor, which describes succinctly the particular risk being addressed. This short summary can then be readily lifted into the summary section;
  - listing and trading arrangements;
  - key selected financial information;

---

[58] See Prospectus Directive Regulation Article 24.

- key structural provisions of the debt securities or programme (including the type of debt securities, the form of their issuance, currencies, arrangements for guarantees, interest, maturity, denominations, whether there is a negative pledge or cross-default provision and governing law);
- particulars of any ratings of debt securities;
- selling restrictions.
- The final sentence of Article 11(1) of the Prospectus Directive makes it clear that the summary section cannot incorporate information by reference. This, together with the general preference of regulators that the summary doesn't simply cross-refer to other sections in the prospectus or base prospectus, means that in practice the summary should be drafted so that it can be read and the key points understood without the reader having to thumb through other parts of the prospectus or base prospectus. In other words, it needs to stand alone in its own right. This makes sense, even though it is a drafting challenge within the prescribed word limit, since the suspicion has to be that many investors will, despite the warnings, base their investment decisions solely or principally on the basis of reading the summary alone. Added to this, where the prospectus or base prospectus has been passported from one jurisdiction to another, it is only the summary that has to be translated into the host member state's official language, assuming that the prospectus or base prospectus is otherwise written in a language which is 'customary in the sphere of international finance'.[59]

3.5.4 Risk factors

Before implementation of the Prospectus Directive in 2005, the inclusion of a 'risk factors' section in prospectuses and similar documents was not formally required, but was becoming standard market practice, particularly where any kind of US offering of the underlying securities was contemplated. In this sense, by requiring the inclusion of risk factors relating to the issuer and the securities being offered, the Prospectus Directive formalized what was already, for the most part, market practice. The requirement of the Prospectus Directive Regulation is to include 'prominent disclosure of risk factors that may affect the issuer's ability to fulfil its obligations under the securities to investors'[60] and *'prominent disclosure of risk factors that are material to the securities being offered … in order to assess the market risk associated with these securities'.*[61] **3.64**

It is therefore fairly normal to split the risk factor section into two main headings, namely (i) those risk factors relating to the issuer and its business generally and, separately, (ii) those risk factors relating to the particular types of securities. So far **3.65**

---

[59] See Prospectus Directive Article 19(2).
[60] See Prospectus Directive Regulation Annex IV(4) and Annex IX(3).
[61] See Prospectus Directive Regulation Annex V(2) and Annex XIII(2).

as risk factors relating to the issuer(s) and any guarantor(s) are concerned, it is difficult to be prescriptive as to content since, as noted above, a properly prepared risk factor section should be specific to the particular issuer(s) or guarantor(s) concerned. However, the following guiding principles are suggested:

- Drafting risk factors for a particular issuer or group's prospectus or base prospectus ought to be (and usually is) a challenging exercise. The temptation, of course, is to gather a large pile of recent precedent prospectuses (whether or not the issuers operate in the same market sector or industry as the prospective issuer), and to set to work with scissors and glue. This may result in a risk factors section having the required apparent length and sheer number of risk factors, but the result of such an exercise may well be to include risks that aren't real or important for that particular issuer or guarantor and quite possibly to omit the ones that are.
- Regulators are increasingly aware of and are discouraging the inclusion of 'standard form' risk factors. The UKLA has published a warning to this effect.[62] It has reminded issuers that 'the risk factors should be specific to the company, its industry and should be relevant to the type of securities being offered'. It has stated that 'these disclosure requirements are important to emphasise, as we are of the view that there has been an increasing tendency for risk factors' sections to include more generic, standardised risk factors, which do not appear to be directly relevant for the company or the issue that is the subject of the document'. The UKLA has also stated that whilst it won't normally question an issuer's judgment as to what risks are or are not relevant to disclose, it 'will challenge risk factors in certain situations as part of its *day-to-day* vetting [of the prospectus]'. The UKLA has given examples of circumstances where it might challenge risk factors and, whilst a number of these circumstances are more relevant to equity issuance than debt securities (for example, the inclusion of risk factors that appear to qualify working capital statements), some are nevertheless equally relevant to debt securities. They include:
  - where the UKLA believes that sufficient prominence is not given to material risks;
  - where there is disclosure elsewhere in the document that seems to clearly present a risk to the issuer, which has not already been addressed in the risk factor section; and
  - where the risk factors are simply statements of fact that contain no explanation of the risk in the context of the issuer's business or the issue of the securities in question.
- Based on the above two points:
  - Avoid generic 'standard form' statements and stating the obvious. For example, all businesses face the risk of employees resigning and having

---

[62] See List! Issue No. 21 (May 2009).

difficulty replacing them or obtaining suitably qualified employees. Does it really need to be stated? In some very particular cases the answer may well be 'yes', but the point (and other similarly generic points) should be questioned and tested, rather than mindlessly included because it is contained in other prospectuses.

- Identify and focus on the risks facing that particular company and business, for example, the market in which it operates, intellectual property considerations, competition, financing and more recently counterparty risk, the ability to raise borrowings for working capital or to refinance maturing debt and its liquidity position generally. Discuss specific risks facing the business with appropriate senior management. Ask them what keeps them awake at night!

- Don't use the risk factor section as a substitute for specific disclosure elsewhere in the prospectus or base prospectus. The risk factor section is intended to identify factors that might affect the business in the future, but which are not currently doing so. If any of the risks are currently affecting the business (or it is likely that they will soon do so) then this should be disclosed specifically as part of the business description.

3.5.5 Information incorporated by reference

Before implementation of the Prospectus Directive in 2005, some regulatory authorities (for example, Luxembourg's CSSF) allowed incorporation by reference into prospectuses not just of historic information, but also of prospective information. So for example, the then equivalent of a programme base prospectus could state that it incorporated by reference not just existing historical financial information but also future financial information as and when it was published by the issuer, a useful facility which avoided formal updating whenever new financial information was published during the life of a programme and which is an approach that continues in the case of programmes listed on the Luxembourg Stock Exchange's Euro MTF market. **3.66**

In contrast, some jurisdictions, such as the United Kingdom, did not permit incorporation of information by reference at all. The approach of the Prospectus Directive is somewhere between these two positions. Under the Prospectus Directive, a prospectus or base prospectus can incorporate by reference[63] information contained in another document (provided that the conditions referred to below are met in relation to those documents), but may not incorporate information by reference prospectively. So future financial information in relation to an issuer (and indeed any other relevant information) arising in the future, must, if necessary, be incorporated into the prospectus or base prospectus by means **3.67**

---

[63] See Prospectus Directive Article 11 and Prospectus Directive Regulation Article 28.

of a supplement in accordance with the provisions set out in Article 16 of the Prospectus Directive.[64]

3.68 As might be expected, incorporation by reference is most normally used as the method of complying with the requirement to include two years of audited historical financial information in relation to the issuer(s) and any guarantor(s).[65]

3.69 General practice is that the information incorporated by reference is set out in the prospectus or base prospectus in tabulated form,[66] making it clear exactly what is incorporated from the specified documents and where in those documents the information is to be found. It is also normal to state that any information included in documents incorporated by reference but not specifically set out in the cross-reference list included in the prospectus or base prospectus, is included for information purposes only.[67] To be able to incorporate information from other documents by reference into the prospectus or base prospectus, those documents must either:

- have been approved by the competent authority of the home member state (or by the competent authority of another home member state in relation to that issuer[68]); or
- have been filed with that authority.[69]

3.70 These requirements mean that various types of document (or information contained within them) can be incorporated by reference, the most relevant of these being:[70]

- annual and interim financial information together with audit reports and financial statements;
- merger or de-merger documentation;
- previously approved and published prospectuses or base prospectuses;
- regulated information;[71]
- circulars to security holders.

3.71 It should be noted that the information to be incorporated by reference must be up to date or if it isn't, the prospectus or base prospectus must identify out-of-date information and update it.[72] Where an issuer wishes to carry out a further (or 'tap')

---

[64] See Section 3.7, 'Prospectus Supplements'.
[65] See Prospectus Directive Regulation Annex IV(13) and Annex IX(11).
[66] Note the requirement for a cross-reference list in Prospectus Directive Article 11(2).
[67] Note the requirement to do this is set out in Prospectus Directive Regulation Article 28(4).
[68] See paragraph 2.2 of List! Issue No. 12 (February 2006).
[69] See Prospectus Directive Article 11(1).
[70] See Prospectus Directive Article 28.
[71] 'Regulated information' is defined in Prospectus Directive Regulation Article 2(12) and includes information which is required to be disclosed by issuers under the Directive 2001/34/EC or the Market Abuse Directive (2003/6/EC).
[72] See Prospectus Directive Regulation Article 28(3).

issue of debt securities under a programme which is to be fungible with an earlier issue, the terms and conditions of the original securities may be set out in an earlier base prospectus that has expired. If the terms and conditions in the new base prospectus are not the same as those in the earlier base prospectus, a fungible issue is not possible by reference to the current terms and conditions. In these circumstances the old terms and conditions can and should be incorporated into the current base prospectus by means of a supplement to the current base prospectus.[73] It would appear to be insufficient, for example, to simply refer to the old terms and conditions in the final terms issued under the current base prospectus.

3.5.6 Financial information

The nature of the financial information to be included in a prospectus or base prospectus differs depending upon whether (i) the issuer is incorporated in a member state or in a 'third country' or (ii) whether the debt securities (in the case of a stand-alone issue) have a denomination of less than EUR 50,000 (or its equivalent in other currencies) or (in the case of a programme) whether the base prospectus contemplates that the debt securities to be issued under the programme will (a) have such denomination and either (b) be offered to the public (other than pursuant to an exemption from the need for a Prospectus Directive compliant prospectus) or admitted to trading on an EEA regulated market. Whichever of these circumstances apply, audited historical financial information covering the latest two financial years (or such shorter period that the issuer has been in operation) together with the audit report for each year is required.[74] The differences that arise as a result of the denominations of the debt securities are primarily around whether or not the financial statements that are included must be prepared and audited in accordance with IAS/IFRS or whether they can be prepared and audited according to some other accounting standards.[75]

3.72

A question that sometimes arises, particularly for special purpose issuers or new finance subsidiaries acting as an issuer, is what accounts should be provided where the issuer concerned has not actually been in existence for two full financial years. Taking into account the applicable rules in relation to audited historical financial information and interim unaudited financial information referred to above, the position would seem to be that:

3.73

• If the issuer is newly incorporated or has been recently incorporated but has not 'been in operation'[76] since incorporation, then all that is required is a statement to that effect. No audited or unaudited financial information is required.

---

[73] See CESR FAQ No. 8 and UKLA's List! (October 2008).
[74] See Prospectus Directive Regulation Annex IV(13) and Annex IX(11).
[75] For a discussion of this point, see later in this Section generally.
[76] See, for example, the introductory wording to Annex IV(11.1).

There is a question as to what 'been in operation' means. No doubt the point could be debated at length, but if the issuer has done nothing other than coming to existence (including issuing shares and appointing directors) then it should be possible to conclude that it has not been 'in operation'. However, if it has incurred liabilities or obligations or otherwise conducted business, then it may well be more difficult to say that it has not been 'in operation' and accounts will be required.

- If the issuer has not been in existence for a full financial year but has been 'in operation' (as discussed above) for at least a part of that time, then audited financial information relating to the period from commencement of those operations until the latest practicable date before publication of the prospectus or base prospectus should be included. This is clearly something of an inconvenient outcome and so in such a situation the practical advice may be (if at all possible) to use a different SPV or issuer that has not been 'in operation'!

- If the issuer has been in operation for a full financial year, then audited financial information will be required for that period.

- If the issuer has been in operation for more than one financial year but less than two financial years, then audited financial information will be required for the complete financial year. In addition, in the case of debt securities having a denomination of less than EUR 50,000 (or its equivalent in other currencies), that is, in circumstances where the prospectus or base prospectus is being prepared in accordance with Annex IV of the Prospectus Directive Regulation:

  - If the date of the prospectus or base prospectus is later than nine months after the end of the most recent financial year then interim financial information covering at least the first six months of the second financial year must be included in the prospectus or base prospectus.[77] The interim financial information may be audited or unaudited.

  - If the date of the prospectus or base prospectus is earlier than nine months after the end of the last financial year and in the meantime the issuer has actually published quarterly or half-yearly financial information, then that financial information must in any event be included.[78] Note that there is no requirement to include such information; it only needs to be included if it actually has been published during that period. It should also be noted that an issuer of retail debt securities may well be under an obligation to publish half-yearly financial information under Article 5(1) of the 'Transparency Directive'.[79] This obligation will arise if the issuer already has outstanding debt securities with a denomination of less than EUR 50,000 (or its equivalent

---

[77] See Prospectus Directive Regulation Annex IV (13.5.2).
[78] See Prospectus Directive Regulation Annex IV (13.5.1).
[79] Directive 2004/109/EC.

in other currencies) and which are admitted to trading on an EEA regulated market (subject to limited exceptions for issuers of debt securities that are guaranteed by the issuer's home member state or by a regional or local authority). The issuer may, of course, in any event be obliged to publish half-yearly financial information if its share capital is admitted to trading on an EEA regulated market.

In the case of debt securities having a denomination of EUR 50,000 (or its **3.74** equivalent in other currencies) or greater or, in the case of a base prospectus, where the debt issuance programme only allows for debt securities with a denomination of EUR 50,000 (or its equivalent in other currencies) or more to be offered to the public (other than on an exempt basis) or admitted to trading on an EEA regulated market, then the prospectus or base prospectus must contain audited historical annual financial information on the basis set out above. However, in these circumstances, there is no requirement in Annex IX to the Prospectus Directive Regulation equivalent to that in Annex IV[80] for the inclusion of interim (i.e. half-year or quarterly) financial information, whether audited or unaudited and whether or not it has been published.

In the case of both wholesale and retail debt securities or debt issuance pro- **3.75** grammes, the last year of audited historical financial information included in the prospectus or base prospectus must not be older than 18 months from the date of the prospectus or base prospectus.[81]

For an issuer incorporated in a member state, the financial information must be **3.76** prepared and audited in accordance with international accounting standards (IAS or IFRS), to the extent that the issuer is required to do so in accordance with the IAS Regulation.[82] Article 4 of the IAS Regulation requires a company incorporated in a member state to prepare its consolidated accounts in accordance with IAS if it has any securities admitted to trading on a member state regulated market. If the issuer concerned has no subsidiaries, then it will not be required to prepare its accounts in accordance with IAS under the IAS Regulation unless the laws of its member state separately require it to do so. Otherwise, the audited historical financial information of the issuer must be prepared and audited in accordance with its own national accounting standards (for example, in the case of the UK issuer, in accordance with UK GAAP).

The position of so-called 'third country issuers' (i.e. those not incorporated or **3.77** established in an EU member state) is rather more complex and has been the subject of some political debate over the last few years and differs depending upon

---

[80] See Prospectus Directive Regulation Annex IV(13.5.2).
[81] See Prospectus Directive Regulation Annex IX (11.4) and Annex IV (13.4).
[82] EC No 1606/2002.

whether the debt securities concerned have a denomination of EUR 50,000 (or its equivalent in other currencies) or more, in which case the position is rather more flexible. The practical point is that issuers from countries outside the EC (for example, from the United States, Canada, Japan, Australia, Korea and others) do not necessarily (though some may) prepare their consolidated accounts in accordance with IAS. Since London and Luxembourg have been popular destinations for the listing of debt securities issued by companies incorporated in jurisdictions outside of the EU (including those previously mentioned), it might be argued that the position of such companies was not sufficiently addressed when the Prospectus Directive was implemented.

3.78 In the case of securities having a denomination of less than EUR 50,000 (or its equivalent in other currencies), there is some flexibility built into the wording of Article 13.1 of Annex IV of the Prospectus Directive Regulation, since it allows for the relevant financial information of 'third country issuers' to be prepared in accordance with IAS '*or to a third country's national accounting standards equivalent to these standards*'. The key word in this provision is 'equivalent' and it is that word which has given rise to discussion (and some political debate) over recent years.

3.79 Following implementation of the Prospectus Directive, transitional provisions were included in Article 35 of the Prospectus Directive Regulation. In December 2007, an EC regulation was adopted[83] which provided a mechanism for the determination of 'equivalence'. Recital 3 of that regulation made it clear that equivalence was to be determined not just on the basis of the adequacy of the third country accounting standards concerned, but also by reference to whether IAS was an accepted accounting standard for the purpose of accessing the financial markets of those third countries. The full history of IAS equivalence, whilst interesting, is not directly relevant to this Chapter. What is more relevant is the outcome. As at October 2009 the accounting standards of the United States and of Japan are treated as 'equivalent' to IAS for the purposes of the Prospectus Directive Regulation.[84] In addition, the accounting standards of China, Canada, South Korea and India are treated as 'equivalent' for the purposes of the Prospectus Directive Regulation for a transition period until the end of 2011.

3.80 If the issuer does not prepare its accounts in accordance with IAS or equivalent (or if the issuer is incorporated in a member state and the IAS regulation is not applicable to that member state's national accounting standards), then the issuer must include two years of audited historical financial information which has been restated to IAS.

---

[83] EC No 1569/2007.
[84] Commission Decision 2008/961/EC.

In the case of debt securities having a denomination of EUR 50,000 (or its equivalent in other currencies) or more, Annex IX(11) provides much greater flexibility for 'third country' issuers and states that such issuers can include audited financial statements which have been prepared to (a) IAS/IFRS or (b) the third country's 'equivalent' national accounting standards[85] or (c) a third country's accounting standards provided that (i) a prominent statement is included in the prospectus or base prospectus warning that the financial statements have not been prepared according to IAS/IFRS and that there may be differences had the financial information been so prepared (ii) immediately following such financial statements there is a section that sets out on a narrative description basis the differences between IAS/IFRS and the accounting principles actually adopted by the issuer in preparation of the relevant financial statements and (iii) a similar warning statement and narrative of 'significant departures' is included in relation to applicable auditing standards.[86]

3.81

The downside of not including financial statements in the prospectus or base prospectus that have been prepared and audited in accordance with IAS/IFRS (or 'equivalent') is that a warning and a narrative of differences between IAS/IFRS and actual accounting and auditing standards has to be included. This formulation at least allows for the possibility of issuance of wholesale debt securities under the Prospectus Directive by third country issuers that have not adopted IAS/IFRS (or 'equivalent' accounting and audit standards). This is a better outcome than in the case of a third country issuer wishing to issue debt securities with a denomination of less than EUR 50,000 (or its equivalent in other currencies) whose choices are to adopt IAS/IFRS (or 'equivalent'), restate its accounts to IAS/IFRS (or 'equivalent') or not issue on this basis at all.

3.82

3.5.7 Use of proceeds

Where debt securities are issued on a stand-alone basis, there will often be little to say other than that funds are being raised for *'general corporate purposes'* or similar wording. On occasion, an issuance of debt securities may be for a particular purpose, for example in connection with funding an acquisition or for repaying existing debt and if this is the case then the purpose of the issue should be described. A description other than the *'general corporate purposes'* formulation is even less likely for a base prospectus, since for the most part it is unlikely that at the time of establishing or updating a programme the issuer will know the purpose of future drawdowns. The intended use of proceeds of any particular issuance of

3.83

---

[85] See above as to the meaning of 'equivalent'.
[86] See Prospectus Directive Regulation Annex IX (11.1).

debt securities under a programme will be of more relevance for disclosure in the final terms relating to that issue.[87]

3.5.8 Form of the notes

3.84 In the early days of issuances in the Euromarkets, bonds were initially represented at closing by a temporary global note that was exchanged for definitive notes in the form of individually security-printed certificates in the denomination of the notes. This was the case even though the definitive notes would then be held in the vaults of the common depositary for Euroclear and Clearstream, Luxembourg. Security printing of bond certificates was good business in those days!

3.85 In more recent years, market practice has changed and whilst most programmes still provide for the issue at closing of a temporary global note, instead of exchanging the temporary global note into definitive notes (as in the old days), they now provide for a exchange into definitive notes or for exchange into a permanent global note. In turn, the choice whether to exchange from a temporary global note into a permanent global note is subject to a further choice in relation to the permanent global note. That choice is either that (i) the permanent global note can be exchanged at the option of the issuer or the holder of the notes into definitive notes at any time or, more normally, (ii) the permanent global note can only be exchanged into definitive notes in certain specified limited circumstances. These limited circumstances are typically if (i) Euroclear or Clearstream, Luxembourg closes or (ii) if an event of default occurs under the terms and conditions of the debt securities. Programmes will typically provide for notes to be in either bearer or registered form. Since notes are invariably held through clearance systems, there is in practice little distinction between the two forms, though practice in the Euromarkets has been generally to issue bearer notes.

3.86 In the case of a stand-alone issue of debt securities, the prospectus will specify in this section which route for global notes and definitive certificates has been adopted. The normal approach is that a temporary global note is issued at closing of the issue which is to be exchanged after 40 days (subject to certification of non-US beneficial ownership) for a permanent global note. The permanent global note will typically be exchangeable into definitive notes only in the limited circumstances described above. In the case of a base prospectus, this section will set out the available options and the actual option selected will be specified when completing the final terms for a particular debt issuance under the programme.[88] Most issuances under programmes will also typically select the temporary global note to permanent global note which is only exchangeable into definitive notes in the specified limited circumstances option. No doubt this is all to the considerable chagrin of security printers.

---

[87] See Section 3.5.11.
[88] See Section 3.5.11.

The circumstances in which a temporary or permanent global note may provide for exchange at the option of noteholders into definitive notes is likely to be dictated by tax considerations of the issuer and/or holders of the debt securities and is outside the scope of this Chapter.

3.87

Regulation S which was promulgated in April 1990 by the US Securities and Exchange Commission provides a 'safe harbour' under which offerings of securities can be made outside the United States without triggering a registration requirement under the United States Securities Act of 1933, as amended. The two main requirements which need to be observed so as to be able to take advantage of the safe harbour are that (i) the offering of the debt securities is an 'offshore transaction'[89] and (ii) that there are no 'directed selling efforts'[90] in connection with the offering of those debt securities into the United States.

3.88

There are further requirements depending upon whether under Regulation S the issuer is a Category 1, Category 2 or Category 3 issuer. For all practical purposes, only Category 1 and Category 2 may be applicable to non-US (or non-US owned) issuers of debt into the Euromarkets. A non-US, non-governmental issuer is a Category 1 issuer under Regulation S if the issuer concerned reasonably believes that there is *'no substantial US market interest'*[91] in respect of its debt securities. If the issuer is not confident that it is Category 1, then it will normally treat itself as Category 2 and in fact this is the normal default position for non-US issuers to adopt in their programmes. The consequence of being a Regulation S, Category 2 issuer, is that further offering restrictions and procedures need to be adopted over and above those referred to earlier. These are (in summary):

3.89

- adoption of procedures to prevent the debt securities being sold to US persons during the period of 40 days from the later of the closing date of the offering and its commencement;
- the inclusion of prescribed selling restrictions and warnings in the prospectus or base prospectus.

---

[89] Generally, an offer or sale of securities is made in an 'offshore transaction' if made outside the United States and either (a) the buyer (who may be a US person) is (or is reasonably believed by the seller to be) outside the US when the buy order is originated or (b) the transaction is executed on the physical trading floor of a foreign securities exchange outside the US.

[90] 'Directed selling efforts' are generally activities undertaken for the purpose of, or that could reasonably be expected to have the effect of, conditioning the US market for the securities being offered in reliance on Reg S (for example, mailing printed material to US investors and advertising the offering in the US).

[91] Generally, there is no 'substantial US market interest' in a non-US issuer's debt securities if the issuer reasonably believes that when the offering began (a) its debt securities were held by fewer than 300 US persons, or (b) less than $1 billion in aggregate principal amount of its debt securities were held of record by US persons or (c) less than 20% of the aggregate principal amount of its debt securities were held of record by US persons.

3.90   The Tax Equity and Fiscal Responsibility Act of 1992 ('TEFRA') is aimed at limiting tax evasion by encouraging US investors to hold debt securities in registered rather than in bearer form. No TEFRA restrictions are necessary if the debt securities are issued in registered form. For non-US issuer debt issuance programmes, the main choice for TEFRA purposes is between 'TEFRA C' and 'TEFRA D' respectively the so-called 'C rules' and 'D rules'. Briefly, the C rules should only be used if all parties are satisfied that there is no intention to place any of the debt securities into the United States and it is unlikely that there will be any interest in the debt securities in the United States. Generally, the D rules require that an issuer of bearer debt securities ensures that 'reasonable arrangements' are in place to prevent bearer debt securities being sold to US persons in connection with the primary offering of those debt securities, that specific legends be endorsed on the debt securities themselves and that there should be no payment of interest in the United States. Compliance with the 'reasonable arrangements' requirement involves:

- no offer of the debt securities during the 'restricted period' (generally, the period commencing on the earlier of the closing date of the offering and its commencement and ending 40 days following the closing date) in the US or to a US person;
- the debt securities must not be sold in definitive form within the US during the restricted period; and
- certification must be provided before the first actual payment of interest on the debt securities that the security is owned by a non-US person.

3.91   The default position, therefore, is that most Regulation S offerings of bearer debt securities by non-US issuers are carried out as a Regulation S Category 2 issuer under TEFRA D. This results in the normal approach of having a temporary global note which is exchangeable into the permanent global note after a restricted period of 40 days from closing of the issuance against certification of non-US ownership and during which time no interest can be paid to investors.

3.92   It is the consequences of the Regulation S and TEFRA D rules set out above that account for the need for temporary global notes, lock-up periods and certification of non-US ownership which are described in the section of the prospectus headed 'Form of the Notes'.

3.93   There is a further choice in relation to temporary and permanent global notes that will be described in this section of the prospectus or base prospectus. A debt issuance programme may well provide for a choice of form of global notes and this choice will be to issue debt securities under the programme in the form of either *'new global notes'* (or 'NGNs') or *'classic global notes'* (or 'CGNs').

3.94   The reason for the distinction is that if it is intended that the debt securities should be capable of being recognized as 'eligible collateral' for Eurosystem monetary policy operations (which an issuer may wish to be the case as eligibility may increase the attractiveness of the debt securities to certain investors), then, among other requirements, bearer debt securities must be issued in the form of NGNs.

The criteria as to whether a particular debt security is eligible collateral for Eurosystem purposes are (broadly) that the debt security must be Euro denominated (though the rules have been relaxed at least until 31 December 2009 to include debt securities denominated in US dollars, Japanese yen and pounds sterling[92]), meet 'high credit standards' and be issued by an issuer established within the EEA or a non-EEA G10 country. The debt securities must also be deposited with a central securities depository (CSD) which fulfils the minimum standards established by the European Central Bank.[93] When the NGN structure was introduced in July 2006, it was thought that NGNs would fairly quickly replace CGNs for most bearer debt instruments and become the default structure for issuance, whether or not the debt securities themselves were capable of constituting eligible collateral. Whilst there appears to have been a continued trend towards use of NGNs, their use has not become invariable, particularly where the debt securities concerned do not otherwise constitute eligible collateral.

3.95

Classic global notes: A classic global note is executed by the issuer of the debt securities and 'authenticated' by the fiscal agent (or the trustee if there is one). The temporary global note becomes 'live' only once it has been both executed by the issuer and authenticated by the fiscal agent (or trustee). Once it has been issued and authenticated, the temporary global note is physically held by a financial institution that is a 'common depositary' for the relevant clearing system or systems where the debt securities are to be traded, typically Euroclear and Clearstream, Luxembourg. The common depositary holds the temporary global note on behalf of the relevant clearing systems and so, through the clearing systems, for the accounts of participants in the clearing systems. These accounts may in turn be held for the account of the underlying investors in (or beneficial owners of) those debt securities.

3.96

The temporary global note is exchanged after 40 days into a permanent global note which is held by a common depositary in the same way on behalf of the relevant clearing systems[94] in place of the temporary global note.

3.97

New Global Notes: Like CGNs, NGNs are issued initially in temporary global form and are exchanged in the same way for a permanent global note, also in NGN form. An NGN physically looks very similar to a CGN, save that instead of

3.98

---

[92] See ECB/2009/16.

[93] As to eligibility generally, see 'The Implementation of Monetary General Policy in the Euro Area—Documentation on Eurosystem Monetary Policy Instruments and Procedures' as published by The European Central Bank. The ECB's website also contains a list of eligible securities.

[94] See also Section 3.5.9.

being authenticated by the fiscal agent (or trustee) it is instead 'effectuated' by a common safe keeper (or 'CSK') appointed by the clearing systems.

3.99   Upon closing of the issue of the relevant debt securities, the NGN in temporary global form is not delivered to a common depositary but instead is delivered to the relevant CSK. The CSK holds the temporary global note for the clearing systems. The temporary global note is exchanged for the permanent global note, also in NGN form in the same way as a CGN and is similarly held by a CSK for the clearing systems.

3.100   Legally, therefore, the main differences between a CGN and an NGN are that:

- A CGN is held by a common depositary (which is a third party financial institution) on behalf of the clearing systems, whereas an NGN is held by one of the clearing systems (i.e. the CSK) itself.
- In the case of a CGN, the physical CGN as held by the common depositary is conclusive as to the amount of debt securities that it represents, whereas in the case of an NGN, the records of the clearing systems in respect of the particular debt securities is definitive as to their amount outstanding.

3.5.9 Summary of provisions relating to the debt securities while in global form

3.101   A prospectus or base prospectus will sometimes, but not always, include a section with this heading or with a similar heading. It may not be included in some prospectuses or base prospectuses as the subject matter covered may be dealt with elsewhere or in the terms and conditions of the debt securities themselves. The reason for this section is that the terms and conditions of the debt securities are generally written for definitive securities, that is, they assume that the debt securities will be in the form of individual bearer certificates that are held physically by individual noteholders. As mentioned earlier,[95] this approach does not match the normal modern default position of, essentially, the debt securities being held in clearance systems in permanently dematerialized form.

3.102   If it does appear, the purpose of this section in the prospectus or base prospectus may address all or some of the following matters:

- A statement that references to 'noteholders', or similar, in the terms and conditions of the debt securities should be understood as a reference to the holder of the global note being the common depositary (if the global notes are in CGN form) or the common safe keeper (if the global notes are in NGN form). The point being made is that in respect of those debt securities, whilst they are

---

[95]   See Section 3.5.8.

represented by global notes then the only person with a direct claim in respect of those notes against the issuer is the common depositary or the common safe keeper (as the case may be). The economic holders of the debt securities are of course the holders of accounts in the clearance systems that have been credited with an interest in the debt security. However, such persons are typically stated as only having a claim in respect of such debt securities against the clearing system and not as against the issuer. This approach changes in two instances: (i) for the holding of meetings[96] of holders of the debt securities where procedures are put in place (typically through electronic voting instructions) to allow the underlying economic holders of the debt securities to participate in and vote at meetings and (ii) in certain circumstances where the global notes become void and are replaced by the provisions of a deed of covenant in the circumstances described below.

The approach differs slightly depending upon whether the debt securities are constituted by a trust deed or fiscal agency agreement[97] since where there is a trustee, obligations under the debt securities will be owed by the issuer to the trustee and (unless the trustee defaults in its obligations) cannot be enforced directly by holders of the debt securities.

• In the case of a fiscal agency arrangement, a description of the provisions for exchange of a temporary global note into a permanent global note (or in limited circumstances, directly into definitive notes) and for the exchange of the permanent global note into definitive notes. Broadly, the exchange mechanics are described and it is then noted that if:

  • the relevant exchange of global note (that is, the temporary global note being exchanged into a permanent global note or definitive notes or a permanent global note being exchanged into definitive notes) does not occur, or

  • the temporary or permanent global note has become due and payable (for example by reason of an event of default),

then the temporary global note or permanent global note (as relevant) becomes void and the obligation represented by it is replaced by an undertaking in a deed of covenant that is executed by the issuer at the time of closing of the issuance of the debt securities (and delivery of the temporary global note). The undertaking in the deed of covenant is by the issuer in favour of account holders in the relevant clearing systems as if definitive notes had been issued and delivered to them. This is intended to provide beneficial owners of the debt securities with a direct claim against the issuer without having to proceed through clearance system accounts or through the holder of the global note. Again, the position differs depending upon whether the debt securities

---

[96] See Section 3.5.10, 'Meetings'.
[97] See Section 3.3.5, 'Trustee or Fiscal Agent'.

are constituted by a trust deed or a fiscal agency agreement and the mechanism providing for global notes to become void and be replaced by obligations under a deed of covenant are not needed where obligations are in any event owed to a trustee on behalf of holders of the debt securities. It can be seen that where debt securities are constituted by a fiscal agency agreement, whilst it is clear that legally the issuer is indebted by the amount of the debt securities, it may be less than clear in practice exactly to whom those sums are owed (to the holder of the global note, to account holders in the clearing systems under the deed of covenant or to their underlying customers, the ultimate beneficial and economic holders of the debt securities concerned).

• Finally, some of the terms and conditions of the debt securities are amended in the provisions of the global notes themselves to address changes needed to reflect the fact that the debt securities are held in global form rather than in definitive individual form. These changes are described in this section if they are not separately addressed in the terms and conditions of the debt securities themselves. The changes may address a number of matters, in particular the method by which notices are given to holders. Whilst the debt securities are represented by a global note which is held by a common depository or CSK for the clearance systems, any requirement in the terms and conditions of the debt securities for the giving of notices by way of publication in national or international newspapers (which may well be appropriate while the debt securities are held in individual certificate form but isn't relevant when the debt securities are permanently locked into clearance systems) is normally suspended and replaced by the giving of a notice through the procedures of the clearance systems themselves. This change is of course subject to compliance, in any event, with the requirements of any stock exchange on which the relevant debt securities are listed, a point that may or may not be reflected in the amended notice provisions but is nevertheless true.

3.5.10 Terms and conditions of the debt securities

3.103 A detailed discussion of each of the possible terms and conditions of a debt security under a stand-alone issue or under a debt issuance programme is beyond the scope of this Chapter. Instead, set out below is a short summary and discussion of some of the main features most likely to be found in the terms and conditions of debt securities, whether set out in the base prospectus for a programme or in a prospectus for a stand-alone issue.

3.104 The general scheme of terms and conditions of debt securities may well be that they are written so as to apply to individual definitive notes. Indeed, historically, this is what happened. They were written to be printed on the reverse of the definitive bond certificates. Now that the practice of the market has moved almost entirely to the issuance of permanent global certificates, their function is similar save that there are a few variations that apply whilst they are in global form.[98] This is not necessarily the case, and the trend is probably to move to terms and conditions that address both global and definitive form. For the most part, the differences in approach are relatively minor and in any event do not affect the substance of the terms and conditions of the debt securities.

In the context of a debt issuance programme, the terms and conditions are also written so that they are 'universal' in the sense that they can be used for the different types of debt securities that are to be issued at different times under the programme. On their own, the terms and conditions are meaningless. They have to be brought to life and made specific for each issuance of debt securities under the programme. To do this, a set of 'final terms' is drawn up for each issuance.[99] The final terms for each issuance either fill in blanks in the terms and conditions (for example, the amount of the particular issuance or the rate of interest payable on the debt securities, if any) or activate provisions of the terms and conditions (for example, the provisions for calculating a fixed rate of interest, relevant day count conventions etc.). These commercial provisions will be specifically incorporated within the terms and conditions of a stand-alone issue of debt securities where there will be no separate 'final terms' or similar.

3.105

The key elements of the terms and conditions of debt securities that will appear in virtually all Euromarket stand-alone debt issues or in programmes are as set out below.

3.106

• Form, denomination and title

This section will state whether the notes are in bearer or registered form and will state presumptions as to ownership—normally the holder in the case of a bearer debt security or the registered holder in the case of a registered debt security.

3.107

• Status and guarantee

This condition will address whether the debt securities are intended to be, for example, senior or subordinated.[100] In the case of debt issuance programmes for financial institutions, subordinated notes may well be split into undated subordinated notes and dated subordinated notes (which under UK regulations would be intended to constitute supplementary regulatory capital in the form of Upper Tier 2 and Lower Tier 2 capital respectively) and may even include undated subordinated capital notes that are intended to constitute Tier 1 capital (which in

3.108

---

[98] See Section 3.5.9.
[99] See Section 3.5.11.
[100] See Sections 3.2.2 and 3.2.4.

the UK would be in the form of hybrid innovative Tier 1 capital[101]). If there is a guarantee of the debt securities or of the programme, reference will be included to that guarantee in this section of the terms and conditions.

- Negative pledge

3.109 A 'negative pledge' is an undertaking by the issuer and any guarantor that whilst debt securities remain outstanding neither the issuer nor any guarantor will create 'security' over other 'indebtedness'. The purpose of a negative pledge, in general, is to ensure that if indebtedness is raised in the debt capital markets on an unsecured basis, then other creditors will not be provided with senior ranking claims (at the expense of the holders of the debt securities) against that issuer through the grant of a security interest over its assets to those other creditors.

3.110 Not all debt securities will include a negative pledge in their terms and conditions, as some issuers may be unwilling to accept such restrictions on their capital raising abilities. This has historically been the case, for example, for some banks and other financial institutions. Most corporate issuers, however, will have included a negative pledge in the terms and conditions of their debt securities.

3.111 Unless an issuer is in the position of being able to reject the requirement of a negative pledge altogether, the next best starting point (from an issuer's perspective) is that the negative pledge should only apply to 'relevant indebtedness'. Relevant indebtedness is typically defined as '*indebtedness in the form of bonds, notes or other similar instruments which are or are capable of being listed or traded on a stock exchange or securities market*'. In other words, the negative pledge applies only to instruments similar to those being issued or which are likely to be issued under a debt issuance programme and so achieves parity of treatment for holders of traded debt securities of that issuer. A negative pledge formulated in this way would not typically apply, for example, to bank lending under a loan facility, which could therefore be secured in favour of those lenders without there being a breach of the terms and conditions of the debt securities. This formulation may also be limited in its application within members of the group of companies of which the issuer (or any guarantor) is a part. So, for example, the negative pledge may only be expressed to apply to the issuer, any guarantor and possibly other specified subsidiaries or types of subsidiaries. Whilst these various formulations generally provide issuers and their groups with a significant degree of flexibility in the way that they carry out other borrowing activities, some financial institutions have found, when they have wished to introduce covered bond programmes, that such programmes (which may well involve the issuance of traded debt securities which are backed or secured by underlying pools of mortgages)

---

[101] See Section 3.2.8.

are restricted even by these limited types of negative pledge provisions. The consequence in some cases has been a need to amend the negative pledge provisions for future issues and to obtain the consent of bondholders through the holding of meetings[102] to the amendment of the negative pledge provisions then existing.

This limited 'relevant indebtedness' approach to the negative pledge is just one **3.112** approach, albeit a relatively favourable one, for an issuer. In practice, the exact form of the negative pledge will depend upon various factors including the negotiating position of the issuer. For example, it is quite likely that 'indebtedness' may well be more widely defined and catch other categories of indebtedness than just 'relevant indebtedness'. If this is the case then the focus of the drafting of the negative pledge from an issuer's perspective may well be to carve out from the definitions of 'security' or of 'indebtedness' (or both) as many specific forms of indebtedness or security as is reasonable and acceptable to investors. The negative pledge may also be significantly different if the specific debt securities (in the case of a stand-alone issue) are secured or if debt securities issued under a programme are to have the benefit of security over assets of the issuer or other members of its group.

- Interest provisions

This section of the terms and conditions will set out the mechanics for calculating **3.113** the amount of interest to be paid on the debt securities and also the dates on which interest is to be paid. In the case of a debt issuance programme, the vital information enabling an investor to work these things out will be contained in a combination of the terms and conditions and, in particular, the final terms for the particular issuance.

Broadly, the interest provisions will be divided into two sections dealing respec- **3.114** tively with debt securities that have a fixed rate of interest and those which are to have a floating rate.[103]

- Redemption

Most debt securities will specify a date when they are due for scheduled repayment **3.115** and this will be specified in the redemption provisions or in the relevant final terms for the issue of debt securities under a programme.

The redemption provisions will also provide the mechanics for redemption in **3.116** other circumstances. These mechanics are switched on if the final terms for the

---

[102] See 'Meetings' below in this Section.
[103] See Section 3.2.3.

particular issue specify that they should apply and might typically include some or all of the following:

- early redemption at the option of the issuer or 'issuer call';
- early redemption at the option of holders of the debt instruments (typically designated as a 'put option' in the final terms) and which may be linked, for example, to a change of control of the issuer (or any guarantor);
- redemption for tax reasons. The tax-related circumstances that might give rise to a call option on the part of the issuer will depend on the nature of the debt securities concerned and might include:
- if an obligation on the part of the issuer to make a withholding from interest payments on account of tax arises (with a consequent obligation to 'gross-up' the interest payment[104]);
- if the interest payments cease to be deductible from the issuer's income for tax assessment purposes.

3.117 Whenever there is provision for early redemption at the option of the issuer, there are normally two questions to be considered. First, when can the early redemption be effected? Second, what amount must the issuer repay to holders of the debt securities?

3.118 The answer to the first question will normally depend upon the interest rate calculation basis that is applicable at the time of the redemption. So, for example, if the interest rate basis is a floating rate calculation, then the redemption may normally only be effected on the last day of an interest period. If the applicable interest rate basis is fixed rate, then it is more normal for redemption (subject to minimum and maximum notice periods as specified in the terms and conditions) to be at any time.

3.119 The answer to the second question similarly depends on the applicable interest rate basis, but it is likely to have been subject to rather more detailed negotiations. As a broad proposition, if the applicable interest rate basis is fixed rate, then investors might expect to receive compensation in the form of a 'make-whole' (or similarly described) redemption amount should redemption of the debt securities occur ahead of the scheduled redemption date. This is because the current fixed rate of interest on the debt securities may well not reflect market rates at the time of redemption and (particularly where the specified fixed rate on the debt security is higher than current market rates) the investor may well have paid a premium above par for the debt securities when acquiring them in the market. In these circumstances, the 'make-whole' amount will represent the discounted value of the fixed coupon for the remainder of the period from the date of early redemption

---

[104] See 'Taxation' below.

until the date of scheduled redemption. Depending upon market rates, this could be an unattractively expensive call option for an issuer! The issuer may of course also argue that if changes occur that are outside of its control and which make servicing the debt represented by the debt securities unreasonably more expensive, then it should be entitled to redeem the debt securities without additional cost to itself. This approach may lead to negotiation and compromise around the circumstances where a 'make-whole' is payable and where it is not.

• Taxation

The Eurobond market is essentially a 'gross' interest market. What this means in practice is that investors expect to receive interest or coupons on debt securities without any withholding having been made on account of taxation, whether by the issuer or any of its paying agents.   **3.120**

To the extent that any such withholdings are required to be made, the terms and conditions of the debt securities invariably provide that the issuer will pay additional amounts so that the net amount received by the holder of the debt security remains that which it would have received had no withholding on account of taxation been made. In other words, economically, the debt securities remain as gross instruments. Under current United Kingdom taxation law,[105] a UK issuer can pay interest on Eurobonds on a gross basis, provided that they are listed on a 'recognized market'.[106] HM Revenue & Customs provide a list of recognized markets which include the London Stock Exchange's Main Market and its Professional Securities Market ('PSM'), the Luxembourg Stock Exchange's regulated market and its Euro MTF market, the Channel Islands Stock Exchange ('CISX') as well as most other European regulated markets and the New York Stock Exchange.   **3.121**

This is the so-called 'quoted Eurobond exemption' and applies provided the relevant debt security is listed on a recognized market at the time of an interest payment. Is isn't necessary for the debt security to have been listed throughout its life and in some cases debt securities are not listed until sometime after issue, though before the first interest payment is made.   **3.122**

The obligation on the issuer to gross up interest payments should it be required to make a withholding on account of taxation is subject to a number of customary exceptions. These are typically listed in the terms and conditions and are mostly market standard. These include: **3.123**

• a withholding which is made by or on behalf of a holder of the debt security who is liable for the tax withheld by reason of some connection with the jurisdiction requiring the withholding to be made. So, for example, if a

---

[105] Section 882 of the Income Tax Act 2007.
[106] Within the meaning of section 1005 of the Income Tax Act 2007.

payment is made by the issuer (or its paying agent) in a particular country where the person receiving such payment is tax resident and laws of that country accordingly require the issuer to make a withholding on account of tax, then there will be no obligation to gross-up the interest payment;

- where the withholding is imposed on a payment of interest to an individual which is required to be made under various EU measures aimed at tax avoidance. Broadly, the measures implemented under the European Savings Tax Directive[107] permit interest payments to be made gross (i.e. not subject to any withholding on account of taxation) provided that the member state where the payment is made exchanges information with other member states in relation to those payments. However, three member states have elected not to exchange information—these are Austria, Luxembourg and Belgium, and payments made by issuers or paying agents in those countries to individuals will be subject to withholding;
- where the holder could have avoided the need for withholding by presenting the relevant debt security to another paying agent or where the withholding arises by virtue of late presentation.

- Events of default

3.124 Events of default (or events, which if they happen, entitle the holder to require early repayment) are among the most important of the provisions in the terms and conditions of debt securities and, consequently, probably the most keenly negotiated.

3.125 They typically include:

- failure to pay principal or interest when due. This event of default is normally expressed not to apply until a defined grace period (during which time the issuer can remedy what would otherwise be an event of default) has expired. The permitted number of days' grace is a matter of negotiation between the issuer and the underwriters or dealers and is normally just a few days. Sometimes the grace period permitted for interest payments is rather longer than for payment of principal amounts;
- failure on the part of the issuer (or any guarantor) to observe any of its respective other obligations under the terms and conditions of the debt securities. Again, there is typically a grace period—rather longer than in relation to a payment default—with the grace period sometimes only running from the date that the failure is bought to the attention of the issuer or guarantor;
- default in the payment by the issuer or any guarantor of any other outstanding indebtedness. This is the so-called '*cross-default*' provision. It has the effect, for

---

[107] Directive 2003/48/EC.

the benefit of investors in the issuer's debt securities, of ensuring that if one type of indebtedness of the issuer is in default and capable of being called for repayment early (or 'accelerated')—possibly whether or not that other indebtedness is actually being accelerated by the other creditors, then so too are the debt securities. From an investor perspective this is an important provision as it means that otherwise the investor in the debt securities might find itself unable to take any action to recover amounts potentially owing to it under its debt securities whilst other creditors are enforcing their claims against the issuer in relation to other indebtedness. In these circumstances, the holder of the debt securities might otherwise find that all of the issuer's available assets had been used in payment of the other creditors before it was itself able to take any action. In reality, the position is unlikely to be so simple and it is quite possible that default and enforcement under some other obligations would in any event trigger other insolvency or similar events of default set out in the terms and conditions of the debt securities or be contrary to the insolvency laws applicable to the issuer. Nevertheless, the cross-default provision is regarded as important to investors in achieving for them equality in bargaining power compared to other creditors. This provision is normally the subject of discussion and negotiation around two particular points: first, what amount of other indebtedness must be in default for the provision to trigger and second, what does 'indebtedness' mean for these purposes? The amount that needs to be exceeded for the cross-default provision to be triggered (the cross-default threshold amount) is a matter of negotiation and the issuer will of course want it to be as high as possible whereas investors will want it to be lower. If the issuer has other debt securities outstanding or loan arrangements with banks in each case with similar provisions, then a starting point will be to look and see what the cross-default thresholds are in those instruments or loans and adopt a similar approach. On the other hand, an issuer is likely nevertheless to want to push that number gradually higher over a period of time. Similarly, an issuer will wish to define 'indebtedness' for the purposes of the cross-default provision as narrowly as possible (and in particular, possibly to confine the definition to real 'borrowings' rather than simply to include all amounts owed to third parties).

• insolvency and bankruptcy events: These events will be broadly drafted (though with specific reference to the insolvency laws of the place of incorporation of the issuer or any guarantor) to catch both involuntary and voluntary insolvency events. An issuer will normally wish to confine the event of default to genuine insolvency events rather than, for example, tactical steps using insolvency laws or procedures taken by litigants or others. It is therefore usual for there to be a grace period to allow an issuer or guarantor to discharge the insolvency proceedings before the event of default is triggered. An issuer may also wish to make provision for solvent restructurings, though this is likely to require the consent of holders of the debt securities at a meeting.[108]

- cessation of business: The events of default will specify that there will be an event of default if the issuer (or a guarantor) ceases to carry on its business, unless that cessation of business has been approved by resolution of a meeting of holders of the debt securities. An issuer will wish to make sure that ceasing to carry on just a small part of its business will not necessarily trigger the event of default and will therefore wish to include wording to the effect that there is only an event of default if it ceases to carry on 'all or a substantial part' of its business, or even better, if it ceases to carry on 'all or substantially all' of its business so that in either case, closing down a relatively small division within its overall business will not, for example, necessarily constitute an event of default. Similarly, an issuer will wish to ensure that this event of default does not inadvertently catch disposals on arm's-length terms.

3.126 If an event of default occurs, the exact consequences will depend upon whether the debt securities are constituted by a trust deed or by a fiscal agency agreement. If they are subject to a trust deed, then the events of default provision will typically state that following an event of default the trustee may in its discretion call an event of default (in which case all of the debt securities outstanding at that point become repayable) or that it will call an event of default if it is instructed to do so by the holders of a specified proportion (often one-quarter) of the outstanding debt securities of that series. In the case of payment events of default or insolvency related events of default, it is normally mandatory for the trustee to declare an event of default and accelerate the outstanding debt securities. In the case of other events of default, the terms and conditions may also require that, for the relevant event to enable the trustee to accelerate the outstanding debt securities, the trustee must also specify that the occurrence of the relevant event is, in its opinion, 'materially prejudicial' to the interests of the holders of the debt securities.

3.127 On the other hand, if there is no trustee, then the occurrence of any of the events of default (allowing for the passing of any permitted grace periods) will normally entitle any holder (whatever amount of bonds it holds) to call an event of default and so accelerate repayment of any of its affected debt securities. Whilst this means that the entire outstanding series of the debt securities doesn't necessarily become repayable (some holders may decide not to accelerate their debt securities and require repayment), in these circumstances the issuer does not have the benefit of the need for a trustee to determine material prejudice, at least in some cases. The role of the trustee can potentially be useful to an issuer, particularly where any

---

[108] See 'Meetings' above.

relevant event is fairly minor or of limited or no consequence to holders of the debt securities.

The terms and conditions or, in the case of an issue under a debt issuance pro-   **3.128**
gramme, the final terms, will specify what amount is payable if and when there is
an event of default. This may be the par value of the debt security, which in turn
may in some cases be relevant to a trustee or holders in the context of determining
materiality of the underlying occurrence giving rise to the particular event of
default, and accordingly, whether or not to actually call the event of default and
accelerate repayment of the debt securities.

• Meetings

The terms and conditions set out in the prospectus or base prospectus will   **3.129**
normally include a relatively short section describing the key provisions relating
to the convening, conduct and powers of a meeting of holders of the debt
securities.

A detailed discussion of the law, conduct and mechanics of meetings is beyond the   **3.130**
scope of this Chapter, but it is nevertheless an important subject, particularly if
the issuer is encountering any kind of financial stress and needs to reach any kind
of compromise or arrangement with the holders of its debt securities. Euromarket
debt securities are typically (but not always) issued in bearer form, and in any case,
whether bearer or registered, are invariably held and traded on an anonymous
basis through clearance systems. It is therefore quite difficult, in practice, for an
issuer to be able to enter into any kind of meaningful direct discussions or negotiations with bondholders. There are specialist service providers who aim to identify
holders of debt securities for issuers, and they perform a very useful function. It
may well be possible to identify some holders of significant stakes, but in the case
of a relatively widely held series of debt securities, it is unlikely that the issuer, even
with the assistance of the specialist service providers, will be able to identify more
than at best a significant minority of holders.

This means that it is not possible, usually, for an issuer to agree changes to the   **3.131**
terms and conditions of its debt securities on a bilateral basis as it would, say,
when negotiating with its lending banks. The terms and conditions might provide
for powers of amendment with the written approval of holders of the debt securities, but the required percentage to be able to effect such amendments that are
binding upon all holders is likely to be holders representing at least 90 per cent
and in many cases 100 per cent of all the debt securities of that series. Even at the
90 per cent level, this is likely to be extremely challenging to achieve, and in reality
an issuer will have little choice but to resort to amendment to the terms and conditions through the mechanism of the convening and holding of a meeting of
holders and the passing of relevant resolutions. A resolution passed at a meeting of
holders of debt securities, provided that the relevant quorum was present at that

meeting and the resolution was passed by the requisite majority of those voting, is binding on all holders, whether or not they attended that meeting and whether or not they voted in favour of the proposed resolution. It may well be possible to effect changes to the terms and conditions of debt securities through other statutory compromise or arrangement methods (for example, pursuant to a scheme of arrangement in the United Kingdom[109] or similar proceeding elsewhere), but consideration of such statutory arrangements is not considered further in this Chapter and in any event the outcome is unlikely to differ significantly from what can be achieved through the meeting provisions that are applicable to the particular series of debt securities under their terms and conditions.

3.132 The meeting provisions that appear in the terms and conditions and which therefore appear in the prospectus or base prospectus, are a very short summary of the full provisions that appear either (if the series of debt securities or programme is constituted by a fiscal agency agreement) in a schedule to the fiscal agency agreement or (if the series of debt securities or programme is constituted by a trust deed) in a schedule to the trust deed. Even within those documents, they are relegated to a distant schedule and occasionally a close reading suggests that they might not have received the detailed attention that they possibly deserved!

3.133 The main mechanical complication in relation to bondholder meetings arises from the fact that most bonds are represented by bearer global notes or registered global notes in respect of which the beneficial interests are held anonymously through the clearing systems. The aim of the meeting provisions in the fiscal agency agreement or trust deed is to facilitate the enfranchisement of underlying beneficial holders. The clearing systems have effective and efficient electronic systems which distribute notices of meetings and proposed resolutions to underlying account holders (and through those account holders, to ultimate beneficial holders) and, in turn, gather voting instructions that are then passed back electronically through the clearing systems to whoever is coordinating voting arrangements for the particular meeting. Often, meetings (particularly those that are relatively uncontroversial) are held almost on a 'virtual' basis, with all voting being carried out electronically through the use of 'block voting instructions' with the only attendees at the meeting being the issuer and its various advisers! If the subject matter of the meeting is more controversial, underlying beneficial holders are able if they wish to attend the meeting by arranging for instructions to be sent electronically through the clearing systems which result in the issue of a 'voting certificate' (which is a kind of form of proxy). Whether voting is carried out through the block voting instruction or in person through a voting certificate, an important function of the procedures that are implemented by the clearing systems is that the debt securities that are being voted are immobilized within the

---

[109] Under section 895 of the Companies Act 2006.

clearing systems whilst the voting procedure is underway, either at the original meeting or, if that first meeting is inquorate (which is often the case), at any adjourned meeting. This procedure is important so as to prevent multiple voting in respect of the same debt securities.

Other points to note in respect of these meeting provisions in view of the **3.134** following:

Quorum requirements:

- the meetings provisions will normally summarize the quorum requirements for bondholder meetings. These can vary slightly, but will distinguish between the quorum required for regular business and that required for 'special business' or 'reserved matters'. The quorum for regular business is likely to be two or more persons representing more than half of the outstanding debt securities at an initial meeting or, if that initial meeting is not quorate, two or more persons whatever the amount of debt securities they hold or represent at any adjourned meeting. The quorum for a meeting to consider special business is likely to be two or more persons representing at least three-quarters (or sometimes two-thirds) of the outstanding debt securities or, if that initial meeting is not quorate, two or more persons representing at least one-quarter (or, correspondingly, sometimes one-third) of the outstanding debt securities at an adjourned meeting.

Special business:

- what constitutes 'special business' will be defined in the relevant schedule to the fiscal agency agreement or trust deed. It will almost invariably include proposals to change the core commercial terms of the debt securities, including their currency, the date for repayment and the rate of interest payable, as well as a long list of other 'entrenched' matters. If an issuer is encountering financial difficulties and looking to reschedule or otherwise significantly change the terms of the debt securities, it is quite likely (indeed probable), that to do so will involve 'special business'.

What majority is required to pass a resolution?

- Most meaningful business to be considered at a meeting of holders of the debt securities will require a resolution to be passed as an 'extraordinary resolution'. To be passed, an extraordinary resolution will require votes in favour by at least three-quarters of that series of debt securities represented at the meeting.

Who can vote at a meeting of holders of the debt securities?

- The answer to this question is not necessarily as simple as it at first seems. The schedule to the fiscal agency agreement or the trust deed constituting the debt securities will likely state that quorum requirements and voting provisions are by reference to debt securities that are 'outstanding'. The word 'outstanding' is invariably a defined term (even though it may be used with a lower case 'o' and therefore not appear to be defined) but with the definition to be found somewhere else in the trust deed or fiscal agency agreement. For these purposes, the expression 'outstanding' is normally defined to exclude debt securities that are held by the issuer or any subsidiary of the issuer. The definition may also exclude debt securities that are held by an 'affiliate' (which is potentially a broader expression and may well not be defined) of the issuer or that are held by any person who holds the debt securities 'for the benefit of' (again, on an undefined basis) the issuer or any of its subsidiaries. This definition of 'outstanding', particularly where it refers to affiliates or third parties who hold for the benefit of the issuer, can be very difficult to apply in practice, but the consequence of the definition is that any such securities should be excluded from being counted in the quorum or voting and if they are not excluded, any resolutions passed at a meeting may well be invalid.

3.135 There is one further consideration that might sometimes complicate meeting procedures for debt securities where the debt securities concerned are expressed to be governed by English law. There are English common law principles that apply to the conduct of meetings generally and, in particular, which address the circumstances in which holders of the debt securities are entitled to vote their holdings any way they think fit on a proposed resolution.[110] The starting point is, of course, that holders of debt securities are free to vote in favour of or against a resolution entirely as they wish. However, in limited circumstances this may not necessarily be the case. For example, a holder may be precluded from voting in a particular way if to do so would not be in the interests of the class of holders of that series of debt securities as a whole, and where voting by that holder is as a result of some improper or unfair motive such as fraud, bad faith, an intention to oppress the minority holders or a collateral purpose such as the enrichment of the majority at the expense of the minority holders.

3.136 This area of English law is uncertain and it is difficult to express a general principle. However, by way of illustration, one example might be where an issuer pays a particular holder (but does not at the same time make at least the possibility of such an incentive payment available to all holders) to vote in favour of a resolution, where the passing of that resolution is otherwise not in the interests of holders of that series of debt securities as a whole. In these circumstances, there is at least a risk that the resolution would be set aside by court as having been improperly passed. Considerable care should therefore be given to the terms of any voting

---

[110] See for example *Redwood Master Fund Ltd v TD Bank Europe Ltd* [2006] 1 BCLC 149.

incentives offered to holders of debt securities when convening meetings, since it is possible (though the precise scope of this rule of English common law is unclear) that otherwise the payment of improper incentives to holders might, in relevant circumstances, invalidate the passing of a resolution at a meeting where that holder voted.

One point that isn't always recognized in the context of meetings to approve changes to the terms and conditions of debt securities, is whether the proposed changes are sufficiently significant that they might amount to, in effect, an offering of new securities and so, without anything further, might infringe the securities laws of various jurisdictions. A solution to this difficulty that is common in the context of exchange offers to holders of debt securities (that is, an offer of new debt securities or a mixture of cash or new debt securities to holders of existing debt securities) is to exclude potentially 'difficult' jurisdictions from the exchange offer, or at least to prevent holders (or certain classes of holders) in those jurisdictions from being able to receive the new debt securities. It should be noted that this solution is not likely to be possible where what is being proposed is a meeting of holders, since all holders are entitled to notice of and to attend and vote at meetings of holders of those debt securities and cannot be disenfranchised. Jurisdictions where this point should at least be considered typically include the United States and Italy. **3.137**

• Further issues

Where an issuer has already issued a tranche of debt securities, this provision in the terms and conditions of the debt securities permits an issuer to issue a further tranche which has identical terms and conditions, including as to interest and redemption. The idea is that the further tranche or tranches are consolidated with the original tranche into a single series, so as to increase the size of that series of debt securities as a whole. **3.138**

Such issues are commonly referred to as 'tap issues' and are executed so that the original tranche plus any subsequent tranches can trade together (which enhances the liquidity of the series as a whole) on a fungible (i.e. wholly interchangeable) basis. If the tranches are to be fungible, which is an essential part of them being capable of being treated as a single series going forward, they will need to have identical rights in all respects. In this context two particular issues can typically arise: (i) how to deal with interest entitlements where the additional tranche is issued other than on an interest payment date for the original tranche and (ii) how to deal with any requirement for a temporary global note arising from the Regulation S/TEFRA rules?[111] **3.139**

---

[111] See Section 3.5.8.

3.140 One possible solution to the problem of a tap issue taking place otherwise than on an interest payment date (which would otherwise mean that the holder would be entitled to full payment of interest for the current interest period notwithstanding that the further tranche of the debt security had not been in existence for that length of time), is for the new investors to 'pre-pay' at the time of subscription for the new tranche of the debt securities an amount equivalent to the interest that has accrued between the interest payment date preceding the date of the tap issue, up until the date of the tap issue itself. This amount, together with interest for the period from the date of the tap issue until the next interest payment date, will be represented by the aggregate coupon paid to all holders of that series of debt securities on the next interest payment date. An alternative approach is for the tap issue tranche not to become fungible with the original tranche of the series until after payment of the first amount of interest on the tap issue (and this should be specifically provided for in the 'Further Issues' section of the terms and conditions of the debt securities), which will therefore be of a lower amount for the tranche representing the tap issue than for the original tranche of the series.

3.141 If, as is often the case, the further series of debt securities has initially to be represented by a temporary global note which is only exchangeable for a permanent global note after the 40-day lock-up period,[112] then there isn't realistically any way of achieving fungibility of the original tranche of the series with the new tap issue tranche until such time as the temporary global note has been exchanged into the permanent global note within the clearance systems in the usual way.

• Notices

3.142 The notices provision of older bonds often provides for notices to holders to be given by publication in newspapers. These notices are still sometimes seen and no doubt have been a good source of revenue for newspapers such as the *Financial Times* over the years.

3.143 A more modern approach is to provide for newspaper notices but (i) only if the rules of any stock exchange on which the debt securities are listed so require and (ii) subject to that, not for such time as the debt securities concerned are represented by a global note and held through the clearance systems. Most stock exchanges do not require notices to be given by way of newspaper and instead require notices to be given through designated information services (such as a Regulatory Information Service (or 'RIS') in the United Kingdom. In practice, notices to holders of debt securities are given by way of regulatory announcement and through the clearance systems. For more recent debt securities, notices in

---

[112] See Section 3.5.8.

newspapers are not normally required unless they are for some reason held in definitive bearer form. Since some terms and conditions are written with definitive securities in mind, they may appear to require newspaper publication. However, these provisions are typically overridden in the terms of the global notes, as set out in the section of the prospectus or base prospectus which describes certain provisions of the debt securities whilst they are in global form.[113]

• Substitution

The terms and conditions may or may not include provision for substitution. **3.144** There is likely to be such a provision where the issuer or issuers are finance subsidiaries or special purpose vehicles having the benefit of a parent or group guarantee or other support arrangements, since the identity of the issuer in these circumstances is of relatively little importance to an investor. In these circumstances, the terms and conditions will normally provide mechanical provisions permitting the substitution of the issuer with another issuer provided that the economic consequences to investors (for example, in particular, provisions relating to withholding tax) are not disadvantageous and provided that guarantee or other support arrangements extend to the new issuer as they did to the previous issuer (or where the guarantor or other support provider becomes the issuer itself or the debt securities are guaranteed by the original issuer).

The terms and conditions may also provide for substitution in other circum- **3.145** stances. In particular, if the credit rating of the substitute issuer is at least as good as the original issuer and otherwise the substitution would have no adverse economic effect on investors. However, this is a less common approach.

• Governing Law

In the Euromarkets, the governing law of debt securities that are to be issued on **3.146** an international basis is generally English law. This is not always the case and the domestic law of the place of incorporation of the issuer (or the guarantor or other support provider, if there is one) may be the governing law, particularly if the debt securities concerned are primarily aimed at investors in the issuer's domestic market. Sometimes, there may be a split governing law clause such that the general terms and conditions of the debt securities are expressed to be governed by, say, English law but specific provisions that are closely based upon the law of place of incorporation of the issuer (for example, in particular, subordination provisions) may well be expressed to be governed by the law of the issuer's place of incorporation.

---

[113] See Section 3.5.9.

3.5.11 Form of final terms

3.147 As discussed above,[114] in the case of terms and conditions as set out in a base prospectus for a debt issuance programme, it is the final terms that bring a particular issuance of debt securities under that programme to life.

3.148 The form of final terms included in a Euromarkets base prospectus generally uses one or more of the suggested forms published by the International Capital Market Association ('ICMA') and contained in the IPMA Handbook. These forms are accompanied by helpful notes as to their use. There are separate pro-forma final terms contained in the IPMA Handbook which are suggested for use in debt issuance programmes for:

- debt securities with a denomination of less than EUR 50,000 (or its equivalent in other currencies) which are to be admitted to trading on an EEA regulated market and/or which are to be offered to the public in the EEA;[115]
- debt securities with a denomination of EUR 50,000 (or its equivalent in other currencies) or more, that are to be admitted to trading on an EEA regulated market;[116]
- debt securities to be admitted to trading on the London Stock Exchange's Professional Securities Market ('PSM') and where the debt securities are not to be offered to the public within the meaning of the Prospectus Directive;[117] and
- debt securities that are to be admitted to trading on other markets that are not EEA regulated markets and where the debt securities are not to be offered to the public within the meaning of the Prospectus Directive.[118]

3.149 In the case of a retail debt issuance programme, the starting point for the final terms to be included in the base prospectus will therefore be the form set out in Section 7(II)(b) of the IPMA Handbook. This form of final terms is largely self-explanatory and is divided into three main sections:

- *Introduction*: the introduction to the form of final terms provides, within its drafting, a series of alternative scenarios for the issuance of debt securities. These are:
  - where the debt securities will be admitted to trading on an EEA regulated market and may be offered to the public in various jurisdictions in the EEA in two different ways: (i) an offering in some jurisdictions to the public (but on the basis that such offering is carried out taking advantage of one or more of the exemptions set out in the Prospectus Directive (an 'exempt offering'),

---

[114] See Section 3.5.10.
[115] Section 7(II)(b) of the IPMA Handbook.
[116] Section 7(II)(c) of the IPMA Handbook.
[117] Section 7(II)(d) of the IPMA Handbook.
[118] Section 7(II)(e) of the IPMA Handbook.

for example by confining any offering to qualified investors ('QI's)[119] and in addition (ii) an offering in one or more EEA member states in circumstances that do not take advantage of any of such exemptions (a 'non-exempt offering'). If a non-exempt offering is to be made in any EEA member state other than the one that approved the base prospectus for the retail programme, then to be able to offer the debt securities to the public it will be necessary to 'passport' the base prospectus into that member state. This can be done at the time the base prospectus is originally approved by the home member state or passporting can be requested at any time during the one-year life of the base prospectus.[120]

- where the debt securities will be admitted to trading on an EEA Regulated Market but the offering of the debt securities will be carried out in one or more EEA member states wholly on an exempt basis, for example by confining the offer of the debt securities to QIs.

Of course, it is quite possible to issue debt securities having a denomination of **3.150** EUR 50,000 or more (or its equivalent in other currencies) under a retail programme, and if this is the case then the introduction to the final terms (as well as certain other sections of the final terms) can be modified to reflect the simplified regulatory position resulting from the higher denomination of the debt securities. Some programmes include two forms of final terms, one for use for issuances of debt securities having a denomination of less than EUR 50,000 (or its equivalent in other currencies) and one for use with debt securities having a denomination of EUR 50,000 or more (or its equivalent in other currencies). Alternatively, the base prospectus may include just one form of final terms annotated appropriately to show which items need to be amended or are not relevant where the denomination of the debt securities is EUR 50,000 or more (or its equivalent in other currencies).

- *Part A—Contractual terms*: the 'contractual terms' section of the form of final terms, sets out placeholders of the commercial provisions of a particular tranche or series of debt securities that are to be issued under the debt issuance programme. These particulars include the principal amount, currency, issue price, coupon (and whether it is fixed or floating and if so, how it is calculated), redemption provisions (including any put or call options) and any other general provisions relevant to the debt securities.
- *Part B—Other Information*: the 'other information' section of the form of final terms sets out details of the debt securities being issued that are not commercial terms as such and includes details of any listing, any rating, reasons for the offer

---

[119] See Prospectus Directive Article 3(2)(b).
[120] See Prospectus Directive Article 9(2) and 18(1).

of the debt securities including the proposed use of proceeds (and details of any expenses) and operational information such as ISIN/Common Code numbers, relevant clearing systems and whether the debt securities are to be in classic or new global note form. Finally, this section of the form of final terms may contain a section headed 'Terms and Conditions of the Offer' and this section is intended to address certain items that are required by the Prospectus Directive Regulation where offers of the debt securities being issued are to be made in one or more EEA member states on a non-exempt basis.[121]

3.151   For the purposes of any particular issuance of debt securities under a programme, the form of final terms as set out in the base prospectus is completed with the commercial terms and other information and, when executed by the issuer, they are then attached to the temporary and permanent global notes for the programme and form the legal contract that creates the particular debt securities.

3.152   There are two particular areas of complexity that have arisen in the context of issuance of debt securities under programmes since the introduction of the Prospectus Directive. Since preparation and publication of final terms is the key act that brings about an issuance of debt securities under a programme, it is inevitable that those complexities should be reflected in the form of the final terms set out in the base prospectus and then completed for a particular issuance. The two areas of particular complexity are:

- What is the relationship between final terms and a prospectus supplement in the context of a debt issuance programme? In particular, to what extent can final terms for any particular issuance of debt securities add to the original base prospectus rather than simply completing commercial terms that are identified in the terms and conditions in the base prospectus as requiring completion in the relevant final terms?[122]
- The Prospectus Directive Regulation requires disclosure of the terms and conditions of 'the offer'.[123] Matters to be disclosed include any conditions of the offer, the amount of the offer and the time period during which the offer is open. A practical difficulty with the wording of the Prospectus Directive Regulation is that it isn't clear (in the context of a public offering of debt securities) to which of several possible offers the disclosure requirement relates. So for example, debt securities might be offered by the issuer to underwriters and in turn by underwriters to other financial institutions who in turn might offer them to their underlying retail and other clients.[124]

---

[121] The particular relevance of this section of the form of final terms is discussed further in Section 3.9 below.

[122] This subject is discussed further in Section 3.7 below.

[123] See Prospectus Directive Regulation Annex V(5).

[124] This subject ('retail cascades') is discussed further in Section 3.9.6 below.

3.5.12 Business description

Annex IV of the Prospectus Directive Regulation sets out the various types of information in relation to the issuer under a retail offering that need to be included in the prospectus or base prospectus.[125] It should be noted that Annex IV needs to be applied to each issuer (if there are more than one permitted under the programme) as well as for any guarantor.[126] It is normal to set out the descriptions of each issuer and any guarantor in separate sections in the base prospectus. There is no right or wrong way to present a description of the business of an issuer. Each issuer will have its own preferred way of presenting and describing what it does. Indeed, many issuers will have various public documents in which descriptions of its business appear including in their annual reports, public filings (if any) in the United States and in existing prospectuses or other documents in relation to offerings of other securities, whether equity or debt. The general aim of issuers of this kind will be, within the constraints of applicable regulatory requirements and the need for disclosure to be fully up to date when published, so far as possible to maintain consistency in the presentation of information across all of the issuer's disclosure documentation. It should also be noted that whilst Annex IV of the Prospectus Directive Regulation prescribes certain information that must be included in a prospectus or base prospectus, there is nothing to stop an issuer including further information as long as, of course, it is accurate and not misleading and provided that the core information required by Annex IV is fully covered. An issuer may well wish to do this so as to ensure consistency of disclosure across different markets. **3.153**

The information required by Annex IV breaks down into a number of general categories: **3.154**

- the general business description that would cover the history of the issuer;[127]
- a description of the business that it presently carries on—this is likely to be the most substantial part of the business description;[128]
- formal information which will include its name, place and number of registration, date of incorporation, legal form and the issuer's position within a group, if relevant;[129]
- general statements about the issuer's business and financial position:
  - a statement that there has been no material adverse change in the prospects of the issuer since the date of its last published audited financial statements;[130] and

---

[125] See Appendix 3.
[126] See further Section 3.5.13.
[127] Prospectus Directive Regulation Annex(IV)(5.1).
[128] Prospectus Directive Regulation Annex(IV)(6).
[129] Prospectus Directive Regulation Annex(IV)(7).
[130] Prospectus Directive Regulation Annex(IV)(8.1).

- a description of any significant change in the financial trading position of the group since the most recent audited or unaudited published financial information, or a statement there has been no such change.[131]
- selected financial information, which usually takes the form of key line items from the most recent audited balance sheet, profit and loss statement and cash flow statement;[132]
- disclosure of major shareholders, to the extent of controlling stakes;[133]
- various other miscellaneous items, including details of issued share capital, names, addresses and particulars of membership in a professional body of the issuer's auditors;
- a description of any 'material contract' to which the issuer is a party.[134] Material contracts are contracts other than in the ordinary course which could result in any group member being under an obligation or entitlement that is 'material' to the ability of the issuer to perform its obligations under the debt securities.

There are two quite difficult judgement criteria here:

- First, when is a contract outside of 'the ordinary course of business'? Contracts of this kind are probably easier to identify in reality than their criteria are to define in abstract. However, as a general principle, if a contract is part of the normal day-to-day business of an issuer or relates to that day-to-day business, then it is likely to be in the ordinary course. However, if it is of a one-off nature (for example, the acquisition or disposal of another business) then it is less likely to be in the ordinary course.
- Second, at what point could a contract materially affect the ability of the issuer to perform its obligations under the debt securities? Again, this is a matter of judgment and discussion, but in many cases if an issuer is well capitalized and in good financial health with its business performing normally, it may conclude that no individual contract to which it (or any other group member) is a party could itself materially affect the ability of the issuer to perform its obligations under the debt security. It should be noted that this requirement is not by reference to materiality in the abstract as is the case for the comparable provision relating to equity,[135] but is specific to the issuer's ability to perform its obligations under the debt securities. Nevertheless, this will not always be the case, and the point should always be considered carefully by an issuer with its professional advisers.
- legal and arbitration proceedings (including, to the extent the issuer knows of them, any threatened proceedings) during the previous 12 months must be

---

[131] Prospectus Directive Regulation Annex(IV)(13.7).
[132] Prospectus Directive Regulation Annex(IV)(3).
[133] Prospectus Directive Regulation Annex(IV)(12).
[134] Prospectus Directive Regulation Annex(IV)(15).
[135] Prospectus Directive Regulation Annex(I)(22).

disclosed if they may have (or have in the recent past had) significant effects on the issuer and/or group's financial position or profitability. If there is no such litigation, then that must be stated. Again, there is quite a difficult judgment call in determining what legal or arbitration proceedings to disclose. The general rule, of course, is that if there is any doubt then disclosure should be made. Nevertheless, an issuer will frequently ask what 'significant' means for these purposes and there is no easy answer. Any form of calculation of a threshold amount, for example as a percentage of turnover, profits or market capitalization, will be somewhat arbitrary. As a practical matter though, it is recognized that many companies, by virtue of their size or the particular nature of their businesses, are likely to have a significant number of legal proceedings of one kind or another outstanding at any given time, and some realistic assessment of their individual significance may need to be made.

- Certain documents must be made available for inspection. These include the constitutional documents of the issuer, all financial information and other experts' reports included or referred to in the base prospectus and the financial information for the two years prior to publication of the base prospectus. Such documents are often kept available for inspection variously at one or more of the registered office of the issuer, the office of a paying agent or through the website of the issuer and/or the website of the stock exchange upon which the debt securities are to be listed. The precise arrangements for inspection will depend upon the approach of the regulatory authority in the jurisdiction of the home member state approving the base prospectus.

3.155 Annex IX of the Prospectus Directive Regulation sets out the various types of information in relation to the issuer under a wholesale offering that need to be included in the prospectus or base prospectus. Again, it should be noted that Annex IX needs to be applied to each issuer (if there are more than one permitted under the programme) as well as for any guarantor.[136]

3.156 The general scheme of Annex IX is very similar to that of Annex IV and so won't be repeated here. However, there are some differences between the two Annexes that reflect the lesser disclosure requirements of Annex IX in the context of a wholesale rather than a retail offering.

3.157 The differences are set out in Appendix 2 to this Chapter. However, the main differences are that if the prospectus or base prospectus is being prepared under Annex IX, there is no need to include within it a summary[137] or selected financial

---

[136] See further Section 3.5.13.
[137] See Prospectus Directive Article 5(2).

information and the description of the issuer's business can be shorter (only a 'brief description'[138] is required).

3.158   The base prospectus or prospectus will need to include disclosure in relation to Annex V (if it relates to a retail offering) or Annex XIII (if it relates to a wholesale offering).[139] These Annexes address the 'Securities Note' aspect of the prospectus or base prospectus and require disclosure in relation to the securities themselves. Compliance with the disclosure requirements of these Annexes will be mostly contained in the terms and conditions of the debt securities or (in the case of a base prospectus for a programme), the final terms for the particular debt securities being issued.

3.5.13 Guarantors

3.159   An issue of debt securities, whether a stand-alone issuance or under a debt issuance programme, may well include one or more guarantees from one or more guarantors which are usually other companies within the same group of companies as the issuer of the debt securities. There are broadly two circumstances where guarantees might be provided by other group members:

- where the issuer is a special purpose company or finance subsidiary, in which case it would be normal for the debt issue to be guaranteed by the company or companies in the group that constitute the principal credit. This would often include the holding company of the group but, if different, could also include the group's main operating company or companies.
- where the issuer is the holding company of the group but the principal credit is regarded as being elsewhere in the group.

3.160   Of course, there are many possible variations on the above approach. Where the issuer is the holding company, upstream guarantees may be provided by several other companies within the group. This would be the case, for example, if the issuer were a holding company of a variety of operating companies or other companies holding a significant portion of the group's assets. The same may be true in relation to downstream guarantees, where the guarantee may be provided by not just one, but several other companies within the group.

3.161   If the primary credit for a particular debt issuance is not the issuer itself or, even if it is, if that credit is supported by guarantees from other members of the group, then it is logical that the prospectus or base prospectus for that debt issuance should contain information in relation to the guarantor or guarantors. The question is,

---

[138] Annex IX(5.1.1).
[139] See Appendix 3.

what information is required to be provided in relation to each guarantor and, in particular, what is the approach where there are multiple guarantors?

As a starting point, Annex VI of the Prospectus Directive Regulation (which **3.162** applies whether the offering is retail or wholesale) requires:

- a description of the guarantee (and any other arrangement amounting substantively to a guarantee, such as surety, keep well agreements, mono-insurance policies or similar);[140]
- the terms and conditions of such guarantee;[141] and
- information about the guarantor (or, if there is more than one, each guarantor) 'as if it were the issuer of that same type of security that is the subject of the guarantee'.[142]

This means that the prospectus or base prospectus must contain both a descrip- **3.163** tion of the guarantee arrangements themselves, and the same information about each guarantor as is provided in relation to the issuer. Physically, this information can be provided in the prospectus or base prospectus by including a separate section about the guarantor or (if relevant) about each guarantor. An alternative approach is to combine much of the information relating to the guarantor or each guarantor, for example the business description, with information relating to the issuer in relevant sections. In fact, where the issuer is a finance subsidiary or other special purpose company, the principle credit will be the guarantor or guarantors and the main focus of the prospectus or base prospectus will be in relation to it (or them) rather than the issuer, which may well only merit a small amount of space, especially if it has been newly incorporated for the purpose of the issue!

Whichever approach is used, each item in Annex IV (in the case of a retail issue or **3.164** programme) or Annex IX (in the case of a wholesale issue or programme) of the Prospectus Directive Regulation must be clearly and specifically addressed in the prospectus or base prospectus in respect separately of each of the issuer and any guarantor. As a practical matter, the regulatory authority of the relevant EEA home member state reviewing the prospectus or base prospectus will likely require the submission of separate checklists demonstrating compliance with Annex IV or Annex IX (as relevant) in relation to the guarantor (or each guarantor) in just the same way as for the issuer.[143]

Perhaps the main question in relation to what information is required in a pro- **3.165** spectus or base prospectus in respect of a guarantor or guarantors, relates to what financial information is required to be included. The starting point set out in the

---

[140] AnnexVI(1).
[141] AnnexVI(2).
[142] AnnexVI(3).
[143] See Section 3.6 below.

Prospectus Directive Regulation[144] is that the included financial information should be the same as if the guarantor were the issuer of the relevant securities. In the case of a guarantor of a retail offering of debt securities, this would mean that two years (assuming that the guarantor has been in operation for at least that period of time) of audited consolidated financial statements of the guarantor (or each guarantor) prepared according to IAS/IFRS or to an 'equivalent'[145] standard (in the case of a guarantor from a 'third' country) are required to be included in the prospectus or base prospectus.

3.166   In fact, the position is not quite this simple in two particular respects:

- *Multiple guarantors*: if (i) the issuer and all guarantors together represent substantially all of the assets of the group and (ii) the consolidated financial statements of the holding company of the group are included in the prospectus or base prospectus, then it can be seen that the inclusion in the base prospectus of individual accounts by each guarantor may well add little information compared to the group's consolidated financial statements. On this basis, a number of regulatory authorities may be willing to allow the omission of separate financial statements for each guarantor[146] provided that the issuer and the guarantor or guarantors together represent substantially all of the assets of the group and are reflected in the consolidated financial statements of the group holding company which are contained in or incorporated by reference into the prospectus or base prospectus.

- *Applicable accounting and audit standards*: the starting point in the Prospectus Directive Regulation is again, on a literal reading, that a guarantor's accounts that are required to be included in the prospectus or base prospectus should be prepared as though it were an issuer, that is in accordance with IAS/IFRS (or 'equivalent') or, if not applicable, to a member state's national accounting standards. Under the IAS Regulation,[147] a company is required to prepare its accounts in accordance with IAS/IFRS if it (i) prepares consolidated accounts and (ii) has securities admitted to trading on an EEA regulated market. However, a company that does not itself have securities admitted to trading on an EEA regulated market is not required under the IAS Regulation to prepare its consolidated accounts in accordance with IAS/IFRS. To require it to do so simply because it is a guarantor of debt securities of another company (even if it a member of its group) which are admitted to trading on an EEA regulated market, would be

---

[144] Prospectus Directive Regulation Annex VI(3).

[145] See 'Financial Statements' in Section 3.5.6.

[146] Presumably under the 'not pertinent' provisions of the Prospectus Directive Regulation Article 23(4) or the 'minor importance' provisions in the Prospectus Directive Article 8(2)(c).

[147] EC No 1606/2002.

imposing a requirement beyond that of the IAS Regulation. The position in relation to the required accounting standards of a guarantor's consolidated accounts is therefore different to those of an issuer and an EEA guarantor may therefore include consolidated accounts in the prospectus or base prospectus that are not prepared in accordance with IAS/IFRS, an approach that an issuer would not itself be entitled to adopt.[148]

Logically, the position for a guarantor incorporated outside the EEA, i.e. in a third country, should be substantially the same. There is no obligation under the Transparency Directive[149] for guarantors to prepare and file financial information prepared in accordance with IAS or 'equivalent' on a continuing basis. On this basis, there would seem to be little purpose in requiring a non-EEA guarantor to prepare financial information in accordance with IAS or 'equivalent' for the purposes of the prospectus or base prospectus, where there is no obligation on it to prepare accounts on that basis (or indeed, any other basis) going forwards. However, this apparently logical position is not supported by the wording of Annex IV of the Prospectus Directive Regulation.[150]   **3.167**

3.5.14 Taxation

The requirements of the Prospectus Directive Regulation[151] to include informa-   **3.168**
tion on taxation in a prospectus or base prospectus for debt securities have caused some confusion since their implementation. In particular, there was some confusion as to whether any disclosure was required to be made by the issuer in relation to the tax treatment of investors in its debt securities. The Prospectus Directive Regulation is reasonably clear that the only information that is required to be disclosed is that in relation to withholding taxes. The CESR FAQs[152] confirm that view though they comment that 'a statement in the tax section of the prospectus inviting investors to seek appropriate advice on their specific situation is strongly recommended'. A more complete taxation section may be provided if that is thought helpful for marketing purposes, but is not required and most taxation sections in a prospectus or base prospectus will therefore be fairly short and only address withholding on account of taxation in the place of incorporation of the issuer, where any public offering is being made and where the debt securities concerned are being admitted to trading.

---

[148] See List! No 13 (September 2006).
[149] Directive 2004/109/EC.
[150] See Paragraph 13.1 of Annex IV.
[151] Annex V(4.14).
[152] CESR FAQ 45.

3.6 Approval Process for the Prospectus or Base Prospectus

3.6.1 Introduction

3.169 The detailed approval process for a prospectus for a stand-alone issue or for debt issuance programme base prospectus will vary depending upon the home member state that is to actually approve the prospectus. As a general point, it is not worth submitting a draft base prospectus to the approving authority unless it is in reasonably final form. Of course, changes can always be made to the prospectus after it has been submitted for approval at any time up until formal approval of the base prospectus for publication purposes. Small changes probably won't much affect the timing of approval, but more substantial changes may well delay the process.

3.170 The Prospectus Directive[153] gives the reviewing authority ten working days to respond (with approval or more likely questions and comments) to a draft prospectus that has been submitted to it. This time limit will only start running if the submission formalities have been observed (see below). Further, the ten-working-day period only applies to an issuer that already has securities admitted to trading on a regulated market and that has previously offered securities to the public.[154] Many issuers under debt issuance programmes are likely (though not necessarily) to fall within this category and so are likely to be able to take advantage of the 'fast-track' approval process. If not, then the review time limit extends to 20 working days.

3.171 However, before assuming that a prospectus or base prospectus can be submitted to a regulatory authority and approved within two weeks (or four weeks for a new issuer), issuers should be aware that the approval clock is set back to zero each time the reviewing authority makes comments on the draft base prospectus that are reflected in a revised draft, from the time that the revised draft is resubmitted to the reviewing authority.[155] So the original ten-working-day limit can in practice extend out for a rather longer period if the reviewing authority does in fact respond with comments and questions, as it inevitably will even in respect of the best draft document.

3.172 In fact, many regulatory authorities will respond to a revised draft prospectus or base prospectus rather more quickly than the first draft, so that the timetable does not in reality expand by 10 working days for each resubmission. In the final stages of revising and resubmitting the base prospectus, the reviewing authority may

---

[153] Prospectus Directive Article 13.
[154] Prospectus Directive Article 13(3).
[155] Prospectus Directive Article 13(4).

well be prepared to respond within a short period—within the same day if changes are relatively minor and the process is nearing its conclusion. As a rule of thumb, if the issuer and its advisers resubmit a draft prospectus or base prospectus within a day or so of receiving comments from the reviewing regulatory authority, and assuming that the prospectus has been properly prepared so that it complies in all substantial respects with the regulatory requirements, then an issuer can expect its base prospectus to be approved, in the ordinary course, within four to five weeks of first submission to the reviewing regulatory authority. This is not an absolute, and is only a guide. Approval times may be shorter if (for whatever reason) the reviewing regulatory authority staff are not particularly busy and it is also likely to be an easier and quicker process if the draft base prospectus closely follows the form and content (other than updating) of a prospectus previously approved by that authority. For example, the annual update of a debt issuance programme base prospectus with the same regulatory authority is likely to be a quicker process than the approval process for a debt issuance programme that is being newly established. Some regulatory authorities commit to provide comments on the first and subsequent drafts more quickly than they are strictly required to do and it may therefore be possible to shorten the above indicative timing.

3.6.2 Which stock exchange and reviewing authority?

An initial question to be answered is which stock exchange should be chosen as the principle stock exchange for a stand-alone prospectus or base prospectus for a debt issuance programme? As previously noted, provided the debt securities concerned have a denomination of at least EUR 1,000 (or its equivalent in other currencies), the issuer is free to choose whichever member state it wishes as its home member state. This choice will in practice be driven by the location of the chosen stock exchange for the listing (assuming the debt securities are to be listed) and this in turn will determine which regulatory authority reviews and approves the draft prospectus or base prospectus. So, for example, if the issuer were to select the Luxembourg Stock Exchange as the principle market for its offering or programme, it would be usual for the base prospectus to be submitted for approval to the Commission de Surveillance du Secteur Financier ('CSSF'), in which case Luxembourg would be the home member state for the purposes of the prospectus or base prospectus. It is important to realize that this would be a choice of home member state solely for the purposes of that offering or debt issuance programme. The issuer would be free to choose any other EEA member state as its home member state for the approval of a prospectus relating to other securities. This is of course subject to the mandatory home member state rules[156] that apply in the case of equity and low-denomination debt (i.e. debt securities having a denomination

3.173

---

[156] Prospectus Directive Article 2(1)(m).

of less than EUR 1,000 (or its equivalent in other currencies) where the home member state will be where the issuer has its registered office. Subject to this, issuers of debt securities are free to choose any stock exchange and any EEA member state as the home member state for the purposes of reviewing and approving the prospectus or base prospectus.

3.6.3 Approval process formalities

3.174 Each home member state regulatory authority will have its own detailed procedures and requirements for the review and approval process of a draft prospectus or base prospectus. As noted above, the Prospectus Directive sets out basic provisions on timing of the approval process.[157] Beyond that, the detailed procedures will be as specified by the relevant regulatory authority.

3.175 By way of example, the UK Listing Authority ('UKLA') requires:

- Submission of the draft of the prospectus or base prospectus itself,[158] which must be in a 'substantially complete form'.[159] The UKLA is the only regulatory authority that requires the draft prospectus or base prospectus (other than in the case of an update) to be annotated in its margins with cross references that match the annotated content in the prospectus or base prospectus to the relevant requirements of the Annexes to the Prospectus Directive Regulation. So, for example, alongside any disclosure in relation to litigation involving the issuer, there will be an annotation 'AIV 13.6'. The practical and logistical challenge of running these annotations against a changing draft and at the same time matching those annotations against the contents of the checklist (see below) should not be underestimated, particularly in the context of the time pressures that are often imposed on advisers by their clients. As a final complication, the UKLA requires revised drafts of prospectuses to be marked to show changes from the previous draft, but in a way that distinguishes between changes that have been made to address comments on the previous draft by the UKLA reader from other changes made in the new draft.[160] Since there can be any number of intermediate drafts between the previous form submitted to the UKLA and the revised draft submitted to the UKLA in response to its comments, tight version control of the draft prospectus or base prospectus is essential.
- The relevant review request form (Form A).[161]

---

[157] Prospectus Directive Article 13.
[158] Prospectus Rule 3.1.1(2).
[159] Prospectus Rule 3.1.1.
[160] Prospectus Rule 3.1.5(2).
[161] Prospectus Rule 3.1.1(1).

- If the order of contents of the draft prospectus or base prospectus does not exactly match that required by the relevant Annexes of the Prospectus Directive Regulation, a checklist demonstrating compliance with the relevant Annexes of the Prospectus Directive Regulation.[162] The checklist must be submitted with the draft prospectus or base prospectus and with each subsequent revised draft listing the items in the Annexes and indicating against each one exactly where in the draft prospectus the information required by that item in that Annex can be found. Whilst a prospectus or base prospectus that follows precisely the order set out in the relevant annexes brings with it the significant advantage of not having to file a checklist with the reviewing authority, so doing will involve a conscious decision to forsake elegant prose in favour of dispensing with the checklist requirement. The result can be a rather stilted and reader-unfriendly document. Checklists are therefore, for the most part, a somewhat tedious fact of life for those involved in the prospectus approval process with regulatory authorities.
- A 'non-applicable' letter (if relevant) setting out items that have not been included in the prospectus or base prospectus (as otherwise required by the relevant Annexes) on grounds that they are not applicable to the particular prospectus or base prospectus.[163]
- A copy of any document which contains information that is to be incorporated by reference into the prospectus or base prospectus. As with the draft prospectus, each document must be annotated in the margin to demonstrate which provision of the applicable Annexes of the Prospectus Directive Regulation it addresses.[164]
- If the issuer wishes to omit from its prospectus or base prospectus items of information that are otherwise required by applicable Annexes to the Prospectus Directive Regulation, a written submission must be made to the relevant regulatory authority stating what is to be omitted, the particular reasons for the issuer wishing to omit that information and the justification (by reference to section 87B(1) of the Financial Services and Markets Act 2000 which implements Article 8 of the Prospective Directive) for the omission. The permitted justifications are that:
  - disclosure would be contrary to the public interest;
  - disclosure would be 'seriously detrimental' to the issuer (which is only permitted as a ground of omission if so doing would be unlikely to mislead the public); and
  - the information omitted is only of minor importance in the context of the particular offer.

---

[162] Prospectus Rule 3.1.1(3).
[163] Prospectus Rule 3.1.1(4).
[164] Prospectus Rule 3.1.1(5).

Historically, omissions of this kind have been relatively uncommon. A point to note if there is a permitted omission, then the passporting procedure for the prospectus or base prospectus will need to include the fact of omission in the home member state's Certificate of Approval together with the justification for any such omission. Whilst Article 18 of the Prospectus Directive does not appear to contemplate that a host member state might be able to review the fact of omission and the justification for so doing, there is a possibility that having to address omissions in passporting procedures might complicate or delay passporting procedures. It is worth noting that Article 23(4) of the Prospectus Directive Regulation permits the omission of information which is otherwise required where that information '*is not pertinent to the issuer, to the offer or to the securities to which the prospectus relates*'. No doubt the operation of this provision should be discussed in any given case with the regulatory authority concerned.

- Contact details of persons who can answer questions on the documentation.[165]
- Payment of review fee.[166]

3.176 The above submission formalities are based upon those of the UKLA and as set out in its Prospectus Rules and may be varied in practice. The procedures for other regulatory authorities differ in detail and mechanics. For example in Luxembourg, is it relatively normal (though not essential) for the entire submission process with the CSSF to be handled by a Luxembourg listing agent. Nevertheless, the substance of the above procedures is likely to be largely reflected in the procedures of most regulatory authorities.

3.6.4 Review and approval process

3.177 The approval process, once an initial draft of the prospectus or base prospectus has been submitted for approval as described above, is an iterative one.

3.178 Within (hopefully) the 10-business-day or 20-business-day (as applicable) time limit mentioned above, the reviewing regulatory authority will respond to the issuer or its advisers with a list of its written comments or questions on the draft prospectus or base prospectus that was submitted to it for review.

3.179 It is difficult to generalize about what comments the reviewing authority might raise, and much depends of course on the quality (generally in the compliance sense) of the draft document submitted for review, but here are a few likely ones:

- Simple failure to address each item required by the relevant Annexes. This should not happen, of course, if the checklist is properly compiled and on its face demonstrates that each item has been addressed in the draft document.

---

[165] Prospectus Rule 3.1.1(9).
[166] Prospectus Rule 3.1.3(1)(b).

Whilst the checklist process may be regarded as a tedious one, it is a required part of the Prospectus Directive Regulation.[167]

- Discrepancy between the reference provided in the checklist and the apparent content in the cited location within the draft prospectus or base prospectus. The reader of the document at the regulatory authority is unlikely to be willing to spend much time searching other pages for compliance with incorrect cross-references. A poorly completed checklist can delay the entire prospectus approval process.

- In the case of submissions to the UKLA, discrepancies between margin annotation and the apparently annotated contents of the prospectus or base prospectus. Again, the UKLA reader is unlikely to be willing to spend time puzzling over whether the draft document really addresses the margin annotation.

- The reviewing authority generally won't comment on whether risk factors are relevant to the particular issuer or whether additional risk factors should be included.[168]

- Questions are often raised around the incorporation by reference tables if, as is often the case, incorporation by reference is utilized in a prospectus or base prospectus. However, advisers have become more familiar with the likely requirements of the regulatory authorities in relation to incorporation by reference procedures in recent times, and by, in particular, providing detailed tabulation of information incorporated by reference, comments from regulatory authority readers are fortunately becoming less frequent on this subject.

- A prospectus or base prospectus for debt securities is not required to include profit forecasts or pro-forma financial information. However, if either of these are included, they must comply (in the case of a profit forecast) with Annex IV(9) of the Prospectus Directive Regulation or (in the case of pro-forma financial statements) with Annex II of the Prospectus Directive Regulation (save for the requirement to include an auditor's report). Both should in any event comply with the relevant recommendations set out in CESR Guidance. Detailed comments and questions on both profit forecasts (and their underlying assumptions and methodology) and pro-formas, if either of them are included in the document, are almost invariable.

- Where an issuer makes statements or claims about its competitive position, then the Prospectus Directive Regulation[169] requires any such statement or claim to be substantiated. To do so may require reference back to independent third-party sources. If those sources are public (and generally made) then they can be referred to in the prospectus or base prospectus without anything further. However, if they are not public then the approval of that third party

---

[167] Prospectus Directive Regulation Article 26(3).
[168] However, see the recent comments of the UKLA referred to in Section 3.5.4.
[169] Prospectus Directive Regulation Annex IV(6.3) and Annex IX(5.1.2).

will be required, something which is not always necessarily forthcoming, or forthcoming without payment of a fee! The choice in these circumstances will be to pay the fee or delete or modify the claim

- Certain statements required by the relevant Annexes to the Prospectus Directive Regulation require a particular form of words to be included in the prospectus or base prospectus. So, for example, Paragraph 8.1 of Annex IV requires there to be a statement that 'there has been no material adverse change in the prospects of the *issuer* since the date of its last published audited financial statements'. In contrast, Paragraph 13.7 of the same Annex requires a description of 'any significant change in the financial or trading position of the *group* which has occurred since the end of the last financial period for which either audited financial information or interim financial information has been published, or an appropriate negative statement'. So there is plenty of scope for confusion and mistakes are frequently made, not least because of differences in the formulations of the wording which are difficult to understand. So for example:
  - one of these rules requires a statement in relation to the issuer;[170] the other requires a statement in relation to the group.[171]
  - one requires a statement to be made in respect of the period since the date of the latest audited accounts;[172] the other requires a statement to be made from the date of the latest audited accounts or the most recent interim accounts, whichever is the most recent.[173]
- Paragraph 13.6 of Annex IV requires, in relation to legal and arbitration proceedings, disclosure of proceedings 'during a period covering at least the previous 12 months which may have, or have had in the recent past, significant effects on the issuer and/or group's financial position or profitability, or provide an appropriate negative statement'.

3.180 It is possible, of course, that the differences in the formulation of these paragraphs in Annex IV (and indeed, in corresponding paragraphs in other Annexes to the Prospectus Directive Regulation) are deliberate and reflect their particular subject matter and implementation of a coherent policy decision, and are not designed simply as a trap for the unwary!

3.181 Following receipt of comments from the reviewing regulatory authority, the issuer or its advisers amend the draft prospectus or base prospectus to reflect those comments and re-submit a revised draft prospectus or base prospectus to the reviewing regulatory authority. This revised draft will need to be accompanied by a revised checklist (because all those page numbers in the cross-references to the draft

---

[170] Annex IV(8.1).
[171] Annex IV(13.7).
[172] Annex IV(8.1).
[173] Annex IV(13.7).

prospectus or base prospectus will likely have changed). The revised draft will also need to be accompanied by a response to the questions, comments or requests for explanation or further information which were made by the regulatory authority, either pointing out where changes have been made to the draft or explaining why changes or further information requested to be made or included by the regulatory authority have not be fulfilled.

The precise manner in which responses are communicated back to the reviewing regulatory authority will depend on the procedures of that particular authority. The UKLA provides its comments on a draft prospectus or base prospectus through a 'comment sheet'. It expects the comment sheet to be returned to it with the revised draft prospectus with a written addition to each comment raised indicating compliance with the comment, providing further information or explaining why a particular change has not been made. On the other hand, the CSSF typically responds to draft documents submitted for review through the listing agent by a series of comments, questions or requests and these will be responded to individually by the listing agent. **3.182**

Finally, after several drafts and redrafts of the prospectus or base prospectus have been submitted and resubmitted and after the iterative process of comments, questions and responses between the issuer, its advisers (including in Luxembourg, the listing agent) and the reviewing regulatory authority have finally run their course, the regulatory authority will finally confirm that it has no further comments or questions on the draft prospectus or base prospectus. At this point, the prospectus or base prospectus is ready for formal approval. **3.183**

3.6.5 Approval of a prospectus or base prospectus

Again, the exact rules and procedures for the approval of a draft prospectus or base prospectus for publication (and therefore allowing any particular public offering of debt securities or admission to trading of debt securities on an EEA regulated market) will vary depending upon the regulatory authority concerned. **3.184**

Regulatory authorities will only approve a prospectus or base prospectus that is dated and will only approve it on the day that matches the date appearing on the prospectus. This may seem obvious, but actually can cause practical timing difficulties if outstanding comments by the regulatory authority are still being resolved or if, as is now fortunately rarely the case, the regulatory authority concerned is unwilling to indicate precisely when final formal approval might be forthcoming. It is fair to say that most regulatory authorities now understand the practical time constraints within which issuers are operating and are generally cooperative (within their own regulatory and resource constraints) so as to help an issuer meet a targeted publication date for its prospectus or base prospectus. **3.185**

3.186 Final approval of the prospectus or base prospectus can be indicated by a letter to the issuer (as is the practice of the Luxembourg CSSF) or by an approval stamp appearing on the front page of the prospectus or base prospectus (as is the practice of the UKLA).

3.6.6 Publication requirements

3.187 Once a prospectus or base prospectus has been approved by the relevant regulatory authority, it must be published '*as soon as practicable*'.[174] In practice, this normally means the same day as its approval. It must not be published until it has been approved.[175]

3.188 The permitted mechanics (and only permitted methods) by which publication may take place are set out in the Prospectus Directive and are:

- newspaper advertisement where the newspaper concerned is widely circulated in the member state(s) in which the offer to the public is being made or admission to trading is being sought.[176] This method of publication is unlikely to be much used in practice due to (i) its expense (ii) the impracticality of publishing today's monster prospectuses in a newspaper (there would be no room left for any news) and (iii) the lead time necessary to coordinate such publication.
- in printed form available to the public at 'the offices of the market on which the securities are being admitted to trading, or at the registered office of the issuer and at the offices of the financial intermediaries placing or selling the securities, including paying agents'.[177] This is a more likely method of publication from an issuer's perspective, though it still has some practical drawbacks. Many stock exchanges are unlikely to be willing to provide facilities for members of the public to obtain hard copies of prospectuses. This means that it may well be necessary to resort to the fallback position of public availability from the issuer's registered office (which should not be difficult) *and* from the offices of financial intermediaries and paying agents. Again, the financial intermediaries and paying agents may be reluctant to provide public facilities of this kind, even when it is pointed out to them that they are unlikely to be faced with queues of clamouring investors. Nevertheless, this route of publication is a realistic one should others be unavailable for any reason.
- 'In an electronic form on the issuer's website and, if applicable, on the website of the financial intermediaries placing or selling the securities, including paying agents.'[178] The obvious drawback with this method of publication is that even

---

174 Prospectus Directive Article 14(1).
175 Prospectus Directive Article 13(1).
176 Prospectus Directive Article 14(2)(a).
177 Prospectus Directive Article 14(2)(b).
178 Prospectus Directive Article 14(2)(c).

though an issuer may well wish to include the prospectus or base prospectus on its website (subject to regulatory restrictions), financial intermediaries and paying agents are unlikely to be willing to provide website facilities for issuers. Whilst there may be scope for debate as to exactly what 'if applicable' means in any particular case, generally this is unlikely to be an attractive method of publication.

- 'In electronic form on the website of the competent authority of the home member state if the said authority has decided to offer this service.'[179] Some regulatory authorities (such as Ireland) helpfully provide such a facility and automatically file an approved prospectus or base prospectus on their website. Others (such as the UKLA) do not provide such a facility.
- 'In an electronic form on the website of the regulated market where the admission to trading is sought.'[180] Where filing on the website of the regulatory authority of the home member state isn't possible, this is the usual alternative method of publication (for example in the United Kingdom through an RIS announcement).

It should be noted that regulatory authorities may well have other formal filing **3.189** requirements—for example the UKLA requires prospectuses to be made available at its document viewing facility ('DVF'), though it should also be noted that filing with the DVF does not of itself constitute formal publication for Prospectus Directive purposes. Some issuers also may believe that maintaining a prospectus or base prospectus on its website itself constitutes sufficient publication. As can be seen from the methods highlighted above, it does not and one of the other methods should also be used, normally by filing the approved prospectus or base prospectus onto the website of the regulatory authority or stock exchange concerned.

Where documents are incorporated by reference into a prospectus or base pro- **3.190** spectus, those documents must also have been published by one of the methods set out above.[181]

Prospectus supplements and final terms in respect of debt securities issued under **3.191** a programme's base prospectus must also be published by one of the methods specified above.

3.7 Prospectus Supplements

3.7.1 When is a supplement to the base prospectus required?

Article 16 of the Prospectus Directive, which sets out when a supplement to **3.192** a prospectus is required, has been one of the most debated of its provisions,

---

[179] Prospectus Directive Article 14(2)(e).
[180] Prospectus Directive Article 14(2)(d).
[181] Prospectus Directive Article 14(5).

particularly in the context of debt issuance programmes. Whilst the provisions of Article 16 are just as important and, in some cases, as difficult to apply in offerings of other types of securities, there are particular complications for debt issuance programmes that make the practical operation of Article 16 even more challenging.

3.193 These particular difficulties arise in the context of debt issuance programmes for two main reasons:

- First, whilst under Article 9 of the Prospectus Directive all prospectuses have a theoretical life of 12 months, in practice (though, admittedly, practice does vary between different markets within the EU) a prospectus other than a base prospectus is only likely to be used for a particular single offering (or conceivably, several offerings over a relatively short period of time) and is unlikely in reality to be 'live' for the full 12-months theoretical period. Whilst this might also be the case, in practice, for debt issuance programmes, in the case of frequent issuers under such programmes it will not be the case and they will wish to keep the base prospectus fully up to date throughout its life (in other words, on a continuous basis) with as little 'down time' for the debt issuance programme as possible. This is because an issuer under a debt issuance programme, particularly in volatile or fragile market conditions, may well want to be able to move quickly to get a debt issuance away at short notice so as to be able to take advantage of perhaps fleetingly favourable market conditions. Senior management of such an issuer are likely to be unimpressed by a response from the issuer's legal department or external legal advisers that a favourable market window can't be accessed within the preferred timetable because the base prospectus requires a supplement!

- The second main reason for a particular focus on Article 16 of the Prospectus Directive in the case of debt issuance programmes, arises from the mechanical aspects of actually carrying out an issuance by means of preparation, publication and filing of final terms. The ability to issue debt securities under a programme simply by preparing and publishing final terms,[182] has to be considered against the provisions of Article 16, and in particular in respect of the point at which information relating to the particular drawdown under the programme cannot simply be included in the final terms for that drawdown but must be included in the base prospectus by way of preparation and publication of a supplement under Article 16. This point is considered in more detail below.[183]

3.194 The debate around the operation of Article 16 is not just a theoretical one. If a decision is taken not to supplement the base prospectus and that decision is wrong,

---

[182] Prospectus Directive Article 5(4).
[183] See Section 3.7.2.

then the base prospectus will no longer comply with the Prospectus Directive and will expose the issuer to potential liability. If the relevant information is contained in the final terms rather than in a prospectus supplement, there is a possibility that the regulatory authority with whom those final terms are filed for the purposes of the drawdown, may reject the final terms as demonstrating non-compliance with the Prospectus Directive. Finally, and importantly, if a decision is taken that a supplement to the base prospectus is required, the preparation and approval process for that supplement inevitably involves the time taken to prepare the supplement, submit it to the relevant reviewing regulatory authority, possibly receive comments on the supplement from that authority, implement those comments and resubmit to the reviewing regulatory authority, obtaining approval of the supplement and finally publication of that supplement in accordance with the Prospectus Directive.[184]

Finally, and in some cases at least, most importantly, the publication of a prospectus supplement triggers 'withdrawal' or 'walk-away' rights for investors under Article 16(2) of the Prospectus Directive. That paragraph states that 'investors who have already agreed to purchase or subscribe for the securities before the supplement is published shall have the right, exercisable within a time limit which shall not be shorter than 2 working days after the publication of the supplement, to withdraw their acceptances'. The practical application of Article 16 is not necessarily that easy to construe. Who are 'investors' for these purposes? They may well include underwriters or dealers under a debt issuance programme though this is likely to be something of an academic debate since the underlying documents (and in particular the underwriting agreement or dealer or programme agreement) will likely specifically provide that the obligations of the underwriters or dealers to purchase the relevant debt securities will be subject to the condition that no supplement to the prospectus or base prospectus is required to be published or has been published prior to closing of the drawdown. **3.195**

Alternatively, Article 16 may entitle placees for the debt securities found by the underwriters or dealers to withdraw from their commitments, though from the issuer's perspective whether or not this is the case is also likely to be pretty academic due to the provisions of the underwriting agreement or dealer or programme agreement referred to earlier. **3.196**

The short point is that the publication of a supplement to the prospectus or base prospectus during the course of an offering is something that an issuer (as well as the underwriters or dealers) will be very keen to avoid. In the case of a base prospectus for a programme, this means that any supplement will have to have been **3.197**

---

[184] See Section 3.8.

prepared, approved and published before the launch of any issue of debt securities under the programme, giving rise to the timing implications described earlier.

3.7.2 What factors might require a supplement to a prospectus or base prospectus?

3.198 Article 16(1) of the Prospectus Directive states that:

> every significant new factor, material mistake or inaccuracy relating to the information included in the prospectus which is capable of affecting the assessment of the securities and which arises or is noted between the time when the prospectus is approved and the final closing date of the offer to the public or, as the case may be, the time when trading on a regulated market begins, shall be mentioned in a supplement to the prospectus.

3.199 This is no doubt a perfectly appropriate definition of when a prospectus supplement is needed. Rightly, but unhelpfully for legal and other advisers, it leaves as a matter of judgment whether the new factor, mistake or inaccuracy is '*significant*' or '*material*'. The further test that such an event is '*capable of affecting the assessment of the securities*' doesn't really add anything to the paragraph.

3.200 Leaving aside mistakes or inaccuracies (which would bring with them their own particular problems), there are two main types of 'new factor' that need to be considered in the context of a prospectus or base prospectus and any final terms. These are, first, developments affecting the issuer or its business generally and, second, particular matters that affect the securities which are proposed to be issued under a debt issuance programme and which go beyond what is already provided for or anticipated in the base prospectus.

3.201 The rules for determining whether a supplement to a prospectus is needed for a development that affects the issuer or its business generally is no different for a base prospectus than a stand-alone prospectus. In practice, the question is of more relevance for a base prospectus because of the greater likelihood of it occurring (see above). There may also be a different result for any given new development depending on whether the prospectus concerned relates to equity compared to debt. It is quite difficult to formulate a coherent test for any distinction in the operation of Article 16 between equity and debt other than to note that as a general proposition the significance or materiality test may be more sensitive in the context of equity than for debt where, in theory at least, the main concern of a holder of debt securities is to determine how likely (or otherwise) it is that the issuer will be able to meet its obligations under those debt securities.

3.202 If an issuer of debt securities or an issuer under a debt programme already has debt or other securities admitted to trading on an EEA regulated market, then it will also be required to disclose 'inside information' under the Market Abuse Directive as implemented in relevant member states. For example, an issuer with debt securities admitted to trading on the London Stock Exchange's regulated market will be required to comply with the ad hoc disclosure provisions of DTR 2 of the Disclosure and Transparency Rules of the FSA.

The language in Article 16 of the Prospectus Directive is of course different to the ongoing disclosure obligations in relation to 'inside information' for the purposes of the Market Abuse Directive.[185] Nevertheless, as a broad proposition, it is likely that any information which is required to be disclosed on an ongoing basis under the Market Abuse Directive[186] will also need to be included into a live prospectus or base prospectus by means of a prospectus supplement under Article 16 of the Prospectus Directive. Whilst theoretically the same may be true the other way round, since Article 16 requires a supplement in relation to new factors which are '*capable of affecting the assessment of the securities*', it is not necessarily the case that an Article 16 prospectus supplement would also trigger a requirement to disclose the subject matter of that supplement as inside information under the Market Abuse Directive. This is the case not least because supplements may deal with routine matters that are not price sensitive or may incorporate by reference, for example, annual or half-year financial statements or interim management statements that have already been announced under the relevant provisions of the Transparency Directive.[187]

3.203

Whilst the following is by no means intended to be exhaustive, here are some examples of when a prospectus or a base prospectus in relation to a debt issuance programme may require a supplement to be prepared and published under Article 16 of the Prospectus Directive:

3.204

- significant business acquisitions or disposals;
- changes (negative or positive) in the business or prospects or ratings of the issuer;
- subject to what is said below, publication of annual financial statements, interim financial statements or interim management statements;
- details of a new development giving rise to an ad hoc 'inside information' announcement under the Market Abuse Directive;
- new litigation, or developments (such as findings, settlement or withdrawal) of litigation already disclosed in the prospectus or base prospectus.

Of course, not all matters that have changed since the date the prospectus or base prospectus was originally published will need to be reflected in a supplement, since not everything contained in the prospectus is 'significant' and therefore changes in such circumstances may well not merit publication of a supplement

3.205

---

[185] Directive 2003/6/EC.
[186] Market Abuse Directive Article 6(1).
[187] Directive 2004/109/EC.

and can instead (in the case of a base prospectus) wait until the time of the next normal annual or other update of the debt issuance programme as a whole.

3.206 The second category of 'significant new factor' which may be required to be included in a base prospectus can arise as a result of particular features of securities that are proposed to be issued under the debt issuance programme. If the base prospectus does not already envisage the issuance of those securities or of debt securities of that class, then it may be necessary to supplement the base prospectus to provide for such issuance.

3.207 For example, if an issuer proposes to issue subordinated debt securities under its debt issuance programme and the base prospectus does not already envisage the issuance of subordinated debt and set out terms and conditions effecting subordination, then the base prospectus for that programme may well have to be updated to address the possibility of issuance of subordinated debt. Changes are also likely to be needed to the summary (if there is one) and risk factors (since subordinated debt carries its own particular risks compared with senior debt). Changes will also need to be made to the terms and conditions of the debt securities as set out in the base prospectus to include subordination and any other relevant provisions. The addition of subordinated debt to a debt issuance programme that previously only contemplated senior debt is probably an example of where a base prospectus needs to be amended by way of supplement under Article 16 of the Prospectus Directive rather than through, for example, simply the addition of subordination language in the final terms for those debt securities. However, it is fully acknowledged that practice may vary considerably on this point as between different practitioners and within different legal markets and there is no absolute right or wrong answer on the point.

3.208 By way of contrast, another example might be where the particular debt securities proposed to be issued are to have a coupon which is to be calculated by reference to a formula that is not already envisaged or set out in the terms and conditions in the base prospectus. In this circumstance, many practitioners would probably say that it is sufficient for the final terms in relation to that particular issue of debt securities to set out that formula for the calculation of the coupon and that a supplement to the base prospectus is not necessary.

3.209 The practical difficulty is in determining the point at which, on the one hand, particular information (such as the formula referred to earlier) merely 'completes' the base prospectus (and so can be included in the final terms without anything further being required) or, on the other hand, the point at which the information becomes a 'significant new factor' which arguably cannot be dealt with simply by inclusion in final terms (for example, provisions for the issuance of subordinated debt as referred to above) and which therefore also needs to be dealt with by way of supplement to the base prospectus. There is one other practical solution to this, the issue of a so called 'drawdown prospectus' which is considered further below.

The practical difficulty in determining when a prospectus supplement or draw-   **3.210**
down prospectus (see below) is required is that there is an inherent contradiction between the Prospectus Directive and the Prospectus Directive Regulation on the point. On the one hand, both deliberately allow for the possibility of debt issuance programmes and recognize the need for flexibility as to what securities can be issued under that programme in the future. Specifically, the Prospectus Directive Regulation[188] states that 'the issuer ... may omit information items which are not known when the base prospectus is approved and which can only be determined at the time of the individual issue ...'. On the other hand, the Prospectus Directive Regulation[189] also says that 'with respect to base prospectuses, it should be set out in an easily identifiable manner which kind of information will have to be included as final terms'. As an observation, it isn't necessarily easy for a base prospectus to anticipate the information items which are not known when the base prospectus is approved. The question therefore is, to the extent that a base prospectus does not anticipate a particular feature of the debt securities to be issued, at what point is it sufficient for that feature to be included in the final terms or alternatively at what point must a supplement to the base prospectus or drawdown prospectus be prepared and published?

It seems reasonably clear that splitting a prospectus into two for the purposes of a   **3.211**
debt issuance programme (i.e. into a base prospectus and final terms) is derogation from the general requirement that a prospectus should contain all information that is material to an investor. To this extent, it seems clear that information is permitted to be included in final terms that would otherwise have been required to be included in the prospectus at the time of original publication or by way of prospectus supplement or drawdown prospectus. The practical difficulty is that common sense dictates that at some point a minimum level of information must be contained in the base prospectus. Little explicit guidance is to be found in either the Prospectus Directive or the Prospectus Directive Regulation as to where that particular line is to be drawn.

It is tempting to say that any information that amounts to a 'significant new   **3.212**
factor' for the purposes of Article 16 of the Prospectus Directive must be incorporated into a prospectus supplement. However, on its own, this approach cannot be right as much of the information that is generally permitted to be included in final terms (such as the offer price, principle amount, coupon etc.) is clearly significant.

---

[188] See Article 22.
[189] See Recital 26.

3.213 CESR has published in its FAQs some guidance on this point.[190] The response to the question in its FAQs is to acknowledge the practical difficulties and inconsistency of application of the relevant rules and to emphasize flexibility and pragmatism of approach (but not to the point of abuse) by regulatory authorities. The FAQ also helpfully states that: 'It should also be noted that the [Prospectus] Directive is intended to regulate disclosure of information rather than to regulate products that are appropriate to be offered to the public. Thus, there is usually no need to require information specific to a certain underlying or redemption structure to be vetted by the competent authorities.' CESR's views have been endorsed by the UKLA in List!,[191] where the UKLA notes that it is primarily a decision for the issuer to make, but also states that it 'reserves the right in all cases however to challenge an issuer's view that a supplement is not required where we think it is appropriate to do so'.

3.214 Subject to the above, and in the absence of a definitive answer on the point, but fully acknowledging the absence of a definitive 'right answer' in any particular case, the following general guidance is suggested:

- Final terms should only include information taken from the various securities note Annexes of the Prospectus Directive Regulation, and in particular only those Annexes for which the base prospectus concerned was approved.[192] So for example, final terms should not be used for the purposes of issuing a derivative debt instrument if the base prospectus wasn't drawn up and approved in compliance with Annex XII of the Prospectus Directive Regulation.
- Final terms should not be used to update or change disclosure about the issuer or any guarantor under the debt issuance programme and should not be used to make general changes to the prospectus or base prospectus; they should only deal with the specific debt securities being issued.
- Similarly, a prospectus supplement should only be used to make generic changes to the prospectus or base prospectus and should not directly relate to a specific issuance of debt securities under the programme.
- Subject to the next two points below, final terms can be used to include information that could not have been known at the date of the prospectus or base prospectus, for example issue price, coupon rate, maturity date and other similar information.
- Information that could not have been known at the date of the prospectus or base prospectus can only be included in the final terms if the prospectus or base prospectus makes it clear (or at least envisages) that information of that type will, or can be, included in final terms under the debt issuance programme.

---

[190] CESR FAQ 57.
[191] List! Issue No 18 (March 2008).
[192] See Prospectus Directive Regulation Article 22(4).

So a particular formula for the calculation of a coupon can be included (because most debt issuance programmes will allow for such matters to be set out in the final terms) whereas a whole new class of security (for example subordinated debt) probably cannot be dealt with in final terms alone.

- Final terms should not include information that ought to be reflected in either the summary (if there is one) or in the risk factors. These sections of the prospectus or base prospectus should only be updated by way of a supplement.
- Modifications (including additions, deletions and/or amendments) to existing terms and conditions for a particular issue should be possible by way of inclusion in the final terms only.
- Additional provisions or mathematical formulae for the calculation of coupon payments or redemption amounts can be dealt with in the final terms only.
- Where coupon or principal amounts are calculated by reference to a description of the index, basket, underlying issuer, security or other instrument concerned (including any relevant historic data) should, in principle, be capable of being addressed in the final terms alone.
- If in doubt, publish a supplement to the prospectus or base prospectus or carry out the issuance through a drawdown prospectus.[193]

All of this is, to some extent at least, a question of degree and common sense. If the **3.215** terms and conditions of the debt securities contained in the base prospectus do not contain any provisions for a particular type or class of security in circumstances where it would be normal to have standard or 'boilerplate' provisions for that type of security, then it is probably right that the base prospectus should first be updated by a prospectus supplement to include those basic terms and conditions that can then be completed by the relevant final terms. However, it probably is not necessary to provide all possible permutations or variations of the terms and conditions and it should be possible to vary those standard provisions by deletion or addition, significantly if relevant.

There are two main reasons why a prospectus supplement may not be an ideal **3.216** solution for a particular issuance of debt securities. Clearly, if the prospectus or base prospectus needs to be updated generally in relation to a significant new factor (for example, a significant change in the business of the issuer or a guarantor) then that change must be reflected in a supplement to the prospectus or base prospectus. However, if the significant new factor relates to the particular securities which are proposed to be issued and application of the above analysis suggests that otherwise final terms would not in themselves be sufficient and a supplement would be required, then a possible alternative is to prepare a so-called 'drawdown prospectus'.

---

[193] See below in this section.

3.217 The idea of a drawdown prospectus is that:

- it avoids any possible trigger of withdrawal rights under Article 16(2) of the Prospectus Directive, since it is not a supplement to a prospectus or base prospectus;
- it can be used where changes generally to the base prospectus are not appropriate, for example, where there needs to be particular disclosure of risk factors in relation to the proposed securities on a 'one-off' basis and which are not relevant to the debt issuance programme as a whole.

3.218 A drawdown prospectus is a self-standing prospectus in its own right which broadly comprises a front cover, the final terms (which include the significant new factors concerned) and incorporate the base prospectus by reference. The approval process is essentially the same as for a base prospectus, but on a fast-track basis.

3.8 Approval Process for a Prospectus Supplement

3.219 In principle, the approval procedure for a supplement to a prospectus or base prospectus is the same as for the original prospectus.

3.220 However, many regulatory authorities will be willing to try to fast-track the approval process for prospectus supplements, recognizing that either they are of a relatively routine nature (for example, recording the publication of financial statements and incorporating them by reference into the base prospectus) or need to be dealt with on an urgent basis (for example, in respect of business developments ahead of a proposed issuance or during an offer period).

3.221 By way of example, the UKLA offers a 'same day supplement' (or 'SDS') service for the approval of certain supplements. The same day service is available for:

- incorporation by reference of SEC filings (such as forms 8-K, 10-Q, 10-K);
- incorporation by reference of interim financial statements and annual report and accounts;
- supplements to increase the facility amount of a debt issuance programme, to update the tax section of the base prospectus and to incorporate by reference documents previously approved by the UKLA.

3.222 The procedure for same day supplement approval with the UKLA is that the final form supplement must be submitted to the UKLA electronically no later than 2pm on the day the supplement requires approval (and the supplement will be dated that day) together with:

- a copy of any document(s) being incorporated by reference into the base prospectus by the supplement (as applicable);
- a completed SDS form (available from the UKLA's website);

- proof of payment of the vetting fee;
- Form A (which is an application for approval and is also available from the UKLA's website);
- Document publication form specifying how the supplement is to be published (and which is also available on the UKLA's website).

There is no need to provide any check list in the case of approval of the supplement.

The procedures for approval of a supplement other than a same day supplement by the UKLA are similar, save that the normal response times of four clear working days for the first draft and two clear working days for each subsequent draft will apply. **3.223**

It should be noted that once a supplement to a prospectus or base prospectus has been approved, it must be published in one of the ways set out in the Prospectus Directive.[194] **3.224**

3.9 Distribution Arrangements

3.9.1 Introduction

If the denomination of the debt securities is less than EUR 50,000 (or its equivalent in other currencies) and they are to be offered to the public other than on the basis of one or more of the various exemptions available under the Prospectus Directive (a *non-exempt offering*), then it will be necessary to prepare a prospectus or base prospectus which complies with the requirements of the Prospectus Directive and is approved by the relevant home member state. **3.225**

If the securities concerned have a denomination of EUR 50,000 or more (or its equivalent in other currencies) or if the denomination is below EUR 50,000 (or its equivalent in other currencies), are to be offered in the EEA solely on the basis of one or more of the available exemptions[195] under the Prospectus Directive (an *exempt offering*) and are not to be admitted to trading to an EEA regulated market, then there is no requirement under the Prospectus Directive to prepare a Prospectus Directive compliant prospectus or to obtain approval for such a prospectus. Whatever the denomination of the debt securities, if they are to be admitted to trading on an EEA regulated market, then it will still be necessary to prepare a Prospectus Directive compliant and approved prospectus for the purposes of that admission to trading. **3.226**

---

[194] Prospectus Directive Article 14(2).
[195] See Section 3.9.5 and further, generally, Section 3.1 and Chapter 3.

3.227   It should be noted that individual countries may have their own rules restricting distribution of offering materials relating to debt or other securities which operate in addition to or in parallel with any requirements under the Prospectus Directive.

3.228   For example, in the United Kingdom, the Financial Services and Markets Act 2000 ('FSMA') restricts the communication of financial promotions in the United Kingdom. An Offering Circular, Listing Particulars or Information Memorandum (however it is described or called) in relation to debt securities is likely to constitute a financial promotion for FSMA purposes, and should not therefore be distributed in the United Kingdom other than:

- by a person who is an authorized person under FSMA;
- where the Offering Circular, Listing Particulars or Information Memorandum has been approved by an authorized person; or
- otherwise in compliance with exemptions such as those set out in the Financial Services and Markets Act 2000 (Financial Promotions) Order 2005[196] which broadly permits distribution of such materials to 'investment professionals' and 'high net worth companies'.[197] The exemption order does contain other exceptions such as 'certified high net worth individuals' but these are not necessarily very easy to utilize in practice and are rarely used.

3.229   There are a number of ways of carrying out an offering for both stand-alone issues or issues under programmes. Outline steps and an illustrative timeline for a bond issue on either a stand-alone basis or under a debt issuance programme is set out in Appendix 1 to this Chapter. The types of offering are broadly as follows (and are each discussed in more detail below):

- through a single dealer (in the case of a programme) or underwriter or through a syndicate of dealers or underwriters;
- on a wholesale basis (that is, debt securities having a minimum denomination of EUR 50,000 or its equivalent in other currencies) or on a retail basis (that is, with the debt securities having a denomination of less than EUR 50,000 or its equivalent in other currencies);
- an offering which is carried out on an exempt basis (that is, regardless of their denomination, the debt securities are only offered to qualified investors within the EEA or pursuant to another exemption in the requirements of the Prospectus Directive);
- the offering of the debt securities is carried out on a non-exempt or 'true retail' basis (that is, the debt securities are offered to the public generally in one or more EEA jurisdictions);

---

[196]   SI 2005 No 1529.
[197]   See Sections 19 and 49 of the Exemption Order.

- through a combination of an exempt offer and true retail offer;
- on a private placement basis, not necessarily involving a dealer under the programme or any underwriter.

3.9.2 Single dealer or underwriter offer

At the risk of generalizing, an offering through a single dealer or underwriter is likely to be made to a relatively small group of institutional investors. It is also likely (but not necessarily the case) that the size of the offering will be smaller than for a multiple dealer or underwriter syndicate. Of course, some of this may not necessarily be the case and it is quite possible for a single dealer or underwriter to carry out just about any other kind of offering as well, though it is likely to be stretching resources to carry out a multi-jurisdictional exempt and non-exempt offering on a single dealer or single underwriter basis. **3.230**

The documentation for a trade of this kind can be very simple (particularly in the case of a single dealer under a debt issuance programme). **3.231**

Documentation under a debt issuance programme for a single dealer trade may involve nothing more than an exchange of commercial terms, amount, timing and pricing (between the issuer concerned and the dealer). The rest of the documentation is, of course, already in place under the programme so that nothing further is required to be agreed other than the commercial terms and a set of final terms. **3.232**

Programmes are not committed (that is, pre-underwritten) in any way, so it is possible that a single dealer under a programme may nevertheless require other documentation as a condition of carrying out the trade. These documents could include a formal agreement (probably based on the form of syndication agreement attached to the programme agreement) and possibly legal opinions and accountants' comfort letters. All this will be a matter of negotiation between the issuer and the dealer concerned at the time. The final terms relating to the trade will be issued and published so as to deal with Prospectus Directive and stock exchange listing formalities, and will be attached to the master global note for the programme so as to record their actual issuance. Finally, assuming that the debt securities concerned are to be held through Euroclear and Clearstream, Luxembourg, the normal related documents delivered at closing would also be necessary. **3.233**

3.9.3 Offering through multiple dealers or underwriters

An issuer of debt securities may well want to involve more than one dealer (where the issuance is under a debt issuance programme) or more than one underwriter (where the issue of the debt securities is on a stand-alone basis). This may be for any number of reasons. The issuer may believe that more than one dealer or **3.234** underwriter should be involved because the transaction is of a size that requires their combined resources. If the issuance involves marketing into different jurisdictions and/or different types of investors, then particular dealers or underwriters may be more appropriate to handle the marketing into those jurisdictions or to those types of investors. The issuer may also take the view, particularly where it is a larger trade, that the involvement of several dealers or underwriters will provide a level of 'price tension' so that the issuer is able to execute the trade at better pricing levels.

3.235　The documentation for a syndicated trade under a debt issuance programme would typically involve the following:

- a signing and closing agenda. This sets out the steps involved in executing the trade, all the documentation that needs to be produced and executed through to closing of the trade, and allocates responsibility to the various parties and advisers for their preparation and execution;
- signed and duly completed final terms which will be attached to the global notes for the programme (to constitute the trade) and filed (assuming that the debt securities are to be listed) with the relevant stock exchange;
- a syndication agreement made between the issuer and the dealers under the programme that are participating in that particular trade. This will be based closely upon the standard form of syndication agreement set out as a schedule to the dealer agreement for the programme;
- legal opinion(s) (as to valid execution of documentation and such documentation constituting legally binding obligations of the parties);
- auditors' comfort letter(s); and
- formal closing documents.

3.9.4 Wholesale offering

3.236　An offering through a single dealer or underwriter or through multiple dealers or underwriters may well be of debt securities that have a denomination of at least EUR 50,000 (or its equivalent in other currencies). As noted above, as long as this is the case, the debt securities can be offered anywhere in the EEA without having to be concerned about compliance with the Prospectus Directive, at least for the purposes of the offering.

3.237　Care should however be taken that there are no other laws or regulations that might be applicable to marketing the debt securities within the EEA or in countries outside the EEA.[198]

---

[198] See Section 3.9.1.

3.9.5 Exempt and non-exempt offering

If the denomination of the debt securities is less than EUR 50,000 (or its equiv- **3.238**
alent in other currencies), the offering can be carried out on either an exempt or
non-exempt basis or through a combination of the two.

An exempt offering is one which is carried out in a manner which takes advantage **3.239**
of the exceptions from the need to publish an approved prospectus in the
jurisdiction(s) where the exempt offering is taking place.

The main exemptions from the obligation to publish a prospectus that are avail- **3.240**
able under the Prospectus Directive (in addition to the exemption which relates
to debt securities having a denomination of at least EUR 50,000 or more or its
equivalent in other currencies[199]) and that are useful in the context of an offering
of debt securities[200] are as follows:

- the offer is addressed only to qualified investors;[201]
- an offer to fewer than 100 persons (natural or legal) in any EEA member
  state;[202]
- an offer where the minimum consideration is EUR 50,000 (or its equivalent in
  other currencies).[203]

It should be noted that these exceptions can be combined. In other words, if an **3.241**
offering is made to more than 100 individual investors in an EEA member state,
then provided that the number of investors to whom the offer is made that are not
qualified investors[204] is less than 100, that offer is still an exempt offer. Care needs
to be taken when using the fewer-than-100-persons exemption, particularly when
a syndicate of dealers or underwriters is involved. One of those underwriters or
dealers should be nominated to monitor observance of the fewer-than-100-persons
limit so that the exemption isn't inadvertently breached by each of the dealers or
underwriters in a syndicate offering the debt securities to 99 persons in a particular
EEA jurisdiction!

The principal documentation for an offering, that is, the prospectus or base pro- **3.242**
spectus and the underwriting agreement or dealer agreement, will contain 'selling
restrictions' that will reflect the nature of the particular offering. In particular,
where the denomination of the debt securities being offered is less than EUR
50,000 (or its equivalent in other currencies), the underwriters or dealers concerned will undertake with the issuer to observe specified selling restrictions that

---

[199] Prospectus Directive Article 3(2)(c).
[200] See further, generally, Chapter 1 and Section 3.1.
[201] Prospectus Directive Article 3(2)(a).
[202] Prospectus Directive Article 3(2)(b).
[203] Prospectus Directive Article 3(2)(c).
[204] As defined in Prospectus Directive Article 2(1)(e).

will ensure compliance with the Prospectus Directive. Their purpose is to ensure that the issuer (and indeed, any other party to the offering) is not obliged to prepare and publish a Prospectus Directive compliant prospectus either at all (if the debt securities are not being offered to the public or admitted to trading on an EEA regulated market) or (if they are) only to the extent specifically contemplated by the offering. A standard set of suggested selling restrictions that address retail and wholesale offerings are included in the IPMA Handbook.

3.243   For the most part, the Eurobond market has been traditionally viewed as an institutional investor market. However, in some EEA countries, there is a long-standing tradition of investment in debt securities by true retail investors. This has been for a number of reasons, including the fact that the bearer bond market generates interest payments that are free of withholding tax, and that, historically at least, were paid to whoever the bearer of the bond or coupon might be. Whilst interest payments are still typically paid on a 'no-withholding' basis, the potential for receiving interest on an anonymous bearer basis (with the consequent possibility of that payment being free of tax in the hands of that recipient) have been significantly reduced due to the implementation of the EU Savings Tax Directive.

3.244   Nevertheless, there is still an active true retail market in some EEA jurisdictions and international offerings of debt securities are sometimes structured so as to be able to tap these domestic investment pools. Since the underlying investors are true retail investors, and since the scale of such an offering would normally mean that taking advantage of the fewer-than-100-persons Prospectus Directive exemption would be inappropriate, the normal approach is for such an offering to take place on a non-exempt basis by passporting the prospectus or base prospectus for the offering. The prospectus (in the case of a stand-alone offering) or base prospectus (in the case of an offering from a programme) is published in each jurisdiction where the offering is to take place before the offering begins in that jurisdiction.

3.245   The documentation required for a non-exempt multi-EEA jurisdiction offering therefore includes the following:

- the prospectus or base prospectus which has already been prepared and approved by the regulatory authority of the home member state for that offering or debt issuance programme;
- assuming that the prospectus or base prospectus itself is written in a language which is 'customary in the sphere of international finance',[205] a translation of the summary section of the prospectus or base prospectus into the official

---

[205] Prospectus Directive Article 19(2).

language of any host EEA member state where the prospectus or base prospectus is being passported for the purposes of the retail offering;

- final terms for the particular trade. These will need to be published and filed with the regulatory authority of the home member state in the usual way, and as a matter of good practice, even if not strictly required by the Prospectus Directive, should also be filed with the regulatory authority of each host member state;
- a syndication (or underwriting) agreement between the issuer and the dealers or underwriters;
- legal opinion(s);
- auditors' comfort letter(s);
- formal closing documents.

3.9.6 Retail cascades

A fairly standard structure for the offering of debt securities on a non-exempt basis to true retail investors might be: **3.246**

- the issuer offers the debt securities to one or more dealers or underwriters;
- the dealers or underwriters offer the debt securities to and place them with institutional counterparties in a number of specified EEA member states;
- those institutional counterparties (and possibly other intermediaries), in turn, offer the debt securities to and place them with retail investors,

in each case, normally, for the purposes of retail offerings in specified retail public offer jurisdictions (where the prospectus or base prospectus will have been approved and published or passported) and for a specified period of time, which will in practice define for the benefit of the issuer the period during which the prospectus or base prospectus needs to be kept 'live' and therefore supplemented, to the extent necessary.

Whilst from a broad perspective the above steps look like a single offering of debt   **3.247**
securities for the purposes of the Prospectus Directive, a close look at each of the steps (as is the unfortunate habit of debt capital markets lawyers) suggests that there is scope for confusion and difficulty as to whether, and if so how, the prospectus or base prospectus and final terms for the trade should address each stage of the so-called 'retail cascade' offering described above.

There are two main difficulties that potentially arise under the Prospectus Directive   **3.248**
from this so-called retail cascade. These are:

- do any of the above offers (other than that by the issuer to the underwriters or dealers) require preparation of a separate prospectus by any person?
- to what extent does the issuer's prospectus or base prospectus and final terms have to address any of the offers other than its own to the underwriters or dealers?

3.249   In relation to the first question, there really isn't a clear answer. Common sense suggests that the issuer's prospectus or base prospectus and final terms:

- should 'cover' (in the sense that no person should be required to prepare and publish a further prospectus and that the issuer should be 'liable' for the contents of its prospectus) its own initial offer to the underwriters and dealers as well the offer by the underwriters and dealers to other institutional intermediaries, provided those offers are made within the time period permitted by the issuer and specified in the prospectus or the final terms;
- should similarly 'cover' offers to retail investors by those institutional intermediaries arranged by the underwriters or dealers, at least during the period permitted by the issuer and in the public offer jurisdictions specified by the issuer, since in general terms, such offerings are likely to have been in the contemplation of the issuer when structuring the offer with the underwriters or dealers concerned;
- should not 'cover' offers:
  - by institutional intermediaries other than those arranged by the dealers or underwriters (since the issuer has no actual or implicit knowledge of them);
  - by any person after the specified 'cut-off' date (since the issuer will wish to end any obligation it may otherwise have to keep the prospectus or base prospectus up to date after that time);
  - in any jurisdiction other than one of the specified public offer jurisdictions.

3.250   It is not at all clear that the above common-sense result is the one reached on a literal reading of the Prospectus Directive.

3.251   In relation to the second question mentioned above, the difficulty stems principally from Paragraph 5 of Annex V to the Prospectus Directive Regulation. This paragraph requires a description of the 'terms and conditions of the offer'. The question again is, what is 'the offer' for the purposes of a retail cascade of the kind described above, and therefore what needs to be described in the issuer's prospectus or final terms?

3.252   Paragraph 5 of Annex V requires that in relation to the offer, among other things, the following are also described:

- any conditions of the offer, the total amount of the offer, the time period during which the offer is open (and the application process in relation the offer);
- the price at which the debt securities will be sold pursuant to that offer;
- the names and addresses, to the extent known to the issuer, of the 'placers' in the various countries where the offer takes place.

3.253   In the context of the normal structure of a non-exempt true retail cascade offering described above, the close-looking debt capital markets lawyer might conclude that for the purposes of Paragraph 5 of Annex V, actually there are at least three different offers involved in getting the debt securities to the true retail investors.[206]

If the requirements of Paragraph 5 of Annex V are looked at against each of these **3.254**
potential offers, it can be seen that the final terms would become unwieldy, and in any event it may be impossible to provide all the information that is technically necessary since it may not be known to the issuer at the time of publication of the final terms. For example, the 'terms of the offer' of an institutional intermediary would probably be the standard business terms on which that intermediary deals with its customers and the price might well vary on a transaction-by-transaction basis and as between different intermediaries. Little purpose would be served (even if it were possible) by including such information in the prospectus or final terms. It may also be that offers by intermediaries are made over a period of time, at different prices, so that the issuer would simply be unable to include that pricing information in the final terms documenting the particular trade, because it was not available at the time of publication. On the other hand, if the identity of the institutional intermediaries (or 'placers') are known to the issuer at the commencement of the offering (which they may or may not be), then the names of those intermediaries should be included in the final terms for the offer.

At a practical level, the information in the prospectus or base prospectus and final **3.255**
terms that an investor would be most interested in, is the disclosure information in relation to the issuer, its business and prospects and the terms and conditions of the particular debt securities, all as recorded in the issuer's prospectus or base prospectus and the final terms, and the price at which the issuer sells the debt securities to the initial dealers or underwriters. Whilst a retail investor might well be interested in the terms on which other retail investors are buying the debt securities from other intermediary distributers, none of that should legitimately be a concern of the issuer or its prospectus or base prospectus or the final terms. Its disclosure obligations in respect of such matters should logically end at the point of the dealers or underwriters.

The practical solution to this problem, which has been adopted by the FSA in the **3.256**
UK, is to utilize Article 23.4 of the Prospectus Directive Regulation which allows otherwise required information to be omitted if 'the information is not pertinent to the offer'. This approach is set out in the UKLA's publication List!.[207] Instead of setting out the information which might, on a strict reading, otherwise seem to be required by Article 5 of Annex V, the approach taken is, relying upon Article 23.4

---

[206] These might be (i) the offer to the dealers/underwriters, (ii) offers by the dealers/underwriters to their institutional counterparties in the public offer jurisdictions and (iii) offers by those counterparties to their retail clients.
[207] List! Issue No 16 (July 2007).

of the Prospectus Directive Regulation, that the final terms for a non-exempt offering include a section addressing Paragraph 5 of Annex V, but the main sense of which is to label items as 'N/A' or to refer investors to the institutional intermediary (or other placer or distributor) from whom they are considering acquiring the debt securities concerned for the relevant information.

3.257   The price (though it is a relatively small price) of adopting this approach is that the UKLA requires the prospectus or base prospectus checklist (submitted during the approval process for the base prospectus[208]) to note that Article 23.4 of the Prospectus Directive Regulation is being invoked. Further, the UKLA requires a prominent statement on the front page of the prospectus or base prospectus stating that an investor (because not all authorized distribution agents are identified therein) should check with the distributor of the securities whether the distributor is acting in association with the issuer as part of the offer to which the prospectus or base prospectus relates. It should also state that if the distributor is not acting in association with the issuer, then the investor may not have recourse against the issuer in respect of information in the prospectus.

3.258   The approach to this retail cascades issue in jurisdictions other than the United Kingdom, to the extent relevant, appears to be based around either not acknowledging that a problem exists at all, or if it is recognized, through implementation of the common sense and pragmatic approach referred to above, though without being formalized by the inclusion of any equivalent to the legends required by the UKLA.

3.9.7 Clearance systems

3.259   In most cases, investors are likely to want to hold debt securities in dematerialized electronic form rather than in any physical certificated form. This is likely to be true even where the issuance is by way of private placement.

3.260   There are a wide variety of clearance systems that are capable of dealing with debt instruments. The choice will, to some extent, depend upon the country of incorporation of the issuer, the nature of the offering (for example, true domestic retail or international institutional investors) and the stock exchange, if any, on which the debt instruments are to be listed. In the case of an institutional Eurobond offering, the most commonly used clearance systems are Euroclear Bank SA /NV and Clearstream Banking, Société Anonyme (respectively, more commonly called Euroclear and Clearstream, Luxembourg). Even where debt instruments are initially entered into clearance systems other than these two, it is often possible to trade securities through Euroclear and Clearstream, Luxembourg through sub-accounts with the other clearance systems and vice versa.

---

[208]   See Section 3.6.3 above.

Appendix 1

Outline steps and illustrative timeline for a debt securities issue—stand-alone issue

Timing	Step	Comments
D-30	Prepare documentation for issue: • offering circular/prospectus; • the subscription agreement. This sets out the underwriting arrangements for the bonds and will need to have been negotiated and finalized in time for signing; • the trust deed or (if there is not to be a trustee) the fiscal agency agreement. This will need to have been finalized in time for closing of the transaction; • agency agreement; • supporting documentation including any accountants' comfort letter(s) and legal opinion(s).	Strictly, timing of documentation can be fairly flexible. If it is intended that the debt securities should be listed at or shortly after closing, then sufficient lead time should be left to allow for preparation of the prospectus and its approval by the relevant regulatory authority. On the other hand, if listing is not needed until, for example, before the due date of the first payment, then preparation of the prospectus and listing of the bonds can be left until later.
D	Launch of the offer. Invitation telex dispatched.	Issue goes lives in the market at this point.
D+7	Signing of the subscription agreement	
D+10	Closing: • execution of the trust deed or fiscal agency agreement; • execution of temporary and permanent global notes and delivery to common depository or common safekeeper;[209] • delivery of other conditions precedent, for example, any accountants' comfort letter(s) and legal opinion(s); • payment of the proceeds of the issue of the debt securities to the issuer; • debt securities listed on relevant stock exchange.	

Issue of debt securities under a debt issuance programme[210]

Timing	Step	Comments
D	Agree terms. Dispatch of invitation telex.	
D+7	Signing of syndication agreement.	The syndication agreement is in a prescribed form and set out in the dealer agreement relating to the debt issuance programme.

---

[209] Where the debt securities are to be issued in new global note form.

[210] This timeline assumes that the base prospectus for the debt programme is up to date at the contemplated time of the debt issuance.

Issue of debt securities under a debt issuance programme *(Continued)*

Timing	Step	Comments
D+10	Closing: • filing of final terms with relevant stock exchange; • final terms attached to master global note for the programme; • delivery of any other conditions precedent (for example, accountants' comfort letter(s) and legal opinion(s)); • payment of net subscription proceeds to the issuer.	

Appendix 2

Summary of main differences between Annex IV and Annex IX of the Prospectus Directive Regulation

Contents of the prospectus/ base prospectus	Annex IV ('retail offering')	Annex IX ('wholesale offering')
Front cover	Yes	Yes
Table of contents	Yes	Yes
Responsibility statement, notices, disclaimers	Yes	Yes
Summary of the base prospectus	Yes	Not required[211]
Risk factors	Yes	Yes
Information incorporated by reference[212]	Optional	Optional
Use of proceeds	Yes	Yes
Expenses	Yes	Yes[213]
Forms of the debt securities	Yes	Yes
Terms and conditions of the debt securities	Yes	Yes
Form of final terms	Yes	Yes
Description of issuer(s)	Yes	Yes, but abbreviated[214]
Description of any guarantor	Yes	Yes
Selected financial information	Yes	Not required
Financial information[215]	Yes—two years' IFRS or 'equivalent'	Yes—two years' IFRS or 'equivalent' or (in the case of third country issuers) local GAAP with a narrative of differences from IFRS

[211] A summary can be included, but if it is, it must comply with the requirements of Prospectus Directive Article 5 (including the required introductory language to the summary).

[212] The Prospectus Directive and Prospectus Directive Regulation (and associated Annexes) permit the incorporation by reference of certain information typically financial information, provided it complies with Prospectus Directive Article 11.

[213] But note that the level of disclosure required for a wholesale offering is more limited than for a retail offering.

[214] Prospectus Directive Regulation Annex IX states that for wholesale programmes the description of the issuer's principle activities should be 'brief' unlike the equivalent provision in Annexe IV.

[215] Can be incorporated by reference.

Summary of main differences between Annex IV and Annex IX of the Prospectus Directive Regulation *(Continued)*

Contents of the prospectus/ base prospectus	Annex IV ('retail offering')	Annex IX ('wholesale offering')
Taxation	Yes	Not required
Subscription and sale	Yes	Yes
General Information	Yes	Yes

Appendix 3

Overview of Annexes to the Prospectus Directive Regulation relevant to an issue of debt securities under a prospectus or base prospectus[216]

Annex IV

Disclosure requirements for the registration document[217] where the debt securities have a denomination of less than EUR 50,000 (or its equivalent in another currency)

Annex paragraph number	Subject
1.	Identity of those responsible for the prospectus or base prospectus and responsibility statement.[218]
2.	Details about the issuer's auditors.
3.	Selected historical financial information.[219]
4.	Risk factors.[220]
5.1	Information about the issuer:[221] • history; • legal information (name, incorporation and domicile details); • recent events relevant to solvency.
5.2	Principal investments since date of last financial information and proposed future investments and sources of funds.
6.	Business description:[222] • business activities; • new products or activities; • principal markets.
7.	Organizational/corporate structure.

---

[216] Note that this Appendix is a summary of the relevant Annexes and is not exhaustive. It is intended to give an overview of the scope of the disclosure requirements set out in the Annexes.

[217] See Section 3.5 above for a description of the components of a prospectus or base prospectus.

[218] See Section 3.5.2. The responsibility statement is normally given by the issuer concerned on a corporate basis.

[219] These will be key line items from the financial information included in (or incorporated by reference into) the prospectus or base prospectus. See Paragraph 13 below and Section 5.7.

[220] See Section 3.5.4.

[221] See Section 3.5.12.

[222] See Section 3.5.12.

Disclosure requirements for the registration document where the debt securities have a denomination of less than EUR 50,000 (or its equivalent in another currency) *(Continued)*

Annex paragraph number	Subject
8.	Trend information:[223] • description of any material adverse change in the issuer's prospects since last audited financial statements, or a negative statement; • known trends or uncertainties material to the issuer's prospects for at least the current financial year.
9.	Profit forecasts or estimates, if any, and if so, principal assumptions and an accountants' report on such forecast or estimate.
10.	Details of administrative, management and supervisory bodies: • names of members and functions; • potential conflicts of interest, or a negative statement.
11.	Board practices: • committee; • statement of compliance (or otherwise) with applicable corporate governance regime.
12.	Identity of major shareholders.[224]
13.1 through 13.5	Financial information:[225] • two years' audited consolidated IFRS (or 'equivalent') accounts not more than 18 months old (or if IFRS is not applicable, prepared according to the relevant member state's GAAP); • half-year or quarterly interims, if published; • audit information.
13.6	Description of any issuer and/or group material litigation, or a negative statement.[226]
13.7	Description of any significant change in the issuer's financial or trading position since the last audited or interim accounts, or a negative statement.[227]
14.	Description of the issuer's share capital and objects.
15.	Description of group contracts which are not ordinary course and could be material to the issuer's obligations under the debt securities.[228]
16.	Experts' statements or reports, if any.
17.	Details of documents on display: • memorandum and articles of association; • reports, valuations, statements of experts referred to in the prospectus or base prospectus; • two years' group historical financial information; • place the documents are available for inspection.

---

[223] See Section 3.5.12.

[224] The text of this paragraph actually requires disclosure of whether the issuer is 'owned or controlled' and if so, by whom as well as details of any arrangements addressing abuse of control.

[225] See Section 3.5.6.

[226] See Section 3.5.12.

[227] See Section 3.5.12.

[228] See Section 3.5.12.

Annex V

Disclosure requirements for the securities note[229] where the debt securities have a denomination of less than EUR 50,000 (or its equivalent in another currency) omitting information already covered in Annex IV

Annex paragraph number	Subject
3.1	Interests of natural and legal persons in the issue including conflicting interests.
3.2	Reasons for the offer and use of proceeds.[230] Estimate of total expenses of the offer (broken into each intended principal use in order of priority) and estimated net proceeds.
4.	Description of the securities:[231] • type/class/form; • ISIN number; • currency; • ranking and rights; • interest provisions. Indication of yield and how calculated; • explanation of any underlying derivative; • issue date and maturity date; • any withholding tax.[232]
5.1	Terms and conditions of the offer:[233] • amount, time during which the offer will be open; • reduction of subscriptions/method of returning any excess amounts; • any minimum or maximum subscription amount; • time for payment and delivery of the securities; • how offer results will be announced.
5.2	Distribution arrangements.[234]
5.3	Issue price or how it will be determined.[235]
5.4	Underwriting arrangements including names of global coordinator(s) and placers (if known to the issuer).[236]
5.6	Listing and trading arrangements
5.7	Additional information: • if mentioned, capacity of advisers; • credit ratings of issuer and/or securities.

---

[229] See Section 3.5 above for a description of the components of a prospectus or base prospectus.

[230] See Section 3.5.7.

[231] In the case of an issue under a programme, this information will be covered partly in the base prospectus and partly in the final terms.

[232] See Section 3.5.14.

[233] In the case of an issue under a programme, this information will be covered partly in the base prospectus and partly in the final terms. See Section 3.9.6 as to how this information is provided or addressed in the case of 'retail cascades'.

[234] See Section 3.9.

[235] See Note 233.

[236] See Note 233.

Annex VI

Disclosure requirements for guarantees/guarantors

Annex paragraph number	Subject
1. and 2.	Description of any guarantee or other similar support arrangement.
3.	Description of the guarantor as though it were the issuer.[237]
4.	Where documents relating to the guarantee can be inspected.

Annex IX

Disclosure requirements for the registration document[238] where the debt securities have a denomination of EUR 50,000 (or its equivalent in another currency) or more

Annex paragraph number	Subject
1.	Identity of those responsible for the prospectus or base prospectus and responsibility statement.
2.	Details about the issuer's auditors.
3.	Risk factors.[239]
4.	Information about the issuer:[240] • history; • legal information (name, incorporation and domicile details); • recent events relevant to solvency.
5.	Brief description of principal activities.[241]
6.	Organizational/corporate structure.
7.	Description of any material adverse change in the issuer's prospects since last audited financial statements, or a negative statement.[242]
8.	Profit forecasts or estimates, if any, and if so, principal assumptions and an accountants' report on such forecast or estimate.
9.	Details of administrative, management and supervisory bodies: • names of members and functions; • potential conflicts of interest, or a negative statement.
10.	Identity of major shareholders.[243]

---

[237] See Section 3.5.13, in particular in relation to financial information for a guarantor.

[238] See Section 3.5 above for a description of the components of a prospectus or base prospectus.

[239] See Section 3.5.4.

[240] See Section 3.5.12.

[241] See Section 3.5.12.

[242] See Section 3.5.12.

[243] The text of this paragraph actually requires disclosure of whether the issuer is 'owned or controlled' and if so, by whom as well as details of any arrangements addressing abuse of control.

Disclosure requirements for the registration document where the debt securities have a denomination of EUR 50,000 (or its equivalent in another currency) or more *(Continued)*

Annex paragraph number	Subject
11.1 through 11.4	Financial information:[244] • two years' audited consolidated IFRS (or 'equivalent') accounts not more than 18 months old (or if IFRS is not applicable, prepared according to the relevant member state's GAAP). For 'third country issuers' the financial information can be prepared in accordance with other GAAP, in which case a narrative description of differences from IFRS must be included. • audit information (in the case of a third country issuer, including a narrative of differences from IFRS, if relevant).
11.5	Description of any issuer and/or group material litigation, or a negative statement.[245]
11.6	Description of any significant change in the issuer's financial or trading position since the last audited or interim accounts, or a negative statement.[246]
12.	Description of group contracts material to the issuer's obligations under the debt securities.[247]
13.	Experts' statements or reports, if any.
14.	Details of documents on display: • memorandum and articles of association; • reports, valuations, statements of experts referred to in the prospectus or base prospectus; • two years' group historical financial information; • place the documents are available for inspection.

Annex XIII

Disclosure requirements for the securities note where the debt securities have a denomination of EUR 50,000 (or its equivalent in another currency) or more, omitting information already covered in Annex IX

Annex paragraph number	Subject
3.	Interests of natural and legal persons in the issue including conflicting interests.
4.	Description of the securities:[248] • total amount of securities being admitted to trading; • type/class/form; • ISIN number;

---

[244] See Section 3.5.6.
[245] See Section 3.5.12.
[246] See Section 3.5.12.
[247] See Section 3.5.12.
[248] In the case of an issue under a programme, this information will be covered partly in the base prospectus and partly in the final terms.

Disclosure requirements for the securities note where the debt securities have a denomination of EUR 50,000 (or its equivalent in another currency) or more, omitting information already covered in Annex IX *(Continued)*

Annex paragraph number	Subject
	• currency; • ranking and rights; • interest provisions and yield; • issue date and maturity date.
5.	Listing and trading arrangements.
6.	Estimate of total expenses related to admission to trading.
7.	Additional information: • if mentioned, capacity of advisers; • credit ratings of issuer and/or securities.

4

PRIVATE PLACEMENTS[*]

4.1 Introduction

This Chapter sets out a summary of the legal and regulatory framework within **4.01**
which European issuers and existing investors offer securities to investors by way
of private placements in Europe and the United States.

---

[*] The author of this chapter would like to acknowledge the valuable contribution of Ben Lyon, Senior Associate of Herbert Smith LLP, to the drafting of this chapter.

4.02   In its simplest form, a private placement is an offer of transferable securities to specified persons, which does not involve an offer of securities to the public, or otherwise trigger the requirement to prepare a prospectus. The categories of specified persons to which private placements are normally made include authorized financial institutions, placement agents, banks or investment funds or firms, pension funds, life insurance companies, and, in some cases, high net worth individuals and other significant or large corporate investors.

4.03   The relevant European financial regulators and capital market participants generally accept that European securities laws should allow sophisticated parties to transact in a space relatively free of regulation, so long as those parties are recognized as having the ability to undertake financial transactions without requiring supervisory protections. The premise of a private placement, therefore, is that experienced market participants can arrange such investment transactions among themselves without any need for the regulatory protections that have been put in place to safeguard retail investors, such as disclosure requirements, regulatory authority approvals, rules on distribution and marketing, and conduct of business rules.

4.1.1 Legislative background

4.04   As discussed in Part 1, the EEA member states, through the implementation of the Prospectus Directive, legislated to harmonize securities laws across the EEA. Such harmonization is intended to move the EEA towards the creation of an integrated pan-EEA securities market. Consequently, the ability of EEA member states to impose, directly or indirectly, any additional regulation on issuers and capital markets participants, or to grant dispensations from Prospectus Directive requirements, is quite limited.

4.05   The key impact of the Prospectus Directive is that it requires the publication of a Prospectus Directive compliant prospectus in relation to any offer of securities to the public in the EEA or admission of securities to trading on an EEA regulated market. The Prospectus Directive also introduced a scheme of exemptions to the requirement to publish a prospectus, and it is the existence of such exemptions that enables private placements of securities to be conducted in the EEA in the absence of a prospectus. Accordingly, private placements represent a less regulated segment of European capital markets than their fully regulated and documented cousins, which is appropriate given the level of sophistication of the parties typically involved.

4.06   Elsewhere in the world, private placements are supported with tailored, codified regimes. Jurisdictions such as the United States, Japan and Australia operate successful legislated private placement regimes, which contribute depth, fluidity and dynamism to their financial markets. Across the EEA, private placement regimes are not properly codified at the national level and this lack of legal certainty provides a barrier to cross-border pan-European private placements. For instance, the lack of common understanding of private placements across the EEA may make it uneconomical to privately place securities in certain EEA member states. This has the effect of depriving sophisticated investors of potentially valuable investment opportunities. Furthermore, in the absence of a clear legal framework, offerors may be deterred from approaching suitable investors.

There are considerable potential benefits to be achieved by establishing a common   **4.07**
EU-level understanding of private placements to facilitate transactions between sophisticated investors. The efforts of the European Commission ('EC') to harmonize private placement regimes across EEA member states (as well as improving other legislation relevant to private placements) are described in Section 4.10 below.

4.2 Reasons for a Private Placement over a Prospectus Directive Compliant Offer

There are a number of stages in an issuer's life cycle during which it might wish to   **4.08**
raise additional capital, either through debt financing, or the issue of equity or debt securities. During an issuer's early growth phase it might need initial funding to ensure that its business plan can be realized. A more mature issuer might wish to raise funds to pursue an acquisition opportunity or retire maturing debt.

A private placement has several advantages over a conventional offer of trans-   **4.09**
ferable securities made under a prospectus. These advantages can benefit not only issuers but also existing shareholders who may wish to exit or sell their shareholdings in an issuer.

The first such advantage is the ability to avoid the burdensome investor prote-   **4.10**
ction rules in Europe for entities looking to raise capital, namely the reporting obligations and the expensive and time-consuming requirement to produce a prospectus. Without the need to produce a prospectus, transaction costs are reduced and private placements can be carried out in a much shorter time frame. This makes private placements particularly attractive to smaller companies look-ing to raise funds quickly or seasoned capital market issuers wishing to transact quickly.

Second, since only a small number of sophisticated investors will invest in a pri-   **4.11**
vate placement, the parties have a greater opportunity to enter into discussions in respect of the investment and the relative rights and protections each party requires. Such an arrangement is more flexible than a public offering of securities made pursuant to a prospectus since the needs of each party can be taken into

account, resulting in an investment that is focused on the specific requirements of both the issuer and the offerees. This may not be possible when accessing a pool of less sophisticated (and typically unidentified) investors, which potentially can be the case with retail or public offers.

4.12 Third, private placements can generally be made in respect of most types of transferable securities, providing issuers with the option to raise capital by issuing securities of several varying types, including securities which, in terms of risk, may be considered less suitable for wider retail offers. Furthermore, the terms of these securities can be tailored to the specific needs of the issuer or the offeree, depending on the nature of the capital raising.

4.13 In light of the above advantages, it is clear why private placements are attractive to sophisticated market participants. On the other hand, such parties need to ensure that they fully appreciate the risks they are undertaking. Whilst these investors may still have recourse to criminal, civil and contractual remedies, they cannot benefit from the protective rules found in the Prospectus Directive, so they are undoubtedly left more exposed than in the case of a public offering.

4.3 Private Placements in the Context of the Prospectus Directive

4.14 Private placements usually fall within the meaning of an 'offer of securities to the public'. However, the Prospectus Directive provides a range of exemptions from the obligation to produce a prospectus, some of which can be used for private placements, thereby enabling parties to conduct private placements without preparing a prospectus.

4.4 Regulatory Framework

4.15 The Prospectus Directive seeks to protect investors by requiring consistent standards of disclosure within prospectuses, and by establishing a single competent authority in each EEA member state to approve such prospectuses.

4.16 The Prospectus Directive is supplemented by the Prospectus Regulation, which details the required contents of prospectuses, the format, incorporation by reference, publication of prospectuses and the advertisement regime.

4.17 The Prospectus Directive is a 'maximum harmonisation' directive, while the Prospectus Regulation is directly applicable into the law of each EEA member state. Consequently, this greatly restricts the ability of EEA member states to impose on issuers or offerors, directly or indirectly, any additional content requirements for prospectuses (or to grant dispensations from Prospectus Directive or Prospectus Regulation requirements) in connection with public offers or the admission of securities. There are, however, two important limitations on the impact of the Prospectus Directive:

(a) the Prospectus Directive only relates to the prospectus itself and does not govern admission criteria or continuing obligations for regulated markets; and

(b) the application of the Prospectus Directive to admission of securities to trading is limited to the admission of securities to trading on a regulated market (as set out under the heading 'Prospectus directive exemptions').

Since the Prospective Directive does not govern admission criteria or continuing **4.18** obligations for regulated markets, EEA member states are free to impose super-equivalent or 'gold plated' requirements in those areas. For instance, in the United Kingdom, the Financial Services Authority has imposed super-equivalent require-ments for listing in the Listing Rules issued by the United Kingdom Listing Authority.

Listed companies in the EEA must also comply with the requirements of the **4.19** Market Abuse Directive, which promotes prompt and fair disclosure of relevant information to the market by obliging a listed company to notify the market as soon as possible of any inside information which directly concerns it. Furthermore, listed companies in the EEA must comply with the Transparency Directive, which requires listed companies to disclose certain information to the market, including periodic financial reporting and the notification of the acquisition or disposal of major shareholdings.

4.4.1 Prospectus Directive exemptions

4.4.1.1 *The prospectus requirement*

The Prospectus Directive sets out when a prospectus is required to be prepared or **4.20** published. In short, subject to certain exemptions, a prospectus must be produced and approved by a competent authority whenever there is an offer of securities to the public in the EEA[1] and/or an admission of securities to trading on a regulated market in the EEA.

Accordingly, there are two triggers for the requirement to publish a prospectus: the **4.21** 'public offer' trigger and the 'admission to trading' trigger. Most private placements

---

[1] Prospectus Directive Article 2(1)(d) defines an 'offer of securities to the public' widely, as a communication to persons in any form and by any means, presenting sufficient information on the terms of the offer and the securities to be offered, so as to enable an investor to decide to purchase or subscribe to these securities.

will trigger at least the 'public offer' requirement to produce a prospectus, and many will also trigger the 'admission to trading' requirement. Accordingly, issuers conducting a private placement may well need to find applicable exemptions to enable them to avoid both prospectus triggers and, thereby, avoid the requirement to prepare a prospectus in connection with their proposed placement.

4.22   Article 3(2) of the Prospectus Directive describes the types of offer to which the obligation to prepare a prospectus does not apply:

   (a)   an offer of securities addressed solely to qualified investors; and/or

   (b)   an offer of securities addressed to fewer than 100 natural or legal persons per member state, other than qualified investors; and/or

   (c)   an offer of securities addressed to investors who acquire securities for a total consideration of at least EUR 50,000 per investor, for each separate offer; and/or

   (d)   an offer of securities whose denomination per unit amounts to at least EUR 50,000; and/or

   (e)   an offer of securities with a total consideration of less than EUR 100,000, which limit shall be calculated over a period of 12 months.

4.23   EEA member states construe the public offer trigger in different ways. In Germany, for example, the competent authority, the Bundesanstalt für Finanzdienstleistungsaufsicht (the 'BaFin') considers a rights issue, where shares are offered exclusively to existing shareholders, not to be a public offer, provided that persons other than existing shareholders are excluded from trading in the rights. In this regard, the BaFin considers existing shareholders to be a definable group of persons who are already well informed about the issuer and therefore do not represent the general public. While the competent authority for Austria, the Finanzmarktaufsichtsbehörde, agrees with the BaFin on this point, it is unclear whether the BaFin will maintain its view, as most other regulators in the EEA member states and the Committee of European Securities Regulators ('CESR') are not of the same opinion.

4.24   It should be borne in mind that in the context of a rights issue the issuer would still be obliged to publish a prospectus if the relevant securities were subsequently admitted to trading on a regulated market (unless, of course, an exemption were available).

4.25   **4.4.1.1.1 Qualified investors**   As set out in Article 3(2)(a) of the Prospectus Directive, if an offer is addressed solely to qualified investors there is no requirement to publish a prospectus in respect of the offer.

4.26   'Qualified investor' is defined in Article 2(1)(e), and means:

   (a)   legal entities which are authorized or regulated to operate in the financial markets, including: credit institutions, investment firms, other authorized or regulated financial institutions, insurance companies, collective investment schemes and their management companies, pension funds and their management companies, commodity dealers, as well as entities not so authorized or regulated whose corporate purpose is solely to invest in securities;

(b) national and regional governments, central banks, international and supranational institutions such as the International Monetary Fund, the European Central Bank and the European Investment Bank;

(c) other legal entities which do not meet two of the following three criteria: an average number of employees during the financial year of less than 250, a total balance sheet not exceeding EUR 43,000,000 and an annual net turnover not exceeding EUR 50,000,000;

(d) certain natural persons: subject to mutual recognition, a member state may choose to authorize natural persons who are resident in that state and who expressly ask to be considered as qualified investors if these persons meet at least two of the following criteria:

　(i) the investor has carried out transactions of a significant size on securities markets at an average frequency of, at least, ten per quarter over the previous four quarters;

　(ii) the size of the investor's securities portfolio exceeds EUR 0.5 million;

　(iii) the investor works or has worked for at least one year in the financial sector in a professional position which requires knowledge of securities investment;

(e) certain small and medium-sized enterprises ('SMEs'): subject to mutual recognition, an EEA member state may choose to authorize SMEs which have their registered office in that member state and who expressly ask to be considered as qualified investors.

4.27 In respect of (d) and (e), Article 2(3) obliges the competent authority in each EEA member state to establish and maintain a register of natural persons and SMEs considered as qualified investors. The purpose of the register is to facilitate the issuance of securities without the requirement to publish a prospectus. The register is available to all issuers, and each natural person or SME wishing to be considered as a qualified investor is required to register.

4.28 In the United Kingdom, the Financial Services Authority levies a charge on those persons who wish to register as 'qualified investors' and on those issuers who request to view the register. Registration is valid for a year and renewable after that.

4.29 **4.4.1.1.2 Placement to brokers/financial intermediaries** If a private placement of securities is made to a broker or financial intermediary who is himself a qualified investor under Article 2(1)(e) of the Prospectus Directive, the exemption will not be available if that broker then offers the securities to clients who are not qualified investors. If, however, the broker is a 'discretionary broker' whose terms of engagement allow him to make the decision to purchase securities without reference to those clients, in the United Kingdom at least, the Financial Services Authority has confirmed that such an offer should not be treated as an offer to the underlying client.

4.30 Issuers and offerors in private placements may seek to address the problem of offers to brokers or financial intermediaries who do not operate on a discretionary basis by requiring the broker or financial intermediary to represent that the relevant securities are neither being acquired on a non-discretionary basis on behalf of, nor being acquired with a view to their offer or resale to, persons in circumstances which may give rise to an offer of securities to the public (other than their offer or resale to qualified investors).

4.31 **4.4.1.1.3 Fewer than 100 persons per EEA member state** As set out in Article 3(2)(b) of the Prospectus Directive, the requirement to publish a prospectus does not apply if the offer of equity securities is addressed to fewer than 100 natural or legal persons per EEA member state, other than qualified investors.[2]

4.32 This exemption to the Article 3(1) 'public offer' trigger in the Prospectus Directive has been implemented inconsistently across the EEA. Some EEA member states have implemented the exemption as applying to fewer than 100 persons for that particular EEA member state (for example, the United Kingdom, France, the Netherlands and Ireland), regardless of how many persons the offer has been addressed to in other EEA member states. Other EEA member states (for example, Liechtenstein) have implemented the exemption in such a way that it will not be available in that EEA member state if, in respect of any other single EEA member state, the offer has been addressed to over 100 natural or legal persons in that other EEA member state.

4.33 Accordingly, to determine whether this exemption is applicable to a particular transaction, it is necessary to consult the local legislation of the relevant EEA member state.

4.34 In the EEA generally, legislation treats offers by financial intermediaries as offers by the issuer. Thus, in the EEA, issuers and offerors wanting to limit their offers to fewer than 100 natural or legal persons per EEA member state and who are using financial intermediaries, may choose to impose a selling restriction on the intermediary, obliging them to first obtain the issuer's or offeror's consent before selling to anyone other than a qualified investor, as this person would count towards the 99-person limit.

4.35 **4.4.1.1.4 Other public offer exemptions** In addition to the exemptions set out in Article 3(2) of the Prospectus Directive and described above in paragraph 4.26,

---

[2] It is important to note that this exemption relates to the number of persons actually approached with the offer of securities, not the final number of investors who accept the offer.

certain other types of offer are exempt from the requirement to publish a prospectus. These can be found in Article 4(1) of the Prospectus Directive; however, they are not generally relevant in the context of a private placement.

4.4.1.2 *Admission to trading on a regulated market*

As previously mentioned, Article 3(3) of the Prospectus Directive requires the publication of a prospectus when certain types of securities are admitted to trading on a regulated market. **4.36**

The definition of 'regulated market' in the Prospectus Directive refers to the meaning provided under MiFID. Some EEA member states are seeking to remove their second markets from the list of 'regulated markets' or to create new markets that are not classified as 'regulated markets' specifically to avoid the need for potential offerors to publish a prospectus in connection with an application for admission of securities to trading on such markets. **4.37**

Pursuant to Article 47 of MiFID, each EEA member state is obliged to maintain an updated list of regulated markets authorized by it and to forward that list, and any changes to it, to the EC for publication in the Official Journal of the European Union and on the EC's website. **4.38**

4.4.1.2.1 Exemptions from the requirement to publish a prospectus in connection with admission to trading A listed company undertaking a private placement will need to obtain admission of the new securities to trading on the relevant regulated market, so it will need to ensure that the private placement is structured to fall within one of the exemptions set out in Article 4(2) of the Prospectus Directive. **4.39**

Of these Article 4(2) exemptions, the most relevant to private placements is Article 4(2)(a) which applies to the admission to trading of securities representing, over a period of 12 months, less than 10% of the number of securities of the same class already admitted to trading on the same regulated market. **4.40**

The other exemptions provided by Article 4(2), which are generally not relevant to private placements, include: **4.41**

(a) shares resulting from the conversion or exchange of other securities, provided that those shares are of the same class as shares already admitted to trading on the same regulated market;
(b) shares issued in substitution for shares of the same class already admitted to trading on the same regulated market, if the issuing of such shares does not involve any increase in the issued capital;
(c) shares offered free of charge to existing shareholders, provided that those shares are of the same class as shares already admitted to trading on the same regulated market and that a document is made available containing

information on the number and nature of the shares and the reasons for and details of the offer;

(d) securities offered in connection with a takeover by means of an exchange offer, or offered in connection with a merger, where a document equivalent to a prospectus has been produced; and

(e) securities offered to employees provided that those securities are of the same class as securities already admitted to trading on the same regulated market and that a document is made available containing information on the number and nature of the securities and the reasons for and details of the offer.

4.42   **4.4.1.2.2 Less than 10% of the issued share capital**   As set out in Article 4(2)(a) of the Prospectus Directive, a prospectus is not required for the admission to trading of securities, where those securities are shares representing, over a period of 12 months, less than 10% of the number of shares of the same class already admitted to trading on the same regulated market.

4.43   This exemption is calculated on an aggregated basis over a 12-month period, ending with the date on which the relevant admission is to take place.

4.44   Generally, any securities that have benefited from the application of another exemption from the requirement to produce a prospectus in respect of admission to trading should not be counted in this calculation. So, for example, securities admitted under the convertibles and exchangeables exemption set out in Article 4(2)(g) (see Section 4.4.1.2.3 'Convertibles and exchangeables') would be disregarded for the calculation of the 10% limit.

4.45   In Europe, it is common for companies to 'whitewash' previous issues of securities. If a company has already issued securities representing 9% of its share capital using this exemption and plans to issue securities representing a further 1.5% of its share capital, it will trigger the requirement to produce a prospectus. It can whitewash the previous 9% issued by specifically stating in its prospectus that the prospectus is intended to cover both the new shares to be issued and the previous issues that relied on the 10% exemption. Going forward, therefore, the previous issues can then be ignored when calculating whether the company is within its 10% limit.

4.46   When calculating whether the 10% exemption is available in a particular case, for the numerator, those securities issued over the past 12 months are disregarded if they have either:

(a) been issued pursuant to an exemption other than the 10% exemption; or

(b) been issued pursuant to (or whitewashed in) a prospectus.

4.47   All other securities issued over the past 12 months are counted towards the 10% limit, including those that were previously issued pursuant to the 10% exemption.

For the denominator, all securities in issue at the time the calculation is performed must be counted, regardless of whether they were issued using any exemption or pursuant to a prospectus. **4.48**

By way of example, a company has the following share capital history: **4.49**

(a) 1 July—100 shares in issue;
(b) 1 August—issues 5 shares—exempt under Article 4(2)(a) from requirement to produce a prospectus (10% exemption);
(c) 1 September—issues 50 shares—a prospectus is produced which does not specifically cover the issue of 5 shares in August; and
(d) 1 October— wants to issue 10 further shares.

The calculation is therefore: 15/155 (i.e. taking into account the August shares and the October shares but ignoring the September shares which were issued pursuant to a prospectus). **4.50**

If the company had whitewashed the August issue in the September prospectus, the calculation would have been 10/155 (i.e. only taking into account the October issue). **4.51**

CESR has published guidance[3] that confirms that the 10% calculation should be adjusted for any procedure that affects the number of shares admitted to trading such as a share split for example. **4.52**

4.4.1.2.3 Convertibles and exchangeables   As set out in Article 4(2)(g) of the Prospectus Directive, shares are exempt from the obligation to publish a prospectus where those shares: **4.53**

(a) result from the conversion or exchange of other securities or from the exercise of the rights conferred by other securities; and
(b) are of the same class as other shares that are already admitted to trading on the same regulated market.

Accordingly, there is no requirement that the original securities that are being converted or exchanged must themselves have been previously admitted to trading, or have been the subject of a prospectus. **4.54**

CESR has provided guidance on the application of this exemption. If an issuer has previously issued a convertible bond, the exemption will apply and the underlying shares (i.e. the shares into which the bonds have been converted) can be admitted to trading without the need for an additional prospectus, provided that the issuer already has shares of the same class as the underlying shares admitted to trading on that regulated market. **4.55**

---

[3] CESR's guidance is entitled 'Frequently asked questions regarding Prospectuses: Common positions agreed by CESR Members 8th Updated Version – February 2009'.

4.56   CESR has suggested, however, that the relevant competent authorities should consider relying on national legislation to take enforcement action or to cancel transactions in cases where the issuer appears to be abusing the exemption i.e. interposing an artificial convertible to avoid the production of a prospectus in relation to the underlying securities that it desires to list.

4.57   CESR has confirmed that this exemption does not apply to cases where non-transferable securities are converted into shares, since the Prospectus Directive requirement for a prospectus applies only to transferable securities.

4.4.1.3 Combining exemptions

4.58   Across the EEA, it is not generally possible to combine the exemptions to the 'public offer' trigger that are set out in Article 3(2)(a)–(e) of the Prospectus Directive. However, the qualified investor exemption (Article 3(2)(a)) and the fewer-than-100 persons exemption (Article 3(2)(b)) can be combined on an aggregate basis, allowing a private placement to be offered to both qualified investors and up to 99 persons in each member state who are not qualified investors.

4.59   When combining exemptions to avoid the 'public offer' trigger, an issuer must be careful not to fall outside the exemptions in respect of the 'admission to trading' trigger. For instance, the issuer may wish to restrict the number of shares that it issues in the United Kingdom so that it can rely on the exemption under Article 4(2)(a) in respect of the admission to trading of shares representing, over a period of 12 months, less than 10% of the number of shares of the same class already admitted to trading.

4.5 Pre-emption Rights

4.5.1 General

4.60   Pre-emption rights across the EEA member states are set out in the Second Council Directive on the coordination of safeguards which, for the protection of the interests of members and others, are required by member states of companies (Directive 77/91/EEC) (the 'Second Council Directive'). The Second Council Directive seeks to protect holders of equity securities in public companies by providing existing shareholders in a company the right to subscribe for their pro rata share of any new securities which that company issues for cash.[4] It is a right of first

---

[4] Where a company issues new securities for non-cash consideration, the obligation to offer these new securities to existing shareholders is not triggered. Therefore the use of non-cash consideration can be used to circumvent statutory pre-emption rights—a 'cashbox' structure utilizes non-cash consideration and is described in paragraphs 4.68–4.76.

refusal that the Second Council Directive grants to existing shareholders, which means that when a company wants to issue securities, it must first offer those securities to the existing shareholders in proportion to their existing shareholdings. The Second Council Directive further provides that pre-emption rights may be misapplied only by shareholders at a general meeting of the company.

The reason for a right of pre-emption is to protect shareholders against the dilu- **4.61**
tion of their shareholdings. A shareholder's existing percentage shareholding will be preserved if he exercises his right to buy the proportion of securities that are being offered to him on a pre-emptive basis. Without such a right of pre-emption the shareholder would suffer value leakage of his investment.

A company wishing to undertake a private placement is likely to be restricted **4.62**
in its ability to issue securities to placees of its choice, since the pre-emption rights oblige the company to first offer the securities to existing shareholders. Pre-emption rights, therefore, can be a significant barrier to large-scale private placements in the EEA.

4.5.2 Disapplication of pre-emption rights

In order to conduct a private placement, pre-emption rights in respect of the **4.63**
shares to be placed must be disapplied. In the United Kingdom, most listed companies propose resolutions at their annual general meetings to disapply statutory pre-emption rights, in accordance with the Second Council Directive as described above.[5] Disapplying pre-emption rights and obtaining authority to allot shares annually in this way provides an issuer with the flexibility to issue shares when it wants and to whom it wants, thus facilitating private placements.

A key factor influencing whether shareholders are likely to pass a resolution to **4.64**
disapply pre-emption rights is whether or not the particular disapplication request would be considered routine in terms of the proposed size and price of the non-pre-emptive offering by the Pre-Emption Group, an interest group representing companies, investors and intermediaries.

According to the Pre-Emption Group, where an issuer seeks authority to conduct **4.65**
non-pre-emptive issues of no more than 5% of ordinary share capital in any one year, with a cumulative limit of 7.5% in any three-year rolling period, such a request for disapplication is considered routine and non-controversial. Similarly, where an issuer seeks authority to conduct non-pre-emptive issuances at a discount of up to 5%, it will be considered routine by the Pre-Emption Group.

---

[5] In the United Kingdom, the directors of an issuer also require authority to allot shares, which will be requested at the annual general meeting, i.e. at the same time as the request to disapply pre-emption rights.

In both cases, the issuer's shareholders will generally give their approval and pass the proposed resolutions.

4.66 The general parameters of what the Pre-Emption Group considers routine are not absolute limits on what an issuer can propose to its shareholders in relation to the disapplication of pre-emption rights. However, where a non-routine request is made, the issuer should present a sufficiently strong business case to justify its proposed course of action.

4.67 A breach of pre-emption rights has no effect on the validity of an issue of shares, but it does render the company and every officer jointly and severally liable to compensate any person to whom an offer should have been made (i.e. existing shareholders) for any loss, damage, costs or expenses the person has sustained or incurred as a result of the relevant share issue.

4.5.3 Cashbox placings in the UK

4.5.3.1 Concept

4.68 An issuer may be unable to obtain the requisite shareholder authority to conduct a private placement by way of a non-pre-emptive offer, particularly in cases where the proposed disapplication of pre-emption rights would not be considered routine by the Pre-Emption Group.

4.69 In such circumstances in the United Kingdom, a cashbox structure can enable an issuer to conduct a private placement without having to comply with pre-emption requirements and without obtaining shareholder approval for the disapplication of pre-emption rights. In summary, in a cashbox structure a company issues new shares to placees in exchange for preference shares in a special purpose subsidiary, whose only material asset is cash. The cash assets of special purpose subsidiary result from the cash consideration paid by the placees to the special purpose subsidiary for the newly issued shares in the company. A cashbox placing, therefore, avoids the expense and timetable implications of a pre-emptive issue. In addition, the availability of merger relief in respect of the cashbox structure allows the creation of distributable reserves for the issuer out of the difference between the issue price and the nominal value of the shares issued.

4.70 In the United Kingdom, the cashbox structure does not trigger statutory pre-emption rights because, as stated above, pre-emption rights are only triggered in circumstances where new shares are issued for cash, whereas cashbox structures involve new shares being issued for non-cash consideration (i.e. shares in the special purpose subsidiary).

4.71 An issuer undertaking a private placement by these means will need to structure the private placement so that it falls within appropriate exemptions to the requirement to produce a prospectus.

4.5.3.2 *Structure*

The issuer must first establish a subsidiary cashbox company, which is likely to   **4.72**
be a company incorporated in an offshore jurisdiction such as Jersey. The share
capital of the cashbox company will consist of ordinary shares and redeemable
preference shares. The ordinary shares of the cashbox company will be held jointly
by the issuer's bank or broker (the 'cashbox subscriber') and the issuer in propor-
tions that allow the creation of distributable reserves, with the issuer holding less
than 90% of the ordinary shares.

The cashbox subscriber then agrees to subscribe for the cashbox company's   **4.73**
preference shares for cash, conditional on the admission and listing of the issuer's
ordinary shares.

In addition, the cashbox subscriber agrees to transfer its cashbox company ordi-   **4.74**
nary shares and its cashbox company preference shares to the issuer in consideration of the undertaking by the issuer to allot new ordinary shares in the issuer
to placees. Merger relief under section 131 of the Companies Act 1985[6] is then
available for the issue of the placing shares, since the issuer secures over 90% of
the cashbox company ordinary shares in pursuance of an arrangement providing for the allotment of its own equity shares (i.e. the placing shares) in consideration for the transfer to it of equity shares of the cashbox company ordinary
shares.

Placees pay the placing price for the new ordinary shares to the cashbox subscriber   **4.75**
and the cashbox subscriber will use these proceeds to pay the cashbox company for
the subscription of its preference shares.

The cashbox structure results in the issuer owning 100% of the ordinary shares   **4.76**
and 100% of the preference shares in the cashbox company, which itself holds the
cash proceeds received from the placees. The cash proceeds are ultimately received
by the issuer upon redemption of the preference shares.

4.5.3.3 *Legal considerations*

Shareholders who are not able to participate in an issue of new shares will suffer a   **4.77**
dilution of their shareholding and a decrease in the value of their investment.
A key consideration for an issuer undertaking a cashbox placing, therefore, is the
risk of shareholders, whose pre-emption rights have been circumvented, challenging the use of the cashbox structure in the courts.

It could be argued that the use of a cashbox structure on its true construction is an   **4.78**
allotment of shares for cash, which, if not made on a fully pre-emptive basis is in
breach of statutory pre-emption rights. Such a breach would have no effect on the

---

[6] The corresponding provision in the Companies Act 2006 came into force on 1 October 2009.

validity of the issue of the shares, but does render the company and every officer jointly and severally liable to compensate any person to whom an offer should have been made for any loss, damage, costs or expenses which the person has sustained or incurred.

4.79   The Association of British Insurers ('ABI'), an influential investor body, has written to the chairmen of companies listed on the London Stock Exchange to express its concern over the use of cashbox structures to circumvent pre-emption rights. The ABI's letter states that it will hold boards to account for the breach of the Pre-Emption Group's principles and its members may vote against the re-election of a director following a cashbox placing.

4.80   Issuers considering using a cashbox structure, therefore, should be aware that its use could be challenged, which could, in turn, lead to reputational damage and liability to investors.

4.6 Structuring a Private Placement

4.6.1 Primary offers of new shares by issuers

4.6.1.1 *General*

4.81   If structured properly, a private placement will fall within an exemption to the Prospectus Directive regime and the issuer will not need to produce a prospectus.

4.82   As previously noted, there are no prescriptive disclosure requirements or process rules that govern private placements, and therefore the level of disclosure provided, and the process followed, in a private placement is fluid. Accordingly, private placements may simply follow the statutory minimum standards for the issue of securities and the associated legal process requirements. Equally, private placements can be undertaken with disclosure and process requirements equivalent to a full prospectus standard. Where a particular private placement will land in this wide spectrum of disclosure and process will depend heavily on the nature and level of sophistication of the parties involved, their expectations, and, to a lesser degree, whether the potential issuer has existing regulatory disclosure obligations (for example, because the issuer is listed on a recognized investment exchange and has an obligation to comply with continuous information disclosure requirements).

4.83   There are a number of examples where the relevant rules in certain EEA member states are slightly more prescriptive. In France, for example, there are country-specific information obligations on a party wishing to carry out a private placement. Article 211-4 of the General Regulation of the Autorité des Marchés

Financiers (the 'GRAMF') obliges offerors and issuers to inform potential investors that:

(i) in connection with the transaction, there will be no prospectus filed with, or approved by, the Autorité des Marchés Financiers (the 'AMF'), the French competent authority;

(ii) the investors must invest on their own account and in accordance with the applicable dispositions of the French Monetary and Financial Code (the 'MFC'); and

(iii) the direct and indirect distribution of the relevant securities to the public may not be carried out except in compliance with the applicable provisions of the MFC.

4.6.1.2 Documentation

While there is no legal requirement to produce a prospectus for a private placement **4.84** that is validly exempt from Prospectus Directive requirements, other disclosure-related provisions, including anti-fraud measures, may apply in respect of any statements and information provided to purchasers of securities in connection with a potential placement.

It is common for issuers to provide potential placees with a disclosure document, **4.85** or, alternatively, to provide such investors with access to a data room containing the relevant information on the company and the securities (or otherwise make such information available) so that investors can conduct their own due diligence.

The use of a disclosure document has become particularly common with issuers **4.86** conducting private placement because of its marketing value. In recent years the level of disclosure typically provided in private placement disclosure documents has become increasingly comprehensive to the point where, while the Prospectus Directive disclosure requirements are rarely followed in full (due to the difficulty in obtaining certain information or the need to conduct the transaction quickly), such disclosure requirements are often used as a benchmark in formulating and assessing the adequacy of disclosure in the context of private placements.

4.6.1.2.1 Disclosure document As discussed above an issuer conducting a pri- **4.87** vate placement may choose to produce a disclosure document (commonly referred to as a 'private placement memorandum' ('PPM') or 'information memorandum' ('IM')), containing details about the company, the terms and conditions of the investment opportunity, risk factors and the company's business strategy.

It has become increasingly common for PPMs or IMs to follow the format of a **4.88** prospectus containing some or all of the following sections:

(i) *Business description*: a description of the issuer's principal products and services, principal markets and methods of distribution or achieving sales and a breakdown of total sales and revenue by categories of activity and geographical markets.

(ii) *Risk factors*: a discussion of the principal factors in respect of the risk involved in the investment opportunity.

(iii) *Financial information*: a description of the key drivers of an issuer's financial position, performance and information on the company's capital resources.

(iv) *Terms and conditions*: the terms and conditions on which the private place-ment of the securities on offer will be made.

4.89   In addition to limiting liability and being used to market the private placement (as discussed above), the disclosure document will also need to provide sufficient information for potential investors to evaluate the investment opportunity and to decide whether to participate in the private placement. The level of disclosure in any form of private placement disclosure document will vary greatly and depend upon the nature of the investment and the nature of the parties involved.

4.90   **4.6.1.2.2 Additional public or listed company considerations**   For a public or listed company, much of the information about the issuer that would be included in a disclosure document (for example, the annual report and financial state-ments) should, in any case, be in the public domain, due to the continuing disclo-sure obligations that apply to the issuer in connection with its listing. Such issuers, therefore, tend not to publish any form of disclosure document when conducting private placements or, if they do, it will be a very limited document containing only the terms and conditions of the securities on offer.

4.91   It is vital that such a company wishing to undertake a private placement does not disclose inside information to potential investors as this might render such investors as 'insiders', thereby precluding their participation in the investment opportunity.

4.92   The Market Abuse Directive defines 'inside information' as:

> information of a precise nature which has not been made public, relating, directly or indirectly, to one or more issuers of financial instruments or to one or more financial instruments and which, if it were made public, would be likely to have a significant effect on the prices of those financial instruments or on the price of related derivative financial instruments.

4.93   Should investors make any investment decision on the basis of inside informa-tion, they may be committing an offence under the Market Abuse Directive. It is therefore imperative that companies disclose inside information to the market as and when they are legally obliged to do so, and not selectively to potential investors.

4.94   **4.6.1.2.3 Additional private company considerations**   Private companies are not listed on a regulated or other market and therefore are not subject to the same reporting and disclosure regime as public or listed companies. For potential investors, this may be the first opportunity to scrutinize detailed information relating to the company. Furthermore, a private company is not subject to the Market Abuse Directive since it is not a listed entity. It can therefore disclose whatever information it wishes to any party, including information that would be deemed to be inside information, if the company were subject to the Market Abuse Directive.

Shareholders of a private company wishing to dispose of their interest in the company may consider a sale of their shares either in connection with an initial public offering (a 'sell down') or the entire company may be sold to one or more institutional investors in a transaction that avoids the need to prepare a prospectus (a private placement). Conducting the private transaction and the public offer in parallel is known as running a dual track process. This is a process in which both exit routes are pursued until a decision is made as to which exit route will achieve the highest value for the shareholders: effectively there are two transactions being conducted in parallel. **4.95**

Since a disclosure document will usually be prepared solely for the purposes of the private placement, and a draft prospectus will be prepared for the initial public offering, it is important for the issuer to ensure that the disclosure document does not conflict with the prospectus. **4.96**

In addition, a private company undertaking a dual track process must be aware that the disclosure of inside information to private investors during the dual track process may prevent the private investors from participating in the initial public offering (should the company decide to go down this route) if such inside information is not included in the prospectus and therefore not available to all investors. However, if the company decides to proceed with the private transaction, the disclosure of inside information to private investors would not prevent such investors' participation. **4.97**

4.6.1.2.4 Non-disclosure agreements   Both private and public companies may require potential investors to sign a non-disclosure agreement before they are involved in a private placement. Where a publicly-listed issuer undertakes, for example, an accelerated book-build placing, (or similar placing in a short timeframe) it is unlikely that any participant in the placing would receive any information about the issuer (other than short notice of the proposed transaction) and it would be unlikely that a non-disclosure agreement would be required. Even though most of the information that a public company will disclose is already in the public domain, there may be sufficient confidential information that does not fall within the definition of inside information that it wishes to protect. Indeed, a public company will want potential investors to sign a non-disclosure agreement in order to keep confidential the very fact that it is considering a private placement. **4.98**

4.99 The non-disclosure agreement makes sure that any confidential information remains confidential. It allows potential investors to disclose confidential information in only a limited set of circumstances (for example, if disclosure of the information is required by law, if the information becomes public by some other means, or if the information is disclosed under regulatory requirements). It is also common for the non-disclosure agreement to include a specific term restricting the ability of the potential investor to deal in the issuer's shares prior to the transaction.

4.100 All EEA member state issuers with securities admitted to trading on a regulated market are subject to the obligation to release inside information in a timely manner, unless an exemption applies. Despite this obligation, a participant in a private placement will want to ensure they do not breach securities trading laws by acting on inside information that has not been properly disclosed and may seek confirmation from the issuer (commonly in the form of a warranty in the transaction documentation) that the issuer has complied with the relevant disclosure obligations. In addition, prior to participation in the private placement the participant may want to terminate the non-disclosure agreement so as to remove any doubt as to whether he is in possession of any inside information.

4.101 Potential investors are not at risk of trading on the basis of inside information where the issuer is not subject to the Market Abuse Directive (i.e. if its securities are not admitted to trading on a regulated market) and, accordingly, it is under no obligation to disclose inside information to the market generally and transactions in its securities are not subject to restrictions based on the existence of inside information.

4.102 An issuer or offeror of securities will need to bear in mind that under Article 15(5) of the Prospectus Directive, when material information is provided by an issuer or an offeror and is addressed to qualified investors or special categories of investors, this material information must be disclosed to all qualified investors or special categories of investors to whom the offer is exclusively addressed. Such material information includes information disclosed in the context of meetings relating to offers of securities.

4.103 This general principle applies irrespective of whether the offer is addressed to qualified investors, to fewer than 100 persons in one member state, or to any other category of persons to whom securities can be offered without the publication of a prospectus. The principle is that material information that is disclosed to certain persons in that category must be disclosed to all such persons.

4.104 **4.6.1.2.5 Subscription documentation** The form of the documentation under which participants subscribe for securities in private placements will depend on the structure of the private placement. In the absence of prescriptive rules on the conduct of private placements, the structure of a particular private placement is likely to be determined by the requirements (including the relative levels of sophistication) of the participants, as well as the general statutory and regulatory requirements that apply to share issues.

Two common private placement structures are: **4.105**

(i)   direct subscription agreement: the issuer agrees to issue securities directly to participants in the private placement. Financial advisers may or may not be involved in the transaction.

(ii) placings through financial institutions: the issuer agrees to issue securities to a financial institution or institutions (which may, or may not, be on an underwritten basis), who in turn place the securities (usually as agent of the issuer) to the placees.

4.6.1.2.6 Subscription agreement The direct issue of securities by a listed **4.106** or non-listed issuer to participants in a private placement by way of direct subscription is likely to be driven by some form of restructuring or other corporate transaction, for example, a private placement to new or existing cornerstone investors. A financial institution such as an investment bank may be involved in negotiating the terms of the private placement, but it is unlikely that the financial institution would take the relevant securities onto its own books—it would be more likely to solicit or source the placees for the securities.

In addition to setting out the price, terms and conditions of the private place- **4.107** ment, the subscription documentation will set out the process for the transaction. It will generally include two sets of warranties:

(i)   warranties from the issuer to the subscribers; and

(ii) warranties from the subscribers to the issuer.

The nature of warranties provided by the issuer to the subscribers will vary widely **4.108** depending on the nature of the transaction. Where the issuer is a listed entity with existing ongoing disclosure obligations, it is likely to provide only minimal warranties. This is because under the issuer's continuous disclosure obligations, all price-sensitive information should have been made public, and the issuer will be reluctant to take on any additional liability (in the form of warranties to subscribers in the public placement), in respect of information already in the public domain.

Where the issuer is not listed, or where the exigencies of the particular transaction **4.109** demand it, the issuer may provide additional warranty cover. Such warranty protection might include matters such as: corporate power and authority to enter into the transaction; valid issuance of securities; compliance with laws; correctness of any due diligence information given to the placees; no inside information that has not been made public; and no breach of European or United States securities laws.

4.110 The warranties given by the participants to the issuer of the securities will typically be limited to the following matters: corporate power and authority to enter into the transaction; compliance with applicable securities laws; and confirmation that they are qualified investors as defined in the Prospectus Directive (or other relevant exemption, which allows them to participate in the transaction without the need for the issuer to prepare a prospectus).

4.111 Depending on the nature of the private placement, participants may be granted additional contractual rights in the definitive transaction documentation. Such additional rights are more common in unlisted issuers, but are sometimes seen in listed issuers attempting to attract new cornerstone shareholders. Such additional rights may include:

(i) the right to appoint directors to the board so that the interests of the participant are represented;

(ii) the right to receive certain information, such as management accounts, board documentation and other financial information (this additional right is seen mainly in unlisted issuers, since listed issuers are required to make price-sensitive information publicly available under their continuous disclosure obligations);

(iii) the right to restrict the issuer from undertaking certain activities and entering into certain types of transactions without the participant's consent. This additional right allows the participant an element of control in the activities of the issuer and provides a layer of protection for the participant's investment; and/or

(iv) pre–emption or anti-dilution rights (see Section 4.5 above).

4.112 In addition, issuers may seek to impose restrictions on participants in private placements in the definitive transaction documentation. Such restrictions may include:

(i) restrictions on passing on information that a participant's nominee director receives in connection with its position;

(ii) limiting or prohibiting trading by the participant in the securities of the issuer for a certain period of time (a 'lock-up' period); and

(iii) following the lock-up period, the obligation on the participant to notify the issuer of its intention to dispose of any part of its shareholding.

4.113 **4.6.1.2.7 Placing through financial institutions** In addition to placings directly between issuers and placees, it is common for financial institutions to be involved in the private placement of listed issuers' securities. Such transactions are usually conducted by issuers whose securities are listed and little or no non-public information is given to potential placees on the basis that listed issuers are under an obligation to disclose all price-sensitive information, in addition to their periodic disclosure requirements.

Such transactions are usually conducted on a short timetable and the financial **4.114** institution's role, in addition to providing transaction advice, is to facilitate the issue of the securities by acting as agent for the issuer and agreeing to place (commonly at an underwritten price) the relevant securities. The securities being issued are commonly taken onto the financial institution's books as agent for the issuer (which avoids transaction or transfer duties or taxes in many jurisdictions), before the financial institution places the securities to placees (typically its clients).

Warranty protection for placees is usually very limited in transaction documenta- **4.115** tion for placements such as these. It would be uncommon for the issuer itself to give any warranties to the placees. Similarly, is unlikely that additional rights would be granted to placees in such a transaction, unlike private placements where the issuer transacts directly with the placees as described above.

Placees in such transactions usually give a suite of warranties that primarily go to **4.116** their ability to participate in the transaction without triggering the requirement to prepare a prospectus.

4.6.2 Secondary offers of existing securities by existing shareholders—block trades

A block trade is a sale of a large block of securities already in issue, usually under- **4.117** taken by institutional investors that have a major securities holding in a company.

A block trade is a form of private placement and its attractiveness is a result of the **4.118** relative speed and low cost at which the sale of securities can be effected, which is partly due to the seller not having to prepare a prospectus.

The parties conducting the block trade will typically seek to rely on the following **4.119** exemptions under the Prospectus Directive:

(i) Article 3(2)(a) of the Prospectus Directive, which exempts an offer of securities addressed solely to qualified investors; and

(ii) Article 3(2)(b) of the Prospectus Directive, which exempts an offer of securities addressed to fewer than 100 natural or legal persons per EEA member state, other than qualified investors.

In addition, the obligation to publish a prospectus for the admission of securities **4.120** to trading usually will not apply since block trades nearly always involve securities that have already been admitted to trading on a regulated market.

Block trades are significantly less documentation-intensive than an issue of new **4.121** equity securities. The main document involved in a block trade is the purchase agreement, which will be short in comparison to an underwriting agreement for an initial public offering (see Chapter 2). Since no prospectus is required, block trades are often referred to as being 'undocumented', in other words, without any form of disclosure document.

4.6.2.1 *Various structures of a block trade*

4.122 **4.6.2.1.1 Accelerated book-build** In an accelerated book-build, the financial institution that is appointed to manage the block trade will sign the purchase agreement with the seller shortly before the transaction is announced. The financial institution may underwrite the block trade, in which case the seller will be guaranteed to raise a minimum amount of money. Alternatively, the financial institution may commit only to using reasonable endeavours to sell the securities, leaving the seller uncertain as to the proceeds it will receive.

4.123 The financial institution will first build a book of demand for the seller, which will inform the discussions between the seller and financial institution as to the price of the private placement, for which the financial institution will receive a commission from the seller. In an accelerated equity offering, the financial institution will usually act as the seller's agent.

4.124 **4.6.2.1.2 Bought deal** A bought deal occurs when the financial institution acting in the private placement purchases securities from the issuer or offeror before it starts to market the investment opportunity to potential investors. The financial institution will generally resell the securities as soon as possible after it acquires them from the seller and, if it is able to resell the securities at a higher price, the financial institution will keep the difference.

4.125 The benefit to the seller is that it is guaranteed the price that it agrees with the financial institution which will carry the financing risk. If the financial institution is not able to sell the securities, it will end up holding them, or have to sell them at a loss.

4.126 **4.6.2.1.3 Private placement with claw-back** In a private placement with claw-back, the securities are privately placed with placees. Initially, therefore, the securities are not initially offered to the existing security holders. Rather, once the securities have been privately placed, the existing security holders are given the opportunity to 'claw back' the securities that are in the hands of the placees. Accordingly, the claw-back complies with pre-emption rights, since the existing shareholders are able to take up their pro rata entitlement. The reason for privately placing the securities prior to the claw-back taking place is to provide the issuer with certainty in terms of the proceeds it will receive.

4.127 Although the private placement component of the transaction will not require a prospectus to be published, the claw-back is effectively an open offer (i.e. to existing security holders) and therefore it is possible that it will constitute a public offer and require the publication of a prospectus, unless the issuer can take advantage of any relevant Prospectus Directive exemptions (as discussed in paragraph 4.26).

4.6.2.2 *Appointment of financial institution*

The financial institution assisting with a block trade may be appointed as the **4.128** seller's agent, or alternatively, the financial institution may purchase the securities from the seller and sell them on to investors as principal. Where the financial institution acts as principal, this will result in a double stamp duty charge in the United Kingdom, as stamp duty will be chargeable on both the transfer to the financial institution and on the on-sale.

In an accelerated equity offering, the seller appoints the manager in advance of the **4.129** block trade and the two parties agree the purchase agreement and conduct due diligence before the block trade is initiated. This approach can also be used for bought deals and back-stopped deals.

Alternatively, and as seen for accelerated book-builds, a selection of financial insti- **4.130** tutions are invited to tender for the position to manage and undertake the transaction, immediately prior to the launch of the block trade. The evening before the launch of the block trade, the financial institutions are sent a confidentiality letter and once this is signed, they will receive the tender documentation. Bids must be submitted within a set deadline (usually a number of hours after the tender documents have been sent). The seller will then negotiate the purchase agreement with the successful financial institution and launch the block trade. The following morning, the transaction will be announced and the financial institution will start the process of building a book for the securities to be sold in the block trade. It is often the case that the book will close before the end of the day.

4.6.2.3 *Block trade timetable: pre-launch*

As explained above, a block trade is an undocumented transaction. A purchaser **4.131** will therefore have to rely on publicly available information on the company, such as annual reports, public information releases or commercially available research reports on the company. Undocumented block trades are therefore suited to securities that are well researched and will usually take place soon after the issuer has published its financial results. It is unusual for a block trade to occur within a few weeks of a scheduled announcement by the relevant company of any material information.

4.7 Liability for Offering Transferable Securities Without an Approved Prospectus

Issuers or offerors of securities who undertake a private placement will rely on one **4.132** of the exemptions in the Prospectus Directive to the obligation to publish a prospectus. If an issuer is mistaken in its reliance on a particular exemption, this will result in the issuer undertaking an offer of securities to the public or admission of securities to trading without the required prospectus, thereby directly contravening the Prospectus Directive (and, most likely, national implementing legislation).

4.133 Article 3 of the Prospectus Directive places the obligation on EEA member states to ensure that any offer of securities to the public or admission of securities to trading on a regulated market is documented with a prospectus. However, the Prospectus Directive does not provide any further information regarding the liability regime in respect of the failure to publish a prospectus when a party is legally required to do so.

4.134 It is therefore a matter for each EEA member state to impose its own liability regime in respect of the Prospectus Directive obligations. A selection of liability regimes across the EEA are summarized below.

4.7.1 United Kingdom

4.135 In the United Kingdom, as is the case throughout the EEA, it is unlawful for transferable securities to be offered to the public or admitted to trading on a regulated market, unless a prospectus is published prior to the public offer and admission to trading.

4.136 In the United Kingdom, where an issuer or offeror has failed to publish a prospectus in breach of national laws implementing the Prospectus Directive and is making an offer of securities to the public, the UK Financial Services Authority (the 'FSA') has the power to require an issuer or offeror to suspend its offer for up to ten days or withdraw its offer of securities to the public.

4.137 Similarly, where an issuer or offeror has requested the admission to trading of securities but failed to publish a prospectus, the FSA has the power to require the issuer or offeror to suspend the request for up to ten days. If the relevant securities have already been admitted to trading, the FSA can require the market operator to suspend trading in the securities (for up to ten days) or to prohibit trading of the securities.

4.138 The FSA also has the power to impose financial penalties on, and make public statements censuring, the issuer, the offeror or the person requesting the admission of transferable securities to trading.

4.139 Furthermore, the failure to publish a prospectus in the absence of a relevant exemption is a criminal offence and can carry a term of imprisonment of up to two years or a fine or both.

4.7.2 France

4.140 In France, where an issuer or offeror fails to publish a prospectus in cases where one is required, the AMF can make use of its general powers of sanction against any party in breach of its legal or regulatory obligations where such breach can negatively affect the protection of the investors or the proper functioning of the market. In these circumstances, the AMF can impose an administrative fine of up to either EUR 10,000,000 or ten times the amount of any profit made by the party in breach.

The AMF can also use its general powers to order the suspension of the trading **4.141** of the relevant securities and, where necessary, bring a claim in summary proceedings before a court of first instance to ensure that the party in breach complies with the orders of the AMF.

In addition, the failure to file a prospectus where required would also be consid- **4.142** ered a civil wrong under the general provisions of tort law, pursuant to which an offeror could be liable to compensate any person that has suffered a loss as a result of the failure to publish a prospectus.

While there is no specific provision under French law that renders the failure to **4.143** publish a prospectus a criminal act, it should be noted that an offeror could be guilty of other criminal offences in the context of the same transaction, for example, if the transaction was marketed or publicized in breach of financial solicitation rules.

4.7.3 Germany

In Germany, the Prospectus Directive was implemented into national law by the **4.144** Securities Prospectus Act (Wertpapierprospektgesetz—'WpPG').

If an offeror or issuer fails to publish a prospectus in breach of the Securities **4.145** Prospectus Act, the BaFin has the power to prohibit the intended offer or issuance. If the BaFin becomes aware of such breach, it is authorized to suspend the offer to the public for a time period of up to ten days.

The failure to publish a prospectus in breach of the provisions of the Securities **4.146** Prospectus Act constitutes a regulatory offence. The BaFin may impose fines on the relevant offeror or issuer of up to EUR 50,000 or EUR 100,000 (depending on the form of breach). If an issuer or offeror fails to comply with a formal ruling of the BaFin prohibiting or suspending the offer, the maximum fine available is EUR 500,000.

Parties that fail to publish a prospectus where one is required may also face civil **4.147** liability to compensate any investors who suffer loss as a result of such failure.

4.7.4 The Netherlands

In the Netherlands, where an offeror or issuer fails to publish a prospectus in the **4.148** absence of a relevant exemption, the Netherlands Authority for the Financial Markets (the 'AFM'), the jurisdiction's competent authority, has the discretionary power to issue an instruction to adhere to a certain line of conduct within a reasonable term. For example, the AFM can order the offeror to suspend its offer for a certain period, during which it must remedy the breach by publishing a prospectus. Where the relevant securities have already been admitted to trading, the AFM can require the market operator to suspend trading in the securities or to prohibit trading of the securities. Dutch securities law, however, specifically provides that any existing agreement between an offeror and a third party will not be invalidated by the offeror's failure to publish a prospectus. In addition to passing orders, the AMF can impose a penalty (last onder dwangsom), an administrative fine (bestuurlijke boete), or both.

4.149 Furthermore, the failure to publish a prospectus where one is required is an economic offence under Dutch law and can carry a term of imprisonment of up to two years, community service, or a fine. In practice, however, it is unlikely that the Public Prosecutor will decide to prosecute.

4.150 Offerors may, however, face civil liability to compensate those who suffer losses as a result of the failure to publish a prospectus.

4.8 Structuring a Private Placement in the United States

4.8.1 US securities laws: register or be exempt

4.151 A fundamental tenet of US federal securities law is that the best way to protect investors is to ensure the disclosure of all of the facts that are material to an investment decision. To that end, US laws provide that public offers and sales of securities in the United States or to US persons outside the United States must either be:

(i) registered with the US Securities and Exchange Commission (the 'SEC') (which must declare the registration statement effective before sales proceed); or

(ii) exempt from registration requirements. There are several exemptions from registration requirements under the US Securities Act of 1933, as amended (the 'Securities Act'), which include, *inter alia*, resales to qualified institutional buyers ('QIBs') (Rule 144A); and private placements by the issuer of the securities (Section 4(2) and Regulation D).

4.152 If an issuer sells securities in violation of the Securities Act registrations requirement and does not fall within an exemption, a buyer of the issuer's securities will have the right to rescind its purchase and recover from the issuer the consideration paid for the securities, even if the buyer is unaffected by the issuer's violation.

4.8.1.1 *Rule 144A: resales of restricted securities to qualified institutional buyers*

Rule 144A is a non-exclusive safe harbour which exempts from registration **4.153** requirements resales of securities issued in a non-public offering to QIBs. The rule addresses the circumstances in which a person who has purchased securities from an issuer in a transaction that was itself exempt from registration under the Securities Act, such as an offshore transaction made in accordance with Regulation S (discussed below), or a private placement made in reliance upon Section 4(2) or Regulation D (discussed below), may resell those securities without destroying the original exemption or otherwise being subject to the Securities Act registration requirements. The rationale behind the Rule 144A exemption is that the benefit of disclosure-based investor protection is outweighed by the benefit of more rapid access to capital markets when securities are exclusively placed with experienced, sophisticated investors.

4.8.1.1.1 Criteria for safe harbour Under Rule 144A, the purchaser may offer **4.154** and resell securities that have been purchased from an issuer in a transaction that was itself exempt from registration under the Securities Act, to any QIB if:

- (i) the securities are not of the same class when issued as any securities of the issuer quoted in NASDAQ or listed on a US stock exchange (the 'fungibility prohibition');
- (ii) the buyer is advised that the seller is relying on Rule 144A (the 'notice requirement');
- (iii) securities to be resold are not those of a company that is registered or is required to be registered under the US Investment Company Act of 1940, as amended (the 'Investment Company Act'); or
- (iv) unless the issuer is a reporting company or is exempt from registration under Rule 12g3-2(b) of the US Securities Exchange Act of 1934, as amended (the 'Exchange Act'), the holder and a prospective purchaser from the holder have the continuing right to receive from the issuer, at or prior to the time of sale by the holder, upon request, specified financial statements of the issuer and information as to its business (the 'available information requirement').

4.8.1.1.2 Eligible purchasers: what is a QIB? Resales under Rule 144A must **4.155** be made exclusively to QIBs. Rule 144A(7)(a)(1) defines a QIB as:

- (i) an institution that owns and invests on a discretionary basis at least US$100 million in qualifying securities (US$10 million if the person is a US broker-dealer);
- (ii) an entity owned by a QIB; or
- (iii) a US broker-dealer buying as agent for, or in a riskless principal transaction for resale to, a QIB. If the person is a bank or a thrift institution it must also have a net worth of at least US$25 million to qualify.

4.156 **4.8.1.1.3 Rule 144A: advantages and disadvantages** Rule 144A offerings have several advantages that make them an appealing alternative for non-US issuers seeking to avoid the time and expense associated with a public offering. As Rule 144A offerings are not subject to lengthy review by the SEC, they can be completed more quickly and at a lower cost than public offerings. Furthermore, the detailed disclosure requirements of the Securities Act and the ongoing periodic reporting requirements and corporate governance regulations of the Exchange Act, do not apply to Rule 144A transactions. Rule 144A also provides access to US capital markets to non-US issuers that would otherwise be considered investment companies under the Investment Company Act and prohibited from engaging in public offerings. Such companies may be permitted to market securities to 'qualified purchasers' (as defined under the Investment Company Act) that are also QIBs under Rule 144A, provided that certain clearing system procedures are implemented.

4.157 However, the benefits resulting from the greater ease of access provided by Rule 144A must be weighed against the costs of engaging in a private placement. For example, a Rule 144A offering is directed at a much smaller group of investors than a public offering. In addition, securities offered under Rule 144A are 'restricted securities' and may only be resold, without registration or an available exemption, by investors to other qualified institutional investors or outside the United States. The combination of these two factors may reduce the size of the transaction and result in less favourable pricing and diminished liquidity.

4.8.1.2 Private placements (non-public offerings)

4.158 Section 4(2) of the Securities Act exempts from registration requirements transactions carried out by an issuer that do not involve a public offering. Although the term 'public offering' is not defined in the Securities Act, the SEC and US courts have interpreted the exemption to be available for offerings conducted in a non-public manner. Generally, the number of persons who are offered the securities, the sophistication of both offerees and purchasers of the securities, and the type of disclosure provided to offerees will be considered in determining whether the issuer has engaged in a public offering.

4.159 Because of the uncertainty in determining whether a public offering has occurred, the SEC adopted Regulation D as a non-exclusive safe harbour for offerings made under Section 4(2). Failure to comply with Regulation D does not preclude issuers from relying on the exemption under Section 4(2). However, most issuers choose to comply with all of the requirements of Regulation D (except with respect to the Form D filing described below).

4.160 Regulation D requires that the following conditions are met:

(i) no general solicitation or advertising;

(ii) no more than 35 offerees or purchasers who are not 'accredited investors';

(iii) compliance with certain information requirements;

(iv) limitation on resales under Rule 144; and

(v) proper notice to the SEC on Form D. Additionally, issuers must assure themselves that private placement purchasers will not act as distributors of the securities (or underwriters) and that such purchasers are aware of the restricted nature of the securities.

Private placements are generally not relied on in circumstances where there is a sizeable placement in the United States because of the more onerous transfer restrictions on secondary sales and also because certain exemptions from the anti-manipulation rules are not available. However, the exemption is useful if there is a small number of offerees with whom the issuer has important relationships (in this case the general solicitation requirement would limit the offerees to those who have a pre-existing relationship with the issuer or banker). **4.161**

4.8.1.2.1 General solicitation and advertising Neither the issuer nor any person acting on its behalf may offer or sell securities by any form of general solicitation or advertising. With certain limited exceptions, the issuer should refrain from offering the securities through advertisements, articles, press releases, mass mailings, notices or other communications published in newspapers, magazines or similar media, broadcast over television or the radio. Any seminar or meeting whose attendees have been invited by any general solicitation or general advertising will also be considered a form of general solicitation or advertising of the kind prohibited under Regulation D. Certain postings on a website also may constitute a general solicitation or advertising and would therefore compromise an issuer's ability to rely on a Regulation D exemption. **4.162**

4.8.1.2.2 Number of offerees/purchasers Regulation D does not limit the number of persons to whom offers may be made (although offerings to a significant number of persons may violate the restriction on general solicitation). Regulation D allows sales to an unlimited number of 'accredited investors' ('AIs') as defined in Rule 501(a). AIs include banks, insurance companies, registered and small business investment companies, certain business development companies, certain employer benefit plans, organizations with total assets in excess of $5 million and certain wealthy individuals (individuals with a net worth or joint net worth with his or her spouse exceeding $1 million, or with individual income in excess of $200,000 ($300,000 joint with spouse), in each of the two most recent years and if the individual has a reasonable expectation of reaching the same income level in the current year). Regulation D also allows sales to no more than 35 non-AIs. **4.163**

Issuers commonly require prospective investors to represent in writing, either in a subscription agreement or a separate investor letter, that the purchaser is an AI. If sales are made to non-AIs, the issuer might ask the purchaser to complete a **4.164** questionnaire that elicits information concerning the level of the investor's financial sophistication. A significant drawback of selling to non-AIs is that the offering becomes subject to considerably more onerous disclosure requirements, as described below.

4.8.2 Liability

4.165   The anti-fraud provisions of the Exchange Act contained in Section 10(b) and its accompanying Rule 10b-5 have become by far the most significant remedy for disclosure violations in securities transactions, both for the SEC and for private litigants. While the provisions themselves do not create a private right of action (the Exchange Act speaks only of civil and administrative remedies by the SEC and possible criminal prosecution), US courts have long held that buyers or sellers of securities have an implied right to recover damages based on violations of Section 10(b) and Rule 10b-5. These provisions continue to apply to offerings regardless of the fact that they are exempt from the registration requirements of the Securities Act.

4.8.2.1 *Broad reach of 10(b) and 10b-5*

4.166   Section 10(b) and Rule 10b-5 are broadly written: Section 10(b) proscribes the use of 'any manipulative or deceptive device or contrivance' in connection with the purchase or sale of any security, while Rule 10b-5 specifies three categories of conduct that qualify as violations. These are:

(i) employing any 'device, scheme, or artifice to defraud';

(ii) making any untrue statement of material fact or failing to state a material fact 'necessary in order to make the statements made, in the light of the circumstances under which they were made, not misleading'; and

(iii) engaging in any 'act, practice, or course of business' which operates as a 'fraud or deceit'.

4.8.2.2 *Remedies (SEC and private litigants)*

4.167   The remedies for violations of Rule 10b-5 differ depending on whether the action was initiated by the SEC or by a private litigant (or group of private litigants). The SEC may impose a number of remedies under Section 10(b) and Rule 10b-5, including:

(i) injunctive relief;

(ii) prohibiting (permanently or temporarily) any person who has violated these provisions from acting as an officer or director of any public company;

(iii) civil penalties; and

(iv) referral to the Department of Justice, which may seek criminal sanctions for wilful violations of the anti-fraud provisions of the Exchange Act.

A private person can recover their out-of-pocket loss, which is generally the difference between the price paid for the security and the 'true' value of the securities, which will normally be deemed to be the market price of the security at the time of the suit. The plaintiff may also seek to rescind the transaction and return the securities to the defendant in exchange for the money originally paid by the plaintiff.

4.168

4.9 Publicity

The ability of an issuer or an offeror of securities to identify and attract investors is crucial for the success of the transaction, and the issuer's or offeror's publicity and marketing efforts are key to this.

4.169

Where an issuer or an offeror of securities planning a private placement relies on the 'qualified investors' exemption to the obligation to publish a prospectus, it is important that the marketing and publicity of the investment opportunity is not addressed to investors other than 'qualified investors'. Similarly, where the 100 persons exemption is relied on, it is essential that the marketing and publicity of the investment opportunity is not addressed to 100 persons or more, other than qualified investors.

4.170

Regardless of which of the above two exemptions is relied on, issuers and offerors of securities will need to be aware of Article 15(5) of the Prospectus Directive which states that when no prospectus is required (i.e. in a private placement):

4.171

> material information provided by an issuer or an offeror and addressed to qualified investors or special categories of investors, including information disclosed in the context of meetings relating to offers of securities, shall be disclosed to all qualified investors or special categories of investors to whom the offer is exclusively addressed.

For private placements, the marketing and publicity efforts not only need to comply with the exemptions of the Prospectus Directive to avoid triggering the obligation to publish a prospectus, but may also need to comply with local laws of individual EEA member states restricting financial promotions.

4.172

There are no pan-European restrictions on publicity in connection with an offering or distribution of securities. Therefore, at the outset of a transaction, local legal counsel will need to advise on publicity and produce publicity guidelines for the issuer or offeror of securities that cover various aspects of the release of publicity:

4.173

(i)   the internal process for the approval of publicity;

(ii) contact with the press;

    (iii)   ordinary course advertisements and product marketing;

    (iv)   release of information to analysts, banks and brokers;

    (v)   communication with employees;

    (vi)   investor roadshow; and

    (vii)   verification of information.

4.174   Local legal counsel will also advise on procedures in respect of 'website blockers'. This is an internet page that investors must pass through to gain online access to any documents relevant to the transaction. Such a website blocker should be worded so as to put the website users on notice that information may not be intended for certain jurisdictions or only intended for certain special categories of investors.

4.175   Relevant issues in respect of marketing a private placement in the United Kingdom and France, including local financial promotion regimes, are highlighted below.

4.9.1 United Kingdom

4.176   United Kingdom legislation places a basic restriction on communicating financial promotions. This restriction does not apply, however, to financial promotions that are issued or approved by persons who are authorized by the FSA pursuant to the Financial Services and Markets Act 2000.

4.177   Therefore, under the basic restriction, financial promotions need to be issued or approved by an authorized person and cannot be communicated by unauthorized persons, unless an exemption is available under the Financial Services and Markets Act 2000 (Financial Promotion) Order 2005 (the 'Financial Promotion Order 2005'). The most relevant exemptions in the context of private placements include:

    (i)   *communications to investment professionals*: this exemption assumes that the investment professionals receiving the financial promotion have sufficient expertise to appreciate the risks involved with investments;

    (ii)   *communications to certified high net worth individuals*: this exemption has a number of detailed limitations and requirements. Of particular relevance is that this exemption is restricted to communications relating to stocks, shares and warrants in an unlisted company;

    (iii)   *communications to certified sophisticated investors*: where the individual is certified by an authorized person as having enough knowledge to be able to understand the risks associated with the description of investment to which the financial promotion relates;

    (iv)   *communications to self-certified sophisticated investors*: a self-certified investor is an individual who has signed a self-certification statement within the previous 12 months; and

(v) *communications to associations of high net worth or sophisticated investors*: this exemption allows financial promotions to associations of high net worth or sophisticated investors, such as investment clubs, or to a member of such an association.

4.9.2 France

Although private placements generally fall within an exemption to the require- **4.178** ment to file a prospectus, in France they are not necessarily exempt from:

(i) the rules on financial solicitation (démarchage bancaire et financier) set out in the MFC; or

(ii) the rules on the marketing of units or shares of collective investment vehicles.

The application of the rules on financial solicitation to private placements depends **4.179** on which Prospectus Directive exemptions an issuer or offeror relies on when conducting the private placement. The MFC provides that the rules on financial solicitation do not apply when a issuer or offeror restricts its marketing to qualified investors. However no exemption is made in cases where the issuer or offeror relies on the 100 persons exemption. Accordingly, in any private placement where the issuer or offeror relies, in full or in part, on the 100 persons exemption (i.e. by marketing the offering only to a restricted circle of investors), the rules on financial solicitation will apply.

The rules on financial solicitation include: **4.180**

(i) the rules regarding the restrictions on persons that are entitled to carry out financial solicitation activities; and

(ii) the prohibition on solicitation to market certain categories of financial products (for example, products for which the maximum level of risk is not known at the time they are subscribed for; products for which the risk of loss may exceed the value of the initial investment; products that require prior authorization for marketing in France where such authorization has not been granted; securities not listed on an EU regulated market or a foreign recognized market (excluding units of collective investment vehicles)).

It is also important to note that private placements are not exempt from the rules **4.181** on the marketing of units or shares of collective investment vehicles. The MFC provides that collective investment vehicles can only be launched in France once they have received the approval of the AMF. In practice it can be very difficult to obtain such approval: the relevant rules under the MFC are highly restrictive in relation to the approval by the AMF of foreign non-UCITS collective investment vehicles, such as hedge funds. The application of these rules, therefore, makes it practically impossible to actively and directly market foreign hedge funds in France, even to qualified investors.

4.10 Current Issues and EEA harmonization

4.10.1 EC consultation on the proposed amendment of the Prospectus Directive

4.182 On 9 January 2009, the EC published a consultation document setting out proposals to improve and simplify the application of the Prospectus Directive. The issues considered include:

(a) the definition of 'qualified investor', which is relevant as to whom offers of private placements can be addressed; and

(b) the revision of 'retail cascade' issue in respect of exempt offers.

4.183 The EC has not yet published the results of this consultation, although CESR has published its comments in relation to the relevant issues.

4.10.1.1 *Definition of qualified investor*

4.184 **4.10.1.1.1 The EC's background position** Under the Prospectus Directive, offers of securities to qualified investors are exempt from the requirement for a prospectus. Practical difficulties may arise from the fact that the concept of qualified investor in the Prospectus Directive is different from the scope of 'professional clients' and 'eligible counterparts' for the purposes of MiFID.

4.185 The EC's European Securities Markets Expert Group ('ESME') has recently completed a detailed and comprehensive analysis of the differences between the concepts of qualified investors in the Prospectus Directive, and of professional investors and eligible counterparts in MiFID, examining the justification, if any, for that difference. The ESME paper stresses that, while the Prospectus Directive is basically 'product-driven', MiFID is in essence 'services-driven'. As a consequence, the exemption for offers to qualified investors in the Prospectus Directive is based on the concept that certain categories of investors need less protection than others when making their investment decisions, while MiFID calibrates the operation of its conduct of business rules by applying differing levels of protection depending on whether the investment firm is providing services to or dealing with a retail client, a professional client or an eligible counterpart.

4.186 These differences may have an impact on issuers wishing to use investment firms as intermediaries for private placements of their securities, as they might operate to restrict issuers' ability to conduct private placements with some classes of experienced individual investors.

4.187 The EC, therefore, has put forward proposals to amend the Prospectus Directive in order to align it with MiFID, by extending the scope of persons to be treated as 'qualified investors' to include those persons that firms consider to be professional clients or eligible counterparties under MiFID.

Such a change (i.e. alignment with MiFID) principally would be for practical **4.188** reasons: since the enactment of MiFID, investment firms have categorized their clients in accordance with the definitions in MiFID, and changing those definitions would impose costs and burdens on those firms. In contrast, it is unlikely that issuers or intermediaries would have to make corresponding changes as a result of an amendment to the definition of qualifying investors in the Prospectus Directive.

The proposed extension to the scope of persons to be treated as qualified investors **4.189** could potentially facilitate the involvement of intermediaries in private placements, because investment firms would be able to define the target of the placement in reliance on their own list of professional clients.

There are cases where the issuer or the offeror might nonetheless want to carry out **4.190** the private placement by itself, without the assistance of an intermediary. Therefore, the EC propose to maintain the system of a central register of qualified investors as established by the Prospectus Directive.

4.10.1.1.2 CESR's reply to the EC's consultation   CESR has responded in **4.191** favour of the EC's proposal to amend the definition of qualified investors to include professional clients and eligible counterparties. Although CESR accepts that the Prospectus Directive and MiFID pursue different objectives, it does not see a rationale for maintaining separate definitions. Furthermore, CESR does not consider that aligning the definitions would create any gap in protection or increased risk for investors.

4.10.1.2 *Exempt offers and the 'retail cascade'*

4.10.1.2.1 The EC's background position   Under the Prospectus Directive, **4.192** the placement of securities through financial intermediaries may require the publication of a prospectus if the final placement by the intermediaries constitutes an offer to the public. Accordingly, even where the original placement to the intermediary falls within a Prospectus Directive exemption, the prospectus obligation is nonetheless triggered by the final placement.

This requirement causes particular problems for issuers where securities are **4.193** distributed by 'retail cascade'. A retail cascade typically occurs when securities are sold to investors (other than qualified investors) by intermediaries and not directly by the issuer itself. This raises two points of uncertainty:

(i) it is unclear how the requirement to produce and update a prospectus, and the provisions on responsibility and liability, should apply in cases where securities are placed by the issuer with financial intermediaries and are subsequently, over a period that could run to many months, sold on to retail investors, possibly through one or more additional tiers of intermediaries; and

(ii) where a prospectus is produced, it is unclear how the disclosure requirements for retail securities apply in relation to the multiple sales by intermediaries that make up the retail cascade.

4.194 This issue only affects issuers in certain EEA markets. This may reflect established differences in distribution patterns (i.e. selling by retail cascade may be common in some markets but not in others), or it may arise from differences in national implementation and application of the final indent of Article 3(2) of the Prospectus Directive.

4.195 The final paragraph of Article 3(2) refers to subsequent resales of securities that were previously the subject of an exempt public offer under an exemption set out in Article 3(2)(a)–(e), such as the 'qualified investor' exemption. The final paragraph of Article 3(2) sets out that such resales are to be regarded as a separate offer and that the definition of 'offer of securities to the public' applies to such resales. The final sentence of Article 3(2) also explicitly states that the placement of securities through financial intermediaries requires the publication of a prospectus if that placement does not fall within one of the exemptions set out in Article 3(2)(a)–(e).

4.196 The final paragraph of Article 3(2) was intended as an 'anti-avoidance' provision, preventing the easy circumvention of the Prospectus Directive requirements. CESR has clarified, for instance, that where financial intermediaries are acting in association with the issuer, they are not required to draw up a new prospectus and they can rely on the prospectus published by the issuer. In respect of supplementing a prospectus, the issuer is responsible for its publication only for the duration of the sub-offer conducted by the intermediaries acting in association. Where the intermediaries are not acting in association with the issuer, they would be expected to draw up and update their own prospectus.

4.197 The EC considers CESR's position, which is based on the concept of association between the issuer and the financial intermediary, as a satisfactory, but only temporary, solution. The EC believes that it does not provide a robust regulatory solution to the problem that would permanently remove the legal uncertainty in terms of information disclosure and responsibilities. For these reasons, following ESME's advice, the EC put forward proposals to delete the last sentence of Article 3(2) of the Prospectus Directive. Such a change could potentially clarify the responsibilities of drafting and supplementing a prospectus as well as the level of information to be included in prospectuses used in a retail cascade scenario.

4.198 **4.10.1.2.2 CESR's reply to the EC's consultation** CESR believes that the EC's proposed changes to the last paragraph of Article 3(2) of the Prospectus Directive would not clarify the responsibilities for publishing and updating the prospectus in a retail cascade scenario. Moreover, CESR has noted that such a deletion could create a regulatory gap in so far as, for instance, it would then be possible to circumvent the obligation to publish a prospectus by approaching fewer than 100 persons at each stage of the cascade, even though, ultimately, a large number of people might subscribe for the securities concerned.

CESR has considered the issue of retail cascade offers and is of the view that in cases where financial intermediaries act in association with the issuer, those financial intermediaries should be able to rely on the issuer's prospectus for their own offers, as long as the prospectus is valid and updated. CESR has suggested to the EC that it should clarify this point through legislation.   **4.199**

4.10.2 The EC's call for evidence regarding private placement regimes in the EU

The absence of a European private placement regime is often perceived as creating legal uncertainty and hindering cross-border business. Private placement regimes are un-harmonized across the EEA member states and the legal uncertainty that this causes is one of the main deterrents to cross-border transactions. Due to these national differences, the legal advice required for cross-border transactions contributes significant costs for each private placement between EEA member states.   **4.200**

The lack of a European private placement regime often compels offerors of financial instruments wishing to undertake cross-border transactions to structure their products so as to take advantage of passporting provisions in the Prospectus Directive. In this way, investments better suited to sophisticated investors are actually being structured and offered to unsophisticated investors. Arguably, a European private placement regime would prevent product originators from offering professional products in retail form since there would be a viable alternative.   **4.201**

Clearly, any private placement regime needs to define the parties who are eligible to participate in private placements. However, there is a tension between making private placements available to as many investors as possible (thereby maximizing their efficiency and flexibility), while restricting private placement opportunities to only those who are experienced and sophisticated enough to make investment decisions without the usual levels of protection.   **4.202**

In 2007, the EC's Directorate-General for Internal Market and Services sought to analyse the national barriers to private placement. It issued a call for evidence regarding private placement regimes in the EU, inviting interested parties to express their views and submit relevant evidence. The call for evidence sought to address the following issues: **4.203**

(i) whether the lack of a common approach to private placement constitutes a material impediment to cross-border financial investments;

(ii) appropriate parameters of a possible private placement regime (in terms of the boundary between public and private offers, eligible participants, and enforcement issues); and

(iii) whether, and how, a private placement regime could be established at European level.

4.204 In particular, the options ranged from taking no action, allowing the industry to regulate itself, member states taking action at a national level, or the EC introducing secondary legislation for a purpose-specific cross-border private placement regime.

4.205 The responses to the call for evidence were inconclusive. Respondents did, however, acknowledge problems in the cross-border distribution of some types of investment products, in particular non-harmonized investment funds. In that context, it was noted that arrangements established under the Prospectus Directive worked well for securities and closed-end funds and it was suggested that these arrangements should be extended to non-harmonized open-ended funds, such as institutional funds and hedge funds.

4.206 At the end of 2008, following the publication of a largely inconclusive impact assessment report on private placement, the EC published a call for tender to analyse the economics and the regulatory background of private placements as well as to examine in detail the obstacles to private placements across borders within the EU and the (additional) costs caused by this. The final report is expected in 2010.

5

LIABILITY FOR LONDON LISTING

5.1 Listing Approval Process

5.1.1 Introduction

In seeking an admission to the Official List of the UKLA (the 'Official List'), **5.01** a company, its directors and a number of its advisers will, directly or indirectly, assume a risk of liability in connection with the listing approval process. As a matter of practice, each of these parties will take steps to reduce and mitigate their liability risk.

Section 1 of this Chapter considers:

(i) the key areas of liability in connection with a primary London listing; and
(ii) how parties seek to mitigate the risk of the potential liabilities.

Similar issues apply in the context of listings in other jurisdictions throughout Europe, but this Chapter focuses solely on law and practice within the United Kingdom.

5.1.2 Key areas of liability

5.1.2.1 Prospectus

As with any European listing, the main focus of potential liability on a London **5.02** listing is the prospectus published by the applicant company. As discussed in

Part 1, any unlisted company that applies for admission of its shares for the first time to the Official List, whether or not the application is accompanied by an offer to the public, will be required to produce a prospectus.[1] The prospectus must be approved by the competent authority of the applicant company's home state (which, for the purposes of this Chapter, is taken to be the United Kingdom) and made available to the public before the request for admission (and any associated offer to the public) is made.

5.03 Any new shares being issued at the time of the float will be subscribed for, and any existing shares being disposed of will be sold, on the basis of the information in the prospectus. As the main 'selling' document, and the document on which buyers and sellers in the after-market are likely to base their trading decisions, those who have responsibility for it may be liable for inaccuracies, or for a failure to disclose all relevant information.

5.04 **5.1.2.1.1 Prospectus liability** The main areas of potential liability for a prospectus are:

    (i) statutory civil liability under FSMA and the Prospectus Rules;

    (ii) tortious liability for negligent misstatement;

    (iii) liability for false or misleading pre-contractual misrepresentation;

    (iv) liability under the market abuse provisions of FSMA; and

    (v) criminal liability under FSMA.

5.05 *5.1.2.1.1.1 Responsibility for the prospectus* The parties in the front line for prospectus liability are those who are responsible for the prospectus.

5.06 FSMA[2] and the Prospectus Rules[3] prescribe that the following parties are 'persons responsible' for the completeness and accuracy of a prospectus issued in connection with an issue of shares:

    (i) the company itself;

    (ii) the directors of the company at the time the prospectus is published;

    (iii) each person who has authorized himself or herself to be named in the prospectus as a director, or as having agreed to become a director (either immediately or at some future time);

    (iv) any other person who is identified in the prospectus as having accepted responsibility for the prospectus; and

    (v) any other person who authorizes the contents of all or any part of the prospectus.

---

[1] If the initial listing occurs as part of a takeover offer or merger, the company may instead prepare an 'equivalent document', which must effectively contain the same information as a prospectus (Prospectus Rules ('PR') 1.2.3(3)/(4)R). If the company is already traded on another regulated market, a summary document might be sufficient (PR 1.2.3(8)R).

[2] FSMA section 84(1)(d).

[3] PR 5.5.

On an initial public offering (IPO), where it is often the case that some of the **5.07**
directors (particularly the non-executive directors) will join the board only
shortly prior to listing and will not have a historic knowledge of the company, it is
important to factor in sufficient time for each director to carry out appropriate
due diligence to enable them to accept responsibility for the prospectus.

It is also important not to be caught out by the requirement that 'proposed' **5.08**
directors must take responsibility, as this can be triggered where an appointment
is still some way in the future. [4] This problem often arises in connection with an
acquisition, where a target director may be invited onto the board of the offeror;
but it can also arise, for example, where a company has not yet recruited its full
complement of non-executives to comply with the corporate governance requirements of the United Kingdom Combined Code on Corporate Governance.

Those taking responsibility under (v) above will include experts (such as reporting **5.09**
accountants and mineral experts), who are required by the UKLA to authorize
and accept responsibility for the contents of their reports if they are included in a
prospectus[5]. While reporting accountants will have standard form engagement
and consent letters—complete with carefully considered divisions of liability—
to deal with this, other experts who are less familiar with the prospectus process
may need advance warning of this obligation.

Where an offer to the public is also being made by a party other than the company— **5.10**
for example, a selling shareholder or a party offering warrants over a company's
securities[6]—that party (and, if relevant, its directors) may also be required to take
responsibility for the prospectus,[7] unless (i) the other party's offer is made in association with the company (i.e. the offer is facilitated by the company—usually
because the company is offering shares at the same time); and (ii) the company is
responsible for the prospectus (and has been the party primarily responsible for
drawing it up).[8]

Where an existing shareholder is selling at the time of an IPO, it will (as a matter **5.11**
of practice) almost invariably be the company that takes responsibility for preparing the prospectus and, in such cases, there is no requirement for the selling
shareholder to take any formal responsibility for the prospectus.

---

[4] PR 5.5.3(2)(b)(ii)R.
[5] PR App 3.1.1, Annex 1, 23.1 sets out the requirement for consent. Reports could include an
accountants' report on a pro-forma (Annex 1, 20.2) or a mineral expert's report on the listing of a
mineral company (CESR Recommendations no 809/2004, paragraph 133(c)).
[6] PR 5.5.3(2)(d)R.
[7] A similar provision (PR 5.5.3(2)(e)R) applies where a person other than the company is
requesting admission to the Official List, which could also be relevant to an issue of warrants.
[8] PR 5.5.7R. This requires that the company has 'authorized' the offer as otherwise the company
does not have responsibility for the prospectus (PR 5.5.5R).

5.12 Under the relevant annexes to the Prospectus Rules,[9] the persons who are responsible for a prospectus must be named in the document and must make the following declaration:

> Having taken all reasonable care to ensure that such is the case, the information contained in the [prospectus] is, to the best of their knowledge, in accordance with the facts and contains no omission likely to affect its import.

5.13 Parties that take responsibility for only part of a prospectus, such as the experts likely to fall within category (v) above, must make a similar statement in relation to the relevant part.

5.14 The overall scope of this category of person responsible (those who have 'authorised the contents of the prospectus') is uncertain. It has become common for the sponsor[10] of the company to require the inclusion in a prospectus of a disclaimer of responsibility that expressly denies that the sponsor has authorized the contents of the prospectus. These disclaimers have been accepted by the FSA and it is therefore supposed that the FSA agrees that sponsors do not have responsibility.

5.1.2.1.1.2 Statutory liability (Section 90 of FSMA)

5.15 **Liability for statements** The persons who are responsible for a prospectus will be *prima facie* liable under section 90 of FSMA to compensate any investors[11] who suffer loss in respect of the securities to which the prospectus relates as a result of:

(i) any untrue or misleading statement in the prospectus; or

(ii) the omission from the prospectus of any matter required to be included by section 87A of FSMA.

5.16 Section 87A—which gives effect to Article 5(1) of the Prospectus Directive, discussed in Part 1—requires the inclusion of such information as is necessary to enable investors to make an informed assessment of:

(i) the assets and liabilities, financial position, profits and losses, and prospects of the company; and

(ii) the rights attaching to the relevant securities.

---

[9] PR App 3.1.1, Annex 1, 1.1/1.2 and Annex III, 1.1/1.2.

[10] The Listing Rules (LRs) require a company that applies for a primary listing of its shares by admission to the Official List to engage as 'sponsor' an appropriately qualified financial adviser, broker or other professional adviser (LR 8.2.1R). The sponsor advises the company and its directors on their obligations under the Listing Rules and the Disclosure and Transparency Rules (the DTRs) and provides assurances to the FSA that those responsibilities have been met.

[11] For these purposes, 'investors' are persons who acquire relevant securities, or who contract to acquire relevant securities or any interest in such securities.

As explained in Chapter 21, this general requirement overlays the specific con- **5.17** tents requirements set out in the annexes to the Prospectus Rules and is not neces- sarily satisfied by mere fulfilment of the more detailed requirements. Accordingly, when drafting the prospectus, the company must at all times consider the wider disclosure objective under section 87A of FSMA in order to guard against the possibility of liability under section 90 of FSMA.

Defences If a prospectus contains an untrue or misleading statement or does **5.18** not contain the information required by section 87A, there are various defences on which the persons responsible for the prospectus may rely. These include in summary:

(i) where information has been omitted on the authority of the UKLA (which is granted very rarely); [12]

(ii) where the court is satisfied that the person responsible (having made such enquiries as were reasonable) reasonably believed that either the statement was true and not misleading, or that the matter in question was properly omitted, and that the responsible person either continued in this belief [13] or took reasonable steps to secure that a correction was published (the 'verifica- tion defence');

(iii) in respect of loss caused by a statement in the prospectus made by an 'expert' (i.e. someone whose professional qualifications or experience give authority to his statements) who has consented to its inclusion in the prospectus, where the court is satisfied that (a) the person responsible reasonably believed that the expert was competent to make the statement and had given its consent to the inclusion of the relevant statement in the prospectus; and (b) the person responsible either continued in this belief or took reasonable steps to secure the publication of a correction; and

(iv) where a correction has been published, or the court is otherwise satisfied that the investor claiming to have suffered loss acquired the securities with knowledge of the false or misleading statement or the omission.

Liability for supplementary prospectus In addition to statutory liability for a **5.19** prospectus itself, section 90 of FSMA imposes liability if an issuer fails to submit a supplementary prospectus in circumstances where one is required.

---

[12] The UKLA is entitled to authorize the omission of information under section 87B of FSMA on the grounds that (i) its disclosure would be contrary to the public interest; (ii) its disclosure would be seriously detrimental to the company but unlikely to mislead the public; or (iii) the information is only of minor importance and is unlikely to influence an informed assessment of the company.

[13] In general, where there has been no correction, the person must either have continued in his or her belief until the time that the relevant securities were acquired by the investor making the claim, or, where the securities were acquired by that investor after such a lapse in time that the person ought in the circumstances to be reasonably excused, at least until the commencement of dealings in the securities.

5.20   A supplementary prospectus must be submitted to the UKLA for its approval (and subsequently published) if, during the period following the UKLA's approval of the underlying prospectus but before the closure of the public offer or the commencement of trading in the securities, there arises or is noted a 'significant' new factor, material mistake or inaccuracy relating to the information included in the prospectus.[14] 'Significant', in this context, means significant for the purposes of an investor making an informed assessment of the matters required to be included in a prospectus by section 87A(2) of FSMA (see 'Liability for statements' above). The obligation to ensure the submission of a supplementary prospectus falls on the company itself (as the party on whose application the prospectus was approved), but those responsible for the prospectus also have a responsibility under section 87G(5) of FSMA to give notice to the company (and should also notify the company's sponsor) of all new facts, mistakes or inaccuracies which give rise to the requirement to publish a supplementary prospectus.

5.21   Failure to comply with these obligations will again expose the relevant party to liability to investors who suffer a loss as a result of the failure. However, a person will not be liable if:

(i)   the court is satisfied that the relevant party reasonably believed that the change or new matter was not such as to call for a supplementary prospectus; or

(ii)   the court is satisfied that the investor claiming to have suffered loss acquired securities with knowledge of the change or new matter.

5.22   **Nature of liability**   Section 90 of FSMA specifies that 'compen-sation' must be paid to investors who suffer loss as a result of (i) an untrue or misleading statement or the omission from the prospectus of information required to be included in it; or (ii) the failure to publish a supplementary prospectus when required, in circumstances where no relevant defences apply.

5.23   Compensation is taken to mean financial compensation, calculated on the tortious measure of loss described at 5.1.2.1.1.3.

5.1.2.1.1.3 Tortious liability

5.24   **Liability for negligent misstatement**   In taking responsibility for a prospectus, a person may also attract common law tortious liability under English law. Such common law liability may arise where a party makes a 'negligent misstatement' to another (i.e. a statement, written or otherwise, which turns out to be false), in circumstances where (i) there is a 'special relationship' between the parties; (ii) it is foreseeable that the recipient of the statement may rely on that statement;

---

[14] FSMA section 87G.

(iii) the recipient does in fact rely on the statement; and (iv) the recipient suffers loss as a result.

As described above, any party that has responsibility for a prospectus must state **5.25** that the prospectus is, to the best of its knowledge, in accordance with the facts and contains no omission likely to affect its import. If the prospectus contains an untrue or misleading statement, or omits material information, then arguably the responsibility statement that covers it may constitute a negligent misstatement on the part of the maker.

The English courts have held that a special relationship exists between the persons **5.26** putting their names behind a prospectus and persons who subscribe or purchase shares directly in reliance on that prospectus.[15] Accordingly, if an initial investor does rely on the responsibility statement (i.e. invests in the company's securities on the basis of the prospectus, believing the information set out in it to be true) and suffers loss as a result, the persons responsible for the prospectus could face liability to compensate the investor.

It is generally considered, however, that the scope of this special relationship does **5.27** not extend beyond initial investors to purchasers in the after-market.[16]

Tortious liability for negligent misstatement is calculated on the basis that the **5.28** claimant should be put into the position in which it would have been had it not relied on the misrepresentation. This means that the claimant is entitled to the difference between the market value of the shares and the price paid. This does not, however, cover the claimant for any loss of profit that the claimant would have earned had the representation been true.

Other non-contractual liability In addition to potential liability arising **5.29** under English law for negligent misstatement, there may be other potential (non-contractual) liability arising under foreign law if securities are offered in other jurisdictions.

Since the introduction of Rome II,[17] it may be possible to mitigate the risk of any **5.30** such liability by including in the terms of any contract to be entered into pursuant

---

[15] See *AI-Nakib Investments (Jersey) Ltd and another v Longcroft and others* [1990] 1 WLR 1390.

[16] This remains the case notwithstanding judicial comments that have suggested that there might be instances in which the requisite special relationship exists between a company producing a prospectus and investors in the after market.

[17] EC Regulation 864/2007 on the Law Applicable to Non-Contractual Obligations ('Rome II'). Since Rome II came into force on 11 January 2009, the courts of all EU member states other than Denmark have, for the first time, to apply the same set of rules to determine the law that will govern non-contractual (principally tortious) obligations arising between parties in most civil and commercial matters.

to the prospectus a provision stipulating that, at least between the company and contracting investors, liability for any tortious claims under the prospectus will be governed by English law.

5.1.2.1.1.4 *Contractual liability*

5.31   **Liability for breach of contract**   Where the admission of a company's shares to the Official List is accompanied by an offer of shares, either by the company or a selling shareholder, the prospectus will form the basis of a contract between the company (and/or the selling shareholder) and those persons who acquire the shares under the terms of the offer.

5.32   An incorrect statement in a prospectus may form the basis of a claim for breach of contract if, in summary, the investor claiming to have suffered loss can show that (i) the statement is a term of the contract; (ii) the term has been breached; and (iii) the investor has suffered loss as a result of such breach. In practice, however, while the investor might be able to demonstrate limbs (ii) and (iii), the courts are not usually prepared to classify statements in a prospectus as terms of the contract between the company and the investor. Accordingly, claims for straightforward breach of contract based on statements in a prospectus are rare or non-existent.

5.33   **Liability under the Misrepresentation Act 1967**   Instead the courts may instead classify statements in a prospectus as representations on the part of those responsible for the prospectus to recipients of the document. If such statements are untrue or misleading, or there is an omission that renders a statement in the prospectus misleading, an investor who bought securities on the basis of the prospectus and consequently suffered loss may have a remedy against the issuing company (and/or the selling shareholder) under the Misrepresentation Act 1967 (the 'Misrepresentation Act').

5.34   Broadly speaking, the Misrepresentation Act offers remedies to a party who has been induced to enter into a contract on the basis of a statement by the contracting counterparty, which later turns out to be false. In such circumstances, the Misrepresentation Act offers the following remedies: (i) rescission of the contract (i.e. the issue or sale of the shares would be cancelled and the company and/or the selling shareholders would be obliged to return to investors the monies paid over); and/or (ii) damages.

5.35   The remedy of rescission is available only to original purchasers or subscribers and will be lost if the subscriber or purchaser affirms the contract by failing to act within a reasonable time of discovering the existence of the misrepresentation. In circumstances where rescission is impossible, a court may in any case require the company to pay damages in lieu of rescission.

Damages under the Misrepresentation Act are calculated on the same tortious **5.36**
basis as set out in section 5.1.2.1.1.3 above. Crucially, however, the investor
would not be required to show that the losses claimed were foreseeable by the
company making the misrepresentation. Consequently, the company would
potentially be liable to compensate the investor for all direct losses caused by the
misrepresentation.

It is a defence to a claim for damages, but not rescission, for the defendant to prove **5.37**
that he believed on reasonable grounds that the statement complained of was true
(i.e. that it was an 'innocent misrepresentation').

5.1.2.1.1.5 *Market abuse*

Market abuse—civil liability Section 4 of Chapter 1 examines the application **5.38**
of the Market Abuse Directive. A person responsible for a London-listing prospectus may commit market abuse under section 118(7) of FSMA, and under the
provisions of the FSA's Code of Market Conduct, if (i) it includes in a prospectus
information which gives, or is likely to give, a false or misleading impression as
to a 'qualifying investment', such as shares; and (ii) such person knew, or could
reasonably be expected to have known, that the information was false or
misleading.[18]

Under section 123 of FSMA, the FSA may choose to impose a civil fine of **5.39**
any amount for market abuse (except where the person concerned has a defence),[19]
or make a public statement that the party concerned has engaged in market
abuse.

The FSA also has the option to apply to the court for (i) an injunction under **5.40**
section 381 of FSMA, which could require the relevant party to take steps to
remedy the market abuse (for example, to correct the misstatement); or (ii) for an
order under section 383 of FSMA that a payment (being the amount of profit
made or losses suffered) be made to the FSA, which the FSA must distribute
among the parties affected.

In addition, under section 384(2) of FSMA, the FSA can itself require the pay- **5.41**
ment of compensation to those who have suffered loss. (The FSA may not exercise

---

[18] In the opinion of the FSA, if a normal and reasonable person would know or should have
known in all the circumstances that the information was false or misleading, then that indicates that
the person disseminating the information knew or could reasonably be expected to have known that
it was false or misleading.

[19] No civil fine may be imposed if there are reasonable grounds for the FSA to be satisfied that
either (i) the person believed on reasonable grounds that he did not commit market abuse; or (ii) the
person took all reasonable precautions and exercised all due diligence to avoid market abuse (section
123(2) of FSMA).

this power (and the court may not make a compensation order) if it is satisfied that either of the factors referred to in footnote 19 apply.)

The FSA has set out,[20] *inter alia*, a non-exhaustive list of factors that it may take into account when deciding on which of the sanctions described above to apply in a particular case. These include (i) whether the person has made a resulting profit; (ii) whether the person has cooperated with the FSA and sought to compensate those who have suffered loss as a result of the conduct in question; and (iii) the party's compliance history.

5.42 **Market abuse—criminal liability** Where a misstatement or omission is not made inadvertently, those taking responsibility for a prospectus could face criminal liability under section 397 of FSMA.

5.43 Section 397 applies to a person who:

    (i) makes a statement, promise or forecast which he knows to be misleading, false or deceptive in a material particular;

    (ii) dishonestly conceals any material facts, whether in connection with a statement, promise or forecast made by him or otherwise; or

    (iii) recklessly makes (dishonestly or otherwise) a statement, promise or forecast that is misleading, false or deceptive in a material particular.

5.44 Such a person is guilty of an offence if he has the purpose of inducing, or is reckless as to whether he may induce, another person:

    (i) to enter or offer to enter into (or refrain from entering or offering to enter into) a 'relevant agreement'[21] (which includes a contract to buy or sell shares); or

    (ii) to exercise or refrain from exercising rights conferred by an investment such as shares.

Therefore, if a person who joins in a responsibility statement in a prospectus is reckless as to whether that responsibility statement is correct and such statement is in fact misleading, false or deceptive, he may be found guilty of a criminal offence if he was also reckless as to whether this would induce an investor to subscribe for, or acquire, shares in the company.

---

[20] DEPP 6.2.1/6.2.2 and 6.4.2. The FSA's Decision Procedure and Penalties Manual ('DEPP') was introduced by the Decision Procedure and Penalties Manual Instrument 2007 (FSA 2007/46) (as subsequently amended).

[21] A 'relevant agreement' is an agreement, the entering into or performance of which by either party constitutes an activity covered by FSMA and which relates to a relevant investment, such as shares.

A person guilty of an offence under section 397 FSMA is liable: **5.45**

(i) on summary conviction, to imprisonment for a term not exceeding six months or a fine not exceeding the statutory maximum,[22] or both; or

(ii) on conviction on indictment, to imprisonment for a term not exceeding seven years or a fine, or both.

5.1.2.1.2 Prospectus liability—other parties

5.1.2.1.2.1 Other parties In addition to those who take direct responsibility   **5.46**
for a prospectus, other parties who are associated with a prospectus may have
concerns about attracting liability. In particular, the company's sponsor and
underwriters may be concerned that they are taken to endorse the prospectus and
its contents by allowing their names to be associated with it, and by acting as the
company's agent in stimulating interest in the offering and securing subscribers
for shares. A selling shareholder may have similar concerns if it is selling shares on
the basis of the company's prospectus.

Sponsors and underwriters Sponsors and underwriters are not generally   **5.47**
'persons responsible' for the prospectus and, therefore, are typically not at risk of
liability under section 90 of FSMA. Nor do such parties typically enter into contracts with investors and therefore they are unlikely to attract liability in relation
to losses suffered by investors for breach of contract or for contractual misrepresentation under the Misrepresentation Act.[23]

However, there are several grounds on which sponsors and underwriters may still   **5.48**
face claims. For example, while this is not a position that has yet been considered
explicitly by the courts, it is possible that an investor could argue that the sponsor
and underwriters have a duty of care to investors to avoid misrepresentations
in the prospectus. However, given that the issuer clearly assumes responsibility for
the content of the prospectus, and, furthermore, given that the sponsors and
underwriters will generally expressly disclaim[24] any such responsibility, it seems
unlikely that such parties would be found liable for negligent misstatement based
solely on the content of the prospectus.[25]

---

[22] The current 'statutory maximum' for a Level 5 fine is £5,000 (section 17, Criminal Justice Act 1991 (as amended)).

[23] In the UK market, the distribution activities of underwriters (in soliciting purchases of the securities being offered) are almost invariably conducted on an agency basis, with the underwriter acting as agent of the company or selling shareholder. As agent, the underwriter is not liable for a breach of contract by its principal.

[24] Disclaimers appearing on the front page of a prospectus are typically in language similar to the following: 'The Sponsor(s) make no representation, express or implied, with respect to the accuracy or completeness of any information contained in this document, and accept no responsibility for, nor do they authorize, the contents of this document.'

[25] For instance, in the context of the scope of an arranger's liability to participants in the syndication of a mezzanine debt facility, the Commercial Court held that the existence of the disclaimer

5.49   Perhaps the greatest risk of liability for sponsors and underwriters arises in the context of comments or recommendations such parties make to potential investors *beyond* those set out in the prospectus. In making such comments, a court could deem that the sponsor or underwriter has assumed responsibility to the recipient as to the correctness of such additional information.[26]

5.50   There is also the possibility that sponsors (but not underwriters) could be found liable in tort for a breach of statutory duty under LR 8.3.3, which requires a sponsor to act with due care and skill (see below at 5.1.2.2.2.1).

5.51   However, in order for tortious liability to arise for breach of a statutory duty, a court must be satisfied that the intention of the legislation,[27] considered as a whole and in the relevant circumstances, was to impose a duty enforceable by an aggrieved individual.[28] Although the courts have yet to rule specifically on this point, existing analogous case law strongly suggests that LR 8.3.3 is *not* intended to confer upon investors a right to sue sponsors if they are found to have fallen below the statutory standard. In particular, it has been held that, where a special statutory remedy by way of penalty or otherwise is prescribed for breach of the legislation in question (as is the case under FSMA and the Listing Rules; see below at 5.1.2.2.2.2), a court will be disinclined to find that tortious liability also exists.[29] In addition, section 150 of FSMA makes breaches of certain rules by 'authorised persons' (such as sponsors) actionable by private persons, but excludes the Listing Rules. Accordingly, it appears unlikely that tortious liability by virtue of breach of statutory duty would apply to a sponsor.

5.52   *5.1.2.1.2.2 Pathfinder prospectus*   The company's underwriters may, however, be more concerned about the risk of liability if a pathfinder prospectus (i.e. an unapproved draft prospectus) is provided to investors as part of the marketing process. Such a pathfinder prospectus is an 'advertisement' for the purposes of the Prospectus Rules,[30] and is also a 'financial promotion' which is covered by section 21 of FSMA.

(in a similar form to that which would typically appear in a prospectus, as set out in note 24 above) in the information memorandum prepared and distributed to the participants by an arranger prevented the participants from claiming that an express or implied representation had been made by an arranger as to the accuracy of the information memorandum—*IFE Fund SA v Goldman Sachs International* [2006] EWHC 2887 (Comm).

[26] For instance, sponsors often accompany issuers to investor roadshow presentations where the sponsor is likely to be in direct contact with potential investors, which potentially could give rise to a duty of care.

[27] Including FSMA, which confers the power upon the UKLA to produce Listing Rules.

[28] See *R v Deputy Governor of Parkhurst Prison, ex p Hague* [1992] 1 AC 58.

[29] See *Lonrho Ltd v Shell Petroleum Co Ltd (No 2)* [1982] AC 173.

[30] PR 3.3.

Under the Prospectus Rules,[31] a pathfinder must therefore include a prominent **5.53** notice making it clear that investors should not subscribe for any shares except on the basis of the finally published prospectus, and the document must be consistent with the information required to be included in the subsequent prospectus.[32]

Under the rules relating to financial promotions, the pathfinder must not be com- **5.54** municated to anyone unless it is (i) approved by an authorized person; or (ii) only communicated to (or directed at) persons who come within a series of exceptions (which include institutional and sophisticated investors).[33]

Despite these restrictions, where a pathfinder is used to create interest among **5.55** investors, it is always possible that changes will have to be made to the pathfinder prospectus before it is approved as a final prospectus by the UKLA and published. Where this is the case, it will be a matter for careful consideration whether the changes need to be specifically drawn to the attention of potential investors who have seen the pathfinder, in order to avoid any argument that they actually invested on the basis of the pathfinder, supplied to them by the underwriters.

5.1.2.1.2.3 Brokers' research Where research on a company whose shares are **5.56** being offered is produced by the sell-side analyst employed by an investment bank or broker involved in the offering process and is circulated among potential investors at around the same time as the prospectus or pathfinder prospectus, the firm that produced the research also takes on a risk of liability.

The firm publishing such research may be exposed to the following heads of **5.57** liability:

  (i) tort (negligent misstatement), if an investor can demonstrate a duty of care on the part of the firm to investors, a breach of that duty and resulting loss among investors;

  (ii) section 397 of FSMA, if the firm deliberately or recklessly makes a misleading statement or dishonestly conceals material facts in connection with a statement for the purpose of inducing another to acquire or dispose of securities;

  (iii) section 118 of FSMA (market abuse), if the research gives a false or misleading impression;

  (iv) the criminal offence of insider dealing (under the Criminal Justice Act 1993), if the firm has inside information and encourages others to deal, or is taken to have disclosed inside information other than in the proper performance of a profession; and

---

[31] PR 3.3.3G.
[32] PR 3.3.2(4)R.
[33] The available exemptions are detailed in the Financial Services and Markets Act 2000 (Financial Promotion) Order 2005 (SI 2005/1529).

(v) the FSA Rulebook, which requires that communications must be fair, clear and not misleading and investment research must be objective and not tainted by conflicts of interest. Breach may give rise to disciplinary action by the FSA, and could even give rise to civil claims under section 150 of FSMA if the reports are sent to private investors.

5.58 5.1.2.1.3 **Level of risk**   Having considered the various types of liability that may potentially arise in respect of a prospectus, it is worth noting that it remains very unusual in the United Kingdom for any party connected with a prospectus to be sued under any of the heads set out above. The paucity of direct experience of litigation in the United Kingdom in this context is probably principally due to the 'loser pays' rule that requires a person bringing a claim to pay the costs of the successful defendant, together with the as yet undeveloped approach to class actions. These factors are a major discouragement to speculative claims. The lack of experience on the part of the judiciary (which makes predicting the outcome of a claim even more difficult) is a further disincentive to investors bringing claims. Finally, it is probably relevant that in a typical IPO the majority of the shares offered will be allocated to institutional investors who are generally disinclined to seek to deal with any perceived deficiencies in the quality of the disclosure through litigation.

5.1.2.2 Dealings with the UKLA

5.59 In the course of an application for admission of its securities to the Official List, a company and its appointed sponsor will both be required to make representations to the UKLA about certain matters covered by the Listing Rules. If these representations are inaccurate or misleading, the person responsible for the representation may be exposed to regulatory sanctions, as discussed in Sections 5.1.2.2.1 and 5.1.2.2.2 below.

5.1.2.2.1   Company obligations

5.60 *5.1.2.2.1.1 Requirements for listing*   Under FSMA, the UKLA may not approve an application for listing unless it is satisfied that the applicant has complied with both the general requirements of the Listing Rules and any special requirements that the UKLA considers appropriate to protect investors.

5.61 The general requirements for listings of all securities are set out in Chapter 2 of the Listing Rules, and those that relate to equity securities such as shares are set out in Chapter 6.[34]

---

[34] Where an entity is an investment vehicle, Chapters 15 or 16 of the Listing Rules will apply to modify these requirements. Where the company is a company applying for a secondary listing, Chapter 14 of the Listing Rules will apply instead. The requirements are also modified in

Key requirements under these Chapters include: **5.62**

  (i)   due incorporation and validity of securities;

 (ii) free transferability (which the UKLA recognizes may be subject to restrictions that are genuinely required by a company to prevent it from breaching law or regulation);

(iii) a minimum capitalization of £700,000;

(iv) audited accounts that cover at least three years and are the latest accounts for a period ended not more than six months before the date of the prospectus;

 (v) an independent business where at least 75% (generally by reference to assets, profitability and market capitalization) is supported by a three-year historic revenue earning record, and where a majority of the company's assets have been under its control for that three-year period; [35]

(vi) a working capital statement, confirming the availability of sufficient working capital for the group's requirements for at least the next 12 months; and

(vii) at least 25% of the company's shares to be held in public hands (i.e. not by persons related to the company, such as its directors or their connected parties, and not by shareholders who hold 5% or more of the issued shares).

The UKLA has the right to impose additional requirements in relation to particular individual companies and also has the right to refuse admission of an issuer's securities to the Official List if it believes that it would be detrimental to investors' interests. **5.63**

5.1.2.2.1.2 Information provided to the UKLA In practice, the sponsor will **5.64** address the company's compliance with these listing eligibility requirements in a letter to the UKLA that it will draft in conjunction with the company and its legal advisers (see below).

In considering an application for listing, the UKLA has powers to require **5.65** additional information from the applicant company. In particular, the UKLA may, *inter alia*:

  (i)   carry out any enquiries and request any further information which it considers appropriate;

 (ii) request that an applicant company answers questions and explains any matter considered relevant to the application for listing; and

---

relation to 'mineral companies' or 'scientific research based companies', and may also be modified by the UKLA in relation to specific other companies.

[35] These provisions might not be satisfied if, for example, the company's business relies for its valuation on admission on future developments rather than its historic record, or there is no record of consistent growth during the period, or the business has undergone a significant change in the scale of its operations (LR 6.1.7G).

(iii) request that any information provided by the applicant company be verified in such manner as it may specify.[36]

5.66 In addition, one of the documents required to be submitted on an application is an 'Application for Admission of Securities to the Official List', which is required to be signed on behalf of the company. The application requires the company to confirm, *inter alia*, that:

(i) all the requirements for listing in the Listing Rules required to be fulfilled before the application is considered have been fulfilled;

(ii) all the documents and information required to be included in the application have been or will be supplied in accordance with the Listing Rules; and

(iii) the company undertakes to comply with the Listing Rules applicable to it.

5.67 Accordingly, in addition to its obligations to its sponsor (see below at 5.1.3.2.2), the applicant company has a direct obligation to the UKLA with respect to the above confirmations.

5.68 *5.1.2.2.1.3 Liability under section 91 of FSMA* The FSA has the power under section 91 of FSMA to impose financial penalties 'of such amount as it considers appropriate' for contraventions of the Listing Rules or the Prospectus Rules by any issuer of listed securities or by any applicant for listing. Moreover, directors of issuers or applicant companies are personally at risk of incurring penalties if they are 'knowingly concerned' in a contravention of such rules by the applicant company.

5.69 The FSA may only exercise these powers after the service of a warning notice, which must state the amount of the proposed penalty and the reasons for its imposition. The company then has a right to make representations to the FSA, following which a decision notice will be issued.

5.70 There is a two-year time limit to the FSA's powers under section 91, commencing on the day on which the FSA first knew of the contravention (which, for the purposes of this section, is the date on which the FSA has information from which the breach could be reasonably inferred).

5.71 The FSA is required to publish a statement of its policy with respect to the imposition of penalties and the amount of such penalties. The FSA policy statement, set out in DEPP 6.5.1G and 6.5.2G, provides a non-exhaustive list of factors that it may consider in determining the penalty, which include:

(i) *deterrence*: when determining the appropriate level of penalty, the FSA will have regard to the principal purpose of deterring persons from committing breaches, and of demonstrating generally the benefits of compliant business;

---

[36] LR 3.2.6G.

(ii) *the nature, seriousness and impact of the breach*: the FSA will consider the seriousness of the breach in relation to the nature of the rule, requirement or provision breached. This also includes consideration of factors such as the loss or risk of loss caused to consumers, investors or other market users; the duration and frequency of the breach and the impact of the breach on the orderliness of the relevant market;

(iii) *the extent to which the behaviour was deliberate or reckless*: the FSA may have regard to whether the person intended or foresaw the consequences of his behaviour or gave consideration to the consequences of the behaviour;

(iv) *whether the person on whom the penalty is to be imposed is an individual*: the FSA may take account of an individual's financial circumstances; and

(v) *the amount of benefit gained or loss avoided by the conduct in question*: it is a principle that a person should not be able to profit from his behaviour and a penalty should provide the person with an incentive to comply with required standards of market conduct.

As an alternative to a financial sanction, the FSA may choose to publicly censure **5.72** the applicant company (and its directors). It is required to take into account the same factors as those set out under the 'Market abuse' heading at 5.1.2.1.1.5 above in reaching this decision.

5.1.2.2.2 Sponsor obligations and liability

5.1.2.2.2.1 Sponsor obligations to UKLA When applying to the UKLA for **5.73** admission to the Official List, a company is required to appoint a sponsor.[37] The sponsor must guide the company in understanding and meeting its responsibilities under the Listing Rules and the DTRs. In addition, the sponsor will correspond and deal with the UKLA on the company's behalf and must provide assurance to the UKLA when required that the applicant company has met its responsibilities under the Listing Rules.[38] In providing these services, the sponsor takes on obligations to the UKLA. It must act with due care and skill and must deal with the UKLA in an open and cooperative way.[39]

In particular, a sponsor is under an obligation not to make an application for **5.74** admission to the Official List on behalf of a company unless, after having made due and careful enquiry, it has come to a reasonable opinion that:

(i) the company has satisfied all requirements of the Listing Rules and the Prospectus Rules relevant to the application;

---

[37] LR 8.2.1R.
[38] LR 8.3.1R.
[39] LR 8.3.3R/LR 8.3.5(1)R.

(ii) the company's directors have established procedures that will enable the company to comply with the Listing Rules and the DTRs on an ongoing basis;

(iii) the company's directors have established procedures that provide a reasonable basis for them to make proper judgments on an ongoing basis as to the financial position and prospects of the company and its group; and

(iv) the company's directors have a reasonable basis on which to make the working capital statement required by LR 6.1.16.[40]

5.75 As part of the documentation to be provided to the UKLA, the sponsor is also required to provide a signed form—the 'Sponsor's Declaration on an Application for Listing'—pursuant to which a duly authorized officer of the sponsor is required to confirm in writing the matters referred to above (including that it has acted with due care and skill and has taken reasonable steps to ensure that the company's directors understand their responsibilities) and in the next paragraph.

5.76 A sponsor is also required to submit a letter to the UKLA setting out how the company satisfies the criteria for listing set out above. Furthermore, it is generally required to ensure that all matters known to it that, in its reasonable opinion, the UKLA should take into account when considering (i) the application for listing; and (ii) whether the admission of the equity securities would be detrimental to investors' interests, have either been disclosed with sufficient prominence in the prospectus or have been otherwise disclosed in writing to the UKLA.

5.77 *5.1.2.2.2.2 Liability for sponsors* The FSA has no statutory power to impose a financial penalty on a sponsor, but FSMA enables the FSA to publish a statement censuring a sponsor where it considers that the sponsor has contravened any applicable requirement under the Listing Rules.[41]

5.78 Where the FSA proposes to publish a statement of censure, it must give the sponsor a warning notice setting out the terms of the proposed statement. If, after considering any representations made by the sponsor in response to the warning notice, the FSA decides to proceed with the proposed statement, it must then give the sponsor a decision notice setting out the terms of the statement. A sponsor to whom a decision notice is given under section 89 of FSMA may refer the matter to the Financial Services and Markets Tribunal for review.

5.79 The FSA also has the power to cancel, at its own initiative, a sponsor's approval to act as such, as conferred by section 88 of FSMA.[42] Chapter 18 of the accompanying FSA Enforcement Guide provides that, when considering whether to cancel

---

[40] LR 8.4.2R.
[41] LR.8.7.19R and section 89 of FSMA.
[42] See also LR8.7.20.G.

a sponsor's approval, the FSA will take into account all relevant factors, including the following:

(i)   the competence of the sponsor;

(ii) the adequacy of the sponsor's systems and controls;

(iii) the sponsor's history of compliance with the Listing Rules;

(iv) the nature, seriousness and duration of the suspected failure of the sponsor to meet (at all times) the criteria for approval as a sponsor set out in LR 8.6.5; and

(v)   any matter that the FSA could take into account if it were considering an application for approval as a sponsor made under section 88(3)(d) of FSMA.

5.1.3 Mitigation/sharing of liability

5.1.3.1 *Prospectus liability*

5.1.3.1.1 Responsible persons

5.1.3.1.1.1 Responsibility statements   In order to ensure that it is clear when and how a company's directors agree to take responsibility for a prospectus, and to confirm to the company that the directors are taking responsibility, it is market practice for each of the directors to sign a personal responsibility letter addressed to the company. On an IPO, letters may also be addressed to the sponsor. Directors will confirm their responsibility by reference to the latest draft of the prospectus that each director has reviewed and approved for these purposes, subject to amendments that are made through an agreed approval process generally involving board/committee sign-off.
5.80

Any person identified as a 'proposed director' in the prospectus, and therefore required to take responsibility for the prospectus, will also sign a similar letter.
5.81

5.1.3.1.1.2 Consent letters   Parties that have prepared and authorized the contents of a report to be included in a prospectus, such as reporting accountants and mineral experts, must take responsibility for the relevant part of the prospectus. They do this by signing a consent letter that also confirms their responsibility. The relevant party will only provide such consent letter once it is satisfied with the form and context of the report as it appears in the prospectus, and with its terms of engagement with the company relating to the provision of the report.
5.82

5.1.3.1.1.3 Verification   To assist the company and its directors in fulfilling their obligations, and to support their reliance on any potentially available defence to liability, a prospectus will be 'verified' before its issue.
5.83

Verification is the process of checking all material statements in the prospectus to ensure that (i) there are reasonable grounds for believing that each statement of fact is true and not misleading; (ii) statements of opinion are identified as such
5.84

and are based on reasonable grounds; (iii) the prospectus gives a true and fair view of the history, business and prospects of the company; and (iv) nothing significant to investors is omitted.

5.85   Verification takes place alongside the drafting of the prospectus; indeed, the process of verification itself will assist with and affect the drafting. Verification should caution those involved in the drafting against the inclusion in the prospectus of statements that cannot be adequately supported by appropriate evidence and of qualitative statements that could be interpreted in different ways.

5.86   The company's lawyers will work with the company to prepare the verification notes. The notes explain to the directors how verification has been conducted and draw their attention to the background information that substantiates key statements in the prospectus. Verification notes are not made public but it is generally market practice for the directors to sign the final version of them at a board meeting, by way of confirmation on the board's behalf of the accuracy and completeness of the prospectus.

5.87   If the verification process is conducted properly, it is generally considered that it will satisfy the verification defence for the purposes of section 90 of FSMA, discussed at paragraph 5.22 above. It should also help to ensure, so far as possible, that liability under the other heads will not arise. Accordingly, although directors may not be personally involved in the detail of the verification process, it is very much in their interests to satisfy themselves that correct control procedures are in place to ensure accurate verification.

5.88   Verification and due diligence will also be of relevance to assist a selling shareholder in satisfying itself as to the accuracy and completeness of the prospectus, especially as a selling shareholder will not generally have the same protections against potential liability as the sponsors/underwriters (see below at 5.1.3.1.2).

5.89   *5.1.3.1.1.4 Reporting accountants*   In addition to the general verification process, specific due diligence will be carried out to support certain statements made in the prospectus. In particular, the statement that the company has sufficient working capital and the 'no significant change' statement[43] will be backed up by work done by the directors and the reporting accountants (see below at 5.1.3.2.1). There are also particular rules that govern profit forecasts and pro-forma statements.[44]

---

[43] PR App 3.1.1, Annex 1, 20.9 requires a description of any significant change in the financial or trading position of the group that has occurred since the end of the last financial period for which either audited financial information or interim financial information has been published.

[44] As regards profit forecasts, see PR App 3.1.1, Annex 1 13.1–13.4. As regards pro-forma statements, see. PR App 3.1.1, Annex 1, 20.2.

5.1.3.1.2 Sponsor/underwriters

5.1.3.1.2.1 Disclaimers As discussed above, the sponsor and underwriters will **5.90** seek to avoid liability in relation to a prospectus by including disclaimers intended to make it clear that those parties do not take any form of responsibility for the prospectus and do not accept any form of liability for its contents.

5.1.3.1.2.2 Underwriting agreement The sponsor and the underwriters will **5.91** also use the underwriting agreement—entered into with the company and (generally on an IPO) its directors—as a means to protect themselves against any liability in relation to the prospectus. An underwriting agreement will invariably include both warranties and an indemnity in favour of the sponsor and the underwriters.

The warranties in an IPO underwriting agreement will generally consist of both **5.92** (i) warranties directly relating to the accuracy of the prospectus and the surrounding public documents; and (ii) warranties relating to the business of the company which are aimed both at backing up the statements made to the UKLA (see above) and also at confirming that there is no further information about the company that needs to be included in the prospectus.

On an IPO, the practice is for the directors of the company to be asked, as a **5.93** minimum, to give certain warranties about the accuracy of the prospectus. The directors' liability under these warranties is generally limited in both time and amount: where a director owns shares in the company, the cap may be set by reference to the value of those shares; a non-executive director may instead have his liability capped at the value of his or her annual fees.

The indemnity in an underwriting agreement is intended by the underwriters to **5.94** ensure, as far as possible, that they have no 'uncovered' liability for the role they take on the IPO. While there will generally be a carve-out from an indemnity for liabilities incurred by the underwriters that are caused by the underwriters' own wilful default or negligence, the practice has arisen that this will not generally apply to liability that arises out of the prospectus, or where the company is actually in breach of the underwriting agreement. The indemnity will not, however, cover all losses arising from a reduction in share price, unless these are caused by company default. This is to avoid the company falling foul of the rules on financial assistance.[45]

---

[45] Sections 677 *et seq* of the Companies Act 2006. Section 677(1)(b)(ii) of the Companies Act 2006 provides that 'financial assistance' includes 'financial assistance given by way of ... indemnity, (other than an indemnity in respect of the indemnifier's own neglect or default)'.

5.95   Given the existence of the indemnity and the protection it offers the underwriters, the function of the warranties in an underwriting agreement is partially that of ensuring that a company and its directors have applied their minds to the right issues. A breach of a warranty, however, will also indicate that a company is in breach of the underwriting agreement, and the company may therefore lose some of the limitations that would otherwise apply to the indemnity.

5.96   Warranties and an indemnity are also likely to be required by the underwriters from a shareholder selling shares in the offer, particularly a shareholder that holds a significant percentage of shares in the company, although this may be strongly resisted by the shareholder. An indemnity given by a selling shareholder is typically limited to matters arising from that shareholder's own default. The extent of the indemnity may become an issue if the company itself is raising no, or very little, new money, because in these circumstances the company may be further constrained from giving a general indemnity by financial assistance considerations.[46]

5.97   *5.1.3.1.2.3 Due diligence*   The sponsor will perform extensive due diligence on the applicant company before making the application for listing on its behalf. In particular, the sponsor will carry out its own business due diligence with the management of the company. The underwriters will also be involved in this process to some degree.

5.98   Due diligence on an IPO will also generally involve the preparation of a so-called 'long form' report by the reporting accountants (see below at 5.1.3.2.1 below), together with some form of legal due diligence. Depending on the nature of the company's business, further reports from other specialists may also be commissioned.

5.99   Where a prospectus is being used to make an offering into the United States, the sponsor and underwriters will seek additional comfort on the contents of the prospectus in the form of a rule 10b-5 letter, generally provided by the lawyers for both the company and the underwriters. A rule 10b-5 letter confirms that nothing has come to the lawyers' attention during their due diligence process that has caused them to believe that the prospectus contains any untrue statement of a material fact or omits to state any material fact necessary to make the statements therein, in the light of the circumstances under which they are made, not misleading. In order to put themselves in a position to give a rule 10b-5 letter, the lawyers

---

[46] An exception to the prohibition on financial assistance in section 678(2) of the Companies Act 2006 allows financial assistance to be given if the giving of such financial assistance for the purposes of the acquisition of shares is only an incidental part of some larger purpose of the company. While the corporate benefits arising from the application of proceeds may be a larger purpose, mere assistance for a selling shareholder is not sufficient of itself.

will carry out a fairly extensive due diligence process in relation to the company and its business.

The main aim of this overall due diligence process is to put the company (and its directors), the sponsor and the underwriters in a position where they have a due diligence defence available if they are sued by others. For the underwriters, this due diligence defence is particularly important for security law reasons in the United States, but will also be relevant for United Kingdom purposes.

5.100

5.1.3.1.3 Brokers As part of the pre-marketing of an IPO, it is usual practice for brokers connected to the issuer's lead underwriter or other members of the underwriting syndicate to publish a research report on the issuer. The aim is to provide an independent and objective view of the issuer, and the report is circulated to the underwriters' institutional clients prior to the offering.

5.101

The brokers publishing such research will be concerned to limit any potential liability arising out of their reports. Methods of minimizing potential liability in respect of such research reports include:

5.102

  (i) limiting their distribution; for example, only to professional investors;

 (ii) the use of appropriate and prominent disclaimers;

(iii) the use of information barriers, to ensure the independence of the compilation of the research report from both the issuing company and the team working on the share offering;

(iv) avoiding profit forecasts and projections in research sourced from the issuing company;

 (v) imposing a blackout period during which research is not distributed. There is no set rule as to how long the period should be, but it is common for investment banks to have internal guidelines stipulating a period of about two weeks prior to launch of the book-building process. The blackout period should continue after the commencement of dealings, for at least 30 days (although in the United States this is extended to 40 days); and

(vi) managing conflicts of interest. There are detailed requirements in Chapter 12 of the Conduct of Business sourcebook and Chapter 10 of the Senior Management Arrangements, Systems and Controls sourcebook, which are part of the FSA Rulebook. For example, brokers should not promise issuers favourable research coverage, investment analysts should not participate in road shows and their reporting and remuneration arrangements should be structured to avoid conflicts.

5.1.3.2 UKLA obligations

The sponsor will also look to cover itself against potential liability for the various representations it is required to make to the UKLA. This is done not only through the underwriting agreement (see Section 5.1.3.1.2.2 above), but also through

5.103

reports and comfort letters addressed to the sponsor from the reporting accountants and other advisers. A number of these comfort letters will also be addressed to the company itself, as part of its supporting documentation.

5.104   **5.1.3.2.1 Reporting accountants**   The reporting accountants will enter into a detailed engagement letter with the company and the sponsor (and possibly at least the lead underwriters, where these are not also the sponsors), which will set out those areas relevant both to the prospectus and the application for listing in relation to which they are carrying out work and giving comfort. The reporting accountants seek to restrict their liability to the company and the sponsor (and other addressees) as far as possible through the terms of the engagement letter.

5.105   In particular, the engagement letter will generally specify that reports will only be provided to the addressees (which will include both the issuer and the sponsor) for the purpose of assisting them in meeting their responsibilities for the contents of the prospectus under common law, the provisions of FSMA, rule 5.5.3(2) of the Prospectus Rules, section 2 of the Misrepresentation Act or (in case of a sponsor) the Listing Rules. However, an engagement letter relating to a prospectus will not, as a matter of practice, include a cap upon the reporting accountants' liability.

5.106   The reporting accountants will give comfort to the addressees of the engagement letter on the following matters:

   (i) the accuracy of financial information extracted from accounts and accounting records of the company and included in the prospectus;

  (ii) any accountants' report included in the prospectus;

 (iii) any pro-forma financial information included in the prospectus;

 (iv) any profit forecast in the prospectus;

  (v) the working capital statement;

 (vi) the 'no significant change' statement; and

(vii) the Sponsor's Declaration on an Application for Listing (see Section 5.1.2.2.2.1 above).

5.107   The accountants' comfort letters will all be issued in reliance upon representation letters addressed by the company to the reporting accountants.

5.108   On an IPO, the reporting accountants will also generally produce a separate 'long form' report on the business of the company. This typically provides a description of the company and its business (including details of its financial and management information systems) and an analysis of its past financial performance and its balance sheet. The long form report provides an additional source to help check that all material information regarding the company and its business is disclosed in the prospectus.

The reporting accountants will generally specify that their reports can only be **5.109** relied upon in respect of the use of the prospectus in the United Kingdom. If the shares are to be offered in the United States, the sponsor and other underwriters will also request a comfort letter from the reporting accountants in form and content governed by the US accounting profession's Statement on Auditing Standards No 72 ('SAS 72 letter'). SAS 72 provides a template for the comfort letter and contains specific instructions and language that should be used by the accountants in various situations.

The SAS 72 letter will generally give negative assurance about certain matters **5.110** since the last audited financial statements produced by the company (such as confirmations that there have been no changes in equity capital, increases in debt, decreases in turnover etc. since that date, other than as disclosed). In particular, the reporting accountants may perform a limited review of subsequent unaudited interim financial statements in accordance with Statement on Auditing Standards No 71 (and will need to carry out such review if 135 or more days have elapsed since the date of the most recent audited financial statements).

If the shares are to be offered in other countries a comfort letter equivalent to the **5.111** SAS 72 letter will generally also be requested.

5.1.3.2.2 Other comfort letters The sponsor will also require the company **5.112** and the company's other advisers (but particularly their lawyers) to provide comfort letters to back up the statements contained in the Sponsor's Declaration on an Application for Listing.

In order to allow the sponsor to fulfil its obligations, the company will be required **5.113** to provide specific confirmation that the company's lawyers have properly briefed the directors on their duties in relation to the company's admission to the Official List. The company will also be required to give a confirmation that supports all of the other provisions of the Sponsor's Declaration, acknowledging that these confirmations can be relied on by the sponsor.

It is market practice also for the company's lawyers (and sometimes its brokers and **5.114** other advisers) to give the sponsors a confirmation that there is no matter relating to the company of which they are aware which is not disclosed in the prospectus and which ought to be drawn to the sponsor's attention. While this confirmation is given expressly in contemplation of the Sponsor's Declaration being entered into by the sponsor in reliance on the letter, it is also generally given without legal liability, and limited to those matters that are customarily the responsibility of the company's lawyers (or the other relevant advisers) on an IPO. Accordingly, these letters are intended to provide a defence for the sponsor, rather than a means of transferring risk or liability onto another party.

5.2 Ongoing Reporting Obligations

5.2.1 Introduction

5.115   Once a company has been admitted to the Official List, it will be obliged to comply with a number of ongoing reporting obligations, the detail of which is set out in the DTRs and the Listing Rules.[47] Section 2 of this Chapter looks at the nature of these obligations and the implications of any breach of such obligations by the listed company.

5.2.2 Listing Principles

5.116   Before examining the detail of the relevant provisions under the DTRs and the Listing Rules, it is worth noting that a listed company must also comply with the general provisions of the Listing Principles set out in Chapter 7 of the Listing Rules. The Listing Principles include requirements that a listed company must:

(i)   take reasonable steps to establish and maintain adequate procedures, systems and controls to enable it to comply with its obligations (Listing Principle 2);[48]

(ii)   communicate information to holders and potential holders of its listed equity securities in such a way as to avoid the creation or continuation of a false market in such listed equity securities (Listing Principle 4); and

(iii)   deal with the FSA in an open and cooperative manner (Listing Principle 6).

5.117   The Listing Principles are enforceable as if they were rules, although the FSA has indicated that it would rarely seek to take enforcement action in respect of a breach of a Listing Principle alone. Nevertheless, where there is an investigation into whether information was announced sufficiently promptly, it is likely that the FSA will consider the adequacy of the procedures, systems and controls that the relevant issuer has put in place for the purposes of the Listing Principles in relation to the information under investigation.

5.118   A listed company will therefore need to consider whether its procedures, systems and controls are adequate to comply with the Listing Principles (in particular,

---

[47]   See Chapter 21 of Part 3.

[48]   For the purposes of Principle 2, a listed company with a primary listing of equity securities admitted to the Official List should have adequate systems and controls to be able to (i) ensure that it can properly identify information which requires disclosure under the DTRs and/or the Listing Rules in a timely manner; and (ii) ensure that any information identified under (i) is properly considered by the directors and that such a consideration encompasses whether the information should be disclosed.

Listing Principle 2). In doing so, it may be useful to take into account the following:

(i)   The procedures need to:
    (a) ensure that information that may be inside information is identified; and
    (b) provide a process for a proper assessment of the relevant information that allows the issuer to take an informed decision as to whether an announcement is required or may be delayed.

(ii) The procedures need to identify different kinds of inside information:
    (a) information about transactions or other strategic projects;
    (b) information about the performance of the business; and
    (c) one-off unplanned events.

(iii) The procedures should provide for formal records to be kept, which may assist in demonstrating that the procedures are operated properly.

(iv) The procedures should be supported by establishing a clear communications policy, which sets out:
    (a) responsibilities for communications; and
    (b) policies for dealing with analysts, rumours and leaks of inside information.

(v)   It may be useful to provide training for relevant individuals to ensure that they understand the procedures and their responsibilities in relation to them.

5.2.3 Key obligations

5.2.3.1 Continuous disclosure obligations

5.119 The DTRs contain a general obligation for an issuer to announce inside information (DTR 2), together with a number of more specific reporting obligations. These apply generally to all issuers of financial instruments admitted to the Official List (both under the DTRs and as a continuing obligation under Chapter 9 of the Listing Rules).[49]

5.120 The DTRs operate alongside the Listing Rules, which also impose a number of specific reporting obligations on issuers that effectively add detail and structure over and above the general requirements of DTR 2. The Listing Rules apply to all issuers of securities admitted to the Official List (or for which an application for such admission has been made), but are amended for companies that have shares listed under LR 14 (secondary listing of companies), LR 15 (closed-ended

---

[49] The DTRs provide that DTR 2 applies to any issuer whose financial instruments are admitted to trading on a regulated market in the United Kingdom (or for which an application for such admission has been made); and DTR 6 applies to any issuer whose home state is the United Kingdom.

investment funds) and LR 16 (open-ended investment companies). The Listing
Rules also apply in an amended form to various types of debt securities under
LR 17 (debt and specialist securities), LR 18 (certificates representing certain securi-
ties) and LR 19 (securitized derivatives), which are beyond the scope of this
Chapter.

5.121 Generally, issuers comply with their reporting obligations under the DTRs
and the Listing Rules by way of notification made to a Regulatory Information
Service ('RIS') in the form of an announcement which the RIS then disseminates.
Where a notification is required at a time when there is no RIS open for business, the issuer is required to distribute the notification to two national UK
newspapers, two UK newswire services and to an RIS for release once it opens. In
addition, if a company has a website it must make any announced 'inside information' available on it by close of the business day following the day the announcement is released. The announcement must be retained on the website for at least
one year.

5.122 The DTRs and the Listing Rules provide that an issuer must take reasonable
care to ensure that any information it notifies to an RIS is not misleading, false
or deceptive, and does not omit anything likely to affect the import of the
information.[50] In addition, the RIS announcement must not be combined with
marketing material in a way that is likely to be misleading.[51]

5.123 Companies with securities also listed on markets in other jurisdictions must
ensure that announcements of inside information, so far as possible, are synchronized. This may necessitate an announcement in the United Kingdom while an
RIS is closed (see above).

5.124 In addition, as a separate requirement, a listed company must also forward to the
FSA, for publication through the FSA's document viewing facility, two copies of
all circulars, notices, reports and other documents to which the Listing Rules
apply, at the same time that they are issued.[52] An RIS must be notified as soon as
possible after a document has been so forwarded to the FSA, unless the full text of
the document itself is provided to the RIS.[53]

5.2.3.2 Periodic disclosure obligations

5.125 DTR 4 requires periodic reporting by listed companies as follows:

   (i) the company must publish an annual report, including its audited financial
statements, a management report and directors' responsibility statements;

---

[50] DTR 1.3.4/LR 1.3.3R.
[51] DTR 1.3.5R.
[52] LR 9.6.1R.
[53] LR 9.6.3R.

(ii) an interim report, covering the first six months of its financial year, including unaudited financial statements, a management commentary and directors' responsibility statements; and

(iii) interim management statements, broadly covering the first and third quarters of the financial year, giving an update on material events during the period and describing the financial position and performance of the company during the period. (This does not necessarily require the publication of financial statements.)

Additional contents requirements for the annual report are contained in LR 9.8.

5.2.3.3 *Shareholder circulars*

The Listing Rules also prescribe disclosures to be included in documents (referred to as 'circulars') sent by a listed company to its shareholders, typically when convening a meeting of shareholders. The general standard required by the rules is that a circular must 'provide a clear and adequate explanation of its subject matter, giving due prominence to its essential characteristics, benefits and risks'.[54] In addition there are specific disclosure requirements for circulars dealing with different matters. The most detailed requirements apply to circulars published in relation to significant transactions by the company that require shareholder approval (known as Class 1 transactions)[55] or to transactions between the company and its directors or significant shareholders (related party transactions).[56] **5.126**

5.2.4 Breach of obligations

5.2.4.1 *Principal sanctions for breach of the Listing Rules or the DTRs*

The FSA can impose the following sanctions on a listed company for breach of the Listing Rules or DTRs: **5.127**

(i) it may require the listed company to pay a financial penalty;

(ii) it may censure the listed company;[57]

(iii) it may suspend the listed company's securities from listing;[58] or

---

[54] LR 13.3.1R.

[55] Chapter 10 of the Listing Rules deals with the categorization of transactions. See LR 13.4 and LR 13.5 for the detailed rules on disclosure required to be included in a Class 1 circular.

[56] Chapter 11 of the Listing Rules deals with related party transactions and the definition of 'related party' (which also includes persons exercising significant influence over an issuer, and associates of other related parties). See LR 13.6 for the detailed rules on disclosure required to be included in a related party circular.

[57] FSMA section 91(1)/(1ZA)/(3).

[58] FSMA sections 77(2) and 89L; LR 5.1.1.R and 5.1.2G.

(iv)   it may require the listed company to provide the FSA with information or to publish information.[59]

5.128   The FSA can also impose sanctions (financial penalties or public censure) on any director (or former director) of a listed company that is in breach of its obligations, if the director was 'knowingly concerned' in the breach. The expression 'knowingly concerned' is not explained further, but there is case law on the meaning of the same expression where it was used in the Financial Services Act 1986.

5.129   In *Securities and Investments Board v Pantell SA (No 2)*,[60] Steyn LJ stated that 'proof of actual knowledge is essential but not enough. Mere passive knowledge will not be sufficient: actual involvement in the contravention must be established.' However, 'concerned' does not mean that the person in question must have an interest (presumably, in the context of the case, a proprietary interest) of his/her own in the subject matter under investigation. In addition, in *Securities and Investments Board v Scandex Capital Management A/S*[61] Millet LJ made clear that a person can be 'knowingly concerned' in a breach by knowing of the facts giving rise to that breach, without knowledge that those facts constituted a breach of the law.

5.130   In the *Pantell* case, at first instance,[62] Browne-Wilkinson VC said that: 'The most obvious example of a person "knowingly concerned" in a contravention will be a person who is the moving light behind [the relevant] company.' He went on to say, in the context of the power to seek restitution from company directors for breach of the legislation, that where a company itself has no value 'it is obviously just to enable the court, as part of the statutory remedy of quasi-rescission, to order the individual who is running that company in an unlawful manner to recoup those who have paid money to the company under an unlawful transaction.'

5.131   The FSA can also impose sanctions (financial penalties or public censure) on a person discharging managerial responsibility, and persons connected with such a person, for breach of the obligations under DTR 3.

5.132   Instances of public sanctions being imposed for breaches of the Listing Rules and DTRs are very rare, as evidenced by the fact that, between the time the FSA took over enforcement of the Listing Rules from the London Stock Exchange in May 2000 and August 2009, the FSA had published only 12 final notices setting out sanctions for breaches of the Listing Rules and DTRs, all but two of which related to failure to make timely disclosure of inside information.

---

[59]   DTR 1.3.1R/1.3.3R and LR 1.3.2R.
[60]   [1993] 1 All ER 134.
[61]   [1998] 1 All ER 514.
[62]   *Securities and Investments Board v Pantell SA and Others (No2)* [1991] 4 All ER 883.

5.2.4.1.1 Financial penalties   Financial penalties are the most common type of **5.133** sanction imposed by the FSA.

The FSA is required to follow its formulated policy[63] in determining the amount **5.134** of financial penalty to be imposed for contravention of the Listing Rules and DTRs. The FSA's stated policy is that the principal purpose of financial penalties includes deterrence against future breaches.

The recent final notices published by the FSA highlight a number of other factors **5.135** that the FSA may consider in determining the level of fines, including (i) the duration, frequency and seriousness of the breach; (ii) whether the breach was deliberate or reckless; (iii) the financial circumstances of the company on which a penalty is to be imposed; (iv) the conduct of the company after the breach (including whether professional advice was sought and followed); (v) the conduct of the company during the FSA investigation; and (vi) the company's previous disciplinary record and compliance history.

The recent cases[64] in which financial penalties have been imposed by the FSA for **5.136** breaches of the Listing Rules and DTRs show the FSA's willingness to reduce the fines by as much as 30% in view of mitigating factors.[65]

The financial penalties imposed by the FSA have not been limited to companies. **5.137** In certain cases, the FSA has imposed fines on company directors who have been knowingly concerned in the relevant breach.[66] To avoid such personal fines, each director must be familiar with the disclosure obligations under the Listing Rules and the DTRs and ensure that, as soon as he or she receives any information that might possibly be categorized as 'inside information', all the details are disclosed to the full board of directors, which must then consider without delay whether an announcement should be issued.

5.2.4.1.2 Public censure   The FSA may impose a statement of public censure **5.138** instead of a fine where its policy allows, which may include: (i) where the company brings a breach to the FSA's attention; or (ii) where the company's lack of financial resources means that it could not pay a financial penalty (for example, where the company is in administration).

---

[63] The FSA statements of policy on imposing financial penalties are contained in the Decision Procedure and Penalties Manual (DEPP 6) and the Enforcement Guide.

[64] See Final Notice issued to Entertainment Rights plc on 19 January 2009 and Final Notice issued to Wolfson Microelectronics plc on 19 January 2009.

[65] Such mitigating factors included full and frank admission to the FSA and cooperation with the FSA investigation, absence of deliberate intention to mislead the market, timely request for professional advice and adoption of recommendations received from the advisers, and absence of previous disciplinary action.

[66] See Final Notice issued to Sportsworld Media Group plc on 29 March 2004 (CEO fined £45,000) and Final Notice issued to Universal Salvage plc on 19 May 2004 (CEO fined £10,000).

5.139 5.2.4.1.3 **Suspension of listing**   The FSA may decide to suspend the listing of a company's securities on the Official List if it considers that the smooth operation of the market is, or may be temporarily jeopardized, or that it is necessary to protect investors.[67] The cases of suspension of listing are rare, but some of the examples of when this power may be used given in the Listing Rules[68] include cases where the issuer has failed to meet its continuing obligations for listing, or has failed to make financial disclosures in accordance with the Listing Rules or is unable to assess accurately its financial position, and cases where there is insufficient information in the market about a proposed transaction.

5.140 In the United Kingdom the admission of securities to listing is separate from their admission to trading on a regulated market. It is a condition of admission of securities to trading on the main market operated by the London Stock Exchange that the securities have been admitted to listing by the FSA, acting as the UKLA. If the listing is suspended, the London Stock Exchange would also suspend trading on the market. However, the FSA's power to suspend a listing is additional to the FSA's power to suspend trading of a company's securities on the London Stock Exchange main market for listed securities (or any other regulated market) in cases of breaches of the disclosure rules contained in the DTRs (as discussed further in Section 5.2.4.2.3 below).

5.2.4.2 *Other sanctions*

5.141 5.2.4.2.1 **Sponsor censure**   The FSA also has the power to censure a sponsor where it considers that the sponsor has contravened any requirement imposed on the sponsor by the Listing Rules.[69] However, the FSA has no statutory authority to impose a financial penalty on the sponsor. If the FSA proposes publishing a statement of public censure in relation to a sponsor it must give the sponsor a warning notice and allow the sponsor to make representations (see also Section 5.1.2.2.2.2).

5.142 5.2.4.2.2 **Cancellation of listing**   The FSA may, in extreme circumstances, cancel the listing of securities following a breach of the Listing Rules.[70]

5.143 In order to cancel the company's listing of securities, the FSA must be satisfied that there are special circumstances that preclude normal regular dealings in such shares; this is therefore an uncommon course of action. The circumstances in which the FSA may cancel the listing of securities include where the securities have been suspended from listing for more than six months or the issuer no longer

---

[67] LR 5.1.1R and section 77 of FSMA.
[68] LR 5.1.2G.
[69] Section 89 of FSMA and LR 8.7.19R.
[70] LR 5.2.1R.

satisfies continuing obligations for listing (for example, if the percentage of shares in public hands falls below 25%).

On 18 July 2007, the FSA published a notice of intended cancellation of listing of the securities in Simon Group Plc as the company no longer satisfied the continuing obligation for listing under LR 6.1.19R that the percentage of shares in public hands must not fall below 25%. The FSA concluded that the fact that only 8.9% of the company's shares were in public hands and that there was no realistic prospect of the percentage being restored in the future amounted to the special circumstances that precluded normal regular dealings in Simon Group Plc's securities.

5.144

5.2.4.2.3 Suspension of securities from trading   In relation to breaches of the DTRs, the FSA can also suspend a listed company's securities from trading if it determines that there are reasonable grounds to suspect the DTRs have not been complied with.[71] This power might be used, for example, where a company fails to make an announcement to a RIS within the applicable time limit or where there is a leak of inside information and the company is unable or unwilling to issue an announcement within a reasonable time.[72] However, use of these powers is also uncommon.

5.145

5.2.4.2.4 Private warning   Instead of taking any of the more formal disciplinary actions set out above, the FSA may instead decide to give the company or relevant person a private warning.[73]

5.146

5.2.4.2.5 Sanctions for market abuse   A listed company that publishes information required by DTR 2 (the ongoing disclosure obligation) that does not comply with the obligation to ensure that the information is not 'misleading, false or deceptive and does not omit anything likely to affect the import of the information'[74] may also thereby commit market abuse on the basis that the information published gives or is likely to give false or misleading representation as to a qualifying investment (as discussed generally in Part 1 and in relation to the prospectus in 5.1.2.1.1.5 above).[75] As described above, the FSA can impose financial penalties for market abuse and may also order that compensation be paid to any investor who suffers loss as a result of the relevant breach. Criminal sanctions

5.147

---

[71] DTR 1.4.1R and section 96C of FSMA.
[72] DTR 1.4.4G.
[73] Enforcement Guide 7.10.
[74] DTR 1.3.4R.
[75] See the Final Notice dated 24 August 2004 in relation to the financial penalty imposed on The "Shell" Transport and Trading Company plc for misreporting of reserves. The misreporting constituted both market abuse and breach of the Listing Rules (containing disclosure obligations equivalent to those now found in the DTRs). The penalty was imposed for the market abuse and not for breach of the Listing Rules.

may apply under section 397 of FSMA if the misstatements in the disclosure are deliberate, dishonest or reckless.

5.2.4.3 *Other liabilities*

5.148   **5.2.4.3.1 Liability for continuous disclosures**   In relation to the obligation to disclose information as it arises, discussed in Section 5.2.3.1 above, and in particular the obligation to disclose all inside information immediately, it is necessary to consider the possibility of claims for:

(i)   failing to make a required disclosure or delay in making the disclosure; and

(ii)   misstatements in any disclosure that is made, including errors, misleading statements or omissions of relevant information.

5.149   It is generally accepted that there are considerable hurdles in the way of a claimant seeking to establish a right to compensation for a delay in making a disclosure. There is no statutory right to compensation (other than, as noted above, the possibility of an order for compensation, if the delay amounted to market abuse). In addition, there should be no liability for breach of statutory duty, if only on the basis that there is a regime for enforcing the rules through regulatory sanctions, which should displace any right to claim.[76]

5.150   Furthermore, any other claim would have to rely on an implied representation by the company that there was nothing to disclose, and such a claim would also face problems in establishing that a duty was owed, given that the representation is addressed to a very wide class of persons (the public) without any special relationship with the company.

5.151   It is less clear that there could be no claim for a misstatement if a disclosure is made. Again, there is no statutory remedy and there should be no liability for breach of statutory duty. However, in this case there is an express representation made by the company and a person who suffers loss as a result may have a claim for negligent misstatement (as noted in *Hall v Cable and Wireless Plc*, referred to in footnote 76). The principal hurdle for the claimant would probably be in establishing that there was a sufficiently clear relationship between the company and existing shareholders, or those who become shareholders by buying shares, to form the basis of a duty of care. The disclosures are published to the world at large, which the courts could conclude was too wide a group. Claims of this sort are not often seen in practice, which suggests that the legal hurdles combined with the practical problems (discussed in Section 5.1.2.1.3 above) may prevent this from being a real risk for companies.

---

[76]   See discussion in 'sponsors and underwriters' at paragraph 47 above. See also *Hall v Cable and Wireless plc* [2009] EWHC 1793 (Comm).

5.2.4.3.2 Liability for periodic disclosures A listed company may also be liable **5.152**
under FSMA for its periodic reports published pursuant to the DTRs (its annual
reports, half-yearly reports and interim management statements).[77] Section 90A
of FSMA provides that a listed company must pay compensation to a person who
has acquired securities and suffered loss as a result of an untrue or misleading
statement in the relevant publication or the omission of any information required
to be included. The listed company will only be liable if a person discharging
managerial responsibilities in relation to the publication either knew that, or was
reckless as to whether, a particular statement was untrue or misleading, or knew
that a particular omission constituted a dishonest concealment of fact. It is
expressly provided that this is the only basis for liability on the part of the company and that *no other person* has any liability, save any liability such other person
may have to the company. These provisions therefore create an important liability
safe harbour in relation to periodic reports. The exception, which leaves liability
to the company unaffected by the provisions, has the effect of preserving the
ability of the company concerned to claim against its directors, auditors or professional advisers. However, the limited scope for liability on the part of the company
significantly reduces the scope for substantial claims by the company against these
parties.

5.2.4.3.3 Proposals for reform of statutory liability In 2006, HM Treasury **5.153**
asked Professor Paul Davies to conduct a review of issuer liability to investors. His
final report (which has yet to be implemented) suggested that:

(i) the fraud standard of liability that applies to periodic reports under section
90A of FSMA should also apply to ad hoc disclosures made in accordance
with the Disclosure Rules and other announcements through an RIS;
(ii) the liability regime should be extended to provide for compensation to be
paid for 'dishonest delay' in making a required ad hoc disclosure. Delay
would be dishonest if the purpose of the delay was fraudulent; and
(iii) both buyers and sellers of shares should be able to claim compensation.

HM Treasury issued a consultation paper in July 2008 with draft legislation to **5.154**
implement these proposals.[78]

5.2.4.3.4 Liability for disclosures in circulars While not free from doubt, **5.155**
and without the benefit of any judicial comment on the question, it is generally
considered that liability for the contents of a shareholder circular extends only
to existing shareholders, whose claim would be limited to the loss suffered as a
result of exercising their governance rights (principally, although perhaps not

---

[77] FSMA section 90A.
[78] 'Extension of the statutory regime for issuer liability' July 2008.

exclusively, in voting at the meeting convened by the circular). This does not, therefore, directly translate into losses suffered as a result of investing in the company. This conclusion is based on the reasoning in *Caparo Industries plc v Dickman*,[79] which held that the auditors of the company had no liability to investors or potential investors generally arising out of their statutory audit opinion. This conclusion presupposes that there is no special relationship created with an investor or shareholder on the basis of which a duty of care could be established.

---

[79] [1990] 2 AC 605.

6

TAKEOVERS AND STAKEBUILDING

6.1 Introduction

6.1.1 The Takeover Directive

6.01 Following the implementation of the EU Directive on Takeover Bids (the 'Takeover Directive'),[1] there is some commonality across the EU on the regulation of takeovers. The Takeover Directive forms an important part of the EU's Financial Services Action Plan, a plan drawn up in 1999 to address issues within the EU's segmented financial markets and the lack of direct access to cross-border financial institutions,[2] with the aim of implementing a set of measures intended to fill gaps and to remove the remaining barriers to a single market in financial services across the EU as a whole. The key aim of the Takeover Directive is to:

> create Community-wide clarity and transparency in respect of legal issues to be settled in the event of takeover bids and to prevent patterns of corporate restructuring within the Community from being distorted by arbitrary differences in governance and management cultures.[3]

6.02 In drafting the directive, the European Parliament and Council also focused on facilitating cross-border takeovers and ensuring that shareholders are given adequate protection.[4] The Takeover Directive is a minimum standards directive and, accordingly, EU member states can broaden its scope and add more stringent rules, if they wish.

6.03 Whilst the Takeover Directive has introduced certain common features across Europe it is not yet the case that there is a standard set of rules. Accordingly, it is not possible for this Chapter to detail a 'standard' takeover in the EU. That said, the Takeover Directive was largely modelled on the UK's takeover regime which has long been regarded as the most sophisticated in Europe. Accordingly, this

---

[1] Directive 2004/25 EC of the European Parliament and of the Council of 21 April 2004 on takeover bids.

[2] 'Financial Services: Implementing the Framework for Financial Markets: Action plan', Communication of the EC Commission COM (1999) 232, 11.05.99, page 3.

[3] Takeover Directive Recital (3).

[4] Takeover Directive Recital (25).

Chapter will explain the UK regime in detail and this case study can serve as a base case for explaining the process for effecting a takeover in the EU in compliance with the principles set out in the Takeover Directive. Whilst, plainly, there will be differences throughout the EU regimes, this Chapter will highlight the core principles and features which, though implemented in a way particular to the UK, are common across the EU.

6.1.2 Framework for the governance of takeovers in the UK

Historically, regulation of takeovers in the UK did not have a statutory footing. **6.04** That changed as part of the UK's implementation of the Takeover Directive and such regulation now has a statutory footing in Part 28 of the Companies Act 2006.

The Takeover Directive requires member states to designate a competent author- **6.05** ity to supervise bids.[5] The UK has designated the Panel on Takeovers and Mergers (the 'Panel') as its competent authority[6] (which preserves the situation prior to the implementation of the Takeover Directive).

The Companies Act 2006 also requires the Panel to make rules giving effect to **6.06** certain provisions of the Takeover Directive[7] as well as affording it general powers to regulate takeover bids, merger transactions and transactions which have or may have, directly or indirectly, an effect on the ownership or control of companies and certain matters relating to each such transaction. The Panel is granted these general powers because the Takeover Directive, as a minimum standards direc-tive, only regulates the takeover of companies admitted to trading on a regulated market.[8] The UK, as a policy decision, considers that the scope of takeover regula-tion should be wider than this. The City Code on Takeovers and Mergers (the 'Takeover Code' or the 'Code') are the rules which have been made by the Panel relating to takeovers and mergers (and which now, accordingly, have a basis in statute). The Code existed long before the implementation of the Takeover Directive and only minor changes to the Code were needed to ensure that it com-plied with the provisions of the Takeover Directive.

6.1.3 The Panel and other relevant bodies

The Panel is an independent unincorporated body which has existed since 1968. **6.07** It has rights and obligations under common law which are supplemented by

---

[5] Takeover Directive Article 4(2).
[6] Companies Act 2006 section 942.
[7] Companies Act 2006 section 943 requires the Panel to make rules giving effect to Takeover Directive Articles 3.1, 4.2, 5, 6.1 to 6.3, 7 to 9 and 13.
[8] Takeover Directive Article 1. The definition of 'regulated market' is in Directive 93/22 EEC of the Council on investment services in the securities field.

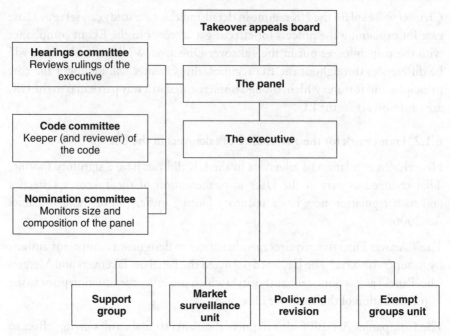

Figure 6.1 Organizational structure of the Panel

relevant statutory powers and obligations. The Panel has up to 34 members at any time. They comprise the Chairman, two Deputy Chairmen and up to 20 other members, each of whom is appointed by the Panel.[9] The remaining 11 members are appointed by various stakeholders who have an interest in the work of the Panel.[10]

6.08   The principal groups that assist with the Code are shown in Figure 6.1 below.

6.1.3.1 The Executive[11]

6.09   The Executive operates independently of the Panel and carries out the day-to-day work of takeover supervision and regulation. It comprises a mixture of direct employees and secondees (who act independently of the body which has seconded them). The secondees are drawn from a mixture of law firms, accountancy firms, corporate brokers, investment banks and other organizations.

---

⁹ Takeover Code Paragraph 3(a)(i)–(iii), Introduction.

¹⁰ Takeover Code Paragraph 3 (a)(iv), Introduction; those bodies which have the right to appoint individuals to the Panel are the Association of British Insurers, the Association of Investment Companies, the Association of Private Client Investment Managers and Stockbrokers, the British Bankers' Association, the Confederation of British Industry, the Institute of Chartered Accountants in England and Wales, Investment Management Association, the London Investment Banking Association (which also has separate representation for its Corporate Finance Committee and Securities Trading Committee) and the National Association of Pension Funds.

¹¹ Takeover Code; information drawn from paragraph 5, Introduction.

The Executive's work involves, either on its own initiative or at the instigation of third parties, the conduct of investigations, the monitoring of relevant dealings in connection with the Code and the giving of rulings on the interpretation, application or effect of the Code.

6.10

6.1.3.2 *The Hearings Committee*[12]

The Hearings Committee comprises the Chairman of the Panel, up to eight other members designated by the Panel (so long as they have never been a member of the Code Committee[13]) and all of the representatives of the bodies who are allowed to appoint individuals to the Panel (as explained above). The Hearings Committee has a statutory basis which provides that a decision of the Panel must be subject to review by a committee of the Panel.[14]

6.11

Its main work is to review rulings of the Executive and to hear disciplinary proceedings when the Executive considers that there has been a breach of the Code. Its rules of procedure are available on the Panel's website and are summarized in the Code.[15]

6.12

6.1.3.3 *The Takeover Appeal Board*[16]

The Takeover Appeal Board is a wholly independent body which hears appeals against rulings of the Hearings Committee. It has a statutory basis which provides that there must be a right of appeal against a decision of the Hearings Committee to an independent tribunal.[17] The Chairman and Deputy Chairman of the Board are appointed by the Master of the Rolls[18] and will usually have been senior members of the judiciary. The other members of the Board are appointed by the Chairman or the Deputy Chairman of the Board and will have relevant knowledge and experience of takeovers. A Board hearing will normally comprise at least five members (although the quorum for Board proceedings is three). The Chairman or the Deputy Chairman will usually preside as chairman of the proceedings in question.

6.13

6.1.3.4 *The Code Committee*[19]

The Code Committee comprises up to 12 members of the Panel who are designated as a member of the Code Committee. The Code Committee is responsible

6.14

---

[12] Takeover Code; information drawn from paragraph 4(c), Introduction.
[13] Takeover Code paragraph 4(d), introduction.
[14] Section 951(1)of the Companies Act 2006.
[15] Takeover Code paragraph 7, Introduction.
[16] Takeover Code; information drawn from paragraph 8, Introduction.
[17] Companies Act 2006 section 951(3).
[18] The Master of the Rolls is the second most senior judge in England and Wales.
[19] Takeover Code; information drawn from paragraph 4(b), Introduction.

for the rule-making functions of the Panel. It is also responsible for keeping most of the Code under review[20] and for proposing, consulting on, making and issuing amendments to those parts of the Code.

6.15   In its structure, therefore, the Panel and its committees, the Executive and the Takeovers Appeal Board ensure that there is a genuine separation of powers, with different individuals performing the executive, legislative and judicial functions relating to relevant takeovers in the UK. A more detailed examination of the Panel's powers is set out at Section 6.1.5 below.

6.1.4 When and to whom does the Code apply?

6.16   The jurisdiction of the Panel and the applicability of the Code to a particular transaction will be determined by reference to the identity of the target company. The Code contains detailed rules which comply with the Takeover Directive rules on jurisdiction and also provide additional rules.

6.17   The test for whether the Code applies will depend on a number of factors relevant to the target company.

6.1.4.1 Companies admitted to trading on a UK regulated market[21]

6.18   If the target entity is a company or a Societas Europaea which has its registered office in the United Kingdom, the Channel Islands or the Isle of Man *and* if any of its securities are admitted to trading on a regulated market in the United Kingdom or on any stock exchange in the Channel Islands or the Isle of Man then the Code will apply.[22]

6.1.4.2 Companies not admitted to trading on a UK regulated market

6.19   **6.1.4.2.1 Where the company is a public limited company**   If the target entity is a company or a Societas Europaea which is a public limited company,[23] has its registered office in the United Kingdom and that company has its place of central management and control in the United Kingdom, then the Code will apply.[24]

6.20   **6.1.4.2.2 Where the company is a private company**   If the target entity is a private company, the conditions relating to a public company (described in

---

[20] The Code Committee is not responsible for Sections 1, 2(a) and (b), 4(a), (b) and (c) 5, 7, 8 and 13 of the Introduction to the Code, which remain the responsibility of the Panel.

[21] Regulated market for these purposes has the meaning given in Directive 2004/39 EC of the European Parliament and of the Council on markets in financial instruments.

[22] Takeover Code paragraph 3(a)(i), Introduction.

[23] A public limited company will have authorized capital of at least £50,000 (of which at least one quarter must be paid up). It may offer its shares to the public. A public limited company will have 'public limited company' or 'PLC' in its name.

[24] Takeover Code paragraph 3(a)(ii), Introduction.

Section 6.1.4.2.1 above) are met and one of the conditions set out below applies, then the Code will apply. The conditions are that:

(i) any of its securities have been admitted to the Official List of the Financial Services Authority during the ten years prior to the relevant date; or

(ii) dealings and/or prices at which persons were willing to deal in any of their securities have been published on a regular basis for a continuous period of at least six months in the ten years prior to the relevant date; or

(iii) any of its securities have been subject to a marketing arrangement as described in section 693(3)(b) of the Companies Act 2006 at any time during the ten years prior to the relevant date; or

(iv) they were required to file a prospectus with the registrar of companies or any other relevant authority in the United Kingdom, the Channel Islands or the Isle of Man to have a prospectus approved by the UKLA at any time during the ten years prior to the relevant date.

In each case, the relevant date is the date on which an announcement is made of a proposed or possible bid for the company or the date on which some other event occurs in relation to the company which has significance under the Code.[25]   **6.21**

Finally, there are some cases where the Panel will share jurisdiction with the regulatory authority in another member state and the Code, accordingly, contains conflicts of law provisions. It is beyond the scope of this Chapter to explore extensively the provisions on dual jurisdiction but the two most common circumstances are where the target company has a UK registered office but is admitted to trading only on a regulated market in another EEA state or the target company has a non-UK registered office but is admitted to trading on a UK regulated market.[26] The Panel should be consulted at any early stage to determine which parts of the Code apply,[27] as the Takeover Directive makes a distinction between matters relating to (a) company law and employee information and (b) matters relating to the bid.[28] Accordingly, different member states may be responsible for supervising different parts of a bid under the Takeover Directive.   **6.22**

By way of summary Figure 6.2 below sets out the main criteria for determining whether the Code applies.   **6.23**

6.1.5 An overview of the Code

The Code is, according to its introduction, to be regarded as a framework for ensuring orderly conduct throughout the course of the takeover.[29] The central   **6.24**

---

[25] Takeover Code paragraph 3(a)(ii), Introduction.
[26] Takeover Code paragraph 3(a)(iii), Introduction.
[27] Takeover Code paragraph 3(d), Introduction.
[28] Takeover Directive Article 4(2)(e).
[29] Takeover Code paragraph 2(a), Introduction.

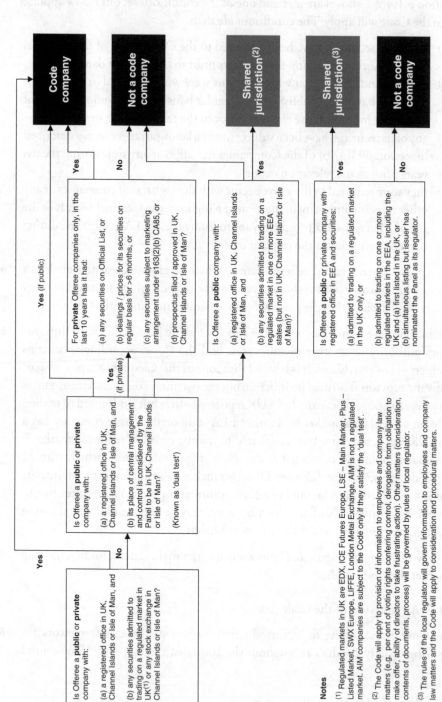

Is Offeree a public or private company with:

(a) a registered office in UK, Channel Islands or Isle of Man, and

(b) any securities admitted to trading on a regulated market in UK[1] or any stock exchange in Channel Islands or Isle of Man?

No → **Is Offeree a public or private company with:**

(a) a registered office in UK, Channel Islands or Isle of Man, and

(b) its place of central management and control is considered by the Panel to be in UK, Channel Islands or Isle of Man?

(Known as 'dual test')

Yes (if public) →

Yes (if private) → **For private Offeree companies only, in the last 10 years has it had:**

(a) any securities on Official List, or

(b) dealings / prices for its securities on regular basis for >6 months, or

(c) any securities subject to marketing arrangement under s163(2)(b) CA85, or

(d) prospectus filed / approved in UK, Channel Islands or Isle of Man?

Yes → **Code company**

No → **Not a code company**

Is Offeree a public company with:

(a) registered office in UK, Channel Islands or Isle of Man, and

(b) any securities admitted to trading on a regulated market in one or more EEA states (but not in UK, Channel Islands or Isle of Man)?

Yes → **Shared jurisdiction**[2]

Is Offeree a public or private company with registered office in EEA and securities:

(a) admitted to trading on a regulated market in the UK only, or

(b) admitted to trading on one or more regulated markets in the EEA, including the UK and (a) first listed in the UK, or

(b) simultaneous listing but issuer has nominated the Panel as its regulator.

Yes → **Shared jurisdiction**[3]

No → **Not a code company**

Yes → **Code company** (if public)

Notes

(1) Regulated markets in UK are EDX, ICE Futures Europe, LSE – Main Market, Plus – Listed Market, SWX Europe, LIFFE, London Metal Exchange. AIM is not a regulated market. AIM companies are subject to the Code only if they satisfy the 'dual test'.

(2) The Code will apply to provision of information to employees and company law matters (e.g. per cent of voting rights conferring control, derogation from obligation to make offer, ability of directors to take frustrating action). Other matters (consideration, contents of documents, process) will be governed by rules of local regulator.

(3) The rules of the local regulator will govern information to employees and company law matters and the Code will apply to consideration and procedural matters.

Figure 6.2 Takeover Panel Jurisdiction

tenet of the Code being the fair treatment of shareholders, the Code is concerned to ensure that shareholders are not denied an opportunity to consider the advantages of a takeover and that shareholders of the same class are treated equally.

The Code comprises six general principles, 38 rules and seven appendices. In addition, the Panel periodically issues practice statements. The general principles, rules, appendices and practice statements are considered in further detail below. **6.25**

6.1.5.1 *General principles*

Article 3(1) of the Takeovers Directive sets out a list of general principles which member states must ensure are complied with when implementing the Takeover Directive. Accordingly, these general principles are mirrored in the general principles set out in the Code. The Panel regards the general principles embodied in the Code as 'essentially statements of standards of commercial behaviour'.[30] The general principles are as follows: **6.26**

(i) All holders of the securities of an offeree company of the same class must be afforded equivalent treatment; moreover, if a person acquires control of a company, the other holders of securities must be protected.

(ii) The holders of the securities of an offeree company must have sufficient time and information to enable them to reach a properly informed decision on the bid; where it advises the holders of securities, the board of the offeree company must give its views on the effects of implementation of the bid on employment, conditions of employment and the locations of the company's place of business.

(iii) The board of an offeree company must act in the interest of the company as a whole and must not deny the holders of securities the opportunity to decide on the merits of the bid.

(iv) False markets must not be created in the securities of the offeree company, of the offeror company or of any other company concerned by the bid in such a way that the rise or fall of the prices of the securities becomes artificial and the normal functioning of the markets is distorted.

(v) An offeror must announce a bid only after ensuring that he/she can fulfil in full any cash consideration, if such is offered, and after taking all reasonable measures to secure the implementation of any other type of consideration.

(vi) An offeree company must not be hindered in the conduct of its affairs for longer than is reasonable by a bid for its securities.[31]

These standards or principles of behaviour are to be adhered to during the course of a bid. Expressed in broad general terms, the exact extent of the scope of the **6.27**

---

[30] Takeover Code paragraph 2(b), Introduction.
[31] Takeover Directive and Takeover Code General Principles.

general principles is deliberately not set out in the Code as the principles are intended to be applied purposively, in the light of their spirit (and not merely their letter) and by reference to their underlying purpose.[32] The importance of the general principles as a basis for underpinning the conduct of the parties to a takeover is borne out by the fact that if the Panel derogates or grants a waiver from a Code rule where the relevant transaction or rule is subject to the requirements of the Takeovers Directive, the Panel is required to ensure that the general principles are respected.[33]

6.1.5.2 Rules

6.28   Article 3(2) of the Takeover Directive also provides that,

> With a view to ensuring compliance with the principles laid down in paragraph 1 [the general principles], Member States:
>
> (a) shall ensure that the minimum requirements set out in this Directive are observed;
> (b) may lay down additional conditions and provisions more stringent than those of this Directive for the regulation of bids.

6.29   The 38 rules of the Code both implement the minimum requirements of the Takeover Directive and 'gold-plate' the Directive by adding additional and more stringent provisions than those contained in the Directive. The rules put flesh on the general principles of the Code and are expressed in more specific terms than the general principles. The language used in the Code rules is not technical and the rules, in the same way as the general principles, must be interpreted according to their underlying purpose, rather than purely on face value.

6.30   In most cases, the rules are supplemented by notes which serve to assist with the interpretation of the rules and should be considered carefully by any practitioner advising on a Code-regulated matter.

6.1.5.3 Appendices

6.31   The appendices form part of the Code and cover matters not dealt with expressly in the main body of the Code rules or the notes. In the case of Appendix 1 (Whitewash Guidance Note) and Appendix 4 (Receiving Agents' Code of Practice) the appendices add detail to and should be read in conjunction with existing rules and the notes to those rules.[34] Other appendices, including Appendix 2 (Formula Offers Guidance Note) and Appendix 7 (Schemes of Arrangement) operate as stand-alone statements.

---

[32] Takeover Code paragraph 2(b), Introduction.
[33] Takeover Code paragraph 2(c), Introduction.
[34] Appendix 1 should be read in conjunction with Note 1 of the Notes on Dispensations from Rule 9. Appendix 4 should be read in conjunction with Rules 9.3 and 10.

6.1.5.4 *Practice statements*

Informal guidance, in the form of practice statements, is issued from time to time by **6.32** the Executive. Such statements assist companies and their advisers with the interpretation of the Code. Practice statements are often published as a result of the consideration by the Executive of the impact of the Code rules and existing guidance on particular factual scenarios which have arisen out of current or recent takeover offers. Practice statements therefore offer practical guidance to the parties to a takeover, detailing the way in which the Executive is minded to interpret the Code given a particular set of facts. Practice statements are not, however, binding on the Panel or the Executive and do not form a part of the Code. The parties to a takeover offer should not rely on them in substitution for liaising directly with the Panel on specific matters ostensibly not covered by the Code, or on matters of Code interpretation.

6.1.5.5 *Interpreting the Code*

Guidance on the interpretation, application and effect of the Code is provided by **6.33** the Executive, which also provides rulings on the same. The Executive may be approached to provide guidance in relation to both general interpretation matters and specific issues. With regard to the latter, it is possible to approach the Executive for guidance on a 'no names' basis where the person seeking the guidance does not provide the names of the parties involved in the takeover. Neither general nor specific guidance provided by the Executive is binding and the parties to a takeover should not rely on such guidance in substitution for obtaining a ruling from the Executive on a named basis.

Further guidance on the interpretation of the Code may be contained in panel **6.34** statements,[35] statements of the Takeover Appeal Board[36] and publications of the Code Committee.

Advance consultation with the Executive must be undertaken by a company or its **6.35** advisers if a waiver or derogation from a rule is sought or there is 'any doubt whatsoever'[37] over whether a particular course of action or conduct breaches the general principles or any rule of the Code. As the Introduction to the Code makes clear, 'to take legal or other professional advice on the interpretation, application or effect of the Code is not an appropriate alternative to obtaining a ruling from the Executive'.[38] Advance consultation with the Executive allows the parties to gain the advantage of either an *ex parte* conditional ruling (which will be issued where the Executive is unable to hear the views of the other parties involved and which is capable of being varied or set aside) or an unconditional ruling (which is

---

[35] Takeover Code paragraph 7(c), Introduction.
[36] Takeover Code paragraph 8(b), Introduction.
[37] Takeover Code paragraph 6(b), Introduction.
[38] Takeover Code paragraph 6(b), Introduction.

binding, absent its being overturned by the Hearings Committee or the Takeover Appeal Board, on those who are made aware of it) in respect of the matter the subject of the consultation. Obtaining a favourable ruling will enable the parties to proceed with a proposed course of action in the knowledge it is not likely to amount to a breach of the provisions of the Code.

6.1.5.6 *Communication with and authority of the Panel*

6.36   As a general rule, persons who are conducting or are involved in a takeover offer must communicate with the Panel in an open and cooperative manner[39] and should promptly provide assistance to the Panel when any requests are made by it.

6.37   All information which is known by the relevant person and which is relevant to the matter the subject of consideration by the Panel should be provided to the Panel. The only exception to this rule is that provision of information or documentation may be resisted on the grounds of legal professional privilege.[40] All those dealing with a takeover must take all reasonable care not to provide incorrect, incomplete or misleading information to the Panel.[41] Furthermore, a person who subsequently becomes aware that information it has supplied to the Panel was incorrect, incomplete or misleading must promptly contact the Panel to correct the position.[42] New information must also be made available to the Panel where this is likely to be relevant to any determination made by the Panel.[43]

6.38   The Panel also has the power to request the supply of information and documents to it where such documents or information are reasonably required in the exercise of its functions.[44] The Panel is obliged to make any such request by way of notice. If such a request is made, documents must, unless the recipient of the request resists the claim on the grounds of legal professional privilege, be supplied within the time and to the place specified in the notice issued by the Panel. Failure to comply with any notice issued pursuant to this power will be a breach of the Code.

6.2 Key Takeover Terms

6.2.1 Introduction

6.39   There are a number of fundamental terms and concepts which frequently occur when considering takeover transactions. These terms are outlined and explained in this Section.

---

[39] Takeover Code paragraph 9(a), Introduction.
[40] Takeover Code paragraph 9(a), Introduction.
[41] Takeover Code Introduction.
[42] Takeover Code paragraph 9(a).
[43] Takeover Code paragraph 9(a).
[44] Companies Act 2006 section 947 and Takeover Code paragraph 9, Introduction.

6.2.2 Offer period

The Code provides that an offer period commences when an announcement is **6.40** made of a proposed or possible offer (with or without terms). It does not matter if a third party has triggered an offer period; the bidder will still have to behave in the same manner as if it had triggered the offer period itself. The Panel treats both an announcement that an interest, or interests in shares carrying in aggregate 30% or more of the voting rights of a company is for sale, and an announcement that the board of the target company is seeking potential bidders as an announcement of a possible offer and they will therefore trigger the commencement of the offer period.[45] An offer period can also be triggered by a company's 'strategic review announcement', specifically where an offer for the company is one of the options which is being considered as part of its strategic review.[46]

An offer period will, in the case of a conventional bid, end on the first closing date **6.41** or, if this is later, the date when the offer becomes or is declared unconditional as to acceptances. If the bid is structured as a scheme of arrangement (a 'scheme'), the offer period will end on the date on which it is announced in accordance with Section 5(c) of Appendix 7 that the scheme has become effective or that the scheme has lapsed or been withdrawn.[47] A scheme is an alternative structure for implementing a public offer whereby a target company enters into a compromise or arrangement with its shareholders and/or creditors, or any class of them. Schemes, and the differences between them and conventional offers, are considered in detail in Section 6.6 below.

6.2.3 Acting in concert

The Panel, through its definition of acting in concert, seeks to, *inter alia*, prevent **6.42** bidders from avoiding their obligations under the Code by using other people to assist them in making the bid, whether directly (through structural control) or formally (such as through an agreement) or informally (such as through moral influence).

The Panel has an automatic presumption that the following people are acting in **6.43** concert unless the contrary is established:

(i) a company, its parent, subsidiaries and fellow subsidiaries, and their associated companies, and companies with which such companies are associated, all with each other (a company will be regarded as an associated company

---

[45] Takeover Code 'Definition of Offer Period'.
[46] Panel Practice Statement No 6.
[47] Ibid.

if a company owns or controls 20% or more of the equity share capital of that company);

(ii) a company with any of its directors (together with their close relatives and related trusts);

(iii) a company with any of its pension funds and the pension funds of any company covered in (i);

(iv) a fund manager with any investment company, unit trust or other person whose investments such fund manager manages on a discretionary basis, in respect of the relevant investment accounts;

(v) a connected adviser with its client and, if its client is acting in concert with a bidder, or with the target company, with that bidder or with the target company respectively, in each case in respect of the interests in shares of that adviser and persons controlling (as explained below), controlled by or under the same control as that adviser (except in the capacity of an exempt fund manager or an exempt principal trader); and

(vi) directors of the target company where the target company is subject to a bid or where the directors have reason to believe that a bona fide offer for the target company may be imminent.[48]

6.44 Even if parties fall outside of these automatic presumptions, they may still be caught by the concert party provisions, as the Panel provides more generally that:

> Persons acting in concert comprise persons who pursuant to an agreement or understanding (whether formal or informal), co-operate to obtain or consolidate control … of a company or to frustrate the successful outcome of an offer for a company. A person and each of its affiliated persons will be deemed to be acting in concert all with each other.[49]

6.45 For these purposes, 'control' means an interest, or interests in shares carrying in aggregate 30% of the voting rights of a company, irrespective of whether such interest or interests give de facto control.[50] An 'affiliated person' is any undertaking in respect of which any person:

(i) has a majority of the shareholders' or members' voting rights;

(ii) is a shareholder or member and at the same time has the right to appoint or remove a majority of the members of its board of directors;

(iii) is a shareholder or member and alone controls a majority of the shareholders' or members' voting rights pursuant to an agreement entered into with other shareholders or members; or

(iv) has the power to exercise, or actually exercise, dominant influence or control.

---

[48] Takeover Code, 'Definition of Acting in Concert'.
[49] Ibid.
[50] Takeover Code 'Definition of Control'.

For the purpose of the definition, a person's rights as regards voting, appointment **6.46**
or removal include the rights of any other affiliated persons and those of any person or entity acting in his own name but on behalf of that person or of any other affiliated person.[51]

Whether or not persons are 'acting in concert' must be assessed in light of the **6.47**
circumstances of each case and it is not possible to create a definitive list of concert party relationships. Some of the more common concert party relationships which may arise are considered below, but this is by no means an exhaustive list.

6.2.3.1 *Affiliates*

A person is deemed to be acting in concert with each of their 'affiliates'.[52] A person **6.48**
is 'affiliated' with an entity when:

(i)   they hold a majority of the voting rights in the entity;
(ii)   they are a shareholder and have the right to appoint or remove a majority of the board;
(iii) they are a shareholder and alone control a majority of the voting rights pursuant to an agreement with other shareholders; or
(iv)   they have the power to exercise, or actually exercise, dominant influence or control over the entity.

6.2.3.2 *Shareholders*

The Panel does not normally regard shareholders who vote in the same manner **6.49**
on a resolution as being concert parties.[53] There will, however, be a presumption that shareholders are acting in concert if they requisition a meeting to consider a proposal which seeks board control of the target.[54] The Panel will consider whether there is any significant relationship or agreement between the new directors and the shareholders proposing them and whether the new directors would be remunerated by any of the shareholders proposing them.[55] If not, the parties would not ordinarily be considered to be acting in concert.[56] If there is a significant relationship, the Panel may go on to consider factors such as:

(i)   the relationship between the new directors and existing directors;
(ii)   the number of board members being appointed or replaced in comparison with the overall size of the board;

---

[51] Takeover Code Note 2 to the 'Definition of Acting in Concert'.
[52] Takeover Code 'Definition of Acting in Concert'.
[53] Takeover Code Note 2 to Rule 2.1.
[54] Ibid.
[55] Ibid.
[56] Ibid.

(iii) the positions held by the board members being replaced and to be held by the proposed new directors;

(iv) the nature of the mandate of the incoming directors; and

(v) whether any shareholder supporting the proposal will benefit from the implementation of the proposal.[57]

6.50 A shareholder will not normally be treated as acting in concert with the bidder by virtue of the fact that it has given an irrevocable undertaking to accept the bid, depending on the scope and nature of the undertaking.[58] An irrevocable undertaking which requires the party giving it to vote on the shares at the bidder's direction in respect of resolutions relating to the implementation of the bid and resolutions which, if passed by the target, could result in a bid condition not being satisfied, are generally acceptable provided that they are given in the context of acceptance of an offer, limited to the duration of the bid and limited to matters which relate to ensuring that the bid is successful.[59] If shareholders supporting the target board's opposition to a bid acquire shares in the target in order to frustrate the bid, they could also be at risk of being made a concert party with the target directors. [60]

6.2.3.3 Directors

6.51 The directors of a company will be presumed to be acting in concert during an offer period or where a bid is imminent, but there will otherwise be no inference that they are acting in concert.[61]

6.52 Where a director proposes to sell shares to a person which would result in that person being obliged to make a mandatory bid, it must be a condition of the sale that the purchaser undertakes to comply with its obligations under Rule 9. The director should also not resign from the target until after the first closing date of the offer or the date on which the offer becomes unconditional, whichever occurs later.

6.2.3.4 Group companies

6.53 If an intra-group reorganization is proposed it may be necessary to consider whether the restructuring could trigger a mandatory bid requirement if shares in the target are transferred from a subsidiary to its parent or another member of the group. The Panel accepts that the concept of persons acting in concert recognizes that the group of concert parties are the equivalent of a single person, but there are

---

[57] Ibid.
[58] Takeover Code Note 9 to the 'Definition of Acting in Concert'.
[59] Panel Practice Statement 22.
[60] Ibid.
[61] Takeover Code Note 3 to Rule 9.1.

circumstances in which the acquisition of shares by one member of the group acting in concert from another member or a third party will result in the acquirer alone having an obligation to make a mandatory bid.[62] The Panel has indicated that it will consider factors such as:

(i) whether the ultimate controller/parent of the group has changed and whether the balance between the interests of the group has changed significantly;

(ii) the price paid for the shares; and

(iii) the length and nature of the relationship between the persons acting in concert.[63]

In other words, if the shareholding of a single member of a group of concert **6.54** parties reaches the thresholds which trigger the mandatory bid requirement, such member could be required to make a mandatory bid.

6.2.3.5 *Employee benefit trusts*

In certain circumstances an employee benefit trust ('EBT') may be presumed **6.55** to be acting in concert with the directors and/or shareholders of a company. The mere establishment and operation of an EBT does not give rise to this presumption, but the Panel will have regard to the circumstances to determine whether on the facts the EBT is acting in concert with the directors or perhaps a controlling shareholder.[64] In determining whether the EBT is acting in concert with another party, the Panel will consider a number of factors including those listed in Note 5 to Rule 9.1 Takeover Code. If the EBT is acting in concert with other parties, the Panel must be consulted in advance of any proposed acquisition of shares by an EBT where the mandatory bid thresholds may be triggered by the EBT and parties acting in concert with it.

6.2.3.6 *Finance providers*

Lending banks are generally not considered to be acting in concert with the **6.56** acquirer of shares as they would not commonly be cooperating with the acquirer 'to obtain or consolidate control of a company' and would therefore not fall within the definition of acting in concert in the Code.

6.2.3.7 *Standstill agreements, break fees and inducements to deal*

A standstill agreement is also not generally indicative of a concert party relation- **6.57** ship between the parties to the agreement, provided that the agreement does not

---

[62] Takeover Code Note 4 to Rule 9.1.
[63] Ibid.
[64] Takeover Code Note 5 to Rule 9.1.

restrict any of the parties from accepting, or agreeing to accept, an offer for the other company's shares at any stage.[65]

6.58   The parties to an arrangement which might constitute an inducement to deal or refrain from dealing are likely to be considered concert parties.[66] This could potentially include parties to a break fee arrangement, so any person entering into a break fee should carefully consider whether its interests will be aggregated with other concert parties in order to avoid triggering the mandatory bid requirement.

6.2.3.8 *Timing*

6.59   Where two or more persons come together to act in concert and their combined existing interests would exceed 30% of the voting rights in the target company, the Panel will not normally require such persons to make a mandatory bid at that point.[67] If, however, the persons acting in concert hold 30% or more but less than 50% of the voting rights in the target, the mandatory bid obligation will be invoked if any of the persons acting in concert subsequently acquire any further interest in the target company.[68]

6.2.4 **Voting rights**

6.60   Voting rights (except in relation to Rule 11 of the Code) means all the voting rights attributable to the capital of a company which are currently exercisable at a general meeting.[69]

6.3 Preparation for Takeover—Bidder

6.3.1 **Early advice**

6.3.1.1 *The importance of early advice*

6.61   The success or failure of a bid will more often than not depend on the tactics used by the bidder. Unless the bidder's strategy is thought through meticulously at the outset of the transaction, the bid may fail or, at least, not proceed in the manner in which the bidder envisaged. The takeover of a public company is likely to entail significant expenditure for any bidder, which may (particularly if the takeover fails to proceed at a late stage) erode shareholder value. A well-advised bidder will therefore want to be appraised of all of the major issues and costs it faces before

---

[65]   Panel Practice Statement: Acting in Concert and Standstill Agreements.
[66]   Takeover Code Note 6 to Rule 8.
[67]   Takeover Code Note 1 to Rule 9.1.
[68]   Takeover Code Note 1 to Rule 9.1.
[69]   Takeover Code 'Definition of Voting Rights'.

committing to such expenditure. In addition, takeover regulation is littered with pitfalls and traps for the unwary and a wrong step may lead to serious consequences for the manner in which the bidder makes its bid. Accordingly, for all these reasons, it is critically important that any bidder takes professional advice at the earliest possible stage.

One caveat to this is that the Panel emphasizes the vital importance of secrecy **6.62** before an announcement can be made.[70] This is on the basis that it is a general principle of both the Takeover Directive and the Code that false markets must not be created in the securities of the offeree company, of the offeror company or of any other company concerned by the bid.[71] The Panel therefore requires an announcement to be made if negotiations or discussions are about to be extended to include more than a very restricted number of people (outside those who need to know in the companies concerned and their immediate advisers).[72] The Panel views 'a very restricted number of people' as being no more than six people.[73] This includes people such as providers of finance. Accordingly, a bidder might very quickly use up the six people with whom it may enter into discussions. This could, for example, prevent it from discussing irrevocable undertakings with shareholders.

The Panel does, however, have the discretion to allow the bidder to approach **6.63** a wider group of people for the purposes of, *inter alia,* seeking irrevocable undertakings.[74] The Panel has stated that it is likely to consent to more than six parties being approached only in limited circumstances and that it will need to be satisfied that secrecy will be maintained.[75] Given the potential for leaks once shareholders have been approached, a leak announcement should be prepared, as an announcement is required in the following two circumstances:

(i) when, following an approach to the target company, the target company is the subject of rumour and speculation or there is an untoward movement in its share price;[76] and

(ii) when, before an approach has been made, the target company is the subject of rumour and speculation or there is an untoward movement in its share price and there are reasonable grounds for concluding that it is the potential

---

[70] Takeover Code Rule 2.1.
[71] Takeover Directive Article 3(1)(d) and Takeover Code General Principle 4.
[72] Takeover Code Rule 2.2(e).
[73] Panel Practice Statement No 20: 'Rule 2—secrecy, possible offer announcements and pre-announcement responsibilities' paragraph 7.2.
[74] Takeover Code Rule 2.2(e).
[75] Panel Practice Statement No 20: 'Rule 2— secrecy, possible offer announcements and pre-announcement responsibilities' paragraph 7.3.
[76] Takeover Code Rule 2.2(c).

bidder's actions (whether through inadequate security or otherwise) which have led to the situation.[77]

6.64 Accordingly, the number of people involved should be kept to a minimum for as long as possible. The advisers that usually need to be consulted at the outset of a bid are a financial adviser, accountants and lawyers. Corporate brokers may also be involved. Initially, only key contacts at these advisers should be informed of the bid, so as to minimize the risk of the bid being leaked.

6.3.1.2 *Key initial considerations for the bidder*

6.65 Whilst the key issues for a bidder will vary from bidder to bidder and from transaction to transaction, there are a number of issues which are likely to be important for most bidders to consider at the outset of a bid. This will apply whether the bid is in the UK or elsewhere in the EU.

6.66 The key issue for the bidder will, and should be, the price which it is prepared to pay to acquire the target. Whilst a takeover may make strategic sense, it can ultimately only be judged a success if it makes economic sense; *viz.* it enhances shareholder value over the medium to long term. In the heat of a transaction, it is all too easy to be dragged into a bidding war without considering whether or not the transaction makes economic sense. The bidder should therefore consider, before making a bid, the maximum price at which the transaction would still be economically defensible. Allied to price will be the consideration which the bidder offers for shares in the target. Amongst other things, the bidder will need to consider the extent to which it needs third party financing and whether or not the same is readily available, whether in the form of equity or debt and whether it is commercially viable for the bidder to offer shares and/or loan notes in itself as all or part of the consideration. Some of these options may have a significant impact on the proposed timescale of the bid (particularly if the option requires shareholder approval or the production of a prospectus) which the bidder will have to consider carefully if it wishes to conclude the transaction swiftly. In some cases, extensions to the timetable will be simply unavoidable; for example, where the rules of the relevant listing authority require the transaction to be approved in advance by the bidder's shareholders.

6.67 The likely response of the target's board to an approach from the bidder will invariably be a highly significant issue as it will inform whether the bid is likely to involve either a recommended bid or a hostile bid—each of which has different consequences. The bidder should also take an informed view as to whether or not there is likely to be a competitive situation. Some bidders will have a greater

---

[77] Takeover Code Rule 2.2(d).

tolerance than others for competitive situations and some will have a policy of not entering competitive situations at all. A competitive situation is likely to increase costs significantly (as the process is likely to be more protracted and involve a tactical battle with the other bidder(s)) and potentially reduces the likelihood of success of the bid.

The bidder should also examine any potential impediments to the bid. An obvi-   **6.68** ous impediment to the success of a bid would be a shareholder with a blocking stake; for example a stake held by a competitor or by a family with emotional ties to the business. The shareholder register should therefore be analysed as early as possible to identify such issues. Antitrust law may also hinder the bid, e.g. if the combined market share of the newly merged entity in relevant markets would be significant. Accordingly, a full competition analysis should be undertaken at an early stage.

Many of these factors will inform the bidder's approach to the form of acquisition   **6.69** structure, most importantly whether the bid will proceed as a takeover offer or a scheme of arrangement. Whilst schemes of arrangement are peculiarly English law creations it is frequent for national law to have alternative methods for effecting a takeover. The difference between takeover offers and schemes of arrangement are discussed in Section 6.6.6 of this Chapter.

6.3.2 Advisers

A bidder will require a significant amount of professional advice throughout the   **6.70** course of a bid. It will therefore be important for the bidder to build a team of trusted professional advisers with sufficient expertise and capacity to handle the demands of the transaction. The type of advisers which the bidder will need to appoint vary from transaction to transaction dependent on the nature of the 'in-house' expertise of the bidder, the target's business and the bidder's objectives but the core advisers common to the majority of bids and their roles on a bid are as follows.

6.3.2.1 *Financial adviser*

The financial adviser will provide strategic advice on tactics to be used during the   **6.71** bid. It will also provide general financial advice such as assisting with the valuation of the target (which will inform the price at which the bidder will make its bid) and advising on appropriate funding structures. If the consideration offered is new equity in the bidder or the bidder proposes to raise cash to fund the bid through an equity issue, the financial adviser may act as sponsor and/or underwriter (as may be appropriate). Where documents require approval (whether for the purposes of financial regulation or otherwise) the financial adviser will usually give such approval. Finally, the financial adviser will often be mandated to coordinate the advice of and manage the other advisers to the bidder.

6.3.2.2 *Brokers*

6.72 Brokers will assist to a certain extent with bid tactics, in particular in relation to market purchases and will effect such purchases where instructed to do so. They will also coordinate meetings with and give presentations to the institutional investors in the target with a view to ascertaining and advising on market reaction. Brokers are also assigned responsibility for liaison with relevant stock exchanges and listed authorities (including making any necessary application for listing).

6.3.2.3 *Lawyers*

6.73 The bidder's lawyers will also advise on strategy, tactics and structuring. They will also draft the offer documentation produced in connection with the bid and perform a verification exercise on those documents and any announcements or other communications made during the transaction. Their core role will also include advising on compliance with relevant law and practice, such as the Takeover Code, the Listing Rules of the Financial Services Authority, other regulatory law and institutional guidance.

6.74 Where the bidder is raising finance for the transaction, its lawyers will draft and negotiate the relevant documentation. For equity issues this could include any prospectus necessary for offering and listing the equity and they will negotiate the terms of any underwriting agreement with underwriters' counsel. For debt financings the lawyers will negotiate the debt documentation with lenders' counsel.

6.75 Finally, the bidder's lawyers will carry out a legal due diligence exercise on the target and produce a legal due diligence report addressed to the bidder. The due diligence process is considered further at Section 6.3.4 below.

6.3.2.4 *Accountants*

6.76 Accountants will conduct financial due diligence on the target and will produce a financial due diligence report addressed to the bidder. They will also provide the relevant financial information to be inserted into the offer documents and will assist with the verification of such information.

6.3.2.5 *PR advisers*

6.77 PR advisers are responsible for managing the bidder's corporate image throughout the process. This involves advice on tactics and how the bid will be perceived in the market and the wider world. They will advise on announcements and other media communications and use their media contacts to ensure that the bidder and its offer for the target is viewed in as favourable a light as possible.

6.78 The role of PR advisers may have particular significance on competitive and hostile deals and also on deals where there is particular sensitivity e.g. political sensitivity relating to the ownership of a target company.

6.3.3 Websites

One of the general principles of the Takeover Directive and the Code is the **6.79** prevention of false markets.[78] This principle has its practical manifestation in rules of the Code requiring the prompt and equal dissemination of information to the market. These rules have recently been supplemented to take account of the increased use of the internet as a principal method of information dissemination and accordingly all bidders (as well as the target company) now have to maintain a website. This is probably not a significant issue for many bidders but it will be a departure for e.g. private equity firms who have not generally used websites as part of the bid process in the past. Bidders, if they do not already have their own website, should arrange for one to be set up. The purpose of the website is to provide a single point of reference for all documents, announcements and other information published by the bidder in relation to its bid. All of the relevant information should be uploaded to the website from the time of publication (although the Panel accepts that delays may occur and has therefore set a deadline of noon the day following publication as the deadline for the upload of documents to the website).

Plainly, this in an additional item of housekeeping for bidders to address at the **6.80** outset.

In addition to the logistical issues, bidders also need to give consideration to the **6.81** foreign securities laws issues that arise from making documents relating to the bid available over the internet. Care needs to be taken to ensure the offer is not inadvertently made (through the website) into a jurisdiction where it unlawful to do so. The bidder will therefore have to consider employing blocking devices or asking the relevant individual to confirm their identity and jurisdiction to avoid these inadvertent breaches.

6.3.4 Due diligence

6.3.4.1 *Purpose and approach*

Bidder due diligence on the target has several purposes. The bidder will, through **6.82** its due diligence, seek to assess accurately: (i) whether the target holds the assets which the bidder thought it held; (ii) whether the target has any hidden liabilities; and (iii) whether the target is performing in line with the bidder's expectations and whether it is likely to continue to do so in the future. Analysis of these issues will inform the bidder's assessment of whether or not it should make a bid for the target and, if it does make such a bid, on what terms. A bidder will need to conduct due diligence prior to making a firm announcement of a takeover bid.

---

[78] Takeover Directive Article 3(1)(d) and Takeover Code General Principle 4.

This is because once such an announcement has been made, the Takeover Panel will insist that the bid which is the subject of that announcement be made. The Takeover Panel will not allow the completion of due diligence to be a condition or pre-condition to an announced bid, as the Takeover Panel only permits very limited pre-conditions (see Section 6.5.4.4 of this Chapter for further details). Accordingly, the bidder will need to be satisfied at the time of announcement of the bid that it is prepared to make a bid for the shares in the capital of the target at (or above) the level of consideration specified. The due diligence exercise will aid the bidder in satisfying itself that such is the case.

6.3.4.2 *Different approach from private company acquisitions*

6.83 There is a fundamental difference in approach between a due diligence process in the acquisition of a private unlisted company and that in the acquisition of a Code-governed entity. As a general proposition, far less due diligence information will be made available by the target entity in a Code process. There are three core arguments put forward by listed target companies for taking this different, more limited approach.

6.84 The first justification is that public companies are subject to more stringent requirements as to the timing and content of their financial statements. The target's accounts provide the key financial information on the target and are critical in making an assessment of the value of the target. The target's latest set of audited accounts will be available publicly from the files at Companies House but (depending on where the target is in its reporting cycle) more recent financial information may be available. Companies listed on the Official List must also make public annual financial reports (containing audited financial statements, a management report and responsibility statements) within four months after the end of each financial year. Half-yearly reports (containing a condensed set of financial statements, an interim management report and responsibility statement) must be made public within two months of the half year. Finally, interim management statements (containing an explanation of material events and transactions that have taken place during the relevant period and their impact on the financial position of the issuer and its controlled undertakings, as well as a general description of the financial position and performance of the issuer and its controlled undertakings during the relevant period) must be made public twice a year: once in the first six-month period and once during the second six-month period. The net result is that the bidder will have access to four publicly available reports in any financial year and therefore the information to which it has access will be reasonably current.

6.85 Second, listed entities are bound by additional regulation regarding the publication of price sensitive information. A company listed on the main market of the London Stock Exchange will be required to comply with the Disclosure and

Transparency Rules which are the UK's rules implementing the Transparency Directive.[79] Similar obligations exist for companies listed on the London Stock Exchange's Alternative Investment Market ('AIM'). Broadly, and subject to limited exceptions, the listed target must notify a regulatory information service as soon as possible of any price sensitive information which directly concerns that company. Price sensitive information is essentially information which, if generally available, would be likely to have a significant effect on the Company's share price.

The Code requires that any information given to one bidder must, on request, **6.86** be given equally and promptly to another offeror or bona fide potential offeror.[80] This applies no matter how unwelcome the bid may be. This rule will significantly influence how a target company approaches due diligence and highlights the difference from private sales. In the context of a private sale, a vendor may choose to withhold certain information (such as key supplier contracts) from trade bidders, as receipt of that information may confer a competitive advantage on such trade bidder, whereas there would be fewer concerns in giving such information to a private equity bidder with no competing business in its portfolio. A listed company target is not afforded the luxury of making such a distinction. Accordingly, it frequently adopts a position of minimum disclosure. The bidder should therefore be prepared not to receive full information from a target in a situation where the target believes there could be competition or where trade competitors may look at the target (the threshold of bona fide potential bidder is a low one) with the real intention of just gathering information on its operations.

Accordingly, a target will seek to reduce the amount of confidential due diligence **6.87** information it provides to a bidder to the minimum possible. That is not to say that detailed due diligence is not carried out. Rather that more thought needs to be given by a bidder in order to target its efforts in a way to maximize the value of the process.

6.3.4.3 *Bidder's approach, scope and materiality*

In contrast to the target's approach, the bidder's approach to due diligence will be **6.88** driven by whether the bid is hostile or not. If the bid is hostile, the bidder will only have access to publicly available information and certain information which the target is required to give it by law. If the target is not hostile then it is a matter of negotiation. The bidder's requirements may be driven by a number of factors: its lending bank requirements, its fee tolerance, materiality and timing.

---

[79] Directive 2004/109/EC of the European Parliament and of the Counsel of 15 December 2004 on the harmonisation of transparency requirements in relation to information about issuers whose securities are admitted to trading on a regulated market and amending Directive 2001/34/EC.
[80] Takeover Code Rule 20.2.

6.89   There is no set approach to conducting a due diligence exercise; however, it is important to ensure that the due diligence exercise is conducted in an efficient, coordinated manner and that there is no duplication of work between advisers. Accordingly, it is usually advisable for one of the advisers, generally the financial adviser, to coordinate the due diligence process.

6.90   As part of coordination of the process the bidder and its advisers should seek to agree the scope of the due diligence and the level of materiality. Scoping the due diligence will involve (broadly) allocating areas of review to the relevant advisers and deciding on whether to exclude certain matters from the scope of review. This may just be a commercial decision for the company but it is possible that the lending banks will also have their own minimum requirements which need to be factored in. Plainly, to the extent this is the case, it is better to know these requirements at the outset.

6.91   Whilst the allocation of diligence may vary from transaction to transaction, each of the bidder, the financial adviser and the accountants would usually carry out a review of financial information such as accounts and profit forecasts. Lawyers will review the contractual arrangements which the target has in place, as well as its legal compliance. The financial adviser or the bidder generally conduct commercial due diligence, although sometimes this is delegated to a specialist commercial diligence provider. Other diligence providers which could be engaged include environmental consultants, actuaries (in relation to pension funds), human resources and benefits consultants and tax consultants.

6.92   The level of materiality which the bidder sets for the due diligence exercise will largely be driven by transaction value. Where transaction value is very large, there clearly will be little value in addressing issues of low value. Materiality should ideally be set at a level which is not so high that the bidder does not have sufficient information from which to formulate its bid nor at a level which is so low that the bidder is overwhelmed by the information which is required. The due diligence work product of each of the bidder's advisers will generally be set out in the form of a due diligence report which is addressed to the bidder. Report providers should be made aware that they may be required to address their reports to third parties, such as debt providers and underwriters subsequently.

6.3.4.4 *Public sources*

6.93   In addition to the public information described in paragraphs 6.84 and 6.85 above, there are a number of public sources from which the bidder can gather diligence information.

6.94   Information which the relevant listing authorities require the target to make public is also a useful source of information. For example, the Listing Rules made by the Financial Services Authority provide that companies listed on the Official List must make certain notifications via a regulatory information service, including in relation to capital, board changes and directors' details, lock-up arrangements, shareholder resolutions, change of name, change of accounting reference date and certain material transactions. Copies of circulars, notices, reports or other documents to which the Listing Rules apply must also be forwarded to the Financial Services Authority for publication through its document viewing facility. If the target company is listed in more than one country, the different rules should be borne in mind. For example, the disclosure obligations in the United States are very different to those in the UK and a wealth of information can be found searching the US EDGAR system.

Other information which is publicly available and generally useful includes infor-   **6.95**
mation in the press, reports on the target and its industry by research analysts and consumer and other market research. Subscription services providing newswire information and document retrieval can also provide relevant information. Other registers, e.g. real estate and intellectual property registers, can be searched for information on the target's assets.

6.3.4.5 Other legal rights to information

Anyone has the right under the UK Companies Act 2006 to require that a UK   **6.96**
company disclose its shareholder register and its 'register of interests disclosed'.[81] The shareholder register is extremely useful for identifying potential barriers to the takeover and for providing a list of contacts.

The register of members will record the registered holders of the shares but clearly   **6.97**
that may not give the whole picture. Therefore the Companies Act 2006 gives public companies the ability to serve notice on any person whom the company knows or has reasonable cause to believe (a) is interested in the company's shares, or (b) was interested in the company's shares at any time during the three years immediately preceding the date on which the notice was issued.[82] The definition of being interested in shares is wide[83] and catches more interests than the Disclosure and Transparency Rules. The responses to these notices therefore offer the target a useful insight into its true shareholder base and these responses are contained in the 'register of interests disclosed'.

In reality these provisions are infrequently used. In recommended transactions,   **6.98**
information is shared without the need to invoke statutory rights and in hostile deals, making such requests is unlikely to be appropriate pre-announcement, as it would alert the target to the possibility of a bid.

---

[81] Sections 116(2) and 811(2) of the Companies Act 2006.
[82] Section 793 of the Companies Act 2006.
[83] Sections 820 to 825 of the Companies Act 2006.

6.99   In any event, the bidder's brokers will be able to ascertain a fairly accurate picture of the target register through other sources without requiring the use of these statutory powers.

6.3.4.6 *Private sources*

6.100   If the bidder has not been received with hostility, it may have access to the target and its advisers and will, accordingly, be in a position to make a due diligence request to the target. Again, it is important to ensure that the bidder's advisers do not duplicate requests, as this will waste resources and may slow down the process. One adviser should therefore be mandated to coordinate the due diligence request list and to ensure that information gathered is shared between the advisers.

6.101   The request should focus on the key value items.

6.3.4.7 *Confidentiality and equality of information*

6.102   Before the target releases confidential information to the bidder, it will insist that the bidder signs a confidentiality agreement. The terms of the confidentiality agreement will depend partly on whether or not there is a competing bid situation.

6.103   If there is no competing situation then the parties are free to agree the terms of the confidentiality agreement. Accordingly, it could include 'standstill' obligations on the potential bidder and detailed non-solicitation provisions. As set out in paragraph 6.86 above, however, any information given to one bidder must, on request, be given equally and promptly to another offeror or bona fide potential offeror.[84] As an anti-avoidance measure, the Code prohibits the target company from requiring excessive protections in a confidentiality agreement as the price for releasing the information. Accordingly, if there are subsequent requests for due diligence information, the only conditions that may be attached to the passing of information to competing bidders are those relating to (i) the confidentiality of the information; (ii) reasonable restrictions forbidding the use of the information passed to solicit customers or employees and (iii) the use of information solely in connection with an offer or a potential offer.[85] The conditions must not be more onerous than those imposed on any other bidder or potential bidder.[86]

6.104   It is important to note that the equality of information principle does not give subsequent potential bidders the right to (a) new information or (b) simply to ask for everything that has been given to the first bidder. The subsequent bidder must

---

[84] Takeover Code Rule 20.2.
[85] Takeover Code Note 2, Rule 20.2.
[86] Takeover Code Note 2, Rule 20.2.

make requests or ask questions and the obligation on the target is to respond to these to the extent it has done so already.

Accordingly, a subsequent bidder or potential offeror should frame its request in the widest possible terms to ensure all possible requests are covered. This is a marked contrast to the first bidder who may have submitted a very targeted request. **6.105**

A first bidder in a process may seek to include in the confidentiality agreement an obligation on the target not to provide any additional information to a third party thereby contractually defining the extent of the due diligence. An alternative structure which is more palatable to a target is that any additional information provided by the target to a third party will also be provided automatically to the bidder. **6.106**

6.3.4.8 *Implications for dealing*

The bidder may decide to buy shares in the target before the bid is announced (known as stakebuilding (for a fuller discussion see Section 6.3.6 below). The due diligence process presents certain issues for dealing. If, through its due diligence, the bidder receives non-public information from the target which would be price-sensitive information i.e. it would, if made public, have a significant effect on the price of the target's shares and the bidder wishes to stakebuild, its directors will have to rely on a statutory defence to the criminal offence of insider dealing to do so. The defence which they would have to establish is one of the following: (i) that they did not expect its dealing to result in a profit; (ii) that they believed that the information was sufficiently widely disseminated for the seller of the shares not to be prejudiced by not having such information or (iii) that they would have made the purchase even if they did not have the information. The burden of proof is on the bidder's directors and so they may find it difficult to establish a defence. Similar considerations exist in relation to the civil offence of market abuse. Insider dealing and market abuse are more fully considered at Sections 6.3.6.1.1 and 6.3.6.1.2 below. It is, accordingly, prudent not to deal in these circumstances without detailed consideration of the circumstances by the bidder's advisers. This usually becomes less of an issue on or around the time of announcement of the offer as the share price is likely to be maintained by the existence of the offer at this time, rather than price-sensitive information. **6.107**

6.3.4.9 *Antitrust*

A key due diligence issue will be to establish whether any filings need to be made with the relevant competition authorities. **6.108**

A detailed analysis of antitrust law is beyond the scope of this Chapter, but work needs to be carried out pre-announcement to ensure that all requisite clearances **6.109** are identified and a view taken that it will be possible to obtain these clearances within the offer timetable.

6.110   An early approach to the relevant antitrust authorities is recommended as such authorities are often prepared to have early-stage discussions on a confidential basis. Once the lawyers have decided where the main antitrust issues lie, the bidder (in conjunction with its advisers) will have to determine whether or not to make its bid subject to antitrust clearance and, if so, in which jurisdictions. In some jurisdictions, the bidder will have no choice as to whether or not the bid is subject to antitrust clearance, such as in Germany where, if the notification thresholds are met, closing of the transaction is prohibited if antitrust clearance has not been received from the *Bundeskartellamt*. In others, it may take the view that no condition is necessary, whether because notification only (rather than clearance) is required or there is no real risk of the transaction being prohibited or otherwise.

6.111   In the UK, the Code generally allows bidders to make bids conditional upon antitrust clearance in the UK and under the EC Merger Regulation (the 'ECMR')[87] and in other jurisdictions where clearance is material.[88]

6.112   Under the Code, if the bid falls within the statutory provisions for possible reference to the UK Competition Commission or falls within the scope of the ECMR, it must be a term of the bid that such bid will lapse upon any of (i) a referral to the Competition Commission; (ii) if the European Commission initiates proceedings or (iii) if the European Commission refers the bid to a competent authority in the UK and there is a subsequent reference to the Competition Commission, should such event take place before the first closing date or when the bid is declared unconditional as to acceptances, whichever is earlier.[89] The Code also provides that where the bid is referred to the UK Competition Commission or the European Commission initiates proceedings, the offer period will end. A new offer period is, however, deemed to begin at the time when the competition reference period ends.[90]

6.3.4.10 Management issues

6.113   Where it is proposed that the management of the target be involved in the transaction on the bidder side, e.g. as part of a management buy-out or similar transaction, they have a potential conflict of interest. Management deals are dealt with in more detail in Section 6.1 of this Chapter. For the purposes of due

---

[87]   Council Regulation (EC) No 139/2004.
[88]   Takeover Code Rule 12.1(c) and Rule 13.3(b).
[89]   Takeover Code Rule 12(1)(a) and (b).
[90]   Takeover Code Rule 12.2.

diligence, however, it is clear the potential conflict of interest could result in management frustrating the bid of a competing bidder. Although the management of the target company involved in the MBO will not consider the merits of any competing bid, as this will fall to the independent directors of the target company, they could nonetheless be in a position of advantage if they refuse to assist in the compilation of due diligence materials to be provided to a competing bidder. The Code seeks to prevent this type of behaviour. As explained above, the Code provides that the target should provide equality of information to competing bidders.[91] To assist this process, the Panel expects the directors of the target who are involved in making the bid to cooperate with the independent directors of the target and its advisers in the assembly of this information.[92]

6.3.4.11 *Funding*

A bidder is likely to consider a number of options to fund the acquisition of the target. The simplest method of funding is through existing cash on the bidder's balance sheet. If the bidder is a listed company, it might raise funds through the issue of new securities (either as part of the consideration or to raise cash for the acquisition through a rights issue or a placing or open offer). Third party debt is also frequently used, whether under existing or new debt facilities. Often a combination of these funding methods will be used. The situation is somewhat different where the bidder is a newly incorporated special purpose vehicle ('SPV') (which would generally be the case where the bidder is a private equity house). In these circumstances, the SPV is unlikely to have any existing cash or debt facilities and accordingly, will generally seek to fund the acquisition through new equity subscription and subordinated debt from the private equity sponsor and third party debt.

6.114

6.3.4.12 *Certainty*

It is a fundamental principle of the Takeover Directive that the funding of a bid must be certain.[93] This has long been the case in the Code (which reflects the General Principle in the Takeover Directive). This is enshrined in General Principle 5 which provides that:

6.115

> an offeror must announce a bid only after ensuring that he/she can fulfil in full any cash consideration, if such is offered, and after taking all reasonable measures to secure the implementation of any other type of consideration.

The Panel takes the view that bids cannot be subject to a financing condition because this would potentially lead to speculative bids and market manipulation.

6.116

---

[91] Takeover Code Rule 20.2.
[92] Takeover Code Note 3 to Rule 20.2.
[93] Takeover Directive Article 3(1)(e).

Accordingly, funding is something that the bidder will need to consider well in advance of announcing a firm intention to make a bid. This is endorsed by Rule 2.5(a) of the Code, which provides that a firm intention to make a bid should not be announced until the bidder has every reason to believe that it can and will be able to implement its bid. It is difficult to see how a bidder could form this view unless it has financing in place before making the announcement. Responsibility for forming that view also rests with the bidder's financial adviser.[94]

6.117   Supporting the certain funds principle is the Code's requirement for cash confirmation. If the bid is for cash or includes an element of cash, both the announcement of firm intention to make an offer and any subsequent offer document must include confirmation by the financial adviser or another appropriate third party that resources are available to the bidder sufficient to satisfy full acceptance of the bid.[95]

6.3.4.13 *Liability for the cash confirmation*

6.118   The cash confirmation process is taken very seriously by the financial advisers involved in UK public bids given the potential financial liabilities and reputational damage if a cash confirmation is incorrectly given. If the cash confirmation is unreasonably given by the financial adviser, *viz*, it failed to act responsibly or failed to take all reasonable steps to assure itself that the cash was available, then the financial adviser may be required to advance the sums of money itself.

6.119   The Panel also has a number of sanctions open to it if a financial adviser fails to act responsibly or failed to take all reasonable steps to assure itself that the cash was available. These sanctions include:

(i)   the issue of private or public censure of that adviser;

(ii)   withdrawal of rights or the imposition of conditions on rights afforded to that adviser by the Panel;

(iii)   reporting of the adviser's conduct to a regulatory authority or a professional body; and

(iv)   issuing a 'cold-shouldering' statement stating that the adviser is someone who, in the Panel's opinion, is not likely to comply with the Code (this has the effect that other financial institutions and professionals may not be able to work with the adviser).[96]

6.120   Clearly, the imposition of any one of these sanctions would be extremely embarrassing for and potentially damaging to the business of the relevant financial adviser.

---

[94]   Takeover Code Rule 2.5(a).
[95]   Takeover Code Rule 2.5(c) and Rule 24.7.
[96]   Takeover Code paragraph 11, Introduction.

It is also a criminal offence to knowingly or recklessly fail to comply with rules about bid documentation.[97] The offence is punishable with a fine.

An example of a case where the Panel took action against a party for a failure under the cash confirmation provisions was in the takeover of Focus Dynamics Plc by Corporate Resolve Plc where the cash confirmation was given by a partner of the bidder's auditors. The Panel issued a statement criticizing the auditor for his failure to exercise due care in providing a cash confirmation,[98] the Panel noting his failure to review any detailed underwriting agreement or binding facility letter and his failure to investigate the ability of the lender to procure funds from its investors. In reaching its decision, the Panel stated that:

6.121

> the onus on the adviser confirming the availability of finance for an offer is particularly high when, as in this case, the offeror's own resources are inadequate to finance the offer. In such circumstances it is necessary to have an irrevocable and effective commitment from a party upon whom reliance can reasonably be placed.

6.3.4.14 *Not an absolute guarantee*

Although the Code provides that resources have to be made available to a bidder sufficient to satisfy full acceptance of the bid, the Panel recognizes that, commercially, providers of finance will not give an unconditional commitment to fund. Accordingly, it accepts that what is required is for the bidder, its financial advisers and the finance providers to agree that for a particular period (generally around four to seven months), the finance will be conditional only on no serious events occurring.

6.122

In a certain funds debt facility, only the breach of a very restricted set of warranties and only a very restricted set of defaults—the most serious events—can prevent funding. Examples would include breaches of warranties as to the status and authority of the bidding vehicle(s) and the enforceability and ranking of the various agreements, breaches of certain fundamental protections (such as providing third party security), the insolvency of any of the bidding vehicles or any illegality.

6.123

This is significantly narrower than under a standard facility agreement, where it would be usual for a list of conditions precedent to be satisfied and for there to be no breach of any warranty nor any default under any of the funding documents before drawdown takes place.

6.124

---

[97] Companies Act 2006 section 953. Appendix 6 to the Code sets out what is 'bid documentation' for the purposes of section 953.

[98] Panel Statement 2001/2: 'Corporate Resolve Plc/Focus Dynamics Plc'.

6.3.4.15 Process

6.125   The Panel's guidance on how the financial adviser is to satisfy itself that cash is available is minimal. It states that:

> it is a matter of judgement, in each case, for the party giving a cash confirmation to satisfy itself that there will be funds available to meet the offer. In making that judgement, the party giving the cash confirmation will be influenced by a variety of matters such as the standing of the bidder and the extent and nature of its relationship with the bidder.

6.126   There is, accordingly, no set manner in which a financial adviser will satisfy itself before giving a cash confirmation. All major financial advisers will, however, have internal policies and procedures relating to cash confirmations. As well as following these policies and procedures, financial advisers will almost invariably instruct external lawyers to carry out a due diligence exercise on whether the legal documents provide funding on a certain basis.

6.127   The due diligence exercise carried out in relation to the cash confirmation will partly depend on the instructions given to the lawyers but set out below are some issues which the financial advisor (in conjunction with its lawyers) ought to consider.

6.128   **6.3.4.15.1 Existing cash**   If the financial adviser knows the bidder well, it will usually want confirmation from the bank(s) holding the cash that the cash is unencumbered and that the bank(s) are not aware of any reason why the funds cannot be used for the reasons contemplated. If the bidder is not well known to the financial adviser, the financial adviser may request that the funds are transferred to an escrow account where they can only be drawn to fund the bid (and require the financial adviser's consent to withdrawal). If the financial adviser is particularly concerned, it is likely to request that the cash is deposited with it during the certain funds period. The financial adviser will also want the bidder to confirm that the funds will not be used for any other purpose.

6.129   **6.3.4.15.2 Existing debt facilities**   The bidder's existing debt facilities are unlikely to have been drafted on a certain funds basis. Accordingly, the financial adviser will have to focus on the drawdown mechanics, the covenants and termination rights and the right to repayment. The financial adviser may request written confirmation from the bidder of the amount of available funds and that it is not aware of any reason likely to prevent drawdown of these funds or otherwise to accelerate the facility. Some financial advisers may further seek a drawdown of the facilities into an escrow account or an account with the financial adviser.

6.130   **6.3.4.15.3 New debt facilities**   Any new facilities agreements will need to be reviewed to ensure that they are drafted on a certain funds basis. In particular, that: all conditions precedent are within the bidder's control and in agreed form;

all major defaults and major representations (for which the lender can terminate) are within the bidder's control and in the case of insolvency, relate only to the company making the bid; the lenders are prevented from cancelling, accelerating and setting off (unless there has been a major default); that no other documents impact on the financing documents (such as mandate letters) and if they do, confirmation should be requested that they contain no provisions which would enable a lender to vary the terms of the facility documents. The lawyers to the financial adviser will usually want to see: signed versions of each of the facilities agreements; a conditions precedent satisfaction letter to those conditions precedent which are conditions precedent to signing; and any intra-group funding documentation.

The financial adviser will usually also want the bidder to confirm in writing that: **6.131**

  (i) it has the power and authority to enter into the financing documents;

 (ii) the conditions precedent to drawdown are within its control and will be delivered promptly;

(iii) there is no major default or breach of a major representation and that the bidder is not aware of any circumstances which could give rise to such a breach/default;

 (iv) it will comply with the provisions of the finance documents and will not amend them; and

  (v) it will not cancel the facilities.

6.3.4.15.4 Currencies If the funding is in currencies other than sterling, the **6.132**
financial adviser should satisfy itself that appropriate hedging is in place to convert the relevant currency into sterling and the signed hedging documents should therefore be reviewed. An alternative (although often more costly) approach is to ensure that there is sufficient headroom to cover any currency fluctuations during the certain funds period. This is not without risk and therefore currency hedging is much the preferable route.

6.3.4.15.5 Issues involving private equity sponsor funds As private equity **6.133**
sponsors rely on commitments from their investors which can be drawn down under the terms of the relevant limited partnership agreements, financial advisers will usually do due diligence on each of the investors. They will usually want to:

  (i) understand the levels of their original commitments, funds drawdown and outstanding commitments;

 (ii) know if any investors in the fund have ever failed to honour their commitments;

(iii) see a copy of the private equity sponsor's commitment letter, together with a confirmation that the private equity sponsor has signed the commitment letter without making material amendments; and

(iv) obtain an opinion/letter from the private equity sponsor's lawyers as to the strength of funding obligations.

6.134 The financial adviser will also require an equity commitment letter from the private equity sponsor confirming that: it will be able to comply with its obligations to fund the bidding vehicle; it will do all that it should in connection with the drawdown of funds from investors (e.g. the issue of drawdown notices); and that those funds will be available to finance the bidding vehicle on an unconditional basis—this will usually include an undertaking to comply with the terms of the investment agreement and not to amend the agreement without the financial adviser's consent. In an extreme case, the financial adviser might request that a private equity sponsor draws down its full equity commitment and places it in an escrow account prior to announcement. This, however, has traditionally been resisted by private equity sponsors.

6.135 **6.3.4.15.6 Confirmation letters** Financial advisers will usually require confirmation letters from the company making the bid and any parent company or private equity sponsor. The substance and form of the letter will vary from deal to deal but would generally include the following:

(i) each of the matters highlighted above in respect of different types of funding;

(ii) that the bidder has sufficient funds to satisfy the cash consideration;

(iii) that the funds are unencumbered;

(iv) that the funds will only be used to fund the bid; and

(v) that all appropriate corporate approvals and consents have been obtained.

6.136 On the basis of a satisfactory outcome of this process the offer documentation can publicly state that the financial adviser is satisfied as to cash confirmation. The language used is very straightforward and is generally a statement in a similar form to that set out below:

> X Bank is satisfied that resources are available to Bidder sufficient to satisfy full acceptance of the Offer.

6.3.4.16 Due diligence

6.137 Funding using new debt finance can create a number of issues in relation to due diligence. As mentioned in paragraph 6.90 above, lenders will normally want to rely on the due diligence conducted on behalf of the bidder. They will therefore require the bidder to procure that the providers of due diligence to the bidder address their due diligence reports to the lender(s). This will simply be a process issue and the bidder should therefore ensure at an early stage that all of its advisers are aware that they will have to address their due diligence report to any finance providers.

Lack of information on the target and its subsidiaries can create issues for the bid- **6.138**
der in relation to debt facilities. The lender(s) are likely to request that the bidder
will procure that specific security and guarantees are given by the target company
and its group. If the bidder does not have sufficient information to understand
whether or not the relevant security and guarantees can be given (particularly in
relation to overseas subsidiaries and assets) then it will not be able to agree to this
obligation. The bidder will therefore try to seek as much flexibility as possible in
relation to the security and guarantee arrangements in case they cannot be put in
place in a particular manner. The lender and the bidder will often, as a compromise,
agree a qualified procurement obligation based on certain agreed fundamental
principles of security.

The facilities agreement(s) will have a number of covenants and events of default **6.139**
in them. A bidder may not have sufficient diligence information on the target
company and its subsidiaries to be able to tell whether or not it will be in breach
of these provisions of the facilities agreement immediately on closing of the
bid (i.e. when the target and its subsidiaries become subsidiaries of the bidder).
To address this issue, the bidder is often granted a grace period (usually between
30 and 90 days) known as the 'clean-up' period. In this period, a matter will not
usually be treated as an event of default if it is capable of remedy, steps are being
taken to address the matter and the matter has not arisen as a result of the action
of the bidder.

6.3.4.17 *Financial assistance and security*

A significant issue that frequently arises for lenders on a bid is how they get secu- **6.140**
rity over the assets of the target company and its subsidiaries. This is particularly
the case on private equity bids where the bidding entities have little or no intrinsic
value in themselves.

It is unlawful for UK public companies or their subsidiaries to give financial assist- **6.141**
ance and to do so is a criminal offence. The Companies Act 2006 provides that:

> where a person is acquiring or proposing to acquire shares in a public company, it is
> not lawful for the company, or a company that is a subsidiary of that company, to
> give financial assistance directly or indirectly for the purpose of that acquisition
> before or at the same time as the acquisition takes place.[99]

Neither the legislation nor case law provide a definitive definition of what consti- **6.142**
tutes financial assistance. The Companies Act 2006 does, however, set out four
'heads' of financial assistance (which are considered in more detail in Section
6.3.5.1.1 below).[100] If an action does not fall within one of these four heads, it will

---

[99] Companies Act 2006 section 678.
[100] Companies Act 2006 section 677.

not constitute financial assistance. One of the key heads of financial assistance is financial assistance given by way of guarantee, security or indemnity.[101] It will therefore not be possible for a lender to take security over the assets of the target company and its subsidiaries whilst the target is a public company. If the bid is reliant on secured lending, the lenders will only be able to take security over the assets of the target company and its subsidiaries once the target company has been acquired, de-listed and re-registered as a private company.

6.143   The lack of ability to take security over the assets of the target company and its subsidiaries leaves the lender potentially exposed for a significant period of time. Lenders generally try to mitigate this risk by entering into security arrangements in several phases. One conventional approach is as follows: a lender (or a syndicate of lenders) would firstly take a debenture over the bidder and its assets. This debenture is typically put in place at the time the announcement of a firm intention to make a bid for the target company is made. If the bidder is a trading company, this will give the lender some protection, as that company will have assets. If, however, the bidder is a special purpose vehicle, it is unlikely to have substantial assets and therefore the bidder will get very little initial protection (equally however, the special purpose vehicle should have limited liabilities). When the bid becomes unconditional the lender will, by virtue of having a debenture over the bidder, bring into the security net those shares which are held by the shareholders who accept the bid.

6.144   As soon as the bid becomes unconditional, the lender may enter into a second debenture (although this is not always the case), this time given by the target company and its subsidiaries (which the bidder, now having control of the target company can procure that they enter into). This debenture cannot, however, take full security over the assets of the target company and its subsidiaries as the target company is still a public company at this stage and therefore the grant of security would still be financial assistance. Instead, it will cover working capital advances made from the lender to the target company and its subsidiaries only. Securing working capital advances does not constitute financial assistance because the purpose of working capital advances is not to facilitate the acquisition of the shares in the target company *viz*, it is not acquisition finance.

6.145   When the bidder acquires 90% of the shares in the target that were the subject of the offer, it can begin a compulsory acquisition process to acquire the remaining shares in the company (this is known as the 'squeeze-out' process and further details of the process are set out at Section 6.10 of this Chapter). Once it controls 100% of the target company, the bidder will be able to re-register it as a private company without the risk of any minority challenge. It is at this point that the

---

[101]   Companies Act 2006 section 677(1)(b)(i).

lender(s) can take full security over the assets of the target company and its subsidiaries (through a further debenture or accession to a previous debenture).

It is possible to delist and reregister the target company without acquiring 100% **6.146**
of the target. These steps could be taken once the bidder has acquired in excess of 75% of the target's share capital. The statutory processes are longer and there is a residual risk of a challenge by a minority but lending banks are generally willing to permit the level of acceptances required under the offer to be dropped from 90% (i.e. the level that permits the compulsory purchase process) to 75%.

It normally takes between 60 and 180 days from the bid being declared uncondi-   **6.147**
tional for full security to be taken. A lender will clearly not want the process to go on indefinitely and therefore usually negotiates a provision in the facilities agreement which provides that there will be an event of default if the security given by the target company and its securities does not extend to all indebtedness under the facilities agreement by a given date.

This process will be slightly different where the bid is effected by way of scheme of   **6.148**
arrangement because there will be no need to effect the squeeze-out and therefore the target company can be reregistered as a private company almost immediately following the court approving the scheme of arrangement. Schemes of arrangement are considered in Section 6.6 of this Chapter and are popular with lenders because of this lack of uncertainty of success within the structure.

6.3.5 Deal protection

When formulating its bid tactics a bidder will wish to do all it can to maximize its   **6.149**
chances of success. There are many different ways of doing this during the process with both the target company and the target company's shareholders. Equally, the bidder will want to derive some cost protection such that if its bid is ultimately unsuccessful it will receive recompense for the wasted time and costs which it has incurred in working on the bid.

6.3.5.1 *Break fees*

A break fee is, according to the definition in the Code: **6.150**

> an arrangement which may be entered into between an offeror or a potential offeror pursuant to which a cash sum will be payable by the offeree company if certain events occur which have the effect of preventing the offer from proceeding or causing it to fail.[102]

By their very nature, break fees arise only where the bid is not hostile. There are   **6.151**
several reasons why a bidder might seek to enter into a break fee arrangement.

---

[102] Takeover Code Note 1 to Rule 21.2.

Firstly, a bidder is likely to incur significant costs during the course of a bid and it will want to seek some cover for those costs if the bid does not proceed through no fault of its own (albeit that for legal reasons, the break fee cannot be structured as an indemnity for costs, as is explained below). A break fee is also a useful way of persuading the target to continue to negotiate with the bidder and to think twice before entertaining bids from other bidders. Other bidders will also need to take account of the fee in their financial models as, if they are successful, it will be paid by their new subsidiary.

6.152 The vast majority of break fee arrangements are entered into at the time that the announcement of a firm intention to make an offer is made. The rationale is that this is the point where significant costs are incurred (principally, the commitment fees on any lending). It is also easier for the target's board to justify at this stage. In effect, a bid at a sufficiently high level has been made and put the company into play—if something better comes along then that will benefit shareholders and so it is acceptable to compensate the first bidder.

6.153 The timing of this type of break fee will not, however, work for all bidders. The main problem arises for private equity bidders who will usually use a 'newco' structure (which has no assets) to make the acquisition. If the board withdraws its recommendation of a private equity bidder's bid prior to the announcement of a firm intention to made a bid is made, the newco will have incurred wasted costs with no way of paying them (i.e. the fund will need to pick up the abort costs). In these circumstances, the private equity house may try to argue for the break fee arrangement to be entered into at an earlier stage (i.e. before detailed due diligence and other significant activities which incur cost take place).

6.154 The Panel must be consulted at the earliest opportunity if a break fee is proposed and the target board and its financial adviser must confirm to the Panel in writing that they believe the fee to be in the best interests of shareholders.[103] The Panel considers that these confirmations must either be given separately by the target's board and the financial adviser or a single confirmation signed by, or on behalf of, both the target's board and the financial adviser. A letter from the financial adviser on behalf of the board will not be acceptable.[104] The Panel has set out in a practice statement the matters which it expects to see addressed in those written confirmations.[105]

6.155 The Panel will also normally require all agreements relevant to the break fee to include the following wording:

---

[103] Takeover Code Rule 21.2.

[104] Panel Practice Statement No. 23: 'Rule 21.2—inducement fee arrangements and other agreements between an offeror and the offeree company', paragraph 4.2.

[105] Ibid, paragraph 4.3.

Nothing in this agreement shall oblige [the target company] to pay any amount which the Panel determines would not be permitted by Rule 21.2 of the City Code on Takeovers and Mergers.[106]

6.3.5.1.1 Legality There are a number of legal issues connected with the structuring of a break fee. One key legal issue will be to ensure that the break fee does not constitute financial assistance (the concept of financial assistance is explained at Section 6.3.4.17 above). The three heads of financial assistance which are most likely to be relevant in the context of a break fee are: (i) financial assistance by way of gift; (ii) financial assistance by way of guarantee, security and indemnity; and (iii) any other financial assistance given by a company the net assets of which are thereby reduced to a material extent.[107]   **6.156**

Before dealing with these three heads, it is important to address the theoretical argument that a break fee cannot constitute financial assistance because its payment will only occur where shares are not acquired and so cannot be said to be 'for the purpose of' an acquisition. On a plain reading of section 678, this argument seems to have some force. The case law, however, in particular the Court of Appeal decision in *Chaston v SWP Group Limited*,[108] does not seem to support an outcome-orientated analysis of financial assistance. In any event, at the time when the break fee is to be agreed, it could be argued that the bidder would not proceed with the acquisition without the break fee in place and therefore the break fee could be said to be for the purposes of the acquisition. Accordingly, it will be difficult for any bidder taking a reasonably prudent approach to conclude categorically that a break fee arrangement is not financial assistance *ab initio*.   **6.157**

The bidder and the target company will therefore have to structure the break fee arrangement so that it does not fall within any of the heads of financial assistance set out in section 677 of the Companies Act 2006.   **6.158**

The break fee must firstly not be a gift. This is easily addressed by expressly stating the consideration for the break fee in the relevant agreement. If the break fee is agreed at the time the bid is announced, it can simply be expressed as being granted in consideration for the bidder making that bid. If it is agreed prior to the bid being announced, then the likely consideration will be the bidder agreeing to undertake negotiations, investigations and due diligence prior to a bid being made.   **6.159**

The break fee must not be a guarantee, security or an indemnity. The indemnity provision is most likely to be relevant in connection with a break fee. It is tempting   **6.160**

---

[106] Panel Practice Statement No. 23: 'Rule 21.2—inducement fee arrangements and other agreements between an offeror and the offeree company', paragraph 2.5.
[107] Companies Act 2006 section 677.
[108] [2002] All ER (D) 345, CA.

for a bidder to use break fees as a method of covering its costs and expenses of making the bid. If the quantum of the break fee is referable to such costs and expenses incurred by the bidder then it will very likely be categorized as an indemnity. The break fee should instead be a pre-determined fee which is not referable to the costs and expenses incurred by the bidder. When agreeing the break fee, the parties will, however, almost certainly have the likely costs and expenses of the bidder in mind.

6.161 The break fee must not materially reduce the net assets of the target company. This is an issue that goes to the quantum of the break fee and is, accordingly, discussed at paragraph 6.169 below.

6.162 Care should also be taken to ensure that the break fee arrangement is structured so as not to be a penalty. A penalty is a where a fixed or pre-determined amount is payable upon a breach of contract and that amount is not a reasonable pre-estimate of contractual loss. A penalty is unenforceable at law.[109] The break fee arrangement should therefore be drafted so as to be predicated on a contingent event rather than a breach of contract.

6.163 Before entering into a break fee arrangement, the directors of the target company will also need to consider their fiduciary duties. Section 172 of the Companies Act 2006 provides that:

> a director of a company must act in a way he considers, in good faith, would be most likely to promote the success of the company for the benefit of its members as a whole.

6.164 If a company enters into any agreement which conflicts with this duty, that agreement will be unenforceable at law.[110] When considering a break fee arrangement, the directors of the target company will have to weigh the merits of securing an offer from the bidder (which, from the target company's point of view, a break fee arrangement is usually designed to elicit) against the potential effect it will have on a higher bid being made (as rival bidders may be deterred from making a bid by the existence of the break fee). Given the extent of the duty, a properly advised target board should seek to set a break fee at the minimum level which is likely to secure an offer from the bidder. The directors will not be liable if they exercise the duty in good faith. In order to show that they have done this, they should carefully minute their discussions relating to the break fee arrangement. Directors also have a duty to exercise independent judgment under the Companies Act.[111] Arguably, a director would be constrained in considering the merits of any subsequent competing offer by the break fee arrangement and would therefore

---

[109] *Dunlop Pneumatic Tyre Co Ltd v New Garage and Motor Co Ltd* [1915] AC 79, HL.
[110] *Fulham Football Club v Cabra Estates Plc* [1992] BCC 863.
[111] Companies Act 2006 section 173(1).

not be judging that offer wholly independently. This argument should be rebutted by section 173(2)(a) of the Companies Act 2006, which provides that the duty is not infringed by a director 'acting in accordance with an agreement duly entered into by the company that restricts the future exercise of discretion by its directors'. A break fee arrangement would be an example of such an agreement.

6.3.5.1.2 Quantum Rule 21.2 of the Takeover Code provides that a break fee: **6.165**

> must be de minimis (normally no more than 1% of the value of the offeree company calculated by reference to the offer price).

The Panel considers that the purpose of this rule is to prevent the possible payment of an inducement fee from frustrating a competing bid.[112]

The Panel has produced a practice statement[113] clarifying how a break fee   **6.166**
should be calculated. In that statement, it appears implicit that the Panel will generally consider a 1% break fee acceptable. This is supported by a Panel decision in the *BAA/Ferrovial* transaction where Goldman Sachs complained to the Panel that the break fee agreed between BAA and Ferrovial could not be regarded as *de minimis* because of its absolute size, notwithstanding that it did not exceed 1% of the offer price. The Panel, however, ruled that the break fee was *de minimis*. In determining the maximum amount payable in respect of a break fee, the Panel considers that:

(i)   the 1% limit can be calculated on the basis of the fully diluted equity share capital of the target company but only taking into account those options and warrants that are 'in the money';

(ii) any VAT payable on the break fee should be included in the calculation (unless it is recoverable by the target company);

(iii) if the bid is a securities exchange offer, the value of the bid for the purposes of working out the break fee is by reference to the value of the bid set out in the firm intention to make an offer announcement and will not change as a result of subsequent price movements.[114]

The Panel also recognizes that a break fee arrangement can be agreed before the   **6.167**
announcement of a firm intention to make a bid.[115] In these circumstances, it permits the 1% limit to be calculated either by reference to the expected value of the offer at the time the break fee is agreed or the value of the target company by reference to the offer price as stated in a subsequent firm bid announcement.[116]

---

[112] Panel Practice Statement No. 23: 'Rule 21.2—inducement fee arrangements and other agreements between an offeror and the offeree company'.
[113] Ibid.
[114] Ibid, paragraph 3.1.
[115] Ibid, paragraph 3.2.
[116] Ibid.

6.168   Finally, the Panel provides some welcome clarification on the threshold where break fees are paid to more than one bidder. It acknowledges that a target company can agree break fees with two or more bidders, each up to the relevant 1% limit, notwithstanding that, in certain circumstances, the aggregate amount payable by the target company in respect of all such inducement fees might exceed 1% of the value of the target company. The drafting set out in paragraph 6.155 above ensures that multiple payments in breach of the rules are avoided.

6.169   Financial assistance will also have an impact on the quantum of a break fee. As explained above, if a break fee materially reduces the net assets of the target company, then it will constitute financial assistance and be unlawful.[117] A further restriction applies to public companies in so far as they may only pay a break fee out of distributable profits[118] (although a detailed examination of the accounting mechanisms for determining distributable profits is beyond the scope of this Chapter). Accordingly, if a break fee is to be paid, it will be necessary to determine whether it materially reduces the net assets of the target company. Net assets for these purposes are the aggregate of the target company's assets, less the aggregate of its liabilities. Leading counsel have opined that a reduction in net assets of 1% or less is not likely to be material. This, however, is not the same test as under Rule 21.2 of the Code. Rule 21.2 of the Code is predicated on the value of the target company, whereas the financial assistance 'test' relies on net asset value. Accordingly, the application of each test may give an altogether different result.

6.170   The Listing Rules made by the FSA (which apply to all companies listed on the Official List of the FSA) provide another restriction on the quantum of break fees. Parties should be careful to avoid the break fee being classified as a class 1 transaction. The consequences of a class 1 transaction are that shareholders will have to approve the arrangement at a general meeting in advance of the arrangement being put in place and a circular will have to be sent to shareholders explaining the arrangement. Prior shareholder approval could cause major timetable issues, as a bidder may be reluctant to make a bid or commence due diligence in earnest (as the case may be) until it has entered into the break fee arrangement. The circular which has to be sent to shareholders is an onerous document which requires a significant amount of disclosure and must be approved in advance by the FSA. Given the resources that producing the circular will use up (when they could otherwise be employed in furthering the bid process), the break fee should be structured, if possible, to ensure that it is not a class 1 transaction. A break fee will be treated as a class 1 transaction if the total value of the break fees in aggregate exceeds 1% of the value of the target company calculated by reference to the

---

[117] Companies Act 2006 section 677(1)(d)(i).
[118] Companies Act 2006 section 682(1).

bid price.[119] The test for working out the bid price is exactly the same as under the Code[120] and so, theoretically at least, if a break fee is acceptable under Rule 21.2 of the Code, it should not be a class 1 transaction. There is one caveat to this. In addition to the specific rule on break fees, the Listing Rules also has general rules on class tests. Chapter 10 of the Listing Rules sets out four 'class tests' being: (i) the gross assets test; (ii) the profits test; (iii) the consideration test; and (iv) the gross capital test. It is beyond the scope of this Chapter to set out the details of those rules but broadly, they (in the case of a break fee) compare the break fee against certain measures which value the listed company, giving rise to percentage ratios. If any of the four tests give rise to a percentage ratio in excess of 25%, the transaction will be a class 1 transaction. Parties will therefore have to be mindful of this rule as well as the specific rule on break fees.

6.3.5.1.3 Trigger events   The trigger events for payment of a break fee will vary   **6.171**
from transaction to transaction and will depend greatly on the bargaining power of the respective parties. The bidder should, however, consider including some of the following triggers (if they are appropriate to the transaction):

  (i) the bid does not become unconditional in all respects (this will be generally where there is a higher competing bid);
  (ii) the board of the target company does not recommend the bidder's bid or subsequently withdraws its recommendation;
  (iii) the shareholders of either the target or the bidder fail to pass the necessary resolutions to give effect to the bid;
  (iv) a substantial shareholder fails to accept the bid; and
  (v) the target board, in breach of a non-solicitation agreement between the bidder and the target, solicits discussions with a third party with a view to that third party making a bid.

A well-advised target board will wish to restrict the triggers to the payment of a   **6.172**
break fee to situations where another bid has been successful so that, as a matter of economics, it is the successful bidder that is bearing the cost of the break fee.

6.3.5.1.4 Shareholder break fees   Although break fees arrangements are usu-   **6.173**
ally entered into between the bidder and the target company, it is not unheard of for major shareholders to enter into break fee arrangements with the bidder. They will most often be used where a major shareholder will receive a significant sum of money on completion of the bid and such shareholder is therefore prepared to enter into the arrangement in order to secure a bid from the bidder. Break fees arrangements given by shareholders cannot, because they are not given by the

---

[119] LR 10.2.7(1)R.
[120] LR 10.2.7(2)R.

target company or any of its subsidiaries, constitute financial assistance (see the discussion above).

6.174   The main legal issue that the bidder should be concerned with is that, by entering into the break fee arrangement, the target company shareholder is not treated as acting in concert with the bidder. The meaning of 'acting in concert' is discussed at Section 6.2.3 of this Chapter. If the shareholder indemnifies the bidder or enters into an arrangement which may be an inducement to deal or refrain from dealing, that is likely to mean that such shareholder is acting in concert with the bidder.[121] This is likely to arise where either the break fee arrangement provides cost cover or the shareholder agrees to pay break fees if it does not accept the bidder's bid at a certain level. If the shareholder is acting in concert with the bidder, the principal consequences are, *inter alia*, under Rules 6, 9 and 11 of the Code. These consequences are set out at Section 6.3.6.2 below. In these circumstances, the shareholder will also be an associate of the bidder for the purposes of Rule 8.[122] The consequences of this are also set out at Section 6.3.6.3.1 below.

6.175   **6.3.5.1.5   Reverse break fees**   Reverse break fees are, as the name implies, break fees payable from the bidder to the target. They are likely to be used in a situation where there is a risk of the bidder's bid failing, for example, where the bid has to be approved by the bidder's shareholders or where there is a possibility of that bid not being cleared by the antitrust authorities. They are also more frequent in transactions involving parties of similar size.

6.176   **6.3.5.1.6   Implications for the bid**   The Code provides that any break fee must be fully disclosed in the announcement of an intention to make a firm bid.[123] Any documentation relating to the payment of a break fee must also be made available for inspection from the time the offer document is published until the end of the offer period.[124] The offer document must state where the documentation is so available and the place (being a place in the City of London or such other place as the Panel may agree) where inspection can be made. A copy of each document on display must, on request, promptly be made available to any competing bidder or potential bidder.[125] Accordingly, competing bidders will have full disclosure of any break fee arrangement.

6.3.5.2 Non-solicitation

6.177   In a private M&A transaction a vendor can deal with its asset as it chooses and therefore is entitled to grant a period of exclusivity to a particular bidder. The

---

[121]   Takeover Code Note 6 to Rule 8.
[122]   Ibid.
[123]   Takeover Code Rule 21.2.
[124]   Takeover Code Rule 26(m).
[125]   Takeover Code Note on Rule 26.

fiduciary duties of a target board mean that they should not do this. They should leave themselves available to be able to deal with any approaches from third parties if that is in the best interests of shareholders.

Accordingly, a well-advised target board will never agree to more than a period of non-solicitation. Whilst not granting the bidder exclusivity, it will give the bidder comfort that the target board is not actively soliciting bids from other potential bidders. **6.178**

6.3.5.3 *Confidentiality undertakings from the target*

In addition to the target seeking confidentiality undertakings from the bidder prior to providing due diligence information, a well-advised bidder will also want confidentiality obligations from the target. A bidder will want to ensure that its identity, offer and the status of the negotiations between it and the target are kept confidential. It may also be providing reverse due diligence (e.g. if there is to be share consideration) and should seek to protect that information. **6.179**

6.3.5.4 *Irrevocables*

6.3.5.4.1 Purpose of irrevocables Obtaining irrevocable undertakings is a cornerstone of deal protection for a bidder. An irrevocable undertaking is a legally binding commitment from a shareholder of the target to accept an offer or to vote in favour of a scheme of arrangement. **6.180**

A bidder will want to gather irrevocable undertakings because it sends a positive message about the bid to the market, other shareholders and potential competitors. Accordingly, they therefore increase the bidder's chances of meeting the acceptance condition on a conventional bid or the 75% threshold on a scheme of arrangement. **6.181**

6.3.5.4.2 Hard, soft and semi-soft irrevocables For the reasons set out below, bidders will usually seek to gather irrevocable undertakings in the 24-hour (or 48-hour) period prior to the announcement of a firm intention to make a bid. Irrevocable undertakings generally take one of the following forms: **6.182**

(i) *hard irrevocable*: a hard irrevocable is an irrevocable undertaking with no provision for release and which therefore continues to bind the shareholder until the offer lapses;
(ii) *soft irrevocable*: a soft irrevocable is an irrevocable undertaking with provision for release if a higher competing bid is announced; and
(iii) *semi-soft irrevocable*: a semi-soft irrevocable is an irrevocable undertaking with provision for release if a higher competing bid is announced and that competing bid exceeds the bidder's bid by a certain margin e.g. X pence or Y%.

6.183 An additional feature of soft and semi-soft irrevocables is that bidders are sometimes granted a 'matching' right. This provides that, if there is a higher competing bid, the bidder has a given a short period to match or beat that bid and, if it does, the irrevocable undertaking continues to bind the person giving it.

6.184 In a recommended transaction, one would expect directors of the target who hold shares to be prepared to give hard irrevocables. In essence they are standing behind their recommendation to other shareholders. As a general proposition, institutional investors will be far more unlikely to offer a hard irrevocable. This is because they will prefer to retain the flexibility to accept a higher bid.

6.185 **6.3.5.4.3 Content of irrevocables** A bidder will usually have two forms of irrevocable undertakings: one for shareholders who are also directors of the target company and one for any other shareholders of the target company. Although the content of an irrevocable undertaking will vary depending on the bidder, the transaction, and the relative negotiating positions of the bidder and target shareholders, the following are examples of what might typically be found in an irrevocable undertaking:

(i) Attached to the document will usually be the draft press announcement which should provide the primary reference point for the terms of the bid, which will be referred to in the irrevocable.

(ii) The primary obligation in the document will be the undertaking to either accept the bid (within a given period) or to vote in favour of the scheme (as applicable).

(iii) There will also be a number of anti-avoidance provisions, principally not to withdraw any acceptance of the bid and not to transfer or encumber the shares (except pursuant to the bid).

(iv) The bidder may also seek certain other behavioural undertakings from the shareholders such as not soliciting a bid from a third party and not acquiring any other shares in the target.

(v) To ensure that the irrevocable will actually secure shares in the target for the bidder, the shareholder should represent that it has beneficial title to the shares the subject of the undertaking and that it has the capacity to transfer the shares together with all rights attaching to the shares to the bidder free from all encumbrances and other third party rights.

(vi) There should be included various obligations (including the provision of information) to help the bidder comply with its regulatory obligations and the shareholder should consent to the details of his irrevocable undertaking being disclosed in the announcement to make a firm bid.

(vii) Finally, the document sometimes contains a power of attorney from the shareholder in favour of the bidder so that the bidder may enforce its undertakings under the agreement and execute a form of acceptance in relation to the shareholder's shares in the target company.

The directors of the target giving irrevocable undertakings will sign up to the same   **6.186**
undertakings as other shareholders but may also give certain additional undertakings relevant to their position as directors of the target. They may undertake to
recommend and not withdraw their recommendation of the bid. They will also be
asked to provide all information in their possession to assist the bidder in complying with the Code and its other regulatory obligations. Most controversially,
directors are sometimes asked to warrant certain issues relating to the target, such
as the target's accounts and information in the draft firm intention to make a bid
announcement. This is usually resisted but is ultimately a matter of commercial
bargaining power.

6.3.5.4.4 Letters of intent/statements of support   Many institutional share-   **6.187**
holders, as a matter of policy, will not give irrevocable undertakings. Some will
provide letters of intent or statements of support. Although, as the name implies,
letters of intent are not legally binding but instead set out an intention to accept
the bid or vote in favour of a scheme of arrangement (as applicable) they, nonetheless, provide the bidder with some comfort that the particular shareholder is not
hostile to the bid in principle. Non-binding letters of intent or support (unlike
irrevocable undertakings) are not 'interests in shares' for the purposes of Rule 5
of the Code (restrictions on acquisitions) but they are required to be publicly
disclosed like irrevocables pursuant to Rule 8 (see Section 6.3.6.3.1 below).
Details of Rule 5 of the Code are set out in Section 6.3.6.2.1 below.

6.3.5.4.5 Legal and regulatory issues relating to irrevocables

6.3.5.4.5.1 The Companies Act   It is important to ensure that any irrevocable   **6.188**
undertaking is either for:

(i)   no consideration and executed as a deed;
(ii)   for consideration of negligible value; or
(iii)   for consideration consisting only of a promise by the bidder to make
the bid.

This is because, on a conventional bid, the shares the subject of the irrevocable   **6.189**
undertaking can only count towards the 90% threshold for compulsory purchases
(as explained at Section 6.3.6.2.4 below) if the consideration is in one of the three
forms set out above.[126] The analysis is the same for a scheme of arrangement;
unless the consideration is in one of those three forms, there is a risk that those
shares subject to the irrevocables will be held to form a separate class of shares by
the court. In these circumstances, the bidder's chance of passing the scheme will
be reduced as a majority in number of shareholders, representing at least 75%

---

[126] Companies Act 2006 section 975(2).

in value of the members present and voting either in person or by proxy at the relevant meeting (in both cases excluding any shares subject to irrevocables which do not comply with any of the relevant forms) will have to vote in favour of the scheme for the scheme to be passed.

6.190   *6.3.5.4.5.2 The Code*   The Code's rules requiring secrecy affect the ability of a bidder to seek irrevocables. These requirements were discussed at paragraph 6.62 above. Accordingly, the bidder may need the consent of the Panel before approaching shareholders to obtain irrevocable undertakings.

6.191   The identity of the shareholder will also be relevant before a bidder is able to approach it to seek an irrevocable undertaking, as Rule 4.3 of the Code provides that if the bidder intends to contact a private individual or a small corporate shareholder with a view to seeking an irrevocable undertaking, it must consult the Panel in advance. The bidder will need to satisfy the Panel that adequate time and information will be given to that shareholder to decide whether or not it should give the irrevocable along with the opportunity to obtain independent advice, if necessary.[127]

6.192   The gathering of irrevocable commitments (above a certain level) will, *prima facie*, fall within Rule 5 of the Code. Rule 5 prevents bidders from acquiring interests in shares which carry more than 30% of the voting rights in the target or if the bidder already holds between 30% and 50% of the voting rights, from acquiring any further interests in shares in the target (Rule 5 is explained in more detail at Section 6.3.6.2.1 below). If a bidder wishes to gain irrevocable commitments which would take its voting rights above 30% or which would increase its share of the voting rights where it already holds between 30% and 50%, then it will have to seek to take advantage of one of the exceptions to these restrictions. The two main exceptions which a bidder is likely to rely on are:

(i) the irrevocable undertaking is gathered at any time before the bidder announces a firm intention to make a bid and either the bid will be publicly recommended or the irrevocable is sought with the consent of the target board and is conditional upon the announcement of a firm intention to make a bid;[128] and

(ii) the irrevocable undertaking is gathered after the bidder has announced a firm intention to make a bid, as long as the bid is not subject to a pre-condition and one of the following applies:

(a) the target board agrees to the acquisition;

(b) the bid has been publicly recommended by the target (this applies even if that recommendation is subsequently withdrawn);

---

[127] Takeover Code Note on Rule 4.3.
[128] Takeover Code Rule 5.2(b).

(c) after the first closing date of the bid or any competing bid (generally 21 days after the offer document has been posted) the bid or competing bid (as applicable) has been cleared by the relevant antitrust authorities, or the relevant bid is outside the scope of the relevant antitrust laws; and

(iii) the offer is unconditional in all respects.[129]

If the bidder can take advantage of one of these exemptions, there is a potential for a 'shut-out' which is where sufficient shareholders sign up to irrevocable undertakings such that the bid can be declared unconditional as to acceptances from the outset. If the bidder's share of the voting rights goes above 30% of the voting rights in the company as a result of gathering irrevocable undertakings, the bidder will not necessarily be obliged to make a mandatory offer under Rule 9 of the Code (as it would be so obliged if it bought shares) (Rule 9 is described in detail in Section 6.7 of this Chapter). The Panel does not consider (other than for the purposes of Rule 5 of the Code) the bidder to have an interest in the shares to which the irrevocable undertaking relates, so long as the voting undertaking is given in the context of an irrevocable commitment to accept the bid, it is limited to the duration of the bid or, if earlier, until the irrevocable commitment otherwise ceases to be binding and it is limited to matters which relate to ensuring that its bid is successful.[130] **6.193**

The bidder must, however, disclose any irrevocable undertakings gathered by midday on the business day after they are gathered (details of the manner of disclosure outlined by Rule 8 are set out at Section 6.3.6.3.1 below). The bidder will also be required to disclose any irrevocable undertakings in its announcement of an intention to make a firm bid[131] and in the bid documentation.[132] As a result, bidders will typically ensure that irrevocables are signed immediately before the announcement to make a firm bid is made. **6.194**

Driven by Article 3(1)(a) of the Takeover Directive and General Principle 1 of the Code (which each provide that all holders of securities of a target company of the same class must be afforded equal treatment), the Code provides that where the bidder or its financial adviser has, *inter alia*, met with a shareholder for the purpose of gathering irrevocable undertakings, the bidder's financial adviser must confirm in writing to the Panel that no new information or significant **6.195**

---

[129] Takeover Code Rule 5.2(c).
[130] Panel Practice Statement No. 22: 'Irrevocable Commitments, Concert Parties and Related Matters', paragraphs 2.5 and 3.3.
[131] Takeover Code Rule 2.5(b)(iv).
[132] Takeover Code Rule 24.2(d)(x).

opinions have been provided to the shareholder which will not be set out in the announcement of a firm intention to make a bid.

6.196   *6.3.5.4.5.3 Insider dealing and market abuse*   When approaching shareholders to seek their entry into irrevocable undertakings, the bidder will have to make such shareholders insiders for the purposes of the insider dealing and market abuse regimes (both of which are described more fully at Sections 6.3.6.1.1 and 6.3.6.1.2 below). The bidder should be sensitive to certain shareholders not wanting to be made insiders, as their ability to deal will be restricted. This is another reason for delaying approaching shareholders until late in the process as they will not wish to be insiders for prolonged periods of time.

6.197   *6.3.5.4.5.4 Financial promotion*   An approach to a shareholder to enter into an irrevocable undertaking may be a financial promotion pursuant to section 21 of the Financial Services and Markets Act 2000 (unless it falls within an exemption contained in the Financial Promotion Order,[133] such as where the approach is made to an investment professional). A financial promotion is where a person, in the course of business, communicates an invitation or inducement to engage in investment activity.[134] This is an unlawful criminal act, punishable by a maximum sentence of two years' imprisonment.[135] It will not be an offence, however, if the communication is made by an authorized person or is approved by an authorized person.[136] Accordingly, if it is not exempt pursuant to the Financial Promotion Order, the approach should either be made by or approved by an FSA-authorized person. This will most likely be the corporate broker to the bidder.

6.3.6 Stakebuilding

6.198   Stakebuilding is a process pursuant to which a bidder acquires interests in the target company (either off or on market) outside of the formal bid structure. There are several reasons why a bidder might consider stakebuilding. Firstly, stakebuilding is a signal of intent to the board of the target. It aims to ensure that the target board takes an approach from the bidder seriously and seeks to focus the minds of the directors of the target on their fiduciary duties. If stakebuilding takes place in a competitive situation, it can be used to put pressure on other bidders. It may dissuade a potential bidder from making a bid in the first place or it might make existing bidders reconsider whether they want to proceed with their bid given that there is a clear expression of intent that there is a competing bidder who is taking the bid seriously. In some cases, stakebuilding by a bidder can frustrate

---

[133] The Financial Services and Markets Act 2000 (Financial Promotion) Order, SI 2005 No 1529.
[134] FSMA 2000 section 21(1).
[135] FSMA 2000 section 23(1).
[136] FSMA 2000 section 21(2).

the bid of another bidder. For example, on a conventional bid structure, if a bidder acquires 10% or more of the issued share capital of the target, it could prevent a rival bidder from taking advantage of the squeeze-out provisions contained in the Companies Act and may be a strong dissuading tactic. Similarly, if one bidder's bid is structured as a scheme of arrangement, the other bidder could acquire sufficient shares in the market to either block or make it very difficult for a special resolution to be passed approving the scheme. Stakebuilding can also potentially reduce the overall cost of the transaction through the bidder buying shares at a price which is lower than the final offer price.

Stakebuilding can also confer advantages on a bidder if it is not successful in acquiring the target. If the bidder acquires shares in the market at a price which is lower than the final bid price, it will make a profit on those shares where they are acquired by the successful bidder pursuant to its bid. This should provide cover for some or all of the costs incurred by the unsuccessful bidder in making its bid. A bidder should be careful, however, to ensure that this is not its principal motivation for stakebuilding as this may give rise to insider dealing and market abuse issues (as explained below). **6.199**

Stakebuilding usually takes place prior to and around the time of announcement of a bid. This is because once a bid is announced, the share price of the target company is likely to rise having been rebased on the bid price. If the market expects a competing bid the price may be significantly higher than the bid price. Accordingly, prior to the announcement of a bid is the best time to acquire shares for a price below the bid price. Once an announcement of a bid or possible bid has been made, the disclosure requirements become more onerous (as explained below) and it is therefore more difficult to stakebuild by stealth. The other main opportunity a bidder may have to stakebuild is when a revised or final bid is made, when the share price of the target company drops below the bid price to reflect the time value of money. **6.200**

Before a bidder engages in stakebuilding, it is very important that it takes extensive professional advice. At certain times, stakebuilding will not be permitted at law and, if carried out, could result in both criminal and civil penalties. Even if stakebuilding is permitted at law at the relevant time, it could have serious consequences for the bidder's bid as a whole, as a number of consequences flow from stakebuilding under the relevant regulations. **6.201**

6.3.6.1 *Permissibility*

The two principal offences which might prevent a bidder from stakebuilding are the criminal offence of insider dealing and the civil offence of market abuse. The bidder will also need to be mindful of overseas securities laws and antitrust issues when stakebuilding. These issues are examined below. **6.202**

6.203   **6.3.6.1.1 Insider dealing**   Insider dealing is a criminal offence punishable by a maximum sentence of seven years' imprisonment.[137] It is an offence which can only be committed by individuals[138] and in the context of stakebuilding, the relevant individuals are likely to be the directors of the bidder and potentially those advisers which advise the directors to deal. The insider dealing offence is committed when an individual who has information as an insider deals in securities on a regulated market[139] (or uses a professional intermediary to do so) that are price-affected securities in relation to the information.[140] There are also offences relating to encouraging another person to deal on the basis of inside information, and improper disclosure of inside information.[141]

6.204   In view of the insider dealing offence, it will be critical for the bidder to establish whether or not it is in possession of inside information before stakebuilding. A bidder will only have inside information if the information that it has meets the following four requirements:[142]

(i)   the information must relate to the securities of the target or to the target itself—so information about an industry in general or about macro-economic conditions will not be inside information;

(ii)   that information is specific and precise—so vague rumour will not constitute inside information;

(iii)   that information has not been made public ('made public' is fairly broadly defined); and

(iv)   if it were made public it would be likely to have a significant effect on the price of the target company' securities—if the bid has been made public (and there has been no intention formed to increase that bid) then there is significantly less likelihood of the information being price-sensitive as the target's share price will most likely be sustained by the bid price and may therefore not be affected by information which would normally affect the share price.

6.205   A person will have information as an insider if the information is inside information and he knows that it is inside information and that he has it from an insider source and he knows that it is from an inside source.[143] An inside source will include where the direct or indirect source of the information is a director, employee or shareholder of the target or where an individual has access to the information

---

[137]   Criminal Justice Act 1993 ('CJA') section 61(2).
[138]   CJA 1993 section 52(1).
[139]   Regulated markets are listed in the schedule to the Insider Dealing (Securities and Regulated Markets) Order 1994, SI 1994 No 187.
[140]   CJA 1993 section 52(1).
[141]   CJA 1993 section 52(2).
[142]   CJA 1993 section 56.
[143]   CJA 1993 section 57(1).

by virtue of his employment, office or profession.[144] It is clear, therefore, that knowledge that the bidder is going to make a bid for the target is *prima facie* inside information which those individuals within the bidder who know about the bid have as insiders. The bidder may, however, be able to take advantage of the special bid defence described below.

A special bid defence to the insider dealing offence is potentially available to those stakebuilding. An individual is not guilty of insider dealing if he shows that he acted in connection with a bid which was under consideration or the subject of negotiation, with a view to facilitating the accomplishment of the bid.[145] An individual must also demonstrate that the information he had as an insider was market information arising directly out of his involvement in the bid.[146] In the context of a bid, the 'market information' test will generally be satisfied by an individual demonstrating that he had, at the time of dealing, knowledge that the bidder was going to make or it was considering making a bid. Accordingly, even if stakebuilding takes place pre-announcement of the bid, the individual's knowledge that the bidder is contemplating making a bid for the target company will not, in itself, constitute inside information. If a bidder otherwise has price sensitive information (for example through its due diligence) then the insider dealing offence is likely to be more relevant, as at this time the share price of the target company will not be supported by the bid price and therefore inside information is more likely to have an effect on the price of the target for shares.

6.206

If an individual connected with the bidder is *prima facie* caught by the insider dealing legislation and is unable to fall within the special bid defence when the bidder is seeking to stakebuild, he will need to consider the other defences to insider dealing. There are three alternative defences which such an individual can seek to rely on. He will need to demonstrate that either:

6.207

(i) he did not expect the dealing to result in a profit attributable to the information; or

(ii) he believed on reasonable grounds that the information had been disclosed widely enough to ensure that the seller would not be prejudiced by not having the information; or

(iii) that he would have done what he did even if he had not had the information.

The burden of proof is on the individual accused of insider dealing to establish that a defence applies. This can be difficult to establish in a bid situation, particularly

6.208

---

[144] CJA 1993 section 57(2).
[145] CJA 1993 para 3(a) Schedule 1.
[146] CJA 1993 para 3(b) Schedule 1.

if on an unsuccessful bid a bidder has made a profit from the sale of shares in the target.

6.209 **6.3.6.1.2 Market abuse** The civil law offence of market abuse is derived from the Market Abuse Directive.[147] Unlike insider dealing it can apply to the bidder as well as to individuals. The offence of market abuse[148] involves certain prescribed behaviour which occurs in relation to qualifying investments (which are very widely defined and include swaps, derivatives and futures, as well as securities)[149] admitted to trading on a prescribed market.[150]

6.210 Stakebuilding in a UK target will almost certainly involve qualifying investments on a prescribed market. Whether stakebuilding will constitute market abuse will therefore turn on whether or not the bidder's behaviour falls within any of the seven prescribed heads of behaviour prescribed by the Financial Services and Markets Act 2000. In summary, those heads of behaviour are as follows:[151]

  (i) insider dealing;
  (ii) improper disclosure of inside information;
  (iii) misuse of information;
  (iv) transactions which manipulate the market;
  (v) employing manipulating devices;
  (vi) dissemination of information likely to give a false or misleading impression; and
  (vii) misleading behaviour and distortion of the market.

6.211 Insider dealing is likely to be the most relevant of the heads of market offence abuse in the context of stakebuilding. Insider dealing under the market abuse regime is committed when an insider deals or attempts to deal in a qualifying investment or related investment on the basis of inside information relating to the investment in question.[152] 'Inside information' has a broadly similar definition to the definition in the insider dealing regime and is information of a precise nature which:

  (i) is not generally available;

---

[147] Directive 2003/6/EC of the European Parliament and of the Council of 28 January 2003 on insider dealing and market manipulation (Market Abuse).

[148] The offence is defined in FSMA 2000 section 118(1).

[149] Qualifying investments are those specified by Article 5 of the Financial Services and Markets Act 2000 (Prescribed Markets and Qualifying Investments) Order 2001, SI 2001 No 996, which draws its definition from the definition of 'financial instrument' from Article 1(3) of the Market Abuse Directive.

[150] Prescribed markets are those specified by Article 4 of the Financial Services and Markets Act (Prescribed Markets and Qualifying Investments) Order 2001, SI 2001 No 996 which prescribes that most markets in the UK are qualifying markets.

[151] FSMA 2000 section 118(2)–(8).

[152] FSMA 2000 section 118(2).

(ii) either relates to the securities of a company or the company itself; and

(iii) would, if generally available, be likely to have a significant effect on the price of the qualifying investments or on the price of related investments.[153]

A bidder's knowledge that it is going (if not announced) to make a bid would fall within the definition of inside information and would therefore *prima facie* constitute market abuse. **6.212**

Unlike insider dealing, market abuse has no statutory defences. The FSA's Code of Market Conduct,[154] however, amongst other things, specifies descriptions of behaviour which either amount to market abuse or do not amount to market abuse. This effectively creates 'safe harbours' for certain types of behaviour which would otherwise be viewed as market abuse. The Code of Market Conduct makes clear that, in the context of a bid, behaviour based on inside information does not, of itself, amount to market abuse.[155] There are two caveats to this safe harbour. Firstly, the inside information which the bidder has must be of the relevant type *viz*, either information that the bidder is going to make or is considering making a bid for the target or information the bidder may obtain through due diligence.[156] Secondly, the stakebuilding must be for the purpose of the bidder gaining control of the target company. The FSA has indicated two factors which are indicative of whether this test has been met: (i) whether the transactions concerned are in the target company's shares or (ii) whether the transactions concerned are for the sole purpose of gaining control of the target or effecting the merger.[157] Notwithstanding these two caveats, it should be relatively straightforward for a bidder to demonstrate that it falls within this safe harbour, provided that its motivation is genuinely to acquire control of the target. **6.213**

6.3.6.1.3 Shares v derivatives   An economic alternative to sharebuying is to stakebuild through a derivative product known as a contract for difference ('CFD'). A CFD is an instrument which gives its holder economic exposure (either long or short) to the change in price of an underlying share without having to hold that underlying share. They can either be settled in cash or settled physically. CFDs have become very popular in recent years and the FSA has noted that some commentators believe that between 20% and 40% of turnover in the cash equities market is now driven by activity in related derivative products and that in bid situations, the figure is likely to be towards the top of that scale.[158] **6.214**

---

[153] FSMA 2000 section 118C.

[154] Made pursuant to FSMA 2000 section 119 FSMA.

[155] Code of Market Conduct, MAR 1.3.17C.

[156] Code of Market Conduct, MAR 1.3.18G.

[157] Code of Market Conduct, MAR 1.3.19G.

[158] FSA Consultation Paper CP07/20, 'Disclosure of Contracts for Difference: consultation and draft Handbook text' (November 2007).

6.215 Historically, one of the main benefits of CFDs was that if cash-settled and not physically-settled, no disclosure of the CFD interest was required under the Disclosure and Transparency Rules. This allowed parties to acquire large exposures without disclosure. Although the voting rights were not conferred on the party acquiring CFDs (unless the CFD is physically settled), they are nonetheless a useful method of tying up shares in the capital of the target. This is because a broker writing a CFD will usually hedge its exposure to the underlying shares by purchasing underlying shares in the market. This largely ensures that those shares cannot be bought by competing bidders. As brokers hold the underlying shares to hedge their position, it is easy for a bidder to subsequently agree with a broker that a cash-settled CFD can be amended to be settled physically. The shares which the broker would otherwise sell in the market to cash-settle the CFD are simply transferred to the bidder. Whether the broker is prepared to amend a cash-settled CFD to a physically-settled CFD will largely be a relationship matter but the key point is that it is only at the point of amendment that the party would have an announceable interest in the shares.

6.216 That position on disclosure is now of historic relevance only as the Disclosure and Transparency Rules have now been extended to cover long interests held through cash-settled CFDs.[159]

6.217 The key disadvantage of using CFDs is that neither the special bid defence to insider dealing afforded to bidders nor the market abuse safe harbour applies to dealings in CFDs. In December 1996, following the extensive use of CFDs by Trafalgar House in its bid for Northern Electric, the Securities and Investment Board (the predecessor organization to the FSA) issued a guidance document stating that CFDs should not be entered into on the basis of inside information where they would provide a cash benefit only and would not facilitate the accomplishment of a takeover. A similar analysis applies to the market abuse safe harbour. This is supported by the Code of Market Conduct which makes clear that there are two criteria that the FSA will take into account in determining whether or not a person's behaviour is for the purpose of gaining control of the target company or his proposing a merger of that company.[160] As set out in paragraph 6.213 those are (i) whether the transactions concerned are in the target's shares or (ii) whether the transactions concerned are for the sole purpose of gaining that control or effecting the merger. It is difficult to make the case that a bidder entering into a cash-settled CFD fulfils either criterion. The Code of Market Conduct also expressly confirms that, in the FSA's view, a bidder entering into a transaction that provides merely an economic exposure to movements in the price of the target

---

[159] See paragraph 6.266 below.
[160] Code of Market Conduct, MAR 1.3.19E.

company's shares on the basis of inside information concerning the proposed bid is *prima facie* market abuse.[161] Although the safe harbours in the insider dealing and market abuse legislation may not be available when dealing in CFDs, this does not mean that it is impossible to stakebuild using CFDs. Rather, care needs to be taken and professional advice must always be sought before doing so.

There are also some ancillary benefits to stakebuilding using CFDs. Firstly, unlike an acquisition of shares, no stamp duty is payable on a cash-settled CFD (although it is evidently payable on physically-settled CFDs). Bidders can also make money from CFDs as an arbitrage tool. Most bidders using CFDs in a bid would take a long position, hoping that the market price of the underlying share increases above a reference point. The bidder would then make money from the increase in price, which covers the costs of its bid. This method, however, gives rise to significant insider-dealing and market-abuse issues.

6.218

6.3.6.1.4 US law   A detailed assessment of US securities law is beyond the scope of this Chapter but under the laws of the United States, it is generally illegal for a bidder to acquire shares in the target outside of a bid when the bid is pending (i.e. to stakebuild).[162] This rule applies even where the target is a UK company and traded only on markets in the UK. This is because the Securities Exchange Act of 1934 has extra-territorial effect. The bidder may be able, however, to take advantage of an exemption. If the bid is an exempt bid pursuant to the Tier I exemption, it will also be exempt from the prohibition on stakebuilding, as long as certain conditions are met.[163]

6.219

The Tier I exemption is available to bids for target companies which are 'foreign private issuers'[164] where the percentage of the target company's shares sought in the bid held by US persons does not exceed 10% and certain conditions on equal treatment and communication of the bid are met.[165] The conditions which the bidder will have to meet (if it falls within the Tier I exemption) in order to be exempt from the prohibition on stakebuilding are:

6.220

(i)   the offer document sent to US holders must '*prominently* disclose the possibility of any purchasers, or arrangements to purchase, or the intent to make

---

[161]   Code of Market Conduct, MAR 1.3.2E.

[162]   Rule 14e-5, Securities Exchange Act of 1934.

[163]   Rule 14e-5(b)(10), Securities Exchange Act of 1934.

[164]   The term 'foreign private issuer' means any foreign (i.e. non-US) issuer other than a foreign government except an issuer meeting the following conditions: (i) more than 50% of the issuer's outstanding voting securities are directly or indirectly held of record by residents of the US; and (ii) any of the following: (a) the majority of the executive officers or directors are US citizens or residents, (ii) more than 50% of the assets of the issuer are located in the US, or (iii) the business of the issuer is administered principally in the US (Rule 3b-4 of the Securities Exchange Act of 1934).

[165]   Rule 14d-1(c) of the Securities Exchange Act of 1934.

such purchases' and the manner in which any further information about such matters will be disclosed;

(ii) all purchases of target company shares must comply with the rules in the target company's jurisdiction of origin and primary listing; and

(iii) the bidder must disclose information in the US about any such purchases or arrangements to purchase in a manner comparable to the disclosure of these matters made in the subject company's jurisdiction of organization and primary listing.

6.221 If the bidder cannot fit within the Tier I exemption, it might consider making separate US and non-US bids. In a dual offer that is eligible for the narrowly-tailored Tier II exemption, the bidder may make purchases pursuant to the concurrent non-US bid and may also acquire shares outside the offer, so long as certain conditions are satisfied.[166] If the Tier II exemption is not available, the non US offer could potentially be construed as an arrangement to purchase securities outside the US offer (and therefore a breach of Rule 14e-5). In this scenario bidders would have to seek individual relief from Rule 14e-5 by way of a no-action letter from the US Securities and Exchange Commission.

6.222 **6.3.6.1.5 Antitrust** Many of the considerations set out at Section 6.3.4.9 above will also be applicable to stakebuilding. Antitrust law does not just apply where all of the shares in a target company are acquired by the bidder. Most antitrust law on mergers applies where a concentration is increased and therefore the acquisition of only a small number of shares might either trigger a mandatory notification or otherwise arouse the interest of antitrust authorities. Bidders should therefore consult antitrust lawyers before engaging in any stakebuilding.

6.3.6.2 *Implications of stakebuilding*

6.223 When a bidder is considering whether or not to stakebuild and, if so, to what extent, it should be advised on the implications under a number of headings.

6.224 **6.3.6.2.1 Mandatory bids** Although Rule 5 of the Takeover Code contains a general prohibition on a bidder and its concert party acquiring more than 30% of the voting rights in the target,[167] (see paragraph 6.192 above), there are three key exemptions[168] available to bidders which apply at different times and each allow a

---

[166] Rule 14e-5(b)(11) and Rule 14e-5(b)(12) of the Securities Exchange Act of 1934.
[167] Takeover Code Rule 5.1(a).
[168] The exemptions are contained in Takeover Code Rule 5.2.

bidder and its concert parties to acquire in excess of 30% of the voting rights in the target. The table below sets out the available exemptions:

Timing	Conditions
At any time[169]	(i) the acquisition must be from a single shareholder and be the only such acquisition within any period of seven days; and (ii) the bidder must not have announced a firm intention to make an offer where that offer is subject to pre-conditions.
Immediately before the bidder announces a firm intention to make an offer[170]	(i) the acquisition must be publicly recommended by the board of the target company or the acquisition must be made with the agreement of the board of the target company; and (ii) the acquisition must be conditional upon the announcement of the bid.

After the bidder has announced a firm intention to make a bid[171]	(i) the bid must not, at the time of acquisition, be subject to a pre-condition;
	(ii) one of the following must apply:
	  (a) the target board agrees to the acquisition;
	  (b) the offer has been publicly recommended by the target (this applies even if that recommendation is subsequently withdrawn);
	  (c) after the first closing date of the bid or any competing bid (generally 21 days after the offer document has been posted) the bid or competing bid (as applicable) has been cleared by the relevant antitrust authorities, or the relevant bid is outside the scope of the relevant anti-trust laws; and
	  (d) the offer is unconditional in all respects.

6.225 As the table demonstrates, it is much easier for a bidder to rely on the exemptions in a recommended bid situation as opposed to a hostile bid situation. If a bidder relies on the exemptions in Rule 5 to acquire in excess of 30% of the voting rights in the target, then the provision of Rule 9 of the Code (mandatory offers) will apply to the bidder. A full discussion of the implications of Rule 9 are set out in Section 6.7 of this Chapter, but in broad terms, the bidder must make a bid to acquire the entirety of the equity share capital of the target. The bid for the target must be in cash or offer a full cash alternative at a price which is not less than the highest price paid by the bidder for shares of the same class during the 12 months prior to the announcement of the bid, the only condition allowed (unless the Panel consents) to the acceptance of sufficient shareholders of the offer for the bidder to hold 50% of the voting rights in the target. The Panel will also not allow a mandatory bid to be made by Scheme of Arrangement without its prior consent (paragraph 2, Appendix 7). Acquiring more than 30% of the voting rights in the target has serious implications for both the structure and content of the offer and

---

[169] Takeover Code Rule 5.2(a).
[170] Takeover Code Rule 5.2(b).
[171] Takeover Code Rule 5.2(c).

a bidder should, accordingly, carefully consider whether the provisions of Rule 9 will unduly restrict its commercial aims before acquiring in excess of 30% of the voting rights in the target.

6.226   **6.3.6.2.2 Equal treatment on quantum of consideration**   Rule 6 of the Code provides a floor for the consideration of a bid if the bidder or its concert parties have been stakebuilding during the relevant period. For these purposes, the relevant period is the period commencing three months before the offer period commences (which is the date on which an announcement is made of a proposed or possible bid for the target) and ending on the date on which the bid closes for acceptance.[172]

6.227   If the bidder or its concert parties acquire interests in shares in the relevant period prior to an announcement of a firm intention to make a bid and the bidder subsequently goes on to make a bid for the target, its offer to shareholders of the same class must not be on less favourable terms.[173] This does not mean that the bidder has to make a cash bid, even if interests in shares have been acquired in cash; the consideration must simply be at least equal to the highest relevant price paid.[174] However Rule 6 must be read alongside Rule 11 of the Code, which does regulate when a cash alternative is required (see paragraph 6.234 below).

6.228   If the bidder or its concert parties acquire interests in shares in the relevant period at above the bid price after an announcement of a firm intention to make an offer, the bidder must increase its bid to not less than the highest price paid for the interest in shares so acquired[175] and (immediately after the acquisition) announce that a revised bid will be made in accordance with Rule 6. Wherever practicable, the announcement should also state the nature of the interest, the number of shares concerned and the price paid.[176]

6.229   Rule 6 interacts with Rule 11 (requirement to make a bid with certain types of consideration) in so far as the Panel will generally regard a bidder as having complied with Rule 6 if it has complied with the provision of Rule 11 where it is required to do so.[177]

6.230   The Code provides details of how the highest price should be calculated (which varies depending on whether the interest is in the form of shares, derivatives or options). In the case of shares, the price paid is the price at which the bargain between the purchaser and the vendor is struck, excluding any stamp duty and

---

172 Takeover Code Rule 6.1(a).
173 Takeover Code Rule 6.1.
174 Takeover Code Note 3 to Rule 6.
175 Takeover Code Rule 6.2(a).
176 Takeover Code Rule 6.2(b).
177 Takeover Code Rule 6.1(a).

commission payable. If the bidder is proposing to acquire voting rights attaching to shares or general control of them at above the bid price, the Panel must be consulted in advance.[178]

The principal rationale for the rule is found in General Principle 1 of the Code **6.231** (which is derived from a General Principle of the Takeover Directive[179]) which provides that all holders of securities of the target of the same class must be afforded equal treatment. The Panel regards this general principle as fundamental to the operation of the Code and, indeed, the Panel is afforded the discretion to extend the start of the relevant period to a date prior to the date three months prior to commencement of the offer period if in the view of the Panel, there are circumstances which render such a course necessary in order to give effect to General Principle 1[180] (albeit that the Panel is unlikely to exercise such discretion unless the vendors or other parties to the relevant transaction are directors of, or other persons closely connected with, the bidder or the target company).[181] This background informs the Panel's strict interpretation of the rule. The rule will therefore apply whether or not the bidder was considering making a bid at the time when it acquired interests in shares in the target. The definition of the offer period is also interpreted strictly so that references to the 'offer period' in the rule are interpreted as any time when the company is in an offer period, whether or not the offer period was triggered by the bidder. Accordingly, if a competing bidder made a firm announcement of a bid well before the bidder had even contemplated making a bid, the relevant period could run from three months before the announcement of that rival bid.

It is not difficult to envisage circumstances where Rule 6 would operate harshly **6.232** on a bidder. A bidder could, for example, have bought shares in the market a considerable time before making a bid and in the meantime, the value of the target may have fallen significantly due to one or a combination of macro-economic factors and factors specific to the target. The Panel does have discretion to adjust Rule 6 but it will only do so in exceptional circumstances.[182] If an application is made to adjust Rule 6, the Panel has stated that the factors it will consider taking into account include:

(i)   whether the relevant acquisition was made on terms then prevailing in the market;

(ii) changes in the market price of the shares since the relevant acquisition;

(iii) the site and timing of the relevant acquisition;

---

[178] Takeover Code Note 4 to Rule 6.
[179] Takeover Directive Article 3(1)(a)T.
[180] Takeover Code Rule 6.1.
[181] Takeover Code Note 2 to Rule 6.
[182] Takeover Code Rule 6.1 and Note 1 to Rule 6.

    (iv) the attitude of the offeree board;

    (v) whether interests in shares have been acquired at high prices from directors or other persons closely connected with the bidder or the target; and

    (vi) whether a competing bid has been announced for the target.

6.233   **6.3.6.2.3 Equal treatment on form of consideration** Guided by General Principle 1 of the Code,[183] which provides that all shareholders should be treated equally, Rule 11 of the Code provides that bidders must offer the same type of consideration that they and their concert parties have used when stakebuilding.

6.234   Rule 11 firstly provides that a bidder must make a cash offer (or include a full cash alternative) at not lower than the highest price paid by the bidder or its concert parties for:

    (i) interests in any class of the target's shares in the offer period and in the 12-month period prior to the offer period where those interests in aggregate carry 10% or more of the voting rights of that class and the bidder has acquired them for cash; and

    (ii) interests in any class of the target's shares in the offer period where the bidder has acquired such shares for cash.[184]

6.235   If neither (i) nor (ii) apply then there will be no obligation to make a cash offer. (ii) is subject to (i), so if the price paid for interests in the target's shares in the 12-month period prior to the offer period commencing is higher than the price of any purchases made during the offer period and interests have been acquired which carry 10% or more of the voting rights of a class, the highest price paid in that prior period will be the reference price for the cash offer.

6.236   Rule 11 contains a number of quirks. As in the case of Rule 6, the term 'Offer Period' refers to any offer period relating to the target, not just one triggered by the bidder. In determining whether the rule applies, 'cash' also has a much wider definition than might be expected. If the bidder acquires interests in the target's shares where the bidder offers securities in exchange for such interests, such securities will be treated as cash on the basis of the value of the securities at the time of exchange unless the counterparty to the transaction is required to hold such securities until either the bid has lapsed or the bid consideration has been posted to accepting shareholders.[185] This wider definition of cash does not apply to the obligation to make an offer in cash or offer a cash alternative where that word bears its natural meaning.

---

[183] Derived from Takeover Directive Article 3(1)(a).
[184] Takeover Code Rule 11.1(a).
[185] Takeover Code Note 5 to Rule 11.1.

The Panel also has the discretion to compel the bidder to make a cash offer even where the bidder is not strictly caught by the provisions of Rule 11, if it would give effect to General Principle 1 (equality of treatment of shareholders).[186] The Panel, however, will generally only exercise this discretion where counterparties to the relevant stakebuilding transactions are directors of or persons closely connected with the bidder or the target.[187]   **6.237**

Rule 11 applies a similar (although not identical) regime where the bidder has stakebuilt by exchanging securities for interests in shares in the target. If during the offer period or in the three-month period prior to the offer period, the bidder acquires interests in shares of any class carrying 10% or more of the voting rights currently exercisable at a class meeting of that class, the bidder will be required to offer such securities to all other holders of that class.[188] The number of securities offered for each target share must be equal to the greatest number of securities received in exchange for an interest in a share of the target during the offer period or the three months prior to the offer period (and not calculated on the basis of value).[189] Given the definition of 'cash' in Rule 11 (as explained above), the bidder may have to make a cash offer as well as a securities offer as a result of stakebuilding through exchanges of securities.   **6.238**

It might be thought that a bidder could circumvent the provisions of Rule 11 by acquiring shares in the target partly in consideration for cash and partly in consideration for securities. For example, a bidder might, prior to the commencement of the offer period, be able to acquire interests in 9.99% of target shares for cash consideration and 9.99% of target shares for consideration by way of securities (supposing that such securities do not fall within the definition of cash) leaving the bidder with interests in almost 20% of the target company but no technical requirement to comply with Rule 11. The Panel, however, recognizes this loophole and states that the Panel may apply its discretion to apply Rule 11 to uphold General Principle 1 where interests in shares carrying 10% or more of the voting rights of a class have been acquired in the previous 12 months for a mixture of securities and cash. The Panel should therefore always be consulted in such cases.[190]   **6.239**

As under Rule 6, a bidder may apply to the Panel for a ruling that the highest price should not apply in a particular case.[191] The Panel has the discretion to agree an   **6.240**

---

186 Takeover Code Rule 11.1(c) T.
187 Takeover Code Note 4 to Rule 11.1.
188 Takeover Code Rule 11.2.
189 Takeover Code Note 1 to Rule 11.2.
190 Takeover Code Note 5 to Rule 11.2.
191 Takeover Code Rule 11.3.

adjusted price and the factors which it might take into account when considering such an application include:

   (i)   the size and timing of the relevant acquisitions;

   (ii)   the attitude of the board of the offeree company;

   (iii)   whether interests in shares had been acquired at high prices from directors or other persons closely connected with the bidder or the target; and

   (iv)   the number of shares in which interests had been acquired in the preceding 12 months.[192]

6.241   6.3.6.2.4 **Effect on bid**   Stakebuilding can, in certain circumstances, achieve the opposite effect to that which the bidder intends to achieve and prevent the bidder from acquiring control of 100% of the target.

6.242   On a conventional bid, a bidder will seek to utilize the compulsory acquisition provisions within the Companies Act 2006. These provisions are described in detail in Section 6.10 of this Chapter but in summary, they allow a bidder who has acquired or unconditionally contracted to acquire at least 90% in value of the target's shares and at least 90% of voting rights of the shares in each case subject to the offer, to acquire compulsorily, the remaining shares which it has not acquired pursuant to the bid.[193] If, however, a bidder and its associates have acquired shares before the making of the bid (i.e. the posting of the offer document), those shares are not shares to which the bid relates and accordingly cannot count towards the 90% threshold. It may therefore be much more difficult for the bidder to reach the thresholds which allow it to effect the squeeze-out. In contrast, shares acquired after the bid has been made (whether or not the shares are acquired though the bid or otherwise) may be counted towards the 90% target.[194]

6.243   A similar analysis applies on a scheme of arrangement. A court may sanction a scheme of arrangement if a majority in number representing 75% in value of the members or class of members, present and voting either in person or by proxy vote in favour of the arrangement at a meeting convened for the purpose.[195] For these purposes, a court will treat a bidder's shareholding as forming a different class of shares (notwithstanding that they have the same rights as the other shares) as their holders have different interests from other shareholders. Accordingly, the bidder's shares do not count towards the relevant thresholds. Indeed, by purchasing shares, the bidder is reducing the size of the stake necessary to block the transaction.

---

[192] Takeover Code Note on Rule 11.3.

[193] Companies Act 2006 section 979(1).

[194] Companies Act 2006 section 979(8).

[195] Companies Act 2006 section 899(1).

6.3.6.3 Disclosure

The Takeover Directive sets out a broad obligation on member states to establish   **6.244**
a disclosure regime in relation to bids. It provides that:

> Member States shall ensure that a bid is made public in such a way as to ensure
> market transparency and integrity for the securities of the offeree company, of the
> offeror or any other company affected by the bid, in particular in order to prevent
> the publication or dissemination of false or misleading information.[196]

This provision is complied with in the UK both through the Code and other
legislation as described below.

6.3.6.3.1 Rule 8   Rule 8 of the Code is a rule which requires disclosure of deal-   **6.245**
ings during an offer period. In the context of stakebuilding, it applies in three
main circumstances: (i) to dealings by bidders and their associates for their own
account;[197] (ii) to dealings by bidders and their associates for discretionary and
non-discretionary clients;[198] and (iii) to dealings by anyone over 1% or more.[199]
There are also rules regarding dealings in interests in the bidder's shares but this is
beyond the scope of this Chapter.

If a bidder deals in relevant securities during an offer period, it must make public   **6.246**
disclosure of such dealing. For the purposes of the rule, 'relevant securities' includes
securities of the target company which are being bid for or which carry voting
rights, equity share capital of the target company and securities of the target
company carrying conversion or subscription rights into any of the foregoing.[200]
Rule 8 requires disclosure of such dealing to be made no later than 12 noon on the
business day following the date of the transaction by submission of the relevant
information to a Regulatory Information Service in typed format by electronic
means or electronic delivery.[201] A copy must also be faxed or e-mailed to the
Panel.[202] The disclosure should follow a particular format, being set out in speci-
men disclosure forms which are available on the Panel's website.[203]

Most of the matters which are required to be disclosed are straightforward, such   **6.247**
as price paid for the relevant securities. One of the more interesting disclosures,
however, is details of relevant securities in which the person disclosing (i.e. the
bidder) is interested. This goes wider than simply dealings in relevant securities.
An interest in relevant securities could, for example, cover a cash-settled long

---

[196] Takeover Directive Article 8(1).
[197] Takeover Code Rule 8.1(a).
[198] Takeover Code Rule 8.1(b) and Rule 8.2.
[199] Takeover Code Rule 8.3.
[200] Takeover Code 'Definitions, Relevant Securities'.
[201] Takeover Code Notes 3 and 4 on Rule 8.
[202] Takeover Code Note 4 on Rule 8.
[203] Takeover Code Note 5 on Rule 8.

contract for difference, as the Code makes clear that a person who has long economic exposure, whether absolute or conditional, to changes in the price of securities will be treated as interested in those securities. The Code provides that a person will be treated as having an interest in securities if:

(i) he owns them;

(ii) he has the right (whether conditional or absolute) to exercise or direct the exercise of the voting rights attaching to them or has general control of them;

(iii) by virtue of any agreement to purchase, option or derivative he:

    (a) has the right or option to acquire them or call for their delivery; or

    (b) is under an obligation to take delivery of them, whether the right, option or obligation is conditional or absolute and whether he is in the money or otherwise; or

(iv) he is party to any derivative:

    (a) whose value is determined by reference to their price; and

    (b) which results, or may result, in his having a long position in them.[204]

6.248 Dealings by associates of bidders on their own account also need to be disclosed in the same manner.[205] The Panel explains in the Code that it is not possible to define what an associate is (largely because of the almost endless permeations of relationships in an offer). The Code, instead, sets out the menace which the rule is trying to address; that is to catch all persons (whether or not acting in concert) who directly or indirectly are interested or deal in relevant securities of the target in a bid and who have an interest or potential interest, whether commercial, financial or personal.[206] The Code then gives examples of people who will usually be associates, including directors and members of the bidding group, pension funds and employee benefit trusts of that group, any investment company managed by an associate on a discretionary basis, any company having a material trading arrangement with the bidder and any connected advisers and members of their group. This last point is often particularly important as it will usually cover the bidder's financial adviser and broker, as well as their groups. Financial advisers and brokers generally have proprietary trading desks and therefore any dealings in the target company by these desks will be caught. Most investment banks have systems in place to monitor these trades and therefore it should be relatively easy to establish what needs to be disclosed.

6.249 Dealings on behalf of clients by the bidder and any of its associates on behalf of clients will also fall to be disclosed.[207] Although such dealings will be effected

---

[204] Takeover Code Definitions, Interests in Securities.

[205] Takeover Code Rule 8.1(a).

[206] Takeover Code 'Definitions, Associate'.

[207] Takeover Code Rule 8.1(b) and Rule 8.2.

by the bidder in some circumstances (for example, where the bidder is a fund manager or an investment bank), it is most likely to be applicable to the bidder's financial adviser or broker. The manner of disclosure will depend on whether the dealing is on behalf of discretionary clients or non-discretionary (i.e. execution-only) clients. Dealings in relevant securities on behalf of discretionary clients must be disclosed in the same manner as own-account dealings, unless the associate dealing is an exempt fund manager.[208] An exempt fund manager is a person who has been approved as such by the Panel.[209] Dealings in relevant securities on behalf of non-discretionary clients or on behalf of discretionary clients by exempt fund managers must be disclosed in the same manner as own-account dealings but they must be privately disclosed instead of publicly disclosed.[210] Private disclosure means that the dealings should be notified to the Panel only (by fax or by e-mail) and not notified to a regulatory news service.

6.250 The Code also applies to situations where any person (whether or not an associate) is interested (directly or indirectly) in 1% or more of any class of relevant securities of the target company or as a result of any transaction will be interested in 1% or more.[211] In such circumstances, all dealings in any relevant securities of the target must be publicly disclosed by 3.30pm on the business day following the date of the transaction in otherwise the same manner as dealings on own-account.[212] This rule may be relevant for a bidder when stakebuilding if it has not yet made a firm announcement of a bid nor an announcement of a potential bid but the company is nonetheless in an offer period (i.e. a competing bidder has made a bid). The Rule does create the somewhat curious position that if the bidder or one of its associates has established interests in relevant securities (even if it is a significant stake), it will not have to announce that interest under Rule 8 unless and until it deals in relevant securities in the offer period. The Panel recognized this in Panel Statement 2007/15,[213] stating that a number of respondents to a previous consultation paper had argued that since one of the main purposes of Rule 8.3 is to assist shareholders in determining where voting control of a company lies, persons with interests of 1% or more in relevant securities at the commencement of an offer period should be required to disclose their positions at that time. Whilst recognizing the logic of the argument, the Code Committee noted that it would be a significant step as it would extend disclosure obligations to people who have not dealt in relevant securities. Accordingly, the Code Committee has asked the Executive to analyse the extent and nature of the interest in relevant securities

---

208 Takeover Code Rule 8.1(a).
209 Takeover Code 'Definitions, Exempt Fund Manager'.
210 Takeover Code Rule 8.2.
211 Takeover Code Rule 8.3.
212 Takeover Code Note 3 on Rule 8.
213 Panel Statement 2007/15, 'Derivatives and Options Regime 2007 Review'.

which the adoption of this suggestion would reveal. The Code Committee has not yet reported on the outcome of this analysis.

6.251   **6.3.6.3.2 Disclosure and Transparency Rules**   Whilst Rule 8 of the Code only applies during an offer period, the Disclosure and Transparency Rules (the 'DTRs') require notification of certain types of stakebuilding (beyond certain levels) at all times, whether or not a listed company is in an offer period.

6.252   The DTRs are made by the FSA under Part VI of FSMA and implement the European Transparency Directive.[214] As a result of the Transparency Directive, there are now similar regimes for the disclosure of major shareholdings across the European Union (albeit that some member states' interpretation of the Transparency Directive has proved to be particularly idiosyncratic).

6.253   In the UK, the voteholder and issuer notification parts of the DTRs apply to:

(i)   a company with shares admitted to trading on a regulated market and where the home member state is the United Kingdom;[215] and

(ii)   a public company as defined in section 4(2) of the Companies Act 2006 and any other body corporate incorporated in and having a principal place of business in the United Kingdom whose shares are admitted to trading on a prescribed market.[216]

6.254   If a bidder is stakebuilding in a target which falls into either of those two categories, it must consider whether or not it has an obligation to notify its acquisitions (and disposals) under the DTRs. The purpose of the notification regime is to identify both to the company and to the market the persons controlling the way in which voting rights are exercised. Accordingly, the notification obligation arises for the bidder if it acquires or disposes of shares or certain financial instruments and, as a result of the acquisition or disposal, the percentage of voting rights it holds in the target company (either as shareholder or through its direct or indirect holdings of relevant financial instruments) reaches, exceeds or falls below certain disclosure thresholds.[217] Those disclosure thresholds will depend on whether the target company is a UK issuer or a non-UK issuer.

6.255   A company is a non-UK issuer if its shares are admitted to trading on a regulated market and its home member state is the United Kingdom but it is neither a public company within the meaning of section 4(2) of the Companies Act 2006 nor

---

[214] Directive 2004/109/EC of the European Parliament and of the Council of 15 December 2004 on the harmonisation of transparency requirements in relation to information about issuers whose securities are admitted to trading on a regulated market and amending Directive 2001/34/EC.

[215] DTR 5.1.1(1)R.

[216] DTR 5.1.1(2)R.

[217] DTR 5.1.2R.

a company which is otherwise incorporated in, and whose principal place of business is in the United Kingdom.[218]

The disclosure thresholds for shareholdings in UK issuers are 3% and each whole   **6.256**
percentage figure above 3%,[219] whereas the disclosure thresholds for non-UK
issuers are set at 5, 10, 15, 20, 25, 30, 50 and 75%.[220]

If the bidder is obliged to make a notification and the target is admitted to trading   **6.257**
on a regulated market, the bidder must submit its notification to each of the issuer
and the FSA[221] using the prescribed Form TR-1 (which can be found on the
FSA's website).[222] If the target is admitted to trading on a prescribed market,
the notification only has to be made to the target[223] (and not to the FSA) and the
notification does not have to be made using Form TR-1 (although it is advisable
to use Form TR1 so as to ensure that all of the relevant information is included).
A notification, whether the target company is admitted to trading on a regulated
market or a prescribed market, must contain the following information:

(i)   the resulting situation in terms of voting rights;
(ii) the chain of controlled undertakings through which voting rights are
      effectively held, if applicable;
(iii) the date on which the threshold was reached or crossed; and
(iv) the identity of the shareholder, even if that shareholder is not entitled to
      exercise voting rights and of the person entitled to exercise voting rights on
      behalf of that shareholder.[224]

If the notification arises from the holding of financial instruments, it must include   **6.258**
the following information:

(i)   the resulting situation in terms of voting rights;
(ii)   if applicable, the claim of controlled undertakings through which financial
       informants are effectively held;
(iii) the date on which the threshold was reached or crossed;
(iv)   for instruments with an exercise period, an indication of the date or time
       period when shares will or can be acquired, if applicable;
(v)   date of maturity or expiration of the instrument;
(vi)   identity of the holder; and
(vii) name of the underlying issuer.[225]

---

[218] DTR 5.1.1R.
[219] DTR 5.1.2(1)R.
[220] DTR 5.1.2(2)R.
[221] DTR 5.1.2R and DTR 5.9R.
[222] DTR 5.8.10R.
[223] DTR 5.1.2R.
[224] DTR 5.8.1R.
[225] DTR 5.8.2R.

6.259   For financial instruments having similar economic effects to (but which are not) qualifying financial instruments (as explained in paragraph 6.266 below) the person making the notification must do so on a delta-adjusted basis, that is, in relation to the underlying shares referenced, only in the proportion which is equal to the delta of the instrument at any particular point in time.[226]

6.260   The notification must be made within two trading days of the trade if made to a UK target and within four trading days if made to a non-UK issuer.[227]

6.261   A UK-issuer (unless it is admitted to trading on a prescribed but not a regulated market) then must make public all of the information contained in the notification by no later than the end of the trading day following receipt of the notification.[228] A non-UK issuer and any other issuer whose shares are admitted to trading on a prescribed but not a regulated market has the same obligation save that it must comply with the obligation by no later than the end of the third trading day following receipt of the notification.[229]

6.262   The timings of the notifications do allow a bidder a limited period of time to stakebuild above the thresholds before the target (and the market) is informed of their dealing. The DTRs, however, serve to put a significant barrier in the way of the bidder building up a significant stake over the medium to long term. Absent the DTRs, a bidder would probably not want to buy a significant number of shares in the market over a short period of time as this would most likely drive the share price up. Instead, it might consider making smaller purchases over a longer period of time, building up a significant stake without moving the price. The disclosure required under the DTRs makes it much more difficult for a bidder to do this. Bidders may, therefore, be forced into doing the vast majority of their stakebuilding in a very short window, most likely at or around the time of announcement of its bid.

6.263   The indirect shareholding rules in the DTRs seek to prevent the circumvention of the notification rules through the establishment of structures or arrangements which would otherwise escape notification if the rules only related to direct shareholdings. In the context of a bid, the three most important forms of indirect shareholding are (i) through a chain of controlled undertakings;[230] (ii) where a third party holds voting rights in his own name on behalf of a person;[231] or (iii) a concert party holding.[232] The DTRs provide that a person must aggregate its

---

[226] DTR 5.8.2(4)R.
[227] DTR 5.8.3R.
[228] DTR 5.8.2(1)R.
[229] DTR 5.8.12(2)R.
[230] DTR 5.2.1(e)R.
[231] DTR 5.2.1(g)R.
[232] DTR 5.2.1(a)R.

holdings with those of any undertaking controlled by it. A 'controlled undertaking' is defined as in section 420 of the FSMA (excluding section 420(2)(b)) by reference to section 1162 and Schedule 7 to the Companies Act 2006. Under section 1162(2) and (4), a person controls an undertaking where it:

(i) holds the majority of the voting rights;

(ii) is a member of the undertaking and has the right to appoint or remove a majority of the board of directors;

(iii) has the right to exercise dominant influence or control over the undertaking:

(a) by virtue of provisions contained in the undertaking's memorandum or articles; or

(b) by virtue of a control contract; or

(iv) is a member of the undertaking and controls alone, pursuant to an agreement with other shareholders or members, a majority of the voting rights in the undertaking; or

(v) if it has the power to exercise or actually exercises, dominant influence or control over it; or

(vi) it and the subsidiary are managed on a unified basis.

The definition means that a bidder acquiring shares through one or more vehicles will still have to disclose its true identity. The bidder cannot be hidden behind other purchase vehicles. The bidder cannot similarly have a third party purchase the shares for it without having to disclose that interest. Finally, the 'concert party' interest is where a third party holds voting rights in the target and the bidder concludes an agreement with them, which obliges them to adopt, by concerted exercise of the voting rights they hold, a lasting common policy towards the management of the target company. **6.264**

If the bidder acquires financial instruments rather than shares in the target, then some additional factors need to be taken into account before it can be established that their acquisition falls due for notification. Firstly, the instruments need to be qualifying financial instruments or have similar economic effect to a financial instrument.[233] Financial instruments is very widely defined by Section C of Annex 1 of MiFID and includes any transferable securities, options, futures, swaps, forward rate agreements and any other derivative contracts. To be qualifying financial instruments, the instruments must result in an entitlement, on the bidder's own initiative alone, under a formal agreement (which means an agreement which is binding under applicable law) to shares to which voting rights are attached, already issued of the target.[234] Secondly, the bidder must enjoy, **6.265**

---

[233] DTR 5.3.1(1)R.
[234] DTR 5.3.2(1)R.

on maturity either the unconditional right to acquire the underlying shares or the discretion as to his right to acquire such shares or not. [235]

6.266 Previously, the obvious lacuna in the legislation was that that it did not catch stakebuilding using certain derivative instruments such as cash-settled CFDs as they do not confer voting rights or the right to acquire voting rights. This has now been remedied by the inclusion within the DTRs of financial instruments which have a similar economic effect to qualifying financial instruments. Accordingly, CFDs are now discloseable under the DTRs.

6.267 Although it is not an offence in itself for a bidder to fail to disclose an interest in shares, the FSA has the power to impose such penalty as it considers appropriate on a bidder if it considers that the bidder has contravened the disclosure and transparency rules.[236] The FSA also has other powers under Part 6 of FSMA to make public information that shareholders are required to publicize but fail to do so and to call for information and documents. Accordingly, a bidder should always take advice as to whether it should make disclosure of dealings in shares or financial instruments in the target under the DTRs.

6.268 **6.3.6.3.3 The Companies Act**   The bidder may be forced into making a disclosure following a request from the target. Under section 793 of the Companies Act 2006, the target is permitted to give notice to any person that it knows or has reasonable cause to believe to be interested in its shares or to have been so interested at any time during the three years immediately preceding the date on which the notice is issued (the 'relevant period').[237] This also has the potential to prevent the bidder from hiding behind nominee companies.

6.269 The notice served by the target may require a person to do any of the following:[238]

(i) confirm or deny that it is interested in the company's shares or that it has been so interested in any time in the last three years;

(ii) provide details of the identity of persons interested in the shares in question in the pelevant period and whether persons interested in the same shares are or were parties to:

(a) an agreement to which section 824 of the Companies Act applies (section 824 relates to an agreement between two or more persons that includes provision for the acquisition by any one or more of them of interests in shares of a public company); or

(b) an agreement or arrangement relating to the exercise of any rights conferred by the holding of the shares;

---

[235] DTR 5.3.2(2)R.
[236] FSMA 2000 section 91(1B).
[237] Companies Act 2006 section 793(1).
[238] Companies Act 2006 section 793(2)–(6).

(iii)   if the relevant person's interest is a present interest and another interest in the shares subsists or another interest in the shares subsisted during the relevant period, to give, so far as lies within the knowledge, such particulars set out in (ii) (a) and (b) above with respect to that other interest as may be required by the notice; and

(iv)   where the person's interest is a past interest, to give (so far as lies within his knowledge) particulars of the identity of the person who held that interest immediately upon his ceasing to hold it.

The addressee of the notice has to respond within such a reasonable time as may be specified in the notice.[239] Failure to comply with such a notice or if, in reply to a notice, the addressee of the notice makes a statement that he knows to be false in a material particular or recklessly makes a statement that is false in a material particular, is a criminal offence,[240] punishable by up to two years' imprisonment.[241] The target also has a remedy if the addressee fails to comply with the notice. The target may apply for an order directing that the shares the subject of the notice be subject to restrictions.[242] The effect of a court order to this effect is that any transfer of the shares is void, no voting rights are exercisable in respect of the shares, no further shares may be issued in right of the shares or in pursuance of an offer made to their holder and except in a liquidation, no payment may be made of sums due from the target on the share, whether in respect of capital or otherwise.   **6.270**

6.4 Preparation for Takeover—Target

6.4.1 Introduction

A listed company must be ready to respond to a takeover approach at all times. In some cases, the target will be in charge of the bid process (such as where it solicits potential purchasers for the target). In other circumstances, the approach may be entirely unexpected. Often the first time that the target will become aware of a potential bid is when the bidder telephones the chairman of the target to inform him that the bidder intends to make a bid. Following an approach, the target will have to react very quickly, firstly in deciding whether or not to recommend the bid and then, if it does not recommend the bid, defending any hostile bid.   **6.271**

The defence of a hostile bid is considered more fully in Section 6.8 of this Chapter but, in essence, a target's defence to a hostile bid will be based primarily on financial information. This information should be prepared in advance of a bid, as a   **6.272**

---

[239] Companies Act 2006 section 793(7).
[240] Companies Act 2006 section 795(1).
[241] Companies Act 2006 section 795(2).
[242] Companies Act 2006 section 794(1).

target will only have 14 days to publish its defence document after an offer document is published. Clearly, this information may have to be updated at the relevant time but the target should, at all times, be satisfied that it has processes in place which enable this information to be pulled together at relatively short notice.

6.4.2 Ongoing process—the 'black book'

6.273 The start of a bid process can be chaotic and such an atmosphere is not conducive to clarity of thought. Accordingly, many listed companies have a defence manual (known as a 'black book') prepared by a combination of its lawyers and financial advisers which sets out at a high level the action required and the issues which need to be addressed by the board of a listed company and its advisers prior to or in the event of an announcement of a bid for that company. The black book cannot be expected to cover every eventuality, as every takeover is different and it is impossible to predict with any accuracy the sequence of events in any given takeover. The black book, nonetheless, provides administrative and logistical help and a broad overview of the possible defence strategies which might be used.

6.274 Although a black book will have to be tailored for each listed company, an example of the types of information that could be covered is set out in the table below:

PART A: process management	
• Key do's and don'ts:	This section might cover matters such as secrecy, proper conduct in the transaction, announcement and disclosure obligations, dealings in securities and misleading information.
• Initial phone call:	This section is intended to assist the chairman or chief executive in dealing with an initial approach. It should contain key do's and don'ts and scripted responses to various scenarios (perhaps including decision trees).
• Principal contact list:	This section should simply be a list of the addresses, telephone numbers and email addresses of the key individuals within the company and advisers to the company who would need to be alerted on a bid.
• Telephone cascade:	This section should set out in as an efficient manner as possible how each member of the defence team is to be contacted about the bid.
• Board agendas:	An agenda should be prepared for the initial board meeting (broadly covering the bid, strategy and administration) and a standing agenda for daily bid committee meetings.
• Outline timetable/ action list:	A detailed timeline should be set out which assumes that the target will reject the bid. It should set out key milestone dates such as the last date for the dispatch of a defence document. A very detailed timetable should be prepared for the day on which an approach is received.
• Key responsibilities:	This section should allocate key responsibilities between the board committee, the chairman, the chief executive and other relevant individuals.
• Responses to media:	Some brief responses to media questions in relation to bids should be formulated.

(Continued)

PART B: situation analysis

• Valuation position:	The target's financial adviser should prepare a current valuation of the target (this must be kept up to date).
• Summary of potential bidders:	This section should analyse potential bidders, including synergies and their strengths and weaknesses.
• Bid response options:	This section should set out factors which should help to determine the target's response and set out each of the likely options.

PART C: supplementary materials

• Public announcements:	Draft alternative announcements covering the situation where the target is uncertain as to its reaction to an offer and where the target is rejecting the offer should be included as well as an announcement of the number of securities in issue at the start of the offer period.
• Employee communication:	An email should be included to be sent by the chief group executive to all employees as soon as an announcement has been made.
• Shareholder communication:	A letter specifying the matters set out in Rule 2.6 of the Code should be included.
• Directors' responsibility statements:	As the directors may have to take responsibility for a number of documents in the offer period, responsibility statements should be included.
• Directors' powers of attorney:	A number of documents may have to be signed during the offer period and therefore (as the directors may be away or unavailable) it is important that they give a power of attorney. A form of power of attorney should be included in the black book.
• Memorandum on legal and regulatory obligations during a bid:	This section should be a non-exhaustive outline of the legal and regulatory requirements on a bid as it is very important that the directors are informed of these at the beginning of the offer period.

6.275 All listed companies should regularly review their black book to ensure that it is up to date on all matters. Sections that will be particularly important to update include contact details and valuations.

6.4.3 Advisers

6.276 The target will appoint advisers in the same manner as the bidder (see Section 6.3.2 of this Chapter for details of those advisers) and those advisers will provide a broadly similar role for the target.

6.277 The only key difference is that the target is required under the Code to obtain competent independent advice on any offer.[243] The person providing such advice is known as a Rule 3 adviser. The Panel requires the Rule 3 adviser to have a sufficient degree of independence from the bidder to ensure that the advice given is properly objective.[244] The Code also requires that the Rule 3 adviser has no

---

[243] Takeover Code Rule 3.1.
[244] Takeover Code Note 1 to Rule 3.3.

conflict of interest with either the bidder or the target.[245] Appendix 3 to the Code gives guidance to potential Rule 3 advisers to help them to establish whether or not there is a conflict of interest.

6.4.4 Financial preparation

6.278 One of the key battlegrounds on a hostile bid will concern arguments surrounding the financial performance of the target. The target should therefore at all times have all of the relevant information to hand or processes to enable that information to be pulled together at relatively short notice.

6.279 A target may have to produce a profit forecast and perhaps an asset valuation on a hostile bid (principally to demonstrate that the bid undervalues the target). In order to enable it to do this at short notice, it should review regularly its budgets for the coming year and ensure that its business plan is up to date. This will enable it to give solid reasons for any profit forecast. The target should speak to its financial advisers to ensure that its business plans are realistic and, along with its assumptions underlying the forecasts (such as interest rates and exchange rates), continue to be accurate. The target's auditors should also confirm that they are happy with the basis on which a profit forecast is to be prepared. Finally, the target should identify any public statements which might be profit forecasts, as they would have to be reported on in the course of a bid.

6.280 A target is only likely to have to prepare an asset valuation where, although the bid is above the prevailing market price, it undervalues the assets of the target. It should produce a preliminary rough valuation of each part of the business separately on a break-up basis. The target should also have an independent valuer in mind if it needs to produce an asset valuation on a bid.

6.281 The target should also consider regularly compiling alternative methods of valuing the target, such as long-term shareholder value or benchmarking against sector, as these measures may give more favourable comparisons, which can be used in defence documents.

6.282 The target should also consider certain other matters as part of its financial preparations. It should review regularly its accounting policies to ensure that they are neither too bullish nor too conservative as the bidder may challenge them. If the target is a company which requires a significant amount of capital expenditure and investment, this should be reviewed regularly. The target should also review more complicated financial matters such as pension funding. Finally, it should consider how quickly financial information such as management accounts and projections can be produced.

---

[245] Takeover Code Rule 3.3.

6.4.5 Relations with major shareholders, analysts and the press

A target board should keep good relations with its shareholders at all times. If rela- **6.283**
tions between the board and its key shareholders are good then such shareholders
are more likely to follow the target board's recommendation if a bid is made. The
target board can seek to do this by consulting regularly with its shareholders,
whether through investor days, presentations to institutional shareholders or one-
on-one meetings. It should seek to provide shareholders with transparency and
clarity in relation to the target's business and its shares and note and seek to address
(if appropriate) any concerns which such shareholders raise.

Analysts may have a significant effect on the perception of the target company in **6.284**
the market as they can either help to support the target company's valuations
through the research notes which they produce or create a more negative impression of the target in the market (including amongst the target company's shareholders who will ultimately decide the outcome of the bid). Accordingly, the
target should seek to establish good relations with the analysts which follow it,
including being open with them, providing them with sufficient information and
reviewing the research notes which they produce. The target should consider
whether it will focus on a smaller group of influential analysts or keep a wider
circle.

For similar reasons, the target needs to maintain good relations with the press, as **6.285**
adverse publicity may lessen the chances of the target company board being able
to defend the bid successfully. Whilst seeking to achieve positive press coverage,
the target company board should avoid contradictory or inaccurate information
appearing in the press. It will also not want unauthorized information to be disclosed, neither will it want to have information in the press which has unintended
consequences (such as an inadvertent profit forecast). Accordingly, the target
company should appoint a press spokesman who has been trained on these issues
to deal with the press.

6.4.6 Market monitoring

A target should monitor trading in its shares as this may give it some prior warning **6.286**
that an approach is likely to be forthcoming. The target should enlist the help of
its registrars and brokers to see who is purchasing shares and interests in shares
and look out for unusual trading patterns and market movements. This may help
alert the target to stakebuilding, although stakebuilding ahead of an announcement of an intention to make a firm bid for the target is less common now than it
has been historically.

As well as examining who is buying shares in the market, the target should moni- **6.287**
tor the shareholdings of substantial shareholders. If they are selling, it may be an
indication that they are unhappy or they would accept a bid. The target would be

well advised in these circumstances to arrange a meeting with or otherwise contact that shareholder to gain comfort that the shareholder would not support a bid.

6.288   There are number of provisions at law which may help the target to monitor who has interests in its shares.

6.4.6.1 *Section 793 of the Companies Act*

6.289   If new shareholders are entered onto the register and their identity is not immediately apparent (for example, if the shares are held through a nominee account), the Companies Act allows the company to send a notice to the legal holder requiring it to, *inter alia*, confirm who holds the beneficial interest in the target's shares. Section 793 requests are discussed in detail at Section 6.3.4.5 of this Chapter.

6.4.6.2 *Inspection of registers*

6.290   Section 116 of the Companies Act allows anyone to inspect a company's share register. A target must respond to a request to inspect its register within five days of the request being made[246] (unless it can demonstrate to a court that the request is for an improper purpose).[247] Similarly, anyone may request a copy of the register of interests disclosed pursuant to section 793 notices[248] (this is also subject to court approval if the company makes an application on the grounds of improper purpose for the request).[249] If the target's registrars receive a request for inspection of either register, it should pass such request to the target immediately.

6.291   If the target identifies a potential bidder through these processes, it should instruct its brokers to investigate further whether that party is actually preparing a bid. This will include following market rumour and unusual patterns of trading or movement in the target's share price. Indications can also be given by the potential bidder having cancelled presentations with its analysts or delayed or changed the date of its results. Contra-indicators include directors of the potential bidder dealing in the potential bidder's shares, as they are likely to be prevented from doing this if the bidder is considering making a bid because of the market abuse and insider dealing regimes.

6.4.7 Duties of the target board

6.292   The duties of the target board will be relevant in considering a bid. These are discussed in detail in Section 6.8 of this Chapter.

---

[246] Companies Act 2006 section 117(1).
[247] Companies Act 2006 section 117(3).
[248] Companies Act 2006 section 811(1).
[249] Companies Act 2006 section 812(4) and (5).

6.4.8 Defensive tactics

The post-bid aspects of defensive tactics are discussed in Section 6.8 of this Chapter. Pre-bid, the defensive tactics of a target will largely involve the financial preparations set out above. The target should also examine its other strengths and weaknesses, such as threats and opportunities and likely changes to market share. **6.293**

One other specific defensive tactic which a target may consider from the outset is the use of a 'poison pill'. The term 'poison pill' is not a term of art but rather is used in practice to describe any issue that can be used to dissuade a bidder from launching a bid. The term originated in the United States where such frustrating action is more popular. In particular, the term 'poison pill' often refers to structural changes to the company's constitution which take effect on a change of control and are detrimental to the bidder's efforts. The term could, however, catch anything that could be adverse to the bidder's efforts to achieve a change of control. For example, the target board agreeing to a termination right on a change of control in a material contract. **6.294**

It is a general principle of the Takeover Directive that the board of the target must not act in a way to deny target shareholders the opportunity to decide on the merits of a bid.[250] The principle has long existed in the Code and is embodied within Rule 16. Rule 16 is considered further in Section 6.9.8 of this Chapter. Rule 16 applies however, only when a bid is existence or in contemplation. Outside of that timeframe, however, issues still arise. **6.295**

Before the target enters into any arrangement, the directors of the target will have to consider their fiduciary duties. In particular, the directors have a duty to promote the success of the target company for the benefit of its members as a whole.[251] The generally accepted position is that this is a duty to promote long-term value for shareholders. It is relatively easy to show this in the context of a wider agreement, for example, where the target company concedes a change of control provision in a major commercial contract or a debt facility because those documents clearly have corporate benefit. The motivation of the directors in seeking to enter into an arrangement which could be considered a 'poison pill' is not a relevant consideration. In *Criterion Properties Plc v Stratford UK Properties LLC & Others*,[252] the High Court found on the facts that the joint venture agreement was clearly to subject the applicant to a contingent crippling of its commercial interests in order to deter an unwanted predator. The House of Lords held that the conscience of the directors was not a relevant consideration at law; the matter could only turn **6.296**

---

[250] Takeover Directive Article 3(1)(c).
[251] Companies Act 2006 section 172.
[252] [2004] UKHL 28.

on whether the directors had either actual or apparent authority to conclude the agreement.

6.297 It is questionable as to whether arms-length commercial contracts actually work in practice as poison pills, as the counterparty to the agreement will usually want to retain the benefit of the agreement. It would only be in circumstances where the counterparty was looking to terminate the agreement and the agreement was fundamental to the business that it would work well in practice. The one exception is debt where the lending banks may wish to use the change of control as an exit mechanism or a mechanism to renegotiate a deal. In practice however, this is less of a poison pill as most bidders will presume that the target debt will need to be re-financed and will have built that into their model and financing.

6.298 Entrenched rights in the target company's articles of association are much more likely to be effective. To insert such provisions, the target's shareholders will have to approve the changes by special resolution. In the UK, institutional shareholders have been reluctant to approve such arrangements because they often consider it in their interests for the target company to be subject to a bid (they are, therefore, generally hostile to defensive steps). Accordingly, such structural poison pills are not at all common in UK companies.

6.5 The Offer Process

6.5.1 Contractual offer and acceptance

6.299 Traditionally, takeover bids undertaken in the UK have been made by way of contractual offer by the bidder to target shareholders (although schemes of arrangement are now more commonly used; see Section 6.6.6 below for a description of the principal differences between an offer and a scheme of arrangement).

6.5.1.1 *Contract formation*

6.300 In the UK, formation of a legally binding contract is incumbent upon the presence of four key elements: offer, acceptance, consideration and intention to create legal relations. Contract formation is defeated by the absence of any one of these elements.

6.5.1.2 *Offer*

6.301 An offer is a promise by one party to enter into a legally binding commitment. The offer itself must be capable of acceptance and be sufficiently certain so that a court is capable of enforcing its terms.

6.302 In a takeover bid, the offer by the bidder to target shareholders to purchase their shares is made by way of offer document. The offer document sets out the terms of the bid, including, amongst other terms, the price being offered by the bidder for target shares (on a price per share basis) and the form that the consideration will take. The contents of an offer document are considered in further detail at Section 6.5.4.7 below.

6.5.1.3 *Acceptance*

6.303 A binding contract will only be formed when an offer is accepted. Target shareholders must accept the bidder's offer, in accordance with the acceptance procedure contemplated by the offer document in order to take advantage of it. As with an offer, acceptance must be sufficiently certain so that a court is capable of enforcing it.

6.304 As an offer is only binding once the target shareholder has communicated its acceptance of the offer to the bidder, target shareholders should be careful to comply with the precise acceptance procedure contained in the offer document.

6.5.1.4 *Consideration*

6.305 Consideration must pass between contracting persons in order for a contract to be enforceable unless the contract is made by way of deed. A deed is enforceable notwithstanding an absence of consideration.

6.306 In the context of a contractual takeover bid, consideration is provided by the bidder who promises to pay an amount per share to each accepting target shareholder. Target shareholders make a reciprocal promise by accepting the offer, thereby contracting to sell their shares (or a portion of them) to the bidder on the terms and at the price stated in the offer document.

6.5.1.5 *Intention to create legal relations*

6.307 Without an intention of the parties to create legal relations, there can be no contract.

6.308 Although intention is usually assessed on an objective standard, namely whether a reasonable person would regard the contract as legally binding,[253] there is, in relation to commercial contracts, a rebuttable presumption that the parties intend to be legally bound.[254] In the context of contractual takeover offers, disputes are rare over whether or not there existed, at the moment of acceptance of the contract, an intention to create legal relations.

6.5.1.6 *Termination of contractual offers*

6.309 As an offer is usually revocable, termination can be effected in a variety of ways, including lapse of time, rejection of the offer by the recipient or withdrawal of the

---

[253] *Merritt v Merritt* [1970] 1 WLR 1211.
[254] *Edwards v Skyways* [1964] 1 All ER 494.

offer (at any time up to the time at which it is accepted) by the person who made the offer. Failure to satisfy a condition precedent to a bid may also constitute effective termination of the bid.

6.310   In the context of a takeover, a bid may lapse or be rejected by target shareholders. Although acceptances of the offer by target shareholders may in certain circumstances be withdrawn, the bidder may not withdraw a contractual offer unless a condition is invoked.

6.5.2 Alternative structures: schemes of arrangement

6.311   Schemes of arrangement are discussed in Section 6.6 of this Chapter.

6.5.3 Role of the target board

6.312   The most significant decision facing the directors of the target will be whether or not to recommend the bid to their shareholders. In determining whether or not to make such a recommendation, the target's directors must try to balance their statutory duty to act in the best interests of the company with the interests of the current shareholders in the target. The difficulty facing the target's directors in balancing the short-term interests of the target's current shareholders and the longer-term interests of the company itself is explored in greater detail in the context of hostile offers at Section 6.8.4.1 of this Chapter.

6.313   The Takeover Directive requires the target to draw up and make public a document setting out its opinion of the bid and the reasons on which it is based, including its views on certain specified matters.[255] These provisions are reflected in the Code. Accordingly, once the target's board has reached a decision on whether or not to recommend the bid, target directors must circulate to target shareholders their opinion on the bid.[256] This must include the views of the target board on the effects of the implementation of the bid on all of the target's interests, including employment and the bidder's strategic plans for the target, including the repercussions of such on the employment and locations of the target's places of business. The target board must state its reasons for forming its opinion. In addition, the statement circulated by the target board must include the substance of any advice given to the board by its independent financial adviser.

6.314   Practically, where the directors of the target decide to recommend the bid, the target board's opinion, views and advice will be contained in the offer document itself and the target's directors must take responsibility for that information. In circumstances in which the board's views on the bid are split however, the directors

---

[255] Takeover Code Article 9(5).
[256] Takeover Code Rule 25.1.

in the minority should also publish their views.[257] The target board's obligations in respect of hostile takeover situations are examined at Section 6.8.4.1 of this Chapter.

6.5.4 Process

6.5.4.1 Overview

It is of crucial importance to both target and bidder that the moment at which the target enters an offer period is identified with certainty, as it is from that moment that many of the rules set out in the Code take effect. A discussion of the meaning of offer period is set out at Section 6.2.2 of this Chapter.   **6.315**

A list of all those companies currently in an offer period is available on the Panel's website (http://www.thetakeoverpanel.org.uk).   **6.316**

6.5.4.2 Leak announcements

Notwithstanding that secrecy must be maintained before an announcement and that all persons must conduct themselves so as to minimize the chances of an accidental leak of information,[258] there can be situations in which the fact of or information about a potential bid finds its way into the market. Equally, the target may find itself the subject of market rumour or may experience an unexpected and marked fluctuation in its share price. The bidder must therefore make sure it is aware of when an announcement of a bid or a potential bid is required and it must be ready to release such announcement without delay.   **6.317**

The circumstances in which an announcement is required are as follows:[259]   **6.318**

(i)   when a firm intention to make a bid (which is not or is no longer subject to any pre-conditions) is notified to the target board from a serious source, irrespective of the attitude of the board to the bid;

(ii)   immediately upon an acquisition of any interest in shares which gives rise to an obligation to make a bid under Rule 9 (mandatory offers);

(iii)   when, following an approach to the target, the target is the subject of rumour and speculation or there is an untoward movement in its share price;

(iv)   when, before an approach has been made, the target is the subject of rumour and speculation or there is an untoward movement in its share price and there are reasonable grounds for concluding that it is the potential bidder's actions (whether through inadequate security or otherwise) which have led to the situation;

---

257 Takeover Code Note 2 to Rule 25.1.
258 Takeover Code Rule 2.1.
259 Takeover Code Rule 2.2(a) to (f).

(v)   when negotiations or discussions relating to a possible bid are about to be extended to include more than a very restricted number of people (outside those who need to know in the parties concerned and their immediate advisers); or

(vi)   when a purchaser is being sought for an interest, or interests, in shares carrying in aggregate 30% or more of the voting rights of a company or when the board of a company is seeking one or more potential bidders, and:

(a)   the company is the subject of rumour and speculation or there is an untoward movement in its share price; or

(b)   the number of potential purchasers or bidders approached is about to be increased to include more than a very restricted number of people.

6.319   With the exception of 6.318 (i) and 6.318 (ii) above,[260] the circumstances highlighted above describe situations in which an external influence or an otherwise seemingly inconsequential action of either the bidder or the target may trigger the requirement to announce. Announcements made in these circumstances are known as 'leak announcements'.

6.320   As detailed above at 6.318 (v),[261] an announcement is required when negotiations or discussions are about to extend to include more than a very restricted number of people. Further details of what this means are set out at Section 6.3.1 of this Chapter.

6.321   In circumstances where there is rumour in the market, there is no requirement for an announcement to be made confirming that there is no truth to the rumour or speculation that an offer might be made for the target.[262]

6.322   Whether an announcement is required in accordance with any of the limbs of Rule 2.2 of the Code depends on whether there has been an untoward movement in the target's share price. The Panel will determine whether this is the case in light of all the relevant facts and not solely by reference to the absolute percentage movement in price of the target's shares.[263] It is therefore crucial to consult with the Panel in such cases.

6.323   The Panel should, however, as a general rule of thumb, in relation to the circumstance detailed at 6.318 (iii) above,[264] be consulted at the latest when the target becomes the subject of any rumour or speculation or where there is a price movement of 10% or more above the lowest share price since the time of the

---

[260]   Takeover Code Rule 2.2 (a).
[261]   Takeover Code Rule 2.2(e).
[262]   Panel Practice Statement No 20, paragraphs 4.11 and 5.12.
[263]   Takeover Code Note 1 to rule 2.2.
[264]   Takeover Code Rule 2.2(c).

approach or the day on which the bidder first actively considered making an offer. Equally the Panel may consider a price spike of, for example, 5% in one day as untoward.[265]

6.324 Similarly, in respect of the circumstances detailed at 6.318 (iv) and (vi) above,[266] the Panel should be consulted at the latest when the target becomes the subject of any rumour or speculation or where there is a material abrupt movement in its share price after the time when:

(i) in the case of 6.318 (iv) above,[267] a bid was first actively considered; or
(ii) in the case of 6.318 (vi) above,[268] either the potential seller or the board started to seek one or more potential purchasers or bidders.

6.325 From a practical perspective, in order to effectively calculate movements in the target's share price for the purpose of ascertaining whether an announcement is required, the bidder (or where it has been appointed, its financial adviser) must ensure that it has established:

(i) the date on which the bidder first actively considered making a bid for the target; and
(ii) the target's share price on that day.

6.326 Establishing the above parameters will set the 'floor' price from which the bidder or its financial adviser will be able to calculate movements in the target's share price. In respect of assessing daily price spikes, the previous day's closing price for the target shares should be used.

6.327 Prior to an approach, it is the bidder's and its financial adviser's responsibility to monitor whether a requirement to announce arises and to consult with the Panel is necessary.[269] Following an approach, this responsibility shifts to the target (which will adopt the date of approach as the date from which to calculate share price movements). In circumstances in which the bidder's proposals are unequivocally rejected, the primary responsibility for monitoring whether an announcement is required reverts to the bidder.[270] Where there is any doubt as to which party is responsible, the Panel should be consulted.[271]

6.328 In assessing for the purpose of ascertaining responsibility what constitutes 'an approach', the Executive have stated that although each case will turn on its own

---

265 Takeover Code Note 1 to Rule 2.2.
266 Takeover Code Rule 2.2(d) and rule 2.2(f).
267 Takeover Code Rule 2.2(d).
268 Takeover Code Rule 2.2(f).
269 Takeover Code Rule 2.3.
270 Panel Practice Statement No 20, paragraph 3.3.
271 Panel Practice Statement No 20, paragraph 3.3.

facts, it will interpret the term broadly.[272] Normally, it will consider an approach to have taken place when a director or representative of, or an adviser to, a target is informed by, or on behalf of, a potential bidder that it is considering the possibility of making a bid for the target.[273] This is the case, even if the approach constitutes a preliminary stage, informal contact where the potential terms of the bid are no more than broadly indicative.[274]

6.329   Where an announcement obligation arises but where the bidder is not yet ready to announce a 'firm intention' to make a bid, the announcement of a possible bid[275] may be made. Alternatively, where the bidder does not intend to make a bid,[276] a statement to that effect may be made.

6.330   If an announcement of a possible bid is to be made, the announcement obligation will be satisfied by the release of a brief announcement stating that talks are taking place or that a potential bidder is considering making a bid.[277] The announcement should, however, include a summary of the provisions of Rule 8 of the Code (Disclosure of dealing during the offer period).

6.331   Any person making a statement that he does not intend to make a bid for a company must do so in clear and unambiguous terms and[278] in any event where a statement of an intention not to make a bid is contemplated, the person making that statement should be reminded of the consequences flowing from it. Importantly, following such an announcement, neither the person making the statement, nor any person who acted in concert with him (or any person subsequently acting in concert with him) may within six months from the date of the statement, *inter alia*, announce a bid or potential bid for the target which would result in the bidder or persons acting in concert with it being interested in shares carrying 30% or more of the voting rights of the target.[279]

6.5.4.3 Bid timetable

6.332   The announcement of a firm intention to make a bid will, provided that there are no pre-conditions to the posting of the offer document requiring satisfaction, start the offer timetable. This section examines the bid timetable as it relates to an offer being made by way of offer document. The process of and timetable

---

272 Panel Practice Statement No 20, paragraph 3.2.
273 Panel Practice Statement No 20, paragraph 3.2.
274 Panel Practice Statement No 20, paragraph 3.2.
275 Takeover Code Rule 2.4.
276 Takeover Code Rule 2.8.
277 Takeover Code Rule 2.4.
278 Takeover Code Rule 2.8.
279 Takeover Code Rule 2.8 (a).

relating to conducting a takeover by way of scheme of arrangement is considered in Section 6.6 of this Chapter.

An outline offer timetable is set out below, beneath which a more detailed discussion of the main milestones of the bid timetable is set out. In the table below 'D' represents the day on which the offer document is posted. **6.333**

Date	Offer
D – 28	Announcement of transaction.
D	Offer document posted.
D + 21	First closing date of bid. This is the earliest date the offer could become wholly unconditional. (Bidder acquires board and practical control of target once bid is unconditional.)
D + 24	Practically the earliest that compulsory acquisition notices could be posted (if bid has become unconditional and 90% requirement satisfied by D + 21). Typically this would be achieved somewhat later even on a recommended bid.
D + 39	Latest date on which new information can be published by target.
D + 42	Acceptances of offer can now be withdrawn unless offer is unconditional as to acceptances.
D + 46	Latest date on which any revised offer document may be posted.
D + 60	Latest possible date for the bid becoming or being declared unconditional as to acceptances.
D + 65	Practically the earliest date that compulsory acquisition of non-accepting shares could be completed (if bid has become unconditional and 90% requirement satisfied by D + 21).
D + 74	Earliest day on which the bid may close (assuming the offer becomes or is declared unconditional as to acceptances on Day 60).
D + 81	Latest possible date for the bid becoming or being declared unconditional in all respects.
D + 95	Final date for paying target shareholders if bid declared wholly unconditional on D + 81.
D + 125	Practically the earliest date that compulsory acquisition procedure could be completed, if bid declared unconditional on D + 81.

6.5.4.3.1 Announcement of the Transaction   The Takeover Directive makes clear the importance of the timely announcement of a bid. It requires member states to ensure that, **6.334**

> a decision to make a bid is made public without delay and that the supervisory authority is informed of the bid.[280]

In relation to announcing a bid, it is important for a bidder to understand that once a 'firm intention' to make a bid has been made, the bidder is bound by it and must consummate the bid except in very limited circumstances.[281] In fact, the **6.335**

---

[280] Takeover Directive Article 6(1).
[281] Takeover Code Rule 2.7.

bidder will be permitted to withdraw its bid only where, in accordance with Rule 13 (Pre-conditions in firm offer announcements and offer conditions), it is allowed to invoke a pre-condition to the making of a bid or would be permitted to invoke a condition to the bid if one were made.[282] As such the bidder should announce a firm intention to make a bid only after the most careful and responsible consideration[283] and only then once the bidder has every reason to believe that it can and will continue to implement the bid.[284]

6.336   Any announcement of a firm intention to make a bid (a 'Rule 2.5 announcement') must be drafted in clear and concise language[285] and must include:[286]

    (i) the terms of the offer;

    (ii) the identity of the bidder;

    (iii) details of any relevant securities of the target in which the bidder or any person acting in concert with it has an interest or in respect of which he has a right to subscribe, in each case specifying the nature of the interests or rights concerned (including details of any short positions (whether conditional or absolute and whether in the money or otherwise) and any short positions under derivatives or otherwise);

    (iv) details of any relevant securities of the target in respect of which the bidder or any of its associates has procured an irrevocable commitment or a letter of intent;

    (v) details of any relevant securities of the target which the bidder or any person acting in concert with it has borrowed or lent, save for any borrowed shares which have been either on-lent or sold;

    (vi) all conditions (including conditions relating to acceptance levels, any admission to listing or admission to trading, or increase in capital) to which the offer or the making of an offer is subject;

    (vii) details of any agreements or arrangements to which the bidder is party which relate to the circumstances in which it may or may not invoke or seek to invoke a pre-condition or a condition to its offer and the consequences of its doing so, including details of any break fees payable as a result;

    (viii) details of any arrangement which exists between the bidder and the target or an associate of the bidder or of the target in relation to relevant securities;

    (ix) a summary of the provisions of Rule 8 (Disclosure of dealings during the offer period); and

---

[282]   Takeover Code Rule 27.
[283]   Takeover Code Rule 2.5(a).
[284]   Takeover Code Rule 2.5(a).
[285]   Takeover Code Note 1 to Rule 2.5.
[286]   Takeover Code Rule 2.5(b).

(x) details of any arrangement for the payment of an inducement fee or similar arrangement.

In addition to the above criteria, if the bid is for cash or partly for cash, the announcement should include a statement from the financial adviser or another appropriate third party that sufficient resources are available to the bidder to satisfy full acceptance of the bid.[287]   **6.337**

Following a Rule 2.5 announcement, the target must ensure that a copy of the announcement (or a circular summarizing the terms and conditions of the bid) is sent to target shareholders and persons with information rights, as well as the Panel.[288] In practice, where a circular summarizing the terms of the Rule 2.5 announcement is sent out, the target should also make the full text of the announcement available by, for example, publishing it on its website.[289]   **6.338**

In addition, the target and the bidder must make the Rule 2.5 announcement readily available to their employee representatives or, where there are none, to the employees themselves.[290]   **6.339**

6.5.4.3.2 Posting of the offer document   The Takeover Directive provides that member states must ensure that,   **6.340**

> an offeror is required to draw up and make public in good time an offer document containing the information necessary to enable the holders of the offeree company's securities to reach a properly informed decision on the bid.[291]

In the UK, the offer document must be posted to target shareholders within 28 days of the announcement of the bid and, with this in mind, from the moment of announcement, the bidder will (in collaboration with the target where the bid is recommended), begin preparing the offer document. The contents of the offer document are examined in detail at Section 6.5.4.7 below.   **6.341**

On the day of posting the offer document, the bidder must put the offer document on display[292] and must announce that the offer document has been posted, as well as details of where the document can be inspected.[293] The offer document must also be made readily available to the employee representatives, or where there are none, the employees of the bidder and target.[294]   **6.342**

---

287 Takeover Code Rule 2.5(c).
288 Takeover Code Rule 2.6(b).
289 Takeover Code Note 1 to Rule 2.6.
290 Takeover Code Rule 2.6(b).
291 Takeover Directive Article 6(2).
292 Takeover Code Rule 30.1 and Rule 26.
293 Takeover Code Rule 30.1.
294 Takeover Code Rule 30.1(b).

6.343 As soon as practicable after the posting of the offer document and in any event within 14 days of its being posted, the target board must publish a circular[295] containing its opinion on the offer together with the substance of any advice it has received from its independent advisers. The contents requirements of the target board's opinion are examined in detail at Section 6.8.6.2.1 of this Chapter. The target board must also, on the day of posting, put the circular on display and announce the posting of the circular.[296] Provided such opinion is provided in good time before circulation, a separate opinion from the employee representatives on the effects of the bid must be appended to the circular.[297] In a recommended bid, the requirement that the target board post a circular dealing with the above matters will be satisfied by the posting of the offer document itself as the offer document will contain a letter from the target's chairman dealing with all necessary disclosures.[298]

6.344 The date on which the offer document is posted is the reference point for calculating the remainder of the timetable. This date is also important because it is the date from which market share purchases are calculated in accordance with the statutory compulsory acquisition procedure[299] (which is considered in more detail in Section 6.10 of this Chapter).

6.345 **6.5.4.3.3 Initial period of the offer**   The Takeover Directive states that,

> Member states shall provide that the time allowed for acceptance of a bid may not be less than two weeks nor more than ten weeks from the date of publication of the offer document.[300]

6.346 In the UK, the offer must remain open for a minimum of 21 days from the date of posting the offer document.[301] The date on which the initial 21-day offer period expires is known as the first closing date.

6.347 **6.5.4.3.4 Effect of first closing date**   The first closing date is an important reference date in the offer timetable for two reasons. First of all, it is the date from which the last date for satisfaction of all conditions to the bid is calculated. It is also the date from which the period during which accepting shareholders may withdraw their acceptance is calculated. The effect of the first closing date on the satisfaction of conditions is examined below whilst withdrawal rights are considered at Section 6.5.4.3.11 below.

---

[295] Takeover Code Rule 30.2.
[296] Takeover Code Rule 30.2.
[297] Takeover Code Rule 30.2.
[298] Takeover Code Note to Rule 30.2.
[299] Companies Act 2006 section 979.
[300] Takeover Directive Article 8(1).
[301] Takeover Code Rule 31.1.

As the last date for satisfaction of all conditions, save for acceptances, is the later **6.348** of 21 days from:

(i) the first closing date; and

(ii) the offer becoming unconditional as to acceptances,[302]

the bidder may, where there is concern over the time required to fulfil certain conditions (other than the acceptance condition), wish to adopt a later first closing date than the minimum 21 days from posting the offer document. This is particularly likely where the bid is recommended by the target board, and is therefore likely to become unconditional as to acceptances on or before the first closing date, but it is likely that satisfaction of other conditions will not be obtained within 21 days from first closing. Unless, however, there are specific and pressing concerns in relation to a particular condition, the bidder will wish to elect for the earliest possible closing date in order to ensure the takeover is effected in the shortest period possible.

6.5.4.3.5 Extending the offer period If the bid is not contested, the bid may **6.349** become unconditional as to acceptances by or before the first closing date. If this is the case, the offer may remain open for a further 21 days from the first closing date for the satisfaction of any further conditions.[303] In any event, the offer must, after it has become or is declared unconditional as to acceptances, remain open for acceptance for not less than 14 days after the date on which it would otherwise have expired.[304]

If the bid has not become unconditional as to acceptances by the first closing **6.350** date, which is common in the case of a competitive offer situation, there is no minimum period to the next closing date. Although there is no obligation to extend an offer the conditions of which have not been met by the first (or any subsequent) closing date,[305] the offer period may be extended and it is usual for the bidder to extend the offer incrementally for 14-day periods at a time. The bidder must, where the bid is not yet unconditional as to acceptances, stipulate a revised closing date.[306] If the bid has become unconditional as to acceptances, the bidder may make a statement that the offer will remain open until further notice.[307]

---

[302] Takeover Code Rule 31.7.
[303] Takeover Code Rule 31.7.
[304] Takeover Code Rule 31.4.
[305] Takeover Code Rule 31.3.
[306] Takeover Code Rule 31.2.
[307] Takeover Code Rule 31.2.

6.351   As a general matter, a bidder should retain caution in respect of making firm statements concerning the duration of its offer or stating that its offer will not extend beyond a specific time as the bidder will be bound by any such statement.[308] The Panel takes a wide view as to what constitutes a firm statement and it is clear that using the expression 'present intention' in relation to offer periods should be avoided by the bidder as it may present a misleading picture to target shareholders.[309]

6.352   There are three exceptions to the rule that the bidder will be bound by a firm statement detailing the duration of the offer. These exceptions are available only if the bidder has expressly reserved the right, at the time the statement was made, to set it aside. They are, broadly:[310]

  (i)   where a competitive situations exists (see below for further detail on competitive situations);
  (ii) where the binding of a bidder to a 'no extension' statement would otherwise prevent the posting of an increased or improved bid recommended for acceptance by the target board; and
  (iii) where the target has, after Day 39, announced the existence of material new information.

6.353   **6.5.4.3.6 Announcement of acceptance levels**   An announcement of acceptance levels is required to be made no later than 8 am on the business day following the day on which an offer is due to expire, or becomes or is unconditional as to acceptances, or is revised or extended.[311] The earliest date on which such an announcement will be made is, therefore, the business day following the first closing date.

6.354   The deadline for announcing acceptance levels is important because, if the bidder, having announced the bid to be unconditional as to acceptances, fails by 3.30 pm on the day following such announcement to comply with the requirement so to announce such acceptance levels, any accepting shareholder will immediately thereafter be permitted to withdraw their acceptance.[312] This right of withdrawal is capable of termination not less than eight days after the date on which an acceptance levels announcement should have been made in accordance with the acceptance levels announcement requirements.

---

[308] Takeover Code Rule 31.5.
[309] Takeover Code Note 1 to Rule 31.5.
[310] Takeover Code Notes 3, 4 and 5 to Rule 31.5.
[311] Takeover Code Rule 17.1.
[312] Takeover Code Rule 17.2.

An announcement of acceptance levels must contain the following:[313]   **6.355**

(i)   the number of shares for which acceptances of the offer have been received (including details of the extent to which acceptances have been received from persons acting in concert with the bidder or in relation to which irrevocable commitments had been obtained);

(ii) details of, broadly, any relevant securities in the target held by the bidder (or anyone with whom the bidder is acting in concert) or in respect of which the bidder (or anyone with whom the bidder is acting in concert) has a right to subscribe;

(iii) details of any relevant securities in the target in respect of which the bidder or any of its associates has an outstanding irrevocable commitment or letter of intent; and

(iv) details of any relevant securities in the target which the bidder or any person acting in concert with it had borrowed or lent, save for any borrowed shares which have been either on-lent or sold.

In the case of each of the above limbs, both the figure and the percentage that figure represents as a proportion of the total securities in the target must be presented.   **6.356**

The announcement must also contain a prominent statement of the total numbers of shares which the bidder may count towards the satisfaction of its acceptance condition. It must also specify the percentages of each class of relevant securities represented by these figures.[314]   **6.357**

6.5.4.3.7 Last date for revision of the offer   As the Code stipulates that any revised offer must be kept open for at least 14 days following the date on which the revised offer document is published,[315] the latest date on which any revised offer document can be published is Day 46, being 14 days from Day 60 (the last day that a bid may become or may be declared unconditional as to acceptances). This ensures that target shareholders have enough time to assess the terms of the bid and determine whether or not they wish to accept it. A bidder should therefore take care not to put itself in a position in which it would be required to revise its offer in the 14 days ending on Day 60.[316]   **6.358**

This rule may be significant in securities exchange offers in the context of the publication of new material information which may have the effect of increasing   **6.359**

---

[313] Takeover Code Rule 17.1(a) to (d).
[314] Takeover Code Rule 17.1.
[315] Takeover Code Rule 32.1.
[316] Takeover Code Note 3 to Rule 32.1.

the value of the offer. Indeed, announcements containing such information are usually prohibited after Day 46.[317]

6.360 It should also be remembered that the revision of an offer document will not restart the offer timetable or otherwise affect the timetable for compulsory acquisition (which is considered in more detail in Section 6.10 of this Chapter).

6.361 **6.5.4.3.8 Last day on which the bid becomes or is declared unconditional as to acceptances** Except with the consent of the Panel, a bid may not become or be declared unconditional as to acceptances after midnight on the 60th day following the day on which the initial offer document was published.[318] The Panel will only consent to waive this rule:

(i) in a competitive situation; or

(ii) if the target board consents to an extension; or

(iii) as provided for in Rule 31.9; or

(iv) if the bidder's receiving agent requests an extension in order to issue the certificate required by Note 7 to Rule 10; or

(v) when withdrawal rights are introduced under Rule 13.5.

6.362 In respect of Rule 31.9, which prohibits, except with the consent of the Panel, any announcement by the target board of material new information after the 39th day following publication of the initial offer document,[319] the Panel, where it consents to such an announcement being made, will normally be prepared to grant an extension to both Day 46 and Day 60.[320]

6.363 In terms of process, except with the consent of the Panel, the Day 60 announcement (covering whether the bid is unconditional as to acceptances or whether it has lapsed) should be made by 5 pm and should include the details stated above in the context of an announcement as to acceptance levels.[321]

6.364 **6.5.4.3.9 Latest possible date for the bid becoming or being declared unconditional in all respects** As stated above, the last date for satisfaction of all conditions, save for acceptances, after which the bid must lapse, is the later of 21 days from:

(i) the first closing date; and

(ii) the bid becoming unconditional as to acceptances.[322]

---

[317] Takeover Code Note 1 to Rule 32.1.
[318] Takeover Code Rule 31.6.
[319] Takeover Code Rule 31.9.
[320] Takeover Code Rule 31.9.
[321] Takeover Code Rule 17.1(a) to (d).
[322] Takeover Code Rule 31.7.

In practice, the drop-dead date for satisfaction of all conditions is therefore Day 81, being 21 days from the 60th day following the day on which the initial offer document was published.

6.5.4.3.10 Final date for payment of consideration to target shareholders   **6.365**
Except with the consent of the Panel, the consideration for the offer must be sent to accepting target shareholders within 14 days of the later of:

(i) the first closing date of the bid;

(ii) the date the bid becomes or is declared wholly unconditional; or

(iii) the date of receipt of an acceptance complete in all respects.[323]

This means that practically, the drop-dead date for making payment to accepting   **6.366** shareholders is Day 95, being 14 days after the date on which the bid becomes or is declared wholly unconditional (which may itself be as late as Day 81).

6.5.4.3.11 Withdrawal rights   Provided that the bid has not become or   **6.367** been declared unconditional as to acceptances, an accepting shareholder must be entitled to withdraw its acceptance at any time from the date which is 21 days after the first closing date.[324] This will usually be 42 days after posting of the offer document. Day 42 therefore usually represents the first day on which shareholders may withdraw their acceptance as, until that date, an acceptance is irrevocable.

The right to withdraw acceptance must be exercisable until the earlier of: **6.368**

(i) the time that the bid becomes or is declared unconditional as to acceptances; and

(ii) the final time for lodgement of acceptances which can be taken into account in accordance with Rule 31.6.

In addition, the Panel may permit accepting shareholders to withdraw their   **6.369** acceptances on such terms as the Panel considers appropriate in circumstances in which the target is not permitted to invoke, or to cause or permit the bidder to invoke a condition.[325]

As well as the withdrawal rights contained in the Code, accepting shareholders   **6.370** may take advantage of additional withdrawal rights in circumstances in which, where the consideration offered for the target's shares comprises (in whole or in part) securities for which a prospectus is published, a supplementary prospectus is published.[326] Where a supplementary prospectus is published, accepting

---

[323] Takeover Code Rule 31.8.

[324] Takeover Code Rule 34.

[325] Takeover Code Note 2 to Rule 13.5.

[326] Prospectus Regulations (2005) (SI 2005 No 1433) and FSMA 2000 section 87Q(4).

shareholders may, broadly, withdraw their acceptance within two days of the publication of the supplementary prospectus.

6.371 The time at which, during the offer period, the rights of withdrawal on publication of a supplementary prospectus either fall away or are incapable of being invoked by an accepting shareholder is not clear. Consequently, there has been some debate over the potential detrimental impact of such rights being invoked in circumstances in which a bid has been declared unconditional as to acceptances but has not yet become wholly unconditional. Although, arguably, the right of withdrawal is lost upon the bid becoming or being declared unconditional, this is by no means certain. The Executive has, therefore, recommended that a bidder intending to offer securities as consideration for the offer (i) considers the consequences of withdrawal rights arising where a supplementary prospectus is required and (ii) attempts as far as possible to arrange matters so that the offer becomes wholly unconditional simultaneously with it becoming or being declared unconditional as to acceptances.

6.372 6.5.4.3.12 **Compulsory acquisition procedure**   The ability of the bidder to take advantage of the statutory 'squeeze-out' provisions is discussed in Section 6.10 of this Chapter.

6.373 6.5.4.3.13 **Competitive Situations**   A competitive situation may arise at any stage of the bid process. Tactically, however, competitors will often wait until towards the end of the original bidder's timetable to announce its own bid in view of the fact that, without the consent of the Panel, the original bidder cannot, after Day 46, revise the terms of its offer.[327]

6.374 Helpfully, the Executive has confirmed that in circumstances in which a rival offer is announced after Day 46 of the existing bidder's timetable, an extension to Day 60 (the date after which a bid may not become or be declared unconditional as to acceptances) may be granted.[328] In order to benefit from such an extension, the Executive states that the target board must consent to it and no unreserved 'no extension' or 'no increase' statement must have been made by the bidder.[329] If an extension is granted, the original bidder will be able to revise its own bid in light of that of the competitor.

6.375 Express 'no extension' or 'no increase' statements which have been included in documents or announcements issued in connection with the bid without a specific reservation of the right to extend usually prevent a bidder from extending its offer beyond its existing timetable.[330] In a competitive situation, however, where

---

[327] Takeover Code Rule 32.1.
[328] Panel Practice Statement 8 to the Code.
[329] Ibid.
[330] Takeover Code Rule 31.5.

the bidder has expressly reserved its right to withdraw a 'no extension' statement at the time that statement was made, the bidder may choose not to be bound by it and to extend its offer provided that:

(i)   notice to this effect is given as soon as possible (and in any event within four business days after the day of the firm announcement of the competing offer) and shareholders are informed in writing at the earliest opportunity; and

(ii) any target shareholders who accepted the offer after the date of the no extension statement are given a right of withdrawal for a period of 8 days following the date on which the notice is posted.[331]

Where a competing bid has been announced, both bidders will normally be bound by the timetable established by the publication of the competing offer document.[332]   **6.376**

Competitive situations also force the target to consider in greater detail the process of the takeover offer. Arising out of the general principle of equality of treatment of the target shareholders, competing bidders are afforded similar equality of treatment in terms of the information provided to them.[333] Issues arising from this rule are discussed at paragraph 6.86 of this Chapter.   **6.377**

6.5.4.3.14 Auctions   If a competitive situation continues to exist in the later stages of the offer period, the Panel will normally require revised bids to be announced in accordance with an auction procedure.[334] The Panel will determine and issue the rules of such auction and in so determining will consider applying any alternative procedure as is agreed between competing bidders and the target board.[335] The Panel may, as part of the auction rules it prescribes, impose a final time limit for announcing revisions to competing offers.[336] In addition, it will usually grant an extension to Day 60.[337]   **6.378**

In order to ease the burden of continual offer document revision and circulation, the auction procedure will normally state that any revised offer document need not be circulated to target shareholders (and other persons with information rights) before the expiry of a set period after the last revision to either competing offer is announced.[338]   **6.379**

---

[331] Takeover Code Note 3 to Rule 31.5.
[332] Takeover Code Note 4 to Rule 31.6.
[333] Takeover Code Rule 20.2.
[334] Takeover Code Rule 32.5.
[335] Takeover Code Rule 32.5.
[336] Takeover Code Note 2 to Rule 32.5.
[337] Takeover Code Note 4 to Rule 31.6.
[338] Takeover Code Rule 32.5.

6.380 It is usual for an auction established by the Panel to include rounds of bidding over a course of days. The Panel can, however, adopt an accelerated auction procedure where circumstances necessitate this. The Panel, in consultation with the bidding parties, adopted such an alternative approach in relation to the bids by Tata Steel UK Limited and CSN Acquisitions Limited for Corus Group plc. The Corus auction rules[339] provided for a maximum of nine rounds to take place between 4.30 pm (UK time) on 30 January 2007 and 2.30 am (UK time) on 31 January 2007. The timing of the auction ensured that all rounds of bidding would take place when the three stock markets on which the bidders' and target's shares were traded (London, Mumbai and New York) were closed, thereby ensuring that the relevant markets were not affected by increased speculation.

6.381 Copies of all auction rules published by the Panel, together with statements confirming the outcome of each completed auction can be found on the Panel's website at <http://www.thetakeoverpanel.org.uk/statements/panel-statements>.

6.382 **6.5.4.3.15 Bringing matters to a conclusion** The successful bidder, following the bid becoming or being declared to be unconditional in all respects will, as noted above, make payments of the relevant consideration to each accepting shareholder. If necessary and possible, the bidder will also begin and complete the statutory compulsory acquisition procedure to ensure that it obtains 100% of the target's issued share capital.

6.383 If the bidder is ultimately unsuccessful in its bid because, for example, the bid has not become or been declared wholly unconditional and has been withdrawn or the offer has, in certain circumstances, lapsed, the bidder will find itself subject to certain restrictions vis-à-vis the target.[340] These restrictions are borne out of the general principle that a target company must not be hindered in the conduct of its affairs for longer than is reasonable by a bid for its securities.[341]

6.384 Specifically, in circumstances in which an offer has been announced or been made but has not become or been declared wholly unconditional and has been withdrawn or has lapsed otherwise than pursuant to Rule 12.1 (competition commission and European commission), neither the bidder, nor any person who acted in concert with the bidder in the course of the bid nor any person who is subsequently acting in concert with any of them, may, without the consent of the Panel, within 12 months from the date on which the original bid is withdrawn or lapses, either:

    (i) announce an offer or possible offer for the target (including a partial offer which could result in the bidder and persons acting in concert with it

---

[339] Panel Statement 2007/3.
[340] Takeover Code Rule 35.1.
[341] Takeover Code General Principle 6.

being interested in shares carrying 30% or more of the voting rights of the target);

(ii) acquire any interest in shares of the target if the bidder or any such person would thereby become obliged under Rule 9 (mandatory offers) to make an offer;

(iii) acquire any interest in, or procure an irrevocable commitment in respect of, shares of the target if the shares in which such person, together with any persons acting in concert with him, would be interested and the shares in respect of which he, or they, had acquired irrevocable commitments would in aggregate carry 30% or more of the voting rights of the target;

(iv) make any statement which raises or confirms the possibility that an offer might be made for the target; or

(v) take any steps in connection with a possible offer for the target where knowledge of the possible offer might be extended outside those who need to know in the bidder and its immediate advisers.[342]

In circumstances in which a competing bid has been announced, the Panel may permit the original bidder dispensation from compliance with the restrictions detailed above. **6.385**

In addition to the above restrictions, in circumstances in which an offer lapses, all documents of title and other documents lodged with forms of acceptance must be returned as soon as practicable (and in any event within 14 days of the lapsing of the offer).[343] **6.386**

6.5.4.4 Conditionality

Conditionality in a bid process results in there being less certainty that the takeover will ultimately be successful for the bidder. Despite this, and with the exception of offers made in pursuance of Rule 9 of the Code (mandatory offers), a degree of conditionality is permissible under the Code and can be introduced into a deal by either the bidder or, less often, by the target board. **6.387**

6.5.4.4.1 Pre-conditions and conditions A pre-condition is, in essence, a form of condition. It is detailed in the announcement of the bid as an event, circumstance or happening to which the posting of the offer document is made subject. Its presence or otherwise in the offer process is therefore controlled by the bidder only. **6.388**

By contrast, a condition is contained within the offer document and is a consent, approval or other event or circumstance to which the bid itself is subject. **6.389**

---

[342] Takeover Code Rule 35.1.
[343] Takeover Code Rule 31.10.

6.390   **6.5.4.4.2 Pre-conditions**   The Panel must be consulted in every case in which a bidder proposes to include in its announcement a pre-condition to the posting of the offer document[344] and the Panel will only allow the same in limited circumstances. A bidder should therefore be minded of this during its preparations prior to announcing the bid and preparing the offer document.

6.391   The limited circumstances in which the Panel generally permits the incorporation into the announcement of pre-conditions relate to pre-conditions concerning references made to the Competition Commission or the need to obtain other material official authorization or regulatory clearance in relation to the transaction.[345]

6.392   As such, except with the consent of the Panel, no bid may be subject to a pre-condition unless the pre-condition:

   (i)   relates to a decision that there will be no reference to the Competition Commission or initiation of proceedings by the European Commission;

 (ii)   relates to a decision that there will be no reference to the Competition Commission or initiation of proceedings by the European Commission or, if there is such a reference or initiation of proceedings, a decision by the relevant authority to allow the offer to proceed (the decision may, in each case, be stated to be on terms satisfactory to the bidder); or

(iii)   involves another material official authorization or regulatory clearance relating to the offer and:

     — the offer is publicly recommended by the board of the target; or

     — the Panel is satisfied that it is likely to prove impossible to obtain the authorization or clearance within the Code timetable.[346]

6.393   **6.5.4.4.3 Conditions**   Conditions are usually incorporated into the bid by the bidder. The typical categories of condition affecting UK takeovers are:

   (i)   the acceptance condition;

 (ii)   UK or EC competition clearance condition;

(iii)   other legal or regulatory conditions, for example the need to obtain shareholder consent under the class consents regime under the Listing Rules;[347] and

(iv)   other conditions designed to benefit the offeror, for example conditions relating to the status or performance of the target's business.

---

[344] Takeover Code Rule 13.3.
[345] Takeover Code Rule 13.3.
[346] Takeover Code Rule 13.3.
[347] LR 10.2.2R and 10.5.1R.

Whilst it is usual for conditions in the offer document to have been requested by the bidder, the target may request the benefit of some conditionality. This is particularly the case where consideration for the bid is to be satisfied, in whole or in part, by an issue by the bidder of securities in itself to target shareholders. The target board will want to ensure that the bid will not proceed in the event that the bidder's securities are worth materially less than at the time that the target board had recommended the takeover. **6.394**

A bid must not normally be subject to conditions and pre-conditions which depend solely on subjective judgments by the directors of the bidder or target (although conditions relating to competition clearance included in the offer document pursuant to Rule 12.1 are excepted from this restriction). Neither should the bid be subject to conditions or pre-conditions the fulfilment of which is in the hands of the bidder or target.[348] Only in circumstances where it is not practicable to specify all the factors on which the satisfaction of a condition may depend may the Panel be prepared to accept an element of subjectivity. This is most likely to occur in relation to conditions involving official authorizations or regulatory clearances. **6.395**

6.5.4.4.4 Conditions relating to financing Bids must not normally be subject to conditions or pre-conditions based on financing, although there are two circumstances in which the Panel may permit the inclusion of such conditions. **6.396**

The first circumstance is where a bid is being made for cash (or includes an element of cash) and the bidder proposes to finance the cash consideration by means of a fresh issue of securities. In these circumstances, the bid must be made subject to any legal or regulatory requirements necessary for the issuance of such securities (for example, the requirement to obtain shareholder approval) or their listing or admission to trading.[349] The Panel will not allow such conditions to be capable of being waived.[350] **6.397**

Although only used exceptionally, the second circumstance is where it is not reasonable, due to the likely lengthy period required in order to obtain regulatory clearance or another material official authorization, for the bidder to maintain committed financing. In such circumstances, it will be necessary for the pre-condition to be waived or satisfied, or the bid withdrawn, within 21 days after the satisfaction (or waiver) of any other pre-condition permitted and the bidder and its financial adviser must, before the bid is announced, confirm in writing to the **6.398**

---

[348] Takeover Code Rule 13.1.
[349] Takeover Code Note to Rule 13.3.
[350] Takeover Code Note to Rule 13.3.

Panel that they are not aware of any reason why the bidder would not be able to satisfy the financing condition within that 21-day period.[351]

6.399 **6.5.4.4.5 Relationship with the timetable** As the posting of an offer document is dependent on the satisfaction of any pre-conditions contained in the announcement of a bid, the inclusion of pre-conditions is likely to result in the extension of the offer timetable. Equally, the inclusion of conditions within the offer document may cause the offer timetable to become elongated.

6.400 The Panel's reluctance to permit (i) the inclusion of pre-conditions in the offer announcement to the making of the bid and (ii) conditions to the posting of an offer document is therefore clear: to permit the same is to sanction a potential extension to the period of time during which, as a result of the bid, the future of the target and its business remains uncertain. The Panel must therefore balance General Principle 6 of the Code, which reflects the provisions of Article 3(1)(f) of the Takeover Directive which states that a target must not be hindered in the conduct of its affairs for longer than is reasonable by a bid for its securities, with the potential advantages for the company of attracting the bid and allowing it to progress, albeit with conditions.

6.401 **6.5.4.4.6 Obligation to satisfy conditions** The bidder is obliged, following the announcement of a firm intention to make a bid, to use all reasonable efforts to ensure the satisfaction of any conditions or pre-conditions to which the bid is subject.[352]

6.402 Furthermore, both the bidder and the target are each under a general obligation not to invoke, and in the case of the target not to cause or permit the bidder to invoke, any conditions.

6.403 A bidder may waive conditions (other than the acceptance condition) if it has reserved the right to do so and if the bid would otherwise at that stage be wholly unconditional.

6.404 **6.5.4.4.7 Ability to invoke conditions** As the invocation of a condition will cause the bid not to proceed, to lapse or be withdrawn, restrictions are placed on both the bidder's and the target's ability to do so.[353] Whenever a party wishes to invoke a condition, the Panel must be consulted.

6.405 Except in the case of the acceptance condition and any UK or EC competition condition, the bidder may not invoke a condition unless the circumstances which give rise to the right to invoke the condition or pre-condition are of material

---

[351] Takeover Code Note to Rule 13.3.
[352] Takeover Code Rule 13.4(b).
[353] Takeover Code Rule 13.4 and Rule 13.5.

significance to the bidder in the context of the bid. This restriction is replicated in respect of conditionality protections benefiting the target which are contained in the offer document.

The level of materiality which must be satisfied before the bidder, or target (as the case may be), can rely on the benefit of the condition is to be assessed by reference to the facts of each case at the time the relevant circumstances arise.[354] To the party wishing to invoke the condition, these facts must be of material significance in the context of the bid.
   6.406

In the context of a condition based on a material adverse change to the business or prospects of the target, guidance from the Executive states that the above test would be satisfied only where there had been:
   6.407

> an adverse change of very considerable significance striking at the heart of the purpose of the transaction in question, analogous … to something that would justify frustration of a legal contract.[355]

Given that the materiality threshold for invocation of a condition is high, it is unlikely that a bidder will be able to invoke a condition based on a material adverse change to the business or prospects of the target following announcement of the bid.
   6.408

More generally, when determining whether certain circumstances give rise to the ability to invoke a condition, the Panel has stated that it will consider whether the condition:
   6.409

  (i) was the subject of negotiation with the target;
  (ii) was expressly drawn to the target shareholders' attention in the offer document or announcement, with a clear explanation of the circumstances which might give rise to the right to invoke it; and
 (iii) was included to take account of the particular circumstances of the target.[356]

A bidder should therefore be minded that, for example, negotiation of a condition with the target and/or drawing the condition to the attention of the target's shareholders may increase the likelihood of being permitted by the Panel to invoke a condition.
   6.410

A target's ability to invoke or to cause the bidder to invoke a condition will not necessarily be restricted to those circumstances in which the Panel would permit a bidder to invoke a condition.[357] Indeed, the Panel will, in deciding whether or not to allow the target to invoke (or cause or permit a bidder to invoke) a condition,
   6.411

---

[354] Panel Practice Statement No 5.
[355] Ibid.
[356] Ibid.
[357] Takeover Code Note 1 to Rule 13.5.

take into account all relevant factors.[358] The Panel's discretion is further evidenced by their ability, where a target is not permitted to invoke (or cause or permit a bidder to invoke) a condition, to instead determine both:

   (i) that accepting shareholders should have the right to withdraw their acceptances on such terms as the Panel considers appropriate; and

   (ii) the effect of this right of withdrawal on the Code timetable.[359]

6.412   The effect of the Panel's right is significant as it may result in withdrawals of acceptance sufficient to cause the bid to cease to be unconditional as to acceptances. The possibility of this occurring should be incorporated into the terms of the bid.[360]

6.5.4.5 *Partial offers*

6.413   **6.5.4.5.1 Advantages and disadvantages**   Partial offers are not a regularly occurring feature of the UK's takeover landscape. Whilst they are a tool through which a bidder may increase its stake in a target, the regime can be restrictive in terms of a bidder's ability otherwise to acquire shares in a target, particularly in respect of partial offers which, if successful, would provide the bidder with between 30% and 50% of the voting rights in the target. Equally, the costs of launching a partial offer which will result in the bidder obtaining less than 30% of the voting rights in the target may outweigh the cost of buying up the same shares directly in the market.

6.414   A partial offer, however, offers the advantage that it affords a potential bidder a method of obtaining, in a single move, a sizeable interest in the target. This may result in the bidder obtaining negative control of the target without having to undertake a concerted and potentially lengthy programme of share acquisition in the market. Depending on the bidder's rationale for purchasing shares in the target, the partial offer route may therefore be preferable to potentially driving up the price of the target's shares by purchasing in the market and disclosing its interests in target shares to the market as purchases are effected.[361]

6.415   The decision as to whether a bidder chooses to launch a partial offer will therefore depend on a number of factors including the bidder's rationale for the acquisition of shares, the composition of the target's shareholder base, the availability of the bidder's funds, the bidder's appetite for continued disclosure to the market and the bidder's and bidder's advisers' views of the effect that the bidder's increasing

---

[358] Takeover Code Note 2 to Rule 13.5.
[359] Takeover Code Note 2 to Rule 13.5.
[360] Takeover Code Note 2 to Rule 13.5.
[361] DTR 5.

interest in the target will have on the market, in terms of both price and sentiment.

6.5.4.5.2 Requirement for Panel consent   A potential bidder will require Panel consent to make an offer for part only of the target's share capital.[362] In determining whether or not to consent, the Panel will examine the total share interest in the target which would be obtained by the bidder if the bid was ultimately successful.

6.416

Where the proposed offer could not result in the bidder and persons acting in concert with it being interested in shares carrying 30% or more of the voting rights of the target, consent will usually be granted.[363]

6.417

In the case of an offer which could result in the bidder and persons acting in concert with it being interested in shares carrying 30% or more but holding less than 100% of the voting rights of the target, the Panel will not normally consent if the bidder or persons acting in concert with it have acquired, selectively or in significant numbers, interests in shares in the target during the 12 months preceding the application for Panel consent or its interests in shares have been acquired at any time after the partial offer was reasonably in contemplation.[364]

6.418

6.5.4.5.3 Additional requirements   Where an offer is made which will result in the bidder and persons acting in concert with it being interested in shares carrying more than 30% but less than 100% of the voting rights of the target, the bidder should be aware that the following may affect the success of the partial offer:

6.419

(i) the precise number of shares the subject of the offer must be stated and the offer may not be declared unconditional as to acceptances unless acceptances are received for not less than that number;[365] and

(ii) the offer must be conditional, not only on the number of acceptances received, but also on approval of the offer being given in respect of over 50% of the voting rights held by shareholders who are independent of the bidder and persons acting in concert with it (although this requirement may be waived if over 50% of the voting rights of the target are in the hands of one shareholder).[366]

In addition, if the partial offer could result in the bidder alone or with persons acting in concert with it holding shares carrying over 50% of the voting rights of

6.420

---

362 Takeover Code Rule 36.1.
363 Takeover Code Rule 26.1.
364 Takeover Code Rule 36.2.
365 Takeover Code Rule 36.4.
366 Takeover Code Rule 36.5.

the target, the offer document must contain a specific and prominent reference to this and to the fact that, if the offer succeeds, the bidder (and persons acting in concert with it) will be able to acquire, subject to the 12-month prohibition, further shares in the target without incurring an obligation to make a subsequent offer for the whole of target.[367]

6.421   **6.5.4.5.4 Restrictions on acquisition of shares in target**   In circumstances in which the Panel grants consent to a bidder to make a partial offer for the target, the bidder and persons acting in concert with it will be subject to restrictions on its or their acquisition of further shares in the target. These provisions are restrictive and their implications should be considered at the outset of a potential bidder's consideration of a partial offer.

6.422   Specifically, the bidder and persons acting in concert with it are, unless the partial offer will result in the bidder gaining less than 30% of the voting rights of the target (in which case Panel consent will normally be granted),[368] subject to the following:

   (i)   the absolute prohibition on the acquisition of target shares during the offer period;[369] and
   (ii)   in the case of a successful partial offer, and absent the Panel's consent, the prohibition on the acquisition of target shares by the bidder or any person acting in concert with it both during the offer period and during a period of 12 months after the end of the offer period.[370]

6.5.4.6 Disclosure

6.423   **6.5.4.6.1 General**   It is a general principle of both the Takeover Directive and the Code that target shareholders must be provided with information sufficient to enable them to make a properly informed decision on the merits of the takeover offer. The Takeover Directive further provides that,

> Member states shall ensure that a bid is made public in such a way as to ensure market transparency and integrity for the securities of the offeree company, of the offeror or of any other company affected by the bid, in particular in order to prevent the publication of false or misleading information.[371]

6.424   Accordingly, the Code contains a number of rules which regulate the provision of information and the contents of documentation circulated during a takeover offer.

---

[367]   Takeover Code Rule 36.6.
[368]   Takeover Code Note 2 to Rule 36.3.
[369]   Takeover Code Rule 36.3.
[370]   Takeover Code Rule 36.3.
[371]   Takeover Directive Article 8(1).

6.5.4.6.2 Code rules concerning information provided during the offer period   **6.425**
The Code stipulates that the issuer of any document (whether that be a company
or an adviser) produced during the offer period must ensure that in relation to
each document and statement made 'the highest standard of care and accuracy' is
adopted. Furthermore, the information provided must be adequately and fairly
presented.[372] Practically, this means that directors and other officials of the companies involved in the takeover offer must be advised at an early stage by their
financial and other advisers of their obligations under the Code and the potential
implications of their discussions and remarks. The Panel regards the financial
advisers as responsible to the Panel for guiding their clients, with relevant public
relations officers being responsible for the information released during the offer
period.[373]

Bearing in mind the general principle contained in both the Takeover Directive   **6.426**
and the Code not to create a false market in the securities of either the target or the
bidder,[374] misleading statements should be avoided by the parties to a takeover.[375]
The obligation is wider than merely preventing factually inaccurate statements
from entering the public domain. Rather, the parties and their advisers must take
care not to issue statements which, whilst not factually inaccurate, may mislead
shareholders and the market or may create uncertainty.[376]

To further the general principle relating to equivalence of treatment of sharehold-   **6.427**
ers of the same class,[377] the Code rules state that all information about companies
involved in an offer must be made equally available to all offeree company shareholders as nearly as possible at the same time and in the same manner.[378] Whilst,
in theory, this principle is easy to grasp, its practical implications must be grappled
with at an early stage and a procedure for ensuring compliance adopted. Meetings
of representatives of the bidder or target and shareholders have the potential to be
problematic and will require the attendance of a representative of the financial
advisers or corporate brokers to the bidder or target (as applicable).[379] According
to Code guidance, the attending advisers will be required, not later than by
12 noon on the business day following the day of the meeting, to confirm to the
Panel that no material new information was forthcoming and no significant new
opinions were expressed at the meeting.[380] Where such new information does

---

[372] Takeover Code Rule 19.1.
[373] Takeover Code Note 1 to Rule 19.1.
[374] Takeover Directive Article 3(1)(d) and Takeover Code General Principle 4.
[375] Takeover Code Rule 19.3.
[376] Takeover Code Rule 19.3.
[377] Takeover Directive Article 1(a), and Takeover Code General Principle 1.
[378] Takeover Code Rule 20.1.
[379] Takeover Code Note 3 to Rule 20.1.
[380] Takeover Code Note 3 to Rule 20.1.

emerge at the meeting, shareholders must be updated with the relevant information by way of circular (which may be supplemented by publication of the relevant information in a national newspaper if the bid is in its final stage) as soon as possible thereafter.[381]

6.428 Accordingly, then, with respect to the provision of information during the offer period, the bidder should generally operate on the basis that it should treat target shareholders in the same manner as it would treat its own shareholders,[382] thereby always seeking to act fairly and to ensure the timely provision of all relevant information.

6.429 **6.5.4.6.3 Material changes to information provided** As a separate matter, target shareholders and persons with information rights must also be informed of any material changes to information previously published by the relevant company during the offer period[383] or, where there have been no such changes, shareholders should be informed of this.[384]

6.5.4.7 *Contents of offer document*

6.430 The offer document is the means by which, traditionally, takeover offers in the UK have been effected. As it is the principal means by which target shareholders are provided with sufficient information to make a properly informed decision about the bid, it is a document of substantial size. It is prepared by the bidder, but if the offer is recommended by the target board, the target will also contribute to its preparation. As the offer document must be posted to shareholders within 28 days of an announcement of a firm offer it is important to ensure that as part of the bidder's deal preparation a reasonable and considered timeframe is drawn up for its preparation.

6.431 **6.5.4.7.1 General terms of the offer** The Takeover Directive provides minimum contents requirements for the contents of the offer document.[385] The offer document should include:

— the terms of the bid;
— the identity of the offeror and, where the offeror is a company, the type, name and registered office of that company;
— the securities or, where appropriate, the class or classes of securities for which the bid is made;
— the consideration offered for each security or class of securities;

---

[381] Takeover Code Note 3 to Rule 20.1.
[382] Takeover Code Rule 23.
[383] Takeover Code Note 1 to Rule 23 and Rule 27.1.
[384] Takeover Code Rule 27.1.
[385] Takeover Directive Article 6(3).

—the compensation offered for the rights which might be removed as a result of the restrictions on the transfer of shares being lifted as a result of the offer;

—the maximum and minimum percentages or quantities of securities which the offeror undertakes to acquire;

—details of any existing holdings of the offeror, and the persons acting in concert with him/her, in the offeree company;

—all the conditions to which the bid is subject;

—the offeror's intentions with regard to the future business of the offeree company and, in so far as it is affected by the bid, the offeror company and with regard to the safeguarding of the jobs of their employees and management, including any material change in the conditions of employment, and in particular the offeror's strategic plans for the two companies and the likely repercussions on employment and the locations of the companies' places of business;

—the time allowed for acceptance of the bid;

—where the consideration offered by the offeror includes securities of any kind, information concerning those securities;

—information concerning the financing for the bid;

—the identity of persons acting in concert with the offeror or with the offeree company and, in the case of companies, their types, names, registered offices and relationships with the offeror and, where possible with the offeree company; and

—the national law which will govern contracts concluded between the offeror and the holders of the offeree company's securities as a result of the bid and the competent courts.

6.432 The prescribed contents are not particularly extensive but the bidder should also consider that member states also have a general duty to ensure that the offer document contains the information necessary to enable the holders of the target's securities to reach a properly informed decision.

6.433 In the UK, the precise content of offer documents varies from transaction to transaction. Their general form and content are nonetheless relatively consistent as a result of the disclosures prescribed by the Code. As can be seen below, the Code incorporates the contents prescribed by the Takeover Directive but also goes significantly further than the Takeover Directive. With respect to general terms, the offer document will always include, but such inclusions shall not be limited to, the following:[386]

   (i) the terms of the offer, including:
      (a) the consideration offered for each class of security;

---

[386] Takeover Code Rule 24.2(d).

    (b) the price at which an offer for the target's shares is being made;

    (c) the total consideration offered; and

    (d) the particulars of the way in which the consideration is to be paid;[387]

  (ii) the details of each class of security for which the offer is made, including whether those securities will be transferred with or without dividend;

  (iii) the date on which the offer document is despatched;

  (iv) the name and address of the bidder (including, if it is a company, its registered office);

  (v) the identity of any person acting in concert with the bidder and, if known, details of the same in relation to the target;

  (vi) all conditions (including the acceptance condition) to which the offer is subject;

  (vii) detailed particulars setting out the procedure[388] and deadline[389] for acceptance of the offer;

  (viii) the middle market quotations for the securities to be acquired and, in the case of a securities exchange offer the securities offered, for the first business day in each of the six months immediately before the date of the offer document, for the last day before the commencement of the offer period and for the latest available date before posting the offer document;

  (ix) details of any irrevocable commitment or letter of intent which the bidder or any of its associates has procured in relation to target securities;

  (x) in the case of a securities exchange offer:

    (a) full particulars of the securities being offered, including the rights attaching to them;

    (b) the effect of full acceptance upon the bidder's assets, profits and business;

  (xi) a summary of the provisions of Rule 8 of the Code (disclosure of dealings during the offer period); and

  (xii) details of any inducement fee or similar arrangement.

6.434   The way in which the offer is to be financed is of critical importance to target shareholders as they may be concerned about both the bidder's ability to pay the consideration and the effect of the bidder's financing package on the target's business following completion of the takeover. The offer document must therefore contain a description of how the bid will be financed and the sources of that finance. It must also name the principal lenders or arrangers of that finance. If the bidder intends to rely on the revenues generated in the target's business to

---

[387] Settlement of consideration, including the date by which it should be paid, is dealt with in Takeover Code Rule 31.8.
[388] Takeover Code Rule 24.2(d)(vii).
[389] Takeover Code Rule 24.6.

satisfy the payment of interest or repayment of security or any other liability associated with the financing of the bid, a description of the arrangements contemplated will also be required.[390]

6.5.4.7.2 Bidder's intentions as regards target The offer document must contain the following information concerning the bidder's intentions as regards the future business of the target, as stipulated by Rule 24 of the Code: **6.435**

(i) the bidder's intention as regards the future business of the target;
(ii) the bidder's strategic plan for the target and the likely repercussions of this on the employees and the location of the target's business;
(iii) the bidder's intentions as regards the redeployment of the fixed assets of the target;
(iv) the long-term commercial justification for the proposed offer; and
(v) the bidder's intentions with regard to the continued employment of the employees and management of the target and its subsidiaries, including any material change in the conditions of employment.[391]

If the bidder's business is to be affected by the takeover, the bidder is also required to disclose information concerning its intentions as regards its own future business, its strategic plans, including repercussions in respect of its own employees and the locations of its business and its intentions concerning the continued employment of its employees and management, including any material change in the conditions of employment.[392] **6.436**

In addition, if the bid is a securities exchange offer, the bidder is required to disclose the effect of the takeover, or any associated transaction on its directors' compensation package. If there is to be no effect, this must be stated.[393] **6.437**

6.5.4.7.3 Financial information The largest section of the offer document is dedicated to the provision of financial information relating to the bidder[394] and the target.[395] **6.438**

The scope of the financial information required to be presented within the offer document is dependent upon (i) the status of the bidder, specifically whether the bidder is incorporated under the Companies Act 2006 (or its predecessor acts) and has its shares admitted to the Official List or to trading on AIM and (ii) the form of consideration being offered by the bidder, specifically whether it is cash only, or includes an issue of securities in the bidder. **6.439**

---

[390] Takeover Code Rule 24.2(f).
[391] Takeover Code Rule 24.1.
[392] Takeover Code Rule 24.1.
[393] Takeover Code Rule 24.4.
[394] Takeover Code Rules 24.2(a) and (b).
[395] Takeover Code Rule 24.2(e).

6.440   Where the bidder complies with the above-mentioned requirements as regards its corporate status and the consideration comprises an issue of shares in the bidder, comprehensive disclosure of financial information is required pursuant to Rule 24.2(a) of the Code.

6.441   Where the bidder complies with the above-mentioned requirements as regards its corporate status and the consideration offered is cash only, the disclosure requirements are pared down to producing figures for turnover and profit and loss before taxation for the last two years for which information has been published, together with a statement of the net assets of the company (as shown in the last published audited accounts), the names of the company's directors, and the nature of the business and its financial and trading prospects.[396]

6.442   Particularly important is the disclosure required where the offer is for cash or includes an element of cash. In such circumstances, a 'cash confirmation' statement is required to be included within the offer document.[397] A discussion of cash confirmation is set out at Sections 6.3.4.12 to 6.3.4.15 of this Chapter.

6.443   **6.5.4.7.4 Disclosure of interests and dealings**   The offer document must set out comprehensive details of the interests (or an appropriate negative statement where there are no such interests) held in target securities by each of the bidder (including any short positions held by it under a derivative instrument or otherwise), its directors, any person acting in concert with it and any person with whom the bidder or any person acting in concert with it has any indemnity or option arrangement relating to the relevant securities.[398]

6.444   Where bidder securities are to form part of the consideration for the target, the holdings in bidder securities of the bidder directors and any person acting in concert with it and any person with whom the bidder or any person acting in concert with it has any indemnity or option arrangement relating to bidder securities must also be disclosed.[399]

6.445   In addition, where the bidder or any person acting in concert with it has borrowed or lent relevant securities in the target or, in the case of a securities exchange offer, the bidder, details of these securities, save to the extent that they have been on-lent or sold, must be incorporated into the offer document.[400]

6.446   Finally, a disclosure is required setting out the details of any dealings in relevant securities of the target, or in the case of a securities exchange offer, the bidder,

---

[396]   Takeover Code Rule 24.2(b).
[397]   Takeover Code Rule 24.7.
[398]   Takeover Code Rule 24.3(a).
[399]   Takeover Code Rule 24.3(a)(i) and (ii).
[400]   Takeover Code Rule 24.3(a)(iv).

during the period beginning 12 months prior to the offer period and ending with the latest practicable date prior to posting the offer document. Where no such dealings have taken place, a negative statement to that effect must be incorporated.[401]

Disclosures relating to dealings are usually presented in tabular form within the offer document. **6.447**

6.5.4.7.5 Responsibility statements Responsibility must be accepted by the directors of the bidder and, where appropriate, the directors of the target in respect of the information contained in each document issued to shareholders or each advertisement published in connection with a bid.[402] A statement of responsibility should therefore be contained within the offer document. The statement should include not only an assumption of responsibility for the information contained within the offer document, but also a confirmation that, to the best of the directors' knowledge and belief (and having taken all reasonable care), the information contained therein is in accordance with the facts and, where appropriate, that nothing has been omitted which is likely to affect the import of such information. Unless Panel consent has been obtained permitting the exclusion of one or more directors, all directors should be included within the scope of this statement.[403] **6.448**

6.5.4.7.6 Other disclosures Unless otherwise agreed by the Panel, the offer document must also contain details of whether or not any special arrangements have been entered into between the bidder or any persons acting in concert with it and any of the directors, recent directors, shareholders or recent shareholders of the target, or any person interested in or recently interested in the target shares or having any connection with or dependence on the bid.[404] If such agreements, arrangements or understandings exist, full particulars of such must be disclosed. **6.449**

Whether the form of consideration will necessitate disclosure in the offer document, or elsewhere should also be considered. As noted at paragraph 6.136 above, a confirmation by an appropriate third party that the bidder has sufficient funds to satisfy full acceptance of the offer must, for example, be included within the offer document where the offer is for cash or includes an element of cash.[405] Further, where securities are to be offered as consideration and those securities are to be admitted to listing on the Official List or to trading on AIM, the relevant admission to listing or admission to trading condition should, except with the **6.450**

---

[401] Takeover Code Rule 24.3(c).
[402] Takeover Code Rule 19.2(a).
[403] Takeover Code Rule 19.2(b).
[404] Takeover Code Rule 24.5.
[405] Takeover Code Rule 24.7.

consent of the Panel, be in terms which ensure that it is capable of being satisfied only when the UKLA or stock exchange (as the case may be) has decided to admit the securities to listing or trading. Equally, it is necessary for the bidder to consult the Panel if securities are to be offered as consideration and it is intended that those securities should be admitted to listing or to trading on any other investment exchange or market.[406] Where shares which are not admitted to trading are offered as consideration, the offer document should contain an estimate, provided by a relevant adviser, of the value of such securities.[407]

6.451 The Panel also requires a statement confirming whether or not, following the acquisition of target shares by the bidder, those securities will be transferred to another entity. If such a transfer is contemplated, the names of those who are party to the agreement, arrangement or understanding in pursuance of which such a transfer will be effected must be included in the offer document, together with particulars of all interests in the securities of the target held by such persons (or a statement that no such interests are held).[408]

6.5.4.8 *Profit forecasts and asset valuations*

6.452 Profit forecasts and asset valuations may be made in the context of a takeover by either the bidder or the target. They are commonly used by the target in hostile situations as a defence tactic.

6.453 **6.5.4.8.1 Profits forecast** The Code interprets the term 'profit forecast' widely.[409] A profit forecast may therefore be a figure, or any statement which contains either a floor or ceiling on, the prospective profits of a company over a specified period. Equally, profit forecasts may be made, notwithstanding the absence of the word 'profit', by the provision of data through which it is possible to calculate the likely profits of a company for a period. For example, the Panel would regard a statement that 'performance in the second half-year is expected to be similar to our performance and results in the first half-year' as a profit forecast.[410]

6.454 Any profit forecast must be prepared with due care and consideration by the directors (who are solely responsible for it) and the financial advisers must satisfy themselves that the forecast has been prepared in this manner by the directors.[411]

6.455 The assumptions, including commercial assumptions, upon which the profit forecast is based must be included within the document containing the

---

[406] Takeover Code Rule 24.9.
[407] Takeover Code Rule 24.10.
[408] Takeover Code Rule 24.8.
[409] Takeover Code Rule 28.6.
[410] Takeover Code Rule 28.6.
[411] Takeover Code Rule 28.1.

profit forecast.[412] The disclosure of such assumptions should be detailed enough to provide a relevant person with enough useful information to be able to form a view as to the reasonableness and reliability of the forecast.[413] As such, the assumptions should be specific and not vague.[414]

Although the responsibility for the profit forecast and assumptions falls to the directors, other advisers must also be comfortable with the assumptions used and the policies adopted in the preparation of the forecast. The financial adviser, for example, has a duty not only to discuss with the directors the assumptions upon which the forecast is based but to satisfy itself that the forecast has been made with due care and consideration.[415] Equally, the auditors must review and be comfortable with the accounting policies and calculations which form the basis of the profit forecast. It is important that such advisers perform their reviews thoroughly because, as mentioned above and with the exception only in the case of an offer solely for cash,[416] both the auditors and the financial adviser must report on the forecasts.[417]   **6.456**

It is important to remember that where a profit forecast has been made prior to the commencement of the offer period, that forecast must be reviewed, repeated and reported on publicly to the shareholders. The directors in question should, if appropriate, state that the forecast remains valid for the purpose of the offer and that the financial advisers and accountants who reported on the forecast have indicated that they have no objection to their reports continuing to apply.[418] The Panel will only permit deviation from the obligations to confirm or revise an existing profit forecast in exceptional circumstances and where it does so permit this, a full explanation as to why the requirements of the Code are not being met must be provided.[419]   **6.457**

As a practical matter, it is therefore prudent for the relevant advisers to ascertain from the outset of their instructions whether or not the client has already issued a profit forecast and, if it has not, whether it wishes to make one within the offer document. In either case, the verification or preparation of the forecast will represent an additional, and not insignificant, work-stream for the target or the bidder and their respective advisers.   **6.458**

---

[412] Takeover Code Rule 28.2.
[413] Takeover Code Note 1(a) to Rule 28.2.
[414] Takeover Code Note 2 to Rule 28.2.
[415] Takeover Code Note 1(c) to Rule 28.2.
[416] Takeover Code Rule 28.3(a).
[417] Takeover Code Rule 28.3(b).
[418] Takeover Code Rule 28.5.
[419] Takeover Code Rule 28.3(e).

6.459   6.5.4.8.2 **Asset valuation**   If a target's business lends itself to valuation based on net assets, an asset valuation may be produced. Any asset valuation prepared in relation to a takeover offer must be supported by the opinion of a named independent valuer,[420] and the basis of valuation must be clearly stated.[421] Only in exceptional circumstances and with the consent of the Panel may such a valuation be qualified or special assumptions be relied upon.[422]

6.5.4.9 *Other documents*

6.460   6.5.4.9.1 **Prospectus**   A prospectus is required pursuant to sections 85(1) and 85(2) of the Financial Services and Markets Act 2000 if securities are offered to the public or are admitted to trading on a regulated market.

6.461   If the purchaser is offering share consideration which falls into either of these two limbs, it will be required to produce a prospectus complying with the Prospectus Rules of the Financial Services Authority and the guidance produced by the Committee of European Securities Regulators.

6.462   The obligations under the Prospectus Rules are extensive and significant time and cost will be incurred in producing a prospectus. Accordingly, the bidder should consider whether the ability to offer consideration shares is outweighed by the disadvantage of having to produce the prospectus.

6.463   6.5.4.9.2 **Forms of acceptance and CREST**   Traditionally, target shareholders have accepted a takeover offer by completing and returning to the bidder a hard copy form of acceptance. This is still the required method of acceptance for shareholders whose shares are held in certificated form.

6.464   Where target shares are held in uncertificated form by a shareholder, because settlement of the company's shares is operated through CREST and the shareholder has opted not to retain its shares in certificated form, the bidder must provide for hard copy and CREST acceptance mechanisms as part of its offer.

6.465   Euroclear UK & Ireland Limited, the company which operates CREST, has issued guidance on the operation of CREST in a takeover process as well as wording which may be incorporated into the offer documentation, where an uncertificated settlement process is to be adopted.[423]

6.466   Transfer of legal title in CREST shares occurs simultaneously with electronic settlement in CREST.[424]

---

[420] Takeover Code Rule 29.1.
[421] Takeover Code Rule 29.2(a).
[422] Takeover Code Rule 29.2(a).
[423] CREST, Corporate Actions Standardization (Version 4).
[424] Uncertificated Securities Regulations 2001 (SI 2001 No 3755).

6.6 Using a Scheme of Arrangement as an Alternative to a Takeover Offer

6.6.1 What is a scheme of arrangement?

In certain circumstances, it may be appropriate to consider whether to implement **6.467** an acquisition by way of a scheme of arrangement (a 'scheme') as opposed to a conventional takeover offer. A scheme is a process whereby a target company enters into a compromise or arrangement with its shareholders and/or creditors, or any class of them. In the UK a takeover by way of a scheme is governed by the procedure in Part 26 of the Companies Act 2006 as well as by the Code.

The court procedure for implementing a scheme in the UK is set out in Part 49 **6.468** of the Civil Procedure Rules 1998, Practice Direction 49 (Applications Under the Companies Acts and Related Legislation) and Chapter 20 of the Chancery Guide.

This Section examines the procedure for effecting a scheme and compares the **6.469** benefits and disadvantages of using a scheme in comparison with an offer.

6.6.2 Overview of the process for undertaking a scheme of arrangement

6.6.2.1 *The scheme process*

6.6.2.1.1 Identification of classes of shareholders and creditors The scheme **6.470** must be approved at a court-ordered meeting of the shareholders and creditors of the target or at separate meetings of each class of shareholder and/or creditor of the target.[425] For the purposes of this Chapter such meeting or meetings are together referred to as the 'scheme meeting'.

The constitution of classes of shareholders and creditors is a critical issue as **6.471** the court cannot sanction the scheme unless meetings of the correct classes of shareholders and creditors have been held.

It is primarily the target's responsibility to identify whether different classes of **6.472** shareholders and creditors exist and to convene properly constituted meetings of each class.[426] Whilst the composition of a class will depend on the circumstances in each case, the general test established by Bowen LJ in *Sovereign Life Assurance Co v Dodd* [1892] 2 QB 573 is that a class 'must be confined to those persons whose rights are not so dissimilar as to make it impossible for them to consult together with a view to their common interest'. This test was expanded in *Re Hawk Insurance Company Ltd* [2001] 2 BCLC 480 where Chadwick LJ stated that in

---

[425] Companies Act 2006 section 896(1).
[426] *Practice Statement (Companies: Schemes of Arrangement)* [2002] 3 All ER 96.

addition 'those whose rights are sufficiently similar to the rights of others that they can properly consult together should be required to do so'. The overall outcome of these tests is that unless significant dissimilarities in rights exist, all members and creditors should be capable of forming the same class.

6.473 A common concern is whether shareholders who have given irrevocable undertakings to vote in favour of a scheme should be classified as a separate class of shareholder, as this would negate the benefit in obtaining the undertaking. This matter has not to date been the subject of a challenge and practice in recent years has evolved in favour of obtaining such undertakings. This practice could, however, come under scrutiny by a court if the scheme would not have been approved but for the acceptances of the shareholders who had given undertakings to support it. The nature of the undertaking will also be relevant, including its scope, the time period it is given for, the consequences of breach and the ability for the undertaking to lapse if the circumstances change materially. Even if the court concludes that the mere giving of an irrevocable does not constitute a separate class it may be relevant to the court's overriding obligation to consider the fairness of the scheme when deciding whether to sanction it or not.

6.474 If the target is concerned about the division of classes it should bring any issues which may arise to the attention of the court as early as possible.[427] The court will consider the constitution of the classes and give appropriate directions for the resolution of any issues when it grants the target leave to convene the scheme meeting.[428] This may include affording anyone affected by the meeting a period of time to object to the scheme meeting being convened.[429]

6.475 6.6.2.1.2 **Application to the court**   The target must apply to the Companies Court for a court order seeking:

(i) directions for convening the scheme meeting;
(ii) court sanction of the scheme if it is approved by the relevant members and/or creditors of the target at such scheme meeting; and
(iii) a direction that the target shall file a copy of a report to the court by the chairman of the relevant meeting.[430]

6.476 The application is made by filing a claim form[431] supported by a witness statement by a director of the target which includes statutory information about the target (such as details of its incorporation, registered office and share capital) and key

---

[427] *Practice Statement (Companies: Schemes of Arrangement)* [2002] 3 All ER 96.
[428] Ibid.
[429] Ibid.
[430] Companies Act 2006 section 896 and New Practice Direction 49 paragraph 7.
[431] New Practice Direction 49 paragraph 5.

information relating to the scheme[432] such as its purpose, the proposed location and constitution of the scheme meeting, the proposed chairperson of the scheme meeting and any advertisement in respect of the scheme meeting. The witness statement will also attach the scheme, the draft explanatory statement (otherwise known as the 'scheme circular') to be sent to members and/or creditors, draft notices convening the scheme meeting and proxy forms for use at the scheme meeting.

6.6.2.1.3 Convening the meeting   The court has a discretion as to whether or not to grant leave to the target to convene a scheme meeting, but would ordinarily not refuse the target's application unless it had reason to believe that the necessary level of shareholder approval for the scheme could not be obtained. The hearing is generally before a registrar, unless there are complex substantive issues in which case it may be referred to a judge.   **6.477**

The court will make an order on the claim form approving the form of the explan- **6.478** atory statement, the notice convening the scheme meeting, the advertisement of the scheme meeting (if any) and the proxy form to be used at the scheme meeting and setting a date for the scheme meeting. If there are any issues associated with the constitution of classes of shareholders and/or creditors, the court will consider these issues and give any directions on the composition of the classes which it considers necessary. The claim form is then adjourned until after the scheme meeting has been held.

The target is responsible for sending the notice and proxy form, in the form **6.479** approved by the court, to its shareholders and/or creditors summoning the scheme meeting and publishing the advertisement in the form approved by the court (if required).

The notice and advertisement (if any) must be accompanied by an explanatory **6.480** statement which explains:

(i)   the effect of the compromise or arrangement;
(ii) any material interests of directors of the target company; and
(iii) the effect on those interests of the compromise or arrangement to the extent that they differ from the effect of like interests on other members or creditors.[433]

The bidder and target commonly jointly prepare and issue to shareholders and **6.481** creditors a composite document known as the 'scheme document' or 'scheme circular', containing the notice of meeting, explanatory statement, a joint letter from the bidder and target recommending the scheme to shareholders and the

---

[432] New Practice Direction 49 paragraph 7.
[433] Companies Act 2006 section 897(1).

terms of the scheme. The scheme document must also satisfy the same content requirements as for an offer, which are prescribed by the Code and discussed in detail in Section 6.5 above.

6.482   As is the case with an offer, the Code requires the scheme to contain a condition that it will lapse if a reference is made to the Competition Commission or merger-regulation proceedings are initiated.[434]

6.483   The scheme meeting must be held no earlier than 21 days after the posting of the scheme circular, subject to any longer notice requirements contained in the target's articles of association.[435] Unless the Panel grants an extension, the scheme circular must be posted to shareholders within 28 days of the initial announcement of the proposed scheme.[436]

6.484   **6.6.2.1.4 Scheme meeting**   At the scheme meeting, if a majority in number representing 75% in value of the members or creditors or class of members or creditors present and voting agree to the scheme, then the company may make a further application to the court for a court order sanctioning the scheme.[437] Any votes in respect of shares held by the bidder and/or its associates will not be included when tallying the votes. The votes will be conducted on a poll to ensure that the value of the shares is correctly tallied.

6.485   As soon as practicable after the results of the scheme meeting are known, and by no later than 8.00 am the following business day, the target must make an announcement of the results of the scheme meeting.[438] In addition, the chairman of the scheme meeting is required to report to the court on the conduct and outcome of the meeting, including the number and value of shareholders who attended and who did not attend, the number of votes for and against and details of any proxies which were rejected.

6.486   A witness statement by the appropriate person (such as the company's registrar, the printers and/or the mailing house) confirming the proper despatch of the scheme documents to shareholders and a witness statement verifying the chairman's report on the meeting must be filed with the court before the meeting at which the court will consider sanctioning the scheme.

6.487   **6.6.2.1.5 Court sanction of the scheme**   The court will consider whether to sanction the scheme at a second court hearing in respect of the claim form.[439] In determining whether to exercise its discretion to sanction a scheme, the court

---

[434] Takeover Code Rule 12.1(a)(ii).
[435] Takeover Code Rule 3 of Appendix 7.
[436] Takeover Code Rule 30.1(a).
[437] Companies Act 2006 section 899.
[438] Section 5, Schemes Appendix.
[439] Companies Act 2006 section 899.

will consider whether the approval of the scheme is 'reasonable'. The test of reasonableness was stated by Maugham J in *Re Dorman Long & Co Limited* [1934] 1 Ch 635 to be 'whether the proposal is such that an intelligent and honest man, a member of the class concerned and acting in respect of his interests, might reasonably approve'. An independent adviser's recommendation of the scheme may be taken into account by the court as evidence that the scheme is reasonable.

The court will also consider whether the procedural and content requirements **6.488** relating to the issue of the notice of meeting and explanatory statement and other regulatory requirements were strictly complied with, and may refuse to sanction the scheme if there has been a procedural error or material failure to comply with the law. In particular, the court will consider whether the explanatory statement is fair and contains the necessary information to enable shareholders and/or creditors to determine how to vote. If the court considers that a matter was not disclosed which would have affected shareholders' views, it may refuse to sanction the scheme.[440] If a material matter arises after the explanatory statement is posted to shareholders but before the scheme meeting, the target should send details of the matter to shareholders before the scheme meeting. It may be necessary to adjourn the scheme meeting to allow shareholders sufficient time to consider the new information, depending on the circumstances. If a material matter arises after shareholder approval of the scheme is obtained, the target should again send details of the matter to shareholders but may also need to re-apply to the court to reconvene the scheme meeting and issue a revised scheme circular if it is a matter which would affect the way in which shareholders vote.

Schemes are often considered to afford the bidder less flexibility than an offer due **6.489** to the court process involved. No revision to a scheme can be proposed less than 14 days before the scheme meeting, or after the scheme meeting, without the Panel's consent.[441] The Code Committee of the Panel has indicated that the Panel should normally consent to a revision of a scheme in the 14 days before the scheme meeting if the target board and independent adviser (appointed under Rule 3 of the Code) each confirm to the Panel that:

(i)   in their opinion the revision is in the best interests of the target shareholders;
(ii) in their opinion, it is in the target shareholders' best interests for the revision to be considered without adjournment of the meeting;
(iii) in its opinion, the resolutions to approve and give effect to the revised scheme are likely to be passed if the scheme meeting is not adjourned; and
(iv) that they have received legal advice that the proposed revision would not be likely to result in the court refusing to sanction the scheme.[442]

---

[440] *Re Jessell Trust Limited* [1985] BCLC 119.
[441] Takeover Code section 7 Appendix 7.
[442] Takeover Panel Response Statement 2007/1 paragraph 7.5.

6.490   The target's board must also undertake to apply for an adjournment if it no longer believes the resolutions are likely to be passed.[443]

6.491   The court will also consider whether each class of member and/or creditor was fairly represented, as if only a single member of a class voted at the scheme meeting this would not be representative of the interests of the class.

6.492   Although the court has a discretion as to whether or not to approve a scheme, it would normally be reluctant not to approve a Scheme if it has been approved by the requisite shareholder and/or creditor majorities and there are no other compelling circumstances to do so (such as new material developments or material non-disclosures in the scheme circular). The court may also impose conditions on its sanction of the scheme.

6.493   If the scheme is sanctioned by the court it becomes binding on all shareholders and creditors of the relevant classes and the company with effect from the time it is delivered to the Registrar of Companies.[444] The target must make an announcement once the scheme has been sanctioned by the court and when the scheme becomes effective.[445]

6.6.3 Timetable

6.494   The table below sets out a timetable for implementing a scheme. The timetable can be compared with the offer timetable set out at Section 6.5.4.3 of this Chapter.

Day (D)	Scheme
Up to D −28	Court timetable agreed with Companies Court and Chancery Listings.
D −28	Earliest day to release press announcement.
D −9	Issue Part 8 claim form, and supporting witness statement, seeking an order of the court to convene shareholders' meeting.
D −3	Last day for material alterations to the scheme document.
D −2	• Court hearing of the claim form, order granted to convene shareholders' meeting. • Submit scheme document and drafts of the order, notice of scheme meeting and forms of proxy for the shareholders meetings to the Registrar.
D	• Post scheme document and proxy forms to shareholders. • Convene scheme meeting and extraordinary general meeting to consider other issues ('EGM').
D +24	Scheme meeting and EGM held, resolutions passed.

---

[443] Takeover Panel Response Statement 2007/1 paragraph 7.5.
[444] Companies Act 2006 section 899(4).
[445] Takeover Code section 5, Schemes Appendix.

(Continued)

Day (D)	Scheme
D +25	• Present petition to the court; • Issue application notice for directions to be given to fix the date of the hearing of the petition and the reduction.
D +32	Hearing of application for directions, order granted for hearings to sanction the scheme and reduction.
D +33	Advertise notice of petition hearing as directed by the court.
D +43	Hearing of petition to sanction the scheme, final order granted.
D +45	Hearing to confirm the reduction of capital, order granted and minute stamped.
D +46	• Registration of order sanctioning the scheme and the order confirming the reduction of capital and minute with Registrar of Companies. • Scheme becomes effective.
D +47	Advertise notice of reduction of capital as directed by the court.

6.6.4 Types of scheme

There are two main types of scheme of arrangement; a reduction scheme and a transfer scheme. A reduction scheme involves a reduction of capital, whereby the shares of the target are cancelled, the bidder pays the consideration to target shareholders for the cancellation of their shares and the reserve created by the cancellation is applied in paying up the new shares issued by the target to the bidder. A transfer scheme is effected by way of the transfer of the target's shares to the bidder. Alternatively, a hybrid scheme can be used, which comprises a combination of reduction and transfer schemes, whereby some shareholders roll over their shares for loan notes in the bidder in order to obtain capital gains tax relief under section 136 of the Taxation of Chargeable Gains Act 1992 and the balance of the shares are cancelled for cash. **6.495**

The reduction scheme is more common as it gives rise to stamp duty savings due to the fact that there is no transfer of shares. **6.496**

In a reduction scheme, the standard procedure for effecting a reduction of capital (contained in sections 641 to 653 of the Companies Act 2006 in the UK) is carried out contemporaneously with the scheme process. As a scheme meeting may, however, only consider matters relating to the approval of the scheme, a separate general meeting of the target company is required to consider the reduction of capital. These meetings are invariably held on the same day, one after the other. The scheme document will contain notices for both meetings. **6.497**

In a reduction scheme, a second hearing of the claim form is required at which the target seeks an order from the court to publish an advertisement in a newspaper in respect of the scheme meeting. **6.498**

6.499   The final court hearing at which the court determines whether to sanction the scheme is also often split into two sessions with a short gap of two or more days between the sessions. Whilst this is not necessary, an advantage of holding the reduction of capital meeting after the scheme meeting is that optionholders have the opportunity to exercise their options in the period between the sanction of the scheme and the court order confirming the reduction of capital, so that the shares issued on exercise of the options are included in the scheme and reduction of capital. The first session is used to deal with the approval of the scheme and the second session is used to confirm the reduction of capital. In this scenario, the scheme will become effective on the date on which the court order confirming the reduction of capital and minute of the reduction are delivered to the Registrar of Companies.

6.6.5 Other applicable regulations

6.6.5.1 *UK Listing Rules*

6.500   If the bidder is a listed company it will also be subject to the Listing Rules and may be required to obtain shareholder approval if the merger constitutes a Class 1 transaction under the Listing Rules.[446] The UK Listing Authority has indicated that it would not normally expect to review the scheme circular unless there are unusual features or circumstances. The provisions of Listing Rule 13 relating to contents of circulars will still apply however and if the target's shares will be delisted the target company will need to comply with Listing Rule 5, which sets out the requirements for delisting.

6.6.5.2 *Prospectus Rules*

6.501   The FSA has indicated that a scheme would not ordinarily involve an offer to the public which requires a prospectus to be issued under the Prospectus Rules as the transaction is effected through a court procedure under which the members and/or creditors vote on the compromise or arrangement.[447] If, however, the scheme involves the issue of a new class of shares in the bidder which will be admitted to trading on a regulated market (such as the Main Market of the London Stock Exchange) or an increase of 10% or more of a class of shares that are already admitted to trading on a regulated market, a prospectus would be required.[448] In contrast, if the bidder made a share-for-share exchange offer, the bidder would need to prepare a prospectus in addition to the offer document on the basis that there would be an offer to the public of securities in the bidder.[449]

---

[446]   LR 10.2.2R.
[447]   List! Issue No 10 (June 2005) (Prospectus Directive and Role of Sponsor).
[448]   Prospectus Rule 1.2.3R.
[449]   List! Issue No. 10 (June 2005) (Prospectus Directive and Role of Sponsor).

6.6.6 Differences between an offer under the Takeover Code and a scheme of arrangement

The tables below consider some of the principal advantages and disadvantages of using a scheme as opposed to an offer. **6.502**

6.6.6.1 *Advantages of a scheme in comparison with an offer*

Offer	Scheme
No remaining minority	
Compulsory acquisition of non-accepting shares is only possible if the bidder receives acceptances in respect of 90% or more in value and voting rights of the shares the subject of the offer. Shares acquired by the bidder before the offer is made are disregarded for the purposes of the 90% calculation.	If the scheme is approved, all shareholders will be bound and no minority interests will remain.
Timeframe for obtaining 100% control is shorter	
The timetable may initially be shorter as the minimum period during which the offer must remain open for acceptances is 21 days from when the offer document is posted to the offer. If, however, after an offer a bidder has to go through the compulsory acquisition procedure in order to obtain 100% ownership of the target, this would add at least an additional six weeks to the overall process from the date on which the 90% threshold is attained.	Although the timetable for implementing a scheme depends somewhat on the court's schedule, as a general estimate a scheme may take four to six weeks longer for control to pass to the bidder, from the date of announcement to the date on which the scheme becomes effective, than the shortest possible period of an offer from the announcement date to the earliest date it could be declared wholly unconditional. A scheme, however, ensures 100% control once effective so the timeframe for acquiring 100% control may be faster than an offer which goes through the compulsory acquisition process to reach 100% control.
Security for debt finance can be put in place more rapidly and with more certainty	
The ability of a finance provider to obtain security from the target in respect of any debt finance provided to the bidder to fund the acquisition can only be assured once the bidder has 100% control over the target and either converts it to a private company or carries out a whitewash, as the giving of security by the target would constitute unlawful financial assistance in connection with the acquisition of its shares. There will be a delay of at least six weeks after the compulsory acquisition threshold is reached before either the privatization or whitewash can be carried out.	Actions that would be permitted if the target were a private company can be approved by the court as part of the scheme,[450] or the re-registration of the target as a private company can be carried out very shortly after the date on which the scheme becomes effective, allowing the security to be put in place earlier than for an offer.

---

[450] Companies Act 2006 section 681(2)(e).

(Continued)

Offer	Scheme

No stamp duty liability on a reduction scheme

Stamp duty is levied at approximately 0.5% of the consideration paid by the bidder for the shares in the target.	If a scheme is structured as a reduction scheme, there would not be any stamp duty liability as the shares in the target are cancelled and re-issued, rather than transferred, which is not a dutiable event.
	If, however, the scheme is structured as a transfer scheme whereby the shares in the target are transferred to the bidder, a stamp duty liability may still arise.

Scheme may benefit from helpful exemptions under US securities laws and other overseas securities laws

If less than 10% of the target's shares are owned by US persons, the offer can be made into the US pursuant to the Tier 1 exemption from the US tender offer rules. However, if between 10% and 40% of the target's shares are held by US persons, then under Tier II most US tender offer rules apply and a US registration statement will be required.	A scheme may benefit from exemptions under the securities laws of other jurisdictions which would not be available if the transaction was structured as an offer. For example, a scheme is not subject to the US tender offer regulations and a registration statement under section 3(a)(10) of the US Securities Act of 1933 is not needed.
	Jurisdictions which do not generally regard a scheme as a tender offer, or which provide an exemption for it, include Australia, Canada, Japan, Russia, South Africa, Hungary, Ireland, the Netherlands, Poland, Portugal, Romania, Slovak Republic and Spain.

Trading in target shares

Accepting shareholders must submit share certificates or transfer shares into escrow. Institutions often wait as long as practicable before accepting to preserve flexibility.	Target shareholders can usually continue trading up to the final court hearing date.

Prospectus requirement (on securities exchange offer)

Preparation and approval by FSA of a prospectus, or equivalent document, to accompany the offer document would normally be required where securities are offered as consideration.	The FSA currently takes the view that the requirement for a prospectus or equivalent document does not apply where securities are issued pursuant to a scheme as there is no offer to the public (NB a prospectus may nonetheless be needed in order to obtain a listing of the consideration shares).

6.6.6.2 Disadvantages of a scheme in comparison with an offer

Offer	Scheme

Higher acceptance level for control

The bidder may set the minimum acceptance condition at any level giving it more than 50% voting control, so a lower threshold is required for the bidder to obtain an interest in the target.	Approval is 'all or nothing'. A majority in number of shareholders actually voting, representing at least 75% in value of shares actually voted is required, so the initial threshold required in order for a scheme to succeed is higher than for an offer. In addition, shares held by the bidder cannot be voted.

(Continued)

Offer	Scheme

Schemes tend to be more expensive

| As there are no court procedures involved costs can be minimized. | The court process inevitably increases the cost of implementing a scheme, although the stamp duty saving may negate the increased cost making it overall more economical to undertake a scheme than an offer. |

Schemes cannot be used in a hostile scenario

| An offer can be hostile or recommended. | A scheme can realistically only be completed with the cooperation of target directors, therefore is not practical in a hostile situation. |

Undertakings to vote

| Before making an offer which is recommended by the target board, it is common for the bidder to obtain undertakings from major shareholders and director shareholders of the target that they will accept the offer in respect of the shares they hold and these shares can be counted towards the 90% compulsory acquisition threshold. | There has in the past been some degree of uncertainty as to whether shareholders who have given undertakings to vote in favour of a scheme could be deemed by the court to be a separate class of shareholder, resulting in the need to requisition a separate meeting of shareholders of that class to approve the scheme. Alternatively, binding commitments to vote in favour could prejudice the fairness of the scheme in the eyes of the court. |

Lack of flexibility

| It is relatively easy to change terms of an offer, subject to limitations imposed by the Code. | It is more complicated to change the terms of a scheme in a material way (except a simple price increase) without restarting the timetable due to the court process involved. NB It is possible to switch from a scheme to an offer.[451] |

Court sanction is required

| No court approval needed. | Court approval is needed and the decision as to whether to sanction the Scheme is at the court's discretion, although the court would usually be reluctant to reject a scheme approved by the required majorities, absent compelling circumstances (such as material conflicts of interest, failures in disclosure or new developments). There is also a risk that the court hearing could provide a forum for opposition to the merger, causing delay or disruption. In practice contested hearings are infrequent and the court would normally deal with any objections quickly. |

Process is driven more by the target

| The bidder issues the offer document and normally leads on its preparation and in driving the offer process, although on a recommended | The scheme circular and court filings can only be issued by the target, giving it more control over the process and leaving the bidder open to the |

---

[451] Takeover Code section 8, Appendix 7.

(Continued)

Offer	Scheme
offer target directors are responsible for certain sections and the document will typically be a joint effort.	risk that the target may withdraw the scheme before it becomes effective if, for example, a higher rival bid is received.
It is not usual to sign a formal agreement for the deal, except as regards ancillary matters such as break fees or non-solicitation ('no-shop').	This can to some extent be mitigated by the parties agreeing the relevant timetable deadlines and actions to be taken in the 'cooperation' or 'implementation' agreement before the scheme is announced.

<table>
<tr><td colspan="2" align="center">Market purchases by the bidder do not contribute to acceptance levels</td></tr>
<tr><td>Only purchases of target shares made by the bidder after posting of the offer document (not simply after announcement of the offer) will count towards the 90% compulsory acquisition threshold.</td><td>Share purchases would usually be counterproductive, as shares acquired cannot be voted in favour of the scheme. However a strategic purchase may still be advantageous to 'neutralize' shares that might be voted against or sold to opponents instead.</td></tr>
</table>

6.6.7 Ownership and control

6.503 In considering whether to structure the transaction as a scheme or a contractual offer, the level of shareholder support the bidder predicts that it will receive and the bidder's goal in terms of ownership control of the target company will be key considerations.

6.6.7.1 *Obtaining 100% ownership of the target*

6.504 The main advantage of a scheme is that a lower acceptance level is required in order to obtain 100% ownership of the target and certainty that there will be no remaining minority shareholders. In order for a scheme to be implemented, approval of shareholders who hold at least 75% by value of the shares voted at the scheme meeting must be obtained. In contrast, under an offer a bidder must receive acceptances in respect of 90% of both the value and voting rights of the shares to which the offer relates before it becomes entitled to use the compulsory acquisition procedure (the compulsory acquisition procedure is discussed in detail in Section 6.10 of this Chapter) to acquire the balance of the shares and bring its ownership interest in the target company to 100%. As a result, a lower level of shareholder support is required in order for a bidder to obtain 100%. ownership of a target when using a scheme in comparison with an offer.

6.505 If any shareholder in the target company holds a 'blocking stake' of 10% or more of the value and voting rights of the shares, although this holding would prevent a bidder reaching the compulsory acquisition threshold of 90% under an offer, the bidder may still be able to acquire a 100% ownership interest in the target under a scheme if the relevant approval thresholds are met.

6.6.7.2 *Obtaining a majority interest in the target*

An offer may proceed on an unconditional basis once the bidder receives accept-   **6.506**
ances in respect of more than 50% of the voting rights only (regardless of value) in
respect of the shares to which the offer relates.[452] Bidders who are not seeking
100% ownership of a target or who are not confident of achieving the approval
threshold required for a scheme may prefer to use the offer process as a means
of becoming a majority shareholder in the target, even though they may not ultimately end up owning the whole of the target if the 90% compulsory acquisition
threshold is not reached. Alternatively, if a bidder is not prepared to tolerate any
minority shareholders remaining after the merger, a scheme would be preferable
as it ensures 100% ownership if approved.

6.7 Mandatory Offers

6.7.1 When is a mandatory offer required?

It is a general principle of the Takeover Directive that if a person acquires control   **6.507**
of a company, the other holders of securities must be protected[453] (this is also
enshrined in General Principle 1 of the Takeover Code). This general principle is
fleshed out by Article 5 of the Takeover Directive which provides that,

> where a natural or legal person, as a result of his/her own acquisition or the acquisition
> by persons acting in concert with him/her, holds securities of a company as referred to
> in Article 1(1) which, added to any existing holding of those securities of his/hers and
> the holdings of those persons acting in concert with him/her, directly or indirectly give
> him/her a specified percentage of voting rights in that company, giving him/her con-
> trol of that company, Member States shall ensure that such person is required to make
> a bid as a means of protecting the minority shareholders of that company ...[454]

It is up to each member state to determine the percentage of voting rights that
constitutes control.[455]

Article 5 of the Takeover Directive has been implemented in the UK by the Code   **6.508**
providing that, except with the consent of the Panel, it is mandatory pursuant to
Rule 9 of the Code for a person to make an offer for all of the equity share capital
of a company if:

(i) such person acquires an interest in shares which, when aggregated with the
     interests in shares held by persons acting in concert with them, would carry
     30% or more of the voting rights in the company;[456] or

---

[452] Takeover Code Rule 10.
[453] Takeover Directive Article 3(1)(a).
[454] Takeover Directive Article 5(1).
[455] Takeover Directive Article 5(3).
[456] Takeover Code Rule 9.1(a).

(ii) a person, together with persons acting in concert with them, holds 30% or more but less than 50% of the voting rights in a company and either such person or any person acting in concert with them increases the percentage of voting rights in which they are interested.[457]

6.509 This obligation is not one to be taken lightly and if there is any doubt as to whether or not a person will trigger the mandatory bid obligation they should consult the Panel for guidance at the earliest opportunity.

6.7.2 Terms on which a mandatory offer must be made

6.510 When acquiring shares in a public company, investors should be careful not to permit their interests in voting shares to reach the thresholds in Rule 9 of the Code or they will be required to make an offer for the entire company. Even if the investor is considering making an offer for the entire target company, it should take care to avoid the mandatory offer obligations as the terms on which a mandatory offer under Rule 9 of the Code must be made are significantly more restrictive than the terms on which a voluntary offer or scheme can be proposed, as Rule 9 of the Code imposes limitations on the minimum offer price and level of conditionality permitted.

6.7.2.1 *Consideration*

6.511 Article 5 of the Takeover Directive provides that a bidder making a mandatory offer must, unless the consideration offered consists of liquid securities admitted to trading on a regulated market, include a cash alternative.[458] The directive also allows member states to provide that cash consideration must be offered, at least as an alternative in all cases. The UK has taken this stricter line and, accordingly, a mandatory offer made under Rule 9 of the Code must be in cash or accompanied by a cash alternative,[459] whereas a voluntary offer can be made in any form of consideration, including shares in the bidder. [460]

6.512 The Takeover Directive provides that a mandatory offer must be made at a price not less than the highest price paid by the bidder or any person acting in concert with the bidder for any interest in shares of the relevant class during a period prior to the announcement of the offer determined by the relevant member state.[461] The directive allows member states to specify a period of not less than six months but not more than 12 months.[462] In the UK, the relevant period has been set

---

[457] Takeover Code Rule 9.1(b).
[458] Takeover Directive Article 5(5).
[459] Takeover Code Rule 9.5(a).
[460] Takeover Code Rule 6.1.
[461] Takeover Directive Article 5(4).
[462] Ibid.

at 12 months.[463] In a voluntary offer, the 12-month rule would only apply if the bidder and persons acting in concert with it acquired 10% or more of the voting rights in the class of shares under offer during the 12-month period before the announcement of the offer.[464] Generally, the minimum offer price in a voluntary offer is calculated by reference to the most favourable terms offered by the bidder for shares in the target in the three months prior to the announcement of the offer.[465] In addition, regardless of whether the offer is made on a mandatory or voluntary basis, if during the offer period the bidder or any person acting in concert with it acquires shares above the offer price, the offer price must also be increased to not less than the highest price paid for such shares and the bidder must announce the acquisition.[466]

The Takeover Directive allows member states some flexibility in adjusting the price at which a mandatory offer is made. It provides that: **6.513**

> Provided that the general principles laid down in Article 3(1) are respected, Member States may authorise their supervisory authorities to adjust the price referred to in the first sub-paragraph in circumstances and in accordance with criteria that are clearly determined. To that end they may draw up a list of circumstances in which the highest price may be adjusted either upwards or downwards ... They may also determine the criteria to be applied.[467]

Accordingly, in the UK, the Panel may allow an adjustment to the minimum price at which a mandatory offer must be made in certain circumstances. In determining whether to permit such an adjustment, the Panel will take into account: **6.514**

  (i) the size and timing of the relevant acquisitions of shares in the target;

 (ii) the attitude of the board of the target;

(iii) whether interests in shares had been acquired at high prices from directors or persons closely connected with the bidder or target;

 (iv) the number of shares acquired in the preceding 12 months;

  (v) if the offer is being made to save a company from financial distress; and

 (vi) the circumstances in which the obligation to make the offer arose, in particular if it arose simply because someone was given a gift of shares triggering the thresholds or because a shareholding interest was magnified as a result of a redemption or buy-back by the company of its shares.[468]

---

[463] Takeover Code Rule 9.5(a).
[464] Takeover Code Rule 11.1(a).
[465] Takeover Code Rule 6.1.
[466] Takeover Code Rule 6.2 in respect of a voluntary offer and Takeover Code Rule 9.5(b) in respect of a mandatory offer.
[467] Takeover Directive Article 5(4).
[468] Takeover Code Note 3 to Rule 9.5.

6.515   Absent a dispensation granted by the Panel, the form and price of a mandatory offer are more restrictive than for a voluntary offer and the bidder will therefore try to avoid triggering the mandatory bid obligation in order to retain as much flexibility as possible in relation to the form of consideration and price of the offer.

6.7.2.2 Conditions

6.516   The Takeover Directive provides that, in relation to mandatory bids, member states may make further provisions intended to protect the interests of holders of securities, so long as those provisions do not hinder the normal course of a bid.[469] In the UK, one such provision relates to conditions to the bid. Except with the consent of the Panel, the only condition to which a mandatory offer may be subject is that the bidder receives acceptances from shareholders which will result in the bidder and persons acting in concert with it holding 50% or more of the target's voting rights.[470] If the bidder and persons acting in concert with it hold 50% or more of the target's voting rights before the mandatory offer is made, the bid should be unconditional.[471] The Panel will not normally grant any dispensations to permit the offer to be subject to additional conditions, except in exceptional circumstances such as where a regulatory consent is required before the offer document is posted to shareholders.[472]

6.517   In contrast, in a voluntary offer the bidder has freedom to make the offer subject to whatever conditions it considers necessary to protect its interests, subject to the requirements that the conditions do not depend on the subjective judgment of the bidder's board in order to determine whether or not they have been triggered[473] and the offer cannot be declared unconditional unless the bidder holds shares which carry over 50% of the voting rights in the target.[474] The type of conditions commonly imposed by the bidder are discussed at Section 6.5.4.4 of this Chapter.

6.518   Importantly, the bidder normally makes a voluntary bid subject to a condition that it receives 90% or more acceptances so that the bidder can use the compulsory acquisition procedure to acquire the minority non-assenting shareholders at the conclusion of the offer, or 75% acceptances so that it may unilaterally pass special resolutions and can de-list the target. As this type of condition cannot be imposed in a mandatory offer, the bidder is exposed to the risk that it will be a

---

[469]   Takeover Directive Article 5(6).
[470]   Takeover Code Rule 9.3(a).
[471]   Takeover Code Note 1 to Rule 9.3.
[472]   Takeover Code Note 3(b) to Rule 9.3.
[473]   Takeover Code Rule 13.1.
[474]   Takeover Code Rule 10.

majority shareholder but unable to use the compulsory acquisition procedure to acquire 100% ownership of the target or unable to pass special resolutions.

A bidder making a mandatory offer cannot impose conditions which allow it to withdraw its offer if material circumstances arise after the offer is made which could affect the bidder's willingness to proceed with the offer. The bidder therefore loses its ability to protect its interests and is exposed to the risk that it may be forced to acquire an entity which has become undesirable due to a matter which has arisen after the offer was made. In a mandatory offer, the bidder will only be able to rely on the limited protection afforded by the prohibition in Rule 21.2 of the Code on the target carrying out certain actions which might frustrate the offer in order to protect its interests. As a result, the bidder will be concerned to avoid triggering the mandatory bid obligation so as to retain the flexibility to make the offer subject to conditions which allow the bidder to protect its interests.

6.519

As for a voluntary offer, the Code requires that terms of any mandatory bid must, if relevant, provide that it will lapse if the transaction is referred to the Competition Commission or proceedings are initiated by the European Commission before the later to occur of the first closing date or the date on which the offer is declared unconditional as to acceptances, or the date of the scheme meeting in the case of a scheme.[475]

6.520

6.7.2.3 Form of the offer

The offer must be made by the person who makes the acquisition which triggers the mandatory bid requirement.[476] However, if such person is a member of a group of persons acting in concert, the obligation may also attach to the principal member or members of the group, depending on the circumstances.[477] Therefore, when conducting a stakebuilding exercise it is important to consider which entities in a group of companies may be required to make the offer if the mandatory bid obligation is triggered.

6.521

A mandatory offer cannot be made by way of scheme, except in limited circumstances where the Panel may give consent to do so. Accordingly, the advantages of implementing a scheme as opposed to an offer,[478] such as the certainty of obtaining 100% ownership of the target and possible stamp duty savings, are not generally available to a bidder that has been required to make a mandatory offer.

6.522

---

[475] Takeover Code Rule 12.
[476] Takeover Code Note on Rule 9.2.
[477] Takeover Code Rule 9.2 and Takeover Code Note on Rule 9.2.
[478] The advantages of a scheme as opposed to an offer are discussed in detail in Section 6.6 of this Chapter.

6.523 A mandatory offer must be made for all of the equity securities in the target as well as any other class of transferable securities carrying voting rights, but need not be extended to treasury shares.[479] The bidder is also not required to extend the offer to other concert parties.[480] Offers for different share classes must be comparable and the Panel should be consulted in advance in such cases.[481] In contrast, when making a voluntary offer the bidder can select the classes of shares to which it wishes to extend the offer.

6.7.3 Calculating the mandatory offer thresholds

6.7.3.1 *Acting in concert*

6.524 In calculating whether the mandatory offer thresholds in Rule 9.1 of the Code have been triggered, the interests of the person acquiring shares in the target and persons acting in concert with such person are aggregated. As the terms on which a mandatory bid can be made are less favourable to the bidder than those on which a voluntary offer can be made, it is of critical importance when stakebuilding in the target to ascertain which parties are classified as concert parties to ensure that their aggregated interests in voting shares in the target do not trigger the mandatory bid obligation. An explanation of the term 'acting in concert' is set out at Section 6.2.3 of this Chapter.

6.7.3.2 *Calculating the percentage thresholds*

6.525 In addition to determining whose interests must be taken into account in calculating whether the mandatory bid thresholds have been triggered, it is also critical to determine the types of interests which will be classed as 'interests in shares' and thereby included in the calculation of the percentage of voting rights acquired by a person and their concert parties for the purposes of Rule 9.1 of the Code. The notes to Rule 9.1 provide guidance on this issue and this Chapter examines some of the types of interests which are included in and excluded from the calculation of the mandatory bid thresholds.

6.526 **6.7.3.2.1 Interests in shares which are excluded from the calculation of the bid thresholds** Securities convertible into, or rights to subscribe for, shares in the target company are not taken to be 'interests in shares' for the purposes of Rule 9.1 and are therefore excluded from the calculation of the percentage of voting rights held by a shareholder.[482] Any securities issued on the conversion or exercise of such rights, however, will be included in the calculation of the interest in shares

---

[479] Takeover Code Rule 9.1.
[480] Panel Statement 2003/15.
[481] Takeover Code Rule 9.1.
[482] Takeover Code Note 10 to Rule 9.1.

held for the purposes of Rule 9.1.[483] If a proposed conversion or exercise of rights would trigger the mandatory bid obligation, the Panel should be consulted in advance of the conversion to determine whether an offer obligation arises and the price at which the offer should be made.[484] The Panel would not ordinarily require a mandatory offer to be made following the exercise or conversion of securities if the issue of such convertible securities was approved by a vote of independent shareholders in the whitewash procedure described at Section 6.7.4.1.1 below.[485]

Voting shares which have been allotted but are not yet issued (e.g. under a rights issue when the shares are represented by renounceable letters of allotment) are likely to be relevant for the purpose of calculating the percentage thresholds under Rule 9.1[486] and the Panel should be consulted prior to an acquisition of such shares. **6.527**

An irrevocable undertaking to acquire shares or to accept a takeover offer is generally not considered to be an 'interest in shares' for the purposes of the mandatory bid provisions.[487] As a result, obtaining irrevocable commitments in respect of over 30% of the voting rights in the target's shares will not trigger the requirement to make a mandatory bid. **6.528**

If a person or group of persons acting in concert together hold more than 30% of the voting rights in a company but subsequently reduce their interest (whether by dilution, disposal of shares or otherwise), provided that such persons still hold 30% or more of the voting rights they may acquire further shares without making a mandatory offer, provided that: **6.529**

(i) such persons may only acquire up to an additional 1% of the voting rights in the company in any 12-month period; and

(ii) the percentage of shares in which they are interested does not exceed the highest percentage of shares in which they were interested in the previous 12 months. [488]

If the 30% threshold for a mandatory bid will be exceeded but the acquirer's interest will soon thereafter be reduced below 30% again, for example due to the dilutionary effect of a placing, the Panel will consider waiving the mandatory bid requirement.[489] Similarly, if a company redeems or purchases its own voting shares, any resulting increase in the percentage of shares held by a person or **6.530**

---

[483] Takeover Code Note 10 to Rule 9.1.
[484] Takeover Code Note 10 to Rule 9.1.
[485] Takeover Code Note 10 to Rule 9.1.
[486] Takeover Code Note 14 to Rule 9.1.
[487] Panel Practice Statement No 22 paragraph 3.2.
[488] Takeover Code Note 11 to Rule 9.1.
[489] Takeover Code Note 7, Rule 9.1.

persons acting in concert will be treated as an acquisition for the purposes of Rule 9.[490] The Panel will, however, normally waive any resulting obligation to make a mandatory bid provided that the whitewash procedure in Appendix 1 to the Code is followed,[491] unless the acquirer is a director of the target or acting in concert with a director.

6.531   **6.7.3.2.2 Interests included in the calculation of the bid thresholds**   Interests in shares across a group of companies (being a company and any person controlling, controlled by, or under the same control as, that company) are aggregated for the purpose of calculating the thresholds in Rule 9.1 of the Code.[492] In a group company scenario, a person who acquires a direct majority interest in a company may also thereby acquire indirect control over a second company due to the shareholding interest (direct or indirect) of the first company in the second company. In this situation, the Panel should be consulted but will not ordinarily require a mandatory offer to be made unless:

   (i) the second company has a more significant presence in comparison with the first company, taking into account factors including whether the value of the assets or profits of the second company are more than 50% of the first company; or

  (ii) the first company was acquired in order to secure control of the second company.[493]

6.532   In the group company context, shares held by recognized intermediaries acting in a client service capacity can be excluded from the calculating of interests in shares.[494] The Panel may also consent to a principal trader acquiring shares without making a mandatory bid provided that the target company is not in an offer period and the principal trader does not at any time hold more than 3% of the voting rights of the target company.[495]

6.533   A shareholder who has borrowed or lent shares will be treated as holding the voting rights in respect of such shares, except where they have been sold or on-lent.[496] Such shareholder or persons acting in concert with them must consult with the Panel before acquiring or borrowing shares which, when taken together with their existing holdings, would result in the obligation to make a mandatory bid being triggered.[497]

---

[490] Takeover Code Rule 37.1.
[491] Takeover Code Rule 37.1.
[492] Takeover Code Note 16 to Rule 9.1.
[493] Takeover Code Note 16 to Rule 9.1.
[494] Takeover Code Note 16 to Rule 9.1.
[495] Takeover Code Note 16 to Rule 9.1.
[496] Takeover Code Note 17 to Rule 9.1.
[497] Takeover Code Note 17 to Rule 9.1.

The Panel should be consulted if a person receives a gift of an interest in shares **6.534** which takes their aggregate interest above the mandatory bid threshold.[498]

6.7.4 Conversion of a voluntary offer to a mandatory offer

The requirement to make a mandatory offer is not an alternative to a voluntary **6.535** offer or scheme. If the mandatory offer requirement is triggered by the acquisition of shares in a target made during the course of a voluntary offer or scheme, the bidder must convert the offer or scheme into a mandatory bid which complies with the terms of Rule 9 of the Code, with the Panel's prior consent. Once the mandatory offer obligation is triggered, an offer under Rule 9 must be announced immediately.

Where no change in the consideration is involved, the bidder may simply notify **6.536** shareholders of:

(i) the number of shares in which the bidder and persons acting in concert with it are interested;

(ii) the fact that the only condition remaining is that the bidder and persons acting in concert with it acquire 50% or more of the target's voting rights; and

(iii) the period for which the offer will remain open following the posting of the offer document.

As a mandatory offer must remain open for at least 14 days,[499] the bidder will not **6.537** be able to exceed the mandatory offer thresholds in the last 14 days of a voluntary offer ending on the date on which the offer is able to become unconditional as to acceptances.

As a mandatory bid cannot be made by way of a scheme, the bidder under a **6.538** scheme may not trigger the mandatory bid obligation unless the Panel has given its prior consent to the mandatory offer being effected by way of a scheme.[500]

6.7.4.1 *Dispensations from the mandatory bid requirements*

6.7.4.1.1 Whitewash In certain circumstances which would ordinarily trigger **6.539** the mandatory bid obligation, such as an issue of securities as consideration for an acquisition, a cash subscription or in cases involving the underwriting of an issue of shares, the Panel will generally waive the obligation to make a mandatory bid if the matter has been approved by a majority of the independent shareholders of the target on a poll at a shareholders' meeting.[501] Appendix 1 to the Code sets out

---

[498] Takeover Code Note 10 to Rule 9.1.
[499] Takeover Code Note 4 to Rule 32.1.
[500] Takeover Code Section 2, Appendix 7.
[501] Takeover Code Note 1 on the dispensations from Rule 9.

the whitewash procedure which must be undertaken and describes the content requirement of the circular to be sent to shareholders. Amongst other things, shareholders must be given information relating to the number and percentage of shares in which the subscriber will acquire an interest and must specifically be informed if the subscriber will acquire more than 50% of the voting rights in the target and will not be required to comply with the mandatory bid obligations going forward. Shareholders must also be provided with competent independent advice on the proposal.

6.540 **6.7.4.1.2 Majority shareholder approval** If holders of shares carrying 50% or more of the voting rights in the target indicate in writing that they would not accept an offer if one was made under the mandatory offer provisions, the Panel would ordinarily waive the requirement to make an offer, as the target will not be able to reach the minimum 50% acceptance level required for the offer to become unconditional as to acceptances.[502] Similarly, if a single shareholder holds shares carrying 50% or more of the voting rights in the target, the Panel may waive the requirement for a mandatory offer.[503]

6.541 **6.7.4.1.3 Inadvertent mistake** If a person inadvertently triggers the mandatory bid obligation, the Panel may grant a waiver from the requirement to make an offer if such person disposes of sufficient shares in a limited timeframe to unconnected persons so as to reduce their interest below 30%.[504]

6.542 **6.7.4.1.4 Enforcement of security** Where shares are charged as security for a loan and the lender enforces the security and takes possession of the shares, the Panel will not ordinarily require a mandatory offer to be made by either the lender or purchaser, provided that the lender disposes of sufficient shares to unconnected persons to reduce its interest to below 30% within a reasonable period of time in a manner satisfactory to the Panel.[505]

6.543 **6.7.4.1.5 Rescue of a distressed company** Where a company is in severe financial distress and needs to issue or sell shares without shareholder approval in circumstances which would trigger a mandatory bid requirement, the Panel may waive the mandatory bid obligation provided that approval of the matter is obtained from independent shareholders as soon as possible after the event and some other protection for independent shareholders which the Panel considers satisfactory is proposed by the target.[506]

---

[502] Takeover Code Note 5 on dispensations from Rule 9.
[503] Takeover Code Note 5 on dispensations from Rule 9.
[504] Takeover Code Note 4 on dispensations from Rule 9.
[505] Takeover Code Note 2 on dispensations from Rule 9.
[506] Takeover Code Note 3 on dispensations from Rule 9.

6.8 Hostile Offers

6.8.1 Introduction

An offer from a bidder which is unsolicited and not recommended by the target's **6.544** board is known as a hostile offer. This Section considers the issues which a bidder and target may have to contend with when faced with a hostile offer. The same rules apply as for a recommended offer; there are, however, a number of additional issues for the bidder and the target to consider.

6.8.2 Making a hostile offer

6.8.2.1 Approaching the target

In the initial investigation phase of a possible acquisition, one of the matters a **6.545** bidder will need to consider is how the target is likely to respond to an approach and whether there would be any advantage in attempting to negotiate with the target in advance of making an offer.

A bidder may decide to contact the target in advance of a proposed bid, even if **6.546** it has no pre-existing relationship with it, in the hope of negotiating the terms on which the offer will be recommended by the target board. The benefit which might be obtained from having the target board's support of the offer will need to be weighed against the possible disadvantage of putting the target's board on notice of an intended approach by the bidder, giving the target more time to prepare its response to the offer and perhaps also more scope to take action which could frustrate the offer. If the target's board supports the offer, the bidder may also be able to negotiate a non-solicitation agreement whereby the target agrees not to solicit rival bids and/or a break fee arrangement whereby the target agrees to pay the bidder a pre-agreed amount if the target withdraws its recommendation of the bid. If negotiations with the bidder are not successful, the bidder will then need to consider whether to proceed with a hostile bid, how it will react to any competing bids which may emerge and whether it would be prepared to increase the offer either to gain the support of the target board or in response to a rival bid.

Where a bidder expects strong resistance to an offer from the target, the bidder **6.547** may benefit from only informing the target of its intention to make a bid immediately before the bid is announced.[507] This could minimize the target's ability to take certain action to deter the offer or make the offer less attractive to

---

[507] Takeover Code Rule 1(a) requires the offer to first be made to the board of the target, but does not specify how much notice should be given, so in practice the board can be informed immediately before the announcement of the offer.

shareholders, as the target's activities will immediately be regulated by the Code after the board is informed that the bidder intends to make an offer. Actions which could have been taken by the target before it became aware of the bidder's intention to make an offer, such as the issue of shares or the acquisition or disposal of a material asset, can only be undertaken with shareholder approval after the board of the target becomes aware that a bona fide offer might be imminent. As the target may be caught off guard by a surprise offer it will have less time to carry out such actions and prepare its response to the offer.

6.8.2.2 *Information on the target*

6.548   If the target does not welcome the bidder's approach, it will not be willing to voluntarily provide additional information to the bidder which could assist it to make the offer or contribute to the level of positive acceptances. The bidder will therefore only have recourse to publicly available information on the target in order to make and price its offer and may be exposed to the risk that the information is out of date, deficient in a material manner or generally insufficient to allow the bidder to properly formulate its offer.

6.549   In a competitive bid situation the target is obliged to make information given to one bidder available on specific request to other bidders or bona fide potential bidders.[508] This obligation is considered more fully at paragraph 6.86 of this Chapter. As any request made under this rule will alert the target to a potential bid, the bidder will need to consider the most appropriate time for the request, which may be after the offer is announced.

6.8.3 Preparing to receive a hostile offer

6.550   If a company is concerned that it may become a potential takeover target there are several things it can do in order to make sure it is prepared to promptly and effectively defend an offer if one is received, which are discussed in detail in Section 6.4 of this Chapter. Most importantly, the potential target should have a defence manual of the kind described in Section 6.4 of this Chapter which the directors can immediately turn to if a bid is received and will contain key contact information in respect of the target and its advisers, the first steps to take if an offer is received and draft announcements dealing with different scenarios which may arise.

6.551   Immediately after a bid is received a committee of the target should be appointed to deal with the target's response to the bid, the running of the defence, drafting press announcements and the defence document and managing press and shareholder relations.

---

[508] Takeover Code Rule 20.2.

6.8.4 Defending a hostile bid

There are two main regimes which govern the actions a target's board may take in **6.552** response to an unwelcome bid. First, the directors must consider their general fiduciary duties, which arise under common law but in the UK have also been embodied in the Companies Act 2006. Second, it is a general principle of the Takeover Directive (and accordingly the Code) that the board of the target company must not deny the holders of securities the opportunity to decide on the merits of a bid.[509] The Takeover Directive adds flesh to the general principle by providing that the target may not take certain action which may result in the frustration of the bid unless it obtains shareholder approval.[510] This provision is reflected in the Code.[511]

Several other regulatory regimes, such as the prohibitions on market abuse, mar- **6.553** ket manipulation and insider dealing may also impact on the actions of the target board in response to a bid. The potential impact of these regulations is, however, beyond the scope of this Chapter.

6.8.4.1 *Directors' duties in responding to an offer*

In considering how to respond to an offer, the directors must at all times consider **6.554** their fiduciary and common law duties, which have now been codified in the Companies Act 2006. In the context of a takeover, the most relevant duties will be the duties of the directors to:

(i)   act within their powers;[512] and
(ii) promote the success of the company.[513]

The duty to act within powers obliges the directors of a company to act in accord- **6.555** ance with target's constitution (which comprises the memorandum and articles of association for companies incorporated in the UK) and only exercise their powers for the purpose for which they were conferred.[514] If the target directors attempt to use a power conferred on them by the memorandum or articles of association of the target for the purpose of frustrating a takeover bid (for example by exercising the power to allot shares or acquire or dispose of assets in a manner which would trigger a condition of the offer), this could fall outside the scope of the proper purpose for which such power was granted to the directors and render

---

[509] Takeover Directive Article 3(1)(c) and Takeover Code General Principle 3.
[510] Takeover Directive Article 9(2).
[511] Takeover Code Rule 21.
[512] Companies Act 2006 section 171.
[513] Companies Act 2006 section 172.
[514] Companies Act 2006 section 171.

the directors in breach of their fiduciary duties, even if the directors are acting to promote the success of the company.

6.556 The duty to promote the success of the company requires the directors to act in the way they consider, in good faith, would be most likely to promote the success of the company for the benefit of the members as a whole.[515] The 'success of the company' is determined by reference to a long-term increase in value of the company. The phrase 'members as a whole' is not defined but generally requires directors to consider the interests of both current and future members. The Companies Act 2006 prescribes six specific factors which the directors must take into account.[516] Relevantly, during a takeover offer there is often an inherent tension between the short-term interests of the existing shareholders in receiving immediate value for their investment and the long-term interests of the company if the merger with the bidder proceeds. There can be circumstances where, although the offer price is fair and reasonable, target directors do not consider the offer to be in the long-term interests of the company as ownership by the bidder could damage the target's business. This may be due to a range of factors such as perceived reputational issues associated with the bidder, an increased financial burden on the target post-merger or a potential adverse impact on the target's business as a result of integration with the bidder's business. The directors must take account of all relevant circumstances and make a judgment, in good faith, as to how the short-term interests of existing shareholders and long-term interests of the company should be balanced.

6.557 In considering a takeover offer, directors must also have regard to the interests of the company's employees[517] and must include in the response document the board's opinion in respect of the effects of the offer on employment.[518] The bidder must include a proposal for the treatment of employees and a statement of its intentions with regard to the continued employment of staff and management, in the offer document.[519] This will be the starting point of the target's assessment of the impact of the offer on employees. If the target is insolvent the interests of creditors must also be taken into account.[520]

6.8.4.2 *Frustrating action*

6.558 In response to a hostile bid, the target could potentially use a range of devices in an attempt to deter the offer or force a higher offer from the bidder. Such actions will often result in an offer condition being breached or rendered incapable of

---

[515] Companies Act 2006 section 172.
[516] Companies Act 2006 section 172(1).
[517] Companies Act 2006 section 172(1)(b).
[518] Takeover Code Rule 25.1(b).
[519] Takeover Code Rule 24.1(e).
[520] Companies Act 2006 section 172(3).

satisfaction, enabling the bidder to withdraw its offer. As the frustrating action and/or the triggering of the offer condition would deny target shareholders the opportunity to consider the offer, regulations have been imposed on the action which a target may take during an offer to ensure that target shareholders are given a fair opportunity to consider the merits of the offer and determine the future of the target.

Article 3 of the Takeover Directive, which is also embodied in General Principle 3 of the Code, regulates the conduct of the target and requires the board of the target to act in the interests of the company as a whole and not to deny target shareholders the opportunity to decide on the merits of the bid. **6.559**

Article 9 of the Takeover Directive restricts frustrating action being taken by the target in member states which have adopted this article. Article 9 is implemented in the UK by Rule 21.1 of the Code which provides that when an offer has been made or when the target has reason to believe that an offer might be imminent, the target board cannot, without the approval of shareholders in general meeting: **6.560**

(i)   take any action which may result in any offer or bona fide possible offer being frustrated or in shareholders being denied the opportunity to decide on its merits; or

(ii) specifically take any of the following actions:
(a)   issue any authorized but unissued shares or transfer or sell, or agree to transfer or sell, any shares out of treasury;
(b)   issue or grant options in respect of unissued shares;
(c)   create, or issue, or permit the creation or issue of, any securities carrying rights of conversion into or subscription for shares;
(d)   sell, dispose of or acquire, or agree to sell, dispose of or acquire, assets of a material amount; or
(e)   enter into contracts otherwise than in the ordinary course of business.

The restrictions on frustrating actions apply from the point at which the target's board has reason to believe that a bona fide offer 'might be imminent'.[521] Depending on the circumstances, a call from a bidder asking the target to meet to discuss a possible acquisition may be sufficient contact to trigger the application of Rule 21.1 of the Code. **6.561**

6.8.4.3 Exceptions to the shareholder approval requirement

If there is any doubt as to whether the target is the subject of the restrictions on frustrating actions, the Panel should be consulted.[522] The Panel will generally be prepared to waive the requirement for the target to hold a shareholders' meeting **6.562**

---

[521] Takeover Code Rule 21.1.
[522] Takeover Code Rule 21.1.

to seek approval of the relevant action if the bidder consents to the action[523] or if shareholders holding 50% or more of the voting rights in the target state that they approve the proposed action and would vote in favour of any resolution to that effect proposed at a general meeting.[524] Such waivers, however, are unlikely to be obtained in a hostile bid situation.

6.563　The Panel will also be prepared to waive the requirement to seek shareholder approval where the proposed action is being undertaken pursuant to a pre-existing contract or obligation, or the decision to take that action was made before the offer period and has either been partly or fully implemented or has not yet been implemented but is in the ordinary course of the target's business.[525]

6.564　Where the Panel dispenses with the need to seek shareholder approval or if shareholder approval of the frustrating action is obtained, the bidder may become entitled to withdraw its offer, either because the Panel permits the withdrawal or because the action would trigger a bid condition entitling the bidder to withdraw its offer.[526]

6.8.4.4 Determining whether an action is a 'frustrating action'

6.565　There are five key matters which are expressly deemed to be 'frustrating actions' in Rule 21.1. However, this list is not exhaustive and there are a range of actions which may also be classified as 'frustrating actions' depending on the circumstances in each case. Some of the more common types of frustrating actions are considered in more detail below.

6.566　**6.8.4.4.1 New share issues**　A target may seek to make a bonus issue or rights issue as an alternative means of returning value to shareholders. A decision, however, by the target board to issue further shares during an offer period could potentially frustrate a bid[527] as a bidder seeking to acquire 100% of the target would need to revise its offer to extend to the new shares issued and may also need to adjust the offer price. As shareholder approval is required to issue new shares during the offer period,[528] the choice between receiving value by participating in the new share issue or participating in the offer is left in the hands of the target shareholders.

6.567　**6.8.4.4.2 Dividends**　A target may wish to pay an interim dividend as an alternative method of returning value to shareholders than accepting the offer.

---

[523] Takeover Code Note 1 to Rule 21.2.
[524] Takeover Code Note 10 to Rule 21.1.
[525] Takeover Code Rule 21.1.
[526] Takeover Code Note 5 to Rule 21.1.
[527] Takeover Code Rule 21.2(b)(i).
[528] Takeover Code Rule 21.2(b)(i).

The Panel must be consulted in advance of any proposal by the target to declare and pay an interim dividend otherwise than in the ordinary course of the target's business during an offer period, as such action is considered by the Panel to be contrary to the general prohibition on frustrating actions in the Takeovers Directive and the Code.[529] However, the board may declare an intention to pay a dividend after the offer has lapsed without requiring such approval.

6.8.4.4.3 Options Although the issue or grant of options in respect of unissued shares is generally prohibited by Rule 21.2(b)(iii) without prior shareholder approval, the Panel will normally consent to the grant of options during the offer period in accordance with normal practice of the target, such as a grant of options under a share option scheme at such times and in such number as is consistent with past practice of the target.[530] The Panel will also normally consent to the issue of shares on the exercise of options during the offer period.[531]   **6.568**

6.8.4.4.4 Acquisitions or disposals of assets In relation to the prohibition on disposals or acquisitions of assets 'of a material amount' during the offer period without prior shareholder approval set out in Rule 21.1(b)(iv), the Panel has stated that what is 'material' is determined by having regard to (where appropriate):   **6.569**

  (i) the aggregate value of the consideration to be received or paid in comparison to the market capitalization of the target;

 (ii) the value of the assets to be disposed of or acquired in comparison with the target's assets as a whole; and

(iii) the operating profit attributable to the assets to be disposed of or acquired in comparison with that of the target as a whole.[532]

The Panel generally considers values of 10% or more to be material, although values of under 10% can still be deemed material depending on the importance of the asset.[533]   **6.570**

6.8.4.4.5 Variations to the terms of directors' employment Amendments to, or new, service agreements with a director of the target will generally be considered to be otherwise than in the ordinary course of business and actions which require shareholder approval during the offer period, particularly if the terms of the service agreements are significantly improved.[534]   **6.571**

---

[529] Takeover Code Note 3 to Rule 21.1.
[530] Takeover Code Note 7 to Rule 21.1.
[531] Takeover Code Note 7 to Rule 21.1.
[532] Takeover Code Note 2 to Rule 21.1.
[533] Takeover Code Note 2 to Rule 21.1.
[534] Takeover Code Note 6 to Rule 21.1.

6.8.5 Defence strategy

6.8.5.1 Common grounds of defence

6.572 The best way for a company to defend a hostile takeover bid is to mount a strong defence and show persuasive evidence as to why shareholders should not accept the offer. The target's defence strategy should be well considered and focus on the main arguments against a merger with the bidder in order to have the strongest impact on target shareholders.

6.573 **6.8.5.1.1 Bid at an undervalue**   One of the most significant grounds of defence to an unwelcome offer is that the bidder has undervalued the target. The target's board will commonly assert that the bidder has opportunistically made the offer at a stage of the company's development when the benefits of current business strategies have not yet translated into profits or been reflected appropriately in the company's share price. Alternatively, the target may consider that its share price is underperforming due to prevailing poor market conditions which will in time stabilize and return greater value to the shareholder. The target will need to convince shareholders that it is in their interests to hold on to their shares in order to receive greater returns in the future, rather than selling to the bidder for an immediate return.

6.574 Profit forecasts, independent asset valuations and other financial information can be highly persuasive tools in supporting the target's assertion that it has been undervalued by the bidder, especially where published information may be out of date at the time the bid is made. As discussed at Sections 6.8.6.2.3 and 6.8.6.2.4 below, the regulations governing publication of such information must be strictly complied with. It may also be useful for the target to present valuations of the business, or various parts of the business, and a comparison with other similar business in the same industry to highlight the comparative performance of the target.

6.575 **6.8.5.1.2 Insufficient premium for control**   Even if the offer is at a premium to the prevailing market value of the shares when the offer is made, the target may criticize the offer price on the ground that the premium offered for control of the target is too low. It may be relevant for a target to adduce evidence of the share price at different points in time before the offer was made in order to support this assertion, if the share price at the time of the offer was not representative for any reason.

6.576 **6.8.5.1.3 Insufficient rationale for the merger**   The target may be able to find flaws in the bidder's rationale for the merger where there are insufficient synergies or efficiencies of scale in cost or economy to commercially justify a merger.

6.577 **6.8.5.1.4 New business strategy or model for growth**   The board of the target may decide to introduce a new business strategy in order to defend the bid.

This could include introduction of new management or the divestment or re-structuring of certain divisions of the target's businesses. Target directors may also be able to present a model for future capital growth or income and increase in value linked to the new business strategy which shows more favourable returns than those being offered by the bidder.

6.8.5.1.5 Return of value to shareholders The target's board may be in a posi- **6.578** tion to adduce evidence of a strong history of delivering value to shareholders in support of an argument that the target should maintain its independence from a bidder. It may be useful to present the rates of return analysed in different ways, such as at various time periods, or by different measures (such as gross return, capital value or income return) or in comparison with the relevant stock indices in support of this assertion.

The target's board may also announce a new initiative to return value to share- **6.579** holders by way of an interim dividend or a bonus share issue. As discussed above, unless shareholder approval is obtained, such measures could only be imple- mented after the offer period has ended due to the restrictions on carrying out frustrating actions. If undertaken with prior Panel and shareholder consent during the bid period, however, the payment of a dividend or bonus share issue could frustrate an offer. Directors must also comply with their directors' duties in determining whether to declare a dividend and Part 23 of the Companies Act regulating the payment of dividends.

6.8.5.1.6 Attack on the bidder If the consideration being offered comprises **6.580** shares in the bidder, the target will often try to attack the value of the bidder, as this will in turn affect the value of the offer. The target can use publicly available information on the bidder in order to find weaknesses in its business strategy or performance or inconsistencies with statements made in the offer document.

6.8.5.2 *Defensive actions by the target*

As well as responding to the bid, there are certain actions a bidder may take to **6.581** strengthen and/or defend its position, subject to the prohibition on frustrating actions.

6.8.5.2.1 Major acquisition or disposal by the target If the target completes **6.582** a major acquisition or disposal before the end of the offer period, the merits of the bid could be significantly impaired. The value of the target may be affected by the change in its asset portfolio, which may in turn make the offer price inade- quate, or the target may generally be less attractive to the bidder as the nature of the business may have changed. As mentioned in Section 6.8.4.2 above, any such material acquisition or disposal needs to be subject to shareholder approval.[535]

---

[535] Takeover Code Rule 21.1(b)(iv).

The bidder will commonly reserve the right to withdraw the offer if a material acquisition or disposal is made. Directors must also consider their duties and may not undertake the acquisition or disposal for an improper purpose such as blocking or frustrating the bid.

6.583   **6.8.5.2.2 Change of control clauses in the target's key contracts**   If any of the target's material contracts contain change of control clauses which would entitle the counterparty to terminate the contract if the offer is successful, the risk of such a clause being enforced by the counterparty may significantly detract from the potential benefits being offered by the bidder.

6.584   **6.8.5.2.3 Investigation by regulatory authorities**   A target company which is the subject of an unwelcome offer may be able to utilize the antitrust and other regulatory processes to its advantage, depending on the circumstances. Although the target cannot control the outcome of any proceedings, it may encourage the Competition Commission or European Commission to investigate the proposed merger and may take an active role in making submissions and providing evidence in opposition to the proposed merger. The offer will lapse if regulatory proceedings are commenced, as this is a compulsory term of the offer.[536]

6.585   **6.8.5.2.4 Litigation**   The commencement of litigation, either before or during the offer period, could potentially frustrate an offer. In determining whether to bring such litigation, the target's directors must consider their duties and balance the possible benefit of commencing proceedings to protect the company against the possible detriment to shareholders of frustrating an offer. The target would need to seek shareholder approval before commencing litigation during the offer period.

6.586   **6.8.5.2.5 White knights**   If the target board is not opposed to a merger, but does not consider the offer from a particular bidder to be the best available option to the company, the target's board may seek a rival bid from its preferred bidder (known as the 'white knight') on more favourable terms. Similarly, the target may approach several potentially interested parties in an attempt to 'auction' the target to identify the highest bidder. As discussed above, in deciding whether it is appropriate to seek rival bidders and in assessing any rival bids received, the directors must comply with their duties to act in the way which they consider, in good faith, would be most likely to promote the success of the company for the benefit of the members as a whole. In determining whether to recommend the offer from the white knight over the original bidder, directors must have regard not only to the comparative offer prices, but also to the prospects of the business post-merger and any other benefits offered by each bidder, although the price will often be the most important consideration.

---

[536] Takeover Code Rule 12.1.

6.8.5.2.6 White squires The target's board may be able to rely on the support **6.587**
of a friendly shareholder (know as a 'white squire') who is prepared to increase
their stake in the target to a 'blocking stake' of either (i) greater than 10% of
the shares the subject of the offer which could prevent the bidder from using the
compulsory acquisition procedure to acquire 100% ownership of the target or
(ii) 25% of the shares the subject of the offer which would prevent the target being
able to pass a special resolution without the white squire's approval.

The white squire could increase its interest by purchasing existing shares or **6.588**
through the issue of new shares. Shareholder approval must be obtained before
any new shares are issued to the white squire during the offer period.[537] As with
all new share issues, the directors will need to ensure that they have the relevant
authority to allot the shares and that any pre-emptive rights over new share
issues are disapplied.[538] The directors will also need to ensure that they comply
with their duties to exercise their powers for a proper purpose when issuing the
shares. The directors must believe that a strategic alliance with the white squire
would promote the success of the company, as if the sole reason for the issue of
the shares is to block the bid, it is not likely to be a proper purpose for which the
directors may exercise their powers. If the white squire acquires shares on market
it will need to comply with the various disclosure regulations discussed in detail at
Section 6.3.6.3 of this Chapter.

If the white squire, or indeed any other major or institutional shareholder, has **6.589**
made a clear statement to the target that it will not accept the bid, and they are
prepared to confirm this position to the Panel, the target may be able to use the
support of these shareholders as a tool to encourage others to reject the bid.

6.8.5.2.7 Market purchases by friendly parties Whilst it is not possible for a **6.590**
subsidiary to hold shares in its parent company in the UK, it is possible for sister
companies to hold shares in each other. Accordingly, a fellow group company
could acquire shares in the target, effectively acting as either a white knight or a
white squire, to block the bid. However, as such companies will be deemed to
be 'acting in concert' with each other, they must take care to ensure that their
aggregate interests in voting shares do not exceed the mandatory bid thresholds in
Rule 9 of the Code. The target cannot purchase its own shares during an offer
without shareholder approval.[539]

Subject to the insider dealing and market abuse regimes, directors of the target are **6.591**
free to acquire shares on market to prevent such shares being acquired by the bidder or sold into the offer by the holder, subject to the share dealing and disclosure

---

[537] Takeover Code Rule 21.1(b)(i).
[538] Companies Act 2006 sections 549 and 570–573.
[539] Takeover Code Rule 37.3(a).

requirements discussed at Section 6.3.6.3 of this Chapter, but will be treated as acting in concert with the target and must ensure that their shareholding percentages to not exceed the mandatory bid thresholds (discussed at paragraph 6.508 of this Chapter). Financial advisers and stockbrokers to the target, and certain parties connected with or controlled by them, are not, however, permitted to acquire interests in the target's shares during the offer period.[540]

6.592 Section 6.3.6 of this Chapter contains a general discussion of the regulatory regime governing acquisitions of shares in an offer period.

6.593 **6.8.5.2.8 Pacman defence**   The so-called 'pacman defence' refers to situation where the target responds to a hostile bid by making a bid for the bidder. This is not common practice in the UK, but is more commonly used in the US. The target would need to seek shareholder approval before making the bid pursuant to Rule 21.1 of the Code.[541]

6.594 **6.8.5.2.9 Poison pills**   As discussed at Section 6.4.8 of this Chapter, a 'poison pill' is a mechanism put in place by a target to deter or frustrate a bid, although this technique is rare in the UK. Shareholder approval would likely be required to put in place a poison pill during an offer period, as it would not be a transaction in the ordinary course of the target's business.[542] In the case of a poison pill which grants special share rights over a new issue of shares, shareholder approval of the creation of the new class of shares and their subsequent issue would be required.

6.595 **6.8.5.2.10 Lobbying support in defence of the bid**   The target board may seek to lobby opposition to the bid from a range of parties, such as institutional investors, major shareholders, analysts, political groups, the financial media and perhaps employees and union groups, depending on the circumstances. The rules governing communications with these parties, including the Listing Rules, Financial Services and Markets Act 2000 and Rule 20 of the Code should be complied with at all times.

6.8.6 Responding to a bid—key documents and timetable

6.8.6.1 *Press announcement*

6.596 When an offer has been made the target must as soon as possible announce details of all classes of relevant securities of the target in issue and the number of shares in each such class.[543]

---

540 Takeover Code Rule 4.4.
541 Takeover Code Rule 21.
542 Takeover Code Rule 21.1(b)(v).
543 Takeover Code Rule 2.10.

6.8.6.2 Defence document

In the immediate aftermath of an announcement of a hostile offer for the target, the target's board will, to the extent it has not anticipated the making of the bid, need to deal with a number of issues, not least of which will be to appoint relevant external advisers and respond formally, by means of public announcement, to the bid announcement. **6.597**

In addition to these, and other, workstreams, the target board should begin preparation of its defence strategy and its circular to shareholders. The circular, which must be sent to shareholders and persons with information rights,[544] will, in effect, constitute the target's first defence document and must be dispatched as soon as practicable and, at the latest, 14 days following the posting of the offer document.[545] In addition, at the time of circulation, the circular should promptly be made available to employee representatives of the target (or, if none, the employees themselves)[546] and, on the day of its publication be put on display in accordance with Rule 26 of the Code. If received in good time before publication of the circular, appended to the circular must be a separate opinion from the employee representatives as to the effect of the offer on employment matters.[547] **6.598**

The defence document will seek to weaken the offer in an attempt to encourage the target's shareholders to reject the offer. As well as containing the target board's arguments defending an acquisition, such as those outlined in Section 6.8.5.1 above, the defence document must cover certain matters prescribed in the Code, which are discussed in further detail below. In presenting the defence document, target directors must present information accurately and fairly and meet prospectus standards in all documents sent to shareholders.[548] **6.599**

6.8.6.2.1 Opinion on the offer The defence document must contain sufficient information and advice to enable shareholders to reach a properly informed decision as to the merits or demerits of the offer and should not withhold relevant information.[549] The defence document must contain the target board's opinion on the offer and its reasons for such opinion.[550] Where a target board is split in its views on an offer, the views of both the majority and minority should be presented.[551] If a director has a conflict of interest their view should not be **6.600**

---

[544] Takeover Code Rule 30.2(a).
[545] Takeover Code Rule 30.2.
[546] Takeover Code Rule 30.2(a).
[547] Takeover Code Rule 30.2(b).
[548] Takeover Code Rules 19.1 and 19.3.
[549] Takeover Code Rule 23.
[550] Takeover Code Rule 25.1(a).
[551] Takeover Code Note 2 to Rule 25.1.

included in the board's opinion on the offer and the nature of the conflict should be explained to shareholders.[552]

6.601 The target board's opinion must specifically cover:

(i) the effect of the offer on the company's interests and in particular employment; and

(ii) the bidder's strategic plans for the company and likely repercussions on employment and the target's place of business.[553] In addition, the defence document must append a separate opinion from the nominated employee representative as to the effect of the offer on employment.[554]

6.602 The defence document must also include the substance of advice given to the target board by its independent adviser and may also include a recommendation or opinion from the adviser, subject to their consent being given.[555]

6.603 If any of the target board hold shares in the target, they must state whether they intend to accept or reject the offer in respect of the shares they hold.[556]

6.604 **6.8.6.2.2 Financial information** In addition to the above, central to the target's defence will be the financial information it presents in respect of the target and its business.

6.605 As a minimum, the circular prepared by the target must contain all known material changes in the financial or trading position of the target since the last published audited accounts or a statement that there are no material changes.[557]

6.606 Practically, the target should therefore ascertain whether there are any existing profit forecasts (or statements which could constitute such) in respect of the target in the market as these will need to be reported on within the defence document.

6.607 **6.8.6.2.3 Profit forecast and valuation** In addition to the above information, the target may wish to include as a means by which to rebut the offer, a profit forecast or, where relevant, asset valuation which can be used to reveal that the bidder has, in its takeover offer price, undervalued the target.

6.608 The profit forecast must be prepared with due care and consideration by the directors of the target in collaboration with the target's accountants (who must be comfortable with the target's forecasting bases and procedures).[558] The legal context to producing a profit forecast is examined at Section 6.5.4.8 of this Chapter.

---

552 Takeover Code Note 3 to Rule 25.1.
553 Takeover Code Rule 25.1(b).
554 Takeover Code Rule 30.2(b).
555 Takeover Code Rule 25.1(a).
556 Takeover Code Rule 25.3(a)(ii)(v).
557 Takeover Code Rule 25.2.
558 Takeover Code Rule 28.1.

The profit forecast will be compiled on the basis of a review of the business plan in light of the budget for the current financial year. From a practical perspective, it is therefore prudent for the target, if it anticipates that it will be the target of an unwanted takeover bid, to put in place procedures for reviewing the budgets and business plan and the assumptions on which the target's forecasting is based. **6.609**

As value is central to defending a takeover bid, the target board must justify in its defence document its own valuation of the target. In preparing its valuation defence, the target will usually consider a number of different valuation mechanisms, including sector comparison and desk valuations. The target may also seek support from its financial adviser (in relation to determining the offer price at which the target board should be prepared to recommend an offer) and independent valuers to the extent that asset valuations are key to supporting the target's valuation. **6.610**

6.8.6.2.4 Asset valuations Asset valuations can be important for companies which are more likely to be valued on an assets basis as opposed to a profits basis, such as mining and property companies. If a valuation of assets is given in connection with the defence, the valuation must state the effective date at which the assets were valued and be supported by the opinion of a named and appropriately qualified independent valuer.[559] The basis of the valuation, which will generally be market value, must be clearly stated and qualifications or assumptions are generally not permitted unless they are fully explained.[560] The valuation must include a statement regarding any potential tax liability which would arise if the assets were to be sold at the amount of the valuation and a comment on the likelihood of such liability crystallizing.[561] **6.611**

The Panel has indicated that in exceptional cases where the target is the subject of an unexpected offer and cannot commission an independent valuation in time to release its defence document, the Panel may waive strict compliance with that requirement and permit informal valuations to be included where on balance shareholders' interests are best served by doing so.[562] **6.612**

6.8.6.2.5 Interests and dealings The Code stipulates that the first major circular prepared by the target board in connection with the offer must include comprehensive share disclosures.[563] Specifically, the following details must be **6.613**

---

[559] Takeover Code Rules 29.1 and 29.4.
[560] Takeover Code Rule 29.2(a).
[561] Takeover Code Rule 29.3.
[562] Takeover Code Rule 29.6.
[563] Takeover Code Rule 25.3.

incorporated (or, except in respect of (ii)(g) below, a negative statement to the contrary included):[564]

   (i) details of any relevant securities of the bidder in which the target or any of its directors has an interest or in respect of which it or he has a right to subscribe, in each case specifying the nature of the interests or rights concerned;[565]
   (ii) the same details as above in respect of any relevant securities of the target in relation to each of:
       (a) the directors of the target;
       (b) any company which is an associate of the target (as defined by reference to paragraph (1) of the definition of associate contained within the Code);
       (c) any pension fund of the target or of a company which is an associate (as defined by reference to paragraph (1) of the definition of associate contained within the Code) of the target;
       (d) any employee benefit trust of the target or of a company which is an associate (as defined by reference to paragraph (1) of the definition of associate contained within the Code) of the target;
       (e) any connected adviser to the target, to a company which is an associate (as defined by reference to paragraph (1) of the definition of associate contained within the Code) of the target, or a person acting in concert with the target;
       (f) any person controlling, controlled by or under the same control as any connected adviser falling within (e) above (except for an exempt principal trader or an exempt fund manager); and
       (g) any person who has an arrangement of the kind referred to in Note 6 on Rule 8 with the target or with any person who is an associate of the target by virtue of paragraphs (1), (2), (3) or (4) of the definition of associate contained within the Code.

6.614   In addition, in the case of a securities exchange offer, the disclosures must cover the same details as in (i) above in respect of any relevant securities of the bidder in relation to each of the persons listed in (ii)(b) to (g) above.[566] Also, details of any relevant securities of the target and (in the case of securities exchange offer only) the bidder which the target or any person acting in concert with the target has borrowed or lent, save for any borrowed shares which have been on-lent or sold should be included.[567]

---

[564] Takeover Code Rule 25.3(b).

[565] Short positions (whether conditional or absolute and whether in the money or otherwise), including any short position under a derivative or similar arrangement must also be disclosed according to Rule 25.3(a)(i) of the Code.

[566] Takeover Code Rule 25.3(a)(iii).

[567] Takeover Code Rule 25.3(a)(iv).

Finally, if the target or any of its directors has dealt in relevant securities of either **6.615**
the bidder or the target between the start of the offer period and the latest practicable date prior to the publication of the circular then relevant disclosures (including the dates on which the transactions occurred) or an appropriate negative statement must be made.[568] Equally if any person referred to above at (ii)(b) to (g) above has dealt in relevant securities of the target (or, in the case of a securities exchange offer, the bidder), similar details must be included in the circular.[569]

Importantly for target shareholders, the circular must contain a disclosure detail- **6.616**
ing whether the directors of the target intend, in respect of their own beneficial shareholdings, to accept or reject the offer.[570]

6.8.6.2.6 Directors' service contracts The defence document should also **6.617**
include particulars of all service contracts of any director or proposed director of the target with the target or any of its subsidiaries. If, within six months of the date of the circular, the existing service contracts have been altered or new service contracts have been entered into, the circular should, in addition, contain details of the preceding service contracts.[571]

The details to be disclosed in relation to directors' service contracts are compre- **6.618**
hensive and include, but are not limited to:

 (i) the name of the director;
 (ii) the date of the contract, together with its unexpired term and details of any notice periods;
 (iii) full particulars of the director's remuneration; and
 (iv) any compensation payable on early termination of the contract.[572]

If there are no service contracts or, within six months of the date of the circular, **6.619**
the terms of the service contracts have not been altered or no new service contracts have been entered into, the circular should state this.[573]

6.8.6.2.7 Responsibility statements As stated at Section 6.5.4.7.5 of this **6.620**
Chapter, responsibility must be accepted by the directors of the target in respect of the information contained in each document they issue in connection with an offer for the target.[574] The defence document will therefore contain an appropriate responsibility statement.

---

[568] Takeover Code Rule 25.3(c).
[569] Takeover Code Rule 25.3(c).
[570] Takeover Code Rule 25.3(a)(v).
[571] Takeover Code Rule 25.4.
[572] Takeover Code Notes to Rule 25.4.
[573] Takeover Code Rule 25.4.
[574] Takeover Code Rule 19.2(a).

6.621 **6.8.6.2.8 Material contracts and irrevocable commitments**   The first defence document must also contain a summary of each material contract entered into by the target or any of its subsidiaries during the period beginning two years before the commencement of the offer period.[575] For the purpose of assessing materiality, the Code states that any contract entered into by the target not in the ordinary course of business will be caught.[576]

6.622 Details of any irrevocable commitment or letter of intent which the target or any of its associates has procured in relation to relevant securities of the target (or, if appropriate the bidder) should also be disclosed.[577]

6.8.6.3 Bid timetable

6.623 An example bid timetable is included at Section 6.5.4.3 of this Chapter, but in the context of a hostile bid this timetable may vary depending on the target share-holders' response to the offer.

6.624 In terms of key dates for the target, the board of the target has up to 14 days from the date on which the bidder posts its offer document to respond to the bid by issuing its defence document.[578] The target may continue to release new informa-tion by way of supplementary defence circulars until Day 39.[579] Between Days 14 and 39 the target commonly meets with its institutional shareholders, advisers and analysts to muster support for the defence of the offer.

6.625 The bidder may revise the offer to improve the terms up to Day 46 after posting the offer document, provided it has not restricted its ability to do so in the offer document. It may also extend the offer period (usually in 14-day increments) if the minimum acceptance condition has not been met within the initial offer period, which must be at least 21 days.[580]

6.626 The minimum acceptance condition must be satisfied by Day 60 after posting the offer document.[581] If sufficient acceptances have not been received by this date, the bidder may reduce the level of the minimum acceptance condition and declare the offer unconditional as to acceptances at a lower level, provided that the minimum level of acceptances remains above 50%.

6.627 Once an offer has become unconditional as to acceptances it must remain open for at least 14 days,[582] although the bidder may wish to extend this period in order

---

[575] Takeover Code Rule 25.6.
[576] Takeover Code Rule 25.6.
[577] Takeover Code Rule 25.6(b).
[578] Takeover Code Rule 30.2.
[579] Takeover Code Rule 31.9.
[580] Takeover Code Rule 31.1.
[581] Takeover Code Rule 31.6.
[582] Takeover Code Rule 31.4.

to attain further acceptances. If the acceptance condition has been satisfied on or before Day 60, the remaining bid conditions must be satisfied or waived within 21 days of the later of the first closing date or the date that the offer is declared or becomes unconditional as to acceptances otherwise it will lapse.[583]

6.9 Additional Issues with Public to Private Transactions

6.9.1 Introduction to public to private transactions

A 'public to private' or a 'take private' transaction involves a private equity funded **6.628** bidder or consortium of bidders making an offer for a target company whose shares are publicly traded which, if successful, would result in the target becoming privately owned. Typically, a private equity house will establish a new company to make the offer and some or all of the target's management team will roll over all or part of their shareholding in the target for shares in the newly formed bidder. The funding structure of the bidder commonly comprises a mixture of share capital subscribed by the management team, share capital and loan notes subscribed by the private equity house and bank debt provided by a third party lender.

Whilst such transactions will also be regulated by the Code, this Section examines **6.629** some of the additional issues which commonly arise in the context of a public to private transaction due to the unique nature of certain aspects of the transaction such as the identity of the bidder, the relationship between the bidder and the target's management team and the investment requirements of the private equity house and lender.

6.9.2 Conflicts of interest

Some or all of the target's management team will often have some involvement in **6.630** managing the combined entity post-merger and may even be contemporaneously on the board of both the target and the bidder. This gives rise to an inherent conflict of interest as such directors will be obliged to satisfy their director's duties to both the bidder and target. During a takeover the interests of the bidder and target are likely to diverge considerably as the bidder will be interested to obtain the target for the lowest price possible whilst the target will be concerned to extract the most favourable offer at the highest price from the bidder. Members of the management team may easily find themselves in a position where they are unable to satisfy their duties to both sides at the same time.

---

583 Takeover Code Rule 31.7.

6.631 Directors are required to avoid situations where they have, or can have, an interest that conflicts or may conflict with the company.[584] It is generally not necessary for a director on the board of both the target and the bidder to resign from one or both boards due to the offer. However, where a director has a conflict of interest they should not normally be joined with the remainder of the target board when it expresses its opinion on the offer to shareholders and the nature of the conflict of interest should be explained to shareholders.[585] The most common way of avoiding a conflict of interest arising is for the target to establish an independent committee comprising its independent board members to consider the offer and make an unbiased recommendation to shareholders as to whether or not to accept the offer. A board member will generally be regarded as 'independent' and permitted to form part of the independent committee if they will have no continuing role (whether in an executive or non-executive capacity) in either the bidder or target if the offer is successful.[586] The independent committee should be appointed at an early stage as it will be responsible for several pre-bid matters such as determining whether to permit management to devote time to the business of the bidder, permitting the bidder to conduct due diligence on the target and negotiating the terms of the offer with the bidder.

6.632 The target is required to obtain competent independent advice on the offer and make the substance of that advice known to shareholders.[587] This is of particular importance where the transaction involves a management buy-out[588] as the target's shareholders are entitled to independent and unbiased advice on the offer. The independent adviser should therefore be appointed as early as possible in the process and their independence should be beyond question.[589] If none of the target's management are independent and the target is incapable of establishing an independent committee, the target's independent adviser may also be asked to step in and fulfil the role which the independent committee would have played in determining whether or not to recommend acceptance of the offer to shareholders.

6.9.3 Management's service agreements

6.633 Members of the target's management team will often require waivers from the terms of their service agreements which require all of the directors' time to be devoted to the business of the target. The independent committee of the target should take the decision as to whether such dispensation should be granted.

584 Companies Act 2006 section 175(1).
585 Takeover Code Note 3 to Rule 25.1.
586 Takeover Code Note 4 to Rule 25.1.
587 Takeover Code Rule 3.1.
588 Takeover Code Note 1 to Rule 3.1.
589 Takeover Code Note 1 to Rule 3.1.

6.9.4 Break fees

The benefits of a break fee and the regulation surrounding them are considered at   **6.634**
Section 6.3.5.1 of this Chapter. The same logic and rationale applies in a private
equity-led management buy-out, except that the commercial need for a break
fee is greater. Private equity houses are more unwilling than other buyers (such as
trade buyers) to commit significant resources to a newly created bid unless they
have some form of cost protection should, ultimately, they not be successful.

In addition to the break fee agreed on announcement, private equity houses may   **6.635**
try to argue for earlier protection for the work done by them prior to announcement (as described at paragraph 6.153 of this Chapter).

6.9.5 Due diligence

Due diligence in public bids is considered at Section 6.3.4 of this Chapter. The   **6.636**
same considerations will also apply to 'take private' transactions. The identity of
the parties, however, causes some additional issues.

As a general proposition, private equity houses and their lending banks will need   **6.637**
more due diligence than a trade buyer. A trade buyer will generally be more
familiar with the target company, the market place, its competitors and other
similar matters. That will be a relevant factor when it decides what level of due
diligence it needs. It is probable that the private equity house will not have that
level of industry knowledge and therefore a higher level of due diligence will be
needed.

The independent committee of the target company needs to be able to control   **6.638**
information flow: (i) to stop management giving out information improperly,
(ii) to be able to comply with Rule 20.2 of the Code, which requires equality of
information to be given to competing bidders (an explanation of Rule 20.2 is set
out at paragraph 6.86 of this Chapter) and (iii) to use the relevant information to
assess bid value.

The independent directors are assisted in this by Rule 20.3 of the Code which   **6.639**
requires that on a management buy-out or similar transaction, the bidder or
potential bidder must, on request, promptly furnish the independent directors of
the target company or its advisers with all information which has been furnished
by the bidder or potential bidder to external provides of finance (whether equity
or debt) for the buy-out.

6.9.6 Concert parties

It is important to establish at the outset which parties will be treated as acting in   **6.640**
concert with the bidding vehicle, as this could have a bearing on the structure and
terms of the offer. The Panel must be consulted at an early stage to determine

which parties will be treated as concert parties. This classification is important for a number of reasons, some of which are discussed below.

6.9.6.1 Definition of 'acting in concert'

6.641 The definition of 'acting in concert' is discussed in detail in Section 6.2.3 of this Chapter. In the context of a public to private transaction, the private equity house and management team will be regarded as acting in concert with the bidder as they have an arrangement to cooperate to obtain control of the target. In addition, other members of the private equity house's group of companies who are 'affiliated' with it are deemed to be acting in concert with each other. A company is deemed to be 'affiliated' with another where such other company either (i) has a majority of the voting rights in the company, (ii) may appoint and remove a majority of the board of the company, (iii) controls a majority of the voting rights pursuant to an agreement with the other members of the company, or (iv) exercises or has the power to exercise dominant influence or control over the company.[590] There is also a rebuttable presumption that the private equity house will be acting in concert with its other group companies including its parent, subsidiaries, fellow subsidiaries and each of their 'associated companies' (for this purpose ownership or control of 20% or more of the equity share capital of the company is regarded as the test of associated company status).[591] Close relatives of the management team will also be presumed to be acting in concert with the bidder.[592]

6.642 As discussed in Section 6.7 of this Chapter, if the bidder acquires an interest in the target's shares which, when aggregated with the interests of its concert parties, would carry 30% or more of the voting rights in the target, the bidder must make a mandatory bid.[593] The private equity house and management team will wish to avoid this mandatory bid obligation as they will not want the offer to be subject to the restricted terms on which a mandatory bid must be made, details of which are outlined at Section 6.7.2 of this Chapter. It is therefore important that the private equity house identifies all concert parties and their shareholdings in the target (including shares held by other members of the private equity house's group of companies) before the offer is announced so that the mandatory bid obligation is not inadvertently triggered by an acquisition of securities during the offer period. Stakebuilding in the target will also have an impact on the offer price, as explained at Section 6.7.2 of this Chapter.

---

[590] Takeover Code Note 2 to the 'Definition of Acting in Concert'.
[591] Takeover Code 'Definition of Acting in Concert'.
[592] Takeover Code 'Definition of Acting in Concert'.
[593] Takeover Code Rule 9.1.

6.9.7 Information about the bidder in the announcement and offer document

Section 6.5 of this Chapter describes the general content requirements of the offer **6.643** document. It is important to remember, however, in the context of a public to private transaction, where the bidder is invariably ultimately controlled by a private equity fund manager which is part of a larger group of companies, that certain information about the ultimate parent company of the bidder (or such other company controlling the bidder as the Panel determines is appropriate) must also be disclosed.[594] The Panel should be consulted to determine the level of information required and from which parties.

As discussed at paragraph 6.448 of this Chapter, the directors of the bidder and **6.644** target must include a statement in each document they issue to shareholders taking responsibility for the information in the document.[595] Where the bidder is controlled by another party such as a private equity fund manager, the Panel must be consulted and may require the ultimate parent company (or such other company controlling the bidder as the Panel determines is appropriate) to also give the responsibility statement.[596] The Panel's goal is to ensure that persons with the appropriate level of seniority take responsibility for the document issued to shareholders to the same extent as the directors of the bidder and target. In respect of the target, whilst only the independent committee should take responsibility for the recommendation to shareholders in respect of the offer,[597] all directors of the target should take responsibility for the remainder of the document relating to the target.

6.9.8 Special deals

One of the general principles stemming from the Takeover Directive[598] and **6.645** the Code[599] is that all shareholders should be afforded equivalent treatment. In keeping with the general tenets of this principle, a bidder and its concert parties are prohibited from making any arrangements with shareholders (or persons interested in shares carrying voting rights) and from dealing, or entering into arrangements to deal, in shares of the bidder or entering into arrangements which involve acceptance of an offer, either during an offer period or when an offer is

---

[594] Takeover Code Rule 24.2 and Note 1 to Rule 24.2.
[595] Takeover Code Rule 19.2.
[596] Takeover Code Note 5 to Rule 19.2.
[597] Takeover Code Note 3 to Rule 25.1.
[598] Takeover Directive Article 3(1)(a).
[599] Takeover Code General Principle 1.

reasonably in contemplation if there are favourable conditions attached which are not extended to all shareholders.[600]

6.9.8.1 *Management rollovers*

6.646   This could cut across the commercial reality of a take private transaction where a private equity house will often insist that the target's management team who will have an ongoing role in the combined entity post-merger take a stake in the bidder to ensure that they are properly incentivized to continue in their roles after the merger. This will commonly be structured as a rollover of some or all of management's shares in the target for shares in the bidder in order to obtain capital gains tax relief.[601] As the private equity house will not wish to offer the same opportunity to all target shareholders, there is a *prima facie* breach of the principle of equal treatment.

6.647   The Code, however, recognizes that the incentivization of management is a legitimate objective and may justify a deviation from the general principle. Accordingly, the Panel retains a right to consent to special deals with management. In determining whether or not to consent to proposed special arrangements with management, the Panel will primarily be concerned to ensure that management will bear the risks associated with their equity shareholding in the bidder and not just benefit from the rewards.[602] For example, the Panel will normally not find an option arrangement which guarantees the original offer price as a minimum to be acceptable as management is not exposed to the risks associated with the investment.[603] Similarly, arrangements which guarantee a minimum price on management leaving the business will be closely scrutinized. The Panel will also examine the proposed special arrangements to ensure that management are simply receiving their consideration in a different form compared to the other shareholders and are not effectively receiving a higher value for their shares in the target.

6.648   The arrangements with management must be approved by independent share-holders in a general meeting taken on a poll.[604] The Panel will also require the independent adviser to the target to state that the arrangements with management are fair and reasonable.[605] Any special arrangements must also be disclosed in the offer document.

---

[600] Takeover Code Rule 16.
[601] Pursuant to Taxation of Chargeable Gains Act 1992 section 135.
[602] Takeover Code Note 4 to Rule 16.
[603] Takeover Code Note 4 to Rule 16.
[604] Takeover Code Note 4 to Rule 16.
[605] Takeover Code Note 4 to Rule 16.

6.9.9 Certain funds

Certain funds on take private transactions are covered in Sections 6.3.4.11 to 6.3.4.15 of this Chapter. **6.649**

6.10 Close-out Procedures

6.10.1 Introduction

The Takeover Directive provides a squeeze-out right, stating that, following a bid **6.650** made to the holders of the target's securities for all of their securities,

> Member States shall ensure that an offeror is able to require all the holders of the remaining securities to sell him/her those securities at a fair price. Member States shall introduce that right in one of the following situations:
>
> (a) where the offeror holds securities representing not less than 90% of the offeree company's capital carrying voting rights and 90% of the voting rights in the offeree company, or
> (b) where, following acceptance of the bid, he/she has acquired or has firmly contracted to acquire securities representing not less than 90% of the offeree company's capital carrying voting rights and 90% of the voting rights comprised in the bid.[606]

For these purposes, the consideration offered in the bid will be presumed to be **6.651** fair where, through acceptance of the bid, the bidder has acquired securities representing not less than 90% of the capital carrying voting rights comprised in the bid.[607] Member states are at liberty to increase the threshold in case (a) but only up to 95%.[608]

The Takeover Directive also provides a sell-out right, namely that holders of **6.652** remaining securities shall have the right to require the bidder to buy his/her securities from him/her under the same circumstances as described in relation to the squeeze-out procedure detailed above.[609]

Both the squeeze-out right and the sell-out right have been incorporated into UK **6.653** law in the Companies Act 2006. At the end of a takeover offer, if the bidder has received sufficient acceptances to satisfy the compulsory acquisition thresholds prescribed by the Companies Act 2006, it will be entitled to acquire the remaining shares in the target from any shareholders who did not accept the offer, whether by choice or simply because they failed to respond. A bidder wishing to fully

---

[606] Takeover Directive Article 15(2).
[607] Takeover Directive Article 15(5).
[608] Takeover Directive Article 15(2).
[609] Takeover Directive Article 16(2).

integrate the target into its group will not want any minority shareholder of the target to remain after the offer and will commonly use the compulsory acquisition process if it is available to them. Non-assenting shareholders will also have a converse right to be bought out in similar circumstances in order to protect against shareholders being involuntarily trapped as minority holders in a company controlled by the bidder. The procedures governing the exercise of these rights are contained in Chapter 3 of Part 28 of the Companies Act 2006.

6.654   After the takeover, scheme and any compulsory acquisition procedures have been completed, the bidder can consider other actions to integrate the target into its group, such as re-registering it as a private company and/or amending its articles of association to entrench the power of the majority shareholder.

6.10.2 Squeeze-out procedure

6.10.2.1 Entitlement to use the 'squeeze-out' procedure

6.655   A bidder is entitled to use the 'squeeze-out' procedure if it has, by virtue of acceptances of a 'takeover offer', acquired or unconditionally contracted to acquire 90% or more in value of the shares to which the offer relates and, where the shares to which the offer relates are voting shares, 90% or more in voting rights carried by those shares.[610] The squeeze-out procedure also operates in the same manner in relation to the compulsory acquisition of other forms of securities admitted to trading on a regulated market, such as convertible securities and debentures.[611]

6.10.2.2 'Takeover offer'

6.656   The first element of this test is whether there has been a 'takeover offer'. The Companies Act 2006 prescribes the following two conditions which must be satisfied in order for an offer to be classified as a 'takeover offer' for the purposes of the squeeze-out provisions:

(i)   the offer must be to acquire all of the shares, or all of at least one class of shares, in the target other than those held by the bidder; and

(ii) the terms of the offer must be the same in relation to all of the shares, or the class of shares, to which the offer relates.[612]

6.657   In respect of the first limb of this test, the offer must be for the entire issued share capital or class of share capital as at the date of the offer or as at a specified future date if the offer extends to shares allotted or converted into shares of the class subject to the offer after the date of the offer.

---

[610] Companies Act 2006 section 979(1) to (4) inclusive.
[611] Companies Act 2006 section 990.
[612] Companies Act 2006 section 974(1), (2) and (3).

In certain circumstances the Panel may be prepared to allow the bidder to offer **6.658** a special deal to certain shareholders. For example, in a public to private transaction the Panel may permit the bidder to offer the target's management team the opportunity to exchange part or all of their target shares for shares in the bidder in order to incentivize them to develop the business of the post-merger entity. If the offer provides for some shareholders to receive a special deal this would result in the offer not being on the same terms in respect of all of the shares and therefore falling outside the definition of a 'takeover offer', which would in turn prevent the bidder from being able to use the compulsory acquisition procedure. The bidder could enter into a contract with such a shareholder outside the terms of the offer in order to prevent the offer falling outside the definition of a 'takeover offer' so as to ensure the availability of the 'squeeze-out' procedure.

There may be circumstances where a takeover offer is not made to foreign **6.659** shareholders due to prohibitions imposed by foreign laws. The offer is still, however, capable of falling within the first limb of the definition of a 'takeover offer' provided that:

(i) those shareholders have no registered address in the UK;
(ii) the offer was not communicated to those shareholders in order to avoid contravention of a foreign law; and
(iii) either the offer is published in the London Gazette or the offer can be inspected or obtained at a place in an EEA state or on a website and a notice specifying the location of the offer is published in the Gazette.[613]

Similarly, the bidder may be prohibited from offering a particular form of consid- **6.660** eration, such as shares in the bidder, in certain jurisdictions or the conditions on which such consideration may be offered may be unduly onerous on the bidder. In such cases the bidder will commonly offer a cash alternative to foreign shareholders who are not entitled to accept the share-for-share exchange offer and so long as the alternative form of consideration is of 'substantially equivalent value', the offer is still capable of being on the same terms within the second limb of the definition of 'takeover offer'.[614] Alternatively, the bidder could offer to sell the consideration shares to which the foreign shareholders would have been entitled in the market and provide them with the proceeds of sale.

6.10.2.3 Calculating the 90% threshold

When calculating the 90% threshold any shares owned by the bidder or its **6.661** 'associates', or which the bidder has contracted to acquire, as at the date of the

---

[613] Companies Act 2006 section 978(1).
[614] Companies Act 2006 section 976.

offer are excluded from the calculation.[615] Shares acquired by the bidder or its associates during the offer period at equal to or below the final offer price are, however, still counted in the 90%.[616] Therefore, a bidder may prefer to wait until after the offer is made before engaging in a stakebuilding exercise in order to make the compulsory acquisition threshold easier to attain. There are also other considerations the bidder will need to keep in mind when acquiring shares during an offer period, such as price implications and disclosure requirements.

6.662 Shares acquired by an 'associate' of a bidder are treated in the same way as shares acquired by a bidder for the purposes of the compulsory acquisition process. An 'associate' is defined in the Companies Act 2006 as including nominees, holding companies, subsidiaries and sister companies of the bidder, companies in which the bidder has a 'substantial interest' (being where the company or its directors are accustomed to acting in accordance with the bidder's directions or instructions, or where the bidder is entitled to exercise or control the exercise of one-third or more of the voting power in general meetings of the company) and parties to a share acquisition agreement with the bidder.

6.663 Shares the subject of irrevocable undertakings are also still included in the calculation of the 90% threshold provided that the undertaking is a deed for no consideration or for no consideration other than the obligation of the bidder to make the offer.[617]

6.664 The thresholds are calculated based on the number of shares to which the original offer relates. Therefore if the offer is made for shares in issue as at the date of the offer, the 90% threshold is calculated by reference to such number of shares. If the offer also extends to shares allotted during the time the offer is open for acceptance, then the 90% threshold is calculated in respect of the number of shares in issue at any given time. Similarly, if there are convertible securities in issue and the offer extends to securities converted before a specified date or the close of the offer, the new shares allotted on the exercise of the convertible securities before such date would be included in the calculation of the 90% threshold.

6.665 If convertible securities were exercised or new shares allotted after the offer closed but before the date on which the compulsory acquisition process began, it is possible that whilst the 90% threshold would be met and the bidder would be entitled to commence the compulsory acquisition process, the bidder could subsequently be diluted below 90% and become disentitled to use the process. A cautious approach would be to calculate the 90% threshold on a fully diluted basis in this scenario to ensure that the bidder remains entitled to use the compulsory

---

[615] Companies Act 2006 section 974(2) and (4).
[616] Companies Act 2006 section 979(8) to (10).
[617] Companies Act 2006 section 975(2).

acquisition procedure. Alternatively, if the bidder wishes to acquire all the convertible securities in issue it can make an offer for such securities, which would be treated as a separate class.[618]

6.666 The bidder can, but is not obliged, to take into account treasury shares when calculating the thresholds.

6.10.2.4 Court order to use compulsory acquisition procedure

6.667 Where a bidder has not attained sufficient acceptances to meet the thresholds for using the compulsory acquisition procedure, it may still apply to a court for an order that it be permitted to use the procedure.[619] To grant the order, the court will need to be satisfied that: (i) the bidder has after reasonable enquiry been unable to trace one or more of the persons holding shares to which the offer relates; (ii) the requirements of the subsection relating to the service of notices would have been met if the person, or all the persons in (i) had accepted the offer; and (iii) the consideration offered is fair and reasonable.[620]

6.668 **6.10.2.4.1 The process** The bidder may exercise its right to compulsorily acquire shares held by shareholders who did not accept the offer (referred to as the 'non-assenting shareholders') by following the procedure prescribed by the Companies Act 2006.

6.669 **6.10.2.4.2 Notices** The bidder must first serve a notice in the prescribed form on shareholders who did not accept the offer which states, amongst other things, that the bidder wishes to acquire their shares.[621] A copy of the notice must also be sent to the target accompanied by a statutory declaration in the prescribed form by a director of the bidder stating that the conditions for exercising its right to use the compulsory acquisition procedure and giving the notice have been satisfied.[622]

6.670 The bidder may serve the compulsory acquisition notice on shareholders at any time between the offer becoming unconditional and three months after the day on which the offer closes for acceptances where the offer was pursuant to the Takeover Directive (or six months in the case of a non-Takeover Directive offer, such as an offer for a company whose securities are admitted to trading on the AIM Market of the London Stock Exchange).[623] As the bidder is obliged to inform non-assenting shareholders of their right to be bought out under the sell-out

---

618 Companies Act 2006 section 989.
619 Companies Act 2006 section 986(9).
620 Ibid.
621 Companies Act 2006 section 980(1).
622 Companies Act 2006 sections 979 and 980.
623 Companies Act 2006 section 980(1) and (2).

provisions described below[624] within one month of the offer closing, the bidder will often issue the compulsory acquisition notice before the deadline for informing shareholders of their right to be bought out in order to avoid sending two notices.

6.671 Regardless of whether the non-assenting shareholder accepts the compulsory acquisition notice, their shares will be acquired by the bidder six weeks after the notice is issued unless a court order prohibiting the acquisition is issued in the meantime.

6.672 **6.10.2.4.3 Consideration**   Where the original offer contained a choice of consideration, the same options must be made available to shareholders under the compulsory acquisition procedure. However, if the bidder is no longer able to provide one of the forms of consideration or the consideration was provided by a third party who is no longer either bound or able to provide it, the bidder must provide an equivalent cash alternative, even if the option of receiving cash was not available under the original offer.[625] If the bidder was restricted from offering certain forms of consideration to foreign shareholders, as described above, the same restrictions may apply to the offer to compulsorily acquire the balance of the minority shares. The compulsory acquisition notice must give particulars of the choice of consideration and specify which form of consideration will be provided if the shareholder does not make an election. Shareholders have six weeks from the date of the compulsory acquisition notice within which to reply to the bidder and elect the form of consideration they wish to receive.

6.673 Where the original offer is still open for acceptance when the compulsory acquisition notice is given, shareholders may accept the original offer and receive their consideration sooner in accordance with the terms of the original offer. This will often be explained to shareholders in a covering letter from the bidder.

6.674 **6.10.2.4.4 Acquisition**   Six weeks after the date of the compulsory acquisition notice the bidder must acquire the shares the subject of the compulsory acquisition notices by sending the target a copy of the compulsory acquisition notice, the consideration due to the non-assenting shareholders and signed, stamped stock transfer forms signed by a person nominated by the bidder on behalf of the shareholder. The target is obliged to hold the consideration in trust in a separate interest-bearing account for the non-assenting shareholders[626] and to register the shares into the bidder's name. Any shares in CREST will be removed from the CREST system and the transfers will take place outside CREST in the usual way. Any consideration which is not claimed by a non-assenting shareholder must

---

[624] Companies Act 2006 section 984(3).
[625] Companies Act 2006 section 981(5).
[626] Companies Act 2006 section 982.

remain in trust for 12 years after which time the target must pay the money into court. The target is also obliged to make reasonable attempts to locate the non-assenting shareholder in order to provide them with the consideration due to them.

6.10.2.4.5 Court order If a shareholder wishes to challenge the bidder's use of **6.675** the compulsory acquisition process or terms of the compulsory acquisition notice, they may apply to the court within six weeks of the date of the compulsory acqui- sition notice for an order that either the bidder is not entitled to acquire their shares or that the terms of the acquisition should be different to those proposed by the bidder.[627] The onus will be on the shareholder to convince the court that the compulsory acquisition process should not be permitted to proceed, for example because of a breach of the Code or other material procedural requirement or because shareholders have not been provided with sufficient information about the offer.

6.10.3 Sell-out procedure

6.10.3.1 *When the right arises*

A shareholder who has not accepted a takeover offer has a right to require the **6.676** bidder to acquire its shares once the bidder has, by virtue of acceptances of a 'takeover offer' (as explained at Section 6.10.2 above), acquired or uncondition- ally contracted to acquire 90% or more in value of the shares in the target and 90% or more of the voting rights carried by those shares.[628] If the takeover offer only related to a particular class or classes of shares, the test is applied in respect of that class or each of the classes, as applicable.[629]

6.10.3.2 *Procedure*

Within one month of the shareholder's right to be bought out being triggered, the **6.677** bidder must give shareholders who have not accepted the offer notice in the pre- scribed form of their right to be bought out and the timeframe within which such right can be exercised, unless a compulsory acquisition notice of the type described at Section 6.10.2.4.2 above has already been issued.[630] If the notice is given before the offer has closed for acceptances, this must be expressly stated in the notice.[631] Shareholders must be given up to three months from the earlier of the date on which the offer closes for acceptances and the date of the notice in which to

---

[627] Companies Act 2006 section 986.
[628] Companies Act 2006 section 983.
[629] Companies Act 2006 section 983(4).
[630] Companies Act 2006 section 984(3).
[631] Companies Act 2006 section 984(3).

exercise their right to be bought out, by written communication addressed to the bidder.[632]

6.678 Where a shareholder exercises its right, the bidder is bound to acquire its shares on the terms of the initial offer or such other terms as may be agreed.[633] The same factors taken into account in the section entitled 'Consideration' referred to above are relevant where there is a choice of consideration or a form of consideration offered under the original offer is no longer available.[634]

6.10.3.3 Comparing the squeeze-out and sell-out procedures

6.679 An important difference in calculating the 90% threshold for the purposes of the squeeze-out and sell-out provisions, is that in respect of the sell-out procedure all shares (or where there are different classes of shares, all shares of each relevant class) are taken into account, regardless of whether the offer related to them or whether the bidder and its associated and connected persons held them at the date of making the offer or acquired or agreed to acquire them during the offer period (irrespective of price). This may result in the threshold being triggered earlier than the compulsory acquisition threshold referred to at Section 6.10.2.3 above if the bidder has an existing stake in the target when the offer is made.

6.680 Finally, the bidder only has one month from triggering the threshold to serve a sell-out notice, but has up to three months to serve a squeeze-out notice. Therefore, the bidder may have to serve a sell-out notice followed by a squeeze-out notice if it does not reach the squeeze-out notice threshold within a month after reaching the sell-out notice threshold.

---

[632] Companies Act 2006 sections 984(1) and (2).
[633] Companies Act 2006 section 985(1).
[634] Companies Act 2006 sections 985(3), (4) and (5).

7

SPECIAL CONSIDERATIONS FOR
NON-EU ISSUERS*

7.1 Introduction

This Chapter covers considerations of particular importance to issuers organized **7.01** under the laws of a jurisdiction other than a member state[1] in connection with securities offerings and admissions to trading in one or more member states.

---

* The author is a partner of Cravath, Swaine & Moore LLP. The views expressed in this Chapter are those of the author and not necessarily the views of Cravath, Swaine & Moore LLP. The author acknowledges the research assistance of Katerina Kousoula, an associate at the firm, in connection with the preparation of this Chapter.

[1] Throughout this Chapter, references to a 'member state' means a country that is a member of the European Economic Area (the 'EEA'), and references to a 'non-EU issuer' mean an issuer organized under the laws of a jurisdiction other than a member state, excluding an asset-backed issuer and government issuers.

The Chapter focuses on the applicable requirements under the Prospectus Directive,[2] Transparency Directive[3] and the Market Abuse Directive.[4] Certain requirements of certain exchange-regulated markets are also addressed as they are an alternative for a non-EU issuer to consider in listing securities with the EEA.

7.02 In particular, the following principal topics are covered:

- the rules and considerations relating to the choice by an issuer of a home member state, which will act as the principal regulator within the EEA with respect to securities offerings and applicable ongoing reporting requirements;
- Prospectus Directive and Market Abuse Directive requirements applicable to securities offerings and the application of those requirements (including coordination with non-EU regulation) in multi-jurisdictional offerings; and
- ongoing reporting requirements under the Transparency Directive and Market Abuse Directive and coordination of those requirements with applicable non-EU disclosure requirements.

7.03 Although this Chapter generally focuses on the provisions of the directives described above, these directives do not in and of themselves apply directly to issuers of securities.[5] Instead, the directives require member states to enact laws implementing (or transposing) those directives in the relevant member state. As a result, there are variations in how the member states have transposed and interpreted the directives (even in the case of directives that are intended to promote maximum harmonization among the member states). Therefore, it is necessary in practice to confirm in the relevant member state(s) exactly how the relevant provision has been transposed and interpreted.[6]

---

[2] Directive 2003/71/EC of the European Parliament and Council of 4 November 2003 on the prospectus to be published when securities are offered to the public or admitted to trading and amending Directive 2001/34/EC [2003] OJ L 345/64.

[3] Directive 2004/109/EC of the European Parliament and Council of 15 December 2004 on the harmonization of transparency requirements in relation to information about issuers whose securities are admitted to trading on a regulated market and amending Directive 2001/34/EC [2004] OJ L 390/38.

[4] Directive 2003/6/EC of the European Parliament and Council of 28 January 2003 on insider dealing and market manipulation (market abuse) [2003] OJ L 96/16.

[5] On the other hand, regulations under these directives (such as the Prospectus Regulation) have the direct force of law without the need for member state transposition.

[6] A useful resource in this regard with respect to the Transparency Directive is a survey undertaken by the Committee of European Securities Regulators ('CESR') on transposition of the Transparency Directive. See 'Summary of Responses to Questionnaire on Transposition of the Transparency Directive', September 2008 conducted by CESR (the 'CESR TD Transposition Study'), available at http://www.cesr.eu/index.php?docid=5337. Annex II to the CESR TD Transposition Study (available at http://www.cesr.eu/index.php?docid=5339) summarizes the responses from each member state that responded to CESR.

7.2 Choosing a Home Member State

For an issuer that is not organized under the laws of a member state that wishes to **7.04** offer securities in one or more member states or have its securities admitted to trading on certain markets within the EEA, the choice of a home member state for the purposes of the Prospectus Directive or the Transparency Directive is a decision to be considered at the outset.

This Section discusses the role of the home member state under the Prospectus **7.05** Directive, the rules and processes for a non-EU issuer choosing a home member state and key considerations that a non-EU issuer should take into account in making a choice. This Section concludes with a brief discussion of the choice of the home member state under the Transparency Directive, which choice is frequently (but not always) driven by the choice of home member state under the Prospectus Directive.

7.2.1 Choice of home member state under the Prospectus Directive

The Prospectus Directive is intended to establish a consistent regulatory regime **7.06** across the EEA in which the competent authority in a single member state (the home member state) has authority for approving prospectuses and applying the Prospectus Directive with respect to 'offers to the public'[7] of securities in the EEA and admissions to trading of securities on any regulated market[8] located in the EEA. For equity securities[9] and low-denomination non-equity securities,[10]

---

[7] An 'offer to the public' means 'a communication to persons in any form and by any means, presenting sufficient information on the terms of the offer and the securities to be offered, so as to enable an investor to decide to purchase or subscribe to these securities'. Prospectus Directive Article 2.1(d). As discussed below, certain offers are exempt from the requirement to publish a prospectus, such as offers addressed to 'qualified investors' (as defined in Prospectus Directive Article 2.1(e)), offers made to fewer than 100 persons (other than qualified investors) in each member state, offers with a minimum total consideration per investor of at least EUR 50,000 or minimum denomination per security of at least EUR 50,000 (which is only available for non-equity securities). Prospectus Directive Article 3.2.

[8] A 'regulated market' is defined in Article 4.1(14) of Directive 2004/39/EC of the European Parliament and of the Council of 21 April 2004 on markets in financial instruments amending Council Directives 85/611/EEC and 93/6/EEC and Directive 2000/12/EC of the European Parliament and of the Council and repealing Council Directive 93/22/EEC [2004] OJ L 145/1 ('MiFID'). Although the Prospectus Directive continues to refer to 'regulated market' as defined in an earlier directive, MiFID has replaced that directive in its entirety. MiFID Article 69.

[9] 'Equity securities' means 'shares and other transferable securities equivalent to shares in companies, as well as any other type of transferable securities giving the right to acquire any of the aforementioned securities as a consequence of their being converted or the rights conferred by them being exercised, provided that securities of the latter type are issued by the issuer of the underlying shares or by an entity belonging to the group of the said issuer'. Prospectus Directive Article 2.1(b).

[10] 'Low-denomination non-equity securities' are non-equity securities with a minimum denomination of less than EUR 1,000 per security (or, if denominated in a currency other than euro, its equivalent in that currency). Prospectus Directive Article 2.1(m). The equivalent of EUR 1,000

the Prospectus Directive contemplates a single home member state for all issues by an issuer. For high-denomination non-equity securities,[11] the issuer of the securities has the ability to select a different home member state for each issue of securities.[12] Depositary receipts are treated for the purposes of the Prospectus Directive as non-equity securities.[13] Although technically equity securities, certain home member states have treated preference shares as 'debt' since they can be more debt-like in character than equity-like.[14]

7.07 The distinction in treatment between low-denomination non-equity securities and high-denomination non-equity securities has created some complications in connection with debt issuance programmes. A base prospectus for a debt issuance programme that contemplates both low-denomination non-equity securities and high-denomination non-equity securities could only be approved by the competent authority of the issuer's home member state for low-denomination non-equity securities.[15] However, if the issuer intended to offer non-equity securities only in another member state or have non-equity securities under the programme admitted to trading on a regulated market in another member state, it would be required to passport the base prospectus to those other member states.[16] Issuers can avoid this concern by having separate debt issuance programmes for low-denomination non-equity securities and high-denomination non-equity securities.

7.08 Another complication that has arisen in practice relates to certain types of structured products that are non-equity securities and do not have denominations (e.g. 'certificates' structures that have been used in the German market for retail investors).

7.09 In light of these complications, the European Commission included in its proposal for the review of the Prospectus Directive the elimination of the distinction between low-denomination non-equity securities and high-denomination non-equity

---

should be determined at the time the draft prospectus is submitted to the competent authority in the home member state. Question 13 of the 'Frequently asked questions regarding Prospectuses: Common positions agreed by CESR Members', 9th updated version, September 2009 (the 'CESR Q&As') published by CESR, available at http://www.cesr.eu/index.php?docid=6041. The CESR Q&As represent the views of the CESR members on the questions addressed and do not bind the European Commission as an institution, and the European Commission would be entitled to take a position different to the positions contained in the CESR Q&As in any future judicial proceedings concerning the relevant provisions.

[11] 'High-denomination non-equity securities' are non-equity securities with a minimum denomination of at least EUR 1,000 per security (or, if denominated in a currency other than euro, its equivalent in that currency). Prospectus Directive Article 2.1(m).

[12] Prospectus Directive Article 2.1(m)(ii).

[13] Prospectus Directive Recital 12; question 39 of the CESR Q&As.

[14] Annex to the European Securities Markets Expert Group Report (the 'ESME Prospectus Report') on the Prospectus Directive, 5 September 2007, page 6 available at http://ec.europa.eu/internal_market/securities/docs/esme/05092007_annex_en.pdf.

[15] Question 46(a) of the CESR Q&As.

[16] Ibid.

securities.[17] The elimination of this distinction has been supported, by among others, the European Securities Markets Expert Group ('ESME').[18] If this proposal is ultimately adopted, then issuers would be able to select a home member state on an issue-by-issue basis for all non-equity securities. As of the date of writing, this change has not yet been implemented, so the distinction remains relevant.

7.2.1.1 Role of the home member state

The competent authority of the home member state under the Prospectus **7.10** Directive is the entity responsible for reviewing and approving the prospectus. In addition, the home member state is generally the member state in which a prospectus is first published.

The Prospectus Directive is a 'maximum harmonisation' measure, meaning **7.11** that member states cannot impose higher standards (so-called 'super-equivalent' standards) for the disclosure contained in the actual prospectus. However, a home member state may impose additional requirements for admission to trading on a regulated market in that member state (including continuing disclosure obligations) that would not apply under the Prospectus Directive alone.[19] Part 3 provides greater detail on the additional obligations and requirements imposed by particular member states.

Once approved by the home member state, a prospectus is permitted to be used **7.12** in other member states under the passporting regime provided for in Article 18 of the Prospectus Directive. Given the maximum harmonization nature of the Prospectus Directive, other member states generally do not have latitude to impose additional requirements on an issuer that wishes simply to use a passported prospectus in that member state (as opposed to admitting securities to trading on a regulated market in that member state).[20] Host member states into which a prospectus is passported under the Prospectus Directive do not have the ability to intervene in the publication of the prospectus, although they do have the authority to enforce compliance with the advertising requirements of the Prospectus Directive.[21] Host member states also do not have the ability to require publication of a notice of passporting of a prospectus into that member state.[22]

---

[17] Proposal for a directive of the European Parliament and of the Council amending Directives 2003/71/EC on the prospectus to be published when securities are offered to the public or admitted to trading and 2004/109/EC on the harmonisation of transparency requirements in relation to information about issuers whose securities are admitted to trading on a regulated market (Prospectus Directive), 23 September 2009 ('PD Review Proposal'), available at http://ec.europa.eu/internal_market/securities/docs/prospectus/proposal_240909/proposal_en.pdf.

[18] ESME Prospectus Report Section 3.2.

[19] Prospectus Directive Recital 15.

[20] Prospectus Directive Article 17.1.

[21] Prospectus Directive Article 15.6.

[22] See question 2 of the CESR Q&As for a discussion of this subject.

7.2.1.2 Rules governing choice of home member state

7.13   Non-EU issuers have the ability to choose their home member state for purposes of offers to the public and admissions to trading on a regulated market of their equity securities and low-denomination non-equity securities.[23] By contrast, the home member state for equity securities and low-denomination non-equity securities for an EU issuer is the member state in which its registered office is located.[24] Both EU and non-EU issuers have flexibility to choose a home member state for issues of high-denomination non-equity securities.[25]

7.14   For a non-EU issuer that has not previously made an offer to the public[26] of its equity securities or low-denomination non-equity securities in any member state or had its equity securities or low-denomination non-equity securities admitted to listing on a regulated market in a member state, its home member state for the purposes of the Prospectus Directive will be either:

*   the member state in which its equity securities or low-denomination non-equity securities are intended to be offered in an offering to the public for the first time after 31 December 2003;[27] or
*   the member state in which the first application for admission to trading on a regulated market of its equity securities or low-denomination non-equity securities on a regulated market is made after 1 July 2005.

7.15   The issuer of the securities or the person requesting admission to trading has the right to choose between the two alternatives above. In the event that a person other than an issuer chooses a home member state with respect to such issuer's equity securities and low-denomination non-equity securities as part of seeking admission of those securities to trading on a regulated market without the issuer's involvement and the issuer has not previously chosen a home member state, then the issuer will have the ability to override that choice of a home member state when it first makes an offer to the public of its securities or requests the admission of securities to trading on a regulated market and will have the ability to choose between the two alternatives mentioned above at that time.[28] Since the Prospectus Directive does not

---

[23]   Prospectus Directive Article 2.1(m)(iii).

[24]   Prospectus Directive Article 2.1(m)(i).

[25]   Prospectus Directive Article 2.1(m)(ii).

[26]   For purposes of selection by a non-EU issuer of its home member state for equity securities and low-denomination non-equity securities, an offer made between 31 December 2003 and 1 July 2005 will only be an 'offer to the public' if it would have been treated as such under the legislation in force in the country where the offer was made at the relevant date.

[27]   If there is a simultaneous offer to the public in multiple member states, the issuer would have the ability to choose among those member states.

[28]   The ability of non-EU issuers to make a subsequent overriding election in this situation is provided for in Prospectus Directive Article 2.1(m)(iii), although the Prospectus Directive does not specify a procedure for making such an election.

provide for an issuer to change its home member state with respect to equity and low-denomination non-equity securities in the future, non-EU issuers that still have the ability to choose a home member state for equity or low-denomination non-equity securities should make a considered decision about the choice.

Non-EU issuers that offered to the public in a member state equity securities or **7.16** low-denomination non-equity securities after 31 December 2003 have already effectively chosen their home member state based on the criteria described above with respect to such securities.[29]

A non-EU issuer that has not offered to the public equity securities or low- **7.17** denomination non-equity securities after 31 December 2003 but had such securities admitted to trading on a regulated market on 1 July 2005 (the deadline for transposition of the Prospectus Directive) had the right under Article 30 of the Prospectus Directive to make a one-time election of its home member state for purposes of equity securities and low-denomination non-equity securities.[30] To make that election, the issuer was required to give notice of its election to the competent authority in the elected home member state by 31 December 2005. Issuers in this situation were permitted to choose their home member state from among the following:

• any member state in which the issuer's equity securities or low-denomination non-equity securities were admitted to trading on a regulated market; and
• if the issuer had made an offer to the public of its equity securities or low-denomination non-equity securities after 31 December 2003, a member state in which such offer was made.

If an issuer did not give notice of an election of a home member state by the **7.18** deadline and subsequently gives notice after the deadline, the relevant competent authority should accept the notice and treat it as if made on time so long as the election would have been permitted if timely made. For an issuer that failed to give notice of an election by the deadline and did not offer to the public in a member state its equity securities and low-denomination non-equity securities after 31 December 2003 and whose equity securities and low-denomination non-equity securities are admitted to trading on a regulated market in only a single member state, its home member state is automatically the member state

---

[29] Non-EU issuers should consider the fact that an employee share offering for which a prospectus (including a short-form prospectus for an employee share scheme) under the Prospectus Directive is prepared constitutes an 'offer to the public' and that would have had the effect of fixing the issuer's home member state. For further discussion of employee share schemes, please refer to Section 7.3.6 below.

[30] 'Note of the Internal Market Directorate General on the determination of home member state for third country issuers with traded securities', 3 October 2005, available at http://ec.europa.eu/internal_market/securities/docs/prospectus/art-30-1_en.pdf.

in which such securities are admitted to trading.[31] An issuer that did not give timely notice of such an election that subsequently makes an annual update filing under Article 10 of the Prospectus Directive[32] with a competent authority in a member state will be treated as having given notice of an election to have that member state as its home member state.[33]

7.19 A public offer of high-denomination non-equity securities will not result in an issuer choosing a home member state for future issuances of securities. The home member state for purposes of that issue of securities will be the home member state in which those securities were first offered to the public.

7.20 Similarly, the admission of securities, whether equity or non-equity, to trading only on an exchange-regulated market will not result in a choice of home member state. As a practical matter, the familiarity of an issuer with securities admitted to trading on an exchange-regulated market may lead the issuer to choose the member state in which the exchange-regulated market is located as a home member state in a future situation in which the choice arises.

7.21 For ease of reference, the following table summarizes the situation for non-EU issuers based on the situation in which they find themselves:

Characteristics	Possible home member states
No public offer in a member state after 31 December 2003 *and* no equity or low-denomination non-equity securities admitted to trading on a regulated market in a member state on 1 July 2005.	Issuer choice: member state in which public offer of such securities is first made or member state in which such securities are first admitted to trading.
Public offer of equity or low-denomination non-equity securities in a member state after 31 December 2003 and securities admitted to trading on a regulated market in a different member state on 1 July 2005.	Issuer choice: member state in which public offer was first made *or* member state in which securities admitted to trading.
Public offer of equity or low-denomination non-equity securities in a member state after 31 December 2003 but no securities of that type admitted to trading on a regulated market in a member state on 1 July 2005.	Automatic: member state in which public offer was first made.
No public offer of equity or low-denomination non-equity securities in a member state after 31 December 2003 but had such securities admitted to trading on a regulated market in a member state on 1 July 2005.	Automatic: member state in which such regulated market is located.

[31] Question 12 of the CESR Q&As.

[32] Ongoing disclosure requirements under Prospectus Directive Article 10 are discussed in Section 7.4.2 below.

[33] Question 12 of the CESR Q&As.

(Continued)

Characteristics	Possible home member states
Public offer of equity or low-denomination non-equity securities in a member state after 31 December 2003 and securities of that type admitted to trading on a regulated market on 1 July 2005 in the member state in which the public offer was first made.	Automatic: member state in which public offer was first made.

7.2.1.3 *Key considerations in choosing a home member state*

The Prospectus Directive imposes limits on an issuer's choice of a home member **7.22** state to a member state in which the issuer intends to make an offer to the public or to have its securities admitted to trading on a regulated market.[34] In an offer to the public in multiple member states (including a global offering), this would not become a meaningful limitation. However, if the first offer to the public of equity securities or low-denomination non-equity securities in the EEA occurs only in a single member state, the issuer will not have the ability to choose another member state as its home member state for these securities. Such a situation could arise in a global offering of equity securities in which securities are only offered to the public or admitted to trading on a regulated market in a single member state.

In choosing a home member state, an issuer should also recognize that the designa- **7.23** tion of a home member state is on an issuer-by-issuer basis. For issuers that intend to use a special purpose vehicle or finance subsidiary to issue securities, that vehicle will have its own home member state, which could differ from the home member state of the parent entity. Choice of a home member state by an issuer that issues non-equity securities guaranteed by another entity does not result in a choice of home member state for the guarantor. For example, for a non-EU issuer that sets up a debt issuance programme with a Luxembourg finance subsidiary, Luxembourg will be the home member state for the finance subsidiary (since that is the member state in which its registered office is located) and the home member state for the parent, if it is also an issuer under the programme, would be determined as described above.

With respect to high-denomination non-equity securities, these considerations **7.24** are somewhat less significant because the choice will relate only to a single issue of these securities. However, from a practical perspective it would be desirable for an issuer to minimize the number of home member states for high-denomination

---

[34] An issuer that selects a home member state for a prospectus needs to have an intent to offer securities to the public in that member state or have those securities admitted to trading on a regulated market in that member state. Otherwise, that issuer may face the possibility of action by the competent authority of that member state if it fails to do so during the period that a prospectus is valid. Question 46(b) of the CESR Q&As.

non-equity securities (i.e. the number of competent authorities with which it needs to interact), absent specific reasons to do so.

7.25 Set forth below is a summary of some of the key considerations of which non-EU issuers should take account in choosing a home member state.

- *Review process of competent authority in the member state.* What has the review practice of the competent authority been in terms of implementing the Prospectus Directive? How extended and difficult has the process of getting prospectuses approved by that competent authority been? Does the competent authority have a 'fast track' procedure that may be available to the issuer?
- *Frequency of dealing with non-EU issuers.* If a competent authority has more experience dealing with non-EU issuers, including issuers organized in the jurisdiction in which the issuer is organized, then it is more likely to have already identified potential issues and conflicts and have established views on them.
- *Additional requirements and obligations.* As described in further detail in Part 3, various member states have imposed additional requirements to be admitted to trading on a regulated market in that member state. In particular, consider if any particular governance requirements may apply if a particular home member state is chosen.[35]
- *Language.* In what language(s) does the competent authority in the member state permit a prospectus to be used with investors to be prepared? In what language(s) will the competent authority accept a prospectus for purposes of the review process? Under the Prospectus Directive, the competent authority in an issuer's home member state determines the language in which an issuer can prepare prospectuses.
- *Liability.* Who is liable for the contents of the prospectus under the member state's legislation? The Prospectus Directive requires member states to ensure that responsibility for the information given in a prospectus attaches to a clearly identified person (normally the issuer). However, the Prospectus Directive does not create a harmonized liability regime, which can result in the same information being subject to different liability regimes, depending on the home member state where the prospectus is approved, and possibly also on the member state where it is being used, if, under the relevant conflict of law rules, the host member state's regime for civil liability applies. For example, in the United Kingdom only the issuer is liable for a prospectus used for a primary

---

[35] Of particular note in this regard is the requirement under Chapter X of Directive 2006/43/EC of the European Parliament and of the Council of 17 May 2006 on statutory audits of annual accounts and consolidated accounts, amending Council Directives 78/660/EEC and 83/349/EEC and repealing Council Directive 84/253/EEC [2006] OJ L 157/87 (the 'Statutory Audit Directive') to have an audit committee. The directive does not specify whether a member state can impose this requirement only on issuers incorporated in that member state or whether a member state can impose this requirement on all issuers for which that member state is the home member state.

offering of securities, while in Germany the issuer and the underwriters would be liable. There can also be differences in the extent to which selling security-holders and guarantors may be liable for the contents of a prospectus.[36]

- *Likelihood of future offerings/listings.* What is the likelihood that the issuer will make further offers to the public or seek admission of securities to trading on a regulated market in a member state? This is particularly relevant in the context of high-denomination non-equity securities where there is a likelihood of multiple offers to the public over time of different securities. The principal consideration is that using the same home member state repeatedly allows the issuer to establish an ongoing relationship with the competent authority and build up experience in understanding how the competent authority approaches questions.

- *Transparency Directive considerations.* How does the member state approach non-EU issuers under the Transparency Directive? Does the member state impose any super-equivalent reporting requirements on issuers for which it is the home member state? What reporting does the member state require from debt-only issuers? As discussed below, for the purposes of the Transparency Directive, an issuer's home member state for equity and low-denomination non-equity securities under the Prospectus Directive will generally be the issuer's home member state for purposes of the Transparency Directive.

- *Experience with securities of the type.* If making a choice in the context of a particular issue of high-denomination non-equity securities with unique features (such as derivative securities and other structured products), does the competent authority have experience in reviewing prospectuses for securities of that type?

7.2.2 Choice of home member state under the Transparency Directive

The triggering event for the application of the Transparency Directive to an issuer is the admission of its securities to trading on a regulated market in a member state. While the admission of debt securities to trading on a regulated market triggers ongoing reporting obligations, an issuer that has only wholesale debt securities (i.e. debt securities with a minimum denomination in excess of EUR 50,000 per unit[37] (or a nearly equivalent amount in another currency)) admitted to trading on a regulated market is not subject to the periodic reporting obligations provided for in the Transparency Directive.[38]

7.26

---

[36] Questions 47 and 48 of the CESR Q&As.

[37] Note that for securities denominated in another currency a sufficient cushion is usually included to address the possibility of fluctuations in exchange rate in the future (e.g. $100,000 has been used as a minimum denomination for debt denominated in US dollars).

[38] Transparency Directive Article 8.1(b). As discussed in Section 7.4.1.3 below, this exemption does not exempt such an issuer from all informational requirements contained in the Transparency Directive.

7.27 For a non-EU issuer that has equity securities or low-denomination non-equity securities admitted to trading on a regulated market, its home member state for purposes of the Transparency Directive is its home member state under the Prospectus Directive.[39] For a non-EU issuer that only has high-denomination non-equity securities admitted to trading on regulated markets in the EEA, the issuer has the ability to choose its home member state for purposes of the Transparency Directive from among the member states in which it has securities admitted to trading.[40] A choice by an issuer of a home member state under the Transparency Directive will remain valid for at least three years unless the issuer's securities are no longer admitted to trading on a regulated market.[41] Disclosure of the choice of home member state for Transparency Directive purposes is required.[42]

7.28 The Transparency Directive is a 'minimum harmonisation' measure, meaning that member states are free to impose additional requirements on the issuers for which they are the home member state. However, the Transparency Directive does not provide for host member states to impose more onerous requirements on issuers. The extent to which member states have imposed various super-equivalent requirements are described in Part 3.

7.3 Coordinating Offering Aspects

7.3.1 Overview

7.29 Non-EU issuers that wish to offer securities both outside the EEA and in one or more member states will inevitably need to confront the question of how to coordinate compliance with the multiple regulatory regimes that may be applicable to the offering. Sections 7.3.2 and 7.3.3 address the Prospectus Directive requirements in a situation in which an issuer includes one or more member states and uses a prospectus approved under the Prospectus Directive or on a private placement basis. Sections 7.3.4 and 7.3.5, respectively, address implications with respect to merger and acquisition transactions and rights offerings involving non-EU issuers. Issues relating to employee share schemes are addressed in Section 7.3.6. Finally, the impact of the Market Abuse Directive on stabilization activities in connection with an offering is addressed in Section 7.3.7.

---

[39] Transparency Directive Article 2.1(i)(i).
[40] Transparency Directive Article 2.1(i)(ii).
[41] Ibid.
[42] Article 2 of Commission Directive 2007/14/EC of 8 March 2007 laying down detailed rules for the implementation of certain provisions of Directive 2004/109/EC on the harmonisation of transparency requirements in relation to information about issuers whose securities are admitted to trading on a regulated market [2007] OJ L 69/27 (the 'Transparency Implementation Directive').

This Section is intended to highlight the issues that may arise for a non-EU issuer   **7.30**
in connection with various types of offerings but is not a comprehensive discussion
of the offering process in the EEA. For further detail regarding the basic mechanics
of equity offerings or debt offerings, please refer to Chapters 2 and 3 of this Part 2.

A non-EU issuer contemplating undertaking an offer to the public of securities in   **7.31**
the EEA or having its securities admitted to trading on a regulated market in the
EEA needs to consider a series of questions at the outset of the process. How these
questions are answered will suggest an appropriate approach to the regulatory
regime established by the Prospectus Directive.

These questions include: **7.32**

- *Existing presence in the EEA*: Has the issuer previously issued a prospectus under
  the Prospectus Directive? Does the issuer already have securities admitted to
  trading on a regulated market in the EEA? Does the issuer have employees in
  the EEA to whom it is likely to wish to grant equity-based compensation?
- *Nature of transaction*: Are securities to be offered to the public as part of the
  transaction or is it a secondary listing only? The competent authorities in
  certain member states have established a 'fast path' procedure for secondary
  listing by issuers that are obligated to file reports with the US Securities and
  Exchange Commission (the 'US SEC') under US reporting standards (including foreign private issuers reporting on Form 20-F).
- *Type of securities*: What type of securities are involved? Are the securities equity,
  debt or something else? If the securities are not equity, then what is the desired
  minimum denomination of the securities?
- *Breadth of target market*: How broad is the target market for the issuer's securities?
  Are the securities intended for institutional-only purchasers or is there likely to be
  significant retail demand as well? Is the transaction targeted to potential purchasers in one or a small handful of member states or is there a desire to market broadly?
  In the case of a listing, what types of investors already hold the issuer's securities?
- *Nature of offering and likelihood of future offerings*: What is the expected length
  and frequency of offerings? Is it a one-off transaction or is the issuer likely to
  undertake other transactions in the future? Is it a continuous or shelf offering
  that will extend over a significant period of time?
- *Listing of securities*: Is there a desire to list the securities? If so, is there a market
  reason to choose a regulated market over an exchange-regulated market? Listing
  securities on an exchange-regulated market generally does not implicate the
  Transparency Directive but would subject the issuer to whatever requirements
  are imposed by the market on which the securities are listed and the member
  state in which such market is located.
- *GAAP*: What is the issuer's home country GAAP? Does the issuer report in any
  other GAAP?

7.33 Before discussing the approach to offering documentation, it is necessary to be aware of the types of transactions to which the Prospectus Directive does not apply[43] and the types of transactions which are exempt from the obligation to publish a prospectus.[44] These are relevant as an alternative to compliance with the Prospectus Directive.

7.34 Below is a summary of the exclusions from the Prospectus Directive:

- units issued by collective investment undertakings, other than the closed-end type;
- non-equity securities issued by a member state, legal or regional authorities of a member state, public international bodies of which one or more member states are members, the European Central Bank or the central bank of a member state;
- shares in the capital of a central bank of a member state;
- securities unconditionally guaranteed by a member state or one of its local or regional authorities;
- securities issued by certain non-profit organizations;
- certain securities issued by credit institutions, including non-equity securities issued in a continuous or repeated manner;
- non-fungible shares of capital that provide the holder with the right to occupy an apartment or other immovable property that cannot be sold without losing such right; and
- securities included in an offer in which the total consideration is less than EUR 2,500,000, calculated over a period of 12 months.[45]

7.35 Set forth below is a summary of the types of offers to the public covered by the Article 3 exemptions:

- an offer of securities addressed solely to 'qualified investors';[46]
- an offer of securities addressed to fewer than 100 natural or legal persons per member state, other than qualified investors;

---

[43] Prospectus Directive Article 1 excludes certain types of securities entirely from the scope of the Prospectus Directive. An issuer relying on an exclusion from the Prospectus Directive will need to consider what non-Prospectus Directive legislation is applicable in the member states in which it is offering securities.

[44] Prospectus Directive Articles 3 and 4 provide for exemptions from the obligation to publish a prospectus. If an exemption applies, then no prospectus is required and compliance with non-Prospectus Directive legislation should not be required.

[45] Prospectus Directive Article 1.2.

[46] The term 'qualified investor' is defined in Prospectus Directive Article 2.1(e). In practice, there has been some complexity for financial intermediaries around the definition of this term because it is not the same as the terms 'professional client' and 'eligible counterparty' as defined in MiFID. In particular, natural persons have to ask to be listed on a register as qualified investors, as opposed to the approach under MiFID in which a financial intermediary can make a determination as to the status of a client based on objective information provided by that client. In order to address these issues, the PD Review Proposal contains a proposal to amend the Prospectus Directive to align these definitions.

- an offer of securities addressed to investors who acquire securities for a total consideration of at least EUR 50,000 per investor;
- an offer of securities whose denomination per unit amounts to at least EUR 50,000; and
- an offer of securities with a total consideration of less than EUR 100,000, calculated over a period of 12 months.[47]

Set forth below is a summary of the types of offers to the public covered by the Article 4 exemptions: **7.36**

- shares issued in substitution for shares of the same class already issued, if the issuing of such new shares does not involve any increase in the issued capital;
- securities offered or allotted in connection with an exchange offer, provided that a document equivalent to a prospectus is made available to investors;
- securities offered or allotted in connection with a merger, provided that a document equivalent to a prospectus is made available to investors;
- shares offered or allotted free of charge to existing shareholders and share dividends of the same class as the shares in respect of which such dividends are paid, provided that a document is made available containing information on the number and nature of the shares and the reasons for and details of the offer; and
- securities offered or allotted to existing or former directors or employees by their employer which has securities already admitted to trading on a regulated market or by an affiliated undertaking, provided that a document is made available containing information on the number and nature of the securities and the reasons for and details of the offer.[48]

Set forth below is a summary of the types of admissions to trading on a regulated market covered by the Article 4 exemptions: **7.37**

- shares representing, over a period of 12 months, less than 10% of the number of shares of the same class already admitted to trading on the same regulated market;
- shares issued in substitution for shares of the same class already admitted to trading on the same regulated market, if the issuing of such new shares does not involve any increase in the issued capital;
- securities offered or allotted in connection with an exchange offer, provided that a document equivalent to a prospectus is made available to investors;
- securities offered or allotted in connection with a merger, provided that a document equivalent to a prospectus is made available to investors;

---

[47] Prospectus Directive Article 3.2.
[48] Prospectus Directive Art. 4.1.

- shares offered or allotted free of charge to existing shareholders and share dividends of the same class as the shares in respect of which such dividends are paid, provided that such shares are of the same class as shares already admitted to trading on the same regulated market and a document is made available containing information on the number and nature of the shares and the reasons for and details of the offer;
- securities offered or allotted to existing or former directors or employees by their employer or by an affiliated undertaking, provided that such shares are of the same class as securities already admitted to trading on the same regulated market and a document is made available containing information on the number and nature of the securities and the reasons for and details of the offer;
- shares resulting from the conversion or exchange of other securities or from the exercise of the rights conferred by other securities, provided that such shares are of the same class as the shares already admitted to trading on the same regulated market; and
- securities already admitted to trading on another regulated market, subject to certain conditions, including that the securities have been admitted to trading on that other regulated market for at least 18 months.[49]

7.3.2 Offering or admission to trading on a regulated market with an approved prospectus

7.38 A non-EU issuer that wishes to conduct an offering that includes investors in one or more member states pursuant to an approved prospectus will need to plan in advance in order to be able to conduct a well-functioning offering process. This Section outlines some of the issues that such an issuer will need to confront in order to be able to undertake an offering of this type. This Section also addresses technical listing transactions.

7.3.2.1 *Overall approach to offering documentation*

7.39 Unless the Prospectus Directive does not apply or there is an available exemption under the Prospectus Directive, an issuer will need to prepare a prospectus that complies with the requirements of the Prospectus Directive for the type of securities to be offered and the issuer's history in order to be able to offer securities to the public in the EEA.

7.40 **7.3.2.1.1 Single offering document or multiple offering documents** One of the initial questions to be considered is how to structure the offering documents that will be used in the various jurisdictions in which securities will be offered.

---

[49] Prospectus Directive Art. 4.2.

As discussed below, the approach to structuring the offering document will be influenced by a combination of legal, practical and marketing considerations. Because the approach to the structure of the offering document can influence the entire drafting process and there is no single correct approach to the question, the issuer, the underwriters for the offering and their respective counsel should agree early on the approach to these questions. In particular, if there are to be multiple versions of the prospectus, it is important to determine what version will function as the master and the stage of the drafting process at which other versions will be created from the master (later is typically better than sooner).

Of note in this regard is the view expressed by CESR[50] that a prospectus is required **7.41** to be in the order prescribed in the Prospectus Regulation[51] (i.e. table of contents, summary, risk factors and other information called for by the schedules and building blocks contained in the Prospectus Regulation). Although this order is consistent with US SEC requirements and typical practice in the United States, it may differ from the typical offering document structure in another jurisdiction. Note also that Article 25.4 of the Prospectus Regulation permits the competent authority of the home member state to require a cross-reference table when a prospectus does not present information in the order contemplated by the schedules and building blocks contained in the Prospectus Regulation.[52] While a cross-reference table is not an inordinate burden to prepare, this requirement should be kept in mind when thinking about how best to organize a document to be used in the EEA and elsewhere.

An initial consideration that a non-EU issuer will need to consider in approaching **7.42** the preparation of an offering document is the possibility that the law of jurisdictions outside the EEA in which the offering will be conducted will require the inclusion of information in the offering document that differs from the information required to be included by the Prospectus Directive (or vice versa). Assuming that is the case, the issuer and the underwriters will need to make a judgment about whether it is preferable to use a single offering document for all jurisdictions (subject to the discussion of language requirements in Section 7.3.2.3 below) or

---

[50] Question 9 of the CESR Q&As. Note that the response by CESR indicates that it would be permissible to include a cover page about the issuer and the issue of securities to which the prospectus relates prior to the table of contents.

[51] Commission Regulation (EC) No 809/2004 of 29 April 2004 implementing Directive 2003/71/EC of the European Parliament and of the Council as regards information contained in prospectuses as well as the format, incorporation by reference and publication of such prospectuses and dissemination of advertisements [2004] OJ L 149/1 (the 'Prospectus Regulation').

[52] Prospectus Regulation Article 25.4.

confront the practical headaches of producing multiple versions of the offering document for use in the EEA and elsewhere.[53]

7.43　If an issuer is contemplating using multiple offering documents in order to address differing disclosure requirements, a question that will naturally arise is whether differential disclosure to investors in different jurisdictions increases the likelihood of a claim that one of the offering documents is misleading because it omits material information. Offering participants will need to consider this question carefully in the context of the specific information that is contemplated to be omitted from one of the versions of the offering document. These concerns typically result in only minor differences between the various versions of an offering document (e.g. differences in order or format), leaving aside language. One common structure is to prepare a common offering document for use in all jurisdictions and then prepare one or more 'wrappers' for use in connection with the common offering document in jurisdictions that require additional immaterial information that offering participants wish not to include in the common offering document.

7.44　If the issuer chooses to prepare multiple offering documents, then it should include a legend in each version of the offering document explaining where that offering document can be used and advising recipients of the fact that the offering is being conducted with other offering documentation in other jurisdictions and, if applicable, that such offering documentation is in a different format and may contain different information. However, in this situation, an issuer should still ensure that there are not material differences between the different versions of the offering document.

7.45　**7.3.2.1.2 Structure of prospectus**　The Prospectus Directive and Prospectus Regulation contemplate the possibility of either a single prospectus (intended to be used for a single offering) or a tripartite document consisting of a summary, registration document and securities note.[54] Such a structure may be useful for circumstances in which an issuer wishes to undertake multiple offerings of

---

[53] Note that in global offerings that include registration under the US Securities Act of 1933 (the 'US Securities Act') of offers and sales of securities in the United States, it may be desirable for US legal reasons to have a separate essentially identical prospectus that is used only for offers and sales in the United States and to US persons.

[54] Although it is common for large issuers to use shelf registration statements for equity offerings in the US market, it has been fairly uncommon in the EEA. One reason may be that in the US system an issuer's registration statement is constantly updated by periodic filings under the US Securities Exchange Act of 1934 (the 'US Exchange Act') without the need for regulatory approval, while under the Prospectus Directive a supplemental prospectus, which requires the approval of the competent authority of the home member state, may be required to update a registration document.

securities over a period of time.[55] Another type of offering in which the tripartite prospectus structure may be useful is an offering with a substantial retail component in which there may be a desire to be able to send the summary to retail investors separate from the full registration document. If the offering is to be conducted outside the EEA as well, these two approaches give some flexibility to structure a consistent offering document in all jurisdictions.

For an offering of non-equity securities (including warrants) intended to be offered under an 'offering programme',[56] the Prospectus Directive and Prospectus Regulation also provide for a base prospectus/final terms offering structure.[57] This structure allows an issuer to file a base prospectus that includes all information other than the terms of specific offerings of securities, which would be included in final terms filed with the competent authority of the home member state. The base prospectus structure is available for repeated offerings under debt issuance programmes in which different series of non-equity securities with different economic terms are offered in separate offerings over an extended period of time. Only the base prospectus would be subject to approval by the competent authority of the home member state. A base prospectus for an offering programme is not required to specify a maximum amount of securities to be offered under the programme,[58] and the prospectus would remain valid (assuming it is updated as needed through supplemental prospectuses) for 12 months.[59] The European Commission has proposed amending Article 9 to provide that a base prospectus would remain valid for 24 months.[60]   **7.46**

Article 22 of the Prospectus Regulation outlines the basic requirements with respect to the information to be contained in the base prospectus and the information to be contained in the final terms. As a general matter, the base prospectus is intended to include information about the issuer and the risks and considerations common to all securities to be offered under the offering programme to which that base prospectus relates, while final terms should contain information about the terms of a specific issue of securities (i.e. information from the applicable securities note schedule to the Prospectus Regulation).[61]   **7.47**

---

[55] This structure is somewhat similar to shelf registration in the United States, although it differs in that the summary and securities note are required to be approved by the competent authority and periodic filings under the Transparency Directive do not update the registration document. Material changes that occur between approval of a registration document and an offering of securities would need to be included in a supplemental prospectus under Prospectus Directive Article 16.1 or in the securities note for the offering. Prospectus Directive Article 12.2.

[56] Prospectus Directive Article 2.1(k) defines an 'offering programme'.

[57] Prospectus Directive Article 5.4.

[58] Question 36 of the CESR Q&As.

[59] Prospectus Directive Article 9.2.

[60] Section 5.3.8 of the explanatory memorandum included in the PD Review Proposal.

[61] Question 57 of the CESR Q&As.

Final terms are not intended to be used to include material updates, which should instead be disclosed through a supplemental prospectus (subject to review and approval by the competent authority of the home member state) under Article 16 of the Prospectus Directive.[62]

7.3.2.2 *Resale prospectuses*

7.48   Article 3.2 of the Prospectus Directive raises the possibility that resales of securities sold in an exempt offering (e.g. to qualified investors) might constitute an offer to the public for which a prospectus may be required unless an exemption is available. In the most typical situation (i.e. a purchaser that at a future date wishes to resell securities it purchased in an exempt offering to a small number of purchasers), the purchaser could rely on the fewer-than-100-offerees exemption in Article 3.2 of the Prospectus Directive. Alternatively, the purchaser could resell the securities into the market through a normal course broker or dealer transaction and rely on the fact that it is not making an offer to the public.

7.49   The last sentence of Article 3.2 goes beyond simply requiring the analysis of each subsequent resale as a separate offer and provides that a placement of securities through financial intermediaries will be subject to the obligation to publish a prospectus if the final placement is not to an exempt offeree.[63] In practice, this language has proved problematic in situations in which an issuer or the primary underwriters for an offering of securities sells the securities to one or more financial intermediaries who in turn resell those securities to the ultimate purchasers (typically, retail investors). In order to address possible issues arising out of this method of distribution, the issuer and its primary underwriters should consider imposing offering restrictions on financial intermediaries that will function in this role. The issuer and primary underwriters may also need to conduct due diligence on financial intermediaries that purchase in an offer to ascertain their investment intent and their knowledge of the applicable requirements and exemptions.

7.50   This subject has been addressed most extensively in the context of a 'retail cascade' distribution of debt securities. Given that offerings of debt securities by non-EU issuers are typically targeted to institutional investors, concerns about a retail cascade are unlikely to be a particularly significant issue for non-EU issuers. This issue could also conceivably arise in the context of an equity offering in which there is retail distribution over an extended period of time.[64]

---

[62] Ibid.

[63] Prospectus Directive Article 3.2.

[64] Unlike the US federal securities laws, the Prospectus Directive and Prospectus Regulation do not impose an explicit ongoing prospectus delivery requirement for a specific period of time.

In retail debt offerings, a common method of distribution is a so-called retail **7.51** cascade in which an issuer sells to intermediaries in an exempt offering, because such intermediaries are typically qualified investors, and those intermediaries then distribute the purchased securities to retail investors over a period of time ranging from days to months at varying prices. The requirement of Article 3.2 of the Prospectus Directive to create a prospectus for these offers can create practical problems for both the issuer and the selling financial intermediaries. One such problem is that it may leave the issuer obligated to publish supplemental prospectuses for an indeterminate period of time until the distribution is completed. A second issue is that an issuer will likely not have details at the outset of the retail cascade of the particular offers that will be made by the selling parties in the distribution.

CESR has published views on how the relevant Prospectus Directive provisions **7.52** should be applied to retail cascade offers.[65] Where there is an offer consisting of other sub-offers from intermediaries to the ultimate investor, intermediaries should be able to rely on the prospectus drawn up by the issuer without having to draw up a separate prospectus, in particular where the issuer has consented to this. Therefore, where the intermediaries are acting in association with the issuer, an additional prospectus should not be required. On the other hand, intermediaries not acting in association with the issuer would be required to prepare a separate prospectus, which from a practical perspective would necessarily incorporate by reference from the issuer's prospectus.

The issuer would be responsible for preparing any supplemental prospectuses **7.53** required during the period when the sub-offers from the intermediaries acting in association with the issuer are ongoing (and, therefore, the issuer would have an incentive to limit the time period during which such offers were being made). Intermediaries not acting in association with the issuer would be required to update their own prospectus. Finally, information relating to the sub-offers will not be available at the time of the publication of the prospectus. Such information which relates to allocation, distribution and pricing will be provided by the intermediaries to the ultimate investor. Such information on the subsequent sub-offers may be omitted on the basis of Article 23.4 of the Prospectus Regulation. The intermediaries would be expected to supply the information to the investor at the time of any sub-offer. Issuers should insert a bold notice in a suitable place in the prospectus informing investors that such information would be provided at the time of any sub-offers.

In response to concerns raised about the impact of Article 3.2 of the Prospectus **7.54** Directive on retail cascade distributions, the European Commission has proposed

---

[65] See question 56 of the CESR Q&As.

the addition of language to Article 3.2 to clarify that no additional prospectus is required in connection with subsequent resales so long as a valid prospectus is available for use and the issuer or the person responsible for drawing up the prospectus consents to its use.[66] As of the date of writing, this proposal has not yet been implemented.

7.3.2.3 Language requirements

7.55 Under the Prospectus Directive, when an offer to the public or admission to trading on a regulated market is sought only in the home member state, then the prospectus is required to be drafted in a language accepted by the competent authority of the home member state.[67]

7.56 If the prospectus is to be used in one or more host member states but not the home member state, then it must be prepared in a language accepted by the competent authorities in the host member states *or* a language customary in the sphere of international finance.[68] In this situation, a host member state may require that the summary of the prospectus be translated into the official language(s) of that host member state.[69] English is generally considered to be a language customary in the sphere of international finance.[70]

7.57 For purposes of review by the competent authority of the home member state, a copy of the prospectus in a language accepted by that competent authority or a language customary in the sphere of international finance is required to be prepared.[71] In a situation in which the prospectus is intended to be prepared in a language that is not accepted by the competent authority of the home member state (e.g. because the prospectus is intended to be used principally in another member state and was prepared in the official language of the host member state),

---

[66] Section 5.3.4 of the explanatory memorandum included in the PD Review Proposal.

[67] Prospectus Directive Article 19.1.

[68] Prospectus Directive Article 19.2.

[69] CESR has prepared a summary of the requirements for the translation of summaries and languages accepted by competent authorities of member states for purposes of the review of prospectuses, available at http://www.cesr.eu/index.php?docid=5607. There is some variation among the competent authorities in member states with respect to when a translation of the summary is required.

[70] Neither the Prospectus Directive nor the Prospectus Regulation specify which languages are 'customary in the sphere of international finance', although English has been accepted as qualifying. The competent authority in the United Kingdom, the Financial Services Authority (the 'UK FSA') has identified criteria to be used in determining which languages it would regard as customary in the sphere of international finance and indicated that it was certain that English satisfied its criteria but would require issuers seeking to use another language to demonstrate compliance with the criteria on a case-by-case basis. See UK FSA Policy Statement 07/8, June 2007, page 6, available at http://www.fsa.gov.uk/pubs/policy/ps07_08.pdf.

[71] Prospectus Directive Article 19.2. In general, most (but not all) competent authorities accept prospectuses drafted in English for review.

then it may be necessary to prepare a translation of the prospectus simply for purposes of competent authority review.

If the prospectus is to be used in both the home member state as well as in other member states, then the prospectus is required to be drawn up in a language accepted by the competent authority of the home member state and shall also be made available either in a language accepted by the competent authorities of each host member state or in a language customary in the sphere of international finance.[72] The competent authority of each host member state may only require that the summary be translated into its official language(s).[73] **7.58**

Finally, in the case of admission to trading on a regulated market of non-equity securities with a minimum denomination of at least EUR 50,000 (i.e. wholesale debt securities), the prospectus is required to be prepared in a language accepted by the home and host member states or a language customary in the sphere of international finance.[74] **7.59**

It is permissible under the Prospectus Directive to incorporate documents by reference into a prospectus that are in a different language than the prospectus itself.[75] In order to do so, the incorporated document must comply with the language requirements of the Prospectus Directive and the competent authorities in the relevant member states. In particular, language issues with respect to incorporated documents can become a stumbling block if the prospectus is intended to be passported into another jurisdiction—the incorporated document must be in a language accepted by the competent authorities of the host member states into which the prospectus is being passported. **7.60**

The Prospectus Directive and Prospectus Regulation do not specify the quality of the translation in the event that a portion of the prospectus is translated in connection with passporting. However, CESR has made clear its view that the persons responsible for the prospectus are responsible for the quality of the translation and that the competent authorities in a host member state bear no responsibility for the translation.[76] CESR has further stated its view that a competent authority in a host member state is not permitted to hold up the passporting process in order to permit it to check the quality of any translations.[77] CESR recommends the insertion in a translation of a prospectus a statement that **7.61**

---

[72] Prospectus Directive Article 19.3.

[73] Prospectus Directive Articles 19.2 and 19.3.

[74] Prospectus Directive Article 19.4.

[75] Question 7 of the CESR Q&As. This question and response also make clear that incorporation of a translation of a document filed with the competent authority of the home member state is permissible, subject to complying with Prospectus Directive Articles 11 and 13.

[76] Question 33 of the CESR Q&As.

[77] Ibid.

the document is a translation of the approved prospectus made under the sole responsibility of the persons responsible for the approved prospectus.[78]

7.62 Issuers that are contemplating the possibility of having a prospectus translated should not underestimate the time that may be required to complete that exercise on a document the size of a typical prospectus.[79] In addition to the simple mechanics of having the prospectus translated, there will need to be time allowed in the schedule for double-checking to ensure consistency across versions of the prospectus.

7.63 Offering participants should also give careful consideration to the timing of translation of a prospectus. There will need to be a balance struck between translating too late, in which case the translation holds up the timetable, and translating too early, in which case changes will need to be made simultaneously in multiple versions of the prospectus (which is a practical burden and increases the likelihood of inconsistencies).

7.3.2.4 *Prospectus content requirements*

7.64 **7.3.2.4.1 Non-financial disclosure** In terms of the detailed content required to be included in the prospectus by the Prospectus Directive and Prospectus Regulation, the disclosure requirements are generally based on the International Organization of Securities Commissions ('IOSCO') disclosure standards.[80] To further facilitate common disclosure in offerings and listings that include both EEA and non-EEA jurisdictions, the Prospectus Directive contemplates the possibility that competent authorities would accept prospectuses for non-EU issuers prepared in accordance with international standards set by international securities commission organizations, including IOSCO.[81]

7.65 If the competent authority in the home member state is, in fact, willing to accept a prospectus prepared in accordance with the IOSCO standards, this can create significant synergies in preparing a prospectus that would otherwise be required to be prepared in accordance with those standards. The most obvious benefit would be for non-EU issuers whose home country disclosure requirements are based on the IOSCO disclosure requirements.[82] Another possible area of benefit is that a non-EU, non-US issuer conducting a simultaneous offering in the United States and the EEA could benefit from the fact that the US disclosure standards

---

[78] Ibid.

[79] Given its limited size (i.e. 2,500 words), the requirement to translate a summary should impose a more modest burden than translation of a prospectus running to hundreds of pages.

[80] Prospectus Directive Article 7.3; Prospectus Regulation Recital 2.

[81] Prospectus Directive Article 20.1(a).

[82] The IOSCO disclosure standards are available at http://www.iosco.org/library/pubdocs/pdf/IOSCOPD81.pdf.

applicable to a registration statement by such an issuer[83] are also based on the IOSCO disclosure standards.

Notwithstanding an equivalence determination, the authority to approve a prospectus prepared in accordance with a non-EU issuer's home country legislation still requires the competent authority to review the completeness of the prospectus. This means that a full review process by the competent authority in the home member state should still be expected. As of December 2008, no competent authority has made any blanket or unconditional determinations as to the equivalence of the disclosure requirements of any non-EU country with the requirements imposed under the Prospectus Directive and Prospectus Regulation.[84] In order to improve the situation, the European Commission has asked the members of CESR to agree on a common procedure for determining equivalence.[85] The equivalence assessment began in December 2008 with the requirements of the United States and Israel, and CESR is expected to make further statements on the assessment in due course.[86]

7.66

7.3.2.4.2 Financial statements The requirements applicable to the financial statements to be included in a prospectus approved under the Prospectus Directive are a critical initial item for a non-EU issuer to consider. A non-EU issuer contemplating an offering or admission to trading needs to determine up front whether and to what extent it will need to restate its existing financial statements into another set of generally accepted accounting principles in order to be able to comply with the requirements of the Prospectus Directive. The amount of time required to restate financial statements and have them audited is substantial, and an issuer would not want to discover once its transaction process is underway that it needs to undertake a costly and time-consuming exercise with respect to its financial statements.

7.67

The schedules to the Prospectus Regulation require inclusion in a prospectus of financial statements prepared under International Financial Reporting Standards ('IFRS') as adopted by the European Union[87] or an equivalent system of accounting principles. Unlike the regime in the United States applicable to

7.68

---

[83] Registration Statements on Form F-1 and Form F-3 under the US Securities Act. Form 20-F, which serves as both a form of annual report as well as a registration statement under the US Exchange Act in connection with a listing on an exchange in the United States, is also based on the IOSCO disclosure standards.

[84] See CESR Statement, 'Assessment on the Equivalence of Prospectuses from non-EEA Jurisdictions' (Article 20.1 Prospectus Directive), 17 December 2008, available at http://www.cesr.euindex.php?docid=5428.

[85] Ibid.

[86] Ibid.

[87] Regulation 1606/2002 of the European Parliament and of the Council of 19 July 2002 on the application of international accounting standards [2002] OJ L 243/1.

foreign private issuers, the Prospectus Regulation does not generally provide for reconciliations of financial statements prepared under a different system of financial accounting principles to IFRS (in lieu of requiring a restatement of all required financial statements into IFRS). There is an exception to this general principle for prospectuses relating to issuances of wholesale debt securities, in which a reconciliation suffices. Therefore, for issuers that do not prepare financial statements in their home country in accordance with IFRS, the requirement to restate their financial statements into IFRS imposes a significant practical burden to undertaking an offering that requires approval of a prospectus by a member state. These financial statement requirements apply to both current period financial statements as well as all historical financial statements required to be included in the prospectus.[88]

7.69 Issuers in a number of jurisdictions are not subject to the above requirements based on an amendment to the Prospectus Regulation as of 1 January 2009, which provides that financial statements prepared under generally accepted accounting principles in the United States and in Japan are 'equivalent' for purposes of the Prospectus Directive.[89] This determination arises out of the ongoing process of convergence between these GAAPs and IFRS. As a result, issuers that prepare financial statements under these accounting principles will not need to restate their financial statements into IFRS in order to include them in a prospectus under the Prospectus Directive. This determination follows a several-year period during which the European Commission had treated financial statements prepared under these GAAPs as equivalent so long as certain additional disclosures were included with them (referred to as 'remedies'). These additional disclosures are not required for issuers reporting under US GAAP or Japanese GAAP.

7.70 This amendment to the Prospectus Regulation also provides that financial statements prepared in accordance with generally accepted accounting principles in the People's Republic of China, Canada, the Republic of Korea and the Republic

---

[88] The schedules to the Prospectus Regulation generally require issuers to include three years of historical financial statements in a prospectus for shares or depositary receipts and two years of historical financial statements in a prospectus for debt or derivative securities. See the Schedules to the Prospectus Regulation. The financial statements required for these periods include balance sheets, statements of comprehensive income, statements of changes in equity and statements of cash flows. If interim financial statements have been published since the date of the most recent audited financial statements, they are required to be included in a prospectus. If the date of the registration document is more than nine months after the end of the most recent audited financial year, then financial statements covering at least the first half of the financial year are required to be included (even if they have not have not otherwise been published). Interim financial statements are not required to be audited or reviewed. See the Schedules to the Prospectus Regulation.

[89] Article 1.1 of Commission Regulation (EC) No 1289/2008 of 12 December 2008 amending Commission Regulation (EC) No 809/2004 implementing Directive 2003/71/EC of the European Parliament and of the Council as regards elements related to prospectuses and advertisements [2008] OJ L 340/17.

of India will be accepted in prospectuses for financial years ending no later than 31 December 2011. Therefore, issuers that prepare financial statements in accordance with GAAP in one of those jurisdictions will be able to use those financial statements in a prospectus under the Prospectus Directive without the need to restate or include additional disclosures about the differences in GAAP through the end of 2011. Once these jurisdictions converge to IFRS, the temporary exemption will cease to apply. Although the European Commission has not made any commitments in this regard, it would be reasonable to expect that there will be further developments in the future to provide for permanent equivalence in one or more of these jurisdictions.

A non-US issuer that is preparing a prospectus under the US securities laws or that reports under the US Exchange Act, as a 'foreign private issuer' should be able to realize substantial practical benefits from reporting in either US GAAP or IFRS. Under rule changes implemented by the US SEC in 2008, non-US issuers have the ability to include financial statements prepared in accordance with IFRS as issued by the International Accounting Standards Board (the 'IASB') without a reconciliation to US GAAP in US Exchange Act periodic reports and registration statements under the US Securities Act. At present, IFRS as adopted by the European Union differs from IFRS as issued by the IASB chiefly with respect to the approach to hedge accounting for certain financial instruments in IAS 39, 'Financial Instruments: Recognition and Measurement'. In this regard, IFRS as adopted by the European Union offers greater flexibility than IFRS as issued by the IASB.[90]   **7.71**

7.3.2.4.3 Auditor requirements   A non-EU issuer needs to determine very early in the process of any proposed offering or admission to trading on a regulated market in the EEA whether its existing auditor will be able to audit financial statements to be included in the prospectus for the offering and, if applicable, in annual reports to be filed in the future under the Transparency Directive. This subject needs to be addressed at the outset because a change in auditors would radically alter the timetable for an offering or listing and could lead to a modification to the proposed transaction to eliminate the need to replace the issuer's existing auditors.   **7.72**

Under the Statutory Audit Directive, the auditors of financial statements of non-EU issuers that have securities (other than solely wholesale debt securities)   **7.73**

---

[90] Issuers should note that there is a transitional provision that allows issuers incorporated in a member state to use the increased flexibility with respect to hedge accounting in IAS 39 as adopted by the European Union. This transitional provision, by its terms, does not apply to other foreign private issuers. Therefore, if a non-EU issuer is utilizing this increased flexibility, it would need to either reconcile to US GAAP or seek relief from the US SEC to permit it to rely on the transitional provision.

admitted to trading on a regulated market will be required to be registered with the competent authorities of the issuer's home member state. This requirement should apply only to financial statements of an issuer following that issuer's admission to trading on a regulated market (i.e. not to a prospectus for the admission of those securities to trading on a regulated market). Nevertheless, a change in auditors between the initial admission to trading and the first annual report would be burdensome for an issuer and would expose the issuer to the risk that a new auditor is unwilling to step in or that the auditor finds problems in its audit (and potentially exposes the issuer to claims of misleading disclosure). The Statutory Audit Directive is still in the process of transposition in a number of member states.

7.74   Article 46.2 of the Statutory Audit Directive requires the European Commission to assess the equivalence of the oversight and quality assurance and enforcement systems in the home countries of non-EU auditors. Once these equivalence determinations have been made, then member states can exempt non-EU auditors from the requirements of the Statutory Audit Directive. The European Commission has not yet made final assessments of equivalence but has provided transitional relief for auditors based in certain countries for financial years starting during the period from 29 June 2008 through 1 July 2010.[91]

7.75   **7.3.2.4.4 Incorporation of documents by reference**   Article 11 of the Prospectus Directive permits an issuer to incorporate in a prospectus material approved by or filed with the competent authority of the issuer's home member state, except in a prospectus summary. Documents that can be incorporated by reference into a prospectus include annual and interim financial information, previously approved prospectuses and regulated information.[92] Unlike in the integrated disclosure system in the US system, information arising after the date of the prospectus cannot be incorporated by reference.

7.76   Issuers should note that the competent authorities of certain member states may require copies of documents incorporated by reference into a prospectus to be distributed with copies of the prospectus into which those documents have been incorporated (including in the case of prospectuses passported into that member state). The German competent authority (BaFin) previously had such a requirement but has eliminated it.

---

[91] Commission Decision 2008/627/EC of 29 July 2008 concerning a transitional period for audit activities of certain third country auditors and audit entities [2008] OJ L 202/70. The 34 countries covered by the transitional relief are: Argentina, Australia, Bahamas, Bermuda, Brazil, Canada, Cayman Islands, Chile, China, Croatia, Guernsey, Jersey, Isle of Man, Hong Kong, India, Indonesia, Israel, Japan, Kazakhstan, Malaysia, Mauritius, Mexico, New Zealand, Pakistan, Russia, Singapore, South Africa, South Korea, Switzerland, Taiwan, Thailand, Turkey, Ukraine, United Arab Emirates and the United States.

[92] See Section 7.4.1.8 below for a discussion of the requirements under the Transparency Directive with respect to disclosure of 'regulated information'.

7.3.2.4.5 Responsibility statements and due diligence The Prospectus **7.77**
Directive provides that responsibility for the information given in a prospectus
attaches at least to the issuer, its administrative, management and supervisory
bodies, the person offering the securities (i.e. a selling securityholder) and any
guarantor, as the case may be.[93] In a situation in which a person other than the
issuer is seeking to have securities admitted to trading on a regulated market, that
person is responsible for the contents of the prospectus in connection with that
admission to trading. Each of the persons responsible are required to be identified
as such in the prospectus and to make a responsibility statement to the effect that,
to the best of their knowledge, the information contained in the prospectus is in
accordance with the facts and that the prospectus makes no omission likely to
affect its import.[94]

Unlike most other elements of the Prospectus Directive, the liability provisions **7.78**
are not subject to maximum harmonization, which has resulted in member states
imposing liability for disclosure contained in a prospectus on different persons.
An issuer planning to publish a prospectus in a member state should investigate
its approach to liability and consider appropriate due diligence/verification
procedures to allow the persons responsible in that member state for the contents
of the prospectus to have an appropriate degree of comfort, especially if securities
are being offered in a member state in which the underwriters have liability for the
contents of the prospectus.[95] When thinking about an appropriate due diligence/
verification process, offering participants should also take into account the laws of
any member state into which the prospectus is being passported.

7.3.2.4.6 Wholesale debt securities Under the applicable requirements, a **7.79**
non-EU issuer of wholesale debt securities could avoid the need to publish a
prospectus under the Prospectus Directive in connection with an offering of
wholesale debt securities by having its wholesale debt securities admitted to
trading only on exchange-regulated markets.[96] In practice, however, a number of
large non-EU issuers have chosen to have their wholesale debt securities admitted
to trading on regulated markets and, therefore, have been required to publish
prospectuses.

In the event that an issuer publishes a prospectus in connection with the **7.80**
admission to trading of wholesale debt securities, the Prospectus Directive and
Prospectus Regulation permit the issuer to reduce significantly the amount of

---

[93] Prospectus Directive Article 6.1.
[94] Ibid.
[95] For example, Germany.
[96] Prospectus Directive Article 3.2(d).

disclosure included in the prospectus, reflecting a presumption that wholesale debt securities are typically marketed to institutional investors.[97]

7.81 With the emergence of significant exchange-regulated markets for debt issuers (e.g. the Global Exchange Market (GEM) in Dublin (the successor to the Alternative Securities Market)), Euro MTF in Luxembourg and the Professional Securities Market in London, issuers of wholesale debt securities have the option of choosing to only have their securities admitted to trading on an exchange-regulated market. For a non-EU issuer that does not otherwise have securities admitted to trading on a regulated market, this approach would avoid triggering the application of the Transparency Directive or the Market Abuse Directive.[98]

7.82 Issuers choosing to have their securities admitted to trading only on an exchange-regulated market would still be subject to the requirements of those exchange-regulated markets and any applicable requirements of national law in the jurisdiction in which the exchange-regulated market is located, which may be equivalent (or nearly so) to obligations under the Transparency Directive and the Market Abuse Directive.

7.3.2.5 *Coordinating approval processes*

7.83 A key element for offering participants to focus on in establishing an offering or listing timetable is how to approach regulators in the relevant jurisdictions to ensure that the offering document is approved at roughly the same time, so that sales can be made concurrently. In addition to focusing on how long it will take to achieve final approval of the prospectus, offering participants also need to determine what regulatory approval is needed in order to market the offering to the intended audience. In addition to approval of a prospectus by the competent authority in the relevant jurisdictions, issuers will need to obtain approval from the relevant listing authority or exchange if the securities are to be admitted to trading on a market (whether regulated or exchange-regulated).

7.84 Offering participants will want to conduct an offering process to ensure that securities are not sold to purchasers at different times in different jurisdictions, since the possibility of secondary trading may adversely impact the offering

---

[97] For example, an issuer of wholesale debt securities is not required to prepare a summary of the prospectus. Prospectus Directive Article 5.2. The schedule applicable to such a prospectus also permits reduced disclosure. See Prospectus Regulation Annex IX.

[98] Commission services of the European Commission has requested feedback on the question of whether the Market Abuse Directive should continue to be limited in application to issuers with securities admitted to trading on a regulated market or whether it should also cover exchange-regulated markets and multilateral trading facilities. The call for evidence indicates that such an expansion is being considered. Section 2.1.1 of 'Review of Directive 2003/6/EC on insider dealing and market manipulation (Market Abuse Directive)', April 2009 ('MAD Review Call for Evidence').

process as a whole. Finally, if the securities are being listed on an exchange (whether a regulated market or an exchange-regulated market), the issuer will also need to consider the timeline for the listing process.

7.3.2.5.1 Time periods for approval Under the Prospectus Directive, the **7.85** competent authority of the home member state has a period of ten working days from the submission of a complete draft prospectus to the competent authority.[99] This period is extended to 20 working days in the case of an issuer that does not have securities admitted to trading on a regulated market and has not previously offered securities to the public.[100] Notwithstanding these time periods, failure of a competent authority to give a decision within these time periods does not constitute the approval of a prospectus.[101]

In practice, the above time periods cannot be relied upon by an issuer in planning **7.86** its offering schedule. It frequently takes significantly longer to achieve final approval for a prospectus from the date of first submission, in particular to deal with queries from the competent authority. The required length of time will vary from member state to member state as well as based on the type of securities covered by the prospectus. A June 2008 Study on the Impact of the Prospectus Regime on EU Financial Markets indicated that based on survey responses it takes an average of five weeks to clear a prospectus for an equity offering and three weeks for a prospectus for an offering of non-equity securities and base prospectus for an offering programme.[102] Offerings of wholesale debt securities and medium term note programmes have typically moved on faster timetables. In light of the wide variation among member states in terms of time necessary to receive approval of a prospectus, it is important in constructing an offering timetable to get an up-to-date sense of the time periods that the competent authorities in the relevant home member state have been taking to approve prospectuses for offerings of the type contemplated.

7.3.2.5.2 Coordinating marketing and prospectus approval Under Article 13 **7.87** of the Prospectus Directive, a prospectus may not be published prior to its approval by the home member state and is required to be published[103] prior to the beginning of the offer to the public of securities. Unlike in the United States, it is

---

[99] Prospectus Directive Article 13.2.

[100] Prospectus Directive Article 13.3.

[101] Prospectus Directive Article 13.2.

[102] See pages 35–36 of the 'Study on the Impact of the Prospectus Regime on EU Financial Markets' (the 'CSES Report'), available at http://ec.europa.eu/internal_market/securities/docs/prospectus/cses_report_en.pdf.

[103] Prospectus Directive Article 14 of the Prospectus Directive sets forth the requirements for publication of a prospectus. In a situation in which an offering is made on a private placement basis outside the EEA, offering participants will need to ensure that the means of publication does not impair the ability to rely on the relevant exemption.

necessary to complete the regulatory approval process prior to commencing a marketing exercise to the public. In the United States, it would be typical to undertake the marketing exercise based upon a red herring that typically would not have received final sign-off from the US SEC and could be subject to further comment.

7.88 Within the EEA, prior to approval of the prospectus, marketing can only be undertaken on the basis of a draft or preliminary prospectus on an exempt basis, typically only to institutional investors that are qualified investors. Pre-marketing to institutional investors on the basis of a draft prospectus (typically referred to as a 'pathfinder' or red herring) is common, particularly in initial public offerings of equity. If this approach is followed, then the prospectus approved by the competent authority of the home member state would be the final prospectus for liability purposes and would be the prospectus used to market to retail investors. As discussed below, a pathfinder would be subject to the advertising requirements contained in the Prospectus Directive.

7.89 In an offering in which there is a desire to extend the marketing efforts to retail investors or to engage in broader publicity efforts, then an approved prospectus needs to be obtained prior to engaging in these efforts. This prospectus can contain a price range for the offering and needs to contain a fixed number of securities to be offered.[104] The final pricing can then be notified to the competent authority after the pricing of the offering without the need for a supplemental prospectus that would trigger a new approval period or create withdrawal rights on the part of prospective purchasers in the offering.

7.90 One question that exists with respect to a price range prospectus is the exact information that is required by the Prospectus Directive and the Prospectus Regulation to be included in that prospectus relating to the pricing. The issue arises out of the fact that Article 8.1 of the Prospectus Directive and Item 5.3 in Annex III of the Prospectus Regulation (which contains the requirements for the securities note for shares) do not have identical requirements with respect to the price information required to be disclosed. The principal question relates to what information needs to be disclosed about how the final price for the securities being offered would be determined in a situation in which a maximum price is included in the approved prospectus. The CESR Q&As suggest that in such a situation information about how the final price would be determined would need to be included only if there is not an established and liquid market with respect to the

---

[104] If the prospectus does not contain a maximum price and fixed number of securities to be offered, then withdrawal rights under Prospectus Directive Article 8.1 would apply once those terms are finalized. See Question 58 of the CESR Q&As.

securities being offered (e.g. in an initial public offering).[105] The need to disclose information about how the price would be determined differs from typical US disclosure practice in which it is sufficient simply to include a price range in a prospectus used in marketing.

In an initial public offering of a class of shares not previously admitted to trading **7.91** on a regulated market, an approved prospectus is required to be available to purchasers not less than six working days prior to the end of the offer.[106] This period runs from the date the prospectus is approved by the competent authority in the home member state. In a situation in which the offering is marketed to institutional investors on the basis of a draft prospectus (referred to as a 'pathfinder') and then marketed to retail investors following approval, the offering would need to remain open for a minimum of six working days from the date of formal regulatory approval.

Issuers have at least two other potential approaches to coordinating marketing **7.92** with the six-day rule. The first is to use a price range prospectus as described above and have the prospectus approved prior to beginning marketing. A second possible approach is to limit participation in the offering to qualified investors and gain approval of the prospectus for purposes of having the shares being offered admitted to trading on a regulated market.[107] Issuers facing the question of the preferred approach to use should discuss the issue with their underwriters to identify any potential marketing considerations.

7.3.2.5.3 Listing authority process   In an offering in which the securities being **7.93** offered are intended to be traded on a market (regardless of whether it is a regulated market or an exchange-regulated market), it is highly advisable early in the process to get in contact with the relevant authority for that market. This is important to get current feedback on the timeframe for completing the listing/ admission process and review process that the relevant authority would employ. While the Prospectus Directive restricts member states from imposing additional requirements on the prospectus itself, authorities operating markets are permitted to impose additional requirements as a condition to admission to trading.

Depending on the market, these additional requirements may be fairly time- **7.94** consuming to address and can impact the disclosure that needs to be made to offerees in the offering. For example, as described above in Chapter 5 of this

---

[105] Question 58 of the CESR Q&As.
[106] Prospectus Directive Article 14.
[107] Note that in the United Kingdom, the competent authority does not impose this six-day rule on admissions to trading on a regulated market. Issuers contemplating listing on a regulated market in another member state should confirm whether the competent authority in that member state imposes this six-day rule on those transactions.

Part 2, there are additional requirements that would need to be met in order to obtain a primary listing on the main market of the London Stock Exchange. Issuers should also determine whether a financial institution is required to act as a sponsor of the listing and confirm with their proposed sponsor what additional work the sponsor will need to undertake in connection with that role.

7.95   On the other hand, a listing of global depositary receipts on the London Stock Exchange would not require additional information beyond that required by the Prospectus Directive. Such a listing also does not require the involvement of a sponsor.[108]

7.96   Please refer to Part 3 for additional details on additional requirements in member states.

7.3.2.6 Supplemental prospectuses

7.97   Article 16 of the Prospectus Directive requires an issuer to supplement an approved prospectus whenever a significant new factor or material mistake or inaccuracy relating to information contained in the approved prospectus that is capable of affecting the assessment of the securities to which the prospectus relates arises between the approval of the prospectus and the completion of the offering to which the prospectus relates.[109] An issuer may be called upon to make a judgment as to whether a development or new piece of information constitutes a 'significant new factor' and so triggers the obligation to publish a supplemental prospectus. Given the requirement for approval by the competent authority and the triggering of withdrawal rights (as described below), it would be expected that a supplemental prospectus would be an unusual event, absent a change in the terms or timing of the offering.[110]

7.98   In connection with the consultation on the review of the Prospectus Directive, the European Commission has noted that Article 16 of the Prospectus Directive leaves room for divergent application and has generated intense debate.[111]In order to address one of the principal issues that have arisen in this regard, the European Commission has proposed clarifying that the obligation to publish a supplement

---

[108] The UK FSA recently undertook a consultation that addressed, among other things, the segmentation of the listing regime in the United Kingdom with respect to depositary receipts. See Consultation Paper 08/21, 'Consultation on the amendments to the Listing Rules and feedback on DP08/1' (A review of the structure of the Listing Regime), December 2008.

[109] Prospectus Directive Article 16.1.

[110] The publication of a profit forecast by an issuer would be presumed to require a supplemental prospectus, at least in the context of an equity offering. Question 20 of the CESR Q&As. On the other hand, the correction of mistakes and inaccuracies that are not material would not require publication of a supplemental prospectus.

[111] Section 5.3.10 of the explanatory memorandum included in the PD Review Proposal.

to a prospectus ends as of the earlier of the final closing of the offering period and the admission of the securities to trading on a regulated market.

If a supplemental prospectus is required, then the issuer is required to receive the **7.99** approval of the competent authority of the home member state, which has seven working days to approve the supplemental prospectus.[112] If a supplemental prospectus is required in connection with an offering in which a prospectus has been passported to other member states, then the supplemental prospectus will also need to be similarly passported. Article 16.1 of the Prospectus Directive requires a supplemental prospectus to be published in the same manner as the original prospectus.[113]

Given the potential for a significant delay as a result of a supplemental prospectus, **7.100** an issuer would generally wish to avoid having to prepare a supplemental prospectus if at all possible. For example, an issuer should time its offering to avoid the occurrence of an event (such as the scheduled publication of an updated profit forecast) during the pendency of an offering that would require a supplemental prospectus.

In the context of a continuous offering (e.g. in connection with an offering **7.101** programme), a supplemental prospectus is the intended method of updating the base prospectus or registration document to reflect material changes. Practically, the need for approval by the competent authority of the home member state can result in the issuer being blacked out of using the offering programme for a period of time while that approval is obtained. For large well-known issuers, the Prospectus Directive provides less flexibility than the current US system in which approval by the US SEC of the supplemental disclosure contained in a periodic filing would not be required.

A further consequence of a supplement to the prospectus is that it creates **7.102** withdrawal rights for at least two working days after its publication.[114] In a situation in which a supplemental prospectus is required during the offering period, these withdrawal rights may have little practical significance. For example, in a registered offering in the United States by an issuer that is required to amend its

---

[112] Prospectus Directive Article 16.1.

[113] Ibid.

[114] Prospectus Directive Article 16.2. Issuers should confirm how the relevant member state(s) have applied the period to exercise withdrawal rights. The two competing interpretations are: (i) investors have two working days following publication to give notice of the exercise of withdrawal rights; and (ii) the decision to exercise withdrawal rights merely has to be made during the two-working-day period after publication and have a longer period of time to give the issuer notice of that decision. Note also that the European Commission has proposed to harmonize the period for withdrawal rights by amending Article 16.2 to harmonize the time period across member states of a minimum of two working days after publication to exercise. Section 5.3.10 of the explanatory memorandum included in the PD Review Proposal. The European Commission also proposes to clarify that an issuer may voluntarily extend the period of withdrawal rights.

prospectus during the roadshow for a material event, market practice is to require a period of time for potential purchasers to digest the information prior to pricing. Therefore, the issuer can accommodate the required period for withdrawal rights prior to the pricing of the offering. As discussed in Sections 7.3.4 and 7.3.5 below, these withdrawal rights can cause significantly more problems in the context of merger and acquisition transactions and rights offerings.

7.3.2.7 *Publicity restrictions*

7.103   **7.3.2.7.1 Advertising**   Article 15 of the Prospectus Directive imposes certain limitations on the publication of advertisements in connection with an offer to the public or an admission to trading on a regulated market.[115] In particular, advertisements in connection with an offer to the public are required to be identified as such and contain a prominent statement that the advertisement is not a prospectus and that a prospectus has been or will be published and indicate where investors are or will be able to obtain a copy of the prospectus.[116] Article 34 of the Prospectus Regulation clarifies the means by which advertisements may be disseminated to the public beyond traditional print media, including electronic and oral communications.[117] In addition, all written or oral information concerning an offer to the public or admission to trading on a regulated market (whether or not for advertising purposes) is required to be consistent with the information contained in the prospectus.[118]

7.104   These broad requirements are in contrast to the publicity in connection with securities offerings in the United States in which there has traditionally been quite limited advertising and publicity based on a concern that advertising or publicity constituted an impermissible offer of securities. Revisions to these rules as part of the Securities Offering Reform in 2005 have significantly increased the ability of issuers, especially well-known seasoned issuers (referred to as WKSIs), to engage in publicity in connection with an offering in the form of free-writing prospectuses, although issuers are still subject to prospectus liability under the US Securities Act for these communications.[119]

7.105   Potentially of more significance to issuers and underwriters is an obligation to ensure that all material information conveyed to investors is included in the prospectus. In particular, Article 15.5 of the Prospectus Directive requires that

---

[115] The term 'advertisements' is defined in Prospectus Regulation Article 2.9 as 'announcements: (a) relating to a specific offer to the public of securities or to an admission to trading on a regulated market; and (b) aiming to specifically promote the potential subscription or acquisition of securities'.

[116] Prospectus Directive Articles 15.2–15.3.

[117] Prospectus Regulation Article 34.

[118] Prospectus Directive Article 15.3.

[119] See Rules 163 and 164 under the US Securities Act, 17 CFR § 230.163 and 17 CFR § 230.164.

material information addressed to investors, including information disclosed in roadshow presentations and sales meetings, is required to be included in the prospectus or a supplemental prospectus. Even absent this specific requirement, issuers and underwriters have had reason to take care to limit the extent to which information is disclosed in roadshows that goes beyond the information contained in the prospectus. In light of this express requirement, issuers and underwriters need to take special care to ensure that all material information discussed in roadshows and sales meetings is contained in the prospectus as approved by the competent authority of the home member state. The potential consequence under the Prospectus Directive if there is a discrepancy that is discovered during the offering and after approval of the prospectus is that the issuer will need to publish a supplemental prospectus that will need to be approved by the competent authority, which may have the effect of delaying the offering process.

One further issue that issuers and financial intermediaries participating in an offering will need to be cognizant of in connection with marketing materials is the application of MiFID to information provided by financial intermediaries. Article 19 of MiFID requires that information provided by financial intermediaries to clients and potential clients be fair, clear and not misleading. This general rule is applied specifically in the context of marketing material, and requires that it be identifiable as such and must be clearly distinguished from other general information provided to the public.[120] In practice, marketing materials distributed by financial intermediaries in connection with an offering will need to be vetted to ensure that they comply with MiFID. **7.106**

In the event that an offering in the EEA is part of a global offering that is not being registered under the US securities laws (e.g. an offering with a prospectus in the EEA combined with a distribution to qualified institutional buyers in the US in reliance on Rule 144A), the issuer and underwriters will need to ensure that any advertising undertaken in the EEA complies with the advertising safe harbours under the US Securities Act.[121] Practically, press releases and advertising relating to the offering will need to be bifurcated between limited versions for release in the United States and more expansive versions used outside the United States. Non-US, non-EU issuers should also consider any applicable restrictions on advertising under home country law. **7.107**

7.3.2.7.2 Pre-marketing documents Draft prospectuses used in the pre-marketing of offerings constitute advertising (since they are communications **7.108**

---

[120] MiFID Article 19.2.

[121] Rule 135c under the US Securities Act creates a safe harbour for limited press releases in connection with unregistered offerings. Rule 135e under the US Securities Act provides a safe harbour for press releases and other advertising made outside the US in connection with an exempt offering. 17 CFR § 230.135e.

'aiming to specifically promote the potential subscription or acquisition of securities')[122] and, therefore, should contain legends and otherwise comply with the advertising requirements described above.

7.109 **7.3.2.7.3 Research** In contrast to concerns arising under the US securities laws, research by financial intermediaries participating in an offering is generally considered not to be a prospectus. While research of this type is considered not to be an offer to the public under the Prospectus Directive, it is required to comply with certain independence procedures and prominently disclose the involvement in the offering of the institution preparing the research.[123] Appropriate independence procedures include maintaining an 'ethical wall' between analysts preparing research reports and persons involved in the offering to ensure that analysts do not receive material non-public or price-sensitive information about the issuer in the offering. Investment firms also typically have internal compliance guidelines that may impose additional restrictions.

7.110 Prudent issuers should limit their involvement in research so as to avoid being seen as having adopted that research, which could result in that research constituting advertising by the issuer. Issuers should also avoid providing prospective investors with analyst projections and other information not included in the prospectus, as that information could be seen as advertising by the issuer, which is subject to the rules described above.

7.111 Issuers and offering participants in global offerings will also need to ensure that research activities in connection with the portion of the offering to be conducted in the EEA does not result in an impermissible offering or solicitation either in the EEA or outside it. This is typically achieved by imposition by the lead underwriters of restricted and blackout periods on research by syndicate members and strict legending and distribution requirements on research produced by offering participants to ensure that it is not used in ways that constitute impermissible solicitation.[124] See Section 4 of Part 1 for additional discussion of MiFID generally.

7.3.2.8 Passporting of prospectuses

7.112 Articles 17 and 18 of the Prospectus Directive set out the framework for the passporting of a prospectus approved by the competent authority of the home

---

[122] Definition of 'advertisement' contained in Prospectus Regulation Article 2.9.

[123] Article 5 of Commission Directive 2003/125/EC of 22 December 2003 implementing Directive 2003/6/EC of the European Parliament and of the Council as regards the fair presentation of investment recommendations and the disclosure of conflicts of interest.

[124] For example, in global offerings it would be typical to limit research reports that can be distributed to investors in the United States (including qualified institutional buyers) to research that can be distributed in reliance on the safe harbour contained in Rule 138 or 139, as applicable, under the US Securities Act. 17 CFR §§ 230.138–230.139. Research guidelines may also include procedural requirements designed to reduce the risk of impermissible distribution of research reports.

member state into other member states. Under Article 18 of the Prospectus Directive, the competent authority is obliged within three working days after a request to provide a certificate of approval of the prospectus to each other member state into which the prospectus is desired to be passported. This period can be shortened to one working day after approval by the competent authority of the home member state if the draft prospectus is accompanied by a request for this certificate.

The competent authority in each host member state into which the prospectus is being passported will then need to respond to the certificate of approval from the competent authority of the home member state, which should typically occur within a relatively short period of time.[125] The passporting timetable imposes some practical barriers to be overcome in the case of a simultaneous offering in multiple member states in that it may take several days from the date the home member state approves the prospectus for the prospectus to be available for use in the other member states in which it is to be used. An issuer contemplating such an offering should investigate whether the competent authorities in the relevant member states to be included in the offering would accommodate an expedited passporting procedure, or it should allow time in its offering timetable for the passporting process to be completed.

7.113

An alternative to passporting a prospectus into multiple home member states in connection with an offering in multiple member states is to have a prospectus approved in the home member state and offer the securities on an exempt basis in other member states. This avoids the potential delay and complication of passporting into a member state if securities are only going to be offered on an exempt basis in that member state.

7.114

7.3.2.9 Secondary listing on a regulated market

Non-EU issuers with equity listings in their home country or on a market outside the EEA may wish to have their shares admitted to trading on a regulated market in the EEA outside the context of an offering to the public. Under the Prospectus Directive, a listing transaction of this type requires a prospectus.[126]

7.115

A second situation in which a non-EU issuer might wish to engage in a listing transaction would be following an offering made to investors on a private placement basis. This approach might be followed in order to facilitate a capital raising based on more limited information than would be required in a full prospectus

7.116

---

[125] For example, the UK FSA has undertaken informally to respond to passport requests from other member states within 24 hours of receipt. See UKLA Factsheet No 4, October 2008.

[126] Prospectus Directive Article 3.3. Note that the exemptions contained in Prospectus Directive Article 3.2 are not applicable to a transaction in which securities are admitted to trading on a regulated market.

and would allow additional time for a non-EU issuer to prepare the complete prospectus and gain approval of the competent authority in the home member state. In this situation, the issuer and its financial advisers will need to be careful to ensure that it complies with the private placement requirements and does not take actions that would constitute an offer to the public of the privately placed securities.

7.117 The competent authorities in Belgium, France, the Netherlands and Portugal have established a 'fast path' procedure for review and approval of a prospectus for a technical listing by a non-EU issuer listed on the New York Stock Exchange and subject to the US Exchange Act reporting regime either as a US domestic issuer or as a foreign private issuer.[127] This fast path procedure is available to an issuer for a pure secondary listing and a listing following a private placement in the EEA (including in connection with a registered initial public offering in the United States). The competent authorities of the relevant member states have undertaken to conduct an expedited approval process of the listing prospectus. It is not available to an issuer that already has securities admitted to trading on a regulated market in the EEA.

7.118 The fast path procedure would allow a non-EU issuer meeting the above criteria to list shares on a regulated market in the EEA essentially based on US documentation (either US Exchange Act filings within the prior 12 months or the issuer's US prospectus for its registered initial public offering) with a short wrapper (including a cross-reference table to the Prospectus Regulation requirements). This fast path procedure has been used by Cliffs Natural Resources, a US domestic issuer, and Companhia Vale do Rio Doce, a Brazilian foreign private issuer, in connection with a secondary listings on Euronext Paris and Satyam Computer Services Limited, an Indian issuer, in connection with a registered initial public offering in the United States and a secondary listing in Amsterdam.

7.119 Issuers choosing to utilize a fast path procedure should be aware that having securities admitted to trading on a regulated market in the EEA will subject the issuer to ongoing disclosure requirements under the Transparency Directive and the requirements of the Market Abuse Directive.

7.3.3 Offering without an approved prospectus in the EEA

7.120 There are two principal categories of offerings that need to be considered in this connection: (a) an offering of wholesale debt; and (b) a global offering (whether debt or equity) in which investors in the EEA only participate on a private placement basis.

---

[127] See Fast Path Listings using SEC Documents prepared by NYSE Euronext, available at http://www.euronext.com/fic/000/033/111/331110.pdf.

7.3.3.1 *Wholesale debt securities*

An issuer is permitted to offer wholesale debt securities to the public in the EEA **7.121** without the need for a prospectus so long as those debt securities are not admitted to trading on a regulated market. If there is a desire to list the wholesale debt securities in order to enable a broader range of institutional investors to participate in the offering, the wholesale debt securities can be listed on an exchange-regulated market such as the Global Exchange Market ('GEM') in Dublin, Euro MTF in Luxembourg and the Professional Securities Market in London.[128] A wholesale debt offering would have the effect of excluding the retail market in the EEA, although this is likely to be a relatively minor concern for a non-EU issuer that is more focused on tapping the institutional market. A further consideration for a non-EU issuer is whether a wholesale debt offering can practically be combined with an offering outside the EEA, where minimum denominations are typically much smaller (e.g. $1,000 per note in the United States).

An offering of wholesale debt securities in the EEA can be made using the same **7.122** documentation as used elsewhere in the world (e.g. the prospectus from a US registration statement) without triggering the obligation to publish a prospectus under the Prospectus Directive so long as those wholesale debt securities are not admitted to trading on a regulated market in the EEA. An offering of this type also would not trigger Transparency Directive and Market Abuse Directive obligations and would not result in a non-EU issuer selecting a home member state for equity securities and Transparency Directive purposes.

Issuers should note that although listing on an exchange-regulated market does **7.123** not technically trigger the application of the Transparency Directive and the Market Abuse Directive by their terms, the principal exchange-regulated markets impose certain similar obligations on issuers. For example:

- the Professional Securities Market requires annual reports and audited financial statements within six months after the end of the fiscal year (although those financial statements are not required to be prepared in accordance with IFRS) and requires compliance with portions of the Market Abuse Directive relating to disclosure of inside information and insider lists;[129]
- Euro MTF in Luxembourg imposes requirements with respect to equal treatment of security holders and requires disclosure of material developments which may affect in a significant way the issuer's ability to meet its commitments

---

[128] Another alternative that domestic US issuers have utilized is listing debt securities offered in the EEA on the New York Stock Exchange.

[129] See Listing Rule 17.3 in the UK FSA Handbook, available at http://fsahandbook.info/FSA/html/handbook/LR/17/3.

and requires compliance with the portions of the Market Abuse Directive relating to insider dealing and market manipulation;[130] and

- the GEM requires annual reports and audited financial statements to be published no later than the latest time required under home country law (although those financial statements are not required to be prepared in accordance with IFRS), imposes certain disclosure requirements under the Transparency Directive relating to changes in securities and communications with security holders and requires compliance with portions of the Market Abuse Directive relating to disclosure of inside information and insider lists.[131]

7.124   Issuers contemplating admission to trading on an exchange-regulated market should consider these requirements in light of weighing these markets as an alternative to admission to trading on a regulated market.

7.3.3.2 *Global offering with EEA private placement*

7.125   A second category of offerings that could be undertaken without the need for an approved prospectus is a global offering of equity securities or debt securities with a minimum denomination of less than EUR 50,000 (or its equivalent) in which participation within the EEA is limited in order to ensure the availability of an exemption and securities are not admitted to trading on a regulated market. In an offering of this type, offering restrictions and restrictions on publicity are of critical importance because the private placement exemption is dependent on offers not being made to impermissible offerees, even if the offering is made outside the EEA on a basis that does not require publicity restrictions.[132] For example, an issuer that is a well-known seasoned issuer under the US Securities Act that undertakes an offering on a registered basis under the US securities laws has a great degree of flexibility to communicate with prospective purchasers and there are effectively no restrictions on the number or type of offerees that can be solicited.

7.126   This approach would be typical in a global equity offering in which there is a desire to sell to institutional accounts in the EEA, which are qualified investors, and possibly to a limited number of other investors (fewer than 100 in any member state). A second type of offering in which this approach would be followed is an offering of debt securities that are not wholesale debt securities, which would be typical if market practice in the primary markets for the

---

[130] See Chapter 10 of the Rules and Regulations of the Luxembourg Stock Exchange, Edition 2009/03, available on the website of the Luxembourg Stock Exchange (http://www.bourse.lu); Chapter II of the Luxembourg law of 9 May 2006 on market abuse, available at http://www.cssf.lu/uploads/media/Law_090506_marketabuse.pdf.

[131] See Global Exchange Market Listing and Trading Rules, available at http://www.ise.ie/index.asp?locID=596&docID=561.

[132] See Chapter 4 of this Part 2 for a more detailed discussion of private placements in the EEA.

debt offering was to use a smaller minimum denomination (e.g. a US dollar-denominated offering).

In an offering with this structure, the underwriting or purchase agreement for the intermediaries selling in the EEA would need to include selling restrictions to ensure that the underwriters or placement agents do not engage in activities that would result in the loss of the exemption. **7.127**

The offering document used worldwide should also include a legend describing these selling restrictions. Set forth below is an example of this type of legend from a global offering of debt securities in which no prospectus was published under the Prospectus Directive: **7.128**

> In particular, each underwriter has represented and agreed that:
>
> In relation to each Member State of the European Economic Area which has implemented the Prospectus Directive (each, a 'Relevant Member State'), with effect from and including the date on which the Prospectus Directive is implemented in that Relevant Member State (the 'Relevant Implementation Date'), it has not made and will not make an offer of Notes to the public in that Relevant Member State, except that it may, with effect from and including the Relevant Implementation Date, make an offer of Notes to the public in that Relevant Member State at any time:
>
> (a) to legal entities which are authorised or regulated to operate in the financial markets or, if not so authorised or regulated, whose corporate purpose is solely to invest in securities;
> (b) to any legal entity which has two or more of (1) an average of at least 250 employees during the last financial year; (2) a total balance sheet of more than €43,000,000 and (3) an annual net turnover of more than €50,000,000, as shown in its last annual or consolidated accounts;
> (c) to fewer than 100 natural or legal persons (other than qualified investors as defined in the Prospectus Directive) subject to obtaining prior consent of the representatives of any such offer; or
> (d) in any other circumstances falling within Article 3.2 of the Prospectus Directive,
>
> provided that no such offer of Notes shall require the issuer to publish a prospectus pursuant to Article 3 of the Prospectus Directive.
>
> For the purposes of this provision, the expression an 'offer of Notes to the public' in relation to any Notes in any Relevant Member State means the communication in any form and by any means of sufficient information on the terms of the offer and the Notes to be offered so as to enable an investor to decide to purchase or subscribe for the Notes, as the same may be varied in that Relevant Member State by any measure implementing the Prospectus Directive in that Relevant Member State and the expression 'Prospectus Directive' means Directive 2003/71/ EC and includes any relevant implementing measure in each Relevant Member State.

7.3.4 Merger and acquisition transactions

In light of the broad scope of application of the Prospectus Directive and the definition of the phrase 'offer to the public', issuers engaging in merger and acquisition **7.129** transactions in which all or part of the consideration consists of securities need to consider carefully whether the Prospectus Directive may apply to that transaction and, if so, the available exemptions. The likelihood of the need for compliance or an exemption from the Prospectus Directive would increase substantially if the company being acquired is listed in the EEA or otherwise has a significant number of shareholders in the EEA. This Section does not address the Takeover Bids Directive or the issues that would arise in connection with a merger or acquisition of an EU issuer. See Chapter 6 of this Part 2 for a discussion of those issues.

7.3.4.1 Absence of an offer to the public

7.130 The initial question to be considered is whether the transaction constitutes an offer to the public of securities. In considering that question, the form of the transaction is likely to be significant. For example, an exchange offer extended to persons in the EEA, will constitute an offer to the public of the securities that form part of the consideration in the exchange offer absent an exemption.[133]

7.131 A situation that is less clear but would still likely constitute an offer to the public absent an exemption is a US-style merger or consolidation in which securityholders have the right to vote on the transaction and possibly the right to exercise dissenters' or appraisal rights under applicable corporate law. The exemption contained in Article 4.1 of the Prospectus Directive, which is discussed in greater detail below, refers to but does not define a 'merger'. In addressing this question, the CESR Q&As also do not answer the question of whether every stock-for-stock merger actually constitutes an offer to the public of securities.[134] However, the CESR Q&As do make clear the view that there is scope for flexibility in interpreting what constitutes a 'merger' under the exemptions, which suggests that competent authorities have flexibility to treat other types of business combinations (e.g. an amalgamation under Canadian law) as a 'merger'. The right of securityholders to vote on the transaction and the availability of dissenters' or appraisal rights would seem to increase the likelihood that competent authorities will regard such a transaction as an offer to the public that requires compliance with the Prospectus Directive or an exemption (because investors are effectively making an investment decision in determining how to vote or exercise dissenters' or appraisal rights).

7.132 Another possible situation is a transaction involving a plan or scheme of arrangement in which securityholders would have the right to vote but judicial approval

---

[133] The exemption contained in Prospectus Directive Article 4.1(b) is also available for debt-for-debt exchange offers in addition to acquisition transactions involving shares. Summary record of the 3rd Informal Meeting on Prospectus Transposition, 26 January 2005, p. 6, available at http://ec.europa.eu/internal_market/securities/docs/prospectus/summary-note-050126_en.pdf.

[134] Question 30 of the CESR Q&As.

is also required to complete the transaction. A plan or scheme of arrangement of this type may not constitute an offer to the public of the securities to be offered, although there appears to be some difference in views among the competent authorities in various member states on that question.[135]

When considering these questions, it is advisable to discuss the particular form of transaction being considered with counsel in the member state(s) in which there are known to be substantial numbers of securityholders because the views of the relevant competent authority on the subject, to the extent known, will necessarily inform the approach to be taken. **7.133**

7.3.4.2 *M&A-specific exemptions*

The Prospectus Directive contains exemptions from the obligation to use an approved prospectus in connection with a 'merger'[136] or an 'exchange offer,'[137] so long as a disclosure document that contains information that is regarded by the competent authority in the member state in which the securities are being offered or sold as containing information equivalent to a prospectus is available. These exemptions cover both offers to the public (to the extent that the transaction is considered to involve an offer to the public) and the admission of the securities being used as consideration to trading on a regulated market. **7.134**

Although these exceptions on their face would seem to exempt non-EU issuers from the need to worry about the Prospectus Directive, the scope of the relief they provide depends on how the relevant competent authorities apply the concept of an equivalent disclosure document. To date, competent authorities have tended to take a fairly narrow view of equivalent disclosure documents and have required the documents to be all but identical to a prospectus. For a non-EU issuer that is preparing an offering document that complies with the US registration statement and proxy statement requirements, it may be able to satisfy the competent authorities by simply adding a wrapper to the document to add any additional information the competent authorities require. On the other hand, this may be a significantly bigger burden for a non-EU issuer that does not prepare financial statements in US GAAP, IFRS or Japanese GAAP and under applicable law is only obligated to produce a less fulsome offering document. **7.135**

---

[135] Although it is not binding guidance, the UKLA has stated that it is inclined to agree with market participants that a scheme of arrangement in which transferable securities are used as consideration does not constitute an offer to the public. See UKLA List! (June 2005). The competent authorities in other member states may take a different view, however. This subject could have particular importance to non-EU issuers organized under the laws of other countries which contemplate a similar type of transaction (e.g. Australia, Canada and New Zealand).

[136] Prospectus Directive Articles 4.1(c) and 4.2(d).

[137] Prospectus Directive Articles 4.1(b) and 4.2(c).

7.136 Unlike a prospectus approved by the home member state that is passported into other member states, the equivalent disclosure document for a merger or exchange offer is required to be approved by the competent authority in each member state in which it is to be used.[138] If there are substantial numbers of target company securityholders in multiple member states, then the need to get the approval of the competent authority in each such member state may make trying to use an equivalent offering document unattractive.

7.137 Two final considerations that need to be taken into account in thinking about whether to use an approved prospectus or rely on an exemption are (a) the possibility of additional withdrawal rights as a result of the issuance of a supplemental prospectus and (b) limits on the ability to use the prospectus prior to its approval by the competent authority of the home member state. The extent to which these considerations are significant will depend on the home country law applicable to the parties involved in the transaction.

7.138 As discussed above in Section 7.3.2.6, the issuance of a supplemental prospectus gives offerees the right to withdraw their acceptance of the offer for at least two working days after the date of publication of the supplemental prospectus. In an exchange offer, additional withdrawal rights may not be a material concern for an acquirer if there are already withdrawal rights applicable to the offer. For example, the securityholders of a company that is the subject of an exchange offer that is subject to the full US tender offer rules will have withdrawal rights throughout the offer period until securities tendered are accepted for payment.[139] In the context of a merger or similar business combination in which a shareholder vote is being obtained, these withdrawal rights should be regarded as the right to withdraw or change a vote or a proxy prior to the time the shareholder vote is actually obtained.

7.139 As described above in Section 7.3.2.5, a preliminary or draft prospectus cannot be used other than with a limited number of investors or qualified investors. In the context of an exchange offer, this may be more limiting than what is allowed under the law of the jurisdiction in which the subject company of the offer is organized. For example, in the United States an exchange offer may be commenced prior to completing the US SEC approval process although tendered securities may not be accepted prior to effectiveness of the registration statement. Whether this is a material concern will depend on the extent to which there are retail securityholders to whom it is important to make available a prospectus quickly.

---

[138] Question 31 of the CESR Q&As.

[139] In the context of the UK Takeover Code, these withdrawal rights are understood to expire as of the time a takeover bid becomes 'wholly unconditional' and securities are unconditionally allotted to tendering securityholders but would still operate with respect to a takeover bid which is 'unconditional as to acceptances', which typically only occurs once a majority of shares sought in the bid are tendered. Takeover Panel Statement 2005/29, available at http://www.thetakeoverpanel.org. uk/wp-content/uploads/2008/12/2005-29.pdf.

7.3.4.3 Other exemptions

In the event that an issuer desires not to have to get a prospectus approved or **7.140**
undertake the process of gaining approval of equivalent disclosure documents by
competent authorities in one or more member states, there are other possible
exemptions which may be available in connection with a business combination
transaction.

One possible approach would be limiting the participants in the transaction in **7.141**
the EEA to qualified investors.[140] In order to rely on this exemption, appropriate
legends and selling restrictions disclosure would need to be included in the
offering document and the parties to the transaction would need to take care not
to engage in activities that could be seen as extending the offer to other investors.
Although this type of approach would avoid the need to obtain approval of a
prospectus or approval of an equivalent disclosure document, it would need to
be confirmed that this type of approach would be consistent with home country
laws and practice applicable to the companies involved in the transaction.[141] Even
if an exclusion of investors who are not qualified investors comports with that
law, exclusion may not be feasible for practical reasons (e.g. if the shares held by
such investors are needed to meet the threshold for a squeeze-out or compulsory
acquisition).

Another possible exemption that non-EU issuers might consider is the exemption **7.142**
for offers to fewer than 100 offerees in a single member state. In the context of a
straightforward securities offering, this exemption can be policed fairly easily by
ensuring that communications are made only to a specified number of offerees.
However, in a business combination transaction an initial difficultly will be determining the number of shareholders of the company being acquired. In addition,
there is likely to be no practical way to limit the number of offerees because

---

[140] Note that this type of approach would not be available if the securities being issued in
the transaction were to be admitted to trading on a regulated market unless investors other than
qualified investors were paid cash rather than receiving the securities (i.e. a vendor placement procedure), assuming such a procedure is permitted under applicable law.

[141] For example, a prohibition on tenders from a category of securityholders would not be
permitted in an exchange offer subject to section 14(d) of the US Exchange Act because of the
applicability of the 'all holders' rule (Rule 14d-10) thereunder. Rule 14d-10 under the US Exchange
Act, 17 CFR § 240.14d-10. On the other hand, the US SEC has stated that it is permissible for an
offeror not to distribute tender offer materials into a jurisdiction (i.e. the offer is not being made into
the jurisdiction) and in certain circumstances it may be permissible in connection with an exchange
offer to use a vendor placement. See Commission Guidance and Revisions to the Cross-Border
Tender Offer, Exchange Offer, Rights Offerings, and Business Combination Rule and Beneficial
Reporting Rule for Certain Foreign Institutions, 73 FR 60050, 9 October 2008. For an issuer
engaging in a transaction in which a shareholder vote is required, it should consider whether not
soliciting proxies or votes from certain shareholders would comply with home country law and the
listing requirements of other stock exchanges on which they may be listed.

the number of shareholders of the parties to the transaction in each member state cannot be controlled and may fluctuate during the pendency of the transaction.[142] This problem would be exacerbated if the securities of the company to be acquired are listed on an exchange.

7.3.4.4 *Loan notes*

7.143   In certain cash offers, the securityholders of the subject company have the right to elect to receive notes in lieu of all or a portion of the cash consideration payable in the offer (so-called loan notes). If the loan notes are able to be transferred, then the ability of the subject company shareholders to elect to receive notes will likely constitute an offer to the public that would require a prospectus under the Prospectus Directive. To avoid the need for a prospectus in a situation in which a prospectus is not otherwise being prepared (since the transaction is a cash offer), the solution seems to be to make the loan notes non-transferable and not to admit the loan notes to trading on a regulated market.[143]

7.3.5 Rights offerings

7.144   A capital raising through a rights offering by a non-EU issuer is another situation in which the Prospectus Directive may be applicable to non-EU issuers. In general, the competent authorities in the EEA regard a rights offering as an offering of the securities underlying the rights for which the 'free offer' exemption contained in Article 4.1(d) is not available.[144] However, it is also the case that the competent authorities in Germany and Austria take the view that there is no offer to the public if the rights themselves cannot be traded to anyone other than existing shareholders.[145]

7.145   Unlike merger and acquisition transactions, the Prospectus Directive does not contain an analogous exemption for rights offerings that would allow an issuer to use an equivalent disclosure document. Therefore, a non-EU issuer with a significant number of shareholders in the EEA that is contemplating undertaking a rights offering will have the following options: using a prospectus approved by the home member state; excluding shareholders (to the extent permitted under home country law) from the rights offering and selling the rights that would otherwise be allocable to those shareholders and giving them the cash resulting from those sales; or relying on the private placement exemption. For the same reasons discussed above in the context of merger and acquisition

---

[142] This would not be the case if the company is closely held by a small number of securityholders who have agreed not to transfer or there are otherwise effective transfer restrictions on the securities.

[143] See UKLA List! (June 2005).

[144] Prospectus Directive Article 4.1(d); question 63 of the CESR Q&As.

[145] Question 63 of the CESR Q&As.

transactions, the 100-offeree exemption will most likely not be workable in a rights offering.[146]

A further issue to consider in the context of a rights offering is the possibility of withdrawal rights arising as a result of a supplemental prospectus. Under Article 16 of the Prospectus Directive, potential purchasers in an offering of securities are required to have a period of at least two working days to withdraw their subscription to the offer following the publication of a supplemental prospectus.[147] In the context of a rights offering, the application of withdrawal rights could cause substantial confusion if a supplemental prospectus is published prior to the end of the subscription period for the rights. Issuers should consider whether there is a need to disclose the possibility of withdrawal rights in their rights offering timetable. On balance, it would seem the better course not to disclose the risk unless and until a supplemental prospectus is in fact needed.[148] Issuers should also consider the possible need for disclosure in the initial prospectus with respect to whether the issuer or the underwriters bear the risk of holders of rights exercising withdrawal rights.

7.146

In the UK, the competent authority has provided non-binding guidance on this issue to the effect that withdrawal rights expire upon a shareholder paying up the subscription price for a right in full.[149] From a practical perspective, this approach is workable because it avoids the potential nightmare scenario of subscribers exercising withdrawal rights after they have subscribed for shares (and potentially traded the shares allotted into the market).

7.147

7.3.6 Equity share schemes for employees in the EEA

A key area of focus for multinational non-EU issuers that have employees in the EEA is the extent to which they need to have an approved prospectus in connection with various types of equity compensation schemes for those employees. Initially, this was an area of great concern that led many such employers to question whether they would have to cease offering equity-based compensation to employees in the EEA unless they could rely on an exemption contained in the Prospectus Directive for offers to employees by issuers admitted to trading on a regulated market.[150]

7.148

---

[146] Note that questions 42 and 43 of the CESR Q&As address issues relating to material being sent by a custodian to a client in a member state in which a public offering is not being made in a rights offering and whether shareholders in an excluded member state can subscribe.

[147] Prospectus Directive Article 16.2.

[148] Note question 21 of the CESR Q&As, which indicates that a supplemental prospectus needs to include disclosure with respect to withdrawal rights.

[149] See UKLA List! (September 2005).

[150] Prospectus Directive Article 4.1(e).

7.149 A 2006 survey for Linklaters on employee share schemes found that:

- compliance was considered to be expensive, with costs (excluding management time) ranging from $1,000 to $1,000,000;
- 20% of respondents were considering changing or withdrawing their employee share schemes; and
- 90% of respondents believed that competent authorities in the EEA should accept non-EU listing documents as a base for offering employee share schemes.[151]

7.150 In an update to the survey in June 2008, Linklaters reported as follows:

- The Prospectus Directive has impacted firms' employee share schemes due to increased legal and administration costs, distortion of compensation due to different exemption conditions and potential liability if they offer employee share schemes that do not comply with the Prospectus Directive.
- Some global employers have removed or reduced their employee share schemes and others are in the process of doing so.
- Employee share schemes are offered mostly in 'old' member states, as compared to the new accession member states. This is not due to lack of experience with market economy practices but due to differences in interpretation and application of regulations.[152]

7.151 In its review of the Prospectus Directive, the European Commission has proposed changes to the employee share scheme exemption to address some of the concerns noted above.[153] In particular, there is a proposal to amend Article 4.1 of the Prospectus Directive to eliminate the requirement that the securities being offered to the employee be admitted to trading on a regulated market, although the requirement for a document would remain in place.[154] If this amendment is implemented, then non-EU issuers would be able to freely issue securities to their employees so long as the requisite document was made available.

7.152 As an interim measure, CESR has established a short-form prospectus disclosure regime for offers to employees by issuers with securities admitted to trading on a market.[155]

---

[151] Linklaters study 'Unintended Consequences: How the EU's Prospective Directive is threatening the employee share plans for workers of non-EU companies' cited on page 41 of the CSES Report (see n 102).

[152] Linklaters study 'How the EU's Prospectus Directive is Adversely Affecting Employee Share Plans' cited on page 42 of the CSES Report.

[153] Section 5.3.5 of the explanatory memorandum included in the PD Review Proposal.

[154] Ibid.

[155] This regime is described in the response to question 71 of the CESR Q&As, which is discussed in greater detail below in Section 7.3.6.4.

7.3.6.1 *Non-transferable options*

A common form of equity compensation of employees is the grant of stock options **7.153** with an exercise price equal to fair market value on the date of grant. These options are typically non-transferable, only become exercisable after a vesting period and are subject to forfeiture in certain situations upon termination of employment. Except as described below, the competent authorities in the EEA have taken the view that non-transferable options granted to employees do not fall under the Prospectus Directive, as the Prospectus Directive only applies to transferable securities.[156] Under this interpretation, local law would govern the grant, so advice on any local law issues relating to the grant would need to be sought.

Even if the grant itself is not subject to the Prospectus Directive, the question **7.154** would remain whether the ability to exercise the option would constitute an offer of the underlying security that would require a prospectus absent an exemption. CESR has stated that the exercise of such options by employee share schemes does not constitute an offer to the public within the meaning of the Prospectus Directive.[157]

However, the competent authorities in several member states appear to take a **7.155** different view with respect to the grant and exercise of options of this type. For instance, the competent authority in Germany has stated that it is possible to structure the grant of non-transferable options in a manner such that the Prospectus Directive would not apply but that the question of whether there is an offer to the public of the underlying securities would depend on the circumstances at the time the options become exercisable.[158] The competent authority of Poland takes the view that the grant of non-transferable options requires either an approved prospectus or an information document of the type required by Article 4.1(d) of the Prospectus Directive.[159]

7.3.6.2 *Awards of restricted stock*

Another common form of equity compensation is the award of equity securities **7.156** to employees without the requirement to pay any consideration but subject to restrictions that prevent the sale of such securities for a period of time and subject to forfeiture in the event that the grantee leaves under certain circumstances prior to vesting. These grants may either not constitute an offer (because there is no choice on the part of the offeree)[160] or may be an exempt offer (because the

---

[156] Question 5 of the CESR Q&As; UKLA List! (June 2005).
[157] Question 5 of the CESR Q&As.
[158] Ibid.
[159] Ibid.
[160] Question 6 of the CESR Q&As.

consideration is zero).[161] A question in this regard in connection with an employee equity compensation arrangement is whether there is 'hidden' compensation paid by the employee (in the form of a lower salary). CESR and commission services of the European Commission have stated that hidden compensation should not be found unless there is an express relinquishment of quantifiable benefits on the part of an employee.[162]

7.3.6.3 *Other possible exemptions*

7.157 Article 4.1(d) of the Prospectus Directive provides an exemption from the obligation to deliver a prospectus in connection with the offer of securities to current or former directors or employees by an issuer with securities admitted to trading on a regulated market if an information document meeting certain requirements is delivered.[163] An initial question that arises with respect to this exemption is whether it is a requirement that the securities being offered to employees be admitted to trading on a regulated market or if it is sufficient that the issuer have some type of securities admitted to trading. At present, there appear to be some differences in view between competent authorities on the subject. The competent authority in the United Kingdom regards it as sufficient for the issuer to have any type of securities admitted to trading on a regulated market.

7.158 A second issue is that the issuer must have securities admitted to trading on a 'regulated market' and admission to trading on an exchange-regulated market or a market outside the EEA is not sufficient for the exemption to be available. Practically, this exemption would be available for large multinationals that have a secondary listing of their shares on one of the regulated markets in the EEA. However, it will not be available for a company that only has securities admitted to trading on an exchange-regulated market either because it is smaller or, assuming the admission to trading of any securities is sufficient, because it has only listed debt securities and there was no market reason to have its securities admitted to trading on a regulated market.

---

[161] If the consideration for the offer is zero, then either the exclusion in Prospectus Directive Article 1.2(h) or the exemption contained in Article 3.2(e) should be available. Note that the exclusion in Article 1.2(h) (which applies to offers with consideration of less than EUR 2,500,000) is treated differently from the exemption in Article 3.2(e) (which applies where the consideration is less than EUR 100,000). Under the exemption, local law does not apply, while under the exclusion local law would apply. Therefore, it would be preferable for an issuer that can do so to rely on the exemption.

[162] Question 6 of the CESR Q&As.

[163] Prospectus Directive Article 4.1(e). The informational document is required to provide information on the number and nature of the shares and the reasons for and details of the offer. It seems likely that a Registration Statement on Form S-8 (for a US domestic issuer or a foreign private issuer that has in place such a form) and the related prospectus delivered to plan participants would be sufficient to satisfy these requirements.

A second possible exemption is to rely on the fewer than 100 offerees in any member state exemption.[164] This would be particularly attractive to an employer that does not have more than 100 employees in any member state to whom it wishes to grant equity compensation.

7.159

7.3.6.4 *Approved prospectus*

In the event that it is determined that it is necessary to have an approved prospectus in connection with the granting of employee equity compensation, then presumably a non-EU issuer would look to whatever disclosure document it is required to prepare in connection with employee equity compensation in the home jurisdiction. For US domestic issuers, this would be a Registration Statement on Form S-8 and the prospectus delivered to participants in the equity compensation scheme to which the Form S-8 relates. Given the limited amount of information typically included in these documents in the United States, it would be a substantial undertaking to prepare a full prospectus based on these documents and therefore it would be desirable to structure the employee equity compensation arrangements for employees in the EEA to fit within one of the excluded or exempt methods discussed above.[165]

7.160

In an effort to reduce the burden on issuers that are required to prepare a prospectus in connection with an issuance of shares in connection with employee share schemes, CESR has established a short-form prospectus regime. This regime is available to issuers with securities listed on a market (not limited to regulated markets) and would allow the issuer to omit certain information in a prospectus to be used in connection with an offer to employees.[166] A prospectus would still be required to be approved by the competent authority in the home member state and once approved could be passported into other member states.[167] Issuers should note that a competent authority would still have the ability to require the issuer to include information that CESR has specified as able to be omitted.[168]

7.161

7.3.7 Stabilization activities

Securities admitted to trading on a regulated market in the EEA will be subject to the provisions contained in the Market Abuse Directive with respect to stabilizing

7.162

---

[164] Prospectus Directive Article 3.2(b).

[165] Notwithstanding the expense of doing so, a number of US incorporated multinational issuers have gone through the exercise of getting a prospectus approved for employee equity compensation for employees in the EEA.

[166] Question 71 of the CESR Q&As describes the short-form disclosure regime and lists the items that can be omitted.

[167] Ibid.

[168] Ibid.

activities in connection with an offering of those securities. Issuers and under-writers of offerings in such securities should be cognizant that such provision may differ from home country rules and may impact the actions that can be taken during the pendency of an offering.

7.163 In order to benefit from a safe harbour under the Market Abuse Directive for stabilizing activities in connection with an offering, the prospectus for that offer-ing is required to include certain disclosures with respect to the possibility of stabilizing activities, including:

- the fact that stabilization may be undertaken, there is no assurance it will be undertaken and may be discontinued at any time;
- the fact that stabilization transactions are aimed to support the market price of securities;
- the period during which stabilization may occur;[169]
- the identity of the stabilization manager; and
- the existence, size and terms and conditions for the exercise of the overallot-ment facility or greenshoe option.[170]

7.164 The details of all stabilization transactions are required to be reported to the competent authority of the market in which such stabilizing activities were undertaken within seven trading days, and certain information is required to be disclosed to the public within one week of the end of the stabilization period.[171]

7.165 The Buy-Back Regulation limits the price at which stabilizing activities can be executed in shares and other securities equivalent to shares to the offering price and stabilization of the shares underlying convertible and exchangeable debt securities cannot exceed the market price of those underlying securities when the final terms of the offer of the convertible and exchangeable debt securities were publicly announced.[172] The Buy-Back Regulation also imposes certain limits related to overallotment facilities and greenshoe options (including limiting naked short positions by the underwriters to 5% of the original offer and limiting the greenshoe option to 15% of the original offer).[173]

---

[169] Art. 8 of Commission Regulation (EC) No 2273/2003 of 22 December 2003 implement-ing Directive 2003/6/EC of the European Parliament and of the Council as regards exemptions for buy-back programmes and stabilisation of financial instruments [2003] OJ L 336/33 (the 'Buy-Back Regulation') limits the period of time during which stabilizing activities may be undertaken in reliance on the safe harbour. The period is 30 days from the date of commencement of trading on a regulated market or adequate public disclosure of the final price in the case of an initial public offering.

[170] Buy-Back Regulation Article 9.1.

[171] Buy-Back Regulation Articles 9.2–9.3.

[172] Buy-Back Regulation Article 10.

[173] Buy-Back Regulation Article 11.

For an issuer that has its equity securities admitted to trading on an exchange-regulated market, the Buy-Back Regulation does not technically apply (since those markets are not 'regulated markets'). However, the laws of the jurisdiction in which the exchange-regulated market operates, in addition to the rules of the relevant exchange-regulated market, may impose requirements with respect to an issuer that buys back its own securities.[174]   **7.166**

In connection with a global offering that includes a public offering in the United States (to which Regulation M[175] under the US Exchange Act applies) and an offering of securities admitted to trading on a regulated market in a member state, the underwriters will need to ensure that their stabilizing activities comply with both regimes, since both have extraterritorial application. Issues that have arisen include the impact of the time difference between the United States and Europe making it difficult to make pre-stabilization disclosure in the EEA (for example in the case of debt securities which are offered after the close of business in Europe) and the 5% limit on overallotment facilities, which is not applicable in the United States. Market participants have also identified conflicts between the stabilization regime under the Buy-Back Regulation and the stabilization regime in Japan.[176]   **7.167**

7.4 Coordinating Ongoing Disclosure Requirements

This Section discusses compliance by a non-EU issuer with ongoing disclosure requirements under the Transparency Directive,[177] Market Abuse Directive and Article 10 of the Prospectus Directive.   **7.168**

This Section does not discuss additional ongoing disclosure requirements that may be imposed by the listing or admission standards of regulated markets and exchange-regulated markets on which an issuer has securities admitted to trading. Therefore, non-EU issuers would need to investigate these requirements as well when evaluating the ongoing obligations they are taking on when listing securities within the EEA.   **7.169**

---

[174] For example, Part V of the Irish Companies Act 1990, relating to market abuse, applies to issuers listed on the Irish Enterprise Exchange, and the United Kingdom has imposed super-equivalent requirements in its transposition of the Market Abuse Directive to make it applicable to the Alternative Investment Market ('AIM').

[175] 17 CFR §§ 24.100 et seq.

[176] See Market Abuse Directive Level 3 Paragraph 50 —third set of CESR guidance and information on the common operation of the Market Abuse Directive to the market, 15 May 2009 (the 'Third CESR MAD Guidance').

[177] It is important to recall that the Transparency Directive is a 'minimum harmonisation' directive and, therefore, member states may impose 'super-equivalent' requirements on issuers for which they are the home member state. These super-equivalent requirements are discussed in greater detail for various member states in Part 3.

7.4.1 Transparency Directive

7.170   As a general matter, the Transparency Directive imposes certain minimum ongoing reporting obligations on non-EU issuers with securities admitted to trading on a regulated market. As discussed in detail below, the scope of these ongoing reporting obligations can differ depending on whether the securities admitted to trading are wholesale debt securities and whether another exemption from the full disclosure requirements is applicable. The Transparency Directive does not impose reporting obligations on a guarantor of debt securities that are admitted to trading on a regulated market. In addition to ongoing issuer reporting obligations, the Transparency Directive imposes reporting obligations on major shareholders of issuers with shares admitted to trading on a regulated market.

7.4.1.1 *Equivalence of non-member state reporting*

7.171   The Transparency Directive contemplates the possibility that member states will determine for non-EU issuers that home country requirements are equivalent to the reporting obligations under the Transparency Directive.[178] Equivalence determinations would allow non-EU issuers that comply with those home country requirements to comply with their Transparency Directive obligations simply by disclosing home country reports as regulated information under the Transparency Directive. The Transparency Implementation Directive sets forth criteria that need to be met by third-country requirements in order to be considered equivalent to the Transparency Directive requirements.[179]

7.172   The United Kingdom has determined that US domestic issuers that are subject to reporting requirements under Section 13(a) of the US Exchange Act satisfy various reporting obligations under the Transparency Directive and has reached a similar conclusion with respect to issuers incorporated in Switzerland with respect to certain Transparency Directive requirements.[180] The consequence of this equivalence determination is that a listing on a regulated market by a US domestic issuer subject to US Exchange Act reporting requirements would not require the issuer to report under the Transparency Directive, although it would have other consequences (such as the Market Abuse Directive applying to the issuer). To date, the United Kingdom has not made equivalence determinations for general Transparency Directive purposes with respect to any other non-EEA country.

7.173   Non-EU issuers that are subject to US Exchange Act reporting obligations with securities admitted to trading on regulated markets in other member states

---

[178]   Transparency Directive Article 23.1.

[179]   Transparency Implementation Directive Articles 13–22.

[180]   See 'Equivalence of non-EEA Regimes', available at http://www.fsa.gov.uk/Pages/Doing/UKLA/company/non_eea/index.shtml.

practically should be able to satisfy their periodic reporting obligations under the Transparency Directive through those filings. In order to do so, the non-EU issuer will likely need to disclose those US Exchange Act reports as regulated information (including notifying the competent authority of the home member state) and comply with other home member state requirements.

7.4.1.2 *Minimum reporting obligations under the Transparency Directive*

As discussed in greater detail above in Section 3 of Part 1, the Transparency **7.174** Directive imposes certain minimum ongoing reporting obligations on issuers with securities admitted to trading on a regulated market. These obligations include annual reporting, half-yearly reports and interim management statements or quarterly reports.

7.4.1.2.1 Annual reports An issuer is required to file its annual report with its **7.175** home member state[181] within four months after the end of its fiscal year. This annual report is required to consist of (a) audited financial statements prepared in accordance with IFRS or an equivalent set of accounting principles,[182] (b) a management report and (c) a responsibility statement that the financial statements included in such report give a true and fair view of the issuer and the undertakings consolidated with the issuer in such report.[183]

Financial statements. The obligation to produce the required financial state- **7.176** ments should generally not be burdensome for non-EU issuers who report under generally accepted accounting principles considered to be equivalent to IFRS for purposes of the Transparency Directive (which is discussed in greater detail below). For non-EU issuers who do not otherwise report in IFRS or generally accepted accounting principles considered to be equivalent to IFRS, the ongoing obligation to restate financial statements represents a substantial and expensive undertaking and may lead such an issuer, to the extent it is permitted to do so under home country regulation, to switch to IFRS or generally accepted accounting principles considered equivalent. The acceptance by the US SEC of IFRS as promulgated by the International Accounting Standards Board without the need

---

[181] See Section 7.2.2 above for a discussion of a home member state for purposes of the Transparency Directive.

[182] See Section 7.4.1.6 below for a discussion of accounting principles that have been deemed equivalent to IFRS (including US GAAP).

[183] Issuers with a registered office in the EEA with securities admitted to trading on a regulated market are also required to make certain disclosures with respect to compliance with or departures from any corporate governance code applicable to it. Recital 10 to Directive 2006/46/EC of the European Parliament and of the Council of 14 June 2006 amending Council Directives 78/660/EEC on the annual accounts of certain types of companies, 83/349/EEC on consolidated accounts, 86/635/EEC on the annual accounts and consolidated accounts of banks and other financial institutions and 91/674/EEC on the annual accounts and consolidated accounts of insurance undertakings [2006] OJ L 224/1.

for a reconciliation should help facilitate such a switch where such a change is permitted by the issuer's home country law.

7.177 The financial statements to be included in the annual report are required to be audited by an auditor meeting the Statutory Audit Directive requirements described above in Section 7.3.2.4.

7.178 **Management report.** The management report required to be included in the annual report is required to provide a fair review of the development of the issuer's business and of its financial position and a description of the principal risks and uncertainties that it faces as well as an indication of the following information:

- important events that have occurred since the end of the fiscal year;
- the issuer's likely future development;
- a discussion of the issuer's activities in the field of research and development; and
- certain information with respect to repurchases by the issuer of its own shares or shares held by the issuer's subsidiaries and related-party transactions.[184]

7.179 In practice, a non-EU issuer that prepares a US-style management's discussion and analysis or an operating and financial review as contemplated by the IOSCO disclosure standards for home country reporting purposes should be able to use that document to cover the majority of the management report requirements, possibly with the addition of a few specific disclosures.

7.180 **Responsibility statement.** The responsibility statement requires the responsible persons within the issuer to certify, to the best of their knowledge, that:

- the financial statements give a true and fair view of the assets, liabilities, financial position and profit or loss of the issuer and the undertakings included in the consolidation taken as a whole; and
- the management report includes a fair review of the development and performance of the business and the position of the issuer and the undertakings included in the consolidation taken as a whole, together with a description of the principal risks and uncertainties that they face.[185]

7.181 The Transparency Directive does not specify which persons within an issuer are required to give the responsibility statement. In the case of the United Kingdom, the view of the competent authority is that the directors of the issuer will usually be giving the responsibility statement. Certain member states have provided

---

[184] The requirements applicable to annual reports are set forth in Article 46 of the Fourth Council Directive 78/660/EC of 25 July 1978 on the annual accounts of certain types of companies [1978] OJ L 222/11, and Article 36 of the Seventh Council Directive 83/349/EEC of 13 June 1983 on consolidated accounts, [1983] OJ L 193/1.

[185] Transparency Directive Article 4.2(c).

specificity about the persons required to give responsibility statements in their transposition of the Transparency Directive.[186]

The substance of the responsibility statement differs somewhat from the require- **7.182** ments applicable to issuers that are subject to the Sarbanes-Oxley Act in the United States. In addition, unlike the required management certifications under the Sarbanes-Oxley Act in the United States, the Transparency Directive is not explicit about which persons are required to give the responsibility statement.

In order for the responsible persons within an issuer to give the required responsibil- **7.183** ity statement, the issuer should establish an internal process by which the responsible persons can gain comfort that the responsibility statement which they will be required to make is accurate. For an issuer that is required to include Sarbanes-Oxley certifications in its filings with the US SEC, all that should be required is an expansion of the internal process to ensure that the specific elements of the responsibility statement are included in the process and potentially the expansion of the addressees of that process to ensure that the persons giving the responsibility statement under the Transparency Directive have the benefit of that process.

7.4.1.2.2 Half-yearly reports   Issuers are required to publish as soon as possible **7.184** and in any event no later than two months after the end of the half-yearly period a half-yearly report including a condensed set of financial statements, which must be prepared in accordance with IFRS or generally accepted accounting principles considered equivalent, a management report and a responsibility statement.

Financial statements. Issuers that prepare half-yearly financial statements other **7.185** than in accordance with IFRS are subject to the following specific requirements under the Transparency Directive:

• the balance sheet and statement of profit and loss in half-yearly reports are required to include each heading and subtotal included in the most recent annual financial statements;[187] and
• comparative half-year balance sheets and profit and loss statements and limited explanatory notes.[188]

There is no requirement that the financial statements in a half-yearly report be **7.186** audited or reviewed, but if an audit or review takes place, then the audit or review report is required to be included in the half-yearly report.[189] This requirement differs from practice in the United States where financial statements in quarterly reports filed by US issuers are required to be reviewed (but not audited) and a

---

[186]   See Annex II to the CESR TD Transposition Study.
[187]   Transparency Implementation Directive Article 3.2.
[188]   Transparency Implementation Directive Articles 3.2–3.3.
[189]   Transparency Directive Article 5.5.

review report included only if the issuer refers in its report to the fact that the financial statements have been reviewed.[190] As a result, US issuers typically do not refer to their quarterly financial statements as having been reviewed. If the financial statements have not been audited or reviewed, that fact must be disclosed.[191]

7.187 **Management report.** The management report for the half-yearly report is required to include the following information:

- an indication of important events during the first six months of the year and their impact on the condensed financial statements; and
- a description of the principal risks and uncertainties for the remaining six months of the year.[192]

7.188 **Responsibility statement.** The responsibility statement required to be included in the half-yearly reporting is essentially equivalent in scope to the responsibility statement that is required to be included in the annual report.[193]

7.189 **Major related-party transaction disclosure.** For an issuer with shares admitted to trading on a regulated market, the half-yearly report is also required to include information on major related-party transactions:

- related-party transactions that have taken place during the first six months of the current financial year that have materially affected the financial position or performance of the issuer; and
- changes to related-party transactions described in the most recent annual report that could have a material effect on the financial position or performance of the issuer during the first six months of the current financial year.[194]

7.190 Issuers with shares admitted to trading on a regulated market in the EEA that are not required under home country reporting requirements to disclose related-party transactions in their interim reports will need to modify their reporting procedures to ensure that these transactions are identified for disclosure in half-yearly reports under the Transparency Directive.

7.191 **7.4.1.2.3 Interim management statements** The Transparency Directive imposes interim financial reporting obligations on issuers whose shares are admitted to trading on a regulated market in the form of a requirement to publish interim management statements twice a year. This requirement will not apply if an issuer reports quarterly (whether as a result of home country legislation, listing standards or of the issuer's own initiative).[195] In most member states, issuers have

---

[190] Article 10-01(d) of Regulation S-X, 17 CFR § 210.10-01(d).
[191] Transparency Directive Article 5.5.
[192] Transparency Directive Article 5.4.
[193] Transparency Directive Article 5.2(c).
[194] Transparency Directive Article 5.4.
[195] Transparency Directive Article 6.2.

the option to publish either interim management statements or a quarterly report.[196] Member states generally have not imposed a requirement to publish interim management statements on debt-only issuers.[197]

Interim management statements are required to be published no earlier than ten **7.192** weeks into and no later than six weeks before the end of each half-yearly period.[198] The interim management statements are required to describe material events that have taken place during the relevant period and their impact on the financial position and performance of the issuer and its controlled undertakings as well as a description of the financial position and performance of the issuer and its controlled undertakings during such period.[199]

The Transparency Directive does not specify any particular content requirements **7.193** for interim management statements and practice by issuers varies. A non-EU issuer that is not otherwise required to report on a quarterly basis would need to look to market practice in the home member state to get a sense of the level of detail disclosed by comparable issuers in that member state with respect to interim management statements. Issuers that choose to prepare a quarterly report in lieu of interim management statements are required by a majority of member states to include information comparable to that included in a half-yearly report for the period covered by the quarterly report.[200]

7.4.1.3 *Other ongoing requirements under the Transparency Directive*

Non-EEA disclosures. Non-EU issuers are required to disclose information that **7.194** is disclosed outside the EEA which may be of importance to investors within the EEA as regulated information.[201] This requirement applies to disclosures of information, even if the information would not otherwise constitute 'regulated information'.[202] For an issuer that already discloses significant information through mechanisms (such as news services) that include the EEA, this requirement

---

[196] See responses to question 95 in Annex II to the CESR TD Transposition Study.
[197] See responses to questions 96–97 in Annex II to the CESR TD Transposition Study.
[198] Transparency Directive Article 6.1.
[199] Ibid.
[200] See the CESR TD Transposition Study.
[201] Transparency Directive Article 23.3.
[202] 'Regulated information' is defined in Transparency Directive Article 2.1(k) as 'all information which the issuer, or any other person who has applied for the admission of securities to trading on a regulated market without the issuer's consent, is required to disclose under this Directive, under Art. 6 of the Market Abuse Directive, or under the laws, regulations or administrative provisions of a member state adopted under Art. 3(1) of this Directive'. Prospectuses are generally not considered regulated information. Note also that there is a division of views among member states over whether information required to be disclosed by issuers with shares admitted to trading on a regulated market is regulated information. See responses by member states to question 147 in Annex II to the CESR TD Transposition Study.

should not have a significant practical impact unless disclosure through a specified mechanism or service in the EEA is required by the home member state.

7.195   If the issuer does not typically disclose information through mechanisms that are followed or known in the EEA, the home member state requires disclosure of regulated information through specific mechanisms or services that the issuer does not use for general disclosures, or the disclosure of significant information is made in a regulatory filing outside the EEA, then the issuer should disclose significant information in the same manner it uses for regulated information in order to comply with this obligation. For example, making an announcement through a newswire service that only has subscribers located in the United States would likely not be regarded as constituting sufficient dissemination of the information in the EEA. In practice, this may require an issuer to establish a process to monitor disclosures to ensure that significant information disclosed elsewhere is treated as regulated information.

7.196   **Notice of certain events.** Article 16 of the Transparency Directive requires issuers to make disclosures with respect to the following events without delay (which requirement is in addition to any disclosure obligation they may have under the Market Abuse Directive):

- for an issuer with shares admitted to trading on a regulated market, changes to the rights of the issuer's classes of shares or to the terms of derivative securities issued by the issuer and giving access to the issuer's shares;
- for an issuer with other securities admitted to trading on a regulated market, changes to the rights of holders of those securities; and
- new loan issues,[203] including any guarantee or security in respect thereof.[204]

7.197   **Equal treatment of securityholders.** Article 17 of the Transparency Directive imposes certain equal treatment obligations on issuers with shares admitted to trading on a regulated market. These obligations include a general obligation to ensure equal treatment for all holders of shares who are in the same position.[205] There are also specific obligations to make proxies, notices and other information relating to shareholder meetings available to shareholders through facilities in the home member state, the appointment of a paying agent and conveyance of information to shareholders through electronic means, so long as the decision to

---

[203] Although there is some variation among member states, most member states have interpreted the phrase 'new loan issue' to include all issuances of debt securities admitted to trading on a regulated market. Some member states have interpreted this phrase more broadly and do not require that the debt securities be admitted to trading on a regulated market. See responses to questions 132–133 in Annex II to the CESR TD Transposition Study.

[204] Transparency Directive Article 16.

[205] Transparency Directive Article 17.1.

use electronic communications is approved by shareholders.[206] The provisions relating to electronic communication of information to shareholders allows for deemed consent to electronic delivery of information by shareholders to the extent they do not respond in the negative to a request for a consent to such use.[207]

Article 18 imposes similar obligations on issuers whose debt securities (including issuers of wholesale debt securities) are admitted to trading on a regulated market.[208]   **7.198**

7.4.1.4 *Financial statement equivalence and exemptions*

The European Commission has determined, effective as of 1 January 2009, that generally accepted accounting principles in the United States and in Japan are equivalent to IFRS for purposes of annual and half-yearly reports required under the Transparency Directive.[209] In the same decision, the European Commission also determined that financial statements prepared in accordance with generally accepted accounting principles in the People's Republic of China, Canada, the Republic of Korea and the Republic of India are equivalent to IFRS for purposes of reporting under the Transparency Directive for financial years ending no later than 31 December 2011.   **7.199**

There are several temporary exemptions available to non-EU issuers, which are now of less significance to non-EU issuers given the equivalence determinations described above.   **7.200**

The first is an exemption provided for in the Transparency Directive itself, which exempted non-EU issuers preparing financial statements in accordance with 'internationally accepted standards' from the obligation to restate their financial statements into IFRS in annual and half-yearly reports for fiscal years before 2007.[210]   **7.201**

Second, the Transparency Directive permitted but did not require member states to provide for a ten-year exemption from half-yearly reporting for issuers that as of 1 January 2005 had only debt securities admitted to trading on a regulated market in the EEA. This exemption was not applicable to any issuer that had any securities admitted to trading since 1 January 2005 or issuers that had equity securities admitted to trading.[211]   **7.202**

---

[206] Transparency Directive Article 17.2–17.3.
[207] Transparency Directive Article 17.3(c).
[208] Transparency Directive Article 18.
[209] Commission Decision 2008/961/EC of 12 December 2008 on the use by third countries' issuers of securities of certain third country's national accounting standards and International Financial Reporting Standards to prepare their consolidated financial statements [2008] OJ L 340/112.
[210] Transparency Directive Article 23.2.
[211] Transparency Directive Article 30.4.

7.203   Third, there is an exemption in the Transparency Directive from the obligation to include IFRS financial statements in half-yearly reports available to issuers that have only debt securities admitted to trading on a regulated market in the EEA and issuers that have securities admitted to trading outside the EEA and in connection therewith have been using internationally accepted standards since a financial year that started prior to 19 July 2002.[212]

7.204   Fourth, the Transparency Directive permits member states to allow non-EU issuers that only had debt securities admitted to trading on a regulated market on 1 January 2005 and have not had any securities admitted to trading since that date to prepare annual financial statements in accordance with accounting standards other than IFRS if that member state acknowledged that financial statements prepared in accordance with those accounting standards gave a true and fair view of the issuer's assets and liabilities, financial position and results.[213] This exemption ceased to be applicable once the European Commission determined the equivalence of other accounting standards to IFRS.

7.4.1.5 *Global depositary receipts*

7.205   It has been common for non-EU issuers from countries such as China and Russia that wish to list in the EEA to have global depositary receipts admitted to trading on a regulated market (such as the London Stock Exchange) rather than directly listing their shares. One of the principal benefits of having global depositary receipts admitted to trading (rather than shares) is that the Transparency Directive imposes reduced ongoing reporting obligations on the issuer of the underlying shares.[214] In particular, an issuer of shares underlying global depositary receipts would be obligated to produce annual reports meeting the requirements described above but would not be required to produce half-yearly reports or interim management statements. An issuer of shares underlying global depositary receipts would also be subject to ongoing disclosure obligations under Article 16 of the Transparency Directive as described above.

7.206   Issuers of global depositary receipts that have those receipts admitted to trading on a regulated market may also be taking on super-equivalent reporting obligations imposed by that market in addition to those imposed by the Transparency Directive. Issuers contemplating having global depositary receipts admitted to trading on a regulated market should investigate what those requirements may entail.

7.207   One additional matter that an issuer of depositary receipts which is having its depositary receipts admitted to trading on a regulated market should consider is

---

[212] Transparency Directive Article 30.1.
[213] Transparency Directive Article 30.3.
[214] Transparency Directive Article 2.1(d).

the possible need to issue an additional prospectus if additional depositary receipts are admitted to trading on the regulatory market. Since the number of depositary receipts can fluctuate based on deposits and withdrawals of the underlying securities, an issuer of depositary receipts will not be able to control the number of depositary receipts. Although there is an exemption in Article 4.2 of the Prospectus Directive for the admission of additional securities of the same class to trading on a regulated market, there is a 10% limit during a 12-month period.[215] In order to address this potential issue, issuers frequently have excess depositary receipts admitted to trading at the outset so as to minimize the likelihood that a prospectus will be needed to admit additional depositary receipts.

7.4.1.6 *Wholesale debt securities*

Non-EU issuers that only issue wholesale debt securities in the EEA and choose to have their securities admitted to trading on an exchange-regulated market, such as Euro MTF in Luxembourg, the Irish GEM or the Professional Securities Market, rather than a regulated market, would not be subject to the Transparency Directive as a whole. The ongoing disclosure requirements for wholesale debt issuers in this position are those imposed by the exchange-regulated market on which those debt securities are admitted to trading. Issuers of wholesale debt securities are also permitted to disclose any regulated information required to be disclosed under the Transparency Directive in either a language accepted by the competent authority of the issuer's home member state or a language customary in the sphere of international finance (at the issuer's election).[216]   **7.208**

Non-EU issuers that choose to have their wholesale debt securities admitted to trading on a regulated market and do not have other securities admitted to trading on a regulated market are exempt from the obligations to produce annual, half-year or interim management statements under the Transparency Directive.[217] These issuers are, however, required to comply with the obligations under Articles 16 and 18 of the Transparency Directive described in Section 7.4.1.3 above.   **7.209**

7.4.1.7 *Convertible and exchangeable securities*

Convertible and exchangeable securities are not treated as 'debt securities' for purposes of the Transparency Directive.[218] On the other hand, there is no definition of the term 'shares' in the Transparency Directive, so these securities are not clearly covered by that term either (unless and until there is a conversion or exchange). Based on this lack of clear coverage, issuers of these securities should only be   **7.210**

---

[215] Prospectus Directive Article 4.2(a).
[216] Transparency Directive Article 20.6.
[217] Transparency Directive Article 8.1(b).
[218] Transparency Directive Article 2.1(b).

required to prepare annual reports unless the home member state has expressly provided otherwise in its transposition of the Transparency Directive.[219] Issuers of these securities should confirm the treatment in the relevant member state.

7.4.1.8 *Disclosure requirements for regulated information*

7.211   **7.4.1.8.1 Disclosure generally**   Regulated information is required to be disclosed by the issuer or the person who applied for admission to trading of the issuer's securities without the issuer's consent in a manner ensuring that it is capable of being disseminated to as wide a public as possible in the home member state, in any host member state in which the information is required to be disclosed[220] and in the other member states.[221] In particular, regulated information is required to be communicated to the media in unedited full text.[222] The competent authorities of some member states have specified mechanisms that are required to be used to disseminate regulated information. For example, the United Kingdom and Ireland require the use of a 'Regulated Information Service'. As a result, a non-EU issuer may be required to disseminate information through an additional mechanism beyond that used in its home country.

7.212   In the case of annual, half-yearly and interim reports this obligation may be satisfied by posting the information on a website that is in addition to the officially appointed mechanism (e.g. the issuer's website) and making an announcement to the media.[223] Issuers are required to ensure that annual and half-yearly reports remain publicly available for at least five years.[224]

7.213   Paper-based dissemination (in addition to electronic dissemination) of certain regulated information, such as annual reports, is required in various member states and is permitted in all member states other than the Netherlands.[225] See Part 3 below for more detailed discussion of the requirements adopted in the relevant member state.

7.214   In any event, an issuer is required to disclose regulated information to the media in a manner which minimizes the risk of data corruption and unauthorized access.[226] To address possible issues with respect to unauthorized communication of regulated

---

[219] For example, in the United Kingdom, issuers of convertible securities are only required to prepare annual reports. See Annex 3 to UK FSA Policy Statement 06/11, Implementation of the Transparency Directive, available at http://www.fsa.gov.uk/pubs/policy/ps06_11.pdf.

[220] In the case of an issuer with securities admitted to trading on a regulated market only in a host member state, the disclosure of regulated information is required in the host member state rather than in the home member state. Transparency Directive Article 21.3.

[221] Transparency Implementation Directive Article 12.2.

[222] Transparency Implementation Directive Article 12.3.

[223] Note that issuers are not permitted to charge investors for providing copies of regulated information. Transparency Directive Article 21.1.

[224] Transparency Directive Articles 4.1 and 5.1.

[225] See responses to questions 122–124 in Annex II to the CESR TD Transposition Study.

[226] Transparency Implementation Directive Article 12.4.

information to the media, the issuer is required to be able to disclose to the competent authority of the home member state certain detailed information regarding the disclosure of regulated information, including the person who communicated the information and security validation details. Given these specific requirements, non-EU issuers need to ensure that they have in place a system for tracking and recording this information to be able to respond to inquiries from the competent authority.

The obligations to disclose regulated information as described above should not impose significant practical burdens on non-EU issuers. An issuer will need to ensure that it makes disclosures to appropriate media sources within its home member state. In thinking about the timing of disclosure of regulated information, issuers should be cognizant of time differences; it would be the better practice to time significant disclosures to be made at a point in time when the issuer's securities are not being traded on a regulated market or in the home market. For a US issuer, that would suggest that significant disclosures are better made after the close of trading in the United States. **7.215**

7.4.1.8.2 Filing obligations   Regulated information is also required to be filed with both the competent authority of the home member state and the 'officially appointed mechanism' in the home member state for the central storage of information disclosed by issuers under the Transparency Directive.[227] The purpose of the officially appointed mechanism is to ensure that there is widespread access throughout the EEA to regulated information filed with the home member state. Over time, it is expected that these two filing requirements would be combined in member states to allow a single filing to suffice for both. **7.216**

To date, the implementation by member states of the officially appointed mechanism has varied somewhat and a number of member states have implemented interim solutions. For example, one interim solution consists of links on the competent authority's website to the websites of the issuers for which such member state is the home member state,[228] while other member states have implemented a searchable database of filings.[229] The method by which an issuer discloses information to the officially appointed mechanism also varies between member states, with approximately half of member states allowing electronic submission.[230] **7.217**

Issuers will also need to establish a mechanism for filing regulated information with the competent authority and officially appointed mechanism. In member states that require paper filings with the competent authority and/or the officially **7.218**

---

[227] Transparency Directive Article 21.1.
[228] For example, Belgium.
[229] For example, France, the Netherlands, Luxembourg and Spain.
[230] See responses to questions 148–149 in Annex II to the CESR TD Transposition Study.

appointed mechanism, this may require an issuer to think further ahead than an electronic system in which filings can easily be made on a same-day basis. These considerations should become less significant if member states shift to electronic-based filing systems.

7.219   From an investor and issuer perspective, an issue that arises is that there is no central pan-European repository for regulated information. Such a repository would substantially increase the ability of investors to access that information and would avoid the need to search out information in the home member state.[231] Although a formal pan-European central depository is not yet in place, CESR has set up a network of national storage mechanisms for shares listed on regulated markets through a database on its website as an initial step.[232]

7.4.1.9 Language requirements

7.220   Similar to the Prospectus Directive, the Transparency Directive imposes requirements with respect to disclosures required thereunder. As discussed in Section 7.3.2.3 above, a non-EU issuer that contemplates having securities admitted to trading on a regulated market should consider carefully the languages accepted by the competent authority of the member state that it selects as its home member state for Transparency Directive purposes.

7.221   If the issuer only has securities admitted to trading on a regulated market in the home member state, then disclosure under the Transparency Directive is required to be made in a language accepted by the competent authority of the home member state.[233] In this situation, there is variation among member states. A number of significant member states allow either all issuers or issuers incorporated outside that member state to use English or a language customary in the sphere of international finance for disclosure of regulated information. In particular:

- Belgium allows an issuer that does not have a place of business in Belgium to choose from among one of the national languages and a language customary in the sphere of international finance;
- France allows any issuer to choose between French and a language customary in the sphere of international finance;

---

[231] The European Commission has called for the creation of such a system and has invited CESR to reflect by September 2010 on the possibility of such a network. See 'Commission Calls for Easier Public Access to Financial Information on Listed Companies', 15 October 2007, available at http://europa.eu/rapid/pressReleasesAction.do?reference=IP/07/1494&format=HTML&aged=1&language=EN&guiLanguage=en.

[232] The CESR MiFID database is available at http://mifiddatabase.cesr.eu.

[233] Transparency Directive Article 20.1.

- Germany allows an issuer incorporated elsewhere to choose between German and English;
- Italy and Spain each allow an issuer incorporated elsewhere to choose between the national language(s) and a language customary in the sphere of international finance;
- Luxembourg allows any issuer to choose from among Luxembourgish, French, German and English; and
- The Netherlands allows the use of English by any issuer if approved by shareholders.[234]

7.222 If, on the other hand, an issuer has securities admitted to trading on regulated markets in both the home member state and one or more host member states, then the issuer is required to disclose regulated information:

- in a language accepted by the home member state; and
- at the choice of the issuer, either in a language accepted by the competent authorities in each host member state in which the issuer has securities admitted to trading or a language customary in the sphere of international finance.[235]

7.223 In the third possible case, an issuer that has securities admitted to trading in one or more host member states but not in its home member state, the issuer is required to disclose regulated information, at the choice of the issuer, either in a language accepted by the competent authorities in each host member state in which the issuer has securities admitted to trading or a language customary in the sphere of international finance.[236] The home member state may also require an issuer in this situation to disclose regulated information, at the choice of the issuer, in a language accepted by the competent authority of the home member state or a language customary in the sphere of international finance.[237]

7.224 Issuers are not required to disclose regulated information in compliance with the above language requirements when the issuer's securities are admitted to trading on a regulated market without the issuer's consent. Instead the obligation falls on the person who, without the issuer's consent, requested the admission.[238]

7.4.1.10 Disclosure of major holdings

7.225 The Transparency Directive also imposes a reporting regime on persons that acquire voting shares above certain thresholds and separately on persons that acquire voting rights above similar thresholds for issuers that have shares admitted

---

234 See responses to questions 137–139 in Annex II to the CESR TD Transposition Study.
235 Transparency Directive Article 20.2.
236 Transparency Directive Article 20.3.
237 Ibid.
238 Transparency Directive Article 20.4.

to trading on a regulated market in a member state. For a non-EU issuer and its major holders,[239] this regime may result in reporting obligations beyond those imposed by home country law. Holders of depositary receipts are treated as 'shareholders' for purposes of the major holder reporting regime.[240]

7.226   Although the bulk of the practical impact of the major holder reporting regime will be felt by major holders of non-EU issuers, the regime does impose certain obligations on the issuer that it may not be subject to under home country law. As discussed below, the Transparency Directive imposes obligations on the issuer with respect to disclosure of changes in the total number of outstanding voting rights and prompt publication of any notifications it receives from a major holder that a reporting threshold has been crossed.

7.227   If an equivalence exemption is not applicable to a non-EU issuer with shares admitted to trading on a regulated market, the issuer should consider carefully the extent to which the Transparency Directive regime may differ from the regime in their home country. For example, the regime differs in several important respects from the US beneficial ownership reporting system under sections 13(d) and 13(g) of the US Exchange Act. Unlike the US system, a holder is required to disclose a reporting threshold being crossed based on changes in the total number of outstanding voting rights (whereas the US system only requires notification based on an acquisition or disposition by the reporting person). The Transparency Directive requires the issuer to make public information contained in a notification from a major holder, while the US regime requires the major shareholder to make a public filing with the US SEC and does not require issuer action.

7.228   In practice, a non-EU issuer that is subject to the major shareholding notification regime will need to ensure that its public relations and investor relations staff are aware of the significance of a notification under that regime and inform them of the need to make a public disclosure in response to such a notification.

7.229   **7.4.1.10.1 Equivalence determinations**   As with ongoing reporting obligations, the Transparency Directive contemplates the possibility that competent authorities in member states could conclude that home country legislation with respect to non-EU issuers would be equivalent with respect to reporting of major shareholdings.[241] To date, the UK FSA has made an equivalence determination with respect to home country legislation for issuers organized under the laws of the

---

[239] For purposes of this discussion, the term 'major holder' is used to refer to shareholders and vote holders that exceed the Transparency Directive minimum threshold.
[240] Transparency Directive Article 2.1(e)(iii).
[241] Transparency Directive Article 23.1.

United States, Japan, Israel and Switzerland.[242] Therefore, an issuer incorporated in one of those jurisdictions for which the UK is the home member state is exempt from the major holder reporting regime under the Transparency Directive.

7.4.1.10.2 Reporting thresholds The Transparency Directive requires disclo- **7.230**
sure by a shareholder or vote holder of the acquisition or disposal of shares or voting rights of an issuer that results in the shareholder or vote holder acquiring shares representing at least 5% of the voting rights applicable to the issuer's shares, although a handful of member states have imposed lower initial thresholds in their transposition of the Transparency Directive (as low as 2%).[243] The Transparency Directive specifies further disclosure thresholds at 10%, 15%, 20%, 25%, 30%, 50% and 75% of the voting rights.[244]

In addition to requiring disclosure of acquisitions that result in one of the **7.231**
disclosure thresholds being reached or exceeded, the Transparency Directive also imposes a disclosure obligation if, as a result of a disposition, a major holder falls below one of the thresholds.[245] Major holders are also required to disclose if one of the reporting thresholds is crossed as a result of events that result in changes in the breakdown of voting rights.[246] In order to allow shareholders and vote holders to determine when reporting thresholds have been crossed, an issuer is required to disclose its total number of voting rights and capital at the end of each calendar month in which a change in the total number of voting rights occurred.[247]

For purposes of calculating voting rights, all shares of the issuer with voting rights **7.232**
are taken into account (including shares in respect of which voting rights have been suspended).[248] In most member states, treasury shares are also taken into account in determining voting rights.[249] Ownership of depositary receipts confers ownership for these purposes of the shares underlying those depositary receipts.[250]

In addition to acquisitions of shares with voting rights, Article 10 of the **7.233**
Transparency Directive imposes similar reporting obligations on persons that are

---

[242] See Equivalence of non-EEA Regimes, available at http://www.fsa.gov.uk/Pages/Doing/UKLA/company/non_eea/index.shtml.

[243] Transparency Directive Article. 9.1; see also CESR TD Transposition Study.

[244] Ibid. Certain member states have also adopted different thresholds above the initial reporting threshold. For example, the United Kingdom requires disclosure of each increase or decrease of 1% once an initial 3% threshold has been exceeded. CESR TD Transposition Study.

[245] Ibid.

[246] Transparency Directive Article 9.2. A shareholder would be required to determine that one of the reporting thresholds had been crossed based on information about total voting rights that the issuer is required to disclose under Transparency Directive Article 15.

[247] Transparency Directive Article 15.

[248] Transparency Directive Article 9.1.

[249] See responses to questions 28–29 in Annex II to the CESR TD Transposition Study.

[250] Transparency Directive Article 2.1(e)(iii).

entitled to acquire, dispose of or exercise the right to vote voting shares of an issuer in any of the following cases (or combination of them):

- agreements to act in concert with respect to voting;
- temporary transfers of voting rights for consideration;
- pledges that allow the pledgee to exercise the voting rights, which the pledgee declares an intent to exercise;
- having a life interest in shares with voting rights;
- control of an entity that holds or can exercise voting rights in a manner described above;
- deposit of shares that gives the depositary the right to exercise discretion in the absence of specific direction by the depositor;
- voting rights held by a third party in its own name on behalf of another person; and
- being granted a proxy with respect to voting rights which the grantee may exercise at its discretion in the absence of specific instruction from the grantors of the proxies.

7.234   **7.4.1.10.3 Notification procedures and common reporting form** The Transparency Directive contemplates a two-step notification process. In the first step, the holder of voting rights notifies the issuer within a specified period of time that a reporting threshold has been crossed.[251] The Transparency Directive imposes a four trading day deadline for this notification, although certain member states have imposed more stringent deadlines in transposing the Transparency Directive.[252] In the second step, an issuer that receives a notification from a holder of voting rights that a reporting threshold has been crossed is required within three trading days to make that notification public.

7.235   In an effort to eliminate a multiplicity of notification forms, CESR has prepared a common form of major shareholder notification.[253] As discussed below, the UK FSA has adopted rules that will require disclosure of certain swaps and derivatives under the major shareholding notification regime, which will result in a divergence between the notification form in use in the UK and elsewhere, unless and until there is a convergence between the UK and other member states in the treatment of these types of instruments.

7.236   In addition to the matters covered by the common notification form, two member states (France and Denmark) require disclosure of investor objectives once

---

[251] Transparency Directive Article 12.2.
[252] These deadlines range from immediately after a transaction in which a reporting threshold is crossed to within three trading days. See responses to question 48 in Annex II to the CESR TD Transposition Study.
[253] Standard Form TR-1.

voting rights in excess of 10% are reported. Similar disclosure requirements became applicable in Germany as of 31 May 2009.[254]

Notifications under the major shareholdings regime are required to be permitted to be made in a language customary in the sphere of international finance.

7.237

7.4.1.10.4 Treatment of derivative securities The UK FSA has recently adopted rules requiring inclusion of certain derivatives relating to shares of a company (including, but not limited to, contracts for difference) in the determination of whether the notification threshold of 3% has been exceeded.[255] Under these rules, subject to certain exceptions related to client-serving intermediaries, financial instruments (including swaps) that have a similar economic effect to shares or certain other instruments that entitle the holder to acquire shares are treated as equivalent to ownership of the underlying securities.[256] These rules become effective as of 1 June 2009.

7.238

The treatment of derivative securities under major holder notification regimes generally has received a great deal of attention in the past several years. Hedge funds and other investors acquiring ownership interests through derivatives that do not convey formal ownership of the securities to which they are referenced has been a principal reason for the recent focus on this subject. In particular, the treatment of cash-settled total return swaps has been an area of focus in the United States (principally as a result of the litigation arising out of a proxy fight involving CSX Corporation)[257] and the Chairman of the US SEC has recently stated that the US SEC is examining whether ownership of equity swaps should be required to be reported under the US Exchange Act beneficial ownership reporting requirements.[258] Over time, it would be reasonable to expect other jurisdictions to at least consider following a similar approach to that taken by the UK FSA.

7.239

7.4.1.10.5 Exemptions Article 9 of the Transparency Directive also contains various exceptions to the major holders reporting regime for custodians, market

7.240

---

[254] Commission Staff Working Document, 'Report on more stringent national measures concerning Directive 2004/109/EC on the harmonisation of transparency requirements in relation to information about issuers whose securities are admitted to trading on a regulated market', 10 December 2008, page 28, available at http://ec.europa.eu/internal_market/securities/docs/transparency/report_measures_122008_en.pdf.

[255] See UK FSA Policy Statement 09/3, 'Disclosure of Contracts for Difference', March 2009, available at http://www.fsa.gov.uk/pubs/policy/ps09_03.pdf.

[256] Ibid.

[257] *CSX Corp. v Children's Inv. Fund Management (UK) LLP*, 2008 WL 2372693 (SDNY 2008).

[258] See Testimony Concerning Regulation of Over-The-Counter Derivatives by Chairman Mary L. Schapiro, US SEC before the Subcommittee on Securities, Insurance, and Investment Committee on Banking, Housing and Urban Affairs, United States Senate, 22 June 2009, available at http://www.sec.gov/news/testimony/2009/ts062209mls.htm.

makers (subject to satisfaction of certain conditions) and certain shares held in the trading book of a credit institution or investment firm.[259]

7.241 **7.4.1.10.6 Notification of issuer acquisitions and dispositions** An issuer of shares admitted to trading on a regulated market is also required to disclose acquisitions and dispositions of its own shares, either on its own or through a person acting on its behalf, when the amount of shares acquired or disposed of exceeds 5% or 10% of the issuer's total voting rights.[260] Such disclosure is required to be made within four trading days of the acquisition or disposition.[261] Non-EU issuers should keep in mind this potential additional disclosure requirement in connection with significant buy-back programmes (such as an accelerated share repurchase programme) or a significant offering of shares (including treasury shares).

7.4.1.11 Liability

7.242 Article 7 of the Transparency Directive requires that the issuer or the management, supervisory or administrative boards of an issuer take liability for the information included in a periodic report under the Transparency Directive.[262] In the transposition of the Transparency Directive by member states, most member states have imposed liability only on the issuer for periodic reporting, although certain member states have imposed liability on either or both the issuer's management and administrative board.[263]

7.243 In light of the existence of liability for errors and omissions in periodic reporting, issuers should establish some type of due diligence or verification mechanism for periodic reports. Possible approaches could include meetings with the relevant members of management to review the filings and focusing in particular on any potentially sensitive disclosures. Internal certificate 'roll-up' procedures could also be used by senior management to get comfort on the accuracy of disclosures contained in periodic reports. Issuers that file periodic reports with the US SEC would very likely already have a verification regime in place. Such issuers should consider whether any modifications to that verification regime would be appropriate.

7.4.2 Article 10 of the Prospectus Directive

7.244 Article 10 of the Prospectus Directive requires each issuer whose securities are admitted to trading on a regulated market to file at least annually with its home

---

[259] Transparency Directive Article 9.4–9.6.
[260] Transparency Directive Article 14.1.
[261] Ibid.
[262] Transparency Directive Article 7.
[263] The responses to questions 115–118 in Annex II of the CESR TD Transposition Study include details on the persons responsible for periodic reports in a number of member states.

member state a document that contains or refers to all information that the issuer has published or made available to the public over the preceding 12 months in any member state *or any other country* in compliance with applicable law.[264] This requirement does not apply to an issuer whose only securities admitted to trading on a regulated market are wholesale debt securities. Issuers are required to file this information with the competent authority of their home member state after the publication of their financial statements. Article 27.3 of the Prospectus Regulation requires the annual update document to contain a statement that some of the information contained or referred to in the document is out of date.

In practice, issuers can comply with this requirement by simply filing a list of all such announcements and filings. **7.245**

This continuing disclosure requirement overlaps with the obligations imposed by the Transparency Directive and overlaps with the requirements thereunder. This annual disclosure requirement was expected to be superseded by the continuing reporting obligations contained in the Transparency Directive but in fact has not been eliminated. The European Commission has proposed that Article 10 of the Prospectus Directive be eliminated entirely, although that has not yet occurred.[265] **7.246**

7.4.3 Market Abuse Directive

7.4.3.1 Overview

By its terms, the Market Abuse Directive applies to any issuer that has securities admitted to trading on a regulated market, whether the conduct occurs within or without the EEA.[266] Whether a particular competent authority will in fact seek to apply this directive to conduct entirely outside its borders but related to a security admitted to trading on a regulated market within its borders will likely depend on the general legal principles of the member state on the requisite nexus between the conduct and such member state. Although it remains to be seen whether in fact competent authorities will in fact take steps to enforce the Market Abuse Directive extraterritorially, issuers with securities admitted to trading on a regulated market in a member state need to consider the possibility of issues arising under the Market Abuse Directive. These concerns become more significant as the proportion of the worldwide trading in the issuer's securities that occurs in the EEA increases (e.g. if the principal trading market for an issuer's shares is in the EEA and there is only limited trading in the issuer's home market). An enhanced presence in the EEA in terms of employees and assets also seems likely **7.247**

---

[264] Prospectus Directive Article 10.
[265] Section 5.3.9 of the explanatory memorandum included in the PD Review Proposal.
[266] Market Abuse Directive Article 10.

to increase the possibility of enforcement action, even if the conduct occurred entirely outside the EEA.

7.248 As a technical matter, the Market Abuse Directive does not apply to issuers that only have securities admitted to trading on exchange-regulated markets. Nevertheless, such issuers may in fact be made subject to similar or equivalent market abuse rules by the rules of the exchange-regulated market to which their securities are admitted to trading or by the laws of the jurisdiction in which such exchange-regulated market is located. For example, the United Kingdom enacted super-equivalent provisions in transposing the Market Abuse Directive to make it applicable to AIM.[267]

7.4.3.2 *Ad hoc disclosures*

7.249 The Market Abuse Directive requires an issuer with any type of securities admitted to trading on a regulated market to disclose publicly 'inside information'[268] as soon as possible,[269] subject to a limited exception permitting issuers to delay disclosure of such information so long as the delay is not likely to mislead the public and the issuer can maintain the information in confidence.[270] The reporting requirement under the Market Abuse Directive is continuous and imposes an exacting timeframe for disclosure (as soon as possible).

7.250 **7.4.3.2.1 Definition of inside information** An initial question an issuer will face is what constitutes 'information of a precise nature'. Despite efforts to provide clarity on how this concept should be applied in practice, it will inevitably require an issuer and its counsel to make judgments about when information is sufficiently precise (much as the determination of 'materiality' of information under the US securities laws requires judgments to be made).

7.251 CESR has provided guidance on this issue along the lines set forth below that may be helpful in determining how the competent authorities evaluate this determination:

---

[267] See Section 10 of the Statutory Instrument 2005 No 381, The Financial Services and Markets Act 2000 (Market Abuse) Regulations 2005, available at http://www.hm-treasury.gov.uk/d/MAD_regs240205.pdf.

[268] 'Inside information' is defined for the purposes of an issuer of securities as 'information of a precise nature which has not been made public, relating, directly or indirectly, to one or more issuers of financial instruments or to one or more financial instruments and which, if it were made public, would be likely to have a significant effect on the prices of those financial instruments or on the price of related derivative financial instruments'. Market Abuse Directive Article 1.1. There is also language in the Market Abuse Directive defining 'inside information' with respect to commodity derivatives and with respect to intermediaries charged with executing orders that are not addressed in this discussion.

[269] Market Abuse Directive Article 6.1.

[270] Market Abuse Directive Article. 6.2.

- for information concerning a process which occurs in stages, each stage and the overall process may be of a precise nature;
- information need not be comprehensive to be of a precise nature and information concerning alternative proposals may be precise;
- information that an investor would be able to assess with confidence how the information would impact the price of an issuer's securities is specific enough to enable a conclusion to be drawn about its impact on prices of the issuer's securities; and
- information that is likely to be exploited immediately following it becoming known is specific enough to enable a conclusion to be drawn about its impact on prices of the issuer's securities.[271]

The next question an issuer will need to consider is whether the information would be likely to have a 'significant price effect'. In considering this element of the definition of inside information, an issuer would need to consider how similar pieces of information have in the past had a significant impact on the price of the issuer's securities. Issuers also should not rely on a fixed threshold or quantitative criteria alone in determining whether the anticipated impact of a piece of information on the price of the issuer's securities is likely to be significant.[272]   **7.252**

7.4.3.2.2 Delay of disclosure   The Market Abuse Directive permits an issuer to delay disclosure of inside information, at its own risk, in order not to prejudice its legitimate interests and provided that the delay is not likely to mislead the public[273] and the issuer can ensure confidentiality of the information.[274]   **7.253**

An issuer's legitimate interests may justify delaying disclosure in the types of circumstances in the following non-exhaustive list:[275]   **7.254**

- negotiations in process where the outcome or normal process of those negotiations would be likely to be affected by disclosure;
- decisions taken or contracts approved that are subject to further internal approvals if the disclosure of that information prior to approval would jeopardize the correct assessment of the information by the public;
- confidentiality agreements in a competitive situation;

---

[271] Market Abuse Directive Level 3 Sections 1.6–1.8 — second set of CESR guidance and information on the common operation of the Market Abuse Directive to the market, July 2007 (the 'Second CESR MAD Guidance').

[272] Second CESR MAD Guidance Sections 1.13–1.14.

[273] CESR has stated in guidance that it does not agree with the argument that any delay in disclosure is likely to mislead the public. Second CESR MAD Guidance Section 2.12.

[274] Market Abuse Directive Article 6.2.

[275] Note that Section 2.2.2.1 of the MAD Review Call for Evidence notes that the conditions under which disclosure of inside information may be delayed may be revisited, in particular with respect to a situation in which the financial viability of the issuer is at risk.

- product development, patents and inventions where the issuer needs to protect its rights, except that significant events on major product developments (such as clinical trials) should be disclosed; and
- impending developments that could be jeopardized by premature disclosure.[276]

7.255 There is some divergence among member states in their approach to the question of whether an issuer that elects to delay disclosure of inside information in reliance on this provision of the Market Abuse Directive is required to disclose to the competent authority the fact that it has elected to delay disclosure. A limited number of member states have gone further and required that an issuer that elects to delay disclosure must disclose to the competent authority the basis on which it has concluded delay of disclosure is warranted.[277] Even if disclosure is not required, an issuer that elects to delay disclosure should consider recording the rationale for deciding to delay disclosure.

7.256 An issuer that elects to delay disclosure of inside information should implement procedures to ensure that the information disclosure of which has been delayed is restricted to individuals that need to know the information and should be prepared to issue a statement in the event a leak is discovered.

7.257 7.4.3.2.3 **Required method of disclosure** An issuer that concludes that it has inside information that it is required to disclose under the Market Abuse Directive is required to disclose that information as 'regulated information' under the Transparency Directive. See Section 7.4.1.8 above for discussion of the Transparency Directive disclosure mechanisms.

7.258 7.4.3.2.4 **Practical implications** In the normal course of events, the obligation to disclose price-sensitive information as soon as it becomes precise may not be of much practical significance for the typical issuer. Issuers typically make periodic disclosure of their earnings and financial position. Assuming these disclosures are made in a timely manner, then likely the only practical consequence of the Market Abuse Directive would be a requirement to ensure that the information is appropriately disclosed as regulated information under the Transparency Directive.

7.259 Issuers are likely to face trickier questions under the Market Abuse Directive when there are non-routine corporate events that give rise to material non-public information, such as merger and acquisition discussions. In these situations, the

---

[276] Commission Directive 2003/124/EC of 22 December 2003 implementing Directive 2003/6/EC of the European Parliament and of the Council as regards the definition and public disclosure of inside information and the definition of market manipulation [2003] OJ L 339/70; Second CESR MAD Guidance Sections 2.8–2.9.

[277] Section 7 of the 'Report on CESR Members' Powers Under the Market Abuse Directive and its Implementing Measures', June 2007, available at http://www.cesr.eu/index.php?docid=4671.

Market Abuse Directive reporting obligations may be more stringent than home country requirements and could impose a shorter period for public disclosure. Non-EU issuers should evaluate carefully the extent to which the disclosure requirements under the Market Abuse Directive may require more and quicker disclosure than under home country law and ensure that they implement disclosure controls and procedures to ensure compliance.

For example, a US domestic issuer would only be required by the US Exchange Act **7.260** to disclose publicly material non-public information if (a) it is subject to a specific reporting requirement (e.g. it is filing a periodic report or the information relates to an event that specifically requires a Current Report on Form 8-K), (b) it is choosing to disclose such information and is required to make public disclosure to avoid concerns under Regulation FD[278] with respect to selective disclosure of the information or (c) it is engaged in an activity that gives rise to an affirmative duty to disclose (e.g. a buy-back or securities offering). A further issue for a US domestic issuer would be the timing of disclosure—the Market Abuse Directive contemplates immediate disclosure while the deadline for filing a Current Report on Form 8-K is most typically four business days. In order to avoid the odd situation of disclosure of material information in the EEA preceding disclosure in the home country, an issuer would need to accelerate the timing of its disclosure in the United States.

7.4.3.3 *Rumours*

The question of what issuers are required to do under the Market Abuse Directive **7.261** in response to market rumours arises naturally out of the broad obligation imposed on issuers to disclose price-sensitive information as soon as possible. Issuers generally are not required to respond to speculation or market rumours which are without substance and can implement a policy of not commenting on market rumours with respect to false rumours.[279] This applies to rumours contained in publications as well as rumours spread by word of mouth through market participants.

However, a more thorny question arises in connection with rumours that are **7.262** accurate in that they may be evidence of a leak. CESR has stated its view that if a publication or rumour relates explicitly to a piece of information that is inside information within the issuer, the issuer is 'expected' to respond to the publication or rumour as the information is sufficiently precise to indicate a leak and indicate that confidentiality can no longer be maintained.[280] In this situation, an issuer

---

[278] Regulation FD under the US Exchange Act, 17 CFR §§ 243.100, et seq. Regulation FD generally prohibits selective disclosure of material non-public information, subject to certain exceptions.

[279] Third CESR MAD Guidance Paragraphs 65 and 67.

[280] Third CESR MAD Guidance Paragraph 69.

following a 'no comment' policy would not be acceptable—the issuer would be required to disclose the inside information.

7.263　If this approach is adopted by the competent authorities in the EEA, then this view could expose issuers to 'fishing' expeditions by market participants in an effort to prompt a confirmation. Non-EU issuers with securities listed on a regulated market need to consider carefully their approach to responding to rumours in light of this view, if it is adopted, as it may well contrast with practice in their home country. This would certainly be the case for US domestic issuers, where it is typical practice to apply a consistent 'no comment' policy with respect to market rumours and speculation, unless there are facts indicating that the company is sufficiently entangled with a leak.[281]

7.264　A non-EU issuer for whom the Market Abuse Directive imposes requirements with respect to rumours different to those in its home jurisdiction will need to consider carefully in light of the specific facts and circumstances how to proceed. It is likely to be a difficult conclusion to reach that a non-EU issuer that only has a secondary listing of its shares on a regulated market in which there is limited trading is in fact required to disclose information about confidential negotiations in response to an accurate rumour with respect to those negotiations when the issuer's home country law would not require such disclosure.

7.4.3.4 Selective disclosure

7.265　The Market Abuse Directive prohibits selective disclosure of inside information by issuers to third parties, subject to an exception for disclosures to parties bound by a duty of confidentiality based on law, regulation, articles of association or a contract.[282] There is also a similar prohibition on selective disclosure by persons acting on behalf of the issuer, unless the disclosure is in the normal exercise of such person's employment, professions or duties and there is complete and effective public disclosure of the information (which is required to be simultaneous if the disclosure is intentional and prompt if it is unintentional).[283]

7.266　In general, the prohibitions on selective disclosure are consistent with the require-ments applicable to US issuers subject to Regulation FD.

---

[281] In the US market, many issuers adhere to a strict 'no comment' policy, even in the face of accurate rumours on the basis that the issuer has no general affirmative duty to disclose material non-public information. The listing standards of both the New York Stock Exchange and the Nasdaq technically impose an obligation on issuers listed thereon to make affirmative disclosure in response to rumours, but the consequence of violation of those listing standards is delisting.

[282] Market Abuse Directive Article 6.3.

[283] Ibid.

7.4.3.5 Share buy-back programmes

The Market Abuse Directive creates a safe harbour for repurchases by issuers of their shares[284] without the need for concern that their purchases constitute market abuse. This safe harbour is subject to a number of conditions and requirements. The safe harbour is non-exclusive, and transactions by an issuer outside the safe harbour should not in themselves be deemed to constitute market abuse.[285]

7.267

Non-EU issuers that have only a secondary listing of their shares in the EEA will need to evaluate the extent to which the requirements of the safe harbour are consistent with home country requirements and, to the extent the safe harbour requirements are more onerous, whether compliance with the safe harbour with respect to purchases outside the EEA is warranted in light of the facts and circumstances. Those facts and circumstances would include the likelihood that the buy-backs would impact the price of the issuer's shares on a regulated market in the EEA and the number of shares held by persons in the EEA (and, therefore, the likelihood of sales into the buy-back programme).

7.268

This safe harbour is only available to buy-backs conducted to reduce the capital of the issuer or to obtain shares to satisfy the issuer's obligation to deliver shares (a) upon conversion or exchange of debt instruments convertible or exchangeable into the issuer's shares or (b) under employee stock options or other employee equity compensation arrangements of the issuer or an associated company.[286] Although these are common reasons an issuer may establish a buy-back programme, non-EU issuers may not be subject to limitations of this type under home country law and, therefore, the safe harbour may be unavailable to them. An issuer relying on the safe harbour is also required to comply with certain maximum price[287] and volume limitations[288] on its purchases under the programme.

7.269

---

[284] Note that the safe harbour does not expressly apply to depositary receipts, so an issuer contemplating buying depositary receipts would need to be comfortable that its actions did not otherwise constitute market abuse.

[285] Buy-Back Regulation Recital 2.

[286] Note that the competent authorities of certain member states (e.g. France) have identified as an accepted market practice a buy-back programme the purpose of which is to acquire shares to be held in treasury for the purpose of acquiring another company in the future. If the company determines in the future that the shares are no longer needed for this purpose, then it can dispose of them. CESR has a section of its website that tracks accepted market practices. See http://www.cesr-eu.org/index.php?page=contenu_groups&id=51&docmore=1#doc.

[287] The purchase price cannot be higher than the highest independent bid on the regulated market. Buy-Back Regulation Article 5.1.

[288] An issuer is not permitted to purchase more than 25% of the average daily volume of its shares in any one day on the regulated market on which the purchase is carried out. The average daily volume is calculated based on the average daily volume in the month preceding the month of public disclosure of that programme and fixed on that basis for the authorized period of the programme. Where the programme makes no reference to that volume, the average daily volume figure must be based on the average daily volume traded in the 20 trading days preceding the date of purchase.

7.270   In addition, an issuer cannot engage in any of the following activities if it wishes to benefit from the safe harbour:

- sell its own shares during the life of the programme;
- trade during a closed period under the law of the member state in which the trading occurs; or
- trade while in possession of inside information of which the issuer has elected to delay disclosure.

7.271   The above prohibitions do not apply if: (a) the issuer has in place a time-scheduled buy-back programme; or (b) the buy-back programme is lead-managed by an investment firm or a credit institution which makes its trading decisions in relation to the issuer's shares independently of, and without influence by, the issuer with regard to the timing of the purchases.

7.272   An issuer is required to make prior public disclosure of details of the buy-back programme (including the maximum amount that can be used to purchase shares under the programme, the maximum number of shares to be acquired and the time period for which the programme has been authorized).[289] Subsequent changes to the programme must be subject to adequate public disclosure in member states.

7.273   In addition to up-front disclosure of the programme, an issuer is required to disclose purchases under the buy-back programme to both the competent authority of each regulated market on which the shares have been admitted to trading and the public. Public disclosure is required to be made no later than the end of the seventh trading day following the date of execution of such transactions.[290]

7.274   The obligation to make public disclosure of all purchase transactions under the buy-back programme may make the safe harbour less attractive to a non-EU issuer who is not required under home country law to make such disclosures. For example, Rule 10b-18 under the US Exchange Act does not require issuers to disclose purchases and it is not customary for issuers conducting buy-backs in the United States to make such transaction-level disclosures. Issuers that are subject to the reporting requirements of the US Exchange Act are required in their periodic reports to include certain specified disclosures with respect to share repurchases

---

Buy-Back Regulation Article 5.2. In certain situations of extreme low volume, the issuer can exceed the 25% limit provided certain conditions are met. Buy-Back Regulation Article 5.3.

[289] Buy-Back Regulation Article 4.2. The language of the Buy-Back Regulation refers to disclosure to the public in each member state in which the shares are admitted to trading on a regulated market, which has created some confusion as to exactly what is required. However, CESR has stated in paragraph 56 of the Third CESR MAD Guidance its view that it is sufficient to disclose the initial information about a buy-back programme as regulated information.

[290] With respect to disclosure of trade-specific information, CESR has stated in paragraph 56 of the Third CESR MAD Guidance that this information is not required to be disclosed as regulated information and it is sufficient to disclose the information through public press release.

during the period covered by the periodic report, although that disclosure is only required to be made quarterly (for US domestic issuers) or annually (for foreign private issuers) and then only a summary of purchases on a monthly basis during the relevant period is required to be disclosed.[291]

There is an ambiguity with respect to the mechanism by which an issuer is required **7.275** to make adequate public disclosure of inside information, which arises as a result of a technical issue resulting from the enactment of the Transparency Directive. The portion of the Buy-Back Regulation relating to the disclosure of information relating to buy-back programmes, which was adopted in December 2003, refers to portions of an earlier directive that were repealed by the Transparency Directive in December 2004. In an effort to address this ambiguity and provide clarity to market participants, CESR has clarified in guidance that disclosure of information through the Transparency Directive mechanism would be sufficient.[292]

7.4.3.6 Debt buy-backs

As noted above, the regulatory safe harbour does not apply to buy-backs by issuers **7.276** of their debt and issuers are required to analyse the permissibility of these buy-backs under general principles relating to market manipulation. The Market Abuse Directive does not create hard and fast rules from which issuers can draw comfort with respect to transactions of this type. However, market practice for issuer buy-backs of high yield debt in the EEA has tended to follow US practice applicable to self-tenders for debt.

7.4.3.7 Notification of managers' transactions

Under the Market Abuse Directive, 'persons discharging managerial responsibility'[293] **7.277** ('PDMRs') of an issuer and persons 'closely associated'[294] with PDMRs are required

---

[291] See Item 703 of Regulation S-K under the US Securities Act and US Exchange Act, 17 CFR § 229.703 and item 16E of Form 20-F under the US Exchange Act.

[292] Third CESR MAD Guidance Paragraphs 54–56.

[293] This concept is defined in Article 1.1 of Commission Directive of 29 April 2004 implementing Directive 2003/6/EC of the European Parliament and of the Council as regards accepted market practices, the definition of inside information in relation to derivatives on commodities, the drawing up of lists of insiders, the notification of managers' transactions and the notification of suspicious transactions [2004] OJ L 162/70 (the '2004 MAD Implementation Directive'). The concept of a PDMR generally covers members of the board of directors (including management and supervisory boards) and senior executives that have regular access to inside information and having the power to make managerial decisions affecting the future development and business prospects of an issuer.

[294] This concept is defined in Article 1.2 of the 2004 MAD Implementation Directive and generally covers spouses, partners equivalent to spouses, dependent children, relatives living in the same household and entities controlled by or for the benefit of a person discharging managerial responsibilities.

to notify the competent authority of the issuer's home member state for purposes of equity securities and low-denomination non-equity securities under the Prospectus Directive of transactions for their own account in the issuer's shares and financial instruments linked to them. These notifications are required to be made available to the public. The Market Abuse Directive also gives member states the ability to implement a *de minimis* exclusion (or a delayed reporting obligation) for the first EUR 5,000 of transactions in a fiscal year by PDMRs and persons closely associated with that PDMR.[295]

7.278   In concept, this regime is similar to reporting under section 16 of the US Exchange Act, although the scope of persons covered is not identical. Unlike section 16 of the US Exchange Act, the Market Abuse Directive does not contain a short-swing profit recovery mechanism that makes profits resulting from short-term trading recoverable by the issuer as being the product of the misuse of inside information. Instead, the notifications serve as a more general reporting mechanism designed to assist competent authorities in policing management profiting from inside information. Unlike section 16, a competent authority would be required to prove misuse of inside information in violation of the Market Abuse Directive.

7.279   For issuers that are subject to section 16 reporting obligations, complying with these obligations should simply be a matter of modifying the existing system for notification of transactions in the issuer's securities under section 16 as needed to cover the relevant individuals. However, since relatively few non-US issuers are in fact subject to section 16 of the US Exchange Act, compliance with these notification obligations may require creation of an entirely new system unless home country law already imposes reporting obligations similar to Section 16.

7.280   Issuers should be aware that there is some variation in reporting deadlines for transactions by PDMRs among member states. The most typical deadline for filing notifications of such transactions is five trading days.[296]

7.4.3.8 Insider trading

7.281   **7.4.3.8.1 Legal standard for insider trading**   Non-EU issuers should be aware of the fact that the Market Abuse Directive imposes a stricter standard on trading on inside information than is currently the law in the United States. Under the Market Abuse Directive, it is market abuse for a person to trade on information that the person knows or ought to have known constitutes inside information.

---

[295]   MAD Implementation Directive 2004 Article 6.2. Note that the language in the 2004 MAD Implementation Directive is ambiguous as to whether the EUR 5,000 threshold was for all PDMRs of an issuer or for each PDMR. Although the latter interpretation would be more practical, issuers should confirm how the ambiguity has been addressed in the relevant member state(s).

[296]   'Report on CESR Members' Powers Under the Market Abuse Directive and its Implementing Measures', June 2007, Section 9, available at http://www.cesr-eu.org/popup2.php?id=4671.

Unlike in the United States, the prohibition on trading on insider information under the Market Abuse Directive does not require a breach of a duty.

In light of the difference in legal standards, non-EU issuers subject to the Market Abuse Directive should review their insider trading policies to ensure that they appropriately reflect the difference in standards. **7.282**

7.4.3.8.2 Insider lists The Market Abuse Directive requires issuers to maintain **7.283** a list of all persons working for them that have access to 'inside information relating, directly or indirectly, to the issuer, whether on a regular or occasional basis'.[297] This requirement applies by its terms to persons worldwide and not just to persons located in the EEA. The issuer is required to produce its insider list upon request to the competent authority in any member state in which it has securities admitted to trading on a regulated market.[298]

This requirement to maintain lists of persons with access to material non-public **7.284** information extends to persons outside the issuer, such as legal and financial advisers, consultants and public relations and investor relations firms. Third-party service providers will need to work with an issuer to coordinate the preparation and maintenance of insider lists for the service provider.

Insider lists are required to contain a substantial amount of detail (although the **7.285** amount of detail varies among member states), including information about why each person has access to inside information and the date the list was created or updated. The issuer is required to obtain from each person included on an insider list an acknowledgement of the legal and regulatory duties entailed by being given access to inside information and the sanctions for the misuse of such information.[299]

Given the breadth of the universe of persons that may potentially need to **7.286** be included on an insider list, non-EU issuers and their outside advisers who have access to inside information need to consider carefully whether they have an appropriate mechanism for capturing this information. Although these lists may be maintained as a matter of practice in the home country, there may not be a specific home country requirement to maintain these lists (as there is not in the United States). In that situation, they are unlikely to be as far-reaching as those required under the Market Abuse Directive. Non-EU issuers in evaluating their

---

[297] Market Abuse Directive Article 6.3.

[298] Issuers with securities admitted to trading on regulated markets in multiple member states have to comply with the insider list requirements in each member state in which they have securities admitted to trading on a regulated market. It is possible that the burden of complying with differing insider list requirements in different member states will be eliminated in the future. See Section 2.2.4.1 of the MAD Review Call for Evidence.

[299] MAD Implementation Directive 2004 Article 5.5.

mechanisms also need to ensure that they update these lists on an ongoing basis[300] and appropriately maintain records of the lists.[301]

7.4.3.9 *Short sales*

7.287   The events of the autumn of 2008 prompted numerous jurisdictions, including various member states, to impose limits on the ability to sell short securities of certain issuers.[302] Within the EEA, these measures were implemented in an uncoordinated manner and have prompted questions as to whether short-selling should be addressed across all member states and whether those limits should be addressed through amendments to the Market Abuse Directive.[303] This is an area that seems highly likely to be subject to further evolution in the near future at the level of member states, if not through EEA-wide regulation.

---

[300] Issuers are required to update these lists 'promptly' to reflect changes, additions and deletions. MAD Implementation Directive Article 5.3.

[301] Issuers are required to retain these lists for five years. MAD Implementation Directive 2004 Article 5.4.

[302] CESR has compiled a list of the measures adopted by various member states. See 'Measures adopted by CESR Members on short selling', 22 September 2008, updated 1 July 2009, available at http://www.cesr-eu.org/popup2.php?id=5238.

[303] MAD Review Call for Evidence Section 2.3.4.

PART 3

MEMBER STATE REGULATION

8

AUSTRIA

8.1 Listing Securities in Austria

8.1.1 The capital market in Austria

The Austrian capital markets are located principally in Austria's capital city, **8.01** Vienna, which also plays host to Austria's only stock exchange, the Vienna Stock Exchange (the 'VSE').

The Austrian market is dominated by domestic players from various sectors, such **8.02** as banking, insurance and heavy industry. Compared to the international capital markets and stock exchanges of, say, the United States and the United Kingdom, the Austrian market is small and therefore is unlikely to be the preferred place for primary listings of international companies. Despite this, the Austrian Trade Index—the index of the most actively-traded and highest capitalized securities on the VSE (see Section 8.1.3.1.1)—outperformed many of the international indices in respect of growth of stock prices during 2007 and the first half of 2008. A key factor behind this growth was the success of Austrian companies making significant investments in the Central Eastern European countries, particularly within the new member states of the EU, such as Bulgaria, Romania, Hungary, Slovakia, Czech Republic and Poland.[1] During the second half of 2008, however, the onset of global financial crisis contributed to a marked slump in activity on the Austrian market, a trend that was seen in many other jurisdictions.

8.03   The regulation of the Austrian market, as in all other EU jurisdictions, is based on the key EU directives: the Prospectus Directive, the Transparency Directive, the Market Abuse Directive, the Takeover Directive[2] and MiFID, which are described in detail in Part 1. Austria's competent authority for the supervision of financial institutions and markets is the Austrian Financial Market Authority (the 'FMA').

8.1.2 The Austrian Financial Market Authority

8.04   The FMA is responsible for the supervision of credit institutions, insurance undertakings, pension funds, employee provision funds, investment funds, investment service providers, companies listed on the Vienna Stock Exchange, as well as stock exchanges themselves. Its responsibilities also include, *inter alia*, the supervision of public offers of securities, the approval of prospectuses and monitoring listed companies' compliance with rules and continuing obligations in connection with their listings.[3]

8.05   The FMA is organized as an independent, autonomous and integrated supervisory body. It is empowered to impose penalties on parties in breach of any of the relevant rules. The FMA also has the power to issue binding regulations regarding specific aspects of Austrian securities and capital markets law and has laid down a range of detailed provisions that supplement general statutory provisions.[4] As an official authority in Austria, the FMA is obliged to cooperate with other official authorities, both in Austria and in other jurisdictions, for instance, with respect to criminal proceedings against foreign issuers or Austrian companies listed abroad.

8.06   The FMA regularly engages with listed companies and capital markets legal practitioners to conduct preliminary and informal discussions and to exchange information outside the scope of formal proceedings. For instance, it is a well established practice for companies planning to list in Austria to inform the FMA of their intention to file a prospectus for approval sufficiently well in advance of doing so, in order to allow the FMA to allocate its resources appropriately and

---

[1] Especially listed stock corporations such as Erste Group Bank AG, Raiffeisen International Bank-Holding AG and WIENDER STÄDTISCHE Versicherung AG Vienna Insurance Group extraordinarily grew by increasing their investments in CEE countries.

[2] Directive 2004/25/EC of the European Parliament and of the Council of 21 April 2004 on takeover bids, [2004] OJ L 142/12.

[3] For details see Section 8.3 below.

[4] For details see Section 8.1.4.3 below.

thus to attain approval quickly.[5] The FMA can then provide guidance to the prospective issuer on its proposed transaction. Accordingly, maintaining a good working relationship with the FMA can prove to be an important factor in a successful offering and listing in Vienna.

8.1.3 The Vienna Stock Exchange

The VSE is the only stock exchange in Austria. It is also the only general **8.07** commodities exchange in Austria.[6] The VSE is operated by the Wiener Börse AG, an Austrian stock corporation organized under private law and owned by more than 55 shareholders, the majority of which are Austrian banks and industrial companies.[7] In December 2004, the US Securities and Exchange Commission granted the VSE the status of a 'Designated Offshore Securities Market' in accordance with the US Securities Act.

The VSE's responsibilities and competencies are regulated by the Austrian Stock **8.08** Exchange Act ('SEA')[8] which, *inter alia*, provides for the scope of VSE's regulatory licence, trading supervision, trading rules, and the different types of trading systems.[9]

The VSE is supervised by the FMA, specifically through the Exchange **8.09** Commissioner appointed by the Federal Ministry of Finance, and the Federal Ministry of Economics and Labour. The VSE is not equipped with regulatory powers and its role is limited to ensuring the execution of exchange trading and acting as intermediary for market participants by operating trading systems.

The SEA provides for two types of admission to the VSE: the first tier market **8.10** ('official market' —*Amtlicher Handel*) and the second tier market ('semi-official market' —*Geregelter Freiverkehr*).[10] These markets are separated into a number of trading segments, which are discussed below at Section 8.1.3.1. Both the official market and the semi-official market of the VSE have been recognized as regulated markets under MiFID.

To obtain and maintain a listing on the VSE, companies must fulfil certain listing **8.11** criteria set out in the SEA. In the prime market trading segment of the VSE

---

[5] For details on this slot system established by the FMA see Section 8.2.3.1 below.
[6] There are only specific commodity exchanges for agricultural products in Vienna, Graz and Linz-Wels.
[7] For details see http://www.wienerborse.at/about/shareholders.
[8] Stock Exchange Act—Bundesgesetz vom 8 November 1989 über die Wertpapier- und allgemeinen Warenbörsen und über die Abänderung des Börsesensale-Gesetzes 1949 und der Börsegesetz-Novelle 1903 (Börsegesetz 1989—BörseG); BGBl. I Nr. 555/1989 of 29 November 1989, as amended.
[9] For a synopsis of the SEA see Section 8.1.4.1 below.
[10] For details see Section 8.1.5.1 below.

(defined below), companies must also satisfy certain additional non-statutory criteria set out by the VSE. Securities that meet the relevant criteria are admitted to trading on the VSE and included in the appropriate trading segment.[11]

8.12 In addition to the official market and semi-official market (both regulated markets), Wiener Börse AG operates an unregulated third market ('unregulated third market') in the form of a multilateral trading facility (an 'MTF') within the meaning of the Securities Supervision Act ('SSA')[12]. Wiener Börse AG is permitted to operate the unregulated third market on the basis of a special FMA approval, and the VSE has set its own set of FMA-approved rules for market participants. Certain provisions set out in the SEA are also applicable to the unregulated third market such as the statutory offence of 'misuse of insider information' and the administrative offence of 'market manipulation'.

8.1.3.1 Vienna Stock Exchange market segmentation

8.13 Securities admitted to listing on the VSE are traded in various trading segments. In order to be traded in a specific segment, an issuer and its securities must meet the applicable statutory listing criteria, as well as certain non-statutory criteria (*inter alia* additional market rules issued by the VSE). The equity market (official and semi-official market) is divided into the following four segments: 'prime market', 'mid market', 'standard market continuous' and 'standard market auction'. The VSE has issued a number of market rules relating to these specific market segments, with which issuers must comply in connection with their listings.

8.14 **8.1.3.1.1 The prime market** The prime market represents the highest-ranking market segment of the VSE and is comprised of shares that are admitted to listing on the official market or the semi-official market. Companies admitted to the prime market are required to fulfil not only the eligibility and continuing obligations regime prescribed under the SEA,[13] but also a range of more stringent admission and disclosure requirements, which are set out in the prime market Rules.[14]

---

[11] For details see Section 8.1.3.1 below.

[12] Securities Supervision Act—Bundesgesetz, mit dem ein Bundesgesetz über die Beaufsichtigung von Wertpapierdienstleistungen (Wertpapieraufsichtsgesetz 2007—WAG 2007) erlassen wird sowie das Bankwesengesetz, das Börsegesetz 1989, das Investmentfondsgesetz, das Kapitalmarktgesetz, das Finanzmarktaufsichtsbehördengesetz, das Konsumentenschutzgesetz und die Gewerbeordnung 1994 geändert werden; BGBl. I Nr. 60/2007 of 31 July 2007, as amended.

[13] For details about the eligibility for the official and semi-official market see Section 8.1.5.1 below. For details about the continuing obligations for the official and semi-official market see Section 8.3 below.

[14] Prime market Rules—Regelwerk Prime Market 2008, http://www.wienerborse.at/static/cms/sites/wbag/media/de/pdf/marketplace_products/regelwerk_primemarket.pdf

For example, all issuers listed on the prime market must comply with the Austrian **8.15**
Code of Corporate Governance.[15] To verify this, each issuer must include a
declaration of commitment on compliance with the Austrian Code of Corporate
Governance (including explanations as to any deviations) in its annual report
pertaining to fiscal years beginning after 31 December 2008. The annual report
must be published on the issuer's website.

As of August 2009, the prime market comprised the shares of 50 issuers, of **8.16**
which 20 companies are included in the Austrian Traded Index ('ATX')[16]. The
ATX consists of the most actively-traded (most liquid) and the highest-capitalized
securities in the prime market. The ATX is calculated, disseminated and licensed
by the VSE on a real-time basis. The composition of the ATX is reviewed every
year in March and September. With every review, no more than three stocks
may be changed in the composition of the ATX. The *ATX Prime* comprises the
securities of all companies presently listed on the prime market segment.[17]

To provide additional liquidity, securities traded in the prime market segment **8.17**
must be serviced by a specialist trader, which has agreed on a permanent basis to
enter firm quotes into XETRA, the electronic trading system used by the VSE.
Additional liquidity providers other than the designated specialists are permitted
to act as market makers in securities already serviced by at least one specialist. The
market makers' commitments must meet certain minimum requirements set up
by the VSE.[18]

**Overview of transparency and disclosure obligations applicable to prime market
listings[19]**

Requirements	
Admission	Official market or semi-official market
Stock category	Ordinary shares
Free float of stocks	Free float higher than 25% and at least EUR 20m or free float below 25% and over EUR 40m

---

[15] Austrian Code of Corporate Governance as amended in January 2009; http://
www.wienerborse.at/corporate/pdf/CG_Code_engl_2009draft_tr_fin.pdf. For further discussion
see Section 8.3.6 below.

[16] For details of the ATX see http://www.indices.cc/indices/details/atx

[17] For details of the ATX Prime see http://www.indices.cc/indices/details/atpx/. In June 2009,
the VSE launched a new index, the ATX Fundamental, which comprises the companies included
in the ATX and is weighted according to certain fundamental ratios: http://en.indices.cc/indices/
news/atxfnd_launch_090616.html

[18] For details of the obligations of market makers see www.wienerborse.at/members/marketmaker/

[19] Slightly adjusted table from VSE homepage http://en.wienerborse.at/listing/aktien/
zulassung/index.html

Overview of transparency and disclosure obligations applicable to prime market listings *(Continued)*

Requirements	
Publication of financial statements	At the latest, four months after the end of the reporting period pursuant to the Prime Market Rules
Publication of interim reports	At the latest, two months after the end of the reporting period pursuant to the Prime Market Rules
Ad hoc disclosure	Link to an electronic system (ad hoc disclosure)
Corporate events calendar	Mandatory publication at the beginning of the financial year (German and English)
Language	German and English
Austrian Code of Corporate Governance	Inclusion of the declaration of commitment on compliance with the Austrian Code of Corporate Governance in the annual report

8.18   **8.1.3.1.2 The mid market**   The mid market segment comprises companies that are admitted to listing on the official market or semi-official market and that do not meet all listing criteria required for trading in the prime market. Mid market segment companies are required to meet certain non-statutory listing criteria as well as the applicable rules under the SEA and the Mid Market Rules.[20]

8.19   A notable requirement in connection with mid market segment listings is the requirement that issuers must appoint a capital market coach ('CMC'), whose function is to advise the issuer on its compliance with all duties and obligations imposed by the relevant rules.

8.20   Shares listed on the mid market are traded only once per day. For market making purposes, a market maker must be engaged by the issuer to assume the obligation to enter binding buy and sell prices during the trading phase as nostro orders and to conclude trades in such orders.

8.21   The transparency and disclosure obligations applicable to issuers of shares traded in the mid market segment differ depending on whether the shares are admitted to the official market, semi-official market or the unregulated third market.

---

[20] Mid market Rules—Regelwerk Mid Market http://www.wienerborse.at/static/cms/sites/wbag/media/de/pdf/marketplace_products/regelwerk_midmarket.pdf

Overview of transparency and disclosure obligations applicable to mid market listings[21]

Requirements		
Admission to listing or inclusion in trading	Official market/semi-official market	Third market as an MTF (inclusion)
Share category	Ordinary shares	Ordinary shares
Period of existence	Minimum of three years/ minimum of one year	One year
Accounting standards	IFRS	National accounting standards or IFRS
Publication of annual financial statements (audited)	At the latest, four months after the end of the reporting period pursuant to Article 82, paragraph 8 Stock Exchange Act, accounting according to IFRS (for consolidated statements)	Publication within five months after the end of the reporting period
Publication of half-year financial statements	At the latest, two months after the end of the reporting period pursuant to Article 82, paragraph 8 Stock Exchange Act, accounting according to IFRS (for consolidated statements)	Publication within three months after the end of the first half-year
Publication of interim reports or quarterly reports for 1Q and 3Q	Interim reports: at the latest six weeks after the end of the reporting period pursuant to Article 82, paragraph 8 Stock Exchange Act or optionally quarterly reports: at the latest two months after the end of the reporting period according to IFRS (for consolidated statements)	No
Ad hoc disclosure	Yes, written advance notification to Wiener Börse and FMA and disclosure pursuant to Article 82, paragraph 8 Stock Exchange Act	Publication of price-sensitive company information
Corporate events calendar	Yes	Yes
Language	German or the language accepted in the respective host member state or is commonly used in international financial circles[22]	German or English
Annual information talk with CMC	Yes	Yes

---

[21] Slightly adjusted table from VSE homepage http://en.wienerborse.at/listing/aktien/zulas-sung/index.html

[22] SEA Article 85 regulates the acceptable language, among others as follows: (i) if the securities have been admitted to trading only on a regulated market in Austria as home member state, then the prescribed information must be published in German; (ii) if the securities have been admitted to listing on a regulated market in Austria as home member state as well as on a regulated market in one or several host member states, then the regulated information shall be published in (x) German and (y) depending on the choice of the issuer either in a language accepted by the competent body in the concerned host member state or in a language that is commonly used in international financial circles.

8.22   **8.1.3.1.3 The Standard Market**   The Standard Market segment consists of all companies admitted to listing on the official market or semi-official market that do not meet the criteria for the prime market or for the mid market. A standard market segment listing does not require any additional transparency or disclosure obligations beyond those set out in the SEA.

8.23   The standard market segment is divided into two segments: standard market continuous and standard market auction. Shares listed on the standard market continuous segment are traded continuously, while shares listed on the standard market auction segment are traded once a day only.

8.24   To provide additional liquidity, stocks traded in the standard market continuous segment must be serviced by a specialist trader, which has agreed on a permanent basis to enter firm quotes into XETRA. Additional market makers are permitted to provide further liquidity. The market makers' commitments must meet certain minimum requirements prescribed by the VSE.[23]

8.1.3.1.4   Market making by market segment

Overview of market making by market segment[24]

	Trading procedure	Liquidity provider
Prime market	Continuous trading (with opening auction, intra-day and closing auction)	Specialist mandatory, further market makers possible
Mid market	Single intra-day auction (market making is obligatory)	Mandatory capital market coach
Standard market continuous	Continuous trading (with opening auction, intra-day and closing auction)	Specialist mandatory, further market makers possible
Standard market auction	Single intra-day auction (market making is possible)	Liquidity providers possible for the auction
Other securities	Single intra-day auction (market making is possible)	Liquidity providers possible for the auction
	Continuous trading with an opening auction and a closing auction	Mandatory market maker

8.1.4 Legislative overview

8.25   The Austrian securities market is regulated by a number of key pieces of legislation, the most important of which are the SEA and the Capital Markets Act ('CMA'),[25]

---

[23] For details of the obligations of market makers see http://www.wienerborse.at/members/marketmaker/

[24] See VSE homepage http://en.wienerborse.at/listing/aktien/zulassung/index.html

[25] The Capital Market Act —Bundesgesetz über das öffentliche Anbieten von Wertpapieren und anderen Kapitalveranlagungen und über die Aufhebung des Wertpapier-Emissionsgesetzes (Kapitalmarktgesetz - KMG) sowie über die Abänderung des Aktiengesetzes 1965, des Genossenschaftsgesetzes, des Nationalbankgesetzes 1984, des Kreditwesengesetzes und des Versicherungsaufsichtsgesetzes; BGBl. Nr. 625/1991 of 6 December 1991, as amended.

which are supplemented and clarified by a number of regulations and circular letters issued by the FMA.[26] In addition, the Austrian Takeover Act[27] ('Takeover Act') applies in the context of takeovers of listed companies. Listed companies are also encouraged to comply with a voluntary Code of Corporate Governance.

8.1.4.1 The Stock Exchange Act

The SEA remains the principal piece of legislation through which Austria imple- **8.26**
ments the EU directives relating to listing, admission to trading on a regulated market, market abuse (including insider trading rules), and the ongoing and ad hoc disclosure obligations for the issuer and its directors and shareholders.

The SEA comprises: **8.27**

(i) provisions relating to the stock exchange, for example, the issuance of licences, the membership of the stock exchange, official brokers and dealers, surveillance of trading and trading rules;

(ii) provisions that implement parts of the Market Abuse Directive and the Transparency Directive. These provisions—which concern the disclosure of inside information, the publication of periodic financial reports, the notification of major holdings of voting rights, the dissemination of regulated information and communications with shareholders—constitute a significant part of the continuing obligations regime to which companies must adhere as long as they are admitted to the official or semi-official market; and

(iii) provisions for the processes and conditions for admission to listing of shares and other securities, including certificates (typically, Austrian depositary certificates), bonds and warranties, on the official market and semi-official market, and certain of the continuing obligations of issuers vis-à-vis the stock exchange and the public.

8.1.4.2 The Capital Market Act

The content and publication requirements in relation to prospectuses are gov- **8.28**
erned exclusively by the CMA, which implements[28] the Prospectus Directive in Austria.

---

[26] For details see Section 8.1.4.3 below.
[27] Austrian Takeover Act—Bundesgesetz betreffend Übernahmeangebote sowie über Änderungen des Börsegesetzes und des Einführungsgesetzes zu den Verwaltungsverfahrensgesetzen 1991 (Übernahmegesetz - ÜbG); BGBl. I Nr. 127/1998 of 14 August 1998, as amended.
[28] The Prospectus Directive was implemented by the federal act: Bundesgesetz, mit dem das Kapitalmarktgesetz, das Börsegesetz, das Investmentfondsgesetz, das Wertpapieraufsichtsgesetz und das Finanzmarktaufsichtsbehördengesetz geändert werden; BGBl I 78/2005 of 28 July 2005.

8.29 The CMA applies to all public offers of securities within Austria and governs exclusively the necessity, content and publication requirements of a prospectus in the event of a public offer of securities or the admission of securities to trading on a regulated market of the VSE. In addition, the CMA comprises the rules for advertisements during public offers and the special liability for the content of the prospectus for (i) the issuer; (ii) prospectus auditors or any other person whose services were used to audit the prospectus; and (iii) auditors of the annual accounts if the accounts form an integral part of the prospectus and the auditor has given an audit opinion.

8.1.4.3 FMA regulations

8.30 The FMA is subject to several laws, in particular, the SEA and the CMA. It is empowered to issue regulations, principally to specify the broader provisions contained under the SEA and the CMA. In practice, the regulations offer important guidance to issuers on how to comply with the relevant legislation in connection with their listings.

8.31 The FMA has issued regulations in the following key areas:

    (i) *Disclosure and Reporting Regulation:*[29] This regulation lays down principles as to how to structure and publish ad hoc publications and directors' dealing reports. The regulation also stipulates how issuers should publish statutorily required information.

    (ii) *The Transparency Regulation:*[30] This regulation deals with the statutory minimum content of interim reports, notification of considerable change of shareholdings, and provisions concerning the participants involved in the process. It also elaborates on the equivalency of such reports and notifications for issuers whose registered offices are located outside the EU.

    (iii) *The Issuer Compliance Regulation:*[31] This regulation sets out measures issuers must take in order to prevent disclosure or abuse of inside information, It stipulates how inside information is to be processed and transmitted internally within the issuer. It also establishes the requirements for issuers to implement an internal compliance directive and to appoint a compliance officer. It also provides rules for the treatment of directors' dealings reports.[32]

---

[29] Disclosure and Reporting Regulation (Veröffentlichungs- und MeldeV) Austrian Federal Law Gazette II 2005/109.

[30] Regulation of the Austrian Financial Market Authority concerning interim reports, reports about changes of major shares and the equality of mandatory information from third countries—Transparency Regulation (TransparenzV) Federal Law Gazette II 2007/175.

[31] Issuer Compliance Regulation (Emittenten-ComplianceV) Federal Law Gazette II 2007/213.

[32] For details see Section 8.3.3 below.

(iv) *Publication Regulation 2002:*[33] This regulation concerns the publication requirements applicable to share buy-backs.

(v) *The regulation concerning the temporary prohibition of naked short selling*[34] *and the regulation concerning the transmission of reports of short selling suspicions:*[35] These regulations provide for the temporary prohibition of naked short selling of shares listed in the prime market,[36] as well as certain reporting obligations with respect to short selling for professional market participants.

8.1.4.4 FMA guidance

The FMA issues non-binding circular letters, which provide guidance on the application of the CMA and the SEA. Notable examples are the circular letter regarding questions on the transformation of the Prospectus Directive ('PD-Circular Letter')[37] and the circular letter on ad-hoc disclosure requirements and reports on directors' dealings.[38]   **8.32**

The FMA can also be contacted by an issuer and/or its legal advisers to discuss specific issues by email or telephone. Any guidance the FMA provides by email or over the telephone is also non-binding and (again) only indicates the FMA's application of the regulations to the given case. The FMA should only be contacted in this way in cases where no clear answer is yielded by the statutes, CESR-Recommendations, literature or past practice.   **8.33**

8.1.4.5 The Austrian Takeover Act

8.1.4.5.1 Overview The Austrian Takeover Act regulates public offers for the acquisition of shares of Austrian companies whose securities are admitted to trading on a regulated market of an Austrian stock exchange ('target company').   **8.34**

---

[33] BGBl II 2000/5; Publication Regulation 2002 (VeröffentlichungsV 2002) Federal Law Gazette II 2000/5.

[34] Second regulation concerning the temporary prohibition of naked short-selling (LeerverkaufsverbotsV); Federal Law Gazette II 2008/412.

[35] Regulation concerning the transmission of reports of short selling-suspicions (Short Selling VerdachtsübermittlungsV); Federal Law Gazette II 2008/329.

[36] Erste Group Bank AG, Raiffeisen International Bank-Holding AG, UNIQA Versicherungen AG and WIENER STÄDTISCHE Versicherung AG Vienna Insurance Group.

[37] Circular Letter of the FMA dated 29 March 2007 in respect to questions relating to the implementation of the Prospectus Directive in the Capital Market Act and Stock Exchange Act (Rundschreiben der Finanzmarktaufsicht vom 29.03.2007 zu Fragen der Umsetzung der Prospektrichtlinie in Kapitalmarktgesetz und Börsegesetz); available on the homepage of the FMA: www.fma.gv.at

[38] Circular Letter of the FMA dated 6 March 2006 as amended on 5 April 2007 on Ad Hoc Disclosure Requirements and Reports on Directors' Dealings (Rundschreiben der Finanzmarktaufsichtsbehörde vom 06.03.2006 in der Fassung vom 05.04.2007 betreffend Ad-hoc Publizität und Directors' Dealings-Meldungen); available on the homepage of the FMA: http://www.fma.gv.at/cms/site/EN/einzel.html?channel=CH0096

The purpose of the Takeover Act is to ensure that public offers for target companies are carried out fairly and that shareholders of target companies are treated equally in such circumstances. If a bidder acquires a controlling interest in the company, the Takeover Act also seeks to ensure that shareholders have an opportunity to sell their shares at a fair price. The Takeover Commission supervises compliance with the Takeover Act and for parties in breach of the Takeover Act, it has the power to impose fines, suspend voting rights and, in the case of severe breaches, to suspend other shareholders' rights.

8.35 Any public offer for the shares of a target company must be prepared in accordance with the Takeover Act and be submitted to the Takeover Commission prior to its publication. Generally, a bidder must not disclose its intention to launch a public offer until it has notified the Takeover Commission. If, however, rumours of the bidder's intention lead to significant changes in the price of the target company's shares prior to the bidder notifying the Takeover Commission, the bidder is required to immediately publish its intention to offer for the shares and within ten trading days of such publication submit the offering documents to the Takeover Commission.

8.36 *8.1.4.5.2 Offers and controlling interests* The Takeover Act differentiates between voluntary offers, mandatory offers and voluntary offers to gain 'control' of the target company. Under the Takeover Act, an interest is 'controlling' if it confers more than 30% of the voting rights in the target company.[39]

8.37 Any person who acquires a controlling interest in a target company must notify this to the Takeover Commission and must prepare an offer ('mandatory offer') to purchase all remaining shares in the target company within 20 trading days of acquiring the controlling interest.[40] Acquisitions of less than 30% of the voting rights do not trigger a mandatory offer; however, if a secured blocking minority (26%) but not the threshold of 30% voting rights in the target company is exceeded for whatever reason, the shareholder can only exercise voting rights corresponding to the secured blocking majority (i.e. 26%)—the shareholder's voting rights exceeding 26% of the total voting rights in the target are statutorily suspended. Upon request by the acquirer, the Takeover Commission can explicitly revoke the suspension and may establish other conditions and obligations instead.

8.38 In addition, passive acquisition of control does not trigger a mandatory offer, provided that the shareholder acquiring control did not expect or intend to acquire such control at the time of acquiring the shares[41] (for example, if control is acquired as a result of

---

[39] Takeover Act section 22 (2).
[40] Takeover Act section 22.
[41] Takeover Act section 22b.

the break-up of a controlling shareholder consortium). In such circumstances, only 26% of the voting rights can be exercised, unless the Takeover Commission, upon request by the relevant shareholder, explicitly revokes this restriction.

Under certain circumstances, the extension of an existing controlling interest **8.39** ('creeping-in') also triggers an obligation to make a mandatory offer. This applies where a person with a controlling interest, but not a majority of the voting rights, of a target company, acquires an additional 2% or more of the voting rights within a period of 12 months commencing with the first purchase of additional shares.[42]

Every voluntary offer aimed at acquiring a controlling influence, by the operation **8.40** of section 25a(2) of the Takeover Act, in a target company is conditional on the bidder acquiring more than 50% of the outstanding shares with permanent voting power ('voluntary offer to gain control').[43] Accordingly, if the bidder fails to acquire more than 50% of the outstanding shares in connection with its offer, the entire offer will fail. In such cases, the bidder cannot acquire shares from those shareholders that accepted the offer, and, furthermore, it is blocked for a one-year period (see 8.1.4.5.9) from acquiring a controlling interest in the target company or launching a second voluntary offer to gain control.

8.1.4.5.3 Mandatory offers versus voluntary offers

Aspects of offer	Mandatory offer	Voluntary offer to gain control	Voluntary offer
Shares to be acquired	All shares of the target company listed on a stock exchange	All shares of the target company listed on a stock exchange	No restriction
Controlling interest required	Yes	No	No
Applicable to parties acting in concert	Yes	Yes	Yes
Market test[44]	No	Yes	No
Independent expert	Yes	Yes	Yes
Price building rules	Yes	Yes	No
Increases of offer consideration	Yes	Yes	Yes

---

[42] Takeover Act section 22 (4).
[43] Takeover Act section 25a (2).
[44] The principle of the market test is a way to ascertain the fair price. Takeover Act section 25a (2) provides for a market test.

(Continued)

Aspects of offer	Mandatory offer	Voluntary offer to gain control	Voluntary offer
Payment	Within 10 trading days after the offer became binding	Within 10 trading days after the offer became binding	No statutory rules
Sell-out period	Yes	Yes	Yes
Breach sanctioned by administrative fines	Yes	Yes	Yes

8.41   **8.1.4.5.4 'Parties acting in concert'**   The Takeover Act prevents bidders from circumventing its provisions by the use of special purpose vehicles or associated companies to acquire shares in a target, which would—but for the anti-avoidance measures—enable the bidder to avoid triggering the relevant ownership percentage thresholds. It does so by taking a broad and economic approach to the concept of a controlling interest, which it applies to all persons acting together. Accordingly, if several parties acting in concert acquired more than 30% of the voting rights in a target company, they would be required to make a mandatory offer as if they were one single party.

8.42   Parties acting in concert are defined as any persons (i) cooperating with the bidder on the basis of an agreement aiming at acquiring or exercising control over the target company, in particular by concerting votes, or (ii) cooperating with the target company in order to impede the success of the takeover offer. It is assumed under the Act that parties are acting in concert, if (a) a party holds a direct or indirect controlling interest in one or more other companies, or (b) parties reach an agreement on the exercise of voting rights regarding the election of supervisory board members of the target company.[45]

8.43   **8.1.4.5.5 The breakthrough**   The articles of association of a company incorporated under the laws of Austria and whose securities are admitted to trading on a regulated market of an Austrian stock exchange can stipulate that during a takeover process certain restrictions on transfer and voting rights with respect to its shares are not applicable.[46] This can help to facilitate a takeover. Irrespective of whether the articles of association of a target company contain such restrictions, the acquirer of an interest of at least 75% of the share capital can call a shareholders' meeting within six months of the takeover process in order to amend the

---

[45] Takeover Act section 1(6).
[46] Takeover Act section 27a. Prior to October 2009 none of the relevant companies had amended its articles accordingly to allow such breakthrough.

articles of association, for instance, to abolish any transfer restrictions, voting right restrictions and delegation rights, or to change the members of the supervisory board. In any such meeting, any restrictions on voting rights (for instance, which are set out in the target's articles of association or in a shareholders' agreement) will automatically be disapplied pursuant to provisions under the Takeover Act.

Once a bidder's intention to make an offer becomes known to the management **8.44** board and the supervisory board of the target company, such boards require the consent of the shareholders' meeting for all defence measures, i.e. measures designed to hinder the offer or its success. In particular, the issuance of securities in order to prevent the bidder from acquiring the requisite percentage of voting rights to establish control requires the consent of the shareholders' meeting even if the management board was already authorized by a previous shareholders' meeting to increase the company's share capital but has not initiated the capital increase prior to the announcement of the bidder's intention to make an offer.

8.1.4.5.6 The minimum offer price While the price for a voluntary offer **8.45** can be freely determined, the minimum price offered in a mandatory offer or a voluntary offer to gain control is determined by the Takeover Act.[47]

The minimum price must be: **8.46**

(i) at least equal to the average stock exchange price estimated according to the respective trading volume during the preceding six months before the day on which the bidder announced its intention to make an offer; and

(ii) at least equal to the highest share price that the bidder or a legal entity acting jointly with the bidder has paid or agreed to pay during the 12 months prior to the bidder's publication of the intention to make an offer.

If the consideration that the bidder has paid or agreed to pay for shares of the **8.47** target company during the 12 months prior to publication of the intention to make an offer was provided in a form other than cash, or only partly in cash, the total value of the consideration forms the basis of the calculation for the minimum offer price. When determining the total value, payments effected or promised and any other financial advantages will be included if they bear a financial relation to the acquisition of the shares. Furthermore, the minimum price of the offer will be determined in accordance with the general principle of equivalent treatment of all shareholders if:

(i) the obligation to make a Mandatory Offer arises through the acquisition of shares or other rights in a company which (a) owns, directly or indirectly,

---

[47] Takeover Act section 26.

a controlling interest in the target company; and (b) holds (in addition to the shares of the target company) other assets or has debts;

(ii) the consideration paid or promised by the bidder within the preceding 12 months was fixed taking into account special circumstances (for instance, if the seller of shares agrees to undertake special liabilities towards the acquirer); or

(iii) the circumstances have changed significantly in the preceding 12 months (for example, if the target's share price has changed unexpectedly and significantly due to factors other than the publication of the intention to make a takeover offer).

8.48 Furthermore, any mandatory offer must include an alternative offer that provides for a cash payment where the consideration offered is in a form other than cash (for instance, in case the bidder offers shares as consideration).

8.49 A bidder may submit an improved offer (for instance, with an increased offer price) during the acceptance period, provided the original offer has not failed. Equally, other bidders may submit competitive bids during the acceptance period for the original offer. Such improved or competitive offers are governed by the same rules that apply to the original offer.[48]

8.50 The bidder and all parties acting in concert with the bidder may not acquire securities of the target company on better terms than those of the offer. Violation of these rules can lead to suspension of voting rights and to penalties imposed by the Takeover Commission.[49]

8.51 **8.1.4.5.7 The offer document** The offer document for voluntary offers and mandatory offers must be examined by a qualified independent expert before it is submitted to the Takeover Commission and delivered to the target company. The bidder must publish the offer documents and the expert's findings not before the 12th and not later than the 15th trading day after receipt by the Takeover Commission, provided the Takeover Commission has not prohibited the publication of the offer.[50] The target's management and supervisory boards must issue a statement regarding the offer immediately after the publication of the offer document.

8.52 The offer document, as a minimum, must include the following information:[51]

(i) the terms of the offer;

(ii) particulars of the bidder;

---

48 Takeover Act section 15.
49 Takeover Act section 16.
50 Takeover Act section 11.
51 Takeover Act section 7.

(iii) the consideration offered for each security and the method of valuation used for determining the consideration;

(iv) the shares in the target company already held by the bidder or the parties acting in concert or the shares they are entitled to, or obligated to acquire in the future;

(v) all conditions and rights of withdrawal the offer is subject to;

(vi) the bidder's intentions regarding the future business of the target company;

(vii) the conditions under which the bidder will finance its offer; and

(viii) information on any parties acting in concert with the bidder.

8.1.4.5.8 Acceptance period The acceptance period for a takeover offer must **8.53** be not less than two weeks and not more than ten weeks, calculated in each case from the date of the publication of the offer document. However, in certain instances, such as in the case of a mandatory offer, there is a follow-up period of three months after the publication of the results of the offer, within which the target's shareholders may still accept the bidder's offer. This enables such shareholders to make their acceptance decision on the basis of the preliminary results of the offer.[52]

8.1.4.5.9 Exclusion periods Pursuant to section 21 of the Takeover Act if a **8.54** bidder fails in an offer, it is excluded from making any further offer for the shares of the target company for a period of one year following the publication of the result of the failed offer. During this exclusion period the bidder is also prohibited from acquiring shares in the target company (by means other than a fully-fledged takeover offer) that could trigger an obligation to make a mandatory offer (see Section 8.1.4.5.2).

Similarly, if a bidder issues a public statement declaring that it will not make **8.55** an offer or acquire a controlling interest in a target company, it also triggers an exclusion period of one year, during which the bidder may not make an offer or acquire a controlling interest in the relevant company.[53] Potential bidders, therefore, should avoid public statements (for instance, in response to inquiries from journalists, or from shareholders in shareholder meetings) that include information about the existence or absence of an intention to make an offer.

Furthermore, this exclusion period applies in any case in which a bidder states **8.56** publicly that it intends to make a takeover offer (or even that an offer cannot be ruled out). It must file the relevant offer documents with the Takeover Commission

---

[52] Takeover Act section 19 (3).
[53] Takeover Act section 21 (3).

within a period of ten (with granted extension of this period up to 40) trading days of the statement.

8.57 The Takeover Commission may reduce the one-year exclusion period upon application of the bidder. It is most likely to grant a reduction in the context of an intended friendly takeover if the target company confirms vis-à-vis the Takeover Commission that a reduction of the exclusion period is not detrimental to its business.

8.58 **8.1.4.5.10 The Takeover Commission** The Takeover Commission observes compliance with the Takeover Act and is authorized to penalize violations of the Act. In addition to other civil and administrative sanctions, violations of the Takeover Act can result in the suspension of all voting rights of the violator's shares and—in the case of serious violations—suspension of other shareholder rights. The Takeover Commission, which can also officially institute proceedings against parties if suspects are in breach of relevant provisions, is not itself subject to any supervising authority.

8.1.4.6 Squeeze-out of minority shareholders

8.59 Under the Squeeze-Out Act,[54] a shareholder that has more than 90% of the total nominal capital of a listed company has the right to demand exclusion of the remaining shareholders from the company by paying adequate compensation in cash. This right is not restricted to cases of a successful takeover offer.

8.60 In such circumstances, the minority shareholders cannot block the shareholder exclusion as such, but can induce a separate review procedure for assessing the adequacy of the cash compensation offered for the minority interests. If a squeeze-out is implemented subsequent to a takeover in which more than 90% of the outstanding shares involved in the offer were acquired, it is assumed that cash compensation amounting to the highest amount paid during such offer is adequate. In such cases, therefore, the chances of minority shareholders being permitted to initiate a separate review procedure to assess the adequacy of the cash compensation are significantly reduced.

8.1.5 Eligibility for listing

8.61 To conduct a listing in the official market or semi-official market of the VSE, the applicant must submit an application to the VSE.[55] Depending on the extent of

---

[54] Squeeze-Out Act—Gesellschafter-Ausschlussgesetz (Übernahmerechts-Änderungsgesetz 2006), BGBl. I Nr. 75/2006 of 9 June 2006.
[55] SEA section 72.

the particular applicant's conformity with the applicable requirements,[56] it will be admitted to the official market or the semi-official market.

8.1.5.1 *The application for admission to listing*

8.1.5.1.1 General Applications for admission to listing of a security or of an **8.62** issuing programme on the official market or the semi-official market are to be made in writing to the VSE by the issuer and must be co-signed by a stock exchange member, i.e. a stock trader admitted by the VSE pursuant to the SEA.

The application must contain the name and registered office of the applicant, the **8.63** type and denomination of the securities, and the total offer size (which the applicant must describe) by stating the number of the securities to which the application relates, as well as the nominal value of the securities or, in cases where no-par value securities are to be admitted, the expected market value of the securities to be admitted).

In practice, in order to ensure that the issuer complies with all applicable **8.64** obligations, the advisers should discuss the application with the VSE prior to its submission. In particular, any doubt about the interpretation of specific provisions can be discussed on a case-by-case basis (indeed, through such discussions, the VSE may agree to dispense or modify certain provisions for the admission).

The VSE must reach a decision on an application within ten weeks of its complete **8.65** submission. This period does not include any time the issuer takes to provide additional information requested by the VSE.

8.1.5.1.2 The application The application for admission to listing of a **8.66** security or of an issuing programme on the official market and on the semi-official market must be accompanied by the following documents:[57]

(i) an excerpt from the commercial register in which the issuer is registered that is not older than four weeks;

(ii) a valid copy of the issuer's articles of association or partnership agreement;

(iii) any official authorization certificates required for the pursuit of its business activities or the issue of securities (for instance in Austria the establishment of a credit institution or insurance company requires prior authorization of the FMA);

(iv) verification that all legal requirements for the issue of securities have been complied with (for instance, if an Austrian company intends to admit shares

---

[56] Evidence of adherence to certain continuing obligations set out in the SEA and in all related regulations is a prerequisite for admission to the official market and the semi-official market. See Section 8.3 below.

[57] SEA section 72.

issued in connection with a capital increase, the applicant must provide an excerpt from the commercial register because the capital increase of an Austrian company does not become valid until it is registered with the commercial register);

(v) the issuer's annual audited accounts (with auditors' statement) and the financial reports (a) for the past three complete business years if shares are to be admitted to listing on the official market for the first time;[58] or (b) for the last completed business year in all other cases;

(vi) the approved prospectus including, where relevant, a confirmation by the FMA of having received a passport notification;

(vii) if security certificates are to be printed, two sample prints of the security certificates for each denomination of securities for which admission is sought; and

(viii) if the securities are to be secured by a global certificate, a declaration of the issuer stating the central depository in whose custody the global certificate shall be held.

8.67   **8.1.5.1.3 Admission to the official market**   The official market is regulated by the VSE's most stringent admission requirements and publicity guidelines and continuing obligations.

8.68   The VSE will only grant admission to the official market if it is satisfied that the applicant meets the full suite of eligibility requirements under the SEA:[59]

(i) The establishment and the bylaws or articles of association of the issuer must comply with the law of the country in which the issuer has its registered office.

(ii) The total number of securities for which admission is sought must be at least 20,000; the total nominal value of the shares must be at least EUR 2.9 million and for other securities (for example, bonds), at least EUR 725,000. In the case of securities with no monetary denomination, the issuer must be able to confirm that the probable total value will be at least EUR 725,000.[60] This requirement does not apply if the issuer already has securities admitted to listing and it applies to enlarge its current listing.

---

[58] If the company has not existed in its current legal form for the full three-year period the applicant can for instance provide the annual audited accounts of another company to fulfil the three years requirement if (a) the applicant is the universal successor to this other company; and (b) the accounting principles of the other company have been maintained.

[59] SEA section 66a.

[60] In the case of non-voting preferred shares issued by Austrian stock corporations whose ordinary shares are not admitted to listing on the official market, the nominal value of the preferred shares must be EUR 1 million.

(iii) A sufficient number of the securities for which admission is sought must be in public hands (free float). This requirement will be satisfied if at least a total nominal value of EUR 725,000 is owned by the public, or, in the case of securities with no monetary denomination, at least 10,000 shares are in public hands or are offered to the public for purchase. This requirement does not apply if the relevant securities have already been admitted to official listing on a foreign stock exchange.

(iv) The application for admission to listing must refer to all shares of the same category already issued by the issuer (for instance, voting stocks) or to all other securities of the same issue (for instance bonds); shares that cannot be traded for a certain period of time due to applicable legislation may be exempt from the admission.

(v) The issuer must have complied with all laws, decrees and official notices (whether Austrian or otherwise) applicable to the issuance of the securities. If required, the securities must have been registered in the appropriate public register.

(vi) In case of securities with a minimum denomination of less than EUR 50,000 that grant holders the right to convert or subscribe to other securities, the securities to which the right of conversion or subscription refers must be admitted to listing on the stock exchange before or at the same time as the securities that grant the conversion or subscription right.[61]

(vii) In case of an initial admission to listing of shares, the applicant must have existed for at least three years and must have published financial statements for the three full financial years preceding the application in accordance with applicable law.[62] The VSE may grant an exception to the three-year track record requirement if it considers the admission to listing to be in the interests of the issuer and of the public, and the applicant makes available to the public documents that contain information equivalent to that of the financial statements for the past three years. However, in any event, the applicant must have published the financial statements for one full financial year.

---

[61] This requirement may be waived if the issuer furnishes proof that the owners of the securities that grant such right to conversion or subscription have all the information at their disposal that they need to reach an informed judgment of the value of the securities to which the right of conversion or subscription refers, which may be assumed if the securities to which the right of conversion or subscription refers are admitted on an internationally recognized securities exchange and the prospectus for the admission to listing of the respective securities meets the requirements of CMA section 7 (see Section 8.2 below).

[62] If the company has not existed in its current legal form for the full three-year period the applicant can for instance provide the annual audited accounts of another company to fulfil the three-years requirement if (a) the applicant is the universal successor to this other company and (b) the accounting principles of the other company have been maintained.

8.69 **8.1.5.1.4 Admission to the semi-official market** The requirements for the admission to listing of securities and issuing programmes to the semi-official market are largely the same as those for the official market. Notable differences include the following:[63]

(i)   The total number of securities to be listed must be at least 10,000. Such securities must have a total nominal value of at least EUR 725,000. In the case of admission of securities with no monetary denomination, the issuer must be able to certify that the market value is expected to be at least EUR 362,500.

(ii) The securities must have the appropriate free float among the public or if this free float is to be achieved through an initial listing, the adequate number of securities must be made available for stock exchange trading. Where shares are admitted to trading, the free float requirement is assumed to be satisfied if at least a total nominal value of EUR 181,250 is owned by the public. Where shares are admitted, at least 2,500 shares must be owned by the public or offered to the public for purchase.

(iii) An applicant whose shares are to be admitted for the first time must have existed for a period of at least one year and have published financial statements in accordance with applicable regulations for the complete financial year preceding the application. If the applicant is the successor of another company and the accounting is continuous, the period of existence of the original company will be included into the one-year time period.

8.1.5.1.5 Overview of admission criteria for official market/ semi-official market

Admission criteria according to the Stock Exchange Act[64]

	Regulated markets	
	Official market	Semi-official market
Total nominal value	Minimum of EUR 2.9m	Minimum of EUR 725,000
Free float nominal value	Minimum of EUR 725,000 (par value shares)	Minimum of EUR 181,250
Free float in number of shares	Minimum of 10,000 no-par-value shares	Minimum of 2,500 no-par-value shares
Period of existence	Minimum of three years	Minimum of one year
Financial statements	For the three preceding full business years	For the preceding full business year
Prospectus	Pursuant to Article 74, SEA	Pursuant to Article 74, SEA

---

[63] SEA section 68.

[64] Slightly adjusted table from VSE homepage http://en.wienerborse.at/listing/aktien/zulassung/index.html

8.1.5.1.6 Admission of certificates Certificates (such as depositary receipts) **8.70**
that represent shares may be admitted to listing on the official market or semi-
official market if the relevant conditions outlined above are met and the issuer of
the certificates guarantees to fulfil its obligations toward the certificate holders in
the relevant offer document or purchase contract.[65]

8.1.5.1.7 Admission of non-dividend bearing securities (programmes) There **8.71**
is no separate admission procedure for non-dividend-bearing securities issued
within the scope of an issuing programme that has been admitted to listing on the
official market or semi-official market, provided the relevant securities are issued
within 12 months of the publication of the programme prospectus.

Official market listings of programmes commence without separate application **8.72**
after the applicant has submitted to the VSE the terms and conditions of the
concrete non-dividend-bearing shares[66] provided the requirements set out in
8.1.5.1.3. (ii)–(vii) are met.

Semi-official market listings of programmes commence without separate appli- **8.73**
cation after the applicant has submitted to VSE the terms and conditions of the
issuing programme, provided the issuer meets the requirements set out in
8.1.5.1.3. (iv)–(vii) and 8.1.5.1.4. (i) and (ii).

8.1.5.1.8 Foreign issuers If shares of an applicant whose registered office is **8.74**
located in a country outside the EU are not listed in the company's home country,
nor in the country where they are mainly traded, they will only be admitted to the
VSE if the applicant provides a plausible explanation as to why its securities are
not listed in either of these countries (in particular, confirming that it is not for
reasons of investor protection).[67]

8.2 The Prospectus

8.2.1 Applicable law

The law relating to prospectuses in Austria is closely based on the Prospectus **8.75**
Directive, which sets out maximum standards of harmonization, and the
Prospectus Regulation, which is directly applicable in Austrian law. Accordingly,
the Austrian rules regarding prospectuses bear a close resemblance to those in
other member states across the EU.

---

[65] SEA sections 66a (6) and 68 (2).
[66] SEA sections 66a (7) and 68 (4).
[67] SEA section 71.

8.76 The CMA, which implements the Prospectus Directive and the Prospectus Regulation, is the key piece of legislation concerning the content and publication requirements for prospectuses in Austria.

8.2.2 Requirement for a prospectus and exemptions

8.77 As is the case throughout the EU, there are two triggers to the requirement to produce a prospectus: (i) when securities are offered to the public in Austria; and (ii) when securities are admitted to trading on a regulated market in Austria.[68] Austrian companies often offer securities to the public in connection with an application for the same securities to be admitted to the VSE. In this situation, a single prospectus can serve for both purposes.

8.2.2.1 Public offer versus private placement

8.78 An offer of securities to the public in Austria must be accompanied by a prospectus, which has been prepared in accordance with the CMA and approved by the FMA (or by a competent authority of another EU member state). Such prospectus must be published at least one banking day in advance of a relevant public offer.[69]

8.79 The CMA, in accordance with the Prospectus Directive, defines a public offer as a communication to the general public in any form whatsoever that contains adequate information on the terms and conditions of an offer (or an invitation to subscribe) for securities, and on the securities themselves, to enable potential investors to make an informed investment decision or subscription to securities. This definition also applies to the placement of securities by financial intermediaries.[70]

8.80 Private placements, which typically involve a limited number of sophisticated investors, generally fall within an exemption to the requirement to publish a prospectus in accordance with the Prospectus Directive and Prospectus Regulation. However, it is market practice for offerors to produce an offering memorandum in order to describe and market the investment opportunity. Such offering memorandum does not require the approval of the FMA. However, where securities are offered for the first time, certain notification requirements apply;[71]

---

[68] FSMA sections 85 and 86, implementing the Prospectus Directive.

[69] CMA section 2.

[70] CMA section 1 (1) (1). The public offer definition comprises not only securities but also investments. Investments are pursuant to CMA section 1(1)(3) property rights for which no securities are issued, arising out of direct or indirect investments of the capital of several investors for their collective account and collective risk or for the collective account or risk together with the issuer if the administration of the capital invested is not overseen by the investor himself. Investments in the meaning of this federal act are all transferable, securitized rights that are not securities within the meaning of the CMA. Money market instruments with maturities shorter than twelve months are not subject to the obligation to publish a listing prospectus pursuant to Article 2.

[71] CMA section 13.

in particular, the offeror must inform Oesterreichische Kontrollbank AG ('OeKB' in its capacity as notification office) as soon as possible after the details of the private placement have been fixed by the issuer, setting out the identity of the offeror, the planned issuing date, the total volume of the offering and the circumstances that enable the private placement to qualify for an exemption from the obligation to publish a prospectus pursuant to section 3 of the CMA.[72]

8.2.2.2 *Exemptions*

As discussed above in the context of private placements, a series of exemptions **8.81** apply to the obligation to publish a prospectus. These exemptions, which are set out in the Prospectus Directive and have been implemented into Austrian law by the CMA and the SEA, are considered in detail in Part 1.

8.2.3 Preparing a prospectus

8.2.3.1 *The FMA approval process—dealing with the FMA*

The FMA must approve any prospectus before its publication. The FMA will **8.82** approve the prospectus—by means of an official approval notification—if it is complete, coherent, clear and complies with the CMA. However, the FMA will not approve the content of the prospectus for which the issuer and certain other individuals are responsible (see Section 8.2.7). To begin the approval process, applicants must file an application with the FMA, including, *inter alia*, a signed prospectus and a cross-reference list (if the prospectus is not drawn up exactly in the manner required under the Annexes to the Prospectus Regulation).

Within ten working days of receipt of the application, the FMA must announce **8.83** whether it needs more information (which it is entitled to do if it considers it necessary for investor protection), or if the prospectus is approved. This period is extended by statute to 20 working days if the prospectus is filed for an initial public offer. If the FMA does not react within the relevant periods the prospectus will not automatically be deemed approved.[73]

Focusing in particular on the procedure relating to the prospectus, first, a prospec- **8.84** tus must be signed by the applicant and filed with the FMA, even if it is not completed. The FMA will, within the 10- or 20-working-days period, review the document and provide the applicant with a detailed order of revision in writing. After amending the prospectus, the applicant must re-file the prospectus. This procedure continues until the FMA informs the applicant that the prospectus is

---

[72] The Oesterreichische Kontrollbank AG has issued a form for the notification which is available at http://www.oekb.at/de/kapitalmarkt/meldungen/emissionskalender/seiten/default.aspx

[73] CMA section 8a (3) and (4).

finalized and fit for approval. Then a final version (four copies), duly signed by the applicant, must be filed and generally will be approved within a couple of hours.

8.2.3.2 Language

8.85 Any prospectus published in Austria must be prepared in German or English.[74] The prospectus summary must be drafted in a generally understandable language, which, in practice, is usually German or English (although one could argue that German is more suitable for Austrian offers, certainly from a consumer protection point of view). Indeed, it is common practice for the terms and conditions of bonds offers, for example, to be drawn up in both English and German, irrespective of which language is used for the summary or the rest of the prospectus.

8.2.4 Prospectus contents

8.2.4.1 The information necessary

8.86 The CMA implements Article 5 of the Prospectus Directive, essentially on a word-for-word basis. Accordingly, a prospectus must contain the information necessary to enable investors to reach an informed decision on the issuer and the securities offered.[75] Beyond this fundamental disclosure obligation, the prospectus must be drawn up pursuant to Articles 3 to 24 of the Prospectus Regulation and the annexes thereto.

8.2.4.2 Derogations

8.87 In certain cases, the FMA has the power to grant—upon request of the issuer, the offeror or the person applying for the admission of the securities to a regulated market—derogations from the general duty of disclosure or from the specific content requirements under the CMA. It may exercise this power where: (i) the disclosure of the relevant information would be contrary to the public interest; (ii) the disclosure of the relevant information would be seriously detrimental to the issuer, provided that omission would not be likely to mislead the public with regard to the facts and circumstances essential for reaching an informed assessment of the issuer, offeror or guarantor, if any, and of the rights attached to the securities to which the prospectus relates; or (iii) the relevant information is of minor importance only and would not influence the assessment of the financial position and prospects of the issuer, offeror or guarantor.

---

[74] Circular Letter from the FMA dated 29 March 2007 regarding questions related to the implementation of the PD in the Capital Market Act and Stock Exchange Act (Rundschreiben der Finanzmarktaufsicht vom 29.03.2007 zu Fragen der Umsetzung der Prospektrichtlinie in Kapitalmarktgesetz und Börsegesetz); available on the homepage of the FMA: http://www.fma.gv.at.

[75] CMA section 7(1).

8.2.4.3 *Responsibility statements*

The prospectus must include a statement that the directors of the company **8.88** accept responsibility for all the information in the prospectus and that to the best of their knowledge and belief (having taken all reasonable care to ensure that such is the case) the information contained in this document is in accordance with the facts and does not omit anything likely to affect the import of such information.

Responsibility in the context of the prospectus is discussed in further detail in **8.89** Section 3 of Chapter 1.

8.2.5 Prospectus publication

8.2.5.1. *Method of publication*

In the context of prospectus publication requirements, the CMA more or less **8.90** copied Article 14 (1) and (2) of the Prospectus Directive into Austrian law.[76]

Accordingly, a prospectus is deemed duly published if: **8.91**

(i) it is published (in full) in the Amtsblatt zur Wiener Zeitung (Austria's official gazette) or in a newspaper distributed throughout Austria;[77]

(ii) it is made available in printed form free of charge at the market where the securities will be admitted for trading or at the registered office of the issuer,[78] or at the offices of the financial intermediaries, including paying agents;

(iii) it is published in electronic form on the issuer's website and as the case may be on the website of the financial intermediaries, including paying agents;

(iv) it is published in electronic form on the website of the regulated market on which the securities are to be admitted to trading;

(v) it is published in electronic form on the website of the FMA (or of a third party retained by the FMA), if the FMA has decided to provide such services.[79]

---

[76] CMA section 10 (2) and (3).

[77] A prospectus may only be published in a newspaper other than the Amtsblatt zur Wiener Zeitung if it fulfils the conditions stipulated in section 5 of FMA's minimum content, publication and language regulation (*Verordnung der Finanzmarktaufsicht über die Mindestinhalte von Prospekte ersetzenden Dokumenten, über die Veröffentlichung von Prospekten in Zeitungen und über die Sprachenregelung,* Official Gazette II No 236/2005), i.e. a newspaper that is published on working days and is regularly available throughout Austria and exceeds the following thresholds on average per year: (i) 100,000 copies print run and (ii) 75,000 newspapers distributed in Austria.

[78] The English version of Article 14 (2) b of the Prospectus Directive states that a printed form of the prospectus shall be made available at the registered office of the issuer *and* at the offices of the financial intermediaries, including paying agents. The German version however contains a translation error and thus provides that the prospectus shall be made available at the registered office of the issuer *or* at the offices of the financial intermediaries, including paying agents. As a result of the copy and paste method applied by the Austrian legislator this error was also incorporated in CMA section10 (2) (2).

[79] So far the FMA has neither decided to operate such a website itself nor to delegate such services to a third party.

8.92 In the PD-Circular Letter,[80] the FMA stated that in order for publication to be deemed valid in Austria the prospectus must be available in Austria or, at least, obtainable in Austria. This suggests that for the purpose of a public offer in Austria it is not sufficient to make the prospectus available solely at the registered office of an issuer outside of Austria, without making it available at the registered office of, for example, a financial intermediary within Austria at the same time.

8.93 Publication in electronic form is not required if the issuer publishes the prospectus in a newspaper or in other printed form in accordance with Article 14(2)(a) or (b) of the Prospectus Directive.

8.94 In addition, in respect of prospectuses approved by the FMA, the FMA must be informed in advance of how the prospectus is being published and where it will be available.[81] Furthermore, Austria exercised the option under Article 14(3) of the Prospectus Directive to require the publication of a notice stating how the prospectus has been made available and where the public can obtain it. According to the relevant provision of the CMA, such notice may be published either in a newspaper or in electronic form on the internet.[82] However, this provision contradicts Article 31 of the Prospectus Regulation, which requires such notice to be published merely in a newspaper. This apparent conflict has been resolved in favour of the Prospectus Regulation, which has direct effect in Austria, and accordingly the publication requirement will be satisfied by a notice in a newspaper.

8.95 According to the PD-Circular Letter the obligation to publish such notice only applies to a prospectus or a base prospectus, but not to the publication of the final terms of an offer or any supplementary prospectus.[83]

8.96 The OeKB, in its capacity as notification office, must, without undue delay, be provided with regulated information on any securities that are offered for the first time in Austria. The notification must include the following details: issuer, prospective date of the issue, total volume, minimum denomination, maturity, information on the identification of the investment (ISIN or other identification) and, if applicable, details of the circumstances that enable the offer to qualify for an exemption to the obligation to publish a prospectus. The information will be included in the so-called 'issuing calendar', which is administered by OeKB to monitor issues of securities and other investments[84] in Austria to provide an overview of expected capital market activity. Public as well as private placements

---

[80] See Section 8.1.4.4 above.

[81] CMA section 10(3). In the PD-Circular Letter the FMA clarifies that this requirement does not apply to prospectuses passported into Austria.

[82] CMA section 10 (4).

[83] CMA section 7(4) and (5). This follows Article 5 (4) and Article 8 (1) of the Prospectus Directive.

[84] CMA section 13.

are subject to this notification requirement. An exemption only exists for offers of investment fund units pursuant to Article 1(2)(a) and (c) of the Prospectus Directive, offers of certain participation certificates,[85] offers of shares pursuant to Article 4(1)(d), Article 3 (2) (e) of the Prospectus Directive, and certain offers of securities to existing or former employees.

8.2.6 Supplementary prospectuses

8.2.6.1 Requirement for a supplementary prospectus

If a significant new factor arises or a material mistake or inaccuracy is discovered in the approved prospectus between the time of the approval of the prospectus and the completion of the offer or the admission to trading, the issuer must prepare a supplement to the prospectus to correct the problem. This supplement must be published immediately in the same way as the prospectus itself[86] and simultaneously filed with the FMA. The FMA must approve the supplement within seven working days.[87]   **8.97**

Since prospectus supplements must be published immediately they are typically sent out to the market without the approval of the FMA. The rationale for this is that the public should be informed of the relevant facts prior to the completion of the offer or the admission to trading, which would not be possible if prior approval of FMA was required.   **8.98**

8.2.6.2 Right to withdraw

Where an issuer publishes a supplement, investors who have already agreed to purchase or subscribe to the securities prior to the publication of the supplement, have a right to withdraw from the deal, even if such investors agreed to purchase or subscribe to the securities prior to the event that triggered the requirement for the supplement. The right to withdraw acceptances is open to investors for two working days following the publication of the supplement. If the investor is a consumer pursuant to the Consumer Protection Act,[88] this period is extended to one week.   **8.99**

8.2.7 Prospectus liability

The CMA provides for a special joint and several liability, which applies to individuals and legal entities (see below) who have assumed responsibility (see Section 8.2.4.3) for the prospectus or parts of it for the correctness and integrity of the   **8.100**

---

[85] The exemption applies to participation certificates within the meaning of § 6 Bundesgesetz vom 18. Feber 1982 über die Errichtung und Verwaltung von Beteiligungsfonds (Beteiligungsfondsgesetz), Official Gazette I No. 111/1982 as amended.

[86] For detail of the publication requirements see Section 8.2.5 above.

[87] CMA section 6 (1).

[88] Consumer Protection Act —Konsumentenschutzgesetz; BGBl. Nr. 140/1979 of 30 March 1979, as amended.

prospectus ('prospectus liability').[89] The key aim of this liability regime is to protect investors by ensuring that the disclosure in a prospectus is not incorrect or misleading, and that it satisfies the fundamental disclosure obligation laid down in Article 5 of the Prospectus Directive.

8.101 In cases of prospectus liability, investors have the right to claim damages commensurate with the losses they suffered when relying on the accuracy or integrity of the information contained in the prospectus (or any other information required to be published pursuant to the CMA in connection with the offering, and which is relevant for assessing the offered securities or investments).

8.102 Prospectus liability may attach to the following individuals or legal entities:

    (i) any issuer who is responsible for any incorrect or incomplete information in the prospectus;[90]

    (ii) prospectus auditors for any incorrect or incomplete information in the prospectus attributable to their gross negligence;

    (iii) any persons who have accepted the investor's offer to purchase the securities as an intermediary (irrespective of whether the intermediary acts in its own name or on behalf of a third party), if the intermediary (a) is professionally engaged in trading or mediating of securities and (b) knew (or was unaware due to gross negligence) of the incorrectness or incompleteness of the information in the prospectus or of the audit;

    (iv) the auditor of the annual accounts who has provided an audit opinion, knowing of the incorrectness or incompleteness of the information pursuant to (i) above and knowing that the annual accounts confirmed by him form part of the prospectus.

8.103 Prospectus liability may not be excluded or limited in advance. In cases where the inaccuracy in the prospectus is deemed to be unintentional, compensation is likely to be limited to the purchase price (including fees and interests) paid by the investor bringing the relevant claim. Prospectus liability claims are also limited in time: claims must be filed with the court within five years of the relevant public offer.

8.2.8 Sanctions

8.104 In connection with public offers of securities or other investments that require a prospectus, the CMA provides for sanctions in relation to the following forms of prohibited conduct (criminal offences):

---

[89] CMA section 11.

[90] In the case of securities or investments of foreign issuers the party making an offer, which is subject to the obligation to publish a prospectus within Austria shall also be liable.

(i)   offering securities without timely publication of a prospectus (or supplements to the prospectus);

(ii) providing incorrect or misleading information in, or omitting material information from, a published prospectus or a supplement thereto; or

(iii) providing incorrect or misleading information in, or omitting material information from, the financial reports published in a prospectus.

Any party found to have committed any of these criminal offences under the CMA is liable to a maximum penalty of two years imprisonment or a monetary fine of up to an amount equal to the individual's income for 360 days (provided that the offence is not subject to more severe sanctions according to other applicable laws, for example, in the case of fraud).[91]   **8.105**

In addition, the CMA prescribes a fine of up to EUR 50,000 for the following administrative offences committed in connection with public offers of securities that require a prospectus:[92]   **8.106**

(i)   offering of securities, if the relevant prospectus, any supplements thereto, or any related publications do not comply with the provisions of the CMA;

(ii)   in the case of an issuer or prospectus auditor, providing incorrect or misleading information in a prospectus or supplements thereto or in the relevant financial reports, or signing off a prospectus without having obtained the required insurance coverage;[93]

(iii) violating the rules relating to advertisements and financial promotions;

(iv)   in the case of an offeror of debt securities that require the publication of a rating, failing to publish the rating or failing to deliver the rating information to the notification office in due time;

(v)   failing to provide OeKB with the required information for the issuing calendar (even if not related to a public offer);

(vi)   failing to provide the notification office with the prospectus and its supplements in a timely manner;

(vii) offering debt securities without a required licence;

(viii) in the case of an auditor, signing off on a prospectus, supplement thereto or financial reports while being barred from doing so (for example, due to a conflict of interest);

(ix)   failing to comply with certain orders of the FMA;

---

[91] CMA section 15.

[92] CMA section 16.

[93] For the auditing of prospectuses relating to securities or other investments auditors have to obtain insurance indemnity in the amount of EUR 3.65 million per year. For the auditing of prospectuses relating to real estate funds (*Veranlagungsgemeinschaft in Immobilien*) auditors have to obtain insurance coverage in the amount of EUR 18.2 million per year.

    (x) failing to immediately forward the auditor's check mark for prospectus supplements to the notification office;

  (xi) failing to comply with certain information requirements; or

 (xii) violating the advertisement or prospectus publication rules pursuant to chapter V of the Prospectus Regulation.

8.2.9 Passporting

8.107   Prospectuses (including any supplements) approved by the EU home member state of a foreign issuer are valid for a public offer or admission to trading of securities in Austria provided that the FMA was appropriately notified in accordance with Article 18 of the Prospectus Directive.[94] Where a prospectus is passported to Austria, it is not necessary to draw up a German translation of the summary if the prospectus has been drawn up in English.

8.108   In addition, OeKB must be provided with the same information for the issuing calendar on the securities offered in Austria as in case of a private placement (see Section 8.2.2.1).

8.3 Continuing Obligations

8.3.1 Applicable law

8.109   Companies listed on the official market or semi-official market must, for the duration of their listing, comply with certain additional obligations laid down principally in the SEA and in regulations issued by the FMA. The ultimate source for many of these obligations is the Transparency Directive, which was implemented in Austria in 2007 and the Market Abuse Directive, which was implemented in Austria in 2005. The Transparency Directive and the Market Abuse Directive are discussed in detail in Part 1.

8.3.2 Disclosure and control of inside information, market abuse and market manipulation

8.3.2.1 *Misuse of insider information*

8.110   The SEA prohibits the misuse of inside information in connection with securities that are admitted to trading on a regulated market in Austria, as well as the misuse of inside information in Austria in connection with securities that are admitted to trading on a regulated market in other EU member states.

---

[94] CMA section 8b.

8.3.2.2 *Identifying inside information*

Pursuant to the implementation of the Market Abuse Directive 'inside information' **8.111** is defined as information of a precise nature which has not been made public, relating, directly or indirectly, to issuers of financial instruments or to financial instruments[95] and which, if it were made public, would be likely to have a significant effect on the price of those financial instruments or on the price of related derivative financial instruments, because a reasonable investor would be likely to use such information as part of the basis of his investment decision ('inside information').

8.3.2.2.1 Primary and secondary insiders   An insider is any person who is in **8.112** possession of inside information.

The SEA differentiates between primary insiders and secondary insiders. Primary **8.113** insiders are members of an issuer's management and the supervisory board and other persons who are in possession of inside information due to their profession, function, responsibilities or shareholding. Primary insiders are also persons who gain inside information by violating criminal laws. Secondary insiders are persons who, without falling into the category of primary insider, obtain inside information from a primary insider or a third person.

Primary and secondary insiders are prohibited from using inside information for **8.114** their own or a third party's account by (i) acquiring or disposing of the relevant securities; (ii) giving recommendations concerning the purchase or sale of such securities to third parties and (iii) communicating inside information, unless required by law. In any of these cases it is not necessary for the primary insider to act with the intention of gaining a pecuniary advantage for himself or a third person—it is sufficient if the primary insider is shown to be grossly negligent as to whether the information in question was inside information.

The misuse of inside information is a criminal offence punishable by imprison- **8.115** ment for up to five years.

8.3.2.2.2 Obligations to prevent misuse of inside information   In order to **8.116** prevent the misuse of inside information, issuers are obliged to take the following measures:[96]

(i) inform their employees and other persons providing services to the issuer of the prohibition on the misuse of inside information;
(ii) issue internal directives for the communication of information within the company and monitor compliance thereto; and

---

[95] The term 'financial instrument' includes securities, money market instruments, futures, forward rate agreements and commodity derivatives.
[96] SEA section 82 (5).

(iii) take appropriate organizational measures to prevent the misuse of inside information or its disclosure to third parties.

8.117   Evidence of adherence to these obligations—which the issuer must provide to the FMA by delivering its internal compliance directive[97]—is a prerequisite for admission to the official market and the semi-official market.

8.118   **8.3.2.2.3 Corporate compliance**   The Issuer Compliance Regulation[98] enacted by the FMA, regulates in further detail the measures issuers must take if their securities are admitted to trading on the official market or the semi-official market. This regulation provides, *inter alia*, for blackout periods, during which persons working in confidential areas (i.e. areas within the company where persons have access to inside information on a regular or occasional basis) are prohibited from trading in the issuer's securities.

8.119   In addition, the circle of persons within confidential areas with access to inside information must be minimized, and confidential areas must be organizationally separated from other areas within the company to reduce the danger of an abuse or an improper distribution of inside information. In particular, an issuer must (i) establish effective arrangements to deny access to such information to persons other than those who require it for the exercise of their functions within the company; (ii) take the necessary measures to ensure that any person with access to such information acknowledges the legal and regulatory duties entailed and is aware of the sanctions attached to the misuse or improper dissemination of such information; and (iii) implement measures that allow immediate public disclosure in case the issuer is not able to ensure the confidentiality of the relevant information.[99]

8.120   When an issuer, or a person acting on its behalf or for its account, discloses inside information to any third party in the normal exercise of his employment, profession or duties, complete and effective public disclosure of that information must be made, either simultaneously (in the case of an intentional disclosure) or as soon as possible (in the case of a non-intentional disclosure). However, the obligation to publish inside information in this manner does not apply if the recipient of the information is under a duty of confidentiality.

8.121   The issuer must keep a record ('insider list') of those of its employees who regularly or occasionally have access to inside information. The insider list must be regularly updated and transmitted to the FMA upon request. Furthermore, it must be archived by the issuer for at least five years after it was completed or last

---

[97] For details see Section 8.3.2.2.3 below.
[98] See Section 8.1.4.3 (iii) above.
[99] SEA section 48d (2) (2).

updated. The persons responsible for maintaining insider lists must ensure that those who have access to inside information sign a written acknowledgement of the obligations that arise in relation to inside information and of the sanctions that apply in the event of misuse of inside information or the improper dissemination of such information.

A violation of these rules constitutes an administrative offence in relation to which the FMA may impose a fine of up to EUR 30,000.   **8.122**

8.3.2.3 *Market manipulation*

Under the SEA, market manipulation is defined as transactions or orders to trade that:[100]   **8.123**

(i) give, or are likely to give, false or misleading signals as to the supply of, demand for, or price of financial instruments; or
(ii) secure, by a person, or persons acting in collaboration, the price of one or several financial instruments at an abnormal or artificial level.

Market manipulation also includes transactions or orders to trade that employ fictitious devices or any other form of deception or contrivance and the dissemination of information through the media, including the internet, or by any other means, which gives, or is likely to give, false or misleading indications as to financial instruments. This includes the dissemination of rumours and false or misleading news, where the person who made the dissemination knew, or ought to have known, that the information was false or misleading.   **8.124**

An exemption applies where the person who entered into the transactions or issued the orders to trade can establish that his reasons for doing so were legitimate and that the relevant transactions or trades conform to accepted market practices on the regulated market concerned.[101]   **8.125**

Market manipulation is an administrative offence and is subject to a fine by the FMA of up to EUR 50,000. Furthermore, the party in violation must forfeit any pecuniary advantage gained.   **8.126**

8.3.2.4 *Ad hoc disclosure*

8.3.2.4.1 General   The requirement on issuers to make ad hoc disclosures is designed to increase transparency in the market, to ensure that investors have equal access to important information and, in particular, to limit the opportunities for misuse of inside information. The immediate publication of a new fact   **8.127**

---

[100] SEA section 48a (1) (2).
[101] With regard to accepted market practices the FMA has issued a regulation on market practice: Market Practices Regulation—http://www.fma.gv.at/cms/site/DE/detail.html?doc=CMS115 7110891041&channel=CH0095

makes inside information accessible to all market participants, which, in turn, prevents its misuse in connection with transactions in listed securities. The FMA's Disclosure and Reporting Regulation regulates the form, content and type of the publication and the transmission of ad hoc disclosures.[102]

8.128　The statutory provisions on ad hoc disclosure build on the concept of inside information.[103] Accordingly, issuers are obliged to 'disclose to the public without delay any insider information which is directly related to them'. Disclosure must be made through an electronic information dissemination system that ensures the publication of the information with a reputable news provider such as Reuters, Bloomberg or Dow Jones Newswire.

8.129　Any announcement of inside information must also be reported to the FMA and the VSE and disclosed through the information portal of the OeKB (Issuer-Information-Center Austria). In addition, an issuer must make all ad hoc inside information disclosed to the public available on its website (typically, in a 'Publications' section, which must be easily accessible by the public) for at least six months following the announcement.

8.130　**8.3.2.4.2 Changes to disclosed inside information**　Material changes to disclosed inside information must be announced immediately following the occurrence of the relevant changes in accordance with the same procedure followed for the original announcement.

8.131　**8.3.2.4.3 Delaying disclosure of inside information**　Issuers may delay the public disclosure of inside information in order not to prejudice their legitimate interests, provided that (i) such omission would not be likely to mislead the public and (ii) the issuer is able to ensure the confidentiality of such information. The issuer is obliged to inform the FMA without delay of its decision to delay the public disclosure of inside information.[104]

8.3.3 Disclosure and publication of directors' dealing

8.132　Persons discharging managerial responsibilities ('PDMRs') within an issuer in Austria must report to the FMA all of their dealings in the issuer's securities (or the securities of related companies admitted for trading on regulated markets), including dealings in related derivatives.[105] PDMRs must also publish details of any such dealings on the FMA's website.

---

[102]　For details see above Section 8.1.4.3.(i).
[103]　For details see Section 8.3.2 above.
[104]　SEA section 48d (2).
[105]　SEA section 48d (4).

PDMRs are, in particular, members of a company's management board and the **8.133**
supervisory board. The same rules apply to related parties of PDMRs, for example, spouses, common law spouses, dependent children and any other family
members who have lived in the PDMR's household for at least one year. Such
related parties may also include legal entities, fiduciary institutions or partnerships which are managed or which are directly or indirectly controlled by a PDMR,
or which have been established for the benefit of a PDMR or whose business
interests, to a large extent, are similar to those of a PDMR.

PDMRs must notify the FMA of all relevant dealings within five business days of **8.134**
the closing of the relevant trade, although such notification may be postponed if
the total volume of the trades does not exceed EUR 5,000 (on an aggregate basis
per calendar year). The Disclosure and Reporting Regulation regulates the form,
content and type of disclosure and transmission of PDMRs (including directors')
dealings notifications.[106]

Violations of notification requirements constitute an administrative offence in **8.135**
relation to which the FMA may impose a fine of up to EUR 30,000.

According to the FMA's Issuer Compliance Directive, all notifications concerning **8.136**
PDMRs' dealings must be disclosed to the person who is responsible for compliance in the company, who must keep a register of such dealings. The publication
can also be made through the FMA's website by agreement between the FMA and
the person obliged to notify dealings in the particular issuer's securities.

8.3.4 Major shareholding notifications

Disclosures of material ownership interests—measured in terms of the propor- **8.137**
tion of voting rights—of individual shareholders of a listed company are intended
to make the influence of such shareholders transparent to the public.

8.3.4.1 *Applicable provisions and extent of applicability*

The SEA imposes obligations on voteholders and issuers to make notifications **8.138**
regarding changes in the percentage of voting rights in the issuer beyond specified
thresholds. It applies to issuers whose securities are admitted to trading on a
regulated market and whose EU home member state is Austria.

8.3.4.2 *Notifications and publication of major shareholdings*

Natural or legal persons acquiring or disposing directly or indirectly of an owner- **8.139**
ship interest in an issuer whose EU home member state is Austria, and whose
shares are listed on a regulated market, must notify the FMA, the VSE and the
company whose securities have been acquired or disposed of about the interest

---

[106] For details see above Section 8.1.4.3(i).

held, if the acquisition or disposal results in such shareholder's voting rights equalling, exceeding or falling below a specified percentage threshold. Furthermore, a shareholder must notify the FMA, the VSE and the relevant company following an acquisition of shares or financial instruments which results in an unconditional entitlement to acquire further issued shares of the issuer to which voting rights are attached, if this acquisition or disposal results in such shareholder's voting rights equalling, exceeding or falling below a specific percentage threshold. The company, in turn, must disclose such information to the market.[107]

8.140 In addition, issuers must also make notifications if they acquire or dispose of their own shares, either themselves or through a person acting in his own name but on behalf of the issuer.

8.3.4.3 Notification thresholds and notifiable interests

8.141 The requirement to notify the FMA, the VSE and the relevant company of movements in a listed issuer's shareholding is triggered if a person directly or indirectly acquires or disposes (or is unconditionally entitled to acquire or dispose) of an ownership interest in the issuer and acquisition or disposal results in that shareholder's voting rights in the issuer equalling, exceeding or falling below 5%, 10%, 15%, 20%, 25%, 30%, 35%, 40%, 45%, 50%, 75% and 90%.[108] The percentage share of voting rights is calculated on the basis of the total number of voting shares even if the exercise of certain of all these voting rights is suspended.[109]

8.142 The notification to the FMA, the VSE and the relevant company of the acquisition or the disposal of voting rights must contain the following details: (i) the number of voting rights after the acquisition or disposal; (ii) the date on which the threshold was attained or exceeded; (iii) the name of the relevant shareholder and of any person that is entitled to exercise the voting rights in that shareholder's name; and (iv) if applicable, the chain of the controlled companies through which the voting rights could in fact be exercised.[110]

8.3.4.4 Notification and publication deadlines

8.143 The relevant shareholder must notify the issuer immediately and in any event no later than two trading days beginning on the day subsequent to the day on which the shareholder:

(i) gained knowledge of the acquisition or disposal;
(ii) gained knowledge of its right to exercise the voting rights;

---

[107] For details of the publication requirements see Section 8.3.4.4.
[108] SEA section 91 (1). In December 2009 the legislator is discussing an amendment to the disclosure threshold by introducing the requirement for disclosure when 2% of the total voting rights is reached, exceeded or fallen below which will come into force during 2010.
[109] SEA section 91 (1a).
[110] SEA section 92a.

(iii) should have gained knowledge of (i) or (ii), irrespective of the day on which the acquisition, disposal or right to exercise the voting rights becomes effective; or

(iv) has been informed of an increase or decrease of issued shares (i.e. voting rights) by the issuer.

Once the issuer has been notified of the acquisition or disposal of voting rights and in any event, no later than two trading days following receipt of such notification, it must disclose the information to the market in German through a suitable media outlet that can ensure the dissemination of the information throughout the EU, such as Bloomberg or Reuters. The issuer must provide this information simultaneously with supporting disclosure documentation to the FMA, VSE and OeKB's Issuer-Information-Center Austria.   **8.144**

At the end of each calendar month during which an increase or decrease of issued shares has occurred, the issuer must disclose to the public the total number of voting rights and capital in respect of each class of its issued shares and the total number of voting rights attached to any shares that the issuer holds in treasury.   **8.145**

8.3.5 Periodic financial reporting

8.3.5.1 *Annual and semi-annual reports*

With respect to periodic financial reporting, the SEA implemented into Austrian law the key provisions of the Transparency Directive. Accordingly, companies listed in Austria must produce an annual financial report, which must contain: (i) annual audited financial statements prepared in accordance with IFRS or equivalent accounting standards; and (ii) an annual management report and a semi-annual report (containing: (i) interim financial statements prepared in accordance with IFRS or equivalent accounting standards; and (ii) a half-year management report). The specific requirements relating to annual and semi-annual reports are discussed in Section 1.3 of Chapter 1.   **8.146**

8.3.6 The Austrian Code of Corporate Governance[111]

8.3.6.1 *General*

The Austrian Code of Corporate Governance provides Austrian companies listed on the VSE with a framework for the management and control of their operations. The code provides for standards of good corporate management in accordance with both international best practice and key provisions of Austrian corporation   **8.147**

---

[111] This chapter comprises a summary of the Preamble of the Austrian Code of Corporate Governance, available at http://www.wienerborse.at/corporate/pdf/CG_Code_engl_2009draft_tr_fin.pdf

law that are relevant in the corporate governance context. In particular, it is designed to increase the level of transparency with which listed companies operate.

8.148 The Austrian Code of Corporate Governance is based on the provisions of Austrian law (principally, corporation law, securities law and capital markets law), EU recommendations relating to supervisory board members, and on the principles set out in the OECD Principles of Corporate Governance.

8.149 In addition to important statutory requirements under Austrian law, the Austrian Code of Corporate Governance contains rules based on common international practice. Beside mandatory L-rules (see below), which are applicable for all issuers, issuers that do not comply with C-rules (see below) must state this and provide reasons for non-compliance. The Austrian Code of Corporate Governance also contains rules (i.e. R-rules, see below) that go beyond these requirements and should be applied on a voluntary basis.

8.150 The Code comprises the following categories of rules:

(i)   Legal requirement (L): these rules are mandatory legal requirements.
(ii) Comply or explain (C): these rules should be followed and any deviations therefrom must be explained.
(iii) Recommendation (R): these are recommendations, non-compliance with which requires neither disclosure nor explanation.

8.3.6.2 Commitment, corporate governance report

8.151 Austrian companies are called to voluntarily adhere to the principles set out in the Austrian Code of Corporate Governance by publishing a declaration of compliance on their websites. Such declaration is mandatory only for Austrian companies admitted to the prime market of the VSE.[112]

8.152 In respect of financial statements pertaining to fiscal years beginning after 31 December 2008, all companies with shares admitted to trading on the official or semi-official market of the VSE must include in such financial statements a specific corporate governance report containing the following information:[113]

(i)   nomination of a Corporate Governance Code generally recognized in Austria or at the respective place the issuer is already admitted;
(ii) information on where the report is publicly available;
(iii) where the issuer deviates from the Comply or Explain rules of the Austrian Code of Corporate Governance, an explanation of all deviations; and
(iv) if relevant, an explanation of why the issuer has opted not to adhere to a corporate governance code.

---

[112] For details regarding admission to the prime market see above Section 8.1.3.1.1.
[113] Entrepreneur Act section 243b and 906 —Unternehmensgesetzbuch (Handelsgesetzbuch); dRGBl. S 219/1897 zuletzt geändert durch BGBl. I Nr. 70/2008 of 7 May 2008, as amended.

Issuers that are subject to the company law of another EU member state and are listed on the VSE are required to adhere to a corporate governance code recognized in the EU or EEA. Such issuers must identify on their website (i) the particular corporate governance code to which they adhere; and (ii) the relevant applicable company law. **8.153**

Companies that are subject to the company law of a third country and listed on the VSE are required to comply with the Austrian Code of Corporate Governance, according to the terms of the Code itself. **8.154**

9

BELGIUM*

9.1 Jurisdiction Overview

9.1.1 Legislative overview

9.01 The Prospectus Directive has been implemented into Belgian national law by the statute of 16 June 2006 regarding the public offering of investment instruments and the admission to trading of investment instruments on a regulated market (the 'Prospectus Statute').

9.02 A more detailed technical elaboration on the minimum information, the form and the publication of a prospectus can be found in the Prospectus Regulation. This Prospectus Regulation specifies the Prospectus Directive and applies in Belgium, just as in any other member state, directly without the need for implementation.

9.03 The statute of 2 August 2002 regarding the supervision of the financial sector and the financial services (the 'Financial Supervision Statute') is also relevant in the field

---

* The author would like to express his gratitude to Kris Verdoodt, Bert Van Ingelghem and Bregtje Van Bockstaele for their valuable contribution in preparing this chapter.

of public offers and admittance to trading of securities on a regulated market. Among other matters the Financial Supervision Statute deals with the following:

(i)   the conditions and procedure for market undertakings to obtain a permit to organize a Belgian regulated market;

(ii) the principles applicable to the market rules of a regulated market;

(iii) market abuse and market manipulation; and

(iv) the organization, functioning and powers of the Belgian Banking, Finance and Insurance Commission ('*Commissie voor Bank-, Financie- en Assurantiewezen*'/ '*Commission Bancaire, Financière et des Assurances*') (the 'CBFA'), the competent authority for the supervision of the financial sector and financial services in Belgium.

After a market consultation procedure conducted by the CBFA, the Royal Decree   **9.04**
of 17 May 2007 relating to primary market practices (the 'Primary Market Practices Decree') was adopted. The Primary Market Practices Decree was amended on 30 July 2008 after a new consultation procedure during which the first applications of the Primary Market Practices Decree were assessed. Based on international best practices, the Primary Market Practices Decree aims to provide a comprehensive set of rules in relation to: (i) the equitable treatment of retail investors; (ii) stabilization, over-allotment and adjustment of the offer size; (iii) the prohibition against granting certain advantages in the pre-offer period; and (iv) the disclosure of information on market demand during and after the IPO.

As is the case for all member states, the recommendations by the Committee of   **9.05**
European Securities Regulators (the 'CESR') for the consistent implementation of the Prospectus Regulation are an important source for Belgian practice. Furthermore the CBFA, as the regulatory authority, has issued a number of circular letters and has adopted certain practices in relation to the application of the prospectus legislation.

The Belgian legislation on the continuing obligations of issuers whose shares   **9.06**
are admitted to trading on a regulated market has been updated following the implementation of the Transparency Directive. The applicable laws are the Financial Supervision Statute, the Royal Decree of 14 November 2007 regarding the obligations of issuers of securities admitted to trading on a regulated market ('Transparency Decree I') and the Royal Decree of 5 March 2006 on market abuse (the 'Market Abuse Decree').

With regard to the disclosure of major shareholdings, the Transparency Directive   **9.07**
has been implemented into Belgian law via the statute of 2 May 2007 regarding the disclosure of material holdings in issuers whose shares are admitted to trading on a regulated market (the 'Transparency Statute') and the Royal Decree of 14 February 2008 regarding the disclosure of material holdings ('Transparency Decree II'). The Belgian Companies Code ('*Wetboek van Vennootschappen*'/

'*Codes des Sociétés*') (the 'Companies Code') and Transparency Decree I also contain some relevant provisions relating to the notification obligations.

9.08 With regard to public takeovers, the Takeover Directive has been implemented into Belgian national law by the statute of 1 April 2007 (the 'Takeover Statute'), which has been further detailed by the Royal Decree of 27 April 2007 regarding public takeover bids (the 'Takeover Decree') (dealing with public takeover bids in general) and the Royal Decree of 27 April 2007 regarding public squeeze-out bids (the 'Squeeze-out Decree') (addressing a particular type of squeeze-out bid). General principles and important rules of takeover law are set forth in the Takeover Statute. Detailed rules and procedures can be found in the Takeover Decree and the Squeeze-out Decree.

9.1.2 Competent authority: Belgian Banking, Finance and Insurance Commission

9.09 The CBFA is the single Belgian authority in charge of supervising most financial institutions and financial services offered to the public. The CBFA was established to ensure the protection of savers, public confidence in financial products and services and the proper operation of markets in financial instruments.[1] The CBFA has thus been entrusted with a wide variety of responsibilities and powers.

9.10 The CBFA is the authority that: (i) supervises the proper operation, integrity and transparency of the financial markets (by supervising the organization of the markets and behaviour of market participants); (ii) approves the prospectus whenever a public issue of investment instruments or the admission to trading on a regulated market takes place in Belgium; (iii) monitors compliance with the rules on public takeover bids, including those regarding anti-takeover protection and defensive measures; and (iv) monitors the compliance with the Transparency Statute and both Transparency Decree I and Transparency Decree II, of information disseminated by listed companies and the disclosure of large shareholdings. In that capacity the CBFA can impose certain corrective measures. It can: (i) require an issuer to publish a rectification in case it deems that certain information is missing in the prospectus or that a significant item in the prospectus is incorrect or potentially misleading (failing such rectification the CBFA can publish it on its own initiative); (ii) publish warnings where it deems that information published by a listed company is incorrect or insufficient; (iii) suspend trading; (iv) issue injunctions; and (v) impose administrative fines in certain cases (including coercive fines to enforce its injunctions). The above demonstrates that the CBFA plays a key role in the Belgian financial markets. Hence, it is of major importance to keep the CBFA in the loop of any proposed transactions or publications in a

---

[1] For more details see Financial Supervision Statute Article 45.

timely fashion. In that respect it is common to organize an informal 'kick-off' meeting with the CBFA well in advance of formally introducing files to the CBFA, in order to discuss the transaction structure and the proposed timeline.

9.1.3 Belgian regulated market: Euronext Brussels and the Belgian Derivatives Market

9.1.3.1 *Euronext markets in Belgium*

Euronext Brussels NV is the market operator for the following two Belgian regulated markets:[2] Euronext Brussels[3] and the Belgian Derivatives Market. Euronext Brussels NV is governed by the Financial Supervision Statute and has been registered as a market undertaking in accordance with that statute. As a market undertaking Euronext Brussels NV is supervised by the CBFA.[4]   **9.11**

Euronext Brussels NV also operates the following non-regulated markets (multilateral trading facilities): Alternext, the Free Market ('*Vrije Markt*'/'*Marché Libre*'), the Public Auctions ('*Publieke Veilingen*'/'*Ventes Publiques*'), the Trading Facility and Easynext.   **9.12**

Given that the regulated markets are subject to the most detailed scope of regulation, this contribution will only focus on rules applicable to regulated markets and/or to companies listed on a regulated market.   **9.13**

9.1.3.2 *Euronext as a pan-European stock exchange*[5]

Euronext Brussels NV holds a licence as market undertaking granted by the CBFA and operates under its supervision. However, given the fact that Euronext NV operates exchanges in five European countries, regulation of Euronext Brussels and its constituent markets is conducted in a coordinated fashion by the respective national regulatory authorities pursuant to memoranda of understanding relating to the cash and derivatives markets. Those memoranda provide a framework to coordinate supervision of the markets operated by the Euronext group.   **9.14**

---

[2] Apart from the market for linear bonds, split securities and treasury certificates, these are the only regulated markets in Belgium.

[3] Euronext Brussels is the commercial denomination of the regulated market operated by Euronext Brussels NV and includes the former First Market, Second Market and New Market and the Public Debt Instruments Market.

[4] Financial Supervision Statute Article 3, §2.

[5] For more information see Euronext's website http://www.euronext.com and more in particular NYSE Euronext's Form 10-K for fiscal year ended 31 December 2008, pages 20–24 which can be found at https://materials.proxyvote.com/Approved/629491/20090210/10K_34570.PDF.

9.2 Listing Securities in Practice

9.2.1 Listing Rules

9.2.1.1 Euronext rule book applicable to Euronext Brussels

9.15   The market rules applicable to Euronext Brussels and the Belgian Derivatives Market consist of two books. Book I contains the harmonized rules, including rules of conduct and enforcement rules that are designed to protect the markets, as well as rules on listing, trading and membership. Book II—Specific Rules for Euronext Brussels—contains all non-harmonized market rules for Euronext Brussels and the Belgian Derivatives Market.

9.16   The notices adopted by Euronext for the enforcement of Book I apply to all Euronext markets (unless otherwise specified), while those for the enforcement of Book II are specific to local jurisdictions.

9.17   Market rules of a Belgian regulated market should at all times comply with the general principles set forth in Article 5 of the Financial Supervision Statute. Hence, in order to secure compliance with the Financial Supervision Statute, the CBFA needs to approve both the market rules of Book I[6] and the market rules of Book II and any changes which are made thereto. The most recent changes to the Euronext Rule Books were approved by the CBFA on 17 March 2009.

9.2.1.2 Admission to listing and listing requirements

9.18   **9.2.1.2.1 Admission to listing**   Chapter 6 of Euronext Rule Book I sets forth the requirements and procedures for the admission to listing (and delisting) of securities on Euronext Brussels as well as the continuing obligations of issuers whose securities are admitted to listing with their consent.

9.19   In its capacity as the registered market undertaking organizing the Euronext Brussels regulated markets, Euronext Brussels NV is the competent authority for the purpose of Directive 2001/34/EC of 28 May 2001 on the admission of securities to official stock exchange listings and on information to be published on those securities. Thus, Euronext Brussels decides on the admission to listing on a Euronext Brussels regulated market (though without prejudice to the need to obtain the CBFA's approval of an admission prospectus).[7]

---

[6] Given that Euronext Rule Book I contains harmonized rules, changes to Euronext Rule Book I should also be approved by the competent authorities in France, the Netherlands, Portugal and the United Kingdom.

[7] Financial Supervision Statute Article 7, §2.

9.2.1.2.2 Listing requirements   Some flexibility has been built into the appli-   **9.20**
cation of the listing requirements of Euronext Rule Book I[8] as Euronext Brussels
NV may derogate from the admission conditions, insofar as such derogation
applies to all issuers that find themselves in similar circumstances.[9] On the other
hand, Euronext Brussels NV may make the admission of a financial instrument
dependent on any specific condition that it deems appropriate for the protection
of the interests of investors.

9.2.2 The prospectus

9.2.2.1 Scope of application of the Prospectus Statute

The Belgian Prospectus Statute has a broader scope than the European Prospectus   **9.21**
Directive due to the fact that the Prospectus Statute also applies to investment
instruments that do not fall within the scope of the Prospectus Directive.

As a result, two types of rules co-exist in Belgium. On the one hand, there is a har-   **9.22**
monized regime for the transactions covered by the Prospective Directive, i.e.:

(i)   public offers of securities in Belgium for a total consideration of EUR
      2,500,000 or more (optional if less than such amount);[10] and
(ii) admissions of securities to trading on a Belgian regulated market.[11]

On the other hand, the Prospectus Statute governs the following non-harmonized   **9.23**
transactions:[12]

(i)   public offers of securities in Belgium for less than EUR 2,500,000 (unless
      the harmonized regime is opted for);
(ii) all public offers in Belgium of investment instruments other than securities
      in the sense of the Prospectus Directive; and
(iii) all admissions to trading on a Belgian regulated market of investment instru-
      ments other than securities in the sense of the Prospectus Directive.

The main impact of the different regimes relates to the contents of the prospectus.   **9.24**
Given the fact that the non-harmonized transactions are rather uncommon, we
will not further elaborate on those in this Chapter.

---

[8] The main listing requirements and the additional listing requirements per category of securities (shares, corporate bonds, securities issued by investment funds and investment companies and
trackers) can be found in, respectively, Rules 6601–6608 and Rules 6701 and 6707/2 of Euronext
Rule Book I.
[9] Rule Book II Rule B-3301/2 .
[10] It should be noted that certain offers which fall outside the scope of the Prospectus Directive
(as set forth in Prospectus Directive Articles 1, 2) also fall outside the scope of the Prospectus
Statute.
[11] A prospectus is required for an admission to listing on a regulated market even if such admission is not connected to a public offer.
[12] Prospectus Statute Article 43.

9.25 The Prospectus Statute also applies to the prospectus and promotional communications concerning public offers of securities and admissions of securities in other European countries, when Belgium is the home member state of the relevant issuer.[13]

9.2.2.2 Exemptions and safe harbours

9.26 In line with the Prospectus Directive, the Prospectus Statute contains a number of exemptions to the obligation to publish a prospectus for a public offer or an admission to trading on a regulated market.[14]

9.27 Furthermore, securities can be offered and sold to investors in Belgium without triggering public offer disclosure and prospectus registration requirements if the offer does not qualify as a public offer in accordance with the safe harbour provisions.[15]

9.28 In addition, informing existing holders of securities in Belgium of the launch of a public offer abroad, or allowing them to subscribe as part of such offer, does not in principle constitute a public offer in Belgium.[16] Offers or attributions for free are not offers within the meaning of the Prospectus Statute, but, in principle, are subject to the publication of limited information (not to be approved by the CBFA).[17]

9.2.2.3 Definition of public offer

9.29 The criteria to determine whether an offer is public in Belgium are based on the Prospectus Directive and the Prospectus Statute.

9.30 Under Belgian law, a public offer is defined as: a communication to persons in any form and by any means, presenting sufficient information[18] on the terms of the offer and the securities to be offered, so as to enable an investor to decide to purchase or subscribe to these securities.[19] This definition is identical to the definition given in Article 2.1(d) of the Prospectus Directive. The Prospectus Statute however adds one element to this definition. It states that the offer needs to be effected by a person who is capable of issuing or transferring the securities (or by a person representing such person). Hence communications made by third parties such as journalists, analysts (independent from the members of the banking syndicate) or

---

[13] Prospectus Statute Article 15, §1, 2°.

[14] For more details see Prospectus Statute Article 18, §1 and §2.

[15] Those safe harbour provisions are identical to the safe harbour provisions in the Prospectus Directive and can be found in Prospectus Statute Article 3, §1.

[16] Prospectus Statute Article 3, §4.

[17] Prospectus Statute Article 73.

[18] The information provided is deemed sufficient whenever the principal features of the offer are described and the price is given or determinable.

[19] Prospectus Statute Article 3, §1.

investment firms cannot constitute a public offer in case such persons do not represent the issuer or offeror.

9.2.2.4 Content of the prospectus

9.2.2.4.1 General The prospectus must contain all necessary information **9.31** which, in light of the particular nature of the issuer and of the securities offered, enables the investors to make an informed assessment of the assets and liabilities, the financial position, the results and the prospects of the issuer and guarantor (if any) and of the rights attaching to such securities. This information should be presented in an easily analysable and comprehensible form.[20]

Given that the Belgian Prospectus Statute is based on the European Prospectus **9.32** Directive, which provides for a far-reaching harmonization, and that the European Prospectus Regulation applies directly in Belgium, there are no fundamental differences between the Belgian rules applicable to the content of a prospectus compared to those of other EU member states. Hence, only a number of topics for which the Belgian situation is particular will be covered herein.

9.2.2.4.2 Price information The Prospectus Statute determines that in case **9.33** the final offer price and the final number of securities offered to the public cannot be included in the prospectus, the prospectus should mention (i) the criteria and/ or conditions on which the determination of the final offer price and the final number of offered securities will be based *and* (ii) the maximum price. If no maximum price can be mentioned, the prospectus should mention that subscriptions can be withdrawn within two working days after publication of the final offer price.[21]

This is more stringent than the Prospectus Directive and the Prospectus Regulation, **9.34** since they leave the choice to mention either (i) the arrangements and time for announcing to the public the definitive amount of the offer, (ii) the maximum price, *or* (iii) the right to withdraw subscriptions within two days after publication of the final offer price.

In case the offer price is established through a bookbuilding procedure, the pro- **9.35** spectus or the press release issued just prior to the offer period usually only contains a price range as the final price is determined after the offer period. Given the Belgian rule that in the absence of a maximum offer price investors are entitled to withdraw their subscriptions, Belgian market practice became that the prospectus (or the pre-offer press release) explicitly mentions that the top of the price range is

---

[20] Prospectus Statute Article 24, §1.
[21] Prospectus Statute Article 27.

also the maximum offer price. Thus, issuers tend to prefer a potentially lower issue price over the risk connected with the potential withdrawal of subscriptions.

9.36 **9.2.2.4.3 Working capital statement** The Prospectus Regulation requires that the prospectus for an offer of shares contains a working capital statement. It should be stated that in the issuer's opinion the working capital is sufficient for the issuer's requirements for the 12 months as from the date of the prospectus.[22] If no such clean statement can be given, the prospectus should mention how the issuer proposes to provide the additional working capital needed.

9.37 In Belgium, the question has arisen whether the proceeds of the offer can be taken into account when assessing the issuer's working capital needs. Contrary to the views held in other member states, the initial position of the CBFA was that the proceeds of the offer can as a principle not be taken into account.[23] However, in some more recent cases[24] the CBFA has taken the view that, in a case where prior to the prospectus approval date a hard underwriting agreement is entered into between the issuer and the banking syndicate in connection with the public offer, the proceeds of such offer can be taken into account up to the amount of the hard underwriting commitment when providing the working capital statement. The same reasoning applies in a case where certain reference shareholders commit to exercise their preferential subscription rights within the framework of a rights issue.

9.38 The CESR is currently assessing this issue. The general expectation is that the CESR will take the view that offer proceeds can under no circumstances be taken into account for the working capital statement and that it may be the case that a qualified working capital statement must be included in the prospectus whereby the offer is to be mentioned as a measure to provide additional working capital.

9.39 **9.2.2.4.4 Summary** Unless the prospectus relates to the admission to trading on a regulated market of non-equity securities having a denomination of at least EUR 50,000, the prospectus should include a summary which shall, in a brief manner and in non-technical language, set forth the essential characteristics and risks associated with the issuer and the securities.[25]

---

[22] Prospectus Regulation section 3.1 of Annex III. For the 12-month period, see CESR's recommendations for the consistent implementation of the Prospectus Regulation of January 2005, page 25.

[23] However, the upcoming public offer, and the likelihood of its success, could serve as a measure proposed by the issuer to provide for additional working capital within the framework of an unqualified working capital statement in the prospectus.

[24] See for example the listing prospectus published by Hansen Transmissions NV in December 2007 and the public offering prospectus published by Picanol NV in June 2009.

[25] Prospectus Statute Article 24, §2.

In addition, the summary shall contain a warning that:[26] **9.40**

(i)   it should be read as an introduction to the prospectus;
(ii) any decision to invest in the securities should be based on consideration of the prospectus as a whole by the investor;
(iii) if a claim relating to the information contained in a prospectus is brought before a court, the investor might, under the national legislation of the member state where the court is located, have to bear the costs of translating the prospectus before the legal proceedings are initiated; and
(iv) nobody can be held liable merely on the basis of the summary except if the contents thereof are misleading, incorrect or inconsistent when read in conjunction with the other parts of the prospectus.

9.2.2.5 Supplement to the prospectus

In the event of important new developments, material errors or inaccuracies that   **9.41**
could affect the assessment of the securities, and which occur or are identified between the time of the approval of the prospectus and the final closing of the public offer, or, if applicable, the time at which trading on a regulated market commences, the issuer will need to publish a supplement to the prospectus.[27] This supplement will be published on the websites of the issuer and the lead manager. The issuer must ensure that this supplement is published as quickly as possible. Investors who have already agreed to purchase or subscribe to securities before the publication of the supplement to the prospectus, have the right to withdraw their subscription for two working days after the publication of the supplement.

9.2.2.6 Form of the prospectus

The issuer may draw up the prospectus as a single document or in separate docu-   **9.42**
ments. A prospectus composed of separate documents shall divide the required information into:

(i)   a registration document, which shall contain the information relating to the issuer;
(ii) a securities note, which shall contain the information concerning the securities to be offered to the public; and
(iii) a summary.[28]

The registration document may be approved by the CBFA at any time in anticipa-   **9.43**
tion of future public offers or admissions to trading. Once the issuer has obtained

---

[26] Prospectus Statute Article 24, §2.
[27] Prospectus Statute Article 34 .
[28] Prospectus Statute Article 28.

such CBFA approval of a registration document, it only needs to establish a securities note and a summary for a specific offer. In such case, only the securities note and the summary have to be approved by the CBFA right before the offer. If, on the contrary, the registration document has not yet been approved by the CBFA in anticipation of future public offers or admissions to trading, it has to be approved by the CBFA together with the securities note and the summary, right before the offering.

9.44   A still more flexible solution compared to working with a registration document and securities note, is that for the following types of securities, the prospectus can, at the choice of the issuer, consist of one base prospectus containing all relevant information concerning the issuer and the securities offered to the public:[29]

(i)   non-equity securities, including warrants in any form, issued under an offer programme; and

(ii)   non-equity securities issued in a continuous or repeated manner by credit institutions provided certain conditions are met.

9.45   If the base prospectus (or any supplement thereto) does not include the final terms of the offer, the latter shall be filed with the CBFA and shall be duly made available to the public, as soon as possible before the beginning of the trading. Such final terms do not need to be approved by the CBFA. The formula to publish a base prospectus supplemented with final terms offers a flexible solution for issuers willing to set up a continuous issue programme of certain types of securities.

9.2.2.7   Use of languages

9.46   The Prospectus Statute provides that the prospectus can be established in Dutch, French or another language customary in the sphere of international finance and which is accepted by the CBFA, i.e. English. In case the prospectus entirely or in part relates to a public offer of securities on the Belgian territory, a summary of the prospectus in Dutch and in French has to be available.[30]

9.47   However, given that Belgium is a federal country with three language communities (the Flemish community, the French community, the German community), the Belgian Constitution grants the exclusive power to the communities to adopt rules on the use of languages for documents of companies which are 'prescribed/imposed' by the law and the regulations. Both the Flemish community and the French community have issued legislation applicable to companies with a seat of exploitation in the Flemish Community or the French Community respectively. The basic principle of this legislation is that documents which are prescribed

---

[29]   Prospectus Statute Article 29.
[30]   Prospectus Statute Article 31.

or imposed by the law and the regulations, should be published in Dutch or French respectively. Non-compliance with the respective language regimes leads to a nullity sanction.

In that context, discussion has arisen as to whether the Prospectus Statute can lawfully allow an issuer with a seat in the Flemish community or the French community to publish a prospectus in English with only a summary in Dutch and French.[31]   **9.48**

Some legal scholars have taken the view that a prospectus is a document prescribed by law which is subject to the language regime of each of the communities where the issuer has a seat of exploitation. That would mean that an issuer with a seat of exploitation in both the Flemish community and the French community would have to publish the entire prospectus in both Dutch and French. The flexibility granted by the Prospectus Statute would thus be in vain. In case a frustrated investor should invoke non-compliance with the Belgian language regimes, the prospectus could be declared null and void, which would entail subscriptions received based on such annulled prospectus also being null and void. Hence non-compliance with the Belgian language regime(s) could in the view of these legal scholars endanger the entire transaction.   **9.49**

However, there are good arguments for the statement that the use of languages as set forth in the Prospectus Statute (pursuant to which issuers are entitled to publish a prospectus in English with a summary in Dutch or French) can be applied without taking into account the specific Belgian language regimes set out above. Those arguments are primarily based on the fact that the language regime set forth in the Prospectus Statute is based on a precise, clear and unconditional provision of the Prospectus Directive (i.e. Article 19, §2, of the Prospectus Directive), which thus has direct effect in Belgium. Hence Belgian national law should be interpreted by the courts in conformity with European Community law. In addition, against the background of the achievement of the European internal market, Recital 35 of the Prospectus Directive states that the obligation for an issuer to translate the full prospectus into all the relevant official languages discourages cross-border offers or multiple trading. To facilitate cross-border offers, where the prospectus is drawn up in a language that is customary in the sphere of international finance, the host or home member state should only be entitled to require a summary in its official language(s). Hence if Belgian legislation were applied in such a way that an entire translation of the prospectus in Dutch and/or French were required, it would not comply with one of the basic principles of the Prospectus Directive.   **9.50**

---

[31] In case an issuer has a seat in several communities their respective language legislation is to be applied cumulatively.

9.2.2.8 Approval process

9.51   As a kick-off for any envisaged public offer or admission to trading on a regulated market, the practice is widely established to organize a meeting with the CBFA once the plan to effectuate an offer has crystallized. Usually during such kick-off meeting, a presentation is given on the issuer's business and a timeline is agreed upon with the CBFA. Furthermore, the CBFA requests to be kept informed of any milestone that has been achieved in such process. The prospectus approval process is an interactive process between the issuer/offeror and the CBFA where some informal contacts and informal filings of drafts of the prospectus take place prior to the official filing of the draft prospectus with the CBFA for approval.

9.52   After the issuer/offeror has notified the CBFA of its intention to make a public offer in Belgium, it has to file the following documents with the CBFA: the draft prospectus; information on the underwriting process; information on lock-up agreements regarding the securities for which the admission to trading is sought (if any); special reports required under Belgian corporate law (if any); to the extent the prospectus refers thereto, the special reports provided by any specialist or expert; and any other document that might be relevant for the review of the prospectus.

9.53   Once the file is complete, the CBFA has 10 working days (or 20 working days if the CBFA has not approved any prospectus of the issuer during the last 10 years, which is always the case for an IPO) to approve or reject the prospectus.

9.54   If the CBFA fails to notify the issuer/offeror of a decision within the said time limit, special procedures apply and the application shall be deemed to be rejected.

9.55   The CBFA's approval should not be considered an opinion on the opportunity or the quality of the transaction, nor on the status of the issuer. With respect to prospectuses, the CBFA is entrusted (only) with the supervision of and control over the quality of the information contained in the prospectus.

9.56   The approved prospectus and/or registration document is valid for 12 months after its approval, to the extent that it is duly updated and completed by any required supplements.

9.57   In addition to the requirement to have a prospectus approved by the CBFA in accordance with the Belgian legislation, specific requirements may be imposed by the regulated market authority in case listing is sought. Those requirements depend upon the type of securities being listed and the segment of the market on which it will be listed.

9.2.2.9 *Marketing documentation*

Advertisements and marketing materials produced in the framework of a public **9.58** offer in Belgium or listing on a Belgian regulated market should comply with the following requirements:[32]

(i) They shall state that a prospectus has been or will be published and indicate where investors will be able to obtain it.

(ii) The information contained therein shall not be inaccurate, or misleading.

(iii) The information contained therein shall be consistent with the information contained in the prospectus, if already published, or with the information required to be in the prospectus, if the prospectus is published afterwards.

On 5 March 2009 the CBFA adopted recommendations regarding advertisements **9.59** in respect of public offers and admissions to trading on a regulated market.[33] These recommendations were made based on the following considerations:

(i) Advertisements are not intended to replace the prospectus or the final terms of the offer. The CBFA therefore recommends that the place where investors can obtain the prospectus and the final terms of the offer be clearly and visibly mentioned.

(ii) It is also desirable that advertisements should contribute, together with the prospectus and the summary, to a better understanding of the investment instrument being offered. This is the case when the information is presented in a reasonably clear manner.

(iii) Care should be taken that the information provided in advertisements is correct and does not disguise, diminish or obscure important items, statements or warnings.

Based on these general considerations the CBFA has made recommendations **9.60** relating to: the name to be given to a security, the identification of the type of security, the identification of the issuer, the mentioning of risk factors, the presentation of the yield of bonds and other debt securities, capital redemption in case of bonds and other debt securities, examples included in the advertisement, indications of past performance, simulated past performance (pro-forma information), information on future performance, tax matters, charges, negotiability, liability and the mentioning of the name of the competent authority.

In all events, advertisements and marketing documents shall be clearly recogniz- **9.61** able as such. Advertisements and marketing materials produced in the framework

---

[32] Prospectus Statute Article 58.
[33] Communication CBFA_2009_11 of 5 March 2009, 'Recommendations of the CBFA regarding advertisements and other documents and announcements relating to an operation referred to in Title VI of the Prospectus Statute'.

of a public offer shall be approved by the CBFA prior to being made available to the public. The CBFA reviews the advertisements and marketing materials within five working days after receipt of the documents.

9.62 It is to be noted that the notion of advertisements is broader in the Prospectus Statute than in the Prospectus Directive since the former also purports to 'all other documents and notices relating to a public offer or admission to trading'.[34] Hence there could be some (theoretical) doubt as to whether certain documents that are not advertisements under the Prospectus Directive e.g. certain documents on an issuer's intranet, documents spread among the IPO team, etc. do qualify as advertisements under the Prospectus Statute and should thus comply with the above requirements. In practice, however, this does not entail important discussions.

9.2.3 Primary market practices (rules of conduct)

9.2.3.1 Introduction

9.63 As mentioned above,[35] certain primary market practices are laid down in the Primary Market Practices Decree.

9.64 The Primary Market Practices Decree replaces the CBFA's previous circular letter D2/F/2000/4. As laid down in a Royal Decree, such practices have become 'hard law', whereas the CBFA's circular letter contained administrative best practice recommendations which were applied by the CBFA with a certain degree of flexibility and was thus considered 'soft law'. It can be questioned whether this is the right approach. Stock market practices have over time proven to be subject to quite some evolution and the CBFA will have no flexibility in applying the provisions of the Primary Market Practices Decree. Moreover, as a rule of law, amendments to the Primary Market Practices Decree can only be made after a relatively lengthy consultation procedure.

9.2.3.2 Scope of application

9.65 The Primary Market Practices Decree applies to all public offers of securities effected in Belgium to the extent a prospectus is required pursuant to the Prospectus Statute and such prospectus is to be filed in advance with the CBFA for approval.[36]

9.66 This means that the Primary Market Practices Decree applies to all public offers, both primary and secondary offers, irrespective of whether such offer concurs with an admission to trading on a regulated market.

---

[34] Prospectus Statute Article 58, §1.
[35] See Section 9.9.1.1 above.
[36] Primary Market Practices Decree Article 2.

9.2.3.3 *Equitable treatment of retail investors*

9.2.3.3.1 Qualification of retail investors   Retail investors are defined in the   **9.67**
Primary Market Practices Decree as all investors which do not qualify as qualified
investors under the Prospectus Statute.

9.2.3.3.2 10% retail tranche   The Primary Market Practices Decree provides   **9.68**
that each public offer which is not restricted to one specific group of investors should include a minimum retail tranche of 10%. The CBFA can however
derogate from this provision with a duly motivated decision. The 10% tranche
should be calculated based on the initial offer size, irrespective of the actual
take-up.

The purpose of this provision is that for offers which are clearly also aimed at retail   **9.69**
investors, those investors would not be frustrated in their expectations during the
allocation process. Clearly, the 10% retail tranche should only be complied with
if the retail investor demand exceeds 10%. If there is insufficient retail demand, a
claw-back can in principle be applied.[37]

9.2.3.3.3 Closing of retail tranche prior to closing of the institutional tranche   **9.70**
not allowed   As a principle the retail tranche offer cannot be closed prior to the
institutional tranche except under the following conditions:[38]

(i)   the possibility of closing the retail tranche first has been included in the
     prospectus;
(ii) the circumstances that may give rise to such early closing of the retail tranche
     have been described in the prospectus; and
(iii) measures have been taken to warrant confidentiality of the order book until
     all tranches have been closed.

The main reason why the retail tranche would be closed a few days prior to the   **9.71**
institutional tranche is probably that the logistics for the closing of the retail
tranche are more complex (centralization, review of acceptance notices, etc.).
Even when complying with the above-mentioned conditions for the early closing
of the retail offer, it would still be feasible to provide for the possibility of closing
the retail offer for logistical reasons.[39] However, in practice it seems that in
the majority of cases the prospectus states that the offer period for retail and

---

[37] A clawback can in any case only be applied in accordance with the terms set forth in the
Prospectus (pursuant to Prospectus Regulation section 5.2 of Schedule III).
[38] The Primary Market Practices Decree explicitly mentions that the institutional tranche can be
closed prior to the retail tranche.
[39] However, it should be noted that in case a supplement to the prospectus is published, investors
have the possibility to revoke their acceptance of the public offer within two business days, even if
the retail tranche has already been closed.

institutional investors will be the same and thus excludes an early closing of the retail tranche.

9.72   **9.2.3.3.4 Allocation**   In case of oversubscription of a public offer, issues of allocation may arise. Such issues may concern the allocation to the different tranches (retail v institutional) but may also relate to unequal treatment of investors belonging to the same tranche (eg preference for subscriptions made through the banking syndicate, preference for the syndicate members' own clients, etc).[40]

9.73   In order to address such issues, the legal framework applicable in Belgium imposes a number of allocation prohibitions on the members of the banking syndicate in order to avoid abuse. In addition, it provides for disclosure of certain aspects of the allocation process both in the prospectus and after the offer period.[41]

9.74   *9.2.3.3.4.1 (a) Prohibitions*   In order to avoid abuse by the members of the banking syndicate, members of the syndicate are not allowed to directly or indirectly acquire for their own account securities that are offered within the framework of a public offer in case the public offer has entirely been subscribed for or in case of oversubscription, except within the framework of a hard underwriting commitment.

9.75   Furthermore, the members of the syndicate cannot allocate instruments to third parties if such allocation would result in direct or indirect advantages for the members of the syndicate.[42] This prohibition, which is based on the 'Handbook of Rules and Guidelines' issued by the Financial Services Authority in the United Kingdom, aims at preventing (i) allocations to clients as a result of which such clients would be incited to pay excessive remunerations for other services or to enter into a high number of service agreements; (ii) preferential allocations to leaders of clients or potential clients of the syndicate members as a *quid pro quo* for future assignments in the field of corporate finance, and (iii) all allocations which are, either explicitly or implicitly, subject to the receipt of orders or the provision of any other service.[43]

9.76   *9.2.3.3.4.2 (b) Disclosure requirements*   As pre-allotment disclosure, the Prospectus should contain information on the following elements:[44]

---

[40] CESR, 'Stabilisation and Allotment: a European Supervisory Approach', CESR/02/020b, April 2002, pages 15–16.

[41] For the practical aspects of such publication see under (b) hereunder.

[42] Primary Market Practices Decree Article 7, §2.

[43] Report to the King in relation to the Primary Market Practices Decree, *Belgisch Staatsblad* 18 June 2007, 32.928.

[44] Prospectus Regulation section 5.2 of Annex III.

(i) the division into tranches of the offer including the institutional, retail and issuer's employee tranches and any other tranches;

(ii) the conditions under which the claw-back may be used, the maximum size of such claw-back and any applicable minimum percentages for individual tranches;

(iii) the allotment method or methods to be used for the retail and issuer's employee tranche in the event of an over-subscription of these tranches;

(iv) a description of any pre-determined preferential treatment to be accorded to certain classes of investors or certain affinity groups (including friends and family programmes) in the allotment, the percentage of the offer reserved for such preferential treatment and the criteria for inclusion in such classes or groups;

(v) whether the treatment of subscriptions or bids to subscribe in the allotment may be determined on the basis of which firm they are made through or by;

(vi) a target minimum individual allotment if any within the retail tranche;

(vii) the conditions for the closing of the offer as well as the date on which the offer may be closed at the earliest; and

(viii) whether or not multiple subscriptions are admitted, and where they are not, how any multiple subscriptions will be handled.

Furthermore, the Prospectus Statute provides that the result of a public offer of shares should be made public.[45] In addition, pursuant to the Primary Market Practices Decree, the following information is to be disclosed as post-allocation disclosure within five working days after the closing of the offer period: **9.77**

(i) the aggregate number of the allotted instruments;

(ii) the results of the allocation;

(iii) the allocation within the different tranches;

(iv) the result of the use of the over-allotment facility;

(v) the result of the application of the claw-back;

(vi) the percentage of the offer which benefited from a preferential treatment; and

(vii) the final offer price.

Such disclosure can either be made through a publication (i) in one or more daily newspapers which are distributed in the entire country or are published in a considerable edition or (ii) by posting it on the website of the issuer, the offeror or the intermediary. **9.78**

9.2.3.3.5 Offer price The Primary Market Practices Decree provides that for public offers of shares, the terms and conditions of such offer and, most importantly, **9.79**

---

[45] Prospectus Statute Article 63.

the final price of the offer, should be identical for the retail tranche and the tranche reserved for institutional investors. However, a limited price reduction can be granted to the retail investors (e.g. employees).

9.2.3.4 Over-allotment, stabilization and adjustment of the offer size

9.80　**9.2.3.4.1 Over-allotment and stabilization**　The over-allotment facility is defined in the Primary Market Practices Decree as the clause in the underwriting agreement or the lead management agreement which allows the acceptance of subscriptions for a higher number of financial instruments than initially offered.[46] Thus, the over-allotment facility allows the lead manager to address the situation where market demand exceeds the offer size. Usually in order to address such potential excess demand, a stock lending is granted by one or more major existing shareholders to the lead manager (who usually also acts as the stabilizing manager).

9.81　After the over-allotment has taken place, the lead manager's short position is usually hedged by granting him a greenshoe option. The greenshoe option is defined as the option granted by the issuer or the offeror to the lead manager allowing him to acquire an extra number of financial instruments in order to cover over-subscriptions during a certain term after the offer period at the offer price.[47] In case the greenshoe option is exercised (which will in practice only occur in case the stock price has gone up since the offer)[48] the initial size of the offer will increase.

9.82　In accordance with best practices set forth by the CESR, the Primary Market Practices Decree provides that, except in a case where the CBFA grants an exemption,[49] the over-allotment facility and the greenshoe option should be limited to 15% of the amount of the public offer which has effectively been subscribed to.[50] Furthermore, any position of the lead manager due to him exercising the over-allotment facility and which is not covered by the greenshoe option (i.e. the so-called 'naked short position') should not exceed 5% of the amount of the offer. Pursuant to Section 5.2.5 of Annex III to the Prospectus Regulation, the prospectus

---

[46] Primary Market Practices Decree Article 1, 7°.

[47] Primary Market Practices Decree Article 1, 8°.

[48] If the stock price is lower than the offer price, the lead manager can buy the instruments on the secondary market in order to deliver shares lent in accordance with the stock lending. In that case, notwithstanding that the over-allotment facility has been exercised, the size of the offer does not increase.

[49] It should be noted, however, that an exemption from the 15% threshold granted by the CBFA in accordance with the Primary Market Practices Decree would not constitute an exemption from Article 11, (d) of Regulation 2273/2003 which also sets forth the 15% threshold. Thus, in such case the safe harbour provided for by Regulation 2273/2003 would not apply.

[50] Regulation 2273/2003 however provides that these percentages should be calculated on the basis of the initial size of the offering and not on the amount effectively subscribed to. Hence, there is some doubt in Belgium as to which calculation basis should be used.

should contain information on the existence, size, existence period and the conditions for the use of both the over-allotment facility and the greenshoe option.

The combination of the over-allotment facility and the greenshoe option allows the lead manager flexibility to perform market stabilization actions. Such stabilization actions mainly have the effect of providing support for the price of an offer of the relevant securities if they come under sales pressure. Sales pressure generated by short term investors can thus be alleviated and an orderly market in the relevant securities can be maintained. However, given the potential market manipulation issues connected with stabilization actions, stabilization has been regulated on the European level by the Market Abuse Directive and Commission Regulation (EC) 2273/2003 of 22 December 2003 implementing Directive 2003/6/EC of the European Parliament and of the Council as regards exemptions for buy-back programmes and stabilization of financial instruments ('Regulation 2273/2003'). Regulation 2273/2003 provides for a safe harbour in respect of stabilization transactions which meet the conditions set forth in it.

9.83

The purpose of Regulation 2273/2003 was not that stabilization transactions which do not meet the conditions set forth in it, should as a principle in themselves be deemed to constitute market abuse.[51] However, following the fact that the Primary Market Practices Decree repeats the conditions set forth in Articles 9.3 (disclosure of certain information regarding stabilization) and 10 (no stabilization above the offer price) of Regulation 2273/2003,[52] such provisions acquire a mandatory character. Thus, the particular situation arises in Belgium that no other stabilization transactions are allowed than those falling within the scope of safe harbour provided for in Regulation 2273/2003. Hence, the Belgian legislation on stabilization is more stringent than the European legislation.

9.84

9.2.3.4.2 Adjustment of the offer size   The Primary Market Practices Decree provides that, except in case of an exemption granted by the CBFA and without prejudice to the over-allotment facility, the number of shares offered in excess of the initial offer size cannot exceed (i) 15% of the amount of the initial offer in case of a transaction with dilution of the existing shareholders or (ii) 25% in case of a transaction without dilution of the existing shareholders (i.e. a transaction in which the preferential subscription rights of the existing shareholders are not cancelled). The prospectus should mention the possibility of increasing the offer size. If, however, the issuer or the offeror wishes to increase the size of the offer in excess of those limits, a supplement to the prospectus should be published (which would trigger the possibility for investors to withdraw their subscriptions).[53]

9.85

---

[51] Regulation 2273/2003 Recital (2).
[52] Primary Market Practices Decree Article 5.
[53] Primary Market Practices Decree Article 10.

9.86   **9.2.3.4.3 Prohibition on grant of certain advantages in the pre-offer period**
The Prospectus Regulation requires disclosure of any material disparity between
the public offer price and the effective cash cost to members of the administrative,
management or supervisory bodies or senior management, or affiliated persons,
of securities acquired by them in transactions during the year prior to the offer, or
which they have the right to acquire.[54]

9.87   In order to discourage transactions whereby persons knowing of an upcoming
IPO would be entitled to acquire shares at a price below the offer price, the Primary
Market Practices Decree contains a mandatory lock-up for a period of one year
after the first listing for each person who, in the year preceding the first listing, has
acquired shares with a discount vis-à-vis the offer price to be paid within the
framework of the IPO.[55] Such lock-up does however not apply if the acquisition
at a discount would entail the obligation to launch a public takeover bid or if the
shares thus acquired would be transferred within the framework of a public takeover bid. Furthermore such lock-up would not apply in a case where such shares
were admitted to listing on a foreign regulated market or foreign multilateral trading facility or on any other market in respect of which the CBFA assesses that it
provides for equivalent safeguards for investors.

9.88   This one-year lock-up is however alleviated depending on the discount and the
time of acquisition as follows:

(i)   for acquisitions within three months prior to the IPO at a discount of up to
20% vis-à-vis the offer price, the acquirer can opt for (a) a lock-up of 100%
of such shares for a period of six months, (b) a lock-up of nine months for
two-thirds of such shares or (c) a lock-up of 12 months for one-third of those
shares; and

(ii)   for acquisitions between 12 months and three months prior to the IPO at a
discount of up to 30% vis-à-vis the offer price, the acquirer can opt for (a) a
lock-up of 100% of such shares for a period of six months, (b) a lock-up of
nine months for two-thirds of such shares or (c) a lock-up of 12 months for
one-third of those shares.

9.89   **9.2.3.4.4 Disclosure of information on market demand**   In case of a public
offer of shares, information on the market demand which is publicly disclosed
during or at the end of the offer period should not be misleading (i.e. either by
being untrue or incomplete). If the amplitude of market demand is mentioned,

---

[54] Prospectus Regulation section 5.3.4 of Annex III.
[55] Primary Market Practices Decree Article 11, §1. It should be noted that the CBFA can grant
an exemption from this mandatory lock-up.

only subscriptions at or above the offer price or subscriptions within the price range can be mentioned.[56]

As soon as the issuer/offeror has knowledge thereof, he should communicate the following information to the CBFA: the final market demand (including the entire demand and the breakdown of the demand in the retail tranche and the institutional tranche); the amount of the offer which has directly or indirectly been subscribed to by parties related to the issuer or the offeror and the amount to which the members of the banking syndicate (or their related parties) have subscribed. This information has to be communicated to the CBFA only. It does not have to be publicly disclosed. The Prospectus Statute provides only that the result of public offers of shares is to be published.[57]   **9.90**

9.3 Continuing Obligations/Maintaining a Listing in Practice

9.3.1 Disclosure requirements

9.3.1.1 Regular and ongoing disclosure requirements

9.3.1.1.1 Applicable law   In accordance with what is required by the Transparency Directive, the Belgian legislation on the continuing obligations of issuers whose shares are admitted to trading on a regulated market has been updated. The applicable laws are the Financial Supervision Statute, the Market Abuse Decree and the Transparency Decree I as explained in Circular FMI/2007-02, issued by the CBFA, regarding the obligations of issuers listed on a regulated market (update as of September 2008) ('CBFA Circular FMI/2007-02').   **9.91**

In principle, the new Belgian disclosure regime applies to companies for which Belgium is the home member state in accordance with Article 10, §3, of the Financial Supervision Statute.[58] An unofficial list of these issuers can be found at   **9.92**

---

[56] Primary Market Practices Decree Article 12.

[57] Prospectus Statute Article 63.

[58] Pursuant to Financial Supervision Statute Article 10, §3, Belgium is considered as the home member state for the following issuers:

    1° in the case of an issuer of shares or an issuer of debt securities the denomination per unit of which is less than EUR 1,000:

        a) issuers with their registered office in Belgium; or

        b) issuers with their registered office in a State that is not a member of the EEA which must file their annual information with the CBFA in accordance with the provisions of Title X of the Prospectus Statute;

    2° as regards issuers not falling under 1°, those issuers which have chosen Belgium from among the member states of the EEA where they may have their registered office and the member states which have admitted their financial instruments to trading on a regulated

http://www.cbfa.be/eng/gv/info/li/dBeginFrmEmittenten.asp. In general all relevant issuers must make available to the public all information necessary to ensure the transparency, integrity and proper working of the market. The information must be true, accurate and fair and must allow investors to make an informed assessment of the financial position, the business and the results of the company.[59]

9.3.1.1.2 Disclosure towards securities holders

9.93   *9.3.1.1.2.1 Obligations of issuers*   Articles 6, 7 and 8 of Transparency Decree I impose the following general obligations:[60]

(a) equal treatment of all securities holders who are in the same position;

(b) insurance that all the facilities and information necessary to enable securities holders to exercise their rights are available in Belgium[61] and that the integrity of data is preserved;

(c) provision of a proxy form, on paper or, where applicable, by electronic means, to each person entitled to vote at the general meeting of shareholders or debt securities holders.

9.94   *9.3.1.1.2.2 Timing*   The above-mentioned information must be made available to security holders as soon as possible unless the Companies Code prescribes a specific timing (the latter is only applicable for Belgian issuers).

9.3.1.1.3 Disclosure of inside information

9.95   *9.3.1.1.3.1 Obligations of issuers*   The obligations relating to inside information are applicable to those issuers whose financial instruments are admitted to trading on a Belgian regulated market.[62] All issuers must disclose any inside information that directly or indirectly relates to them.[63]

---

market situated or operating on their territory, it being understood that such an issuer can only choose one of these member states.

[59] Transparency Decree I Article 5 .

[60] The CBFA may exempt issuers whose registered office is in a third country from these obligations, provided that the law of the third country lays down equivalent obligations or provided such an issuer complies with equivalent obligations of the law of a third country.

[61] This includes information on the agenda of the general meeting, the procedure to participate, information on the financial institution designated as agent through which securities holders may exercise their financial rights in Belgium and information regarding the rights attaching to the holding of securities and, among other things, information concerning the allocation and payment of dividends and the issue of new shares, including information on any arrangements for allotment, subscription, cancellation or conversion, and information on the payment of interest, the exercise of any conversion, exchange, subscription or cancellation rights, and repayment (reference is made to Transparency Decree I Article 7, §2).

[62] Certain other issuers (as defined in §3 of Financial Supervision Statute Article 10) should also, subject to certain exceptions, transmit such inside information to the CBFA.

[63] Financial Supervision Statute Article 10.

9.3.1.1.3.2 Identifying inside information Inside information is any informa- **9.96**
tion of a precise nature which has not been made public, relating, directly or
indirectly, to one or more issuers of financial instruments or to one or more financial instruments and which, if it were made public, would be likely to have a significant effect on the prices of those financial instruments or on the price of related
derivative financial instruments. It is in the first instance the issuer's responsibility
to judge whether or not certain information is to be considered inside
information.[64]

9.3.1.1.3.3 Timing and contents of disclosure Subject to certain limited excep- **9.97**
tions, inside information should be disclosed immediately in order to ensure that
the information reaches all market players. The disclosure of inside information
may be delayed (at the sole responsibility of the issuer) in case such disclosure may
prejudice the issuer's legitimate interests, provided that such delay would not be
likely to mislead the market and provided that the issuer is able to ensure the confidentiality of that information.[65] The issuer must inform the CBFA without
delay of its decision to delay disclosure.

Selective disclosure to third parties is allowed if said third parties are subject to a **9.98**
duty of confidentiality to the issuer, regardless of whether such duty is based on a
statute, on regulations, on articles of association or on a contract. If no such duty
of confidentiality exists, any information disclosed to any third party, by an issuer,
or a person acting on his behalf or for his account, in the normal exercise of his
employment, profession or duties, must be made public simultaneously. Where
the inside information has been disclosed to a third party unintentionally, the
issuer must immediately make the information public.

The information must be precise, true and sincere and must also include financial **9.99**
data (insofar as available to the issuer).[66]

9.3.1.1.3.4 Precautionary measures against market abuse
Insider lists Issuers have to keep lists with persons who have access to inside **9.100**
information.[67] The precise contents of such lists are set forth in the Market Abuse
Decree. The lists do not have to published, but must be kept for five years, and the
CBFA may request a copy of them.

---

[64] A (non-exhaustive) list of examples is given in the CBFA Circular FMI/2007-02, page 17.
In case of inside information relating to a takeover or transfer, the legal transparency requirements
sometimes contravene contractual confidentiality clauses (e.g. a clause on confidentiality as regards
the agreed price). In such cases, the legal requirements prevail over the contractual limitations.
[65] Financial Supervision Statute Article 10.
[66] CBFA Circular FMI/2007-02, page 18.
[67] Financial Supervision Statute Article 25bis.

9.101 **Disclosure of transactions by persons with managerial responsibilities** Another precautionary measure against market abuse is the obligation for persons with managerial responsibilities and persons who are closely affiliated with such persons, to notify the CBFA of the transactions for their own account in the financial instruments issued by the issuer with whom they are so connected.[68]

9.3.1.1.4 Disclosure of periodic information[69]

9.3.1.1.4.1 Annual reporting

9.102 **Annual financial report** The annual financial report must as a minimum include the following information:

(i) Audited financial statements (statutory accounts under Belgian GAAP and consolidated accounts under IAS/IFRS).

(ii) Statutory annual report and consolidated annual report in accordance with Articles 96 and 119 of the Companies Code. In addition these reports need to contain certain information on anti-takeover protection mechanisms pursuant to Article 34 of the Transparency Decree I.

(iii) Statements made by the persons responsible within the company, whose names and functions shall be clearly indicated, to the effect that, to the best of their knowledge:

   (a) the financial statements prepared in accordance with the applicable set of accounting standards give a true and fair view of the assets, liabilities, financial position and profit or loss of the company and the undertakings included in the consolidation taken as a whole; and

   (b) that the annual report includes a fair review of the development and performance of the business and the position of the group together with a description of the principal risks and uncertainties that they face.

(iv) The audit report on the statutory and consolidated financial statements executed by the statutory auditor.

9.103 In practice, the annual financial report may contain more information, e.g. information on the business strategy, information on foreign currency or raw material prices that have influenced the results, etc.

9.104 It should be made available to the public in print form (in a brochure) at no cost to the investor within four months after the close of the financial year (in addition to publication on the website).

9.105 **Optional annual bulletin** If it wishes to do so, the issuer can publish an annual bulletin during the period after the drawing up of the financial statements by the

---

[68] Ibid.
[69] The Belgian Transparency Decree I imposes annual, half-yearly and quarterly reporting.

board and the release of the annual financial report.[70][71] The CBFA believes that it is best practice to publish the results as soon as the financial statements have been drawn so as to limit the risks of insider trading.[72]

If the issuer opts for the release of an annual bulletin, the bulletin must cover at least the following:

9.106

(a) financial information;[73]
(b) an explanatory note;[74] and
(c) information on external control.[75]

9.3.1.1.4.2 Half-yearly financial report The half-yearly financial report must include at least the following information:[76]

9.107

* the summarized set of financial statements drawn up in accordance with IAS 34;
* the half-yearly management reports including at least (i) an indication of important events that have occurred during the first six months of the financial year, and their impact on the condensed set of financial statements, together with (ii) a description of the principal risks and uncertainties for the remaining six months of the financial year, and (iii) material related-parties transactions and their impact on the condensed set of financial statements;
* statements made by the persons responsible within the company, whose names and functions shall be clearly indicated, to the effect that, to the best of their knowledge:
  (a) the summarized set of financial statements prepared in accordance with the applicable set of accounting standards give a true and fair view of the assets,

---

[70] Transparency Decree I Article 11.
[71] The publication of such annual bulletin used to be mandatory in Belgium.
[72] CBFA Circular FMI/2007-02, page 27.
[73] This is information on the results of the company based on the financial statements reflecting the same accounting line items and subtotals as those mentioned in the financial statements, with comparables for the previous financial year, and the proposed dividend and/or interim dividend that has already been distributed.
[74] This is a note explaining the important events in the development of the business and the results of the company and its financial position as well as the particular factors that had an impact on it with a comparison with the previous financial year. If it is difficult to provide comparable information because of structural changes to the business, pro-forma financials can be included. To the extent possible, the explanatory note should also relate to the expected developments in the current financial year.
[75] Audit information, namely whether or not the financial statements have already been audited and if not the current status of the auditing activities. If the audit has been completed, the form of the audit declaration should be mentioned. If a qualification has been made, the full declaration should be reflected. If the preliminary results have not been audited, the statement must also give details of any likely modification that may be contained in the auditors' report required to be included with the annual financial report.
[76] Transparency Decree I Article 13.

liabilities, financial position and profit or loss of the company and the undertakings included in the consolidation taken as a whole; and

(b) that the half-yearly management report includes a fair review of the development and performance of the business and the position of the group, together with a description of the principal risks and uncertainties that they face;

• information on the external control. If the financial statements have been audited (in full or limited), the audit report must be reproduced in full. If the half-yearly financial statements have not been audited or reviewed by auditors, the company must make a statement to that effect in its report.

9.108 The half-yearly financial report must be published within two months after the end of the first six months of the financial year.

9.109 *9.3.1.1.4.3 Interim statements or quarterly reporting* Pursuant to Article 14 of Transparency Decree I, issuers have the option, either:

(a) to publish an interim statement by its management during the first six-month period of the financial year and another statement by its management during the second six-month period of the financial year, or

(b) to publish quarterly financial reports.

9.110 The interim statements should cover the period from the start of the ongoing half year until the date of its publication. The statement includes:

• an explanation of material events and transactions that have taken place during the relevant period and their impact on the financial position of the group;

• a general description of the financial position and performance of the group during the relevant period.

9.111 The interim statements should be published in the period between ten weeks after the start of the ongoing half year and six weeks before the end of the ongoing half year.

9.112 As an alternative, issuers may decide to publish quarterly reports insofar as these reports are published no later than two months after the end of the first and the third quarter of the financial year, and, *mutatis mutandis* for the relevant quarterly reporting periods, have been prepared in accordance with the rules laid down for the half yearly financial report,[77] or which have been prepared in accordance with equivalent rules of the regulated market.

9.113 *9.3.1.1.5 Additional ongoing information* In addition, certain issuers must make public the following information pursuant to the Transparency Decree I and the Prospectus Statute:

---

[77] See above under 9.3.1.1.4.2(b).

- any change in the rights attached to the various classes of shares, including changes in the rights attached to derivative securities issued by the company itself and giving a right to acquire shares of that company (this applies to different types of issuers depending on the information concerned—as indicated by Article 15 of Transparency Decree I). Such information must be published immediately;
- all special reports required by the Companies Code (this applies to Belgian issuers for which Belgium is the home member state—as indicated by Article 16 of Transparency Decree I). The special reports must be published on the issuer's website within the terms stipulated by the Companies Code;
- all proposals for amendment of the articles of association (this applies to issuers for which Belgium is the home member state—as indicated by Article 16 of Transparency Decree I). Without prejudice to the generally applicable corporate law rules, the proposals must be published on the website immediately and ultimately on the date the shareholders' meeting has been convened;
- yearly publication of a document containing all information (or referring to such information) that has been published in the last twelve months (the issuers to whom this applies are indicated in Articles 65 and 66 of the Prospectus Statute). Such yearly information must be published within 20 business days after the publication of the yearly financial report. The CBFA recommends that issuers at least publish this information on their website.[78]

9.3.1.1.6 Legal requirements relating to publication and storage

9.3.1.1.6.1 Publication Issuers have to disclose regulated information (as discussed above) in a manner that ensures:

9.114

(i)   fast access to such information on a non-discriminatory basis;
(ii) the capability of being disseminated to as wide a public as possible; and
(iii) the capability of being disseminated as close to simultaneously as possible in Belgium and the other member states.

The issuers may not charge investors any specific cost for providing the information.

9.115

The issuers shall use such media as may reasonably be relied upon for the effective dissemination of information to the public throughout the EEA. The CBFA recommends that the issuers should use as many distribution channels as possible. It is however not necessary to make use of the media in every single country of the EEA.[79] With regard to inside information, the Transparency Decree I contains a special provision pursuant to which all reasonable measures should be taken in order to

9.116

---

[78] CBFA Circular FMI/2007-02, page 41.
[79] CBFA Circular FMI/2007-02, page 43.

guarantee that the inside information is disclosed as close to simultaneously as possible to all classes of investors in all members states where the issuers have requested or accepted the admission of their financial instruments to trading on a regulated market.[80]

9.117   The information has to be communicated to the media in unedited full text. However, certain information of considerable size (such as the financial reports) may be communicated to the media through an announcement indicating on which website the information in question is available. In addition, the yearly financial report has to be published in the form of a brochure (see above).

9.118   The issuers must make clear in the document itself[81] that the information published is regulated information. The CBFA recommends that the information (and especially periodical information and inside information) is communicated to the media after market closure and ultimately 30 minutes prior to the opening of the markets.[82]

9.119   Issuers whose securities are admitted to trading exclusively on a regulated market in one host member state other than Belgium (the latter being the home member state), shall be exempted from complying with the Belgian publication provisions of Articles 35 to 37 of Transparency Decree I when publishing regulated information.

9.120   *9.3.1.1.6.2 Storage*   Until now a central storage mechanism (as required by the Transparency Directive) has not been created in Belgium. As an interim solution, the CBFA publishes hyperlinks on its website to the websites of the issuers, which will be used as a storage device. The hyperlinks can be found at http://www.cbfa.be/eng/gv/info/links/dBeginFrmLinksWebsite.asp. As these issuers' websites will be the sole storage mechanisms during the interim period, every issuer has to have a website that complies with the conditions set forth in the Transparency Directive.[83]

9.121   9.3.1.1.7 **CBFA measures in case of non-compliance**   The CBFA can take the following measures against an issuer who does not comply with its obligations as set forth above:

- order an issuer to publish certain information, or if the issuer still refuses to publish, publish the relevant information at the issuer's expense;

---

[80]   Transparency Decree I Article 35, §2.
[81]   CBFA Circular FMI/2007-02, page 44.
[82]   CBFA Circular FMI/2007-02, page 44. For further specific guidelines relating to the timing of disclosure, reference is made to the CBFA Circular FMI/2007-02, pages 44–47.
[83]   Transparency Decree I Article 41. For an overview of the information that should be published on the website, reference is made to the list in the CBFA Circular FMI/2007-02, pages 51–52.

- publish a warning relating to a certain issuer (but only after having heard the issuer's comments);
- order a preliminary disclosure to the CBFA of certain information in order to perform a preliminary control; and
- suspend or prohibit the trade in certain financial instruments.

Further, the CBFA can impose coercive damages. It may also impose an adminis- **9.122**
trative fine on an offender.

9.3.1.2 Disclosure of major shareholdings

9.3.1.2.1 Applicable law   With regard to the disclosure of major sharehold- **9.123**
ings, the Transparency Directive has been implemented into Belgian law through
the Transparency Statute and the Transparency Decree II. The Companies Code
and the Transparency Decree I also contain some relevant provisions relating to
the notification obligations. The CBFA issued the 'Practitioners' guide on the
application of the notification obligation of major shareholdings' (update as of 15
June 2009) (the 'CBFA Practitioners' Guide').

9.3.1.2.2 Notification—issuers concerned   The new disclosure obligations **9.124**
apply in respect of participations in companies for which Belgium is the home
member state. Belgium is the home member state for issuers having their registered office in Belgium whose shares (or related depositary receipts) are admitted
to trading on a regulated market located in the EEA and for issuers having their
registered office outside the EEA whose shares (or related depositary receipts) are
admitted to trading on a Belgian regulated market and which are required by the
Prospectus Statute to file annual information with the CBFA. Similar notification
obligations apply to issuers who are admitted to Alternext.

An unofficial list containing the names of companies for which Belgium is the **9.125**
home member state is published on the website of the CBFA at http://www.cbfa.
be/eng/gv/ah/li/dbeginfrmemittenten.asp.

9.3.1.2.3 Notification—instruments concerned   In order to determine whether **9.126**
disclosure obligations are triggered, the following types of instruments must be
taken into consideration:

(i) voting securities—whether or not they represent the capital of the issuer;[84]
(ii) voting rights (including the right to exercise such voting rights) exercisable
     by a person other than the holder of the relevant voting securities and result-
     ing from any of the following situations:[85]
     - agreement on the temporary transfer of the voting rights;

---

[84] Transparency Statute Article 6 .
[85] Transparency Statute Article 7.

- pledge agreement (provided that the pledgee controls the voting rights);
- 'usufruct' (provided that the beneficiary of the 'usufruct' controls the voting rights);
- deposit agreement (provided that the depositary can, in the absence of specific instructions, exercise at its discretion the voting rights);
- proxy arrangement (provided that the proxyholder can, in the absence of specific instructions, exercise at its discretion the voting rights); and

(iii) certain financial instruments that are assimilated to voting securities, i.e. financial instruments that give their holder the right to acquire existing voting securities (i.e. voting securities already issued), such as options, futures, swaps, forward rate agreements and any other derivative contracts, (a) provided that they result in an entitlement to acquire existing voting securities, on the holder's initiative alone, under a formal agreement, and (b) under the conditions that:
- the holder has the unconditional right to acquire the underlying voting securities; and
- the holder can exercise this right at its own discretion.[86]

9.127 **9.3.1.2.4 Notification—instruments excluded** In order to determine whether disclosure obligations are triggered the following instruments are not to be taken into consideration: (i) convertible bonds, (ii) subscription rights, and (iii) capital securities without voting rights.[87] However, pursuant to Article 15, §1 of the Transparency Statute the issuer must publish information on the total number of capital securities without voting rights. Further, any person subject to notification[88] must include in their notification the number of capital securities without voting rights held by them.[89] The same applies to convertible bonds and subscription rights. The issuers must publish information on the total number of bonds convertible into voting securities or rights to subscribe to voting securities to be issued and on the total number of voting rights that might be created after conversion of the bonds or exercise of the subscription rights. The persons subject to notification must also include information on the convertible bonds or subscription rights held by them any time when submitting their notification.

9.3.1.2.5 Notification—thresholds and trigger events

9.128 *9.3.1.2.5.1 Notification thresholds* There are two kinds of notification thresholds, those stipulated by law[90] and those stipulated in the articles of association of

---

[86] Transparency Statute Article 6, §7 and Transparency Decree II Article 6.
[87] The old Belgian law explicitly made the transparency regulations applicable to these kinds of instruments.
[88] See Section 9.3.1.2.6.
[89] Transparency Decree II Article 16.
[90] Transparency Statute Article 6.

the issuer.[91] Notification thresholds have been set at 5%, 10%, 15% or 20% and every additional 5%, except for companies listed on Alternext where the notification thresholds are 25%, 30%, 50%, 75% and 95%. Additional notification thresholds of 1%, 2%, 3%, 4% and 7.5% may be introduced by the issuers in their articles of association. Those additional thresholds are available on the CBFA website at http://www.cbfa.be/eng/gv/ah/not/dbeginfrmemittenten.asp. Companies listed on Alternext are not allowed to introduce such additional thresholds.

Pursuant to Article 9 of the Transparency Statute, the percentage of a person's **9.129** reportable interests is calculated by dividing the reportable interests (the sum of the voting securities, the voting rights and the assimilated financial instruments) attributable to that person (the numerator) by the total number of outstanding voting rights of the issuer (the denominator).[92] Issuers are required to publish their denominator on their website. The CBFA also holds a list of denominators on http://www.cbfa.be/nl/gv/ah/li/dBeginFrmEmittenten.asp.

9.3.1.2.5.2 Trigger events   The events possibly triggering a notification duty are: **9.130**

(i)   a direct or indirect acquisition or transfer of reportable interests;[93]
(ii) the (direct or indirect) holding of voting rights at the time of an initial public offer;[94]
(iii) a passive crossing (e.g. in the event of dilution following a capital increase or in the event of cancellation of own shares);[95]
(iv) conclusion, amendment or termination of an agreement to act in concert;[96]
(v)   update of the notification made with respect to assimilated financial instruments;[97] and
(vi) additional thresholds being introduced by the issuer.[98]

In principle, the notification duty is triggered when a relevant threshold (see **9.131** above) is reached and/or crossed (in either direction). A person reaching a threshold and subsequently crossing it only has to notify once.[99] Also, when a threshold is crossed in one direction and then crossed in the other direction in the course of

---

[91] Transparency Statute Article 18.
[92] All voting rights shall be taken into consideration notwithstanding the possibility that the exercise thereof is suspended.
[93] Transparency Statute Article 6.
[94] Ibid.
[95] Ibid.
[96] Ibid.
[97] Where assimilated financial instruments have not been exercised by their maturity date and, as a consequence, the (direct or indirect) holding of reportable interests falls below a threshold, the notification made with respect to such assimilated financial instruments must be updated. Transparency Decree II Article 14.
[98] Transparency Statute Article 18.
[99] *Parl. St.*; Kamer, DOC 51, nr. 2963/1, 21.

four trading days (i.e. the notification term), the reporting entity must notify both crossings, but this can be done through a single notification.[100]

9.132   Contrary to the general rule requiring a threshold crossing, the following events are subject to specific disclosure and notification requirements, even though no threshold is crossed:

(i) Notifications made with respect to the acquisition of assimilated financial instruments must be updated on an annual basis (on each 31 December) in the event that such instruments have not been exercised by their maturity date.

(ii) Notifications made with respect to the acquisition of assimilated financial instruments must be updated on an annual basis (on each 31 December) in the event that such instruments have been exercised.

(iii) When the amendment to an agreement to act in concert involves a change in the nature of such agreement a notification has to be made.

9.133   *9.3.1.2.5.3 Special cases*   In certain cases[101] voting rights (including the right to exercise such voting rights) exercisable by a person other than the holder of the relevant voting securities are to be taken into consideration when establishing a notification obligation.[102]

9.134   It is not entirely clear whether or not under the application of Article 7 of the Transparency Statute, a temporary transfer of voting rights (whereby the temporary loss of actual voting rights is compensated by the (temporary) acquisition of potential voting rights) triggers a separate notification obligation.[103] According to some legal scholars such exchange of actual voting rights for potential voting rights no longer triggers a notification duty (as no threshold is crossed). The reverse is explicitly arranged for in the Transparency Decree. When assimilated financial instruments are exercised (a 'potential voting right' attached to an existing voting security becomes an 'actual right') only a yearly update is required, as no thresholds are being crossed.

---

[100] Transparency Decree II Article 19.

[101] See 9.3.1.2.3(ii).

[102] Transparency Statute Article 7.

[103] Pursuant to the preparatory works relating to the Transparency Statute, the transfer of voting rights without transferring the relevant securities triggers a notification duty if any of the relevant thresholds is crossed (by either the transferor, the transferee or both). See *Parl. St.*; Kamer, DOC 51, nr. 2963/1, 26. The specific situation of a temporary transfer is not addressed in the preparatory works.

Some specific cases, such as a proxy for representation on one shareholders' meeting, are addressed specifically in the Transparency Decree II. In such case and subject to certain conditions a single notification at the moment the proxy is granted suffices and no additional notification is necessary upon termination of the proxy (Transparency Decree II Article 8).

9.3.1.2.6 Notification —persons subject to notification

9.3.1.2.6.1 General Any (legal) person directly or indirectly acquiring, trans- **9.135**
ferring or holding reportable interests might be subject to a notification duty in
any of the circumstances set forth above in Section 9.3.1.2.5. Reportable interests
are deemed to be held indirectly in the following three situations:

- reportable interests held, acquired or transferred by a third party acting for the
  account of that person (irrespective of whether that third party acts in its own
  name or in the name of that person);
- reportable interests held, acquired or transferred by a company controlled by
  that person; or
- the acquisition or transfer of a controlling interest in a company that, in turn,
  holds reportable interests in an issuer.[104]

'Control' means the power, in law or in fact, to exercise a decisive influence on the **9.136**
appointment of the majority of an undertaking's directors or on the orientation
of its policies.[105] The law lists five non-rebuttable presumptions of 'legal control'
that will apply to an undertaking qualifying as a subsidiary[106] and one rebuttable
presumption of 'de facto control'.[107]

The reportable interests held by parties acting in concert must also be aggregated. **9.137**
Persons acting in concert are defined in Article 3, 13° of the Transparency
Statute as:

- the natural or legal persons acting in concert within the meaning of Article 3,
  § 1, 5°, a) of the Takeover Statute; [108]

---

[104] The parent company of an EEA or non-EEA management company or investment firm
offering portfolio management services is exempted from aggregating the reportable interests of its
management company or investment firm subsidiaries if certain conditions, such as independence
for the exercise of voting rights and CBFA notification, are met.

[105] Article 5 *juncto* 7 of the Companies Code.

[106] Control flows from (i) the possession of the majority of the voting rights; (ii) right to appoint
or dismiss the majority of an undertaking's directors; (iii) power of control pursuant to the undertaking's articles of association or to arrangements entered into with the undertaking; (iv) majority
of the voting rights on the basis of an agreement concluded with other shareholders; and (v) joint
control, i.e. control that a limited number of shareholders exercise when they have agreed that decisions on the orientation of the undertaking's policies cannot be adopted without their joint consent
(Companies Code Article 5 et seq.).

[107] The exercise by a shareholder of the majority of the votes cast at the two most recent general
shareholders' meetings of the company (Companies Code Article 5, §3).

[108] Natural or legal persons who cooperate with the offeror, the offeree company or any other
person on the basis of an agreement, either express or tacit, either oral or written, aimed either at
acquiring control of the offeree company, at frustrating the successful outcome of a bid or at maintaining the control over the target company.

- the natural or legal persons that have concluded an agreement to adopt, by concerted exercise of the voting rights they hold, a lasting common policy towards the issuer in question;
- the natural or legal persons that have concluded an agreement to hold, acquire or dispose of securities to which voting rights are attached.

9.138 The CBFA has stated that an agreement regarding the concerted exercise of their voting rights[109] does not necessarily result in identical voting behaviour of all parties involved. Other than as stipulated in Article 10, (a) of the Transparency Directive, the agreement regarding the concerted exercise of their voting rights does not have to contain an obligation for the parties to adopt a lasting common policy towards the management of the issuer in question.[110]

9.139 *9.3.1.2.6.2 'Shared' notification duties* In any of the situations described in Section 9.3.1.2.6.1 the notification duty may fall upon several persons, depending on whether the reportable interests are held (i) through a third party, (ii) by a controlled entity or further to a change of control, or (iii) by persons acting in concert.

9.140 **Interest holdings through a third party** The notification duty first falls upon the person for the account of which the third party acts.[111] When determining whether or not someone acts for someone else's account, one must take into account who actually holds the voting rights.

9.141 However, a distinct notification duty falls upon the third party itself insofar as the third party acts in its own name and reaches (or crosses) a threshold. In such a case, two persons (provided that each of their respective holdings reach (or cross) a threshold) may be subject to a notification duty in relation to the same reportable interests. If so, to avoid the publication of misleading information,[112] those persons must establish a single joint notification.[113]

9.142 **Interest holdings through a controlled entity/following a change of control** Any person acquiring direct reportable interests in an issuer must disclose such acquisition through proper notification. In principle this also applies to controlled entities.

9.143 The person having (direct and/or indirect) control over such entity is in such a case considered as acquiring, indirectly, the reportable interests acquired by the controlled entity and is therefore also subject to a notification duty. Such notification duty applies throughout the chain of control (and, potentially, up to the ultimate controlling person(s)) so that the person(s) who, in turn, control(s) the controlling entity will also be subject to a notification duty.

---

[109] See Section 9.3.1.2.5.2 above.
[110] See Annual Report CBFA 2007, page 58.
[111] Transparency Statute Article 6.
[112] Report to the King in relation to Transparency Decree II, *Belgisch Staatsblad*, 4 March 2008, 13040.
[113] Transparency Decree II Article 12.

In other words:[114]   **9.144**

- a controlled entity whose holdings reach (or cross) a threshold is subject to a notification duty; and
- the controlling entity thereof (including any intermediary in the chain of control up to, and including, the ultimate controlling entity) is also subject to such notification duty so that, in practice, the controlling entity must aggregate its direct and indirect reportable interests in order to determine whether a threshold is reached (or crossed) at its own level.

However, it should be noted that: **9.145**

- when the ultimate controlling entity is a parent company, such controlling entity may file the notification on behalf of its subsidiary(ies).[115] According to the CBFA, in order for the controlled entity to be released from its notification duty, the notification made by the parent company must contain all the information that should be contained in a distinct notification made by the controlled entity:[116] and
- in any event, the parent company (or ultimate controlling entity) can be appointed as agent by the controlled entity(ies) to make the required notification(s) on their behalf.[117] In such case, the parent company will make a joint notification on behalf of the controlled entity(ies) in which it will give all the information that otherwise should have been mentioned in distinct notification(s) made by each of the controlled entities.

In practice, therefore, a controlled entity may choose amongst the following   **9.146**
options in order to fulfil its notification duty:

- a separate notification made by the controlled entity itself;
- a joint notification made (on a voluntary basis) by the controlled entity and the parent company (or the (ultimate) controlling entity);[118]

---

[114] Transparency Decree II Article 10. See the CBFA Practitioners' Guide, page14.

[115] Transparency Statute Article 11, §1. Please note that there are two important exceptions whereby a parent company—subject to certain conditions—is not obliged to aggregate its holdings with the holdings managed by its subsidiaries. These exceptions refer to the parent undertakings of certain management companies and investment firms as described in Transparency Statute Article 11, §2-5.

[116] The CBFA Practitioners' Guide, page 14.

[117] Persons subject to a notification duty may always appoint an agent to submit a mandatory notification on their behalf (Transparency Decree II Article 12, §4). This does not release those persons from their own responsibility (Transparency Decree II Article 12, §4).

[118] Two or more persons subject to a notification duty may always opt for a single joint notification (Transparency Decree II Article 12, §2). This does not release those persons from their own responsibility. Such joint notification is mandatory in two cases: (i) a third party acting in its own name but on behalf of someone else and (ii) persons acting in concert.

- a notification made by the parent company pursuant to Article 11, §1 of the Transparency Statute (whereby the controlled entity is exempted from its obligation to notify); or
- one notification made by the parent company (or ultimate controlling entity) acting as agent.

9.147 It is recommended by the CBFA that controlling and controlled entities make one notification.[119]

9.148 Furthermore, where a person acquires (or transfers) control over an entity, such person is considered as indirectly acquiring (or transferring) reportable interests in the issuer concerned irrespective of whether either that person or the entity (over which the control is acquired) actually acquires (or transfers) reportable interests in the issuer concerned. The fact that a person acquires the control over an entity holding reportable interests in an issuer is sufficient to be considered as an indirect acquisition (or transfer) at the level of the acquiring (or transferring) entity, which is therefore subject to a notification duty.

9.149 **Agreement to act in concert** The parties to an agreement to act in concert are jointly subject to the notification duty, irrespective of the importance of their respective holdings[120] and must disclose their reportable interests through a single joint notification.[121]

9.150 The relevant parties are subject to a notification duty if either (i) the percentage of reportable interests to which the agreement applies, or (ii) the percentage of reportable interests held by one of the parties involved, reaches or crosses any relevant threshold. It should be noted that the notification duty applies irrespective of whether or not the threshold is crossed through a transfer or acquisition. In other words, the notification duty is also applicable when an agreement to act in concert is entered into, is modified or is terminated (without any transfer of voting rights having taken place).

9.151 **Special cases**

(a) Voting rights

With respect to the acquisition or transfer of voting rights and to the extent that their respective holdings reach, exceed or fall below a threshold, the notification duty falls on:

- the transferor and the transferee;

---

[119] The CBFA Practitioners' Guide, page 15. It should be noted that a joint notification does not release the controlled entities (subject to a notification duty) from their responsibility to provide in such notification accurate and complete information regarding their (own) holdings.
[120] Transparency Decree II Article 11.
[121] Transparency Decree II Article 12.

- the pledgor and the pledgee;
- the persons granting the 'usufruct' and the beneficiary thereof;
- the shareholder and the depositary/custodian; and
- the principal and the agent/proxyholder.

In each of the above situations, the persons subject to a notification duty (e.g. the principal and the agent) may choose to make a joint notification. **9.152**

Should the above persons decide to make separate notifications, it is recommended by the CBFA that each of them refers to the notification to be made by its counterparty (for example the agent refers to the principal in its notification and vice versa) in order to clearly identify the relationship between them.[122] **9.153**

(b) Interests held by a collective investment scheme (CIS)

When interests are held by a collective investment scheme ('CIS'), the notification duty falls, in principle, on the CIS in question. **9.154**

However, if the CIS has, directly or indirectly, entrusted a third party (management company) with the power to exercise the voting rights attached to the voting securities held by it, and provided that such third party may, in the absence of specific instructions, exercise at its discretion the voting rights, the notification duty shall fall upon such third party only and not on the CIS.[123] **9.155**

If, in turn, the third party delegates the intellectual management of all or part of the portfolio under management, the notification duty shall then fall upon the person entrusted with the intellectual management. **9.156**

9.3.1.2.6.3 *Exemptions and special cases*

Custodians   A custodian with whom voting securities have been deposited will be subject to the notification obligations to the extent it can exercise the voting rights at its discretion in the absence of specific instructions from the shareholder.[124] The custodian will not be subject to the notification obligations if it can exercise the voting rights only upon and in accordance with written voting instructions (including instructions provided by email). **9.157**

Clearing and settlement   Reportable interests acquired for the sole purpose of clearing and settlement within the usual three-day settlement cycle do not need to be reported by the entity or person who holds such interest for clearing and settlement purposes.[125] **9.158**

---

[122] The CBFA Practitioners' Guide, page 16. See also Report to the King in relation to Transparency Decree II, *Belgisch Staatsblad* 4 March 2008, 13038.

[123] Transparency Decree II Article 9, § 2.

[124] Transparency Statute Article 10, § 2.

[125] Transparency Statute Article 10, § 1.

9.159 **Market making**   Market makers are exempted from notification duty when they hold, acquire or transfer, in their capacity as market makers, reportable interests that reach, exceed or fall below the 5% threshold or any other lower threshold provided that certain conditions, including prior CBFA notification, are met.[126]

9.160 **Voting rights held in trading book**   Voting rights held in the trading book of a credit institution or investment firm shall not be taken into account in the calculation of the proportion of voting rights held by those credit institutions or investment firms, provided that certain conditions are met.[127]

9.161 **Voting securities provided to or by members of the ESCB**   Under certain conditions the notification duty shall not apply to voting securities provided to or by members of the European System of Central Banks (the 'ESCB') in carrying out their functions as monetary authorities, including voting securities provided to or by members of the ESCB under a pledge or repurchase or similar agreement for liquidity granted for monetary policy purposes or within a payment system.[128]

9.3.1.2.7 Notification—timing, form and content

9.162 *9.3.1.2.7.1 Timing*[129]   Any disclosure must be made as soon as possible and, at the latest, within a time period of:

(i) four trading days, beginning on the trading day following (1) the date on which the person subject to the notification requirements knows or should have known of the existence of the triggering event, in case of an acquisition or transfer of reportable interests,[130] or (2) the date on which the person subject to the notification requirement was informed of the event resulting in a passive threshold crossing, or (3) the date on which the agreement to act in concert was concluded, modified or terminated, or (4) the maturity date of the assimilated financial instruments in case the assimilated financial instruments were not exercised, insofar as a relevant threshold has been crossed.

(ii) ten trading days after the additional thresholds introduced in the articles of association have been disclosed in the case of new thresholds being introduced in the issuer's articles of association (after 1 September 2008).

---

[126] Transparency Statute Article 10, § 3 and Transparency Decree II Article 20.

[127] Transparency Statute Article 10, § 4.

[128] Transparency Statute Article 10, § 5.

[129] In each situation described below, the trading days to be taken into consideration are Euronext Brussels trading days. The list of Euronext Brussels trading days is available on the following website: http://www.euronext.com/editorial/documentation/wide/documents-1690-EN.html.

[130] The persons concerned are irrefutably presumed to have known of the acquisition or transfer of reportable interests at the latest on the second trading day following the day of the transaction.

Notifications made with respect to the acquisition of assimilated financial instru- **9.163**
ments as referred to in Section 9.3.1.2.5.2 must be made within ten trading days
as from (each) 1 January.

When a threshold is crossed in one direction and then crossed in the other direc- **9.164**
tion in the course of four trading days, the reporting entity must notify both crossings, but this can be made through a single notification.

9.3.1.2.7.2 *Form and content*

Notification form   The notifications to the CBFA and to the issuer may be made **9.165**
in Dutch, French or English.

The CBFA has produced a notification form (Form TR-1 BE) available at http:// **9.166**
www.cbfa.be/eng/gv/ah/circ/pdf/TR-1BE.xls. This form consists of two parts:
Part I, which must be transmitted to both the CBFA and the issuer, and Part II,
which must be transmitted to the CBFA only.

Addressees of the notification   Notifications must be addressed to both the **9.167**
issuer concerned and the CBFA. For each notification filed a fee is due to the
CBFA. It is possible to send a notification in draft form to the CBFA for a verification that the form has been adequately completed.

Notifications can be sent to both the issuer and the CBFA electronically. For that **9.168**
reason, the CBFA asks issuers to mention on their website the name of a contact
person as well as an email address.

9.3.1.2.8 Notification—publication   Pursuant to Article 23, § 1 of Trans- **9.169**
parency Decree II the relevant issuers have to publish (i) all notifications received
and all notifications submitted by them in relation to reportable interests held by
them, (ii) the total number of voting rights issued by them (the 'denominator') and
(iii) the additional thresholds in accordance with their articles of association
(this last obligation only applies to Belgian issuers).[131] The information has to
be published on the relevant issuers' websites and in accordance with what is set
forth in Articles 35 to 37 of Transparency Decree I.

The publication has to occur within three trading days after the issuer has received **9.170**
the notification.[132] [133] For the publication of its own notifications a term of four
trading days (the regular notification term) applies. Belgian issuers further have to
publish their shareholding structure on a yearly basis in the annual financial report.

---

[131] Issuers whose securities are admitted to trading exclusively on a regulated market in one
host member state other than Belgium (the latter being the home member state), shall be exempted
from complying with the Belgian publication provisions of Transparency Decree II Article 23,
§ 1 (Article 23, § 1 *in fine*).
[132] Transparency Statute Article 14.
[133] Without prejudice to the rules relating to inside information.

9.171 The denominator has to be updated and reported to the CBFA at the end of each calendar month during which a change in the numbers has occurred.[134]

9.172 **9.3.1.2.9 Notification—sanctions** Different types of sanctions may apply in the event of failure to comply with reporting requirements.

9.3.1.2.9.1 Civil sanctions

(i) *Sanctions affecting the shareholders' rights:*[135] the owners of reportable interests are admitted to vote in the shareholders' meetings only if they have fulfilled their notification duty at least 20 days prior to the meeting.[136]

(ii) *Judicial orders:*[137] the President of the competent Commercial Court may, for a period of up to one year, suspend the possibility to exercise part or all of the rights attached to the relevant securities.[138] The President may also (1) order the suspension of a shareholders' meeting already convened and/or (2) order the relevant securities to be sold to a third party.

9.173 *9.3.1.2.9.2 Administrative sanctions* The CBFA can order a person to submit a notification, and if such person keeps failing its obligation, the CBFA can impose coercive damages. Such coercive damages may amount to a maximum of EUR 50,000 per day and EUR 2,500,000 in total.[139] In addition, the CBFA may also, in the event of a breach of the disclosure rules, impose an administrative fine ranging between EUR 2,500 and EUR 2,500,000.[140]

9.174 *9.3.1.2.9.3 Criminal sanctions* Deliberate refusal to make the required notifications or supplying incorrect or incomplete information to the CBFA are criminal offences subject to imprisonment from one month to one year and/or to criminal fines between EUR 50 and EUR 10,000.[141]

9.175 **9.3.1.2.10 Notification—special cases** The acquisition and/or disposal of capital securities and voting rights in credit institutions, insurance companies, investment firms, fund management companies and financial holding companies are subject

---

[134] Transparency Statute Article 15.

[135] Companies Code Article 545.

[136] If the board of directors, within the 20 days preceding a shareholders' meeting, receives a notification or learns that a notification should have been made, it may postpone the meeting for three weeks (Companies Code Article 534).

[137] Companies Code Article 516.

[138] The competent Commercial Court may declare void part or all of the decisions of a shareholders' meeting if the suspended voting rights have been illegally exercised and if, without such voting rights, the attendance or voting quorums would not have been met.

[139] Transparency Statute Article 23, §5.

[140] Transparency Statute Article 27.

[141] Transparency Statute Article 26. Such amounts of the criminal fines are to be multiplied with the applicable factor which varies from time to time.

to special CBFA approval requirements. Furthermore, the acquisition of securities during a takeover may also trigger specific notification obligations.[142]

9.3.2 Market abuse

The Market Abuse Directive (and its implementing directives) have been imple- **9.176** mented into Belgian national law by the Financial Supervision Statute, which has been further detailed by the Market Abuse Decree, the Royal Decree of 5 March 2006 on fair presentation of investment recommendations and the disclosure of conflicts of interest, and the Royal Decree of 21 August 2008 containing certain rules on MTFs. This Section deals with the repressive rules against market abuse, i.e the prohibitions against abuse of inside information and market manipulation. The preventive rules have been addressed under Section 9.3.1.1.3 above.

9.3.2.1 *Abuse of inside information*

There are two separate sets of rules against the abuse of inside information: as an **9.177** administrative offence[143] and as a criminal offence.[144] Administrative offences are subject to administrative fines imposed by the CBFA, while criminal offences may be punished with criminal sanctions in court.

9.3.2.1.1 Common rules and concepts Both sets of rules share the same defi- **9.178** nition of inside information.[145] In line with the Market Abuse Directive, inside information has been defined as 'information of a precise nature which has not been made public, relating, directly or indirectly, to one or more issuers of financial instruments or to one or more financial instruments and which, if it were made public, would be likely to have a significant effect on the prices of those financial instruments or on the price of related derivative financial instruments'.[146] In line with EC Directive 2003/124 of 22 December 2003, the Financial Supervision Statute further specifies what should be understood by a 'precise nature' and 'likely to have a significant effect on the prices'.

In line with the Market Abuse Directive, both the criminal and the administrative **9.179** prohibition apply to financial instruments admitted to trading (or for which an application for admission is pending) on a Belgian regulated market or on one of four designated Belgian MTFs (Alternext, Vrije Markt/Marché Libre, Trading Facility and Easynext), regardless of whether the prohibited type of abuse took place in or outside of Belgium. The Belgian rules also apply to financial instruments

---

[142] See Section 9.4.2.5.2.2.
[143] Financial Supervision Statute Article 25.
[144] Financial Supervision Statute Article 40.
[145] Financial Supervision Statute Article 2, 14°.
[146] In line with the Market Abuse Directive, a separate definition is provided for inside information in relation to derivatives on commodities.

with a listing elsewhere in the EEA, but only if the prohibited type of abuse took place in Belgium. Over-the-counter dealings are covered by the criminal and the administrative prohibition. The prohibitions also apply to financial instruments that are not admitted to trading, but whose value depends on financial instruments that do have a listing.

9.3.2.1.2 Criminal offence

9.180 *9.3.2.1.2.1 Prohibited actions* The description of prohibited actions is modelled on the terms of the Market Abuse Directive. No one who has information which he knows or ought to have known constitutes inside information may:

- use the information by acquiring or disposing of, or trying to acquire or dispose of, for its own account or for the account of a third party, either directly or indirectly, financial instruments to which that inside information relates;
- disclose inside information to any other person unless such disclosure is made in the normal course of the exercise of his employment, profession or duties;
- recommend or induce another person, on the basis of inside information, to acquire or dispose of financial instruments to which that information relates.

9.181 Excluded from the scope of this rule are transactions conducted in the discharge of an obligation that has become due to acquire or dispose of financial instruments if that obligation results from an agreement concluded before the relevant person acquired inside information.

9.182 *9.3.2.1.2.2 Scope* The prohibition applies to any person who has inside information:

- by virtue of its membership of the administrative, management, or supervisory bodies of the issuer or a company with 'close connections' to the issuer;
- by virtue of its holding in the capital of the issuer;
- by virtue of its having access to the information through the exercise of its employment, profession or duties;
- by virtue of its criminal activities.

9.183 If a prohibited transaction has been carried out by a company or legal entity, or a prohibited order has been placed by such company or legal entity, all individuals who are involved in the decision to carry out that transaction or place that order will be exposed to criminal sanctions as well.

9.184 The aforementioned persons could be referred to as 'primary insiders'. The prohibition also applies to 'secondary insiders', i.e. any person, other than the persons referred to above, who has inside information while that person knows or ought to have known that the information (i) constitutes inside information, and (ii) originates (directly or in directly) from a primary insider.

9.3.2.1.3 Administrative offence

9.3.2.1.3.1 Prohibited actions The administrative prohibition covers the **9.185**
same types of abuse as the criminal prohibition. However, there is one important
exception, regarding the prohibition against dealing in the relevant financial
instruments:[147] an insider will commit an administrative offence as soon as he
deals in the relevant financial instruments, regardless of whether he 'used' the
inside information in doing so. This means that the CBFA, contrary to the public
prosecutor in criminal cases, will not have the burden of proving that the insider
acted on the information.

9.3.2.1.3.2 Scope The administrative prohibition applies to anyone who has **9.186**
inside information, and knows or ought to have known that its information
constitutes inside information. Hence, the administrative prohibition is broader
in scope than the criminal one. The administrative prohibition does not distinguish between primary and secondary insiders. Those who are primary insiders
for the purposes of the criminal offence will be subject to the administrative prohibition regardless of whether they obtain the information by virtue of their
capacity, function or activities. Those who are secondary insiders for the purposes
of the criminal offence will be subject to the administrative prohibition regardless
of whether they know that primary insiders are (directly or indirectly) at the source
of their information.

9.3.2.2 Market manipulation

In relation to market manipulation, there are also two separate sets of rules: mar- **9.187**
ket manipulation is punishable as an administrative offence[148] and as a criminal
offence.[149] Administrative offences are subject to administrative fines imposed by
the CBFA, while criminal offences may be punished with criminal sanctions in
court.

Similar to the rules on inside information, and in line with the Market Abuse **9.188**
Directive, both the criminal and the administrative prohibition apply to financial
instruments admitted to trading (or for which an application for admission is
pending) on a Belgian regulated market or on one of four designated Belgian
MTFs (Alternext, Vrije Markt/Marché Libre, Trading Facility and Easynext),
regardless of whether the prohibited type of manipulation took place in or outside
of Belgium. Belgian rules also apply to financial instruments with a listing
elsewhere in the EEA, but only if the prohibited type of manipulation took place

---

[147] See the first bullet point under 9.3.2.1.2.1.
[148] Financial Supervision Statute Article 25.
[149] Financial Supervision Statute Article 39.

in Belgium. Over-the-counter dealings are covered by the criminal and the administrative prohibition.

9.189   **9.3.2.2.1 Criminal offence**   The following types of manipulation are covered by the criminal prohibition:

   (i)   carrying out or attempting to carry out a transaction, or placing or attempting to place an order to trade, disseminating or attempting to disseminate information or rumours, through any deceptive means, where such transactions, orders or information:
   - give or could give false or misleading signals as to the supply of, demand for or price of financial instruments; or
   - have an abnormal influence on the activity on the market, the price of a financial instrument, the volume of trading in a financial instrument, or the level of a market index.

9.190   **9.3.2.2.2 Administrative offence**   The description of prohibited actions is modelled on the terms of Articles 1, 2, (a)–(c) of the Market Abuse Directive.

9.191   In line with EC Directive 2003/124 of 22 December 2003, the Market Abuse Decree provides more details on possible signals of (i) manipulative behaviour related to false or misleading signals and to price securing, or (ii) manipulative behaviour related to the employment of fictitious devices or any other form of deception or contrivance.

9.192   The Market Abuse Decree also gives further effect to the exemption for buy-back programmes and stabilization of financial instruments, as instituted by EC Regulation 2273/2003.

9.3.3   Obligations pursuant to the Corporate Governance Code

9.193   Pursuant to the preamble to the Belgian Corporate Governance Code (the 'Corporate Governance Code') disclosure is essential for corporate governance and crucial to allow effective external monitoring. Through disclosure, the Corporate Governance Code seeks to achieve a high level of transparency. The Corporate Governance Code applies to companies incorporated in Belgium whose shares are admitted to trading on a regulated market (the 'listed companies'). The Corporate Governance Code is soft law and is based on the 'comply or explain' principle. A copy of the English version of the Corporate Governance Code can be found at http://www.corporategovernancecommittee.be/en/corporate_governance_code/final_code/.

9.194   An extensive description of the precise contents of the obligations imposed by the Corporate Governance Code falls outside the scope of this Chapter. Through the Corporate Governance Code, transparency is mainly achieved through disclosure via two different documents: the Corporate Governance Charter,[150] posted on the company's website, and the Corporate Governance Statement,[151] a specific section of the annual financial report.

9.4 Public Takeover Bids

9.4.1 Structuring the deal

Most Belgian listed companies are controlled by one or several reference share- **9.195** holders. These reference shareholders will very often control the decision-making in the board, or will at least have the power to appoint and remove the majority of the board members. Therefore, a successful public takeover of a Belgian listed company will almost always require the support of its reference shareholders. As a result, unsolicited public takeovers are not very common in Belgian public M&A practice, and hostile takeovers even less so.

There are generally two ways for a bidder to secure the support of the reference **9.196** shareholders: it can either acquire their reference shareholding first, and launch a public bid after that; or it can launch a public bid straight away and secure the interest of the reference shareholders through an irrevocable undertaking to tender their shares in the bid. In the first scenario, the public bid will usually be a mandatory one, because the acquisition of the reference shareholding will typically trigger a takeover obligation. In the second scenario the public bid will usually not be compulsory but 'voluntary'.

There is some discussion among legal scholars regarding the enforceability of an **9.197** irrevocable undertaking to tender, or at least of the ancillary undertakings that typically go with such undertaking (i.e. commitment of the reference sharehold-ers not to accept a counter-bid; option for the bidder to acquire the reference shareholding, which can be called if the reference shareholders fail to comply with their commitment to tender). Because of this discussion, the bidder will not be entirely certain that it will acquire the shares of the reference shareholders unless it acquires these shares prior to the public bid. This is a clear advantage of

---

[150] Pursuant to the preamble to the Corporate Governance Code, in its Corporate Governance Charter, 'the company must describe the main aspects of its corporate governance, such as its gov-ernance structure, the terms of reference of the board and its committees as well as other important topics. The Corporate Governance Charter should be updated regularly.'

[151] The Corporate Governance Statement should state 'that the company has adopted this Code as its reference code. It should also include more factual information relating to corporate governance: e.g. the provisions it does not comply with and the reasons for non-compliance, the remuneration report, a description of the main features of the internal control and risk management systems and a description of the composition and operation of the board.'

structuring the takeover in accordance with the first scenario (mandatory bid). The disadvantage of the first scenario is that a mandatory bid can (as a rule) not be made subject to any conditions, such as achieving a particular acceptance rate. Voluntary bids, on the other hand, may be subject to conditions, and this is the main advantage of structuring the bid in accordance with the second scenario.

9.4.2 Voluntary bids

9.4.2.1 *Scope of the rules on voluntary bids*

9.198 **9.4.2.1.1 Principles**   The scope of the Belgian takeover rules is defined in a very complex patchwork of provisions (Article 4 of the Takeover Statute). To determine whether or not the Belgian rules on voluntary bids apply, the central question is whether information in relation to the bid is being publicly spread in Belgium. Once it is determined that Belgian rules apply, two further criteria will be used to determine whether all or only some aspects of the bid will be governed by Belgian law: the location of the registered office of the target company, as well as the place where its securities have a (principal) listing.

9.199 The scope of the rules on voluntary takeovers could be summarized as follows:

- *'Mandatory' application*: a voluntary bid to acquire securities will always be subject to the Belgian takeover rules, if each of the following conditions is satisfied: (i) the voting securities of the target company are listed on a Belgian regulated market, and (ii) the bid falls within the scope of the Takeover Directive.
- *'Contingent' application*: if the target company does not have a listing on a Belgian regulated market, or if the bid does not fall within the scope of the Takeover Directive, a voluntary bid will be subject to the Belgian takeover rules, if the bidder (or persons acting in concert[152] with the bidder, or persons acting for the account[153] of the bidder or its concert parties) publicly spreads information in relation to the bid in Belgium. Application of Belgian law will in such cases be 'contingent' on the bidder's (free) choice to specifically target Belgian investors.
- *Full v partial application*: the fact that a voluntary bid falls within the scope of the Belgian takeover rules, does not automatically mean that each and every one of its aspects will be governed by Belgian law: certain cross-border bids will only be governed by Belgian law in some of their aspects.

---

[152] Parties are considered to be acting 'in concert', if they have an agreement (express or implied, verbal or in writing) with the aim of (a) acquiring or maintaining control over a target company, or fending off a takeover bid on that company, or (b) adopting a sustained common policy in respect of the target company through a concerted use of voting rights (Takeover Statute Article 3, 5°).

[153] Anyone who (directly or indirectly) receives compensation or benefits in the context of the bid, will be deemed to be acting 'for the account' of the bidder or a concert party of the bidder (Takeover Statute Article 6, §2).

9.4.2.1.2 'Mandatory' application   A voluntary bid to acquire securities **9.200** will always be subject to the Belgian takeover rules if the bid falls within the scope of the Takeover Directive and the voting securities of the target company are listed on a Belgian regulated market. In such case, the bid must be open for acceptance in Belgium.[154] Opening a bid for acceptance in Belgium will require the publication of a prospectus in Belgium, and will therefore inevitably lead to the public spreading of information in relation to the bid in Belgium. The Belgian takeover rules apply as soon as information in relation to the bid is being spread publicly.

9.4.2.1.3 'Contingent' application   If the target company does not have a list- **9.201** ing on a Belgian regulated market, or if the bid does not fall within the scope of the Takeover Directive, a voluntary bid to acquire securities will be subject to the Belgian takeover rules if the bidder (or persons acting in concert with the bidder, or persons acting for the account of the bidder or its concert parties) choose to publicly spread information in relation to the bid in Belgium.

- *'Information in relation to the bid'*: Belgian rules will apply if the information either (i) contains sufficient details on the terms of the bid in order to enable securities holders of the target company to decide whether or not to accept it, or (ii) amounts to an advertisement of the bid.
- *'Publicly' spread*: the information must be spread 'publicly', otherwise the bid will not qualify as a 'public' bid. This requires that information is spread among at least 100 persons (who are not 'qualified investors'[155]).

Belgian rules only apply if the bid relates to 'securities'. This is, however, by no **9.202** means a restrictive criterion, because the concept of 'securities' has a very broad definition in the Belgian takeover rules, and includes among others: shares, convertible instruments, debt securities and real estate certificates.[156]

It should be noted that in cases where there is no 'mandatory' application of **9.203** Belgian rules, there is some room for 'forum shopping': if in these cases the bidder chooses not to publicly spread any information in relation to its bid in Belgium, the Belgian takeover rules will not come into play.

9.4.2.1.4 Full v partial application: cross-border bids   As a rule, Belgian law **9.204** will govern all matters of a voluntary takeover bid (and not just some), if by virtue of the above criteria the bid falls within the scope of the Belgian takeover rules. The CBFA will monitor all aspects of the bid.

---

[154] Takeover Statute Article 4, §4.
[155] The concept of 'qualified investors' is defined in Prospectus Statute Article 10.
[156] Specific rules apply to takeover bids on real estate certificates or other debt instruments (Takeover Decree Article 46 et seq.).

9.205 As required by the Takeover Directive, there are exceptions to this principle: the Takeover Statute provides some conflict of law rules for certain cross-border bids, which are essentially based on the question (i) where the registered office of the target company is located, and (ii) where its securities have a (principal) listing.

9.206 These conflict of law rules do not apply to takeover bids which are not governed by the Takeover Directive: if such a bid falls within the scope of the Belgian rules, every aspect of it will be governed by Belgian law. Needless to say this still leaves quite some room for conflict of laws.

9.207 For voluntary bids falling within the scope of the Takeover Directive, the following conflict of law rules apply:

- as long as the target company has its registered office and a listing in Belgium, all matters of the bid will be governed by Belgian law;
- if the target company has its registered office in Belgium, but its 'principal listing'[157] in another EEA member state and no listing in Belgium, Belgian law will govern aspects of employee information and matters of company law (including defensive measures); in addition, if any announcements are made in Belgium in relation to the bid, these will have to comply with Belgian requirements and will be subject to approval by the CBFA; if the bid is open for acceptance in Belgium, a prospectus will have to made available in Belgium, and the prospectus recognition procedure will apply;
- if the target company has its registered office in another EEA member state than Belgium, and a 'principal listing' in Belgium but no listing in its home country, Belgian law will govern matters relating to the bid price and bid procedure (including takeover prospectus and announcements);
- if the target company has its registered office and its principal listing in another EEA member state than Belgium, Belgian law has only limited implications: if any announcements are made in Belgium in relation to the bid, these will have to comply with Belgian requirements and will be subject to approval by the CBFA; if the bid is open for acceptance in Belgium, a prospectus will have to made available in Belgium, and the prospectus recognition procedure will apply.

9.208 **9.4.2.1.5 Excluded from the scope** The following bids are excluded from the scope of the Belgian takeover rules: (i) offers for securities issued by investment

---

[157] If the target company has a listing on an EEA regulated market, that will be considered to be its 'principal listing'. If the target company has a listing in more than one EEA member state, the 'principal listing' will be the one where it has been admitted first. If the target company has been listed in more than one EEA member state simultaneously, it will designate which one is to be considered as its principal listing (Takeover Statute Article 3, 14°).

companies which are not of the closed-ended type, (ii) offers for securities issued by central banks of EEA member states.

9.4.2.2 *Bid requirements, terms of the bid*

9.4.2.2.1 Bid requirements A public takeover bid must satisfy the following requirements:[158] **9.209**

- the bid must extend to all securities with a voting right or 'giving access to voting right'[159] not yet held by the bidder or parties acting in concert with the bidder (under the previous takeover rules, it was possible to offer to acquire a maximum of 10% of voting securities, but that option no longer exists under the current rules);
- if a different price is being offered for different types or classes of securities, price differences must be justified by the terms and features of the respective types or classes;
- the terms of the bid should normally allow the bidder to achieve its intended result;
- the bidder must commit to completing its bid (which it may subject to the satisfaction of certain conditions precedent);
- the funding of the bid must be secured. When the offer is for cash, the amount that would have to be due assuming a 100% tender rate, must either be held in escrow with a bank, or must be covered by an unconditional and irrevocable bank guarantee. Only banks operating under a Belgian licence will qualify. In case the bidder offers securities instead of cash, it will have to establish that it holds the securities that will be offered, or at least that it has power to issue or acquire them in sufficient numbers and within the required timeframe, or that it has the power (by law or in fact) to cause another company to issue such number of securities within such timeframe;
- the bidder must engage a professional paying agent;
- the bid must be in line with the requirements of the Takeover Statute and Takeover Decree.

The bidder must show that the bid requirements are satisfied at the time of the formal takeover filing. The CBFA will use the (brief) time span between formal takeover filing and formal announcement to run a preliminary compliance check on the bid requirements.[160] **9.210**

---

[158] Takeover Decree Article 3.

[159] 'Securities giving access to voting rights' are securities carrying a right to acquire newly issued voting securities, where the issuer of the securities giving access to voting rights and the issuer of the relevant voting securities are one and the same entity (Takeover Statute Article 3, 9°).

[160] See Section 9.4.2.4.1 below.

9.211 **9.4.2.2.2 Bid price** The takeover rules do not interfere directly with the price of a voluntary offer: it is left to the discretion of the bidder to determine the value or amount of the consideration, and to the market to determine whether the offered price is acceptable.

9.212 The same is true for the type of consideration that is offered (cash, securities, combination of both). However, there are certain instances where a person who launches a so-called 'consolidation offer' (i.e. an offer launched by a bidder who already controls[161] the target company) must offer a cash alternative if it chooses to offer securities.[162]

9.213 Fairness opinions were not specifically required by the terms of the previous take-over rules. In practice, however, the CBFA tended to insist on them in certain cases, typically in consolidation offers. Under the current takeover rules, fairness opinions have become a statutory requirement in consolidation offers.[163] Because the legislator only required an opinion in the case of consolidation offers, it has been argued in the legal doctrine that the CBFA has no power to require them in other situations.

9.214 There are a few more provisions that deal with pricing indirectly. First, there is the above-mentioned[164] requirement that the terms of the bid price should nor-mally allow the bidder to achieve its intended result: this requirement applies to the bid price, but it is generally accepted that the CBFA only has a very marginal room for appreciation in that respect. Furthermore, there is the bid requirement that if a different price is being offered for different types or classes of securities, price differences must be justified by the terms and features of the respective types or classes.[165] Finally, the offered price will have to be adequately justified in the takeover prospectus, in order to satisfy the general principle that a prospectus must contain the information required to ensure that target securityholders are able to take an informed decision in respect of the bid.[166]

9.215 **9.4.2.2.3 Conditions precedent** Voluntary bids may be subject to conditions precedent. Typical conditions precedent are antitrust clearings or the achievement of a particular acceptance rate. Generally speaking, a bidder will mathematically be able to control the board of the target if it acquires over 50% of the target's voting securities. Transactions or decisions that technically require an amendment

---

[161] A party has 'control' over the target, if it has the power, in law or in fact, to exercise a decisive influence on the appointment of the majority of its directors or on the orientation of its policies (Companies Code Article 5). See also in Section 9.3.1.2.6.1(a).
[162] See Section 9.4.2.5.3.3.
[163] See Section 9.4.2.5.3.3.
[164] See Section 9.4.2.2.1.
[165] See Section 9.4.2.2.1.
[166] See Section 9.4.2.4.2.1.

of the articles of association—such as issuing new shares or convertible instruments (other than through authorized capital), decreasing the share capital, and most corporate restructurings—require 75% of the voting securities. The approval of share buy-back programmes and amendments of the corporate purpose require 80% of the voting securities. The squeeze-out threshold will normally be at 95%.[167]

A bidder has a fair degree of discretion in attaching conditions to its bid. As a **9.216** general principle of law, the bidder may not hide behind conditions whose satisfaction is at its exclusive discretion. In addition, a number of restrictions follow from the bid requirements outlined in Section 9.4.2.2.1 above: (i) a bid cannot be subject to finance, and (ii) conditions should normally allow the bidder to achieve its intended result (i.e. conditions which are (very) unlikely to materialize will not qualify—tender rates of 95% are accepted as valid conditions by the CBFA). Specific restrictions apply to anti-trust clearings: a bid may only be subject to obtaining approval in phase 1 of the antitrust review. If the antitrust review goes into phase 2, the bidder must either withdraw its bid, or pursue the bid at its own risk.

9.4.2.3 *Preparation of the bid*

9.4.2.3.1 General As explained in Section 9.4.1 above, unsolicited public **9.217** takeovers are the exception in Belgium. Most bidders will seek support from the target company and/or its reference shareholders before initiating formal takeover proceedings. The odd thing about the Belgian takeover rules, though, is that they seem to be written on the assumption that a takeover bid does come unsolicited. The Takeover Statute and the Takeover Decree do not specifically deal with a number of delicate issues that typically arise in the preparatory stages of a negotiated takeover, such as (i) whether due diligence is possible on a listed target company, and if so on what conditions, (ii) whether the fact that a takeover is under preparation must be disclosed, and if so at what stage, (iii) the enforceability of certain commitments undertaken in relation to the bid by the board and/or the reference shareholders of the target company, (iv) whether stakebuilding is allowed in the preparatory stages.

In the absence of tailored provisions in the Takeover Statute or Takeover Decree, **9.218** all of these sensitive issues are governed by general principles and rules of company law and financial law, and create a fair amount of discussion in legal doctrine and 'grey' areas in public M&A practice.

There is a consensus in public M&A practice that due diligence on a listed target **9.219** company is possible, but on stricter conditions than for privately held companies.

---

[167] See Section 9.4.2.6.2.1.

It is also generally acknowledged that, as a rule, the fact that a bid is under consideration or preparation will constitute 'inside information' (which, as a rule, should be disclosed) as soon as parties have reached a binding agreement on the principal terms of their deal. There is, however, unsettled scholarly debate around pre-bid stakebuilding, and the prudent approach, therefore, is not to engage in any such action until the bid has been announced.

9.220 9.4.2.3.2 **'Put up or shut up'**   If statements that are made by any person (or its intermediaries) raise questions with the public as to whether that person has the intention to launch a public takeover bid on a particular target company, the CBFA has the power to request that person to state his intentions.[168] The CBFA will determine within how many days the suspected bidder must issue its statement, provided that this term may not exceed ten working days.

9.221 The suspected bidder will have two options. The first one is to issue a public statement to confirm its intention to launch a takeover bid. In that case it will be obliged to initiate formal takeover proceedings (by introducing a formal takeover file with the CBFA[169]), within a term to be fixed by the CBFA. The other option is not to issue such a statement, in which case it will be prohibited from launching a takeover bid on the relevant target company within the next six months. If the suspected bidder chooses the first option, it should be noted that the CBFA does not have the power to issue a takeover injunction in case the suspected bidder fails to comply with its obligations. The CBFA can only impose an administrative fine up to a maximum of EUR 2.5 million. In addition, there might be claims for damages by third parties. If the suspected bidder chooses the second option, it will be exempted from the standstill requirement if it can establish that there has been a substantial change in circumstances, in the situation of the target company, or in the shareholder structure of any of the entities involved.

9.222 It is important to note that a 'put up or shut up' request may go entirely unnoticed. The CBFA may decide to keep the request confidential (although it has the right to make an announcement as well). In addition, if the suspected bidder is not prepared to confirm its bidding intentions, it has no obligation to announce this in a public statement (unless, as the case may be, it would be obliged to do so by virtue of its general disclosure obligations as a listed company).

9.223 The 'put up or shut up' rule did not exist under the previous takeover rules. It effectively creates the power for the CBFA to intervene in the preparatory stages leading up to a public takeover bid. Those powers come into play as soon as rumours circulate that can be tracked back (directly or indirectly) to the suspected

---

[168] Takeover Decree Article 8, §2.
[169] See Section 9.4.2.4.1.

bidder or its intermediaries. Therefore, it will be essential for a potential bidder to protect the confidentiality of preparatory proceedings, and to put every measure in place to avoid accidental disclosure, also with its advisers. As soon as information starts to leak, the suspected bidder may face a 'put up or shut up' request from the CBFA, which will effectively put it out of control over the process.

9.4.2.3.3 Announcement

9.4.2.3.3.1 Principle: Formal Announcement by the CBFA is first announcement   **9.224**
The CBFA has a legal monopoly in terms of announcements regarding public takeover bids. As a rule, it will be the first one to announce a public takeover bid, in a formal announcement to be made on the next working day following receipt of a formal takeover filing from the bidder (the 'formal announcement'[170]). The rule is that no one is allowed to make any announcement in respect of a public takeover bid if and as long as the CBFA has not made its formal announcement.[171]

9.4.2.3.3.2 Exception: early announcement   In reality, the formal announcement   **9.225**
of the CBFA will often not be the first one. The reason is that preparing a formal takeover file takes quite some time and effort, mainly because it must include a draft prospectus and evidence of secured funding.[172] In many 'negotiated' takeover deals, there will be a signed agreement between the bidder on the one hand and the target company and/or its reference shareholders on the other, before the formal takeover file is ready. In such circumstances, it will be advisable or even required (under disclosure obligations of listed companies) to issue a public statement well ahead of the formal takeover filing (and the formal announcement due on the next working day). However, even then, the CBFA has full control over such 'early announcements', as they must be cleared by it in advance. The CBFA may also take the initiative to request certain parties to issue early announcements. If required to protect the proper functioning of the financial markets, the CBFA may request anyone involved in a possible takeover bid to make such announcement. If such a person fails to comply with the request of the CBFA, the CBFA may issue the announcement itself.[173]

Early announcements to protect the proper functioning of the financial markets   **9.226**
are not the only exception to the principle that the formal announcement by the CBFA is the first one. If a suspected bidder publicly confirms its bidding intentions further to a 'put up or shut up' request from the CBFA,[174] that confirmation

---

[170] See Section 9.4.2.4.1.
[171] Takeover Decree Article 8, §3.
[172] See Section 9.4.2.4.1.
[173] Takeover Decree Article 8, §1.
[174] See Section 9.4.2.3.2.

will also be an 'early announcement': it will precede the formal announcement, because the suspected bidder will not be required to introduce a formal takeover file immediately.

9.4.2.4 Bid procedure

9.227 **9.4.2.4.1 Formal filing, formal announcement**   The formal takeover filing by the bidder marks the start of the formal takeover proceedings. The takeover file must be introduced with the CBFA.[175] The CBFA runs a preliminary compliance check on the bid requirements, and if it thinks the bid is compliant, it will issue a formal announcement on the next working day following receipt of the takeover file.[176] Unless there has been an early announcement,[177] this formal announcement will be the first one.

9.228 The formal takeover filing constitutes in a way the point of no return for the bidder, and has important consequences: as part of the takeover filing, the bidder will have to commit to completing the takeover proceedings, and from this point on, the bidder will only be able to withdraw from the bid under very strict conditions.[178] In a voluntary bid, the bidder will be free to determine exactly when it will be introducing its formal takeover file (unless it has confirmed its bidding intentions further to a 'put up or shut up' request, in which case the CBFA will have imposed a deadline for the formal filing[179]).

9.229 The takeover file will have to include all elements to enable the CBFA to perform its preliminary compliance review on the bid requirements. Furthermore, the file will have to include a draft prospectus and evidence of secured funding.[180] In the event of a 'consolidation' bid,[181] the mandatory fairness opinion will have be part of the file as well.

9.230 **9.4.2.4.2 Prospectus**   A takeover bid cannot open for acceptance until the takeover prospectus of the bidder has been approved by the CBFA and published.[182]

9.231 *9.4.2.4.2.1 Contents, language, publication*   The prospectus must specify the terms of the offer, and in addition provide all information required to enable the target's securityholders to make an informed decision in relation to the bid. A typical takeover prospectus will have three main sections: (i) a section on the terms and rationale of the bid, (ii) a second section with information on the

---

175 Takeover Decree Article 5.
176 Takeover Decree Article 7.
177 See Section 9.4.2.3.3.
178 See Section 9.4.2.5.3.1.
179 See Section 9.4.2.3.2.
180 See Section 9.4.2.2.1.
181 See Section 9.4.2.2.2.
182 Takeover Statute Article 11 et seq.

bidder (and its group of companies), and (iii) a third section with information on the target company (and its group of companies). It must also include a summary and a responsibility statement.[183] Since a takeover prospectus is normally not as sizeable as an issue prospectus (if the takeover bid is for cash), the drafting process is usually markedly shorter.

As a rule, a takeover prospectus will have to be published in Dutch and in French. Only if the bidder shows that the target company usually publishes financial information in only one of those languages (i.e. Dutch or French), or in a language which is 'customary in international financial circles' (i.e. English), the CBFA may accept that the prospectus is published in the relevant language only. Stricter rules apply to the summary of the prospectus. The summary must always be available in Dutch and French, except when all announcements, public communication and advertisements issued by the bidder are published in one of those languages only (i.e. Dutch or French), in which case that language will be sufficient. An English summary only is not possible. **9.232**

The prospectus must be posted on the website of the bidder (if it has one) and its paying agent(s). In addition, the bidder may publish the prospectus in a Belgian newspaper (which is never done in practice), and through printed copies made available at the counters of the paying agent. The bidder may choose to publish the prospectus through the websites only, but in such case every securityholder will have the right to request a paper copy free of charge. **9.233**

9.4.2.4.2.2 Approval, recognition As explained in Section 9.4.2.4.1 above, the formal takeover file must include a draft takeover prospectus. The CBFA has ten working days to approve or reject the prospectus or request further information. If further information is required, another term of ten working days applies. In practice, it usually takes about three to four weeks to process a takeover prospectus. Time can be won by submitting an 'informal' draft prospectus before the formal filing (the CBFA has a very flexible approach in this). **9.234**

If a public takeover bid is open for acceptance in Belgium, but (by the terms of the Takeover Directive) monitored by the regulator of another EEA member state, the takeover prospectus (in the form approved by the foreign regulator) may be published in Belgium after it has been recognized by the CBFA. The scope of the CBFA's review is much more limited in the 'recognition' procedure (compared to the 'acceptance' procedure). In a recognition procedure, the CBFA may only require that additional information is provided to explain specific formalities that need to be observed in order to accept the bid and receive payment in Belgium, or to explain the Belgian tax treatment of the consideration offered in the bid. If a **9.235**

---

[183] See Section 9.4.2.4.2.4.

bidder for securities without a listing in Belgium chooses to open the bid for acceptance in Belgium, he will also be able to process the prospectus through the recognition procedure.

9.236 *9.4.2.4.2.3 Input from target company* On the day when the CBFA issues its formal announcement of the bid, it must also forward a copy of the draft prospectus (which is part of the formal takeover file) to the board of the target company. The board will have five working days to inform the CBFA and the bidder of any incomplete or misleading sections in the draft prospectus. The board will have a second opportunity to give its comments on the prospectus, this time in the form as approved, in its memorandum in reply.[184]

9.237 *9.4.2.4.2.4 Responsibility* The prospectus must specify who takes responsibility for it and must contain a responsibility statement by these persons, confirming that the information provided in the prospectus is true and complete. These persons are jointly and severally liable for any damage caused by false, misleading or incomplete information in the prospectus. If anyone can establish the damage he suffered and the existence of false, misleading or incomplete sections in the prospectus, the burden of proof will be on the responsible persons to show that the former were not caused by the latter.

9.238 **9.4.2.4.3 Memorandum in reply** The board of the target company must formally and publicly respond to the bid, in a so-called 'memorandum in reply'. The memorandum in reply may not be published until approved by the CBFA.[185]

9.239 *9.4.2.4.3.1 Contents, language, publication* A memorandum in reply has three main sections: (i) a first section with any comments the board of the target may still have on the prospectus (in the form as approved), (ii) a second one setting out the position of the board in relation to the bid, and (iii) a third one with details of any restrictions on the transfer of the securities of the target. When stating its position in relation to the bid, the board must provide details on (i) the consequences of the bid, taking into account the interests of the target company, its securityholders, creditors and staff (including the overall rate of employment), (ii) its opinion on the strategic intentions of the bidder, and their likely impact on the target's results, head count, and places of business, and (iii) the details of any securities holdings of board members (or securityholders represented by board members) and the board members' intention whether or not to accept the bid.

9.240 The same rules on the use of languages apply as for the prospectus.[186]

---

[184] See Section 9.4.2.4.3.
[185] Takeover Statute Article 22 et seq. Takeover Decree Article 26 et seq.
[186] See Section 9.4.2.4.2.1.

The memorandum in reply may be published as part of the prospectus, or sepa- **9.241**
rately (in which case the same rules of publication apply as for the prospectus).

9.4.2.4.3.2 Approval   The board of the target must file a draft memorandum in **9.242**
reply with the CBFA within five working days from the receipt of the approved
prospectus (as soon as the prospectus is approved, the CBFA must send a copy to
the board). The CBFA has five working days to approve or reject the memorandum in reply, or request further information. If further information is required,
another term of five working days applies. Time can be won by submitting an
'informal' draft memorandum in reply before final approval of the prospectus.

The CBFA even accepts that both the prospectus and the memorandum in reply **9.243**
are submitted for simultaneous approval (of course, the memorandum in reply
will then have to refer to the final draft of the prospectus, i.e. the one in the form
as submitted for approval). If the approval procedures can be coordinated like
that, the approval of the memorandum in reply will have no impact on overall
timing of the process.

9.4.2.4.3.3 Responsibility   Regarding responsibility for the contents of the **9.244**
memorandum in reply, the same rules apply—*mutatis mutandis*—as for the
prospectus.[187]

9.4.2.4.4 Acceptance period   The acceptance period of the bid must not be **9.245**
shorter than two weeks or longer than ten weeks.[188] Mandatory extensions apply
in certain circumstances, i.e. (i) in case an extraordinary shareholders' meeting of
the target has been called to resolve on defensive measures, (ii) in case the bidder
acquires securities of the target, during the acceptance period, at a price higher
than the bid price (or commits to doing that), or (iii) in the event of a public
counter-bid.[189]

The acceptance period may start as soon as the memorandum in reply has been **9.246**
approved. However, if the memorandum in reply is not approved within five
working days from the approval of the prospectus, the bidder may open the acceptance period nonetheless. This will avoid the board of the target company obstruct-
ing proceedings by deliberately dragging the approval process of the memorandum
in reply.

Securityholders who have tendered their securities are free to revoke their tender **9.247**
at any time during the acceptance period.[190]

---

187 See Section 9.4.2.4.2.4.
188 Takeover Decree Articles 30–31.
189 See Section 9.4.2.4.5.
190 Takeover Decree Article 25, 1°.

9.248 **9.4.2.4.5 Counter-bid**   In the event of a public counter-bid, the takeover rules protect the competition between the two bidders:[191] the acceptance period of the initial bid will be extended to expire on the same day as the acceptance period of the counter-bid. All securities holders who have accepted the initial bid will be free to withdraw their acceptance and tender their securities to the counter-bidder. In order to obtain the benefit of protected competition, the counter-bid must satisfy a number of conditions:

- the price of the counter-bid must be at least 5% higher than the price of the initial bid;
- the counter-bid cannot be subject to conditions which are more restrictive than those attaching to the initial bid (with the exception that a counter-bid may always be subject to (phase 1) antitrust approval, even if the initial bid was not subject to any such condition);
- the counter-bidder will have to ensure that the formal announcement of its counter-bid is made at the latest two working days prior to the expiry date of the acceptance period of the first bid (which means that, to be safe, the counter-bidder should introduce a formal takeover filing with the CBFA at least three working days prior to that expiry date).

9.249 As a rule, the target company will have to provide the same information to the initial bidder and the counter-bidder. If the initial bidder was given the opportunity to conduct due diligence on the target company, this means that the counter-bidder (even a hostile one) must be given the same access to information. In its position in relation to the counter-bid (part of the memorandum in reply), the board of the target will have to compare the counter-bid to the initial bid. The board has no obligation to express a preference for either of the bids, but if it chooses to do so, it must take into account the interests of the target company, its securityholders, creditors and staff (including the overall rate of employment).

9.250 **9.4.2.4.6 Employees**   The employees of the bidder and the target company must be informed as soon as the bid has been announced.[192] In practice, employees will normally be informed just before the announcement, in order to preserve constructive relations with them (by avoiding that they learn about the bid through the media). The prospectus (in the form as approved) must be made available to the employees of the bidder and the target company (or their representatives). Also the position of the board of the target in relation to the bid must be made available.

---

[191] Takeover Decree Article 37 et seq.
[192] Takeover Statute Articles 42–45.

The works council of the target company (if there is one) has the right to interview **9.251**
the representatives of the board of the bidder in a special hearing session. In such
a session, the bidder must provide details on its industrial and financial policies,
as well as on its strategic intentions for the target company, and their likely impact
on the target's head count and places of business. The works council also has the
right to adopt a position in relation to the bid, and may require the board of the
target to include its position in the memorandum in reply.

9.4.2.5 *Specific obligations/restrictions during the bid period*

9.4.2.5.1 'Bid period' and 'parties to the bid'   A number of specific obligations/ **9.252**
restrictions apply to certain persons involved in takeover proceedings.[193] Most of
these apply during the 'bid period', and to some or all of the 'parties to the bid'.

The 'bid period' starts on the day of the first announcement (i.e. depending on the **9.253**
circumstances, the formal announcement by the CBFA, or an early announcement to protect the proper functioning of the markets, or an early announcement
triggered by a 'put up or shut up' request[194]). The bid period ends on the day of the
announcement of the results of the bid (or on the day when the bid lapses on
grounds of non-satisfaction of any condition attached to it). For the bidder and
parties acting in concert with it, the obligations and restrictions of the bid period
will apply as soon as the bidder introduces a formal takeover filing, or as the case
may be, as soon as the bidder submits an early announcement to the CBFA for
approval.

'The parties to the bid' include (i) the bidder and the target company, (ii) the **9.254**
members of their board, (iii) the securityholders of the target company, and (iv)
the persons acting in concert with any of the aforementioned.

9.4.2.5.2 **Obligations/restrictions applying to all parties to the bid**

9.4.2.5.2.1 *Communication*   During the entire bid period, all parties to the bid **9.255**
must refrain from spreading false or misleading statements, announcements or
documents in relation to the bid.

The CBFA may require from any party to the bid to disclose (to the CBFA, or even **9.256**
to the public) all agreements that may have a substantial influence on the assessment, the process or the outcome of the bid.

9.4.2.5.2.2 *Dealings in securities*   Subject to rules on inside dealing, there is no **9.257**
restriction on dealings in securities of the target or the bidder (or in case of an
exchange offer, on dealings in securities offered as consideration).

---

[193]   Takeover Decree Article 9 et seq.
[194]   See Section 9.4.2.3.2.

9.258 Certain (but not all) parties to the bid have a duty to inform the CBFA of any dealings in the aforementioned securities. The duty to inform applies to the bidder, the target company, the members of their board, the persons acting in concert with the bidder or the target company, as well as the persons holding at least 1% of the voting securities of the bidder or the target company. The information is due on the day on which the transaction took place. The CBFA will post this information on its website.

9.4.2.5.3 Obligations/restrictions applying to the bidder

9.259 *9.4.2.5.3.1 No withdrawal or modification of the bid* The formal takeover filing to the CBFA marks the 'point of no return' for the bidder: from this point on, the bidder will only be able to modify or withdraw the bid under very strict conditions.

9.260 The bidder will be entitled to modify or withdraw its bid, subject to the approval by the CBFA, in case the target company takes one of the following defensive measures: (i) the issue of new securities with voting rights or access to voting rights, (ii) the substantial modification of its asset base or its liabilities, (iii) the commitment to obligations without consideration. There is a *de minimis* exception: the issue of new securities representing less than 1% of the securities with voting rights or access to voting rights will not entitle the bidder to modify or withdraw its bid.

9.261 Apart from defensive measures by the target company, the following circumstances also allow the bidder to withdraw its bid: (i) the formal filing of a valid public counter-bid, (ii) the absence of a required clearing from an administrative authority, (iii) the non-satisfaction beyond the power of the bidder of any condition precedent attached to the bid, and (iv) subject to approval by the CBFA, exceptional circumstances that obstruct completion of the bid, on objective grounds and beyond the power of the bidder.

9.262 *9.4.2.5.3.2 Increasing the bid price* In case the bidder (or parties acting in concert with the bidder) acquires securities of the target company during the acceptance period, at a price higher than the bid price (or commits to doing that), the bidder must increase the bid price accordingly. In such event, the acceptance period will be extended.[195]

9.263 *9.4.2.5.3.3 Consolidation bid* In the event of a consolidation bid, the bidder will have to include in its formal takeover file a fairness opinion in respect of the bid price. The fairness opinion must be rendered by an independent expert appointed by the independent directors of the target company. The takeover rules provide specific criteria to secure the independence of the expert. The expert must

---

[195] See Section 9.4.2.4.4.

prepare its own valuation of the securities of the target company, and in case of an exchange offer, of the securities that will be offered in return. The expert will also analyse the valuation used by the bidder. The fairness opinion will be prepared at the expense of the bidder.

Further restrictions apply in case of an exchange offer. A cash alternative must be offered in the following instances: (i) if the securities that are offered as consideration do not have adequate liquidity or are not admitted to trading on a regulated market within the EEA; or (ii) if the bidder (or persons acting in concert with the bidder) acquired (or committed to acquiring) securities of the target, for cash, at any time during the bid period or during 12 months preceding the announcement of the bid. A *de minimis* exception applies to purchases (for cash) of securities representing less than 1% of the voting securities of the target company.   **9.264**

9.4.2.5.4 Obligations/restrictions applying to the target company   The target company must inform the CBFA of any defensive measures taken during the bid period, including in particular (but without limitation) any issue of new securities with voting rights or access to voting rights, but with the exception of any solicitation of alternative bidders.   **9.265**

9.4.2.6 *After the acceptance period*

9.4.2.6.1 Announcement of results, settlement   The bidder must announce the results of the bid within five working days from the end of the acceptance period. Within the same time period, the bidder must announce whether the conditions precedent attached to the bid (if any) have been satisfied, and if not, whether or not it waives the conditions that have remained unsatisfied. Payment and settlement must occur within ten working days from the date of announcement of the results.[196]   **9.266**

9.4.2.6.2 Re-opening of the bid   The bidder will have to reopen the bid in the following instances: (i) if as a result of the bid, it holds more than 90% of the voting securities of the target; or (ii) if the bidder applies for delisting of the target company within three months from the end of the acceptance period; or (iii) if before the end of the 'bid period',[197] the bidder has committed to acquiring securities of the target company at a higher price than the bid price.[198]   **9.267**

---

[196] Takeover Decree Articles 32–34.
[197] See Section 9.4.2.5.1.
[198] Takeover Decree Articles 35–36.

9.268   *9.4.2.6.2.1 Squeeze-out/sell-out*   The bidder may reopen the bid to squeeze out the remaining minority holders of securities with voting rights or access to voting rights, if each of the following conditions is satisfied:[199]

- as a result of the bid or its reopening, the bidder (together with persons acting in concert with the bidder) holds more than 95% of the voting capital of the target company and more than 95% of its voting securities;
- the securities tendered in the bid represent more than 90% of the voting capital comprised in the bid.

9.269   In the event the bidder chooses to use its squeeze-out right, the bid must be re-opened, on the same terms, within three months from the end of the acceptance period, and for a minimum of 15 working days. Upon settlement of the squeeze-out proceedings, the bidder will acquire legal title, by operation of law, to 100% of the securities with voting rights or access to voting rights, including those that were not tendered. The price for securities not tendered in a squeeze-out is kept on deposit with a specific administrative institution (*Deposito- en consignatiekas—Caisse des dépôts et consignations*).

9.270   In addition, if the conditions for a squeeze-out are satisfied, the remaining minority holders of securities with voting rights or access to voting rights have a right to sell their securities to the bidder at the price of the bid. This 'sell-out right' must be exercised within three months from the end of the acceptance period.

9.271   **9.4.2.6.3 Restrictions after the bid period**   If within the first year after the end of the 'bid period',[200] the bidder acquires securities of the target company on terms that are more favourable to the sellers than the terms of the bid, the bidder must pay the price difference to all securityholders who had accepted the bid.[201]

9.4.2.7 Anti-takeover protection and defensive measures

9.272   Belgium used the opt-out right of Article 12, 1 of the Takeover Directive, and did not implement the provisions of Articles 9 (obligations of the board of the target) and 11 (breakthrough) of the Takeover Directive. In accordance with Article 12, 2 of the Takeover Directive, Belgian companies have the possibility to opt back into Articles 9 and/or 11. Companies that use the opt-in provision, have the right to opt out again in case a bid is launched on their securities by a bidder who does not observe the principles of Articles 9 and/or 11.

---

[199] Takeover Decree Articles 42–44.
[200] See Section 9.4.2.5.1.
[201] Takeover Decree Article 45.

9.4.3 Mandatory bid

9.4.3.1 Scope of the rules on mandatory bids

9.4.3.1.1 Mandatory application A mandatory takeover bid will always be governed by Belgian law, in the following instances: **9.273**

- the target company has its registered office in Belgium and its voting securities have a listing on an EEA regulated market or on one of two designated multi-lateral trading facilities ('MTFs') organized by Euronext Brussels (Alternext and Vrije Markt/Marché Libre); or
- the voting securities of the target company are listed on a Belgian regulated market, and the bid falls within the scope of the Takeover Directive; or
- the target company has its registered office in another EEA member state than Belgium, but its 'principal listing' in Belgium, and no listing in its home country.

9.4.3.1.2 Contingent application In cases where there is no mandatory application of Belgian law, the Belgian takeover rules will still apply if the bidder chooses to open the mandatory bid for acceptance in Belgium. The bidder will have the obligation to open the bid for acceptance in Belgium, if it publicly[202] spreads information in relation to the bid in Belgium.   **9.274**

9.4.3.1.3 Full v partial application As is the case for voluntary bids, Belgian law will—as a rule—govern all matters of a mandatory bid (and not just some), if by virtue of the above criteria the bid falls within the scope of the Belgian takeover rules. The CBFA will monitor all aspects of the bid.   **9.275**

As required by the Takeover Directive, there are exceptions to this principle. The Takeover Statute contains some conflict of law rules for cross-border bids, which are essentially the same as those for voluntary bids.[203] A conflict of law rule specifically designed for mandatory bids, though, is that Belgian law determines the 'trigger' of a takeover obligation if the target company has its registered office in Belgium (even if it has no listing in Belgium).   **9.276**

9.4.3.2 Trigger

9.4.3.2.1 Direct trigger An obligation to launch a public takeover bid on a particular company will be triggered by anyone who—directly or indirectly—acquires voting securities of a company whose registered office is located in Belgium and whose securities are admitted to trading on an EEA regulated market or on any of the two designated MTFs organized by Euronext Brussels (Alternext, Vrije Markt/Marché Libre), and as a result of such acquisition holds more than   **9.277**

---

[202] See Section 9.4.2.1.3.
[203] See Section 9.4.2.1.4.

30% of all voting securities of that company.[204] The takeover bid must be made for all securities with voting rights or access to voting rights.

9.278 Any holdings or acquisitions of voting securities by parties acting in concert with or as intermediary of a particular person will be added to that person's personal holding of voting securities.

9.279 **9.4.3.2.2 Indirect trigger** It is not possible to avoid a takeover obligation by acquiring shares in the holding company of the target. A takeover obligation will also be triggered by a person who, as a result of the acquisition of voting securities, holds 'control' in a 'holding entity'.[205] A 'holding entity' is defined as an entity that satisfies each of the following the conditions:

- it holds more than 30% of the voting securities in a target company;
- its stake in the target company represents either (i) more than 50% of its net assets, or (ii) more than 50% of its average net results of the last three financial years.

9.280 **9.4.3.2.3 Exemptions** No takeover obligation will be triggered by an acquisition of voting securities:[206]

- in the context of a voluntary bid;
- from an entity that is affiliated to the acquirer;
- by an acquirer who can establish that an unrelated third party holds control or at least a larger interest than its own in the target company;
- in the context of an issue of new shares, decided by the shareholders' meeting of the target company in a specific situation of financial distress (i.e. where net assets of the target have dropped below 50% of its share capital);
- in the context of a rights issue, decided by the shareholders' meeting of the target company;
- in the context of a merger (amalgamation), on the condition that the acquirer did not have the majority of votes in the shareholders' meeting that approved the merger;
- leading to a temporary holding of not more 32% of the voting securities, on the condition that the excess percentage of voting securities is transferred within the next 12 months and the voting rights attached to the excess securities are not used;
- as a result of a death, a gift (between individuals or to certain foundations), or further to patrimonial arrangements between spouses;

---

204 Takeover Statute Article 5; Takeover Decree Articles 49–50.
205 Takeover Decree Article 51.
206 Takeover Decree Article 51.

- by a financial intermediary, as a result of an underwriting arrangement or the enforcement of a surety right, on the condition that the excess percentage of voting securities are transferred within the next 12 months and the voting rights attached to the excess securities are not used;
- in the context of certain certification structures.

9.4.3.3 *Applicable rules*

In principle, the rules applicable to a voluntary bid also apply to a mandatory one. There are, however, a few exceptions, which are outlined in this Section 9.4.3.3.[207]

9.281

9.4.3.3.1 Terms In a voluntary offer, the bid price is essentially a matter left to the discretion of the bidder.[208] This, of course, is not the case for mandatory offers. The mandatory bid price may not be lower than the higher of: (i) the highest price paid by the bidder (or any person acting in concert with the bidder) for securities of the target company at any time during 12 months preceding the announcement of the bid, or (ii) the weighed average trading price of the relevant securities in the 30 calendar days preceding the trigger of the takeover obligation.

9.282

The mandatory bid price may consist, at the discretion of the bidder, of cash, securities, or a combination of both. If the bidder chooses to offer securities, it will have to offer a cash alternative in the following instances: (i) if the offered securities do not have adequate liquidity or are not admitted to trading on an EEA regulated market, or (ii) if the bidder (or persons acting in concert with the bidder) acquired (or committed to acquiring) securities of the target, for cash, at any time during the bid period or during 12 months preceding the announcement of the bid.

9.283

A mandatory bid may, as a rule, not be subject to any condition precedent.

9.284

9.4.3.3.2 Procedure The bidder must introduce a formal takeover filing with the CBFA within two working days from the trigger of a takeover obligation. This tight timing requires careful preparation and deal management, because the formal takeover file must include a draft prospectus and evidence of secured funding. The CBFA will issue its formal announcement on the next working day. The bidder must ensure that the acceptance period of the bid starts within 40 working days from the trigger of the takeover obligation.

9.285

---

[207] Takeover Decree Articles 53–57.
[208] See Section 9.4.2.2.2.

9.286   **9.4.3.3.3 Other specific provisions**   The following rules do not apply to mandatory takeover bids:

- the grounds for withdrawal or modification:[209] since it is mandatory, it is not possible to withdraw the bid or modify its terms;
- the specific rules and requirements in case of a consolidation bid:[210] there is a statutory minimum price for mandatory bids, and separate cash alternative requirements apply;
- the requirement to announce whether or not any conditions precedents are satisfied and/or waived:[211] mandatory bids cannot, as a rule, be subject to any conditions precedent.

9.287   There is also an important difference with the rules on voluntary bids in terms of squeeze-out thresholds: a mandatory bidder may re-open the bid to squeeze out the remaining minority securityholders as soon as the 95% threshold (of voting capital and voting securities) is achieved. The 90% threshold (of the voting capital comprised in the bid) does not apply in case of a mandatory bid.

9.4.4 Squeeze-out bids

9.288   There are two types of squeeze-out procedures: (i) those that follow after a voluntary or mandatory bid as a result of which the bidder has reached applicable squeeze-out thresholds (these squeeze-out proceedings are actually nothing but a re-opening of the initial voluntary or mandatory bid, on the same terms), and (ii) those where the bidder had not first launched a voluntary or mandatory bid, or at least not one as a result of which it reached the required thresholds. The first type of squeeze-out proceedings have been addressed under Section 9.4.2.6.2.1 above. This Section 9.4.4 only deals with the second type, which is governed by a separate Royal Decree, the Squeeze-Out Decree.

9.289   Upon settlement of any type of squeeze-out proceedings, the bidder will acquire legal title, by operation of law, to 100% of the securities with voting rights or access to voting rights, including those that are not tendered. The price for securities not tendered in a squeeze-out bid is kept on deposit with a specific administrative institution (*'Deposito- en consignatiekas'/'Caisse des dépôts et consignations'*).

9.4.4.1 Scope of the rules on squeeze-out bids

9.290   The rules on squeeze-out bids apply to companies who have sourced their funding publicly (also if none of its securities are listed).

---

[209] See Section 9.4.2.5.3.1.
[210] See Section 9.4.2.5.3.3.
[211] See Section 9.4.2.6.1.

9.4.4.2 *Squeeze-out threshold*

A squeeze-out bid will only be open to a bidder who already owns 95% of the vot- **9.291**
ing securities in the target company.

9.4.4.3 *Applicable rules*

The rules governing squeeze-out bids are generally modelled on those governing **9.292**
voluntary and mandatory bids, with some exceptions. The following are the most
important specific rules applying to squeeze-out bids:

- Squeeze-out bids may only be for cash: it is not possible to offer other securities
  as consideration.
- An independent expert will have to prepare a fairness opinion on the terms of
  the squeeze-out bid.
- The securities holders of the target company have a right to object to the terms
  of the bid. They have to address their objections to the CBFA. The CBFA has
  the right to require the bidder to take certain measures in order to protect the
  interests of the securityholders, and it will not approve the prospectus as long as
  the bidder fails to comply with the requests of the CBFA.

10

DENMARK*

10.1 Process and Timing of Prospectus Approval

10.1.1 Jurisdiction overview

10.1.1.1 Offerings of securities in Denmark

10.01 The prospectus regime in Denmark is divided into three tiers according to the nature of the securities offering in question, as illustrated in Table 10.1. Of the three tiers only 'tier 1' is a direct consequence of the implementation of the Prospectus Directive.

* Special thanks to Simon Bjørnholt of Kromann Reumert for drafting Section 10.4 on Market Stabilization Transactions and Overallotment Facilities and Section 10.5 on Takeover Bids and Defensive Measures.

Table 10.1 Overview of the Danish prospectus regime

	Type of offering	Applicable legislation
Tier 1	Offerings of securities with an aggregate value above EUR 2,500,000 and of securities which are listed or admitted to trading on a regulated market	Prospectus Directive Prospectus Regulation (2004/809/EC) CESR's recommendations The Danish Securities Trading Act, Chapter 6 Executive Order No 885/2009 Guidelines No 9318/2005
Tier 2	Offerings of unlisted securities with an aggregate value between EUR 100,000 and EUR 2,500,000	The Danish Securities Trading Act, Chapter 12 Executive Order No 1231/2007 Guidelines No 9320/2005
Tier 3	Offerings of unlisted securities with an aggregate value below EUR 100,000	Not encompassed by the Prospectus Regulation. The Danish Marketing Act and other acts may be applicable

Tier 2 encompasses legislation concerning 'smaller unlisted offerings'. This legislation is based principally on the desire of the Danish legislature to ensure that investors in smaller unlisted offerings are afforded a minimum standard of protection. Generally, the legislation applicable to tier 2 is similar to that applicable to tier 1. However, there are certain differences attributable to the fact that the tier 2 regulation is not based on the Prospectus Directive; for example, the prospectus passporting regime is inapplicable to tier 2 offerings and the Danish Financial Services Authority (in Danish '*Finanstilsynet*'—the 'FSA') is not bound by the Prospectus Directive in relation to tier 2 legislation. **10.02**

Tier 3 deals with smaller offerings that have an aggregate value below EUR 100,000. The Prospectus Directive removes the requirement to publish a prospectus for such offerings, which are therefore only subject to the provisions of the Danish Marketing Practices Act (Act No 1389 dated 21 December 2005 as amended), the Danish Contract Act (Act No 781 dated 26 August 1996 as amended) and other general pieces of legislation. **10.03**

10.1.1.2 Competent authority

The FSA is the competent authority for securities offerings in Denmark.[1] As such, it is responsible for approving prospectuses prepared in connection with tier 1 and tier 2 offerings. The FSA is also the competent authority for the procedure under the EU prospectus passporting regime which is discussed below, at 10.3. **10.04**

For the approval of a tier 1 prospectus, including any supplements, the Danish FSA charges a fee of DKK 32,500 (approximately EUR 4,365). An approval of a tier 2 prospectus is free of charge. **10.05**

---

[1] The Danish Securities Trading Act (Consolidated Act No 795 of 20 August 2009).

10.06 While the FSA is responsible for approving prospectuses for offerings of securities to be listed and/or admitted to trading on a regulated market in Denmark, it is customary for the relevant Danish regulated market to request further information and/or amendments to the prospectus before the securities are listed or admitted to trading.

10.1.1.3 Regulated markets in Denmark

10.07 The Danish Securities Trading Act distinguishes between (i) a stock exchange and (ii) an authorized market. Both of these are types of market and both constitute a 'regulated market' and are within the purview of the Prospectus Directive. Denmark's regulated markets include:

- NASDAQ OMX Copenhagen (Stock Exchange or in Danish '*fondsbørs*'); and
- The Danish Authorized Market Place.

10.08 By way of alternative, issuers may list on First North, a multilateral trading facility (an 'MTF') constituted by Danish securities regulation and operated in Copenhagen by the NASDAQ OMX group. Being a non-regulated market, admission of securities to First North is considered an admission of unlisted securities within the ambit of the tier 2 regulation. Companies traded on First North are subject to the rules of First North and not the legal requirements of a regulated market.

10.1.2 Listing securities in practice

10.1.2.1 The obligation to publish a prospectus

10.09 Generally, an issuer of securities to the public in Denmark is required under the Danish prospectus regime to publish a prospectus in relation to the offering if it has an aggregate value of more than EUR 100,000. In accordance with the Danish Securities Trading Act,[2] an offer of securities to the public means: 'a communication to natural or legal persons in any form and by any means, presenting sufficient information on the terms of the offer and the securities to be offered, so as to enable an investor to decide to purchase or subscribe to these securities'.

10.10 In this context, the issuer must actively take steps to make 'sufficient information' on the terms of the offer available to the Danish public. Such information could include, *inter alia*, information on the characteristics, terms and price of the securities and how and when to subscribe for the securities. If the issuer publishes information or statements or in any other way makes publicity efforts which have

---

[2] Section 2(b) .

the effect of arousing public interest in an issuer or its securities in advance of a proposed offering, such steps are likely to constitute an offer to the public unless the communication contains only general information about the relevant securities and is clearly not intended to form a part of an offering.

10.1.2.2 *Exemptions from the obligation to publish a prospectus*

The obligation to publish a prospectus is qualified pursuant to two categories of exemptions, depending on whether the securities in question are listed or not. For the purposes of the Danish rules, unlisted securities include securities that are listed or admitted for trading outside the EU/EEA. **10.11**

Although the exemptions follow from two different sets of rules[3]—the exemptions apply equally to tier 1 and tier 2 offerings. Table 2 below illustrates the applicable exemptions under Danish law. **10.12**

Table 10.2 Exemptions from the obligation to publish a prospectus under Danish law

Unlisted securities

- An offer of securities addressed solely to qualified investors.
- An offer of securities addressed to fewer than 100 natural or legal persons per member state or EEA state, other than qualified investors.
- An offer of securities addressed to investors who acquire securities for a total consideration of at least EUR 50,000.
- An offer of securities whose denomination per unit amounts to at least EUR 50,000.
- An offer of securities with a total consideration of less than EUR 100,000, calculated on an assessment basis over a period of 12 months.
- Shares issued in substitution for shares of the same class already issued, if the issuing of such new shares does not involve any increase in the issued capital.
- Securities offered in connection with a takeover bid, provided that a document is available with information equivalent to that in a prospectus.
- Securities offered, allotted or to be allotted in connection with a merger, provided that a document is available with information equivalent to that in a prospectus.
- Shares offered, allotted or to be allotted free of charge to existing shareholders, and dividends paid out in the form of shares of the same class as the shares in respect of which such dividends are paid, provided that a document is made available with information on the number and nature of the shares and the reasons for and details of the offer.
- Securities offered, allotted or to be allotted to existing or former directors or employees by the issuing company provided the securities are offered or allotted by the issuing company or by an affiliated undertaking, cf. section 5(1)(9) of the Danish Financial Business Act. If the unlisted securities in the offering have an aggregate value above EUR 2,500,000, the exemption only applies if the employer already has securities admitted to trading on a regulated market. A document must be made available with information on the number and nature of the securities and the reasons for and details of the offer.

---

[3] Executive Order No 885/2009 for tier 1 offerings and Executive Order No 1231/2007 for tier 2 offerings.

Table 10.2 Exemptions from the obligation to publish a prospectus under Danish law *(Continued)*

Listed securities

- Shares representing, over a period of 12 months, less than 10% of the share capital of the issuer of the same class already admitted to trading on the same regulated market.
- Shares issued in substitution for shares of the same class already admitted to trading on the same regulated market, if the issuing of such shares does not involve any increase in the issued capital.
- Securities offered in connection with a takeover bid, provided that a document is available with information equivalent to that in a prospectus.
- Securities offered, allotted or to be allotted in connection with a merger, provided that a document is available with information equivalent to that in a prospectus.
- Shares offered, allotted or to be allotted free of charge to existing shareholders, and dividends paid out in the form of shares of the same class as the shares in respect of which such dividends are paid, provided that the said shares are of the same class as the shares already admitted to trading on the same regulated market and that a document is made available with information on the number and nature of the shares and the reasons for and details of the offer.
- Securities offered, allotted or to be allotted to existing or former directors or employees by the issuing company provided the securities are offered or allotted by the issuing company or an affiliated undertaking of the employer, cf. section 5(1)(9) of the Danish Financial Business Act, and provided that the said securities are of the same class as the securities already admitted to trading on the same regulated market and that a document is made available with information on the number and nature of the securities and the reasons for and detail of the offer.
- Shares resulting from the exchange of other securities or from the exercise of the rights conferred by other securities, provided that the said shares are of the same class as the shares already admitted to trading on the same regulated market.

10.1.2.3 The roles of the FSA and NASDAQ OMX Copenhagen in the listing process

10.13 As described above, the FSA is the competent authority responsible for approving prospectuses for offerings of securities in Denmark. The FSA checks whether the applicant company has complied with all formalities under the Prospectus Regulation and the Danish Executive Orders. In practice, the applicant submits its prospectus for approval to the Danish FSA and, simultaneously, to the relevant regulated market on which the securities are to be listed.

10.14 Matters of a more technical nature regarding the admission to trading and listing of the securities are typically resolved between the issuer's advisers and the regulated market (NASDAQ OMX Copenhagen) or the alternative market (First North), as the case may be. The relevant market also determines whether the applicant is required to include any additional information in the prospectus and also coordinates the timetable for listing.

10.15 The prospectus submission process is typically handled by the investment bank assisting the issuer with the offering. Generally, it will submit the prospectus by email on the applicant's behalf, together with a timetable detailing all relevant dates in respect of the offering together. Identical documents are sent to the Danish FSA and to NASDAQ OMX Copenhagen.

10.1.2.4 The Danish FSA's prospectus approval process

Under the Danish FSA's guidelines, prospectuses must be sent to the FSA by email (to the appointed contact person)[4] or by post at the following address: Finanstilsynet, Århusgade 110, DK-2100 Copenhagen OE, Denmark.

10.16

While the prospectus does not have to be complete at the time of the first filing, the FSA will not review a prospectus if material sections have not been completed. The issuer's interim accounts may be excluded (since they are often prepared simultaneously with the prospectus) but sections such as risk factors, information about the issuer and business overview must be included.

10.17

To the extent that the prospectus has not been drafted in the same order as set out in the Prospectus Regulation,[5] the issuer must submit a cross-reference table that notes the deviations and states the pages of the prospectus on which each of the items mentioned in the Prospectus Regulation can be found.[6]

10.18

The Danish FSA will provide the issuer with notice of its decision regarding approval of the prospectus within ten trading days after receiving the request for approval of the prospectus.[7] The time limit is prolonged to 20 trading days if the offer relates to securities that have not previously been admitted to trading.

10.19

In addition, if the application for approval to the Danish FSA is not complete or if the Danish FSA needs further information, the ten-day time period will not start running until the missing documents have been provided to the Danish FSA.

10.20

The Danish FSA will check whether all required information has been included in the prospectus in accordance with the Prospectus Regulation. Although the Danish FSA is not under an obligation to review the actual descriptions in the various sections of the prospectus, in practice, it is likely to provide detailed comments, including highlighting any inconsistencies in the prospectus.

10.21

The Danish FSA sends its comments on the prospectus to the issuer's contact person. The expectation is that the issuer will amend the prospectus in accordance with the Danish FSA's comments. The Danish FSA also requires that any comments provided by the relevant market following its review are incorporated into the prospectus. After revising the document, the issuer must submit to the Danish

10.22

---

[4] The issuer must appoint one person as its contact person as regards communication with the Danish FSA. Often this person will be the investment bank assisting the issuer with the offering but it may well be the issuer itself, the issuer's legal counsel or other advisers. The Danish FSA, in turn, appoints one person to act as the issuer's contact person.

[5] (2004/809/EC).

[6] Prospectus Regulation Article 25(4).

[7] For the purposes of calculating the time period for approval, a request for approval received later than 9am Danish time by the Danish FSA is considered to have been received on the next trading day.

FSA a mark-up of the prospectus, reflecting all changes made, including any deletions.

10.23 If the Danish FSA has no comments on the revised prospectus, it will report this to the issuer's contact person who will then arrange for the complete prospectus, including signed declarations,[8] to be sent to the Danish FSA for final approval.[9]

10.24 The Danish FSA approves a prospectus on the basis of a declaration signed by the issuer's management ('*direktionen*') (provided the board of directors ('*bestyrelsen*') have provided the management with a power of attorney to do so). The declaration must state that the management and the board of directors have taken all reasonable care to ensure that, to the best of their knowledge, the information contained in the prospectus is in accordance with the facts and that no information likely to affect the import thereof has been omitted.

10.25 The Danish FSA will send the issuer (typically by email) a letter approving the prospectus, with a copy to the issuer's contact person and to the relevant market.

10.26 While it is not a requirement, the Danish FSA suggests that the issuer prepares a timetable for the offering. This timetable should be submitted to the Danish FSA and the relevant regulated market for its comments on the timing of the listing. The timetable should take into consideration the necessary period to process the application for approval of the prospectus, as well as the period required for subsequent amendments to the prospectus to incorporate the comments of the Danish FSA. The timetable should also allow for deadlines (if any) in connection with the publication of the prospectus.

10.1.2.5 NASDAQ OMX Copenhagen—admission requirements

10.27 The issuer must submit to NASDAQ OMX Copenhagen an application for the admission of shares to trading. The application must state (i) the reason for the admittance application; (ii) how the proceeds will be spent; (iii) the issuer's share capital/number of shares (with information about share classes and an indication of differences between share classes, if applicable); (iv) the size of the share offering, broken down by new and existing shares, and specifications as to the type of offering; (v) the names of the financial intermediary/intermediaries handling the share offering on behalf of the issuer; and (vi) how the issuer fulfils the requirements for admittance to trading and if necessary, admission to the official list as described in Section 10.1.2.6 below.

---

[8] In accordance with the Prospectus Regulation Annex I section 1.2, the prospectus must include a declaration by those responsible for the prospectus. For further requirements under Danish law with respect to declarations in a prospectus, see Section 10.2 below.

[9] The signed declaration pages may be submitted by fax or email.

The following documents must accompany the application: **10.28**

  (i) a draft prospectus;

 (ii) the issuer's accounts for the past three fiscal years;

(iii) a timetable for the admission to trading and the share offering;

(iv) the issuer's latest registered set of articles of association;

 (v) a subscription/sales form;

(vi) documentation evidencing the issuer's registration with the Danish Commerce and Companies Agency or other authority of registration; and

(vii) a copy of the issuer's internal rules (described in this Section below).

According to sections 4.1 and 4.2 of the Rules for Issuers of Shares on NASDAQ **10.29**
OMX Copenhagen, an issuer must prepare internal rules that govern (i) trading
in its own shares (and related financial contracts); and (ii) trading by board members, general managers and other employees of the issuer, for their own or any
third party's account, in the issuer's securities that have been admitted for trading
(and any financial instruments attached thereto).

In addition, the Danish Securities Trading Act requires each company with securi- **10.30**
ties listed on a regulated market and its parent company to prepare internal rules
governing (i) trading by board members, directors and other employees in the
company's shares (and related financial contracts); (ii) the treatment of inside
information; and (iii) the company's disclosure obligations.

With respect to an issuer's reporting obligations, the Rules for Issuers of Shares **10.31**
on NASDAQ OMX Copenhagen require that, in advance of seeking admission
to trading, a company must establish adequate procedures, controls and systems,
including systems and procedures for financial reporting, to enable compliance
with its obligation to provide the market with timely, reliable, accurate and up-to-
date information. This requirement is often part of the verification procedure
discussed in Section 10.1.2.7.

10.1.2.6 Conditions for admission of securities to the Official List

Admission of securities to trading on a regulated market in Denmark is a pre- **10.32**
requisite for admission of the securities to the Official List; however, securities
admitted to trading are not automatically admitted to the Official List.

The conditions for admission of securities to the Official List are set out in **10.33**
Executive Order No 1069.[10] The Danish FSA is the decision-making authority in
this context. It may reject an application for admission to the Official List if it
deems that the issuer's situation is such that the official listing would be detrimental to investors' interests. It may refuse to admit a security already admitted to the

---

[10] Issued on 4 September 2007.

official list in a country within the EU (or in a country with which the EEC has entered into an agreement for the financial area), if the issuer has failed to comply with the obligations pursuant to its listing in that country. The Danish FSA may also impose any such condition for the admission of a security to the Official List as it considers necessary for investor protection.

10.34 The Danish FSA must notify the issuer of a decision within six months of receipt of its application. Failure to give a decision within the time limit is deemed to be a rejection of the application.

10.35 In order to be admitted to the Official List, the issuer and its shares must meet a number of conditions, set out in Annex 1 to Executive Order 1069/2007, including the following:

(i) the foreseeable market capitalization of the shares represents at least EUR 1 million. If the market capitalization cannot be assessed, the company's capital and reserves, including profit or loss, from the last financial year, must be at least EUR 1 million;

(ii) the company must have published or filed its financial statements in accordance with national law for the three accounting years preceding the application for admission to the Official List (the Danish FSA may derogate from this condition if it is deemed to be in the interests of the company or of investors and where the Danish FSA is satisfied that investors have the necessary information available to be able to reach an informed judgment on the company and its securities);

(iii) the shares must be freely transferable;

(iv) a sufficient number of shares must be distributed to the public[11] in one or more countries within the European Union or in countries with which the Community has entered into an agreement for the financial area no later than the time of admission (this condition does not apply where shares are to be distributed to the public through the regulated market. In that event, admission to the Official List may be granted only if the Danish FSA is satisfied that a sufficient number of shares will be distributed through the regulated market within a short period); and

(v) the application for admission to official listing must cover all the shares of the same class already issued.

---

[11] According to the Rules for issuers of shares on NASDAQ OMX Copenhagen, it is a general requirement and a prerequisite for exchange trading that a 'sufficient number' of shares must be distributed to the public. In addition, the company shall have a 'sufficient number' of shareholders. In general, companies with at least 500 shareholders each holding shares with a value of around EUR 1,000 will be considered to fulfil the requirement regarding the number of shareholders.

Where applications for admission to the Official List are to be made simultane- **10.36**
ously or within short intervals of admission of the same securities to official listing
in another EU member state or countries with which the EU has entered into an
agreement for the financial area), the issuer must specify this in the application.
Similarly, if the securities in question have already been admitted to official listing
in another EU member state, this must be specified in the application.

Executive Order 1069/2007 sets out additional requirements for admission to the **10.37**
Official List of bonds, convertible bonds, exchangeable bonds and bonds with
warrants, which are beyond the scope of this Chapter.

Once securities have been admitted to the Official List, various obligations are **10.38**
imposed on the issuer. These include:

(i)   in the event of a new public issue of shares of the same class as those already
      admitted on the Official List, the company must (if the new shares are not
      automatically admitted) apply for their admission to the same listing, either
      within a year after their issue or when they become freely negotiable;
(ii) the general meetings of the company must be open to the press; and
(iii) the Danish FSA may require the company to publish information required
      by the Danish FSA in such a form and within such time limits as the Danish
      FSA considers appropriate. This includes 'inside information', as defined in
      the Danish Securities Trading Act. The purpose of this provision is to protect
      investors and to ensure the smooth operation of the market.

The Danish FSA may publicly censure any issuer that fails to comply with these **10.39**
obligations. It may also decide to suspend the issuer's listing if it considers that
the smooth operation of the market is, or will be, jeopardized, or that investor
protection so requires. Furthermore, the Danish FSA may decide to withdraw an
issuer's official listing if it deems that, owing to special circumstances, normal
regular dealings in its securities are no longer possible. The issuer may also request
a withdrawal of its official listing, which the Danish FSA will grant unless it
believes that the discontinuation of the official listing is not in the interest of
investors, the issuer's creditors, or the securities market in general.

10.1.2.7 *Verification of a prospectus*

While there is no legal requirement to verify a prospectus, the process of verification **10.40**
is typically undertaken by an independent lawyer appointed by the investment
bank assisting the company with the offering in order to ensure that the prospectus
complies with the relevant rules and adequately conveys the required information
to potential investors. The process of verifying prospectuses, which is generally
carried out on the basis of the first draft of the prospectus filed with the Danish
FSA and NASDAQ OMX Copenhagen, is primarily based on market practice
and, consequently, it is subject to continuous change.

10.41   Verification does not entail a complete due diligence review and typically only covers documentation provided by the issuer. The verification lawyer will focus primarily on potential liabilities and key risks facing the issuer. The verification lawyer will often participate in the last few prospectus drafting sessions in order to understand the specific issues and risks pertaining to the issuer in question but will not normally participate in the actual writing of the prospectus.

10.42   The verification lawyer will typically prepare a number of questions to be answered by the company (the board of directors and the management), its external auditors and its legal counsel, the answers to which will then be discussed at a meeting. If the prospectus is revised pursuant to this process then a marked-up version showing the changes must be filed with the Danish FSA and NASDAQ OMX Copenhagen.

10.43   After the meeting the verification lawyer will circulate a verification document including all questions and answers discussed at the meeting. The company's board of directors, management, external auditor and legal counsel will be asked to sign the verification document. The verification document is not a public document but will often state that the investment bank is entitled to make use of the document in the event that claims are put forward against the bank and/or the company with respect to the prospectus and/or the offering.

10.1.2.8 *Publication of a prospectus*

10.44   Once the prospectus has been approved by the Danish FSA and the relevant regulated market the issuer must make the prospectus available to the public as soon as practically possible and in any case before the public offering commences or the securities are admitted to trading. In the case of an initial public offering of a class of shares not already admitted to trading, the prospectus must be publicly available at least six business days before the end of the offer period.[12]

10.45   The prospectus is deemed to have been made available to the public when published in one of the following ways:

   (i)   by insertion in one or more newspapers circulated widely in Denmark;
   (ii)   in printed form made available, free of charge, to the public at the offices of the market on which the securities are being admitted to trading, as well as at the registered office of the issuer and at the offices of the entities acting as financial intermediaries in the sale of the securities;
   (iii)   in electronic form on the issuer's website and, if applicable, on the website of the financial intermediary for the sale of the securities; or
   (iv)   in electronic form on the website of the regulated market where admission to trading is sought.

---

[12] See Danish Executive Order 885/2009 section 24.

The Danish FSA publishes on its website a list of all prospectuses that have been **10.46** approved within the past 12 months, detailing the date of the approval, the name of the issuer and the type of securities listed. Such prospectuses are also made available on the FSA's website.

10.1.3 Continuing obligations

10.1.3.1 Disclosure obligations

Issuers of securities listed on a regulated market in Denmark must inform the **10.47** public as soon as possible of inside information that directly concerns the issuer. This general disclosure obligation is set out in section 27 of the Danish Securities Trading Act, which implements Article 6(1) of the Market Abuse Directive.

The NASDAQ OMX Copenhagen rules for issuers of shares last updated on **10.48** 1 July 2009 (the 'NASDAQ Rules') are almost completely harmonized with the rules applicable to issuers listed on the NASDAQ OMX-exchanges in Stockholm, Helsinki, Copenhagen and Iceland. The NASDAQ OMX Rules include a general disclosure obligation similar to that under section 27 of the Danish Securities Trading Act. In addition, the NASDAQ Rules require listed companies to fulfil a number of specific disclosure obligations, which include the publication of annual and interim financial reports, information regarding issue of share-based incentive programmes and investments and a number of specific events.

There is no obligation for a company listed on NASDAQ OMX Copenhagen to **10.49** publish forecasts and forward-looking statements. However, when a company discloses a forecast, it must provide information regarding the assumptions or conditions underlying the forecast. Furthermore, where a company expects that its financial result or financial position will deviate significantly from a previously announced forecast, and such deviation is price sensitive, the company must disclose the deviation, noting the previous forecast and contrasting it with the actual result or position.

10.1.3.2 Timing of publication

According to the NASDAQ OMX Rules, publication of inside information must **10.50** be made 'as soon as possible'. NASDAQ OMX Copenhagen's guidance on this rule states that very little time may elapse between the occurrence of the relevant event or decision and the corresponding disclosure. The time gap usually permitted is the time necessary to establish the relevant facts, compile an announcement and disseminate it to the market. A short delay may be permitted if the relevant facts are not sufficiently clear to enable a meaningful announcement (for example, the rule does not require an announcement to be made during an ongoing meeting of the board of directors or other decision-making body—the disclosure may be made after such meeting is over).

10.51 The timing of the publication of inside information is crucial, as illustrated by a March 2009 case. A/S Dampskibsselskabet Torm ('TORM'), a listed company, entered into a written agreement in April 2008 to sell a ship for USD 70 million. The agreement was signed by TORM on 21 April 2008 and by the buyer on 22 April 2008. TORM published a statement on the sale on 25 April 2008 after it had received confirmation from its bank that the buyer had paid the agreed deposit. While TORM argued that it was accepted practice in its line of business that an agreement was not considered to be final until the deposit had been paid by the buyer, the Danish FSA pressed charges against it for violating its obligation to publish inside information immediately (i.e. on 22 April 2008).

10.52 Issuers should note, particularly in the context of the marketing of a public offering, that price-sensitive information cannot be selectively disclosed at meetings (including shareholders' meetings) or at analyst presentations without prior or simultaneous public disclosure of the information.

10.1.3.3 *Information leaks*

10.53 If a company with securities listed on NASDAQ OMX Copenhagen learns that price-sensitive information relating to it has leaked out before it has publicly disclosed such information, the company must promptly make an announcement on the matter. Similarly, if selective disclosure was made inadvertently to a third party not under a duty of confidentiality to the company, the company must promptly disclose the information to the public. However, in situations where the information concerning the company was selectively disclosed but not by the company, the company must assess whether such information is price-sensitive and whether a disclosure obligation has arisen due to the general prohibition on selective disclosure of inside information. The company's assessment must take into consideration the accuracy of the information, as well as whether it constitutes price-sensitive information. If the company concludes that such information is largely accurate and in fact price-sensitive in relation to the company's securities, it is likely that the information has been leaked, in which case the company must prepare an announcement as soon as possible.

10.54 Market rumours or media speculation regarding the company may occur even if information has not leaked from the company. The company is not obliged to monitor market rumours or respond to inaccurate or misleading information communicated to the market by a third party. In such cases the company may legitimately respond to questions relating to the rumour with 'no comment'. However, when an untrue rumour has a significant effect on the price of the company's securities, the company may consider making an announcement in order to provide the market with correct information and to promote orderly price formation. If orderly trading is substantially affected by such rumours, NASDAQ OMX Copenhagen will consider whether it needs to take action, such as suspending trading in the company's securities. In some instances, NASDAQ OMX Copenhagen has approached listed companies and requested them to publish a statement in relation to the rumours.

If market rumours are largely accurate then the company concerned is usually obliged to make an announcement to the public. For example, in case of a leak, an issuer may be obliged to inform the market of ongoing negotiations even though they are not finalized. It should be noted, however, that this issue is currently disputed in Denmark. While the NASDAQ OMX rules appear to trigger a duty to make an announcement in the case of a largely accurate rumour relating to ongoing negotiations, a recent ruling held that a disclosure obligation under the Securities Trading Act does not arise, even in case of a leak, until a final decision among the parties of the negotiation has been made.[13]

10.55

10.1.3.4 *Information to NASDAQ OMX Copenhagen only—public offers and publication of significant information*

Where a company with securities admitted to trading on NASDAQ OMX Copenhagen has made internal preparations to make a public tender offer for securities of another listed company, the company preparing the offer must notify NASDAQ OMX Copenhagen when it has reasonable grounds to believe that its preparations will lead to a public tender offer being made. Furthermore, if a company with securities admitted to trading on NASDAQ OMX Copenhagen has been informed that a third party intends to make a public tender offer to its shareholders, and such public tender offer has not been disclosed, the company must notify NASDAQ OMX Copenhagen when it has reasonable grounds to assume that the intention to make a public tender offer will go ahead. The information

10.56

---

[13] In response to a clarification sought by the Danish Securities Council ('*Fondsrådet*') on listed companies' obligation to comment on rumours, the Danish Ministry of Economic and Business Affairs requested the Danish FSA to approach the European Commission to investigate whether the Danish legislation complies with the Market Abuse Directive. In response, the European Commission stated that matters or events that precede the signature of a contract or the finalization of negotiations may constitute inside information that shall be published as soon as possible. It is expected that a bill will be presented in the Danish Parliament later this year to amend the Securities Trading Act in case of leakages.

The background to this request involved a company's appeal against a reprimand from the Copenhagen Stock Exchange (now NASDAQ OMX Copenhagen). The Copenhagen Stock Exchange had reprimanded the company for not publishing information regarding ongoing negotiations for the sale of a subsidiary even though detailed information on these negotiations had been leaked to the press. The Danish Commerce and Companies Appeals Board ('*Erhvervsankenævnet*') withdrew the reprimand on the ground that while the company had initiated an auction process for sale of the subsidiary no final decision regarding a sale had been made. This decision was contrary to the practice of the Danish FSA according to which companies were obligated to publish price sensitive information on negotiations if information was leaked— regardless of whether the negotiations were finalized or not.

will be used by NASDAQ OMX Copenhagen to monitor trading in order to detect unusual price movements and to prevent insider trading.

10.57   There are no formal requirements regarding the manner of notification to the NASDAQ OMX Copenhagen and notice is normally made by telephone to the surveillance department.

10.58   If a listed company intends to disclose information that it anticipates will have a significant effect on the price of its securities, the company must notify NASDAQ OMX Copenhagen prior to disclosure. The object of this rule is to enable NASDAQ OMX Copenhagen to consider if any special measures need to be taken. For example, NASDAQ OMX Copenhagen may briefly suspend trading in the company's securities and cancel pending orders in order to provide the market with an opportunity to evaluate the new information. Companies need not provide information in advance where the information is to be included in a scheduled report, such as its periodic financial statements, since the market is already braced for the company to announce price sensitive information on such occasion.

10.1.3.5 Corporate governance

10.59   A company with securities listed on NASDAQ OMX Copenhagen must disclose its compliance with the corporate governance code in the jurisdiction where its registered office is situated, according to local practice. If the company is not subject to a corporate governance code of its home country, it must apply the corporate governance code that is applied on NASDAQ OMX Copenhagen.

10.60   Companies subject to the Danish corporate governance code must include in their annual report a statement on how they address the Danish Recommend-ations for Corporate Governance 2005, as amended on 10 December 2008 (the 'Recommendations'). Such companies must adopt the 'comply-or-explain' prin-ciple when preparing this statement, i.e., they must either comply with the Recommendations or explain the reason for non-compliance.

10.61   The Recommendations overlap to an extent with the disclosure requirements that apply to companies admitted for trading.

10.2 Particular Content Requirements

10.2.1 Prospectus declarations

10.62   NASDAQ OMX Copenhagen requires that a prospectus include a declaration from the company's financial intermediary with the following wording:

> In our capacity as intermediaries, we hereby confirm that the issuer and the issuer's auditors have made available to us all the information requested and deemed

necessary by us. The data provided or disclosed to us, including data on which financial information, market information, etc., are based, have not been independently verified by us; however, we have reviewed the information and have compared it with the information contained in the prospectus and have found nothing that is incorrect or inconsistent.

The company's auditors must make a declaration in the prospectus confirming **10.63** that the prospectus contains all facts relating to the company that are known to the auditors and which are likely to affect the investors' and their investment advisers' assessment of the company's assets and liabilities, financial position, results and outlook for the future. NASDAQ OMX Copenhagen will approve declarations made in the following terms:

> In pursuance of the rules and regulations of the NASDAQ OMX Copenhagen A/S, we hereby confirm that the prospectus contains all material facts relating to XX that are known to us and which, in our opinion, may affect the assessment of the company's and the group's assets and liabilities, financial position and results (as stated in the said consolidated accounts).

While NASDAQ OMX Copenhagen only requires that the above declarations **10.64** are included in prospectuses relating to initial public offerings, the Prospectus Regulation requires a similar declaration in any securities prospectus by the persons responsible for the prospectus (which will include the auditors) and therefore in practice there is little difference.

10.3 Passporting Requirements

10.3.1 The EU prospectus passport under Danish law

10.3.1.1 Introduction

As the Prospectus Directive only applies to offerings of securities that are listed or **10.65** admitted to trading on a regulated market within EU/EEA (i.e. in Danish terms, tier 1 offerings) with an aggregate value above EUR 2,500,000 the distinction between the three tiers (outlined under Section 10.1.1.1 above) is essential in the context of the Danish legislation regarding the EU prospectus passport.

To enable the cross border passporting of prospectuses within the EU/EEA the **10.66** EU prospectus passport requires all EU/EEA member states to mutually recognize tier 1 (or equivalent) offering prospectuses approved by the competent authority in any other EU/EEA member state.

The Danish regulations of relevance to the EU prospectus passport are primarily **10.67** encompassed in chapters 5, 8 and 9 of the Danish Executive Order No 885/2009. Furthermore, the Prospectus Regulation lays down certain provisions regarding the content of the prospectus to be passported which are directly applicable under Danish law.

10.3.1.2 *Tax description*

10.68   To be eligible for passporting into Denmark, the prospectus must meet certain minimum requirements, including a description of the rules on withholding tax in the home member state as well as that of the member state in which the securities are being offered (in this case Denmark).[14]

10.3.1.3 *Danish summary*

10.69   The prospectus may be published in English and/or Danish but if the prospectus is only published in English, the summary must be translated into Danish.[15]

10.70   The summary should be easy to read, brief and generally should consist of no more than 2,500 words. It must convey the essential characteristics of, and the risks associated with, the issuer and its securities, and any underwriters. Furthermore, the summary must clearly state the following:[16]

- the summary should be read as an introduction to the prospectus;
- any decision to invest in the securities should be based on consideration of the prospectus as a whole;
- where a claim relating to the information contained in the prospectus is brought before a court, the plaintiff investor may have to bear the costs of translating the prospectus before any legal proceedings are initiated; and
- civil liability attaches to those persons, whether natural or legal, who have drafted the summary including any translation thereof, and applied for its notification, in cases where the summary is misleading, inaccurate or inconsistent when read together with the other parts of the prospectus.

10.3.1.4 *The filing procedure and commencement of a public offer in Denmark*

10.71   When an issuer with a registered office in a country within either the EU or a country with which the Community has entered into an agreement for the financial area, wishes to passport a prospectus into and commence a public offering in Denmark, the filing procedure is as follows:

(i)   the prospectus, including any supplements, must be filed with the competent authority of the relevant EU/EEA member state in which the issuer has its registered office;

---

[14] Prospectus Regulation Article 6 and Schedule III, Item 4.11, which stipulates that the prospectus must contain (i) information on taxes on the income from the securities withheld at source, and (ii) indication as to whether the issuer assumes responsibility for the withholding of taxes at source.

[15] Danish Executive Order No 885/2009 section 29(5).

[16] Danish Executive Order No 885/2009 section 15(3).

(ii) the competent authority of the relevant EU/EEA member state must approve the prospectus and any supplements;[17]

(iii) the issuer must request the competent authority of the relevant EU/EEA member state to issue a certificate of approval, which must state that the prospectus, together with any supplements, complies with the Prospectus Directive;

(iv) the issuer must request the competent authority of the relevant EU/EEA member state to send the certificate of approval to the Danish FSA along with a copy of the prospectus and any supplements and a Danish summary of the prospectus. (Note that the prospectus must be valid at the time of filing);[18]

(v) the Danish FSA will then confirm its receipt of the certificate of approval, the copy of the prospectus and any supplements and the Danish summary to the competent authority of the relevant EU/EEA member state;

(vi) the Danish FSA will issue a prospectus certificate (free of charge), stating that the Danish FSA has received the necessary documents under the EU prospectus passport regime;[19] and

(vii) the public offering may commence as soon as the prospectus certificate is received from the Danish FSA and the prospectus and any supplements, are deemed to be published in Denmark.

10.3.1.5 *Use of a prospectus approved in non-EU countries for offerings in Denmark*

Even if a prospectus is drawn up in accordance with the legislation of a country **10.72** outside the EU, provided the relevant issuer has its registered office in such a country, the Danish FSA may still approve a prospectus for a tier 1 offering in Denmark if certain conditions are met.[20] The Danish FSA will approve such prospectus if the following conditions are satisfied:

(i) Denmark is the issuer's home member state;

(ii) the prospectus has been drawn up in accordance with international standards set by international securities commission organizations, including the IOSCO disclosure standards; and

(iii) the information requirements under the law of the country in question (a country outside the EU or of a country with which the EU has not entered into an agreement for the financial area), including requirements relating to financial information, are equivalent to Prospectus Directive requirements.

---

[17] Danish Executive Order No 885/2009 section 30.

[18] A prospectus is valid for a period of 12 months from the time of publication in the relevant EU/EEA member state, cf. Danish Executive Order no. 885/2009 sections 21–23.

[19] The Danish FSA publishes a list of prospectus certificates issued within the last 12 months on its website: http://www.finanstilsynet.dk.

[20] Danish Executive Order No 885/2009 section 32.

10.73 The prospectus approval procedure is otherwise the same as that applicable to the EU/EEA prospectuses.

10.4 Market Stabilization Transactions and Overallotment Facilities

10.74 Stabilization is defined in EC Regulation 2273/2003 ('the Stabilization Regulation') as 'any purchase or offer to purchase relevant securities, or any transaction in associated instruments equivalent thereto, by investment firms or credit institutions, which is undertaken in the context of a significant distribution of such relevant securities exclusively for supporting the market price of these relevant securities for a predetermined period of time, due to a selling pressure in such securities'.[21]

10.75 Stabilization is an optional activity, typically undertaken by investment banks who are involved in an offering, on behalf of the offeror.[22] The process of stabilization attempts to ensure an orderly distribution of newly issued securities into the market place.

10.76 Stabilization transactions are undertaken specifically to affect the market price of the relevant securities. The risk associated with stabilization is that it can have the effect of concealing the true market demand for a security by sustaining a certain price at a potentially artificial level (i.e. there is the potential for price manipulation). However, if a stabilization transaction is conducted according to specific rules it will fall within a *safe harbour*.

10.77 The Stabilization Regulation lays down the rules for public listed companies that wish to trade in their own shares or carry out stabilization activities. Under the Stabilization Regulation, the conditions that must be adhered to in the context of stabilization transactions in order to qualify for the safe harbour from the prohibition on price manipulation include time limitations and price rules, market transparency safeguards and investor information requirements.[23] In addition, the Stabilization Regulation requires the disclosure of ongoing stabilization arrangements to investors, as well as limited public disclosure at the end of the stabilization period. Further details on the proper conduct of stabilization and the applicable safe harbour are provided in Section 10.4.3 below.

---

[21] See Stabilization RegulationArticle 2(7).

[22] Stabilization transactions may also be carried out by the offeror.

[23] Cases where the standards of the Regulation have not been adhered to do not automatically constitute market abuse, see Article 2 of the preamble of the Regulation. In such cases, however, no defence of legitimate stabilization can be raised.

10.4.1 The rationale behind stabilization

The main purpose of stabilization is to counter the negative effect on the price **10.78**
of a new issue of securities caused by initial pressure from selling orders on the
secondary market. Largely, such pressure is generated by short-term investors
disposing of the securities shortly after subscription. This can cause the price of
the securities to fall to a level below the original offering price on the primary
market. Stabilization can alleviate such sales pressure, thereby maintaining an
orderly market in the securities.

An investment bank, on behalf of the issuer, will often manage a significant public **10.79**
offering of securities. It may underwrite the offering, thus guaranteeing the placement of the securities issued under the offering. A significant price drop as a result
of a selling pressure may lead to unsteadiness in the market to the detriment of
investors. Often, the underwriter will require that a right to carry out stabilization
transactions be attached to the offering so as to reduce the risk of a severe loss
on the part of the underwriter should the price of the securities fall due to heavy
selling pressure.

The benefits of stabilization can be considerable for the issuer, the investors and **10.80**
the underwriter. Stabilization encourages new companies, particularly small and
medium-sized operations, to access the capital market and established issuers are
more comfortable raising funds from the securities market through capital
increases when they know there will be some support for the price of their offer.
Stabilization may also lower the cost of funding for the issuer due to the lower risk
associated with the issue. Investors may feel more confident making an investment where there is an expectation that at least for a limited period of time, the
price of the new issue will be actively supported.[24]

The entity that performs stabilization does so by placing purchase orders for the **10.81**
relevant securities or by trading in the securities at the current trading price on the
secondary market. This should have the effect of alleviating any fall in the price
of the securities generated from the increased selling pressure, with the effect of
stabilizing the price of the securities in question.

Stabilization transactions may only be undertaken to support the current trading **10.82**
price of the securities and in any case may not be executed above the initial offering price. Where the securities trade below the offering price, the last independent
transaction (where there is one) is the indicative upper limit for stabilization transactions. Thus, stabilization transactions are not carried out at a price higher than
the latest sales price, and never at a price above the offering price. If done correctly,

---

[24] Investors should not base an investment decision on the assumption that the stabilization
manager will actually undertake stabilization because there is no guarantee that such party will
choose to engage in stabilization activities.

once freed from stabilization the securities should trade at the same level or slightly above the offering price.

10.4.2 Overallotment facilities and greenshoe options

10.83 Where an offering of securities is underwritten, the agreement between the offeror and the investment bank will often be supplemented by a provision concerning overallotment and a so-called 'greenshoe' option. As reflected in the preamble to the Stabilization Regulation, overallotment facilities and greenshoe options are closely related to stabilization.[25]

10.84 When a public offering of securities trades below its offering price, the offering is perceived to be unstable and undesirable. This can lead to hesitant buying and, indeed, further selling of the securities. An overallotment facility enables the investment firm that performs stabilization to buy back securities in the secondary market with the intention of achieving a balanced market, whereas the greenshoe option hedges the overallotment.[26]

10.85 In practice, in the context of an overallotment facility and a greenshoe option, the investment bank, having underwritten the issue, initially oversells the offering to its clients by an additional 15% of the offering size (i.e. the investment bank is selling short). When the offering is priced and the securities become eligible for public trading, the investment bank is able to support and stabilize the offering price by buying back the extra 15% of the pool of securities in the secondary market, at or below the offer price. The investment bank is able to do this without having to assume the market risk of holding a long position as it is simply 'covering' (closing out) its 15% oversell.[27]

10.86 On the other hand, if the offering is successful and demand for the securities is such that the price immediately goes up and stays above the offering price, the investment bank is left having oversold the offering by 15%. If the investment bank were to go into the market to buy back the 15% of the pool of securities, it would have to buy back these securities at a higher price than it sold them at, and would incur a loss on the transaction.

---

[25] See Stabilization Regulation section 19 of the preamble.

[26] It is common to reserve securities amounting up to 15% of the original offer for the overallotment facility.

[27] Should the underwriter make use of the overallotment facility, and the price of the security subsequently drops below the offering price it will be more profitable for the underwriter to cover the overallotments by carrying out stabilization transactions due to the fact that the underwriter thereby observes its stabilization obligations vis-à-vis the offeror and gains a profit corresponding to the difference between the offering price and the lower price as per the time of completion of the stabilization transactions.

This is where the greenshoe option comes into play: the offeror grants the investment bank the option to take from the offeror up to 15% additional securities of the original offering size *at the offering price*. If the investment bank were able to buy back from the market all of its oversold securities at or below the offering price in support of the deal, it would not need to exercise any part of the greenshoe option. But if the investment bank were only able to buy back some of the securities before the price of the securities went above the offering price it would exercise a partial greenshoe option for the rest of the securities. If it were not able to buy back any of the oversold 15% of securities at the offering price (because the price of the securities immediately went and stayed up), it would be able to completely cover its 15% short position by exercising the greenshoe option in full.[28]

10.87

Under Danish company law, an offering of shares with an overallotment facility must be resolved by the board of directors of the offeror pursuant to an authority granted by the general meeting.[29] This is achieved by passing two board resolutions in direct succession. The first resolution provides for increasing the share capital by an amount corresponding to the shares which are expected to be subscribed. The second resolution authorizes a placement in favour of the investment bank underwriting the offering, awarding the bank the right to subscribe to shares corresponding to the number which the investment bank is permitted to overallot. The subscription period during which the relevant investment bank may exercise the overallotment option expires 30 days after the expiry of the subscription period for the principal offering. The subscription price is the same in both instances.

10.88

10.4.3 Stabilization pursuant to the Securities Trading Act

As discussed above, stabilization transactions need to be conducted within the parameters of a safe harbour to avoid the risk of constituting price manipulation or insider trading. The general prohibition on price manipulation is laid out in the Securities Trading Act,[30] which also contains prohibitions on certain specific actions.[31] The Danish Securities Trading Act describes price manipulation as 'transactions or placement of buying or selling orders with the intent to provide incorrect or misleading information in regards to the offering of, the demand for or the price of securities'[32] and 'transactions or placement of buying or selling

10.89

---

[28] Alternatively or in addition to the overallotment facility, which is hedged by the greenshoe option, an overallotment can be undertaken without a hedging device, which results in a naked short option. Transactions to cover such a naked short may constitute stabilization transactions falling under the safe harbour.

[29] See Companies Act section 37.

[30] Act No 795/2009. See section 39(1).

[31] See Securities Trading Act section 38(1).

[32] Securities Trading Act section 38(1)(2).

orders suitable to maintain the price of one or more securities at an artificial level'.[33]

10.90 The Securities Trading Act also provides that stabilization transactions carried out in accordance with the conditions of the Stabilization Regulation do not contravene the prohibition on price manipulation.[34]

10.4.3.1 Stabilization in accordance with the Stabilization Regulation

10.91 The Stabilization Regulation prescribes a set of conditions that alleviate the risk of stabilization transactions being utilized to mislead the market as regards the actual demand for a particular security by maintaining a price for the security at an artificial level.

10.92 In order for a stabilization transaction to benefit from the rules exempting such transactions from the prohibition on price manipulation, it must be carried out in accordance with Articles 8, 9 and 10 of the Stabilization Regulation.

10.93 Firstly, stabilizing activities must be limited in time.[35] The time period in respect of shares and other equivalent securities, in the case of an initial public offer, starts on the date of commencement of trading of the relevant securities on the regulated market and must end no later than 30 days thereafter.[36] In the case of a secondary offer, in respect of shares and other equivalent securities, the time period of 30 days starts on the date of adequate public disclosure of the final price of the relevant securities and must end no later than 30 days after the date of the allotment.[37]

10.94 Secondly, a number of disclosure and reporting conditions must be complied with in order to inform investors that stabilization may be conducted in connection with the offering. The following information must be adequately publicly disclosed by the offeror, or entities undertaking the stabilization transaction on behalf of the offeror, before the opening of the offer period of the relevant securities:[38]

(i) the fact that stabilization may be undertaken, that there is no assurance that it will be undertaken and that it may be stopped at any time;

(ii) the fact that stabilization transactions are aimed at supporting the market price of the relevant securities;

(iii) the period during which stabilization may occur;

---

[33] Securities Trading Act section 38(1)(4).
[34] See Securities Trading Act section 39(4).
[35] See Stabilization Regulation Article 8(1).
[36] See Stabilization Regulation Article 8(2).
[37] See Stabilization Regulation Article 8(3).
[38] See Stabilization Regulation Article 9(1) (a)–(e).

(iv) the identity of the stabilization manager (unless this is not known at the time of publication in which case it must be publicly disclosed before any stabilization activity begins); and

(v) the existence and maximum size of any overallotment facility or greenshoe option, the exercise period for the greenshoe option and any conditions for the use of the overallotment facility or exercise of the greenshoe option.

Furthermore, the following information must be adequately disclosed to the **10.95** public by the offeror, or entities undertaking the stabilization activity on its behalf, within one week of the end of the stabilization period:[39]

(i) whether or not stabilization was undertaken;

(ii) the date on which stabilization started;

(iii) the date on which stabilization last occurred; and

(iv) the price range within which stabilization was carried out, for each of the dates on which stabilization transactions were carried out.

The details of all stabilization transactions must be disclosed to the Danish FSA **10.96** by the offeror (or by a party acting on its behalf).[40]

Where several investment banks or credit institutions undertake the stabilization **10.97** transactions on behalf of the offeror, one of those entities must act as the central point of inquiry for any request from the Danish Financial Supervisory Authority.[41]

Thirdly, in the case of an offer of shares or other securities equivalent to shares, **10.98** stabilization of the relevant security must not, under any circumstances, be executed above the offering price on the primary market.[42]

Besides the limitations that apply to stabilization transactions, the Stabilization **10.99** Regulation sets out a number of limitations that apply to the exercise of the stabilization manager's overallotment facility and greenshoe option (sometimes known as ancillary stabilization). Such ancillary stabilization must be undertaken in accordance with the disclosure and reporting conditions of Article 9 of the Stabilization Regulation. In addition, the following provisions must be complied with:[43]

(i) relevant securities may be overallotted only during the subscription period and at the offer price;

---

[39] See Stabilization Regulation Article 9(3).
[40] See Stabilization Regulation Article 9(2).
[41] See Stabilization Regulation Article 9(5).
[42] The Regulation does not hinder trading above the current trading price on the secondary market.
[43] See Stabilization Regulation Article 11.

(ii) a position resulting from the exercise of an overallotment facility by an investment firm or credit institution which is not covered by the greenshoe[44] option may not exceed 5% of the original offer;

(iii) the greenshoe option may be exercised by the beneficiaries of such an option only where relevant securities have been overallotted;

(iv) the greenshoe option may not amount to more than 15% of the original offer;

(v) the exercise period of the greenshoe option must be the same as the applicable stabilization period; and

(vi) the exercise of the greenshoe option must be disclosed to the public promptly, together with all appropriate details, including the date of exercise and the number and nature of relevant securities involved.

10.5 Takeover Bids and Defensive Measures

10.100 In a takeover bid, a company (the bidder) publicly asks shareholders in another company (the target company) to tender their shares on generally stipulated terms. Takeover bids per se pertain to target companies with many shareholders and, in practice, almost always involve publicly listed companies.

10.101 A company that is publicly listed and has many shareholders may still have a controlling shareholder. This is indeed the case for a great number of listed Danish companies, many of which are controlled by a family trust or the like. A takeover bid for such a company is usually preceded by negotiations between the bidder and the controlling shareholder to acquire the latter's shares. If the parties reach an agreement, a similar offer is then made to the other shareholders. If there is no controlling shareholder in the target company, the takeover bid is made directly to all shareholders.

10.102 The negotiations and discussions preceding a takeover are commonly carried out in concert with the target company's board of directors. Under Danish law the target company's board of directors is permitted to negotiate in respect of a takeover bid, provided that, in doing so, it safeguards the interests of the target company and its shareholders.

10.103 Indeed, the board of directors is obliged to present the shareholders with its opinion on a given takeover bid. If the target company's board of directors does not support a particular bid, it may resolve to treat the bid as hostile and try to defend the company against the bidder.

---

[44] This might also be described as a naked short position.

10.5.1 Duties of the board of directors in connection with public takeover bids

Under Danish law, the duties of the board of directors derive from general company law. Specific provisions in the Companies Act,[45] the Securities Trading Act[46] and the Accounting Act[47] lay out the rules governing the application of measures suitable to defend or frustrate a takeover bid.

10.104

The following discussion focuses on some of the issues likely to be considered by a target company's board of directors in a situation where a public takeover bid for the target company's shares is anticipated or has been made.

10.105

10.5.1.1 *Safeguarding relevant interests*

In the context of a public takeover bid, it is primarily the board of directors that acts on behalf of the target company. When determining its rights and obligations in connection with a public takeover bid, the target company's directors should consider whose interests they are bound to protect. As a general rule, the directors are permitted to exercise extensive discretionary powers, provided they pursue legal objectives in good faith.

10.106

In all circumstances, the board of directors must safeguard the shareholders' interests in their capacity as owners of the target company. In this respect, the shareholders are assumed primarily—or exclusively—to be interested in the bid that is most attractive from a financial point of view. It is less certain whether the directors are allowed (or indeed required) to safeguard other interests that may conflict with this interest. In the event of a takeover bid, the shareholders' interests will generally prevail over those of other parties.

10.107

Danish company law recognizes a public limited company as a separate legal entity that pursues its own interests and is distinct from its shareholders. In this context, it is significant that in some cases the Companies Act requires the board of directors to guarantee proper protection of the corporate interests of the company, which may be in competition with shareholder interests. For example, Section 112 of the Companies Act provides that the shareholders' general meeting cannot pass a resolution to distribute dividends in excess of the amount approved by the board of directors. The Companies Act, therefore, is deemed to allow the board of directors to look beyond the interests of the shareholders and consider those of the company in a wider sense.

10.108

---

[45] Act No 646/2006.
[46] Act No 795/2009.
[47] Act No 647/2006.

10.109   The directors may also be required to consider the interests of other relevant parties, such as the target company's employees. Accordingly, the Danish Executive Order on Takeover Bids[48] ('the Executive Order') requires the board of directors to outline the consequences of any takeover bid for employees in its statement to the shareholders. If one bidder intends to dismiss a large number of employees from the target company after the takeover, while another wants to continue operations, this is an element that may be included in the board of directors' assessment and recommendation to the shareholders.

10.110   In contrast, the board of directors must not take its own interests into account. Accordingly, it may not unfairly prejudice a bid solely because the bidder intended to replace the members of the board of directors and the executive management. Similarly, it will not be relevant to allow for the directors to consider general public interests in the context of a takeover bid (for instance, a public policy desire to maintain Danish ownership of an entity). Although such considerations will not be deemed illegal in all contexts, they are assumed to be of secondary—or no—importance.

10.111   In summary, the board of directors must balance shareholders' interests with other relevant interests, in particular, the wider interests of the company. If, when balancing such interests, the directors find themselves with a conflict of interest and are unable to find a resolution that safeguards both the interests of the company, the shareholders and other relevant parties, the solution may be for such directors to resign. So far, however, there appear to be no instances where this has occurred in Denmark in connection with a takeover bid.

10.5.1.2 Initial response to inquiries

10.112   As discussed above, Danish company law requires the target company's board of directors to safeguard the interests of the company, the shareholders and other relevant parties. Accordingly, a board of directors that receives serious inquiries concerning a possible takeover bid has a duty to assess whether such inquiries are in the company's and/or the shareholders' interests. For the purpose of this assessment, it is not only the company's situation at that point in time that must be considered, but also any realistic forecasts in the company's budgets and business plans, which might indicate whether the company will be able to offer the shareholders the same added value as that generated by the bid price.

10.113   If, based on an assessment of the inquiries received, the directors conclude that the potential offer is not in the shareholders' interests, they may communicate this to the potential bidder(s) without attracting any obligation to subsequently disclose information about the inquiry to the market, or indeed, the target company's

---

[48] Executive Order No 947/2008.

shareholders. However, depending on the firmness of the inquiry, the fact that it has been made may itself constitute inside information about the company, which could trigger an obligation to disclose the inquiries and, in addition, restrict the ability of the target company and others with knowledge of the inquiry to trade in the company's shares. An inquiry which is clearly and irrevocably rejected will generally not constitute inside information, but this is subject to an individual assessment in each case.

In such circumstances, the board of directors should consider whether, despite its opinion that the inquiry or bid is generally not attractive, it would neverthe-less be in the target company's/shareholders' interests to cooperate with the potential bidder. The board should have regard to the likelihood that the potential bidder may announce a bid for the company's shares and the possibility that the bid price may increase following a dialogue, which, through discussions with the management and the performance of a due diligence investigation, would provide the bidder with a greater understanding of and insight into the company. **10.114**

The board of directors might also consider whether it would be in the target company's/shareholders' interests to solicit competing bids through an auction process in order to clarify whether the potential bidder's inquiry is actually the best offer. The directors would not be under any Danish law duty to initiate such an auction process; however, the purpose of such an auction would be to ensure that the target company controls the process (as there is otherwise a greater risk of a subsequent alternative bid) and that bids are made on a properly informed and uniform basis. **10.115**

The fact that the board of directors has received one or more inquiries and has commenced negotiations with potential bidders might, itself, constitute inside information about the company, which under section 27(1) of the Securities Trading Act, must be made available to the public as soon as possible. The company may elect to postpone such public disclosure until it has made a final decision about the takeover bid under the special provision in section 27(6) of the Act, according to which an issuer may, at its own risk, delay public disclosure of inside information 'in order not to prejudice its legitimate interests, provided that such delayed disclosure is not likely to mislead the public, and the issuer guarantees that the information is kept confidential'. The possibility of delaying disclosure does not change the fact that the inquiry constitutes inside information if it is of a firm nature and has not been finally and unconditionally rejected. **10.116**

One reason the company may be interested in disclosing inquiries to the public is that such disclosure could attract further suitors, thereby creating the auction situation described above. Equally, there are examples of a board of directors of a potential target company having announced that it has received inquiries—which **10.117** have then been firmly rejected—in order to discourage other potential bidders from making bids.

10.5.1.3 *Considerations relating to takeover inquiries*

10.118 If a target company's directors expect a potential bidder to make a firm bid that they will recommend the shareholders to accept, further questions will arise.

10.119 A potential bidder will often seek to enter into an exclusivity agreement with the target company in order to ensure that its board of directors does not begin takeover negotiations with other potential bidders. There is no prohibition against such agreements, but particularly in cases where the board believes that there may be several potential bidders, it should seek to avoid exclusivity undertakings, or only accept such undertakings when (i) it is convinced that the bidder with whom the exclusivity agreement is made will make the most attractive bid; and (ii) the exclusivity agreement will in itself facilitate or improve the process and/or the terms of the bid.[49]

10.120 An exclusivity agreement should be drafted so as to permit the board of directors to consider and recommend any competing bid that may be made after public announcement of the initial takeover bid.

10.121 **10.5.1.3.1 Due diligence investigations** Potential bidders will often ask for permission to conduct a due diligence investigation of the target company. The decision to allow a due diligence investigation, including, in particular, the decision to give access to inside information, is outside the powers of the day-to-day management/executive board and must therefore be made by the board of directors. Specifically, the board of directors must decide whether giving access to make such investigation is in the target company's/shareholders' interests which it usually will be because it may well result in the final takeover bid being both higher in value, and subject to fewer conditions.

10.122 **10.5.1.3.2 The duties of disclosure** Section 27 of the Securities Trading Act concerns the disclosure of inside information by Danish-listed issuers. Under section 27(2) of the Act, inside information which is disclosed to a third party (such as a potential bidder) must also be made available to the public. This duty, however, is subject to the following qualifications:

(i) inside information may be disclosed if such disclosure takes place in the normal course of safeguarding legitimate interests[50]; and

---

[49] In foreign takeover transactions, a target company sometimes undertakes to pay a break-away fee if negotiations are terminated. Such payments are not illegal, but are unusual according to Danish standards and should therefore be carefully considered.

[50] See Securities Trading Act section 36.

(ii) the duty to make inside information available to the public at the time of disclosure to the third party does not apply if the receiving party is advised that it is in possession of inside information that may only be used subject to the restrictions provided by the Securities Trading Act, or if the receiving party is otherwise subject to a duty of confidentiality, for example under a secrecy agreement.[51]

In the context of a potential takeover, provided these requirements are met, the **10.123** target company may disclose inside information to a potential bidder without having to make the same information available to the public at the time of disclosure.

In order to ensure that the potential bidder maintains the confidentiality of any **10.124** inside information it receives during the course of its inquiries, the target company should, before granting permission for a due diligence investigation, obtain a letter of confidentiality from the bidder and a statement in which the bidder undertakes to refrain from dealing in the company's shares while in possession of inside information.

10.5.1.3.3 The insider rules The general rule prohibiting insider trading **10.125** under Danish law is set out under section 35(1) of the Securities Trading Act, which provides as follows:

> No sale or purchase of, or inducement to sell or purchase, any security may be made by a person possessing inside information which may affect the transaction.

However, under section 35(2)(i) of the Securities Trading Act, the provision in **10.126** subsection (1) does not apply to

> any purchase of securities which is necessary to complete a public takeover bid for the purpose of gaining control over a company …

Under this exception to the general rule, a bidder may launch a public takeover **10.127** bid without waiting for the target company to publicly announce the inside information the bidder has received during its inquiries into the target company. It should be noted, however, that it is somewhat uncertain whether this exception applies to merger negotiations.

The explanatory notes to section 35(2) explain that in connection with takeover **10.128** negotiations, it is:

> common practice that potential buyers in co-operation with their advisers conduct a detailed investigation (due diligence) of the target company before submitting a non-hostile takeover bid. In connection with such investigation, there is a risk that the potential buyer will gain access to inside information. Consequently, the

---

[51] See Securities Trading Act section 27(2).

potential buyer will be prohibited from trading in the target company's shares until any inside information obtained by the potential buyer has been made available to the public ... The insider trading prohibition, however, does not prevent a public takeover bid from being made in such a situation if the bidder may reasonably assume that the investors' interests are safeguarded otherwise than by public announcement of the inside information.

10.129   The explanatory notes add that shareholders' interests are protected by the rules that require, in certain circumstances, a bidder to make a mandatory bid and prepare an offer document.

10.130   The target company's board of directors may choose to make any inside information provided to the bidder available to the public in connection with the announcement of the bid (a so-called 'disclosure announcement'). This has been common practice in Denmark in circumstances where the target company's board of directors is in favour of a particular bid. Indeed, it may be in the board's own interest to issue such notice because it is otherwise left to the board to determine if the bid takes proper account of the inside information—that is, the information which is unknown to the market and the shareholders. Any failure to establish parity of information will, all other things being equal, increase the risk of the directors incurring liability. It should be stressed that the bidder is under no obligation to ensure that the bid takes into account any inside information—it is merely assumed that it will.[52]

10.131   When the company permits a bidder to conduct a due diligence investigation, it should agree with the bidder if a notice of disclosure is to be issued or not. In such circumstances, all other things being equal, the bidder has no interest in issuing such notice: the more information provided to the outside world, the higher the risk that competing bids will be made. The target company should nonetheless insist on issuing a disclosure announcement.

10.132   **10.5.1.3.4 Scope and contents of the due diligence investigation**   The management of the target company should review the information to be disclosed to any potential bidder in order to assess whether it could be characterized as inside information and to ensure that it has a direct impact on the specific transaction.

---

[52] An example of the board of directors' 'problem' if no notice of disclosure is issued is where the quoted market price is 100, but in the inside information obtained by the bidder the market price is determined to be 300. If the bidder therefore 'only' offers a price of 200 in the takeover bid, this will not constitute a breach of the prohibition against insider trading (Securities Trading Act section 35(1)). If, in this situation, the board of directors does not make the inside information available to the public (including the target company's shareholders) and chooses to recommend the shareholders to accept the bid or merely fails to draw proper attention to the circumstances affecting the price it is possible that the board will be held liable for failing to fulfil its obligation to protect the shareholders' interests as well as the general duty of disclosure in the Securities Trading Act section 27(1).

The bidder will be given access to selected documents and will usually also be **10.133** offered a management presentation, including an opportunity to ask detailed questions. If there is more than one bidder involved, the target company's board should ensure, as far as possible, that all bidders are given access to the same information.

For the purpose of the due diligence investigation, information that could be **10.134** characterized as inside information should be provided (if at all) only when the board considers it highly likely that a takeover bid will actually be made, and only to a limited number of potential bidders. When inside information is provided, it should be pointed out to the potential bidder that the information provided is inside information in order to allow the bidder to decide if it wishes to receive such information.

10.5.1.4 *Statement by the board of directors*

When a takeover bid for the shares of a listed company has been publicly **10.135** announced, the target company's board of directors must[53] provide a statement to the company's shareholders in relation to the bid. The statement must include: '... the board's reasoned opinion on the bid, including the board's views on the effects of implementation of the bid on all the company's interests, notably employment, and on the bidder's strategic plans for the target company and their likely repercussions for employment and the company's establishments as set out in the offer document ...'.

The preparation of the statement requires a detailed analysis of the bid and a **10.136** comparison with the target company's current state and potential. Where relevant, the statement should also consider any conditions stipulated in the bid. According to the legislative history of the Securities Trading Act, the statement must be 'impartial'. In practice the importance of the impartiality requirement is limited because the assessment is partly forward-looking; however, there is no doubt that, when comparing different bids, the board cannot take into account irrelevant preferences for one party over another.

If the directors disagree as to whether the shareholders should be recommended **10.137** to accept the bid, the dissenting opinions may be reflected in the statement by pointing out that the conclusion is backed by a majority of the directors. However, a number of statements published in recent years have included no conclusion at all or have included a recommendation, in either case without any indication of disagreement among the directors.

---

[53] Executive Order on Takeover Bids section 14.

10.138   When assessing the takeover bid, the board should ask the advising investment bank to draw up a fairness opinion. If such fairness opinion has been obtained, the board's statement will usually refer to its conclusion.

10.139   Under section 14(2) of the Executive Order, the statement of the board of directors must be announced to the public before expiry of the first half of the offer period. Under the Executive Order, the directors' statement also must be announced via NASDAQ OMX (the Danish stock exchange). Immediately after announcement, the statement must be posted on a website (typically the company's).[54] In addition, the company must also forward the statement to its registered shareholders, at the bidder's expense.[55] In practice, the statement is usually announced immediately after announcement of the bid. If the board believes it is likely that a competing bid will be made it should consider delaying the announcement of its statement until the competing bid has been made.

10.140   If the bidder changes the terms of the bid in accordance with the applicable rules, the board of directors of the listed company must prepare and publish a supplementary statement to the shareholders, specifying the changes made, within seven days of the announcement of the bidder's revised terms. Similarly, if a competing bid is made, the board of directors must also prepare and publish a statement in relation to such a bid.

10.141   If the directors believe the competing bid is superior to the initial bid, it may withdraw any recommendation already published in relation to the original bid, and make a new recommendation in relation to the competing bid instead. When making a new recommendation, the board of directors should make sure that any exclusivity restrictions that are accepted in relation to the original bid are not drafted so as to prevent the board from recommending a more attractive competing bid.

10.5.1.5 *Liability of the board of directors*

10.142   The target company's board of directors is accountable to its shareholders pursuant to section 140 of the Companies Act, under which the directors may be held liable for any wilful or negligent breach of the Companies Act or the company's articles of association. The board of directors also owes duties to any bidder and, similarly, could incur liability to such bidder. When assessing such liability, the test applied is whether or not the directors have acted reasonably and in good faith to protect legitimate interests of the target company and its shareholders.

---

[54] Executive Order on Takeover Bids section 14(4).
[55] Executive Order on Takeover Bids section 14(5).

There are no reported cases of shareholders in Denmark claiming compensation against members of a board of directors or executive board in connection with a response to a takeover bid, and it can be concluded that directors are afforded fairly extensive discretionary powers in their assessment as to which options best serve the interests of the company and its shareholders.

10.143

10.5.2 Defending or frustrating a takeover bid

Danish law on defensive measures in respect of takeovers is primarily found in sections 81(b) to 81(h) of the Companies Act,[56] which implement key provisions of the Takeover Directive.[57] The Companies Act does not define the nature of frustrating or defensive measures. In practice, such measures consist of any action suitable to frustrate a potential takeover, which is not carried out in the normal course of the target company's business or in conformity with its usual practices.

10.144

Measures utilized to defend a company against a takeover can be divided into two categories: (i) pre-bid measures, which are taken in advance of any bid and serve to prevent or complicate future takeover bids; and (ii) post-bid measures, which are taken to complicate or preclude the implementation of a takeover bid that has already been presented.

10.145

As set out in Section 10.1.3.5 above, companies listed on NASDAQ OMX Copenhagen are subject to the code of corporate governance Recommendations. In relation to takeovers, it is recommended that the board of directors does not implement actions that could frustrate a takeover without prior shareholders' authorization.[58]

10.146

Indeed, a target company's shareholders may pass a resolution requiring the board of directors to obtain prior shareholders' authorization before it may take any action[59] that could result in the frustration of a bid. [60] If such a resolution is passed, it must be communicated to the Danish Commerce and Companies Agency, as well as the Danish FSA.[61]

10.147

---

[56] These rules apply to companies that are publicly listed in an EU/EEA country, see Companies Act Article 81(b).

[57] Directive 2004/25/EC.

[58] See section I(4) of Recommendations for good corporate governance 2005, changed on 10 December 2008.

[59] Other than seeking alternative bids.

[60] See Companies Act section 81(c)(1). The general meeting may pass such a resolution by a majority of two-thirds of all votes cast and capital represented in the general meeting and in accordance with any further requirements provided for in the articles of association (see Companies Act section 81(c)(2)).

[61] See Companies Act section 81(c)(6).

10.148   In such circumstances, the target company's board of directors can convene a general meeting to obtain the requisite authorization by giving notice of at least two weeks, irrespective of whether the articles of association lay down a longer notice period.[62] The obligation of the board of the target company to ask the general meeting for authorization before carrying out any defensive measures does however require that the offeror[63] is subject to a similar obligation to obtain the authorization of its shareholders prior to implementing any defensive measures in relation to a takeover bid.[64]

10.5.2.1 *Defensive measures pursuant to the Companies Act*

10.149   The Companies Act permits companies to be constituted in such a manner that may hinder an attempted change of control. In the context of a takeover bid, certain provisions in a target company's articles of association may prevent a bidder from acquiring sufficient voting capital to enable a successful takeover.

The following measures, each of which is permitted by the Companies Act, are common examples of provisions that could operate to defend or frustrate a takeover bid:

- provisions in the articles of association that lay down limitations on ownership;[65]
- provisions in the articles of association that limit the number of votes each shareholder is allowed to cast at the general meeting, thereby preventing a single shareholder from gaining meaningful control of the company;[66]
- provisions in the articles of association that assign certain shares more votes than others by dividing the shares into share classes;[67] and
- shareholder resolutions that operate to increase the value of the target company, such as the issue of bonus shares[68] or a capital increase at market value, thereby making a takeover more costly.

---

[62] See Companies Act section 81(c)(4).

[63] Or an offeror being directly or indirectly owned by a company which has adopted an equivalent resolution.

[64] See Companies Act section 81(c)(5).

[65] See Companies Act section 79(2)(2).

[66] See Companies Act section 79(2)(4).

[67] Shares may be assigned more votes than others in the ratio of up to 10:1 —see Companies Act section 67(1).

[68] An issue of bonus shares does not always lead to a proportionate decrease in the value of each share.

10.5.2.2 *Defensive measures in contractual agreements*

10.150 A target company may enter into contractual agreements that have the effect of defending or frustrating a takeover bid, in particular, contractual obligations that are triggered in the event of a change of control. Typical examples include the following:

- the target company may enter into a finance agreement in which it undertakes to repay the entire debt on demand in the event of a change of control;
- the target company may enter into material commercial agreements that terminate (or are otherwise substantially altered or jeopardized) in the event of a change of control; and
- the target company may enter into agreements with its management and other employees to pay out significant financial rewards in the event of a takeover.[69]

10.151 For the bidder, such contractual provisions could decrease the value of the target company, hence such provisions commonly are referred to as 'poisoned pills'.

10.152 Contractual agreements among the target company's shareholders can also have the effect of defending or frustrating a takeover bid if, for example, such agreements impose restrictions on the transferability of the target company's shares.

10.5.2.3 *Shareholder measures to facilitate a takeover*

10.153 As discussed above in Section 10.5.2, a target company's shareholders can pass a resolution that requires the board of directors to obtain shareholders' consent before the implementation of any defensive actions in relation to a potential takeover bid.

10.154 The shareholders can go further to clear the way for a takeover bid by adopting a resolution, pursuant to section 81(d) of the Companies Act, which renders ineffective any restrictions on the transfer of shares and voting rights in the target company in the face of a takeover. Such resolution must receive the approval of two-thirds of all votes cast at the general meeting and two-thirds of capital represented on the general meeting and in accordance with any further requirements provided for in the articles of association.[70] If such a resolution is passed it must be communicated to the Danish Commerce and Companies Agency and the Danish Financial Supervisory Authority.[71]

---

[69] A so-called golden parachute.
[70] See Companies Act section 81(d)(2).
[71] See Companies Act section 81(d)(2).

10.155 The implication of such a resolution is that any restrictions on the transfer of shares provided for in the articles of association of the target company or in contractual agreements among the shareholders[72] will not apply vis-à-vis the bidder during the time allowed for acceptance of the bid.[73]

10.156 However, the ineffectiveness of special voting rights and restrictions thereon requires that the offeror has passed an equivalent resolution concerning ineffectiveness of such voting rights and restrictions.

10.5.2.4 Bidder's right to disapply defensive measures

10.157 Even in the absence of such shareholder resolutions, if, following a takeover bid, a bidder holds at least 75% of the capital in a company that has resolved to attach special rights or limitations to the company's shareholding in order to frustrate a takeover bid, such bidder (now the majority shareholder) is entitled to convene a general meeting following closure of the bid in order to amend the articles of association to remove such special rights or limitations and to remove or appoint board members.[74] In such circumstances, the bidder will not be limited by any provisions in the articles of association that give special rights or attach limitations to certain shares or shareholders, for example, provisions (i) concerning rights to appoint board members; (ii) limiting the number of votes each shareholder is allowed to cast at the general meeting; or (iii) assigning more votes to certain shares than others. Essentially a 'one share, one vote' principle would apply at such meeting.

10.158 The rationale behind this special right assigned to the bidder is that the bidder should be able to remove from the articles of association any special restrictions and rights concerning the transferability of the shares and the voting attached thereto that might hinder the bidder in obtaining maximum influence over the company.

10.159 The disapplication of special voting rights and restrictions thereon will take effect at the first general meeting after the expiry of the offer period. The bidder may convene the meeting with at least two weeks' notice, irrespective of whether the articles of association lay down a longer notice period.[75] If the bidder does not take

---

[72] For example, a right for the board to veto the transfer of shares or pre-emption rights contained in shareholders' agreements.

[73] See Companies Act section 81(e)(1). Restrictions on voting rights and the transfer of shares provided for in contractual agreements between the target company and the holders of its shares or between the target company's shareholders being entered into before 31 March 2004 shall continue to apply vis-à-vis the offeror regardless of whether a resolution is passed pursuant to Companies Act section 81(d).

[74] See Companies Act section 81(g).

[75] The ineffectiveness of special voting rights and restrictions thereon requires that the offeror has resolved to an equivalent resolution concerning ineffectiveness of such voting rights and restrictions.

the initiative to amend the articles of association to remove the special rights and restrictions on transferability and voting, such special rights and restrictions become fully effective.

Where special voting rights or restrictions on voting rights in the articles of **10.160** association or contractual agreements are rendered ineffective in the face of a takeover on the basis of a resolution by the general meeting, the bidder must provide equitable compensation for any loss suffered by the holders of those rights, subject to closure of the bid.[76] The offer document must contain information on the compensation offered by the bidder to the shareholders and the basis of calculation for the compensation in question.[77]

10.5.2.5 *Disclosure of frustrating measures in the annual report*

A publicly listed company is under an obligation to disclose in its annual report **10.161** information that could hinder a takeover. Accordingly, the following information should be included in the annual report:[78]

- the structure of the company's capital and details of ownership, including details of the number of shares and their face value;
- details on the number of shares in the company which are not admitted to trading on a regulated market in the EU/EEA;
- where appropriate, details on different classes of shares, including number of shares and their face value;
- details on shareholders that own more than 5% of the votes or the capital of the company;
- information known to the company regarding the rights and obligations attached to each class of shares, restrictions on the transfer of the shares and voting rights;
- rules governing the appointment and replacement of board members and the amendment of the articles of association;
- the powers of board members, and in particular the power to issue or buy back shares; and
- material agreements to which the company is a party and which take effect, alter or terminate upon a change of control of the company following a takeover bid, and the effects thereof, except where their nature is such that their disclosure would be seriously detrimental to the company (this exception does not apply where the company is specifically obliged to disclose such information on the basis of other legal requirements).

---

[76] See Companies Act section 81(h)(1).
[77] See Companies Act section 81(h)(2).
[78] See Accounting Act section 107a.

10.6 Squeeze-outs

10.6.1 Categories of share redemption

10.162 The Danish Companies Act[79] includes provisions on the redemption of shares. The procedure of redemption is covered entirely in sections 20(a) to 20(e).

10.163 The Danish Companies Act provides for four situations in which shares may be redeemed:

(i) the target company's articles of association may be drafted to include a provision stating that the company's shares are subject to redemption. In such a case, the articles of association should state the conditions for redemption and name the person or persons entitled to demand such redemption;

(ii) majority shareholders have a right, governed by sections 20(b) and 20(c) of the Danish Companies Act, to redeem minority shareholders;

(iii) minority shareholders have a right, governed by section 20(d) of the Danish Companies Act, to demand that a majority shareholder redeems its shareholding; and

(iv) a shareholder who, by means of a takeover bid, has acquired a majority shareholding in a company with shares admitted to trading on a regulated market or an alternative market place has a right to demand redemption of shares from the other shareholders, as set out in section 20(e) of the Danish Companies Act.

10.6.1.1 *Redemption provision in the articles of association*

10.164 A company's articles of association may include provisions that govern the conditions on which a shareholder is required to allow redemption of its shareholding in the company. Any such provision must state the conditions for redemption, the name of the person or persons entitled to demand such redemption, and the time limit within which such redemption must be exercised.[80] If the relevant provisions purport to result in a manifestly unreasonable price or contain otherwise manifestly unreasonable terms, they may be overruled in full or in part by an order of the court.[81] If the company's original articles of association do not contain a redemption provision, a shareholders' resolution will be required to make the relevant amendment. Any such resolution (i.e. one which creates a provision in the articles requiring shareholders to allow their shares to be redeemed in

---

[79] Consolidated Act No 649 of 15 June 2006 as amended.
[80] Danish Companies Act sections 20(a) and 19.
[81] Danish Companies Act section 19(1).

situations where the company is not dissolved) is only valid if approved by at least nine-tenths of the votes cast and of the voting share capital represented at the general meeting.[82]

10.6.1.2 Majority shareholders' right of redemption

If a shareholder holds more than nine-tenths of the shares and votes in a company, such majority shareholder and the company's board of directors may, in a joint decision,[83] require that the company's minority shareholders sell their shares to such majority shareholder. When calculating the share ownership and the proportion of voting rights, only shares held directly by the majority shareholder are included. Shares held by the company itself (treasury shares or own shares) are excluded from the calculation.

10.165

If the board of directors refuses to support the squeeze-out of the minority shareholders in this manner, the majority shareholder may call for an extraordinary general meeting in order to replace the board of directors with people who are willing to support the squeeze-out. A voting ceiling in the articles of association may also hinder such a majority shareholder from squeezing out the minority in this fashion.

10.166

Once the majority shareholder has obtained the board's approval and the requisite joint decision has been made, the company will send a notice to the minority shareholders inviting them to transfer their shares to the majority shareholder within a period of not less than four weeks. The notice, which should be made in the same manner as general meetings are called (i.e. by letter or announcement in newspapers), must state (i) the terms of the redemption; (ii) the basis on which the offered price has been determined (it is not required to state the redemption price); (iii) that in the event that the price cannot be agreed upon between the majority shareholder and the minority shareholders, it will be decided by court-appointed experts; and (iv) that unless the court finds special reasons warranting the minority shareholders to reimburse the majority shareholder's expenses in full or in part, the costs of valuation shall be for the account of the majority shareholder.

10.167

Any minority shareholder may object to the offered price at any time in the process, provided the objecting shareholder has not previously accepted the offered price. If the valuation is made by court-appointed experts and results in a redemption price in excess of the price offered by the majority shareholder, the higher price shall apply to all shareholders holding the same class of shares. In this context

10.168

---

[82] Danish Companies Act section 79(2)(3).
[83] A bill published in March 2009 proposed the amendment of this provision to remove the requirement for the board of directors to consent to the redemption.

it is irrelevant who has requested the valuation and who might already have accepted the offered price.

10.169   If not all minority shareholders have transferred their shares to the redeeming majority shareholder before the expiry of the four-week period as requested in the notice, an advertisement should be placed in the Danish Official Gazette, inviting the remaining minority shareholders to transfer their shares to the majority share-holder within a period of not less than three months. The advertisement should be inserted in the first issue of the Official Gazette in the subsequent quarter following the termination of the four weeks' notice and should include the same information as the first notice. In addition, such advertisement should state (i) the date of an expert valuation, if any, or the date on which the court is scheduled to make a decision concerning the redemption price; and (ii) that following the expiry of the period of notice (at least three months), the minority share-holders will lose their right to demand an expert valuation and their shares will be registered in the name of the majority shareholder in the company's register of shareholders.

10.170   With respect to any minority shareholder shares not transferred to the redeeming majority shareholder on expiry of the period of notice as stipulated in the adver-tisement in the Official Gazette, the redeeming majority shareholder must uncon-ditionally and in favour of the relevant remaining minority shareholder(s) deposit the redemption sum equivalent to the number of shares that have not been trans-ferred. At the same time of such deposit, all share certificates representing the shares of the minority shareholders acquired by way of deposit are cancelled. The board of directors of the company shall ensure that new share certificates are pro-vided with an endorsement stating that such certificates have been issued in place of the share certificates that have been cancelled due to the process of redemption. At this point the majority shareholder will hold all shares in the company, other than any held in treasury by the company itself.

10.6.1.3 *Compulsory acquisition requested by a minority shareholder*

10.171   At any point in time when a majority shareholder has acquired more than nine-tenths of the shares in a company and a corresponding proportion of the voting rights (calculated as set out in Section 10.6.1.2 above), any minority shareholder in the company may require the majority shareholder to acquire the shares of that specific minority shareholder.[84] Such redemption request must relate to the minority shareholder's entire shareholding in the company. The rules concerning determination of the redemption price in connection with a redemption required

---

[84] Danish Companies Act section 20(d).

by the majority shareholder applies equally on a redemption required by a minority shareholder.

10.6.1.4 *Majority shareholders' redemption right after a takeover bid*

Following a successful takeover of a listed company, provided the bidder holds more than nine-tenths of the shares and a corresponding proportion of the voting rights (calculated as set out in Section 10.6.1.2 above), such new majority shareholder may demand redemption of shares from minority shareholders as set out in section 20(e) of the Danish Companies Act.   **10.172**

The right to demand redemption under section 20(e) of the Danish Companies Act is similar to the right described in section 20(b),[85] save that (i) the right to demand redemption under section 20(e) is enjoyed by the majority shareholder rather than the minority shareholder; (ii) section 20(e) sets out specific deadlines for the redemption of shares; and (iii) section 20(e) enables a majority shareholder to demand redemption without the approval or participation of the company's board of directors.   **10.173**

A majority shareholder wishing to demand redemption of minority shareholders' shares following a takeover must make the request to do so no later than three months after expiry of the relevant takeover bid. As in the case of redemption under section 20(b), a notice must be delivered to the minority shareholders inviting them to transfer their shares to the majority shareholder within a period of four weeks.   **10.174**

The rules regarding determination of the price for shares as set out in the Danish Securities Trading Act apply equally to redemption requested by a majority shareholder as well as redemption requested by minority shareholders, unless, in the context of section 20(e), a minority shareholder objects to the offered price, in which case the price will be determined by a valuation expert.[86] In such circumstances, the minority shareholders are not required to agree on the price or on whether or not to include a valuation expert. This means that a number of minority shareholders may obtain a price for their shares as determined in accordance with the Danish Securities Trading Act, while other minority shareholders may obtain a price for their shares determined by a valuation expert. In such a situation, a rule of equality will not apply for the minority shareholders.   **10.175**

Section 20(e) states that redemption of shares can be settled as stated in the original offer made by the then offeror (by this point the majority shareholder) or by a cash settlement. While the section does not state specifically how settlement   **10.176**

---

[85] Indeed, pursuant to a March 2009 bill, sections 20(b) and 20(e) are to be combined in one section.

[86] Danish Companies Act section 20(b).

should take place, it has been interpreted as containing a right for minority share-holders to be settled in cash.

10.6.2 Mergers and other possible means of a squeeze-out

10.6.2.1 Merger

10.177 Under Danish law, a merger must be approved by the shareholders at a general meeting by a majority of at least two-thirds of votes cast as well as two-thirds of the voting share capital represented at the general meeting. Such shareholder approval is crucial because a merger entails that shareholders of the non-surviving company will be required to give up their shares, which will be annulled as part of the merger. Such shareholders are entitled to receive a settlement for giving up their shares, either as shares of the continuing company, a cash settlement, a combination thereof or by way of other values.

10.178 The board of directors of the company proposes the type of settlement that the shareholders shall receive for their shares and the shareholders must then at a general meeting of the company decide whether or not to approve the merger, including the means of the settlement.

10.179 If a decision is made to make a cash settlement to shareholders of a company to be dissolved following a merger and the requisite majority of shareholders approve the merger in question, effectively this enables the redemption of the minority shareholders' shares without regard for the rules of redemption set out in section 20(b) of the Danish Companies Act. Accordingly, the minority shareholders could represent more than 10% of the company's share capital and yet would be unable to prevent the redemption of their shares.

10.180 The sole protection available to the minority shareholders in such a situation is provided by section 80 of the Danish Companies Act, which states that the general meeting must not make any decisions that provide certain shareholders with an advantage at the expense of other shareholders or the company.

10.6.2.2 Reduction of share capital to meet a deficit

10.181 A company that has lost funds might discover that its equity capital is lower than its share capital. In such a situation, the board of directors of the company can choose to propose to the shareholders that the share capital is reduced to meet the deficit, provided that the actual deficit at least equals the proposed reduction of the share capital.

10.182 If the deficit is substantial enough to equal the entire share capital of the company, the board of directors can propose to reduce the share capital to DKK 0. When reducing the share capital to DKK 0, all shares in the company are annulled and the shareholders (both major and minority shareholders) will have their shares redeemed.

A reduction of a share capital to DKK 0 must be approved by the shareholders at a general meeting by a majority of at least two-thirds of votes cast, as well as two-thirds of the voting share capital represented at the general meeting.   **10.183**

Following a reduction of share capital, a decision can be made to immediately increase the share capital by the issuance of new shares.   **10.184**

11

FINLAND

11.1 Jurisdiction Overview

11.1.1 Regulatory framework

11.01 The principal statute regulating the Finnish securities market is the Finnish Securities Market Act (495/1989, as amended) (the 'Finnish Securities Market Act'), which regulates both the primary and secondary markets and contains, *inter alia*, provisions concerning offerings of securities, listing and public trading of securities, disclosure obligations of listed companies and their shareholders, take-over bids and insider obligations. The Finnish Securities Market Act delegates power to the Finnish Ministry of Finance to issue decrees to supplement the provisions in the Finnish Securities Market Act, as discussed in more detail below. In addition, the Finnish Penal Code (38/1889, as amended) provides for the imposition of criminal liability in the event of a breach of disclosure requirements, misuse of privileged or insider information or market manipulation.

11.1.2 Finnish Financial Supervisory Authority

11.02 The Finnish Financial Supervisory Authority (the 'FFSA') is the competent authority responsible for the supervision of the Finnish financial and insurance industries. The FFSA in its current form was established on 1 January 2009, through the merger of the Finnish Financial Supervision Authority and the Finnish Insurance Supervisory Authority. The FFSA supervises a range of entities, including banks, insurance and pension companies, investment firms, fund management companies, as well as the NASDAQ OMX Helsinki Oy (the 'Helsinki Stock Exchange'). In administrative terms, the FFSA operates in conjunction with the Bank of Finland, but operates independently in its supervisory role. The objectives and duties of the FFSA are set out in the Finnish Act on the Financial Supervisory Authority (878/2008, as amended).

Pursuant to the Finnish Act on Financial Supervisory Authority and the Finnish **11.03** Securities Market Act, the FFSA is the competent regulatory and supervisory authority for Finland's securities markets. In addition to its supervisory powers, the FFSA issues regulations and guidelines concerning the application of the Finnish Securities Market Act in order to promote predictability, transparency and consistency of application of the Finnish Securities Market Act. The regulations and guidelines are compiled into the FFSA standards, which include both legally binding regulations and non-binding guidelines that are followed by market participants as good securities market practice.

The FFSA may impose administrative sanctions on the entities it supervises or **11.04** other market participants that breach or fail to comply with the provisions of the Finnish Securities Market Act or the FFSA regulations. Such administrative sanctions include fines, public reprimand, public warning, penalty payment (which is imposed by the Market Court upon the FFSA's proposal), prohibition from holding a managerial position and revocation of authorization and suspension of operations. The FFSA may also request a police investigation.

11.1.3 Helsinki Stock Exchange

The requirements for the listing of securities in Finland are set out in the Finnish **11.05** Securities Market Act, the relevant decrees issued by the Finnish Ministry of Finance and the Rules of the Helsinki Stock Exchange.

The markets for public trading of securities in Finland include: (i) the official list **11.06** of the Helsinki Stock Exchange; (ii) the prelist of the Helsinki Stock Exchange; and (iii) the alternative market place NASDAQ OMX First North. The Helsinki Stock Exchange is a subsidiary of the NASDAQ OMX GROUP, Inc.

The official list of the Helsinki Stock Exchange is part of the NASDAQ OMX **11.07** Nordic List ('Nordic List'). Companies listed on the official list are presented on the Nordic List by their market capitalization and industry sector irrespective of the exchange on which they are listed. In addition to the official list of the Helsinki Stock Exchange, the NASDAQ OMX Nordic List comprises exchanges, which are operated and maintained by NASDAQ OMX in Stockholm, Copenhagen, and Reykjavik. Each stock exchange under the Nordic List has its own official list and country-specific listing requirements, although such requirements are largely harmonized.

11.08   The Helsinki Stock Exchange's prelist is a temporary list for shares of an issuer that, as a general rule, has announced its intention to apply for listing of its shares on the official list at a later point. Shares can also be listed on the prelist if they are subject to significant investor interest or if they have a material connection with publicly traded securities. Furthermore, the prelist can be used if there is a significant need to determine the value of the shares in the public markets. The listing rules of the Helsinki Stock Exchange also apply to companies listed on the prelist. Generally, the listing of shares on the prelist is not permitted to continue for longer than one year, but the Helsinki Stock Exchange may extend the listing beyond the one-year period if the requirements for listing on the prelist continue to be fulfilled.

11.09   The NASDAQ OMX First North ('First North') is a Nordic alternative market place for trading in shares. First North does not have the legal status of a regulated market and it is not subject to the EU requirements that apply to regulated markets. First North Finland is operated by the NASDAQ OMX Stockholm AB. Companies listed on First North are subject to the rules of First North and not the legal requirements for admission to trading on a regulated market.

11.1.4 Finnish book-entry securities system

11.1.4.1 Overview

11.10   In a book-entry securities system, physical share certificates are replaced with book-entry securities that are registered to book-entry accounts.

11.11   Companies listed on the Helsinki Stock Exchange are required to use the Finnish book-entry securities system. The Finnish book-entry securities system is centralized at Euroclear Finland Ltd ('Euroclear'), which provides national clearing and settlement, as well as registration services for securities. Euroclear maintains a centralized book-entry securities system for both debt and equity securities.

11.12   Euroclear maintains registers of shareholders of listed companies and book-entry accounts for shareholders that do not wish to use the services of a commercial account operator. The expenses incurred by Euroclear in connection with maintaining the centralized book-entry securities system are borne by the issuers participating in the system and the account operators. The account operators (comprising credit institutions, investment services companies and other institutions licensed by Euroclear to act as account operators) are entitled to make entries in the book-entry register and administer the book-entry accounts.

Each book-entry account is required to contain specified information with respect to the account holder or the custodian administering the assets of a nominee account. Such information includes the type and number of book-entry securities registered and the rights and restrictions pertaining to the account and to the book-entry securities registered in the account. A nominee account is identified as such on the entry. Euroclear and all account operators are bound by strict confidentiality requirements, although certain information, such as the name, nationality and address of each account holder, contained in the register is public, except in the case of nominee registration. The FFSA is entitled to receive certain information on nominee registrations upon request.

11.13

11.1.4.2 *Custody of the shares and nominee registration*

A non-Finnish shareholder may appoint an account operator (or certain non-Finnish organizations approved by Euroclear) to act as a custodial nominee account holder on its behalf. A nominee shareholder is entitled to receive dividends and to exercise all share subscription rights and other financial and administrative rights conferred by the shares held in the nominee's name. A beneficial owner wishing to attend and vote at a general meeting of shareholders must request to be registered temporarily in the shareholders' register by a date specified in the notice to the relevant general meeting of shareholders. If requested, a custodial nominee account holder is required to disclose to the FFSA and the relevant company (whose shares such account holder owns) the name of the beneficial owner of any shares registered in the name of such nominee (when the beneficial owner is known) and the number of shares owned by such beneficial owner(s). If the name of a beneficial owner is not known, the custodial nominee account holder is required to disclose to the FFSA the name of the representative acting on behalf of such beneficial owner and the number of shares held, and to submit a written declaration to the effect that the beneficial owner of the shares is not a Finnish individual or a legal entity.

11.14

Finnish depositaries for both Euroclear Bank, SA/NV, as operator of Euroclear, and Clearstream have nominee accounts within the Finnish book-entry securities system, and accordingly, non-Finnish shareholders may hold their shares through their accounts with Euroclear or Clearstream.

11.15

11.1.5 Self-regulation

The Finnish Securities Market Association is a securities organization established in 2006 by the Confederation of Finnish Industries, the Helsinki Stock Exchange and the Central Chamber of Commerce of Finland. The Finnish Securities Market Association publishes and administers the Finnish Corporate Governance Code, which was published on 20 October 2008, and replaced the Corporate Governance

11.16

Recommendation for listed companies of 2003. The new Corporate Governance Code became effective on 1 January 2009, although certain recommendations will only come into force following a transitional period. The Corporate Governance Code is based on the 'comply or explain' principle.

11.17 The Panel on Takeovers and Mergers of the Central Chamber of Commerce of Finland (the 'Finnish Takeover Panel') has, pursuant to chapter 6, section 17 of the Finnish Securities Market Act, issued a number of recommendations regarding the procedures with which bidders and target companies should comply in connection with takeover bids (the 'Finnish Takeover Code'). The Finnish Takeover Code was issued on 15 December 2006, and is administered by the Finnish Securities Market Association.

11.2 Listing Securities in Practice

11.2.1 Overview

11.18 The preparations for an IPO and listing of an issuer's shares on the Helsinki Stock Exchange typically take between six to eight months and in some cases even longer, particularly, if the issuer is adopting the IFRS accounting standards in connection with the listing process.

11.19 When an issuer is considering listing its shares on the Helsinki Stock Exchange, the issuer and its advisers typically contact and meet with the Helsinki Stock Exchange, the FFSA and Euroclear at a relatively early stage to inform them of the planned project timetable and to bring to their attention any specific questions or issues that have been identified in the preliminary analysis prepared by the issuer and its advisers. In recent years, the importance of preliminary meetings and information exchange with the FFSA has increased after the FFSA started monitoring and supervising financial statements of Finnish public companies prepared in accordance with IFRS. The following description of the Finnish listing process below focuses on the listing of shares on the official list of the Helsinki Stock Exchange.

11.2.2 Helsinki Stock Exchange listing process

11.2.2.1 Listing requirements

11.20 The general listing eligibility criteria for the NASDAQ OMX Nordic List, i.e. the listing requirements for NASDAQ OMX Helsinki, NASDAQ OMX Stockholm, NASDAQ OMX Copenhagen and NASDAQ OMX Iceland, have largely been harmonized. The listing requirements can be divided into general eligibility requirements and requirements concerning the management and corporate governance of the issuer.

Section 2.1.3 of the Helsinki Stock Exchange Rules sets out the requirements for **11.21**
the listing of shares on the official list of the Helsinki Stock Exchange.

The Helsinki Stock Exchange has published explanatory notes on the interpreta- **11.22**
tion and application of the listing requirements. The guidance is not binding, but
rather offers examples of the interpretations the Helsinki Stock Exchange has
adopted.

The general eligibility requirements of the Helsinki Stock Exchange are as **11.23**
follows:

- *Incorporation*: the issuer must be duly incorporated or otherwise validly
  established according to the relevant laws of its place of incorporation or
  establishment.
- *Validity*: the shares of the issuer must comply with the laws of the issuer's
  jurisdiction of incorporation as well as potential registration, consent or other
  similar requirements set out in the laws and regulations applicable to the
  issuer.
- *Transferability*: the shares must be freely transferable.

  The free transferability of the shares is a general precondition for the public
  trading and listing of shares. Any limitations on the transferability of the shares
  included in the issuer's articles of association, or other similar arrangements
  may disqualify an issuer from listing on the Helsinki Stock Exchange.
- *Entire class to be listed*: the listing application must cover all issued shares of the
  class to be listed.

  The listing application must cover all shares of the same class that have been
  issued preceding the first day of listing in connection with an IPO. Subsequent
  issues of new shares are listed in accordance with the practices applied by the
  Helsinki Stock Exchange and the requirements set out in the Finnish Securities
  Market Act.
- *Annual financial statements and operating history*: the issuer and its consolidated
  group of companies must have prepared and made public annual financial
  statements for at least three financial years in accordance with accounting principles applicable to the issuer and its consolidated group. Furthermore, the
  issuer and its consolidated group must have a sufficient operating history in its
  lines of business.

  An issuer that has conducted its current business for at least three years and
  can present financial statements for this period is usually deemed to fulfil the
  operating history requirement, although an issuer may fail to meet such requirement if its business operations have changed materially during such period. In
  the event that an issuer has acquired or divested subsidiaries or businesses
  during such period, such transactions must be reflected in its financial statements. Pro-forma financial information or other financial information

presented for comparative purposes to reflect changes since the publication of the financial statements, should be presented in the prospectus in accordance with applicable regulations, typically for one full financial year and any subsequent interim period. The Helsinki Stock Exchange may require issuers to provide additional comparative information to meet the operating history requirement.

The Helsinki Stock Exchange may grant an exemption from the requirement to provide financial statements for three financial years, but only in cases where sufficient information is available to enable the Helsinki Stock Exchange and investors to reach an informed judgment of the issuer and its shares as an investment. When evaluating companies with less than three years of operating history, the Helsinki Stock Exchange will pay more attention to the information presented about the issuer's business and current operations.

- *Profitability and working capital*: the issuer must demonstrate that is has sufficient earnings capacity on a business group level. An issuer that does not have such earnings capacity may, as an alternative, prove that it has sufficient working capital available for its planned business for a period of at least 12 months after the first day of listing.

The requirement of sufficient earnings capacity is usually met if the issuer can show that it operates a profitable business. The issuer's financial statements must show that it has generated reasonable profits relative to the industry in general, or that it has the capacity to generate such profits. The general rule applied by the Helsinki Stock Exchange is that the issuer must have reported a profit for the most recent financial year. More stringent requirements regarding the quality and scope of the non-financial information set out in the prospectus and the listing application are imposed on an issuer that lacks the required financial history. At a minimum, such an issuer should disclose when it expects to become profitable and how it plans to finance its operations in the meantime.

As for working capital, various means may be used to demonstrate sufficiency of an issuer's working capital to the Helsinki Stock Exchange. For example, cash-flow estimates, planned financing measures, descriptions of planned business actions and investments or an analysis assessment of the issuer's future prospects may be used.

- *Liquidity*: conditions for sufficient demand and supply for the shares to be listed are needed to facilitate reliable price formation. A sufficient number of shares must be held by the public and the issuer is required to have a sufficient number of shareholders. In general, the minimum free float requirement of the Helsinki Stock Exchange is 25% of the issuer's total number of shares outstanding. The requirement for sufficient number of shareholders is generally considered to be fulfilled when the issuer has as least 500 shareholders, each holding shares with an aggregate value of at least EUR 1,000.

- *Market value of shares*: the expected aggregate market value of the shares must be at least EUR 1 million.
- *Overall suitability*: even where all other listing requirements are fulfilled, the Helsinki Stock Exchange may refuse an application for listing if it believes such listing would be detrimental to the securities market or to the interests of investors.

Section 2.1.4 of the Helsinki Stock Exchange Rules sets out management and corporate governance requirements for the issuer. The requirements are as follows: **11.24**

- *Management and board of directors*: the composition of the issuer's board of directors and the senior management must collectively possess sufficient competence and experience required to govern a listed company and ensure that it complies with the obligations.

  Accordingly, the board of directors of an issuer, when assessed as a whole, must be sufficiently qualified. The issuer's management and directors must have a general understanding of the legal requirements and obligations relating to a listed company, and should also be familiar with the issuer and its business. The Helsinki Stock Exchange typically considers the management and board members of an issuer to have sufficient familiarity with the issuer and its business if they have been active in their current positions in the issuer for at least three months and if they have participated in the preparation of at least the most recent financial statements or interim report. It is, therefore, no longer possible to change the entire board of directors of the issuer when the listing becomes effective, an approach that has been used in the past in connection with, for example, spin-off transactions in which a listed company has spun off and listed the shares of one of its subsidiaries which had its own internal board of directors until the listing became effective.

- *Ability to provide information to the market*: the issuer must establish and maintain adequate procedures, systems and controls to enable it to comply with ongoing and periodic disclosure obligations. This should be accomplished well in advance of the listing on the Helsinki Stock Exchange.

  Sufficient organization and routines should be in place prior to the listing and the issuer should have prepared at least one interim report for publication in accordance with the rules of the Helsinki Stock Exchange to demonstrate the adequacy of its procedures, systems and controls. It is recommended that the requisite organization has been in operation for at least two quarters and been involved in the preparation of at least two interim reports or one set of annual financial statements and one interim report prior to the listing. In order to ensure that issuers provide the market with all required information, the Helsinki Stock Exchange encourages issuers to adopt an information policy. Such information policy should be prepared in such a manner that compliance with it is not dependant on any single person and it should also be tailored to fit the circumstances pertaining to the specific issuer.

• *Corporate governance*: the issuer must confirm that it complies with the corporate governance code of its jurisdiction of incorporation. If the issuer is not subject to the corporate governance code of its jurisdiction of incorporation, it must apply the corporate governance code that is applied at the Helsinki Stock Exchange.

Companies domiciled in Finland must comply with the Finnish Corporate Governance Code, which is discussed below.

• *Exemptions from the listing requirements*: the Helsinki Stock Exchange may grant an exemption from a particular listing requirement upon the application of the issuer. However, an exemption will not be granted from the requirement of free transferability of the shares or the requirements concerning the competence of the issuer's management and board of directors. Furthermore, the Helsinki Stock Exchange may only grant an exemption from the requirements regarding the free float and the annual financial statements and operating history if the FFSA has granted the Helsinki Stock Exchange a corresponding permission to grant such exemptions.

11.2.2.2 Listing application

11.25 The process for listing securities on the Helsinki Stock Exchange involves the submission of a listing application by the issuer to the Helsinki Stock Exchange. The requirements for the contents of the listing application are set out in section 2.1.2.2 of the Helsinki Stock Exchange Rules.

11.26 When an issuer files its listing application with the Helsinki Stock Exchange, it must disclose such filing to the market without undue delay, as required by the Finnish Securities Market Act and the Helsinki Stock Exchange Rules. Once an issuer has applied for listing on the Helsinki Stock Exchange, it is treated as a listed company and it must comply with the Helsinki Stock Exchange Rules and the ongoing disclosure obligations and the market abuse provisions set out in the Finnish Securities Market Act, unless it announces the withdrawal of its listing application.[1]

11.27 Pursuant to section 2.1.2.2 of the Helsinki Stock Exchange Rules, the listing application must contain the following information:

• *Outlook statement by the board of directors of the issuer*: the issuer's board of directors must provide a statement on the expected performance of the issuer during the current and immediately following financial year. This requirement

---

[1] Helsinki Stock Exchange Rules section 1.1.11 and Finnish Securities Market Act chapter 2, section 7b and chapter 5, section 14.

is more extensive than the obligation to make a statement on the issuer's current outlook under the ongoing and periodic disclosure obligations. [2] The outlook statement is submitted to the Helsinki Stock Exchange on a confidential basis and the issuer does not have an obligation to disclose it to the market. In practice, issuers usually provide a statement on the outlook of the operational environment for the current and immediately following financial year, and refrain from making any clear statements of their expected financial perform-ance during said years given the extensive time period the statement is expected to cover.

- A list of the 50 largest shareholders of the company and their holdings.
- *A statement confirming that all applicable listing requirements are satisfied*: for a discussion of the listing requirements, see Section 11.2.2.1 above.
- *An extract from the Finnish Trade Register regarding the issuer or a corresponding document and a description of decisions which have not yet been recorded therein*: the extract from the Finnish Trade Register contains basic information regard-ing the issuer, as well as certain other corporate information, including, for example, authorisations to issue shares that have been granted by the issuer's shareholders to its board of directors.
- *The issuer's articles of association as registered with the Finnish Trade Register*: the issuer must submit its articles of association, together with any amend-ments thereto resolved upon by its shareholders but not yet registered and any amendments thereto proposed by the board of directors to a general meeting of shareholders.
- *An extract of the minutes of the meeting of the board of directors of the issuer regard-ing its decision to submit a listing application*: in respect of Finnish companies, the board of directors is the competent corporate body to resolve upon the submission of a listing application. Although a shareholder approval is not needed for the submission of a listing application, a general meeting of share-holders is often required, in order to make the necessary alterations to the issu-er's articles of association and to authorize the board of directors to issue new shares in connection with the listing.[3]
- *Lead manager's opinion*: the Helsinki Stock Exchange requires an opinion issued by the adviser of the issuer that has main responsibility for the listing process, regarding, *inter alia*: (i) the issuer's eligibility for listing; (ii) the issuer's ability to satisfy the prerequisites to operate as a listed company; and (iii) the adequacy

---

[2] For example, pursuant to Finnish Securities Market Act chapter 2, section 5a, issuers must assess in their interim reports the likely development of the issuer during the current financial year, to the extent possible.

[3] Pursuant to Finnish Companies Act (624/2006, as amended) chapter 5, section 27, a majority of two-thirds of the votes cast and shares represented in the general meeting of shareholders is required for any amendments of the articles of association.

of the information contained in the listing application (including the prospectus). Typically, such an opinion is issued by the lead manager, although other advisers, such as auditing firms, may issue the opinion if, for example, the issuer has not engaged any manager or underwriter in connection with the listing.

- *Statement of the executive officers of the issuer*: the listing application must include a statement by the issuer's executive officers that they are familiar with the obligations imposed on listed companies as set out in the Finnish Securities Market Act, other applicable laws and regulations as well as the Helsinki Stock Exchange Rules, and that the issuer is capable of satisfying such obligations. In practice, the statement of the issuer's executive officers must be signed by the members of its board of directors and chief executive officer.

- *Undertaking to the Helsinki Stock Exchange regarding an analysis of the issuer*: the issuer must undertake that, if so requested by the Helsinki Stock Exchange, it will commission an analysis of the issuer and its group. The issuer is responsible for the costs of such analysis.

- *Commitment to enter into an agreement with the Helsinki Stock Exchange*: the issuer must provide a commitment to the effect that it will follow all applicable rules and guidelines of the Helsinki Stock Exchange in connection with its listing. If the issuer is a subsidiary of another company, its parent company will be required to issue a similar commitment. The same requirement applies to the ultimate parent company of the issuer, if the parent company of the issuer is a part of a consolidated group. The detailed contents of such commitment are determined by the Helsinki Stock Exchange.

- *Prohibition on group contribution*: the issuer and its parent company (if any) must agree that the issuer will not make any group contribution payments to its parent company.

- *Receipt of payment of listing fees*: the listing application must include a receipt evidencing the payment of the listing fees in accordance with the applicable price list of the Helsinki Stock Exchange.

- *A description of clearing and settlement arrangements*: if the shares of the issuer are held in the Finnish book-entry system maintained by Euroclear, a reference to this fact will constitute a sufficient description.

- *Approved prospectus*: a prospectus prepared by the issuer and approved by the FFSA needs to be enclosed with the application. Alternatively, the issuer may use a prospectus approved by a competent authority in another EU or EEA member state, duly notified to the FFSA. If an approved prospectus is not required, for example, the issuer is already listed on a regulated market within the EEA and the so-called seasoned issuer exemption[4] is available,

---

[4] Finnish Prospectus Decree chapter 3, section 9, subsection 8 and Prospectus Directive Article 4(2)(h).

an exemption from the obligation to prepare a prospectus granted by the FFSA needs to be enclosed with the application.

- *Exemptions from the contents of the listing application.* The Helsinki Stock Exchange may, at its discretion, grant exemptions from the individual content requirements of the listing application. Such exemptions are not customarily necessary in connection with initial public offerings and/or secondary offerings by listed companies.

11.2.2.3 *Listing Committee of the Helsinki Stock Exchange*

The listing and delisting of shares on the Helsinki Stock Exchange is approved by the Listing Committee of the Helsinki Stock Exchange. The Listing Committee consists of five members appointed by the Board of Directors of the Helsinki Stock Exchange for a term of three years. Each member of the Listing Committee is required to be knowledgeable in business and the securities markets and two of the members of the Listing Committee must represent the business sector and the securities markets. The Listing Committee meets on a monthly basis, typically on the third Friday of each month.[5]   **11.28**

The Listing Committee procedure is a two-step procedure. In the first introductory meeting, the issuer presents itself and its business to the Listing Committee. Typically, the presentation takes place approximately two months prior to the planned date of listing. The listing application is addressed and approved in another Listing Committee meeting that typically takes place a few days prior to the date of listing. The Listing Committee may approve a listing at this stage, on condition that the issuer satisfies the listing requirements. The second Listing Committee meeting does not customarily require attendance by the issuer or its advisers.   **11.29**

Before the introductory meeting with the Listing Committee, companies and their advisers typically meet the staff of the Helsinki Stock Exchange to present the contemplated transaction and its timetable. It is also customary for the staff of the Helsinki Stock Exchange to comment on the draft documentation prior to the first Listing Committee meeting. Draft documentation must be provided to the Helsinki Stock Exchange two weeks before the relevant meeting of the Listing Committee and materials related to the issuer's presentation and the final listing application must be provided one week prior to the relevant meeting.   **11.30**

11.2.2.4 *Secondary listing on the Helsinki Stock Exchange*

Issuers can also apply for a secondary listing on the Helsinki Stock Exchange. As a general requirement, an issuer seeking a secondary listing on the Helsinki Stock   **11.31**

---

[5] However, the date of the meeting can vary provided that the discussions are commenced well in advance of the target date.

Exchange must prove that sufficient demand and supply exist for its shares to enable trading in the shares and reliable price formation. The Helsinki Stock Exchange is considered to be the primary stock exchange of Finnish companies.[6] However, if a Finnish company can show that trading in its shares mainly takes place on a foreign stock exchange, the Helsinki Stock Exchange can approve such a foreign stock exchange as the primary stock exchange and its listing on the Helsinki Stock Exchange becomes a secondary listing. In such cases, a trading volume test is conducted annually, which may result in the Helsinki Stock Exchange becoming the primary stock exchange if the majority of trading takes place there.

11.32 The Helsinki Stock Exchange amended its rules in March 2009 to permit a so-called fast-track secondary listing. Generally, a company that wishes to apply for a secondary listing on the Helsinki Stock Exchange must follow the same listing process as companies seeking a primary listing on the Helsinki Stock Exchange, including the Listing Committee process and requirement for a lead manager's opinion. However, companies that are already listed on an EEA regulated market or a corresponding market maintained by NASDAQ OMX, Deutsche Börse, the London Stock Exchange, NYSE Euronext, Oslo Börs or the Toronto Stock Exchange, may be granted exemptions from certain listing requirements.[7] Such secondary listings are decided by the chief executive officer of the Helsinki Stock Exchange rather than the Listing Committee. In practice, the Helsinki Stock Exchange has granted exemptions from, for example, the requirement of the lead manager's opinion in connection with secondary listings.

11.2.3 Prospectus

11.2.3.1 General remarks

11.33 The Prospectus Directive was fully implemented in Finland on 1 July 2005, principally through amendments to the Finnish Securities Market Act. In addition, being an EU member state, the Prospectus Regulation is directly applicable in Finland. Therefore, the Finnish prospectus rules closely follow the EU prospectus rules, and as such, do not generally contain national interpretations. The FFSA seeks to rely on the European-wide interpretations adopted by CESR.

11.2.3.2 Requirement for a prospectus

11.34 Pursuant to chapter 2, section 3 of the Finnish Securities Market Act, any person who: (i) offers securities to the public; or (ii) applies for admission to public trading of securities, is obligated to prepare a prospectus and make it available to

---

[6] Helsinki Stock Exchange Rules section 2.1.7.1.
[7] Helsinki Stock Exchange Rules section 2.1.7.3.

the public before such offer or admission can take place. In this context, 'offer of securities to the public' means a communication to persons in any form and by any means presenting sufficient information on the terms of the offer and the securities to be offered, so as to enable an investor to decide to purchase or subscribe to these securities.[8] 'Public trading' refers to trading of securities on a regulated market maintained by a stock exchange. In practice, public trading in Finland refers to the Helsinki Stock Exchange, as it is the only stock exchange maintaining regulated markets in Finland. Pursuant to chapter 1, section 2 of the Finnish Securities Market Act, the statute applies to securities that are transferable and in public circulation together with other similar securities.

11.2.3.3 *Prospectus exemptions*

11.2.3.3.1 Overview   The requirement to prepare a prospectus is subject to   **11.35**
exemptions. The prospectus exemptions are set out in sections 7 to 9 of the Decree of the Finnish Ministry of Finance on Prospectus referred to in chapter 2 of the Finnish Securities Market Act (452/2005) (the 'Finnish Prospectus Decree'). Except for a limited number of additional, Finland-specific exemptions,[9] the exemptions from the obligation to prepare a prospectus set out in the Finnish Prospectus Decree are based on the Prospectus Directive, both in relation to an offering of securities and an admission of securities to public trading.[10] In Finland, receiving the benefit of a prospectus exemption always requires the submission of an application to the FFSA and the grant of such exemption by the FFSA.

11.2.3.3.2 Employee offerings   Offerings of securities by an issuer to its   **11.36**
employees in Finland are exempt from the requirements of the Prospectus Directive. Share-based incentive schemes typically have been in the form of stock option programmes although it appears that, during the past few years, the use of stock option programmes has somewhat decreased. It is a customary practice in Finland for employee stock options to become transferable after a certain period of time, and in many cases employee stock options are also listed on the Helsinki Stock Exchange following the expiry of the relevant transfer restriction period.[11] The granting of an exemption by the FFSA in connection with employee offerings—both in relation to an offering of securities and a listing of the securities or shares subscribed for through the exercise or conversion of option rights—requires the relevant issuer to prepare a document that contains information on

---

[8] Prospectus Directive Article 2(1) and the FFSA's standard 5.2a on Securities Offerings and Listing.

[9] Such as the possibility of obtaining an exemption if the securities are offered to finance the operations of a non-profit organization.

[10] Prospectus Directive Articles 3(2) and 4.

[11] This also means that employee stock options in many cases are transferable securities to which the Finnish Securities Market Act and the Prospectus Directive apply.

the number and class of securities offered as well as the reasons for, and the terms and conditions of, the offering.[12]

11.2.3.4 FFSA approval process

11.37 The FFSA must approve a prospectus before it can be made public. The issuer must apply for the approval of the prospectus in writing, and the application must contain the draft prospectus annotated against the relevant Annexes of the Prospectus Regulation in order to ensure that the issuer has satisfied the mandatory prospectus content requirements.

11.38 The FFSA's prospectus review period is 20 business days, if the securities of the issuer have not been offered to the public prior to the application or are not listed on a regulated market within the European Economic Area. This period is shortened to ten business days if such offering has taken place or the securities of the issuer are already listed on a regulated market within the European Economic Area.[13] The date of filing of a prospectus is not included when calculating these review periods.

11.39 The FFSA typically gives written comments on the prospectus filed for approval, and the issuer and its advisers must amend the draft prospectus as required by the FFSA or discuss the FFSA's comments further with its staff. The FFSA may give several rounds of comments, and typically an issuer can expect to receive between two and five rounds of comments on the prospectus.

11.40 Following the completion of the FFSA review process, the FFSA will issue a written approval of the prospectus.

11.2.3.5 Prospectus and marketing materials

11.41 It is not customary in Finland for issuers to prepare a preliminary prospectus excluding pricing related information (a so-called 'red herring') and a separate final prospectus that includes all pricing-related information. Instead, typically only one prospectus is prepared and printed and, in connection with initial public offerings, the printed prospectus only contains a price range. The final subscription or offer price is then announced to investors in a stock exchange release, which is not considered a formal supplement to the prospectus that requires the approval of the FFSA.[14] This approach is made possible by chapter 2, section 3c of the Finnish Securities Market Act, which states that if securities are offered on a conditional basis in such a manner that the final decision on the subscription or

---

[12] Finnish Prospectus Decree chapter 3, section 8, subsection 5 and chapter 3, section 9, subsection 6. The content requirements for such document are set out in more detail in the FFSA's standard 5.2a.

[13] Finnish Securities Market Act chapter 2, section 4.

[14] See also Section 11.2.3.6.

offer price or the final number of securities to be offered has not yet been made, the prospectus can be made available without such information. As soon as such key offering decisions have been made, they must be made public in the same manner as the prospectus was made available.

The Finnish Securities Market Act also provides that if the prospectus does not **11.42**
contain a description of the basis for determining the subscription or offer price and the number of securities to be offered as well as the maximum subscription or offer price, investors have the right to withdraw their subscription or purchase commitments within two business days of the announcement of such information.[15] Therefore, to avoid giving investors such a right to withdraw, it is important that the basis for determining the subscription or offer price and the number of securities to be offered, as well as the maximum subscription or offer price, are set out in the prospectus.

Marketing materials related to an offering of securities or admission to public **11.43**
trading on the Helsinki Stock Exchange must be submitted to the FFSA within two business days of the date of filing of the prospectus.[16] Any marketing materials must include a reference to the prospectus and information regarding the availability of the prospectus. The definition of marketing materials is broad, covering all materials that refer to the securities offering or listing being marketed.[17] Such materials include, for example, press advertisements, posters and campaign letters. In addition, scripts for television and radio commercials need to be submitted to the FFSA and, upon separate request, also the final commercials. Moreover, materials regarding any events with access through invitation only, such as roadshow presentations with limited access, must be delivered to the FFSA, upon its request.

The FFSA does not officially approve marketing materials and from the beginning **11.44**
of 2007, it has generally limited the scope of its review of marketing materials to materials that relate to initial public offerings of shares or to first-time offerings of securities by the issuer in question.

11.2.3.6 *Supplementary prospectus*

Prospectuses need to be supplemented if they contain an error or omission that **11.45**
may be materially relevant to an investor.[18] If a prospectus approved by the FFSA needs to be supplemented due to such an error or omission, investors who have made a subscription or purchase prior to the publication of the supplement are

---

[15] Finnish Securities Market Act chapter 2, section 3c. See also Prospectus Directive Article 8.1.
[16] Finnish Securities Market Act chapter 2, section 4c.
[17] FFSA Standard 5.2a.
[18] Finnish Securities Market Act chapter 2, section 3b.

entitled to withdraw their subscription or purchase order within two business days of the publication of the supplement, or, if so decided by the FFSA for special reasons, within a longer period, although such period may not exceed four business days following the publication of the supplement to the prospectus.

11.46   The obligation to supplement a prospectus is effective until the expiration of the offer or until the listing of the securities in question on the Helsinki Stock Exchange, as applicable. Any supplements to a prospectus need to be approved by the FFSA prior to their publication. The FFSA must approve any supplements to a prospectus within seven business days,[19] but in practice, the FFSA reviews the supplements on an accelerated basis and typically its approval can be obtained on the day of the filing.

11.2.3.7 *Structure of a prospectus*

11.47   For share offerings pursuant to the Prospectus Directive, the prospectus can be prepared either as a single document or as a tripartite document comprising a summary, a registration document and a securities note. To date, the prevailing practice in Finland has been to publish single document prospectuses, and only a handful of issuers have prepared a three-part prospectus in anticipation of a need to access the capital markets several times during the following 12 months. Issuers of non-equity securities may also prepare a base prospectus under an offering programme, which is then supplemented with offering-specific information, including the terms and conditions of the offer, by a document known as final terms.

11.2.3.8 *Contents of a prospectus*

11.48   The general disclosure standard for a prospectus is set out in chapter 2, section 3a of the Finnish Securities Market Act, pursuant to which a prospectus must contain sufficient information to enable investors to make a sound assessment of the securities being offered and the issuer. In accordance with the Prospectus Directive, the prospectus must contain material and sufficient information on the assets, liabilities, financial position, results of operations and prospects of the issuer and any guarantor, as well as rights related to the securities being offered and other factors that have a material effect on the value of the securities. Such information must be presented in a comprehensible and easily understandable form.

11.49   The general disclosure standard set out in the Finnish Securities Market Act must be taken into account at all times when preparing a prospectus. In certain circumstances, it may require the issuer to disclose information over and above the

---

[19] Finnish Securities Market Act chapter 2, section 4.

information specifically required under the Annexes to the Prospectus Regulation. Certain prospectus content requirements in Finland are discussed in more detail below.

11.2.3.8.1 Responsibility statement   A prospectus must contain a responsibil-   **11.50**
ity statement given by the persons responsible for the contents of the prospectus. Such responsibility statement must be given in the form set out in the relevant Annex of the Prospectus Regulation.[20] Any amendments or qualifications to the responsibility statement are generally not permitted by the FFSA. The Prospectus Directive does not regulate whether the issuer or the board members of the issuer are responsible for the prospectus. In its standard 5.2a, the FFSA takes the view that, as a minimum, the issuer is responsible for the prospectus and it must give a responsibility statement. This also means that the directors of the issuer are not required to give the responsibility statement in their own name, although the Finnish corporate decision-making framework requires that the board of directors approves the prospectus on behalf of the issuer.

Prospectus liability is a somewhat open question in Finland, due to the lack of   **11.51**
sufficient court interpretations of the key questions, and it is not entirely clear whether the liability for a prospectus lies with the issuer or the directors or both. The prevailing view among Finnish legal scholars and practitioners is that, while the issuer has a primary liability for the prospectus, its directors may also be held liable for the prospectus.

11.2.3.8.2 Operating and financial review   In recent years, when reviewing   **11.52**
prospectuses, the FFSA has tended to focus on the operating and financial review section of the prospectus as well as the financial information generally contained in the prospectus. This is mainly the result of responsibilities relating to IFRS supervision, which has been within the remit of the FFSA since 2005. Typically, the FFSA does not require the operating and financial review disclosure to exceed the requirements set out in the Prospectus Regulation, but it may nonetheless require detailed and comprehensive disclosure.

11.2.3.8.3 Financial statements   The general requirement to include historical   **11.53**
financial information for each of the last three financial years is also applied in Finland. The financial statements for the last two financial years must be prepared using the accounting policies that are to be applied in the issuer's financial statements for the next following financial year. The FFSA also requires that stand-alone, parent company financial statements of the issuer are included in the prospectus in addition to the issuer's consolidated financial statements. The financial statements can be incorporated into the prospectus by reference, but issuers

---

[20] FFSA standard 5.2a.

should include at least abbreviated financial statements, including income statement, balance sheet and cash flow statement in the form of a comparative table, in the F-pages of the prospectus, as well as corresponding abbreviated interim report information for the quarter last ended together with the information for the comparison period.[21]

11.54 If the issuer does not have the requisite historical financial information, it may apply to the FFSA for an exemption from the requirement to include such information in the prospectus. In such cases, the Helsinki Stock Exchange must apply to the FFSA for an exemption from this requirement, as the Decree of the Finnish Ministry of Finance on Admission of Securities on the Stock Exchange List (940/2007) requires that, in order to qualify for admission into trading on the official list of the Helsinki Stock Exchange, the issuer must have audited financial statements for the last three financial years. The FFSA can grant such an exemption to the Helsinki Stock Exchange if, in the FFSA's view, it is in the interests of investors or the issuer and if sufficient information is available to investors to make a sound assessment on the issuer and the relevant securities. In practice, the FFSA has granted exemptions from the three-year financial history requirement in a situation where the issuer has been formed as a result of a recent transaction, such as a demerger, and, therefore, does not have the requisite financial history as a legal entity. In such cases, the issuer's underlying business has been covered by the audited financial statements of another legal entity and audited carve-out financial statements have been prepared on the basis of such financial statements.

11.55 **11.2.3.8.4 Pro forma financial information** If any significant changes have taken place or will take place in the issuer's operations that result in a situation where the issuer's audited financial statements do not adequately describe the issuer's business, the issuer must prepare pro-forma or other restated financial information for inclusion in the prospectus. The FFSA generally follows the pro-forma financial information requirements set forth in Annex II of the Prospectus Regulation. When assessing whether the 25% significant gross change has taken place triggering the need to present pro-forma financial information, the materiality of the transaction in question is compared against certain key indicators prior to the transaction.[22] The key indicators, which include, for example, total assets, net sales and net profit/loss, are calculated on the basis of the issuer's most recent financial statements or, if applicable, the financial statements that will next be made public. The FFSA may also require presentation of pro-forma

---

[21] FFSA standard 5.2a.
[22] FFSA standard 5.2a.

financial information, if several transactions that have taken place during the financial year result in a 25% significant gross change on an aggregated basis even if none of the individual transactions alone meets the 25% significant gross change test.

The need for pro-forma or other restated information is ultimately decided on a **11.56** case-by-case basis by the FFSA. Accordingly, in cases of doubt, it is advisable to initiate discussions with the FFSA at an early stage regarding the presentation of an issuer's financial information, even if the issuer and its advisers are of the view that pro-forma or other restated financial information is not required to be included in the prospectus.

11.2.3.8.5 Exemptions from individual information requirements The FFSA **11.57** may, for special reasons, decide that certain information referred to in the Prospectus Regulation may be omitted from the prospectus.[23] The FFSA is most likely to do this in cases where the information in question is of minor importance and is not likely to have a material effect on an investor's assessment of the issuer or its securities, or in cases where disclosure of the relevant information would be contrary to the public interest or seriously detrimental to the issuer.

The FFSA may decide that, instead of requiring certain information set out in the **11.58** relevant annexes to the Prospectus Regulation to be included in the prospectus, other corresponding information may be presented instead, provided such corresponding information provides investors with adequate disclosure, taking into account the issuer's operating sector and legal form and the nature of the securities referred to in the prospectus.[24]

11.2.4 Language requirements of a prospectus

A prospectus must be prepared in either Finnish or Swedish,[25] if the securities are **11.59** offered to the public or are to be admitted to public trading solely in Finland.[26] However, the FFSA may, upon application, agree to the use of a language other than Finnish or Swedish. FFSA standard 5.2a provides, that a prospectus can be prepared in English in certain situations, including:

- if the securities are offered to the public or are to be admitted to trading on a regulated market elsewhere than in Finland;
- if the offer or listing in Finland relates to non-equity securities with a minimum denomination or offer lot of at least EUR 50,000; and

---

[23] Finnish Prospectus Decree chapter 3, section 10.
[24] Finnish Prospectus Decree chapter 3, section 10, subsection 2.
[25] Swedish is also an official language in Finland.
[26] Finnish Securities Market Act chapter 2, section 3d.

- if the FFSA deems that a special reason to permit the preparation of an English language prospectus exists, such as:
  - the prospectus is prepared for the purposes of listing shares issued by way of consideration for an acquisition or a private placement provided that the size or nature of the issuer's operations do not change significantly as a result of the acquisition or private placement;
  - the prospectus relates to non-equity securities; or
  - the use of English as the prospectus language does not jeopardize the interests of the relevant investors, taking into account the size, expertise and language skills of the target group.

11.60 If a prospectus is prepared in English for use in Finland, the summary of the prospectus must be prepared in Finnish or Swedish. However, the FFSA does not require the translation of the summary into Finnish or Swedish if the securities concerned are non-equity securities and their denomination or minimum offer lot is at least EUR 50,000. If a prospectus prepared in Finnish or Swedish is passported into a member state of the EEA, it must be translated into English and such translation must be an exact translation of the Finnish or Swedish language prospectus.[27]

11.2.5 Passporting of a prospectus

11.2.5.1 Passporting from Finland

11.61 If securities are to be offered in one or more member states of the EEA and the FFSA is the competent authority to approve the prospectus, the FFSA must, upon the applicant's request, deliver to the competent authorities in the jurisdictions to which the prospectus is being passported, a certificate to the effect that the approved prospectus and any supplements thereto are prepared in accordance with the Prospectus Directive.[28] The FFSA must deliver such passporting certificate within three business days of the request of the applicant, or, if the request is made when the prospectus or a supplement thereto is submitted for approval to the FFSA, within one business day of the approval of the prospectus or a supplement thereto. Furthermore, the FFSA's notification to another competent authority within the EEA must include, if necessary, a translation of the summary in an official language approved by such other competent authority.[29]

---

[27] FFSA Standard 5.2a. This means that, for example, the selling and transfer restrictions will need to be included in the Finnish or Swedish language prospectus as well, unless two English language versions, one for passporting purposes and one for international private placement purposes, are prepared.

[28] Finnish Securities Market Act chapter 2, section 4f.

[29] Ibid.

11.2.5.2 *Passporting into Finland*

A prospectus and any supplements thereto approved by a competent authority in another member state of the EEA are also valid in Finland for the purposes of a public offer or admission to trading on the Helsinki Stock Exchange, if the competent authority that has approved the prospectus has delivered the FFSA with a copy of the prospectus including any supplements together with a certificate that the prospectus has been prepared in accordance with the Prospectus Directive.[30] If the competent authority that has approved the prospectus has granted an exemption from any content requirements of a prospectus, the certificate must refer to such exemptions and reasons therefor. A prospectus being passported into Finland needs to be prepared in English or another language approved by the FFSA. As a general rule, the prospectus being passported into Finland must be prepared in English and the FFSA requires that the summary of the prospectus is translated into Finnish or Swedish.[31]

11.62

11.2.6 Due diligence requirements

The basis for conducting a due diligence review of an issuer in connection with a securities offering and listing is set out in chapter 2, section 2 of the Finnish Securities Market Act. It stipulates that anyone who offers securities or applies for their admission to public trading (or who takes care of such offering or admission on the basis of an assignment)[32] is responsible for making available to investors, on an equal treatment basis, sufficient information in relation to facts that have a material effect on the value of the securities. Other advisers, such as accountants and legal counsel, are not deemed to be responsible to investors on this basis. This interpretation is also confirmed in FFSA standard 5.2a.[33]

11.63

FFSA standard 5.2a states that, while the issuer is primarily responsible for the fulfilment of all applicable disclosure obligations, the manager(s) also have responsibility for disclosure obligations to the extent that they have access to the relevant information. The scope of the managers' responsibility covers the information that they can reasonably be expected to obtain when they sign an engagement letter with the issuer or otherwise accept the assignment to act as managers. Accordingly, managers are generally required to perform a due diligence investigation of the issuer, including business, financial and legal due diligence. The FFSA provides some guidance on the required due diligence in its

11.64

---

[30] Finnish Securities Market Act chapter 2, Section 4e.
[31] Ibid.
[32] In practice, such party which is taking care of a securities offering or listing of securities on the basis of an assignment refers to the manager(s) of an offering.
[33] See Section 11.2.3.8 above.

2002 letter to managers,[34] which focuses on the governance, financial reporting and risk management of the issuer. The matters addressed in the letter, dealing mostly with the issuer's ability to meet the general eligibility criteria for listing and to fulfil its obligations as a public company, are in practice covered by a so-called 'IPO due diligence' typically performed by an audit firm in connection with an IPO.

11.65   In addition, the lead manager's opinion that must be enclosed with the listing application to the Helsinki Stock Exchange creates a need for a due diligence investigation of the issuer.[35] In connection with the introduction of the requirement for a lead manager's opinion, the Helsinki Stock Exchange issued a memorandum in 2002 that contains guidance on the expected scope of due diligence to be performed in connection with an IPO.[36]

11.66   In practice, the level of due diligence that is typically performed in connection with initial public offerings and secondary offerings typically exceeds the minimum standards set out in the FFSA letter and the memorandum of the Helsinki Stock Exchange, particularly in cross-border securities offerings where international standards are likely to be influential.

11.3 Continuing Obligations

11.67   The Transparency Directive and Market Abuse Directive have each been fully implemented in Finland (effective 15 February 2007 and 1 July 2005, respectively) by way of amendments to the Finnish Securities Market Act.

11.68   To supplement the Finnish implementation of the Transparency Directive, the Ministry of Finance issued the Decree of the Ministry of Finance on the Regular Duty of Disclosure of an Issuer of a Security (153/2007) (the 'Disclosure Decree') and the Decree of the Ministry of Finance on the Flagging Obligation and Information to Be Disclosed in connection with the Disclosure and Publication of Holdings (154/2007), which entered into force on 15 February 2007.

11.3.1 Disclosure requirements

11.69   Detailed provisions on the disclosure requirements applicable to issuers of securities and shareholders of listed companies are set out in chapter 2 of the

---

[34] Letter of the FFSA to managers of securities offerings 'Preparatory work preceding a listing', dated 24 October 2002 (diary number 10/269/2002) (available in Finnish only).

[35] Section 11.2.2.2 above provides a more detailed description of the lead manager's opinion.

[36] Memorandum of the Helsinki Stock Exchange on the Scope and Contents of the Due Diligence relating to a Listing, dated 2 April 2002 (available in Finnish only).

Finnish Securities Market Act. The rationale behind the disclosure of information is to provide investors with information necessary to make an informed assessment of the value of the securities and their issuer. Accordingly, issuers of publicly traded securities are obliged to disclose, without undue delay, any decisions and other circumstances that may have a material impact on the value of the securities.[37]

Shareholders of listed companies have an obligation to notify the listed company in question and the FFSA of changes in their holdings if they reach, exceed or fall below certain thresholds as set out in the Finnish Securities Market Act. **11.70**

11.3.1.1 *Periodic reporting requirements*

Periodic reporting requirements refer to an issuer's obligation to provide financial information on a periodic basis. This comprises the publication of interim reports, financial statements and financial statement releases (described below). Provisions regarding periodic reporting requirements are set out in chapter 2, sections 5–6c of the Finnish Securities Market Act and the FFSA standard 5.1 on Disclosure of Periodic Information. **11.71**

11.3.1.1.1 Financial statements, report of the board of directors and auditor's report Finnish listed companies are required to prepare financial statements in accordance with IFRS. The financial statements must provide a true and fair view of the issuer's results of operations and financial position. In accordance with chapter 5, section 3 of the Finnish Companies Act (624/2006, as amended), the financial statements are adopted at the annual general meeting of shareholders of the issuer. **11.72**

Article 4(1) of the Transparency Directive requires issuers to publish financial statements within four months from the end of the financial period. However, in accordance with the Finnish Securities Market Act, the financial statements and the report of the board of directors must be made public no later than one week before the annual general meeting of shareholders of the company, and in any event, within three months of the end of the financial period. In connection with the publication of the financial statements and the report of the board of directors, an auditor's report must also be made public.[38] The content requirements for the report of the board of directors are set out in detail in chapter 3, section 1 of the Finnish Accounting Act (1336/1997, as amended) and in the Disclosure Decree. The supervisory authority regarding compliance with the IFRS in Finland is the FFSA. **11.73**

---

[37] Finnish Securities Market Act chapter 2, section 7.
[38] Finnish Securities Market Act chapter 2, section 6.

11.74   **11.3.1.1.2 Financial statement releases**   Issuers of publicly traded shares or convertible bonds must, immediately upon the completion of their financial statements, publish a financial statement release.[39] The financial statements are deemed to have been completed once the board of directors of the issuer has approved them.[40] Pursuant to section 3.2.2 of the Helsinki Stock Exchange Rules, the financial statement release must be made public within two months from the end of the financial period if it is based on unaudited annual financial statements, and within three months from the end of the financial period if it is based on audited annual financial statements.

11.75   The financial statement release is, effectively, an interim report for the fourth quarter. The contents of the financial statement release and the interim reports are regulated in more detail in the Disclosure Decree and the Rules of the Helsinki Stock Exchange. The financial statement release must give an account of the issuer's business, financial performance and investments, as well as of any changes in its financial position and operating environment during the relevant accounting period. Any irregularities that might have an impact on the issuer's business and financial performance should also be addressed. The explanatory section of the financial statement release must include the proposal of the board of directors to the general meeting of shareholders regarding the disposal of the issuer's profit or loss, as well as an account of the issuer's distributable funds.[41] Furthermore, the financial statement release must also include the proposed dividend per share, information regarding the planned date of the annual general meeting of shareholders and information on where and when the financial statements and the report of the board of directors will be made available to the public.[42] In addition, a stock exchange release containing the financial statement release must include a summary stating the issuer's key figures.[43]

11.76   **11.3.1.1.3 Interim reports and interim management statements**   Issuers of shares listed on the official list of the Helsinki Stock Exchange are generally required to prepare interim reports for the first three, six, and nine months of their financial period.[44] The issuer may, however, decide not to prepare interim reports for the first three and nine months (Q1 and Q3) of the financial period, if it fulfils certain requirements regarding the size or line of its business or if other corresponding requirements are fulfilled. In addition, interim reports must be made public without undue delay, and in any event no later than two months from the

---

[39] Finnish Securities Market Act chapter 2, section 6a.
[40] FFSA standard 5.1 on Disclosure of Periodic Information section 9(4).
[41] Finnish Securities Market Act chapter 2, section 6a.
[42] Helsinki Stock Exchange Rules section 3.2.3.
[43] Helsinki Stock Exchange Rules section 3.2.3.
[44] Pursuant to Finnish Securities Market Act chapter 2, section 5.

end of the reporting period.[45] The date of release must be announced in advance as soon as it has been confirmed.

An interim report comprises an explanatory section and a tabular section.[46] The **11.77** explanatory section should give a general description of the issuer's financial position and results of operations as well as its development during the reporting period. The tabular section should be prepared in accordance with IFRS standards on interim financial reporting, as referred to in the Finnish Accounting Act. The issuer may, however, opt to prepare an abridged tabular section for the first three and nine months of the financial period. The more detailed content requirements for the explanatory section and the abridged table section of an interim report are set out in the Disclosure Decree.

The explanatory section must describe any material events and transactions that **11.78** have occurred during the reporting period and their impact on the issuer's financial position and results of operations.[47] Furthermore, the explanatory section must include details of the principal short-term risks and uncertainties relating to the issuer's business operations. In addition, to the extent possible, it must provide an assessment of the likely development of the issuer during the current financial period and present a clarification of the factors used as a basis for such assessment.

Issuers that opt not to prepare interim reports for the first three and nine months **11.79** of the financial period must provide an interim management statement during the first and second half of the financial period.[48] Pursuant to section 4 of the Disclosure Decree, an issuer may decide to prepare interim management statements instead of interim reports if one of the following preconditions is fulfilled: (i) the market value of the issuer's shares does not exceed EUR 75 million; (ii) in view of the issuer's area of activity and the nature and regularity of its business operations, it concludes that investors receive adequate information regarding the issuer through its interim management statements; (iii) the main area of activity of the issuer is investment activities and the issuer has decided to announce regularly its share-specific net assets and the net asset calculation forming the basis therefor more frequently than at three-month intervals; (iv) the issuer's shares are subject to public trading in another EEA member state and said state does not require companies to publish interim reports for the first three and nine months of the financial period; or (v) the FFSA decides upon application in a

---

[45] Finnish Securities Market Act chapter 2, section 5b.
[46] Finnish Securities Market Act chapter 2, section 5a.
[47] Ibid.
[48] Finnish Securities Market Act chapter 2, section 5c.

corresponding situation, that it is not necessary for investor protection for the issuer to publish interim reports.

11.80   The interim management statement must be made public no earlier than ten weeks after the beginning of the relevant six-month period and no later than six weeks before the end of such period.[49] The date of release must be announced in advance as soon as it has been confirmed by the issuer.

11.81   **11.3.1.1.4 Annual summary**   Issuers of publicly traded securities are required to make public a document containing a summary of the information published during the previous financial period.[50] At a minimum, the annual summary must contain a reference to the information made public by the issuer pursuant to the provisions of the Finnish Securities Market Act and regulations issued thereunder, such as the Disclosure Decree, or the Helsinki Stock Exchange Rules.

11.3.1.2 Ongoing disclosure requirements

11.82   The periodic reporting requirements described above are supplemented by ongoing disclosure requirements. An issuer is required to make public any matters that may have a material impact on the value of its securities. The issuer must disclose such information without undue delay.[51] This ongoing disclosure obligation is cast in broad terms under the Finnish Securities Market Act, which is supplemented with more detailed provisions under the Helsinki Stock Exchange Rules and FFSA standard 5.2b Disclosure Obligation of the Issuer and Shareholder.

11.3.1.3 Major shareholding notifications (flagging notifications)

11.83   Shareholders of a Finnish listed company are required to notify the relevant company and the FFSA if their voting participation in, or their percentage ownership of issued shares of, such Finnish listed company reaches, exceeds or falls below 5, 10, 15, 20, 25, 30, 50 or 66.67% (2/3).[52] This so-called flagging obligation also arises if a shareholder is a party to an agreement or other arrangement which, when executed, causes the shareholder's ownership of shares or voting rights to reach, exceed or fall below the thresholds set forth above.

11.84   The ownership reporting obligation by a shareholder is not limited to directly owned shares only but also includes: (i) shares owned by an entity controlled by the shareholder; (ii) shares owned by a pension foundation or pension fund controlled by (A) the shareholder or (B) an entity in which the shareholder is in control; and (iii) other shares, which the shareholder controls alone or together

---

[49] Ibid.
[50] Finnish Securities Market Act chapter 2, section 10c.
[51] Finnish Securities Market Act chapter 2, section 7.
[52] Finnish Securities Market Act chapter 2, section 9.

with a third party, on the basis of a contract or otherwise (so-called 'acting in concert' provision).

The notification must be submitted to the relevant company and the FFSA **11.85** without undue delay after the time of acquisition or disposition of shares or entering into any contract triggering the notification obligation. If the share acquisition or disposition is made on the Helsinki Stock Exchange, the notification obligation generally arises on the trade date (T) rather than the settlement date.[53] With respect to a contract triggering the notification obligation, the notification must be submitted no later than on the signing date of such contract.

The Finnish shareholder notification requirements are stricter than those set out **11.86** in the Transparency Directive. Whereas Article 9(1) of the Transparency Directive requires that changes in holdings of voting rights are to be notified, the Finnish Securities Market Act requires that both holdings in shares and holdings in voting rights are subject to the flagging obligation. Furthermore, whereas Article 12(2) of the Transparency Directive requires that the notification is to be made as soon as possible, and within four days at the latest, the Finnish Securities Market Act requires that the notification must be made without undue delay, and Finnish market practice is to submit the notification on the day of the transaction that results in the notification obligation.

The information required in a flagging notification is set out in the Decree of the **11.87** Ministry of Finance on the Flagging Obligation and Information to Be Disclosed in Connection with the Disclosure and Publication of Holdings (154/2007).[54] Generally, the notification is not required to contain any qualitative information regarding the shareholding or shareholder's intentions (for example, the purpose for increasing its ownership). However, if the notification obligation arises on the basis of a contract, the shareholder must summarise the contents of such contract

---

[53] The customary settlement cycle on the Helsinki Stock Exchange is T+3 business days.
[54] The notification has to include the following information:
    (i) the full name of the listed Finnish company in question;
    (ii) the reason why the flagging notification is being made;
    (iii) the date when the ownership has reached, exceeded or fallen below one of the applicable thresholds;
    (iv) the actual percentage of the shares owned and voting rights held directly or indirectly, except when the holdings fall below 5%;
    (v) the full name and the corporate register number of the shareholder;
    (vi) the full name and the corporate register number of an entity whose shareholdings are included in the shareholder's ownership and the reasons therefore (if applicable);
    (vii) the manner in which the ownership of shares is divided between the persons/companies referred to in (v) and (vi) above (if applicable);
    (viii) description of the chain of companies through which the shares and voting rights are being controlled;
    (ix) material contents, parties and term of the contract or other arrangement that the shareholder is a party to (if applicable).

(see item (ix) of footnote 54). The flagging notification must be submitted in writing in Finnish, Swedish or English.

11.88   After the Finnish listed company receives a flagging notification, it must disclose the notification to the public.[55] This is accomplished through the issuance of a stock exchange release.

11.89   **11.3.1.3.1 Trading in the issuer's own shares**   Article 14(1) of the Transparency Directive requires that, if an issuer trades in its own shares in such a manner that thresholds of 5 or 10% of the voting rights in such issuer are reached or exceeded, it must announce such holding of its own shares as soon as possible and in any event no later than four trading days following the relevant change. Any trading in the issuer's own shares must be disclosed to the Helsinki Stock Exchange without undue delay and in any event no later than the beginning of the next trading day.[56] The announcement to the Helsinki Stock Exchange must include separately for each share class the number of shares as well as the prices paid per share. The Helsinki Stock Exchange must, in turn, publish such announcement.

11.3.1.4 Enforcement of disclosure obligations

11.90   The FFSA is responsible for enforcing the Finnish disclosure requirements. The primary aim of the FFSA's supervision is to ensure that investors have access to all material and adequate information required in order to make an informed assessment of the issuer and its securities. The FFSA monitors compliance with the reporting requirements retrospectively.

11.91   As for periodic reporting requirements, the FFSA seeks to ensure that all financial reports, interim reports, financial statements and financial statement releases required in accordance with the Finnish Securities Market Act are issued by listed companies within the applicable time periods. The FFSA also enforces compliance with the ongoing disclosure requirements described above at Section 11.3.1.2.

11.3.1.5 Delayed disclosure of information

11.92   Listed companies may delay the disclosure of information for an acceptable reason.[57] Because there is no general obligation for Finnish companies to disclose matters under preparation, the issue of delaying disclosure is generally relevant in cases where a matter has already been resolved and, therefore, should generally be disclosed.

11.93   An announcement may be delayed if three preconditions are fulfilled: (i) as mentioned above, there is an acceptable reason for delaying the disclosure; (ii) such

---

[55] Finnish Securities Market Act chapter 2, section 10.
[56] Finnish Securities Market Act chapter 2, section 10a.
[57] Finnish Securities Market Act chapter 2, section 7.

delay will not jeopardize investors' interests; and (iii) the issuer can ensure that the information remains confidential. The issuer must without undue delay inform the FFSA and the Helsinki Stock Exchange of any delay and the reasons therefor. This notification must also contain the estimated duration of the postponement of the disclosure, if such estimate can be given.

11.3.2 Inside information

Inside information means precise information that has not been made public or is **11.94** not otherwise available to the markets and that is likely to have an effect on the value of securities that are traded publicly or on a multilateral trading facility.[58] Persons who possess inside information are prohibited from using such inside information in securities trading.[59] An insider is also prohibited from using inside information in advising another person in securities transactions. In addition, pursuant to chapter 5, section 2 of the Finnish Securities Market Act, an insider is prohibited from disclosing inside information to another person, unless the disclosure is made in the normal course of the exercise of his employment, profession or duties.

Insider trading under the Finnish Penal Code is a criminal offence and is punish- **11.95** able if committed intentionally or with gross negligence in order to obtain financial benefit for the person possessing inside information or for someone else. The prohibition of insider trading under the Finnish Securities Market Act is more general in scope, and requires no negligence or specific intention to obtain financial benefit. For persons possessing inside information by virtue of their position, employment or responsibilities, the presumption is that trading in the relevant issuer's shares constitutes prohibited use of inside information. Pursuant to chapter 7, section 1 of the Finnish Securities Market Act, the FFSA is the competent authority in respect of supervising compliance with the Finnish Securities Market Act, including the market abuse regulation. The FFSA can impose administrative sanctions for non-compliance, as discussed in Section 11.1.2 above.

A listed company is required to maintain a public register of insider holdings in **11.96** respect of insiders, as defined in chapter 5, section 3 of the Finnish Securities Market Act. Such insiders must declare in a public register of insider holdings their holdings of: (i) shares of the issuer; (ii) securities entitling to shares of the issuer that are subject to public trading; (iii) other securities entitling to such

---

[58] Finnish Securities Market Act chapter 5, section 1.
[59] Finnish Securities Market Act chapter 5, section 2 and Finnish Penal Code chapter 51, sections 1 and 2.

securities; and (iv) securities the value of which is determined on the basis of the said securities, as well as any changes in these holdings.[60]

11.3.2.1 Insider registers

11.97 **11.3.2.1.1 Persons subject to insider disclosure requirements** The Finnish Securities Market Act makes a distinction between so-called primary and secondary insiders. A primary insider is a person who possesses inside information by virtue of his position, employment or responsibilities. He can also have obtained inside information as a result of a shareholding in the issuer. A secondary insider in turn refers to any other person who knew or ought to have known that the information in his possession was inside information.

11.98 Insiders that have an obligation to declare their shareholdings in a public register of insider holdings include:[61]

- members and deputy members of an issuer's board of directors and supervisory board, if any;
- the issuer's chief executive officer and deputy chief executive officer;
- the issuer's auditor, deputy auditor and an employee of an audit organization with main responsibility for the audit; and
- other members of the issuer's management who regularly obtain inside information and have the right to make decisions regarding the issuer's future development and organization of its business activities.

11.99 **11.3.2.1.2 Register of insider holdings** In addition to the insiders themselves, the ownership declaration requirements apply to the insider's spouse or cohabitation partner, persons under his custody, other family members who have lived in the same household for at least one year and companies controlled by any of the above-mentioned persons or in which they exercise influence.[62]

11.100 The declaration on insider holdings must be submitted to the issuer within 14 days of the date the relevant person started to act in a position in relation to which the declaration obligation applies. Any change in information subject to the declaration obligation must be submitted within seven days of the relevant change.[63] Issuers that receive an insider holding notification must record any changes in the insider holdings information to their public register without undue delay.[64]

---

[60] Finnish Securities Market Act, provisions on the public register of insider holdings are set out in the FFSA standard 5.3 'Declarations of insider holdings and insider registers', and the Helsinki Stock Exchange's Guidelines for insiders.

[61] Finnish Securities Market Act chapter 5, section 3.

[62] Finnish Securities Market Act chapter 5, section 3.

[63] Finnish Securities Market Act chapter 5, section 4.

[64] Finnish Securities Market Act chapter 5, section 7; the Helsinki Stock Exchange's Guidelines for insiders state that in practice it is recommended that a company updates changes in the insider register within one week after receiving the notice of the changes, page 7.

Issuers are required to maintain a register of insider holdings. Issuers can also **11.101** outsource the maintenance of the insider register to Euroclear. However, even where an issuer decides to outsource the maintenance of the insider register, it continues to be liable for it. With the help of Euroclear's SIRE system,[65] trading in securities maintained under the book-entry system are entered automatically in a register of insider holdings. The information in the register of persons subject to the declaration obligation is public, except for the social security number and the home address. Regarding persons other than those subject to the disclosure requirement (for example, spouse or cohabitation partner, family members under custody), only information on securities holdings is public and other information, such as name, social security number and address, is not.

11.3.2.1.3 Company-specific insider register   Listed companies are obliged to **11.102** maintain a non-public company-specific insider register,[66] which should contain information on persons who, by virtue of their position and duties, obtain inside information. It should also contain information on persons who obtain inside information from the issuer, for example, on the basis of a contract of employment or otherwise, or who are members of the governing bodies of the issuer. Advisers, including attorneys, who work for and on behalf of the issuer on a particular project, should also be registered in a company-specific insider register. Pursuant to section 9.2(10) of the FFSA standard 5.3, it is deemed sufficient that, in case of external advisers, the company records in its company-specific register the name of the law firm, the lead manager of an offering or other entity providing professional services as well as the name of the attorney or expert who bears main responsibility on such entity's behalf. The external adviser itself should keep a register of all personnel with access to inside information on a particular project. The Helsinki Stock Exchange's Guidelines for Insiders and the FFSA standard 5.3 contain detailed provisions on company-specific registers of insiders and, in particular, for project-specific insider registers.

11.3.2.2 Selective disclosure of inside information

As discussed above, the disclosure of inside information is prohibited pursuant to **11.103** chapter 5, section 2 of the Finnish Securities Market Act. Inside information may, however, be disclosed if the disclosure takes place as part of the ordinary performance of the work, profession or tasks of the person disclosing the information. FFSA standard 5.2b sets forth certain examples of situations where the disclosure of inside information is deemed acceptable.

---

[65] SIRE is a service provided by Euroclear to public companies for outsourcing their insider registers.

[66] Finnish Securities Market Act chapter 5, section 8.

11.3.3 The Finnish Corporate Governance Code

11.104   In accordance with the Helsinki Stock Exchange Rules, listed companies domiciled in Finland must comply with the Finnish Corporate Governance Code. The Finnish Corporate Governance Code follows the so-called 'comply or explain' principle, which means that a listed company should, as a general rule, comply with the Finnish Corporate Governance Code, and if it deviates from the code, it has to explain how it deviates from the code and its reasons for doing so.

11.105   The Finnish Corporate Governance Code entered into force on 1 January 2009, although certain provisions will not enter into full force until the expiry of a transitory period. The Securities Markets Association deemed it necessary to update the code of 2003 due to changes in market conditions and regulations. In particular, transparency has become increasingly important for listed companies and investors and their confidence in the securities market. According to the Securities Markets Association, specially emphasized topics in the updated code include the grounds for management compensation, risks related to companies' operations and the level of risk management.

11.106   Other significant changes to the code relate to risk management, board composition, communication with the shareholders and the corporate governance statement. The importance of the internet as a channel for disclosure is also highlighted.

11.107   The new Finnish Corporate Governance Code increases transparency in relation to management compensation, requiring a listed company to publish information concerning salaries and bonus schemes. The company must also disclose on its websites the principles and decision-making processes behind any bonus schemes for the issuer's chief executive officer and other members of its senior management. For example, information on the determination of the variable components of the management compensation schemes, share-based compensation schemes and voluntary pension arrangements must be disclosed.

11.108   The new Finnish Corporate Governance Code also sets out new requirements on the composition of the board of directors of an issuer. In accordance with recommendation 9, the board of directors must include representatives of both genders. This recommendation does not enter into force until the first annual general meeting of shareholders to be held after 1 January 2010. It is noted in the code that the composition of the boards of directors of many smaller companies does not currently comply with this new requirement and, for such companies, this recommendation functions as a long-term objective. Currently, only one-third of Finnish listed companies have female board members. In addition, in the future, the time a person has acted as a board member of an issuer will be taken into account when evaluating his or her independence from the issuer. A person who has been a board member of an issuer for over 12 consecutive years may, in the

overall assessment, be deemed no longer independent of the issuer. New requirements for the qualifications of committee members have also been introduced.
At least one of the members of an audit committee must have knowledge and
proficiency regarding accounting, bookkeeping or auditing. Furthermore, at least
one of the members of an audit committee must be independent of significant
shareholders. Also, the majority of the members of the issuer's nomination committee and remuneration committee must be independent of the issuer.

Listed companies must issue a separate corporate governance statement in   **11.109**
connection with the financial statements and the related report of the board of
directors.[67] The contents of such statement are regulated under a decree of the
Ministry of Finance (393/2008).

---

[67] Recommendation 51.

12

FRANCE*

12.1 Listing Securities in Paris

12.1.1 The Paris Listing

12.01 Companies that effect and maintain a primary listing (a 'primary listing') of securities on the main market of the NYSE Euronext Paris (the 'Euronext Paris market') must meet certain eligibility criteria and are subject to the full regulatory requirements of the exchange. They are also subject to regulatory supervision by the AMF and more demanding disclosure and corporate governance standards than issuers listed on a multilateral trading system (such as Alternext) or on the unregulated Marché Libre.

12.02 Inclusion in the CAC 40 or SBF 120 indices, which are open to both French and foreign companies with primary listings, hinges on a company's market

---

* The author thanks Charlotte Beroud of the Paris office of Cleary Gottlieb for her extensive contribution to this Chapter.

capitalization and liquidity, as compared to other companies, as well as on certain other eligibility criteria.

In December 2007, new provisions of the AMF General Regulations allowed **12.03** for the creation of a 'professional compartment' of the Euronext Paris market (the 'Professional Compartment').[1] The Professional Compartment is designed for listings without any public offer of securities and allows issuers to be exempt from certain requirements applicable to issuers with a primary listing of shares (both in connection with the admission to listing and as part of the continuing obligations).

12.1.2 The French *Autorité des marchés financiers*

The French *Autorité des marchés financiers* (the 'AMF') is France's 'competent **12.04** authority' within the meaning of the Prospectus Directive.

The AMF is an independent French public authority that resulted from the merger **12.05** of the *Commission des opérations de bourse* and the *Conseil des marchés financiers*. The AMF has the following powers and responsibilities: (i) adopting regulations pursuant to legislative authority set forth in the French Monetary and Financial Code, as amended from time to time (the 'General Regulations') and interpreting such regulations; (ii) overseeing the disclosure of issuers with respect to which it acts as the competent authority, approving the registration of prospectuses and monitoring compliance with certain continuing obligations; (iii) conducting investigations and levying administrative sanctions for violations of its General Regulations; (iv) establishing, interpreting and overseeing the application of rules applicable to tender offers; (v) approving the licensing of regulated investment services providers engaging in asset management activities (portfolio management companies, UCITS management companies, etc), and supervising the activities of such entities, with the power to impose sanctions for rule violations, as well as approving regulated mutual funds and similar collective investment vehicles; and (vi) establishing rules applicable to exchanges.

The AMF's stated purpose, pursuant to Article L. 621-1 of the French Monetary **12.06** and Financial Code, is to see to the protection of investments in financial instruments and any other investments involving a public offer, the disclosure of adequate information to investors and the orderly and fair operation of financial markets. In practice, the AMF exercises its role as France's competent authority regarding admission of securities to listing on the Euronext Paris market through the staff of one of its divisions, the *Direction des émetteurs*, while formal decisions of the

---

[1] General Regulation of the AMF Articles 516-18 and 516-19.

AMF itself are adopted by its Board (the *Collège*), its Chairman or pursuant to a delegation of authority from either of them.

12.1.3 The Paris Stock Exchange

12.07　The Paris Stock Exchange is operated by NYSE Euronext Paris. NYSE Euronext Paris SA runs one principal market in France, the Euronext Paris market (which includes the main board and the Professional Compartment), as well as Alternext.

12.1.3.1 *The Euronext Paris market*

12.08　The Euronext Paris market is the main Paris stock exchange. It is a regulated market, and all companies admitted to it must comply with Euronext's admissions rules. In practice, these standards overlap to a large extent with the eligibility and continuing obligations provisions to which applicants are already bound under the AMF's General Regulations.

12.1.3.2 *Alternext*

12.09　Alternext is designed for small and/or recently incorporated companies, offering a less stringent regulatory environment than the Euronext Paris market.

12.1.3.3 *The Professional Compartment*

12.10　The Professional Compartment provides a platform for the listing of shares as well as specialist securities, including debt securities, convertible or exchangeable securities of any denomination. While all these types of securities could be admitted to listing on the regular market, they are generally not suitable for a retail offering given their specialist nature, and thus an offering through the Professional Compartment's facility to professional or institutional investors could be better suited for such types of securities. Given the recent creation of the Professional Compartment and the fact that the advantages of such a listing are limited for issuers whose shares are already admitted to listing on the main board, to date, this platform has not, however, been particularly used for such specialist securities.

12.11　Note that the Professional Compartment is not a separate market but rather a compartment of the Euronext Paris market, and thus a compartment of a regulated market. Issuers with securities listed on the Professional Compartment are, however, exempt from certain requirements normally applicable in case of listing of securities on a regulated market as a result of specific exemptions provided by applicable French laws and regulations.

12.1.4 Legislative overview

12.1.4.1 *The French Monetary and Financial Code*

12.12　The French Monetary and Financial Code, as amended from time to time, is the principal legislation through which France implements the EU directives relating to listing, admission to trading on a regulated market, and offers of securities to the public. As discussed above, the AMF is empowered under the French Monetary and Financial Code to create rules for these activities, as well as rules governing transparency and other continuing obligations of issuers. These rules constitute a single set of regulations entitled the General Regulations of the AMF (*Règlement général de l'AMF*).

12.1.4.2 *Listing Rules*

In addition to rules set forth in the AMF's General Regulations that apply to the admission to trading on a regulated market, Euronext has established listing requirements that must be complied with by applicants. **12.13**

12.1.4.3 *Prospectus rules*

The prospectus rules set forth in the AMF's General Regulations implement the Prospectus Directive and the Prospectus Regulation. **12.14**

12.1.4.4 *Disclosure and transparency rules*

The disclosure and transparency rules set forth in the AMF's General Regulations implement the Market Abuse Directive and the Transparency Directive. The other sources for disclosure and transparency rules are the French Commercial Code and the French Monetary and Financial Code. **12.15**

These rules constitute a significant part of the continuing obligations to which companies must adhere as long as they are admitted to listing. They govern the disclosure of inside information, the publication of periodic financial reports, the notification of major holdings of shares or voting rights, the dissemination of regulated information and communications with shareholders. In addition, listed companies who are involved in takeovers are regulated by certain provisions of the French Commercial Code as well as provisions of the General Regulations of the AMF relating to tender offer. **12.16**

12.1.4.5 *Other provisions*

In addition to the foregoing rules, listed issuers must comply with a number of other regulatory regimes, including the criminal market abuse regime provided by the French Monetary and Financial Code. Participants must also comply with French solicitation rules provided by the French Monetary and Financial Code in relation to the offer, acquisition or sale of securities in France. **12.17**

12.1.4.6 *AMF guidance*

While the legal and normative status of AMF guidance is not entirely clear, the AMF adopts guidance under various forms (such as recommendations, positions, Q&As and annual reports) which is generally considered an important source of **12.18** interpretation, at least in respect of the AMF's General Regulations as well as certain market practices.

12.2 The Prospectus

12.2.1 Applicable law

12.19 The Prospectus Directive was implemented in France pursuant to French law No 2005-842 of 26 July 2005, which was codified under Articles L.411-1 et seq. and L.621-8 et seq. of the French Monetary and Financial Code. Such rules were recently amended by French Ordinance No 2009-80 of 22 January 2009, which was designed to improve the harmonization of French rules with those of the Prospectus Directive; accordingly, the old French law concept of '*appel public à l'épargne*' and the resulting status of companies having made a public offering (*société faisant appel public à l'épargne*) were abandoned, as further discussed below.

12.20 Article L.412-1 of the French Monetary and Financial Code sets forth the general prospectus requirement applicable in connection with an offer of securities to the public in France or the admission of securities to trading on a French regulated market.

12.21 Title 1 of Book II of the General Regulations of the AMF (as amended on 2 April 2009, following the reform resulting from French Ordinance No 2009-80 of 22 January 2009) provides the regulatory framework for the prospectus requirement in connection with an offer of securities to the public in France or the admission of securities to trading on a regulated market, and thus represents the main source of French rules implementing the Prospectus Directive. In particular, the AMF's General Regulations define the exact scope of the prospectus requirement as well as exemptions therefrom, the filing and AMF approval process, rules applicable to the publication and dissemination of the prospectus, the required content of the prospectus, its prescribed language, and the persons responsible for prospectuses.

12.22 These rules are supplemented by AMF guidelines entitled Instruction No 2005-11 of 13 December 2005, as amended from time to time,[2] relating to disclosure requirements for public offerings, which contain a detailed description of requirements applicable to the filing with and approval by the AMF of the prospectus, the conditions required in order to benefit from certain exemptions from the prospectus requirement,[3] and the warnings that must be included in the summary

---

[2] Including on 6 April 2009, as a result of French Ordinance No 2009-80 of 22 January 2009.
[3] See Section 12.2.2.2 below.

and elsewhere in the prospectus. The required content of the prospectus summary is further detailed in a Recommendation of the AMF dated 4 October 2007.

The developments set forth below do not address French solicitation rules deriving from Articles L.341-1 et seq. of the French Monetary and Financial Code.[4]   **12.23**

12.2.2 Requirement for a prospectus

12.2.2.1 The requirement

In accordance with the Prospectus Directive,[5] French law provides that a company is required to register a prospectus in the following two situations: (i) when transferable securities are offered to the public in France; or (ii) when transferable securities are admitted to trading on a regulated market in France.   **12.24**

The implementation in France of the Prospectus Directive in 2005[6] was limited to the harmonization of prospectus triggers while retaining the French concept of 'appel public à l'épargne'. Under that framework, a company making an 'appel public à l'épargne' (for example, a public offering of securities, whether or not such securities are listed) acquired a status of 'public company' (société faisant appel public à l'épargne), which triggered certain ongoing reporting requirements. The concept of 'société faisant appel public à l'épargne' has been eliminated from French law in connection with the reform resulting from French ordinance No 2009-80 of 22 January 2009 and the notion of 'appel public à l'épargne' has been replaced with the better harmonized notions of 'public offer of securities' and/or 'admission of securities to listing', as the case may be. Accordingly, prospectus requirements under French law are currently triggered by the two following situations, as contemplated by the Prospectus Directive: (i) a public offering of securities in France or (ii) the admission of securities to trading on a regulated market. These definitions match exactly those of the prospectus triggers under the Prospectus Directive.   **12.25**

In order to properly understand the prospectus triggers, a number of terms used above require further explanation.   **12.26**

Securities: While the Prospectus Directive[7] refers to the term 'transferable securities' to trigger the requirement for a prospectus, French law[8] refers to the term 'securities' (titres financiers), which include: (i) equity securities (including shares,   **12.27**

---

[4] Such rules are not applicable to certain transactions relating to financial instruments. In particular, unsolicited contacts with qualified investors do not fall within the scope of solicitation (*démarchage*) rules (Article L.341-2 1° of the French Monetary and Financial Code).

[5] Prospectus Directive Article 1(1).

[6] See Section 12.2.1 above.

[7] Prospectus Directive Articles 1(1) and 2(1)(a).

[8] French Monetary and Financial Code Article L.412-1; General Regulations of the AMF Article 211-1.

whether ordinary or preferred, and securities giving access to equity capital such as warrants or convertible bonds) issued by joint-stock companies (*sociétés par actions*); (ii) debt securities, excluding bills of exchange and certificates of deposit; and (iii) units or shares issued by collective investment undertakings.[9]

12.28 Under French law, only those forms of legal entities that are expressly authorized by law to make public offerings of securities or to issue negotiable securities may do so. If this rule, provided by Article 1841 of the French civil code, is violated, then the securities issued or the contracts entered into are void. Apart from certain legal forms of entities that are specifically authorized by law to that effect,[10] only joint stock companies (*sociétés par actions*) incorporated as *sociétés anonymes* and *sociétés en commandite simple* are legally generally authorized to make public offerings of securities or to issue negotiable securities. A *société par actions simplifiée*— which is a type of limited liability company—may not make a public offering of securities or have its shares admitted to trading on a regulated market; such a company may, however, issue negotiable securities and market them pursuant to private placement rules.

12.29 French law treats as 'securities' (*titres financiers*), and subjects to the same regime, equivalent securities or rights in a financial instrument issued by an entity pursuant to a foreign law.[11]

12.30 Despite the inclusion of units or shares of collective investment undertakings in the definition of securities under French law—although not included in the definition of 'transferable securities' under the Prospectus Directive[12]—French law generally excludes such instruments from eligibility for the benefits of the Prospectus Directive and from the scope of public offering/private placement rules, except for certain specific collective investment undertakings that are treated as companies[13] or unless certain specific conditions allowing such similar treatment are satisfied. In this respect, the AMF has taken the position that shares of foreign limited partnerships may be considered qualifying securities for purposes of public offering rules if the issuing entity is a closed-end entity (i) incorporated in another EU member state or (ii) incorporated in a third jurisdiction and having characteristics similar to those of a French *société anonyme* or *société en commandite par actions*. Failing satisfaction of these conditions, the AMF considers that commercialization in

---

[9] French Monetary and Financial Code Article L.211-1.

[10] Such as, for example, the *société civile de placement collectif immobilier*.

[11] French Monetary and Financial Code Article L.211-41.

[12] Prospectus Directive Article 1(2)(a).

[13] The collective investment schemes include: securitization vehicles, certain specific real estate investment funds (*sociétés civiles de placement immobilier* or *SCPI*), *sociétés d'épargne forestière* and *sociétés d'investissement à capital variable* or *SICAV* (as referred to in Article L.214-1 paragraphs 2), 3), 4) and 6), as a result of the exclusion provided by French Monetary and Financial Code Article L.411-3).

France of the shares of the foreign limited partnership is subject to the prior author-ization regime applicable to the commercialization in France of units of collective investment schemes and that such securities are not eligible for the benefits of French law provisions implementing the Prospectus Directive.[14]

Offer to the public: Subject to certain exceptions, any of the following transactions **12.31** constitute a public offer of securities as defined by Article L.411-1 of the French Monetary and Financial Code: (i) a communication to persons in any form and by any means presenting sufficient information on the terms of the offer and the securities to be offered, so as to enable an investor to decide to purchase or subscribe to these securities; or (ii) the placement of securities through financial intermediaries. This definition conforms to that provided in the Prospectus Directive.[15]

Private placement rules: By way of exception to the definition of an offer to the **12.32** public, the following transactions do not constitute 'offers to the public' under French law and are customarily referred to as private placements. As indicated below, in most instances, such definitions—which are derived from a combina-tion of provisions of the French Monetary and Financial Code and the General Regulations of the AMF[16]—match those of the Prospectus Directive:

(a) Offers of equity securities issued by joint-stock companies or debt securities (excluding bills of exchange and certificates of deposit), which the issuer is legally authorized to offer to the public,[17] if the transaction has one of the fol-lowing characteristics:

  (i) the total amount offered and sold is less than EUR 100,000, or its foreign currency equivalent, calculated over a 12-month period from the date of the first transaction; [18]

  (ii) the total amount offered and sold is between EUR 100,000 and EUR 2,500,000, or their foreign currency equivalent, calculated over a 12-month period from the date of the first transaction, and the transac-tions in question, over the 12-month period, relate to securities account-ing for no more than 50% of the capital of the issuer;

  (iii) investors must acquire the relevant securities for a total consideration of at least EUR 50,000, or its foreign currency equivalent, per investor and per transaction; [19] or

---

[14] AMF Position relating to the commercialization in France of limited partnerships. 7 April 2008.

[15] Prospectus Directive Article 2(1)(d).

[16] French Monetary and Financial Code Article L.411-2-I; General Regulations of the AMF Article 211-2.

[17] In addition, such offers may also be made by French *sociétés par actions simplifiées*.

[18] Prospectus Directive Article 3(2)(e).

[19] Prospectus Directive Article 3(2)(c).

(iv) the transaction relates to securities with a denomination of at least EUR 50,000, or its foreign currency equivalent.[20]

(b) Offers of securities addressed solely to:[21]

(i) persons providing a portfolio of management investment services on behalf of third parties;[22] and/or

(ii) qualified investors or a restricted circle of investors, provided that, in each case, they are acting for their own account.[23]

12.33 Under French law, a 'qualified investor' is defined by Article L.411-2 II 2 of the French Monetary and Financial Code as a person or an entity having the necessary skills and resources to understand the risks inherent in transactions relating to financial instruments. A list of the categories of qualified investors is set forth in Article D.411-1 of the French Monetary and Financial Code.

12.34 A restricted circle of investors is also defined by Article L.411-2 II 2 of the French Monetary and Financial Code and is composed of persons, other than qualified investors, whose number is less than a number currently set at 100 persons.

12.35 *Regulated market*: The French definition of a regulated market is set out in Article L.421-1 of the French Monetary and Financial Code and matches that provided in MiFID, which states that a regulated market is a 'multilateral system operated and/or managed by a market operator, which brings together or facilitates the bringing together of multiple third-party buying and selling interests in financial instruments—in the system and in accordance with its non discretionary rules—in a way that results in a contract, in respect of the financial instruments admitted to trading under its rules and/or systems, and which is authorized and functions regularly and in accordance with the provisions of Title III of MiFID.

12.36 In France, Euronext Paris, the MATIF (international futures regulated market) and the MONEP (regulated market for negotiable options) are the three regulated markets, which were officially recognized by the Minister of Economy, further to a proposal of the AMF.[24] Following a reform enacted in December 2007, NYSE Euronext created a compartment of Euronext Paris customarily

---

[20] Prospectus Directive Article 3(2)(d).

[21] French Monetary and Financial Code Article L.411-2-II.

[22] Collective investment schemes and their management companies are included in the definition of qualified investors set forth in the Prospectus Directive; they represent a distinct category of investors that may be solicited in a private placement in France because, by their nature, they invest on behalf of third parties and would therefore not satisfy the requirement applicable to qualified investors that they must act for their own account.

[23] Prospectus Directive Article 3(2)(a) and (b).

[24] French Monetary and Financial Code Article L.421-4. The AMF establishes the list of the regulated markets (see French Monetary and Financial Code Article D.421-6) in its general annual report.

designated as the 'Professional Compartment', which is a regulated market designed to admit securities without a public offering. Listing of securities on such market either follows a private placement or is a secondary listing of securities with a primary listing on another stock exchange. Accordingly, while the listing of securities on this compartment constitutes a listing of securities on a regulated market, the prospectus requirements are simplified.[25] In addition, ongoing reporting requirements applicable to issuers whose shares are listed on the Professional Compartment are simplified. Secondary trading of securities on the Professional Compartment by a person other than a qualified investor is possible only without prior solicitation and only after special warnings have been given to such person by its broker.

Non-regulated markets in France include Alternext, which is designed for small- and medium-sized entities (SMEs), and the *Marché Libre*. Admission to trading of securities on Alternext may be made pursuant to one of the two following procedures: (i) an offer to the public for a total amount of at least EUR 2,500,000, which triggers the requirement for a prospectus; or (ii) a private placement for a total amount of at least EUR 5 million allocated among at least five qualified investors, which does not trigger the prospectus requirement.[26] Admission to trading on the *Marché Libre* triggers the requirement for a prospectus if the listing involves an offer to the public. **12.37**

12.2.2.2 Exemptions

The circumstances in which a prospectus will be required, as described above, are qualified by a series of exemptions. These exemptions apply in addition to the limitation to the requirements that arise from the scope of the terms 'securities' and 'offer to the public' as defined above in Section 12.2.2.1. **12.38**

12.2.2.2.1 'Public offer' prospectus trigger—exemptions The obligation to publish a prospectus does not apply to offers to the public of the following types of securities:[27] **12.39**

* shares issued in substitution for shares of the same class already issued, if the issuing of such new shares does not involve any increase in the issued capital;[28]

---

[25] The statutory auditors are not required to issue a letter confirming the results of their review of the prospectus (the *'lettre de fin de travaux'*), no sponsor bank is required to issue an affidavit and the prospectus and its summary may be drafted in English, without any translation.

[26] The issuer must however establish an information document in accordance with the market rules established by Euronext.

[27] Prospectus Directive Article 4(1); General Regulations of the AMF Article 212-4.

[28] Prospectus Directive Article 4(1)(a); General Regulations of the AMF Article 212-4 1°.

- securities offered in connection with a takeover by means of an exchange offer, provided that a document subject to the AMF review and containing information equivalent to that of the prospectus,[29] is made available by the issuer;[30]
- securities offered in connection with a merger, a de-merger, or a spin-off, provided that either (i) a document describing the number and nature of the securities and the reasons for and details of the admission is made available by the issuer, if the transaction concerns securities accounting for no more than 10% of the equity capital of the issuer,[31] or (ii) a document subject to the AMF review and containing information equivalent to that of a prospectus[32] is made available by the issuer, if the transaction concerns securities accounting for more than 10% of the equity capital of the issuer;[33]
- shares offered, allotted or to be allotted free of charge to existing shareholders and dividends paid in the form of shares of the same class as the shares in respect of which such dividends are paid, provided that a document describing the number and nature of the securities and the reasons for and details of the offer[34] is made available by the issuer;[35] and
- securities offered, allotted or to be allotted to existing or former directors, company officers[36] or employees by their employer or an affiliated undertaking, provided that such securities are of the same class as those already admitted to trading on a regulated market in an EEA member state and that a document describing the number and nature of the securities and the reasons for and details of the offer[37] is made available by the issuer.[38]

---

[29] Article 11 of the instruction No 2005-11 from the AMF of 13 December 2005 details the required content of such document. It refers to General Regulations of the AMF Article 231-28 relating to disclosures about the legal, financial, accounting and other characteristics of the offeror and the target company in the context of takeover. Annex I to the above-mentioned instruction provides further details on the content of such document.

[30] Prospectus Directive Article 4(1)(b); General Regulations of the AMF Article 212-4 2°.

[31] Article 12 of the instruction No 2005-11 from the AMF of 13 December 2005.

[32] Article 12 and Annex II of the instruction No 2005-11 from the AMF of 13 December 2005 details the required content of such document.

[33] Prospectus Directive Article 4(1)(c); General Regulations of the AMF Article 212-4 3°.

[34] Article 13 and Annex III of the instruction No 2005-11 from the AMF of 13 December 2005 details the required content of such document.

[35] Prospectus Directive Article 4(1)(d); General Regulations of the AMF Article 212-4 4°.

[36] The president of the board of directors (*président du conseil d'administration*), the chief executive officer (*directeur général*), general managers (*directeurs généraux délégués*), the members of the executive board (*membres du directoire*) or the general manager (*gérant*).

[37] Article 14 and Annex IV of the instruction No 2005-11 from the AMF of 13 December 2005 details the required content of such document.

[38] Prospectus Directive Article 4(1)(e); General Regulations of the AMF Article 212-4 5°.

12.2.2.2.2 'Regulated market' prospectus trigger—exemptions The obliga- **12.40**
tion to publish a prospectus does not apply to the admission to trading on a regulated market of the following types of securities:[39]

- shares representing, over a period of 12 months, less than 10% of the number
  of shares of the same class already admitted to trading on the same regulated
  market;[40]
- shares issued in substitution for shares of the same class already admitted to
  trading on the same regulated market, if the issuance of the new shares does not
  involve any increase in the issuer's capital;[41]
- securities offered in connection with a takeover by means of an exchange offer,
  provided that a document subject to AMF review and containing information
  equivalent to that of the prospectus[42] is made available by the issuer;[43]
- securities offered in connection with a merger, a de-merger, or a spin-off, provided that either (i) a document describing the number and nature of the securities and the reasons for and details of the admission is made available by the
  issuer, if the transaction concerns securities accounting for no more than 10%
  of the capital of the issuer,[44] or (ii) a document subject to AMF review and containing information equivalent to that of a prospectus[45] is made available by the
  issuer, if the transaction concerns securities accounting for more than 10% of
  the equity capital of the issuer;[46]
- shares offered, allotted or to be allotted free of charge to existing shareholders and dividends paid in the form of shares of the same class as the shares
  in respect of which such dividends are paid, provided that such shares are
  of the same class as those already admitted to trading on the same regulated
  market and that a document describing the number and nature of the securities
  and the reasons for and details of the admission[47] is made available by the
  issuer;[48]
- securities offered, allotted or to be allotted to existing or former directors,
  company officers[49] or employees by their employer or an affiliated undertaking,

---

[39] Prospectus Directive Article 4(2); General Regulations of the AMF Article 212-5.
[40] Prospectus Directive Article 4(2)(a); General Regulations of the AMF Article 212-5 1°.
[41] Prospectus Directive Article 4(2)(b); General Regulations of the AMF Article 212-5 2°.
[42] See Section 12.2.2.2.1 above for details regarding the content of such document.
[43] Prospectus Directive Article 4(2)(c); General Regulations of the AMF Article 212-5 3°.
[44] Article 12 of the instruction No 2005-11 from the AMF of 13 December 2005.
[45] See Section 12.2.2.2.1 above for details regarding the content of such document.
[46] Prospectus Directive Article 4(2)(d); General Regulations of the AMF Article 212-5 4°.
[47] See Section 12.2.2.2.1 above for details regarding the content of such document.
[48] Prospectus Directive Article 4(2)(e); General Regulations of the AMF Article 212-5 5°.
[49] The term 'company officers' refers to the president of the board of directors (*président de conseil d'administration*), the general manager (*directeur général*), managers (*directeurs généraux délégués*), the members of the executive board (*membres du directoire*) or the manager (*gérant*).

provided that such securities are of the same class as those already admitted to trading on the same regulated market and that a document describing the number and nature of the securities and the reasons for and details of the admission[50] is made available by the issuer;[51]

- shares resulting from the conversion or exchange of other securities, or from the exercise or rights conferred by other securities, provided that such shares are of the same class as the shares already admitted to trading on the same regulated market;[52] and

- securities already admitted to trading on another regulated market, under certain conditions.[53]

12.41 In all other cases, if an issuer wishes its securities to be admitted to an EEA regulated market, it must produce a prospectus complying with the Prospectus Directive.

12.42 **12.2.2.2.3 Other exemptions** By way of exception, French law provides that the offer to the public or the admission to trading on a regulated market of the following types of securities does not trigger the requirement for the issuing entity to produce a prospectus:[54]

(i) securities unconditionally and irrevocably guaranteed or issued by an EU or EEA member state;

(ii) securities issued by a public international organization to which France belongs;

(iii) securities issued by the European Central Bank or the central bank of an EU or EEA member state; and

(iv) securities issued by a collective investment undertaking (subject to certain exceptions); as indicated in Section 12.2.2.1 above, French law generally excludes the commercialization in France of such instruments from the scope of public offering/private placement rules, except for certain specific collective investment undertakings that are treated like companies[55] or unless certain specific conditions allowing such treatment are satisfied.

---

[50] See Section 2.2.2.1 above for details regarding the content of such document.

[51] Prospectus Directive Article 4(2)(f); General Regulations of the AMF Article 212-5 6°.

[52] Prospectus Directive Article 4(2)(g); General Regulations of the AMF Article 212-5 7°.

[53] Prospectus Directive Article 4(2)(h); General Regulations of the AMF Article 212-5 8°.

[54] Prospectus Directive Article 1(2); French Monetary and Financial Code Article L.411-3.

[55] The following collective investment schemes are concerned: securitization vehicles, certain specific real estate investment funds *(sociétés civiles de placement immobilier* or *SCPI)*, *sociétés d'épargne forestière* and *sociétés d'investissement à capital variable* or *SICAV* (as referred to in Article L.214-1 paragraphs 2), 3), 4) and 6), as a result of the exclusion provided by Article L.411-3 of the French Monetary and Financial Code).

12.2.2.3 Employee incentive schemes

The issuance of shares by an issuer to its employees pursuant to an employee incentive scheme may, under certain circumstances described below, trigger a prospectus requirement.

12.43

12.2.2.3.1 'Regulated market' prospectus trigger In principle, the offer of securities to existing or former directors or employees by their employer could be considered an offer of securities to the public, to the extent that it involves a communication of offer terms designed to permit the offerees to make an investment decision or a placement through financial intermediaries, if applicable.

12.44

By way of exception, such an offer would not constitute an offer to the public if the number of employees concerned in France is fewer than 100.

12.45

If the private placement exception is not available, the public offer prospectus requirement is not necessarily applicable since the following exemptions provided by Article 212-5 of the General Regulations of the AMF may be available:

12.46

(i) the securities offered are shares representing, over a period of 12 months, less than 10% of the number of shares of the same class already admitted to trading on the same regulated market;[56] or

(ii) the securities offered are of the same class as those already admitted to trading on the same regulated market.

12.2.2.3.2 'Offer to the public' prospectus trigger In principle, the offer of securities to existing or former directors or employees by their employer could be considered an offer of securities to the public, to the extent that it involves a communication of offer terms designed to permit the offerees to make an investment decision, solicitation or a placement through financial intermediaries, if applicable.

12.47

By way of exception, such an offer would not constitute an offer to the public if the number of employees concerned in France is fewer than 100. In addition, such an offer would also constitute a private placement if (i) the total amount of the offer is less than EUR 100,000; or (ii) the total amount of the offer is between EUR 100,000 and EUR 2,500,000 and the transaction relates to securities accounting for no more than 50% of the equity capital of the issuer.

12.48

If the private placement exception is not applicable, the 'public offer' prospectus requirement is not necessarily applicable since the following exemption provided by paragraph 5°) of Article 212-4 of the General Regulations of the AMF may be available: the securities offered are of the same class as those already admitted to

12.49

---

[56] Prospectus Directive Article 4(2)(a); General Regulations of the AMF Article 212-5 1°.

trading on the same regulated market. Accordingly, this exemption is not available to entities whose shares are not listed on an EEA regulated market.

12.50   In practice, however, securities offered to employees in connection with employee incentive schemes are generally subscribed through employee savings schemes in the form of mutual funds, which is generally considered as excluding any offer to the public, regardless of the number of employees holding shares in the relevant fund, and the offer of interests in mutual funds is not subject to the prospectus requirement but rather to distinct rules applicable to mutual funds.

12.51   In addition, as regards the grant of free shares pursuant to Article L.225-197-1 of the French Commercial Code by French issuers or similar transactions made by foreign entities, the AMF generally considers that in the absence of any consideration paid by the beneficiaries for the subscription or acquisition of such shares, their grant does not constitute an offer of securities and therefore, no prospectus requirement applies. A similar position has been adopted in respect of stock option plans on the basis that they do not constitute transferable securities.[57]

12.2.2.4 Overseas rights issues

12.52   In instances where a foreign company effects a rights issue, the question arises as to whether the issuance of the rights or their exercise by shareholders located in France may constitute a public offering of securities in France or otherwise trigger a prospectus requirement.

12.53   Two situations must be distinguished: (i) the shares of the issuer are listed on a regulated market in France or (ii) no such listing exists or is sought.

12.54   **12.2.2.4.1 The shares of the issuer are listed on a regulated market in France**   If the shares of the issuer are listed on a regulated market in France, an application for listing on the French regulated market of the new shares to be issued in connection with the rights issue will also have to be made. In connection with that listing application, a prospectus will be required, unless an exemption is available.

12.55   In practice, Euronext and the AMF normally require the rights to be listed in France so as to facilitate their trading by the French shareholders. In that case, the holders of such rights would most likely not qualify for a private placement and it would not be possible to restrict their exercise. Accordingly, an offer of securities

---

[57] Position AMF, AMF Monthly Review No 39, September 2007, page 29. CESR has adopted the same interpretation (cf. 'Frequently Asked Questions regarding Prospectuses': 9th updated version—September 2009; questions 5 and 6).

to the public is made in France and, to that effect, a public offer and listing prospectus must be prepared and registered with the AMF.

If the issuer is an entity incorporated in an EU or EEA member state, the prospectus that it prepares in connection with the rights issue and registers in its home member state (or in the member state where the competent regulator is located) may be passported into France. In that case, only the summary of the prospectus must be translated into French.

12.56

If the issuing entity is incorporated in a third country, it may passport into France a prospectus conforming to the requirements of the Prospectus Directive registered in another jurisdiction of the EU or of the EEA where the competent regulator for such issuing entity is located, failing which, if the AMF is the competent authority pursuant to the Prospectus Directive, such issuer must prepare a prospectus in French that conforms to the requirements of the Prospectus Directive. If, however, the securities are admitted to listing in France and there is no public offering of the securities in France—which could be the case, for example, if the shares are admitted to trading on the Professional Compartment of Euronext Paris—the prospectus may be drafted in French or in English (and no translation of the summary into French would be required if the listing is on the Professional Compartment of Euronext Paris).

12.57

12.2.2.4.2 The shares of the issuer are not listed on a regulated market in France and no such listing is sought If the shares of the issuer are not listed on a regulated market in France and no such listing is sought in connection with the rights issue, the questions at stake are (i) whether the rights issue, in and of itself, constitutes a public offer of securities and (ii) whether the exercise of such rights constitutes a public offer of securities in France subject to a prospectus requirement.

12.58

As regards the first question, while there is no definitive authority on the subject, there are serious arguments supporting the view that the issuance and receipt of the rights do not, in and of themselves, trigger a prospectus requirement. The main argument that would support this analysis is that the rights are issued for free and the receipt of the rights does not require that any investment decision be made by the relevant shareholders—while the notion of public offer of securities should be considered as involving an investment decision. In this respect, the information given in connection with the grant of rights could be considered mere information and not a communication of offer terms sufficiently precise so as to permit an investment decision within the meaning of the definition of an 'offer to the public'. In addition, the issuance of the rights is imposed by local company law applicable to the issuer and failing to issue such rights to all shareholders would result in the issuer breaching applicable company law and

12.59

shareholders' patrimonial rights; it could, therefore, be seen as a mere protection of patrimonial rights, with a view to permitting the sale of the rights on the market, and not necessarily an offer of securities if the subscription of the shares is restricted.[58]

12.60 On the other hand, the exercise of the rights and the resulting subscription of the shares may involve a public offering and, thus, the answer to the second question depends on the exact shareholding base of each issuer. If an issuer determines that its shareholder base in France is only composed of (i) qualified investors and/or (ii) a restricted circle of investors, no prospectus requirement would apply since the issuer may be deemed to be making a private placement in France, exempt from the prospectus requirement. Absent such a determination, the exercise of the rights and subscription of new shares by French investors (other than qualified investors participating in a global private placement) may only be permitted if a prospectus is registered in, or passported into, France. It could be argued, however, that if no communication is made in France in respect of the terms of the offer permitting a shareholder to make an investment decision, and if no financial intermediary makes any placement in France, no prospectus should be required.

12.2.3 Preliminary prospectuses

12.2.3.1 *Market practice*

12.61 Since a reform of the prospectus approval procedure that took place in 2002, there is no requirement, under French law, to register a final prospectus that includes the final terms and conditions pursuant to which securities are being issued, provided that such terms and conditions are consistent with the range or indicative terms contained in the prospectus initially registered.

12.62 Accordingly, in the context of French market practice, the notions of preliminary or final prospectuses are generally not relevant. In practice, when a public offer in France is made simultaneously with an international private placement, the preliminary international offering circular prepared for such placement is dated the same date as the French prospectus and the final international offering circular is dated the date when all final terms (including pricing) are determined, i.e. on the date when a pricing press release is published in France in connection with the public offer in France.

---

[58] Note that CESR considers that a rights issue constitutes a public offer and that the mere communication of information regarding the rights by a custodian in a member state other than the member state where the public offer takes place, this communication should not constitute a public offer. (cf. 'Frequently Asked Questions Regarding Prospectuses': 9th updated version; September 2009; questions 63 and 42).

The prospectus that is registered with the AMF and receives its visa upon completion of the approval process is, in principle, the only prospectus prepared in connection with an offer to the public of securities.

12.63

The AMF, however, imposes certain requirements applicable to the terms and conditions set forth in such prospectus.

12.64

As a general rule, the General Regulations of the AMF provide that, if the final offer price and the final number of securities offered is not included in the approved prospectus, the issuer must include: (i) the criteria or basis for determination of such final price and number of securities, or (ii) the maximum offer price.[59] Failing inclusion of such alternative information to the final price and number of securities in the prospectus, acceptance by investors of the acquisition or subscription of the securities offered may be withdrawn by such investors for at least a two-day period following publication of the final price and definitive number of securities offered.

12.65

In connection with an initial public offering, in addition and by way of exception to the foregoing requirements derived from the implementation of the Prospectus Directive, the AMF requires that a price range be included in the prospectus.[60] The extent of the required price range is +/- 10% of an indicative price, with the higher end of the range being a maximum price.[61] The issuer has the option to provide that the lower end of the range is 'imperative' or 'indicative'. If the lower end of the range is imperative, the final price may not be lower than such lower end without a supplementary prospectus being registered; if the lower end of the range is only indicative and the final price is below such lower end, the issuer is required to publish a supplementary prospectus only if such lower price would make the terms and conditions of the offer incompatible with the information contained in the prospectus in respect of the purpose of the offer and the use of proceeds.

12.66

This rule is designed essentially to protect investors and avoid a situation where investors are required to place irrevocable purchase orders absent parameters to determine the size of the free float as well as the amount of dilution, both of which are considered material information in connection with an IPO.

12.67

Generally, when an offer involves a public offering, the AMF requires, in principle, the size of the offer range not to exceed a certain percentage of the number of

12.68

---

[59] General Regulations of the AMF Article 212-17.
[60] AMF Position of 30 June 2009. *Position de l'AMF relative à l'assouplissement de la règle d'encadrement du prix lors d'une introduction en bourse.*
[61] Under the previously applicable position of the AMF published in 2002, the range was +/- 7.5% around an indicative price. Cf. *Commission des Opérations de Bourse. Bulletin mensuel n°370—* July-August 2002, page15 s. '*Mise en œuvre de la seconde étape de la réforme du visa.*'

securities offered: 25% in the case of secondary offers, and 15% in the case of offerings with a primary and a secondary component. Since these requirements are not included in the AMF's General Regulations but are rather the AMF's interpretive positions, the AMF has a certain degree of flexibility to permit exceptions on a case-by-case basis. In practice, the AMF's predecessor authority agreed to certain exceptions to such ranges in light of the exceptional size of certain offerings.[62]

12.2.3.2 *The advertisement regime*

12.69 Advertisements relating to an offer to the public or the admission to trading on a regulated market of securities must be transmitted to the AMF prior to their publication and must be consistent with the information included (or that will be included) in the prospectus[63] and comply with certain other content requirements.[64] In particular, advertisements must refer to the prospectus and specifically refer to the risk factors section of the prospectus. In addition, the AMF may require a mention of certain exceptional characteristics of the offer, the issuer or the guarantor.

12.70 In addition, the prospectus itself must be made available in the same manner as other regulated information,[65] and must also be posted on the AMF website.[66]

12.2.4 Supplementary prospectuses

12.2.4.1 *When a supplementary prospectus is required*

12.71 In addition to the circumstances referred to in Section 12.2.3.1 above, if following the approval of a prospectus but prior to the final closing of the offer or the time when trading on the regulated market begins (whichever is later), a significant new fact, material error or inaccuracy in respect of the information provided in the prospectus that could materially affect the assessment of the securities arises or is identified, the issuer is required to publish a supplementary prospectus that is subject to formal approval by the AMF.[67]

---

[62] The main example of such an exception dates back to 2001, i.e. prior to the publication of the 2002 guidelines referred to above.

[63] General Regulations of the AMF Article 212-29.

[64] General Regulations of the AMF Article 212-28.

[65] See Section 12.3.6.3 below.

[66] General Regulations of the AMF Article 212-27 IV.

[67] Prospectus Directive Article 16(1); French Monetary and Financial Code Article L.621-8-VIII; General Regulations of the AMF Article 212-25-I.

12.2.4.2 *Supplementary prospectuses in practice*

Registering a supplementary prospectus involves delays in an offer; in practice, it is rather exceptional. When such a registration is required, the supplementary prospectus may incorporate by reference certain sections of the base prospectus.

12.72

12.2.4.3 *The 'two day put'*

Investors who have agreed to acquire or subscribe securities before a supplementary prospectus is published are entitled to withdraw their acceptance for a period of at least two trading days after the day on which the supplementary prospectus is published.[68]

12.73

12.2.5 Preparing a prospectus: dealing with the AMF

12.2.5.1 *The AMF approval process*

The AMF must approve any prospectus before its publication. Registration of a prospectus with the AMF is materialized by the so-called visa being granted by the AMF, with a specific number and date.

12.74

The visa is an administrative decision. It must be published on the AMF's official website and third parties may challenge in court such administrative decision within ten days from the date of publication.[69] The Paris Court of Appeals is the competent court to review such challenges, despite the administrative nature of the decision.[70] Pursuant to established case law, the AMF visa does not involve a review or opinion by the AMF with respect to the offer terms or the financial or accounting information included in the prospectus, but merely reflects the verification by the AMF that the prospectus is complete and comprehensible, and that the information contained in such prospectus is consistent.

12.75

Accordingly, the AMF may approve a prospectus only if it complies with the requirements set forth in the General Regulations of the AMF and if the AMF has received all the responsibility statements required from the relevant participants in the transaction. The filing of the draft prospectus must be accompanied by all the information and documents required by the AMF for its review, failing which the AMF is entitled to postpone its review.[71] The AMF issues a notice of filing to the issuer within ten trading days of the date on which the file is complete.

12.76

---

[68] Prospectus Directive Article 16(2); General Regulation of the AMF Article 212-25-II.
[69] French Monetary and Financial Code Article R.621-44.
[70] French Monetary and Financial Code Article L.621-30.
[71] General Regulations of the AMF Articles 212-6, 212-20 and 212-21. See the instruction No 2005-11 from the AMF of 13 December 2005 for detailed information as to the documents to be filed with the AMF together with the draft prospectus.

12.77   The applicable maximum review period by the AMF depends on the circumstances of the offer (e.g. IPO or transaction contemplated by an issuer whose securities are already listed) and the regime applicable to the base prospectus of the issuer. In any case, however, the time period is suspended each time requests for additional information are made to the issuer.

12.78   In principle, in connection with an initial public offering, a complete filing is required to have been made: (i) for the registration document, at least 20 trading days prior to any proposed registration date (i.e. the contemplated launch date of the offer or the preceding business day), and (ii) for the securities note, at least five trading days prior to any proposed registration date.

12.79   In connection with subsequent offer or listing prospectuses, subject to the exceptions described in Section 12.2.5.2 below, the complete filing must be made at least ten trading days prior to any scheduled visa date.

12.80   In addition, before issuing its approval, the AMF may request additional inquiries by the statutory auditors or ask for an audit to be carried out by an external specialist if it considers the due diligence by statutory auditors to be insufficient.

12.2.5.2   *The simplified procedure*

12.81   The conditions of applicability of the simplified procedure depend on whether an issuer has established a *document de référence* and the status of such document.[72]

12.82   For issuers that file a *document de référence* (which qualifies as a registration document within the meaning of the Prospectus Directive) that is subject to the prior review of the AMF and that was registered with the AMF, a complete filing of all documents required for the approval of a prospectus must be made at least five trading days (instead of ten trading days) prior to any scheduled visa date. [73]

12.83   In addition, issuers that file a *document de référence* that is not subject to the prior review of the AMF may also benefit from a simplified procedure for the review and approval of prospectuses (generally referred to as 'fast path') in connection with transactions for which a model standard securities note and summary have been established by the AMAFI[74] and approved by the AMF.[75] If the AMF confirms within two trading days that the simplified procedure applies, the applicable review period is limited to three trading days. In that case, the

---

[72] See Section 12.2.6.1 below.

[73] General Regulations of the AMF Article 212-21. This procedure was created on 12 March, 2008 and is further described in Article 5 of the instruction No 2005-11 from the AMF of 13 December 2005.

[74] *Association française des marchés financiers*, a professional organization that includes French financial markets professionals.

[75] To date, the only approved model standard securities note is that applicable to share issuances with preferential subscription rights. Other model notes are subject to market consultations.

financial services provider that sponsors the transaction must include in its certification transmitted to the AMF in connection with the approval process a confirmation that the securities note and the summary conform in all respects with the model securities note and summary, subject only to exceptions specifically identified by it.

Issuers that file a *document de référence* but that do not opt for the simplified **12.84** procedure—for any reason—may be subject to a reduced review period if they present a duly justified request to that effect.[76]

12.2.6 Structuring a prospectus

Depending on the frequency with which issuers intend to access the capital mar- **12.85** kets, issuers may opt for one of the three prospectus structures available under the Prospectus Directive[77] and the General Regulations of the AMF: (i) the tripartite structure;[78] (ii) the single document or (iii) the base prospectus.[79]

12.2.6.1 *Tripartite document*

If the issuer accesses the markets on a frequent basis, it may decide to produce a **12.86** prospectus consisting of three parts,[80] comprising:

- *Registration document.* The registration document (*document de référence* or *document de base*) [81]—which contains a description of the issuer and its business, together with its financial statements—remains on the shelf throughout the year.[82] Provided it is up to date, only the short securities note and summary (if required) must be produced for each issue made during the year.[83] If applicable, an update of the registration document (*actualisation du document de référence*) is registered or filed, as the case may be, with the AMF. The filing of a *document de référence* is not subject to the prior review of the AMF if an issuer has registered a *document de référence* (i.e. a registration document) at least during the preceding three consecutive years. The review process applicable to updates of a *document de référence* follows that applicable to the issuer's *document de référence*.

---

[76] Article 5 III of Instruction No 2005-11 relating to the information that must be disclosed in connection with an offer to the public or the admission of securities on a regulated market.

[77] Prospectus Directive Article 5.

[78] General Regulations of the AMF Article 212-9.

[79] General Regulations of the AMF Articles 212-31 to 212-33.

[80] Prospectus Directive Article 5(3); General Regulations of the AMF Article 212-9.

[81] The Registration Document is either a *document de référence* or, in case of an initial public offering, a *document de base*.

[82] General Regulations of the AMF Article 212-24.

[83] Prospectus Directive Article 12(1); General Regulations of the AMF Article 212-10.

- *Securities note*. The securities note containing information relating to the securities must be produced when an issue is made. It must contain the information prescribed by the Prospectus Regulation as applicable depending on the type of securities being issued.
- *Summary*.[84] The summary must, in a brief manner[85] and in non-technical language, convey the essential characteristics and risks associated with the issuer, any guarantor (if applicable) and the securities.[86] It must also contain various warning statements, to the effect that it should only be read as an introduction to the prospectus; that any decision to invest in the securities should be based on consideration by the investor of the prospectus as a whole; that the investor may have to bear the cost of any translation of the prospectus required by the relevant courts in its jurisdiction; and that those responsible for the prospectus will only be liable in relation to the summary if it is misleading, inaccurate or inconsistent when read together with the rest of the prospectus.[87] In connection with a passporting of the prospectus, the summary must be translated into the language of the jurisdiction into which the prospectus is being passported.

12.2.6.2 *Single document*

12.87   Issuers who do not plan to access the capital markets more than once within the same year often find the burden of producing a registration document difficult to justify. Such issuers may produce a single prospectus, provided it contains all the elements that would be in a three-part prospectus, including the summary.

---

[84] Pursuant to Prospectus Directive Article 5(3) and General Regulations of the AMF Article 212-8-I, a summary is not required for 'wholesale debt securities' i.e. where debt securities have a denomination of at least EUR 50,000, or the foreign currency equivalent.

[85] The summary normally must not exceed 2,500 words.

[86] Prospectus Directive Article 5(2); General Regulations of the AMF Article 212-8-II. The recommendation from the AMF of 4 October 2007 further details the required content of the summary.

[87] Prospectus Directive Article 5(2); General Regulations of the AMF Article 212-8-III. Article 15 of the instruction No 2005-11 from the AMF of 13 December 2005 provides that such warning must be worded as follows: 'This summary note should be read as an introduction to the prospectus. Any decision to invest in the securities concerned by this transaction should be based on a comprehensive study of the full prospectus. Where a claim relating to the information contained in a prospectus is brought before a court, the plaintiff investor might, under the national legislation of the Member states of the European Community or States party to the European Economic Area Agreement, have to bear the costs of translating the prospectus before the legal proceedings are initiated. Civil liability attaches to the persons who presented the summary note, and any translation thereof, and who requested notification within the meaning of Article 212-42 of the AMF General Regulations only if the content of the summary note is misleading, inaccurate or inconsistent when read with other parts of the prospectus.'

In practice, the use of a single prospectus structure is unusual, largely because it requires the issuer to go through the AMF review process at a time when there is pressure to complete a transaction quickly. While the registration or filing of a shelf registration document is costly, it may take the form of an annual report, with a cross-reference table pointing to the required sections of a registration document (much of the information must be published in any event as part of the annual financial report required by the Transparency Directive and pursuant to additional French legal requirements as to information required to be made available in advance of issuers' annual shareholders' meetings). In addition, registering a shelf registration document for three consecutive years enables issuers to file shelf registration documents in subsequent years that are not subject to the prior review of the AMF.

12.88

12.2.6.3 Programmes

As an alternative to the tripartite format and single document, the Prospectus Directive permits issuers of non-equity securities to produce a base prospectus under an offering programme. A base prospectus must contain all relevant information concerning the issuer and the securities to be offered under the programme other than those which are not known when the base prospectus is approved and can only be determined at the time of an individual issue.[88] This missing information is supplied at the time of each issue under the programme in a document known as final terms.

12.89

This format is typically used for euro-medium-term-notes programmes.

12.90

12.2.7 Prospectus contents

12.2.7.1 The 'necessary information'

Pursuant to Article L.412-1 of the French Monetary and Financial Code, the prospectus must contain the information described in the General Regulations of the AMF that relates to the terms and conditions of the transaction, as well as the organization, financial position and the evolution of the activity of the issuer and, if applicable, any guarantor of the securities being offered or listed.

12.91

Under the Prospectus Directive and the General Regulations of the AMF, the overriding obligation of disclosure in a prospectus is to provide 'the information necessary to enable investors to make an informed assessment of (a) the assets and liabilities, financial position, profits and losses, and prospects of the issuer of the securities and any guarantor; and (b) the rights attaching to the securities'.[89]

12.92

---

[88] Prospectus Directive Article 5(4); General Regulations of the AMF Article 212-32.
[89] Prospectus Directive Article 5(1); General Regulations of the AMF Article 212-7.

Such information must be presented in a form that is comprehensible and easy to analyse.

12.93 In addition, Article 212-7 of the General Regulations of the AMF specifically refers to the Prospectus Regulation requirements as regards the specific contents of the prospectus, and specifies that the AMF will take into account the recommendations of CESR for purposes of its application of such rules.

12.94 Accordingly, the prospectus must be drawn up in accordance with one of the formats and modules set out in Articles 4 to 20 of the Prospectus Regulation or one of the combinations set out in Article 21 of such regulation for the different types of securities.[90] The prospectus must contain the information specified in Annexes I to XVII to the Prospectus Regulation, depending on the type of issuer and the types of securities offered. Annex XVIII to the Prospectus Regulation sets out the combinations of Annexes that must apply to securities that fit within more than one Annex.

12.2.7.2 *Derogations*

12.95 In the following situations described in the Prospectus Directive,[91] the AMF has the authority to grant exceptions and allow issuers not to include certain information in prospectuses: (a) where disclosure would be contrary to the public interest; (b) where disclosure would be seriously detrimental to the issuer, provided that non-disclosure would not be likely to mislead the public; and (c) where the information is of minor importance only for a specific offer or admission to trading on a regulated market, and is not such as to influence the assessment of the financial position and prospects of the issuer or any guarantor.

12.2.7.3 *Forward-looking information and profit forecasts and estimates*

12.96 **12.2.7.3.1 Profit forecasts and estimates** Under the Prospectus Regulation, profit forecasts or estimates may be included in prospectuses in addition to historical financial information.[92] In such a case, a statement setting out the principal assumptions upon which the issuer has based its forecast or estimate and a report from the statutory auditors stating that the forecast or estimate has been properly compiled on the basis stated and that the basis of accounting used for the profit forecast or estimate is consistent with the accounting policies of the issuer must be included in the prospectus.

---

[90] General Regulations of the AMF Article 212-7.
[91] Prospectus Directive Article 8(2); General Regulations of the AMF Article 212-18.
[92] Prospectus Regulation Recital n°8 and paragraphs 13 of Annex I and 9 of Annex IV.

12.2.7.3.1.1 Definition of profit forecasts Under French law, there is no require- **12.97**
ment for an issuer to publish profit forecasts. If an issuer chooses to publish such
forecasts, it must comply with applicable rules derived from the Prospectus
Regulation, as interpreted by the AMF.

Pursuant to the Prospectus Regulation,[93] the term 'profit forecast' means **12.98**
an expression which (i) expressly states or by implication indicates a figure or a
minimum or maximum figure for the likely level of profits or losses[94] for the
current financial period and/or financial periods subsequent to that period, or
(ii) contains data from which a calculation of such figure for future profits or losses
may be made, even if no particular figure is mentioned and the word 'profit' is
not used.

In light of the generality of this definition and the difficulty of distinguishing **12.99**
profit forecasts from other notions (such as business objectives, financial targets or
trends), the AMF has set out certain guidelines in order to determine whether
forward-looking information must be considered profit forecasts within the
meaning of the Prospectus Regulation, as summarized below: [95]

(i) Forward-looking information expressly referred to as profit forecasts by the
issuer are treated as such.

(ii) Certain financial aggregates derived from the issuer's financial statements
such as the operating result and the profit before tax are presumed to be direct
profits forecasts if they relate to a period that is not closed.

(iii) Other indicators such as operating margin, EBITDA, EBITDAR (to the
extent that they relate to a period that is not closed) are presumed to be
indirect profit forecasts, while other forward-looking information such as
turnover forecast may be presumed to be an indirect profit forecast only if
data otherwise made available by the issuer permits, by implication, the
calculation of a likely level of future profits or losses. The time horizon to
which such forward-looking information relates generally determines the
nature of such information: (a) if it relates to the current financial year and
goes beyond published historical interim figures, it should be considered an
indirect profit forecast, provided that, given information and trends otherwise included in the prospectus, such forward-looking information permits

---

[93] Prospectus Regulation Article 2(10).
[94] The AMF indicated in its position dated 10 July 2006 relating to the concept of forecasts that
the terms 'profits or losses' must not only refer to net result, but also to the operating result and that
the term 'result' must refer to consolidated result. Although the CESR recommends referring to the
net profit before tax, the AMF authorizes the issuer to opt for a profit after tax, provided it respects
the transparency of information as to the usual or unusual amount of the income taxes.
[95] Position from the AMF dated 10 July 2006 relating to the concept of forecasts.

the determination of the likely level of profits or losses; (b) if it relates to the financial year N+1, the same interpretation as stated in (a) above applies unless the issuer expressly indicates and justifies that such information may not be used to establish a forecast; and (c) if it relates to the financial year N+2 or subsequent financial years, it would be considered as a forecast only if historical financial statements otherwise provided permit, given the trends information otherwise published, the calculation of the likely level of future profits or losses, and unless the issuer expressly indicates that such information may not be used to establish a forecast.

(iv) With respect to narrative forward-looking information, the following principles apply: (a) sentences such as 'the result will be/should be [notably, appreciably, strongly, slightly] improved' or 'the result will/should [notably, appreciably, strongly, slightly] decrease' should be considered as profits forecasts only if it is possible to determine the likely level of profits or losses using other figures included in the prospectus.

12.100   *12.2.7.3.1.2 Inclusion of profit forecasts in the registration document*   Unless the issuer expressly declares such information outdated, issuers must include in their registration document all forward-looking financial information they have previously published or otherwise disclosed (including in a press release, at a press conference or analyst presentation or otherwise). Issuers must expressly state whether forward-looking information included in the registration document constitutes business objectives (or financial targets) or forecasts. In the latter case, and as noted above, issuers must publish, at the same time, the assumptions underlying such forecasts and a report from the statutory auditors.

12.101   *12.2.7.3.1.3 Inclusion of profit forecasts in the prospectus*   In case a registration document is incorporated by reference into a prospectus, the issuer must determine whether forward-looking information included in such registration document constitutes profit forecasts within the meaning of the Prospectus Regulation, objectives or trend information. If such information constitutes profit forecasts, the issuer must publish, at the same time, the assumptions underlying such forecasts and a report from the statutory auditors, unless: (i) after the determination of such profit forecasts, the issuer has published historical financial information covering, in its entirety or not, the period referred to by the forecasts;[96] or (ii) the issuer decides not to maintain its forecasts.[97]

---

[96] If the issuer does not wish to reiterate its initial forecasts in the prospectus and has not published any new forecasts at the time of the publication of the historical financial statements, it must state in the prospectus that such historical financial statements make the previous forecasts obsolete.

[97] It must then expressly state in the prospectus that forecasts previously published are no longer valid.

12.2.7.3.1.4 Profit estimates The Prospectus Regulation defines a profit esti- **12.102**
mate as a profit forecast for a financial period which has expired and for which
results have not yet been published.[98] Including a profit estimate in the prospectus
requires the indication of the basis upon which such estimate was established and
a report from the statutory auditors concluding that such estimate has been properly compiled on the basis stated.

The AMF has published the five following guidelines in respect of estimated **12.103**
financial information:[99]

(i) Any financial information on the assets, the financial position or the perform-
ances of the issuer published after the end of the financial year (or semester)
and before the publication of the statutory financial statements as approved
by the board of directors[100] for such financial year (or semester) must solely be
referred to as 'estimated financial data or results'. The issuer must avoid any
risk of confusion with the statutory financial statements.

(ii) The prospectus must state the degree of involvement of the board of directors
in the examination of the estimated financial data or results as well as the
scheduled date for its approval of the statutory financial statements.

(iii) The estimated financial data or results must be as coherent and as complete as
possible, given the status of the work on the establishment of the statutory
financial statements. In particular, it must be clear enough to be understood
by investors; it must be presented in aggregates normally used by the issuer; it
must be presented in absolute value and not only in terms of indicators of
progression; it must always be completed with comparable data from the
previous fiscal year, as well as with an indication of the latest estimated financial data or results published, if any; and it must not contain any omission on
significant elements known to the issuer, the absence of which would affect its
pertinence and its sincerity.

(iv) Estimated financial data and results must be established through an accounting process intended to ensure the accuracy of such information. The issuer
must indicate that it has not yet obtained assurances from the auditors that
they will certify the statutory financial statements without qualifications and
must conspicuously state that 'the estimated financial data or results were not
verified by the statutory auditors' or that they are 'under verification'.

(v) If the statutory financial statements as approved by the board of directors vary
significantly from estimated financial data or results published, such difference must be specifically explained.

---

[98] Prospectus Regulation Article 2(11).
[99] Recommendation No 7 from the AMF of October 2004.
[100] Or the executive board, or the manager, depending on the corporate form of the issuer.

12.2.7.3.2 Distinction from other forward-looking information

12.104 *12.2.7.3.2.1 Objectives* The AMF considers that business objectives or financial targets summarize in figures the expected effects of the management's strategy, both in commercial and financial terms, and that they state the goals that the managers have set given their expectations of prevailing economic conditions and which are generally reflected in a business plan.[101] Issuers wishing to publish business objectives or financial targets must be aware that, despite the terminology they may use, such business objectives or financial targets could be considered profit forecasts if the definition of profit forecast is satisfied.

12.105 *12.2.7.3.2.2 Trend information* Trend information is not specifically defined in the Prospectus Regulation. According to the AMF, there are two types of trends: (i) trends relating to recent historical information;[102] and (ii) trends relating to forward-looking information that are reasonably likely to have a material effect on the issuer's prospects for at least the current financial year. The AMF has indicated that trends relating to forward-looking information should preferably be expressed in general or narrative terms when relating to aggregates issued from the income statement so as not to be confused with profit forecasts. In any event, they should not permit the reader to determine with sufficient precision a likely level of future profits or losses. CESR has also indicated that a general discussion about the future or the prospects of the issuer under trend information should not normally constitute a profit forecast or estimate.[103]

12.106 *12.2.7.3.2.3 Future prospects* French law requires an issuer to include information regarding future prospects of the issuer in the annual report.[104] It is not required, however, that such prospects be described in figures. Issuers must be careful in drafting the section of the annual report relating to future prospects in order to avoid a subsequent characterization of such information—for example, in connection with a subsequent registration document or a prospectus—as profit forecasts.

12.2.7.4 Responsibility statements

12.107 Under French law, the disclosure of erroneous or misleading information may be the source of potential liability for the issuer and for various participants in the offer.

---

[101] This concept is not defined in the Prospectus Regulation but was discussed in France by the working group LEPETIT which worked on warning results in April 2000.

[102] Prospectus Regulation Paragraph 12 of Annex I requires the inclusion of 'the most significant trends in production, sales and inventory, and costs and selling prices since the end of the last financial year to the date of the registration document'.

[103] Recommendation No 49 of CESR's recommendation (CESR05-054b) of February 2005.

[104] French Commercial Code Article R.225-102.

First, shareholders may bring a civil action against directors and general managers **12.108** for personal losses or damage they suffered due to their violation of law, breach of the by-laws or mismanagement (*faute de gestion*).[105] The publication of a prospectus containing inaccurate or misleading information (or omitting any requisite information) may, in certain circumstances, constitute such a violation of law and/or mismanagement and therefore trigger the liability of the general manager.

Second, French law provides for criminal sanctions applicable in case of wilful **12.109** disclosure of erroneous or misleading information relating to the condition or prospects of an issuer or of securities admitted to trading on a regulated market, which is intended to have an impact on the market price.[106] Administrative sanctions may also be imposed by the AMF for similar wrongdoings.[107]

More generally, the General Regulations of the AMF provide for a general obliga- **12.110** tion for issuers to disclose information that is exact, precise and fair.[108] Accordingly, disclosing erroneous or misleading information in a prospectus could subject the issuer to sanctions that may be imposed by the AMF.[109]

While such potential liability clearly exists in connection with the disclosure of **12.111** erroneous or misleading information, liability for material omissions derives from applicable provisions of the General Regulations of the AMF relating to the responsibility of issuers.[110] The extent to which liability for the disclosure of erroneous or misleading material information or material omissions could attach to the management or the members of the board of directors of the issuer varies under French case law.

A specific responsibility regime is provided by the provisions of the AMF's General **12.112** Regulations relating to the prospectus, which impose an obligation for the chief executive officer (*directeur général*) of the issuer to include a responsibility statement in the prospectus, confirming that, to the best of his (or her) knowledge, the information contained in the document conforms to reality and does not omit to state a material fact that may affect the information contained therein.[111] A signed copy of the responsibility statement must be transmitted to the AMF prior to its issuance of the visa.

---

[105] French Commercial Code Article L.225-251.
[106] French Monetary and Financial Code Article L.465-2.
[107] General Regulations of the AMF Article 632-1.
[108] General Regulations of the AMF Article 223-1.
[109] General Regulations of the AMF Article 632-1.
[110] General Regulations of the AMF Article 212-14.
[111] General Regulations of the AMF Article 212-14.

12.113   Such statement also specifies that the statutory auditors have reviewed the information contained in the prospectus and, if any reservations or observations were
made by the auditors in connection with the certification of the financial statements included or incorporated by reference therein, or in connection with the
review of the prospectus, such observations and/or reservations must be summarized in the chief executive officer's statement set forth in the prospectus (or, as the
case may be, in the registration document).[112]

12.114   While an issuer's statutory auditors do not issue a responsibility statement that
must be reproduced in the prospectus itself, the statutory auditors must review the
issuer's prospectuses and registration documents and issue a letter to the issuer
(the '*lettre de fin de travaux*') confirming that they have completed a global review
of the information contained in the relevant document.[113] A copy of such letter
must be communicated to the AMF prior to its issuance of a visa.

12.115   Finally, at least one duly qualified financial services provider participating in the
transaction must sign a statement that is not included in the prospectus and which
is only transmitted to the AMF prior to its issuance of the visa.[114] In connection
with an initial public offering and any offer of securities to the public effected
within the three following years, the statement confirms that, after having conducted customary due diligence, such due diligence has not revealed any inaccuracy or material omission such as to mislead an investor. In respect of any prospectus
made available in connection with any offer of securities to the public or admission of securities to trading on a regulated market at any time after such initial
three-year period, the statement signed by the financial services provider is limited
to the terms of the offer and the characteristics of the securities, as described in the
prospectus or the securities note.

12.2.7.5 *Shareholder disclosures*

12.116   Pursuant to the Prospectus Regulation,[115] prospectuses relating to shares must
indicate the name of any person other than a member of supervisory bodies who,
directly or indirectly, has an interest in the issuer's equity capital or voting rights
which is notifiable under the law of the issuer's jurisdiction, together with the

---

[112] This paragraph must not be included in responsibility statements in prospectuses relating
to the admission to trading on a regulated market of debt securities, or the admission to trading of
securities on the professional compartment referred to in Article 516-18 of the General Regulations
of the AMF (i.e., the compartment reserved for issuers applying to admit their securities to trading
on a regulated market without an offer to the public).

[113] Such a '*lettre de fin de travaux*' is not required for a listing on the Professional Compartment
of NYSE Euronext Paris.

[114] The delivery of such a statement is only an option in connection with a listing on the
Professional Compartment of NYSE Euronext Paris.

[115] Prospectus Regulation Paragraph 18 of Annex 1.

amount of each such person's interest or, if there are no such persons, an appropriate negative statement. Under French law, the crossing of the following thresholds must be notified to the AMF and to the issuer: 5%, 10%, 15%, 20%, 25%, 1/3, 50%, 2/3, 90%, and 95%.[116] The by-laws of an issuer may provide for other threshold notifications, with respect to percentages of ownership as low as 0.5% and any multiple thereof.

Prospectuses relating to both shares and debt-securities[117] must, to the extent known to the issuer, state whether the issuer is directly or indirectly owned or controlled and by whom and describe the nature of such control and the measures in place to ensure that such control is not abused, and describe any arrangements the operation of which may, at a subsequent date, result in a change of control of the issuer.

12.117

12.2.7.6 Related-party transactions

Details of related-party transactions[118] that the issuer has entered into during the period covered by the historical financial statements[119] and up to the date of the registration document relating to shares must be disclosed in accordance with IAS 24 'Related-party transactions' by issuers subject to IAS/IFRS, i.e. companies listed on a regulated market.

12.118

CESR recommends[120] that issuers that are not subject to IAS/IFRS follow the definitions of related parties. Such issuers must disclose the following information: the nature and extent of any transactions which are material to the issuer, an explanation of the reasons why a transaction was not concluded at arm's length, if any, and the amount of the percentage to which related-party transactions form part of the turnover of the issuer.

12.119

12.2.7.7 Material contracts

The Prospectus Regulation requires the disclosure of a summary of each material contract, other than contracts entered in the ordinary course of business, to which the issuer or any member of its group is a party, for the two years immediately preceding publication of the registration document relating to shares.[121] In the case of debt securities, the registration document must include a brief description

12.120

---

[116] French Commercial Code Article L.233-7.

[117] Prospectus Regulation Paragraph 12 of Annex IV.

[118] While the Prospectus Regulation refers to the definition of such term contained in IAS 24 'Related party disclosure', French law provides for a legal definition of related-party transactions (French Commercial Code Article L.225-38 for *sociétés anonymes* with a board of directors) that is generally used as a reference by French issuers.

[119] See Section 12.2.8.1 below.

[120] Recommendation No 2c from CESR's recommendation (CESR/05-054b) of February 2005.

[121] Prospectus Regulation Paragraph 22 of Annex I.

of such contracts if they could result in any group member being under an obligation or entitlement that is material to the issuer's ability to meet its obligation to security holders in respect of the securities issued.[122]

12.2.7.8 *Expert reports*

12.121 Where a statement or report attributed to a person as an expert is included in the prospectus, the Prospectus Regulation requires that the issuer disclose such expert's name, business address, qualifications and material interest if any in the issuer. CESR has indicated that a 'material interest' may be derived from the ownership of securities issued by the issuer or any company belonging to the same group or options to acquire or subscribe for securities of the issuer; former employment of the issuer or any form of compensation from the issuer; membership of any of the issuer's body; or any connections to the financial intermediaries involved in the offering or listing of the securities of the issuer. [123]

12.2.8 Financial statements

12.2.8.1 *Historical requirements*

12.122 Audited historical financial information covering the latest three financial years (or such shorter period that the issuer has been in operation) and the audit report in respect of each year must be included in prospectuses.

12.123 Such historical financial information must include at least: (i) a balance sheet; (ii) an income statement; (iii) a statement showing either all changes in equity or changes in equity other than those arising from capital transactions with owners and distributions to owners; (iv) a cash flow statement; and (v) accounting policies and explanatory notes.

12.124 French law strictly applies the rules set forth in the Prospectus Regulation in this respect.

12.2.8.2 *Complex financial histories*

12.125 The Prospectus Regulation contemplates that an issuer's historical financial information might, under certain circumstances, not cover the entirety of the issuer's business undertaking and may be more accurately reflected in information established by another entity. Such situation may occur in particular in the following circumstances: (i) where the issuer has made a significant acquisition not yet reflected in its financial statements; (ii) where the issuer is a newly incorporated holding company; (iii) where the issuer is composed of companies that were

---

[122] Prospectus Regulation Paragraph 15 of Annex IV.
[123] Recommendation No 157 from CESR's recommendation (CESR/05-054b) of February 2005.

under common control but which never formed a legal group; or (iv) where the issuer has been formed as a separate legal entity following the division of an existing business.[124]

Accordingly, Regulation (EC) No 211/2007 of 27 February 2007 amended the Prospectus Regulation by creating a new Article 4bis which provides that where an issuer has a 'complex financial history' or has made a 'significant financial commitment', it must either (i) present the financial statements of that other entity alongside those of the issuer; and/or (ii) present pro-forma financial statements alongside the issuer's financial statements. **12.126**

An issuer has a 'complex financial history' if the following cumulative conditions are satisfied: (i) the issuer's entire business undertaking at the time the prospectus is drawn up is not accurately represented in the historical financial statements; (ii) that inaccuracy will affect the ability of an investor to make an informed assessment as required under Article 5(1) of the Prospectus Directive; and (iii) information relating to the issuer's business undertaking that is necessary for an investor to make such an assessment is included in another entity's financial statements. **12.127**

An issuer has made a 'significant financial commitment' if it has entered into a binding agreement to undertake a transaction which, on completion, is likely to give rise to a significant gross change. **12.128**

New Article 4a of the Prospectus Regulation contemplates that the competent authority may also require inclusion in the prospectus of pro-forma financial information. **12.129**

The competent authority is, however, authorized to modify the requirements in view of a number of factors, including the nature of the securities, the existence of financial information relating to an entity other than the issuer in a form that might be included in a prospectus without modification, the facts of the case and the ability of the issuer to obtain financial information relating to another entity with reasonable effort. The Prospectus Regulation (as amended) further provides that preference must be given to the way of satisfying the requirements that is the least costly or onerous. **12.130**

12.2.8.2.1 Pro-forma financial information   Pro-forma financial information must be included in prospectuses for shares in case of significant gross change in the situation of an issuer due to a particular transaction.[125] **12.131**

---

[124] Recital No 5 to Regulation (EC) No 211/2007 of 27 February 2007 amending the Prospectus Regulation.
[125] Prospectus Regulation Recital 9.

12.132 'Significant gross change' is described in recital No 9 and paragraph 6 of new Article 4a of the Prospectus Regulation as 'a variation of more than 25%, relative to one or more indicators of the size of the issuer's business, in the situation of an issuer due to a particular transaction'. The Prospectus Regulation excepts those situations where merger accounting is required.

12.133 In order to assess whether the change to an issuer's business as a result of a transaction exceeds 25%, CESR recommends[126] assessing the size of the transaction relative to the size of the issuer by using appropriate indicators of size prior to the relevant transaction, such as, in particular, total assets, revenue and profits or losses. Pursuant to such interpretation, a transaction would constitute a significant gross change where at least one of the indicators of change is more than 25%.

12.134 In France, an issuer must establish pro-forma financial statements in particular in case of:[127] significant change in the scope of consolidation (e.g. acquisitions or disposals of subsidiaries), or change in the method of consolidation of a significant subsidiary, or in case of mergers, de-mergers and spin-offs transactions, or takeovers by means of exchange offers.

12.135 Pursuant to Article 222-2 of the General Regulations of the AMF, the AMF also applies 25% as the relevant threshold of variation of the scope of consolidation of the issuer, triggering a requirement to present pro-forma financial information.[128] In that case, the pro-forma financial information that is required must relate, at least, to the current fiscal year.

Pro forma financial information must be covered by a special report of the auditors confirming that such information was adequately prepared on the bases indicated and that the accounting information used conforms to the accounting principles applied by the issuer (General Regulations of the AMF, Article 212-15).

12.136 In most cases, the calculation of the 25% threshold must be made in relation to the previous year, unless such year is atypical, in which case one must refer to the average of the previous financial years. The AMF indicated that in the event that several non-significant variations in the scope of consolidation occur during a financial year, which together cross the 25% threshold, it may be useful to

---

[126] Recommendations Nos 91 and 92 from CESR's recommendation (CESR/05-054b) of February 2005.

[127] General Regulations of the AMF. Article 212-15.

[128] The requirement to present pro-forma financial information does not apply with respect to the issuers whose securities are admitted to trading on the professional compartment of Euronext Paris (referred to in General Regulations of the AMF Article 516-18).

present pro-forma financial statements grouping the impact of all variations in one column.

12.3 Continuing Obligations

12.3.1 Applicable law

As is customarily the case for companies whose shares are listed on the stock exchanges of the main financial markets, French listed companies—and in certain cases, their directors and senior management—must comply with a substantial set of obligations for the duration of the listing, since investors, in the primary and secondary markets, rely on information disclosed by such companies to make their investment decisions.

12.137

While the Transparency Directive has introduced a certain degree of harmonization of transparency rules within the European Union, transparency has been an objective of French securities laws and regulations for at least two decades. In particular, many of the notification requirements applicable in connection with the acquisition of major shareholdings, as well as insider trading and certain related market abuse sanctions, were instituted by French law No 89-531 of 2 August 1989 relating to the security and transparency of financial markets. Since then, applicable requirements have been amended several times, including for purposes of harmonization with various European directives.

12.138

Applicable French rules derive primarily from the following sources:

12.139

- provisions of the French Commercial Code relating to disclosure requirements (in particular in respect of financial information) applicable to commercial companies as well as to obligations applicable to their shareholders and to their directors;
- provisions of the French Monetary and Financial Code relating to disclosure requirements (in particular in respect of financial information) applicable to certain commercial companies whose securities are admitted to listing and those relating to the powers of the AMF and the definition of public offers (and exemptions therefrom);
- the provisions of Book II (entitled 'Issuers and financial disclosure') and Book VI (entitled 'Market abuse—insider transactions and market manipulation') of the General Regulations of the AMF.

The latest amendment to applicable rules results from French Ordinance No 2009-80 of 22 January 2009 relating to French public offering rules and various financial measures (the 'French Public Offer Law') and the resulting amendments to the General Regulations of the AMF, as well as French Ordinance No 2009-105

12.140

of 30 January 2009 relating to share buy-backs, crossings of thresholds and declarations of intent (the '2009 French Transparency Law Amendment').[129] Additional changes to the General Regulations of the AMF were adopted in July 2009 for purposes of adapting the General Regulations of the AMF to be consistent with the 2009 French Transparency Law Amendment.

12.141 Such recent amendments were primarily designed to improve the harmonization of applicable French rules with those deriving from applicable European directives, in particular the Transparency Directive. The intent of the French legislator was also to improve the attractiveness of the Paris market for international investors and create a level playing field for French companies with their European counterparts by eliminating certain French specificities that created an undue burden for French companies.

12.142 One of the important changes introduced by the French Public Offer Law was to eliminate the concept of *société faisant appel à l'épargne*, i.e. the specific permanent status that used to apply to French companies once they had made a public offer of any type of securities, with or without a listing. This reform is described in further detail in Section 12.2 above relating to the prospectus.

12.143 Finally, in addition to the above-mentioned sets of mandatory laws and regulations, the French system is characterized by the existence of a code of conduct (the 'AFEP-MEDEF Code of Conduct') established by the leading organizations of French businesses (AFEP- MEDEF), which describes best practices in the corporate governance area. While such code of conduct is not mandatory, there is growing pressure for French listed companies to apply such non-mandatory rules, failing which the French Government has repeatedly indicated that mandatory rules could be submitted for vote to the Parliament. In addition, the General Regulations of the AMF require French listed companies to publicly disclose the degree of their application of the AFEP- MEDEF Code of Conduct.

12.144 In substance, the main applicable French rules require French issuers to do the following:

- disclose inside information as soon as possible after it arises;
- make periodic financial reports in the prescribed manner;
- notify shareholding details at various specified thresholds (which obligation is imposed on the concerned shareholders as well);
- disseminate various categories of regulated information;
- comply with a variety of corporate governance norms.

---

[129] Certain provisions of the 2009 French Transparency Law Amendment became effective only as of 1 August 2009 or, as the case may be, as of 1 November 2009.

12.3.2 Disclosure and control of inside information

12.3.2.1 *Applicable provisions and extent of applicability*

Provisions of the General Regulations of the AMF relating to the obligations imposed on issuers in respect of disclosure of inside information are applicable to issuers whose securities (whether shares or other securities) are listed on a reguated market or on an organized multilateral trading system,[130] or whose securities are related to a forward contract or a security admitted to trading on a regulated market. Provisions of the General Regulations of the AMF relating to insider trading and other market abuse violations apply substantially to the same types of securities. **12.145**

In addition to Articles 223-1 et seq. and Articles 621-1 et seq. of the General Regulations of the AMF, the main rules applicable to disclosure or use of inside information are contained in the French Monetary and Financial Code. **12.146**

Two key underlying principles of such rules may be summarized as follows: **12.147**

- the relevant issuers must ensure that there is prompt and accurate disclosure of material non-public information equally to all market participants (see discussion below of inside information definition); and
- the information disclosed by an issuer must be accurate, precise and not misleading.

Accordingly, in principle, relevant issuers must disclose inside information by way of a press release as soon as possible, unless circumstances allow, in accordance with applicable rules, delay of such disclosure or selective disclosures. **12.148**

In addition to controlling and disclosing inside information, issuers must compile and maintain insider lists. **12.149**

12.3.2.2 *Identifying inside information*

Since disclosure obligations extend only to 'inside information', the key to satisfying this obligation is for listed companies to be able to properly identify inside information as and when it arises. **12.150**

Under French law, inside information is defined in Article 621-1 of the General Regulations of the AMF as any precise non-public information, relating directly or indirectly to one or more issuers of securities or to one or more securities, and which, if made public, would be likely to have a significant impact on the market price of the relevant securities or of related securities. **12.151**

---

[130] This includes *Alternext*; the obligations do not, however, apply to companies whose securities are listed on the *Marché Libre*.

12.152 Pursuant to such rule, information is deemed to be precise if it contains a set of circumstances or an event that has occurred or may occur, and a conclusion may be drawn as to the possible impact of such set of circumstances or event on the market price of the relevant securities or of related securities.

12.153 The rule further specifies that information that, if made public, would be likely to have a significant impact on the market price of the relevant securities or related securities is information that a reasonable investor would be likely to rely on in connection with its investment decisions.

12.154 The concept of inside information is thus intended to cover a wide variety of circumstances that may have a positive or negative impact on the market price of an issuer's securities. By way of example, the definition may cover the following non-comprehensive list of events or circumstances: (i) financial matters, such as the establishment of the annual accounts or interim financial information, or the determination of the amount of dividends, especially when there is a change in dividend policy, the realization of capital increases or issuances (whether through a fee allocation to shareholders or for a subscription price) of other types of securities; as well as (ii) technical, commercial or accidental events affecting the issuer's activity, such as the development of a manufacturing process, the development or the loss of a specific market, the conclusion of commercial or cooperation agreements, the conclusion or unwinding of a joint venture, an acquisition or a divestiture, a change of control or a change in the management team.

12.3.2.3 *Disclosure of inside information*

12.155 **12.3.2.3.1 Timing of disclosure** Pursuant to Article 223-2 I of the General Regulations of the AMF, issuers must disclose inside information as soon as possible. Applicable rules, however, recognize that issuers may decide, under their responsibility, to delay such disclosure under certain specific circumstances, as further discussed in Section 12.3.2.4 below.

12.156 **12.3.2.3.2 Contents and means of disclosure** Where the disclosure requirement is applicable, issuers must ensure effective and full disclosure of inside information, via a press release. Disclosure is considered full and effective if it can reach the widest possible audience in the shortest possible period of time from the time that it is distributed in France and in the other member states of the European Community or other states parties to the European Economic Area (EEA) agreement.[131] Such requirement is deemed satisfied if the issuer transmits such information electronically to a regulatory information service.[132]

---

[131] General Regulations of the AMF Article 221-4 II.
[132] General Regulations of the AMF Article 221-4 IV.

In addition, Article 223-8 of the General Regulations of the AMF provides for a principle of equivalence of information such that issuers must ensure that information they disclose abroad is disclosed simultaneously in France.   **12.157**

Regulated information published must clearly identify the name of the issuer, the subject of such information and the date and time at which the issuer transmitted it.   **12.158**

Issuers must refrain from providing inside information combined with advertising or commercial materials relating to its activities in such a way that the public could be misled.   **12.159**

Any material change in inside information already disclosed must be disclosed promptly, through the same means as those used for the initial disclosure.   **12.160**

12.3.2.3.3 Simultaneous publication on website and filing with the AMF   Any inside information disclosed via a press release must also be published on the issuer's website[133] and filed electronically with the AMF.[134]   **12.161**

12.3.2.4 *Delaying disclosure*

As indicated above, issuers in possession of inside information must disclose it as soon as possible.   **12.162**

Issuers are only permitted to delay the disclosure of inside information where (i) disclosure would harm their legitimate interests and (ii) the following circumstances apply:

- the omission would not be likely to mislead the public; and
- the issuer is able to ensure the confidentiality of the relevant inside information by controlling access to that information.

With respect to the above first set of circumstances, issuers must be aware of the fact that the more material and the more unexpected the information is, the greater the risk that the issuer is alleged to have misled the public by not disclosing the inside information.   **12.163**

With respect to the above second set of circumstances, Article 223-2 II of the General Regulations of the AMF provides that control of access to inside information may include (without limitation) the following measures: **12.164**

- implementing effective measures preventing access to that information by persons other than those who need to know the information in order to perform their functions within the issuer;

---

[133] General Regulations of the AMF Article 221-3 II.
[134] General Regulations of the AMF Article 221-5.

- taking necessary steps to ensure that every person granted access to that information is aware of the legislative and regulatory obligations associated with
  such access and has been warned of the penalties imposed for unauthorized use
  or disclosure of that information; and
- implementing necessary measures to disclose that information immediately in
  the event that the issuer has been unable to ensure confidentiality.

12.165 For the purposes of assessing whether a delay is permissible, the term 'issuer's
legitimate interests' is to be narrowly construed. In this respect, Article 223-2 III
of the General Regulations of the AMF provides a non-exhaustive set of examples
of situations where the legitimate interests of the issuer are likely to permit delayed
disclosure, including the following:

- Disclosure of negotiations (or any related information) may be delayed where
  the outcome or the ordinary course of such negotiation is likely to be affected
  by public disclosure. For example, when the issuer's financial viability is in grave
  and imminent danger (provided that it is not subject to French bankruptcy
  proceedings), public disclosure could jeopardize existing or potential shareholders' interests by undermining negotiations intended to ensure the issuer's
  financial recovery and, therefore, delay is permitted. This provision is often the
  basis for the delay of disclosure of ongoing negotiations of major transactions;
  in the restructuring area, this provision has also been interpreted as permitting
  a delayed disclosure of certain pre-bankruptcy proceedings that are confidential
  by virtue of applicable law (such as *mandat ad hoc* proceedings[135] or *concilia-
  tion*). While recognizing that the efficiency and success of such proceedings
  greatly depend on their confidentiality, the AMF has recently reminded issuers
  undergoing such confidential proceedings that they must nonetheless disclose
  adequate information about their financial condition.[136] In particular, since
  these proceedings do not involve all of the creditors of a company, their confidential nature results in selective disclosure, thus issuers must exercise particular
  caution in respect of any information relating to such proceedings.
- Disclosure of decisions taken or contracts entered into by the issuer's management which need the approval of another of the issuer's governing bodies to
  become effective can be delayed in situations where public disclosure of the
  information before such approval, combined with a simultaneous announcement that such approval is yet to be obtained, would jeopardize the public's
  correct assessment of information. This provision is intended for companies
  whose organizational structure separates the management body and the

---

[135] Paris Court of Appeal, 1st Chamber, Section H, 13 December 2005, No 2005/13646.
[136] *Recommandation de l'AMF sur l'information financière diffusée par les sociétés en difficulté*,
28 July 2009.

approving body, as this is the case in French *sociétés anonymes* with a management board (*directoire*) and a supervisory board (*conseil de surveillance*).[137]

The existence of a legitimate interest does not, however, allow the issuer to escape all of its information duties and the issuer must carefully assess whether the disclosure of the relevant information is likely to prejudice its legitimate interests or not.   **12.166**

Eventually, issuers must assess at what point it is no longer possible to delay disclosure of inside information despite the existence of a legitimate interest.   **12.167**

12.3.2.5 *Selective disclosure of inside information*

Selective disclosure is only permitted if the person receiving inside information is subject to a duty of confidentiality towards the issuer pursuant to applicable laws and regulations, the issuer's by-laws or by contract. Otherwise, inside information must be disclosed to the general public on an equal basis. In this respect, Article 223-3 of the General Regulations of the AMF provides more specifically that, when an issuer or a person acting in its name or on its behalf communicates inside information to a third party during the ordinary course of that party's work, profession, or functions, it must ensure that such information is fully disclosed to the public either simultaneously, if the communication was intentional, or promptly, if it was unintentional.   **12.168**

It is advisable that the issuers have a clear communication policy in place that clearly identifies the process for communication and the employees responsible for communication, thereby reducing the risk of inadvertent disclosure.   **12.169**

12.3.2.6 *Press speculation and market rumours*

When there is press speculation or market rumour concerning an issuer, the issuer should independently determine whether it has an obligation to disclose information under applicable rules.   **12.170**

If the press speculation or market rumour is largely accurate and the information underlying the rumour is inside information then it is likely that the issuer can no longer delay disclosure as it can no longer ensure confidentiality of the inside information. In such cases, the information must be disclosed as soon as possible. In determining whether the case at hand falls within the situation described above, the issuer must necessarily exercise judgment taking into consideration how concrete the details are in the rumour and how likely it is that a leak of information has taken place.   **12.171**

---

[137] General Regulations of the AMF Article 223-2 III 2°.

12.172 In certain other instances, the issuer can adopt a 'no comment' approach (or 'the company does not comment on rumours'); depending on the circumstances, this might often be preferable to an explicit denial.

12.173 The AMF sometimes contacts issuers to enquire about the facts and circumstances and even, at times, to require a certain type of disclosure, particularly in cases of persistent market rumours.

12.174 France has adopted 'put up or shut up' rules,[138] applicable in case of rumours of a tender offer targeting a French issuer, in addition to the general principle requiring persons preparing a transaction relating to a French issuer to disclose such information as soon as possible, unless confidentiality is necessary to ensure the success of the transaction and these persons are able to keep such information confidential.

12.175 Pursuant to such rules, if the AMF has reason to believe that a person is preparing, alone or in concert, a tender offer for a French listed company—in particular in case of unusual significant market price or volume variations—the AMF may require such persons to disclose their intent within a certain period of time determined by the AMF. If such persons declare their intention to launch a tender offer, the AMF may require them to issue a press release containing the key offer terms (including major agreements involved, any conditions precedent to the filing of an offer, an indicative timetable, as well as an indication of the interest held by the relevant persons in such issuer), or even to launch the tender offer within a certain period of time determined by the AMF.

12.176 Persons failing to declare their intentions within the prescribed time period are deemed not to intend to launch an offer. Such persons, as well as those having declared that they do not intend to launch a tender offer, are prohibited from launching a tender offer on the target for a period of six months, unless they demonstrate that a material change has occurred in the circumstances, the condition or the share ownership of the persons concerned (including the issuer). In addition, during such six-month period, such persons must notify any increase of their interest in the capital or equity securities of the issuer with an indication of their intentions until the expiration of the six-month period, and may not take any action that would result in an obligation for them to launch a mandatory tender offer on the target.

12.3.2.7 *Insider lists*

12.177 Issuers must establish, update and make available to the AMF a list of the persons working for the issuer (under an employment contract or otherwise) having

---

[138] General Regulations of the AMF Articles 223-32 et seq.

regular or occasional access to inside information relating, directly or indirectly, to that issuer, as well as of any third party acting in that issuer's name or on its behalf having regular or occasional access to such information in the context of its professional dealings with that issuer. Such third parties are also required to establish such a list.[139]

These lists must be provided to the AMF, in hard copy or by email, upon the request of the AMF[140] and must contain various details such as the name or corporate name of each person, the reason for their appearing on the list and the relevant dates of the information, as well as an update of the list.[141] Applicable rules require that such lists be kept for at least five years.[142]   **12.178**

Issuers are required to inform the relevant persons of their addition to the list, of the rules applicable to the possession of inside information, in particular the fact that they are subject to the abstention requirements[143] and of the penalties for the violation of such rules.[144] Such information may be given to the relevant persons either on the day they take their functions (permanent insiders) or on the day they are added to the list (occasional insiders).   **12.179**

Issuers are free either to establish a single list of persons with regular or occasional access to inside information or to establish lists of permanent insiders and occasional insiders.[145]   **12.180**

Permanent insiders are persons with regular access to inside information due to their functions. They belong to one of two categories: **12.181**

- Persons working at the issuer, who include, depending on the issuer's size, organizational structure or business, members of the administrative, management or supervisory bodies, as well as any other issuer's employees having regular access to inside information that relates, directly or indirectly, to the issuer. In addition to members of the issuer's corporate bodies, it mainly applies to senior management, particularly members of the financial department, as well as members of the workers' council since it is necessarily informed of and consulted on any planned restructuring transaction.
- Third parties acting in the name or on the behalf of the issuer and having access to inside information in the context of their professional dealings with the issuer, namely professionals regularly dealing with the issuer which

---

[139] French Monetary and Financial Code Article L.621-18-4.
[140] General Regulations of the AMF Article 223-27.
[141] General Regulations of the AMF Article 223-28.
[142] General Regulations of the AMF Article 223-31.
[143] General Regulations of the AMF Articles 622-1 and 622-2.
[144] General Regulations of the AMF Article 223-30.
[145] Position of the AMF on insider lists established by issuers of financial instruments of 18 January 2006, as amended on 14 November 2007.

gives them access to inside information, such as the issuer's usual advisers or companies undertaking functions that the issuer has outsourced. In turn, these third parties must establish their own list, which includes the names of staff members having insider status due to their professional relationship with the issuer.

Since 1 November 2007, statutory auditors acting in the context of their legal duties[146] are no longer subject to this procedure since they are acting pursuant to legislative obligations conferred in the public interest and are therefore not regarded as acting on the issuer's behalf. However, statutory auditors acting pursuant to contractual obligations remain subject to the insider list requirement.

12.182   *Occasional insiders* are persons with access to inside information from time to time, in particular, when involved in preparing a specific transaction. Again, occasional insiders belong to one of two categories:

- Persons working at the issuer, e.g. employees having access to inside information due to their special skills for purposes of a proposed acquisition. This does not extend however to shareholders, except if they were involved in preparing the transaction or if they were aware of the transaction in any manner whatsoever.
- Third parties acting in the name or on the behalf of the issuer and having access to inside information in the context of their professional dealings with the issuer when preparing or carrying out a specific transaction, e.g. service providers such as lawyers and corporate and investment banks, that are working with the issuer on arranging a transaction, or communication agencies chosen to assist in connection with such transaction. It also applies to rating agencies insofar as they are acting at the request of the issuer and have access to inside information relating to the issuer. These third parties prepare their own lists of insiders as well.

12.183   In principle, the above rules do not apply to investment analysts and financial journalists since they are not supposed to have inside information relating to the issuer. Should they come into possession of such information in the context of their professional dealings with the issuer, they would have to be added to the issuer's insider list.

12.3.3 Disclosure of transactions by officers and persons discharging managerial responsibilities

12.184   Article L.621-18-2 of the French Monetary and Financial Code requires that officers and directors of an issuer report to the AMF any transactions they have

---

[146] Pursuant to French Commercial Code Articles L.823-9 et seq.

carried out involving the shares of the issuer for which they exercise their functions or involving related financial instruments, within five trading days from the completion of the reported transaction.

Such requirement applies to officers or directors of the issuer as well as to persons discharging managerial responsibilities ('PDMRs') and persons connected to them.[147] Officers and directors subject to such requirement include members of the board of directors, members of the managing board, members of the supervisory board, the CEO and deputy CEO, the COO, as well as certain members of the senior management determined by each issuer.[148] Members of the executive committee of an issuer are generally included in the list of PDMRs. **12.185**

Issuers subject to the above requirement include issuers whose securities are listed on the Euronext Paris or the Alternext Paris markets, following either a public offering or a private placement of such securities.[149] **12.186**

The rationale behind this requirement is to improve markets' transparency and to make the identification of insider dealings easier. The notification requirement does not exempt declaring persons from their obligation to refrain from carrying out any transaction with respect to the securities of the issuer if they are aware of any inside information relating to that issuer. **12.187**

12.3.3.1 *Identifying PDMRs*

Although the requirement under Article L.621-18-2 of the French Monetary and Financial Code may seem straightforward, difficulties have arisen in interpreting the terms 'PDMR' and 'connected persons'. **12.188**

• *Persons discharging managerial responsibilities*: This category includes any person who has power to make managerial decisions affecting the development and the strategy of the issuer and has regular access to inside information relating, directly or indirectly, to the issuer.[150] The above two criteria are cumulative.

At the time the Market Abuse Directive was implemented into French law, it was decided to let the issuers determine which persons meet the above definition. Therefore, each issuer must establish and update its own list of the

---

[147] See Section 12.3.3.1 below.
[148] French Monetary and Financial Code Article L.621-18-2 a).
[149] General Regulations of the AMF Article 223-22 A; Q&A of the AMF dated 26 May 2009, relating to the requirement of notification of transactions carried out by officers, directors, PDMRs and the persons connected to them.
[150] French Monetary and Financial Code Article L.621-18-2 b).

persons qualifying as PDMR[151] and must communicate such list to the AMF and to the persons appearing thereon.[152]

- *Connected persons*: This category includes any person having close personal relationships with officers, directors or PDMRs within an issuer.[153] Pursuant to applicable regulations, this includes the following persons:[154]
  - the spouse, if not judicially separated, or the civil partner of an officer, director or other PDMR within an issuer;
  - children over whom an officer, director or a PDMR exercises parental authority, or who lives, usually or alternately, with him (or her), or who is in his (or her) effective and permanent charge;
  - any other parent or relative having lived at an officer's, director's or a PDMR's domicile for at least one year at the date of the relevant transaction; and
  - any legal person or entity[155], other than the issuer,
    - (a) whose management or administration is ensured by an officer, director or a PDMR within an issuer, or any connected person, acting in such person's interest;[156]
    - (b) that is controlled, directly or indirectly, by an officer, director or other PDMR within an issuer, or any connected person;
    - (c) that is constituted in the personal interest of an officer, director or other PDMR within an issuer, or any connected person;
    - (d) for which an officer, director or other PDMR within an issuer, or any connected person, receives at least the majority of the economic benefits.

12.3.3.2 Identifying securities subject to notification requirement

12.189 Transactions involving shares of an issuer as well as related financial instruments, whether or not such financial instruments are listed on the Euronext Paris or the Alternext Paris markets, must be disclosed to the AMF.

12.190 The disclosure requirement thus applies to many types of securities, including, without limitation, securities giving access to the share capital of the issuer (e.g. convertible or exchangeable bonds, etc), warrants and certificates.

12.191 However, transactions involving shares of a company that are not listed on the Euronext Paris or the Alternext Paris markets, or involving financial securities,

---

[151] Such list depends on the issuer's size and organization.
[152] General Regulations of the AMF Article 223-24.
[153] French Monetary and Financial Code Article L.621-18-2 c).
[154] French Monetary and Financial Code Article R.621-43-1.
[155] This includes legal persons or entities incorporated under French law or any foreign law.
[156] Therefore, if such company is acting in its own corporate interest without acting in the personal interest of the officer, director or PDMR, no notification is required.

listed or not, which do not relate to the shares of a listed company, do not trigger the notification requirement.

12.3.3.3 *Identifying transactions subject to notification requirement*

The scope of transactions subject to the notification requirement is fairly exten- **12.192**
sive. Pursuant to Article L.621-18-2 of the French Monetary and Financial Code, acquisitions, sales, subscriptions or exchanges of shares of a company as well as transactions involving related financial instruments must be disclosed to the AMF.

By way of example, the AMF has stated[157] that the following transactions trigger **12.193**
the notification requirement:

- the exercise of stock-options;[158]
- sales of securities allocated upon the exercise of stock-options;[159]
- sale and purchase transactions carried out at the end of the year for tax reasons, without any resulting change in the ownership level;
- forward sale or acquisition contracts; [160]
- purchases and sales of options;[161]
- securities loans;
- transactions involving securities issued by entities whose sole assets are securities of the company in which the officers, directors or PDMRs carry out their functions;[162]
- the exercise of options to convert or exchange bonds;[163]
- transactions carried out on behalf of an officer, director or a PDMR by an intermediary pursuant to a mandate;
- the exercise of an option to receive one's dividend in the form of shares, when such option is offered by an issuer.

---

[157] Q&A of the AMF dated 26 May 2009, relating to the requirement of notification of transactions carried out by officers, directors, PDMRs and the persons connected to them.

[158] The grant of stock-options, however, does not trigger such disclosure requirement.

[159] Such transactions are subject to a specific notification requirement, even if such sales are carried out simultaneously to the exercise of the stock-options.

[160] Such transactions must be disclosed to the AMF at the time of conclusion of the purchase or sale of the futures.

[161] Such transactions must be disclosed at the time that the declaring person acquires (or sells) the options and, in case of exercise of such options, upon acquisition (or sale) of the underlying securities.

[162] e.g. shares in mutual funds exclusively dedicated to employees' shareholding.

[163] e.g. convertible bonds or bonds convertible into and/or exchangeable for new or existing shares (known by its French acronym OCEANE).

12.194   By contrast, the AMF has also specified[164] that certain transactions should not be regarded as triggering the notification requirement, such as, for example:

- a grant of free shares to eligible persons in accordance with Article L.225-197-1 et seq. of the French Commercial Code;[165]
- transfers of securities pursuant to a merger, de-merger or spin-off;
- acquisitions of securities by virtue of gifts, distributions and partitions or successions; or
- securities pledges.

12.3.3.4 *Exemption from the notification requirement*

12.195   The notification requirement does not apply when the total value of transactions carried out within a calendar year does not exceed EUR 5,000. Such amount includes transactions carried out by officers, directors and PDMRs as well as transactions carried out on behalf of connected persons. In the event of transactions on financial instruments related to the issuer's shares, such amount applies to the underlying shares.[166]

12.196   The AMF has clarified[167] that once the aggregate value of transactions carried out within a year exceeds EUR 5,000, the declaring person must notify with respect to all transactions carried out within that year, including those amounting to less than EUR 5,000 which were not previously notified in accordance with the foregoing exemption. The notification must expressly state that such transactions were subject to the exemption so that they are not regarded as late notification. In addition, when a declaring person considers that the amount of transactions that it is likely to carry out within a year will exceed the above EUR 5,000 threshold, the notification should be made at the outset.

12.3.3.5 *Form of the disclosure*

12.197   Declaring persons must transmit their notification to the AMF electronically within five trading days from the completion of the reported transaction. Such notifications are published on the AMF's website.[168] Declaring persons must simultaneously transmit a copy of their notification to the issuer.[169]

---

[164] Q&A of the AMF dated 26 May 2009, relating to the requirement of notification of transactions carried out by officers, directors, PDMRs and the persons connected to them.

[165] Following the 'acquisition period' contemplated by applicable law, officers, directors or PDMRs are required to make a disclosure.

[166] General Regulations of the AMF Article 223-23.

[167] Q&A of the AMF dated 26 May 2009, relating to the requirement of notification of transactions carried out by officers, directors, PDMRs and the persons connected to them.

[168] General Regulations of the AMF Article 223-22.

[169] French Monetary and Financial Code Article L.621-18-2, 4th paragraph.

The form and contents of the notification (including information such as nature **12.198** of transaction, date and place, price per security and aggregate amount) is set out in AMF Guidelines No 2006-05 of 3 February 2006.[170]

Notifications are not subject to review by the AMF before their publication. The **12.199** AMF may however control such notifications *a posteriori*.

In addition, Article L.621-18-2 of the French Monetary and Financial Code **12.200** requires that the shareholders' general meeting of the issuer be informed of the reported transactions. Therefore, management's annual report[171] must include a summary statement of the transactions triggering the disclosure requirement carried out within the previous financial year,[172] including nominative information with respect to each officer or director.[173] Issuers may present the above-mentioned transactions in an abbreviated form.

12.3.4 Periodic financial reporting

12.3.4.1 Applicable provisions and extent of applicability

The financial reporting obligations imposed by the Transparency Directive were **12.201** implemented into French law in Articles L.451-1-2 et seq. of the French Monetary and Financial Code, supplemented by Article 222-1 et seq. of the General Regulations of the AMF.

These provisions impose financial reporting obligations on French issuers whose **12.202** shares are admitted to listing on a regulated market of an EEA member state or whose debt securities (with an individual nominal value of less than EUR 1,000) are admitted to listing on such a market. These provisions are also applicable to other French issuers (such as issuers with securities entitling them to a share of the capital of the issuer by way of conversion or otherwise or with debt securities admitted to trading on a regulated market of an EEA member state) as well as foreign issuers with securities of the foregoing type admitted to listing on a French regulated market, if such issuers have elected the AMF as the competent authority to oversee their disclosure obligations. They also apply to foreign issuers with equity securities or debt securities with an individual nominal value of less than EUR 1,000 admitted to listing on an EEA member state regulated market, where the first admission to listing occurred in France.

---

[170] General Regulations of the AMF Article 223-25.
[171] i.e. the report referred to in French Commercial Code Article L.225-100.
[172] General Regulations of the AMF Article 223-26.
[173] Q&A of the AMF dated 26 May 2009, relating to the requirement of notification of transactions carried out by officers, directors, PDMRs and the persons connected to them.

12.203   Applicable rules provide for exemptions, in particular for states, regional or local authorities of states, public international bodies of which at least one member state is a member, the European Central Bank and member states' national central banks. Exemptions are also available for debt issuers where the debt is irrevocably and unconditionally guaranteed by the French state or by French local authority, as well as issuers of debt securities admitted to trading on an EU regulated market issued in minimum denominations of at least EUR 50,000 and without any other securities listed on a regulated market.

12.204   The main financial reporting obligations consist of a requirement to publish annual financial reports, half-yearly reports and interim management statements. The obligation to publish quarterly financial information, however, only applies to the above-mentioned issuers whose shares are admitted to trading on a regulated market within the EEA. Note that, in case of a change in an issuer's scope of consolidation having an impact on its accounts of more than 25%,[174] the issuer must also include pro-forma financial information, at least in respect of the current fiscal year.

12.205   Such reports constitute regulated information and thus must be disclosed to the public accordingly (see Section 12.3.6 below).

12.3.4.2 Consolidated accounts

12.206   Annual and half-yearly financial reports must include consolidated financial statements prepared in accordance with IFRS, when the issuer is required pursuant to Articles L.233-16 et seq. of the French Commercial Code to prepare consolidated financial statements.

12.3.4.3 Annual financial reports

12.207   Annual reports must be filed within four months of each financial year-end and must be publicly available for at least five years. Reports must include audited financial statements, a management report and responsibility statements (also known as management certifications) as well as a copy of the auditors' report.

- *Financial statements*: In the case of an EU issuer that is required to prepare consolidated accounts, its financial statements must include IFRS-compliant consolidated accounts and the issuer's individual accounts prepared in compliance with the law of the member state in which the parent is incorporated. If the issuer concerned is not required to prepare consolidated accounts, then the accounts must be prepared in accordance with local GAAP.

---

[174] As interpreted by CESR. Note that, pursuant to General Regulations of the AMF Article 222-2, this obligation does not apply to issuers whose securities are admitted to listing on the Professional Compartment of Euronext.

- *Management report*: The report must include a fair review of the development of the company's business, results of operations and financial condition together with a description of the principal risks and uncertainties it faces and must give an indication of:
  - prescribed information concerning the share ownership in the company and certain other matters (including matters that may be material in case of tender offer on the company's shares such as, for example, restrictions in the exercise of voting rights or share transfers, rules applicable to changes in the composition of the board or the modification of the by-laws, agreements providing for indemnities payable to board members or employees in case of dismissal without cause or in case of tender offer);[175]
  - prescribed information concerning the acquisition and sale of the company's own shares during the previous fiscal year pursuant to a share buy-back programme (including number of shares and description of nature of transactions);[176] and
  - if the company prepares consolidated financial statements: a description of the company's outstanding debt, key performance indicators (whether of a financial nature or not, including information in respect of environmental matters and employees), a description of the company's use of financial instruments, to the extent relevant, with an indication of the goals of the company in respect of the management of financial risks (including its hedging policy for various types of transactions), and of the company's exposure to liquidity risk, credit risk and treasury risk or to price variations.[177]
- *Responsibility statement by representatives of the issuer*: These statements must be made by the persons responsible at the issuer (who must be named) and state that the financial statements have been established in accordance with applicable accounting principles and give a true and fair view, and that the management report includes a fair review of the development and performance of the business, of the results of operations and of the financial condition of the issuer and the other entities included in the scope of consolidation, as well as a description of the main risks and uncertainties that the issuer faces.
- *Auditors' report*: The report must also include a copy of the auditors' report relating to the financial statements included therein.

The AMF further recommends that issuers publish their annual revenues within **12.208** 60 days from the close of the fiscal year.[178]

---

[175] French Commercial Code Article L.225-100-3.

[176] French Commercial Code Article L.225-211.

[177] French Commercial Code Article L.225-100-2.

[178] *Recommandation de l'AMF relative à la publication par les émetteurs de leur chiffre d'affaires annuel.* 17 December 2008.

12.209 In addition to the annual financial report, companies must make at least the following information available in advance of their annual shareholders' meeting. This information may be included in the annual financial report or in a registration document, as the case may be, if the company decides to present one single annual report to its shareholders' annual meeting:

- interest held by employees in the share capital of the issuer; [179]
- the remuneration and other benefits granted to each director and officer; [180]
- the list of all positions (including directorships) held by each director and officer; [181]
- an indication of the social and environmental consequences of the activities of the company; [182]
- a description of environmentally-sensitive worksites (*installations seveso*); [183]
- a list of the issuer's subsidiaries and interests held in other companies; [184]
- an indication of the notifications of crossings of thresholds received by the company and a description of the share ownership in the company; [185]
- a summary of the outstanding authorizations to increase the share capital; [186]
- a summary of the transactions by PDMRs and connected persons in the company's securities; [187]
- the report of the chairman as to the activities of the board and the report of the chairman relating to internal control. [188]

12.210 Issuers may also decide to include in such a report the amount of fees paid to statutory auditors, thus discharging their obligation to disclose such information within four months from the end of any fiscal year.[189]

12.3.4.4 Half-yearly financial reports

12.211 Under French law, the above-mentioned issuers must publish a half-yearly financial report within two months of the end of the first six-month period of the financial year and the half-yearly report must be publicly available for at least

---

[179] French Commercial Code Article L.225-102.
[180] French Commercial Code Article L.225-102-1.
[181] French Commercial Code Article L.225-102-1.
[182] French Commercial Code Article L.225-102-1.
[183] French Commercial Code Article L.225-102-1.
[184] French Commercial Code Article L.233-6.
[185] French Commercial Code Article L.233-13.
[186] French Commercial Code Article L.225-100.
[187] General Regulations of the AMF Article 223-26.
[188] General Regulations of the AMF Article 222-8. Note that this obligation does not apply to issuers whose securities are listed on the Professional Compartment of Euronext.
[189] 'Recommandation de l'AMF relative à la publication par les émetteurs de leur chiffre d'affaires annuel'. 17 December 2008.

five years. It must include a condensed set of financial statements, an interim management report and responsibility statements, as well as a copy of the auditors' limited review report reproduced in full.

- *Financial statements*: By contrast with the annual financial report, the financial statements that must be included in the half-yearly financial report are not required to include the issuer's individual accounts, and may be presented in a condensed form.
- *Interim management report*: The interim management report must include details of any important events in the relevant period, the principal risks and uncertainties for the remaining six months and (for share issuers only) details of related party transactions.
- *Responsibility statements*: The responsibility statements must confirm that the financial statements have been established in accordance with applicable accounting principles and give a true and fair view of the business, results of operations and financial condition of the issuer and the other entities included in the scope of consolidation, and that the financial report contains a fair description of the items required to be included therein pursuant to Article 222-6 of the General Regulations of the AMF. The responsibility statements must also identify those individuals responsible for the half-yearly report.
- *Auditors' report*: Under French law, semi-annual financial statements of issuers with transferable securities admitted to listing on a regulated market must be subject to a limited review by the auditors. Accordingly, the half-yearly financial report must also include a copy of the auditors' limited review report relating to the financial statements included therein.

12.3.4.5 *Interim management statements*

Companies with shares admitted to trading on a regulated market must disclose the following financial quarterly information within 45 days following the end of the first and third quarter:

12.212

- *Interim management report*: The statement must contain the following information:
  - an explanation of material events and transactions that have taken place since the start of the relevant period and their impact on the issuer's financial condition;
  - a general description of the financial position and performance of the group during that time;
  - an indication of the revenues, broken down by segment of activity, for the relevant quarter as well as each preceding quarter during the fiscal year and a comparison with the same period of the preceding fiscal year.

While the narrative nature of such report has been expressly admitted by the AMF,[190] the content of such report is not specifically defined by applicable rules. Instead, following consultation, the AMF has considered it preferable to allow professional associations of issuers to establish guidelines.[191] These guidelines insist on the purely narrative nature of the information, on their distinction with quarterly accounts, and justify this approach in particular by the drawbacks attached to quarterly financial statements (such as too important a focus on the short-term, quarterly results not being representative, in many instances, especially in case of seasonality or exceptional events occurring during a quarter, and costs associated with the preparation of such quarterly financial information).

12.213 This obligation does not apply to companies that publish full quarterly reports, whether on a voluntary basis or pursuant to applicable local law or the rules of the relevant regulated market. It also does not apply to companies that only have debt securities admitted to trading on a regulated market.

12.3.4.6 Other disclosure requirements (e.g. annual information update)

12.214 See Section 12.3.4.3 above.

12.3.5 Major shareholding notifications

12.3.5.1 Applicable provisions and extent of applicability

12.215 The French Commercial Code contains provisions[192] imposing a requirement on holders of an interest in an issuer to make certain notifications regarding the percentage of share capital and voting rights in the issuer beyond certain specified thresholds, and to make certain additional disclosures regarding certain agreements or financial instruments with similar economic effect.[193] In addition, if certain specific thresholds are met, the persons subject to the notification requirement must also disclose their intentions in respect of the issuer for the following six months. The General Regulations of the AMF[194] provide for implementing rules of such legal provisions.

12.216 These requirements apply in respect of issuers whose shares are admitted to trading on a regulated market and, to a certain extent, to issuers whose shares are admitted to trading on an organized multilateral trading system.

---

[190] AMF press release dated 16 October 2006, relating to the date of applicability of periodic reporting obligations further to the implementation of the Transparency Directive, stating that the report must contain a general description of the financial condition and results of operation of the company and its controlled affiliates, as well as an explanation of material events and transactions having occurred during the relevant interim period.

[191] Position AFEP, ANSA, CLIFF, MEDEF, MiddleNext, SFAF, dated 31 May 2006.

[192] See French Commercial Code Articles L.233-7 et seq.

[193] Such additional disclosure requirement became effective only as of 1 November 2009.

[194] General Regulations of the AMF See Articles 223-11 et seq.

Major shareholding notification requirements and ancillary disclosure require- **12.217**
ments have been amended several times in the recent past, in particular with a
view to the implementation into French law of the Transparency Directive, but
also as a reaction of the Government and of the French regulators to recent hostile
acquisitions of major stakes in French listed companies through the use of certain
undisclosed derivative products. The latest amendments result from French
Ordinance No 2009-105 of 30 January 2009, and a correlative amendment of the
General Regulations of the AMF published on 27 July 2009. The rules described
below are effective as of 1 August 2009 or, as expressly indicated below, as of
1 November 2009.

12.3.5.2 *Filing of major shareholding notifications*

Shareholders of French companies with shares admitted to trading on an EU **12.218**
regulated market are required to notify the company of holdings crossing certain
thresholds in terms of share capital or voting rights. As further described below,
the applicable legal and regulatory framework applies to certain contracts and
financial instruments (such as unconditional options to acquire shares); other
contracts and financial instruments must only be disclosed in connection with a
required notification but do not independently constitute notification triggers.

The notification must also be made to the AMF. In turn, the AMF publishes the **12.219**
information received within three trading days following receipt of complete
notifications. Additional notifications may have to be made to issuers only (and
not to the AMF), if the issuer's by-laws so provide.

In its annual report to shareholders, the issuer must disclose the information it **12.220**
receives.

In order to enable the appropriate notifications of major shareholdings to be **12.221**
made, issuers are required to publish or update, on a monthly basis, the total
number of their outstanding voting rights and shares (including shares whose
voting rights are suspended), in case of changes since the previous publication,
as well as within 15 days from the date of the annual ordinary shareholders'
meeting and from the date that the issuer becomes aware of a change of more
than 5%.[195]

In addition, issuers must also make notifications if they acquire or dispose of their **12.222**
own shares, either themselves or through a person acting in his (or her) own name
but on behalf of the issuer. The legal and regulatory regime applicable to issuers'

---

[195] French Commercial Code Articles L.233-8, R.233-2 and A233-1 and General Regulations
of the AMF Articles 223-11 and 223-16.

share buy-back activities and the resulting notification requirements are not described in this Chapter.

12.3.5.3 *Notification thresholds and notifiable interests*

12.223 Notification is mandated when the share capital or voting rights held as a shareholder reaches, exceeds or falls below 5%, 10%, 15%, 20%, 25%, 33.33%, 50%, 66.66%, 90% and 95%.

12.224 Additional notifications may have to be made to issuers only (and not to the AMF), if the issuer's by-laws provide for additional notification thresholds—which may not relate to shareholdings or voting rights representing less than 0.5%, or multiples thereof.

12.225 In determining whether the threshold has been triggered, the following shares are to be disregarded:[196]

- shares acquired for the sole purpose of clearing or settlement within a settlement cycle not exceeding three trading days;[197]
- shares held by a custodian in such capacity;
- shares held by an investment firm provided the shares are held in its trading book (within the meaning of the applicable capital adequacy directive[198]), voting rights attached to such shares do not exceed 5% and the investment firm ensures that the voting rights are not exercised or used to intervene in the issuer's management;[199]
- shares subject to a collateral arrangement with a central bank of the European System of Central Banks; and
- shares held by a market maker in such capacity provided the percentage of such shares does not exceed 10%, and the market maker ensures that (i) the voting rights are not exercised or used to intervene in the issuer's management and that (ii) it refrains from any influence on the issuer to acquire such shares or to stabilize their market price. The market maker must inform the AMF of the beginning of its activities in respect of a certain issuer or when it ceases such activities, in each case within five trading days.

12.226 Persons making notifications must do so with reference to the aggregate of shares or voting rights held as a shareholder and those treated as such by virtue of applicable law; the latter category is referred to herein as 'indirect holding of shares or voting rights'.

---

[196] French Commercial Code Article L. 233-7.
[197] General Regulations of the AMF Article 223-13 1°.
[198] Directive 2006/49/CE of the Parliament and the Council of 14 June 2006.
[199] General Regulations of the AMF Article 223-13 1°.

Article L.233-9 of the French Commercial Code sets forth the types of indirect **12.227**
holdings of shares or voting rights of a person that must be taken into account for
purposes of the threshold notification requirement, as follows:

1. shares or voting rights held by one or several third parties on behalf of that
   person;
2. shares or voting rights held by companies controlled by such a person
   (where control has the meaning set forth in Article L.233-3 of the French
   Commercial Code); therefore, parent undertakings must aggregate their holdings with the holding of any controlled undertaking, and controlled undertakings are not required to make independent filings if such filings are made by
   the parent undertaking;
3. shares or voting rights held by a third party with whom that person acts in
   concert (within the meaning of Article L.233-10 of the French Commercial
   Code, i.e. with whom that person has concluded an agreement with a view to
   adopting a common policy towards the issuer in question);
4. shares issued and outstanding that such person or any of the above-mentioned
   persons is entitled to acquire, immediately or in the future, upon its own
   initiative, pursuant to an agreement or a financial instrument, as well as voting
   rights that such person may acquire pursuant to the same conditions.

The AMF has interpreted this definition as follows:[200]
- The AMF has set forth the following non-comprehensive list of financial
  instruments covered by this definition: exchangeable bonds, forward contracts, and options (including call and put options, and regardless of the
  strike price as compared to the market price).
- As regards options, the AMF has specified that if the exercise of an option is
  conditional upon a certain threshold level of market price being reached,
  such option must be taken into account in the calculation of the number of
  shares triggering a notification requirement as soon as such threshold share
  price is reached; conversely, until such threshold is reached, the option is
  only disclosed as additional information in the event that the beneficiary is
  otherwise required to make a notification.
- In addition, pursuant to Article L.233-9 of the French Commercial Code,
  financial instruments held by an investment firm are disregarded, provided
  that they are held in its trading book (within the meaning of the applicable
  capital adequacy directive[201]), that they do not give entitlement to shares or
  voting rights in the issuer in excess of 5%, and the investment firm ensures

---

[200] General Regulations of the AMF Article 223-11.
[201] Directive 2006/49/CE of the Parliament and the Council of 14 June 2006.

that the voting rights are not exercised or used to intervene in the issuer's management.

5. shares (or voting rights attached thereto) in which that person has a usufruct (*usufruit*);

6. shares or voting rights held by a third party under an agreement concluded with that person providing for the temporary transfer of the shares or voting rights in question;

7. shares (or voting rights attached thereto) deposited with that person which the person can exercise at its discretion in the absence of specific instructions from the shareholder;

8. voting rights which that person may exercise as proxy where that person can exercise the voting rights at his discretion in the absence of specific instructions from the shareholders.

12.228 Conversely, Article L.233-9 of the French Commercial Code specifies that the following must be disregarded for the purpose of determining whether the threshold has been triggered:[202]

1. shares (or voting rights attached thereto) held (or that may be exercised) by a person in his capacity as the operator of a UCITS scheme, provided that the voting rights may be exercised on a discretionary basis by such operator, without any direct or indirect instructions from that person or from any of its direct or indirect controlling shareholders; the operator must provide the appropriate confirmations to the AMF, upon request, as to the organizational means permitting such independence and, where the person is a client of the UCIT scheme, as to the existence of a written contract establishing a clear independence between the UCIT and the client; and

2. shares (or voting rights attached thereto) held (or that may be exercised) in a portfolio managed by an investment firm in its capacity as portfolio manager on behalf of third parties, subject to similar conditions as those set forth in 1 above.

12.229 Notifications must specify the resulting situation in terms of voting rights, the chain of undertakings through which the voting rights are held, if any, the date as of which the threshold was triggered and the identity of the shareholder and of the person entitled to exercise voting rights on behalf of the shareholder.

12.230 The notification sets forth the number of securities entitling their holder to a share of the capital of the issuer and the voting rights attached thereto.

---

[202] These provisions are supplemented by those of Articles 223-12 et seq. of the General Regulations of the AMF.

Where applicable, the notification must also contain a description of the financial instruments (other than shares) taken into account for the purpose of determining whether a notification requirement has been triggered. **12.231**

In addition, the notification must contain a description of the characteristics of any agreement referred to in 4 above, as well as:

- the maturity date of the financial instrument or agreement;
- if applicable, the date as of which or period during which the shares may be acquired;
- the conditions according to which shares may be acquired pursuant to such instrument or contract, as well as the maximum number of underlying shares (without deduction or set-off of shares that may be sold by such person pursuant to the same or another financial instrument).

As of 1 November 2009, the following additional information must be included in the notification: **12.232**

- the number of shares or voting rights acquired under an agreement providing for the temporary transfer of the shares or voting rights;
- options referred to in 4 above, whose exercise is conditional upon a market price threshold being reached, where such threshold has not been reached;
- shares issued and outstanding underlying a contract or financial instrument providing for cash settlement exclusively and providing such person with a similar economic effect as the holding of shares (including, without limitation, in case of indexation of such financial instrument on the underlying shares); this last category is also intended to include contracts for difference.

12.3.5.4 *Declaration of intentions*

Pursuant to Article L.233-7 VII of the French Commercial Code,[203] in connection with the crossing of the thresholds of 10%, 15%, 20% and 25% of the share capital or voting rights or an issuer, the person crossing such threshold must notify the issuer and the AMF of its intentions in respect of the issuer for the following six-month period. The declaration of intent must specify the mode of financing of the acquisition, whether the person making the declaration of intent acts alone or in concert, whether it contemplates pursuing its acquisitions, whether it intends to acquire the control of the issuer, the strategy that it contemplates for the issuer and the transactions that it intends to implement with a view to its implementation (such as a merger, reorganization, liquidation, transfer of a substantial part of the assets, any proposed change in the activity of the issuer, any proposed modification of the by-laws of the issuer, any proposal to de-list the shares of the **12.233**

---

[203] These provisions are supplemented by the provisions of Article 223-17 of the General Regulations of the AMF.

issuer, any proposed issuance of securities by the issuer), as well as any agreement for the temporary transfer of the shares and voting rights. The declaration must also specify whether the acquirer intends to require its appointment or that of one or several persons to the board of the issuer.[204]

12.234   In case of change of intention within the six-month period following the filing of such declaration of intent, a new declaration, duly justified, must be notified to the issuer and filed with the AMF immediately. This declaration starts a new six-month period during which any change of intention must be notified and filed.

12.3.5.5 *Notification deadlines*

12.235   Notification to issuers and to the AMF must be made as soon as possible and in any event not later than four trading days following the relevant triggering event as described above.

12.3.6 Dissemination of regulated information

12.3.6.1 *Applicable provisions and extent of applicability*

12.236   Articles 221-3 et seq. of the General Regulations of the AMF set out the rules relating to the dissemination of regulated information. As a general principle, issuers must ensure that regulated information is effectively disseminated in full.[205] Such information must be simultaneously filed with the AMF.[206]

12.237   These requirements apply to issuers with securities (*titres financiers*) admitted to trading on a regulated market or on Alternext or the *Marché Libre*.[207]

12.3.6.2 *Regulated information*

12.238   Pursuant to Article 221-1 of the General Regulations of the AMF, where the issuer's securities are traded on a regulated market, 'regulated information' refers to the following documents and information:[208]

- the annual financial report;[209]
- the half-yearly financial report;[210]

---

[204] Pursuant to General Regulations of the AMF Article 223-17 II, the foregoing information does not apply to persons engaging, on a regular basis, in the activity of portfolio management on behalf of third parties, provided that the crossing of the thresholds of 10% or 15% of the share capital or voting rights occurs in connection with the conduct of its activity, that it declares that it does not intend to acquire the control of the issuer nor to request any appointment on the board, and that its activities are conducted independently from any other activity.

[205] General Regulations of the AMF Article 221-3-I.

[206] General Regulations of the AMF Article 221-5.

[207] General Regulations of the AMF Article 221-1-1°.

[208] General Regulations of the AMF Article 221-1-1°.

[209] General Regulations of the AMF Article 222-3.

[210] General Regulations of the AMF Article 222-4.

- the quarterly financial reporting;[211]
- the reports relating to the conditions for preparing and organizing the work of the board of directors or the supervisory board and the internal control and risks management procedures implemented by the issuer;[212]
- the announcement relating to the fees paid to statutory auditors;[213]
- information relating to the total number of voting rights and number of shares making up the share capital of the issuer;[214]
- the description of buy-back programmes;[215]
- the announcement relating to the availability of any prospectus;[216]
- inside information disclosed pursuant to Article 223-2 of the General Regulations of the AMF;
- the announcement relating to the availability of certain information that French law[217] requires to be made available to the shareholders prior to any shareholders' general meeting (including, information relating to the directors, general managers, members of the management board or members of the supervisory board, the draft of the proposed resolutions, the report from the board of directors or the supervisory board, the financial statements, the report from the statutory auditors);
- information relating to any change in the rights attached to various classes of shares, including changes in the rights attached to derivative instruments issued by the issuer and giving access to that issuer's share capital;[218]
- information relating to any change in the terms and conditions of the issuance that may directly affect the rights of holders of financial instruments other than shares;[219]
- information relating to any new debt issues and, in particular, any guarantee or security in respect thereof.[220]

With respect to issuers having their securities traded on Alternext or the *Marché*   **12.239**
Libre, 'regulated information' includes: (i) the announcement relating to the availability of any prospectus[221] and (ii) inside information disclosed pursuant to Article 223-2 of the General Regulations of the AMF.

---

[211] French Monetary and Financial Code Paragraph IV of Article L.451-1-2.
[212] General Regulations of the AMF Article 222-9.
[213] General Regulations of the AMF Article 222-8.
[214] General Regulations of the AMF Article 223-16.
[215] General Regulations of the AMF Article 241-2.
[216] General Regulations of the AMF Article 212-27.
[217] French Commercial Code Article R.225-83.
[218] General Regulations of the AMF Article 223-21.
[219] General Regulations of the AMF Article 223-21.
[220] General Regulations of the AMF Article 223-21.
[221] General Regulations of the AMF Article 212-27.

12.3.6.3 *Dissemination*

12.240 Article 221-3 of the General Regulations of the AMF provides that issuers must ensure that regulated information is effectively disseminated in full.[222] Such dissemination is made in the following two ways:

- Regulated information must be available online on the issuer's website as soon as such information is disseminated;[223] and
- Regulated information must be simultaneously filed electronically with the AMF.[224]

12.241 These requirements are cumulative.

12.242 The dissemination of regulated information pursues the following objectives set forth in Article 221-4 of the General Regulations of the AMF:

- The manner of dissemination must be such that the information is capable of reaching as wide a public as possible and as close to simultaneously as possible in the home member state and other EEA states.
- The information must be communicated in full to the media and in a way that ensures the security of the communication, minimizes the risk of data corruption and unauthorised access, and provides certainty as to the source of the regulated information.
- The communication must identify the issuer, the subject matter of the information and the time and date of the communication.

12.243 Pursuant to Article 221-4-IV of the General Regulations of the AMF, issuers are deemed to comply with the above-mentioned requirements of effective and full dissemination and filing with the AMF of regulated information when they transmit such information electronically to a primary information provider that complies with the above-described dissemination procedures and that is registered on a list established by the AMF. Such primary information provider carries out the filing of the regulated information with the AMF.[225] Issuers do not however have any obligation to use such primary information provider.

12.244 Issuers may, upon request from the AMF, have to communicate to the AMF the name of the person who transmitted the regulated information to the media, the details of the security measures taken, the time and date on which the information was transmitted to the media, the means by which the information was

---

[222] General Regulations of the AMF Article 221-3-I.

[223] General Regulations of the AMF Article 221-3-II. With respect to issuers having their securities listed on Alternext or the *Marché Libre*, regulated information is deemed to have been fully and effectively disclosed when it was published on the issuer's website.

[224] General Regulations of the AMF Article 221-5.

[225] Instruction No 2007-03 from the AMF dated 27 April 2007, relating to the filings of regulated information with the AMF.

transmitted and the details of any embargo placed by the issuer on the information, if any.[226]

In addition to the dissemination of regulated information electronically, an issuer must also make financial disclosure through print media, at a frequency and in a format that it considers appropriate given the type of securities issued, its size and shareholding structure.[227] Such disclosure may include all or part of the regulated information that was disseminated electronically, but it is more concise and flexible in its content than the regulated information communicated to the media in unedited full text. Such disclosure must also not be misleading and must be consistent with the information electronically disseminated.[228]   **12.245**

Exemptions from effective and full disclosure requirement: Article 221-4-V of the General Regulations of the AMF provides that the financial statements and the reports relating to the conditions for preparing and organizing the work of the board of directors or the supervisory board and the internal control and risk management procedures implemented by the issuer may be disseminated by means of an announcement indicating the conditions of availability of such documents.   **12.246**

Exemption from the separate publication of regulated information requirement:[229] In principle, any regulated information must be disclosed in its entirety. However, the General Regulations of the AMF provide for certain exemptions and authorize the inclusion of various regulated information in a registration document or an annual financial report. In order to benefit from such exemption, the issuer must comply with the following two cumulative conditions: (i) the information included in the registration document or the annual report must be published within the required time period; and (ii) the issuer must clarify when it publishes such document the list of regulated information that it contains. With respect to the annual financial report, the issuer may include the announcement relating to the fees paid to the statutory auditors and the report relating to the conditions for preparing and organizing the work of the board of directors or the supervisory board and the internal control and risks management procedures implemented by the issuer.[230] In addition, issuers may be exempted from the separate publication of the annual report and the announcement relating to the fees paid to the statutory auditor if it files and registers with the AMF, within four months of the end of the financial year, a registration document which includes all information   **12.247**

---

[226] General Regulations of the AMF Article 221-4-IV.

[227] General Regulations of the AMF Article 221-4-VI. Recommendation from the AMF dated 20 January 2007, relating to financial communication in print media and dissemination of regulated information by issuers listed on a regulated market.

[228] General Regulations of the AMF Article 221-4-VI.

[229] Guide from the AMF relating to the filing of regulated information with the AMF.

[230] General Regulations of the AMF Article 222-3.

required to be included in the annual report and the amount of the fees paid to the statutory auditors.[231]

12.248   *Filing of regulated information*: Regulated information must be kept available to the public for at least five years from the date of dissemination. Information must be filed at the time of its dissemination, or as soon as possible after such dissemination. Such filing requirement is met if issuers keep regulated information posted on their website under a specific heading for the above-mentioned five-year period. The filing requirement applies as from 20 January 2007 to regulated information disseminated after such date.

---

[231]   General Regulations of the AMF Article 212-13.

13

GERMANY

13.1 Listing Securities in Germany

13.1.1 The Frankfurt Listing

The Frankfurt Stock Exchange (*Frankfurter Wertpapierbörse* - FWB) (the 'FSE') is **13.01** by far the largest German stock exchange with approximately 90% of the total share turnover in Germany. Indeed, based on total share turnover, the FSE is the second largest exchange in Europe, behind only the London Stock Exchange.

The most prestigious category of listing for shares (or certificates representing **13.02** shares) in Germany is the Prime Standard market segment of the FSE (the 'Prime Standard'), which is a sub-segment of the statutory regulated market segment of the FSE (*Regulierter Markt*) (the 'Regulated Market'). A Prime Standard listing is generally comparable to a primary listing on the London Stock Exchange. Accordingly, companies listed on the Prime Standard are subject to the most

835

stringent regulatory requirements applicable to listings on the FSE and in certain cases, these standards are more demanding than the minimum standards laid down in the Transparency Directive, as described in Part 1. Prime Standard listings account for 47% of all regulated market listings in Germany. [1]

13.03 The benefit of listing on the Prime Standard, rather than on another market segment or sub-segment of the FSE, stems from the rigours of its 'super-equivalent' standards, which are set out in the Exchange Rules for the Frankfurt Stock Exchange (*Börsenordnung für die Frankfurter Wertpapierbörse*) (the 'BO FWB'). [2] Companies that list on the Prime Standard often aim to achieve inclusion in one of the FSE indices, including DAX (large cap), MDAX (mid-cap), SDAX (small-cap) and TecDAX (technology issuers). A Prime Standard listing is one of the prerequisites for inclusion in one of these indices.

13.04 A Prime Standard listing, which is only available to issuers of shares, or certificates representing shares, is one of several listing categories offered by the FSE. Listings of securities other than shares or certificates representing shares (in particular, debt securities such as corporate bonds or derivatives) do not involve compliance with super-equivalent regulatory standards; rather, such listings generally require companies to adhere to the minimum standards set out in the applicable EU directives, which are described in Part 1.

13.1.2 The German Federal Financial Supervisory Authority

13.05 The Federal Financial Supervisory Authority (*Bundesanstalt für Finanzdienstleistungsaufsicht*) (the 'BaFin') is in practice the competent authority in Germany for purposes of the German Securities Prospectus Act (*Wertpapierprospektgesetz*) (the 'WpPG'). Although the relevant stock exchange is nominally the competent authority for granting admission of securities to trading on a particular regulated market in Germany, the BaFin is solely responsible for reviewing and approving the securities prospectus. Germany's stock exchanges have no mandate under German law to challenge a securities prospectus that has been approved by the BaFin in connection with the admission of securities to trading.

---

[1] Facts & figures, Prime Standard, General Standard, Entry Standard, XETRA Deutsche Börse Group, May 2009, http://deutsche-boerse.com.

[2] See BörsG section 42 as to the relevant German law. The Transparency Directive was implemented in Germany by the Act Implementing the Transparency Directive (Transparenzrichtlinie Umsetzungsgesetz—TUG), which came into effect on 20 January 2007. Through this Act the provisions of the Transparency Directive were implemented into the German Securities Trading Act (Wertpapierhandelsgesetz) (the WpHG). Germany is permitted to retain super-equivalent standards in this area because the Transparency Directive laid down only minimum standards of harmonization.

In preparation for a listing on the FSE, a company's advisers, particularly its legal   **13.06**
counsel, are likely to have a significant amount of contact with the BaFin in connection with the review of the prospectus and the timing of the approval of the
prospectus, the preparation of which is typically the most important and most
time-consuming part of the process of listing securities on a regulated market. The
ability of an applicant and its advisors to maintain a good working relationship
with the BaFin can be an important factor in whether an application for listing on
the FSE is successful in a timely manner.

In addition to its competencies relating to the approval of securities prospectuses,   **13.07**
the BaFin is the federal financial supervisory authority in Germany with respect
to securities trading. The BaFin's key objectives when discharging its functions are
to ensure the transparency and integrity of the financial market and the protection
of investors. Its principal securities supervision functions include the following:
(i) combating insider dealing; (ii) ad hoc disclosure; (iii) directors' dealings;
(iv) market manipulation; (v) major holdings of voting rights; (vi) rules of
professional conduct and organizational requirements; (vii) corporate takeovers,
(viii) enforcement of financial reporting; (ix) financial analyses (including 'analyst
reports'); (x) supervision of investment companies; and (xi) supervision of
the solvency of financial services institutions. In connection with its mandate,
the BaFin is authorized to create additional rules and impose additional requirements on issuers in connection with their securities listings.[3]

The stock exchange supervisory authorities of each of the German federal states   **13.08**
are responsible for supervising the orderly conduct of trading on Germany's stock
exchanges in accordance with the German Stock Exchanges Act (*Börsengesetz*)
('BörsG'). In particular, they monitor the pricing process in collaboration with
the exchanges' own trading surveillance units. The stock exchange supervisory
authorities are also responsible for the multilateral trading facilities ('MTFs'),
which are operated by the individual stock exchanges. The BaFin cooperates with
the stock exchange supervisory authorities in its role as Germany's national stock
exchange regulator.

13.1.3 The German stock exchanges

Germany has a total of seven stock exchanges. The largest, the FSE, is owned by   **13.09**
Deutsche Börse AG, which also owns the European futures exchange Eurex and
the clearing company Clearstream Banking SA. The Stuttgart Stock Exchange is
the second largest stock exchange in Germany. Germany's oldest stock exchange
is the Hamburg Stock Exchange, which merged with the Hannover Stock
Exchange in September 1999 to form a holding company, BÖAG Börsen AG,

---

[3] WpPG section 21.

which operates the two exchanges. The remaining stock exchanges are the Berlin Stock Exchange, the Munich Stock Exchange, the Düsseldorf Stock Exchange and the Bremen Stock Exchange (the latter being no longer an active exchange but rather a charitable trust).

13.10   Germany is also home to other securities exchanges, such as the Frankfurt-based Eurex, which is a derivatives exchange and clearing house.

13.11   Given its status as the largest stock exchange in Germany, this Chapter will focus on the FSE. It is important to note, however, that the FSE is not the only exchange in Germany that imposes super-equivalent requirements on its members. Other stock exchange regulated market segments, such as the 'M:access' market segment of the Munich Stock Exchange, may impose super-equivalent provisions or additional listing rules on issuers, which should of course be examined carefully in advance of any proposed listing.

13.1.3.1 *Market segments of the FSE*

13.12   When listing securities on the FSE, an issuer can choose between the two statutory market segments, the Regulated Market and the open market (*Freiverkehr*) (the 'Open Market'). Depending on the stringency of the continuing obligations regime that an issuer wants, or is able, to follow, it can choose between two standards of the Regulated Market: the General Standard and the Prime Standard. Both the General Standard and the Prime Standard benefit from the advantages of a full listing and require issuers to meet the minimum standards imposed by the applicable EU directives. As noted above, however, Prime Standard issuers must meet super-equivalent transparency requirements set out in the BO FWB. As noted above, only issuers of shares, or certificates representing shares, which are admitted to the Regulated Market may apply for admission to the Prime Standard.

13.13   Unlike the Regulated Market, the Open Market is not an organized market pursuant to the Prospectus Directive and the Transparency Directive, but rather an 'unofficial regulated market segment', which is governed only by rules and regulations established by the FSE.[4] The entry standard ('Entry Standard'), which was launched in 2005 by the FSE to provide an alternative to EU-regulated segments for small and mid-sized companies seeking access to the capital markets, is a special sub-segment of the Open Market. Issuers admitted to the Entry Standard must comply with a range of post-admission transparency obligations.

---

[4] While the Open Market is not an EU 'regulated market, it is also not an 'over-the-counter' market, since it is regulated by the FSE.

Until the implementation of the Prospectus Directive and establishment of the   **13.14**
BaFin in 2005, the FSE was also the regulator of the German securities industry,
fulfilling many of the functions that are now performed by the BaFin. Today, the
FSE's role in connection with the listing of securities is focused on the verification
of the formal listing requirements contained in the German Stock Exchange
Act (*Börsengesetz*) and the German Stock Exchange Admission Ordinance
(*Börsenzulassungsverordnung*) and the granting of the formal listing approval.

13.1.3.1.1 The Regulated Market

13.1.3.1.1.1 The Prime Standard   The Prime Standard of the FSE requires issu-   **13.15**
ers of shares to meet a range of continuing transparency obligations that exceed
the corresponding requirements for the General Standard. Accordingly, it appeals
particularly to companies aiming to position themselves to attract international
investors.

In addition to the statutory transparency requirements set out in the WpHG and   **13.16**
the relevant sections of the BO FWB, Prime Standard issuers must prepare their
financial reports in English and in German and must hold at least one analyst
conference per year. Furthermore, they are required to prepare quarterly financial
statements in both English and German (although non-German companies can
apply to publish quarterly reports in English only) and to maintain a corporate
action timetable which must be available on the issuer's website.

13.1.3.1.1.2 The General Standard   The General Standard segment is subject to   **13.17**
the minimum statutory requirements that apply to the Regulated Market and is
the listing option of choice for companies seeking a cost-effective listing in an
EU-regulated market and principally targeting domestic investors.[5]

Issuers in the General Standard must meet the minimum standards set out in the   **13.18**
applicable EU directives. Accordingly, the WpHG requires German issuers to publish an annual financial statement within four months of the end of the financial
year, as well as a management report and a balance sheet declaration.[6] The issuer's
annual financial statements and the interim report must be prepared in accordance
with International Financial Reporting Standards ('IFRS')/Internal Accounting
Standards ('IAS') or, in case of a non-EU issuer under certain circumstances,

---

[5] Under most circumstances, the distinction between an issuer organized under the laws of
the Federal Republic of Germany and an issuer organized under the laws of another country that
is listed on a German exchange usually does not make a difference in terms of the standards
that apply to the issuer. However, in certain cases, the distinction can be meaningful. As such
distinctions and their consequences are only meaningful in limited circumstances, this Chapter
does not discuss them.

[6] A balance sheet declaration is a declaration by management confirming the correctness and
competiveness of the financial reports pursuant to WpPG section 264(2) sentence 3 and HGB
section 289(1) sentence 5.

generally accepted accounting principles ('GAAP')—such as US GAAP, Canadian GAAP and Japanese GAAP —that are deemed to be equivalent to IFRS. In addition, German issuers must publish a semi-annual financial statement within two months of the end of the reporting period. Interim reports must be published for the first and third quarters and must give details of material events that have occurred during the reporting period. Post-admission obligations also include the immediate publication of inside information by way of ad hoc disclosures, disclosure of directors' dealings and certain other information, including, for example, changes in the level of holdings in the issuer's share capital when certain ownership percentage thresholds are crossed.[7]

13.1.3.1.2 Exchange Regulated Market

13.19   *13.1.3.1.2.1 The Entry Standard*   The Entry Standard segment of the Open Market is particularly well suited to small and medium-sized companies that want to begin trading their shares quickly and cost-effectively. It imposes fewer formal requirements and fewer post-admission obligations than the Regulated Market. The legal framework governing Entry Standard listings is set out under the 'General Terms and Conditions for the Regulated Unofficial Market' of the FSE. The Entry Standard is open to issuers of shares and certificates representing shares only.

13.20   Issuers that list on the Entry Standard must publish audited annual financial statements, including a management report in German or English, within six months of the end of the reporting period. The financial statements must be prepared in accordance with either national accounting standards (for example, German GAAP as set out in the German Commercial Code (*Handelsgesetzbuch*) ('HGB')) or IFRS. Interim reports must be published no later than three months after the end of the first six months of every financial year. In addition, an issuer listed on the Entry Standard must publish any information that could have an impact on the valuation of its shares. A brief profile of the issuer, its annual update and a current corporate action timetable must be made accessible on the issuer's website.

13.21   *13.1.3.1.2.2 Open Market*   Securities that are not admitted to the Regulated Market, including both equity and debt,[8] are eligible for admission to the Open Market.[9] Issuers listed on the Open Market are subject to less stringent admission and post-admission requirements than those listed on the Regulated Market or on

---

[7] For a more detailed description of post-admission transparency obligations see Section 13.3 below.

[8] General Terms and Conditions for the Regulated Unofficial Market on the Frankfurt Stock Exchange sections 11–13.

[9] General Terms and Conditions for the Regulated Unofficial Market on the Frankfurt Stock Exchange section 11(1).

the Entry Standard of the Open Market. The operating body of the Open Market, Deutsche Börse AG, is responsible for decisions regarding the listing of an issuer's securities on the Open Market.

13.1.3.1.2.3 First Quotation Board and Second Quotation Board The Open Market is split into two sections, the First Quotation Board and Second Quotation Board. All issuers with an initial listing of shares or certificates representing shares in the Open Market are included in the First Quotation Board, while issuers with shares or certificates representing shares already admitted to a domestic or foreign exchange-like market where securities can be purchased or sold are included in the Second Quotation Board.

13.22

13.1.3.2 *Multilateral trading facilities*

A number of off-exchange MTFs operate in Germany and are governed by the WpHG.[10] Financial institutions may establish MTFs, which are not required to be regulated by a stock exchange. MTFs are not EU regulated markets and companies listed on an MTF in Germany are subject only to the transparency requirements set out in sections 31g and 31h of the WpHG. In order to commence trading on a MTF, it is usually sufficient that the relevant security be included in the trading facility by the operator of the MTF. There are also no exchange-specific publication requirements in relation to securities traded on MTFs. Issuers do not have to publish annual reports or financial statements and there is no examination by the German Financial Reporting Enforcement Panel (*Deutsche Prüfstelle für Rechnungslegung DPR e.V.—DPR*).[11] Furthermore, issuers are not required to provide either ad hoc disclosures or directors' dealings reports and investors are not required to make disclosures relating to their voting rights.

13.23

13.1.4 Legislative overview

The listing requirements pertaining to Regulated Market listings of securities are set out principally in the WpPG (which in part replaced the Securities Sales Prospectus Act/Ordinance (*Verkaufsprospektgesetz/-verordnung*) and the Stock Exchange Act/Admission Ordinance (*Börsengesetz/-zulassungsverordnung*)). These key sources are supplemented by various stock exchange and governmental rules and regulations, which impose more detailed requirements on Regulated Market issuers.

13.24

---

[10] WpHG section 31f.

[11] The German Financial Reporting Enforcement Panel operates as the sponsoring organization for an independent body that enforces financial reporting requirements as provided for in WpHG section 37n et seq.

13.1.4.1 *The Securities Prospectus Act*

13.25 The Securities Prospectus Act (*Prospektrichtlinie Umsetzzungsgesetz*) implemented the Prospectus Directive into German law on 1 July 2005. The Securities Prospectus Act provides regulations for the preparation, approval and publication of securities prospectuses. As discussed in Section 13.1.2 above, the Securities Prospectus Act empowers the BaFin to create rules in connection with public offers and securities traded on regulated markets.[12]

13.26 The WpPG consolidated a number of related provisions under the Prospectus Act (*Verkaufsprospektgesetz*), the BörsG and the Stock Exchange Admission Ordinance (*Börsenzulassungsverordnung*) (the 'BörsZulV') into one single statute. The Prospectus Act (*Verkaufsprospektgesetz*) now relates exclusively to non-securities investments, such as shares in German limited liability companies or limited partnerships.

13.27 Before an issuer can offer its securities to the public or have such securities admitted to trading on a regulated market, it must prepare a prospectus in relation to the offering or application for admission and the BaFin must approve such prospectus.[13] The purpose of a prospectus is to provide investors with all material information relating to the issuer and the securities being offered, in order to enable such investors to make an informed investment decision. The BaFin reviews the prospectus, checking its completeness, internal consistency and clarity, but not the accuracy of its contents.

13.28 The WpPG obliges the BaFin to cooperate with competent authorities in other EU member states and implements the Prospectus Directive concept of prospectus 'passporting', under which the BaFin must accept a prospectus, without subjecting it to any further approval process, if such prospectus has been 'passported' into Germany (that is, approved by the competent authority in another EU member state).[14] Pursuant to this process, a certification and copy of the prospectus from the approving competent authority will be sent to the BaFin, verifying that the prospectus was prepared in accordance with the relevant local provisions implementing the Prospectus Directive.[15]

13.1.4.2. *Stock Exchange Act/Admission Ordinance*

13.29 In addition to the requirement to publish a securities prospectus in accordance with the provisions of the WpPG, the admission to trading of shares on the

---

[12] WpPG section 21.
[13] See WpPG section 3.
[14] WpPG section 17(1).
[15] Equally, prospectuses approved by the BaFin may be passported out of Germany into other EU member states.

Regulated Market is subject to the requirements set out in sections 32 BörsG, 1–12 BörsZulV, as well as a review by the management board of the relevant stock exchange.[16]

13.1.5 Eligibility for listing

13.1.5.1 Admission to the Regulated Market

13.1.5.1.1 General Standard—general eligibility criteria The legal bases for the first admission of shares to the Regulated Market of the FSE are regulated in detail in the BörsG, the BörsZulV, the Prospectus Act and the Exchange Rules. The requirements under the BörsZulV[17] include the following: **13.30**

- the anticipated market value of the shares to be admitted (or the equity of the company) must amount to at least EUR 1.25 million;[18]
- the issuer must have existed as a company for at least three years;[19]
- the securities must be freely tradable;[20] and
- a minimum of 25% of the issuer's shares must be in public hands (following admission).

The application for admission to trading to the Regulated Market of the FSE must be filed by the relevant issuer (together with a financial institution[21] that complies with the requirements set forth in section 30 para 2 of the German Stock Exchange Act).[22]   **13.31**

Although the exact procedures and timing regarding the admission of securities to the FSE depend on whether a prospectus is required, the minimum time required for a listing is typically three business days from the date of the application for listing.[23] In practice, depending on the size and complexity of the listing and the current workload of the stock exchange, the FSE listing process is likely to take more time than the minimum time set out in the BörsZulV. Issuers are therefore recommended to contact the FSE before starting the listing application process, in order to plan a suitable timetable.   **13.32**

---

[16] BörsG section 32 and BO FWB section 60(2).

[17] BörsZulV sections 1 to 12.

[18] BörsZulV section 2.

[19] BörsZulV section 3.

[20] BörsZulV section 5.

[21] The financial institution and the issuer are required to make the application together. Both the issuer and the financial institution must sign the application prior to submitting it.

[22] Issuers in the past were required under BörsZulV section 49 to make the admission application publicly available. This is no longer the case following the implementation of MiFID.

[23] See Section 2 for further information regarding exemptions to the requirement for a prospectus.

13.33 **13.1.5.1.2 Prime Standard—general eligibility criteria** Where shares or certificates representing shares are admitted to the Regulated Market of the FSE, the issuer may apply for admission to the Prime Standard sub-segment of the Regulated Market.[24] The issuer's management board must not be aware of any circumstances that could impair the issuer's ability to fulfil the additional obligations that arise from admission to the Prime Standard.[25] For further information regarding the additional obligations to which Prime Standard issuers are subject, see Section 13.3 below.

13.1.5.2 Inclusion in the Regulated Market—secondary listings

13.34 Securities are eligible to be included in the Regulated Market if they are already admitted to trading either:

- on the Regulated Market of another exchange in Germany;
- in another EU member state; or
- in another country that (i) imposes admission requirements and transparency obligations similar to those that apply to securities admitted to the Regulated Market; and (ii) guarantees the exchange of information with competent authorities in other relevant states (i.e. the BaFin) for the purposes of supervising trading.[26]

13.35 In order to avoid being subject to additional German and EU transparency requirements, most non-EU issuers whose securities are admitted to trading in their home member state typically choose to have their securities listed on the Open Market.

13.1.5.3 Depositary receipts—additional eligibility criteria

13.36 Global depositary receipts ('GDRs'), American depositary receipts and Frankfurt global depositary receipts can all be listed and traded on the FSE, which is home to more than 550 depositary receipt programmes.

13.37 Generally, issuers of depositary receipts listed on the FSE must meet the same requirements as issuers of shares. Certain listing requirements that apply to non-EU/EEA issuers of depositary receipts, however, are more lenient. For example, the BO FWB requires Prime Standard non-EU/EEA issuers of depositary receipts to provide semi-annual and quarterly financial reports within three months of the relevant half-year and quarterly periods, which is a month longer than the equivalent periods for German or EU/EEA issuers of GDRs or issuers

---

[24] Exchange Rule for the Frankfurt Stock Exchange section 63(1).
[25] Exchange Rule for the Frankfurt Stock Exchange section 63(4).
[26] BörsZulV section 33.

of other securities. In addition, the FSE often waives or modifies certain listing requirements—for instance, the 25% free float requirement—for non-EU/EEA issuers of depositary receipts.

13.1.5.4 *Debt and other specialist securities—additional eligibility criteria*

There are no further eligibility requirements for listings of debt and other special-   **13.38**
ist securities beyond the criteria set out in Sections 32 BörsG, 1–12 BörsZulV and the BO FWB. However, prospectus requirements do vary according to the type of debt securities being admitted. In particular, the denomination per unit of the relevant securities determines the information required to be provided in the registration document.[27]

13.2 The Prospectus

13.2.1 Applicable law

The German rules regarding prospectuses follow the maximum harmonization   **13.39**
provisions in the Prospectus Directive and the directly applicable provisions in the Prospectus Regulation. Accordingly, they closely resemble the standards applied in other EU member states.

The WpPG implemented the Prospectus Directive in Germany. The WpPG   **13.40**
operates in conjunction with the Prospectus Regulation[28] to provide the legal framework for offers of securities to the public in Germany and admission of securities to trading on the Regulated Market in Germany.

This legal framework, as is the case in other EU member states, is supplemented   **13.41**
at the EU level by CESR's non-binding recommendations on the consistent implementation of the Prospectus Regulation. CESR also provides answers to frequently asked questions relating to the implementation of the Prospectus Regulation. CESR recommendations and answers to FAQs are not legally bind-ing, but are generally treated as binding by market participants in Germany and, in particular, by the BaFin.

---

[27] Prospectus Regulation Article 7 regulates the schedule for the registration document for debt and derivative securities regarding securities with a denomination per unit of less than EUR 50,000, whereas Article 12 regulates that for securities with a denomination per unit of at least EUR 50,000.

[28] WpPG section 7 states that the minimum requirements for the contents of a prospectus are those set out in the Prospectus Regulation.

13.2.2 Requirement for a prospectus

13.2.2.1 *The general requirement*

13.42   In accordance with the corresponding provisions under the Prospectus Directive, the German rules provide that the requirement to publish a prospectus is triggered in two circumstances: (i) when securities are offered to the public and (ii) when securities are admitted to trading on a regulated market. In accordance with the Prospectus Directive, there are a number of exceptions to the requirement to publish a prospectus, which are discussed in Part 1.

13.2.2.2 *Requirement for a prospectus in specific cases*

13.43   There are a number of circumstances, relating to specific types of securities offerings, where the German rules relating to the requirement to publish a prospectus possess certain nuances that merit further exposition. These are described below.

13.44   **13.2.2.2.1 Employee incentive schemes**   Companies with securities already admitted to trading on a regulated market in the EU and/or the EEA may offer securities solely to their existing or former directors or employees without having to publish a prospectus.[29] This is an exemption from the general requirement to publish a prospectus and requires the company instead to make a document available that contains information on the number and nature of the securities being offered and the reasons for and details of the offering. The BaFin currently does not provide detailed guidance regarding the exact content of such a document; rather, it simply refers issuers to the relevant CESR recommendations.[30]

13.45   In the case of an international employee incentive scheme, rather than produce a separate document for each relevant jurisdiction, issuers are permitted to refer eligible employees to documents provided to employees in other jurisdictions in connection with the same scheme, provided that (i) the relevant employees can reasonably be expected to read the document in the relevant foreign language; and (ii) such document complies with the relevant requirements of both the WpPG and the CESR recommendations.[31] In the case of a subsequent listing of the securities without a prospectus, a slightly different standard applies, insofar as section 4(2)(5) WpPG requires the securities allotted to the employees to be 'of the same class as the securities already admitted to trading on the same Regulated Market'. If the relevant securities are not of the same class as those

---

[29]   WpPG section 4(1)(5).

[30]   CESR recommendations for the consistent implementation of the European Commission's Regulations on Prospectuses No 809/2004, paragraphs 173–176 (CESR/05-054b, February 2005). See http://www.cesr-eu.org.

[31]   The relevant requirements are set forth in WpPG section 4(1)(5) and paragraphs 173–176 of the CESR recommendations, respectively.

already admitted to trading, a prospectus may be required, absent another exemption.

13.2.2.2.2 Debt tender/exchange offers   The requirement to produce a pro- **13.46**
spectus in the context of a debt or exchange tender offer depends on the nature of
the consideration to be offered for the relevant securities. When cash is offered for
securities, a prospectus is not required. When other securities are offered in
exchange for the securities, however, a prospectus is required and generally is subject to the same prospectus requirements as if it related to a typical offering and
listing.[32]

13.2.2.2.3 Rights offerings   In connection with a rights offering of a German **13.47**
issuer pursuant to section 186 of the German Stock Corporation Act (*Aktiengesetz*)
(the 'AktG'), various exemptions from the requirement to publish a prospectus
may be available, depending on the contemplated structure of the offering.

Since rights offerings usually involve (i) an offer of newly issued shares; and (ii) a **13.48**
subsequent admission of such shares to trading,[33] it is important to ensure the
availability of statutory exemptions from the obligation to publish a prospectus in
relation to both the offer and the subsequent admission to trading.

In accordance with the standard practice of the BaFin, a rights offering can be **13.49**
made without a prospectus if (i) the offer is first made only to the issuer's existing shareholders (which is a statutory requirement in rights offerings under
section 186 of the AktG); (ii) the rights will not be traded on a stock exchange;
and (iii) the shares not taken up by the existing shareholders during the rights
offering period (known as the 'rump placement shares') are offered under an
available exemption, that is, either to existing shareholders (the 'right to over-
subscribe') or to institutional investors only (a 'private placement').

The BaFin does not base this exemption on one of the statutory exemptions con- **13.50**
tained in sections 3 and 4 of the WpPG, but rather on the reasoning that an offer
of shares to existing shareholders without the possibility to trade the rights on a
stock exchange is in fact an offer made only to 'a limited circle of persons' (*'begrenzter Personenkreis'*) and is therefore not considered to be an offer to the public that
would trigger the obligation to publish a prospectus.

---

[32] However, an exemption from the requirement to publish a prospectus is available under
WpPG sections 3 and 4 if the exchange offer is made to a 'limited number of persons only' (*begrenzter
Personenkreis*), for example if the offer is made only to the issuer's existing shareholders. For further
details, see Section 13.2.2.2.3 below 'Rights offerings'.

[33] German issuers are under an obligation to complete subsequent admissions to trading of
newly issued shares within one year after the issuance of such new shares, pursuant to BörsZulV
section 69(2).

13.51 The subsequent listing of shares issued pursuant to a rights offering does not require a prospectus to be published if one of the exemptions set out in section 4(2) WpPG is available. The following two exemptions are the most likely to apply:

(i) the shares to be admitted to trading represent, over a period of 12 months, less than 10% of the number of shares of the same class already admitted to trading on the same Regulated Market (this exemption is usually not in the best interests of the issuer because it restricts the proceeds of the rights offering); or[34]

(ii) the shares issued in the rights offering can be considered as 'shares resulting from the conversion or exchange of other securities or from the exercise of the rights conferred by other securities'.[35] However, since there are currently no major precedents available where an issuer has relied on this exemption, any issuer seeking to utilize this exemption should discuss the matter in advance with its appointed advisers, as well as with the relevant stock exchange.

13.2.3 Preparing a prospectus

13.2.3.1 Pre-filing contact with the BaFin and the FSE

13.52 When it is clear that a prospectus is required in connection with a proposed listing or offer to the public, the company and its advisers will begin the prospectus drafting process. Any prospectus prepared in connection with an offer to the public or an application for admission of securities to trading must be approved by the BaFin and subsequently filed with the FSE.[36]

13.53 Although not required by German statutory law, it has become market practice to introduce a contemplated capital markets transaction to the BaFin by way of a 'pre-filing' letter before starting the official approval process. This letter is intended to inform the BaFin of the structure of the contemplated transaction, in particular, the proposed timetable. The letter should also raise any important issues that might impact on the prospectus, the timetable, or the transaction as a whole.

---

[34] Since the FSE requires that all shares issued under a rights offering be admitted to trading simultaneously, the admission of the shares to trading in several tranches is not a viable option.

[35] This interpretation of WpPG section 4(2) No 7 was not available in the past but has recently been offered by the FSE as an option to achieve the admission to trading of new shares issued in a rights offering without a prospectus if certain requirements are met.

[36] Although the FSE is formally the competent authority to grant admission to trading of the shares, the BaFin is solely responsible for reviewing and approving prospectuses. The FSE has no mandate under German law to challenge a prospectus previously approved by the BaFin in connection with the admission to trading of securities. For more information, see Section 1.2 'The German Federal Financial Supervisory Authority'.

Ultimately, the letter should give the BaFin sufficient comfort to ensure that any issues that could impact the listing are addressed prior to the first submission of the draft prospectus.

There is no definitive blueprint for a 'pre-filing letter' but the issues raised in pre-filing letters typically include the following: **13.54**

- short introduction of the issuer and the issuer's business (the BaFin usually does not accept pre-filing letters on an anonymous basis); if relevant, structure of the group and shareholders' structure;
- structure of the contemplated offering and/or listing;
- indication of whether the prospectus will need to be passported to another EU/EEA member state;
- timetable for the intended approval process in relation to the prospectus (including the dates for the prospectus filings, review and turnaround periods, target date for the approval of the prospectus) and timetable of the offer/listing;
- description of the issuer's financial history and the historical financial information to be included in the prospectus;[37] and
- any other issue that could have an impact on the approval process or should otherwise be brought to the BaFin's attention before the first filing of the draft prospectus.

The submission of the 'pre-filing' letter is typically followed by a discussion, either in a face-to-face meeting or by way of telephone conference (depending on the importance and the complexity of the matter) between the issuer, its advisers and the BaFin. In this meeting, the issuer and the BaFin usually agree on a preliminary timetable for the transaction and how the major issues raised in the pre-filing letter will be dealt with. In particular, the parties typically agree on the package of financial statements the issuer will present in the prospectus.   **13.55**

The subsequent filing of the first draft of the prospectus must be accompanied by a formal application letter (*Billigungsantrag*), which must include a formal application to approve the prospectus, a power of attorney (if not previously filed) and a cross-reference list to identify specific items of information that are required to be disclosed in the prospectus pursuant to the Prospectus Regulation.[38] The formal application letter typically also makes reference to the previous   **13.56**

---

[37] The advisers may need to elaborate on this point, particularly, in cases where the issuer has a 'complex financial history' and the prospectus would, therefore, not contain the usual set of financial statements for the last three full financial years of the issuer as provided for in the Prospectus Regulation). The issuer or its advisers should also mention to the BaFin in advance if the first submission of the prospectus does not yet contain the entire set of financials to be contained in the final prospectus, as well as the date when a complete document will be made available to the BaFin.

[38] WpPG section 13 sets out the requirements for the filing of the formal application letter.

discussions between the issuer and the BaFin and repeats the agreements during such discussions.

13.57 Depending on the complexity and importance of the proposed listing, approximately two to three weeks prior to the targeted approval date of the prospectus, the issuer should contact the FSE regarding the exact timetable of the admission process.

13.58 If there are any fundamental issues to be resolved in connection with the listing that are extraneous to the prospectus approval process (for example, if a listing of foreign securities is sought), issuers should contact the FSE at the same time as their initial contact with the BaFin.

13.2.3.2 *The BaFin approval process*

13.59 The BaFin must approve any prospectus before its publication. To obtain BaFin approval, applicants must ensure that they follow the correct procedure and that the prospectus contains the required information. The BaFin is not permitted to approve a prospectus unless it is satisfied that (i) Germany is the relevant home member state; (ii) the prospectus contains the necessary information (see Section 13.2.6 below); and (iii) the prospectus complies with all other applicable requirements imposed by BaFin or the Prospectus Directive.

13.60 The BaFin can require the inclusion of additional information if it considers this necessary for investor protection.[39] It can also require the provision of further information or documents, not only by the applicant issuer, but also by its beneficial owners, auditors or any financial intermediary involved in the proposed listing to which the prospectus relates.

13.61 Section 13 of the WpPG provides the timing and procedural requirements for the BaFin's approval of a prospectus. These requirements provide that a prospectus will be approved within 20 business days when prepared in connection with an IPO and within 10 business days in the context of other transactions.[40] In practice, however, the approval procedure and timeline often differs from these stated time periods, primarily due to the BaFin's propensity to require the inclusion of additional information in the prospectus.[41] In the context of an IPO, for example, the BaFin will typically approve the prospectus within six to eight weeks of the initial filing of the document (depending, *inter alia*, on the size of the prospectus and the complexity of the listing).

---

[39] WpPG section 21(1).
[40] WpPG section 13(1).
[41] WpPG section 13(3).

After the initial filing of the prospectus, the process typically will progress as **13.62** follows:

- the BaFin will deliver detailed comments within 10 to 12 business days;
- the issuer and its advisers will prepare a revised draft of the prospectus, which they will submit again to the BaFin, together with a an annotated list of the points the BaFin raised and an explanation of how the issuer has addressed these points;
- the BaFin will take approximately 10 further business days to provide comments on the second filing;
- the issuer will again prepare and submit a revised draft of the prospectus, together with an annotated list setting out the action taken to address the BaFin's comments;
- the BaFin will then usually respond within a couple of business days with minor comments; and
- the issuer will address these final comments, before filing the prospectus for the fourth and last time.

In the context of a rights offering, the above-mentioned time periods are shorter: **13.63** approval can usually be obtained within four to six weeks after the preliminary filing of the prospectus with the BaFin.

13.2.3.3 Prospectus supplement

13.2.3.3.1 When a prospectus supplement is required   If, following the publi- **13.64** cation of a prospectus and prior to the final closing of the offer, or the commencement of trading on the Regulated Market (whichever is later), a significant new factor, material inaccuracy or omission relating to the information provided in the prospectus arises or is identified, which could influence an investor's assessment of the securities, the applicant is required to publish a supplement to the prospectus that is formally approved by the BaFin.[42]

13.2.3.3.2 Supplementary prospectus in practice   Once an issuer and its **13.65** advisers determine that a prospectus must be amended, they must promptly file a supplement with the BaFin. The BaFin then has up to seven business days to comment on and approve the supplement, although issuers can obtain approval within two to three business days if necessary. After approval of a supplement, the issuer and its advisers must deliver the supplement to each investor that received a prospectus. Investors who have agreed to buy securities based on the information contained in the original prospectus have a right to withdraw their acceptance for two business days after the publication of any supplement (the 'two day put').[43]

---

[42] WpPG section 16.
[43] WpPG section 16(3).

13.66 Whether a supplement is required at the point when shares are issued largely depends on the transaction structure the issuer and its advisers have selected. For example, section 8 WpPG allows issuers to use the bookbuilding procedure (which is the process of soliciting and compiling orders for the offered securities into a 'book') in an offering of securities without the obligation to publish a supplement or an additional 'final' prospectus, provided that (i) the maximum purchase price is contained in the prospectus (usually a price range is given); and (ii) the maximum number of shares to be offered is contained in the prospectus. In these circumstances, the issuer is only required to publish the final offer price and offer volume on its website—an approved supplement is not necessary.[44]

13.67 This practice differs from that in other EU member states, such as the United Kingdom, where in the context of bookbuilding, issuers typically use a 'preliminary' prospectus that leaves placeholders for the outstanding information, in particular, the final share price and number of shares to be sold. In Germany, a prospectus containing a price range and the maximum number of shares to be offered is not considered a 'preliminary prospectus' but rather a final document, which does not require a supplement when the shares are eventually priced and issued. The issuer is merely required to publish the offer price and offer volume on its website.

13.68 If the offering involves an international placement with institutional investors, the issuer and the banks will typically provide an amended 'final' offering circular to such investors, which reflects the final share price and actual number of shares sold. The BaFin, however, does not impose any formal approval process in relation to such an offering circular, as the document is not strictly a 'prospectus'.

13.69 In certain transactions, the issuer will publish an initial prospectus that omits both a set price and details of a price range. This is called a 'decoupled' offering, as the price is decoupled from the initial offering. After the underwriters carry out preliminary discussions with investors based on the initial prospectus, the issuer and underwriters will determine a price range. In these circumstances, the issuer will be required to prepare a supplement to the prospectus that must receive the approval of the BaFin, as mentioned above. Such a supplement can include other updates or corrections to the prospectus. In relation to such decoupled offers, however, the BaFin now requires issuers to include in the initial prospectus at least the maximum number of securities to be offered.

---

[44] WpPG Section 14 para 2.

13.2.4 Prospectus contents

13.2.4.1 The 'necessary information'

The overriding disclosure obligation in a prospectus is to provide the information **13.70** necessary to enable investors to make a correct assessment of (i) the assets and liabilities, financial position, profits and losses, and prospects of the issuer and any guarantor of the transferable securities; and (ii) the rights attaching to the transferable securities. The 'necessary information' must be presented in a form that is comprehensible and easy to analyse and must be prepared with regard to the particular nature of the transferable securities and the issuer.[45]

This fundamental disclosure obligation is, of course, the standard laid down by **13.71** the Prospectus Directive. It operates in conjunction with the Prospectus Regulation, which sets out specific information requirements in a 'building block approach', under which different disclosure requirements apply depending on the nature of the relevant securities.[46] As a general rule, the most stringent disclosure requirements apply to equity securities. Where securities fit within more than one Prospectus Regulation annex, generally the requirements of all applicable annexes must be satisfied.

Typically, the 'Strengths and Strategy' section of an equity securities prospectus, in **13.72** which the issuer describes the competitive strengths that set it apart from its competitors as well as its future business strategy, provides disclosure that is not required under the Prospectus Regulation, but which market participants nevertheless generally consider necessary to enable investors to make an informed investment decision.

13.2.4.2 Financial information

A German issuer must publish in the prospectus audited historical financial infor- **13.73** mation relating to the latest three financial years (or such shorter period that the issuer has been in operation) and the audit report for each of these years. An issuer must also publish for such period selected historical financial information providing the key figures that summarize its financial condition.

In the event that the issuer has, during the three-year period, experienced a signifi- **13.74** cant gross change as defined in the Prospectus Regulation, pro-forma financial information is normally required to demonstrate the impact of the relevant transaction that caused the significant gross change on the issuer's assets, liabilities and earnings. When pro-forma financials are used by issuers subject to the German

---

[45] WpPG section 5(1).
[46] WpPG section 7.

WpPG, they must follow the accounting principles of the German Institute of Chartered Accountants (*Institut der Wirtschaftsprüfer in Deutschland e.V.*).[47]

13.75 The complex financial history rules set out in the Prospectus Regulation and the relevant CESR recommendations also apply to companies seeking to offer securities to the public or to have securities admitted to trading on a regulated market in Germany. See Chapter 2 of for a discussion of these requirements.

13.2.4.3 Derogations

13.76 The BaFin has the power to grant derogations from the specific prospectus contents requirements prescribed by to the Prospectus Regulation in certain cases, namely: (i) where disclosure would be contrary to the public interest; (ii) where disclosure would be seriously detrimental to the issuer (provided non-disclosure would not be likely to mislead a potential investor as to any facts, knowledge of which is essential for an informed assessment); and (iii) where the information is merely of minor importance in relation to the issuer and its securities.[48]

13.2.5 The advertisement regime and roadshow materials

13.77 The WpPG prohibits the publication of an advertisement relating to a public offer or the admission to trading of securities, unless such advertisement states that a prospectus has been or will be published and provides details of where investors can obtain such prospectus. Among other things, the advertisement must be clearly recognizable as an advertisement and its content must be accurate, coherent and consistent with the prospectus.[49]

13.78 Any material information provided by an issuer and addressed to qualified investors or special categories of investors, including any information disclosed during meetings relating to an offer of securities, must be included in the prospectus (or in a supplement thereto).[50] In particular, any roadshow materials used by the issuer or the investment banks during the marketing period for the offering must be consistent with the information presented in the prospectus and must not contain any material information that is not reflected in the prospectus.

13.79 These requirements considerably restrict the issuer and the investment banks during the marketing period, particularly in relation to the provision of forward-looking information (such as profit forecasts), which, for liability reasons, typically would not be included in the prospectus. Accordingly, the legal counsel to the issuer and the investment banks, who usually take the lead on the drafting and

---

[47] IDW RH HFA 1.004.
[48] WpPG section 8(2).
[49] WpPG Section 15.
[50] WpPG section 15(5).

reviewing of the prospectus, are often included in the review process of the road-show materials at a relatively early stage to ensure consistency between the two documents.

13.3 Continuing Obligations

13.3.1 Applicable law

The scope of an issuer's post-listing continuing reporting obligations under German law depends on (i) the stock exchange and market segment on which the issuer's securities are admitted to trading; and (ii) the nature of the issuer's listed securities. The Transparency Directive and the relevant German implementing legislation impose post-listing obligations only on issuers whose securities are listed on a regulated market.[51] Furthermore, as a general rule, issuers of equity securities are subject to more stringent ongoing reporting obligations than issuers of debt and other specialist securities. **13.80**

In accordance with earlier sections in this Chapter, the following examination of post-listing continuing obligations will focus on issuers whose securities are listed on the FSE. **13.81**

As explained above, the Regulated Market of the FSE is divided into two market sub-segments: the General Standard and the Prime Standard. Issuers whose securities are listed on the General Standard—which caters to issuers of both equity and debt—must meet the minimum ongoing reporting requirements set out in the relevant German laws implementing the Transparency Directive. Issuers whose securities are listed on the Prime Standard, which is available only to issuers of shares and certificates representing shares, must comply with a scheme of super-equivalent post-admission obligations. **13.82**

The differentiation in General Standard and Prime Standard was introduced not by German statutory rules based on the Transparency Directive, but rather by the private law listing rules (*Börsenordnung*) of the FSE. [52] The more onerous disclosure regime associated with a Prime Standard listing represents international transparency standards and, accordingly, appeals to companies seeking to attract international investors. **13.83**

---

[51] A current list of all regulated markets in the EU is published annually by the European Commission, available at http://eur-lex.europa.eu/.

[52] The Prime Standard's more onerous transparency regime is permitted since both the Transparency Directive and the relevant German laws allow for 'super-equivalent' transparency standards in stock exchange listing rules.

13.84   The key source for post-admission listing obligations in connection with a listing on the Regulated Market is the WpHG, which implemented the provisions of the Transparency Directive into German law in January 2007. The WpHG is supplemented by a number of governmental ordinances, principally, the Ordinance on Notification of Securities Trading and Insider Lists (*'Wertpapierhandelsanzeige- und Insiderverzeichnisverordnung'*) ('WpAIV').

13.85   In addition to the WpAIV, the WpHG operates alongside various German corporate laws and regulations that govern continuing disclosure obligations, including the following:

- the AktG;
- the HGB;
- the WpPG;
- German Corporate Governance Code, as implemented by the Government Commission on the German Corporate Governance Code (the 'Code'); and
- the BO FWB.

13.86   The BO FWB is of particular importance to Prime Standard issuers as it contains the super-equivalent post-admission obligations that differentiate a Prime Standard listing from a General Standard listing.

13.87   German law allows stock exchanges to establish open markets (*Freiverkehr*) for securities that are not admitted to trading on a regulated market, provided that listing and trading rules are made available by the relevant stock exchange to ensure proper trading and settlement in such markets. Issuers whose securities are listed on the Open Market are generally not subject to ongoing reporting obligations.

13.88   In addition to its regular Open Market segment, the FSE operates the Entry Standard, which, as explained in Section 13.1.3.1 above, is a sub-segment of the Open Market. The Entry Standard is governed by the General Terms and Conditions of the Unofficial Regulated Market of the Frankfurt Stock Exchange and requires issuers to comply with more stringent publication requirements than issuers whose securities are listed only in the Open Market. These include the requirement to publish audited annual financial statements and a half-year report in compliance with IFRS, as well as the requirement to present a company profile and corporate news on the company website. The Entry Standard is aimed primarily at small and medium-sized companies and offers an attractive alternative to a listing on an official regulated market but with greater visibility and more stringent admission and post-admission transparency requirements than a listing on the Open Market.[53]

---

[53]   BO FWB section 175.

13.3.2 Disclosure and control of inside information

13.3.2.1 *Key provisions*

Chapter 3 of the WpHG sets out the overriding disclosure obligation of a domestic issuer (*Inlandsemittent*)[54] to publish inside information to the market by way of an ad hoc announcement without undue delay after the inside information has materialized. The aim of this requirement is to ensure prompt and accurate disclosure of material information equally to all market participants. **13.89**

Chapter 3 of the WpHG (along with the WpAIV) also sets out provisions relating to insider trading; delaying the disclosure of inside information; selectively disclosing inside information; the obligation to compile and maintain insider lists; the mechanics of publishing inside information; and measures to control inside information. **13.90**

13.3.2.2 *Identifying inside information*

Insider securities are defined as financial instruments (i) that are admitted to trading on a German stock exchange or that are included in the Regulated Market or the Open Market; (ii) that are admitted to trading on an organized market in another EU or EEA member state; or (iii) whose price is directly or indirectly dependent upon financial instruments that fall within (i) or (ii) above.[55] **13.91**

Inside information is defined as information (i) that is certain; (ii) that is not publicly known; (iii) that relates, directly or indirectly, to the issuer or its securities; and (iv) that could have a significant effect on the market price of the insider securities, if the information were made public.[56] **13.92**

Central to identifying inside information is the question of whether the relevant information could have a significant effect on the market price of the insider securities if it became publicly known. A 'significant effect' is established if a reasonable investor, who is aware of all of the information available at the time of the investor's trading, would find it probable that the market price of the insider securities may be significantly affected by the publication of the information. **13.93**

A non-comprehensive list of types of information that the BaFin considers to have a considerable influence on a security's market price can be found in the BaFin's issuer guidelines.[57] **13.94**

---

[54] As defined in WpHG section 2(7).
[55] WpHG section 12.
[56] WpHG section 13.
[57] These are available at http://www.bafin.de.

13.3.2.3 Disclosure of inside information

13.95 Domestic issuers are under a duty to disclose inside information without undue delay[58] by way of an ad hoc announcement (i) via an appropriate electronic information dissemination system (for example, Business Wire, EquityStory, DGAP, euro adhoc or Hugin Online); and (ii) on the company website (where the relevant information must remain for at least one month).[59] Issuers must also disclose the same information to suitable media outlets (in particular, prominent national and European print media) in order to ensure the dissemination of the information throughout the EU. Any information disclosed in the above manner must also be reported to the company register immediately after publication.

13.96 **13.3.2.3.1 Timing of disclosure** Ad hoc announcements must be published without undue delay after the inside information has materialized, regardless of the relevant stock exchange's trading hours (all current electronic information systems offer the possibility of publishing ad hoc announcements at any time). The issuer is obliged to make all necessary arrangements to enable it to make an ad hoc announcement without undue delay. The issuer must also notify the BaFin and the FSE prior to the publication of the ad hoc announcement.[60]

13.97 When making an announcement, issuers must ensure that the relevant information is not made public on the company website before it has been disseminated via an electronic information system.

13.98 **13.3.2.3.2 Contents of disclosure** An ad hoc announcement must contain a detailed description of the inside information including the date on which the relevant facts materialized. It should be concise, not exceeding 20 lines of text. Information other than price-sensitive information must not be published in an ad hoc announcement (such information can be published through other means, such as a 'corporate news' announcement or a press release). It is standard practice for German issuers to publish a press release with corroborative information shortly after or simultaneously with the publication of an ad hoc announcement.

13.99 Issuers in the Prime Standard market segment must publish inside information in German and English.[61]

13.100 **13.3.2.3.3 Other issues** For a period of six years following the publication of inside information, an issuer must be in a position to provide the BaFin with the following details: (i) the name of the person who sent the information to

---

[58] WpHG section 15 WpHG and WpAIV sections 4 et seq.
[59] WpAIV section 5.
[60] This is typically ensured by the system provider through which the ad hoc announcement is made.
[61] WpHG section 15 and BO FWB section 69.

the media; (ii) the security measures used in conveying the information to the media; (iii) the day and the exact time the information was sent to the media; (iv) the method used to convey the information to the media; and (v) if applicable, information regarding any delay or postponement of the publication.[62]

An update of previous ad hoc announcements is required if the information previously announced has changed to the extent that it could significantly alter an investor's assessment of the issuer and its securities. Furthermore, if inaccurate information has been published, the issuer must prepare and announce a correction without undue delay. **13.101**

13.3.2.4 *Delaying disclosure*

As discussed above, issuers in possession of inside information are generally required to disclose such information as soon as possible. However, under section 15(3) WpHG, an issuer may postpone the publication of inside information under the following circumstances: **13.102**

(i) such postponement is justified by the legitimate interests of the issuer (that is, the issuer's interest in suspending the immediate disclosure of the relevant inside information outweighs the market's interest in immediate disclosure thereof);
(ii) the public is not being mislead due to the postponement; and
(iii) the confidentiality of the insider information can be ensured.

It is common practice for German issuers to have standard documentation in place for compliance with section 15(3) WpHG. **13.103**

13.3.2.5 *Press speculation and market rumours*

Press speculation and market rumours may constitute inside information if, although not necessarily entirely true, they are based at least in part on facts. In determining whether a reasonable investor would trade securities based on such speculation and rumours (i.e. whether the rumour constitutes price-sensitive information), the following factors should be considered: (i) the source of the rumours; (ii) verifiable facts available to investors; and (iii) general market conditions, in particular, conditions in the segment of the market in which the company operates. **13.104**

13.3.2.6 *Insider lists*

Issuers are required to compile and maintain a list of the persons who, on behalf of or for the account of the issuer, have received authorized access to **13.105**

---

[62] WpAIV section 3a (3).

inside information.[63] Insider lists can be set up in relation to specific inside information items, specific projects (*anlassbezogen*) and specific areas of responsibility (*funktionsbezogen*). Issuers must notify anyone placed on an insider list that they are deemed to be 'insiders' and must inform them of the legal implications of their access to inside information.

13.106 Insider lists must not be published, but rather kept for potential disclosure to the BaFin upon request for a period of six years starting with the date of creation of the relevant list. During this period, access to the insider list should be restricted to those persons responsible for the maintenance of the list. With regard to persons acting on behalf of or for the account of the issuer (i.e. parties other than the issuer's own employees), the list must identify the relevant company or entity (for example, the relevant auditors, law firm or bank) and indicate that the issuer has contractually obliged such company or entity to maintain a corresponding insider list itself (and can reasonably assume that such person or entity will comply with such obligation).

13.107 Insider lists must contain the following information:

- information regarding each person at the issuer responsible for maintaining the list;
- information regarding each person that has access to inside information (including, for example, their name, date of birth and private and business addresses);
- the reason for the inclusion of each person in the list;
- the date each person first received access to inside information and date on which each person acknowledges that he or she has access to inside information; and
- dates of when the list was created and updated.

13.108 Each insider list must be updated without undue delay whenever it has become outdated or otherwise incorrect.

13.3.3 Directors' dealings

13.109 Issuers' senior management members (*Personen mit Führungsaufgaben*) and their related parties must notify in writing both the BaFin and the relevant issuer of any trades they conduct in the issuer's shares or derivative instruments linked to such shares (including options) that exceed an aggregate amount of EUR 5,000 within a given calendar year.[64] Such persons must notify the BaFin and the issuer of the relevant trades no later than five business days after the trade date. The notification must contain information regarding the person subject to the notification

---

[63] WpHG section 15b and WpAIV sections 14 et seq.
[64] WpHG section 15 a and WpAIV sections 10 et seq.

obligation and details of the relevant securities transactions. The issuer, in turn, is required to publish the notification on its website no later than on the business day following its receipt of the notification and to report it to the electronic company register. The notification must be available on the issuer's website for at least one month commencing either on the date of publication of the notification or on the date of any amendment to such published notification.

The issuer must provide the BaFin with proof of publication of the relevant notification no later than three business days following publication. The issuer must also make available the information contained in any such notification to media companies (particularly prominent national and European print media) to facilitate the timely dissemination of the information simultaneously throughout the EU.

13.110

The senior management subject to the notification requirement with respect to dealings in the issuer's securities include members of the issuer's management and supervisory boards and other individuals in senior positions within the issuer. Persons closely related to such individuals generally include spouses, children and other relatives, as well as companies and other legal entities that are dependent on members of the issuer's senior management or their closely related persons.

13.111

13.3.4 Periodic financial reporting

13.3.4.1 Applicable provisions

Domestic issuers[65] must publish annual financial statements or consolidated financial statements pursuant to sections 37v et seq. of the WpHG (unless the issuer already has such an obligation pursuant to the HGB), along with semi-annual financial statements and interim management statements.[66] German issuers must also prepare unconsolidated financial statements in view of the fact that dividend payments are based on unconsolidated financial statements under applicable German corporate law requirements.

13.112

The general position is that financial statements must be prepared in accordance with IFRS, although the BaFin may exempt a non-EU issuer from this requirement if its financial statements are prepared in accordance with GAAP that are equivalent to IFRS.[67]

13.113

---

[65] As defined in WpHG section 2(7).

[66] BO FWB sections 65 and 66 apply in addition to the provisions contained in WpHG sections 37v et seq. with respect to the periodic financial reporting of Prime Standard issuers.

[67] The European Commission has recently declared US GAAP and Japanese GAAP equivalent. It has also declared Canadian, Chinese, South Korean and Indian GAAP equivalent on a transitional

13.3.4.2 *Annual financial reports*

13.114   All domestic issuers must publish an annual financial report which should contain, in particular: (i) audited annual financial statements (or, in the case of a group, audited consolidated financial statements); (ii) a management report; and (iii) a declaration by the management confirming the correctness and completeness of the financial reports (see Section 13.1.3.1.1 above).[68] Issuers must publish the annual financial report on the company website immediately after it is approved by the supervisory board and in any event no later than four months after the end of each annual reporting period.

13.115   German issuers must also publish and submit to the BaFin a notification regarding the availability of the annual report, which must be made available to suitable media outlets, in order to ensure the timely and simultaneous dissemination of the information throughout the EU. The issuer must also submit the notification to the electronic company register without undue delay after publication. In addition, Prime Standard issuers must electronically submit their annual financial report to the management board of the FSE.

13.3.4.3 *Semi-annual financial reports*

13.116   All domestic issuers of shares and certain debt securities must publish semi-annual financial reports, which should include (i) condensed interim financial statements (or, in the case of a group, condensed consolidated financial statements) that contain a condensed balance sheet, a condensed profit and loss statement and notes; (ii) an interim management report; and (iii) a balance sheet declaration.[69] The semi-annual financial report need not be audited or made subject to auditor review. Issuers must post the semi-annual financial report on the company website no later than two months after the end of the relevant semi-annual reporting period.

13.117   The relevant issuers must also publish and submit to the BaFin a notification regarding the availability of the semi-annual report in the same manner as required in relation to annual statements, as described above in Section 13.3.4.2.

13.3.4.4 *Interim management statements*

13.118   All domestic issuers of shares must publish interim management statements within the three months prior to the end of each annual or semi-annual reporting period. Such statements, which need not be audited or subject to auditor review,

---

basis until 31 December 2011, as these countries are planning to implement IFRS in the near future. See Commission Regulation (EC) No 1289/2008.

[68] HGB section 264(2) sentence 3; section 289(1) sentence 5; WpHG section 37v; and BO FWB section 65.

[69] WpHG section 37w and BO FWB section 66.

must contain information that enables investors to evaluate the development of the issuer's business operations during the relevant period.

However, issuers may instead choose to publish an interim financial report that **13.119** complies with the requirements set out in the WpHG for semi-annual financial reports (without the requirement to publish a balance sheet declaration). Issuers that opt to produce an interim management statement must post such statement on the company website at least ten weeks after the beginning of the first or second half of the financial year, respectively, and at least six weeks prior to the end of the relevant period.

The relevant issuers must also publish and submit to the BaFin a notification **13.120** regarding the availability of the interim management statement in the same manner as required in relation to annual statements, as described above in Section 13.3.4.2.

A different regime applies to Prime Standard issuers, which are required to publish **13.121** interim financial reports semi-annually as set out in section 37w(2) Nos 1 and 2, (3) and (4) WpHG (but no balance sheet declaration is required).[70]

13.3.4.5 *Super equivalent provisions*

In general, German legislation in the context of ongoing disclosure requirements **13.122** follows the minimum harmonization standards set out in the Transparency Directive. However, alongside the WpHG (the German Securities Trading Act), which implemented the Transparency Directive into German law, certain super-equivalent notification and publication provisions operate in the context of Prime Standard listings. These can be found in the BO FWB.

Notable examples of the super-equivalent standards applicable to Prime Standard **13.123** listings include the following:

- shareholding reporting obligations include a 3% notification threshold and the attribution rules are in some respects stricter than those required by the Transparency Directive;
- certain issuers must adhere to additional rules regarding the publication of information relating to the general meeting; and
- certain requirements of the Code, to the extent issuers comply with its requirements.

13.3.4.6 *Other disclosure requirements*

Issuers must prepare an annual information update containing all the informa- **13.124** tion the issuer has published or otherwise disclosed over the past 12 months,

---

[70] BO FWB section 66.

including disclosures relating to insider information, directors' dealings and disclosures of shareholdings in relation to certain thresholds.[71]

13.125   The annual information update must be submitted to the BaFin within 20 business days after publication of the annual financial report. [72] The document must be published and made available to the public on the company website.[73]

13.126   A Prime Standard issuer is also under a duty to prepare and continuously update a financial calendar for each financial year in German and English, which must be submitted to the Board of Admissions of the FSE in electronic form and published on the company website.[74] Such issuers also have a duty to conduct an analyst meeting at least once a year to announce the figures from the annual financial reports.[75]

13.3.5 Changes in shareholding notifications

13.127   Shareholders with voting interests in an issuer whose registered office is in Germany are under an obligation to notify the issuer and the BaFin if the percentage of voting rights they hold in the relevant issuer changes and, in the process, crosses certain ownership thresholds.

13.3.5.1 *Applicable provisions*

13.128   Any person whose direct or indirect shareholding in a domestic issuer's[76] outstanding voting share capital reaches, exceeds or falls below certain percentage thresholds (3%, 5%, 10%, 15%, 20%, 25%, 30%, 50% or 75%), typically following an acquisition or disposal of the relevant securities, must inform the issuer and the BaFin of the relevant change in voting rights within four business days.[77] If the issuer is a German real estate investment trust (REIT), additional thresholds of 80% and 85% apply.[78]

13.129   Domestic issuers must publish the change in the holdings of voting rights by making the information available to suitable media outlets in order to ensure the timely and simultaneous dissemination of the information throughout the EU no later than three trading days following the receipt of notice from the relevant vote holder. The issuer must simultaneously submit proof of the publication to

---

[71] WpPG section 10.

[72] Article 27(2) of EU Regulation 809/2004. In its consultation on the review of the Prospectus Directive of 10 January 2009, the EU Commission suggested deleting the requirement to publish a single document as currently set forth in section 10 WpPG.

[73] WpPG section 14(2).

[74] BO FWB section 67.

[75] BO FWB section 68.

[76] As defined in WpHG section 2(7).

[77] WpHG section 21.

[78] German REIT Act (Gesetz zur Schaffung deutscher Immobilien-Aktiengesellschaften mit börsennotierten Anteilen) section 11 (May 28, 2007).

the BaFin. Immediately after such publication the issuer must submit the published information to the electronic company register.[79]

Domestic issuers must also publish a change in their own holdings of shares if such holdings, by purchase, sale or by any other means reach, exceed or fall below 5% or 10 % of the total outstanding voting rights. The publication must be made no later than four trading days after the relevant change.[80]

13.130

13.3.5.2 *Filing of changes in shareholding notifications*

At the end of each calendar month during which a change in the percentage of voting rights occurs, a domestic issuer must (i) publish the total number of outstanding voting rights; (ii) provide evidence of such publication to the BaFin; and (iii) submit the change in the holdings of voting rights to the electronic company register without undue delay after publication. Such publication must be made in the same manner as required in relation to publications regarding changes in holdings of voting rights.[81]

13.131

13.3.5.3 *Holdings in financial instruments*

Any person whose direct or indirect holdings of other financial instruments that, under a legally binding agreement, unilaterally grant the holder the right to acquire the issuer's shares with voting rights attached thereto, reaches, exceeds or falls below 5%, 10%, 15%, 20%, 25%, 30%, 50% or 75% of the issuer's voting rights, must immediately inform the issuer and the BaFin about the change in the percentage of the relevant holdings of financial instruments.[82]

13.132

13.3.6 Dissemination of other information

German issuers, and generally also EU-issuers, must publish additional information relating to shareholder rights,[83] including, in particular, the following:

13.133

- *Holders of transferable securities*: a German issuer is under the obligation to make publicly available to its security holders all information that such holders require to exercise their rights in relation to the securities.[84]
- *Electronic Federal Gazette (Bundesanzeiger)*: a German issuer is under an obligation to immediately publish in the electronic Federal Gazette the following:
  - calling of the general shareholders' meeting and the agenda for such meeting; the total number of shares and voting rights at the time the general shareholders'

---

[79] WpHG section 26(1).
[80] WpHG section 26(1).
[81] WpHG section 26a.
[82] WpHG section 25.
[83] Unless exempted from such requirements by the BaFin under WpHG section 30f.
[84] WpHG sections 30a, 30d.

meeting is called and the rights of shareholders regarding participation in such meeting; and

- notifications regarding the distribution and payment of dividends; the issuance of new shares; the agreement on or exercise of, for example, exchangeable rights and subscription rights.[85]

- *Legal foundation*: a German issuer is under an obligation to disclose to the BaFin and the FSE any intended amendments to its articles of association or other legal foundation documents that affect its transferable securities at the latest upon the calling of the board meeting where such amendments are to be decided.[86]

13.134 An issuer must publish without undue delay all changes in the rights attached to ownership of its shares. For example, issuers must publish any change in voting rights relating to its shares. This notification requirement also applies to changes in rights deriving from financial instruments that are linked to derivatives issued by the issuer that confer conversion or acquisition rights relating to the issuer's shares. The issuer must notify the BaFin of any such changes, which should also be submitted to the electronic company register.[87]

13.3.7 Penalties

13.135 If an issuer breaches its various post-admission obligations set out in the WpHG, the BaFin may impose a fine on the issuer of up to EUR 1,000,000. For certain breaches of post-admission obligations, such as insider trading, the WpPG also provides for a range of penalties, including fines and imprisonment of up to five years.[88]

13.136 The FSE may also impose penalties for an issuer's violation of the BO FWB, as well as for breaches of obligations relating to the publication of ad hoc announcements. Such penalties may include revocation of the issuer's inclusion in the Prime Standard market segment.

13.3.8 The German Corporate Governance Code

13.137 The German Corporate Governance Code sets out corporate governance recommendations and suggestions for the management and supervision of German listed companies. The Code is administered by an independent body of corporate executives and academics, initially appointed by the German Minister of Justice

---

[85] WpHG sections 30b(1), 30d.
[86] WpHG sections 30c, 30d.
[87] WpHG section 30e.
[88] WpHG section 38.

in September 2001. The Code is comprised of six main sections relating to (i) shareholders and the general meeting; (ii) cooperation between the management board and supervisory board; (iii) the management board; (iv) the supervisory board; (v) transparency and (vi) reporting and audit of the annual financial statements.

Much like the United Kingdom's Combined Code on Corporate Governance, the Code is not mandatory but rather a 'comply or disclose' regime. Accordingly, German issuers that are admitted to a regulated market must publish a declaration of conformity each year, explaining which of the recommendations of the Code it does not follow.[89] German issuers are not required to make such a declaration regarding any failure to adhere to the suggestions that are found in the Code.

13.138

Summary of applicable continuing obligations

Rule	Obligation	Primary listing of equity
§161 AktG The Code	Corporate governance	Issuer must disclose whether it complies with recommendations under the Code and provide a statement of differences.
§37v WpHG §65 BO FWB	Annual report and accounts	Issuer must publish an annual financial statement at the latest four months after the end of the fiscal year.
§37w WpHG §37x WpHG §66 BO FWB	Semi-annual report	Issuer must publish a semi-annual financial statement on its website at the latest two months after the end of the reporting period, including, *inter alia*, a balance sheet, an income and cash flow statement and an interim report.
37y WpHG Commission Regulation (EC) Nos 1289/2008, 1606/2002	Financial reporting standards	Issuer must prepare financial statements in accordance with IFRS or IFRS equivalent GAAP for non-German issuers.
§30b(2) WpHG	Pre-emption rights notification	Issuer must notify existing shareholders regarding certain follow-on offerings that could dilute shareholdings.
§3 WpHG §13 WpHG §15 WpHG §4 et seq. WpAIV	Inside information: publication to the market as soon as possible and synchronized in all jurisdictions in which the company has securities listed	German issuer is under a duty to disclose inside information without undue delay after it arises via suitable media outlets that can ensure the dissemination of the information across the EU; such inside information must be reported to the company register.
§15b WpHG §14 et seq. WpAIV	Drawing up and maintaining an insider list	German issuer has to maintain a list of the persons who act for or on behalf of the issuer and have authorized access to inside information.

---

[89] AktG section 161.

Summary of applicable continuing obligations *(Continued)*

Rule	Obligation	Primary listing of equity
§15a WpHG §10 et seq. WpAIV	Directors' dealings	German issuer must report trades in shares or in financial instruments linked to the shares by the issuer's executives or/and their related parties as soon as their trades exceed an aggregate amount of EUR 5,000 within a given calendar year by notification in writing to the BaFin by those persons executing trades (both shares and options).
§37x WpHG	Interim management statements	German issuer must publish an interim report at least ten weeks after the beginning and six weeks prior to the end of each of the two halves of the fiscal year.
§26(2) WpHG §26a WpHG	Major shareholder notification	Any person whose shareholding in a German issuer reaches, exceeds or falls below certain percentages of the voting rights must inform the issuer within seven calendar days of a change in the percentage of voting rights; in turn, the issuer must publish the change together with the shareholder's new percentage in a supra-regional stock exchange gazette within nine calendar days after learning of the change.
§10 WpPG	Annual information update	Issuer must publish an 'annual information update' containing or referring to all information that it has made public over the previous 12 months.

14

IRELAND*

* The author is indebted to Patrick Quinlan, Associate, A&L Goodbody, for his assistance and contribution in the preparation and drafting of this Chapter, and would also like to thank his colleagues, Peter Walker and Carol Widger, Partners in the Banking and Investment Funds Departments of A&L Goodbody respectively, for their contributions and comments. The law is believed to be correctly stated as at 20 July 2009. Specific legal advice should be sought before any decision is made or action taken in respect of any matter discussed herein.

14.1 Introduction and Jurisdiction Overview

14.1.1 Markets

14.1.1.1 Introduction

14.01 There has been an official stock exchange in Ireland since the eighteenth century. Between 1973 and 1995, however, the Irish exchange comprised the Irish unit of the International Stock Exchange of the United Kingdom and, during that period, was effectively a constituent part of the London Stock Exchange ('LSE'). The Irish Stock Exchange ('ISE') became an independent entity in 1995 and today is Ireland's 'competent authority' for the purposes of (i) the admission of securities to trading; (ii) the listing rules (the 'Listing Rules') that govern the admission of securities to the official list of the ISE (the 'Official List'); and (iii) setting out and monitoring ongoing requirements applicable to companies with securities so admitted. The ISE is also a 'delegate authority' for the purposes of certain Irish regulations implementing the Transparency, Market Abuse and Prospectus Directives.

14.02 The ISE is a company limited by guarantee, incorporated under, and subject to, the Irish Companies Acts, 1963 to 2009 (the 'Companies Acts'). Membership of the ISE as a company is restricted by its rules[1] and articles of association[2] to trading members (firms which trade on the exchange, deal in Irish government bonds on the exchange or provide settlement or clearing services).

14.03 The ISE, like the LSE, permits the admission of various types of security to listing and trading on its regulated market, known as the 'Main Market'.

14.04 The ISE also operates an 'exchange-regulated' (i.e. regulated by the ISE) equity market, specifically designed for small to mid-sized companies—the Irish Enterprise Exchange ('IEX') and an additional exchange-regulated market for debt and derivative securities, launched in June 2009 —the Global Exchange Market ('GEM').

14.05 Although relatively small in terms of equity listings (41 companies had securities listed on the Main Market as at 20 July 2009), the ISE has been successful in attracting debt listings. In 2007, for example, 984 new debt issuers listed on the Alternative Securities Market (the predecessor to the GEM), while a further 412 listed in 2008.[3] The ISE's commitment to specific turn-around times on all documents submitted by companies applying for admission provides a high degree of certainty when arranging listings of debt and other forms of non-equity offerings.

---

[1] Rules of the Irish Stock Exchange Limited (Release 13—2 February 2009).
[2] Articles of Association of the Irish Stock Exchange Limited as amended and filed at the Companies Registration Office in Dublin.
[3] ISE official reviews for 2007 and 2008.

The ISE has also proven to be responsive to specific inquiries, which provides potential entrants wishing to list debt securities with a high level of comfort.

2008 saw the introduction of a new listing regime for investment funds targeted at 'super-sophisticated investors',[4] as well as a streamlining of the listing rules for closed-ended investment funds.[5] **14.06**

Recently published CESR statistics provide an indication of the relative success of the ISE in this sphere.[6] In the 30-month period to December 2008, 5,533 prospectuses were approved by the competent authority in Ireland (in contrast and by way of example, CESR figures show that during the same period 3,450 prospectuses were approved in the United Kingdom, 1,691 in Germany and 580 in France). **14.07**

14.1.1.2 The Main Market

The Main Market is the principal trading market of the ISE for equity and other securities and is a 'regulated market' within the meaning of MiFID. Securities that have been admitted to the Main Market include ordinary shares, preference shares, government and public sector bonds, corporate debt, exchange traded funds, UCITS and investment funds, debt securities, derivative securities and covered warrants. **14.08**

The Main Market is separate from the Official List, which is not a market of the ISE as such; rather it is the list to which securities are admitted by the ISE in connection with a stock exchange listing in Ireland. Equity securities are both admitted to trading on the Main Market and to listing on the Official List. **14.09**

Main Market companies, unlike their IEX counterparts, are subject to the full rigours of the Listing Rules, the separate Admission to Trading Rules of the ISE (the 'Admission to Trading Rules'), the Transparency Regulations[7] and the Market Abuse Regulations[8] (which are discussed in further detail in Sections 14.1.3.9 and 14.1.3.10 below). As in the United Kingdom, Main Market companies are **14.10**

---

[4] The term 'super-sophisticated investor' includes investment professionals, high net worth individuals and institutions and requires, *inter alia*, a minimum investment (US$500,000) and warranties from the investor as to minimum levels of expertise (ISE Policy Note 1/08). See also Section 14.1.5.4.

[5] ISE Review of Quarter Three 2008. See also Section 14.1.5 for further commentary on the funds regime in Ireland.

[6] CESR document 09-315 entitled 'CESR data on prospectuses approved and passported July 2006 to December 2008'.

[7] Transparency (Directive 2004/109/EC) Regulations 2007 SI 277/2007.

[8] Market Abuse (Directive 2003/6/EC) Regulations 2005 SI 342/2005.

subject to many requirements which are 'super-equivalent'[9] to the minimum standards of regulation prescribed by the directives discussed in Part 1.

14.1.1.3 IEX

14.11 IEX is the ISE's junior market for equity securities, designed for small to medium-sized growth companies, much like the United Kingdom's Alternative Investment Market ('AIM'). IEX was launched on 12 April 2005—partly in response to the success of AIM in the United Kingdom which had attracted a number of Irish companies—as a successor to both the Developing Companies Market and the Exploration Securities Market (on which, collectively, only eight companies were listed at the time). It was established with a view to facilitating the flotation of small to mid-sized Irish companies.

14.12 IEX is a 'multilateral trading facility' as defined in MiFID.[10] IEX has its own set of rules (the IEX Rules for Companies or the 'IEX Rules') which are similar in content to the AIM Rules in the United Kingdom. Indeed, IEX has been modelled very closely on AIM, with reduced admission criteria, no requirement for a prior trading record and no minimum requirement for the number of shares publicly floated. The one notable difference is that all IEX applicants are required to have a minimum market capitalization of EUR 5,000,000.[11] This market capitalization threshold is designed to prevent shell companies from undermining the credibility of the market.

14.13 The key advantages of IEX are considered to be the following:

- Smaller Irish companies can benefit from a presence in their home market.
- IEX companies may qualify for inclusion in the Irish Stock Exchange Quotient ('ISEQ') index (the Irish equivalent of the FTSE 100 index), thereby increasing their visibility to institutional and retail investors; and
- The IEX Rules are largely complementary to the AIM Rules, thereby allowing Irish companies the option of coordinating admission to both markets using the same timetable and essentially the same admission document. Several companies, such as, most recently, Worldspreads Group plc (which was admitted to trading on IEX on 15 May 2008),[12] have taken advantage of this regime. Of the 26 companies listed on IEX as at 20 July 2009, all but two have opted for dual

---

[9] Like the United Kingdom, Ireland has opted to impose standards above the minimum standards required by EU legislation, such as the Transparency Directive, and the Consolidated Admissions and Reporting Directive (Directive 2001/34/EC of the European Parliament and of the Council of 28 May 2001 on the admission of securities to official stock exchange listing and on information to be published on those securities [2001] OJ L184), known colloquially as 'CARD'.

[10] MiFID Article 4(15).

[11] IEX Rule 9.

[12] ISE Review of the first half of 2008.

listing on AIM. It is interesting to note, however, that in its first year of operation (2005/2006), it was reported[13] that, on average, 78% of all trading in the shares of new companies that listed on both IEX and AIM took place on IEX, an indication that the Irish market remains the main source of investment for small to medium-sized Irish companies.

In addition, a number of Irish public limited companies that were previously admitted to the Official List have taken advantage of this 'exchange-regulated' market to 'step down' from the full rigours of the compliance and continuing obligations regime associated with a listing on the Main Market. An example is the homebuilder, Abbey plc, which was granted admission to the predecessor to IEX, the Developing Companies Market, on 16 November 2004 and which is also admitted to AIM. It stepped down from the Main Market in the belief that IEX and AIM were more appropriate for its shares and would encourage greater interest in the company.[14] Another recent example is Fyffes plc, the fruit importer and distributor, which was admitted to IEX and AIM on 10 January 2007. Fyffes also believed that, following a demerger and spin-off of parts of its business, IEX and AIM would be more suitable markets for a company of its size.[15]

14.14

The key points of difference between the IEX Rules and the Listing Rules [16] are as follows:

14.15

IEX	Main Market
No specific admission criteria apply, other than the requirement for an applicant to have a minimum market capitalization of EUR 5,000,000.	Detailed conditions for listing apply.
No trading record is required.	A three-year trading record is usually required.
No minimum number of shares is required to be held in public hands.	A minimum of 25% of shares is required to be held in public hands.[17]
No pre-vetting of IEX admission documents is undertaken by the ISE.	The ISE pre-vets prospectuses prior to circulation.
In most cases, no prior shareholder approval is required for substantial acquisitions and disposals.	Prior shareholder approval is required for substantial acquisitions and disposals.
The Admission to Trading Rules are not applicable.	The Admission to Trading Rules apply.

---

[13] ISE Press Release (Exchange News) issued 12 April 2006.
[14] Abbey plc announcement 15 October 2004.
[15] Fyffes plc shareholder circular 10 November 2006.
[16] The Listing Rules are discussed in detail in Section 14.3.2.
[17] 'Public hands' does not include directors, their connected persons and trustees of any employees' share scheme or pension fund. The ISE may agree to a lower percentage if it is satisfied that the market can still operate properly.

14.16 In addition to the foregoing distinctions, because IEX is not a 'regulated market', Irish companies admitted to IEX are not, by virtue of such admission, subject to the Transparency Regulations or the Market Abuse Regulations. Instead, they are subject to the less onerous disclosure and insider dealing provisions of the Companies Acts. For example, there is no equivalent of the market abuse offence of 'market manipulation' under the Companies Acts, and the main thrust of the relevant provisions is to prohibit any persons connected with a company from dealing in the securities of that company if they are in possession of unpublished price-sensitive information. While the Companies Acts contain detailed disclosure provisions, there is no equivalent for IEX companies, for example, of the reporting obligations in the Transparency Regulations.

14.17 However, it has been indicated[18] that both the Transparency and Market Abuse Regulations will be extended at least in part to apply to companies listed on IEX in the near future, to provide for a uniform disclosure and dealing regime for all companies listed on the ISE's markets.

14.18 IEX companies that propose to make an offer of securities to the public are subject to the regulations implementing the Prospectus Directive in Ireland, namely the Prospectus (Directive 2003/71/EC) Regulations 2005[19] (the 'Prospectus Regulations'), unless an applicable exemption is available (see Section 14.2 below in relation to prospectus requirements).

14.1.1.4 *Global Exchange Market*

14.19 On 11 June 2009, the ISE launched the GEM, a new exchange-regulated market aimed primarily at professional investors, to replace the Alternative Securities Market. Listing on the GEM is achieved through the publication of listing particulars under the Listing Rules, rather than a prospectus.[20] The ISE has produced a combined set of listing and admission to trading rules for the GEM. The new listing rules will apply to all debt products, i.e. bonds, asset-backed securities, derivative securities and convertible bonds listed on the GEM. The rules also set out specific provisions for the listing of convertible securities.

14.20 An issuer might choose to list on the GEM as an alternative to the Main Market as the GEM is not a regulated market and therefore, in general, the specific rules applicable to instruments listed on regulated markets do not apply. Key features of the GEM include the following:

- The listing of debt or derivative securities on the GEM may provide increased marketability for such securities because the GEM is an on-shore European

---

[18] Irish Takeover Panel Consultation Paper—'Proposals to Abolish the Substantial Acquisition Rules', 24 November 2008 as regards the proposed extension of the transparency regime.

[19] SI 324/2005.

[20] Global Exchange Market Listing and Admission to Trading Rules chapter 1 paragraph 1.4.

exchange (certain investors may be restricted in their ability to invest in non-European securities).

- The quoted Eurobond exemption will be available to Irish-incorporated issuers that list their securities on the GEM. Assuming that the technical requirements are complied with, this exemption will allow a relevant issuer to pay all amounts of interest due on the relevant securities free of any withholding tax, irrespective of the jurisdiction of the holders. This is especially attractive to investors based in jurisdictions that do not have any form of tax treaty with Ireland.

- The provision by the ISE of comments on drafts of listing particulars within a short timeframe. (In practice, from the date of first submission, the ISE will require just three business days for their first review and thereafter will only require a further two business days to comment on every subsequent submission.)

- The ISE is expected to take a more flexible view on derogations from the GEM listing rules than it does in respect of the equivalent specialist listing rules for the Main Market.

- The GEM is not available for 'public offers' within the meaning of the Prospectus Regulations. To comply with the rules relating to 'public offers' under the Prospectus Regulations, it is necessary to prepare a prospectus that is approved by the Irish Financial Services Regulatory Authority (known as 'IFSRA' or the 'Financial Regulator'), unless an applicable exemption is available. The listing particulars that are prepared for listings on the GEM do not comply with the higher disclosure requirements of the Prospectus Regulations and are approved by the ISE rather than the Financial Regulator.

Securities admitted to trading on the GEM must also be admitted to the Official List and, accordingly, the Admission to Trading Rules will apply.[21]   **14.21**

14.1.2 Competent authority and delegate authority

The Central Bank and Financial Services Authority of Ireland (the 'Bank') was designated by Irish legislation implementing the Prospectus, Market Abuse and Transparency Directives as the 'competent authority'[22] for the purposes of these Directives and the relevant implementing regulations. The Financial Regulator is the Irish regulatory authority for the financial services industry. It is a distinct division of the Bank, with clearly defined regulatory responsibilities. It has the power to devise and impose rules, policies and codes affecting the financial services industry.   **14.22**

---

[21] Global Exchange Market Listing and Admission to Trading Rules chapter 2 paragraph 2C.5.1.

[22] It should be noted that the Irish Auditing & Accounting Supervisory Authority is the 'competent authority' in the context of certain financial reporting obligations of the Transparency Regulations.

14.23   The Financial Regulator, in accordance with its powers as competent authority, has delegated certain tasks relating to the scrutiny of prospectuses and certain functions under the Irish regulations implementing the Market Abuse and Transparency Directives to the ISE, which is the 'delegate authority' in respect of these tasks. The functions delegated to the ISE include exercising certain powers (such as requiring information and requesting meetings) to ensure compliance with the relevant rules and being the contact point for receiving certain notifications from issuers and other relevant persons.

14.24   As well as being a delegate authority, the ISE itself is the competent authority for the purposes of listing and admission to trading, having being designated as such by regulation 6 of the European Communities (Admission to Listing and Miscellaneous Provisions) Regulations 2007.[23]

14.25   In practice, a company and its advisers will deal with the ISE as delegate authority although the Financial Regulator as competent authority retains certain powers of enforcement and ultimately issues final approval of prospectuses.[24]

14.1.3 Legislative and regulatory framework in outline

14.1.3.1 *Investment Funds, Companies and Miscellaneous Provisions Act 2005 (the '2005 Act')*

14.26   The 2005 Act provided for amendments to certain aspects of the Companies Acts and the implementation of the Market Abuse and Prospectus Directives by statutory instrument.[25] It also permits the Financial Regulator to issue supplementary rules in respect of market abuse and prospectus law.[26] The 2005 Act states that the sanctions available for breaches of market abuse and prospectus law apply equally to breaches of any such rules.[27]

14.1.3.2 *Prospectus Regulations*

14.27   The Prospectus Regulations implemented the Prospectus Directive in Ireland. They provide that a prospectus required to be published in connection with a public offer or an admission to trading on the Main Market must (i) contain, as a minimum, the information prescribed by the Prospectus Regulation;[28] (ii) be approved by the relevant competent authority;[29] and (iii) be published in accordance with the specific requirements of the Prospectus Directive.[30] The Prospectus

---

23 SI 286/2007.
24 Prospectus Rules rules 2.2 and 2.3.
25 2005 Act sections 30 and 46 respectively.
26 2005 Act sections 34(2) and 51(2).
27 2005 Act, sections 34(6) and 51(7).
28 Prospectus Regulations regulation 20.
29 Prospectus Regulations regulations 12 and 13.
30 Prospectus Regulations regulation 44.

Regulations, the Prospectus Directive and the Prospectus Regulation, together with the 2005 Act (as amended), are the primary sources of prospectus law in Ireland. Irish prospectus law applies equally to Irish companies admitted to IEX or AIM that are contemplating a public offering of securities.

14.1.3.3 *Investment Funds, Companies and Miscellaneous Provisions Act 2006 (the '2006 Act')*

The 2006 Act amended the 2005 Act regarding certain provisions relating to liability for prospectuses (principally by exempting guarantors of non-equity securities from statutory civil liability for misstatements in a prospectus, except in relation to statements or omissions relating to the guarantor or its guarantee).[31] The 2006 Act also provided a framework for the introduction of national regulations to implement the Transparency Directive[32] and grants the Financial Regulator the right to issue rules and guidelines.[33] The 2005 Act and the 2006 Act together provide a statutory framework for the implementation of the EU prospectus, market abuse and transparency regimes in Ireland.

14.28

14.1.3.4 *Prospectus Rules and Guidance Notes*

Pursuant to its power to lay down rules for compliance with Irish prospectus law, the Financial Regulator has issued the prospectus rules (the 'Prospectus Rules'). These rules address practical issues such as the procedure for prospectus approval and the passporting of prospectuses. The rules also require that an issuer to whom Irish prospectus law applies must consider the contents of the CESR recommendations for the consistent implementation of the Prospectus Regulation[34] and the regularly updated CESR document titled 'frequently asked questions regarding prospectuses' ('FAQs').[35][36]

14.29

The Financial Regulator has also to date issued five guidance notes in relation to prospectus matters.[37]

14.30

---

[31] 2006 Act section 13.

[32] 2006 Act section 2. See also Section 14.1.3.9 below.

[33] 2006 Act section 22.

[34] CESR 05-054b.

[35] CESR/09-103 (10 February 2009). These documents are available on CESR's website (www.cesr.eu).

[36] Prospectus Rules rule 1.2.

[37] These guidance notes are available at http://www.financialregulator.ie/securities-markets/prospectus/Pages/requirements-guidance.aspx. A sixth guidance note, issued in November 2008 and relating to covered liabilities, was withdrawn as it was superseded by CESR guidance provided in Question 70 of the FAQs published on 17 December 2008.

14.1.3.5 *Companies Acts*

14.31   Although the older provisions of the Companies Acts relating to prospectuses have largely been repealed and replaced by the framework provisions of the 2005 and 2006 Acts, the Companies Acts continue to govern the legal environment for Irish-incorporated issuers. In addition, the somewhat less onerous provisions of the Companies Acts relating to disclosure and insider dealing continue to apply to Irish companies trading on IEX and AIM.

14.1.3.6 *Listing Rules*

14.32   The Listing Rules, which are broadly comparable to the FSA's listing rules, apply to all issuers whose securities are admitted to trading on the Main Market and to listing on the Official List. Notable differences between the Listing Rules and their United Kingdom equivalents are discussed in Section 14.3.2.4 below.

14.33   As noted above, the less rigorous IEX Rules apply to companies admitted to trading on IEX.

14.1.3.7 *MiFID Regulations*

14.34   MiFID was implemented in Ireland on 1 November 2007 by way of three statutory instruments and the Markets in Financial Instruments and Miscellaneous Provisions Act 2007. The statutory instruments are referred to collectively as the European Communities (Markets in Financial Instruments) Regulations 2007 (Nos 1 to 3).[38]

14.35   Although primarily concerned with the regulation of investment firms and intermediaries, MiFID has had a direct impact on the application and scope of the Prospectus Regulations by amending the definition of transferable securities (the definition of which was later the subject of comment by the European Commission). In addition, the implementation of MiFID caused the ISE to introduce separate rules in relation to the admission of securities to trading on the Main Market.

14.1.3.8 *Admission to Trading Rules*

14.36   The Admission to Trading Rules of the ISE became effective in November 2007 in response to the regulations implementing MiFID, which required the ISE to establish and maintain separate rules relating to the admission of securities to trading on its Main Market. The rules were updated in June 2009 to reflect the introduction of the GEM. Accordingly, the concepts of admission to trading and admission to the Official List are distinct, and companies seeking to offer securities to the public and/or have their securities traded on the Main Market, must

---

[38]   SIs 60, 663 and 773 of 2007.

satisfy these rules in addition to those relating to admission of securities to the Official List. In practice, admission to trading and admission to listing are notified to the market by the ISE in a single announcement.

14.1.3.9 *Transparency Regulations and Rules*

The Transparency Regulations implemented the Transparency Directive in Ireland. **14.37**

They are supplemented by rules published by the Financial Regulator in accordance with its powers under the 2006 Act (the 'Transparency Rules') which set out procedural and administrative requirements and guidance in respect of the Transparency Regulations. **14.38**

In addition, the Financial Regulator has recently published a guidance note[39] that clarifies its views in relation to a number of matters which have arisen in respect of the periodic financial reporting obligations of issuers under the Transparency Regulations. In particular, the guidance note highlights certain practical points that issuers should consider when seeking to comply with the transparency regime.[40] See Section 14.3.7 below for further detail on the transparency regime in Ireland. **14.39**

14.1.3.10 *Market Abuse Regulations and Rules*

The Market Abuse Regulations implemented the Market Abuse Directive in Ireland. They are supplemented by rules issued by the Financial Regulator in accordance with its powers under the 2005 Act (the 'Market Abuse Rules') which address some of the practicalities of disclosing inside information[41] and reporting suspicious transactions.[42] The Market Abuse Rules provide that relevant persons must have regard both to the applicable Irish and European legislation and the CESR guidance and information on the common operation of the Market Abuse Directive.[43][44] **14.40**

14.1.4 Categories of listing

14.1.4.1 *Primary*

A primary listing on the ISE is an admission of securities to listing on the Official List, by virtue of which the listed company becomes subject to the full requirements **14.41**

---

[39] 'Guidance Note No 1—Periodic Financial Reporting Obligations pursuant to the Transparency (Directive 2004/109/EC) Regulations 2007' (April 2009).

[40] For example, in relation to how periodic financial information should be published and the format of publication.

[41] Market Abuse Rules rule 5.

[42] Market Abuse Rules rule 8.

[43] CESR/04-505b and CESR/06-562b.

[44] Market Abuse Rules rule 1.2.

of the Listing Rules. A primary listing tends to increase a company's prestige and profile, not least because of the stringent regulatory regime that accompanies such a listing. This in turn can improve a company's credit rating and, accordingly, its ability to borrow. It can also provide a level of comfort to a company's suppliers and customers.

14.42 An Irish company (which must be a public limited company incorporated under the Companies Acts)[45] seeking admission to trading on the Main Market must apply for a primary listing, unless the company has (or intends to have throughout the period of its listing on the Main Market) an overseas primary listing on a recognized stock exchange, and its primary market,[46] in a country other than Ireland.[47] Although unusual, the ISE permitted Irish software company, Iona Technologies plc (which listed on 19 December 1997) to avail itself of this exemption, on the basis that its business was largely US-based. This enabled Iona to obtain a secondary listing on the ISE, while maintaining its primary listing on NASDAQ.[48] The ISE reviews the position of any companies that have benefitted from this exemption on a five-yearly basis to determine whether the exemption is still appropriate.[49]

14.43 A primary listing has traditionally served as an indication of high standards of corporate governance. As in the United Kingdom, companies admitted to trading on the Main Market are subject to a number of obligations that are 'super-equivalent' to the minimum standards of regulation prescribed by the Directives described in Part 1. These super-equivalent requirements, which are generally designed to enhance investor protection, appear throughout the Listing Rules and include provisions concerning related party and substantial transactions (which may require shareholder approval), sponsors (a sponsor must be retained by every Main Market company for the duration of its listing) and compliance with the Combined and Model Codes.[50] Many of these super-equivalent standards will apply to primary and dual primary listed companies only.

14.44 The Listing Rules also impose additional conditions for listing on companies seeking a primary listing of equity securities.[51] This means that a company that is eligible for listing on an exchange in another jurisdiction and has successfully

---

[45] Listing Rule 3.2.1.

[46] The ISE determines what a company's 'primary market' is on a case-by-case basis and will take into account factors such as the proportion of shares in the company held by the public in Ireland, where the majority of the trading in the company's shares takes place and the proportion of the company's turnover generated in Ireland.

[47] Listing Rule 11.4.1.

[48] Iona was taken over by Progress Software Corporation in 2008 and has since been de-listed.

[49] Listing Rule 11.4.3.

[50] See Section 14.3 for detail regarding these codes.

[51] Listing Rule 3.4.

passported a prospectus into Ireland is not automatically guaranteed to be admitted to a primary listing on the Official List.

Many large Irish public limited companies whose equity securities are actively traded have a primary listing on the ISE. One of the most notable exceptions is NTR plc, the utilities group which operates many of Ireland's toll roads and bridges. NTR is currently unlisted and its shares are believed to be traded through a 'grey market' among shareholders which is operated by the company in conjunction with its brokers. Although this 'grey market' is itself unregulated, the Financial Regulator regulates the relevant brokers. A 'grey market' arrangement is often seen as a stepping-stone to a full listing.

14.45

A company with a primary ISE listing may benefit from being quoted on the ISEQ index, subject to the approval of the ISE. New entrants to the market are eligible for inclusion if they meet the following three criteria:

14.46

• the relevant securities must be ordinary shares (or equivalent);
• the relevant securities must be admitted to trading on either the Main Market or IEX; and
• the issuer must be incorporated or have its centre of economic interest in either the Republic of Ireland or Northern Ireland.[52]

Companies that have been included on the ISEQ index for at least two years but whose businesses have developed in such a way that their centre of economic interest could be deemed to be outside Ireland will remain eligible for inclusion, subject to continued compliance with the other relevant ISEQ rules.

14.47

14.1.4.2 Secondary

A company with a primary listing on an overseas stock exchange may apply for a secondary listing on the ISE in order to gain access to another market of investors.[53] The obligations that will apply to the company and its officers following admission to a secondary listing on the ISE are less onerous than would be the case if its primary listing was with the ISE. However, certain additional conditions apply to secondary listings, as discussed further in Section 14.2.2.4 below.

14.48

14.1.4.3 Dual primary

It continues to be possible under Irish law for a company to have a dual primary listing—in other words to have the company's shares admitted to the official lists in both Dublin and London on a primary basis. As previously indicated, until

14.49

---

[52] ISEQ Indices Overview (ISE website).
[53] Listing Rules chapter 11.

1995, the ISE was linked to the LSE. Through an agreement reached between the ISE and the LSE, Irish companies listed in Dublin and London on the date of separation had an opportunity to obtain a dual primary listing on both the Dublin and London exchanges by simplified means. Historically, this preserved the *status quo ante* for certain Irish public companies which, prior to the separation, enjoyed an official listing of their shares on the constituent markets in both Dublin and London.

14.50 The increased regulatory burden associated with a dual primary listing may be such that this is not as attractive an option as it may once have been. However, some Irish companies, including Allied Irish Banks plc, The Governor and Company of the Bank of Ireland and Irish Life & Permanent plc continue to maintain dual primary listings. An example of an Irish company taking a different approach is Aer Lingus Group plc which, in connection with its initial public offering in October 2006, chose to have its equity securities admitted to the Official List by way of a primary listing and to the UKLA's Official List by way of a secondary listing.

14.51 Although it is not common for new applicants to seek a dual primary listing, the Listing Rules continue to expressly cater for this type of listing.[54] The procedure to effect a primary listing simultaneously on the ISE and the LSE is very similar to that involved in applying for a single primary listing on the LSE only. The ISE will separately scrutinize and raise queries on the admission documentation but is likely to maintain a regular dialogue throughout the process with the FSA, with a view to ensuring that matters progress smoothly.

14.1.4.4 *Proposals for change*

14.52 The ISE has announced a proposed separation of its operations into two distinct divisions, one with responsibility for its regulatory and supervisory activities and the other to carry out the commercial, marketing and promotional activities of the ISE (with the promotion of IEX as a market for small and medium-cap companies likely to be a priority).[55] It is unlikely that the proposed separation will lead to any significant changes in the short term in the listing practices and procedures of the ISE. Over the medium to longer term, however, the division of responsibilities may result in greater focus by the ISE on regulation and compliance by listed companies.

---

[54] For example, rule 3.3 of the Listing Rules (Conditions for Listing—Equity Securities Dual Primary Listing).

[55] ISE Announcement, 18 July 2008.

14.1.5 Investment funds: listing in outline

14.1.5.1 *Why list?*

A listing on the ISE is often sought by a promoter of an investment fund[56] who **14.53** wishes to market the fund to institutional investors, such as pension funds or insurance companies, as the regulations governing investments by such institutions often prohibit investment in issuers of unlisted securities. A listing on the ISE should serve to raise the status and prestige of an investment product, thereby increasing its credibility and international profile.

Although a listing on the ISE does not provide liquidity in the units of an issuer **14.54** (there being little dealing in securities of an issuer of this type in practice), an ISE listing is seen as a valuable marketing tool, particularly for targeting institutional investors who are prohibited from investing in anything other than listed securities.

14.1.5.2 *Requirements for listing*

There are specialist listing rules for investment funds which can be found on the **14.55** ISE's website.[57] The main features of the eligibility requirements for listing are as follows:

- as for any ISE listed entity, the applicant fund must appoint a sponsor;[58]
- listing particulars[59] must be approved by the ISE in advance of publication and must include all information necessary to allow potential investors to make an informed assessment on all relevant aspects of the investment fund;[60]
- a listed fund is required to have at least two directors who are independent of the investment manager and investment adviser, and the board of directors as a whole must collectively have appropriate and relevant experience in fund management and property investment (where relevant);[61]

---

[56] For the purpose of the ISE's listing rules for investment funds, a fund is defined as an undertaking which is a company, unit trust, limited partnership or other entity with limited liability, the objective of which is the collective investment of its capital. Investment funds can be open or closed ended. See Section 14.1.5.3 in relation to the requirements for the listing of closed-ended funds.

[57] Principal among these are the 'Investment Funds—Code of Listing Requirements and Procedures of the Irish Stock Exchange' but the ISE has also issued a number of ancillary documents.

[58] Investment Funds—Code of Listing Requirements and Procedures of the Irish Stock Exchange rule 1.1.

[59] Listing particulars are defined in the listing rules for investment funds as any document (including but without limitation any prospectus, placing memorandum or other equivalent document) submitted to the ISE for the purpose of the listing of any class of unit of any fund or sub-fund on the ISE.

[60] Investment Funds—Code of Listing Requirements and Procedures of the Irish Stock Exchange rule 3.1.

[61] Investment Funds—Code of Listing Requirements and Procedures of the Irish Stock Exchange rules 2.17, 2.20 and 7.19.

- a listed fund must appoint a custodian who is responsible for the safekeeping and custody of all of the assets of the fund, including any assets that are charged in favour of a lending bank. The custodian must be a separate legal entity from the investment manager and must be appointed by written agreement with the relevant investment fund;[62]
- where the investment fund is regulated by the Financial Regulator, the ISE will apply a more straightforward set of listing requirements so as to minimize any conflict between the two sets of requirements;[63]
- the ISE has no restrictions on the domicile of a fund; however, if the fund is not domiciled in an EU member state, Hong Kong, the Isle of Man, Jersey, Guernsey or Bermuda, the ISE requires that the fund restrict the sales of its units to sophisticated investors. This condition is met by imposing a minimum initial subscription requirement of US$100,000 or an equivalent in another currency.[64]

14.1.5.3 *Closed-ended funds*

14.56 Unlike open-ended funds, the requirements for the listing of a closed-ended fund on the ISE are governed by the provisions of the Prospectus Regulations. The ISE defines a closed-ended investment fund as one that does not permit the redemption of its units. Action taken by a fund to ensure that the stock exchange value of the units does not vary significantly from its net asset value is regarded as equivalent to such redemption;[65] however, the rules specify that the appointment of a market maker should not be regarded as an action taken by a fund for these purposes.

14.1.5.4 *Super-sophisticated investor fund*

14.57 In August 2008, the ISE introduced a new regime for the listing of investment funds that fall within the definition of super-sophisticated investor fund ('SSF').[66] A number of the normal listing requirements of the ISE, such as investment restrictions, do not apply to SSFs. However, the SSF must demonstrate a general spread of investment risk, both in terms of investments and counterparty exposure. An SSF can be either open-ended or closed-ended.

---

[62] Investment Funds—Code of Listing Requirements and Procedures of the Irish Stock Exchange rule 2.28.

[63] Investment Funds—Code of Listing Requirements and Procedures of the Irish Stock Exchange rule 2.35 for example.

[64] Investment Funds—Code of Listing Requirements and Procedures of the Irish Stock Exchange rule 2.5.

[65] The question of what constitutes such action has not to our knowledge been tested, nor has the Financial Regulator provided any guidance on the point.

[66] See Section 14.1.1.1.

14.1.5.5 *Continuing obligations*

Listed funds are subject to a number of continuing obligations to ensure an orderly   **14.58**
market and that holders of listed units and potential investors have simultaneous
access to the same information, including developments in the nature and conduct of a listed fund. Failure of a listed fund to comply with the continuing obligations may result in the ISE taking disciplinary action, such as censure of the issuer
or its directors or the suspension or cancellation of the listing. The continuing
obligations of a listed fund come under four main categories:

- disclosure;[67]
- notification;[68]
- communication with unit holders;[69] and
- reporting of financial information.[70]

14.2 Listing and Offering Securities in Practice

14.2.1 Introduction

14.2.1.1 *Offering structures*

The means adopted for offering Irish securities to the public are similar to those   **14.59**
commonly adopted in the United Kingdom. In light of the recent global financial
crisis and its impact on current market conditions, however, companies have
become increasingly creative in the way they raise funds. Rights issues, which have
been rare in Ireland over the last decade, are now being considered as a viable
option. The recent rights issue by CRH plc, which raised approximately EUR
1.238 billion net of expenses, has been described as the largest ever corporate
rights issue in Ireland's history.[71] In order to make the process of raising capital
more efficient in difficult market conditions and in keeping with the FSA's
approach in the United Kingdom, the ISE amended the Listing Rules in February
2009 to reduce the subscription period for rights issues[72] from a minimum of
21 days to 10 business days.

---

[67] Investment Funds—Code of Listing Requirements and Procedures of the Irish Stock Exchange rules 8–8.8.
[68] Investment Funds—Code of Listing Requirements and Procedures of the Irish Stock Exchange rules 8.10 and 8.14–8.15.
[69] Investment Funds—Code of Listing Requirements and Procedures of the Irish Stock Exchange rules 8.25–8.32.
[70] Investment Funds—Code of Listing Requirements and Procedures of the Irish Stock Exchange rules 5.23–5.34.
[71] The Irish Times, 20 March 2009.
[72] Listing Rule 6.5.6.

14.60 As in the United Kingdom, key considerations in connection with any public offering are likely to include:

- *the need for a prospectus*—unless an exemption is available, a prospectus will generally be required where an offer of transferable securities is to be made to the public in Ireland, as well as in all situations where 10% or more of a company's issued share capital is being admitted to trading on a regulated market in Ireland;

- *statutory pre-emption*—the Companies Acts contain shareholder pre-emption provisions[73] which restrict the right of directors to allot shares for cash unless the shares are first offered to existing shareholders pro rata to their existing holdings. These provisions are usually disapplied in respect of rights issues and open offers and also in respect of other equity offers up to a certain proportion of the issued ordinary share capital (usually 5%) at each annual general meeting of the relevant company. Accordingly, any offer beyond this will need to be structured in such a way as to either comply with or avoid these provisions. In recent times, Irish public companies, like their United Kingdom counterparts, have considered the use of 'cash box' structures, which do not involve the issue of shares by the issuer for cash and therefore have the effect of avoiding statutory shareholder pre-emption requirements.[74]

  In a typical cash box offer, the issuer incorporates a 'cash box' subsidiary (often a Jersey-incorporated company is used, for tax and other reasons) and an investment bank subscribes for a combination of ordinary shares and redeemable preference shares in that subsidiary. The bank will separately agree with the issuer to carry out and underwrite the placing of shares in the issuer. The bank will use the proceeds of the placing to pay for the shares in the cash box subsidiary, which shares are then transferred to the issuer in consideration of the issue of the placing shares to the placees. Transactions that appear to avoid the statutory pre-emption rights of existing shareholders will usually be scrutinized by the Irish investor community, including the Irish Association of Investment Managers ('IAIM'), an investor representative body, whose objectives are broadly similar to those of the Association of British Insurers and the National Association of Pension Funds in the United Kingdom;

- *the rules applicable to setting offer prices at a discount*—these will apply to most types of offering.[75]

---

[73] These requirements are contained in sections 23 and 24 of the Companies (Amendment) Act 1983.

[74] Section 23(4) of the Companies (Amendment) Act 1983 sets out an exemption where the issue is for non-cash consideration.

[75] Listing Rule 6.5.10. The IAIM has also issued guidance on discounts in non pre-emptive offers ('Shareholders Pre-Emption Rights', available at www.iaim.ie).

14.2.2 Eligibility for listing

14.2.2.1 Eligibility and 'pre-eligibility' letters

Every new applicant seeking the admission of equity securities to the Official List **14.61** must ensure that its sponsor submits a letter (sometimes known as an 'eligibility letter'), explaining how the applicant satisfies the conditions for listing on the Official List.[76] The purpose of this requirement is to give comfort to the ISE in relation to the ability of the applicant to meet these conditions. As described in further detail in Section 14.2.2.5 below, the applicant company's sponsor typically prepares the eligibility letter and submits it to the ISE.

A general practice has emerged in the United Kingdom for applicant companies **14.62** (particularly companies that have a complex financial history) to voluntarily submit a 'pre-eligibility letter' in an attempt to address any potential problems identified by the applicant or its advisers in complying with specific eligibility requirements. There is no equivalent in the Irish context. The ISE is, however, generally open to engaging in informal discussions with companies or their sponsors before an application is made.

14.2.2.2 Key conditions for listing on the Main Market

The key conditions for obtaining a primary or dual primary listing of equity secu- **14.63** rities on the Main Market include the following:[77]

- a prospectus complying with the Prospectus Regulations must be prepared in English, reviewed by the ISE on behalf of the Financial Regulator and, ultimately, approved by the Financial Regulator (or successfully passported in[78] if the applicant for listing is a non-Irish company);[79]
- the securities must be freely transferable and fully paid (although the ISE may allow partly-paid securities to be listed if they are nonetheless freely transferable and investors have been given appropriate information to enable dealings to take place on an open and proper basis);[80]
- the securities must be free from all liens and any restrictions on the right of transfer, other than restrictions imposed by the company for failure to comply with certain security holder disclosure obligations;[81]
- the securities must be eligible for electronic settlement;[82]

---

[76] Listing Rule 2.2.6.
[77] Certain of these conditions are modified for ISE-only primary listings and for listings involving mineral and scientific research-based companies.
[78] See further Section 14.2.9 below.
[79] Listing Rule 3.2.10.
[80] Listing Rules 3.2.4(1) and 3.2.5.
[81] Listing Rule 3.2.4(2).
[82] Listing Rule 3.3.23.

- the company must maintain a public float in one or more EEA member states of 25% (the ISE may relax this requirement in certain circumstances);[83]
- there must be a minimum projected market capitalization for shares of EUR 1,000,000 (the ISE will permit exceptions to this if satisfied that there will still be an adequate market for the shares);[84]
- the company must be validly established under the relevant laws of its place of incorporation or establishment and operating in conformity with its memorandum and articles of association or equivalent documents;[85]
- the company must have published or filed audited consolidated accounts covering a period of at least three years, ending no more than six months before the date of the prospectus (although this condition can be modified or waived if the ISE is satisfied that investors have the necessary information available to them to arrive at an informed judgment about the company and the securities for which listing is sought);[86]
- the company must (i) control the majority of its assets, (ii) be carrying on an independent business as its main activity and (iii) possess a three-year revenue-earning record that supports at least 75% of its business (although this can be waived in the circumstances described above);[87]
- the company must satisfy the ISE that it and its subsidiary undertakings have sufficient working capital available to meet requirements for at least 12 months following the date of publication of its prospectus.[88]

14.64   The ISE has the power to impose additional conditions at its discretion.[89]

---

[83] Listing Rules 3.3.19 and 3.3.20.

[84] Listing Rules 3.2.7 and 3.2.8.

[85] Listing Rule 3.2.1.

[86] Listing Rules 3.3.3 and 3.3.13.

[87] Listing Rules 3.3.4 and 3.3.13.

[88] Listing Rule 3.3.16. The ISE may dispense with this requirement where the applicant already has shares listed (Listing Rule 3.3.17) and for banking, insurance or financial services companies, subject to the satisfaction of certain solvency and capital adequacy conditions (Listing Rule 3.3.18). However, under the Prospectus Regulation, all companies issuing shares are in any case required to include a working capital statement in their prospectus (Annex III, paragraph 3.1). It may be possible under Irish prospectus law (regulation 25 of the Prospectus Regulations and rule 4.11 of the Prospectus Rules), in exceptional circumstances, to seek permission to exclude information required by Irish prospectus law (including, potentially, a working capital statement) where, for example, the disclosure of such information would be: (i) contrary to the public interest; (ii) seriously detrimental to the issuer (provided that the omission will not mislead the public); or (iii) of minor importance only. In such cases, the issuer will be required to make a submission to the ISE setting out the specific information it wishes to omit and the reasons for the omission. It may also be required to warrant that the information that it proposes to omit would not be material to a prospective investor's decision to invest in the relevant securities. The request will be settled with the ISE and then sent to the Financial Regulator for approval. In normal circumstances, the Financial Regulator will adjudicate on the request within five business days (Prospectus Rules rule 4.11(a)).

[89] Listing Rule 3.1.3.

14.2.2.3 *Additional conditions for ISE-only primary listings*

Where a company is seeking a primary listing only on the ISE, it must meet the **14.65** following additional conditions:

- 100% (rather than 75%) of the company's business must be supported by an historic revenue-earning record;[90]
- the company's directors must collectively have appropriate expertise and experience for the management of the business;[91]
- each director should be free of conflicts between duties to the company and private interests and other duties unless the company can show that arrangements are in place to avoid detriment to its interests;[92]and
- the company must be able to carry on its business independently of any 'controlling shareholder' (broadly, a person who either controls 30% or more of the votes in the company or who has the right to appoint a majority of the board of directors) and all transactions and relationships between the company and any controlling shareholder must be at arm's length and on a normal commercial basis.[93]

14.2.2.4 *Secondary listings*

Many of the conditions referred to above apply equally to secondary listings, **14.66** including the requirements relating to sponsors, prospectuses, transferability of shares, minimum market capitalization, due establishment and conformity with constitutional documents. Notably, however, the requirements relating to the publication of accounts and the conditions relating to assets, business activities and working capital do not apply to applicants seeking a secondary listing.[94]

14.2.2.5 *Sponsor regime*

An issuer of equity securities, preference shares or certificates representing equity **14.67** securities seeking a listing on the Main Market is obliged to appoint a sponsor and retain a sponsor for the duration of its listing.[95] The sponsor is responsible for dealing with various matters relating to the application for listing, including ensuring the company's suitability for listing prior to making any submission to the ISE. The sponsor, which must be registered with the ISE in order to fulfil the role, is usually the primary point of contact between the ISE and the applicant company.[96]

---

[90] Listing Rule 3.4.2.
[91] Listing Rule 3.4.3.
[92] Listing Rule 3.4.4.
[93] Listing Rule 3.4.5.
[94] Listing Rule 11.2.1.
[95] Listing Rule 2.3.1.
[96] Listing Rule 2.4.2: the application for registration as a sponsor includes an undertaking from the sponsor to discharge its responsibilities under the Listing Rules and to retain its independence.

14.68 As discussed in Section 14.2.2.1, a sponsor is obliged to submit, with an application for listing, a letter setting out how a new applicant for listing satisfies the various listing requirements set out in the Listing Rules.[97] This letter must be submitted by no later than the date of the submission of the first draft of the prospectus (or, if the ISE is not reviewing the prospectus—where, for instance, an overseas competent authority has responsibility—at a time to be agreed with the ISE). Where a prospectus is required, the sponsor must also submit to the ISE a standard form declaration confirming, *inter alia*, that to the best of its knowledge and belief, it has performed the relevant sponsor duties set out in the Listing Rules.[98]

14.69 In addition, a sponsor must submit to the ISE a prescribed form document confirming its independence from the applicant company.[99]

14.2.2.6 IEX

14.70 Any applicant for listing on IEX will require an 'IEX adviser' (similar to a nominated adviser or 'NOMAD' in the United Kingdom) which it must retain throughout the duration of its listing. The role of an IEX adviser is broadly similar to that of a sponsor on the Main Market. In particular, it is responsible for assessing the 'appropriateness' of an applicant for admission to IEX.[100] The responsibilities of IEX advisers are set out in the ISE's 'Rules for IEX Advisers'. All IEX advisers must be approved by the ISE.

14.71 As noted in Section 14.1.1.3, no specific eligibility requirements apply to companies seeking admission to IEX, save that the expected aggregate market value of all securities to be admitted in any proposed listing must be at least EUR 5,000,000 (and even this condition can be waived if the ISE is satisfied that there will still be an adequate market for the shares).[101]

14.72 However, one important difference between IEX and Main Market requirements is that the IEX admission document, containing prescribed information set out in the IEX Rules and which is required to be published in connection with the applicant's admission to IEX, must be approved by the IEX adviser, rather than by the ISE. The IEX adviser must also make a formal declaration to the ISE that, *inter alia*, the admission document complies with the relevant requirements of the IEX Rules[102] and the admission document itself must contain a statement that the ISE has not itself examined or approved its contents.[103]

---

[97] Listing Rule 2.2.6.
[98] Listing Rule 2.2.7.
[99] Listing Rule 2.2.1(2).
[100] IEX Rule 1.
[101] IEX Rule 9.
[102] IEX Rule 5.
[103] IEX Rules Schedule Two Annex III(e).

The ISE has discretion to impose special conditions on all applicants. Specific **14.73** conditions for new businesses and 'investing companies' are included in the IEX Rules.[104]

14.2.3 Outline of listing procedure

14.2.3.1 Primary and dual primary listings[105]

The typical timeframe for a listing of equity securities in Ireland is between three **14.74** and four months, beginning with the decision to seek a listing to the date of actual listing.

Applicants for a primary listing of equity securities must submit to the ISE a num- **14.75** ber of documents in final form two business days before the ISE's consideration of the application,[106] including:

- a completed application for admission of securities to the Official List and trad- ing on the Main Market (this is a prescribed form document);
- if another EEA state is the home member state, a copy of the prospectus, a cer- tificate of approval of the competent authority of the relevant home member state, and (if applicable) a translation of the summary of the prospectus;
- any circular that has been published in connection with the application, if applicable (for example, if the listing is in connection with financing an acquisi- tion for which shareholder approval is required);
- any supplementary prospectus approved by the relevant competent authority, if applicable;
- written confirmation (by way of board resolution) of the number of securities to be allotted;
- if a prospectus has not been produced, a copy of the regulatory information service ('RIS') announcement detailing the number and type of securities that are the subject of the application and the circumstances of their issue;
- in the case of a new applicant, a copy certificate of incorporation or equivalent document.

If the relevant prospectus includes a working capital statement, the applicant's **14.76** sponsor must also submit written confirmation with the application to the ISE that it has received confirmation from the applicant that its working capital posi- tion is sufficient for at least 12 months.[107]

---

[104] See, for example, IEX Rules 7 and 8. An 'investing company' is defined by the IEX Rules as any IEX company which, in the opinion of the ISE, has as a primary business the investing of its funds in the securities of other companies or the acquisition of a particular business.

[105] No distinction is made by the Listing Rules between primary and dual primary listings in the context of applications.

[106] Listing Rule 4.4.2.

[107] Listing Rule 2.2.10. The requirement includes a statement that the sponsor is satisfied that the applicant's confirmation has been given after due and careful enquiry and that any persons

14.77   If a prospectus has not been produced, the application must contain confirmation that a prospectus is not required and an explanation of why this is the case, including a reference to any specific exemption on which the applicant is relying.

14.78   On the day the ISE is due to consider the application, the applicant must also submit:

- if the application relates to a first listing of a class of shares, a completed shareholder statement;[108] and
- in the case of a placing, open offer and certain other forms of offerings of equity securities, a completed pricing statement, detailing the number of equity shares being placed or offered and the issue or offer price, as applicable.[109]

14.79   Both the shareholder statement and pricing statement are prescribed form documents which are annexed to the Listing Rules.

14.80   Further documents must be submitted as soon as practicable after the ISE has considered the application, including a confirmation of the number of securities allotted.[110]

14.81   The ISE may also request copies of related documents, including the following:[111]

- any agreement to acquire assets, business or shares in consideration for, or in relation to, which the company's securities are being issued;
- any document referred to in the prospectus, circular or other document issued in connection with the securities;
- the applicant's memorandum and articles of association;
- interim accounts and the annual report and accounts of the applicant for each of the periods that form part of the applicant's financial records contained in the prospectus.

14.82   Applicants may apply for block listings of a specified number of their securities where the process of applying for admission of securities is likely to be onerous because, for instance, the applicant plans to make frequent or irregular allotments and if no prospectus is required. The application process is modified in certain respects in relation to such block listings.[112]

---

providing finance have confirmed that the relevant banking facilities exist. See also Section 14.2.2.2 in relation to working capital statements.

[108]   Listing Rule 4.4.3(1). The shareholder statement contains, *inter alia*, details of the equity shares to be admitted, details of existing shareholdings and the number of shares to be in public hands.

[109]   Listing Rule 4.4.3(2).

[110]   Listing Rule 4.4.5.

[111]   Listing Rule 4.4.6.

[112]   Listing Rule 4.5.

14.2.3.2 Secondary listings

It is unusual for an Irish company to seek a secondary listing on the Official List (see Section 14.1.4.1 in this respect). However, those Irish companies that do seek a secondary listing must comply with certain specific rules, including the following: **14.83**

- the ISE will require details from the company's sponsor of any exemptions or derogations from any rules and regulations that would normally apply to a company registered and listed in the other relevant jurisdiction given by the relevant regulatory authority in that other jurisdiction;[113] and
- the ISE will review the case of any Irish company that uses the secondary listing procedure every five years after its listing to assess whether such treatment continues to be appropriate.[114]

Foreign companies seeking a secondary listing on the Official List will be subject to less onerous conditions and continuing obligations.[115] It should be noted however, that all companies maintaining a secondary listing must have a sponsor for the duration of the listing.[116] **14.84**

14.2.3.3 IEX

The requirements for issuers seeking admission to IEX are considerably less onerous than those that apply in the case of an application for admission to the Official List. Certain information set out in the IEX Rules must be provided to the ISE at least ten business days (or 20 business days for companies whose shares are already admitted to trading on certain other recognized stock exchanges (including AIM and the LSE's main market)—known in the IEX Rules as 'quoted applicants') before the expected date of admission.[117] **14.85**

An admission document containing certain prescribed information must be made available publicly (either at a physical location or on the internet), free of charge, for at least one month from the proposed date of admission.[118] An applicant must submit to the ISE a completed application form and admission document, together with a declaration from its IEX adviser to the effect that, *inter alia*, the application is compliant and the applicant and its securities are 'appropriate' for admission at least three business days before the expected date of admission.[119] **14.86**

---

[113] Listing Rule 11.4.2.
[114] Listing Rule 11.4.3.
[115] See generally chapter 11 of the Listing Rules.
[116] Listing Rule 11.1.2.
[117] IEX Rule 2.
[118] IEX Rule 3.
[119] IEX Rule 5.

14.87 A quoted applicant (as referred to above) need not produce an admission document unless otherwise required by Irish prospectus law (for example, in the case of a proposed public offer of securities which does not benefit from an exemption from the requirement to produce a prospectus)[120] but must submit its latest annual report and accounts with the application form.[121]

14.88 Admission to IEX becomes effective when the ISE issues a dealing notice to that effect.[122]

14.2.4 Obligation to publish a prospectus – public offers and listings

14.89 Since the Prospectus Directive is a maximum harmonization directive, the prospectus regime in Ireland broadly follows those provisions described in detail in Part 1.

14.2.5 Some practical considerations

14.2.5.1 Schemes of arrangement

14.90 In the context of the triggers to the requirement to publish a prospectus, the wide definition of 'offer of securities to the public' in the Prospectus Regulations often gives rise to uncertainty as to whether certain transactions require a prospectus. An example is where a United Kingdom listed company with Irish resident shareholders is being taken over by a newly incorporated holding company by way of a court-approved scheme of arrangement under the relevant provisions of United Kingdom legislation. These schemes generally provide for the cancellation of all of the shares held in the existing listed company and the issue of shares in the new holding company to the shareholders of the listed company. Where there are 100 or more shareholders in Ireland who will be affected by the scheme and no other exemption from the requirement to publish a prospectus in connection with an offer to the public is available (as is often the case), the application of Irish prospectus law will need to be considered. While each case will depend on its own particular facts, in many cases a court-approved scheme of arrangement will not constitute an offer to the public as there is no offer capable of acceptance by way of purchase or subscription as required by the Prospectus Regulations (assuming that there are no unusual features such as loan notes or cash being offered as an alternative to the new shares to be issued pursuant to the scheme).

14.2.5.2 DRIPS

14.91 Similarly, other share transactions involving overseas companies with an Irish shareholder base may need to be considered from the perspective of Irish

---

[120] IEX Rule 3.
[121] IEX Rule 5.
[122] IEX Rule 6.

prospectus law; for example, dividend reinvestment plans (or 'DRIPS'). Subject to a review of the terms and method of operation of such plans, it should be possible to structure these so that they benefit from an available exemption from the requirement to publish a prospectus.

14.2.5.3 *Qualified investors*

Another practical point concerns the exemption under which a prospectus is not required if the relevant public offer is only made to 'qualified investors'. The definition of 'qualified investors' includes natural persons and small and medium-sized enterprises ('SMEs') provided that they are entered on a register maintained by the Financial Regulator.[123] In order to be entered on the register, SMEs must comply with a number of formalities and satisfy certain conditions for inclusion on the register. With respect to natural persons seeking registration as a qualified investor, a key condition is that the person must satisfy, *inter alia*, at least two of the following requirements:[124] **14.92**

- a requirement to have carried out transactions of a significant size on securities markets at an average frequency of at least ten per quarter over the four quarters prior to the application;
- a requirement that his securities portfolio exceeds EUR 500,000; and
- a requirement that he works or has worked for at least one year in the financial sector in a professional position requiring knowledge of securities investment.

In addition to this, the Prospectus Rules stipulate that any applicant who is a natural person must include with the application a letter from an accountant or a solicitor *certifying* the applicant's compliance with the foregoing requirements and specifying which of them are fulfilled.[125] This contrasts with the position under the equivalent United Kingdom regime which permits self-certification. **14.93**

Engaging a solicitor or an accountant and requesting such certification will inevitably be costly for the potential qualified investor, as it will involve an element of due diligence and legal formality on the part of the relevant adviser. Any such certificate is also likely to be qualified insofar as it will relate to matters of fact which the certifying professional may not be able to easily verify. As at 20 July 2009, no natural persons or SMEs appeared on the qualified investors register and it is probably unlikely, due in part at least to the nature of the requisite conditions that must be met and the costs of so doing, that this position will materially change in the foreseeable future. **14.94**

---

[123] Prospectus Regulations regulation 2.
[124] Prospectus Regulations regulation 4(2).
[125] Prospectus Rules rule 10. Certification is also required in respect of SMEs that wish to be included on the register although the matters to be certified are different.

14.2.6 Content requirements and prospectus summary

14.95 The Prospectus Regulations echo the provisions of the Prospectus Directive regarding content requirements for a prospectus, which are discussed in Part 1.

14.96 As noted in Section 14.1.3.4 above, the Financial Regulator supplemented the Prospectus Regulations by publishing the Prospectus Rules. These Rules[126] provide that parties making public offers or seeking admission to trading to whom the Prospectus Regulations apply must also have regard to:

- Part 5 of the 2005 Act which includes, for example, provisions in relation to liability for prospectuses and experts' consent to use statements in a prospectus;
- the Prospectus Regulation and the CESR recommendations for the consistent implementation of the Prospectus Regulation;
- the FAQs; and
- the Prospectus Rules and any relevant guidelines issued by the Financial Regulator.[127]

14.97 Accordingly, any company wishing to make an offer into Ireland or to seek admission to trading of its securities on the Main Market will have a relatively heavy burden of compliance. Companies in specific sectors (such as property and mineral companies) should in particular note the additional requirements of the CESR recommendations.

14.98 As required by the Prospectus Directive, the Prospectus Regulations stipulate that a prospectus must also contain a summary that conveys, in non-technical language, the essential characteristics and risks associated with the issuer, any guarantor and the securities being issued.[128] While the preamble to the Prospectus Directive states that the summary 'normally should not exceed 2,500 words', it is worth noting that neither the Prospectus Regulations nor the Prospectus Rules set any limit on the summary.

14.2.7 Approval process, timing and practical issues arising

14.99 Part 7 of the Prospectus Regulations sets out the mechanism for the approval of prospectuses by the Financial Regulator.

14.100 The ISE, in its capacity as delegate authority, reviews and comments on draft prospectuses submitted for approval.

---

[126] In particular, Prospectus Rules rule 1.2.

[127] As at 20 July 2009, the Financial Regulator had issued six formal guidance notes (one of which was subsequently withdrawn) relating to various matters including prospectus summaries and supplements, high yield debt transactions and collateralized debt obligations. It has also issued 'assistance papers' which relate mainly to collective investment schemes.

[128] Prospectus Regulations regulation 21.

In order to have a prospectus approved, an applicant must submit a draft to the ISE with any other information and documents that the ISE may require in accordance with the Prospectus Rules. The Prospectus Rules[129] state that the following draft documents and information must be included with any prospectus application:

14.101

- the prospectus;[130]
- if requested, where the order of items in the prospectus does not coincide with the order in the schedules and building blocks in the Prospectus Regulation, a cross-reference list identifying the pages where each item can be found in the prospectus;
- a letter identifying any items from the annexes and building blocks in the Prospectus Regulation that have not been included in the prospectus because they are not applicable;
- if the applicant is requesting the Financial Regulator to authorize the omission of information from the prospectus, which is possible pursuant to the Prospectus Directive, certain information required by the Prospectus Rules;[131]
- in the case of a prospectus relating to equity securities (other than those issued by collective investment undertakings), the formal notice required under the Prospectus Regulations,[132] in final draft form, stating how the prospectus will be made available and where it can be obtained by the public;
- if the applicant requires the Financial Regulator to provide a competent authority of a relevant host member state with a certificate of approval in accordance with the Prospectus Regulations where the prospectus is approved (i.e. passporting of the prospectus), a letter requesting the Financial Regulator to provide this; and
- any other information that the Financial Regulator or the ISE may require.

If an application for prospectus approval is made in connection with an application for admission to trading on the Main Market and listing on the Official List, all of the documents required in relation to such applications should also be submitted (see Section 14.2.3 above).

14.102

---

[129] In particular, Prospectus Rules rule 4.7.

[130] This will be in draft form at the time of initial submission and in final form on the date on which approval is sought. Any draft prospectus must also contain annotations in the margin to indicate compliance with all applicable requirements of Irish prospectus law (Prospectus Rules rule 4.8).

[131] Prospectus Rules rule 4.11. The issuer will be required to make a submission to the ISE setting out the specific information that it wishes to omit and the reasons for the omission no later than five business days before the approval of the prospectus is required. It may also be required to warrant that the information that it proposes omitting would not be material to a prospective investor's decision to invest in the relevant securities. The request will be settled with the ISE and then sent to the Financial Regulator for approval. In normal circumstances, the Financial Regulator will adjudicate on the request within five business days.

[132] Prospectus Regulations regulation 46.

14.103   The ISE must notify the applicant of its decision within ten working days or, in the case of a new issuer, 20 working days, from the first working day after the date on which it receives the application.[133] If, however, the ISE requests specific documents or information from the applicant in writing, this period starts to run the day after the applicant complies with the request.[134] If the ISE fails to give a decision within the time limits, such failure is not deemed to constitute approval of the prospectus. The ISE will generally revert earlier than anticipated by the timetable set out in the Prospectus Regulations (often within ten working days) with comments (usually on a standard form 'comment sheet'). The process is generally fluid and frequently involves the submission of multiple drafts.

14.104   A number of common errors can arise in the drafting of prospectuses, including:

- risk factors being too generic;
- inadequate presentation of financial information;
- omission of statements required by law;
- inaccurate cross-referencing;
- failure to explain technical terms; and
- inconsistent use of terminology.

14.105   The ISE tends to comment in detail on risk factors and require the company and its advisers to redraft them. While companies frequently outline risks in some detail (and indeed the number of risk factors included in equity prospectuses, and the length of each risk factor, appears to increase with each passing year), they sometimes fail to identify how the risks will directly impact on the issuer and its group or how the risks might be mitigated. In addition, a failure to draft 'company-specific' risk factors has proven to be a recurring issue, and the ISE has noted a tendency for prospectus summaries to fail to adequately reflect the principal risks.

14.106   Looking beyond risk factors, as a general rule, the ISE likes to see significant financial or accounting issues prominently displayed rather than 'buried' in the detail of the financial information. Likewise, unaudited financial information should not be afforded the same prominence as audited information.

14.107   The ISE will also be focused on whether certain statements required by law (for example, in relation to responsibility) are accurately reproduced and whether any necessary statutory references are accurate. Surprisingly, references to the Financial Regulator itself are sometimes found to be incorrect and inconsistent. A failure to explain technical terms, for example, in relation to financial services companies,

---

[133] Prospectus Regulations regulation 35.
[134] Prospectus Regulations regulation 36.

or to use consistent terminology, can also be an issue. In addition, of course, all cross-references within the prospectus to other sections of the document should be checked for accuracy.

14.108 In order to iron out issues such as those described above, issuers should ensure that as complete a draft as possible is submitted to the ISE early in the process.

14.109 After scrutinizing a prospectus, the ISE will issue a recommendation to the Financial Regulator as to whether or not the prospectus has been drawn up in accordance with the Prospectus Regulations and the Prospectus Regulation. Based on this recommendation, the Financial Regulator will decide whether to approve the prospectus and will communicate its decision in writing to the registered office of the relevant issuer or a nominated agent. The Financial Regulator is not permitted to approve a prospectus unless it is satisfied that the issuer has complied with the applicable requirements imposed by it under the Prospectus Regulations and any other provisions of Irish prospectus law.[135]

14.110 In the event that there is a dispute between the applicant and the ISE regarding compliance with the Prospectus Regulations and the Prospectus Regulation, the applicant may refer the matter directly, in writing, to the Financial Regulator.[136] If the Financial Regulator refuses to approve a prospectus, the issuer has 28 days from the date of that decision to appeal to the Irish High Court.[137]

14.111 Once a prospectus is approved, the applicant must immediately file the prospectus with the Financial Regulator[138] and, if the issuer is an Irish company, with the Registrar of Companies in Dublin, within 14 days of its publication.[139] Failure to comply with these requirements is a criminal offence.[140]

14.112 The prospectus must also be published in accordance with the requirements of the Prospectus Regulations in one of a number of specified ways.[141] Usually, an issuer opts to satisfy these requirements by making the prospectus available in printed form, free of charge, at its offices and those of its financial intermediaries (usually stockbroking firms) and/or by making it available in electronic form on the company website. In the case of the publication of a prospectus relating to equity securities, publication in electronic form is mandatory where the prospectus is also published by newspaper insertion or in printed form.[142] An issuer of

---

[135] Prospectus Regulations regulation 37.
[136] Prospectus Rules rule 4.3(c).
[137] Prospectus Regulations regulation 39(2).
[138] Prospectus Regulations regulation 38(1)(a).
[139] Prospectus Regulations regulation 38(1)(b).
[140] Prospectus Regulations regulation 38(2). Regulation 107 sets out the sanctions—in this case, a fine of up to EUR 5,000 or up to 12 months' imprisonment, or both.
[141] Prospectus Regulations regulations 44 and 45.
[142] Prospectus Regulations regulation 45.

equity securities (unless it is a collective investment undertaking) must also publish a formal newspaper notice stating how the prospectus has been made available and where it can be obtained.[143]

14.2.8 Admission to Trading Rules

14.113 A two-stage admission process applies to companies seeking admission to trading of their securities on the Main Market. Until November 2007, when the ISE's new Admission to Trading Rules came into operation, no distinction was made in Ireland between admission to trading and admission to listing. Equity securities are now admitted both to trading on the Main Market and to listing on the Official List. Whereas in the United Kingdom, admission to listing is the responsibility of the FSA and admission to trading is dealt with by the LSE, in Ireland the ISE is responsible for both of these functions.

14.114 A company generally applies to have its securities admitted to listing and trading simultaneously. The ISE will not admit securities to trading until each of the documents required under the Listing Rules for admission to listing has been submitted to the ISE within the appropriate timeframe.

14.115 The Admission to Trading Rules contain their own continuing obligations but these are generally complementary to the continuing obligations in the Listing Rules and do not create any significant additional administrative or compliance burdens.

14.2.9 Passporting in

14.116 As explained in Part 1, an approved prospectus can be passported from one EEA state to another. Under Irish law, the prospectus passport procedure involves the submission by the home state regulator of a copy of the prospectus in question, as well as a certificate of approval of the prospectus by that regulator, to the Financial Regulator in Ireland.[144] The Financial Regulator will acknowledge receipt of these documents directly to the home state regulator and will then publish details of the passported prospectus on the passport notification page of its website, at which point the prospectus is deemed to have been passported. It usually takes two working days from the receipt of the documentation from the home state regulator for the Financial Regulator to publish passport confirmation on its website.

---

[143] Prospectus Regulations regulation 46(1).

[144] Prospectus Regulations regulations 54 and 55. The Financial Regulator may also require a translation of the summary of the prospectus into English or Irish (at the election of the relevant issuer, offeror or person seeking admission to trading, as the case may be).

14.2.10 Passporting out

An Irish company may wish to make a public offer of its securities to persons resident in, and/or seek admission of its securities to trading in, another EU or EEA
member state and will want to avail itself of the 'passporting out' procedure for
these purposes. The procedure is set out in the Prospectus Regulations, subject
to any applicable host state regulations. The company, on submitting the prospectus, simply requests the Financial Regulator to provide the specified host
state regulator with the certificate of approval of the prospectus and a copy of
the prospectus (translated if required).[145] The Financial Regulator will generally
comply with this request within one working day if the request is submitted with
the prospectus and otherwise within three working days.

14.117

The passport procedure will not be available in circumstances where, in connection with a public offer of securities involving a merger or a securities exchange
offer, a compliant prospectus is not drawn up and the issuer instead chooses to rely
on the exemption from the obligation to publish a prospectus contained in regulation 10 of the Prospectus Regulations by making available a document containing
information which is regarded by the Financial Regulator as being equivalent to
that of a prospectus, taking into account any EU requirements.

14.118

14.2.11 Prospectus liability in Ireland

The 2005 Act provides for statutory civil liability for untrue statements in, or
omissions from, a prospectus.[146] While primary liability is likely to fall on the
issuing company, its promoters and directors and any selling shareholders, certain
other prescribed persons and entities could face liability to pay compensation to
persons who acquire any securities on the faith of a prospectus, for loss or damage
sustained by reason of any such untrue statements or omissions. One of the categories included is persons who have 'authorised the issue' of the prospectus. The
expression 'authorised the issue' is not defined in the legislation. However, by
virtue of being involved in drafting the prospectus and in the offer generally, a
person could be said to have 'authorised the issue' of the prospectus, in the absence
of evidence to the contrary.

14.119

The 2005 Act provides that, for the purposes of such civil liability provisions,
underwriters and professional advisers are not deemed to have '"authorised the
issue' of a prospectus and are also not deemed to be promoters of the issuing company.[147] On the other hand, sponsors of an issue, as such, are not covered by this

14.120

---

[145] Prospectus Regulations regulation 56.
[146] 2005 Act section 41.
[147] 2005 Act section 38(5).

exemption and therefore could attract civil liability (although we are not aware of any instances of this having occurred at the time of writing).

14.121　Directors and persons who have 'authorised the issue' of the prospectus are potentially liable to indemnify directors and proposed directors who did not give their consent to be a director (or who gave their consent and later withdrew it), as well as experts whose statements are included in the prospectus, against any damages that they sustain by reason of their names or statements being included in the prospectus.[148] A person who has only given a statement to be included in the prospectus in the capacity of an 'expert' is not deemed to have 'authorised the issue' of the prospectus solely by virtue of this fact.

14.122　There are a number of statutory defences to the civil liability provisions in the 2005 Act,[149] including a 'due diligence' defence, which applies if the person potentially liable had reasonable grounds to believe, and did up to the time of the issue of the securities believe, that an allegedly untrue statement was true or that an omitted matter alleged to be responsible for the loss was properly omitted.

14.123　Separately, the 2005 Act prescribes statutory criminal liability for untrue statements in, and omissions from, a prospectus which, again, applies to any person who 'authorised the issue' of the prospectus.[150] However, the saver for underwriters and professional advisers referred to above in the context of civil liability does not apply. Consequently, to the extent that it can be shown to the satisfaction of an Irish court that an underwriter or sponsor 'authorised the issue' of a prospectus containing untrue statements or material omissions, such underwriters or sponsors could face criminal liability unless a broadly similar (but not identical) 'due diligence' defence to that discussed above in the context of statutory civil liability is successfully pleaded.[151] Persons liable under the criminal provisions may, on summary conviction, be subject to a fine not exceeding EUR 5,000 or to imprisonment for up to 12 months or, on conviction on indictment, to a fine not exceeding EUR 1,000,000 or imprisonment for up to five years, or both.[152]

14.124　For completeness, it should also be noted that all of the parties concerned, by virtue of being involved in the preparation of a prospectus containing a negligent or fraudulent misstatement, could potentially face separate liability under Irish common law.

---

[148]　2005 Act section 44(2).
[149]　2005 Act section 42.
[150]　2005 Act section 48.
[151]　2005 Act section 48(1)(b).
[152]　2005 Act section 48(2).

14.2.12 Responsibility for a prospectus

As required by the Prospectus Directive, Irish prospectus law provides that a **14.125** prospectus must include responsibility statements in respect of the information contained in it.[153] However, somewhat confusingly, there is no direct link in the legislation or the Prospectus Rules between the requirement to include responsibility statements in the prospectus, on the one hand, and the provisions in the 2005 Act which impose statutory liability for misstatements in, or omissions from, prospectuses, as summarized above, on the other hand.

Despite this lack of clarity, responsibility will normally rest with the issuer and its **14.126** directors, any selling shareholders, as well as any other person who is stated in the prospectus as having accepted responsibility for, or who has authorized the contents of, the prospectus. There is no obligation on the underwriters or sponsors under Irish prospectus law to have, or accept, any 'responsibility' for the prospectus or any part thereof or to make any statement of responsibility in the prospectus, provided that they (i) are not seeking admission of the securities to trading on a 'regulated market' (the company would usually do this, albeit through an agent or representative); (ii) do not expressly authorize all or any part of the prospectus or the issue thereof; and (iii) are not stated in the prospectus as having accepted responsibility for all or any part of the prospectus.

Accordingly, while the matter has yet to be tested before an Irish court, it should **14.127** be possible for underwriters and sponsors to lawfully disclaim any representations regarding the accuracy of the prospectus, decline responsibility for the prospectus and declare that they do not authorize the prospectus or the issue of the prospectus or any part thereof. The simplest way to do this, it would seem, is to include statements to such effect in the prospectus itself. [154] By doing so, underwriters and sponsors will put themselves in a strong position to resist any claims in respect of civil and/or criminal liability under Irish law for misstatements in, or omissions from, a prospectus, or to claims for indemnification from directors, proposed directors or experts. This is not to say, of course, that they would thereby achieve immunity from any such claims and, in all probability, underwriters or sponsors (along with the company, the directors and any selling shareholders) would in any event be a likely target for any such claims in the event of a prospectus containing errors, even if any such errors were not the fault or responsibility of the underwriters or sponsors.

Underwriters and sponsors typically utilize other means to protect themselves **14.128** against their potential exposure to liabilities in the event of any claims or proceed-

---

[153] Prospectus Regulations part 6 and Schedule 1.
[154] This approach was followed in the Aer Lingus Group plc initial public offering in 2006.

ings arising in the context of a public offer of securities. In particular, they undertake a detailed due diligence exercise in relation to the issuer's group (which assists in establishing the 'due diligence' defence described above) and an equally detailed verification exercise in relation to the statements of fact, law, opinion and intention contained in the prospectus prior to its approval and publication.

14.2.13 Debt listings in outline

14.2.13.1 Introduction

14.129 In addition to the listing of specialist securities on the GEM, the ISE provides a streamlined and progressive listing regime for various specialist securities on the Main Market.

14.130 In the context of listings of specialist securities, the ISE undertakes to operate within a specified timeline. Such listings are also facilitated by tailored, simplified rules that the ISE has devised for the following types of specialist securities on both the Main Market and the GEM:

- *covered debt securities*: asset covered securities issued pursuant to the Asset Covered Securities Act 2001; these are the Irish equivalent to the widely used German *Pfandbrief* (Main Market only; the new GEM rules do not envisage covered debt being listed);
- *asset backed securities*: these rules cover a vast array of specialist securities which are offered throughout the US, Europe and the Middle East. The securities include, amongst others, collateralized loan obligations, collateralized debt obligations, LPNs (loan performing notes), residential mortgage-backed securities, commercial mortgage-backed securities, various synthetic securities and all forms of trade receivable securities;
- *debt securities*: these rules cover straightforward corporate bonds (guaranteed or not), synthetic bonds, high yield bonds etc.; and
- *derivative securities*: these could include forms of warrants and other derivative notes.

14.131 As provided for under the Prospectus Regulations, the ISE rules referred to above generally provide for the issuance of securities pursuant to programmes (whether single or multi-issue). As the ISE is a European regulated market, its ability to provide an efficient listing of specialist securities has resulted in a vast number of both EU and non-EU resident issuers listing on it. Although by no means the only form of issuer utilizing this process, many of the listed issuers of specialist securities on the ISE are special purpose vehicles ('SPVs').

14.2.13.2 Conditions for listing of specialist securities

14.132 Specific conditions for listing are set out in each of the relevant listing rules for covered debt securities, asset backed securities, debt securities and derivative securities.[155] Although there are differences between the various specialist debt listing rules, there are also a number of common, conditions, including the following:

- the relevant securities must comply with the laws of the issuer's place of incorporation;
- the issuer must be duly incorporated or otherwise validly established according to the relevant laws of its place of incorporation and establishment and be operating in conformity with its constitutional documents;
- the securities to be listed must be freely transferable;
- except where securities of the same class are already listed, the expected aggregate market value of the securities to be listed must be at least EUR 200,000 (other than in the case of 'tap issues'). The issuer must ensure that all holders of debt securities ranking pari passu are given equal treatment in respect of all of the rights attaching to those securities; and
- there must be a trustee or other appropriate independent party representing the interest of the holders of the securities.

Another important issue relating to the listing of specialist securities on the ISE is the requirement for an issuer (subject to certain limited exceptions) to prepare audited financial statements. This has been reinforced by the introduction of the Transparency Regulations, which also require the disclosure of regular financial information (for certain issuers, this can include semi-annual accounts and management statements). **14.133**

14.2.13.3 *Procedure for listing of specialist securities*

Issuers of specialist securities must appoint a listing agent. In order to be eligible, a listing agent must be: **14.134**

- a credit institution under the Second Banking Directive;[156]
- a third country credit institution having its registered office in a state that is a member of the OECD; or
- an organization that is registered as a sponsor with the ISE.

The listing agent must annotate the prospectus against the relevant specialist securities listing rules and provide the prospectus, together with a list of any specific rules that are not applicable to that particular issuer and relevant issuance of securities, to the ISE. The ISE will normally revert within three business days of **14.135**

---

[155] There is now one set of rules for GEM and different sets of rules for Main Market specialist securities.

[156] Second Council Directive 89/646/EEC of 15 December 1989 on the coordination of laws, regulations and administrative provisions relating to the taking up and pursuit of the business of credit institutions and amending Directive 77/780/EEC [1997] OJ L311.

the first such submission.[157] Once the ISE has provided its initial comments on the prospectus, each subsequent submission of the prospectus should be made in the same manner and the ISE will revert within two business days.

14.136   The listing agent will also be required to provide the following, non-exhaustive, list of items to the ISE for the final approval of the prospectus by the Financial Regulator:

- a copy of the complete final prospectus in pdf format;
- a declaration by the relevant listing agent that the prospectus complies with the appropriate listing rules;
- a copy of the board resolution of the issuer approving the issue of the prospectus;
- an application for admission to listing by the issuer;
- information as to who will pay the annual fees of the ISE;
- designation of home member state for the purposes of the Transparency Directive and the Prospectus Directive;
- a formal notice stating how the prospectus or listing particulars have been made available and where it or they can be obtained by the public (unless the securities for which the application is being made are of a class already listed and traded);
- account information; and
- the requisite fee.

14.137   On receipt of the documents, the ISE will liaise with the Financial Regulator with a view to having the prospectus approved for the purposes of the Prospectus Regulations. Once approved, the prospectus will be made available on the website of the Financial Regulator (http://www.financialregulator.ie) as a matter of course, although it is possible for an issuer to request that this is not done.

14.138   There are a number of benefits for issuers and arrangers in having specialist securities listed on the Main Market. These include the ability to avail of the prospectus passport regime and the quoted Eurobond exemption[158] and the fact that a number of investors will have 'investment buckets' which are available solely for investment in notes and other securities listed on a regulated market.

14.3 Maintaining a Listing in Practice

14.3.1 Introduction

14.139   A company with securities admitted to trading on the Main Market must comply with certain continuing obligations set out in the Listing Rules. Main Market

---

[157] The three business days will not include the day of submission.
[158] See Section 14.1.1.4.

companies must also comply with the Market Abuse Regulations and the Transparency Regulations as well as have regard to the Combined Code on Corporate Governance issued by the United Kingdom's Financial Reporting Council. In addition, the Takeover Directive Regulations,[159] the Admission to Trading Rules and the Prospectus Regulations contain certain continuing obligations for Main Market companies. Companies admitted to trading on IEX must comply with the IEX Rules and, as stated above, Irish IEX companies continue for the time being to be subject to the provisions of the Companies Acts in respect of insider dealing and disclosure requirements.[160] Irish companies listed on either the Main Market or IEX must also have regard generally to the provisions of the Companies Acts. If any such listed company is or could be the subject of a takeover approach, the Takeover Rules[161] and Substantial Acquisition Rules ('SARs')[162] will apply.

14.3.2 Listing Rules

14.3.2.1 *Overview*

The Listing Rules are similar in content to the United Kingdom listing rules published by the FSA.[163] They impose a wide range of detailed obligations on listed companies to ensure, principally, timely disclosure to the market of all relevant information and equality of treatment of shareholders. The sanctions for breach of the Listing Rules include the public censure of the listed company, the public or private censure of the listed company's directors and the suspension or cancellation of the company's listing.[164]

14.140

14.3.2.2 *Continuing obligations under the Listing Rules*

Key continuing obligations under the Listing Rules include the following:

14.141

- a requirement to forward to the ISE all circulars, notices, reports or other documents to which the Listing Rules apply;[165]
- notification obligations in relation to major interests in shares;[166]
- notification obligations in relation to capital structure;[167]

---

[159] European Communities (Takeover Bids (Directive 2004/25/EC)) Regulations 2006 SI 255/2006.
[160] Section 14.1.1.3 above.
[161] Irish Takeover Panel Act 1997; Takeover Rules 2007 (as amended).
[162] Irish Takeover Panel Act 1997; Substantial Acquisition Rules 2007.
[163] Like the FSA listing rules, the Listing Rules of the ISE contain a number of obligations that are 'super-equivalent'. In particular, a company listed on the Main Market must comply with super-equivalent eligibility requirements, continuing obligations and rules in relation to sponsors.
[164] Listing Rule 1.5.
[165] Listing Rule 6.6.1.
[166] Listing Rule 6.6.14.
[167] Listing Rule 6.6.4.

- notification obligations in respect of certain directors' details,[168] including in relation to their remuneration;[169]
- notification obligations in respect of all resolutions passed at shareholder general meetings other than those in the ordinary course of business;[170]
- detailed requirements relating to the publication of annual reports.[171]

14.142 Notifications required under the Listing Rules must generally be made by the relevant company to an RIS without delay.

14.143 In addition, as in the United Kingdom, where a relevant listed company undertakes transactions of a certain size, a notification though an RIS may be necessary.[172] Furthermore, where a proposed transaction represents 25% or more of the company's value with reference to its gross assets, profits, market value or gross capital (known as a 'class 1 transaction'), the company must send an explanatory circular to shareholders and obtain their consent to the transaction by way of ordinary resolution.[173] Transactions with 'related parties' (such as persons holding 10% or more of a company's voting shares or persons exercising significant influence over a company) also require prior shareholder approval by way of ordinary resolution.[174]

14.144 There are also extensive obligations in respect of the purchase by a company of its own securities.[175]

14.145 The Listing Rules contain modified continuing disclosure obligations for companies that are incorporated outside Ireland, depending on whether they have a primary or secondary listing in Ireland. For example, overseas companies with a primary listing in Ireland must disclose in their annual reports and accounts whether or not they comply with the corporate governance regime of their country of incorporation.[176]

14.146 Finally, chapter 5 of the Listing Rules contains six Listing Principles that apply to companies with a dual primary listing of equity securities on the main markets of the ISE and the FSA. These include an obligation for listed companies to treat all holders of the same class of listed securities that are in the same position equally in respect of the rights attaching to such securities.[177]

---

[168] Listing Rule 6.6.7.
[169] Listing Rule 6.8.3(8).
[170] Listing Rule 6.6.12.
[171] Listing Rule 6.8.
[172] Listing Rules 7.3 and 7.4.
[173] Listing Rule 7.5.1.
[174] See generally chapter 8 of the Listing Rules.
[175] Listing Rules chapter 9. The IAIM has also issued guidelines on share buy-backs.
[176] Listing Rule 6.8.4(1).
[177] Listing Rule 5.2.1 Principle 5. See also Section 14.3.2.4 below. For a discussion on the subject of dual primary listings, see Section 14.1.4.3 above.

14.3.2.3 *Model Code on directors' dealings*

The Listing Rules provide that all relevant companies must require compliance **14.147**
with the Model Code on directors' dealings in securities, which is set out as an
appendix to chapter 6 of the Listing Rules (the 'Model Code').[178] This is largely
the same as the Model Code set out in the FSA listing rules and regulates the
dealings[179] of 'persons discharging managerial responsibilities' (as defined in the
Market Abuse Regulations)[180] ('PDMRs'), including directors and other members
of a company's senior management, in the shares of Main Market companies.

The Model Code identifies the circumstances in which, even though not expressly **14.148**
prohibited by statute, a PDMR must not deal in his company's securities, including,
subject to certain exceptions, by way of the acquisition or exercise of options.
Broadly, these are the following:

* where there is inside information relating to the company;
* during the 60-day period prior to the preliminary announcement of annual
  results or the publication of an annual financial report (or, if the company
  reports on a half-yearly basis, the period from the end of the relevant financial
  period to the date of publication or, if the company reports on a quarterly basis,
  one month before the announcement of the quarterly results) (a 'close period').

Under the Model Code, a director must notify the chairman (or other designated **14.149**
director) of any intention to deal and obtain approval before dealing.[181] A PDMR
must also seek to prohibit any dealings in securities of the listed company by connected persons[182] and investment managers during a close period.[183] PDMRs are
prohibited by the Model Code from dealing on considerations of a short-term
nature[184] and must also take reasonable steps to prevent any dealings by or on
behalf of any connected person on such a basis.

---

[178] Listing Rule 6.2.7.

[179] 'Dealing' is defined widely under the Model Code and, in addition to the acquisition and disposal of any securities in a company, includes *inter alia* the grant, acceptance, acquisition, disposal,
exercise or discharge of any option; using as security or granting a charge, lien or other encumbrance
over, the securities of a company; or any other right or obligation, present or future, conditional or
unconditional, to acquire or dispose of securities of a company (Listing Rule 6 Appendix 1 paragraph 1(c)).

[180] The definition of 'persons discharging managerial responsibilities' is contained in regulation 12(8) of the Market Abuse Regulations and is very wide. The definition not only covers senior
executives who have regular access to inside information and have the power to make managerial
decisions affecting the future development and business prospects of the issuer but also members of
the 'administrative, management or supervisory bodies of the issuer'.

[181] Listing Rule 6 Appendix 1 paragraphs 3 and 4.

[182] The term 'connected person' is defined in the Listing Rules by reference to the Companies
Act 1990 (section 26) and the Market Abuse Regulations.

[183] Listing Rule 6 Appendix 1 paragraph 21.

[184] Investment with a maturity of one year or less will always be treated as short-term (Listing
Rule 6 Appendix 1 paragraph 8(b)).

14.150   A recent change to the Model Code in Ireland permits PDMRs to deal while in possession of inside information or during a close period, where the dealing results from a stock trading plan that was entered into in advance by the PDMR.[185] A similar exemption was recently introduced in the United Kingdom by the FSA[186] although there are differences in the detail, which are discussed in Section 14.3.2.4 below.

14.3.2.4 Key differences between Irish and United Kingdom listing rules

14.151   As mentioned above, the Irish and United Kingdom listing rules are similar in content and, indeed, until as recently as 2005, the ISE simply adopted the United Kingdom's rules with a set of local amendments (which were known as 'the green pages'). There are however some significant differences, including the following:

- The Listing Principles of the ISE only apply to companies with a dual primary listing on the Official List of the ISE and on the official list of the UKLA[187] while in the United Kingdom, the FSA listing principles apply to all companies with an LSE primary listing.[188] As mentioned in Section 14.1.4.3, a number of Irish listed companies made use of a simplified process at the time of separation of the London and Dublin exchanges to obtain a dual primary listing in both London and Dublin and many retain this status. As such companies were already obliged to comply with the listing principles by virtue of their LSE primary listing; the ISE, to maintain consistency, applied the Listing Principles to these companies in connection with their Dublin listing. The ISE did not deem it necessary to apply the Listing Principles to companies with a primary listing in Dublin only; however, it should be noted that the Listing Rules do impose certain additional conditions on companies that have a primary listing with the ISE only.[189]

- Sponsors have a more prominent role under the Irish rules which, as previously indicated, require a listed company (being an issuer of equity securities, preference shares or certificates representing equity securities) to engage and retain a sponsor for the duration of its listing.[190] The FSA listing rules only require the appointment of a sponsor when certain actions are being taken, such as applications for admission or when a class 1 circular is required[191]

---

[185] This change was introduced with effect from 1 July 2008 and is contained in paragraphs 23 and 24 of the Model Code (Listing Rule 6 Appendix 1).
[186] FSA Trading Plans Instrument 2009 (FSA 2009/12).
[187] Listing Rule 5.1.1.
[188] FSA listing rule 7.1.1.
[189] Listing Rule 3.4.
[190] Listing Rule 2.3.1.
[191] FSA listing rule 8.2.

(although companies may be required to seek the 'guidance' of a sponsor in certain other circumstances).

- The FSA listing rules, unlike their Irish equivalent, do not contemplate secondary listings for domestic companies.[192]

- Under the Irish rules, a company must ensure that, at all times, no more than one-third of its board of directors comprises persons who have been co-opted (that is, appointed by the board by way of resolution of the board of directors).[193] A company in breach of this rule must convene an extraordinary general meeting of shareholders (EGM) in order to take remedial action and may not carry out certain transactions without ISE approval prior to the relevant EGM.[194]

- Under the Model Code, a trading plan set up by a PDMR to allow dealing in securities during certain close periods and periods during which inside information is held requires either that the particular number and price of securities to be dealt in is established in advance or that a written or computer formula calculates the particular security dealing. The PDMR in question must not be permitted to exercise any subsequent influence over relevant dealings.[195] The FSA listing rules, however, subject to the satisfaction of certain conditions, permit discretion to be given to an independent third party to implement a trading plan and make trading decisions on behalf of the relevant persons.[196]

14.3.3 IEX continuing obligations

The key IEX continuing obligations are as follows: **14.152**

- information on new business developments must be notified to the market without delay;[197]
- preparation of half yearly reports;[198]
- preparation of annual accounts;[199]
- any documents sent to shareholders must be available on the relevant company's website and the company must notify their availability through an RIS;[200]

---

[192] Listing Rule 11.4.1.
[193] Listing Rule 6.9(1).
[194] Listing Rule 6.9(2).
[195] Listing Rule 6 Appendix 1 paragraph 23.
[196] FSA listing rule 9 Annex 1 paragraphs 23–26 (see also FSA listing rules glossary definition of 'trading plan').
[197] IEX Rule 11.
[198] IEX Rule 18.
[199] IEX Rule 19.
[200] IEX Rule 20.

- restrictions on dealings: an IEX company must ensure that its directors and certain relevant employees do not deal in any of its IEX securities during a close period;[201]
- substantial transactions,[202] related party transactions[203] and reverse takeovers:[204] an IEX company must issue notification of such transactions without delay;
- provision and disclosure of information: an IEX company may be required to provide information to the ISE in such form and within such limit as the ISE considers appropriate;[205]
- directors' responsibility for compliance: an IEX company must ensure that its directors accept full responsibility, collectively and individually, for compliance with the IEX Rules;[206]
- IEX companies must retain a recognized IEX adviser[207] and a recognized IEX broker[208] at all times.

14.3.4 Debt securities: continuing obligations in outline

14.3.4.1 Continuing obligations

14.153 Issuers with specialist securities listed on the Main Market must comply with a range of continuing obligations. In general, the continuing obligations regime does not vary significantly between the various specialist listing rules and includes the following:

- the requirement to prepare and file audited annual accounts (or in the case of certain retail securities, audited annual accounts together with semi-annual accounts and management statements);
- an obligation to notify the ISE of any 'inside information' pursuant to the provisions of the Market Abuse Regulations;
- an obligation to ensure equality of treatment for all noteholders ranking pari passu in respect of all of the rights attaching to their securities;
- an obligation to publish notices or distribute circulars concerning, *inter alia*, the payment of interest and the exercise of any conversion, exchange, subscription or cancellation of rights and repayment.

14.3.4.2 Common considerations

14.154 The obligation to file published accounts has always been a requirement for issuers listed on the Main Market. For trading companies, it is normally necessary

---

[201] IEX Rule 21.
[202] IEX Rule 12.
[203] IEX Rule 13.
[204] IEX Rule 14. A reverse takeover will also ultimately require shareholder approval.
[205] IEX Rule 22.
[206] IEX Rule 31.
[207] IEX Rule 1.
[208] IEX Rule 35.

to have two years' historical accounts available prior to listing. SPVs are not usually required to provide historical accounts where they are newly incorporated and have carried on no prior trading activity.

The implementation of the Transparency Regulations has not materially changed the level of ongoing disclosure required for new issuers of specialist securities with a denomination of EUR 50,000 and above. There are specific exemptions for the issuers of such specialist debt securities in that they are only required to file annual audited accounts. **14.155**

Issuers of specialist securities with a denomination of less than EUR 50,000 may be required to provide semi-annual accounts and management statements within a specified time frame. Any issuer that fails to comply with this requirement faces sanctions, including de-listing. Compliance in this context can be a particular problem for issuers under multi-issuance programmes. **14.156**

14.3.5 Combined Code

14.3.5.1 Introduction

The Combined Code is the primary source of recommendations for corporate governance for Irish Main Market companies. **14.157**

Although compliance with the Code is not mandatory as such, the Listing Rules require[209] a relevant listed company to include in its annual report a statement of how it has or has not complied with the Code. In addition, before the annual report is published, the listed company must ensure that its auditors review those parts of this corporate governance statement that relate to financial reporting, systems of internal control and audit committee requirements.[210] **14.158**

14.3.5.2 Recent developments

In February 2009, accountancy firm Grant Thornton published its annual corporate governance review report. It stated that almost half of the Irish companies whose shares are admitted to trading on the Main Market admitted to being not fully compliant with the Combined Code, and recommended that new legislation be introduced to incorporate into law key provisions of the Combined Code, in particular, those relating to the role of audit committees and directors. The ISE was understandably unhappy with the findings of the review and pointed out that Ireland and the United Kingdom were the only major markets of Europe to have a corporate governance code of this nature and, furthermore, that the findings of Grant Thornton in the United Kingdom were not dissimilar to those in the **14.159**

---

[209] Listing Rules 6.8.3(6) and (7).
[210] Listing Rule 6.8.6(2).

Irish market.[211] The ISE also noted that the Combined Code specifically states that good governance can be achieved by means other than those outlined in the Combined Code itself.

14.3.6 Market abuse and insider dealing

14.3.6.1 Introduction

14.160 As in the United Kingdom, the two central concepts of Ireland's market abuse regime are insider dealing and market manipulation. While insider dealing has been a statutory offence in Ireland since the implementation of the Insider Dealing Directive[212] by Part V of the Companies Act 1990 (the '1990 Act'), market manipulation was not a statutory offence in Ireland prior to the passing of the Market Abuse Regulations,[213] which implemented the Market Abuse Directive. This is in contrast to the position in the United Kingdom where a comprehensive framework regulating market manipulation has been in place for some time.

14.161 Ireland's market abuse regime closely tracks the provisions of the Market Abuse Directive, which is discussed in detail in Part 1.

14.162 A key point to note is that, at present, the market abuse regime applies only in respect of regulated markets.[214] Accordingly, it does not apply to exchange-regulated markets, such as IEX, which continue to be subject to the old (and slightly archaic) insider dealing provisions of the 1990 Act, referred to in Section 14.1.1.3. As noted above, it is understood that the regime may soon be extended, at least in part, to exchange-regulated markets.

14.163 The penalties on conviction of an offence under Ireland's market abuse regime include fines of up to EUR 10,000,000, imprisonment for ten years, or both.[215] Liability for civil breaches can include compensating affected parties for any

---

[211] ISE Statement, 18 February 2009.

[212] Council Directive 89/592/EEC of 13 November 1989 coordinating regulations on insider dealing [1989] OJ L 334.

[213] However, it was possible to commit the common law offence of 'rigging the market' having regard to the decision in the *De Berenger* case (*Rex v De Berenger* [1814] 105 Eng Rep 536). Actions at common law for fraud or misrepresentation could also arise.

[214] The 2005 Act contained a provision repealing the old Irish insider dealing provisions of the 1990 Act. In Ireland, primary legislation is given effect by statutory instruments known as commencement orders. One of the commencement orders (the Investment Funds, Companies and Miscellaneous Provisions Act 2005 (Commencement) Order, SI 323/2005) that brought the 2005 Act into effect specified that the repeals applied only 'in so far as they relate to a regulated market'. This has been interpreted as meaning that the insider dealing provisions in the 1990 Act, and not the Market Abuse Regulations, continue to apply to Irish IEX or AIM companies (IEX and AIM being exchange-regulated markets).

[215] Market Abuse Regulations regulation 49(2), which applies the sanctions set out in section 32 of the 2005 Act.

losses and accounting to the relevant issuer of the financial instruments for any profit.[216]

While the Financial Regulator is the competent authority in Ireland in respect of market abuse, as explained in Section 14.1.2 it has delegated certain tasks to the ISE. The Financial Regulator has exercised its power under the 2005 Act, referred to above, to issue the Market Abuse Rules. These rules constitute guidance to market participants on compliance with Irish market abuse law.   **14.164**

14.3.6.2 *Enforcement*

Although the market abuse regime has now been in force since 2005, there has been relatively little evidence of significant enforcement action being taken by the Financial Regulator. In April 2008, however, the Financial Regulator reached a settlement with a major national newspaper in relation to a breach of disclosure requirements in the context of a recommendation relating to financial instruments.[217] On the basis that the breach was admitted, was inadvertent and that the responsible party advised that it had reviewed its procedures and practices to ensure more effective compliance with the Market Abuse Regulations, a relatively small fine of EUR 10,000 was imposed. In 2007, an Irish magazine publisher was fined EUR 5,000 for a similar type of breach of the Market Abuse Regulations. To date there have not been any criminal convictions under the Market Abuse Regulations in Ireland, unlike in the United Kingdom where two individuals were recently convicted and given prison sentences (suspended in one case) for insider dealing.[218]   **14.165**

14.3.6.3 *Market abuse and IEX*

Broadly, under the 1990 Act, it is unlawful for any person who is connected with an Irish company to deal (this includes subscription, purchase, sale, etc.) in any securities (this includes shares, debt, options, etc.) of the company if, because of his connection, he has price-sensitive information that is not generally available.[219] There are some exceptions set out in the 1990 Act—for instance a person may in certain circumstances deal in securities of a company between seven and 14 days after the publication of its interim or final results if he gives 21 days' notice to the ISE, which notice is published.[220]   **14.166**

---

[216] 2005 Act section 33, which is applied by Regulations 5 and 6 of the Market Abuse Regulations.

[217] Regulation 18 of the Market Abuse Regulations provides that any person producing a recommendation concerning financial instruments must clearly and prominently disclose the identities of those who have prepared the recommendation.

[218] *R v McQuoid and Melbourne*, Southwark Crown Court, March 2009.

[219] 1990 Act section 108(1).

[220] 1990 Act section 108(10).

14.167   *Fyffes plc v DCC plc* is an important recent Irish case on insider dealing which was heard before the High Court in 2005[221] and the Supreme Court in 2007.[222] It was claimed in the case that Jim Flavin, a non-executive director of Fyffes plc (at the time listed on the Main Market) was in possession of unpublished price-sensitive information received in his capacity as director, at a time when nearly 10% of the shares in Fyffes plc was sold by DCC plc. As well as being a director of Fyffes plc, Mr Flavin was chief executive of DCC plc when the transactions occurred.

14.168   Insider dealing law as set out in the 1990 Act at that time applied to companies listed on the Main Market. Although the Market Abuse Regulations now apply to such companies, as indicated above, the decision of the Supreme Court in the Fyffes case will be directly relevant to IEX companies since the insider dealing rules of the 1990 Act continue to apply to them. The case is also generally relevant to Main Market companies as it illustrates how matters relating to insider dealing are viewed by the Irish Courts.

14.169   The Supreme Court (in overruling in part an earlier decision of the High Court) found that trading reports of Fyffes which had been furnished to Mr Flavin before the Fyffes stake was sold could constitute unpublished price-sensitive information and therefore the insider dealing prohibition would have applied. The trading reports in question showed a worsening trading situation for Fyffes and its shares were traded by DCC plc in advance of an announcement to the market in relation to this worsening situation. The Supreme Court applied a simple and common-sense test of market effect; it also noted that, once the announcement of the worsening trading position was made to the market, Fyffes' share price dropped significantly.

14.170   In *DPP v Byrne*,[223] Mr Byrne was charged with insider dealing under the 1990 Act, having sold shares in a property company in 1997. The evidence presented to the Dublin Circuit Criminal Court was that he had been aware of a planned merger involving the company. The Court found, in the context of the 1990 Act, that a person's intention when dealing must have been to profit by using the relevant information and, in this case, therefore, if the sale had not been motivated by profit, Mr Byrne should be acquitted. Mr Byrne was acquitted after presenting evidence that, when carrying out the transaction, he had been motivated in part by personal circumstances, rather than an intention to make a profit.

---

[221] *Fyffes plc v DCC plc and others* [2005] IEHC 477.
[222] *Fyffes plc v DCC plc and others* [2007] IESC 36.
[223] *DPP v Byrne* [2003] IESC 54.

14.3.7 Transparency and disclosure

14.3.7.1 Introduction

As described in Section 14.1.3.9 above, the Transparency Regulations imple- **14.171**
mented the Transparency Directive into Irish law. The Transparency Regulations
share the Transparency Directive's aim of harmonizing requirements for listed
companies in relation to the provision of financial information, the notification
of major shareholdings and the disclosure of corporate information to shareholders throughout the EU. Indeed, for the most part, the Transparency Regulations
simply transcribe the text of the Transparency Directive without modification.

There is overlap between the Transparency Regulations and the Transparency **14.172**
Rules and, in certain places, the former are materially altered by the latter. In addition, the Financial Regulator has recently published 'Guidance Note No 1 on
Periodic Financial Reporting Obligations pursuant to the Transparency (Directive
2004/109/EC) Regulations' which is intended to clarify a number of matters that
have arisen in respect of financial reporting obligations under the Transparency
Regulations. This Section will concentrate on the Irish implementing legislation,
as the Directive itself is already discussed in Part 1.

The Transparency Regulations currently apply principally to Irish-incorporated **14.173**
legal entities with debt or equity securities admitted to trading on the Main
Market. Consequently, Irish companies whose shares are traded on markets other
than regulated markets, such as IEX or AIM, or whose shares are not traded on a
market at all, are not affected by the Transparency Regulations. However, as mentioned above, it is anticipated that the Minister for Enterprise, Trade and
Employment may extend the ambit of the Transparency Regulations to Irish IEX
and AIM companies in the near future (at least in part).

14.3.7.2 Disclosure obligations

As noted above, the Transparency Regulations are supplemented by the **14.174**
Transparency Rules, which contain additional requirements and guidelines for
compliance with Irish transparency law. In addition to these regulations and rules,
there are a number of other sources of law and regulation in Ireland that contain
disclosure obligations. These include:

- *the Companies Acts*: Irish companies listed on exchange-regulated markets are
  subject to the disclosure rules in the Companies Acts rather than the Transparency Regulations. The Companies Acts also contain certain disclosure
  obligations specifically for company directors, which apply to all companies;
- *the Listing Rules*: Irish Main Market companies are obliged to notify to the
  market any notifications made to them under the Transparency Regulations or
  Companies Acts;

- *the IEX Rules*: IEX companies are also obliged to disclose changes notified to them;
- *the Takeover Rules*: certain disclosure obligations will apply when a company is in an 'offer period';[224]
- *the SARs*: these rules, designed to regulate the speed at which a party can build a stake in an Irish listed company, also contain certain disclosure obligations;
- *the Market Abuse Regulations*: a company must notify the market of certain dealings by PDMRs.

14.175 The Takeover Directive Regulations, the Admission to Trading Rules and the Prospectus Regulations also contain certain disclosure obligations.

14.176 It should also be noted that specific rules apply in relation to certain types of company, such as credit institutions and authorized insurers, for example.

14.3.7.3 Reporting and disclosure under the transparency regime

14.177 The requirements of the Transparency Regulations, in combination with the Transparency Rules, can be divided into two categories: (i) company reporting requirements and (ii) general disclosure obligations.

14.178 **14.3.7.3.1 Reporting** Further to the discussion of the Transparency Directive in Part 1, the requirement under the Transparency Directive to publish an interim management report means that, in Ireland, statements must be published that cover each six-month period in a company's financial year and must explain material events and transactions that have taken place in that period and their impact on their financial position.[225] However, companies that already publish quarterly financial reports are exempt from these requirements.

14.179 As mentioned in Section 14.1.2 above, the Irish Auditing & Accounting Supervisory Authority is the competent authority for monitoring and enforcing compliance with aspects of the Transparency Regulations relating to periodic financial reports and issuers' obligations to ensure the compliance of such reports with the relevant reporting framework.

14.180 **14.3.7.3.2 Disclosure** Part 5 of the Transparency Regulations imposes detailed disclosure obligations in relation to persons who acquire or dispose of shares in Irish issuers which carry voting rights and are admitted to trading on a regulated market. Rule 7.1 of the Transparency Rules materially alters some of these requirements. This would appear to be permitted by virtue of regulation 40(3), insofar as

---

[224] Irish Takeover Rules rule 8. The 'offer period' is the period from the time when an announcement is made of a proposed or possible takeover offer until the first closing date for acceptances or, if this is later, the date when the offer becomes or is declared unconditional as to acceptances or the date on which it lapses.

[225] Transparency Regulations regulation 9.

that regulation authorizes the Financial Regulator by means of supplementary rules to make an issuer or a holder of shares and certain other persons subject to more stringent requirements than those specified in the Regulations. Consequently, reading the two sets of requirements together, the notification obligations can be summarized as follows:

- In the case of an Irish[226] company, a person is obliged to notify the Financial Regulator of the percentage of his voting rights if the percentage of voting rights that he holds as shareholder or through his direct or indirect holding of financial instruments or a combination of such holdings, reaches, exceeds or falls below 3%, 4%, 5%, 6%, 7%, 8%, 9%, 10% and each 1% threshold thereafter up to 100%.[227] Notification must be made within two trading days,[228] beginning on the day after the date on which the person learns, or ought to have learned, of the acquisition or disposal.
- In the case of a 'non-Irish' company whose shares are admitted to trading on the Main Market, the notification obligation is on the basis of thresholds at 5%, 10%, 15%, 20%, 25%, 30%, 50% and 75% (in other words, the thresholds contained in the Transparency Directive) as a result of an acquisition or disposal of shares and financial instruments.[229] Notification must be made within four trading days.[230]
- Although regulation 21(3) provides that the notification to the relevant listed company is to be made not later than four 'trading days' commencing the day after the date on which the person learns, or ought to have learned, of the relevant acquisition or disposal or is informed about changes in the breakdown of voting rights, rule 7.4 of the Transparency Rules amends this, so that the four-trading-day period applies only to (i) non-Irish issuers and (ii) collective investment undertakings of the closed-ended type; the notification must be made within two trading days 'in all other cases'. This in effect means that, if a person acquires the relevant percentage of voting rights in an Irish public limited company with shares admitted to listing on the Official List and/or on the UKLA's official list, the notification of the acquisition or disposal must be made within two trading days and not four trading days.
- A person on whom a notification obligation falls must notify both the Financial Regulator and the relevant listed company.[231]

---

[226] 'Irish' in this context means having a registered office in Ireland.

[227] Transparency Rules rule 7.1.

[228] Transparency Rules rule 7.4. A 'trading day' is defined as a 'day included in the calendar of trading days published by the Financial Regulator on its website www.financialregulator.ie — in fact the calendar of 'trading days' is maintained by the ISE.

[229] Transparency Regulations regulation 14.

[230] Transparency Rules rule 7.4.

[231] Transparency Regulations regulation 21(2)(b).

- The notification requirements apply to persons holding, directly or indirectly, financial instruments that result in an entitlement to acquire already issued shares carrying voting rights.[232]
- Companies are obliged to make public any notification received by them— Irish issuers only have until the end of the trading day after they receive the notification to do so while non-Irish issuers, closed-ended funds and other prescribed entities have three trading days to do so.[233]
- These disclosure obligations will also apply to the chairman of a company who has been granted discretionary voting proxies in general meeting.[234]
- Certain exemptions[235] apply in respect of clearing and settlement, custodian arrangements, market makers, credit institutions or investment firms holding shares in their trading book, collateral arrangements and, in certain circumstances, stock lending.

14.181 As noted above, a number of separate pieces of legislation also contain disclosure obligations and the relationship between the various obligations can be complex. The following points are of particular note:

- If a requirement arises to notify an acquisition or disposal of shares under the Transparency Regulations, the disclosure obligations contained in the Companies Acts do not apply.[236]
- The Transparency Regulations would also appear to operate in such a way as to require disclosure of acquisitions of voting rights by persons engaged in price stabilization activities in the course of an initial public offer, as opposed to at the end of the period during which these activities are carried out. Previously, the obligation to notify any interests in shares acquired during such a period only arose on the first working day following the end of the stabilizing period.
- The Financial Regulator believes that contracts for difference and other financial instruments that have similar effects should be brought within the major shareholding disclosure regime set out in the Transparency Regulations. The new disclosure regime is expected to apply to: (i) issuers whose shares are admitted to trading on the Main Market and whose home member state is Ireland for the purposes of the Transparency Regulations; and (ii) issuers whose shares are

---

[232] Transparency Regulations regulation 15 provides, for example, that voting rights held by a third party on behalf of a person can trigger the disclosure requirements. Regulation 17 extends the requirements to financial instruments such as derivatives where the underlying assets are voting shares.

[233] Transparency Rules rule 7.8.

[234] Transparency Regulations regulation 15(1)(h).

[235] Transparency Regulations regulation 14(5) contains the principal exemptions.

[236] Transparency Regulations regulation 81.

admitted to trading on IEX. At the time of writing draft regulations are being prepared to give effect to the new disclosure regime.

14.3.7.4 *Granting of security*

Further obligations may arise in connection with granting security over shares. On 9 January 2009, the FSA issued a statement confirming that granting security over shares (by the creation of a security interest such as a mortgage or charge) comes within chapter 3 (DTR 3) of the United Kingdom Disclosure and Transparency Rules.[237] Accordingly, the FSA has indicated that PDMRs are required to notify such transactions to their companies, which must in turn notify the market. **14.182**

The question arises as to whether a similar obligation to disclose the grant of security over shares exists in Ireland. The better view is that no such obligation to disclose arises under Irish law, largely because the 'transactions' to which disclosure obligations attach do not expressly include granting security (and, indeed, in the case of the Transparency Regulations, collateral arrangements are excluded). The Financial Regulator has acknowledged that, although it believes that the disclosure of such information is 'within the spirit of the EU Market Abuse Directive', there is no legal certainty on the point. It has therefore issued a consultation paper[238] canvassing the views of market operators and other interested parties as to whether, in their view, the law does or does not require disclosure and, in either case, whether the law should be changed. **14.183**

---

[237] For the text of the FSA press release on 9 January 2009 see: http://www.fsa.gov.uk/pages/Library/Communication/PR/2009/005.shtml.
[238] Financial Regulator Consultation Paper CP 36—'Disclosure of Grants of Security over Shares'.

15

ITALY*

15.1 Listing Securities in Italy

15.1.1 Introduction

15.01   Italian capital markets experienced a relatively slow development in the second half of the twentieth century, as bank financing remained the preferred form of

---

* The contribution of Daniele Colicchio of Cleary Gottlieb Steen & Hamilton LLP to the drafting of this Chapter is acknowledged with thanks.

funding for Italian businesses. It is therefore not surprising that comprehensive rules regarding capital markets and issuers admitted to trading on a regulated market are relatively recent.

The first coherent body of rules relating to issuers of securities admitted to trading **15.02** on a regulated market was contained in law No 216 of 7 June 1974, which also established the Italian Market Authority ('CONSOB'). Soon after, several laws and regulations were passed on different aspects of securities law and capital markets. This process culminated with legislative decree No 58 of 24 February 1998, as amended (the 'Consolidated Financial Act', or 'CFA').

The CFA provides the first comprehensive regulation of capital markets, public **15.03** offerings, financial intermediaries, as well as issuers admitted to trading on a regulated market, and confers wide regulatory powers to CONSOB for its implementation. Pursuant to such regulatory powers, CONSOB has issued specific regulations such as, *inter alia*: (i) Regulation No 11971 of 14 May 1999, as amended (the 'Issuer Regulation', or 'IR') concerning a wide range of areas, including listed issuers and public offerings; (ii) Regulation No 16191 of 29 October 2007, as amended, on the operation, organization and functioning of financial markets (the 'Market Regulation'); and (iii) Regulation No 16190 of 29 October 2007, as amended, on financial intermediaries. The CFA also confers on CONSOB several responsibilities regarding authorization and supervision of financial markets and activities of intermediaries, supervision of issuers' compliance with disclosure and reporting obligations, as well as investigations on insider trading and market abuse.

In recent years, the CFA and the CONSOB Regulations have been subject to **15.04** major amendments, particularly in the context of the implementation of EC directives. Some of these amendments are currently being implemented in the IR, following the transposition of the Transparency Directive (the 'Transparency Directive'), and will come into force gradually, mostly throughout 2009.

15.1.2 The Regulation of capital markets

In the last 15 years financial market regulation has been subject to intense reforms **15.05** that have reshaped the concept and structure of Italian capital markets, including the privatization of exchanges, which now operate regulated markets as joint stock corporations (each an 'operating company') with the authorization and under the supervision of CONSOB.[1]

More recently, Italian laws and regulations were extensively amended with the **15.06** implementation of EC directive 2004/39 (the 'MiFID') and of the rules concerning multilateral trading facilities and systematic internalizers.

---

[1] CFA Articles 61 et seq.

15.07   With respect to regulated markets, the CFA delegates to CONSOB: (i) authorization of joint stock corporations to operate regulated markets; (ii) regulation of the activity of regulated markets, within the general principles set forth in the CFA; and (iii) exercise of extensive supervisory powers on the activities of regulated markets.[2]

15.08   CONSOB's rules on the authorization, operation and supervision of regulated markets, multilateral trading facilities and systematic internalizers are mainly contained in the Market Regulation.

15.09   Pursuant to the CFA, operating companies shall adopt market regulations providing transparent, non-discretional rules and procedures to guarantee correct and orderly trading and objective criteria to allow efficient execution of investment orders,[3] as well as setting forth conditions and procedures for admission to, exclusion and suspension from, the trading of securities, in line with the criteria set forth by CONSOB in furtherance of the MiFID.[4]

15.10   For instance, as discussed in more detail below, Borsa Italiana SpA ('Borsa') has issued a set of general market rules governing all the regulated markets it operates (the 'Borsa Market Rules'), along with more specific regulations (the 'Borsa Instructions').

15.11   Each operating company is responsible for the admission to, suspension and exclusion from trading of securities on its regulated markets. CONSOB, however, retains significant supervisory powers over decisions taken by operating companies.[5]

15.1.3 The financial markets in Italy

15.12   At present, three operating companies exist in Italy: Borsa, TLX SpA and MTS SpA. The following paragraphs will briefly examine the structure of the regulated markets operated by Borsa and TLX SpA.[6]

15.1.3.1 Borsa

15.13   Borsa is currently the largest and oldest operating company in Italy. It was instituted as the Milan Stock Exchange in 1808 during the French domination, as a public institution, along the French model of a stock exchange. Borsa operated as the official Italian public stock exchange until its privatization in

---

[2] Special provisions apply with respect to the authorization of and supervision on regulated markets for: (i) wholesale trading of private and public bonds (other than government securities), money market instruments, derivatives on public securities, interest rates and currencies, (ii) wholesale trading of government securities, and (iii) energy and gas derivatives.

[3] CFA Article 62.2.

[4] CFA Article 62.1-*ter*.

[5] See CFA Article 64.1 and 1-*bis*.

[6] MTS SpA operates a regulated market for government bonds and other fixed income instruments and recently became a fully owned subsidiary of Borsa.

1996–1998, when it was incorporated as a joint stock corporation, Borsa Italiana SpA. Since 2007, Borsa has been part of the London Stock Exchange group.

15.1.3.1.1 The regulated market for equity securities MTA (*Mercato Tele-* **15.14** *matico Azionario*—electronic share market) is the regulated market operated by Borsa for shares, convertible bonds, pre-emptive rights and warrants. Following suppression of the Expandi regulated market on 22 June 2009 MTA is now the only Italian regulated market that admits equity securities as a primary listing venue.[7]

MTA is divided into the following segments, on the basis of type of securities, **15.15** capitalization and/or certain characteristics of the issuers:

• *Blue Chip*—the segment dedicated to issuers with a minimum market capitalization of EUR 1 billion;
• *STAR (Segmento Alti Requisiti—segment of high requirements)*—the segment dedicated to mid-cap issuers (market capitalization between EUR 40 million and EUR 1 billion) with high standards of transparency, corporate governance and floating shares;
• *Standard*—the segment for mid-cap issuers (market capitalization between EUR 40 million and EUR 1 billion); and
• *MTA International*—the segment for trading of shares of foreign issuers already admitted to trading on other EC regulated markets, regardless of their market capitalization.[8]

From 22 June 2009 issuers once listed on the Expandi regulated market were **15.16** automatically admitted on either the Blue Chip or Standard segments, depending on their market capitalization.[9]

Borsa also provides an after-hours market (the 'TAH') dedicated to issuers with **15.17** shares already admitted to trading on the MTA and with particularly high standards of liquidity and market capitalization, i.e. issuers with shares traded on the Blue-Chip segment that make up the FTSE MIB and FTSE Italia Mid Cap indices or with equivalent liquidity and market capitalization (shares of issuers

---

[7] Expandi was the regulated market operated by Borsa dedicated to the trading of shares, bonds, warrants and preemptive rights of small-cap issuers, with minimum market capitalization of EUR 1 million, and float shares of at least 10% of the relevant category of listed shares. Borsa merged the Expandi regulated market into MTA with effect from 22 June 2009.

[8] Borsa Market Rules provide that with respect to shares traded on MTA International, the time frame for settlement of trading may be coincident with that of the foreign regulated market where such shares have their main listing. Therefore, settlement of trading of shares traded on MTA International do not necessary comply with the T+3 time frame (settlement three days after trading), as for other segments of the MTA.

[9] Borsa Notice No 7596 of 4 May 2009. One year thereafter such issuers may apply for trading on the STAR segment.

admitted to the STAR segment may also be traded on the TAH with the assistance of specialists). Covered warrants and certificates traded on the SeDeX regulated market may also be traded on the TAH.[10]

15.18 **15.1.3.1.2 Other regulated markets** Borsa also operates the following regulated markets:

- *ETFplus*—dedicated to units or shares of open-ended funds and exchange traded commodities;
- *MOT*—dedicated to bonds other than convertible bonds, government securities, Eurobonds, foreign bonds, asset-backed securities and other debt securities for fixed income bonds;
- *SeDeX*—dedicated to covered warrant and certificates; and
- *IDEM*—dedicated to futures contracts and options contracts based on securities, interest rates, currencies, goods and related indices.

15.19 With effect from 22 June 2009 Borsa instituted a new regulated market dedicated to investment vehicles (MIV),[11] that is structured into three segments dedicated to, respectively:

- units of closed-end funds;
- shares, convertible bonds, warrants and options of investment companies;[12] and
- shares, convertible bonds, warrants and options of real estate companies.[13]

15.20 **15.1.3.1.3 The multilateral trading facilities: AIM Italia and MAC** Borsa operates a multilateral trading facility, AIM Italia, dedicated to the listing of equity instruments of small and medium-sized enterprises. AIM Italia does not qualify as a regulated market pursuant to MiFID and is characterized by a simplified regulatory regime and a faster admission process.

15.21 Issuers already admitted to trading on AIM Italia may apply for admission to trading on the MTA pursuant to a faster and simplified admission process.[14] Issuers admitted to AIM Italia, like those admitted to the AIM market operated by the London Stock Exchange, must at all times have a nominated adviser (so-called NOMAD), that is responsible to Borsa for: (i) assessing the qualifications of a prospective issuer, (ii) advising and guiding a prospective issuer throughout the

---

[10] Borsa Market Rules Article 4.3.1, as well as Borsa Instructions Articles IA.6.1.1 and IA.6.2.1.

[11] Borsa Market Rules Article 4.6.1.

[12] Investment companies are defined as companies whose exclusive corporate purpose is to invest in majority or minority holdings in listed and unlisted companies or in securities and to perform certain instrumental activities specified in the Borsa Market Rules (Borsa Market Rules Article 1.3).

[13] Real estate investment companies are defined as limited liability companies that engage primarily in real estate investments and/or leasing and meet the requirements set forth in the Borsa Market Rules (Borsa Market Rules Article 1.3).

[14] See Borsa Market Rules Articles 2.4.2 and 2.4.3.

admission process, and (iii) advising an issuer on its obligations pursuant to the AIM Italia market rules.

Borsa also operates another multilateral trading facility for equity instruments of small and medium-sized enterprises, MAC (*Mercato Alternativo del Capitale*— alternative equity market). Access to MAC is limited to professional investors[15] and, in general, admission to trading on MAC follows an institutional offering to 'professional investors'. Trading on the MAC requires, *inter alia*, the appointment of a sponsor and a specialist. **15.22**

15.1.3.2 TLX SpA

TLX SpA is jointly controlled by two of the most important Italian banks, UniCredit SpA and Banca IMI SpA (a subsidiary of Intesa San Paolo SpA), and operates the TLX regulated market (the 'TLX'), as well as the EuroTLX multilateral trading facility, accessible to non-professional investors through brokers. **15.23**

From its establishment in 2000, TXL SpA steadily expanded and in 2008 became, on aggregate, the largest market in Europe for non-governmental bonds.[16] The TLX is also an important secondary market for shares. **15.24**

The TLX and the EuroTLX markets employ a hybrid trading model, both quote- and order-driven, unlike Borsa, which substantially employs an order-driven model. The TLX market rules provide that the admission of both branded and non-branded securities is 'contingent upon a commitment by a market maker to guarantee the liquidity of the securities concerned during continuous trading'.[17] **15.25**

In the following paragraphs we will briefly review the provisions regarding admission to trading on the TLX, whether upon request of the issuer or without the issuer's consent. **15.26**

15.1.3.2.1 Admission upon an issuer's request   The following securities may be admitted to trading on the TLX, both as a primary and as a secondary listing, upon the request of an issuer:[18] **15.27**

- bonds and other debt securities, including convertible bonds, structured bonds, securities issued by sovereign states and atypical bonds;
- covered warrants;
- certificates;

---

[15] 'Professional Investors' are defined in the MAC market rules as the entities and individuals mentioned in Annex II, paragraphs I and II of the MiFID, as well as the majority shareholder of the issuer at the time of admission to trading.

[16] According to data provided by TLX. See company brochure at http://www.eurotlx.com.

[17] TLX Market Rules Articles 2.3, section 2, and 2.23, section 4.

[18] TLX Market Rules Articles 2.1 and 2.3.

- units and/or shares in investment funds;
- asset backed securities; and
- combinations of the securities indicated above.

15.28 **15.1.3.2.2 Admission without an issuer's consent** In addition to the securities that are admissible with the issuer's consent (as outlined above), the TLX may also admit to trading—without the issuer's consent—shares, certificates representing shares and/or other equity securities, provided that such securities are:[19]

(i) issued or guaranteed by Italy or by one of the other member states, or issued by an international organization of a public nature and of which at least one of the member states is a participating member; or

(ii) securities other than those indicated in (i), which are traded on an EC regulated market and whose admission to trading is exempt from the prospectus obligation pursuant to Article 4.2, h) of the Prospectus Directive (see Section 15.2 below).[20]

15.1.4 Admission of shares on Borsa regulated markets

15.29 Borsa has adopted general rules for the admission of securities to the regulated markets it operates, as well as specific rules applicable to certain types of securities, regulated markets, segments, or issuers in certain situations.

15.30 In the following paragraphs we will review the general and specific requirements for admission of shares to trading on the MTA, as well as the specific requirements applicable to companies with a controlling shareholder, investment companies and issuers with controlling interests in non-EC countries. We will also review the regulation for admission to trading on the Borsa regulated markets as a secondary listing, with or without the issuer's consent.

15.1.4.1 *General requirements for admission of securities on Borsa's regulated markets*

15.31 The general requirements for admission to trading of securities, especially shares, are broadly in line with the provisions of EC Directive 2001/34 on the admission of securities to an official stock exchange ('Directive 2001/34').

---

[19] TLX Market Rules Articles 2.21 and 2.23.

[20] In order to be admitted to trading on the TLX, both upon request of the issuer or without the issuer's consent, securities must be: (i) issued in compliance with laws, regulations and all other applicable provisions and remain compliant therewith; (ii) freely negotiable; (iii) suitable for clearing by the settlement and clearing system provided by Article 69 of the CFA or by an analogous foreign system subject to supervision by a competent authority of the home state (See TLX Market Rules Article 2.3, section 1, and 2.23, section 3). As discussed below, similar provisions are set forth by the Borsa Market Rules.

In particular, to be admitted to regulated markets operated by Borsa: **15.32**

- the prospective issuer must be validly incorporated and its by-laws must be fully compliant with applicable laws and regulations;[21]
- the securities to be admitted must be compliant with applicable laws and regulations and must be duly issued pursuant to applicable laws and regulations;[22]
- all securities to be admitted must be freely negotiable;[23]
- all securities must be suitable for clearing by the settlement and clearing system provided by Article 69 of the CFA.[24]

Borsa may refuse admission in case:[25]   **15.33**

- it is plausible that a regular market for the securities will not develop because of the features of such securities;
- the prospective issuer has other securities admitted to listing and does not comply with the obligations deriving from such listing;
- the same securities have already been admitted to listing in another country and the issuer does not comply with the obligations deriving from such listing;[26]
- admission is contrary to the interests of investors, because of the prospective issuer's financial or competitive conditions.[27]

Borsa may, solely in the interest of protecting investors, make the admission of   **15.34**
securities to listing contingent upon special conditions considered appropriate, a
power it does not generally use.[28]

15.1.4.2 Admission of shares to the MTA

15.1.4.2.1 Requirements of the prospective issuer: financial reporting and   **15.35**
business activity[29]   Borsa provides that prospective issuers must have published

---

[21] See also Directive 2001/34 Article 42.

[22] See also Directive 2001/34 Article 45.

[23] The Borsa Market Rules provide that 'securities whose transfer is subject to restrictions are considered freely negotiable when the restrictions do not involve any risk of distortions of the market'. See also Directive 2001/34 Article 46.3.

[24] Alternatively, where applicable pursuant to the rules regarding each segment, by an analogous foreign system subject to supervision by a competent authority of the home state.

[25] Borsa Market Rules Article 2.1.2 section 2.

[26] See Directive 2001/34 Article 14.

[27] In the assessment of such condition, Borsa shall especially take into consideration serious disproportions in the issuer's financial structure, critical competitive position in the issuer's main market sectors, serious inconsistencies in the issuer's business plan and the lack of any concrete basis for such business plan (See Directive 2001/34 Article 11.2).

[28] Borsa Market Rules Article 2.1.2 section 6, which implements Directive 2001/34 Article 12.

[29] The requirements described in this paragraph do not apply in case of issuers with other categories of shares already listed (Borsa Market Rules Article 2.2.1 section 10).

and filed, in compliance with applicable laws and regulations, stand-alone and consolidated financial statements for the last three financial years.[30]

15.36 Borsa may admit issuers that have published and filed annual financial statements for fewer financial years or which have never published and filed annual financial statements, provided that:

- such issuers disclose additional financial information (e.g. pro-forma income statements, balance sheets, related auditor reports);
- Borsa considers such admission in the interests of the issuers and the investors;
- investors are provided with all the information necessary to evaluate the issuer and the securities to be admitted to listing.[31]

15.37 Financial statements for the previous year must be accompanied by a report from an auditor, drawn up in accordance with applicable Italian law or corresponding applicable provisions of foreign law. In case of a negative or qualified opinion, admission will be *ipso facto* rejected. Special provisions apply to prospective issuers with complex financial histories.

15.38 Prospective issuers must conduct a business activity, either directly or through subsidiaries, capable of generating revenues and with managerial independence. As to the managerial independence requirement, Borsa focuses on the existence of hindrances that may prevent the issuer from pursuing the maximization of its economic and financial targets, especially when the issuer is a subsidiary of another listed company or its business is based on a long-term relationship with an important customer. In case of possible hindrances to the managerial independence of an issuer, Borsa demands extensive and continuous disclosure.[32]

15.39 CONSOB has set forth specific rules for the admission to trading of companies with a controlling shareholder and for investment companies, for which satisfaction of the 'managerial independence' requirement may prove problematic. The Borsa Market Rules refer to CONSOB's rules and regulations in this respect.

15.40 15.1.4.2.2 **Requirements of the shares**   To qualify for listing at least 25% of the class of shares to be admitted to listing must consist of float shares, allotted both among professional investors and non-professional investors.[33]

---

[30] Borsa Market Rules Article 2.2.1 section 1.
[31] Borsa Market Rules Article 2.2.1 section 5. This provision is in line with Directive 2001/34 Article 44 .
[32] Borsa Market Rules Article 2.2.1 section 6.
[33] Borsa Market Rules Article 2.2.2 section 1 b), sets forth how to determine float shares. *Inter alia*, controlling shareholdings and shareholdings greater than 2% are disregarded for the determination of the float.

Borsa may also admit issuers with smaller percentages of float shares 'where the **15.41** market value of the shares held by the public suggests the conditions for regular operation of the market can be met by a smaller percentage'.³⁴

Issuers must have an expected minimum market capitalization of EUR 40 million **15.42** to be admitted on the Standard and STAR segments and of EUR 1 billion to be admitted on the Blue Chip segment. As an exception, Borsa may admit companies with a lower market capitalization, provided it is satisfied that an adequate market for such securities may develop.³⁵

As mentioned above, companies once listed on the Expandi regulated market **15.43** were automatically listed on the MTA effective from 22 June 2009. The Borsa Market Rules, as amended following termination of the Expandi regulated market, do not provide—on an ordinary basis—admission to trading of shares of issuers with a market capitalization lower than EUR 40 million.³⁶

15.1.4.3 The admission procedure

Borsa's review period is two months, beginning from the filing of the complete **15.44** application and documentation. However, Borsa may require additional documentation and information throughout the proceeding. In that event, Borsa's review period is interrupted and begins running again once the additional information and documentation has been provided.³⁷

From the filing of the application, a prospective issuer is subject to certain disclo- **15.45** sure obligations towards Borsa, in addition to the reporting and disclosure obligations towards CONSOB and the public pursuant to applicable laws and regulations (see Section 15.3 below). In particular, a prospective issuer must provide Borsa in advance with any notice, announcement, advertisement or marketing materials to be made available to the public, and regarding the listing application and the features of the securities. These materials must mention that the admission procedure is ongoing.

---

³⁴ Borsa Market Rules Article 2.2.2 section 1 b) and section 2. Borsa Market Rules slightly depart from the relevant provision of Directive 2001/34, which does not refer to the market value of the shares but to the 'large number of shares of the same class and the extent of their distribution to the public' (Directive 2001/34 Article 48 co 5). Borsa may also admit issuers whose shares are allotted only among professional investors, where the market value of such shares or the number of such investors suggests that the conditions for regular operation of the market can be met (Borsa Market Rules Article 2.2.2 section 2).

³⁵ Borsa Market Rules Article 2.2.2.1, a).

³⁶ Arguably, such situation contradicts Directive 2001/34 Article 43.3, which provides that member states may impose a requirement of market capitalization higher than EUR 1 million for admission to official listing, provided that 'another regulated, regularly operating, recognised open market exists in that State and the requirements for it are equal to or less than' EUR 1 million.

³⁷ Borsa Market Rules Article 2.4.2 section 2.

15.46 Effectiveness of the admission decision is conditioned upon filing with CONSOB by the prospective issuer of the listing and/or offering prospectus (or publication of a prospectus approved by an EC competent authority and registered in Italy pursuant to the Prospectus Directive).

15.47 In case of admission to trading without a contemporaneous public offer, the admission decision is effective only once Borsa has ascertained that the prospectus is available to the public and has established the first day of trading and the market segment.

15.48 When admission to trading is connected with a public offer, admission to trading is effective only after Borsa is satisfied with the distribution of the securities and has set the first day of trading, which may not occur later than the day set for the payment of the offer shares (i.e. no later than five trading days after the end of the offer period). Delivery of the offer shares shall occur no later than the payment day.

15.49 Borsa provides for special procedures with respect to certain prospective issuers. In particular, as discussed above, admission to the MTA of issuers whose shares are traded on the AIM Italia is subject to a simplified procedure, which provides simplified documentary requirements and a reduced review period of one month. Simplified documentation is also allowed for the admission of private equity backed companies.[38]

15.50 Borsa provides for a special review procedure in the event a prospective issuer has decided to draw up the prospectus as a set of separate documents (the so-called tripartite prospectus). The review procedure is divided into two phases: confirmation of admissibility and admission. During the first phase, with a time limit of two months, Borsa reviews all the documentation available at this stage, including the preliminary registration document.

15.51 The second phase starts when a prospective issuer files an application for admission, and the additional documentation required, which includes the securities note and the summary note. Within 20 days from filing of the complete application and documentation, Borsa will decide upon admission to trading.

15.1.4.4 *Companies with a controlling shareholder, investment companies and issuers with controlling interests in non-EU companies*

15.52 The Market Regulation sets forth specific provisions for the admission to trading of shares in the following situations:

(i) the issuer is a company subject to the direction and coordination powers of another company, as defined under Articles 2497 et seq. of the Italian Civil Code (the 'ICC');[39]

---

[38] Private equity backed companies are defined as companies where at least 30% of the share capital has been held, jointly or severally, by one or more institutional investors for at least the last two years.

[39] Market Regulation Article 37. Articles 2497 et seq. of the ICC provide special obligations for companies exercising direction and coordination on, or subject to the direction and coordination of,

(ii) the issuer is an investment company whose exclusive corporate purpose is the acquisition of interests (including minority interests) in other entities, in fixed maximum amounts, and other ancillary activities.[40]

In case of (i), issuers must be able to deal with customers and suppliers independently from their controlling shareholder, and their board of directors must include a significant number of independent directors.[41]

15.53

In case of (ii), shares of investment companies may be admitted to trading only if the prospective issuers (a) provide quantitative and qualitative information on their investment policies, specifying the criteria adopted for investments and risk management and (b) conduct their investments and activities consistently with such criteria. Such issuers have to disclose, without delay, variations of their investment policies and describe their investment portfolio in their half-yearly and management reports.

15.54

The Market Regulation sets forth other specific obligations that apply to issuers with controlling interests in companies organized under the laws of non-EU countries.[42]

15.55

---

another company. Pursuant to Article 2497-sexies a relationship of direction and coordination between two companies is presumed whenever: (i) companies are consolidated in the annual financial statements, (ii) a company holds the majority of the votes that may be cast at ordinary shareholders' meetings, or so many votes as to exercise a dominant influence on ordinary shareholders' meetings, of another company, or (iii) one company exercises a dominant influence on another company by way of contractual obligations.

[40] Market Regulation Article 38, as recently amended. The Borsa Market Rules (Article 2.2.1 section 8) are not aligned with the current text of the Market Regulation, since they refer to 'investment companies whose equity is composed exclusively of interests in other entities'.

[41] Borsa refers to the Corporate Governance Code for the definition of an 'independent director', as well as to the related requirements set forth for the admission to the STAR segment (Borsa Instructions IA.2.13.6). See Borsa Notice No 22778 of 21 December 2007, and Section 15.3.15 below. The Market Regulation also provides that an issuer subject to the direction and coordination of another company may not be admitted to trading if it: (i) has not complied with the specific disclosure obligations set forth under Article 2497-bis of the ICC; or (ii) implements a centralized treasury policy with other companies of the same group and such policy is inconsistent with its corporate interest.

[42] Market Regulation Article 36. In particular, such prospective issuers shall: (i) make available to the public the financial statements of the relevant controlled companies prepared for purposes of drawing up the consolidated financial statements (which should include at least the balance sheet and income statement); (ii) obtain from the relevant controlled companies the articles of association and composition and powers of the corporate bodies; (iii) ensure that the relevant controlled companies: (a) provide the auditor of the prospective issuer with the information necessary for auditing the annual and interim statements of the prospective issuer; (b) implement an appropriate administrative and accounting system for regular reporting to the management and auditor of the prospective issuer of income statement, balance sheet and financial data necessary for preparation of the consolidated financial statements. Prospective issuers with controlling interests in companies, which are considered not materially significant pursuant to the criteria set forth in the IR, are exempted from such additional requirements (Market Regulation Article 36.2).

15.1.4.5 The STAR segment

15.56 The Borsa Market Rules set forth higher standards for admission of shares to trading on the STAR segment, especially with respect to the number of float shares (which must represent at least 35% of the share capital entitled to vote at an ordinary shareholders' meeting),[43] financial history, corporate governance and reporting obligations.

15.57 In addition, issuers cannot incur losses equal to more than one-third of the share capital[44] and their corporate governance must conform to the principles and criteria set forth in the Corporate Governance Code, a code of conduct prepared by the Corporate Governance Committee of Borsa (the 'Corporate Governance Code'), particularly with respect to the composition of the board of directors, the functioning of its internal committees, the role of non-executive and independent directors, the remuneration of directors and the internal control committee (see Section 15.3.15 below for more details).

15.58 Issuers admitted to the STAR segment must appoint a specialist responsible for supporting the liquidity of their securities.

15.1.4.6 The secondary listing

15.59 The MiFID provides that a 'transferable security that has been admitted to trading on a regulated market can subsequently be admitted to trading on other regulated markets, even without the consent of the issuer'.[45]

15.60 The Borsa Market Rules provide that the following securities may be admitted to trading upon request of any of the issuer, any authorized financial intermediary or Borsa itself:[46]

    (i) securities, including shares,[47] (a) which have been traded on another European regulated market for more than 18 months, (b) for which admission to trading is exempted from the prospectus obligation and (c) which have not been excluded from trading upon the request of an issuer in the last 12 months;

---

[43] A free float of 35% is now required for admission to trading on the STAR segment (Borsa Instructions Article IA.4.1.2).

[44] Borsa Market Rules Article 2.2.3 section 12.

[45] MiFID Article 40.5. CONSOB introduced the possibility of an admission to trading of securities on a regulated market without the consent of the issuer in March 2003 (CONSOB Decision No 14002 of 27 March 2003), before the implementation in Italy of the MiFID.

[46] Borsa Market Rules Article 2.1.2 section 7.

[47] In addition to shares, certificates representing shares and other equity securities, bonds, Eurobonds and other debt securities, structured bonds, asset-backed securities, covered bonds and exchange-traded commodities may be admitted to trading without an issuer's consent.

(ii) securities issued or guaranteed by a member state or an international organization of a public nature in which one or more member states are participating members.

Borsa may reject an admission to trading in the event: (a) it is plausible that a regular market for the securities will not develop because of the features of such securities and (b) the issuer has other securities admitted to listing and does not comply with the obligations deriving from such listing. **15.61**

An admission to trading of shares pursuant to (i) above on the MTA is subject to the following additional requirements:[48] **15.62**

- issuers must be subject to disclosure obligations substantially equivalent to those set forth under Italian law;
- price-sensitive, corporate and periodic disclosures and information regarding the exercise of rights by the holders of such shares must be available to the public in English;
- listing of such securities is not suspended or revoked on the EC regulated market of primary listing for reasons other than technological reasons inherent in the operation of a market;
- shares of foreign issuers must have a par value expressed in Euro, be 'blue chip' and included in a major international or national financial index;[49] and
- any person seeking admission to trading must produce a summary document in Italian describing the issuer and the securities.[50]

15.2 The Prospectus Obligation

15.2.1 Introduction

The Italian Government failed to meet the deadline for the implementation of the Prospectus Directive, which was set on 1 July 2005. The Prospectus Directive is a maximum harmonization directive and is deemed by interpreters as self-enforcing in Italy. To alleviate the possible practical difficulties originating from misalignments between national legislation and the Prospectus Directive, CONSOB **15.63**

---

[48] Borsa Market Rules Article 2.2.45 section 2. Additional requirements are set forth also for the admission of securities pursuant to letter a) above on the MOT segment. In particular, Borsa Instructions Article IB.1.1 requires that such securities 'be issued by companies whose shares are included in a major international or national financial index. Alternatively, the securities or the issuer must have a minimum rating, requested by the issuer and notified to the market, equal to "investment grade" awarded by major credit rating agencies.'

[49] Borsa Instructions Article IB.2.1.2. The Borsa Instructions do not clarify when foreign issuers could be considered 'blue chips' for purposes of Borsa Instructions Article IB.2.1 section 2.

[50] As required by IR Article 56, which transported Prospectus Directive Article 4.2, h) v).

decided to implement significant portions of the Prospectus Directive in the IR, within the limited regulatory authority provided to it by the CFA, as applicable at the time.

15.64 On 28 March 2007 the Italian Government passed legislative decree No 51/2007, which implemented the Prospectus Directive and amended the CFA. This decree also provided CONSOB with wide regulatory authority to implement significant portions of the Prospectus Directive. On 19 March 2009 CONSOB amended the IR—effective from 1 July 2009—(the 'CONSOB Amendment'), fully implementing the Prospectus Directive in Italy and curing certain misalignments of the national regulation with the EC regulation (e.g. with respect to the definition of qualified investors).

15.65 Italian laws and regulations distinguish between different categories of securities, in a complex web of definitions that may sometimes prove hard to grasp. To simplify, when describing Italian laws and regulations in the following paragraphs of Section 15.2, the term 'securities' is used when generically referring to instruments negotiated on the financial markets.

15.2.2 Trigger of the prospectus obligation

15.2.2.1 The 'offer to the public'

15.66 Pursuant to the Prospectus Directive, member states shall require the publication of a prospectus prior to:

- 'any offer of securities to be made to the public';[51]
- 'any admission of securities to trading on a regulated market'.[52]

15.67 The CFA provides an obligation to publish a prospectus in case of any 'offer of financial products to the public'.[53]

15.68 Under the CFA, an 'offer of financial products' to the public is defined as:

> a communication to persons in any form and by any means, presenting sufficient information on the terms of the offer and the financial products to be offered, so as to enable an investor to decide whether to purchase or subscribe to these securities, including the allocation through authorized intermediaries.[54]

15.69 This definition seems to be aligned with the analogous definition of 'offer of securities to the public' under the Prospectus Directive,[55] which constitutes the base for the prospectus obligation ('Member States shall not allow any offer of

---

[51] Prospectus Directive Article 3.1.
[52] Prospectus Directive Article 3.3.
[53] CFA Article 94.
[54] CFA Article 1.1 t).
[55] Prospectus Directive Article 2.1 d).

securities to be made to the public within their territories without prior publication of a prospectus').[56] However, if we then turn to the definition of 'financial products' under Italian law and compare it with the definition of securities under the Prospectus Directive,[57] we understand that the former has a much wider scope.

In fact, under the CFA: 15.70

> financial products shall mean financial instruments and every other form of investment of a financial nature.[58]

Therefore, under Italian laws and regulations, publication of a prospectus is also   15.71
required in connection with an offer to the public of non-transferable securities
(except for offers of non-transferable securities to directors and employees; see
Section 15.2.3.4 below) and other securities not included within the definition of
securities under the Prospectus Directive.

On the other hand, CONSOB does not impose the publication of a prospectus in   15.72
connection with an offer of securities that does not require consideration or any
investment risk for the subscribers, in line with the interpretation provided by
CESR.[59] According to CONSOB's interpretative approach, financial instruments
allotted free of charge should not be considered 'financial products' for purposes
of the obligation to publish a prospectus.[60] With reference to options allotted free
of charge to employees and directors pursuant to employee share schemes, exercise or conversion of such options does not constitute an offer to the public, but
rather the mere exercise of a previous offer.[61]

Before the implementation of the Prospectus Directive, CONSOB based its deci-   15.73
sion as to whether there was an offer to the public on the notions of standard

---

[56] Prospectus Directive Article 3.1.

[57] Prospectus Directive Article 2.1 a).

[58] CFA Article 1.1 u) of the CFA. 'Financial instruments', for purposes of this provision, encompass a large category of securities, which include 'transferable securities' (see below), money market instruments, units in collective investment undertakings, options, futures, swaps, futures contracts on interest rates and derivative contracts, differential financial contracts (CFA Article 1.2). However, bank or postal deposits without the issue of financial instruments are excluded from the definition of 'financial product'.

[59] CESR, 'Frequently Asked Questions regarding Prospectuses: common positions agreed by CESR members—8th updated version' ('FAQs') Question 6. CESR also notes, with reference to employee share schemes, that offers presented as offers of free shares may in fact disguise some forms of 'hidden' consideration, e.g. when shares are offered in lieu of remuneration that the employee would otherwise be entitled to receive.

[60] CONSOB, 'Modifiche alle disposizioni in materia di prospetto relative all'offerta pubblica o all'ammissione alla negoziazione di strumenti finanziari in un mercato regolamentato', 30 March 2009 ('Modifiche'), page132.

[61] Such position reflects the substance of the position of the CESR. CESR FAQs, Question 5.

communication and dissemination to the public. It is plausible that such notions may influence CONSOB's interpretation of the new rules.

15.74 In particular, according to CONSOB's past interpretive approach, communications and conditions of an offer have to be standardized, so that the recipients of an offer may not negotiate or change the conditions of the offer.[62]

15.75 As to dissemination, earlier decisions by CONSOB focused on the dissemination of standard communications to large groups of recipients.[63]

15.76 In more recent decisions, however, CONSOB seemed to take a straight-through approach. Indeed, CONSOB has interpreted dissemination as distribution or transmission to a group of people larger than the offeree threshold provided by the Prospectus Directive.[64]

15.77 CONSOB has also taken a rigorous view of exchange offers, maintaining that rules governing tender offers apply to exchange offers, including cross-border exchange offers of debt securities. CONSOB has in the past refused to grant recognition to offer documents approved in other jurisdictions as the Prospectus Directive mutual recognition principle did not apply to tender and exchange offers. This resulted in offers routinely not being extended to Italian investors. To facilitate cross-border exchange offers of debt securities and tendering by Italian investors, CONSOB recently adopted a new rule whereby, under certain circumstances, it will grant its approval of an exchange offer enacted through a Prospectus Directive compliant offer document approved in another member state.[65]

15.2.2.2 *The admission of securities on a regulated market*

15.78 The CFA[66] and the IR set forth a regulation of the prospectus to be published in case of admission of securities to trading on a regulated market, which closely matches the relevant provisions of the Prospectus Directive. Such obligation only concerns admission to trading on a regulated market of 'EC securities' ('*strumenti finanziari comunitari*'), which correspond to the category of 'securities' adopted by the Prospectus Directive. Such category is narrower than that of 'financial products', which is instead adopted by the CFA and the IR for the application of the general public offerings regime.

---

[62] See CONSOB Notice DEM/3033091 of 20 May 2003 and CONSOB Notice DIN/1055860 of 19 July 2001.

[63] CONSOB Notice DAL/97007063 of 13 August 1997. Standard communications disseminated not to the general public, but to qualified groups of recipients, such as the members of a specific professional category, have been considered an offer to the public.

[64] Prospectus Directive Article 3.2 b). See CONSOB Notice DEM/5017297 of 18 March 2005. At the time of this decision the threshold set forth in the IR was of 200 offerees.

[65] IR Article 37.1-*bis*.

[66] CFA Article 113.

15.2.3 The exemption regime

The CONSOB Amendment resolved certain misalignments between Italian laws and regulations and the Prospectus Directive, especially with respect to the exemptions from the obligation to publish a prospectus.

15.79

In the following paragraphs we will consider some of these exemptions, as implemented in Italy and recently amended.

15.80

15.2.3.1 *The number of offerees*

Pursuant to the IR, the obligation to publish a prospectus shall not apply to offers addressed to fewer than 100 persons, not taking into account 'qualified investors' (for the definition of 'qualified investors', see Section 15.2.3.2 below).[67]

15.81

For the purposes of such exemption, CONSOB considers only the number of offerees resident in Italy, regardless of whether the threshold is exceeded in another member state or not.

15.82

In a relatively recent decision, CONSOB clarified that, in case an offer to the public is divided into different *tranche* reserved to different classes of offerees, CONSOB will not consider each of the different *tranche* separately, but will instead treat them as a series of related transactions and aggregate them into a single offering of securities. In particular, for the purposes of the 100-offeree threshold, purportedly separate offers will be considered as portions of a single offer whenever they are made on the same terms and conditions and are based on the same capital raising transaction, e.g. a shareholders' resolution to increase the company's share capital.[68]

15.83

15.2.3.2 *Qualified investors*

Pursuant to the IR, offers addressed solely to 'qualified investors' are exempt from the Prospectus Directive.

15.84

The definition of 'qualified investor' pursuant to the IR closely matches the definition of 'qualified investor' pursuant to the Prospectus Directive.[69]

15.85

Natural persons resident in Italy and small to medium-sized enterprises with their registered office in Italy—as qualified in the relevant provisions of the Prospectus Directive (which provisions have been integrally transported into the IR)—may ask to be considered as 'qualified investors'.

15.86

---

[67] IR Article 34-*ter*.1 a), which implemented Prospectus Directive Article 3.2 b).
[68] CONSOB Notice No DEM/8036073 of 17 April 2008.
[69] IR Article 34-*ter*.1 b), which implemented Prospectus Directive Article 2.1 e).

15.87 As provided by the Prospectus Directive,[70] CONSOB plans to create an official registry of natural persons and small and medium-sized enterprises considered 'qualified investors'. Such official registry shall be available to all domestic issuers and offerors.[71] Foreign issuers and offerors may have access to such registry, if such option is open to Italian issuers and offerors pursuant to the relevant member state's regulation (as provided by the Prospectus Directive).[72]

15.88 CONSOB clarified that the definition of 'qualified investor' under Article 34-*ter* of the IR is provided only for purposes of the prospectus regulation. Therefore, such definition is distinct from the definitions of 'professional client' or 'eligible counterparties' pursuant to the MiFID and relevant implementing provisions of Italian laws and regulations.[73]

15.2.3.3 *Mergers, de-mergers and takeovers by means of exchange offers*

15.89 The IR[74] provides an exemption from the obligation to publish a prospectus with respect to EC securities offered, allotted or to be allotted in connection with a merger. Provided that a document is available containing information that is regarded by CONSOB equivalent to that of a prospectus, taking into account the requirements of EC legislation. An analogous exemption is provided with respect to 'financial products' offered in connection with a takeover by means of an exchange offer.[75]

15.90 To prevent possible misunderstandings, CONSOB clarified that the exemption hereunder does not mean that any offer or allotment of EC securities addressed to more than 100 recipients in the context of a merger constitutes an offer to the public, which would trigger the prospectus obligation unless the same or another exemption from the prospectus obligation applied. In particular, simple allotment

---

[70] Prospectus Directive Article 2.3.

[71] CONSOB decided not to allow institutional investors, including therefore, the global coordinator of a public offer, access to the official registry of natural persons and small and medium enterprises considered 'qualified investors' pursuant to the Prospectus Directive. Please note, however, that according to the summary record of the European Commission 4th Informal meeting on Prospectus Transposition (8 March 2005): 'Member States may grant access more widely (including to investment firms) if they choose to do so, provided that this is consistent with the law on data protection'.

[72] Prospectus Directive Article 2.1 e) iv) v). As a temporary measure applicable before the institution of the official registry by the CONSOB, natural persons and small and medium enterprises meeting the statutory requirements may be registered in registries kept by issuers and offerors (IR Article 34-*terdecies*).

[73] Likewise, CONSOB distinguished the definition of 'qualified investor' under IR Article 34-*ter*, which implemented the Prospectus Directive, from the definition of 'qualified investor' provided by Ministerial Decree 228/1999 Article 1.1 h) as amended, which Ministerial Decree provides general criteria for the regulation of investment funds (see also CFA Article 37).

[74] Article 34-*ter* 1 k), which closely matches Prospectus Directive Article 4.1 c).

[75] Article 34-*ter* 1 j), which closely matches Prospectus Directive Article 4.1 b). The exemption refers to 'financial products', as defined in the IR (see above for more details).

or offer of EC securities or distribution of documentation to existing sharehold-ers, as required by applicable law in case of a merger (e.g. distribution of the man-agement report pursuant to Article 2501-*bis* and Article 2501-*quinquies* of the ICC), do not constitute an offer to the public and remain outside the scope of the prospectus obligation.[76] An offer to the public occurs only with respect to activities that go beyond what is required pursuant to applicable laws and regula-tions, such as in case the issuers engage in publicity and marketing activities. Therefore, only if the issuers engage in activities that may be qualified as an offer to the public, does a question arise as to whether the exemption hereunder applies. The CESR holds that:

> the exemptions provided in Art. 4.1c) of the PD can be applied to any type of merger or de-merger where a public offer is made according to the PD and about which provision of similar information is required by national legislation.[77]

Accordingly, CONSOB considers the exemption hereunder applicable also in the event of a de-merger, since information to be provided by issuers in case of a merger is similar to the information to be provided in case of a de-merger.   **15.91**

As to the assessment of the equivalence between the document made available in the context of a merger (or de-merger or takeover by means of an exchange offer) and the information to be included in a prospectus, CONSOB decided to endorse a case-by-case approach, rather than issue rules or guidelines.[78]   **15.92**

The exemptions hereunder, and the corresponding interpretive positions endorsed by CONSOB, apply, *mutatis mutandis*, also with respect to the admission to trading of 'transferable securities' ('*valori mobiliari*')[79] on a regulated market   **15.93**

---

[76] CONSOB, Modifiche, page129.

[77] CESR, FAQs, Question 30. This interpretation follows the position of the European Commission, as evidenced in 4th Informal meeting on Prospectus Transposition.

[78] In fact, according to the summary record of the European Commission 4th Informal meeting on Prospectus Transposition (8 March 2005): 'it is up to Member States to decide how to implement the exemptions; for example, whether the determination of whether a document contains informa-tion which is regarded by the CA [Competent Authority] as equivalent to that of a prospectus is done on a case by case basis, or by means of regulations/guidelines issued by the CA defining in advance what information the CA regards as equivalent for a particular purpose'.

[79] 'Transferable securities' ('*valori mobiliari*') is the category introduced in the CFA (Article 1.1-*bis*) in furtherance of the MiFID, which intended to transport the definition of 'transferable securities' under MiFID Article 4.1,18 and includes 'classes of securities which are negotiable on the capital market, such as: (a) shares in companies and other securities equivalent to shares in companies, partnerships or other entities, and depositary receipts, in respect of shares; (b) bonds or other forms of securitised debt, including depositary receipts in respect of such securities; (c) any other securities generally negotiable which gives the right to acquire or sell the transferable securities indicated above; (d) any other securities giving rise to a cash settlement determined by reference to transferable securities indicated above, to currencies, interest rates or yields, commodities, indices or measures.' The category of 'transferable securities' substantially corresponds to the category of securities under the Prospectus Directive, with the exclusion of units of closed investment funds (see also CFA Article 93-*bis*.1 a).

(including the applicability to the case of a de-merger).[80] However, only with respect to the admission of transferable securities on a regulated market, offered, allotted or to be allotted in connection with a merger, the IR provides indications on the content of the informative document, for purposes of the equivalence assessment, and sets forth a specific timeframe for the equivalence assessment by CONSOB. In fact, pursuant to the IR[81] CONSOB shall complete its equivalence assessment within 10 business days from the filing of the relevant document.

15.2.3.4 *Offer or allotment to employees and directors*

15.94   In discussing offers and allotments to employees, the CESR has clarified that 'non-transferable options granted to employees do not fall under the Prospectus Directive as the Directive only applies to transferable securities (Article 2.1a))'.[82]

15.95   Before the CONSOB Amendment, stock option plans that envisaged allotment of non-transferable options for consideration triggered the prospectus obligation in Italy. To correct, in part, the misalignment with the CESR's position, CONSOB introduced a specific exemption for transferable securities offered, allotted or to be allotted to existing or former directors or employees by the issuer or by an affiliated undertaking, provided that such transferable securities could not be traded on capital markets because, *de facto*, totally or partially non-transferable.[83]

15.96   The Prospectus Directive also provides an exemption for:

> securities offered, allotted or to be allotted to existing or former directors or employees by the employer which has securities already admitted to trading on a regulated market or by an affiliated undertaking, provided that a document is made available containing information about the number and nature of the securities and the reasons for and details of the offer.[84]

15.97   The IR, as amended by the CONSOB Amendment, closely mirrors such an exemption.[85]

---

[80] IR Article 57.1 c) and d), which correspond to Prospectus Directive Article 4.2 c) and d). See CONSOB, Modifiche, page 157.

[81] IR Article 57.8.

[82] CESR FAQs, Question 5.

[83] IR Article 34-*ter*.1) n).

[84] Prospectus Directive Article 4.1 e).

[85] IR Article 34-*ter*.1 m). This provision refers to 'financial instruments' ('*strumenti finanziari*'), which corresponds to the definition of securities pursuant to the Prospectus Directive, except for units of closed funds. Before the CONSOB Amendment such exemption pursuant to the IR was more stringent than the analogous provision of the Prospectus Directive. In fact, in order to qualify for the exemption pursuant to the IR, securities offered, allotted or to be allotted had to be of the same class as the securities already admitted to trading on the same regulated market. Such additional requirement is provided by the Prospectus Directive only with respect to the admission to trading of such securities on a regulated market (Article 4.2 f).

15.2.4 The structure and content of the prospectus

15.2.4.1 The base and tripartite prospectuses

The IR[86] has incorporated the provisions of the Prospectus Directive with regard **15.98**
to the base prospectus for (i) offers of non-equity securities, which include any
type of warrant, issued under an offering programme, and (ii) non-equity securities issued in a continuous and repeated manner by credit institutions, in either
case under the same conditions as those set forth in the Prospectus Directive.[87]

The IR provides a regulation of the tripartite prospectus (i.e. a prospectus consist- **15.99**
ing of three separate documents) which closely matches the relevant provisions of
the Prospectus Directive.[88] Unlike the Prospectus Directive, the IR sets forth a
so-called 'fast track' for the approval of the securities note and the summary note
with respect to certain issuers, provided a registration document has already been
approved by CONSOB.

15.2.4.2 The content of the prospectus

The IR[89] refers directly to the provisions and schedules of EC Commission **15.100**
Regulation No 809/2004 when dealing with the content of the prospectus for
offers to the public or for admission to trading on a regulated market of transferable securities.[90] As to the interpretation of the Prospectus Directive and of
Regulation No 809/2004, CONSOB generally follows the positions agreed
within the CESR.[91]

With respect to issuers with a registered office in non-EC countries, the CFA sub- **15.101**
stantially implemented Article 20 of the Prospectus Directive, providing that
CONSOB may, under certain conditions, approve or 'passport' prospectuses drawn
up in accordance with the laws and regulations of such non-EC countries.[92]

In the following paragraphs we will briefly examine certain provisions of the appli- **15.102**
cable Italian laws and regulations, as well as CONSOB's practices regarding the

---

[86] IR Article 6.

[87] Prospectus Directive Article 5.4.

[88] CFA Article 94.4 and IR Article 5.4, which mirror Prospectus Directive Articles 5.3 and 12.

[89] IR Article 5.1 for offers to the public; IR Article 53.1 for admission to trading on a regulated
market.

[90] The content of the prospectus for offers to the public of investment funds is regulated in a
separate section of the IR.

[91] See CONSOB, Modifiche, page 48.

[92] As provided in the Prospectus Directive, the CFA requires, when Italy is the home member
state, that: (a) the prospectus be drawn up in accordance with international standards set by international securities commission organizations, including the IOSCO disclosure standards; and (b) the
information requirements, including information of a financial nature, be equivalent to the requirements of Community regulations. See CFA Article 98-*bis* for offers to the public; CFA Article 113.5
for admission to trading on a regulated market.

content of a prospectus, which may differ from prior Italian practice or other member states' regulations and practices.

15.103   15.2.4.2.1 **The summary note**   The IR has fully incorporated the provisions of the Prospectus Directive[93] regarding the content of the summary note.

15.104   CONSOB has recently clarified that the summary note does not consist in a mere summary of the prospectus, but should be written in non-technical language and should not exceed 2,500 words, as set forth in *Whereas* No 21 of the Prospectus Directive.[94]

15.105   According to CONSOB's interpretation of the Prospectus Directive, except for the summary note, every part of the prospectus may be written in technical language, provided that the prospectus contains a glossary explaining technical words and certain aspects of the business of the issuers that may be unfamiliar to non-specialized readers.

15.106   15.2.4.2.2 **The risk factors**   Neither the Prospectus Directive nor Regulation No 809/2004 provide precise indications on the content of the risk factors section of prospectuses.

15.107   CONSOB developed its practice relying in particular on the indications provided by IOSCO.[95] CONSOB recently summarized some of these practices, together with precise indications on the content and graphic layout of the risk factors section.[96]

15.108   In particular, pursuant to CONSOB's indications:

- The risk factors section should be divided into three parts, the first dedicated to the risk factors relating to the issuer, the second dedicated to the risk factors pertaining to the business of the issuer, the third dedicated to the risks originating from the offer and the securities being offered thereunder.

---

[93] IR Article 5.3 and Prospectus Directive Article 5.2. See also Article 24 of the Commission Regulation No 809/2004, explicitly referred to in the IR.

[94] See CONSOB Notice No DEM/9025420 of 24 March 2009.

[95] International Disclosure Standards for Cross-Border Offerings and Initial Listings by Foreign Issuers, IOSCO (1998), which provides that 'the document shall prominently disclose risk factors that are specific to the company or its industry and make an offering speculative or one of high risk, in a section headed "Risk Factors". Companies are encouraged, but not required, to list the risk factors in the order of their priority to the company. Among other things, such factors may include, for example: the nature of the business in which it is engaged or proposes to engage; factors relating to the countries in which it operates; the absence of profitable operations in recent periods; the financial position of the company; the possible absence of a liquid trading market for the company's securities; reliance on the expertise of management; potential dilution; unusual competitive conditions; pending expiration of material patents, trademarks or contracts; or dependence on a limited number of customers or suppliers. The Risk Factors section is intended to be a summary of more detailed discussion contained elsewhere in the document.' The same provision has been transported in Form 20F by the US Securities and Exchange Commission.

[96] CONSOB Notice No DEM/7105108, of 29 November 2007.

- The paragraphs describing each risk factor should be listed in decreasing order of importance. If risk factors are correlated and material, then they should all be described in the first paragraph.
- Within each paragraph dedicated to a risk factor, the first subparagraph should briefly describe the nature of the risk, whilst leaving the following subparagraphs to describe in detail the risk factor.
- The risk factors section should contain only real and effective risks and not mere menaces or potential and/or not effective risks.

15.2.4.2.3 Indication of the offer price   The price of initial public offers in Italy is often determined through the book building process, whereby the final offer price and the amount of securities to be offered to the public are determined at the end of the offer on the basis of different factors. These factors typically include the quantity and quality of subscriptions by institutional investors in the private placement which accompanies the public offer, the number of subscriptions to the public offer, the characteristics of the issuer and the capital markets' performance.   **15.109**

The book building process is certainly legitimate under the Prospectus Directive, which, in fact, provides that a prospectus may omit any indication of the final offer price and the amount of securities to be offered to the public, provided that: **15.110**

the criteria, and/or the conditions in accordance with which the above elements will be determined or, in the case of price, the maximum price, are disclosed in the prospectus;

or

the acceptances of the purchase or subscription of securities may be withdrawn for not less than two working days after the final offer price and amount of securities which will be offered to the public have been filed.[97]

Therefore, in case the final offer price or the amounts of securities to be offered to the public are unknown, the Prospectus Directive appears to require alternatively an indication of the criteria and/or elements (and the maximum price), or a withdrawal right for subscribers. However, Annex III of Regulation No 809/2004, which sets forth minimum disclosure requirements for shares, seems to suggest that, in case the offer price is not indicated, the prospectus must at least indicate the methods for its determination.   **15.111**

Before the CONSOB Amendment, the IR provided that in cases where the prospectus did not indicate the offer price or the amount of 'financial products'[98]   **15.112**

---

[97] Prospectus Directive Article 8.1 a) and b).
[98] As discussed above, IR provides the prospectus obligation in case of offers to the public with respect to the wide category of 'financial products'.

to be offered to the public, the prospectus had to contain the criteria and conditions on which such prices or amounts would be determined (or, with respect to price, the maximum price). Following the CONSOB Amendment, the IR[99] now provides that in case a prospectus does not contain an indication of the price or amount of 'financial products' to be offered to the public, it may indicate, instead:

- the criteria and conditions in accordance with which the offer price and the amount of 'financial products' to be offered to the public will be determined; and
- with respect to the offer price, the maximum price.

15.113 The prospectus may also omit these requirements, in which case 'the acceptances of the purchase or subscription of financial products may be withdrawn'.[100]

15.114 However, the same option is not available for base prospectuses. The IR,[101] in line with the Prospectus Directive,[102] provides that if the final terms of an offer are not included in either a prospectus or a supplement thereto, the base prospectus shall describe either the criteria and the conditions in accordance with which the offer price and amount of 'financial products' to be offered to the public will be determined or, with respect to the offer price, the maximum price.

15.2.5 The publication of the prospectus and of supplements

15.115 The IR has fully implemented the provisions of the Prospectus Directive regarding publication of the prospectus.[103] In addition, the IR also requires the publication of a notice indicating how the prospectus has been made available and where the public can obtain it, and containing the information required by Article 31 of Regulation No 809/2004.[104]

15.116 CONSOB has recently endorsed certain positions agreed within CESR with respect to the publication of a supplement to a prospectus.[105] In particular, CONSOB disclosed that it would admit corrections of mistakes and inaccuracies in a prospectus, which do not affect assessment of the securities and therefore do not require the publication of a prospectus pursuant to Article 16.1 of the Prospectus Directive.[106]

---

[99] IR Article 7.1.

[100] CFA Article 95-*bis*. See CONSOB, Modifiche, pages 23 and 24.

[101] IR Article 6.3.

[102] Prospectus Directive Article 5.4, in fact, refers only to Article 8.1 a), and not to b).

[103] IR Article 9, which implemented the relevant provisions of Prospectus Directive Article 14.

[104] Prospectus Directive Article 14.3 allows member states to decide whether to require the publication of said notice.

[105] CONSOB, Modifiche, page 42 et seq.

[106] These corrections may be made to the prospectus already approved by the CONSOB, but not yet published, notwithstanding Prospectus Directive Article 14.6, (and corresponding IR Article 9.3),

Issuers will also be allowed to publish a press release, instead of a supplement to **15.117**
the prospectus, to disclose information or events before the closing of the transaction, which, although of interest to investors, do not affect assessment of the
securities and, therefore, do not require the publication of a prospectus pursuant
to the Prospectus Directive.[107]

Moreover, publication of interim financial information by an issuer will not **15.118**
necessarily require the publication of a supplement to a prospectus, provided that
such interim financial information does not contain information that may be
considered relevant for an assessment of the securities (e.g. significant deviations
from financial information contained in a prospectus).[108]

CONSOB has recently disclosed that with respect to offers to the public and/or **15.119**
admission to trading on a regulated market of shares, it may approve—on certain
conditions—a prospectus that does not provide a fixed calendar for the transaction.[109] Thus, issuers and/or offerors are allowed to fix the calendar of an offer even
after the approval by CONSOB, either by disseminating a notice to the public
when publishing the prospectus or, if a prospectus has already been published
(provided that the offer period has not started yet), by issuing a notice in the same
form in which the prospectus has been published. This practice endorsed by
CONSOB allows prospective issuers and/or offerors more flexibility to fix the
date of a transaction and may prove particularly useful in case of uncertain market
conditions or other adverse factors outside the control of the issuer and/or the
offeror which may have an impact on the success of the transaction.

15.2.6 CONSOB's approval of the prospectus

15.2.6.1 *Timing*

The IR, as amended by the CONSOB Amendment, provides time limits for the **15.120**
approval of a prospectus by CONSOB that substantially match those pursuant to
the Prospectus Directive,[110] i.e. ten business days if the public offer involves securities issued by an issuer with securities admitted to trading on a regulated market

---

provides that the text and format of the prospectus published or made available to the public shall
at all times be identical to the original version approved by the competent authority. See CONSOB,
Modifiche, page 44. See also CESR FAQs, Question 23.

[107] Prospectus Directive Article 16.1.
[108] CESR FAQs, Question 19.
[109] CONSOB Newsletter 5/2008. CONSOB requires that the prospective issuer and/or offeror:
(i) indicate in the prospectus that the date may be modified upon occurrence of certain adverse
external factors and that, in case of modifications thereof, the new date shall be disclosed through
a notice; and (ii) file a specific request with CONSOB. The transaction should in any event occur
within a reasonable period of time, normally one calendar month, from the date of the authorization
by CONSOB.
[110] Prospectus Directive Article 13.2 to 4.

or which has previously offered securities to the public, 20 business days with respect to other issuers.[111]

15.121 Pursuant to the IR, the review period starts only when a complete application, together with all the required documentation, is filed with CONSOB. As clarified by CONSOB, the application is not complete if, following a preliminary examination and on reasonable grounds, CONSOB ascertains that entire 'pieces' of information are missing.[112] CONSOB shall complete such preliminary examination of the completeness of the application and, possibly, request missing documentation, within ten days from the filing of the application.

15.122 Such preliminary examination of the completeness of the application is distinguished from a request for supplementary information. In fact, pursuant to the IR CONSOB retains the right to request—on reasonable grounds—supplementary information throughout the entire review procedure.[113] Such supplementary information is to be provided by the issuer and/or offeror within ten business days of CONSOB's request—if the public offer involves securities issued by an issuer with securities admitted to trading on a regulated market or that has previously offered securities to the public—or within 20 business days, with respect to securities issued by other issuers.

15.123 Following preliminary examination, if CONSOB requests that an application be completed or requires—throughout its review period—supplementary information, the time limits for the review by CONSOB are tolled and start running again only from the date such information is provided to CONSOB. However, to prevent the review period from extending indefinitely due to subsequent requests for supplementary information by CONSOB, the IR sets forth a maximum timeline for the review process. Such a timeline is calculated from the date the application and the documentation is complete (therefore, a possible request for supplementary information should not influence such time limit).[114]

15.124 In particular, the review process may not last more than 40 business days if the public offer involves securities issued by an issuer with securities admitted to trading on a regulated market or that has previously offered securities to the public; 70 business days with respect to other securities issued by other issuers.

---

[111] IR Article 8.1 to 5, with respect to an offer to the public of 'transferable securities', applicable to an offer to the public of units of closed investment funds pursuant to IR Article 23, and to the admission of EC Securities to trading on a regulated market, where compatible, pursuant to IR Articles 53.2 and 59.2. Pursuant to the IR, as amended by the CONSOB Amendment, CONSOB's review period in case of request of admission to trading of securities on a regulated market is totally independent from the review proceeding with the relevant operating company.

[112] See CONSOB, Modifiche, page 32.

[113] IR Article 8.4.

[114] IR Article 8.5.

In exceptional circumstances, these terms may be extended for a maximum of five business days.[115] At the end of such review period, CONSOB remains free to reject the application should the information provided be insufficient.

Unlike the Prospectus Directive, the IR provides a fast track for tripartite prospectuses for shares.[116] In particular, CONSOB must approve the securities note and the summary note for shares within five business days from filing thereof, provided that:

- the issuer already has shares admitted to trading on a regulated market;
- the issuer is not subject to an obligation towards CONSOB to update certain information monthly;
- the issuer regularly complies with its reporting obligations; and
- the prospectus does not pertain to securities that have been suspended from trading.

15.125

15.2.6.2 Scope of review of prospectuses for equity securities

The Prospectus Directive defines the approval of a prospectus as the result of a process of 'scrutiny of the completeness' of a prospectus, which implies review of the 'consistency of the information given and its comprehensibility'.[117] The Prospectus Directive, however, does not give precise indications as to the scope of such scrutiny.

15.126

CONSOB has recently set forth certain general principles and guidelines for its review of prospectuses.[118] In particular, CONSOB has clarified that its review does not imply any due diligence on the information contained in a prospectus. Therefore, CONSOB is not responsible for the genuineness of the information contained in a prospectus. Such responsibility falls only upon an issuer, offeror, person asking for admission to trading on a regulated market and a guarantor (as the case may be), as provided by the Prospectus Directive.[119] Pursuant to Italian law, responsibility for the information contained in a prospectus also falls upon lead underwriters ('*responsabili del collocamento*'), as discussed in Section 15.2.7.4 below.[120]

15.127

A review of the completeness of a prospectus by CONSOB is not limited to a mere check-the-box review that the prospectus discusses all the items set forth in

15.128

---

[115] The extension of the review period is limited to exceptional situations occurring during the review period, which are independent from the will of the issuer and/or offeror or person requesting admission to trading, and that may be resolved within the limited maximum extension of five business days. See CONSOB, Modifiche, page 37.

[116] IR Article 8.7.

[117] Prospectus Directive Article 2.1 (q).

[118] CONSOB Notice No DEM/9025420 of 24 March 2009.

[119] Prospectus Directive Article 6.

[120] CFA Article 94.8 and 9.

Regulation No 809/2004. Although CONSOB will not request information beyond what is set forth in Regulation No 809/2004, it may require the disclosure of supplementary information to clarify or complete a prospectus pursuant to the Prospectus Directive.

15.129 CONSOB's review of the 'consistency of the information given' implies a review of information:

- contained in the prospectus, which must be coherent throughout the document;
- contained in the documentation filed together with the prospectus;
- acquired by CONSOB in the course of other different proceedings regarding the issuer. With respect to issuers with securities admitted to trading on regulated markets in Italy and prospective issuers which have requested admission of securities to trading on regulated markets in Italy, such review includes information contained in press releases disseminated to the public and communicated to CONSOB pursuant to applicable reporting obligations.[121]

15.130 CONSOB will not review an issuer's accounts or the consistency of the financial statements with the prospectus.

15.131 CONSOB may not deny approval because a prospectus describes transactions that present irregularities and possible elements of illegality. In such situations CONSOB will confirm that a prospectus provides all necessary disclosure 'to enable investors to make an informed assessment'.[122] CONSOB shall, instead, deny its approval in case the offer itself and/or the admission to trading poses issues of illegality.

15.132 For the purposes of its review of the consistency of the information, CONSOB will not review the information disseminated or made available to the public through press reports or other means of mass communication, except, as discussed above, for information contained in press releases disseminated to the public by an issuer subject to CONSOB's reporting obligations.[123]

---

[121] CONSOB, 'Documento relativo alla definizione dei compiti assegnati alla CONSOB in sede di approvazione dei prospetti relativi a strumenti finanziari rappresentativi di capitale', 30 March 2009, ('Documento'), page 11. Prospective issuers are subject to the disclosure obligations of price-sensitive information from the filing of an application for admission to trading on an Italian regulated market (CFA Article114.12).

[122] Prospectus Directive Article 5.1.

[123] CONSOB shall cooperate and exchange information on an ordinary basis with the Bank of Italy and the Italian insurance authority (ISVAP), when reviewing prospectuses of, respectively, banking and insurance issuers. Cooperation with other public authorities would occur only on an exceptional basis. Claims received from third parties in the course of the review of a prospectus may be considered, on the basis of the source, quality, relevance and quantity of claims. See 'Documento', pages 12 and 13.

15.2.7 The advertisement regime

15.2.7.1 *General principles*

Publicity describing or promoting the prospective issuer's business (so-called **15.133** 'institutional publicity') is always allowed in Italy, even before an offer to the public, provided that it does not contain any reference to the offer and/or listing or any excessively emphatic publicity, especially a mass publicity campaign different from the prospective issuer's prior ordinary practice (which may be deemed by the market authority, CONSOB, as an investment solicitation).[124]

The prospective issuer and/or offeror, as well as the underwriters and the institu-   **15.134** tions participating in the placement of the securities, must ensure correctness, transparency and equal treatment of the potential investors, and must refrain from releasing information inconsistent with a prospectus published in Italy.[125]

Information contained in the Italian prospectus should always be consistent with   **15.135** the information made available to institutional investors. To this end the prospective issuer and/or offeror and the lead manager ('*responsabile del collocamento*') are responsible for ensuring that the information contained in the Italian prospectus is consistent with the information disseminated in the context of an institutional offer, including information contained in 'recommendations' made public by the participants to the offer and any of their respective subsidiaries, controlling entities, or affiliates.[126]

15.2.7.2 *Publicity activities regarding an offering*

Publicity activities regarding an offering are common in Italy and are permitted,   **15.136** provided that:[127]

- the advertisement is clearly recognizable as such;
- the information contained in the advertisement is drafted in a clear and correct manner and is consistent with the information contained in the prospectus;

---

[124] For this reason it is generally preferable to inform CONSOB in advance of any institutional publicity campaign and to file with it the publicity materials in advance.

[125] CFA Article 95 and IR Article 34-*sexies*.

[126] Copy of the 'recommendations' and of the materials used during the institutional offer, such as the offering circular and the slides used during road-shows, must be filed with CONSOB (article 34-*sexies*.3 of the IR). Recommendation is defined as any research or information recommending or suggesting an investment strategy, explicitly or implicitly, concerning one or several securities or the issuers of such securities, including any opinion as to the present or future value or price of such securities, and which are intended for dissemination through the distribution channels or to the public (IR Article 65.2 a)).

[127] See CFA Article 101, which requires that copy of the published advertisements should be simultaneously sent to CONSOB, and IR Article 34-*octies*.

- the information is not misleading as to the features, nature and risks of the securities offered and the proposed investment;
- the advertisement contains a proper disclaimer inviting the potential investor to read the prospectus before subscription; and
- the advertisement indicates the places where the prospectus is available to the public, together with any indication of other means for consulting it.

15.137 Advertisements containing statistical results, studies or elaboration of data must indicate the source of such information.[128]

15.138 Release to the public of information or market research studies and collection of purchase intentions are permissible even before the publication of a prospectus,[129] provided that:

- the relevant information is consistent with the prospectus;
- the relevant documentation is filed with CONSOB simultaneously with its publication;[130]
- there is an express reference to the subsequent publication of a prospectus and where it has been made available; and
- it is expressly stated that purchase intentions do not constitute purchase orders.

15.139 Upon filing an application for listing with Borsa, the prospective issuer is subject, *inter alia*, to the rules and regulations on the disclosure of price-sensitive information (see Section 15.3.3 below for more details).[131]

15.2.7.3 Sanctions

15.140 In the event CONSOB suspects that the CFA or IR provisions on publicity activities have been breached, CONSOB may—as a precautionary measure—suspend the further dissemination of advertisements. If CONSOB determines that an advertisement has been disseminated in breach of the CFA or the IR, it may prohibit its further dissemination. CONSOB may even prohibit the offer to the public, if the offeror fails to comply with its decisions on suspension or prohibition of certain advertisements, and may also impose fines of up to EUR 500,000.[132]

---

[128] IR Article 34-*novies*.2. In the event that an advertisement provides an indication of the returns that may be expected from the proposed investment, the advertisement must (a) specify the reference period for the calculation of the return, (b) clearly represent the risk profile connected to the return, (c) indicate these returns net of taxes or, where this is not possible, specify that they are gross of taxes, (d) include the disclaimer 'Past performance is not indicative of future returns', and (e) in the event that advertisement provides findings from statistics, studies or data processing or make reference to such findings, the sources must be disclosed.

[129] CFA Article 95.1 c) and IR Article 34-*decies*. Such activities may be carried out by the issuer and/or offeror and the lead manager.

[130] Market practice is to send the publicity materials to CONSOB prior to their circulation.

[131] See CFA Article 114, last paragraph, IR Article 65-*duodecies* and CONSOB Notice No DME/6027054 of 28 March 2006.

[132] See CFA Article 101.4 and 191.

15.2.7.4 *Prospectus liability*

The Prospectus Directive requires member states to ensure that responsibility   **15.141**
for the information included in the prospectus attaches 'at least' to an issuer
(or its administrative, management or supervisory bodies), an offeror, a person
asking for the admission to trading on a regulated market or a guarantor, as the
case may be.[133]

In the implementation of such provision, the Italian legislator has set forth a   **15.142**
stricter regime of liability which borrows substantially from foreign regimes but
which will require considerable interpretative work in order to provide a consistent
body of liability rules with the adequate level of incentives for the parties involved
in the offering of securities.[134]

In particular, the CFA provides the cumulative (and not alternative, as suggested   **15.143**
by the Prospectus Directive) liability of the 'issuer, offeror and any possible guarantor, as the case may be, as well as the person responsible for the information
contained in the prospectus, each with respect to the parts of the prospectus of its
pertinence' for damages suffered by any 'investor who has reasonably relied on the
genuineness and completeness of the information contained in the prospectus'.[135]
Thus, liability originates from the reasonable reliance of the investors, which may
be difficult to prove. However, according to a plausible interpretation of the relevant provisions, investors should not be required to prove reasonable reliance,
since reliability is connatural to the concept of a prospectus. Indeed, a prospectus
is intended to be a means of 'increasing confidence in securities and thus of contributing to the proper functioning and development of securities markets'.[136]

In addition to the liability of the entities mentioned above, Italian law also pro-   **15.144**
vides for the concurrent liability of the lead manager for any 'false information or
omissions in the prospectus that are capable of influencing the decisions of a reasonable investor'.[137] Therefore, the lead underwriter is responsible for the entire
prospectus. To this effect, the lead underwriter is required to certify at the filing of
the application that, having exercised due diligence to ensure that the information
contained in the prospectus is true and that there are no omissions that would
distort its meaning, the prospectus does not contain false information or omissions that are capable of influencing the decisions of a reasonable investor.[138]

---

[133] Prospectus Directive Article 6.
[134] CFA Articles 94.8 and 9, amended by legislative decree No 42/2007. Prior to these rules, no
specific regulation regarding prospectus liability existed, and general principles of contract and tort
law applied.
[135] CFA Article 94.8.
[136] Prospectus Directive *Whereas* No 18.
[137] CFA Article 94.9.
[138] IR Annex 1A. Differently from the regulation in force before the CONSOB Amendment,
the lead manager is no longer required to certify that a prospectus is compliant with the schemes

15.145 If at the time of the filing of the application the lead underwriter has not been appointed yet, as may typically happen with respect to base prospectuses or tripartite prospectuses, certification by the lead underwriter may be released in a subsequent phase of the proceeding (e.g. filing of the final terms—in case of a base prospectus—or of the securities note and summary note—in case of tripartite prospectuses). Instead, in case a lead manager is not appointed throughout the proceeding, as may typically happen when the issuer is a credit institution, certification may be released by the issuer and/or the offeror playing the role of lead underwriter.[139]

15.146 Liability hereunder is presumed, though subject to the so-called due diligence defence. Therefore, in case of claims for damages suffered as a consequence of false information or omissions in a prospectus, a defendant has the burden of proving that it has exercised its due diligence to ensure that such information was true and that there were no omissions capable of distorting its meaning. Due diligence defence language in the CFA appears to be similar for issuers and lead underwriters. It is expected that scholars and courts will subsequently provide an interpretation so as to limit the scope of issuers' due diligence defence and to give further guidance on the minimum activities required on the part of underwriters to avail themselves of the defence.

15.3 Continuing Obligations

15.3.1 Introduction

15.147 The current Italian rules imposing continuing obligations on issuers in Italy can be traced to the transposition into national laws and regulations of the Market Abuse Directive (the 'Market Abuse Directive'), the Transparency Directive, together with its implementing Directive 2007/14/EC and, to a lesser extent, the Shareholder Rights Directive. These Directives significantly influenced the nature, quantity, quality and timing of information that issuers (or the entities controlling them) must disclose upon the occurrence of certain significant events or circumstances.

15.148 The CFA sets forth at a statutory level the general continuing obligations, such as the duty to disclose inside information, financial information, information regarding compensation plans, or major shareholdings, while the IR contains regulatory provisions implementing the CFA rules.

---

of Regulation No 809/2004 and/or to sign the application when filing the prospectus with CONSOB.

[139] CONSOB, Modifiche, pages 15 and 16.

The implementation of the Transparency Directive in Italy, which was substantially completed at the regulatory level in April of 2009,[140] brought about significant changes in the way in which issuers must make the required disclosure. On the one hand, it introduced the notion of regulated information, which encompasses the continuing obligations mentioned above without significantly altering them. On the other hand, it introduced the phases of the dissemination, storage and filing of regulated information, which substituted the previous system of disclosure based on parallel disclosure obligations to the public and to CONSOB.

15.149

Due to the complexity of certain organizational requirements for the setting up of effective dissemination, storage and filing systems, as well as the need to adopt further technical and procedural rules, in adopting the new Transparency Directive implementing rules CONSOB provided that they would come into force gradually, mostly throughout 2009.

15.150

At the time of writing this Chapter, in the summer of 2009, the Transparency Directive had just been implemented at the IR level and the process described above had just begun. However, new rules had also just been adopted to modify the implementation of the Transparency Directive at the legislative level, thus requiring CONSOB to modify the IR once more. In particular, upon substantial lobbying and public debate, CONSOB had been mandated by the legislator to change once again the means by which issuers should carry out disclosure of regulated information, with a view to reinstating the general requirement for publication of notices in national newspapers.[141]

15.151

In light of these considerations, the description of the Transparency Directive implementing rules, as well as the interconnections with the other continuing obligations rules contained in the CFA and in the IR, are still partially defective.

15.152

This part is organized as follows. Section 15.3.2 outlines the notion of regulated information and describes the dissemination, storage and filing phases. The next sections outline issuers' most significant continuing obligations and duties with respect to specific types of regulated information, together with a brief overview of CONSOB's supervisory functions and of the possible sanctions in case of non compliance: inside information (Section 15.3.3); forecasts, goals, rumours and recommendations (Section 15.3.4); certain extraordinary transactions (Section 15.3.5); compensation plans (Section 15.3.6); periodic financial reporting (Section 15.3.7); registries of insiders and internal dealing transactions

15.153

---

[140] Legislative decree No 195 of 6 November 2007 amended the CFA, while CONSOB Decision No 16850 of 1 April 2009, significantly amended the IR.

[141] Legislative decree No 101 of 17 July 2009 amended the CFA. See also CONSOB Decision No 17002 of 17 August 2009.

(Section 15.3.8); disclosure of major holdings and potential holdings (Section 15.3.9); restrictions on cross-shareholdings (Section 15.3.10); shareholders' agreements (Section 15.3.11); other disclosure requirements (Section 15.3.12); CONSOB supervisory and monitoring functions (Section 15.3.13); sanctions in case of market abuse or violation of disclosure obligations (Section 15.3.14).

15.154   The final section on corporate governance (15.3.15) provides a general overview of certain Italian corporate law rules, with a particular focus on the recommendations of the Corporate Governance Code.

15.3.2 Regulated information

15.3.2.1 Scope of applicability

15.155   The CFA contains the general statutory provisions imposing disclosure obligations of regulated information on:

- issuers of financial instruments[142] admitted to trading or that have requested admission to trading on a regulated market in Italy;[143]
- issuers of financial instruments that are publicly held;[144]
- the entities controlling them;[145] and
- the persons requesting—without an issuer's consent—admission to trading on a regulated market in Italy of transferable securities that are not admitted to trading on a regulated market in the European Community.[146]

15.156   CONSOB has implemented and clarified in detail the general CFA continuing obligations provisions in the IR and has supplemented the IR with the adoption of several notices and communications. The continuing obligations rules and requirements for issuers admitted to trading on regulated markets operated

---

[142] As already seen in Section 2 above, under CFA Articles 1.1-*bis* and 1.2, transferable securities ('*valori mobiliari*') essentially include shares and debt securities, while the broader category of financial instruments ('*strumenti finanziari*') include, *inter alia*, transferable securities (as just described) and certain financial derivatives. Reference to transferable securities or to financial instruments in this section must be understood as described above. Note that the scope of applicability of certain rules on disclosure of regulated information in Italy is broader than that provided for by the Transparency Directive, as it may apply to issuers of financial instruments, other than shares or debt securities, that do not have Italy as their home member state.

[143] CFA Articles 113-*ter* and IR Article 65-*duodecies*.

[144] Although their financial instruments are not admitted to trading on a regulated market, significant disclosure obligations attach to these issuers (see Section 15.3.2.7).

[145] Under CFA Article 93, 'controlled issuers' are issuers directly or indirectly controlled through: (i) the absolute majority of votes in the ordinary shareholders' meeting; (ii) a relative majority of votes allowing the exercise of a dominant influence in the ordinary shareholders' meeting; (iii) a contract or clause in the by-laws allowing the exercise of a dominant influence; and (iv) shareholders' agreements allowing the exercise of a dominant influence in the ordinary shareholders' meeting.

[146] CFA Article 113-*ter*.6.

by Borsa (i.e. the vast majority of issuers) are complemented by further secondary provisions contained in the Borsa Market Rules and in the Borsa Instructions (see Section 15.3.12.4), as well as in the Corporate Governance Code (see Section 15.3.15).[147]

The disclosure obligations generally described in the following paragraphs apply (unless otherwise provided depending on the specific obligations or requirements) to issuers of transferable securities that are admitted to trading on a regulated market in Italy and that have Italy as their home member state.[148] **15.157**

15.3.2.2 *Categories of regulated information*

Regulated information is any information subject to the continuing disclosure obligations set forth in the CFA and the IR.[149] The CFA and the IR identify the following main categories of regulated information, the most significant of which will be described in detail in the next paragraphs: **15.158**

   (i) inside information;[150]

 (ii) forecasts and quantitative goals;[151]

(iii) rumours and profit warnings;

(iv) investment recommendations;[152]

 (v) information on extraordinary transactions, including, *inter alia*:

     (a) mergers, split-ups and share capital increases through contributions in kind;[153]

     (b) significant acquisitions and sales of assets;[154]

     (c) related-party transactions;[155]

---

[147] As mentioned in Section 15.1, at the time of writing this Chapter three companies operating regulated markets existed in Italy, out of which Borsa was the most significant in terms of issuers admitted to trading on markets regulated by it.

[148] Special rules apply for the continuing disclosure obligations of: (i) issuers of transferable securities admitted to trading on a regulated market in Italy—which is the only host member state—and not in the home member state; (ii) issuers of transferable securities admitted to trading on a regulated market in Italy —which is a host member state—and not in the home member state; (iii) foreign issuers of financial instruments admitted to trading only on a regulated market in Italy; (iv) issuers of transferable securities that have Italy as their home member state and that are admitted to trading on the regulated market of another member state; and (v) issuers of financial instruments admitted to trading on a regulated market in Italy as well as on a regulated market abroad. See IR Articles 112-*bis* et seq.

[149] CFA Article 113-*ter*.1, which includes in the definition of regulated information also the information that must be disclosed pursuant to the rules of non-EC jurisdictions that CONSOB deems to be equivalent to the Italian rules.

[150] CFA Article 114.1. See section 15.3.3.

[151] IR Article 68. See Section 15.3.4.

[152] Article 69-*novies*. See Section 15.3.4.3.

[153] IR Articles 70 and 90. See Section 15.3.5.1.

[154] IR Articles 71 and 91. See Section 15.3.5.1.

[155] IR Articles 71-*bis* and 91-*bis*. See section 15.3.5.2.

(d) purchase or sale of shares;[156]

(e) share capital reductions due to losses;[157]

(vi) compensation plans based on financial instruments;[158]

(vii) periodic financial reporting;[159]

(viii) internal dealing transactions;[160]

(ix) major holdings and potential holdings;[161]

(x) cross-shareholdings;

(xi) shareholders' agreements;

(xii) information regarding the rights of holders of financial instruments;[162]

(xiii) annual information document;[163]

(xiv) compliance with codes of conduct.[164]

15.3.2.3 The dissemination of regulated information

15.159 **15.3.2.3.1 General requirements** Issuers must disseminate regulated information by ensuring fast access to such information on a non-discriminatory basis and in a manner reasonably appropriate to guarantee effective dissemination in all of the European Union.[165] Specifically, pursuant to the CFA and the IR:

- regulated information must be disseminated as widely and promptly as possible, in the European Union;[166]
- regulated information must be communicated to agencies specialized in the dissemination of financial information (which the IR defines as 'media'):[167]

  (a) by ensuring the safety of the communication, by minimizing the risk of data corruption and unauthorized access, and by ensuring certainty as to the source of the regulated information;

  (b) in unedited full text. However, in the case of the annual financial reports, the half-yearly financial reports, the interim management statements, as well as in other cases identified by the IR, this requirement is deemed fulfilled by advising the media of the publication of such documents and of the storage system and website from where they may be retrieved;

---

[156] IR Articles 73 and 93. See Section 15.3.5.3.

[157] IR Articles 74 and 94.

[158] CFA Article 114-*bis* and IR Article 84-*bis*. See Section 3.6.

[159] IR Articles 77 to 83. See Section 3.7.

[160] CFA Article 114.7. See Section 15.3.8.2.

[161] CFA Article 120 and IR Article 116-*terdecies* et seq. See Section 15.3.9.

[162] IR Articles 83-*bis* and 84. See Section 15.3.11.1.

[163] IR Article 54. See Section 15.3.11.2.

[164] CFA Article 124-*bis* and IR Article 89-*bis*. See Section 15.3.15.9.

[165] IR Article 65-*bis*.1, implementing Transparency Directive Article 21 and Commission Directive 2007/14/EC Article 12 .

[166] IR Article 65-*bis*.1 a).1.

[167] IR Article 65-*bis*.1 a).2.

(c) by clearly identifying it as regulated information, the issuer, the subject matter, and the time and date of the communication;

- safety of receipt must be ensured by remedying any failure or disruption in the communication of regulated information as soon as possible (unless these are attributable to the media themselves);[168]
- regulated information must be identified under the appropriate category through the identification code set forth under the IR;[169]
- with respect to the language for the disclosure of regulated information:[170]

(a) when the transferable securities are traded only on regulated markets in Italy and Italy is the home member state, regulated information is disclosed in Italian;

(b) when the securities are traded on the regulated markets of different member states, including Italy, and Italy is the home member state, regulated information is disclosed in Italian and, at the issuer's choice, either in a language accepted by the competent authorities of the host member states or in a language customary in the sphere of international finance;[171]

(c) when the transferable securities are traded on a regulated market in one or more host member states, but not in Italy, and Italy is the home member state, regulated information shall, at the issuer's choice, be disclosed either in a language customary in the sphere of international finance, or in a language accepted by the competent authorities of the host member state, including Italian;

(d) as an exception to the rules under letters a, b and c above, issuers of transferable securities with a denomination per unit of at least EUR 50,000 or, in the case of debt securities not denominated in EUR, equivalent to at least EUR 50,000 at the date of issue, may disclose, at their choice, regulated information in Italian or in a language customary in the sphere of international finance, irrespective of whether Italy is the home member state or a host member state; and

(e) when the transferable securities are traded on a regulated market in Italy, which is a host member state, regulated information is communicated, at the issuer's choice, either in Italian or in a language customary in the sphere of international finance.

15.3.2.3.2 Indirect dissemination through a SDIR or direct dissemination   **15.160**
According to the IR, issuers can disseminate regulated information either directly

---

[168] IR Article 65-*bis*.1 b).

[169] IR Article 65-*ter*.

[170] IR Article 65-*quater*, implementing Transparency Directive Article 20.

[171] In the case of letters a and b above, if the issuer is foreign, it may choose to disclose regulated information in Italian or in a language customary in the sphere of international finance.

or indirectly.[172] Indirect dissemination must occur through a system for the electronic dissemination of regulated information (a 'SDIR') connecting the issuer, the operating company (typically, Borsa), CONSOB and the media. SDIRs are set up and managed in accordance with the rules set forth in the CFA and the IR briefly summarized below.

15.161   SDIRs must establish and maintain an adequate number of connections with media having significant experience and market share in Italy and in the other member states of the European Community. SDIRs must, *inter alia*, receive and disseminate regulated information 24/7, minimize the risk of data corruption and unauthorized access, provide certainty as to the source of the regulated information and grant CONSOB special access rights.

15.162   SDIRs must be authorized by CONSOB and are subject to its supervision. In particular, authorized SDIRs must file with CONSOB an annual report certifying the fulfilment of the operational requirements prescribed by the CFA and the IR.[173] As of the summer of 2009, no SDIR had been authorized by CONSOB, but it is likely that the first SDIRs might be authorized by CONSOB and become operational before the end of 2009.

15.163   When SDIRs become operational, issuers choosing to disseminate regulated information through a SDIR must choose it from a list held by CONSOB, inform CONSOB of the SDIR chosen and inform the SDIR's manager of the name of the person responsible for maintaining the issuer's relations with the SDIR. Furthermore, issuers must disclose on their website the name of the SDIR chosen and, upon request by CONSOB, communicate details of any embargo placed on regulated information.[174]

15.164   At the time of writing this Chapter, and until SDIRs become operational or, in absence of requests by any interested parties, until a date to be set by CONSOB, regulated information is generally disseminated:

- by submitting it to the operating company; and
- through a press release announcing such publication as well as the website from where the documents could be retrieved, to be sent (a) to at least two press agencies and to the operating company (typically, Borsa); or (b) through the electronic system for the transmission of information set up by the operating company (in the case of Borsa, the so-called Network Information System – the 'NIS').

---

[172] IR Articles 65-*quinquies* and 65-*sexies*, implementing CESR's Final Technical Advice on Possible Implementing Measures of the Transparency Directive (CESR/05-439).

[173] IR Articles 116-*quinquies*–116-*octies*.

[174] IR Article 65-*quinquies*.

If an issuer chooses to disseminate regulated information directly, it must disclose **15.165** such choice on its website, adopt the organizational requirements applicable to SDIRs and their managers, certify to CONSOB the adoption of these requirements as well as file with it an annual report certifying their fulfillment.[175] Issuers choosing to disseminate their regulated information directly are subject to CONSOB supervision in this respect.

15.3.2.4 *The storage of regulated information*

Concurrently with its dissemination, regulated information must be stored in an **15.166** authorized storage mechanism (an 'ASM'), set up and managed in accordance with the rules set forth in the CFA and the IR briefly summarized below.[176] ASMs receive regulated information from SDIRs, issuers, CONSOB or the operating company and must adopt an organizational structure that, *inter alia*, ensures sound safety mechanisms, certainty as to the source of the regulated information, and easy access to the public. Regulated information must be made available by ASMs to the public at affordable costs, no later than one hour after its receipt.

ASMs must be authorized by CONSOB and are subject to its supervision. **15.167** In particular, ASMs must file an annual report with CONSOB certifying the fulfilment of the operational requirements prescribed by the CFA and the IR.[177] Similarly to SDIRs, as of the summer of 2009 no ASM had been authorized by CONSOB, but it is likely that the first ASM might become operational before the end of 2009. When ASMs become operational, each issuer will choose an ASM to store all regulated information and shall inform its controlling entities and CONSOB of its choice, as well as disclose the name and address of the chosen ASM on its website.

Pursuant to the Transparency Directive implementing rules, in addition to using **15.168** an ASM issuers must set up a website where they must publish regulated information concerning them no later than the start of trade on the day following its dissemination and keep it accessible for at least five years.[178]

In the interim period prior to the ASMs becoming operational, regulated infor **15.169** mation was temporarily stored in centralized form by means of publication on the website of the operating company (typically, Borsa), which could also incorporate regulated information by reference to the issuers' websites.

---

[175] IR Article 65-*sexies*.

[176] IR Article 65-*septies*.2, implementing Transparency Directive Article 21 and CESR's Final Technical Advice on Possible Implementing Measures Concerning the Transparency Directive—Storage of Regulated Information and Filing of Regulated Information, (CESR/ 06-292), June 2006.

[177] IR Articles 116-*novies*–116-*duodecies*.

[178] IR Articles 65-*bis*.3 and 65-*septies*.5.

15.3.2.5 *The filing of regulated information with CONSOB*

15.170 Concurrently with the dissemination and the storage, issuers must file the regulated information with CONSOB through the relevant ASM[179] or, in certain cases, through an on-line system to which issuers of shares have access (the so-called 'Teleraccolta' system).

15.171 In the interim period prior to the ASMs becoming operational, the obligation to file regulated information with CONSOB was fulfilled, according to the nature of regulated information, through the NIS (or the equivalent transmission system set up by the operating company other than Borsa), the authorized SDIRs, the Teleraccolta system, or by mail, respectively.

15.172 Issuers may comply with their dissemination, storage and filing obligations through a 'one-stop-shop' by simply transmitting the regulated information to their SDIR, which will then take care of transmitting it to the chosen ASM and filing it with CONSOB.

15.173 Generally, issuers must also file regulated information with the relevant operating company (see Section 15.3.12.4 below as regards filing of information with Borsa).

15.3.2.6 *Dissemination, storage and filing in special cases*

15.174 Issuers of financial instruments, other than transferable securities, admitted to trading on a regulated market in Italy must disseminate regulated information either in accordance with the general rules outlined above, or through a press release transmitted to at least two press agencies. The release can be in Italian or in a language customary in the sphere of international finance and must be published on the issuer's website no later than the opening of trade on the day following its dissemination, where it must remain accessible for at least five years.[180]

15.175 Similar provisions apply to entities not admitted to trading on a regulated market that control issuers of transferable securities or of other financial instruments admitted to trading on a regulated market in Italy, with respect to regulated information concerning such subsidiaries.[181]

15.176 Issuers of financial instruments other than transferable securities, and private parent companies, that control issuers of financial instruments admitted to

---

[179] IR Article 65-*septies*.3, implementing Transparency Directive Article 19 and CESR's Final Technical Advice on Possible Implementing Measures Concerning the Transparency Directive – Storage of Regulated Information and Filing of Regulated Information, (CESR/06-292), June 2006.

[180] IR Article 65-*octies*.1.

[181] IR Article 65-*octies*.2.

trading on a regulated market in Italy, must transmit the regulated information concerning their subsidiaries to the subsidiaries' ASMs and make it available on the subsidiaries' websites.

The IR also sets forth appropriate rules to ensure that the above information is filed with CONSOB.   **15.177**

15.3.2.7 *Publicly-held issuers*

Publicly-held issuers (*'emittenti strumenti finanziari diffusi'*) are Italian issuers of   **15.178** shares or debt securities that, although not admitted to trading on a regulated market, are widely held amongst the public. In particular:

- a publicly-held issuer of *shares* is an Italian issuer with more than 200 shareholders collectively owning at least 5% of its share capital (not counting its controlling entities) and which satisfies certain other requirements; and
- a publicly-held issuer of *debt securities* is an Italian issuer of debt securities with more than 200 bondholders and net assets equal to at least EUR 5 million.[182]

Publicly-held issuers are subject to significant accounting and disclosure obliga-   **15.179** tions otherwise not applicable to private companies, including certain disclosure obligations applicable to issuers of financial instruments admitted to trading on a regulated market in Italy such as those relating to inside information and compensation plans, as to which see Sections 15.3.3 and 15.3.6, below.[183]

15.3.3 Inside information

15.3.3.1 *Scope of applicability*

Under the Transparency Directive and Italian laws and regulations implementing   **15.180** it, inside information is a fundamental component of the concept of regulated information and must be disclosed accordingly. The current Italian rules concerning disclosure of inside information can be traced to the transposition of the Market Abuse Directive into national laws and regulations and are briefly summarized in the following paragraphs. They generally apply to (i) issuers of financial instruments admitted, or for which a request for admission has been filed, to trading on a regulated market in Italy, (ii) publicly-held issuers, as defined in Section 15.3.2.7 above, and (iii) their controlling entities.[184]

---

[182] CFA Article 116 of the CFA and IR Article 2-*bis*.
[183] IR Articles 108–112, as well as certain provisions of the ICC.
[184] CFA Articles 114 and 116, as well as IR Article 65-*duodecies*.

15.3.3.2 The notion of inside information

15.181　In accordance with the Market Abuse Directive,[185] the CFA defines inside information as information relating, directly or indirectly, to one or more issuers or to one or more financial instruments, which:

- is of a precise nature;
- has not been made public; and
- if made public, might have a significant effect on the prices of the financial instruments.[186]

15.182　Information is deemed to be of a precise nature if it refers to a set of circumstances that exist or may reasonably be expected to come into existence or to an event that has occurred or may reasonably be expected to occur, and the information is sufficiently specific to allow the drawing of conclusions on the possible effect of the above-mentioned circumstance or event on the price of the financial instruments.[187] Information might thus be of a precise nature even though it is not definitive, as may be the case, by way of example, for ongoing negotiations where the parties have agreed only on the fundamental conditions of the transaction.

15.183　Information that, if made public, might have a significant effect on the price of financial instruments is any information that a reasonable investor would likely use as one of the bases for making his investment decisions.[188]

15.184　A first kind of inside information triggering disclosure obligations includes accounting data and information related to financial reports.[189] In particular, under the IR issuers must disclose:

- accounting data due to be reported in the annual financial statements, the consolidated financial statements and in the half-yearly financial reports, as well as any information and accounting data due to be reported in the interim management statements, when such information is (a) communicated to third parties, unless these parties are bound by confidentiality and the communication is mandatory (e.g. in the case of accounting information and data released to,

---

[185] Market Abuse Directive Article 1.1 defines 'inside information' as 'information of a precise nature which has not been made public, relating, directly or indirectly, to one or more issuers of financial instruments or to one or more financial instruments and which, if it were made public, would be likely to have a significant effect on the prices of those financial instruments or on the price of related derivative financial instruments'.

[186] CFA Article 181.1, implementing Market Abuse Directive Article 1.1.

[187] CFA Article 181.3.

[188] CFA Article 181.4.

[189] IR Article 66.3.

or acquired by, the external auditors in order to carry out their engagements),[190] or (b) sufficiently certain; and

- resolutions by which the appropriate corporate body approves the draft annual financial statements, the dividend distribution proposals, the consolidated financial statements, the half-yearly financial reports and the interim management statements.

CONSOB has issued specific recommendations on the disclosure of inside information. Its general stance is that when there are reasonable doubts as to whether information is price-sensitive, the public should be informed without delay, provided the information is sufficiently complete to allow an accurate evaluation of its impact on the price of the financial instruments.[191] With regard to agreements that are not yet finalized, CONSOB clarified that an early report to the market may be useful only if it ensures a level playing field and, in any event, such disclosure must be clear and concise, as well as comply with the principles of transparency and fairness.[192]

15.185

Disclosure obligations triggered by inside information are equally applicable to all issuers of financial instruments. Neither the CFA nor the IR set forth different quantitative or qualitative disclosure thresholds based on the financial instrument concerned. However, not everything that might be material, say, to a shareholder, is necessarily material to a bondholder. Hence, price-sensitivity of information regarding issuers of debt securities, or of other financial instruments other than shares, is generally regarded as having a higher materiality threshold *vis-à-vis* corresponding information regarding issuers of shares.

15.186

15.3.3.3 *Disclosure of inside information*

In accordance with the Market Abuse Directive,[193] inside information directly concerning an issuer or its subsidiaries must be disclosed without delay by the issuer or its controlling entities.[194] Under the Market Abuse Directive, as duly mirrored in Italian legislation, inside information that issuers must disclose

15.187

---

[190] CONSOB Notice No 6027054 of 28 March 2006. CONSOB clarified that it considers the above-mentioned disclosure rules inapplicable to the communication of information to non-executive directors, as these should not be considered third parties vis-à-vis the issuer.

[191] CONSOB Notice No 6027054 of 28 March 2006.

[192] CONSOB Notice No 6027054 of 28 March 2006. In this regard, CONSOB specifically recommended that in light of the significant media attention listed companies owning football teams should be extremely prudent in their releases pertaining to possible purchases and sales of football players.

[193] Under Market Abuse Directive Article. 6.1 'Member States shall ensure that issuers of financial instruments inform the public as soon as possible of inside information which directly concerns the said issuers.'

[194] CFA Article 114.1, implementing Market Abuse Directive Article 6.1. However, note that the Market Abuse Directive imposes no such obligation upon the controlling entities.

constitutes a narrower category compared to the general notion of inside information applicable under insider trading rules, as outlined in Section 15.3.3.2 above. Indeed, it is generally agreed that the former category includes only inside information *directly* relating to the issuer (or its subsidiaries). Such 'corporate information' consists in any information concerning the issuer's management, its organization, its economic and financial situation, its possible economic developments, as well as any circumstances that may involve specific risks for the issuer. It does not include market information that indirectly reflects on the issuer nor, of course, soft information.

15.188 CONSOB has clarified that if the inside information is disclosed by an issuer, its controlling entities are under no obligation to duplicate such disclosure. However, this does not apply if the controlling entities are also issuers, as defined above, and the information provided by the controlled issuer does not cover all effects on the parent.[195]

15.189 Pursuant to the new rules issuers must disclose inside information by means of a release that is disseminated, stored and filed with CONSOB in accordance with the general rules for disclosure of regulated information.[196] Publicly-held issuers can choose whether to disseminate inside information by means of the general rules, or by sending a release to at least two press agencies. In any case, publicly-held issuers must then send the release to an ASM, or make it public on their website, in addition to filing it with CONSOB.[197]

15.190 As already mentioned, at the time of writing this Chapter the new Transparency Directive implementing rules for the disclosure of regulated information were not yet fully in force and had just become subject to a further amendment. In the meantime, dissemination of inside information generally occurred by sending a release to (i) at least two press agencies and to the operating company, or (ii) the NIS (or equivalent transmission system). The release would then have to be published on the issuers' websites and filed with CONSOB.

15.191 Issuers and the entities controlling them must ensure that: (i) the release contains all elements necessary for a complete and proper assessment of the events and circumstances being disclosed, as well as appropriate references to the contents of previous releases; (ii) every material change to inside information previously made public is also disseminated without delay; (iii) disclosure of inside information is not combined with marketing of an issuer's business in such a way as to mislead the public; and (iv) disclosure to the market takes place, in the most synchronized manner possible, in favour of all categories of investors and in all member states in

---

[195] CONSOB Notice No 6027054 of 28 March 2006. See Section 15.3.3.7 on the disclosure of inside information within corporate groups.

[196] IR Article 66.1.

[197] IR Articles 109 and 111-*ter*.

which an issuer has requested or obtained admission to trading of its financial instruments on a regulated market.[198]

The operating company can set out the minimum content of press releases concerning inside information.[199] The Borsa Market Rules lay down general criteria governing the preparation and the contents of price-sensitive press releases in the event of: (i) approval of financial statements; (ii) qualified auditor opinions; (iii) publication of forecast data or quantitative goals; (iv) resignation or appointment of members of the supervisory and management boards or other key executives; (v) purchase or sale of assets; (vi) capital increases and/or the issuance of convertible bonds; (vii) issuance of bonds; (viii) transactions on treasury shares; (ix) mergers or split-ups.[200]   **15.192**

If inside information is to be disclosed during trading hours, it must be communicated to CONSOB and to the operating company at least 15 minutes prior to its dissemination.[201] CONSOB further recommends that issuers and their controlling entities inform these parties of the intention to submit to the appropriate corporate body material resolutions whose content might be disclosed to the market during trading hours. Such action should be taken suitably in advance, even on an informal basis.   **15.193**

15.3.3.4 *Delaying disclosure of inside information*

Issuers and their controlling entities may, under their own responsibility and under the conditions set forth by CONSOB, delay the disclosure of inside information in order not to prejudice their interests, provided that such a delay does not mislead the public with regard to essential events and circumstances and that the above entities can maintain the confidentiality of the information until it is made public.[202]   **15.194**

Circumstances in relation to which the legitimate interests of the entities subject to disclosure obligations may justify delayed disclosure include those in which disclosure of the information might prejudice the completion of a transaction by the issuer or might, due to the degree of uncertainty surrounding the relevant events or circumstances, lead to the market's incorrect assessment of the situation. Some examples of such circumstances include: **15.195**

• ongoing negotiations or connected circumstances, if disclosure might compromise their outcome or normal development. Specifically, this may occur when, in presence of a serious and imminent threat to the financial solidity of

---

[198] IR Article 66.2.
[199] CFA Article 62 and IR Article 67.
[200] Borsa Instructions section IA2.9.
[201] IR Article 65-*septies*.4.
[202] CFA Article 114.3 and IR Article 66-*bis*, implementing Market Abuse Directive Article 6.2.

the issuer, disclosure might harm negotiations aimed at ensuring its long-term financial recovery;[203] or

- resolutions adopted or agreements entered into by the managing corporate body of the issuer, which are subject to the approval of another body of the issuer (different from the general meeting of shareholders) if disclosure before approval, together with the announcement that the approval process is still ongoing, might compromise the market's proper assessment of the information.

15.196 Issuers or their controlling entities must notify CONSOB promptly of any delay in the disclosure of inside information and of all circumstances connected thereto. After assessing these circumstances, CONSOB may require immediate disclosure of the inside information.[204]

15.197 Entities that delay disclosure of inside information must monitor access to such information in order to ensure its confidentiality by adopting effective measures in this respect.[205]

15.3.3.5 *Selective disclosure of inside information*

15.198 Issuers and their controlling entities, including any agent acting in their name or on their behalf, can communicate inside information to a third party that is subject to legal, regulatory, statutory or contractual confidentiality (e.g. an auditing firm), without being subject to immediate disclosure obligations, so long as such disclosure occurs as a result of the ordinary performance of work, profession, function or office.[206]

15.199 However, if inside information is disclosed to a third party that is not bound by confidentiality, the inside information must be disclosed to the public. The timing of the required public disclosure depends on whether the selective disclosure was intentional or non-intentional; for an intentional selective disclosure, disclosure must be made simultaneously; for a non-intentional disclosure, disclosure must be made without delay.

15.200 With specific regard to meetings with analysts, CONSOB recommends that: (i) issuers and their controlling entities inform CONSOB and the operating company prior to the meeting; (ii) no later than the start of the meeting, issuers and

---

[203] CONSOB has proved cooperative in allowing issuers with ongoing discussions and negotiations with multiple parties to postpone disclosure of agreements entered into that are conditional upon approvals or agreements still pending.

[204] IR Article 66-*bis*.4 and 5.

[205] IR Article 66-*bis*.3.

[206] CFA Article 114.4, implementing Market Abuse Directive Article 6.3. With Notice No 6027054 of 28 March 2006, CONSOB clarified that this exception does not apply to communication other than to the auditors of accounting data due to be reported in the annual financial statements, in the half-yearly financial reports or in the quarterly management statements.

their controlling entities send to CONSOB and to the operating company all information to be made available to the analysts; and (iii) the media be allowed to participate or, if this is not possible, that a press release be disseminated immediately after the meeting.[207]

15.3.3.6 *Disclosure of information at CONSOB's request*

CONSOB may require issuers, their controlling entities, members of their management and supervisory bodies, their executives, their major shareholders[208] or parties to relevant shareholders' agreements[209] to disclose to the public specific information and documents that might constitute inside information, in order to ensure information symmetry on the market. In case of non-compliance with these requests, CONSOB may carry out the disclosure directly, at the expense of the persons who should have effected it. Specific rules apply if the relevant parties oppose CONSOB's request.[210]

15.201

15.3.3.7 *Disclosure of inside information within corporate groups*

Shareholders' access to corporate books and records is limited and essentially aimed at allowing them an informed exercise of their voting rights.[211] Pursuant to the ICC, the CFA and the IR, however, subsidiaries must supply certain information to their parents (in relation, for example, to the preparation of consolidated financial statements),[212] and issuers must set forth organizational guidelines pursuant to which their subsidiaries provide them with the information necessary to comply with mandatory disclosure obligations.[213]

15.202

The disclosure of inside information within corporate groups creates a tension between these corporate law requirements and an issuer's obligation to publicly disclose inside information under the CFA.

15.203

In a case involving an issuer controlled by a municipality, CONSOB was asked whether a discussion regarding the issuer might occur at a public meeting of the municipality without violating the rules mandating disclosure of inside information. CONSOB stated that, as a general rule, the parent[214] of a listed issuer should not be allowed to have selective knowledge of non-public inside information related to the subsidiary, unless such information is communicated to the parent as a result of the

15.204

---

[207] CONSOB Notice No 6027054 of 28 March 2006.
[208] As to which see Section 15.3.9 below.
[209] As to which see Section 15.3.11 below.
[210] CFA Article 114.5 and 6.
[211] ICC Article 2422 and CFA Article 130.
[212] By way of example, ICC Article 2381.5, as well as CFA Articles 150 and 151.
[213] CFA Article 114.2.
[214] Although some debate has developed, the prevailing view asserts that the rules concerning the exercise of direction and coordination ('direzione e coordinamento') within corporate groups pursuant to ICC Article 2497 et seq. have not influenced, modified or contradicted CONSOB's stance.

ordinary performance of work, profession, function or office by managers, officers or employees of the subsidiary, and the parent is subject to legal, regulatory, statutory or contractual duties of confidentiality. CONSOB concluded that discussion of inside information at a public meeting of a municipality did not conform to the rules on the disclosure of inside information. Furthermore, CONSOB stated that inside information concerning the parent may also be relevant for the listed subsidiary, in which case it should be disclosed without delay.[215]

15.3.4 Forecasts, goals, rumours and recommendations

15.3.4.1 *Forecasts and quantitative goals*

15.205 Issuers may (but are not obliged to) release forecast data and quantitative goals, as well as interim management accounts, provided that the disclosure is made in accordance with the general rules for disclosing regulated information.[216] Consistency between the current status of operations and forecast data and quantitative goals previously released must be verified and the public must be informed without delay of any significant change. With respect to such disclosure, CONSOB provided the following clarifications:

- issuers must specify clearly, upon publication of the forecast data, whether such data consists of projections or of strategic objectives set within the business plan; and
- changes in the forecast data must be verified with reference not only to finally approved accounting data, but also to subsequent projections formulated by issuers when updating the previous estimates for the same periods. In any event, issuers must disclose the reasons for the aforementioned changes.[217]

15.3.4.2 *Rumours and profit warnings*

15.206 If information concerning the assets, economic or financial condition of an issuer, its extraordinary financing transactions or its business, is disseminated on the market outside of the rules described above, and as a result of such rumours the price of the issuer's financial instruments changes significantly as compared to the closing price of the previous day, the issuer or its controlling entities must publish without delay a release confirming, denying, correcting or integrating the rumours.[218]

15.207 Financial intermediaries, professional investors and financial analysts often release their assessment of issuers' economic and financial conditions. The overall

---

[215] CONSOB Notice No 6095689 of 1 December 2006.
[216] IR Article 68.
[217] CONSOB Notice No 6027054 of 28 March 2006.
[218] IR Article 66.4.

assessment resulting from the various opinions expressed by analysts, also known as a 'consensus estimate', is usually summarized and made available to the public by the financial press. CONSOB emphasized the relevance of an issuer's verification of, and comment on, the consensus estimate to ensure that investors may formulate realistic expectations, in the event that the consensus estimate differs from the issuer's own projections.[219]

With specific regard to the opportunity to issue profit warnings on the consensus estimate, CONSOB recommends that issuers monitor the market consensus and review potentially material shifts between the results expected by the market and those expected by the issuers and, if necessary, issue profit warnings on the basis of updated internal projections.[220]   **15.208**

15.3.4.3 *Investment recommendations*

The preparation and dissemination of written investment recommendations by issuers, financial companies[221] or the entities controlling them, must comply with certain requirements and such recommendations must be transmitted to CONSOB upon their public dissemination.[222]   **15.209**

In particular, recommendations must: (i) clearly identify the person responsible for their preparation; (ii) clearly distinguish facts from any interpretations, opinions or other non-factual information; (iii) be based on reliable sources, stating any possible doubts as to such reliability; and (iv) clearly indicate all projections and estimates, as well as the hypotheses on which these are based. Publication of recommendations must be as homogeneous as possible in relation to recipients belonging to homogeneous categories.   **15.210**

Issuers and the entities controlling them that produce or disseminate written recommendations pertaining to themselves or their financial instruments must disclose the recommendations in accordance with the rules for the disclosure of regulated information. Finally, the IR sets forth specific rules regarding disclosure of actual or potential conflicts of interests relating to recommendations.   **15.211**

15.3.5 Certain extraordinary transactions

As mentioned in Section 15.3.2.2 above, regulated information includes information that must be disclosed upon the occurrence of certain extraordinary transactions in light of their inherent price-sensitivity. Following is a brief description   **15.212**

---

[219] CONSOB Notice No 6027054 of 28 March 2006.
[220] CONSOB Notice No 6027054 of 28 March 2006.
[221] Under CFA Article 1.1 r), relevant entities include, *inter alia*: investment companies, management companies, certain financial intermediaries and authorized banks.
[222] IR Article 69-*novies*, implementing Market Abuse Directive Article 6.5.

of the disclosure obligations concerning certain extraordinary transactions applicable to issuers of shares admitted to trading on a regulated market in Italy and that have Italy as their home member state.

15.3.5.1 *Mergers, split-ups and significant assets acquisitions or disposals*

15.213   At least 30 days prior to the shareholders' meeting convened to resolve upon a merger or split-up, issuers must publish, in accordance with the general rules applicable to the disclosure of regulated information, as well as make available at their registered office: (i) the plan for the merger or split-up, including the reports of the directors and of the experts, and (ii) the financial statements of the issuers participating in the merger or split-up.

15.214   Enhanced disclosure requirements (mandating publication, prior to the shareholders' meeting, of a separate and additional information document) apply if the above-mentioned transactions are deemed significant pursuant to general criteria set forth by CONSOB, or upon CONSOB's request.[223] Similar rules apply to capital increases through contributions in kind.

15.215   Issuers must also publish an information document if they engage in significant acquisitions or disposals of assets.[224]

15.3.5.2 *Related-party transactions*

15.216   Pursuant to Article 2391-*bis* of the ICC, introduced in 2004, the board of directors of Italian issuers must adopt, in accordance with the general principles set forth by CONSOB, rules aimed at ensuring the transparency and correctness of related-party transactions. As of the summer of 2009, CONSOB had not yet adopted those principles, but had issued a second consultation document outlining its new proposed corporate approval and disclosure rules, to be inserted in the IR, regarding related-party transactions.[225]

15.217   CONSOB's proposed new rules: (i) provide for different corporate approval and disclosure regimes depending on the significance of the related-party transactions (based on quantitative and qualitative criteria); (ii) enhance the role of independent directors with respect to the corporate approval of related-party transactions;

---

[223] IR Article 70. CONSOB Notice No 98081334 of 19 October 1998 sets forth the criteria to determine when the above-mentioned transactions are significant. In particular, a transaction is significant when at least one of the ratios resulting from the comparison of the total assets, the gross profits or the net assets of the companies involved is equal to or greater than 25%. Mergers between two issuers or of an issuer into a private company are always considered significant.

[224] IR Article 71 and CONSOB Notice No 98081334 of 19 October 1998, which sets forth similar criteria to those applicable in case of mergers or split-ups to determine whether a transaction is significant.

[225] CONSOB's Consultation Document on the Regulation Implementing Article 2391-*bis* of the ICC concerning related-party transactions of 3 August 2009.

and (iii) provide for a double disclosure regime for significant related-party transactions (immediate disclosure when the transaction occurs, as well as periodic disclosure).[226]

15.3.5.3 *Buy-back plans*

At least 15 days prior to the ordinary shareholders' meeting convened to authorize the board of directors to carry out the purchase or sale of treasury shares, issuers must publish the board of directors' report to the shareholders requesting such authorization and outlining the main features of the proposed buy-back plan, which include:[227]   **15.218**

- the reasons for the requested authorization;
- the maximum number, category and nominal value of the shares subject to the buy-back authorization;
- the duration of the buy-back (which may not exceed 18 months as regards purchases);
- the minimum and maximum purchase price, as well as the market evaluations on the basis of which these have been determined; and
- the means through which the purchases and (if known) the sales will occur.

15.3.6 Compensation plans

15.3.6.1 *Scope of applicability*

The CFA and the IR set forth specific disclosure obligations relating to compensation plans based on financial instruments issued by an issuer in favour of members of the board of directors, of employees or consultants of the issuer, its parent companies or its subsidiaries (the 'Compensation Plans').[228] These disclosure obligations apply to issuers of financial instruments admitted to trading on a regulated market in Italy, as well as to publicly-held issuers, having their registered office in Italy.   **15.219**

15.3.6.2 *Procedural and disclosure obligations*

Compensation Plans must be approved by the issuer's shareholders. At least 15 days prior to the shareholders' meeting convened to resolve upon a compensation plan,   **15.220**

---

[226] As of the summer of 2009, the disclosure regime applicable to related-party transactions (set forth in IR Article 71-*bis*) was much less stringent and may be summarized as follows. When carrying out (including through subsidiaries) related-party transactions whose purpose, consideration or terms and conditions might have an adverse impact on its assets position or on the completeness and correctness of the information concerning it (including financial information), an issuer must merely publish, post-completion, an information document describing the transaction. Such publication could be avoided altogether if the relevant information had already been disclosed otherwise.

[227] IR Article 73 and Annex 3A. Disclosure shall occur in accordance with the general rules for the disclosure of regulated information. However, dissemination can occur by issuing a press release indicating where the board of directors' report might be retrieved.

[228] CFA Arts 114-*bis* and IR Article 84-*bis*.

an issuer must publish an information document outlining (with different levels of detail depending on the intended beneficiaries of the compensation plans), *inter alia*:

- the reasons for adopting the compensation plan;
- the members of the board of directors and the categories of employees or consultants who will benefit from the compensation plan;
- the terms and conditions of the compensation plan;
- the manner in which prices are determined or the criteria used in determining the prices for the subscription or purchase of the shares; and
- the limitations applicable to the transfer of shares or stock options, with specific reference to the window periods within which subsequent transfers to the issuer or to third parties are either allowed or prohibited.[229]

15.221   The information document must be made available at the issuer's registered office and disclosed in accordance with the general rules applicable to regulated information, as well as published on the issuer's website.[230]

15.222   Similar disclosure obligations and procedures apply, *inter alia*, to:

- resolutions by which the relevant corporate body submits a compensation plan to the approval of the shareholders' meeting, if such resolutions constitute inside information;
- any decisions taken by the relevant corporate body of an issuer with respect to the implementation of compensation plans that have already been approved by the shareholders' meeting; and
- disclosure by issuers of shares with regard to compensation plans approved by a subsidiary, if this information constitutes inside information.

15.3.7 Periodic financial reporting

15.3.7.1 Scope of applicability

15.223   Periodic financial reporting constitutes one of the keystones of regulated information. The transposition of the Transparency Directive into national laws and regulations has affected the content and timing of the approval and disclosure of periodic financial reports. The following paragraphs apply (unless otherwise indicated) to issuers of transferable securities admitted to trading on a regulated market in Italy and that have Italy as their home member state.[231]

---

[229] CFA Article 114-*bis*.

[230] IR Article 84-*bis*.1.

[231] Under IR Article 83, the following rules do not apply, *inter alia*, to issuers of debt securities with a denomination per unit of at least EUR 50,000 or, in the case of debt securities not denominated in EUR, equivalent to at least EUR 50,000.

15.3.7.2 *Responsibility statements and reports*

Issuers must appoint an executive responsible for the preparation of financial statements ('*dirigente preposto alla redazione dei documenti contabili societari*', usually the CFO or the chief accounting officer when different from the CFO), who must:[232]

15.224

- certify in writing that the documents and releases distributed to the market concerning the issuer's accounts, including interim accounts, correspond to the issuer's books, documents and accounting records (the CFO responsibility statement);
- set up adequate administrative and accounting procedures for the preparation of the annual stand-alone and consolidated financial statements, as well as any other financial release; and
- certify in writing, together with the issuer's executive directors, in a report (the responsibility report) to be attached to the audited annual financial statements, the half-yearly financial statements and the audited annual consolidated financial statements (if any), *inter alia*: (i) as to the compliance with the abovementioned administrative and accounting procedures and their appropriateness; (ii) that the financial statements (a) correspond to the issuer's books and accounting records, (b) were prepared in accordance with the applicable international accounting standards, (c) give a true and fair view of the assets, liabilities, financial position and profit or loss of the issuer (and its consolidated subsidiaries); (iii) that the directors' report on operations (a) to the annual financial statements, includes a fair review of the development and performance and the position of the issuer (and its consolidated subsidiaries) together with a description of the main risks and uncertainties they face, and (b) to the half-yearly financial report, includes a fair review of the information described in Section 15.3.7.4 below.[233]

CONSOB has clarified that the rules regarding the executive responsible for the preparation of financial statements, other than those related to the abovementioned certifications, are left to self-regulation by the issuer.[234]

15.225

15.3.7.3 *Annual financial reports*

An issuer's annual financial report includes: (i) the audited stand-alone financial statements; (ii) the audited consolidated financial statements (if any); (iii) the directors' report on operations; and (iv) the responsibility report described in Section 15.3.7.2 above.[235]

15.226

---

[232] CFA Articles 154-*bis* and IR Article 81-*ter*.
[233] See Transparency Directive Article 4.2.(c) and 5.2.(c).
[234] CONSOB Notice DEM/9058755 of 23 June 2009.
[235] CFA Article 154-*ter*.1. See Transparency Directive Article 4.

15.227 The annual stand-alone financial statements are first approved by the issuer's board of directors in draft form and then finally approved by the issuer's ordinary shareholders' meeting within 120 days from the end of the previous financial year.[236] The draft financial statements, the consolidated financial statements and the directors' report on operations must be deposited at the issuer's registered seat and published on its website together with the statutory auditors' report(s) and the auditors' opinion(s) thereon at least 15 days prior to the shareholders' meeting convened to approve the stand-alone financial statements. General disclosure obligations apply in regard of the financial statements.[237] Notice of publication must also be given in a national newspaper.[238]

15.228 Issuers of shares must indicate in the notes to the financial statements, *inter alia*, the compensation granted, in any form (including by subsidiaries) to members of their managing and supervisory boards, as well as (in the aggregate) to general managers and executives with strategic duties.[239]

15.229 The directors' report on operations of an issuer of shares must indicate, *inter alia*, any direct and indirect shareholdings in the issuer or any of its subsidiaries held by members of the management and supervisory boards, the general managers or executives with strategic duties, as well as by their non-separated spouses and minor children.[240]

15.230 The directors' report on operations of issuers of transferable securities admitted to trading on regulated markets must include a section providing information concerning, *inter alia*:[241]

- the issuer's capital structure, including with respect to securities traded on non-EU regulated markets, listing all classes of shares, the percentage of the share capital they represent and their respective rights and obligations;
- any restrictions on transfers of the issuer's securities, including, without limitation, ownership limits or transfer consent requirements from the issuer or from other holders of such securities;
- major holdings;[242]

---

[236] As will be seen in Section 15.3.15 below, Italian corporations may adopt a two-tier corporate governance model. In the two-tier model, annual financial reports are drafted by the management board and approved by the supervisory board (subject to certain exceptions).

[237] IR Article 77.

[238] CONSOB Decision No 17002 of 17 August 2009.

[239] IR Article 78.

[240] IR Article 79.

[241] CFA Article 123-*bis*. The following information may be reported in a separate report from the directors' report on operations as long as both reports are approved by the board of directors and published concurrently. The report must contain additional information concerning compliance with applicable corporate governance codes.

[242] See Section 15.3.9 below.

- holders of securities carrying special control rights;
- any restrictions on voting rights, including, without limitation, percentage limits;
- shareholders' agreements;[243]
- material agreements entered into by the company or its subsidiaries containing change of control provisions not otherwise disclosed, unless such disclosure is prejudicial to the issuer;
- agreements between the issuer and members of its managing or supervisory boards providing for indemnities in case of resignations, dismissals without cause or termination following a tender offer;
- rules governing the appointment and replacement of members of the issuer's managing or supervisory boards, if different from applicable default rules;
- any grant of powers by the issuer's shareholders to the managing board relating to the increase of the share capital, the issue of financial participation instruments or shares buy-backs.

15.3.7.4 Half-yearly financial reports

An issuer's half-yearly financial report includes: (i) the condensed set of financial statements (on a stand-alone or consolidated basis, as applicable); (ii) the directors' interim report on operations; and (iii) the responsibility report described in Section 15.3.7.2 above.[244] CONSOB has recommended external auditors' limited review of half-yearly financial reports,[245] and this has indeed become the common market practice.   **15.231**

Issuers must deposit at their registered seat and publish, in accordance with the general rules for the disclosure of regulated information, the half-yearly financial report together with the auditors' opinion thereon (if any) within 60 days from the end of the first six months of the financial year.[246] Notice of publication must also be given in a national newspaper.[247]   **15.232**

The directors' interim report on operations must indicate important events that have occurred during the semester and their impact on the financial statements, as well as describe the main risks and uncertainties for the remaining six months of the financial year. Issuers of shares must also include in the directors' interim report on operations detailed references to significant related-party transactions.[248]   **15.233**

---

243 See Section 15.3.11 below.
244 CFA Article 154-*ter* and IR Article 81. See Transparency Directive Article 5.
245 CONSOB Recommendation No 10867 of 31 July 1997.
246 CFA Article 154-*ter*.2.
247 CONSOB Decision No 17002 of 17 August 2009.
248 CFA Article 154-*ter*.4 and IR Article 81. See Transparency Directive Article 5.4.

15.3.7.5 *Quarterly management statements*

15.234 Issuers of shares must deposit at their registered seat and publish, in accordance with the general rules for the disclosure of regulated information, un-audited quarterly management statements (that may or may not include un-audited accounting numbers)[249] together with the CFO responsibility statement described in Section 3.7.2 above, within 45 days from the end of the first and third quarters of each financial year. Notice of publication must also be given in a national newspaper.[250]

15.235 Quarterly management statements must contain a general description of the assets position and financial position of the issuer and of its subsidiaries for the period, as well as a description of material events and transactions that have taken place during the period and their impact on the assets position of the issuer and of its subsidiaries.[251]

15.3.8 Registries of insiders and internal dealing transactions

15.3.8.1 *Registries of insiders*

15.236 Issuers of financial instruments admitted to trading on a regulated market in Italy and the entities controlling them, or the persons acting in their name or on their behalf (including outside consultants),[252] must create and update a registry of persons who, due to the work, profession or duties performed, have potential access to inside information directly related to the issuers or their controlling entities (the insiders).[253]

15.237 Insiders' registries must contain information regarding the identity of the insiders and the reasons for their registration, as well as the entry date and the date of each update of the registered information.[254]

15.238 Issuers and the entities controlling them may delegate the creation, management and maintenance of the registry to another company of the group, provided

---

[249] See CONSOB Notice No 8041082 of 30 April 2008.
[250] CONSOB Decision No 17002 of 17 August 2009.
[251] CFA Article 154-*ter*.5 and IR Article 82. See Transparency Directive Article 6.
[252] CONSOB Notice No 6027054 dated 28 March 2006 included amongst those who 'act in the name or on behalf of the issuer or the entities controlling them': (i) outside consultants of the issuers or of the entities controlling them, in connection with transactions involving the issuers, (ii) banks that manage and implement the issuers' financing, where this is considered relevant for the issuers' financial stability or otherwise entails ongoing provisions of services; (iii) qualified persons who have privileged information regarding the issuers in their capacity as members of underwriting consortia for the issuance of financial instruments; (iv) audit firms; and (v) qualified persons acting as sponsors of the issuers.
[253] CFA Article 115-*bis*, implementing Market Abuse Directive Article 6.3.
[254] IR Article 152-*bis*.2.

that internal policies related to the circulation of inside information allow the delegated party to perform the related duties in a timely manner.[255]

Insiders must be timely informed of their inclusion in the registry as well as of the obligations and penalties related to having potential access to inside information.[256] Registered information concerning an insider must be stored for at least five years.[257] **15.239**

15.3.8.2 *Disclosure of internal dealing transactions*

15.3.8.2.1 Scope of applicability Unless otherwise indicated, the following paragraphs apply to Italian issuers of shares admitted to trading on a regulated market in Italy or in the European Community.[258] **15.240**

15.3.8.2.2 Notion of internal dealing transactions Under the CFA and the IR, selected categories of insiders must disclose the purchases, sales, subscriptions and exchanges of shares, or of other financial instruments relating to the shares, of the issuer, including transactions carried out through third parties (internal dealing transactions).[259] **15.241**

The persons subject to the above disclosure duty (significant parties) are:[260] **15.242**

- the members of the management and supervisory boards of the issuer;
- the issuer's general managers;
- the issuer's executives who have regular access to inside information and who may take decisions influencing the issuer's future prospects;
- the above-mentioned persons within any subsidiary of the issuer the book value of which represents more than 50% of the issuer's total net assets; and
- persons holding at least 10% of the voting share capital of the issuer, as well as any of its controlling entities.

Significant parties must also disclose internal dealing transactions carried out by the following persons (connected persons):[261] **15.243**

- persons with close family ties with the significant parties (family members);
- legal entities, partnerships and trusts in which a significant party or a family member performs a managerial function;

---

[255] IR Article 152-*bis*.4.
[256] IR Article 152-*quinquies*.
[257] IR Article 152-*quater*. CONSOB Notice No. 6027054 of 28 March 2006, sets forth detailed guidelines and recommendations regarding insiders' registries.
[258] IR Article 152-*septies*.1.
[259] CFA Article 114.7 and IR Article 152-*septies*.2. See Market Abuse Directive Article 6.4.
[260] IR Article 152-*sexies*.c).
[261] IR Article 152-*sexies*.d).

- legal entities directly or indirectly controlled by a significant party or a family member;
- partnerships between persons whose interests in the issuer are substantially equivalent to those of a significant party or a family member;
- trusts set up in favour of a significant party or a family member.

15.244   Internal dealing transactions include transactions on the following financial instruments:

- the issuer's shares;
- financial instruments that confer the right to subscribe, purchase or sell such shares;
- convertible bonds or other debt instruments convertible into, or exchangeable for, such shares;
- derivative instruments over such shares;
- other financial instruments, equivalent to the issuer's shares and representing such shares;
- shares as well as the above-mentioned financial instruments connected thereto issued by a subsidiary of the issuer and admitted to trading on a regulated market;
- shares issued by any private subsidiary of the issuer the book value of which represents more than 50% of the issuer's total net assets as well as the above-mentioned financial instruments connected thereto.

15.245   **15.3.8.2.3 Disclosure of internal dealing transactions**   A significant party (other than persons holding 10% or more of an issuer's voting share capital) must notify CONSOB (including through the issuer) and the issuer of the internal dealing transactions carried out by such party or its connected persons within five trading days.[262] No later than the trading day following its receipt, the issuer must disclose such information in accordance with the general rules set forth for the disclosure of regulated information.[263]

15.246   Shareholders holding at least 10% of an issuer's voting share capital, or otherwise controlling an issuer, must notify CONSOB and publish (including through the issuer) the internal dealing transactions carried out by them or their connected persons no later than 15 days after the end of the month in which the transaction occurred.[264]

---

[262] To this end, issuers must: (a) set up procedures to identify executives who are required to notify internal dealing transactions; (b) inform the identified executives of their duties; (c) identify a person responsible for receiving, handling and disclosing the information to CONSOB and to the public (IR Article152-*octies*.8).

[263] IR Article 152-*octies*.3.

[264] IR Article 152-*octies*.4. Interim rules applied with respect to the means of disclosure of internal dealing transactions for the period up to when the Transparency Directive implementing rules

15.3.8.2.4 Exemptions from disclosure obligations   The following internal   **15.247**
dealing transactions are exempted from disclosure: (i) transactions carried out by
a significant party and its connected persons the aggregate amount of which is less
than EUR 5,000 in a single calendar year; (ii) transactions occurring between a
significant party and its connected persons; or (iii) transactions carried out by the
issuer or its subsidiaries.

15.3.9 Disclosure of major shareholdings and potential holdings

15.3.9.1 Scope of applicability

Pursuant to the CFA and the IR, actual or potential shareholdings in issuers   **15.248**
exceeding (or falling below) certain thresholds must be disclosed to the market.
These disclosure obligations are aimed at achieving greater transparency with
respect to issuers' ownership structure. Although the Transparency Directive and
implementing Directive 2007/14/EC set forth specific rules and principles concerning the above disclosure obligations, the implementation of such measures in
Italy did not have a significant impact on existing Italian rules. The Italian regulatory framework was already substantially in line with the principles enshrined in
the European Directives, except for certain specific exemptions and for the disclosure obligations that apply to potential holdings (see Section 15.3.9.5 below).

The requirements of the CFA and the IR extend to material holdings held by issu-   **15.249**
ers in non-listed companies and thus go beyond the disclosure obligations set
forth in the European directives.

There follows a description of Italian rules mandating the disclosure of major   **15.250**
shareholdings and potential holdings, as they apply to issuers of shares having
Italy as their own member state.

15.3.9.2 Major shareholdings thresholds

Shareholders must notify the issuer and CONSOB of any transactions that result   **15.251**
in their shareholdings: (i) exceeding or falling below 2%;[265] or (ii) reaching,
exceeding or falling below 5%, 10%, 15%, 20%, 25%, 30%, 35%, 40%, 45%,

---

will have become fully operational. In particular, issuers would effect the disclosure through the
NIS and their websites, and significant shareholders would effect the disclosure by transmitting the
information to at least two press agencies or through the NIS.

[265] No 2% threshold is set forth under the Transparency Directive. Pursuant to CFA Article.
120.2.2-*bis* as introduced in April of 2009, CONSOB may set—for a limited period of time and for
purposes of investors' protection and markets' efficiency and transparency—thresholds lower than
2% for issuers with high market capitalization and a very high shareholders basis. As of June of 2009,
CONSOB had not used this power.

50%, 66.6%, 75%, 90% and 95% of the issuer's voting share capital.[266] The duty to effect the above notifications may arise automatically as a result of a reduction or an increase in the issuer's share capital.[267]

15.3.9.3 *Major shareholdings calculation criteria*

15.252 For purposes of calculating the reportable shareholdings, only voting shares must be taken into account, and the following rules and criteria apply:[268]

- owned shares are attributed to a shareholder even if such shareholder may not vote on them (e.g. if the voting rights attached to the shares have been suspended or are exercisable by a third party);
- non-owned shares are attributed to a non-shareholder if such person may vote on them (including as a result of a pledge, a deposit agreement or a proxy if the voting rights may be exercised at the depositary's or at the proxy's discretion);
- in case of stock lending agreements, shares are attributed to both the lender and—subject to limited exceptions—the borrower;
- if on the same day more transactions occur that are attributable to the same reporting person, the relevant shareholding must be calculated by aggregating such transactions;
- shares held through, or that may be voted on by, subsidiaries, fiduciaries or other intermediaries of the reporting person are counted;
- a subsidiary may opt not to disclose its major shareholding in an issuer if this is reported by its parent company within all direct and indirect shareholdings attributable to it (and *vice-versa*);
- issuers must disclose major holdings in their treasury shares (including those held by their subsidiaries). The parent companies of those issuers, however, do not have to consolidate their subsidiaries' treasury shares within their reportable shareholdings;
- specific disclosure rules apply to shareholders holding less than 2% of an issuer's voting share capital who are parties to shareholders' agreements;[269] and
- special disclosure rules apply if more classes of shares exist and to holders of financial instruments carrying the right to appoint a member of the managing or supervisory body of an issuer.[270]

---

[266] CFA Article 120 and IR Article 117.1. See Transparency Directive Article 9 (which does not refer to the 90% and 95% thresholds).

[267] IR Article 117.2. See Transparency Directive Article 9.2.

[268] IR Articles 117-*bis*, 118 and 119-*bis*. Some of the rules listed in this paragraph derive from the Transparency Directive or from Directive 2007/14/EC. The most significant outcomes of these rules are that (i) the duty to notify may fall on a person or entity that is not a direct shareholder for corporate law purposes (for ease of reference, a reporting person), and (ii) the same shares may be counted more than once.

[269] IR Article 120. See Section 15.3.11, below.

[270] IR Article 122-*bis*.

15.3.9.4 *Major potential holdings or disposals*

Disclosure obligations are also triggered with respect to major holdings of finan- **15.253**
cial instruments that confer the right to (i) acquire (potential holdings) or (ii) sell
(potential disposals), at the holder's mere initiative (that is, with a corresponding
obligation on a third party to sell or acquire, respectively), an issuer's voting
shares.

In particular, holders of potential holdings must notify the issuer and CONSOB **15.254**
of any transactions resulting in their potential holdings: (i) exceeding or
falling below 2%; or (ii) reaching, exceeding or falling below 5%, 10%, 15%,
20%, 25%, 30%, 50%, and 75% of the issuer's voting share capital.[271] Voting
shares that may be acquired by exercising warrants or other conversion rights
count as potential holdings if the conversion right can be exercised within the
following 60 days.[272]

Holders of actual (as described in Section 15.3.9.3 above) or potential holdings in **15.255**
excess of 2% of an issuer's voting share capital must notify the issuer and CONSOB
when their potential disposals: (i) exceed or fall below 2%; or (ii) reach, exceed or
fall below 5%, 10%, 15%, 20%, 25%, 30%, 50% and 75%.[273]

Potential holdings and potential disposals may not be netted against one **15.256**
another. Potential holdings must be notified independently and irrespective of
actual holdings. Similar calculation rules and criteria to those applicable to actual
holdings apply to potential holdings and potential disposals.[274]

15.3.9.5 *Exemptions*

Disclosure obligations regarding actual or potential holdings or potential **15.257**
disposals (as applicable) do not apply to, *inter alia*:[275]

- acquisitions of shares for the sole purpose of clearing and settling (within a
  three-trading-day settlement cycle);
- central counterparts, with respect to shares subject to enforcement procedures,
  for the time required to complete such procedures;
- custodians, if they may vote on the shares they hold only on the basis of
  written or electronic instructions from the shareholders;

---

[271] IR Article 119. See Transparency Directive Article 13 and Commission Directive 2007/14/
EC Article 11.

[272] IR Article 119.

[273] IR Article 119. No such obligations are set forth in the Transparency Directive.

[274] IR Articles 119 and 119-*bis*.

[275] IR Article 119-*bis*. See Transparency Directive Articles 9, 11 and 12, as well as Commission
Directive 2007/14/EC Articles 5 et seq.

- market makers, for holdings below a 10% threshold, provided they meet certain conditions concerning their licence, organization and reporting obligations to CONSOB;
- credit institutions and investment firms, with respect to shares held in their trading books, as defined by Article 11 of Directive 2006/49/CEE, as long as: (i) the relevant holdings do not exceed 5% of the issuer's voting share capital; and (ii) the credit institution or investment firm ensures that the voting rights are not exercised or otherwise used to influence the management of the issuer;
- the European Central Bank or central banks of member states with reference to short-term transactions carried out in the exercise of their functions, provided that the shares are not voted;
- certain management companies with respect to holdings not exceeding 5% of the issuer's voting share capital.[276]

15.3.9.6 *Timing and means of disclosure and sanctions for non-disclosure*

15.258 Major actual or potential holdings, or potential disposals, must be disclosed within five trading days from the triggering transaction—irrespective of the closing date of the transaction—or from the date the issuer disclosed the reduction or increase of its share capital.[277] If different entities not connected by a control relationship are under an obligation to disclose the same holding, the disclosure may be effected by one of them as long as complete information is provided on all direct and indirect holdings of all the entities involved.[278]

15.259 Disclosure to the issuer and to CONSOB is effected through the forms, and following the detailed guidelines and instructions, set forth in the IR. CONSOB then disseminates the information within three trading days of receiving the disclosure.[279]

15.260 If disclosure obligations regarding major holdings are not complied with, the corresponding voting rights may not be exercised. If the voting rights are indeed exercised notwithstanding the suspension, the shareholder resolutions passed with the vote of such shares may be voided by the court.[280]

---

[276] Pursuant to IR Article 119-*ter* (implementing Transparency Directive Article 12) specific disclosure rules apply to the aggregation criteria of holdings held by management companies, financial intermediaries or their controlling entities or sister companies, essentially based on whether the voting rights attached to the shares are exercised independently of their controlling entities or sister companies (and at the clients' written or electronic instructions as far as financial intermediaries are concerned).

[277] IR Article 121. See Transparency Directive Article 12.

[278] IR Article 121.

[279] IR Article 122.

[280] CFA Article 120.

15.3.9.7 *Material holdings of issuers in non-listed companies*

Issuers must notify the participating company and CONSOB of any transactions that result in their holdings in the voting share capital of Italian or foreign companies not admitted to trading on a regulated market exceeding or falling below 10%.[281] For purposes of calculating the above holdings, account must be taken of:[282]

15.261

- shares or quotas directly or indirectly owned (including through subsidiaries, intermediaries or fiduciaries), even if the voting rights are exercisable by a third party;
- non-owned shares or quotas that may be directly or indirectly voted on (including through subsidiaries, intermediaries or fiduciaries), if this allows the issuer to exercise a dominant or significant influence at the subject company's ordinary shareholders' meeting.

Material holdings must be notified: (i) to the subject company, within seven days from the purchase or sale of the shares, quotas or voting rights;[283] and (ii) to CONSOB, within 30 days from the approval of the issuer's annual draft financial statements. Issuers must disclose the above information concurrently with the publication of their draft and final annual financial statements.[284]

15.262

15.3.10 Restrictions on cross-shareholdings[285]

Cross-ownership restrictions limit the ownership by two companies (at least one of which is an Italian issuer of shares listed on a regulated market of the European Community) of one another's voting shares or quotas, with a view to limit potential conflicts of interests by respective management.

15.263

Cross-ownership between two issuers may not exceed 2% of their respective voting share capital, and cross-ownership between an issuer and an unlisted company may not exceed, respectively, 10% of the voting capital of the unlisted company and 2% of the voting share capital of the issuer. The 2% threshold may be increased to 5% pursuant to an agreement authorized in advance by the ordinary shareholders' meeting of each company involved.

15.264

If the above cross-ownership thresholds are exceeded, the last company to exceed the relevant threshold may not exercise the voting rights attributable to any shares or quotas held in excess of the threshold and must sell them within one year. If it does not carry out such sale, it may not exercise the voting rights attached to its

15.265

---

281 CFA Article 120.
282 IR Article 123.
283 IR Article 124.
284 IR Article 126.
285 CFA Article 121.

entire shareholding in the other company. If it is not possible to ascertain which company was the last one to exceed the threshold, the limitation on voting rights and the obligation to sell the excess shares or quotas apply to both companies, unless otherwise agreed between them.

15.266 If a person holds more than 2% of an issuer's voting share capital, such an issuer and its controlling entity may not acquire a holding exceeding 2% of the share capital of another issuer if the latter is controlled by the holder of more than 2% of the former's share capital. In case of non-compliance, voting rights attributable to any shares held in excess of the threshold may not be exercised. If it is not possible to ascertain which entity was the last one to exceed the threshold, the limitation on voting rights applies to both holdings, unless otherwise agreed between them.

15.267 If the voting rights are in fact exercised notwithstanding the suspension described above, any resolutions passed with the decisive vote of such shares or quotas may be voided by the court.

15.268 The foregoing cross-ownership restrictions do not apply when (i) the thresholds are exceeded following a public tender offer to acquire at least 60% of an issuer's ordinary shares, or (ii) a subsidiary purchases shares or quotas representing up to 10% of the share capital of its parent company (whether listed or not) within the limits and conditions set forth in the ICC.[286]

15.3.11 Shareholders' agreements

15.269 Shareholders' agreements are very popular among Italian listed companies and represent a typical way through which Italian companies are controlled. Hence, regardless of their form, shareholders' agreements concerning the exercise of voting rights in Italian issuers of shares admitted to trading on a regulated market in the European Community, or their controlling entities, are subject to significant disclosure rules. Shareholders' agreements must be:[287]

- reported to CONSOB within five days of their execution;[288]
- published in summary form in a national daily newspaper within ten days of their execution;[289] and

---

[286] See ICC Article 2359-*bis*.

[287] CFA Article 122.

[288] Pursuant to IR Article 127, all parties to a shareholders' agreement are jointly and severally bound to report the agreement to CONSOB. Pursuant to IR Article 128 of the IR, certain events affecting reported shareholders' agreements must also be disclosed to CONSOB within five days from their occurrence (e.g. amendments, variations of the parties or in the number or percentages of shares or financial instruments conferred not resulting from an amendment, renewal, withdrawals, termination).

[289] Pursuant to IR Article 130, the summary must include all information necessary to assess it fully, including at least information concerning: the total number of shares and/or financial

• filed with the companies' registry where the company has its registered office within 15 days of their execution.

Failure to comply with the above disclosure requirements renders an agreement **15.270** null and void and the voting rights attaching to the issuer's shares subject to the agreement un-exercisable. If the voting rights are indeed exercised notwithstanding the suspension, the resolutions passed with the decisive vote of such shares may be annulled by the court.[290]

The maximum duration of any such shareholders' agreements is three years (and **15.271** is automatically reduced to three years if longer). The agreements may be renewed upon expiry. If no duration is specified in an agreement, any party may withdraw from it upon six months' notice.[291]

These rules apply to shareholders' agreements which: **15.272**

(i) regulate the exercise of voting rights in an issuer or in its controlling entities;

(ii) require prior consultation for the exercise of voting rights in an issuer or in its controlling entities;

(iii) limit the transfers of shares of the companies mentioned in point (i), above, or of financial instruments which grant the right to purchase or subscribe for such shares;

(iv) provide for the purchase of shares or financial instruments mentioned in point (iii), above;

(v) have as their object or effect the exercise, including joint exercise, of a dominant influence over the companies mentioned in point (i), above; or

(vi) are aimed at favouring or frustrating a public tender offer.

In case of a public tender offer, any party to a shareholders' agreement that intends **15.273** to participate in the tender offer may withdraw from the agreement without notice, but the withdrawal is ineffective if the shares are not subsequently tendered into the offer.

---

instruments subject to the agreement and their percentage in relation to the share capital or their class; the persons or entities that are parties to the agreement and the shares and/or financial instruments they hold; the person or entity that, on the basis of the agreement, controls the issuer or has the power to appoint member/s of the managing or supervising body; the content of the agreement and its duration; its governing bodies, if any, and their powers and composition; withdrawal from and renewal of the agreement; penalty clauses. Pursuant to IR Article 129 the summary is simultaneously sent to: (i) the company whose financial instruments are subject to the agreement, and (ii) the operating company. The summary is also transmitted to CONSOB. Significant amendments and variations to a shareholders' agreement, including renewal, withdrawals, and termination must also be published in summary form.

[290] CFA Article 122.
[291] CFA Article 123.

15.274 Holders (directly or through fiduciaries or intermediaries) of less than 2% of the voting share capital of an issuer who are party to a shareholders' agreement under points (i), (ii) or (v), above, must aggregate the actual holdings of the other parties to the agreement for the purposes of effecting the notifications required for holdings that cross the 5%, 10%, 15%, 20%, 25%, 30%, 50% and 75% thresholds described in Section 15.3.9.3 above.[292]

15.3.12 Other disclosure requirements[293]

15.275 Unless otherwise indicated, the following paragraphs apply to issuers of transferable securities admitted to trading on a regulated market in Italy and having Italy as their home member state.

15.3.12.1 *Modification or exercise of rights of securities holders*

15.276 Issuers must disclose without delay, in accordance with the general rules set forth for the disclosure of regulated information, *inter alia*, any changes in the rights connected to their transferable securities, including bonds.[294]

15.277 Issuers of financial instruments admitted to trading on a regulated market in Italy must publish the information necessary for the holders of such instruments to exercise the rights connected thereto.[295] Notice of publication must also be given in a national newspaper.[296]

15.3.12.2 *Annual information document*

15.278 Issuers must publish, at least once a year, a document containing or referring to all the information made available to the public in the previous 12 months.[297] This disclosure obligation extends to the information disclosed or made available in other member states or third countries in accordance with applicable laws and regulations. The document must also be filed with CONSOB after the disclosure of the annual financial statements.

15.279 The annual information document provides an overview of all regulated information disclosed by the issuer during the year. In practice it usually consists in a table, subdivided by categories of regulated information, in which the issuer lists in

---

[292] IR Article 120. The same disclosure obligation applies to entities controlling the reporting person. The notification must include information regarding the holdings and may be avoided if the information is included in the summary of the agreement mentioned above provided that this is published within the time frame of the disclosure of major holdings.

[293] As to disclosure obligations concerning compliance by issuers with applicable corporate governance codes, see Section 15.3.15.9 below.

[294] IR Article 83-*bis* (substantially replicating Transparency Directive Article 16).

[295] IR Article 84 (substantially replicating Transparency Directive Articles 17 and 18).

[296] CONSOB Decision No 17002 of 17 August 2009.

[297] IR Article 54.

chronological order the regulated information it has disclosed, providing the date of disclosure and the link to the website (usually the corporate website) where such regulated information is available.

15.3.12.3 *Disclosure of information on issuers' websites*

Although the setting up of company websites became mandatory only in 2009, **15.280** with the adoption of the Transparency Directive implementing rules, the use of websites had been common practice for some years, which had prompted CONSOB to issue general recommendations regarding the use of the Internet.[298] In particular, CONSOB recommends that in using their websites issuers should:

- report information and news according to appropriate objectivity criteria aimed at avoiding promotional efforts;
- clearly indicate, on each web page, the date and time of its last update;
- if information is published in Italian and in another language, ensure that the contents are the same in both versions, or indicate any differences;
- in case of errors in the information published, publish a correction as soon as possible, showing any changes made;
- always cite the source of the information when publishing data and information from third parties;
- indicate whether the documents published are complete versions, excerpts or summaries, explaining how the original documents may be obtained; and
- indicate any links to other websites based on principles of correctness and neutrality, so as to allow users to easily realize that they are about to navigate a different website.

15.3.12.4 *Borsa disclosure obligations*

The Borsa Market Rules and the Borsa Instructions contain several disclosure **15.281** obligations that are applicable to issuers of financial instruments admitted to trading on a regulated market operated by Borsa. These disclosure obligations further implement (and, in certain respects, overlap with) those set forth under the CFA and the IR. At the time of writing this Chapter in the summer of 2009, Borsa had not amended the disclosure obligations provisions of the Borsa Market Rules and the Borsa Instructions in order to better tailor them to the new Transparency Directive implementing rules set forth in the IR.

As a general rule, issuers must notify Borsa of all information it deems appropriate **15.282** to ensure that the market operates well. More specifically, according to the Borsa Market Rules and the Borsa Instructions, issuers must provide Borsa and the

---

[298] CONSOB Notice No 6027054 of 28 March 2006. The following recommendations were not repelled by CONSOB following the implementation of the Transparency Directive in Italy and therefore apply insofar as compatible with the new Transparency Directive implementing rules.

market with information regarding, *inter alia*: (i) the annual calendar of corporate events for each financial year;[299] (ii) the distribution of dividends;[300] (iii) extraordinary capital-raising transactions;[301] (iv) any changes in the share capital, amendments to the by-laws, changes of name and changes of the corporate purpose;[302] and (v) significant events and price-sensitive information.[303] Finally, Borsa may also request ad hoc disclosure of specific information.[304]

15.3.13 CONSOB supervisory and monitoring functions

15.3.13.1 *Requests for information by CONSOB*

15.283 In addition to its powers to request additional disclosure of inside information,[305] for purposes of monitoring the fairness and correctness of information disclosed to the public CONSOB may:[306]

- require issuers of financial instruments admitted to trading on a regulated market, their controlling entities and the companies controlled by them, as well major shareholders or parties to relevant shareholders' agreements, to disclose to CONSOB additional information and documentation;
- acquire information, including through hearings, from any of the above entities or persons, as well as from members of corporate bodies, general managers, executives responsible for the preparation of the financial statements, other executives or the external auditors; and
- carry out inspections at the offices of the above-mentioned entities or persons in order to verify and obtain a copy of the relevant corporate documents.[307]

15.284 CONSOB may also require the issuers or entities with a direct or indirect equity interest in the issuers to provide a list of shareholders or of beneficiaries, in case of trust companies (*società fiduciarie*).[308]

15.3.13.2 *CONSOB's monitoring functions*

15.285 CONSOB monitors the regulated information disclosed by issuers of financial instruments admitted to trading on a regulated market in Italy and issuers that

---

[299] Borsa Market Rules Article 2.6.2.1 c).

[300] Borsa Instructions section IA.2.1.2.

[301] Borsa Instructions section IA.2.1.10.

[302] Borsa Instructions section IA.2.3.

[303] Borsa Instructions section IA.2.9. For more details regarding this disclosure requirement, see Section 15.3.3.3 above.

[304] Borsa Market Rules Article 2.6.1.1 and 2.

[305] See Section 15.3.3.6 above.

[306] CFA Article 115.1 and 2.

[307] CONSOB has more stringent powers of inquiry and investigation in connection with its supervisory functions aimed at ensuring that the Market Abuse Directive rules and prohibitions are fully complied with (CFA Article 187-*octies*).

[308] CFA Article 115.3.

have Italy as their home member state, including financial information.[309] In particular, as regards financial information, CONSOB carries out its monitoring functions on a sample basis and in accordance with the principles issued by CESR. The overall number of issuers whose documents are subject to review, equal to no less than a fifth of all issuers, is determined annually by CONSOB taking into account the risks regarding the accuracy and completeness of the information provided to the market by issuers.[310]

15.3.14 Sanctions in case of market abuse or violation of disclosure obligations

15.3.14.1 *Scope of applicability*

The ICC and the CFA set forth sanctions related to market abuse or violation of **15.286** continuing disclosure obligations. The regime of sanctions was significantly amended as a result of the implementation of the Market Abuse Directive into national laws and regulations. The ICC sets forth criminal sanctions applicable to qualified corporate personnel of Italian corporations, including issuers of financial instruments. The CFA sets forth (i) criminal sanctions in case of abuse of inside information (insider trading) and market manipulation, as well as (ii) administrative sanctions relating to, *inter alia*, violations under (i) or violations of the disclosure obligations and requirements described in the preceding paragraphs.

While criminal sanctions may only be imposed by criminal courts, administrative **15.287** sanctions are imposed by CONSOB and may be appealed before a civil court of appeals. Criminal and administrative proceedings can be commenced in parallel—each by the competent authority—and public prosecutors and CONSOB may exchange relevant information. CONSOB may also make use of the services of law enforcement officers in the same manner as public prosecutors do.

The current regulatory framework is relatively recent and no coherent body **15.288** of precedents has yet developed regarding its application.[311] Such regulatory framework will be briefly outlined in the following paragraphs.

---

[309] CFA Article 118-*bis*.

[310] IR Article 89-*quater*.

[311] A recent case involved the equity swap for Fiat shares entered into by the Agnelli family with Merrill Lynch in 2005. The transaction allowed the Agnelli family to retain control of Fiat after a debt-for-equity swap with major Italian banks, without launching a mandatory bid or disclosing purchases that would have influenced the share price. CONSOB has sanctioned the entities involved for failure to disclose the transaction (CONSOB Decision No of 9 February 2007; appealed before the court of appeals of Turin) and the corresponding criminal proceedings are under way.

15.3.14.2 Criminal sanctions

15.289 **15.3.14.2.1 Under the ICC** 'Fraudulent corporate communications' occur when qualified corporate personnel,[312] with the intention of deceiving the shareholders or the public and in order to obtain for themselves or for third parties an unjust profit, report material facts that are false or omit information required to be disclosed by law in the financial statements, reports or other corporate notices directed to shareholders or the public, and regarding the assets, economic or financial position of the issuer or the group to which it belongs, in such a way as to mislead the recipients.[313]

15.290 Perpetrators of fraudulent corporate communications may be punished with imprisonment for up to two years. However, no sanctions apply if the false or omitted information:

- does not significantly alter the representation of the company's or the group's financial position;
- determines a variation not greater than 5% of the year's profit or loss, gross of taxes, or a variation of the net assets not greater than 1%; or
- is due to inadequate estimates differing by no more than 10% from the correct ones.

15.291 'Fraudulent corporate communications to the detriment of a company, its shareholders or its creditors' occur when the conduct outlined above results in economic damage to the company, its shareholders, or its creditors.[314] Perpetrators may be punished with imprisonment from one to four years when the company is an Italian issuer of shares admitted to trading on a regulated market in the European Community. If the fraudulent communications cause *serious* damages to investors, the sanction is imprisonment from two to six years. Damages are considered serious when they involve a number of investors greater than 1/10,000 of the Italian population pursuant to the latest ISTAT census, or if they consist in the destruction or reduction of the value of transferable securities by more than 1/10,000 of the GDP.

15.292 'Frustration of supervisory functions of authorities' occurs when supervised qualified corporate personnel (i) report in the communications to a supervisory authority material facts that are false, or omit or conceal by fraudulent means information, regarding the assets, economic or financial position of the supervised entities, for purposes of frustrating the authority's supervisory functions, or (ii) otherwise

---

[312] Including directors, general managers, the executive responsible for preparing the financial statements, statutory auditors and liquidators.

[313] ICC Article 2621.

[314] ICC Article 2622. Public prosecutors may initiate investigations even in absence of a complaint.

willfully frustrate a supervisory authority's functions. Perpetrators may be punished with imprisonment from two to eight years when the company concerned is an issuer of financial instruments admitted to trading on regulated markets of the EC or is publicly held.[315]

15.3.14.2.2 Under the CFA Pursuant to the CFA, abuse of inside information (i.e. insider trading) occurs when a person who possesses inside information by virtue of such person's membership of the management or supervisory boards of an issuer of financial instruments admitted to trading on a regulated market of the EC, holdings in such issuer, employment, profession, functions (including as a civil servant) or office, or as a result of the commission of another crime:[316]   **15.293**

(i) purchases, sells, or carries out other transactions, directly or indirectly, in such person's interest or on behalf of third parties, related to financial instruments, using such inside information;

(ii) communicates such inside information to third parties, outside the normal scope of such person's work, profession, functions or office; or

(iii) based on such inside information, makes recommendations or induces third parties to carry out any of the transactions under (i), above.

Abuse of inside information may be punished with imprisonment from one to six years and a fine between EUR 20,000 and 3,000,000. Under certain circumstances this fine can be tripled or set at ten times the amount of the gain obtained from the crime.   **15.294**

Market manipulation occurs when a person disseminates false information, simulates transactions or carries out other deceitful conducts that may materially alter the price of financial instruments.[317] Market manipulation may be punished with imprisonment from one to six years and a fine between EUR 20,000 and 5,000,000. Under certain circumstances this fine can be tripled or set at ten times the amount of the gain obtained from the crime.   **15.295**

The assets or gains obtained through insider trading or market manipulation, as well as the assets used to commit these crimes, must be confiscated. If this is not possible, moneys and/or assets of an equivalent value may be confiscated.[318] In addition, insider trading and market manipulation may also result in disbarment from public offices, professions and management positions for a period between six months and two years, as well as the publication of the sentence in at least two national newspapers, one of which must be a financial newspaper.[319]   **15.296**

---

[315] ICC Article 2638.
[316] CFA Article 184.
[317] CFA Article 185.
[318] CFA Article 187.
[319] CFA Article 186.

15.3.14.3 Administrative sanctions

15.297   **15.3.14.3.1 Abuse of inside information and market manipulation**   Insider trading and market manipulation may be punished also as administrative offences (where relevant, in addition to the application of the criminal sanctions provided for the corresponding crime).

15.298   As regards the administrative offence of abuse of inside information, the unlawful conduct substantially coincides with the criminal one. The main difference is that the conduct may also be carried out by persons who merely are in possession of inside information and have knowledge or constructive knowledge of the inside nature of the information. The offence may be punished with an administrative fine varying between EUR 100,000 and EUR 15,000,000. Under certain circumstances this fine can be tripled or set at ten times the amount of the gain obtained from the offence. [320]

15.299   As regards the administrative offence of market manipulation, it partially differs from the criminal offence of market manipulation. The offence may be punished with an administrative fine varying from EUR 100,000 to EUR 25,000,000 (subject to the usual possible increase) and consists in the following conduct:

- dissemination through the media of information and/or rumours providing false or misleading indications regarding financial instruments;
- transactions and/or sale or purchase orders that provide false or misleading indications concerning the offer, demand and/or price of financial instruments;
- transactions and/or sale or purchase orders (including concerted ones) that may set the market price of financial instruments at an artificial level;
- transactions and/or purchase or sale orders through artifices or deceit; or
- artifices that provide false or misleading indications regarding the offer, demand or price of financial instruments.[321]

15.300   In addition to the administrative fines, the above administrative offences may be sanctioned with the temporary suspension (between two months and three years) of the integrity requirements required to discharge certain offices or functions, as well as temporary disbarment from management or supervisory positions in issuers.[322]

15.301   In imposing the administrative sanctions described in this paragraph, CONSOB may avail itself of investigation and procedural tools that are more stringent and powerful than those otherwise available to it.[323]

---

[320] CFA Article 187-*bis*.
[321] CFA Article 187-*ter*.
[322] CFA Article 187-*quater*.
[323] CFA Articles 187-*septes* and *octies*.

15.3.14.3.2 Violations of certain disclosure obligations Any person who does **15.302**
not comply with a request from CONSOB or delays the carrying out of its functions is subject to an administrative fine between EUR 50,000 and 1,000,000
(unless the conduct is punished pursuant to Article 2638 of the ICC, as described
in Section 15.3.14.2.1 above).[324]

Issuers or other entities or persons required to disclose regulated information, or **15.303**
otherwise comply with disclosure obligations, including, without limitation,
those relating to inside information, extraordinary transactions, compensation
plans, periodic financial reporting, registries of insiders and internal dealing transactions, are subject to an administrative fine between EUR 5,000 and EUR
500,000 in case of non-compliance with said obligations.[325]

The omission to disclose major holdings or shareholders' agreements, the viola- **15.304**
tion of the voting rights suspension connected thereto and non-compliance with
cross-ownerships restrictions are subject to an administrative fine between EUR
25,000 and EUR 2,500,000.[326]

15.3.14.4 *Administrative liability of companies*

Pursuant to Legislative Decree No 231 of 8 June 2001, in case of commission of **15.305**
certain crimes by qualified personnel of a company (including its directors, executives, representatives or employees) in the company's interest or to its advantage,
an administrative fine may be levied on the company (in addition to those imposed
on the perpetrators). Such crimes include, *inter alia*, the abuse of inside information and market manipulation,[327] as well as fraudulent corporate communications to the detriment of a company, its shareholders or its creditors, and frustration
of supervisory functions of authorities.

In order to avoid administrative liability, companies must adopt adequate com- **15.306**
pliance programmes aimed at preventing the commission of these crimes and
appoint a compliance officer or body. Although failure to adopt such programmes
is not sanctioned *per se*, the Tribunal of Milan recently established that the
adoption of an adequate organizational programme is part of the directors' duty
of care.[328]

---

[324] CFA Article 187-*quinquiesdecies*.
[325] CFA Article 193.1.
[326] CFA Article 193.2, pursuant to which if the delay in disclosing major holdings does not
exceed two months the applicable fine is between EUR 5,000 and EUR 500,000.
[327] Pursuant to CFA Article 187-*quinquies*, administrative fines may be levied on issuers also in
case of administrative offences of market abuse or market manipulation carried out by their qualified personnel.
[328] Tribunal of Milan, judgment No 1774, of 13 February 2008.

15.3.15 Corporate governance

15.3.15.1 Overview

15.307   In addition to being subject to the ICC rules (applicable to all Italian companies), [329] the CFA and the IR, the corporate governance of Italian issuers of shares admitted to trading on a regulated market in Italy is also governed by the corporate governance codes drawn up by operating companies or trade associations.

15.308   In this section, we will briefly outline certain significant corporate governance rules applicable to issuers of shares admitted to trading on a regulated market operated by Borsa, as well as certain recommendations applicable to them pursuant to the Corporate Governance Code.

15.309   In 2004, a wide-ranging reform of Italian corporate law came into force and brought about significant changes to the corporate governance rules of joint stock companies (the corporate form adopted by most issuers). With effect from 1 January 2004, issuers may adopt one of the following corporate governance models:[330]

- the traditional Italian model, with a board of directors (*'consiglio di amministrazione'*) and a board of statutory auditors (*'collegio sindacale'*), which was the only corporate governance model in existence prior to 2004;
- the two-tier model, with a management board entrusted with management responsibilities (*'consiglio di gestione'*) and a supervisory board entrusted mainly with control and supervisory responsibilities, appointing and removing the members of the management board and approving the company's annual financial statements (*'consiglio di sorveglianza'*); or
- the one-tier model, with a single board of directors and a management control committee (*'comitato per il controllo sulla gestione'*) within the board of directors, composed of independent non-executive directors.

15.310   As the traditional model of corporate governance is still, by far, the most widespread, for ease of reference this section will focus on the rules (and recommendations) applicable to issuers that adopt this model instead of the one-tier or the two-tier models.

15.3.15.2 Board of directors—duties and functioning

15.311   15.3.15.2.1 **Pursuant to the ICC, the CFA and the IR**   Directors are appointed by the ordinary shareholders' meeting for up to three years. The board of directors has full powers of ordinary and extraordinary administration of an issuer's business and may perform all acts it deems appropriate to achieve the issuer's corporate

---

[329]   Corporate governance rules are of course also contained in each issuer's by-laws, which may generally not depart from the above-mentioned statutory or regulatory provisions.
[330]   See ICC Articles 2380 et seq., as well as CFA Articles 147-*ter* et seq.

purpose, except for the actions reserved by applicable law or the issuer's by-laws to a vote of the shareholders at an ordinary or extraordinary shareholders' meeting.

The board of directors may not delegate some of its responsibilities, including those relating to the approval of the draft stand-alone financial statements or the consolidated financial statements, the approval of merger or split-up plans, as well as, if any such power is delegated to the board of directors by the extraordinary shareholders' meeting, share capital increases or the issuance of convertible bonds. **15.312**

The board of directors may generally delegate powers to one or more managing directors ('*amministratori delegati*'), and/or to an executive committee, and/or to one or more ad hoc committees of directors, determine the nature and scope of the delegated powers of each director and committee and revoke such powers at any time. **15.313**

The executive directors prepare the issuer's strategic, industrial and financial plans, ensure, under the supervision of the board of directors, that the issuer's organizational and accounting structure is adequate, and have periodic reporting obligations vis-à-vis the board of directors and the board of statutory auditors.[331] **15.314**

At least every quarter, the directors must report to the board of statutory auditors on their activities, the issuer's most significant transactions on a consolidated basis, and related-party transactions.[332] **15.315**

Directors having an interest in a proposed transaction must disclose their interest to the board, even if it does not conflict with the company's interest. The interested director is not required to abstain from voting on the resolution approving the transaction, but the resolution must state explicitly the reasons for, and the benefit to the company from, the approved transaction. If these provisions are not complied with, or if the transaction would not have been approved without the vote of the interested director, the resolution may be challenged by a director or by the board of statutory auditors if the approved transaction may be prejudicial to the company. A managing director having any such interest in a proposed transaction within the scope of his powers must solicit prior board approval of such transaction. The interested director may be held liable for damages resulting from a resolution adopted in breach of the above rules. **15.316**

Issuers must adopt a slate voting system to appoint the board of directors. Lists may be presented by shareholders representing 0.5% to 4.5% of the issuer's share capital essentially depending on the issuer's market capitalization. Lists must be published in advance of the shareholders' meeting together with the directors' **15.317**

---

[331] ICC Article 2381.
[332] CFA Article 150.

curricula vitae and an indication of those who may be regarded as independent. At least one director must be elected from a minority list (if presented).[333] A list is considered a 'minority list' if it is not connected in any way to the shareholders presenting or voting the list that receives the majority of votes. CONSOB recommended that the shareholders presenting a 'minority list' certify the absence of any connection with the shareholders that individually or jointly control the issuer, or else explain the reasons why specific relationships with the controlling shareholders may be regarded as immaterial for purposes of the above rule.[334]

15.318   Directors may be removed from office at any time by the vote of shareholders at an ordinary shareholders' meeting although, if removed without cause, they may claim damages against the issuer. Directors may resign at any time by written notice to the board of directors and to the chairman of the board of statutory auditors. The board of directors can appoint substitute directors, subject to the approval of the board of statutory auditors, to fill any vacancies and to serve until the next ordinary shareholders' meeting. If more than half of the directors appointed at a shareholders' meeting cease their functions, the shareholders' meeting is immediately convened to appoint a new board of directors.

15.319   Directors' compensation is determined by the ordinary shareholders' meeting. The board of directors, however, in consultation with the board of statutory auditors, may provide for additional compensation of the executive directors.

15.320   **15.3.15.2.2 Certain recommendations of the Corporate Governance Code**
The Corporate Governance Code recommends that the board of directors of an issuer should, amongst other things:

- review and approve the strategic, industrial and financial plans of the issuer and its group, as well as the corporate governance system and the overall group structure;
- assess the adequacy of the issuer's and the group's organizational, administrative and accounting structures as implemented by the executive directors, with particular reference to the internal control system and to the management of conflict of interests;
- establish at least a compensation committee and an internal control committee, which, similarly to other internal committees that the board may choose to appoint, must be composed of at least three directors, should have access to the issuer's resources, be provided with an adequate budget and be able to appoint external advisors;
- grant committees adequate financial resources to carry out their functions;

---

[333]   CFA Article 147-*ter*.1 and 3.
[334]   CONSOB Notice No DEM/9017893 of 26 February 2009.

- determine, upon consultation with the compensation committee and the board of statutory auditors, the executive directors' compensation;
- assess the issuer's business and operations, taking into account the information received from the executive directors and comparing actual versus planned results;
- review and approve, including by issuing guidelines, the issuer's and the group's most significant transactions;
- carry out, at least once a year, an appraisal of the size, composition and functioning of the board of directors and of its committees;
- issue guidelines as to the maximum number of offices directors may hold in other issuers, as well as in financial companies, banks, insurance companies or sizeable companies;
- adopt measures and procedures aimed at ensuring that transactions in which a director has a personal interest, as well as related-party transactions, be resolved upon and carried out in a transparent and proper manner; and
- adopt procedures for the internal circulation of information and its disclosure to the public, with particular regard to price-sensitive information.

15.3.15.3 *Board of directors —composition and independence*

15.3.15.3.1 Pursuant to the CFA   All directors must satisfy certain integrity **15.321** requirements; at least one director, or two in case of boards composed by more than seven members, must be independent according to the independence requirements set forth under the CFA for statutory auditors.[335]

15.3.15.3.2 Certain recommendations of the Corporate Governance Code **15.322** The Corporate Governance Code recommends that boards be comprised of an adequate number of non-executive directors. It further recommends that an adequate number of non-executive directors be independent, that their independence be assessed by the board at least once a year and disclosed to the public in the issuer's annual corporate governance report. Independent directors should meet at least once a year without the other directors.

Under the Corporate Governance Code, directors may not be regarded as **15.323** independent, *inter alia*, when:

- they directly or indirectly control the issuer or may exercise a significant influence over it or are parties to shareholders' agreements through which one or more persons may exercise control or a significant influence over the issuer;
- during the three previous financial years, they have been executive directors or top managers of the issuer, its controlling entity or a strategic subsidiary;

---

[335] CFA Articles 147-*quinquies* and 147-*ter*.4. See Section 15.3.15.6.1, below, for the statutory auditors' independence requirements.

- in the previous financial year, they have had—directly or indirectly—a signifi-cant commercial, financial or professional relationship with (a) the issuer, a subsidiary, or their respective executive directors or top managers, or (b) an entity which, alone or together with other parties to a shareholders' agreement, controls the issuer, or (in case of companies) their respective executive directors or top managers. The board of directors must assess the significance of the rela-tionship on case-by-case basis, including with regard to relationships which, although not economic in nature, may nonetheless be particularly relevant for the interested party;[336]
- they are, or have been in the previous three financial years, employees of any of the entities mentioned in the previous point;
- they receive, or have received in the three preceding financial years, from the issuer, its controlling entity or a subsidiary, significant additional compensation to the base compensation of non-executive directors, including by way of incen-tive plans;
- they have been in office for more than nine of the last twelve years; or
- they are executive directors in a company in which an executive director of the issuer is a director.

15.324 Finally, the Corporate Governance Code recommends that the roles of chairman and chief executive officer not be entrusted to the same person. If not, or if the issuer's chairman also controls the issuer, the board of directors should appoint a lead independent director to serve as point-person to coordinate and voice the non-executive and the independent directors, including by convening meetings of independent directors.

15.3.15.4 The internal control system

15.325 According to the Corporate Governance Code, the board of directors is respon-sible for the issuer's internal control system, consisting of the rules, procedures and organizational structures that allow the issuer to conduct its business in a proper and efficient manner through adequate identification, management and monitoring of the issuer's main risks. The board must set forth the issuer's internal control system's guidelines and assess periodically its adequacy and effectiveness. To this end the board should appoint (i) an internal control committee, (ii) a director in charge of supervising the internal control system, and (iii) one or more internal control officers.

---

[336] On 26 February 2009 CONSOB released for public comment a draft Notice containing recommendations aimed at reinforcing disclosure to the market of the criteria used and facts reviewed in the course of such assessment. On 28 April 2009 CONSOB acknowledged Borsa's intention to amend the Corporate Governance Code to meet CONSOB's recommendations, and the approval of the above-mentioned draft Notice was thus put on hold.

The Corporate Governance Code recommends that the internal control commit- **15.326** tee be composed of non-executive directors, the majority of whom should be independent. Moreover, at least one member should have adequate financial and accounting experience. Pursuant to the Corporate Governance Code, the internal control committee, among other things:

- assists the board in: (i) setting out the guidelines of the internal control system so as to enable the issuer and its subsidiaries to correctly identify, measure, monitor and manage the main risks; (ii) determining criteria which ensure that such risks are compatible with the sound management of the issuer; (iii) assessing, at least once a year, the adequacy and effectiveness of the internal control system; and (iv) describing the key elements of the internal control system in the issuer's annual corporate governance report;
- evaluates, along with the executive in charge of preparing the issuer's financial statements and the external auditors, the correct implementation of accounting principles and their consistency for purposes of drafting the consolidated financial statements;
- reviews the work plan prepared by the internal control officers and their periodic reports;
- evaluates the external auditors' work plan and reviews their reports and management letters;
- supervises the effectiveness of the audit process; and
- reports to the board at least every six months, when the annual financial statements and half-yearly reports are approved, on the activities performed as well as on the adequacy of the internal control system.

The Corporate Governance Code recommends that the internal control officer **15.327** not report to, or be responsible for, operating divisions, and report only to the internal control committee, the board of statutory auditors and the director in charge of supervising the internal control system. The internal control officer should verify that the issuer's internal control system is at all times adequate, fully operational and running and should report periodically on her activities and the way risks are managed.

15.3.15.5 *Compensation of directors and top executives*

The Corporate Governance Code recommends that a significant part of the com- **15.328** pensation of executive directors and executives with strategic responsibilities be tied to the issuer's economic results and/or the achievement of set targets or objectives, while the compensation of non-executive directors should not be tied to the issuer's economic results and should be proportional to the tasks performed by them.

The Corporate Governance Code further recommends that issuers establish a **15.329** remuneration committee, composed of non-executive directors, the majority of whom should be independent. Pursuant to the Corporate Governance Code, the remuneration committee, among other things:

- makes proposals to the board concerning the executive directors' compensation and monitors the implementation of the board's decisions;
- periodically assesses compensation criteria for managers with key responsibilities within the issuer and its subsidiaries, and monitors their implementation; and
- makes proposals to the board concerning the adoption of stock option or stock grant plans.

15.330 As outlined under Section 15.3.6 above, compensation plans based on financial instruments are subject to specific disclosure and approval obligations.

15.3.15.6 *Statutory auditors*

15.331 **15.3.15.6.1 Pursuant to the ICC, the CFA and the IR** Statutory auditors are elected by the ordinary shareholders' meeting for a term of three financial years, may be reappointed, and may be removed only for cause, with the approval of the court having jurisdiction over the issuer.[337] The board of statutory auditors consists of no fewer than three statutory auditors and no fewer than two alternate auditors who automatically replace effective statutory auditors who resign or otherwise cease from their functions.[338]

15.332 Statutory auditors are elected through a slate voting system, in accordance with rules similar to those applicable to directors. At least one auditor must be elected from a minority list (if any such list is validly presented) and the chairman of the board of statutory auditors must be chosen among the auditors elected from a minority list.[339]

15.333 The board of statutory auditors is responsible for monitoring the issuer's activities and, in particular, it supervises:[340]

- compliance with laws and regulations, as well as the by-laws;
- compliance with principles of sound management;
- the adequacy of the organizational structure, the internal control system, as well as the administrative and accounting system;
- the implementation of applicable corporate governance codes; and
- the adequacy of the issuer's directives to its subsidiaries concerning intra-group circulation of information.

---

[337] ICC Article 2400.
[338] CFA Article 148.1.
[339] CFA Article 148.2 and 2-*bis*.
[340] CFA Article 149.

The board of statutory auditors is required to meet at least once every 90 days. **15.334** In addition, statutory auditors attend the meetings of the board of directors, the executive committee and of the shareholders. The statutory auditors may call shareholders' meetings or meetings of the board of directors or the executive committee and carry out inspections, as well as exchange information with the supervisory boards of subsidiaries or with the external auditors.

The board of statutory auditors may report to the competent court serious breaches **15.335** of their duties by the issuer's directors that may be prejudicial to the issuer or to its subsidiaries. The board of statutory auditors must report to the shareholders' meeting convened to approve the annual stand-alone financial statements on its review activities and on any irregularities detected during its review activities. It must also promptly report any irregularities to CONSOB.

An issuer's statutory auditors may not serve in the supervisory boards of more than **15.336** four other issuers and may not hold more than a certain number of executive or non-executive positions with other companies, all of which must be disclosed to CONSOB and to the market.[341]

All statutory auditors must be independent, as well as satisfy certain integrity **15.337** and professional requirements.[342] In particular, the following categories of people may not be regarded as independent, and therefore not serve as statutory auditors:

- spouses, family members or close relatives of the issuer's directors;
- directors of the issuer's subsidiaries, of its controlling entities or of other companies of the group, or spouses, family members or close relatives of such directors; and
- persons who have an employment, professional or economic relationship with the issuer, its subsidiaries or controlling entities or companies of the same group, or with any of the issuer's directors or with any of the persons mentioned in the preceding point, if such relationship may prejudice their independence.

15.3.15.6.2 Certain recommendations of the Corporate Governance Code **15.338** The Corporate Governance Code recommends that statutory auditors act autonomously and independently, including *vis-à-vis* the shareholders that have elected them.[343] Statutory auditors should meet the same independence requirements set forth in the Corporate Governance Code for directors. The board of statutory auditors should assess the independence of its members at least once a year

---

[341] IR Article 144-*terdecies*.
[342] CFA Article 148.3 and 4.
[343] Corporate Governance Code Article 10.P.2.

and disclose its findings in the issuer's annual corporate governance report.[344] Each statutory auditor should inform the other statutory auditors and the chairman of the board of directors of any personal interest such statutory auditor may have in a specific transaction.[345]

15.3.15.7 *External auditors*

15.339 Issuers must appoint a firm of external auditors to verify (i) during the financial year, that the accounting records are correctly kept and accurately reflect the issuer's activities, and (ii) that the financial statements correspond to the accounting records, as verified by the external auditors, and comply with applicable rules.[346]

15.340 External auditors express their opinion on the stand-alone (as well as consolidated, if applicable) financial statements in a report that may be consulted by the shareholders prior to the annual shareholders' meeting. The opinion may be clean, qualified or negative, or the external auditors state they are not in a position to express an opinion. If the opinion is negative, or no opinion may be given, the external auditor must immediately notify CONSOB.

15.341 Although issuers are not under a statutory or regulatory obligation to ask external auditors to review their half-yearly financial statements (on a stand-alone or consolidated basis, as applicable), CONSOB recommends that they do so; in this case, external auditors carry out a limited review.[347] No limited review is generally conducted on quarterly management statements.

15.342 External auditors are appointed by the shareholders' meeting for a period of nine years and a 'cooling off' period is mandated.[348] External auditors must satisfy stringent independence requirements, including as to their network and the partners in charge of the issuer's audit. Indeed, among other things, independence of the external auditor must be evaluated with regard to the 'network' of companies to which the external auditor belongs.

15.343 External auditors may obtain documents and information from the directors as well as carry out inspections, and must inform CONSOB and the board of statutory auditors without delay of any irregularity they ascertain during their activities.[349]

---

[344] Corporate Governance Code Article 10.C.2.
[345] Corporate Governance Code Article 10.C.4.
[346] CFA Articles 155 and 156.
[347] See Section 15.3.7.4 above.
[348] CFA Article 160 of the CFA and IR Article 149-*bis* et seq.
[349] CFA Article 155.

Pursuant to the Corporate Governance Code, the board of statutory auditors **15.344** should monitor the external auditors' compliance with applicable laws and regulations, as well as their independence, including with reference to the non-audit services provided to the issuer and to its subsidiaries by all entities that are part of the auditors' network.[350]

15.3.15.8 *Shareholders' meetings*

15.3.15.8.1 Pursuant to the ICC, the CFA and the IR   Shareholders are enti- **15.345** tled to attend and vote at ordinary and extraordinary shareholders' meetings. Votes may be cast personally or by proxy. Shareholders' meetings may be called by the board of directors (or the board of statutory auditors) and must be called if requested by holders of at least 10% of the voting share capital. Shareholders are not entitled to request that a shareholders' meeting be convened to resolve upon matters which as a matter of law must be resolved upon on the basis of a proposal, plan or report by the board of directors. If the shareholders' meeting is not called despite the request by shareholders and such refusal is unjustified, the competent court may call the meeting.[351]

Ordinary shareholders' meetings resolve upon: **15.346**

- the approval of the annual stand-alone financial statements;
- the appointment (and dismissal) of the directors, the statutory auditors, the chairman of the board of statutory auditors and the external auditors;
- the compensation of the directors, the statutory auditors (unless established in the by-laws) and the external auditors;
- the suits against the directors and the statutory auditors; and
- the other matters provided by the law, including any authorizations required by the by-laws for specific transactions by management.

Shareholders' meetings must be convened at least once a year for the approval of **15.347** the annual stand-alone financial statements and the meeting must be convened within 120 days after the end of the financial year to which such financial statements relate.[352]

Extraordinary shareholders' meetings may be called to resolve upon capital increases or decreases, mergers, split-ups, dissolutions, appointment of receivers, other amendments to the by-laws and similar extraordinary actions.

---

[350] Corporate Governance CodeArticle 10.C.5.
[351] ICC Article 2367.
[352] CFA Article 154-*ter*.1.

15.348   Shareholders collectively holding at least 2.5% of the voting share capital of an issuer can add matters to the agenda of meetings, except for those meetings called to resolve on matters for which a director's proposal or report is necessary.[353]

15.349   **15.3.15.8.2 Certain recommendations of the Corporate Governance Code** Under the Corporate Governance Code, the board of directors should take initiatives aimed both at ensuring that shareholder participation at shareholders' meetings is as broad as possible and at facilitating the exercise of shareholder rights.[354] Furthermore, the board of directors should ensure easy and timely shareholder access to relevant information regarding the issuer, with a view to allowing an informed exercise of shareholder rights. This should be done by providing a specific section in the issuer's website where such information is made available.

15.350   The Corporate Governance Code also recommends that the board of directors propose the adoption of rules governing shareholders' meetings that are aimed at ensuring that the meetings are proper and orderly, as well as at guaranteeing the right of each shareholder to intervene in the discussion.[355] Finally, the board of directors should appoint a person in charge of relations with the shareholders.[356]

15.3.15.9 Compliance with the Corporate Governance Code

15.351   Issuers must publish annually a corporate governance report disclosing the degree of compliance with the Code of Corporate Governance, as well as indicating where the Code of Corporate Governance may be retrieved (the same applies, *mutatis mutandis*, to issuers of transferable securities admitted to trading on regulated markets other than those operated by Borsa, with regard to the applicable codes of conduct). If an issuer chooses not to follow one or more recommendations of the Corporate Governance Code, the corporate governance report must disclose the reasons for this choice. The report must also describe the issuer's corporate governance practices, including those not deriving from any statutory or regulatory obligations.[357]

15.352   In the same report, issuers must disclose: (i) the main characteristics of existing risk management and internal audit systems used in relation to the financial reporting process; (ii) the functioning of the shareholders' meeting, its main powers, shareholder rights and their terms of exercise, if different from those envisaged

---

[353] CFA Article 126-*bis*.
[354] Corporate Governance Code Article 11.P.1.
[355] Corporate Governance Code Article 11.C.5.
[356] Corporate Governance Code Article 11.C.2.
[357] CFA Articles 123-*bis*.2 and 124-*ter* of the CFA, as well as IR Article 89-*bis*.

by legal and regulatory provisions; and (iii) the composition and duties of the management and supervisory corporate bodies and committees.

Directors, members of the supervisory bodies and general managers who fail to **15.353** disclose the issuer's adherence to the Corporate Governance Code (the same applies, *mutatis mutandis*, to other codes of conduct applicable) are sanctioned by CONSOB with a fine between EUR 10,000 and 300,000, and the decision imposing the fine must be published in at least two daily national newspapers, one of which must be a financial newspaper.[358]

---

[358] CFA Article 192-*bis*.

16

LUXEMBOURG

16.1 Listing Securities in Luxembourg

16.1.1 Listing on the Luxembourg Stock Exchange

16.01   The Société de la Bourse de Luxembourg is a commercial company established in 1928 which started to operate a market in securities, the Luxembourg Stock Exchange ('LSE') in May 1929. From the outset, the LSE was geared to serve a global market.

16.02   The LSE is best known for its listing of debt securities. In 2008, it had 32,933 different issues of debt securities listed. This compares to 25,087 on the Irish Stock Exchange, 15,519 on the London Stock Exchange and 4,044 on NYSE Euronext.[1] A very popular feature is the listing of debt securities under debt

---

[1] Source: http://www.world-exchanges.org (World Federation of Stock Exchanges). The source for all subsequent data featured in this Section is the LSE.

issuance programmes. In 2007, there were 466 debt issuance programmes in operation on the LSE and more than 88% of new debt listings made in 2008 were issued under a programme.

Another important segment of the LSE is represented by the listing of shares or units of investment funds. In 2007, the LSE listed securities from 522 issuers representing 7,372 quotation lines (8,166 in 2008). In addition the Global Depository Receipts ('GDR') segment is very active with 222 GDRs listed on 31 March 2009 with issuers mainly from Asia (for instance, Indian issuers represented 63% of GDR issues in 2007). Finally, there were 7,719 warrants and certificates listed on the LSE at the end of 2008. **16.03**

16.1.2 The CSSF

The supervisory authority over the financial sector is the *Commission de Surveillance* **16.04**
du Secteur Financier (hereafter the 'CSSF'), which was established by the Law of 23 December 1998.[2] The CSSF took over the supervisory functions of the banking, investment firms' and investment funds' sector from the Luxembourg Central Bank. It also took over the functions of supervision of the capital markets from the Stock Exchange Supervisory Commission (*Commissariat aux Bourses*). Under the Law of 23 December 1998, the CSSF's duty is *inter alia* to monitor the markets in financial instruments in Luxembourg and those who are active in such markets.

It is the competent authority for the purposes of the Luxembourg laws imple- **16.05**
menting the Prospectus Directive,[3] the Market Abuse Directive,[4] the Transparency Directive[5] and the Takeover Directive.[6]

The CSSF has investigative and injunctive powers. It can take regulatory action **16.06**
and is empowered to impose penalties.

16.1.3 Luxembourg Stock Exchange

The LSE operates two markets: the Regulated Market of the LSE ('Regulated **16.07**
Market' or 'Bourse de Luxembourg Market') and the Euro MTF market.

---

[2] Law of 23 December 1998 creating a supervisory commission of the financial sector.
[3] Council Directive (EC) 2003/71 on the prospectus to be published when securities are offered to the public or admitted to trading and amending Directive 2001/34/EC [2003] OJ L22/28.
[4] Council Directive (EC) 2003/6 on insider dealing and market manipulation (market abuse) [2003] OJ L96/16.
[5] Council Directive (EC) 2004/109 on transparency requirements [2004] OJ L390/38.
[6] Council Directive (EC) 2004/25 on takeover bids [2004] OJ L142/12.

16.08   Prior to the implementation of the Prospectus Directive via the law of 10 July 2005 on prospectuses for securities (the 'Prospectus Law')[7], the LSE carried out the review of prospectuses for admission to listing on the LSE, with the exception of prospectuses of investment funds registered with the CSSF which were reviewed and approved by the CSSF. After implementation of the Prospectus Law, the role of the LSE is now limited to admitting securities to trading on its regulated market.

16.09   The LSE continues to be the authority approving prospectuses which are prepared in connection with a listing on the LSE's Euro MTF market.

16.10   The Regulated Market and the Euro MTF market fall under different regulatory regimes and listing on one or the other of such markets entails different consequences for the relevant issuer. However, the trading system and the market rules and the pre- and post-trade transparency rules are identical.

16.1.3.1 *The Regulated Market*

16.11   The Regulated Market of the LSE is registered on the EU list of regulated markets provided for by the MiFID.[8] Issuers who are listed on the Regulated Market will be subject to the continuing obligations under the law of 11 January 2008 relating to transparency obligations and implementing the Transparency Directive (the 'Transparency Law').

16.12   The admission to trading of securities on the Regulated Market requires a Prospectus Directive compliant prospectus (except for the securities which are outside the scope of the Prospectus Directive).

16.13   Admission to the Regulated Market allows issuers to passport their prospectuses approved in connection with such listing into other EEA member states for purposes of making a public offer or obtaining a second listing.

16.1.3.2 *The Euro MTF Market*

16.14   The Euro MTF market operated by the LSE constitutes a multilateral trading facility for the purposes of the MiFID. The Euro MTF market is a market for securities which are not generally the subject of a retail offering but are typically offered only to professional or institutional investors.

16.15   It was launched in July 2005 to satisfy the needs of those issuers which do not seek a gateway to other European markets or do not prepare financial information in

---

[7] Law of 10 July 2005 on prospectuses for securities, implementing Council Directive (EC) 2003/71.

[8] Council Directive (EC) 2004/39 on markets in financial instruments [2004] OJ L145/1.

accordance with International Financial Reporting Standards ('IFRS') or, in the case of non-EU issuers, in accordance with accounting standards equivalent to IFRS.

The Euro MTF is not an EU regulated market and is therefore outside the scope of the Prospectus Directive and Transparency Directive. **16.16**

Securities listed on the Euro MTF fulfil the listing criteria for securities to be eligible for Euro system operations at the European Central Bank. They also meet the listing requirement for being part of the portfolio of Luxembourg investment funds with UCITS status. The Euro MTF is a recognized market for listing by UK entities in order to achieve certain tax treatments. **16.17**

The LSE approves the prospectuses for admission to the Euro MTF market, in accordance with the rules and regulations of the LSE (the 'LSE Rules'). The LSE Rules provide the LSE with the necessary flexibility so that in appropriate circumstances, the requirements can be adapted to accommodate an issuer's particular situation. **16.18**

16.1.4 Legislative overview

16.1.4.1 MiFID law

The law of 13 July 2007 relating to the markets in financial instruments (the 'MiFID Law') governs the establishment and operation of regulated markets and multilateral trading facilities in Luxembourg. **16.19**

The Grand-Ducal Regulation of 13 July 2007 concerning the official list of financial instruments contains the admissibility rules for securities to be admitted to the official list of the markets operated by the LSE. For equity issuers, these include, *inter alia*, the requirements as to minimum capitalization, how long the issuer must have been in existence, the minimum distribution of shares in the public and free transferability of the shares. For debt issuers, requirements concern, *inter alia*, the minimum size of an issue and the free transferability of the debt securities. **16.20**

16.1.4.2 Prospectus Law

The Prospectus Law implements the Prospectus Directive and applies to the prospectus to be drawn up in connection with offers to the public of securities within the scope of the Prospectus Directive and/or their admission to trading on a regulated market. It also applies to simplified prospectuses to be drawn up in connection with offers to the public and/or admission to listing on a regulated market of securities outside the scope of the Prospectus Directive.[9] It does not apply to prospectuses to be drawn up in connection with a listing on the Euro MTF. **16.21**

---

[9] With the exception of units or shares issued by open-ended investment funds (see Section 16.1.4.7).

16.1.4.3 Transparency Law

16.22 The Transparency Law, together with the Grand-Ducal Regulation of 11 January 2008[10] implementing Commission Directive 2007/14/CE,[11] provides for the continuing obligations of issuers whose securities are admitted on a regulated market. It also contains the rules governing shareholder notifications derived from the Transparency Directive.

16.1.4.4 Market Abuse Law

16.23 The law of 9 May 2006 relating to market abuse (the 'Market Abuse Law')[12] implements the Market Abuse Directive and related EU Commission directives. The prohibitions of the Market Abuse Law regarding insider dealing and market manipulation apply irrespective whether securities are admitted on the regulated market of the LSE or on the Euro MTF market.[13]

16.24 Other rules under the Market Abuse Law applicable to market participants and issuers do not apply in case of securities admitted to the Euro MTF only.

16.25 These other rules include for instance the requirement for an issuer to keep insider lists[14] or the obligation on directors and other persons discharging managerial responsibilities or certain persons connected to them to declare dealings in the shares of the issuer.[15] The obligation to disclose inside information under the Market Abuse Law[16] is also not applicable to issuers listed on the Euro MTF who fall under the disclosure rules regarding significant information provided for by the LSE Rules.[17]

16.1.4.5 Takeover Law

16.26 The Luxembourg law on takeover bids[18] implements the Takeover Directive. It is not applicable in the case of a bid on non-European issuers whether they are listed on the Regulated Market of the LSE or on the Euro MTF.

---

[10] Grand-Ducal Regulation of 11 January 2008 concerning transparency obligations.

[11] Council Directive (EC) 2007/14 laying down detailed rules for the implementation of certain provisions of Directive 2004/109/EC on the harmonization of transparency requirements in relation to information about issuers whose securities are admitted to trading on a regulated market [2007] OJ L69/27.

[12] Law of 9 May 2006 relating to market abuse, implementing Council Directive (EC) 2003/6.

[13] Market Abuse Law Article 4 .

[14] Market Abuse Law Article 16 (2).

[15] Market Abuse Law Article 17 (1).

[16] Market Abuse Law Article 14.

[17] LSE Rules 1001–1005 .

[18] Law of 19May 2006 on takeover bids, implementing Council Directive (EC) 2004/25.

16.1.4.6 *Law on the Financial Sector*

The Luxembourg law on the financial sector[19] governs the licensing and supervision of banks and of investment firms providing investment services. This law has implemented the part of MiFID governing and regulating the provision of investment services with regard to securities.

16.27

16.1.4.7 *The Investment Fund Law*

The law on undertakings for collective investment (the 'Investment Fund Law')[20] implements the EU UCITS Directive.[21] It also regulates non-UCITS funds.

16.28

The prospectuses for investment funds registered with the CSSF who apply for a listing on the Regulated Market and who are outside the scope of the Prospectus Directive (i.e. open-ended funds), are approved by the CSSF. Whilst technically speaking, the LSE is the competent authority to approve the prospectus of an investment fund registered with the CSSF for the purpose of a listing on the Euro MTF; the LSE will in practice accept the prospectus approved by the CSSF under the Investment Fund Law.

16.29

16.1.4.8 *LSE Rules*

The LSE Rules deal with the admission of securities to trading on the markets of the LSE and admission of such securities to the official list of the LSE. In addition to the continuing obligations existing under the Transparency Law and the Market Abuse Law, the LSE Rules provide for certain additional continuing obligations[22] for issuers whose securities are admitted to the Regulated Market which are more technical and relate to the proper operation of the market.[23]

16.30

The LSE Rules provide for the content requirements of prospectuses to be prepared in connection with a listing on the Euro MTF. The LSE Rules contain specific ongoing disclosure obligations for issuers whose securities are listed on the Euro MTF only.[24]

16.31

---

[19] Law of 5 April 1993 on the financial sector.

[20] Law of 20 December 2002 relating to undertakings for collective investments, implementing Council Directive (EEC) 85/611.

[21] Council Directive (EEC) 85/611 on the coordination of laws, regulations and administrative provisions relating to undertakings for collective investment in transferable securities [1985] OJ L375/3.

[22] These additional ongoing obligations relate to information such as (without limitation): any amendment to rights attached to securities, any merger or division of the issuer, any change of transfer or paying agent, any information in relation to dividends, any change of activity or amendment to the articles of association of the issuer or the convening notices for meetings of holders of securities.

[23] LSE Rules 901 to 909.

[24] LSE Rules 1001 to 1005.

16.32 Finally, the LSE Rules govern the operation of the markets of the LSE including the membership of those markets, trading rules and rules of conduct.

16.1.4.9 *Other provisions*

16.33 Luxembourg company law contains criminal law provisions dealing with certain fraudulent activities relating to securities.[25] The following criminal offences would be applicable to any foreign issuer intending to list securities in Luxembourg:

- the escroquerie (fraud) in connection with the payment or subscription of securities is punished by a jail term of one month to five years and a fine of EUR 251 to EUR 30,000;[26] and
- any person who, by any fraudulent means, has caused or attempted to cause the price of securities to fall or rise, shall be subject to a jail term of one month to two years and a fine of EUR 5,000 to EUR 125,000.[27]

16.1.4.10 *CSSF guidance*

16.34 Following a recent change to the Constitution of the Grand Duchy of Luxembourg and a law of 24 October 2008,[28] the CSSF now has the power to adopt regulations (règlements) within the scope of its attributions and missions. These regulations will have the same legislative authority as regulations from the Luxembourg Government adopted by delegation of law. To date the CSSF has not used this power (contrary to the Luxembourg Central Bank, which has obtained an identical power).

16.35 The CSSF typically sets rules through CSSF circulars which are a key source for ascertaining the CSSF position. A number of circulars have been issued by the CSSF in connection with the financial markets' regulations referred to above, which are available on the CSSF website.[29]

16.36 In addition, with respect to the implementation of the Prospectus Law and the Transparency Law, the CSSF has published a list of 'Frequently Asked Questions' which offers guidance on specific issues.

16.37 Finally, an additional source of information consists in the yearly reports of the CSSF in which it may discuss its interpretation and views on regulatory matters. These reports are available on the CSSF website.

---

[25] Articles 164 and 165 of the law of 10 August 1915 on commercial companies, as amended.
[26] Criminal Code Article 496.
[27] Article 165 of the law of 10 August 1915 on commercial companies, as amended.
[28] Law of 24 October 2008 concerning the enhancement of the legislative framework of the Luxembourg financial centre.
[29] http://www.cssf.lu.

16.2 Listing Securities in Practice

16.2.1 The prospectus

16.2.1.1 Requirement for a prospectus

16.2.1.1.1 The requirement   Any person intending to make a *public offer* of securities[30] in Luxembourg must notify the CSSF in advance and must publish a prospectus (or, as the case may be, a simplified prospectus) which must be approved by the CSSF, unless it has been approved by the competent authority in the issuer's home member state, or an exemption is available.[31] Requirements in connection with an application are set out in the Prospectus Law and CSSF Circulars 05/210[32] and 05/226.[33]

16.38

The application to the CSSF needs to include a draft of the prospectus containing all information which, according to the particular nature of the issuer and of the securities offered to the public, is necessary to enable investors to make an informed assessment of the assets and liabilities, financial position, profit and losses, and prospects of the issuer and of any guarantor, and of the rights attached to such securities.[34] The application also needs to comprise any additional information which must be included in the prospectus but which has not yet been included in the submitted draft.

16.39

A prospectus for securities within the scope of the Prospectus Directive will need to contain a summary which must convey the essential characteristics and risks associated with the issuer, any guarantor and the relevant securities, unless the securities offered are wholesale debt securities i.e. securities having a denomination of at least EUR 50,000 (or its equivalent in another currency).[35] There is no requirement for a summary in case of a simplified prospectus for securities outside the scope of the Prospectus Directive. Any document incorporated by reference in the prospectus or simplified prospectus must also be filed with the CSSF.

16.40

No filing is required with the LSE in case of a public offer of securities.

16.41

The same requirements as detailed above will apply in the case of an *application for the admission* of securities, which are within the scope of the Prospectus Directive

16.42

---

[30] A public offer of securities is 'a communication to persons in any form and by any means, presenting sufficient information on the terms of the offer and the securities to be offered, so to enable an investor to decide to purchase or subscribe to these securities' (Article 2 (1) (d) of the Prospectus Directive, as implemented in Article 2 (1) (l) of the Prospectus Law).

[31] Prospectus Law Article 5.

[32] CSSF Circular 05/210 on the drawing-up of a simplified prospectus.

[33] CSSF Circular 05/226 on the general overview of the law on prospectuses for securities.

[34] Prospectus Law Article 8 (1).

[35] Prospectus Law Article 8 (2).

to *trading on the Regulated* Market of the LSE. In that case, a separate application for the admission will also need to be filed with the LSE.

16.43   The admission to listing on the Euro MTF requires the drawing-up of a prospectus to be approved by the LSE. There is in such case no filing with the CSSF unless those securities are also the subject of an offer to the public.

16.44   **16.2.1.1.2 Exemptions**   The Prospectus Law contains the same exemptions as the Prospectus Directive, both in case of a public offer[36] and in case of an admission to the Regulated Market.[37]

16.45   The LSE Rules contain a number of exemptions from an obligation to publish a prospectus in connection with a proposed listing on the Euro MTF as well as partial exemptions from the general content requirements under the LSE Rules.

16.46   **16.2.1.1.3 Takeover bids**   Where the consideration for a takeover bid on a Luxembourg company whose shares are admitted to a regulated market in the EU, consists of or comprises securities, the offer document to be prepared under the Takeover Directive will need to be supplemented by a securities prospectus governed by the Prospectus Directive. The rules of the Takeover Directive and the Prospectus Directive are not identical with regard to the determination of the jurisdiction whose competent authority will need to approve the offer document and the securities prospectus.

16.47   Where the bidder offering its shares in the offer is a Luxembourg company and the target is a Luxembourg company whose shares are listed on the Regulated Market of the LSE, the CSSF will be the competent authority to approve the offer document and the securities prospectus.[38]

16.48   Where the bidder offering its shares is not a Luxembourg company but is established in another EEA member state, the CSSF will not be the competent authority to approve the securities prospectus. The competent authority in this case will be the authority of the jurisdiction of the bidder. If that bidder is established in a third country, its home member state will need to be determined in accordance with the Prospectus Directive.

16.49   Where the target is not a Luxembourg company or the shares of the target are not listed on the regulated market of the LSE, the CSSF will not be the competent authority to approve the offer document.

16.50   In cases where the consideration for a takeover bid only consists of cash and the target is a Luxembourg company whose shares are listed on the Euro MTF only,

---

[36] Prospectus Law Article 5 (2).
[37] Prospectus Law Article 6 (2).
[38] Takeover Law Article 4 (2) (a).

the offer will neither fall under the Takeover Law or under the Prospectus Law. However, if circumstances in its opinion so dictate, the CSSF could scrutinize the offer under its general supervisory powers over Luxembourg financial markets. It would in particular be advisable to engage with the CSSF where the securities in the target have been the subject of a public offer in Luxembourg or could otherwise be considered as having a large Luxembourg retail shareholder base.

16.2.1.1.4 Debt tender offers Where the consideration for a tender offer to the public for debt securities listed on any of the markets of the LSE consists in or comprises securities, it will fall under the scope of the Prospectus Law and require the publication of a Prospectus Directive-compliant prospectus approved by the competent authority of the home member state (as defined in the Prospectus Directive) of the issuer. **16.51**

This would typically be the case with an exchange offer by the issuer of the debt securities or by its parent or one of its affiliates. **16.52**

If the consideration is solely represented by cash, no prospectus or other information document is required as a matter of Luxembourg securities legislation. **16.53**

Depending on circumstances, it would however be advisable to engage with the CSSF or the LSE for information purposes. **16.54**

If the debt securities, which are the subject of the tender offer, are listed on any of the markets of the LSE and in particular when the offer is made by the issuer or a member of the group to which it belongs, the LSE Rules may require the tender offer to be published on the website of the LSE to ensure equal information and equal treatment of all holders of such debt securities. As such a publication may be considered to constitute an offer to the public if the consideration consists in or comprises securities, this aspect needs to be carefully addressed. **16.55**

16.2.1.1.5 Investment funds The prospectuses to be prepared for the purposes of listing shares or units in investment funds are excluded from the scope of the Prospectus Law except in the case of closed-ended funds.[39] **16.56**

The Prospectus Law does not contain a definition of closed-ended funds but the CSSF has indicated that it will only consider funds as closed-ended funds for the purpose of the Prospectus Law where there is *no* right for the investor to require the repurchase of his shares or units. **16.57**

If a closed-ended investment fund resolves at a later stage to permit investors to redeem their shares, the CSSF has indicated that it may for the purpose of the Prospectus Law requalify such fund as an open-ended fund. In such **16.58**

---

[39] Prospectus Law Article 4 (2) (a).

case, the relevant investment fund's prospectus would become subject to review and approval under the Investment Fund Law, rather than the Prospectus Law.

16.59 The review and approval of prospectuses for investment funds registered with the CSSF, other than closed-ended investment funds, will be carried out by the CSSF on the basis of the Investment Fund Law. The public offer of such funds in Luxembourg and their admission to any of the markets of the LSE will be on the basis of that prospectus.

16.60 **16.2.1.1.6 Language** A prospectus can be drawn up in French, German, English or Luxembourgish.[40]

16.61 The CSSF will approve the language version of the prospectus which it has reviewed and commented on. Issuers may also publish translations of the prospectus. However, the CSSF will not separately approve translations even if published in one of the other permitted languages.

16.62 The Prospectus Law allows the CSSF to accept prospectuses in additional languages. However, discussion on this with the CSSF should only be envisaged where the CSSF staff would be sufficiently conversant in the proposed other language and where particular circumstances would justify the exclusive use of such language.

16.63 The CSSF also accepts that documents incorporated by reference are not in the same language as the prospectus itself. For instance the CSSF permits the incorporation by reference in a French language prospectus of a document approved by the United States Securities and Exchange Commission published in the English language. In case of documents in multiple languages, the CSSF will require that the information still be comprehensible.

16.2.1.2 Preparing a prospectus

16.64 There are no particular rules in Luxembourg as regards the preparation of the prospectus or its content since these are based on Commission Regulation 809/2004 (the 'Prospectus Regulation').[41]

---

[40] Prospectus Law Article 20.
[41] Commission Regulation (EC) 809/2004 implementing Directive 2003/71/EC of the European Parliament and of the Council as regards information contained in prospectuses as well as the format, incorporation by reference and publication of such prospectuses and dissemination of advertisements [2004] OJ L149/1.

There is, however, one particularity in case of securities structured via fiduciary contracts. Fiduciary contracts are governed by a law of 27 July 2003[42] and have certain characteristics similar to that of a trust. **16.65**

In capital markets transactions involving a fiduciary, the fiduciary (typically a bank) receives certain assets (typically cash proceeds from a placing), which it then applies in accordance with the fiduciary contract (typically to hold a security, to make a loan or acquire an asset or a pool of assets). The fiduciary securities and their terms represent the fiduciary contract between the holders of the fiduciary securities and the fiduciary. **16.66**

The assets held by the fiduciary are bankruptcy remote. The fiduciary has full ownership over the fiduciary assets but they are not part of its estate in case of insolvency and they cannot be arrested by the fiduciary's personal creditors. **16.67**

These fiduciary securities are transferable securities in the meaning of Article 4.1(18) of the MiFID and can be listed on financial markets. **16.68**

From a legal point of view, there is no restriction as to what type of asset can be held by a fiduciary. The asset can consist of a bank loan made to a borrower but it can also consist of shares and operate in a very similar way to depositary receipts.[43] **16.69**

From a legal point of view, the issuer of the fiduciary securities is the fiduciary. **16.70**

However, because of the legal nature of a fiduciary contract, and in particular, the fact that investors do not take a risk on the financial performance of the fiduciary, the CSSF has issued guidance that the information to be provided in a prospectus on the fiduciary itself will be the information required by item 26 of Annex X of the EU Prospectus Regulation concerning the issuer of depositary receipts. **16.71**

A further point that had to be tackled in respect of fiduciary securities was the determination of the applicable Annex of the EU Prospectus Regulation. The position is that the content requirements will depend on the nature of the assets underlying the fiduciary securities. If the underlying assets consist of shares of an issuer, then Annex X of the EU Prospectus Regulation will apply. If the underlying assets consist of a bank loan to a borrower or in debt securities of an issuer, this will be treated as an issue of debt securities (i.e. in principle Annex IV or V will apply depending on the nominal amount of the fiduciary securities). In each such case the commercial, financial and legal disclosure in the prospectus will be with respect **16.72**

---

[42] Law of 27 July 2003 on the trust and fiduciary contracts, approving The Hague Convention of 1 July 1985 on the law applicable to trusts and on their recognition.

[43] SES, the largest commercial satellite operator is a Luxembourg company listed on the regulated market of the LSE and on Euronext Paris in the form of fiduciary depositary receipts, or FDRs.

to the underlying issuer of the shares or debt securities, or the borrower of the underlying loan.

16.2.1.3 Responsibility for the prospectus

16.73 Under the Prospectus Law, the offeror, or the person who applies for admission of the relevant security to trading on the Regulated Market, or the guarantor, as applicable will be responsible for the prospectus.[44] Such responsibility is typically taken through a statement in the first pages of the prospectus.

16.74 In the case of underwriters or placing agents involved in a primary market transaction in association with an issuer, the responsibility for the prospectus will need to be taken by the issuer.

16.75 In case of an offeror preparing a prospectus to carry out a secondary offering without association with the issuer, responsibility for the prospectus will need to be taken by the offeror.

16.76 In certain jurisdictions the responsibility for the prospectus is taken by the directors of the issuer. Where the responsibility is taken by the issuer itself, the question as to personal liability of directors of the issuer will involve complex questions of international private law. Absent fraudulent intent or intentional omissions, the liability of directors should be a matter to be resolved under the applicable company law principles of the jurisdiction of the issuer. Depending on circumstances and with respect to a prospectus published in Luxembourg, Luxembourg tort rules may also apply.

16.2.1.4 Registration/filing and review process

16.77 **16.2.1.4.1 Prospectus** Under the Prospectus Law, an offeror whose securities are not yet listed on a regulated market, or who has not yet offered securities to the public, will need to submit a prospectus at least 20 business days before the making of the public offer or the admission to trading. In all other cases, the application must be made at least ten business days before the intended date.[45]

16.78 The above periods only begin when a complete file is submitted (i.e. a file containing all the documents referred to in the CSSF circular 05/226, and in particular a prospectus, as described below). For a first-time offeror or an as yet unlisted issuer, or in the case of a transaction of some complexity (such as structured notes), it is advisable to file the prospectus some time in advance.

16.79 The CSSF requires that documents be submitted in an electronic format via the communication platform *e-file* at the following address: http://www.e-file.lu for

---

[44] Prospectus Law Article 9.
[45] Prospectus Law Article 7 (1) and (2).

professionals who have an e-file connection. Alternatively, the application can also be deposited at prospectus.approval@cssf.lu.

Physical means of communication with the CSSF is not excluded but all documentation must always be provided in an electronic format. **16.80**

CSSF Circular 05/226[46] specifies the documents to be provided together with a draft prospectus. The most important document is obviously the prospectus and all the documents incorporated therein by reference. Another important document is the so-called reference table which enables the CSSF to identify the locations in the prospectus which address the detailed requirements of the applicable Annexe(s) of the EU Prospectus Regulation. **16.81**

The CSSF also requires an indication of the expected timetable of the transaction and of the date at which the approval should be forthcoming. The CSSF is generally open to discuss specific timetable requirements in particular for seasoned issuers (i.e. issuers frequently issuing securities). An accelerated timetable requires strict discipline from the issuer and its advisers in the filing and discussion process, the need to as much as possible address all potential disclosure issues in advance of filing and to turn around the prospectus rapidly. A good relationship with the CSSF and an understanding of its requirements is obviously a key element. **16.82**

No offer to the public of securities may be made and securities cannot be admitted to trading on a regulated market until the relevant prospectus has been approved by the CSSF and until it has been published. **16.83**

For securities outside the scope of the Prospectus Directive (other than open-ended investment funds, see Section 16.1.4.7 above), a simplified prospectus must be filed with the CSSF in the case of a public offer,[47] and with the LSE in the case of admission to trading on the regulated market of the LSE.[48] If the documents submitted are complete and no supplementary information is required, the decision of the CSSF[49] or the LSE[50] shall be notified within ten business days of submission, except in the case of a public offer by an issuer which has not previously offered securities to the public where the notification by the CSSF shall be within 20 business days.[51] **16.84**

For securities to be admitted to the Euro MTF market of the LSE, a prospectus must be filed with the LSE. The LSE Rules provide for a minimum ten days **16.85**

---

[46] CSSF Circular 05/226 on the general overview of the law on prospectuses for securities.
[47] Prospectus Law Article 30 (1).
[48] Prospectus Law Article 47 (1).
[49] Prospectus Law Article 31 (2).
[50] Prospectus Law Article 47 (2).
[51] Prospectus Law Article 31 (3).

advance filing in connection with an admission to the Euro MTF market.[52] The LSE is however generally able to accommodate a shorter timetable but on the condition that the prospectus is well prepared (i.e. that it conforms to market standards, that the information therein is accurate and specific and that the document is generally complete). Providing the LSE with reference tables against the LSE Rules will also speed up the review process.

16.86   **16.2.1.4.2 Derogations**   The Prospectus Law allows the CSSF to grant derogations from the general disclosure obligations set out in the Prospectus Law or the detailed requirements of the EU Prospectus Regulation. The CSSF can allow an issuer to omit information if it is of the view that the disclosure of the information would be contrary to the public interest, or where disclosure would be seriously detrimental to the issuer, on the condition that the omission must not be likely to mislead the public with regard to facts and circumstances essential for an informed assessment of the issuer, offeror or guarantor or of the rights attached to the securities to which the prospectus relates or where the information is of minor importance only for a specific offer or admission to trading on a regulated market and is not such as will influence the assessment of the financial position and prospects of the issuer, offeror or guarantor.[53]

16.87   **16.2.1.4.3 Supplementary prospectus**   Every significant new factor, material mistake or inaccuracy relating to any information included in the prospectus shall be disclosed in a supplement to the prospectus. The supplement shall be approved and published in the same way as the initial prospectus, within seven business days.[54] The same rules apply in the case of a simplified prospectus filed with the CSSF in relation to a public offer,[55] and with the LSE in relation to the admission to trading on the regulated market of the LSE.[56]

16.88   Investors who have agreed to purchase or subscribe for securities prior to publication of the supplement to the prospectus shall have the right, exercisable within a period of at least two business days after the supplement's publication, to withdraw their acceptance.[57] Such rule also applies in the case of a simplified prospectus filed with the CSSF in relation a public offer.[58]

16.89   If necessary, the summary of the prospectus must also be supplemented, in the event the supplement to the prospectus has an impact on it.[59]

---

[52] LSE Rules Part 2, Chapter I, Article 2.
[53] Prospectus Law Article 10 (2).
[54] Prospectus Law Article 13 (1).
[55] Prospectus Law Article 39 (1).
[56] Prospectus Law Article 55.
[57] Prospectus Law Article 13 (2).
[58] Prospectus Law Article 39 (2).
[59] Prospectus Law Article 13 (1).

16.2.1.4.4 Listing Process The LSE Rules contain the requirements and 16.90
conditions to be fulfilled and procedures to be followed for the actual admission
to the official list and trading on one of the LSE's markets. This process is typically
handled by a listing agent who often is but need not necessarily be a member
of the LSE.

Where the listing is on the Regulated Market, the LSE will need to be provided 16.91
with the prospectus approved by the CSSF together with the confirmation of
approval.

The LSE will not conduct a parallel or subsequent review of the prospectus 16.92
approved by the CSSF.

The LSE will verify whether the conditions for admissibility to listing as set out in 16.93
LSE Rules and Luxembourg regulations are fulfilled (see Section 16.1.4.1 above).

In their application, issuers will need to provide an undertaking to comply with 16.94
continuing obligations under applicable regulations, as described below.

16.3 Continuing Obligations

16.3.1 Applicable law

As an overarching principle, the Transparency Law provides that issuers must 16.95
ensure the equal treatment of holders of securities ranking pari passu in respect of
all the rights attached to such securities.[60]

Continuing obligations for issuers listed on the Regulated Market of the LSE are 16.96
contained in the Transparency Law and the Market Abuse Law. The Transparency
Law generally provides for various types of 'regulated information' (as described
below) which needs to be disclosed to the public (except with respect to disclosure
of inside information and of directors' dealings, which are dealt with in the Market
Abuse Law), the content of such disclosure and the means by which it needs to
be disclosed and any applicable exemptions from the requirement to disclose
regulated information. It also contains the requirements to file regulated
information with the CSSF and store such information with an officially appointed
mechanism ('OAM').

There are additional disclosure provisions in the LSE Rules but for issuers whose 16.97
securities are listed on the Regulated Market these are more of a technical nature
to ensure proper operation of the market. The LSE Rules contain specific obligations for issuers whose securities are listed on the Euro MTF and who are therefore

---

[60] Transparency Law Article 17 (1).

not subject to the disclosure requirements of the Transparency Law or the Market Abuse Law.

16.98 In addition, in accordance with Article 10 of the Takeover Directive, equity issuers listed on a regulated market in the EEA are required by the Takeover Law to publish the information referenced in such article with regard to the issuer's share capital, voting arrangements and corporate governance, known to the issuer in their annual report.

16.3.2 Regulated information

16.99 The Transparency Law contains provisions regarding the means of publication of regulated information, its filing and storage.

16.100 'Regulated information' consists of the following information:

- the annual financial report;
- the semi-annual financial report;
- the interim management statements or quarterly reports;
- notification of major shareholdings;
- notification required from an issuer if it trades in its own shares and reaches or crosses the 5% or 10% thresholds;
- the publication of the total number of voting rights and capital by equity issuers;
- the additional information referred to in Article 15 of the Transparency Law (which corresponds to Article 16 of the Transparency Directive); and
- 'inside information' as defined in the Market Abuse Law.

16.101 The choice by an issuer of Luxembourg as its home member state (in circumstances where the issuer has an option to choose amongst more than one home member state) must be disclosed, filed and stored in the same manner as regulated information even though it does not constitute regulated information.

16.102 In order to disclose regulated information, issuers must ensure fast access to such information on a non-discriminatory basis. They must therefore use such media as may be reasonably relied upon for the effective dissemination of information to the public in all EEA member states.

16.103 Making regulated information 'merely available', forcing investors to actively seek out the information, does not meet the legal requirements. Publication on the issuer's website is therefore not sufficient. Dissemination must involve the active distribution of information from the issuer to the media with a view to reaching investors, such as a publication in newspapers of international distribution or a communication to press agencies specialized in financial information and a communication to the regulated market on which the securities of the issuer are admitted (other than the LSE), together with the storage of such information with an OAM .[61]

Whilst the Transparency Law typically applies only to issuers whose home member state is Luxembourg, it also applies to issuers whose securities are solely admitted to trading on a Regulated Market in Luxembourg, and where Luxembourg is the host member state. Such issuers must comply with the same publication requirements as if Luxembourg were their home member state.[62]   **16.104**

The LSE operates a dissemination of information system which issuers can use. Using the LSE as a dissemination mechanism will ensure compliance with the legal requirements.   **16.105**

All regulated information must be filed with the CSSF by issuers whose home member state is Luxembourg. This filing must occur at the time of publication. The filing may be sent via email to transparency@cssf.lu. It must be noted that notifications regarding major shareholdings by shareholders in listed equity issuers also qualify as 'regulated information' and must be filed by the investor with the CSSF.   **16.106**

Finally, any regulated information must also be stored with an OAM, which in Luxembourg is the LSE. The CSSF has specified the operation of the OAM in a circular letter of 16 December 2008.[63] The OAM facility of the LSE can be used at the same time as the publication facility of the LSE referred to above.   **16.107**

16.3.3 Language

The Transparency Law contains detailed rules on permitted languages in which regulated information needs to be published, which reflect Article 20 of the Transparency Directive. Acceptable languages in Luxembourg are French, German, English and Luxembourgish.[64]   **16.108**

16.3.4 Inside information

16.3.4.1 Identifying inside information

Article 14 of the Market Abuse Law requires issuers whose securities are traded on a regulated market (or that have applied for admission to trading) to make public any inside information which concerns them as soon as possible.   **16.109**

---

[61] CSSF Questions and Answers on the Transparency Law, dated 19 August 2008.
[62] Transparency Law Article 20 (3).
[63] CSSF Circular letter of 16 December 2008 on the implementation of the officially appointed mechanism for the central storage of regulated information.
[64] Transparency Law Article 19 (5).

For the purpose of the Market Abuse Law, 'inside information' is defined as information which:

- relates to the securities or to the issuer;
- is specific or precise;
- has not been made public; and
- if it were made public, would have a significant effect on the price of the securities.[65]

16.3.4.2 *Disclosure of inside information*

16.110 16.3.4.2.1 (a) **Timing of disclosure** The issuer must publish as soon as possible any inside information which directly concerns it. The issuer shall be deemed to have acted in accordance with such obligations, if, upon the coming into existence of a set of circumstances or the occurrence of an event, even not yet formalized, the issuer has promptly informed the public thereof.[66] The information to the public shall be made through media which may be reasonably expected to disseminate inside information effectively to the public[67] (such as newspapers of international distribution or press agencies specialized in financial information) and stored with an OAM. In this respect, inside information is treated similarly to regulated information.

16.111 16.3.4.2.2 (b) **Delay of disclosure** The issuer may delay public disclosure so as not to prejudice its legitimate interests in certain circumstances provided such omission would not be likely to mislead the public and provided (i) the issuer has put in place the arrangements needed to ensure the confidentiality of such information, (ii) the person receiving the information owes the issuer a duty of confidentiality, and (iii) the issuer is able to ensure the confidentiality of the information.[68] The term 'legitimate interests' covers, among others, situations where negotiations in progress could be affected by a public disclosure or where the decision of a body of the issuer must be approved by another body of the issuer.[69]

16.112 16.3.4.2.3 (c) **Publication on website** Notwithstanding the publication referred to in Section 16.3.4.1 above, Article 14 (4) of the Market Abuse Law requires issuers to make inside information available on their websites for a period of at least three months. Permitted languages are French, German or English.

---

[65] Market Abuse Law Article 1 (1).
[66] Market Abuse Law Article 14 (1).
[67] Market Abuse Law Article 14 (2).
[68] Market Abuse Law Article 15 (1).
[69] Market Abuse Directive—Level 3—Second set of CESR guidance and information on the common operation of the Directive to the market.

16.3.4.3 *Inside information and Euro MTF listing*

The provisions described in Sections 16.3.4.1 and 16.3.4.2 above technically only apply to issuers whose securities are admitted to trading on a regulated market or who have applied for their securities to be so admitted.

16.113

The LSE Rules contain the continuing disclosure obligations for issuers whose securities are admitted to the Euro MTF market. Unlike the Market Abuse Law, the LSE Rules apply a different standard as to what constitutes inside information for issuers of equity securities and debt securities.

16.114

Firstly, an equity issuer listed on the Euro MTF must promptly publish information on any major new developments within its sphere of activities which are not public knowledge and which may, by their impact on its assets or financial position or the general course of its business, lead to substantial movements in the price of its shares or units.[70] Such criteria is not identical to the definition of 'inside information' under the Market Abuse Law, even though both texts use the test of the significant effect on the price of shares that the unpublished information must be likely to have. It is also not clear whether there is a real difference between 'significant effect on the price' as per the Market Abuse Law and 'substantial movements in the price' as per the LSE Rules.

16.115

Secondly, issuers of debt securities listed on the Euro MTF must publish information on any major new development in its sphere of activities which are not of public knowledge and which may affect, in a significant manner, its ability to meet its commitments.[71] This test is clearly much narrower than the test under the Market Abuse Law.

16.116

Notwithstanding these differences, the prohibition on insider dealings in the Market Abuse Law applies where securities are listed on the Euro MTF, and in that respect the definition of inside information of the Market Abuse Law applies. This means that an issuer of securities listed on the Euro MTF who wants to deal in its own securities or allow its management or employees who are privy to inside information (as defined by the Market Abuse Law) to deal in its securities will have to adhere to the potentially stricter standards of the Market Abuse Law in order to avoid prohibited insider dealings.

16.117

This can be particularly relevant for an issuer of debt securities listed on the Euro MTF who wants to repurchase its own debt securities either by private purchases on- or off-market or through a tender offer.

16.118

Finally, the LSE rules contain a super-equivalence rule under which issuers, who must disclose information under market rules from outside the European Union,

16.119

---

[70] LSE Rule 1001.
[71] LSE Rule 1004.

must ensure that equivalent information is made available in Luxembourg,[72] by any means accepted by the LSE Rules, i.e. newspapers, LSE website and issuer website. This super-equivalence requirement only applies to information that may be important for evaluating the securities listed in Luxembourg.

16.3.5 Insider lists

16.120 According to Article 16 of the Market Abuse Law, an issuer who has requested or obtained admission of its securities to trading on a regulated market located or operating in Luxembourg must ensure that it and persons acting on its behalf or on its account prepare and maintain an up-to-date list of those persons working for it who have regular or occasional access to inside information relating directly or indirectly to the issuer. Persons are considered as working for the issuer regardless of whether it is under an employment contract or otherwise (such as external advisers).

16.121 The list must include, in particular, individuals at a higher level of management of the issuer participating in the decision-making process, and individuals working regularly on sensitive subjects such as high-ranking employees in the accounting function or the mergers and acquisitions department.

16.122 The list must also contain those individuals working occasionally on files with sensitive information, such as internal working group members or external advisers. Individuals who may only by accident have access to inside information do not need to be mentioned, except that they would need to be added to the list after they had gained such access.

16.123 Typically, the insider list therefore includes the board members and those persons discharging management responsibilities such as the CEO, the CFO and their immediate staff members (such as assistants and secretaries), the internal auditors and other individuals who have access to sensitive financial data of the issuer (such as databases on budgetary control or balance sheet analysis), individuals working in a unit of the issuer having regular access to inside information and certain external advisers or consultants of the issuer, including without limitation accountants, auditors, attorneys, communication agencies as well as those at rating agencies with whom inside information is shared on a selective basis.

16.124 The insider list must contain (i) the identity (i.e. name, first name and residence) of each person having access to inside information relating to the issuer,[73] (ii) the reason why such person is on the insider list (i.e. the position or office of the

---

[72] LSE Rule 909.

[73] The CSSF accepts for practical reasons, that the addresses of the issuer's employees may be kept and updated on a separate list, held by another department of the issuer (for instance the human resources department). However, these addresses must be specified on the list transmitted to the CSSF (CSSF Circular 07/280 on the Law of 9 May 2006 on market abuse).

relevant person or the fact that he/she worked in a particular file); and (iii) the date on which the insider list was created and updated.

The issuer must advise individuals entered on the list of that fact and of any changes **16.125** made to the list which concerns them. The issuer should take necessary steps to ensure that any person on the list is duly aware of and informed of his/her legal and regulatory obligations and the criminal, administrative or disciplinary penalties laid down on the unlawful use or improper circulation of inside information.

The insider list must be kept up to date and must be available for at least five years **16.126** from the date on which it is drawn up or updated, whichever is the latest (note that no deletions should be made when updating such list). Circumstances when updates to the list should be made include (i) when there is a change in the reason why a person is already on the list, (ii) when any person who is not already on the list is provided with access to inside information and (iii) to indicate the date on which a person on the list no longer has access to inside information.

The CSSF may at any time request the issuer (or the persons acting on its behalf) **16.127** to promptly provide it with a copy of such insiders' list. There is no obligation to submit the insiders' list to the CSSF on the issuer's own initiative or to inform the CSSF of updates to the list.

With respect to issuers who have requested admission of their securities to trading **16.128** on a regulated market located or operating in Luxembourg or whose securities are so admitted and whose securities are also admitted to trading on a stock exchange situated or operating in a country other than Luxembourg, the CSSF may accept a list which is drawn up in accordance with the regulations of such other country to the extent that the criteria set out above are fulfilled.

Insider lists should be submitted to the CSSF in French, German or English.[74] **16.129**

16.3.6 Disclosure of transactions by persons discharging managerial responsibilities

Pursuant to the Market Abuse Law, persons discharging managerial responsibili- **16.130** ties within an issuer having its registered office in Luxembourg and persons closely associated with any such person shall notify to the CSSF and to the issuer, within

---

[74] It should be noted that on a European level it is contemplated to harmonize the requirements for insiders' lists. In particular it is considered that insiders' lists may be submitted in a foreign language either in case of a multi-listed issuer or by a third person acting on behalf of or for the account of an issuer, if required to send its own insiders' list to the competent authority, where relevant in national law, if not using the same language as that of the issuer, provided that this language is customary in the sphere of international finance, such as the English language (Market Abuse Directive—Level 3—Third set of CESR guidance and information on the common operation of the Directive to the market).

five business days of each individual transaction, all transactions conducted on their own account relating to shares of the issuer (or transactions on derivatives or other securities linked to them).[75]

16.131 Persons discharging managerial responsibilities include the members of the board, the managers having a delegation of the day-to-day management as well as other high-level members of management having regular access to inside information and being empowered to take management decisions on future developments and the strategy of the issuer.

16.132 In addition, persons closely associated with a person discharging managerial responsibilities have the same obligation of declaration. This category concerns (i) the spouse or any partner considered by national law applicable to their marriage/partnership as equivalent, (ii) dependent children, (iii) other relatives living in the same household for at least one year, (iv) any legal entity, fiduciary estate or trust or association where managerial responsibilities are discharged by any of the persons described under the two categories (i.e. persons discharging managerial responsibilities with the issuer or closely associated persons) or where the organization is under control of, or the economic interests are substantially equivalent to those of, such a person.

16.133 The declaration has to indicate (i) the name of the issuer, (ii) the name of the person discharging managerial responsibilities, or as the case may be, the name of the closely associated person, (iii) the reason for the notification obligation, (iv) the description of the financial instrument, (v) the nature of the transaction (acquisition or disposal), (vi) the date and place of the transaction and (vii) the price per instrument and the total amount of the transaction.

16.134 The issuer shall ensure that the information pertaining to transactions in shares notified to it by persons discharging managerial responsibilities or closely associated persons is easily accessible to the public as soon as possible, at least in the French, German or English language. This can be effected via publication on the issuer's website.

16.135 It must be emphasized that the above requirement applies whenever the issuer has its registered office in Luxembourg. This therefore also applies to Luxembourg issuers who are listed on a regulated market in another EEA member state but not in Luxembourg.

16.136 Contrary to the Transparency Directive and the Prospectus Directive, the Market Abuse Directive does not contain the concept of home member state. The obligation as to disclosure of directors' dealings under the Market Abuse Law therefore

---

[75] Market Abuse Law Article 17 (1).

does not apply in case of non-Luxembourg issuers whose shares are listed on the regulated market of the LSE even if that is the sole listing. The two following scenarios could occur:

- In the case of a Luxembourg issuer whose shares are listed on another market in the EEA, persons discharging managerial responsibility may fall under the requirement to notify their dealings both under the Market Abuse Law and the regulations of that other jurisdiction. In that case, the highest standard would need to be complied with by those persons.
- In the case of a foreign issuer whose shares are only listed on the regulated market in Luxembourg, where the legislation of the jurisdiction of the registered office of that issuer only applies the requirement to issuers listed in that jurisdiction, there would technically be no obligation on persons discharging managerial responsibilities to declare their dealings.

16.3.7 Periodic financial reporting

16.3.7.1 Issuers within scope

Issuers whose securities are admitted to trading on the Regulated Market of the LSE will be subject to the ongoing disclosure obligations under the Transparency Law (subject to certain exceptions provided for in that law as detailed below) if Luxembourg is the home member state of that issuer. Issuers admitted to the Euro MTF market of the LSE will be subject to the ongoing financial reporting requirements of the LSE Rules (subject to certain exceptions[76]).   **16.137**

Under Luxembourg securities laws, there are no ongoing reporting obligations for issuers whose securities have been offered to the public but not admitted to trading on a regulated market.   **16.138**

The following categories of issuers of securities are exempt from the periodic financial reporting requirements (annual and half-yearly reports, interim managements statements and quarterly financial statements[77]) under the Transparency Law: **16.139**

- states, regional or local authorities of states, public international bodies of which at least one member state of the EU is a member, the European Central Bank and member states' national central banks, regardless of whether they are issuers of shares or debt securities; and

---

[76] The LSE may authorize an issuer not to disclose certain information if such disclosure may affect the legitimate interests of the issuer (LSE Rules 1001 and 1004).

[77] Transparency Law Articles 3, 4 and 5.

- issuers exclusively of debt securities admitted to trading on an EU regulated market issued in minimum denominations of at least EUR 50,000.[78]

16.140   In addition, the obligation to publish semi-annual financial reports is not applicable to issuers whose home member state is Luxembourg and which exclusively issue debt securities which are irrevocably guaranteed by the Luxembourg state or by its local authorities if such issuers were in existence before 31 December 2003.[79]

16.141   Investment funds other than closed-ended investment funds are not subject to the periodic financial reporting obligations under the Transparency Law.[80]

16.142   The CSSF applies the same criteria as explained in Section 16.2.1.1.4 above to determine whether an investment fund is closed-ended or open-ended.

16.143   **16.3.7.1.1 Fiduciary securities**   The determination of who is the 'issuer' in case of fiduciary securities (see Section 16.2.1.2 above) has been the subject of discussions with the CSSF, since the obligation to publish periodic financial information under the Transparency Law applies to the issuer of the relevant securities and this information must relate to that issuer. The difficulty comes from the fact that the fiduciary is the issuer of the fiduciary securities but that financial information with respect to the fiduciary is of no particular interest to holders of fiduciary securities.

16.144   It is noteworthy that the Transparency Directive and the Transparency Law specifically deal with depository receipts representing securities and determine that the 'issuer' will be the issuer of the underlying securities. This principle can be equally applied by analogy to fiduciary structures, where the underlying assets are shares or debt securities of an issuer. Fiduciary structures, however, very often involve an underlying loan which is made by the fiduciary to a borrower or a portfolio of assets which is a situation that is not specifically dealt with by the Transparency Directive and the Transparency Law.

16.145   Relevantly, the CSSF considers the fiduciary securities as a certificate representing the underlying asset. It follows that the first determination to be made is that of the home member state for purposes of the Transparency Law. A depository certificate representing the underlying securities or other assets is considered not to qualify as a share, nor as a debt security. The issuer of the represented security therefore has the option to select the member state of its registered office or the member state of the regulated market where the fiduciary securities are listed.

---

[78] Transparency Law Article 7 (1).
[79] Transparency Law Article 7 (3).
[80] Transparency Law Article 2 (2).

The same reasoning is applied where the underlying asset is not a security but another asset. In cases where the underlying asset consists of a loan, the selection of the home member state must be exercised by the borrower under the loan. Where the underlying asset is represented by a portfolio of assets or where it is, in practice, impossible to determine a legal entity which would fulfil the duties attached to the function of 'issuer', the option is expressed by the fiduciary.

16.146

If Luxembourg is selected as home member state, the following principles will then be applied: firstly, where the underlying asset consists of securities, the principle provided by the Transparency Directive and the Transparency Law with respect to determining the 'issuer' in case of depository certificates will be applied i.e. the 'issuer' for purposes of the Transparency Law will be the issuer of the underlying securities.[81] Secondly, the same principle will be applied in case of fiduciary securities where the underlying asset does not consist of securities. For instance, where the underlying asset is represented by a loan, the borrower will be considered as the 'issuer' for purposes of compliance with the Transparency Law. However, where the underlying asset is represented by a pool of assets or where it is in practice impossible to determine a legal entity which could fulfil the duty of 'issuer', it will be incumbent upon the fiduciary to arrange compliance with the obligations under the Transparency Law.[82]

16.147

The information to be provided in the periodic financial statements (in fact limited to the annual report (see Sections 16.3.7.2.4 and 16.3.7.2.5 below)) will be information with respect to the underlying asset. Where the underlying asset consists of securities or a loan, the financial report of the issuer of the underlying securities or the borrower will have to be established and published in accordance with the Transparency Law. No information pertaining to the fiduciary needs to be published, except if the information relating to the fiduciary could have a significant influence on the price of the fiduciary securities.

16.148

16.3.7.1.2 Euro MTF Issuers admitted to the Euro MTF are subject to the publication requirements of the LSE Rules.[83] Issuers must publish their annual accounts and latest management reports. Issuers who prepare both consolidated and non-consolidated accounts may only publish their consolidated accounts.[84] These accounts must be subject to an independent audit in case of issuers of

16.149

---

[81] The same principles will be applied with respect to the Market Abuse Law. It is price sensitive information relating to the issuer of the underlying shares or debt securities of the borrower under the underlying loan which will be relevant.

[82] In fiduciary structures effecting securitisation, the obligations could in practice be delegated to the administrator or originator.

[83] LSE Rules 1002 and 1003.

[84] LSE Rule 1002 (iii) and Rule 1003 (iii).

shares.[85] Issuers whose shares are admitted to trading on the Euro MTF, must also publish a semi-annual report.[86]

16.3.7.2 Form of reports

16.150 The following Sections discuss the periodic reporting requirements under the Transparency Law in more detail.

16.151 **16.3.7.2.1 Consolidated accounts** The question whether an issuer has to draw up consolidated accounts or is only required to draw up unconsolidated (stand-alone) accounts is to be determined by the law of the registered office of the issuer.

16.152 If that law does not require the issuer to draw up stand-alone accounts, the issuer is not obliged under the Transparency Law to draw up stand-alone accounts but must include in its consolidated accounts, if applicable, information on its minimum capital and equity requirements and on liquidity issues and, for issuers of shares, information on dividend computation and its ability to pay dividends.

16.153 Where the issuer prepares consolidated accounts it is authorized to only publish its half-yearly report in consolidated form.

16.154 **16.3.7.2.2 Accounting standards** European issuers who are obliged under their domestic corporate law or under specific legislation applicable to them (in the case of certain regulated issuers, such as banks and insurance companies) to draw up consolidated accounts, need to draw up such accounts under IFRS as adopted by the European Union. In addition, their unconsolidated accounts must be established under local GAAP in the jurisdiction where the issuer has its registered office.

16.155 For third country issuers, financial statements must be drawn up under IFRS or by using accounting standards that have been declared equivalent. On 12 December 2008, the European Commission granted equivalence to certain third country GAAPs (including Japan and the USA).[87]

16.156 **16.3.7.2.3 Annual financial reports** Issuers of shares, debt securities or other securities will need to publish their annual financial reports in accordance with the Transparency Law within four months of year-end.[88]

---

[85] LSE Rule 1002 (i).
[86] LSE Rule 1002 (ii).
[87] Commission Decision (EC) 2008/961 on the use by third countries' issuers of securities of certain third country's national accounting standards and International Financing Reporting Standards to prepare their consolidated financial statements [2008] OJ L340/112.
[88] Transparency Law Article 3.

Issuers must ensure the annual financial report remains available to the public for five years.

16.157

The annual financial report shall comprise:

16.158

- the audited financial statements;
- a management report; and
- statements made by persons responsible within the issuer, who shall be clearly identified, to the effect that, to the best of their knowledge, the financial statements prepared in accordance with the appropriate accounting standard give a true and fair view of the assets, liabilities, financial position and profit or loss of the issuer and that the management report includes a fair review of the development and performance of the business and the position of the issuer (and, if applicable, the undertakings included in the consolidation taken as a whole), together with a description of the principal risks and uncertainties that they face.

If a consolidated management report has to be produced, it must include a fair review of the business and the position of the issuer.

16.159

The annual financial reports must be audited and the audit reports must be disclosed in full.

16.160

16.3.7.2.4 Half-yearly financial reports Issuers of shares or debt securities must publish a half-yearly report covering the first six months of the financial year.[89] Depository receipts are not considered to constitute shares or debt securities. Issuers of the underlying shares on debt securities therefore do not fall under the requirement to publish half-yearly financial reports. The same principle applies in the case of fiduciary securities (see Section 16.3.7.1.1 above).

16.161

The half-yearly report needs to be published as soon as possible after the end of the relevant period, but at the latest two months thereafter.

16.162

The half-yearly financial report shall comprise:

16.163

- a condensed set of consolidated financial statements;
- an interim management report;
- statements made by persons responsible within the issuer, who shall be clearly identified, to the effect that, to the best of their knowledge, the condensed set of financial statements which has been prepared in accordance with the appropriate accounting standard gives a true and fair view of the assets, liabilities, financial position and profit or loss of the issuer and that the interim management report includes a fair review of the information described in Article 4(4)

---

[89] Transparency Law Article 4.

of the Transparency Law, which comprises, *inter alia*, important events which may have happened during the first six months of the financial year and the influence they may have had on the condensed set of financial reports, and a description of the main risks and uncertainties for the six upcoming months of the financial year.

16.164   Issuers of shares also need to include disclosure on the principal transactions among related parties.

16.165   16.3.7.2.5 **Interim management statements/quarterly reports**   An issuer whose shares have been admitted to a regulated market and whose home member state is Luxembourg must publish interim management statements[90] or quarterly reports.[91] Depository receipts representing shares are not considered shares for the purposes hereof and the issuers of the underlying shares therefore do not fall under the obligation to prepare interim management statements or quarterly reports.

16.166   An interim management statement shall be prepared in a period starting ten weeks after the start of the relevant semester and ending six weeks before the end of that semester. It contains information covering the period comprised between the beginning of the relevant semester and its date of publication. This statement shall provide:

- an explanation concerning important events and transactions that have happened during the relevant period and their impact on the financial situation of the issuer; and
- a general description of the financial situation and the financial results of the issuer during the relevant period.[92]

16.167   Issuers of equity securities of whom Luxembourg is the home member state may also publish quarterly financial reports (instead of interim management statements). If an issuer chooses this option, these reports must be published within 60 calendar days after the end of the first and the third quarter of each financial year. Quarterly reports must contain at least the following information:

- total turnover and turnover by activity, net total result and result per share as well as the corresponding information from the previous financial year; and
- a description of the important events having occurred during the relevant quarter and their influence on the activity and the financial situation of the issuer.[93]

---

[90] Transparency Law Article 5 (1).
[91] Transparency Law Article 5 (2).
[92] Transparency Law Article 5 (1).
[93] Article 4 of the Grand-Ducal Regulation of 11 January 2008 concerning transparency obligations.

16.4 Other Information Required

Issuers must publish certain information for holders of their shares or debt **16.168**
securities in connection with the holding of shareholder or bondholder meetings
and in connection with changes to the rights attaching to their shares or their
debt securities.[94] Issuers must also disclose any new issues of debt securities admitted to trading on a regulated market and collateral securing such debt
securities.[95]

Under the Prospectus Law, an issuer must publish a yearly report containing or **16.169**
referring to all information it has published or made available to the public over
the preceding 12 months in compliance with securities regulations. This obligation does not apply to issuers of non-equity securities with a denomination per
unit of at least EUR 50,000. The CSSF has indicated that where an issuer presents
the information referred to in the Prospectus Law in such a way that it is easily
available and accessible on the website of the issuer or if it has all been stored in an
OAM, such issuer will be deemed to have fulfilled its obligations in this respect
under the Prospectus Law.

Under the Takeover Law, issuers of shares must publish certain information **16.170**
including on the structure of their capital and significant direct and indirect shareholdings, on restrictions on the transfer of securities and voting rights, on shareholder agreements, on changes of control clauses and on golden parachutes. For
issuers whose home member state is Luxembourg, such information is published
in the management report and the annual accounts (and the consolidated
management report, if any).[96]

Issuers must also publicize any amendments to the rights attached to their shares **16.171**
or debt securities.[97] The dissemination of information involves a publication in
newspapers of international distribution or a communication to press agencies
specialized in financial information and a communication to the regulated market
on which the securities of the issuer are admitted (other than the LSE), together
with the storage of such information with an OAM.[98]

---

[94] Transparency Law Articles 16 (2) and 17 (2).
[95] Transparency Law Article 15 (3).
[96] Takeover Law Article 11.
[97] Transparency Law Article 15 (1) and (2).
[98] CSSF Questions and Answers on the Transparency Law, dated 19 August 2008.

16.5 Major Shareholding Notifications

16.5.1 Notification threshold

16.172   The Transparency Law provides that a shareholder who acquires or disposes of shares of an issuer, including depositary receipts in respect of shares, shall notify the issuer of the percentage of voting rights of the issuer held by it as a result of the acquisition or disposal where such percentage reaches, exceeds or falls below any of the following thresholds: 5%, 10%, 15%, 20%, 25%, 33.33%, 50% and 66.66%.[99]

16.173   The same notification requirement applies where the threshold is reached or crossed passively i.e. as a result of a change in the number of voting rights and share capital of the issuer.[100]

16.5.2 Calculation of voting rights

16.174   Voting rights shall be calculated on the basis of all the shares, including depositary receipts in respect of shares, to which voting rights are attached even if the exercise thereof is suspended. This means that treasury shares whose voting rights are suspended, for instance because they are held in treasury by the issuer or by a subsidiary, need to be included in the denominator used to calculate the percentage of voting rights held.

16.175   The notification requirements also apply to a natural person or legal entity to the extent it is entitled to acquire, to dispose of or to exercise voting rights in any of the following cases or a combination of them:

- voting rights held by a third party with whom that person or entity has concluded an agreement, which obliges them to adopt, by concerted exercise of the voting rights they hold, a lasting common policy towards the management of the issuer in question;
- voting rights held by a third party under an agreement concluded with that person or entity providing for the temporary transfer for consideration of the voting rights in question;
- voting rights attaching to shares which are lodged as collateral with that person or entity, provided the person or entity controls the voting rights and declares its intention of exercising them;
- voting rights attaching to shares in which that person or entity has the life interest;

---

[99] Transparency Law Article 8 (1).
[100] Transparency Law Article 8 (2).

- voting rights which are held, or may be exercised within the meaning of the foregoing indents above, by an undertaking controlled by that person or entity;
- voting rights attaching to shares deposited with that person or entity which the person or entity can exercise at its discretion in the absence of specific instructions from the shareholders;
- voting rights held by a third party in its own name on behalf of that person or entity;
- voting rights which that person or entity may exercise as a proxy where the person or entity can exercise the voting rights at its discretion in the absence of specific instructions from the shareholders.[101]

The above voting rights need to be added to the denominator used to calculate the percentage of voting rights held. **16.176**

The above notification requirements also apply to a person who holds directly or indirectly financial instruments which result in an entitlement to acquire, on such holder's own initiative alone, under a formal agreement, already issued shares to which voting rights are attached, of an issuer whose shares are admitted to trading on a regulated market.[102] **16.177**

For the purpose of calculating the voting threshold, voting rights held directly or indirectly or allocated to a person in accordance with the above rules must not be aggregated with voting rights attached to the underlying shares of those financial instruments. However, whenever the relevant threshold of voting rights directly or indirectly held, or with respect to the underlying shares of the financial instruments is independently reached or crossed in either of the two categories, the notification must provide full details on both categories. **16.178**

16.5.3 Exceptions

The Transparency Law provides under certain conditions for exemptions where voting rights attached to certain shares can be disregarded for the determination of the numerator. These comprise shares acquired for the sole purpose of clearing and settlement within a settlement cycle not exceeding three trading days,[103] shares held as custodian where the custodian can exercise the voting rights attached to the shares only pursuant to instructions given to it,[104] shares acquired for disposal by a market maker acting in that capacity to the extent that the 10% **16.179**

---

[101] Transparency Law Article 9.
[102] Transparency Law Article 12.
[103] Transparency Law Article 8 (3) and Article 6 of the Grand-Ducal Regulation of 11 January 2008 concerning transparency obligations.
[104] Transparency Law Article 8 (3).

threshold is not reached[105] and (under certain conditions) shares held in the trading portfolio of a credit institution or investment firm.[106] Certain exemptions with respect to aggregating their holdings are available to management companies or investment firms and their parent undertaking.[107]

16.180   Shares deposited as collateral may be disregarded by the secured party to the extent the secured party does not control the voting rights or does not exercise the voting rights and does not declare that it has the intention to exercise them.[108]

16.181   Shares acquired by a borrower under a stock lending agreement or any similar legal construction can be disregarded from the calculation to the extent they are re-lent or sold or transferred in any other way at the latest on the trading day following the loan (provided settlement occurs within three trading days) provided the borrower has no intention to exercise and does in fact not exercise the voting rights attached to the borrowed shares.

16.182   'Trading days' for the purpose of the Transparency Law means the days on which the regulated market of the LSE is open for trading.[109] This definition also applies for issuers of which Luxembourg is the home member state but whose shares are only admitted to trading on a regulated market outside of Luxembourg.

16.5.4 Notification deadlines

16.183   The notification to the issuer shall be effected as soon as possible, but not later than four trading days after the date on which the shareholder or the natural person or legal entity referred to above:

(a) learns of the acquisition or disposal or of the possibility of exercising voting rights, or on which, having regard to the circumstances, should have learned of it, regardless of the date on which the acquisition, disposal or possibility of exercising voting rights takes effect; or

(b) is informed about an event as a result of which the percentage of the voting rights held by the shareholder in the issues reaches, exceeds or falls below any of the thresholds referred to above (i.e. in case of a passive reaching or crossing of a threshold).[110]

---

[105]   Transparency Law Article 8 (4).
[106]   Transparency Law Article 8 (5).
[107]   Transparency Law Article 11 (3), (4) and (5).
[108]   Transparency Law Article 9 (c).
[109]   Article 8 of the Grand-Ducal Regulation of 11 January 2008 concerning transparency obligations.
[110]   Transparency Law Article 11 (2).

The investor will be deemed to have knowledge of the acquisition or sale or the **16.184** possibility to exercise the voting rights at the latest two trading days after the transaction.[111]

Upon receipt of the notification, but no later than three trading days thereafter, **16.185** the issuer shall make public the information contained in the notification.[112]

16.5.5 Form of notification

The CSSF has determined the content and the form of the notification in its **16.186** Circular 08/349.[113] The notification shall include at least the resulting situation in terms of voting rights, the chain of controlled undertakings through which voting rights are effectively held, the date on which the threshold was reached or crossed and the identity of the shareholder, even if that shareholder is not entitled to exercise the voting rights, and of the natural person or legal entity entitled to exercise voting rights on behalf of that shareholder.

16.5.6 Publication by issuer of total of capital and voting rights

The Transparency Law provides that for the purpose of calculating the thresholds **16.187** of voting rights which trigger a disclosure obligation, the issuer shall make public the total number of voting rights and capital at the end of each calendar month during which an increase or decrease of such total number has occurred.[114] This involves a publication in newspapers of international distribution or a communication to press agencies specialized in financial information and a communication to the regulated market on which the securities of the issuer are admitted (other than the LSE), together with the storage of such information with an OAM.[115] This publication may in turn trigger a notification obligation of investors as referred to in Section 16.5.4 paragraph (b) above.

---

[111] Article 10 of the Grand-Ducal Regulation of 11 January 2008 concerning transparency obligations.

[112] Transparency Law Article 11 (6).

[113] CSSF Circular 08/349 on the information to be notified with respect to major holdings in accordance with the law of 11 January 2008 on transparency requirements for issuers of securities.

[114] Transparency Law Article 14.

[115] CSSF Questions and Answers on the Transparency Law, dated 19 August 2008.

17

THE NETHERLANDS

17.1 Offering and Listing Securities in the Netherlands

17.1.1 Legislative overview

17.01 The rules governing the offering of securities, the listing of securities on a regulated market and the continuing obligations that apply to issuers of such securities can primarily be found in the Netherlands Financial Supervision Act (*Wet op het financieel toezicht*, or 'Wft'). The Wft was enacted on 1 January 2007. It replaced seven separate Acts, each of which contained regulations applicable to one sector or industry only.

17.02 The Wft consists of five parts. Part 5 of the Wft is dedicated to the regulation of conduct of business of market participants generally, and is divided into six subsections. Chapter 5.1 contains the implementation of the Prospectus Directive. The Transparency Directive is implemented in Chapter 5.1a. Other relevant chapters include Chapter 5.3 (disclosure of major holdings in listed companies—see Section 17.3.5) and Chapter 5.4 (regulation and prevention of market abuse—see Section 17.3.3).

Additional rules can be found in over 25 implementing orders. Relevant regula- **17.03** tions for the purpose of this Chapter include the Market Abuse Decree (*Besluit marktmisbruik Wft*), the Transparency Directive Implementing Decree (*Besluit uitvoeringsrichtlijn transparantie uitgevende instellingen Wft*) and the Decree on the Disclosure of Major Holdings in Listed Companies (*Besluit melding zeggenschap en kapitaalbelang in uitgevende instellingen Wft*). In addition, Chapter 5 of the Exemption Regulation (*Vrijstellingsregeling Wft*) contains exemptions to the obligation to publish a prospectus when offering securities to the public or listing securities on a regulated market. See Section 17.2.2 below.

When admitting securities to the listing of Euronext Amsterdam, the regulations **17.04** of Euronext Amsterdam apply in addition to the requirements of the Wft.

In addition to these regulatory requirements, Dutch private law also contains **17.05** a number of provisions that may be relevant in the context of preparing a prospectus or other disclosure documents. Sections 6:194 and 6:195 of the Dutch Civil Code provide for a specific liability regime in relation to the publication of misleading advertisements, which can also be used in disputes involving misleading prospectuses. In October 2008, the Unfair Commercial Practices Act (*Wet op de oneerlijke handelspraktijken*) entered into force. In this Act, the use of misleading advertisements and other commercial statements (including prospectuses) was designated as an unfair commercial practice when dealing with retail clients, and can result in liability in tort. Since the entry into force of the Unfair Commercial Practices Act, the application of Sections 6:194 and 6:195 has been restricted to professionals. Retail investors must now rely on the provisions of the Unfair Commercial Practices Act, which are very similar to Sections 6:194 and 6:195 of the Civil Code.

17.1.2 The AFM

Supervision of the financial markets in the Netherlands is split between two regu- **17.06** lators. The Dutch Central Bank (*De Nederlandsche Bank* or 'DNB') is responsible for securing the stability of the financial markets and the capital adequacy of the financial parties active on those markets. The Financial Markets Authority (*Autoriteit Financiële Markten* or the 'AFM') is responsible for supervising the manner in which parties active on the financial markets conduct their business,[1] including the supervision of the offering and listing of securities in the Netherlands. The AFM is the competent authority for approval of a prospectus. It is also the regulator responsible for supervising ongoing obligations of issuers of securities, including those relating to transparency and market conduct.

---

[1] Wft section 1:25.

17.07   As part of its role as supervisory authority, the AFM has the right to request information from any relevant parties.[2] In addition, it has the ability to give instructions, including to parties that offer securities or seek admission of securities, to either refrain from certain actions or to follow certain instructions of the AFM.[3] The AFM also has the ability to administer fines either as means of enforcement of its instructions[4] or as punitive sanction.[5] As a separate power, the AFM has the right to publish sanctions and to publicly warn investors against certain market parties or practices.

17.1.3 Euronext Amsterdam

17.08   Euronext Amsterdam is part of NYSE Euronext, the international group of stock exchanges, which includes the New York Stock Exchange, the Bourse de Paris, Liffe, Euronext Brussels and the Lisbon Exchange.

17.1.3.1 *Euronext Amsterdam*

17.09   The official market of Euronext Amsterdam is referred to as Euronext Amsterdam. It is part of the integrated market platform of all Euronext exchanges which creates a single pan-European market for equities, closed-end funds, bonds, exchange-traded funds and warrants. It is a regulated market as referred to in the Prospectus Directive.[6]

17.10   Issuers listed on Euronext Amsterdam are divided into three segments (A, B, and C) depending on their markets capitalization. The index for large caps is the AEX, for mid caps the AMX and for small caps the newly created AScX. Companies with sufficient liquidity are quoted on a continuous basis. Securities of the remainder of companies are traded by auctions that occur twice daily. In addition, Euronext Amsterdam has a large-volume derivatives market.

17.11   Euronext Amsterdam is well suited to listing non-Dutch companies. All issuers are traded on the same platform with no distinction between foreign and Dutch issuers. Similarly, foreign issuers can be fully included in the index, unlike in some other foreign indices, when they otherwise qualify.

17.12   Over the last few years, Euronext Amsterdam has proven to be a good listing venue for alternative investment vehicles, such as private equity funds and hedge funds. It has also developed a fast track listing option for SEC-registered issuers, allowing for listing on Euronext Amsterdam within a few days.

---

[2] Wft section 1:74.
[3] Wft section 5:25 in conjunction with section 1:75.
[4] Wft section 1:79.
[5] Wft section 1:80.
[6] MiFID section 47.

The main rules relating to listing and admission on Euronext Amsterdam can be **17.13** found in Euronext Rule Book I ('Rule Book I'), which contains all rules harmonized for the various regulated exchanges of the Euronext Group. Certain additional rules that relate solely to Euronext Amsterdam are found in Rule Book II—General Rules for the Euronext Amsterdam Stock Market ('Rule Book II'). In addition to the two rules books, certain policies of Euronext Amsterdam are set out in announcements.[7]

17.1.3.2 NYSE Alternext

Euronext in Amsterdam, jointly with the other Euronext exchanges, maintains **17.14** the NYSE Alternext market as an unregulated multilateral trading facility ('MTF'). NYSE Alternext is aimed at medium-sized companies seeking to grow through access to the Euro-zone capital markets. Issuers can list their securities on NYSE Alternext in two ways: listing with a concurrent public offering and listing after a private placement.

In either case, companies seeking a listing on NYSE Alternext must enlist the **17.15** services of a listing sponsor which will continue to advise them throughout the listing on NYSE Alternext. The sponsor is obligated to assist the company in meeting its market transparency requirements and fulfilling its other obligations. During the listing process the sponsor must provide Euronext with written confirmation that the applicant complies with the listing rules. It also must certify that it has performed customary due diligence. These certification obligations for the sponsor do not arise in case of a listing on the official market.[8]

17.1.4 Listing criteria

17.1.4.1 Admission to Euronext Amsterdam

An application for admission to Euronext Amsterdam is filed on behalf of an **17.16** issuer by its listing agent. Unlike other Euronext exchanges, Euronext Amsterdam requires the issuer to use a listing agent. The role of the listing agent is to advise the issuer on the admission process and to continue to advise the issuer during the first six months following admission.[9]

The procedure for an application for admission is set out in Chapter 6.2 of **17.17** Rule Book I[10] with a few additional rules for Euronext Amsterdam set out in Chapter 2.7 of Rule Book II. Although the formal period of a decision on

---

7 E.g. Announcement 2004-041 'Policy on delisting shares or depositary receipts'.
8 NYSE Alternext—Non Regulated Market—Rules section 2.2.
9 Euronext Amsterdam Rule Book II section 2701/2.
10 Paragraph 6.2 sets out the procedure and paragraph 6.5 contains a list of documents to be filed.

admission is set at 90 days for a first admission and 30 days for any subsequent admission,[11] in practice this period is much shorter.

17.18 **17.1.4.1.1 General eligibility criteria** Upon admission to listing and thereafter for as long as the securities are listed, the following eligibility criteria apply to all securities for which admission on Euronext Amsterdam is sought:[12]

- The legal position and structure of the issuer must be in accordance with applicable laws and regulations both as regards its formation and its operation under its articles of association.
- The issuer must comply with the requirements of any relevant regulatory authority.
- The securities must be freely transferable and negotiable and adequate procedures must be available for the clearing and settlement of transactions.
- The issuer must ensure that securities of the same class have identical rights as per its articles of association and pursuant to Dutch law and regulations.
- Securities must be validly issued in accordance with applicable laws and regulations governing those securities, the issuer's articles of association and other constituent documentation.
- The form of securities must be in conformity with the requirements of Dutch law and regulations.
- An application for admission to listing must cover all the issuer's securities of the same class issued at the time of the application or proposed to be issued.

17.19 In addition, securities entitling holders to acquire underlying securities are only eligible for admission if, at the time of the application, (i) the underlying securities are admitted to listing on a regulated market or equivalent market outside the European Union or (ii) there are adequate assurances that such underlying securities will be admitted on such market by the time at which the right to acquire them can be exercised.

17.20 **17.1.4.1.2 Additional eligibility criteria** In addition to the general criteria set out in the previous paragraph, further criteria, which depend on the type of security for which admission is sought, are found in Chapter 6 of Rule Book I, with a few additions in Chapter 2.7 of Rule Book II.

17.21 For shares and other similar equity instruments, the criteria are:[13]

- *Sufficient free float*: securities in the hands of the public must be a least 25% of the relevant class unless, in view of the large number of such securities and the extent of their distribution to the public, the market will function with

---

[11] Euronext Rule Book I section 6301.
[12] Euronext Rule Book I paragraph 6.6.
[13] Euronext Rule Book I sections 6702/1 and 6702/2.

a lower percentage. This percentage may not be lower than 5% and must represent a value of at least EUR 5 million calculated on the basis of the offering price.
- *Financial information*: three years under IFRS or equivalent GAAP, and, if the financial year closed more than nine months before the date of the admission to listing, semi-annual accounts.

17.1.4.2 NYSE Alternext eligibility criteria

17.22

Each applicant to NYSE Alternext must have selected a listing sponsor.[14] In addition, it must have published at least two years of financial statements. However, if an offer to the public is made, three years of financial statements will be required because a Prospectus Directive compliant prospectus will have to be prepared.[15]

When application to the NYSE Alternext is made in connection with a public offer, the minimum requirements for admission are:

17.23

- a minimum free float of EUR 2.5 million; and
- the publication of a prospectus approved by the competent regulator.

If companies apply to NYSE Alternext in connection with a private placement, requirements for admission are:

17.24

- the placement of at least EUR 5 million with five or more investors; and
- the publication of an offering circular (i.e., a prospectus not approved by the regulator), prepared by the company and its listing sponsor.

17.1.5 Settlement and custody

The book-entry settlement system operated by Euroclear Nederland is the common settlement system used in respect of securities traded on Euronext Amsterdam. The Euroclear book-entry settlement system facilitates the settlement of securities transactions through electronic book-entry transfer between its accountholders without share certificates or written instruments of transfer. Indirect access to the Euroclear book-entry settlement system is available to other institutions which settle and/or clear through or maintain a custodial relationship with an accountholder of Euroclear Nederland. Euroclear Nederland is subject to supervision by the AFM, the DNB and the Dutch Ministry of Finance.

17.25

Investors in securities will hold ownership of interests (*deelgenootschap*) in these securities pursuant to the Dutch Securities Giro Act (*Wet giraal effectenverkeer*) through their accounts with Admitted Institutions (as defined in section 1 of the Dutch Securities Giro Act). The Dutch Securities Giro Act aims to ensure a

17.26

---

[14] See Section 17.1.3.2 above.
[15] Alternext—Non Regulated Market Rules section 2.2.

properly functioning system for the giro transfer of securities and sets out requirements for Euroclear and its admitted institutions.

17.27 Pursuant to the Dutch Securities Giro Act, Euroclear Nederland holds securities on behalf of its admitted institutions and does not hold securities for itself. An admitted institution's portion of the book-entry deposit must be registered in its name.

17.28 The Dutch Securities Giro Act ensures that the end-investors who hold book-entry interests in the Euroclear book-entry settlement system through an admitted institution benefit from asset protection if the relevant admitted institution were to go bankrupt. In order to benefit from the asset protection offered by the Dutch Securities Giro Act, an institution has to qualify as an admitted institution which means an institution has to be admitted by Euroclear Nederland. Currently, approximately 80 institutions including most Dutch financial institutions and a large number of non-Dutch financial institutions are admitted.

17.2 The Prospectus

17.2.1 Applicable law

17.29 Rules relating to requirement, content and approval process for the prospectus are found in Chapter 5.1 of the Wft. The content requirements for a prospectus are found in section 5:13, which directly incorporates the contents of the Prospectus Regulation into Dutch law.

17.30 The AFM also tends to follow the recommendations of the Committee of European Securities Regulators ('CESR') for the consistent implementation of the European Commission's Regulation on Prospectuses No 809/2004 (the 'CESR Recommendations') and also pays close attention to CESR's Frequently Asked Questions regarding Prospectuses: Common positions agreed by CESR members (Version February 2009) (the 'CESR FAQs').

17.31 Exemptions from the obligation to publish a prospectus are found in sections 5:3 and 5:4 of the Wft and in sections 53 to 55 of the Exemption Regulation.

17.2.2 Requirement for a prospectus

17.2.2.1 The requirement

17.32 As per the Prospectus Directive, there are two situations in which a prospectus is required: (i) in case of an offer to the public in the Netherlands of securities; or (ii) when securities are admitted to trading on a regulated market in the Netherlands. Euronext Amsterdam has been notified to the European Commission as a regulated market. If either of these situations arise, a prospectus is required unless an exemption or exception applies. If both situations arise at the same time, one prospectus can be prepared to fulfil both requirements.

Two elements require further clarification.   **17.33**

Securities: In the Prospectus Directive, securities are defined by the MiFID as   **17.34**
instruments that are 'negotiable on the capital market', including shares and
securities equivalent to shares, bonds and other debt instruments, and certain
derivative instruments.[16] The definition is incorporated in Dutch law by reference
not to 'negotiable on the capital market', but by use of the term 'transferable'.[17]
The relevant legislative history suggests that for the element of transferability to
be met, an instrument must be capable of being transferred and fungible to a
certain degree, thus allowing for trading on a market. If an instrument does not
possess these characteristics, it is not considered a security and hence offers of such
instruments do not trigger the obligation to publish a prospectus.

Certain instruments are expressly carved out of the definition of securities, includ-   **17.35**
ing equity instruments issued by open ended investment funds. In addition,
money market instruments with a maturity of less than 12 months are expressly
exempted from the prospectus obligation.[18] The same applies for certain securities
issued or guaranteed by governments (national or local within the EEA) or
charitable organizations.[19]

Offer to the public: In implementing the definition of 'public offer', the Netherlands   **17.36**
has, on the one hand, arguably limited the definition while, on the other hand,
clarified it. The Prospectus Directive speaks of 'a communication in any form
and by any means (whether or not made through financial intermediaries) that
presents sufficient information on (i) the terms of the offer and (ii) the securities
offered to enable an investor to decide whether or not to purchase or subscribe
for the securities'.[20] The Dutch definition includes a reference not only to an offer
but also to an invitation to make an offer (by a potential purchaser), thus making
clear that the process of book building is deemed to be an offer. At the same time,
the Dutch definition[21] refers to the definition of an offer included in the Dutch
Civil Code.[22] This definition requires that an agreement be entered into, a requirement that the Prospectus Directive does not contain.

An offer is deemed to be 'public' if it is made to more than one person.   **17.37**

---

[16] MiFID section 4(18).
[17] Wft section 1.1.
[18] Wft section 5.1a.
[19] Exemption Regulation Wft section 53(1).
[20] Prospectus Directive section 2(1)(d).
[21] Wft section 5.1 sub (a): a sufficiently concrete offer to more than one person, as referred to in
Section 6:217(1) of the Civil Code, to enter into an agreement to purchase or subscribe for securities, or an invitation to make an offer for such securities.
[22] Dutch Civil Code section 6:217(1).

17.2.2.2 Exemptions and exceptions

17.38 There are a number of exemptions and exceptions to the requirement to publish a prospectus. All of these find their basis in the Prospectus Directive. Below a number of interpretations, definitions and particularities relating to the interpretation and scope of the exemptions and exceptions in the Netherlands are discussed. Shares and options issued as part of incentive schemes will be discussed in more detail in Section 17.2.2.3 below.

17.39 **17.2.2.2.1 Exemption and exceptions relating to the offer of securities to the public** The exemptions and exceptions to the prospectus requirement in case of a public offer are set out below. Please note that 1 to 9 are the exemptions and exceptions set out in the Prospective Directive as implemented in the Netherlands. The other two are additional exemptions or exemptions found in the Exemption Regulation.

1. When the offer is made to qualified investors.[23] The Netherlands has included in this definition persons who meet certain minimum requirements and who have registered the basis of such requirements with the AFM. The AFM does not verify whether the requirements are actually met, but third parties may rely on the register.[24]

2. Where the offer of securities is made to less than 100 persons—not counting qualified investors—per member state.[25]

3. Where the offer involves securities with a denomination of at least EUR 50,000.[26] The AFM has taken the position that for this exemption to be applicable the amount paid at the time of the initial offer must be at least EUR 50,000. In other words, in case of arrangements where part of the purchase price is to be paid at a later stage, the amount paid at the outset will determine whether the EUR 50,000 threshold is met. The other thing to note here is that the use of zero coupon notes with a face value of EUR 50,000 or more as such is allowed, provided the terms and maturity relating to the notes are reasonable.

4. Where the offer involves securities that can only be acquired for a total consideration of at least EUR 50,000.[27] Here too, the amount initially paid must be at least EUR 50,000. Subsequent offers of the same security to the same investors can be offered in any increment.

5. Where the offer of all securities by an issuer has a total consideration of less than EUR 100,000 calculated over a period of 12 months. It is unclear

---

[23] Wft section 5.3(1)(a).
[24] Wft section 1.1 and the Decree definitions Wft.
[25] Wft section 5.3(1)(b).
[26] Wft section 5.3(1)(c).
[27] Wft section 5.3(1)(d).

whether this limit applies for the whole EU or just for the Netherlands.[28] In addition, where the offer of securities within the whole EU by an issuer has a total consideration of less than EUR 2,500,000 calculated over a period of 12 months, an exemption applies. For this latter exemption, the CESR FAQs make it clear that the threshold applies to offers in the entire EU.[29] However, here the threshold is per category of securities (e.g. EUR 2,500,000 for shares and EUR 2,500,000 for bonds). Use of this exemption requires that certain disclaimers are included in any advertisements and documents used in connection with the offer. Unlike the other exemptions, the EUR 2,500,000 exemption cannot be combined with another exemption.

6. Where shares are offered in substitution for shares of the same class (unless the issue involves an increase in issued share capital).[30] At implementation in the Netherlands, it was stated in the legislative history that a marginal increase in the issued share capital would be acceptable.

7. Where shares are offered as part of the consideration in the context of a takeover or merger, provided a document equivalent to a prospectus is produced.[31] The equivalent document does not have to be approved by the AFM, but the AFM is willing to review a document to determine whether it meets the equivalency test.

8. Where shares are offered free of charge and dividends paid in the form of shares of the same class as that to which the dividend relates, provided there is a document describing the number and nature of the shares and reasons for and details of the offer.[32]

9. For shares offered to employees, provided there is a document describing the number and nature of the securities and reasons for and details of the offer.[33] See Section 17.2.3.3 below for a further description.

10. The Exemption Regulation includes a number of additional exemptions that all deal with situations where securities that are offered to the public were previously either the subject of a number of exemptions or for which a prospectus was already published.[34] In addition, and in contravention of the Prospectus Directive, an exemption is granted to the offer of securities that are also admitted to listing under an exemption, but where no exemption for the offer to the public is available. For example, if less than 10% of new shares of a class that is already listed are admitted to trading, no prospectus is required

---

[28] Wft section 5.3(1)(e).
[29] Exemption Regulation Wft section 53(2).
[30] Wft section 5.3(2)(a).
[31] Wft section 5.3(2)(b) and (c).
[32] Wft section 5.3(2)(6).
[33] Wft section 5.3(2)(e).
[34] Exemption Regulation Wft section 54.

for such admission. Under Section 54(2) of the Exemption Regulation, such shares can then also be offered to the public without a prospectus.

11. Finally, under the Exemption Regulation, an offer to the public is exempt if the offer is made to persons who have instructed an appropriately licensed investment manager on the basis of an agreement that leaves the investment decisions solely with such manager and not with the investor.[35]

17.40 **17.2.2.2.2 Exemptions and exceptions relating to the admission to trading on a regulated market**   The exemptions and exceptions to the prospectus requirement in case of admission on a regulated market are set out below.

1. Admission on Euronext Amsterdam of shares or certificates of shares representing, over a period of 12 months, less than 10% of the number of shares or certificates of shares of the same class as is already admitted to trading on Euronext Amsterdam.[36] When calculating the 10%, one uses the number outstanding immediately prior to admission (and not the number outstanding at the beginning of the 12 month period).

2. Exemptions similar to 6 through 9 of Section 17.2.2.2.1 above are also available in case of admission.[37]

3. Shares or certificates of shares that result from conversion or exchange of other securities (such as a convertible or exchangeable bond), provided they are of the same class as the shares already admitted to trading on Euronext Amsterdam.[38] This is a potentially very broad exemption. For example, one could offer a convertible instrument under an exemption to qualified investors and then when such instruments are converted to shares, those shares, irrespective of their number, will be admitted again without the requirement of a prospectus. It is not required that the convertible or exchangeable instruments are listed; only that the instruments qualify as a security. In line with discussions within CESR on the scope of this exemption, the AFM has indicated that it will closely monitor using convertible instruments purely to avoid the requirement of a listing prospectus.

4. Subject to certain conditions, securities that have been admitted for at least 18 months on another regulated exchange within the EU can be admitted to Euronext Amsterdam without the requirement of a prospectus.[39]

17.2.2.3 Employees

17.41 Companies that issue securities to their employees need to ensure that doing so does not require them to publish a prospectus.

---

[35] Exemption Regulation Wft section 55.
[36] Wft section 5.4(a).
[37] Wft section 5.4(b) to (f).
[38] Wft section 5.4(g).
[39] Wft section 5.4(h).

The first question to answer in this respect is whether the offer of securities to employees is a public offer given that either the employee may have no choice in receiving the grant or the offer is for no consideration. It is CESR's view—following discussions with the European Commission—that in many situations the offer will not constitute a public offer, or if it does, it will fall under the EUR 100,000 exemption.[40]   **17.42**

Should, however, the grant constitute a public offer (e.g. because consideration is paid), the Sections below are relevant. Also, if the securities offered are to be admitted to trading on a regulated market, an exemption for the admission of such shares needs to be available.   **17.43**

Employee stock options. In line with the CESR position, employee stock options are not considered securities since they are not transferable. Their offer does not therefore trigger a prospectus requirement. Similarly, their exercise is not considered an offer and also does not trigger a prospectus requirement. If stock options are for shares of a class that is admitted to trading on a regulated exchange, the issuer should also ensure an exemption for admission is available at the time that the options are exercised. If less than 10% of outstanding shares have been admitted over the last 12 months, that exemption will be available. In addition, the exemption for employee shares can be used provided an information document is made available to the employees. There is some debate about the availability of the latter exemption because, according to some, the exercise of   **17.44**

---

[40] According to the answer to Question 6 of the CESR FAQs, after consultation with the European Commission CESR takes the view that: 'In the case of allocations of securities (almost invariably free of charge) where there is no element of choice on the part of the recipient, including no right to repudiate the allocation, there is no "offer of securities to the public" within the meaning of Article 2.1 d) of the Prospectus Directive. This is because the definition refers to a communication containing sufficient information "to enable an investor to decide to" purchase or subscribe for the securities. Where no decision is made by the recipient of the securities, there is no offer for the purposes of the Prospectus Directive. Such allocations will therefore fall outside the scope of the Prospectus Directive.

Offers of free shares, where the recipient decides whether to accept the offer, are properly regarded as an offer for zero consideration. As such, they would fall within the excluded offers under Article 1.2 h), but are also subject to the exemption for offers of less than €100,000 so no prospectus can be required.

This analysis does not prevent competent authorities from assessing whether an offer presented as an offer of free shares in fact disguises a "hidden" consideration. However, the Commission Services take the view that in most cases where free shares are offered in the context of an employee share scheme, where shares are not offered in lieu of remuneration that the employee would otherwise receive, it would be incorrect to find "hidden" consideration in the employment relationship, for example by claiming that the employees would have a higher salary if an equity participation scheme were not available to them. Such reasoning would be speculative, and the "hidden" consideration difficult to prove, let alone quantify. However, if the shares are expressly offered in the place of quantifiable financial benefits in another form, then it might be appropriate to identify consideration to the value of the benefits that the employee would otherwise have been entitled to receive." '

options does not qualify as shares offered or allotted as per the definition of the exemption and hence cannot be brought under the exemption. In our view, however, shares are allotted by way of granting non-transferable options which would make the exemption available. This debate is only relevant if the 10% exemption would not be available (e.g. because the 10% has already been used for the admission of other shares).

17.45   *Employee shares.* If an offer of shares to employees is deemed a public offer, an issuer can avail itself of the employee share exemption, provided the shares offered are of a class that is admitted to trading. This would require the issuer to compile an information document to be made available to the employees to whom shares are offered. The document does not have to be approved by the AFM and does not have to be made publicly available. It is a short document that contains the information as required by the Prospectus Directive.[41]

17.46   In addition, companies that offer shares to fewer than 100 employees in the Netherlands can avail themselves of the fewer than 100 persons exemption. The offer would also be exempt if the overall consideration would be less than EUR 2,500,000 (and no other offers are made in the year the employee shares are offered).

17.47   If shares of a class that is not admitted to trading on a regulated market are offered in the Netherlands to more than 100 employees and the offer constitutes a public offer—i.e. it is an offer for consideration as per the second paragraph of this Section 17.2.2.1—a prospectus requirement arises unless steps are undertaken to avoid the shares qualifying as securities. This may be possible by creating non-transferable depositary receipts for employees in the Netherlands. However, if an issuer opts to publish a prospectus, it may avail itself of the short form regime as is described in Question 71 of the CESR FAQs if it concerns an issuer that has securities listed on a market, including a market outside of the EU.

17.48   If the shares offered—whether free or for some form of implied or explicit consideration—are of a class that is admitted to trading on a regulated exchange, the issuer should also ensure an exemption for admission is available. If less than 10% of outstanding shares have been admitted over the last 12 months, that exemption will be available. In addition, the exemption for employee shares is available provided an information document is made available.

17.49   *Definition of 'employees'.* In the Netherlands, 'employees' for purposes of the special employee exemption, are considered present and former employees of the issuer and its group companies, members of the management board of the issuer and its

---

[41] Prospectus Directive section 4(1)(e).

group companies and also members of the supervisory board of the issuer and its group companies.

17.2.3 Preliminary prospectuses and marketing

Preliminary prospectuses are not typically used for transactions in the Netherlands. Marketing on the basis of a prospectus is usually undertaken once the prospectus is approved by the AFM. Marketing on the basis of a preliminary prospectus or a presentation at a time that an approved prospectus is not yet available, should only be to investors to whom the offer can be made under an exemption or exception. **17.50**

Advertisements in print or other media of an offer or listing of securities are permitted, but only if they refer to the time and place of availability of the full prospectus and conform to certain other content requirements. **17.51**

17.2.4 Supplementary prospectuses

Any significant new factor, material mistake or inaccuracy relating to the information provided in the prospectus that arises or is identified prior to the end of the offer or the date of admission, requires the publication of a supplement to the prospectus.[42] Supplements must be approved by the AFM. The AFM officially has seven days to do so, but in practice takes considerably less time. **17.52**

The requirement for a supplement arises if the new factor or omission is material in the context of the offering (i.e. information that is relevant for the evaluation of the securities offered). It is up to the issuer to make this determination but not every new fact will be relevant. Even the publication of financial results does not automatically mean that a supplement is required. For example, if the results are in line with previous results or in line with previously given guidance, they would not likely give rise to a supplement requirement. **17.53**

Investors who have already subscribed for shares at the time a supplementary prospectus is published are entitled to withdraw their subscriptions during a two business day period following publication of the supplement. **17.54**

17.2.5 Language

The prospectus can be drafted in Dutch or English. If a prospectus is approved in another member state and drafted in a language other than Dutch or English, the summary must be in Dutch.[43] In these latter situations, in practice, the AFM also allows a summary to be drafted in English. **17.55**

---

[42] Wft section 5:23.
[43] Wft section 5:19.

17.2.6 The AFM approval process

17.56 The AFM must approve the prospectus. The prospectus must be filed with the AFM, together with a formal request for approval and all documents that are incorporated by reference. Also filed with the AFM are the reference sheets setting out the contents of the annexes to the Prospectus Directive which indicate where the information required to be included in the prospectus can be found in the document. When filed, the AFM requires the document to be substantially in final form, although it will allow certain elements that are not yet available to be added with a subsequent filing, such as the issuer's latest financial information.

17.57 If an issuer does not yet have a class of securities admitted to trading, the AFM has 20 business days to review a draft prospectus. If an issuer already has securities that are admitted to trading, the period is ten days. In theory, the AFM has the same period for review for each subsequent filing of the draft prospectus. In practice, the review periods tend to be shorter for the subsequent drafts. It is customary at the beginning of a process to get in touch with the relevant department of the AFM to discuss the timetable and any possible disclosure issues (for example, if an issuer has a complex financial history). The AFM welcomes this and is generally willing to agree on a timetable.

17.58 The AFM provides comments on a comment sheet that follows the numbering of the reference sheets. Answers to the AFM comments are provided on the comment sheet which is then re-filed together with an amended draft.

17.59 Once the AFM has indicated it has no further comments on a prospectus, it generally requires one day to issue its formal approval.

17.2.7 Structure of the prospectus

17.60 As per the Prospectus Directive, three prospectus structures are recognized: (i) the single document; (ii) the tripartite prospectus; and (iii) the base prospectus. The choice for a structure is largely driven by the type of transaction.

17.61 Stand-alone equity issuances are invariably undertaken on the basis of a single prospectus which incorporates all required information on the issuer and the securities offered. As an alternative to a stand-alone document, the prospectus can be composed of three parts: the registration document, the securities note and the summary. This form of prospectus is used—albeit not frequently—for large issuers that undertake several offerings of securities during the year. The registration document is approved first and remains valid for 12 months. The securities note and summary are tailor-made for a specific offering or admission and are approved at the time of such offering or admission, allowing for an efficient and quick disclosure process.

A base document can be used for the offering or admission of certain non-equity **17.62** securities.[44] All information, except for terms that can only be finally determined at the time of the actual offer of the securities, has to be included in the base prospectus. The final terms are filed with the AFM but do not have to be approved by the AFM. It is important to ensure that the final terms are limited to terms that were not yet determinable at the time of approval of the base prospectus but are indicated in that base prospectus as terms to be determined. New terms that are not listed as to be determined in the final terms or any other new relevant information, cannot be included in the final terms. The AFM takes a strict approach to this.

17.2.8 Prospectus contents

The general content requirement has been copied from the Prospectus Directive. **17.63** The prospectus must contain all information which, according to the particular nature of the issuer and of the securities offered to the public or admitted to trading on a regulated market, is necessary to enable investors to make an informed assessment of the assets and liabilities, financial position, profit and losses, and prospects of the issuer and of any guarantor, and of the rights attaching to such securities.[45] The relevant section of the Wft goes on by saying that such information includes the information referred to in sections 3 to 23 of the Prospectus Regulation, including the annexes referred to in these sections.

The second paragraph of section 5:13 adds two elements that are not directly **17.64** derived from the Prospectus Directive. The provision states that the information must not contradict other information in the possession of the AFM. It is not clear what information this could extend to. The other element is that the section states that the information must be presented in a manner that makes it comprehensible for a *reasonably informed person acting prudently.* The addition in italics does not derive from the Prospectus Directive.

The AFM has the formal ability to grant dispensation for certain content **17.65** requirements—in line with the Prospectus Directive—if (i) disclosure of such information would be contrary to the public interest; (ii) disclosure would be seriously detrimental to the issuer, but provided the non-disclosure would not be misleading; or (iii) the information is less relevant and would not influence the assessment of the issuer or guarantor.[46] The AFM has been very reluctant until now to use this authority.

---

[44] Wft section 5:16 (i.e., non-equity securities offered or issued under a programme and certain debt securities issued by credit institutions).

[45] Wft section 5:13(1).

[46] Wft section 5:18(3).

17.66 In determining the contents of the prospectus, the AFM very closely follows the text of the annexes and the relevant CESR Recommendations and CESR FAQs. These are discussed in detail elsewhere in this book.[47] Below we set out a number of aspects of the content requirements that appear to have a specific interpretation in the Netherlands or have raised issues in the past.

17.2.8.1 Price

17.67 As per the Prospectus Directive, the final price and final number of securities offered can be left open in the approved prospectus, provided the prospectus sets out criteria or conditions on which the final price and number will be determined. The Netherlands does not permit an issuer to leave these elements open without inclusion of these criteria or conditions but subject to a two-day withdrawal right period as per section 8(1)(b) of the Prospectus Directive. Upon implementation, the Netherlands deemed that the 'or' between (a) and (b) in section 8(1) provided member states with a choice between the section 8(1)(a) and section 8(1)(b). Hence 8(1)(b) was not implemented.

17.68 There is some uncertainty about both the level of disclosure required to describe the manner in which a final price is determined as well as about the question of whether or not a maximum price must be included at all. Given that, from a marketing perspective, the determination of a final price can be a sensitive exercise, issuers and underwriters welcome any flexibility that is available. In the past, a prospectus would have been approved even without a final price but with only a reference to the overall maximum amount of the offering proceeds. However, practice seems to have moved towards a system where a maximum price must be included. Pricing above the price range would require the publication of a supplement. Regarding the level of disclosure of the method of determining a price, the AFM has recently insisted on more detailed disclosure, most likely in light of the discussions within CESR on this topic.[48] Where in the past, a number of fairly generic references for determining the price were deemed to be sufficient; more recently, additional disclosure has been called for.

17.69 Once the final price and number of securities have been determined, they must be filed in a so-called pricing statement with the AFM and published in the same manner as the prospectus was published.

17.2.8.2 Forward-looking information and profit forecasts and estimates

17.70 The AFM actively monitors previous releases by issuers to determine whether profit forecasts or estimates are still outstanding. The AFM applies a fairly wide

---

[47] See Part 2, Chapter 2 (Equity Offerings) and Chapter 3 (Debt Offerings and Programmes).
[48] See Question 58 of the CESR FAQs.

interpretation of profit forecasts and estimates, by putting a strong emphasis on the words 'by implication' in the definition as included in the Prospectus.[49] Issuers are best advised to carefully analyse any guidance they may wish to provide. If guidance has been given and a prospectus is compiled, such guidance should be looked at carefully to determine whether it requires inclusion with all additional requirements as set out in the CESR Recommendations.[50]

17.2.8.3 Responsibility statements

In most cases, the issuer is responsible for the contents of the prospectus, and the **17.71** prospectus must include a statement to that effect. This statement must closely follow the text as prescribed by the Prospectus Directive. There are no rules creating a direct statutory liability for directors of the company or for underwriters or lead managers, and these groups do not have to issue a responsibility statement. However, underwriters will generally be liable for the prospectus or the conduct of the offering generally on the basis of tort law, in particular misleading advertising. Underwriters therefore, in line with international practice, undertake fairly extensive due diligence exercises, which typically involves legal counsel and may also involve outside auditors and other specialists.

Direct liability of directors of Dutch issuers to investors would have to be estab- **17.72** lished on the basis of general tort law and is more difficult to successfully pursue. A director who is responsible for a misleading prospectus could, however, be held liable directly to the issuer, subject to certain conditions being met.

17.2.8.4 Disclosure of financial information

In the area of financial disclosure, the AFM closely follows the annexes as well as **17.73** the CESR Recommendations and comments in the CESR FAQs.

Typically three years' historical financial information is included, the last two of **17.74** which must be audited under IFRS. If the issuer has been in existence less than three years, the information for that shorter period must be included. In addition, if the issuer has a complex financial history, additional disclosure on predecessor entities would be required.

The AFM treats issuers with a complex financial history pragmatically, irrespec- **17.75** tive of the background to such complex financial history. It uses the freedom it has been given following the amendment to the Prospectus Directive to agree with

---

[49] Prospectus Regulation section 2(10): 'profit forecast' means a form of words which expressly states or by implication indicates a figure or a minimum or maximum figure for the likely level of profits or losses for the current financial period and/or financial periods subsequent to that period, or contains data from which a calculation of such a figure for future profits or losses may be made, even if no particular figure is mentioned and the word 'profit' is not used.

[50] CESR's Recommendations paras 38–50.

issuers on tailor-made disclosure that, on the one hand, adequately informs the investors and, on the other hand, takes into account the constraints for issuers in producing additional—often complex—historical information.[51] Issuers are best advised to seek a dialogue with the AFM in the early stages of preparation of a prospectus.

17.2.8.5 *Working capital statements*

17.76 Under Annex III, issuers are required to include a statement as to the adequacy of their working capital for their present purposes through the next twelve months.[52] The AFM takes the very strict view that the issuer must follow the text literally, but more importantly, because the prospectus will be dated—inherently—prior to completion of the offering, the proceeds of the offering can only be included in calculating working capital if the offering is unconditional. Given that underwriting agreements invariably include the usual conditions and hence the completion of the offering is conditional, the proceeds cannot be included in the working capital calculation. This is different in, for example, the UK where the proceeds can be referred to in the statements and taken into account in the underlying analysis.

17.3 Continuing Obligations

17.3.1 Applicable law

17.77 Dutch listed companies are subject to a considerable number of continuing obligations. The purpose of these obligations is as follows:

- *Informing investors of the financial performance of the company.* Pursuant to the Transparency Directive, listed companies must disclose periodic financial information. These obligations are set out in Chapter 5.1a of the Wft and the Transparency Directive Implementing Decree. They entered into force on 1 January 2009. See Section 17.3.2 below.
- *Disclosure of price-sensitive information.* Subject to certain limited exceptions, listed companies are under the obligation to publish price-sensitive information as soon as such information arises. This obligation originates from the Market Abuse and Transparency Directives, and is implemented in Dutch law in Chapter 5.4 of the Wft and the Market Abuse Decree. See Section 17.3.3 below.

---

[51] Commission Regulation (EC) No 2111/2007 of 27 February 2007 amending Regulation (EC) No 809/2004 implementing Directive 2003/71/EC of the European Parliament and the Council as regards financials information in prospectuses where the issuer has a complex financial history or has a significant financial commitment.

[52] Prospectus Regulation, Annex III clause 3.1 and related CESR Recommendations.

- *Disclosure of transactions by directors.* Pursuant to Sections 5:48 and 5:60 of the Wft, managing directors, supervisory directors and other executives[53] of listed companies are required to notify the AFM of transactions in their company's stock or in related financial instruments. See Section 17.3.4 below.
- *Disclosure of major holdings.* Shareholders owning large holdings (greater than 5%) in listed companies are required to report such holdings to the AFM. The company is required to notify the AFM of the amount of its issued share capital and any changes therein. These obligations are set out in Chapter 5.3 of the Wft and the Decree on the Disclosure of Major Holdings in Listed Companies. The obligations originate from the Transparency Directive. See Section 17.3.5 below.
- *Informing Euronext Amsterdam of relevant changes.* Section 6.10 of Rule Book I and Section A-2705 of Rule Book II contain a number of reporting and information requirements, and an obligation to notify Euronext Amsterdam of any changes to the company's capital structure or articles of association that may have an impact on the listing.

17.3.2 Periodic financial reporting

17.3.2.1 Scope

Except for the requirement to publish an annual information update (see Section 17.3.2.5 below), the Dutch disclosure requirements in relation to periodic financial information only apply to issuers of securities that have been admitted to trading on an EU/EEA regulated market, and of which the Netherlands is the issuer's home member state. The Netherlands is an issuer's home member state if, in short, (i) the issuer has its corporate seat in the Netherlands and is listed on Euronext Amsterdam or any other regulated market in an EU/EEA member state, (ii) the issuer has its corporate seat outside the EEA, but has issued securities that are listed on Euronext Amsterdam or any other regulated market in an EU/EEA member state and the AFM has approved the prospectus, or (iii) the issuer has selected the Netherlands as its home member state in accordance with the Transparency Directive. Certain exceptions for debt securities apply. See Section 5:25a(1)(c) of the Wft. **17.78**

17.3.2.2 Annual reports

An issuer must prepare annual financial information and must make it generally available within four months after the end of its financial year. This is one month shorter than the five-month term that applied before implementation of the Transparency Directive on 1 January 2009. An issuer must ensure that the annual **17.79**

---

[53] Section 5:60 of the Wft only.

financial information remains publicly available for at least five years (for example, by making it accessible on the issuer's website).

17.80 The annual financial information must consist of:[54]

(a) the audited annual accounts;

(b) the annual management report; and

(c) a statement of the 'competent persons' of the issuer (usually certain members of the management board) indicating that to their knowledge:

  (i) the annual accounts give a true and fair view (*getrouw beeld*) of the assets, liabilities, financial position and profit and loss of the issuer and its consolidated companies;

  (ii) the annual management report gives a true and fair view of the issuer and its related companies as per the balance sheet date and the state of affairs during the financial year to which the report relates; and

  (iii) the annual management report contains the material risks the issuer is facing.

17.3.2.3 Half-yearly financial information

17.81 Issuers with securities admitted to trading on a regulated market in an EU/EEA member state of which the Netherlands is the home member state are also required to publish half-yearly financial information. The information must be made generally available no later than two months after the end of the first six-month period of its financial year.[55] An issuer must ensure that the information remains publicly available for at least five years.

17.82 The half-yearly financial information must include the same items as the annual financial information, except that the half-yearly accounts information does not have to be audited. The half-yearly management report must mention the fact that the accounts are unaudited.[56]

17.83 In addition, issuers of shares or depositary receipts admitted to trading on a regulated market in the Netherlands must also include an overview of the most important related-party transactions during the six-month period covered by the half-yearly statements.[57] Transactions qualify as 'important' for the purpose of this requirement if such transactions have had a material impact on the financial position or results of the issuer during the relevant period.[58]

17.84 The half-yearly financial information must also contain an overview of the most important occurrences during the first six-month period of the relevant financial

---

[54] Wft section 5:25c(2).
[55] Wft section 5:25d.
[56] Wft section 5:25d(4).
[57] Wft section 5:25d(9).
[58] Transparency Directive Implementing Decree section 3(1)(a).

year and the consequences of these occurrences on the half-yearly accounts, including a description of the most important risks and uncertainties the issuer will face during the remaining six months of the relevant financial year.[59]

An issuer having its corporate seat in the Netherlands and an issuer in an EU/EEA **17.85** member state of which the Netherlands is its home member state, and which is not required to prepare consolidated annual accounts, must include a summary balance sheet and a summary profit and loss statement together with explanatory notes in its half-yearly accounts.[60] The Transparency Directive Implementing Decree provides for a set of minimum requirements with respect to the annual and half-yearly financial information that must be provided by an issuer having its corporate seat in a state which is not an EEA member state and of which the Netherlands is the home member state.[61]

17.3.2.4 Interim (quarterly) statements

An issuer of shares or depositary receipts admitted to trading on a regulated mar- **17.86** ket in an EEA member state and of which the Netherlands is the home member state must prepare and publish interim management statements.[62] This information must be made available in the first half of the financial year and again in the second half of the financial year. The statement must be made generally available between the period starting ten weeks after the beginning of the relevant six-month period and ending six weeks before the end of such six-month period. No interim statements are required if an issuer is already required to make available quarterly financial reports in accordance with applicable law.[63]

The interim statements must contain a summary of all material events and trans- **17.87** actions which occurred during the relevant period, and the impact of such events and transactions on the financial position of the issuer.[64] The interim statements must also contain a general description of the financial position and performance of the issuer during that period.[65]

17.3.2.5 Annual information update

The annual information update requirement has a wider scope of application. It **17.88** applies to *all* issuers of securities admitted to trading on Euronext Amsterdam— irrespective of whether or not the Netherlands is the issuer's home member state—and requires such issuers to prepare and publish a document which

---

[59] Wft section 5:25d(8).
[60] Wft section 5:25d(5)(b) and (6)(b).
[61] Transparency Directive Implementing Decree sections 9 and 10.
[62] Wft section 5:25e(1).
[63] Wft section 5:25e(3).
[64] Wft section 5:25e(2).
[65] Wft section 5:25e(2)(b).

contains or refers to information generally made available during the preceding 12-month period at least once a year.[66]

17.3.2.6 Incidental information requirements

17.89 The incidental information requirements relate to (i) changes in rights attached to shares or to rights to acquire shares, (ii) changes to the rights of the holders of securities other than shares and (iii) price-sensitive information.

17.90 An issuer of shares admitted to trading on a regulated market in an EU or EEA member state *and* of which the Netherlands is the home member state must immediately disclose information on changes to rights attached to a class of shares or to rights to acquire shares (such as options) if such rights have been issued by the issuer.[67] Similarly, issuers of securities other than shares (such as bonds) admitted to trading on a regulated market in an EEA member state and of which the Netherlands is the home member state must immediately make information on changes to the rights of the holders of such securities generally available.[68]

17.91 Issuers of (financial) instruments admitted to trading on a Dutch regulated market or MTF (such as NYSE Alternext) are also required to immediately make price-sensitive information generally available.[69] In exceptional circumstances, an issuer can postpone the disclosure of price-sensitive information if certain conditions are satisfied.[70] See Section 17.3.3 below.

17.3.2.7 Equal treatment

17.92 Effective 1 January 2009, the principle of equal treatment of shareholders or bondholders in the specific context of disclosure of information is now expressly incorporated in the Wft.[71] Issuers of shares or bonds admitted to trading on a regulated market in an EEA member state and of which the Netherlands is the home member state must ensure that shareholders or, as the case may be, bondholders, in similar positions must be treated equally with respect to furnishing specific information. Furthermore, in order to enable shareholders and bondholders to exercise their rights—at shareholder or bondholder meetings—relevant information and sufficient facilities must be made available by the issuer.[72] This information can be made available through electronic means, subject to,

---

[66] Wft section 5:25e(f).

[67] Wft section 5:25h(1).

[68] Wft section 5:25h(2).

[69] Section 5:25i FSA. This information requirement is in fact derived from Article 6 of the Market Abuse Directive, but has been relocated to the Wft chapter implementing the Transparency Directive.

[70] Market Abuse Decree section 14.

[71] Wft section 5:25k and 5:25l.

[72] Wft section 5:25k(3) and (4) and 5:25l(3) and (4).

amongst others, the consent of the general meeting of shareholders or, as the case may be, bondholders.[73]

17.3.3 Disclosure and control of price-sensitive information

In line with section 6(1) of the Market Abuse Directive, issuers with financial instruments listed on a Dutch regulated market are required to immediately disclose any price-sensitive information as soon as such information arises.[74] The obligation also applies to issuers with instruments listed on Dutch MTFs, such as NYSE Alternext.[75] Effective 1 January 2009, and as a result of the implementation of the Transparency Directive, the requirement was moved from the market abuse section (Chapter 5.4) to the transparency obligations chapter (Chapter 5.1a) of the Wft.

17.93

17.3.3.1 Price-sensitive information

Price-sensitive information within the meaning of the Wft is information of a precise nature which has not been made public, and which relates, directly or indirectly, to one or more issuers of financial instruments or to one or more financial instruments and which, if it were made public, would be likely to have a significant effect on the prices of those financial instruments or on the price of related derivative financial instruments. This definition is based on section 1(1) of the Market Abuse Directive.

17.94

In line with Commission Directive 2003/124/EC,[76] information can be deemed to be of a 'precise nature' if it indicates a set of circumstances which exists or may reasonably be expected to come into existence or an event which has occurred or may reasonably be expected to do so and if it is specific enough to enable a conclusion to be drawn as to the possible effect of that set of circumstances or event on the prices of financial instruments or related derivative financial instruments. In addition, information can be qualified as price sensitive if it is information a reasonable investor would be likely to use as part of the basis of its investment decisions.[77]

17.95

The explanatory notes to the Wft mention changes in the composition of the managing or supervisory board of the issuer, planned takeovers and decisions to repurchase its own shares as examples of events that may constitute price-sensitive

17.96

---

[73] Wft section 5:25k(5) and 5:25l(6).

[74] Wft section 5:25i.

[75] Wft section 5:25i(a)(2°).

[76] Commission Directive 2003/124/EC of 22 December 2003 implementing Directive 2003/6/EC of the European Parliament and of the Council as regards the definition and public disclosure of inside information and the definition of market manipulation, [2003] OJ L339/70.

[77] Commission Directive 2003/124/EC section 1(2).

information when not yet made public. In addition, the AFM published the following non-exhaustive list of examples of information that is likely to qualify as price sensitive.[78]

17.97 Important information with respect to the financial position and results of the issuer:

- periodical financial results;
- significant deviations from prior projections;
- the development of important new products;
- substantial changes to credit facilities and security granted under such facilities, including covenant breaches;
- termination of important credit facilities by one or more banks;
- negative net assets;
- auditor changes (other than in the ordinary course of business);
- important claims and litigation.

17.98 Important information with respect to the issuer's business strategy:

- the purchase or sale of material subsidiaries or business lines;
- the entering into or termination of material joint ventures or business alliances;
- major restructurings;
- strategic pricing changes;
- material changes to the issuer's business activities;
- dissolution;
- filing for suspension of payments or application for bankruptcy.

17.99 Important information with respect to the issuer's capital:

- share splits, including reverse splits;
- changes to the rights attached to the relevant classes of shares;
- dividend announcements, including the announcement or change of the ex-dividend date and changes to the dividend policy;
- important changes to the spread of the shares and free float;
- the preparation or implementation of anti-takeover protection.

17.100 Price-sensitive information must be disclosed by (i) preparing a press release which should be released to general and specialist financial media, (ii) posting the press release on the issuer's website and (iii) submitting the press release to the AFM.

---

[78] AFM, 'Publication of Price Sensitive Information', Institutional Brochure [2005] page 7.

17.3.3.2 *Delaying disclosure*

The immediate disclosure of any price-sensitive information that may arise is not **17.101** always in the best interest of the issuer. Examples include confidential merger negotiations which would be frustrated if the negotiations were to become public,[79] or the fact that a contemplated transaction remains subject to approval by the supervisory board or other similar internal governing body.[80]

Disclosure can be delayed if each of the following three conditions are satisfied: **17.102**

- the delay must serve a legitimate interest of the issuer;
- the delay must not be likely to mislead the public;
- the issuer must ensure the confidentiality of the information.

As soon as one or more of these conditions are no longer satisfied, the issuer must **17.103** immediately disclose the information. It is therefore recommended that the issuer prepare a press release in advance to be able to immediately satisfy such disclosure requirement if it appears that confidentiality is no longer safeguarded.

17.3.3.2.1 Legitimate interest   Dutch law does not provide for a definition **17.104** of the concept of 'legitimate interest'. Instead, the Transparency Directive Implementing Decree lists a non-exhaustive number of situations in which the delay of disclosure may be justified.[81] In addition to the two examples provided above (negotiations where the outcome is likely to be affected by public disclosure and pending supervisory board approval), the decree refers to the following situations:

- An information request by the AFM under the Financial Reporting Supervision Act (*Wet toezicht financiële verslaggeving*) in case of doubts with respect to the accuracy of the issuer's financial statements, or a statement by the AFM that such doubts have not been removed by the additional information provided by the issuer.[82]
- If the issuer is a bank or bank holding company: liquidity support provided by the DNB, the undisclosed appointment of a 'silent' trustee (*stille curator*) by the DNB or a request for application of the emergency regulation (*noodregeling*).[83]

17.3.3.2.2 No misleading of the public   The issuer must ensure that no mis- **17.105** leading of the public occurs, other than as a direct result of the fact that disclosure is delayed. This means, *inter alia*, that the issuer may not issue any statements that

---

[79] Transparency Directive Implementing Decree section 4(1)(a).
[80] Transparency Directive Implementing Decree section 4(1)(b). When relying on this provision, the issuer will have to make an effort to obtain such approval as soon as possible.
[81] Transparency Directive Implementing Decree section 4(1).
[82] Transparency Directive Implementing Decree section 4(1)(d).
[83] Transparency Directive Implementing Decree section 4(1)(c).

would qualify as misleading without the information the publication of which is delayed. By way of example, in the event that disclosure of ongoing merger negotiations is delayed in reliance on the delay of disclosure provisions, the issuer may not publicly deny such talks. If the issuer is asked direct questions about the negotiations, a 'no comment' response is usually recommended.

17.106 17.3.3.2.3 **Ensuring confidentiality**   The issuer must ensure that the undisclosed information is maintained confidential by restricting access to such information to persons that require access to such information in the course of their duties.[84] Relevant measures can include signing confidentiality agreements, creating 'Chinese Walls', the use of code names, numbering hardcopies, restricting access to electronic files and similar actions.

17.107 17.3.3.2.4 **No notification**   Pursuant to the Market Abuse Directive, member states may require that an issuer must notify the regulator if and when it relies on the possibility to delay disclosure. Dutch law does not provide for such a notification requirement, however. The issuer can (and must) decide itself whether delay is justified.

17.3.3.3 *Selective disclosure*

17.108 An issuer may share undisclosed price-sensitive information with others if such disclosure is necessary in the ordinary course of business.[85] This will allow an issuer to engage financial and legal advisers, auditors and other third parties to provide services to the issuer in connection with the matter that involves price-sensitive information. The relevant third parties must be subject to appropriate confidentiality obligations or agreements.

17.109 In addition, issuers are allowed to contact large shareholders and, subject to a non-disclosure agreement, ask whether they would be willing to participate in a new issue of shares before such transaction is publicly announced.[86] In the event of an exchange offer, the issuer may also contact large shareholders of the target to request their commitment to tender their shares in the exchange offer.[87] In both cases, the shareholder may only be contacted if the commitment of the shareholder is reasonably necessary for the success of the transaction. Similarly, the major shareholder that is contacted may confirm its participation in the offering or exchange offer (but would be precluded from doing any further transactions prior to announcement or abortion of the transaction).

---

[84] Transparency Directive Implementing Decree section 4(2).
[85] Wft section 5:57(1)(a).
[86] Market Abuse Decree section 3(a).
[87] Market Abuse Decree section 3(b).

These two exemptions already existed prior to the implementation of the Market Abuse Directive in Dutch law, and have been maintained after implementation. The Directive does not expressly mention these exemptions. However, according to the Dutch legislator, paragraphs 18 and 29 of the preamble to the Market Abuse Directive provide a sufficient basis for the two exemptions.[88]

17.110

17.3.3.4 Insider lists

An issuer must prepare a list of employees and other persons working for the company, such as temporary staff, that have access to inside information on a regular or occasional basis.[89] The list must be kept up to date, and must contain the date on which the list was last updated.[90] It must also state why each person appears on the list. If a person is deleted from the list, the person responsible for maintaining the list must record that such person no longer has access to price-sensitive information, and the effective date of such deletion. These data must be retained for at least five years.

17.111

Advisers and other persons acting on behalf of the issuer do not need to appear on the list maintained by the company, but such advisers must maintain lists of their own.

17.112

17.3.4 Disclosure of transactions by directors and executives

Directors and executives ('persons discharging managerial responsibilities' within the meaning of section 6(4) of the Market Abuse Directive) and certain related persons are required to report private transactions in the issuer's shares, or transactions in financial instruments the value of which is determined in whole or in part by the issuer's shares. The obligation only applies to such persons if the issuer's shares are listed on a regulated market or MTF in the Netherlands and the issuer has its seat in the Netherlands or a non-member state.[91]

17.113

The following persons are subject to the reporting requirement:[92]

17.114

- members of the managing board of the issuer;
- members of the supervisory board of the issuer;
- other executives having regular access to inside information relating, directly or indirectly, to the issuer, and having the power to make decisions that may have an effect on the future developments and business prospects of the issuer; and
- related persons of such board members or executives.

---

[88] Appendix to the explanatory notes to the 2005 Market Abuse Decree.
[89] Wft section 5:59(1).
[90] Market Abuse Decree section 10(1).
[91] Wft section 5:60(1).
[92] Wft section 5:60(1)(a)–(d).

17.115 For the purpose of the reporting obligation, related persons include:[93]

- the spouse of the person discharging managerial responsibilities, or any partner of that person considered as equivalent to the spouse;
- dependent children of the person discharging managerial responsibilities;
- other relatives of the person discharging managerial responsibilities who have shared the same household as that person for at least one year on the date of the transaction concerned; and
- any legal person, trust or partnership, whose managerial responsibilities are discharged by a person discharging managerial responsibilities or his or her spouse, dependent child or relative in the same household.

17.116 The transactions must be reported to the AFM within five working days after the transaction date.[94] A person required to report transactions may postpone the first notification in any given calendar year until the total aggregate transaction value exceeds EUR 5,000. Any subsequent transactions after the EUR 5,000 threshold is reached must be reported within five working days.[95]

17.3.5 Disclosure of major holdings

17.117 Shareholders acquiring a substantial holding or voting rights in a Dutch public limited company (*naamloze vennootschap*) that is listed on an EEA regulated market must notify such holding or voting rights to the AFM if certain thresholds are crossed. The notification requirement applies to both direct and indirect holdings or voting power. Potential interests (such as options or convertibles) must also be reported. A similar notification requirement applies with respect to holdings or voting rights in non-EEA issuers the shares or depositary receipts of which are listed on Euronext Amsterdam.

17.3.5.1 Thresholds

17.118 Shareholders must make a notification to the AFM if their holdings or voting rights reach, exceed or fall below one of the following thresholds: 5%, 10%, 15%, 20%, 25%, 30%, 40%, 50%, 60%, 75% and 95%. The percentage a shareholder holds is calculated by dividing the total share capital interest held by such person by the issued share capital (*geplaatst kapitaal*) of the company. Or, in the case of voting rights, by dividing the number of voting rights held by the total number of voting rights attached to the issued share capital.

17.119 In addition, a person or entity acquiring or disposing of a share with special controlling rights attached to it pursuant to the company's articles of association must

---

[93] Market Abuse Decree section 5.
[94] Wft section 5:60(1).
[95] Wft section 5:60(2).

also report the ownership of such share, irrespective of the percentage held. Examples include priority shares or 'golden shares'.

A percentage interest can also change as a result of changes in the issued share capital of the company (commonly referred to as a 'denominator change'). In the event of a denominator change, the shareholder must also notify the AFM if a threshold is crossed as a result. The AFM provides for an electronic alert service notifying major shareholders of reported changes in the issued share capital of the company. **17.120**

17.3.5.2 Public register

All notifications are recorded in a public register maintained by the AFM. Address details of notifying shareholders are not made public. The register can be accessed online at the AFM's website, http://www.afm.nl. **17.121**

17.3.5.3 Allocation of ownership or voting rights

The basic rule is that the person or entity that is the legal owner, directly or indirectly, of the share or voting right is subject to the notification requirement. However, in an effort to ensure that the register adequately reflects the factual/economic reality rather than simply legal ownership, a number of exceptions to the basic rule exist. Important exceptions include the following situations:[96] **17.122**

- Shares owned by subsidiaries and controlled entities are deemed to be held by the parent. The parent must report the interests held by the group as a whole. Subsidiaries and controlled entities do not need to report their interests. This allocation does not apply to voting rights held by subsidiaries that qualify as fund managers or asset managers, to the extent that they can exercise such voting rights at their sole discretion and independent from the parent.
- A pledgee or holder of a right of usufruct with respect to the shares must notify a voting interest if the pledgee or holder is capable of exercising voting rights under applicable law.
- A person whose shares are held by a third party on such person's behalf must notify the interest held by such person through the third party. The third party is not under an obligation to notify.
- A person is deemed to hold the voting rights of a third party with whom such person entered into a voting agreement.
- A person is deemed to hold the voting rights of a third party if the third party holds those voting rights pursuant to a temporary and paid transfer of voting rights.
- The borrower/buyer in a securities lending transaction does not have to notify the transaction if the borrower/buyer transfers the securities before the end of the following trading day or otherwise loses the right to dispose of such securities.

---

[96] Wft section 5:47.

If the borrower/buyer retains the securities after the end of the following trading day, the borrower/buyer must notify the transaction if a threshold is crossed.

- The manager (*beheerder*) of an investment fund is deemed to own the shares and voting rights held by the custodian (*bewaarder*). The custodian is not deemed to own any shares or voting rights.
- A proxy holder is deemed to own the voting rights it can exercise at its sole discretion.

17.3.5.4 Annual update obligation

17.123 No direct notification requirement exists if potential voting rights are converted into actual voting rights by, for example, the exercise of an option or converting a convertible. In order to ensure that the public register will be updated eventually, shareholders are required to update the register once a year with reference to the actual holdings held as at 1 January at midnight. Such update must be provided to the AFM within four weeks after 1 January of each year.[97]

17.3.5.5 Obligations of the issuer

17.124 The issuer is responsible for the reporting of 'denominator changes' (i.e. changes in the issued share capital of the issuer or voting rights attached to it). All changes exceeding 1% must be reported immediately. Smaller changes can be reported in the aggregate once every quarter. 'Potential' denominator changes, for example as a result of the issue of warrants or convertibles, do not have to be reported. Only actual changes in the issued share capital must be notified.

17.125 The issuer must also report the issuance or cancellation of depositary receipts and any shares with special controlling rights attached to it (such as priority shares or 'golden shares').

17.3.5.6 Obligations of directors

17.126 Members of the managing board and of the supervisory board of the issuer must report actual and potential capital and voting interests in the issuer. They must also report any interests they have in a tied issuer (*gelieerde uitgevende instelling*) within the meaning of Section 5:48 Wft.[98]

17.3.6 Penalties and enforcement

17.127 Violation of the provisions of the Wft constitutes an economic offence. In addition, the AFM has broad investigation and enforcement powers ranging from

---

[97] Wft section 5:41.
[98] A tied issuer is a listed company in which the issuer (i) holds an interest which generates at least 10% of the consolidated turnover of the issuer, (ii) qualifies as a group company of the issuer or (iii) holds at least 25% of the issuer.

imposing fines, requesting information, imposing instructions under penalty (*last onder dwangsom*), issuing binding directions (*aanwijzingen*), suspending trading and reversing trades.

17.3.7 The Dutch Corporate Governance Code

17.3.7.1. *The history of the Dutch Corporate Governance Code*

17.128 The Dutch Corporate Governance Code (the 'DCGC') was prepared by the Dutch Corporate Governance Committee and was adopted in 2003 generally in its current form. As with most similar codes, the DCGC was drafted on the basis of the so-called 'comply or explain' principle, and has a statutory basis in section 2:391, paragraph 4 of the Dutch Civil Code ('DCC'). The DCC[99] leaves open the possibility for a Royal Decree requiring information to be included in the directors' report in addition to the information already required by the DCC, and specifically stipulates that such Royal Decree may require listed companies to account for the manner in which they apply a code of conduct which is designated by such decree.

17.129 In December 2004, a Royal Decree was published designating the DCGC as the code of conduct applying to Dutch companies of which shares are admitted to trading on a regulated market in the EU and, consequently, these companies are required to report to what extent they apply the DCGC. This requirement applies for each financial year that started on or after 1 January 2004.

17.130 The scope of the DCGC was not completely clear when it was adopted, and was clarified in the DCGC 2008, which is discussed below.[100]

17.3.7.2 *The Monitoring Committee*

17.131 The Dutch Minister of Finance appointed a Monitoring Committee, which monitors in a general manner application of the DCGC. This committee reports each year and discusses the manner in which the DCGC is applied by Dutch listed companies. In May 2007, the Monitoring Committee recommended that certain changes be incorporated into Dutch law, both the DCC and the Wft. In July 2009, a draft act implementing the recommendations of the Monitoring Committee was sent to the Dutch Parliament.

17.3.7.3 *The Dutch Corporate Governance Code 2008*

17.132 In December 2008, the Monitoring Committee proposed the Amended Dutch Corporate Governance Code (the 'DCGC 2008'). The Dutch Government accepted the recommendations of the Monitoring Committee and announced

---

[99] DCGC section 2:391 paragraph 4.
[100] The DCGC and the DCGC 2008 are available in Dutch and English at www.commissie corporategovernance.nl.

a Royal Decree requiring Dutch listed companies to apply the DCGC 2008 on the basis of comply or explain for all financial years starting on or after 1 January 2009. Directors' reports in respect of financial years that started on or after 1 January 2009 will have to report on the manner in which the listed company applied the new DCGC 2008.

17.133   The DCGC applies to companies organized under Dutch law of which shares or depositary receipts for shares have been admitted to trading on a regulated market or a comparable system, and to all companies organized under Dutch law with a total balance sheet of more than EUR 500 million of which shares or depositary receipts for shares have been admitted to trading on an MTF or a comparable system (referred to below as listed companies).

17.134   **17.3.7.3.1 Excluded from the scope of the DCGC**   The DCGC does not apply to open-end investment companies nor to companies that have issued only bonds that are traded on a regulated market of an MTF.

17.3.7.4 The AFM—enforcement

17.135   In connection with AFM's review of the financial reporting of Dutch listed companies, including their directors' reports, the AFM monitors whether or not the directors' report includes a corporate governance statement. Although initially it was envisaged that the review of corporate governance statements would be limited to checking whether the directors' report included a corporate governance statement, this review is more and more developing towards a check of the consistency of the information in the corporate governance statement against the information that is publicly available on the issuer. The AFM has the power to ask companies for additional information if, based upon publicly available information, it has reason to doubt whether the information complies with the legal requirements, and it may recommend that additional disclosure be made. If the recommendation is not followed by a listed company, the AFM may ask the Enterprise Division within the Court of Appeal at Amsterdam to order the listed company to properly follow the recommendation of the AFM and to amend the directors' report. The AFM is not required to file such request with the Enterprise Division of the Court of Appeal and it is unlikely that the AFM will file such request if the only issue the AFM has with an annual report is criticism of the corporate governance statement. The Enterprise Division has considerable freedom whether or not to issue an order.

17.3.7.5 The DCGC and the DCGC 2008 and Dutch corporate law

17.136   The DCGC and the DCGC 2008 contain principles and best practice provisions that are intended to regulate relations between the management board, the supervisory board and the shareholders of a Dutch listed company. Under Dutch law, the principles and best practices under the DCGC may conflict with the obligations of the members of a management board and a supervisory board. The DCGC and the DCGC 2008 have a strong shareholder focus that may conflict with the obligation of the boards to weigh the interests of all stakeholders (shareholders, employees, creditors and, to a certain extent, customers), in determining and executing the policies of the company. Although generally it is possible to align the requirements of the DCGC 2008 and the requirements of Dutch corporate law, because of the 'comply or explain' nature of the DCGC 2008, the requirements under corporate law will prevail in case of a conflict.

The DCGC and the DCGC 2008 have purposely not been drafted in a 'legal manner'. This may lead to interpretation issues, particularly where there is an apparent conflict between the DCGC 2008 and the law. **17.137**

Prudent boards should be transparent in case of a conflict of the two sets of rules. If a company has stated that it will apply the DCGC 2008 and considers that it is unable to continue to do so as a result of conflicting obligations, it should communicate in a transparent manner what part of the DCGC 2008 it will cease to apply and the reasons for no longer applying such part. **17.138**

17.3.7.6 The DCGC and the DCGC 2008

The DCGC and the DCGC 2008 basically consist of four parts: a part on the management board, a part on the supervisory board, a part on (the general meeting of) shareholders and a part on financial reporting. **17.139**

17.3.7.6.1 General For a proper understanding of the DCGC we note that the archetype in Dutch law for a company having executive and non-executive directors is a two-tier board system consisting of a management board and a supervisory board. In this two-tier system the management board has the central role, with the supervisory board supervising and advising the management board. In recent years, in part as a reaction to internal developments in the arena of corporate governance, the involvement of supervisory boards of Dutch listed companies has increased. **17.140**

A number of listed companies have organized themselves with a one-tier board consisting of executive and non-executive members. Notwithstanding the fact that the responsibility and the risk of potential liability of non-executive members of a one-tier board is larger than the responsibility and risk of potential liability of a member of a supervisory board, the DCGC and the DCGC 2008 treat them both the same. Of course, a company with a one-tier board may explain, like any company with a two-tier board, why it does not apply certain recommendations of the DCGC. **17.141**

For completeness' sake we note that a bill has been submitted to the Dutch Parliament in order to clarify certain issues that may arise under Dutch law in relation to a one-tier board. These issues include amongst others the decisions of the board on the remuneration of executive members, the possibility for the **17.142** board to suspend executive members and the basis on which responsibilities and liabilities are attributed

17.143   17.3.7.6.2 **The management board**   The management board is the corporate organ with primary responsibility for the operational and financial targets of the company and for its strategy. The management board is also responsible for ensuring that the company has adequate internal risk management and control systems that are suitable for the company and for reporting on those systems and the sensitivity of the company to various risks in the directors' report. Dutch law is likely to develop more in the direction of MD&As being included in annual reports.

17.144   Pursuant to the recommendations of the DCGC 2008, members of the management board should be appointed for a maximum period of four years. Because Dutch corporate law does not provide for a maximum term of appointment, this is a principle that a considerable number of companies do not comply with. One of the reasons is that compliance may have adverse consequences for the members of the management board as employees of the company. The DCGC 2008 gives detailed rules for the manner in which the compensation for members of management boards is to be determined. These are probably the rules that are the least fully complied with by Dutch listed companies. Similarly, the recommendation that members of the management board should not be entitled to more than one year's compensation upon their removal from the board is a recommendation that is often not applied. It should be noted that with the increased focus on termination packages and the government entering into the shareholder base of financial institutions companies find it more difficult not to apply this rule.

17.145   We also note that, even where the compensation of members of a management board is determined by the supervisory board, the shareholders meeting of a Dutch listed company has to approve the remuneration policy of the company as well as any management incentive plans.

17.146   The DCGC 2008 introduces the possibility of a company to invoke a response time of up to 180 days in case shareholders ask for an item to be put on the agenda that would change the strategy of the company. If a management board invokes the right to postpone putting an item on the agenda, the management board should engage in constructive discussions with the shareholders involved. This recommendation may be hard to reconcile with corporate law which in principle requires companies to put items on the agenda if qualifying shareholders so request in a timely manner (more than 60 days before the date of the shareholders' meeting) unless it would be contrary to serious interests of the company. It is still too early to say how this direct conflict between the recommendation and the law will be resolved.

17.147   17.3.7.6.3 **The supervisory board**   Members of the supervisory board of most companies are appointed by the shareholders' meeting for a period of up to four years on the basis of a profile of the supervisory board adopted by the shareholders' meeting. It is recommended that supervisory board members do not serve for more than 12 years. By law, employees cannot serve on the supervisory board of the company by which they are employed nor on the supervisory board of a holding company that directly or indirectly controls their employer. The DCGC recommends that the chairman of the supervisory board is not a former member of the management board of the company.

The DCGC recommends that the compensation of supervisory board members **17.148** should not include any shares or option rights. The DCGC also recommends that, outside the ordinary course of business, a company should not make any loans to or provide guarantees for the benefit of members of its supervisory board and, in the ordinary course of business, only after approval by the supervisory board. Any shares held by supervisory board members in the company should only be for long-term investment purposes.

The DCGC introduced, for the first time, a maximum number of supervisory **17.149** boards of which one person should be a member. This recommendation has been generally accepted. However, only memberships of supervisory boards of Dutch listed companies are taken into account for this purpose. Because the arguments supporting limiting the number of board memberships applies in the same manner as far as other demanding functions are concerned, there is a tendency also to consider what other responsibilities candidates for appointment on a supervisory board have when considering whether they would be fit for appointment.

Each supervisory board member should be capable of assessing the overall policy **17.150** of the company and fulfilling the specific duties designated to him or her by the supervisory board. The DCGC recommends that not more than one member of a supervisory board be not independent. The DCGC defines who will not be considered to be independent.

The DCGC recommends that the supervision of the management board by **17.151** the supervisory board should include: (i) the realization of the company's objectives; (ii) the corporate strategy and the risks inherent in its business activities; (iii) the architecture and the effectiveness of the internal risk management and control systems of the company; (iv) its financial reporting process; (v) the compliance by the company with legal requirements; (vi) the relations between the company and its shareholders; and (vii) corporate social responsibility issues that are relevant to the company's business

The supervisory board and each of its members are responsible for obtaining from **17.152** the management board and the external auditor of the company all information that the supervisory board needs in order to adequately carry out its duties. The supervisory board has the right to obtain information directly from staff members of the company or the external auditor and may invite them to attend its meetings.

17.153 The DCGC recommends that if a supervisory board has five or more members it should appoint an audit committee, a compensation committee and a selection and appointment committee. There is now also a legal requirement for listed companies to have an audit committee; for the purpose of that rule, the supervisory board in its entirety may act as the audit committee.

17.154 **17.3.7.6.4 Conflicts of interest** The DCGC recommends that members of a management board and members of a supervisory board should avoid conflicts of interest and apparent conflicts of interest. It also recommends that possible conflicts of interest be disclosed to the supervisory board.

17.155 **17.3.7.6.5 The shareholders and the shareholders meeting** In part as a protection against unwanted influence in their shareholders' meeting as a result of absenteeism of shareholders, certain Dutch companies have adopted a structure providing for the voting shares in the company to be held by a trust that issues non-voting depositary share certificates that are traded. Absent a threat of a hostile takeover and a number of other exceptions, these trusts by law always have to grant a power of attorney to the holders of the depositary receipts to vote the underlying shares in the shareholders meeting, and the trust only votes the shares of the absentee holders of depositary receipts.

17.156 The DCGC also contains certain recommendations on how such a trust should be organized, but these recommendations are only followed to a limited extent.

17.157 While the DCGC has been fairly successful where recommendations were directed to listed companies, their management and supervisory boards, the recommendations to shareholders are not very concrete and individual shareholders have generally not followed these recommendations. In Section 17.3.7.6.2 above the response time of up to 180 days that a company may invoke when shareholders intend to require a matter to be put on the agenda of the shareholders' meeting that may lead to a change of the strategy of the company, has already been discussed. The DCGC 2008 structures this standstill period as a recommendation to shareholders. Whether that recommendation will be followed without a specific legal basis is far from certain.

17.158 **17.3.7.6.6 Financial reporting** The management board is responsible for establishing and maintaining an adequate management information system and for making sure that the quality of all financial reports issued by the company is up to what may reasonably be required of a similar company while taking into account such elements as its type of business, its size, the markets in which it operates, the risks involved in the type of business and that these reports are complete. The supervisory board has to make sure that the management board fulfils its responsibilities in this respect.

It is recommended that the supervisory board nominates the external auditor of **17.159** the company after having received the advice of the management board and of the audit committee, but that the external auditor be formally appointed by the shareholders' meeting. It is recommended that the external auditor attends the shareholders' meeting in which the financial statements are discussed and responds to questions about the auditor's report.

The external auditor will be invited to attend the meeting of the supervisory board **17.160** at which the financial statements and the auditor's report are discussed. The external auditor may, to the extent the auditor is not invited by the audit committee to attend its meetings, request to be allowed to attend meetings of the audit committee.

The internal auditor works under the responsibility of the management board and **17.161** should have direct access both to the external auditor and to the audit committee. If a company does not have an internal audit function, then the audit committee must review each year whether this may be continued.

18

PORTUGAL

18.1 Introduction

18.1.1 General markets overview

18.01 Portuguese law implementing the MiFID[1] sets out the following organized structures for trading of financial instruments: (i) regulated markets as defined under the MiFID; (ii) multilateral trading facilities ('MTFs'); and (iii) systematic internalization by financial intermediaries ('SI').

18.02 For each of these trading structures there are different market players which offer a wide range of financial products.

---

[1] Directive 2004/39/CE of the European Parliament and the Counsel of 21 April (the 'MiFID').

There are currently four regulated markets operating in Portugal:[2] (i) Euronext **18.03**
(formerly known as Eurolist by Euronext Lisbon), the official stock quotations market managed by *Euronext Lisbon—Sociedade Gestora de Mercados
Regulamentados, SA* ('Euronext Lisbon');[3] (ii) the Euronext Lisbon Futures and
Options Market, the derivatives market also managed by Euronext Lisbon;[4]
(iii) the public debt market (MEDIP) managed by *MTS Portugal—Sociedade
Gestora do Mercado Especial de Dívida Pública, SGMR, SA*; and (iv) the Iberian
Electricity Derivatives Market (*Mercado Regulamentado de Derivados do MIBEL*),
managed by the *OMIP—Operador do Mercado Ibérico de Energia*.

As for MTFs, there are two main trading platforms currently operating in Portugal: **18.04**
(i) EasyNext, managed by Euronext Lisbon and (ii) PEX, managed by OPEX—
SGSNM, SA ('OPEX').

In addition, there are currently two further trading structures organized under the **18.05**
former (pre-MiFID) regulations as non-regulated markets, which do not fall into
any of the types of trading structures described above: the *Mercado Sem Cotações*
and the *Mercado de Estruturados*, both managed by Euronext Lisbon. The *Mercado
Sem Cotações* is a market for trading securities that do not fulfil the requirements
for a stock exchange listing on a regular basis. The *Mercado Estruturados* is a
platform for the listing and trading of structured facilities.

This Chapter will focus on the listing of securities on regulated markets in Portugal **18.06**
and the ongoing disclosure obligations imposed on the issuers of such securities.
Reference to the Euronext—the official quotations market in Portugal—and its
management entity (Euronext Lisbon) will be made as appropriate.

18.1.2 Legal regime

The Portuguese Securities Code (*Código dos Valores Mobiliários*, hereinafter the **18.07**
'PSC'), enacted by Decree-Law No 486/99 of 13 November 1999 ('DL 486/99'),[5]
is the key element in the modernization of Portuguese securities law.

---

[2] The list of the regulated markets operating in Portugal is currently set out in the *Portaria*
556/2005, of 27 June 2005.

[3] Euronext Lisbon is part of the NYSE Euronext group resulting from the merger (completed in
April 2007) between the NYSE Group Inc. (the parent company of the NYSE group) and Euronext
NV (the parent company of the Euronext group). NYSE Euronext brings together six derivatives
exchanges and six cash equities exchanges in five countries: USA, France, Belgium, the Netherlands
and Portugal.

[4] i.e. the Lisbon market of NYSE Liffe.

[5] Among other innovations, the PSC transposed the different EC directives related to securities
matters then in force. Likewise, most of the amendments to the PSC enacted after the PSC first
came into force implemented EC directives adopted since then. Any references made herein to the
PSC refer to the provisions of the PSC as amended by Decree-Law No 61/2002 of 20 March 2002;
Decree-Law No 38/2003 of 8 March 2003; Decree-Law No 107/2003 of 4 June 2003; Decree-Law
No 66/2004 of 24 March 2004; Decree-Law No 52/2006 of 15 March 2006 (implementing the

18.08 The PSC constituted a substantial reform of the legal regime then in force, without, however, affecting the continuity of the markets and avoiding systemic disruptions. This reform was driven by five basic principles: codification, simplification, flexibility, modernization and internationalization.[6]

18.09 The legal regime set out in the PSC is supplemented by several other pieces of legislation and further developed in the regulations and instructions issued by the Portuguese securities regulator, the Securities Markets and Exchange Commission (*Comissão do Mercado de Valores Mobiliários*, the 'CMVM') pursuant to its regulatory powers (as further described in Section 18.1.3. below), and in the rules adopted by entities with self-regulation capacity, in particular the management entities of securities markets and securities depositary and settlement systems.

18.10 In addition to these rules and regulations, the CMVM's recommendations and opinions, although they do not have a generally binding regulatory effect, are also considered by market participants for guidance as to the application and clarification of applicable legal provisions.

18.1.3 Supervision—CMVM

18.11 The supervision of the Portuguese securities markets[7] is generally entrusted by law to the CMVM,[8] an independent administrative body. The CMVM's statutory regime is currently set forth in Decree-Law No 473/99 of 8 November 1999.[9]

EU Directive No 2003/6/CE of the European Parliament and the Council, of 28 January and the Directive No 2003/71/CE of the European Parliament and the Council, of 4 November the 'Prospectus Directive'); Decree-Law No 219/2006 of 2 November 2006 (implementing the Directive No 2004/25/CE, of the European Parliament and the Council, of 21 April the 'Takeovers Directive'); Decree-Law No 357-A/2007 of 31 October 2007 (implementing the MiFID); and Decree-Law No 211-A/2008 of 3 November 2008 (implementing the Directive 2004/109/CE of the European Parliament and the Council, of 15 December 2004 the 'Transparency Directive'); and Law No 28/2009, of 19 June 2009.

[6] A brief explanation of these principles is set out in the preamble of DL 486/99.

[7] For this purpose, supervision refers to the control, surveillance and inspection of the activities of securities markets and market participants. Individuals or entities engaging in cross-border activities are subject to the CMVM's supervision provided such activities have some relevant connection with Portuguese regulated markets or MTFs, or involve transactions or financial instruments subject to Portuguese law.

[8] The PSC (Article 372) expressly contemplates self-regulation and internal disciplinary control by certain entities, such as the management entities of exchanges, in the context of securities markets supervision. However, self-regulation must be consistent with and remains subject to the CMVM's supervisory powers.

[9] Decree-Law No 473/99 of 8 November 1999 has been amended by Decree-Law No 232/2000 of 25 September 2000, Decree-Law No 183/2003 of 19 August 2003 and amended and republished by Decree-Law No 169/2008 of 26 August 2008.

Although certain attributions and powers of the CMVM are contained in its stat- **18.12**
ute and in other regulatory provisions, the general legal framework for the CMVM's
supervision of the securities markets is set forth in Articles 352 et seq. of the PSC.

In addition to the supervision of entities subject to its jurisdiction,[10] the CMVM **18.13**
has the power to issue regulations on matters covered by its duties and powers. The
CMVM also organizes an information disclosure system ('IDS') available to the
public on its website (http://www.cmvm.pt) which includes, among other things,
decisions of interest to the public and any other information notified to the CMVM
or approved by it, such as disclosure by regulated entities of inside information and
qualifying holdings and accounts and prospectuses filed with the CMVM.

18.1.4 Portuguese centralized securities depositary system

Securities listed on a regulated market in Portugal must be registered with the **18.14**
Portuguese centralized securities depositary system (*Central de Valores Mobiliários*,
the 'CVM') managed by *Interbolsa—Sociedade Gestora de Sistemas de Liquidação
e de Sistemas Centralizados de Valores Mobiliários, SA* ('Interbolsa') even where they
are registered with a foreign depository and settlement system.[11]

Interbolsa is a joint stock company, the purpose of which is the management of **18.15**
settlement systems and central securities depository systems.

Interbolsa carries out a wide range of activities, focusing on the following three **18.16**
main areas: (i) the CVM; (ii) the settlement systems; and (iii) the National
Numbering Agency in charge of assigning ISIN codes to securities.

18.2 Securities Listings on Regulated
Markets in Portugal

18.2.1 Requirements for listing

18.2.1.1 *General eligibility criteria*

Securities: In order to be listed on a regulated market securities must comply as to **18.17**
their terms and their form with the requirements of their governing law and be
issued in accordance with the law governing the issuer.[12][13]

---

[10] PSC Article 359.
[11] See Sections 18.2.1.3 and 18.2.7 below.
[12] According to Article 3, no 1, of the Portuguese Companies Code (*Código das Sociedades
Comerciais*), companies are deemed to be governed by the laws of the jurisdiction where their principal headquarters are located and their central management is carried out.
[13] When assessing whether the securities to be admitted were issued under terms allowing the
admission to trading, the regulated market's management entity must take into consideration the

18.18 *Issuer.* In addition, the listing of securities on a regulated market operating in Portugal requires the issuer to comply with the following conditions:[14]

(a) being incorporated and validly existing in accordance with its governing law;

(b) showing that it has an adequate financial and economic situation with regards to the nature of the securities to be listed and to the market on which listing is sought;

(c) having carried out its business activity for at least three years;

(d) having published, under applicable law, its annual accounts for the three years prior to the year in which it applies for listing;

(e) ensuring that securities of the same category have identical rights under the issuer's by-laws and applicable legislation; and

(f) ensuring that the securities are freely transferable and negotiable.

18.19 If the issuer has resulted from a merger or demerger, the requirements referred to in (c) and (d) above are considered fulfilled if they are satisfied by one of the merged companies or the demerger company, as applicable. Furthermore, the CMVM may waive the requirements (c) and (d), if it finds that it is advisable in light of the interests of the issuer and investors and the requirement referred to in (b) above, on its own, allows investors to make a clear assessment on the issuer and the securities.

18.20 In addition, Euronext regulations require that adequate clearing and settlement systems in respect of transactions in the securities are available.

18.2.1.2 Additional eligibility criteria

18.21 **18.2.1.2.1 Listing of shares and/or bonds on an official stock quotations regulated market** The PSC (and its supplementary regulations) set forth certain additional eligibility criteria for the listing of shares and/or bonds on an official stock quotations regulated market with respect to the issue size, minimum public float and expected stock appreciation:

(a) Shares

(1) *Minimum public float:* shares may only be admitted to trading if there is an 'adequate level of public dissemination' by the date on which listing

---

characteristics of the different types of financial instruments set out in Articles 35 to 37 of the MiFID Regulation implementing the MiFID.

[14] The requirements referred to in (b), (c) and (d) do not apply to the admission to trading of bonds: (i) representing Portuguese or foreign public debt; (ii) issued by Madeira, the Azores and the Portuguese municipalities; (iii) issued by Portuguese public entities and public funds; (iv) unconditionally guaranteed by the Portuguese state or by a foreign country; (v) issued by public international legal entities and international financial institutions.

commences. An 'adequate level of public dissemination' is deemed to exist[15] (i) if the number of shares publicly held corresponds to at least 25% of the issuer's subscribed share capital represented by such class of shares or (ii) if, due to the high number of shares of the same class and the large number of shares publicly held, a regular functioning of the market in the shares is ensured even though a lower percentage of the shares is publicly held.[16]

(2) *Market capitalization*: the expected market value of the shares to be listed must be at least EUR 1,000,000, or, if market capitalization cannot be determined, the company's shareholders' equity, based on the results of the last financial year, must be at least EUR 1,000,000.[17] This requirement does not apply to the admission to trading of shares of the same class as shares already listed.

(b) Bonds

(1) *Issue size*: only bonds in a principal amount of at least EUR 200,000 may be admitted to trading on a regulated market.

(2) *Convertible bonds*: the admission to trading on a regulated market of bonds convertible into shares or with the right to subscribe for new shares is subject to the prior or simultaneous admission to trading of the shares subject to the right of conversion or subscription, or of shares belonging to the same class. The CMVM may waive this requirement, if such waiver is also permitted under the law governing the issuer and the issuer shows that potential bond-holders have the necessary information to make a reasonable assessment of the value of the shares into which the bonds are convertible.

(3) *Secondary listing*: the admission of bonds convertible into shares or with a right to subscribe for shares already admitted to trading on a regulated market situated or operating in another EU member state where the issuer has its head office are subject to prior consultation by the CMVM with the competent authority of such member state.

18.2.1.2.2 Securities governed by foreign law[18] *Legal opinion*: Except where **18.22** securities are admitted to trading on a regulated market situated or operating in an EU member state, the CMVM may ask the issuer to submit a legal opinion

---

[15] PSC Article 229 No 2. In the case of an application for shares of the same class of shares already listed, the adequacy of the number of shares in public hands is assessed in view of the total number of listed shares.

[16] According to the Euronext Lisbon market rules, the percentage in this latter case must not be less than 5% and represent an amount of at least EUR 5,000,000, calculated on the basis of the offer price.

[17] Euronext Lisbon may require a market capitalization of more than EUR 1,000,000 if there is another regulated market operating in Portugal in which the eligibility criteria for this purpose are the same.

[18] PSC Article 40 provides that the terms and conditions of securities are generally governed by the personal law of the issuer, except if, in relation to bonds and other securities, such terms and

attesting the satisfaction of the general eligibility criteria described in Section 18.2.1.1 above concerning the securities and the valid existence of the issuer in accordance with its governing law.

18.23 *Depositary receipts*: Where the law governing the securities to be admitted to trading does not permit their direct admission to a market located or operating abroad, or the admission of such securities appears to be operationally difficult, certificates evidencing the registration or deposit of such securities may be admitted to trading on regulated markets located or operating in Portugal.

18.2.1.3 Securities issued by foreign issuers—requirement for liaison financial intermediary

18.24 Foreign issuers must appoint a financial intermediary for liaising with the market which must be (i) a credit institution authorized to carry out its activity in Portugal and (ii) a member of the centralized securities depository and settlement systems where the listed securities are to be registered.[19]

18.25 The financial intermediary is responsible for:

(a) submitting the listing application and ensuring compliance with the listing procedures of and liaising with the CMVM, the management entity of the regulated market and Interbolsa;

(b) providing, on behalf of the issuer, the exercise of the economic rights inherent in the listed securities; and

(c) providing, on behalf of the issuer, the information that the issuer is required to provide by law.

18.26 In addition, where the securities to be listed are registered with a foreign depository and settlement system, the financial intermediary is also responsible for ensuring that such securities registered with the management entity of the foreign settlement system are also registered in individual accounts opened with participants in the foreign settlement system, in permanent coordination with such foreign participant.

18.27 In this context, the financial intermediary will enter into an agreement with the issuer and the participant in the foreign depository and settlement system (although if the financial intermediary is also a member of the foreign depository and settlement system, the participation of a foreign participant may not be required). This agreement and any amendments must be submitted to the prior approval of the regulated market's management entity.

---

conditions specify that another law is applicable. The issuer's governing law is also applicable to the terms of securities that grant rights to subscription, acquisition or sale of other securities.

[19] See Section 18.2.7. below.

18.2.1.4 Liquidity provider

The admission to trading on Euronext of warrants, certificates, credit-linked notes, reverse convertible notes and mandatory convertible securities requires the issuer to enter into an agreement with one or more liquidity providers.[20] **18.28**

The liquidity provision agreement must comply with model contractual clauses set forth in an instruction issued by Euronext Lisbon[21] and may adopt two different structures: **18.29**

(a) If the issuer is a member of Euronext Lisbon, it may enter into an agreement with the stock exchange and act as issuer and liquidity provider.

(b) If the issuer is not a member of Euronext Lisbon, it will have to enter into a similar arrangement with the stock exchange, acting as issuer and:

   (i) nominally assuming the role of liquidity provider itself, in which case it will have to appoint a financial intermediary (which must be a member of Euronext Lisbon and will also be a party to the agreement) to carry out any liquidity provision activities on its behalf; or

   (ii) appoint a third party (which must be a member of Euronext Lisbon and will also be a party to the agreement) to act as liquidity provider.

18.2.2 Listing application

Initiative for listing: As a general rule, the admission of securities to trading on a regulated market requires the decision of the market management entity,[22] upon the issuer's request for admission. Foreign issuers must submit their listing application through the financial intermediary they must appoint for liaising with the market, as described in Section 18.2.1.3 above. **18.30**

Additionally, securities may be admitted to trading (i) at the request of the holders of at least 10% of the securities of the same class, and (ii) in case of bonds issued by the Portuguese State, at the request of the *Instituto de Gestão do Crédito Público*. **18.31**

Listing application and documentary requirements: The application for listing is submitted to the regulated market's management entity, together with documents necessary to show compliance with the listing requirements. **18.32**

In particular, prior to listing securities on the regulated market, the issuer must, as a general principle, publish a prospectus (as further described in **18.33**

---

[20] Rule LI 2.7.1. of Regulation II (Non-Harmonised Rules) of Euronext Lisbon.
[21] Instruction LI 2003-03 of Euronext Lisbon.
[22] Securities admitted to trading on a regulated market may be subsequently admitted to trading in other regulated markets and MTFs in Portugal or other member states without the issuer's consent. However, in this case, the securities market management entity of the secondary market must give notice of such further admission to the issuer.

Section 18.2.3. below). The market management entity will send to the CMVM a copy of the listing application together with the documents required for the approval of the prospectus.

18.34 *Representative for relationship with the market:* At the time the application for admission is filed an issuer of securities to be admitted to trading on a regulated market must appoint a representative with appropriate powers for liaising with the market and the CMVM.

18.35 This representative must be a member of a management body, a manager or a person with similar duties within the issuer or the financial intermediary (including the financial intermediary referred to in Section 18.2.1.3. above), if any, pursuant to an agreement subject to approval by the CMVM.

18.36 The representative must be available to be contacted and ensure availability for and promptness in providing clarifications to the market generally and the CMVM, in particular during stock exchange sessions.

18.2.3 Prospectus

18.37 The implementation of the Prospectus Directive into Portuguese law was completed in March 2006.

18.38 Some of the basic features of the Prospectus Directive—such as the obligation to publish a prospectus approved by a national competent authority prior to the public offer and/or admission to trading of securities—had already been included in the PSC in its original version.

18.39 However, the level of harmonization within EU legislation introduced by the Prospectus Directive, particularly regarding the format of prospectuses and the prospectus passporting regime, significantly contributed to the increase in the number of securities publicly offered and/or listed in Portugal by both domestic and foreign issuers.

18.40 From a market practice standpoint, it is also worth noting that the common positions agreed by CESR members in respect of the frequently asked questions regarding prospectuses ('CESR Q&A on the Prospectus Directive') are usually followed by the CMVM[23] and therefore constitute an important tool when preparing a prospectus for approval by the CMVM.

---

[23] http://www.cmvm.pt/NR/rdonlyres/542657CE-77E4-47A2-BF28-2A18F392C8C7/12514/Q_Aprospectus9version.pdf.

The European harmonization of the regulations regarding the issue and trading of **18.41** securities, including through the Prospectus Directive, is discussed in more detail in Part 1.

18.2.3.1 Obligation to publish a prospectus

As a general rule, the circumstances that require a company to prepare a **18.42** prospectus under Portuguese law are essentially those set out in Article 3 of the Prospectus Directive. Accordingly, any offer of securities[24] to the public in Portugal[25] and any admission to trading on a regulated market situated or operating in Portugal[26] is subject to the requirement to publish a prospectus.

If the public offer concerns securities already listed or expected to be listed on **18.43** a regulated market operating in Portugal or any other EU member state, a single prospectus satisfying the requirements for both effects may be approved and used.

---

[24] The legal definition of securities set out in PSC Article 1/1 is given as an 'open-ended' concept. Therefore, (i) shares, (ii) bonds, (iii) equity instruments, (iv) units in collective investment schemes, (v) rights detached from the securities referred to in items (i) to (iv) (provided that such detachment applies to all issues or series, or is foreseen in the issue decision); (vi) asset-backed securities; (vii) warrants; (viii) certificates; (ix) convertible securities (reverse convertibles and mandatory convertible securities); (x) credit-linked notes and (xi) all other documents representing fungible legal situations (i.e. where all legal obligations have the same terms and conditions and the issuer is the same) that may be transferred in the securities markets (transferable securities), are characterized as securities. The securities referred to in item (xi) are classified by the CMVM as 'structured securities', therefore constituting a new legal type of security with different sub-types according to the specific characteristics of each relevant financial product.
Following the implementation of the MiFID into the Portuguese legal system, the legal definition of securities, as far as the scope of the PSC is concerned, was substituted by that of financial instruments, which includes, in addition to the securities listed above, the following instruments: (i) money-market instruments, except for means of payment; (ii) derivative instruments for the transfer of credit risk; (iii) financial contracts for differences; (iv) options, futures, swaps, forward rate agreements and any other derivative contracts relating to (a) securities, currencies, interest rates or yields, or other derivative instruments, financial indices or financial measures which may be settled physically or in cash; (b) commodities, climate variables, freight rates, emission allowances, inflation rates or other official economic statistics that must be settled in cash or may be settled in cash at the option of one of the parties; (c) commodities that can be physically settled provided that they are traded on a regulated market or multilateral trading facility or, not being for commercial purposes, which have the characteristics of other derivative financial instruments under the terms of Article 38 of the MiFID Regulation implementing the MiFID; (v) any other derivative contracts, namely those relating to any of the items indicated in Article 39 of the MiFID Regulation, provided they have characteristics similar to those of other derivative financial instruments set out in Article 38 of the MiFID Regulation. The regulatory regime applicable to public offerings in the PSC remains limited to financial instruments qualifying as securities.

[25] Article 134, No 1 of the PSC implementing Article 3, No 1 of the Prospectus Directive.

[26] Article 236, No 1 of the PSC implementing Article 3, No 3 of the Prospectus Directive. See Section 18.1.1 above.

18.44 According to Article 108 of the PSC, a public offer of securities is deemed to occur in Portugal where an offer is specifically addressed to individuals or legal entities resident or domiciled in Portugal and:

(a) the offer is made in all or in part to unidentified addressees;

(b) the offer is made to all shareholders of a public company (*sociedade aberta*),[27] even if its share capital is represented by registered shares;

(c) the offeror, on or before the launching of the offer, engages in soliciting activities in connection with unidentified addressees, or is engaged in promotion or publicity activities regarding the offer; or

(d) the offer is made to, at least, 100 non-qualified investors resident or domiciled in Portugal.

18.45 However, an offer of securities is deemed to be a private placement when:

(a) none of the requirements for a public offer described above are met;

(b) the offer is made only to qualified investors (as defined by law[28]); or

---

[27] Under Portuguese law, the following companies qualify, for these purposes, as public companies ('*sociedades abertas*'): (i) companies incorporated in the context of an initial public offer specifically made to individuals or entities resident or with a permanent establishment in Portugal; (ii) companies having issued shares or other equity securities publicly offered to individuals or entities resident or established in Portugal; (iii) companies having issued shares or other equity securities that are or have been listed in an official market located or operating in Portugal; (iv) companies having issued shares sold, in an amount exceeding 10% of their share capital, through a public offer made to individuals or entities resident or established in Portugal; and (v) companies incorporated as a result of a split or merger process of a public company.

[28] Pursuant to PSC Article 30/1, qualified investors ('qualified investors') means the following entities: (i) credit institutions, (ii) investment firms, (iii) collective investment schemes and collective investment scheme managing companies, (iv) insurance companies, (v) pension funds and pension fund managing companies, (vi) other authorized or regulated financial institutions, including securitization funds and securitization fund managing companies, other finance companies, securitization companies, venture capital companies, venture capital funds and venture capital funds managing companies, (vii) financial institutions of non-European Union member states that carry out any of the activities referred to in paragraphs (i) to (vi) above; (viii) entities trading financial instruments on commodities; and (ix) national and regional governments, central banks and public debt management entities, supranational or international institutions, including the European Central Bank, the European Investment Bank, the International Monetary Fund and the World Bank.

In addition, for the purposes of certain provisions of the PSC relating to offers of securities and reflecting relevant provisions of the Prospectus Directive (Articles 109/3/c, 112/3 and 134/2/a) and admission to trading (Article 237-A/1/d), the following entities are also deemed qualified investors: (a) legal entities other than those referred to above whose principal corporate purpose is to invest in securities; and (b) companies meeting, according to their latest individual or consolidated accounts, two of the following requirements: (i) an average of at least 250 employees during the last financial year; (ii) a total balance sheet of more than EUR 43,000,000; and (iii) a net turnover of more than EUR 50,000,000. In addition, the following entities may also be considered qualified investors under the PSC, provided they have registered with the CMVM to this end ('Voluntary Qualification'): (a) small and medium-sized companies that have their registered office in Portugal and which, according to their last annual or consolidated accounts, meet only one of the criteria as to number of employees, balance sheet and turnover described above; and (b) individuals who are resident in Portugal and who meet at least two of the following criteria: (i) having carried out

(c) the offer is made by a non-public company to the majority of its shareholders, except in those cases described in paragraph (c) above in relation to public offers.

Publicity and marketing activities are not expressly defined in the Portuguese **18.46** regulations. However, the CMVM construes these concepts very broadly to include any form of communication addressed to prospective investors aimed at promoting the subscription or acquisition of any financial instruments (including securities), including *inter alia* any advertisement campaigns made through the media, contacts made via telephone, mail, or email, personal visits, road shows, etc. For additional information on advertisements please refer to Section 18.2.5. below.

In addition to the aforementioned private placement exemptions and reflecting **18.47** relevant provisions of the Prospectus Directive, the following offers of securities— even if being specifically directed at persons resident or having an establishment in Portugal and otherwise falling under the legal definition of public offers—do not trigger the requirements under Portuguese laws and regulations regarding public offers set out in the PSC and are therefore not subject to the obligation to publish a prospectus:

(i) an offer of securities addressed to investors who acquire securities for a total consideration of at least EUR 50,000 per investor, per each offer;[29]
(ii) an offer of securities with a denomination per unit of at least EUR 50,000;[30]
(iii) an offer of securities with a total consideration of less than EUR 2,500,000, such limit being calculated over a 12-month period;[31] and

transactions of a significant size on securities markets at an average frequency of, at least, ten per quarter over the previous four quarters; (ii) holding a securities portfolio in excess of EUR 500,000; and (iii) working or having worked for at least one year in the financial sector in a professional position which requires knowledge of investment in securities. The CMVM has the power to set, through a Regulation, the form of organization and operation of the register for voluntary qualification, in particular the details required for registration and evidence of the criteria described above, as well as the procedures to be observed for registration and rectification and cancellation thereof. Finally, the CMVM is entitled to grant the status of qualified investors to other entities with special proficiency and experience regarding securities—including issuers—establishing the economic and financial conditions for such qualification through a Regulation. No Regulation has been issued so far by the CMVM regarding this last qualification and the Voluntary Qualification described to above. Likewise, there is no legal definition of non-qualified investors, including high net worth investors. However, this category is deemed to include all of those persons or entities who are not qualified as qualified investors as described above ('non-qualified investors').

[29] PSC Article 111/1(e) implementing Prospectus Directive Article 3.2(c).
[30] PSC Article 111/1(e) implementing Prospectus Directive Article 3.2(d).
[31] PSC Article 111/1(i) implementing Prospectus Directive Article 1.2(h).

(iv) an offer of shares issued in substitution for shares of the same class already issued, if the issuing of such new shares does not involve any increase in the issued share capital.

18.48 In the case of (iii) above, the issuer may prepare a prospectus in accordance with the PSC and any applicable supplementary legislation.

18.2.3.2 *Competent authority*

18.49 The CMVM[32] is the competent authority to approve prospectuses for public offers and/or listings of securities made by for issuers whose 'home member state', pursuant to relevant provisions of the Prospectus Directive as implemented into Portuguese law, is Portugal.

18.50 Portugal will always be the home member state for issuers having their registered office in Portugal, in respect of the issue of (i) shares, (ii) securities giving the right to acquire shares, provided that such securities are issued by the issuer of the underlying shares or by an undertaking belonging to its group, and (iii) other securities with a denomination per unit of less than EUR 1,000.

18.51 However, for offers or listings of certain securities, issuers or offerors may choose a home member state and thereby select which competent authority will have jurisdiction with respect to such offer or listing on a regulated market, between the member state where the issuer has its registered office and the member state where the securities were or will be admitted to trading on a regulated market or offered to the public. This choice is available for a public offer/admission to trading of:

(a) non-equity securities with a minimum denomination per unit of EUR 1,000;
(b) non-equity securities giving the right to acquire any securities or to receive a cash amount, upon conversion or exercise of rights, provided that the issuer of the non-equity securities is not the issuer of the underlying securities or an entity belonging to the group of the latter.

18.52 In the case of non-EU issuers not falling into one of the categories above, the home member state, and thus the competent authority, will be the member state where the securities are intended to be offered to the public for the first time or where the application for admission to trading on a regulated market is made for the first time, at the choice of the issuer or the offeror, as the case may be. In case

---

[32] PSC Article 145 implementing Prospectus Directive Article 21. The CMVM may choose to delegate the approval of a prospectus to the competent authority of another EU member state, upon such authority's prior consent. The delegation of powers is notified to the issuer or the offeror within three business days from the CMVM's decision.

this initial selection of a member state was not made by the issuer, the issuer may subsequently select a different member state as its home member state.

18.2.3.3 *Prospectus exemptions*

Exemptions from the obligation to publish a public offer prospectus: Pursuant to the **18.53** provisions of the Prospectus Directive as implemented in Portugal, the publication of a prospectus is not required where the public offer consists of:

(a) securities to be allotted in connection with a merger to at least 100 shareholders who are not qualified investors, provided that a document containing information which is regarded by the CMVM as being equivalent to information contained in a prospectus is available at least 15 days before the date of the shareholders' meeting;[33]

(b) shares offered, allotted, or to be allotted free of charge to existing shareholders, and dividends paid out in the form of shares of the same class as the shares in respect of which such dividends are paid, provided that a document is made available containing information on the number and nature of the shares and the reasons for and details of the offer;[34] and

(c) securities offered to existing or former directors or employees by their employer which has securities already admitted to trading on a regulated market or by an affiliated undertaking, provided that a document is made available containing information on the number and nature of the securities and the reasons for and details of the offer.[35]

In each of the above cases, the offeror may alternatively prepare a prospectus in **18.54** accordance with the PSC and any applicable supplementary legislation.

The required information described in (a) to (c) must be provided to the CMVM **18.55** before the offer is launched or the relevant event occurs.

Exemptions from the obligation to publish a listing prospectus: The publication of a **18.56** prospectus is not required where the admission to trading on a regulated market is sought for:

(a) shares issued in substitution for shares of the same class already issued, if the issuing of such new shares does not involve any increase in the issued share capital;

---

[33] PSC Article 134/2(a) implementing Prospectus Directive Article 4/1(c).

[34] PSC Article 134/2(b) implementing Prospectus Directive Article 4/1(d). The exemption concerning the offer of shares offered, allotted, or to be allotted free of charge to existing shareholders, is not expressly mentioned in the PSC; however, it is deemed implemented. In this respect, the CMVM shares the views of the CESR Q&A on the Prospectus Directive according to which in such cases there is no offer of securities to the public (as defined in Prospectus Directive Article 1.2.(d)).

[35] PSC Article 134/2(c) implementing Prospectus Directive Article 4/1(e).

(b) securities to be allotted in connection with a merger to at least 100 shareholders who are not qualified investors, as defined under applicable rules, provided that a document containing information which is regarded by the CMVM as being equivalent to information contained in a prospectus is available at least 15 days before the date of the shareholders' meeting;[36]

(c) shares offered, allotted, or to be allotted free of charge to existing shareholders, and dividends paid out in the form of shares of the same class as the shares in respect of which such dividends are paid, provided that the shares are of the same class as shares already admitted to trading in the same regulated market and a document is made available containing information on the number and nature of the shares and the reasons for and details of the offer;[37]

(d) securities offered to existing or former directors or employees by their employer which has securities already admitted to trading on a regulated market or by an affiliated undertaking, provided that the securities are of the same class as securities already admitted to trading in the same regulated market and a document is made available containing information on the number and nature of the securities and the reasons for and details of the offer;[38]

(e) shares representing, over a period of 12 months, less than 10% of the number of shares of the same class as the shares already admitted to trading on the same regulated market;[39]

(f) shares resulting from the conversion or exchange of other securities or from the exercise of the rights conferred by other securities, provided that such shares are of the same class as shares already admitted to trading on the same regulated market;[40]

(g) securities already admitted to trading on another regulated market, if the following conditions are met:[41]

  (i) such securities, or securities of the same class, have been admitted to trading on such other regulated market for more than 18 months;

  (ii) for securities first admitted to trading on a regulated market, the admission to trading on that other regulated market occurred on the basis of

---

[36] PSC Article 236/2(a) implementing Prospectus Directive Article 4/1(c).

[37] PSC Article 236/2(b) implementing Prospectus Directive Article 4/1(d). The exemption concerning the offer of shares offered, allotted, or to be allotted free of charge to existing shareholders, is not expressly mentioned in the PSC; however, it is deemed implemented. In this respect, the CMVM shares the views of the CESR Q&A on the Prospectus Directive according to which in such cases there is no offer of securities to the public (as defined in Prospectus Directive Article 1.2.(d)).

[38] PSC Article 236/2(c) implementing Prospectus Directive Article 4/1(e).

[39] PSC Article 236/2(d) implementing Prospectus Directive Article 4/2(a).

[40] PSC Article 236/2(e) implementing Prospectus Directive Article 4/2(g).

[41] PSC Article 236/2(f) implementing Prospectus Directive Article 4/2(h).

an approved prospectus made available to the public pursuant to Article 140 of the PSC (implementing Article 14 of the Prospectus Directive);

(iii) except in the case of (ii), for securities first admitted to listing after 30 June 1983, listing particulars were approved in accordance with the requirements of Directive 80/390/EEC[42] or Directive 2001/34/EC;[43]

(iv) the ongoing obligations for trading on that other regulated market have been satisfied;

(v) the person seeking the admission of securities to trading on a regulated market under this exemption makes a summary document available to the public in a language accepted by the CMVM;[44] and

(vi) the contents of the summary document comply with Article 135-A of the PSC (implementing Article 5(2) of the Prospectus Directive) and state where the most recent prospectus can be obtained and where the financial information published by the issuer pursuant to its ongoing disclosure obligations is available.

18.2.3.4 *Preparation of the prospectus*

18.57 Drafting a prospectus typically requires intensive drafting work and full coordination between the issuer/offeror (including its auditors), the financial intermediaries involved, and their legal advisers.

18.58 Preliminary drafting work includes, among other things, the selection of the sources of information to be included in the prospectus, agreeing on a timetable for drafting, submission and approval by the CMVM and agreeing on the prospectus structure and its contents.

18.59 **18.2.3.4.1 Structure and contents** The Prospectus must be prepared in accordance with the Portuguese legislation implementing the Prospectus Directive and the Prospectus Directive Regulation.

18.60 *Structure of the prospectus*: Prospectuses may be drafted (1) as a single document, or (2) as a set of the following discrete documents which can be distributed separately:[45]

(i) the *registration document* which contains relevant information regarding the issuer;

---

[42] Council Directive 80/390/EEC of 17 March 1980, coordinating the requirements for the drawing up of scrutiny and distribution of the listing particulars to be published for the admission of securities to official stock exchange listing.

[43] Directive 2001/34/EC of the European Parliament and of the Council of 28 May 2001 on the admission of securities to official stock exchange listing and on information to be published on those securities.

[44] See Section 18.2.3.6 below.

[45] PSC Article 135-B implementing Prospectus Directive Article 5, No 3.

(ii) the *securities note* which contains information regarding the securities to be offered/admitted to trading; and

(iii) the *summary*[46] consisting of a brief description of the registration document and of the securities note, written in non-technical language, including a summary of the risks associated with the issuer, the guarantor (if any) and the securities to be offered and/or admitted to trading.

18.61 The choice of the prospectus structure will mainly depend on the frequency at which the issuer intends to publicly offer and/or request the admission to trading of securities under the same valid prospectus.[47]

18.62 In addition to a unitary or three-part prospectus as described above the issuer, the offeror or the person asking for the admission to trading on a regulated market may as a further alternative also publish a base prospectus, which contains information on the issuer or issuers and the securities to be publicly offered/admitted to trading. A base prospectus structure may be used in respect of:[48]

(i) non-equity securities issued under an offering programme; and

(ii) non-equity securities issued in a continuous or repeated manner by credit institutions, where:

(a) the proceeds from the issuance of such securities are placed in assets which provide sufficient coverage for any liabilities under the securities until their maturity date; and

(b) in the event of the insolvency of the credit institution, the relevant sums are intended, by priority, to repay the capital and interest falling due.

18.63 If the final terms of the securities to be offered or admitted are not already included in either the base prospectus or a supplement to the base prospectus,[49] such final terms must be provided to investors and filed with the CMVM as soon as practicable and, in general,[50] in advance of the beginning of the offer/admission to trading, although the final terms are not separately approved by the CMVM.

18.64 *Contents*: The information that is required to be included in the prospectus depends mainly on the type of issuer and securities to be offered or admitted.

---

[46] The summary is not mandatory for prospectuses for admission to trading on a regulated market of non-equity securities having a denomination of at least EUR 50,000.

[47] See Section 18.2.3.4.3 below.

[48] PSC Article 135-C implementing Prospectus Directive Article 5, No 4.

[49] The base prospectus must be supplemented, if necessary, with updated information regarding the issuer and the securities to be offered to the public, by means of a supplement, as further described in Section 18.2.3.4.4 below.

[50] The CMVM's position is that the exact moment when the final terms must be provided depends on the level of information included in each of the base prospectus and the final terms.

In general, a prospectus must contain complete, true, current, clear and objective **18.65** information that complies with applicable laws and regulations, necessary to enable investors to make an informed assessment of the offer (as the case may be), the terms and conditions of the securities offered or admitted to trading and the assets and liabilities and economic and financial position of the issuer or the guarantor, if any, as well as the prospects for the business and earnings of the issuer and the guarantor, if any.[51]

Minimum contents requirements are provided for in the schedules and building **18.66** blocks set out in the Prospectus Directive Regulation. These schedules and building blocks allow for different combinations where one schedule does not cover all necessary information.

Public offer and listing prospectuses must also include statements by the persons **18.67** who are responsible for their contents[52] that, to the best of their knowledge, the information contained in the prospectus is factually accurate and that there are no material omissions in the prospectus.

Additional information may be included in the prospectus, to the extent appro- **18.68** priate in light of the nature of the issuer and the securities to be offered or admitted.

Omission of information from the prospectus: Upon the issuer's or the offeror's **18.69** request, the CMVM may authorize the omission of certain information from the prospectus, the inclusion of which would otherwise be required, where:

(a) disclosure of such information would be contrary to the public interest;
(b) disclosure of such information would be seriously detrimental to the issuer, provided that the omission would not be likely to mislead the public with regard to any facts and circumstances essential for an informed assessment of the issuer, offeror or guarantor, if any, and of the rights attached to the securities to which the prospectus relates; or
(c) such information is of only minor importance in the context of an offer or admission to trading and is unlikely to influence the assessment of the financial position and prospects of the issuer, offeror or guarantor, if any.

Information incorporated by reference: Issuers may incorporate information in the **18.70** various sections of the prospectus, other than the summary, by reference to external documents, provided such documents have been previously filed with the CMVM.

---

[51] PSC Article 135 implementing Prospectus Directive Article 5.
[52] See Section 18.2.3.7 below.

18.71 **18.2.3.4.2 Submission and approval by the CMVM** *Submission*: The application for the approval of the prospectus must be submitted to the CMVM together with the following documents:

(a) a copy of the resolutions authorizing the issuance and offer of the securities passed by the issuer's and/or offeror's competent corporate bodies, and any required management decisions;

(b) a copy of the issuer's by-laws;

(c) a copy of the offeror's by-laws (where different from the issuer);

(d) a current certificate of company registration of the issuer;

(e) a current certificate of company registration of the offeror (where different from the issuer);

(f) a copy of the management reports and accounts, the opinions of the supervisory corporate bodies and the legal certification of the issuer's accounts for the periods required under the Prospectus Directive Regulation;

(g) a report or statement from an auditor, prepared in accordance with Articles 8 and 9 of the PSC;[53]

(h) the identification code or codes of the securities covered by the approval request;

(i) a copy of the contract with the financial intermediary assisting in the transaction;[54]

(j) a copy of the placing contract and the placing consortium contract, if applicable;

(k) a copy of the liquidity provider agreement, stabilization contract and greenshoe contract, if applicable;

(l) the draft prospectus; and

(m) pro-forma financial information, where required.[55]

---

[53] According to Article 8 of the PSC, annual financial information contained in a prospectus must be covered by a report prepared by an auditor registered with the CMVM. Whenever business plans or forecasts on the economic and financial situation of the relevant entity are included, the auditor's report should clearly address the assumptions used, and criteria applied, as well as their consistency. In the case of interim information or any quarterly or half-yearly financial information that has been the subject of an audit or limited review, the audit or review report should be included, failing which such exclusion should be disclosed.

Only chartered accountants' firms and other auditors qualified to perform their services in Portugal that have the human, material and financial resources necessary to guarantee their reputation, independence and technical competence, may register as auditors with the CMVM. The CMVM may accept a report or written opinion prepared by non-registered auditors subject to appropriate regulation by their home country regulator, provided such auditors present equivalent guarantees of trust under accepted international standards (PSC Article 9).

[54] See Section 18.2.4 below.

[55] Generally, pro-forma financial information is required in case of a significant change in the situation of an issuer due to a particular transaction, with the exception of situations where merger accounting is required.

Instead of filing certain of the foregoing documents the issuer or offeror may indicate that current versions of the documents are already on file with the CMVM. **18.72**

In addition, the application for admission to listing may be submitted before all the necessary requirements have been met, provided that the requesting party indicates how and when any outstanding items will be completed. **18.73**

The CMVM may request the offeror or the issuer to provide any supplementary information it deems necessary to assess the offer. **18.74**

Approval of the prospectus: The approval of the prospectus or the refusal of approval must generally be notified to the issuer or offeror within 10 business days from the date of receipt of the original application or of any supplementary information that the CMVM may have requested from the offeror or third parties. In the case of issuers which have not made any prior public offer for distribution or admission to trading on a regulated market, this delay is 20 business days. **18.75**

The absence of a decision by the end of these time periods is deemed to constitute an implied rejection of the application. **18.76**

The approval of a prospectus is generally refused only where any of the documents filed with the approval application is incorrect or inconsistent with legal and regulatory requirements. Prior to a refusal, the CMVM must notify the issuer or offeror, within a reasonable time, to allow the amendment of any points or issues capable of being corrected. **18.77**

Exclusion of liability: The approval of a prospectus implies no guarantee by the CMVM regarding the information disclosed in the prospectus, the economic and financial position of the issuer or offeror, the feasibility of the offer or the quality of the securities. **18.78**

18.2.3.4.3 Publication and validity   *Publication*: A prospectus may not be published until it has been approved by the CMVM, and the text and format of the prospectus made available to the public must at all times be identical to the original version approved by the CMVM. **18.79**

Upon approval, the final version of the prospectus (mentioning the date of approval) must be filed with the CMVM and made available to the public by the issuer/offeror (as the case may be) as soon as practicable, and in any case, at a reasonable time in advance of, and at the latest at the beginning of, the offer or the admission to trading of the securities involved, depending on the characteristics of the offer and the investors for whom the prospectus is intended. **18.80**

In particular, in the event of a public offer for distribution of securities preceded by a negotiation of rights, the prospectus must be made available to the public no later than the relevant record day (i.e. the last business day before the first day of the rights trading period). **18.81**

18.82   In addition, in the event of an initial public offer of a class of shares not already admitted to trading on a regulated market and shares intended to be admitted to trading on a regulated market for the first time, the prospectus must be available at least six working days before expiry of the offer period.

18.83   The publication of the prospectus must be made through the disclosure options set forth in Article 14 of the Prospectus Directive and in accordance with the Prospectus Directive Regulation.

18.84   *Validity*: Public offer prospectuses and base prospectuses are valid for a period of 12 months after publication, provided that they are updated or completed with any supplements that may be required.[56]

18.85   Likewise, a registration document is valid for a period of up to 12 months from the date of approval of the annual accounts on which it is based.

18.86   **18.2.3.4.4 Supplements to a prospectus**   If, between the date of approval of the prospectus and the final closing of the public offer or, as the case may be, the time when trading on the regulated market commences, any significant new factor, material mistake or inaccuracy relating to the information included in the prospectus arises or is noted and such factor, mistake or inaccuracy is capable of affecting the assessment of the securities, a supplement to the prospectus must immediately be submitted to the CMVM for approval.

18.87   Such supplement must be approved within seven business days and published in the same manner as the original prospectus. The summary and any translations thereof must also be supplemented, if necessary, to reflect the new information included in the prospectus supplement.

18.88   Investors who have already agreed to purchase or subscribe to the securities before the supplement is published will have the right, exercisable within two working days after the publication of the supplement, to withdraw their acceptances.

18.2.3.5 *Prospectus passporting regime*

18.89   Articles 17 and 18 of the Prospectus Directive provide for a 'passporting' facility for issuers wishing to publicly offer securities or admit securities to trading on a regulated market in a member state other than their home member state. Under the passporting facility, a prospectus approved by the competent authority in the home market state may be used for public offers and listings in another member state (the 'host member state') without the need for further approval by the competent authority of the host member state.

---

[56] See Section 18.2.3.4.4 below.

Pursuant to Article 146 of the PSC (implementing Articles 17 and 18 of the **18.90** Prospectus Directive), for a prospectus to be passported into Portugal after being approved by the relevant competent authority, such competent authority (in its capacity as home member state regulator) must submit the following documentation to the CMVM, at the request of the issuer:

(a) a certificate of approval attesting that the prospectus has been drawn up in accordance with the Prospectus Directive and, as the case may be, justifying the exemption of including information in the prospectus;

(b) a copy of the prospectus; and

(c) a translation into Portuguese of the summary included in the prospectus, prepared by and under the responsibility of the issuer (without being subject to the CMVM's approval).

Any documents incorporated by reference in the prospectus must also be sent to **18.91** the CMVM together with the passport notification.

If any new event occurs after the prospectus has been passported into Portugal or **18.92** if the CMVM becomes aware that material mistakes or inconsistencies are contained in the prospectus, the CMVM may advise the home member state regulator of the need for the issuer to provide any additional or new information and publish a supplement as a result.

The issuer must make available to the public the prospectus and the Portuguese **18.93** translation of its summary after the prospectus passport has been received and, in any case, before the beginning of the public offer.

These documents are deemed to be available to the public when published in **18.94** accordance with Article 14 of the Prospectus Directive. According to standard market practice, they are normally made available in electronic form on the websites of the home country regulator and of the CMVM (in the case of the CMVM, this publication is officially promoted by the CMVM, free of charge to the issuer and investors).

For the purposes of international use of a prospectus approved by the CMVM, **18.95** the documents referred in (a) to (c) above (with the translation of the summary to be prepared in accordance with the requirements of the host member state(s)) and the documents incorporated by reference, if any, must be sent by the CMVM to the competent authority of the host member state(s) where the offer/listing of the securities is to take place within three working days of the passporting request addressed to the CMVM by the offeror or, as the case may be, the financial intermediary assisting the public offer.

The procedure described above also applies to the filing of any supplements to the **18.96** prospectus.

18.2.3.6 *Language restrictions*

18.97 Public offer and listing prospectuses published in Portugal may be drawn up, in whole or in part, in a language customary in the sphere of international finance[57] (other than Portuguese), if:

(a) the publication of the prospectus is not legally required;

(b) the prospectus has been prepared in the context of a multi-jurisdictional offer and/or listing; or

(c) where the issuer is governed by foreign law.

18.98 In practice, the CMVM currently only accepts the use of English in addition to Portuguese.

18.99 In the case of (b) and (c) above, the CMVM may require that the summary of the prospectus[58] also be published in Portuguese.

18.2.3.7 *Responsibility attaching to the prospectus*

18.100 *Applicable law*: The Prospectus Directive only seeks minimum harmonization of the various member states' provisions concerning the responsibility attaching to the prospectus, and thus the issue is governed by the internal law of each member state.[59]

18.101 Accordingly, liability for information included in the prospectus is exclusively governed by Portuguese law whenever public offers and listing of securities are specifically addressed to persons resident or established in Portugal,[60] regardless of the law applicable to the issuer and to the relevant securities.[61]

---

[57] PSC Articles 163-A and 238 implementing Prospectus Directive Article 19.

[58] See Section 18.2.3.4.1 above.

[59] Pursuant to Article 6 of the Prospectus Directive, member states must ensure that responsibility for the information given in a prospectus attaches at least to the issuer or its administrative, management or supervisory bodies, the offeror, the person asking for the admission to trading on a regulated market or the guarantor, as the case may be. There are currently no other EU provisions harmonizing the liability for the information included in the prospectus.

[60] According to Article 108 of the PSC, all public offers and listing of securities specifically addressed to persons resident or established in Portugal are governed by the PSC and its supplementary regulations.

[61] PSC Article 40, No 1 provides that the issuer's personal law regulates the terms and conditions of securities, except if, with respect to bonds and other debt securities, another law is designated in the terms and conditions of the securities. In addition, PSC Article 3 provides that the mandatory rules of the PSC (such as those relating to liability for the information included in the prospectus set out in PSC Articles 149 to 154) are directly applicable to all situations that have a relevant connection with the Portuguese territory, as is in particular the case where public offers and listing of securities are specifically addressed to persons resident or established in Portugal.

Requirements regarding information included in the prospectus: As previously **18.102** described,[62] any information included in the prospectus must materially comply with the general principles set forth in Article 135 of the PSC.

Failure to comply with these principles in respect of information included in **18.103** a public offer prospectus may give rise to liability for damages of the following persons or entities (unless they can show that they have acted without fault—negligence, gross negligence or malice):

(a) the offeror;
(b) the members of the management body of the offeror;
(c) the issuer;
(d) the members of the management body of the issuer;
(e) the promoters, in the case of a subscription public offer for the incorporation of a company;
(f) the members of the supervisory body of the issuer, the accounting firms, auditors and any other individuals that have certified or, in any other way, verified the accounting documents on which the prospectus is based;
(g) the financial intermediaries assisting in the offer;
(h) any other entities (including legal advisers) that accept liability for any information, forecast or study included in the prospectus.

The persons referred to in (c), (d), (f) and (h) above may also be liable for damages **18.104** in respect of a listing prospectus.

The liability of any party will be evaluated in light of the highest standards of a **18.105** professional duty of care.

The liability is personal and several, but will be excluded if a potentially liable **18.106** person can show that the injured party—the investor—knew or ought to have known about the deficiency in the contents of the prospectus on the date the order to purchase or subscribe for the relevant securities was given or at any time where the withdrawal of the acceptance was still possible.

In order to make a claim for damages, an injured party is not required to show that **18.107** it would not have invested if it had been aware of the deficiency. However, the injured party is required to show the amount of the losses caused by the deficiency in the contents of the prospectus (which is generally a decline in the value of the securities in question). Likewise, it is possible for the liable party or parties to have the amount of damages reduced by showing that the losses were caused in part by other factors instead of deficiencies in the information in the prospectus.

---

[62] See Section 18.2.3.4.2 above.

18.108 Claims for damages on these grounds must be lodged within six months from the date the injured party becomes aware of the deficiency in the prospectus, or its supplement (in case of a listing prospectus). In any case, there is an outer limit for making claims of two years from the date the result of the offer was published (in case of a public offer prospectus) or from the date the prospectus or the supplement including the deficient information was published (in case of a listing prospectus).

18.2.4 Mandatory use of financial intermediary

18.109 Article 113/1 of the PSC provides that public offers of securities that r equire publication of a prospectus also require the participation of a financial intermediary[63] authorized to provide in Portugal, at a minimum, assistance and placement investment services.[64]

18.110 These services may be provided by the issuer/offeror itself if it is duly authorized to do so in Portugal.

18.2.5 Advertisements

18.111 All marketing materials[65] that are to be published in Portugal in connection with a public offer must be submitted to the CMVM for prior review and approval.

---

[63] According to PSC Article 293, financial intermediaries include: (i) credit institutions and investment firms (including dealer and broker companies, portfolio management companies, money-market and foreign exchange mediation companies, investment consulting companies, multilateral trading facilities management companies and other entities designated as investment companies by law or that, although not designated as credit institutions, provide investment services to third parties or perform investment activities on a regular and professional basis) authorized to conduct financial intermediation activities (as further described below) in Portugal; (ii) managing entities of collective investment schemes authorized to conduct such activities in Portugal; and (iii) entities entitled to conduct activities similar to those referred to in the preceding points and that are authorized to conduct financial intermediation activities in Portugal. The professional exercise of any financial intermediation activity in Portugal is subject to: (a) an authorization by the competent authority (of the country of origin); and, (b) prior registration with CMVM. The CMVM maintains a list of credit institutions and investment firms that carry out independent financial intermediation activities in Portugal, for purposes of the right to provide cross-border services set forth in the MiFID (MiFID Passport).

[64] In general, the professional exercise of financial intermediation activities in Portugal is restricted to financial intermediaries authorized to engage in such activities in Portugal (see above). Financial intermediation activities can also be carried out by other entities that are not qualified as financial intermediaries but are by law deemed equivalent to financial intermediaries for the purposes of provision of financial intermediation activities (expressly indicated in Article 289/3 of the PSC). Following the transposition of MiFID into the PSC, financial intermediation activities include: (i) investment services and certain activities in relation to financial instruments; (ii) ancillary services in relation to investment services and activities; and (iii) management of collective investment undertakings and exercise of depository functions in respect thereof.

[65] See Section 18.2.3.1 above.

Marketing materials may be submitted to the CMVM, including via email, by the issuer or its legal advisers.

In addition, any marketing materials the issuer or offeror intends to use in connection with the marketing of a public offer in Portugal must be in Portuguese or, if in another language, include a full translation into Portuguese. **18.112**

Moreover, such materials must: **18.113**

(i) comply with the principles regarding the quality of information set out in Article 7 of the PSC, and accordingly, must include complete, accurate, updated, clear and objective information that complies with applicable laws and regulations;
(ii) refer to the existence or the availability of the prospectus (i.e. include disclosure indicating where the documentation regarding the public offer is available for inspection); and
(iii) be consistent with the contents of the prospectus.

Marketing materials may include information that is not included in the prospectus, provided that the legal requirements described above are satisfied. **18.114**

As a general rule, no marketing materials may be distributed/published before the approval of the prospectus by the CMVM and the beginning of the offer period. **18.115**

However, the CMVM may authorize advertising prior to the approval of the prospectus if it considers that such approval is likely to be granted and as long as such advertising does not cause disruption to the addressees of the public offer or the markets generally. **18.116**

Marketing materials regarding securities for which only admission to trading is sought are not subject to prior approval by the CMVM, as long as public offer requirements are not triggered. However, the language restrictions and the principles concerning the quality of information described above are still applicable in this case. **18.117**

Material information addressed to qualified investors or special categories of investors: Where no prospectus is required, material information provided by an issuer or an offeror to qualified investors or special categories of investors, including information disclosed in the context of meetings relating to offers of securities, must be disclosed to all qualified investors or special categories of investors to whom the offer is exclusively addressed. Where a prospectus is required to be published, such information must be included in the prospectus or in a supplement. **18.118**

18.2.6 Listing decision

Timing: Pursuant to Article 234 No 1 of the PSC, the regulated market's managing entity must approve or refuse the admission of securities to listing within 90 days **18.119** after submission of the application. The decision is to be immediately notified to the requesting party.

18.120 In practice, this period can be significantly shorter (up to one working week in the case of Euronext), provided that all documents are submitted in compliance with requirements and in a timely manner.

18.121 The admission to trading may only be refused in the following situations (Article 235 of the PSC):

(a) if the requirements for admission set out in the applicable laws, regulations or market rules are not satisfied;

(b) if the issuer is not in compliance with its obligations to which it is subject in other markets, located or operating in Portugal or abroad, where the relevant securities are listed (if applicable); and

(c) if, in the view of the regulated market management entity, it is not advisable to proceed with the admission in the interests of investors and in view of the issuer's particular facts and circumstances.

18.122 In addition, the admission is considered to have been refused if no decision is notified to the requesting party within 90 days following the application for listing.

18.123 *Effects*: The admission to trading covers all securities of the same category.

18.124 In the case of newly issued shares of a class that already has shares admitted to trading, the issuer has a duty to request the admission of such newly issued shares within 90 days of issuance.

18.125 Shares may be admitted to trading immediately after the final registration of the company's incorporation or capital increase in the Commercial Registry Office.

18.126 However, the admission of securities that are publicly offered will only be effective after the closure of the offer.

18.127 *Exclusion of liability*: The decision for admission to listing does not imply any guarantee by the regulated market management entity regarding the information disclosed, the economic and financial position of the issuer, the viability of the issuer and the quality of the securities admitted.

18.2.7 Registration of securities in the Portuguese centralized securities system

18.128 Securities admitted to trading on a regulated market operating in Portugal must be registered with the Portuguese centralized securities system[66] —CVM—by the

---

[66] See Sections 18.1.4 and 18.2.1.3 above.

issuer or through a duly authorized entity, within five business days following the notification of the decision to admit the securities to trading by the regulated market management entity.

In practice, the procedures for the registration of securities with the CVM are usually being completed simultaneously with those required for the listing of the securities, including the approval of the prospectus, if required.   **18.129**

Registration with CVM is approved by Interbolsa, which must notify its decision within four business days of the receipt of the application or its completion with all information required.   **18.130**

The application must be filed together with various documents concerning the issuer and the securities to be registered set forth in the applicable regulations.[67] Interbolsa may waive the requirement regarding one or more of such documents where they are already on file and current, or whenever the legal nature, or the specific characteristics of the issuer or of the securities justify it.   **18.131**

18.3 Ongoing Disclosure Obligations

Public companies (*sociedades abertas*)[68] and, in general, issuers of securities admitted to trading on a regulated market in Portugal are subject to various disclosure obligations, which are mainly set forth in the PSC and CMVM's supplementary regulations[69] implementing the Transparency Directive and the Market Abuse Directive, where the majority of such reporting duties were harmonized and codified at an EU level.[70]   **18.132**

Information must be published within the timeframes and in the manner provided by law.   **18.133**

Failure to comply with applicable disclosure obligations may constitute various administrative offences, which are generally punished by fines imposed by the CMVM.   **18.134**

18.3.1 Qualified shareholdings

Article 16 of the PSC imposes obligations on holders of voting rights and issuers to make notifications regarding the percentage of voting rights held in the issuer once specified thresholds, which are calculated in accordance with Article 20 of   **18.135**

---

[67] Interbolsa Regulation No 3/200 Article 14, as amended.
[68] For a discussion of the concept of '*sociedade aberta*' under Portuguese law, see note 27 above.
[69] CMVM Regulation No 5/2008 on disclosure duties and CMVM Regulation No 1/2007 on corporate governance.
[70] See Part 1 for a discussion of these directives.

the PSC,[71] are exceeded. The notification requirement is triggered by having control over the exercise of voting rights attached to shares, rather than merely by the holding of interests in shares themselves.

18.136 Notification obligations apply with respect to Portuguese public companies (*sociedade aberta*), whether their shares are listed or not, and to foreign issuers having shares (or other securities giving right to subscribe or acquire shares) admitted to trading on a regulated market located or operating in Portugal. Such companies must disclose such information to the market, through the IDS of the CMVM available at http://www.cmvm.pt.[72]

18.3.1.1 *Filing of major qualified shareholding notifications*

18.137 Any individual or entity acquiring direct or indirect holdings, which, in aggregate or together with any shares already held, constitutes a qualified shareholding (as defined below), must:

(i) notify the holding to the CMVM and the issuer; and

(ii) notify to the CMVM and the issuer any circumstances giving rise to the attribution to such person or entity of voting rights attached to shares held by third parties, pursuant to Article 20/1 of the PSC.[73]

18.3.1.2 *Notification thresholds and notifiable interests*

18.138 The notification duty must be complied with by any person or entity whose holdings reach or exceed the following thresholds ('qualified shareholding(s)') of:

(a) 10%, 20%, one-third, one-half, two-thirds, and 90 % of the voting rights corresponding to the share capital of a public company (*sociedade aberta*) governed by Portuguese law;

(b) 5%, 15% and 25% of the voting rights relating to the share capital of:

(i) any public company (*sociedade aberta*) governed by Portuguese law whose shares or other securities giving right to subscribe or acquire its shares are admitted to trading on a regulated market located or operating in an EU member state;

(ii) any company with its statutory office in another EU member state whose shares or other securities giving right to subscribe or acquire its shares are only admitted to trading on a regulated market located or operating in Portugal;

(iii) any company with its statutory office outside of the European Union whose shares or other securities giving right to subscribe or acquire its

---

[71] See Section 18.3.1.4 below.
[72] See Section 18.3.1.6 below.
[73] See Section 18.3.1.4 below.

shares are admitted to trading on a regulated market located or operating in Portugal, and in respect of which the CMVM is the competent authority;[74] and

(c) 2% of the voting rights relating to the share capital of a public company (*sociedade aberta*) governed by Portuguese law whose shares or other securities giving right to subscribe or acquire its shares are admitted to trading on a regulated market located or operating in an EU member state.

A duty to notify also arises (i) where a person or entity reduces its qualified **18.139** shareholding to an amount below any of the notification thresholds described above and (ii) in case of change in the percentage level of one (or more) of the attribution criteria with respect to voting rights, provided that a notifiable threshold is triggered as a result of the change.[75]

18.3.1.3 Exemptions from disclosure obligations

Pursuant to Article 16-A of the PSC, the duty to publicly disclose qualified share- **18.140** holdings does not arise, subject to further conditions provided by law:

(a) in respect of shares traded exclusively for clearing and settlement purposes within a customary and short trading period (typically, three days from the execution of the transaction);

(b) to the holdings of financial intermediaries acting as liquidity providers, which reach, exceed, or fall below, 5% of the voting rights corresponding to the share capital of an issuer, provided that the financial intermediary does not participate in the management of such issuer, nor influence the issuer to acquire such shares or support their price.

In these cases, however, the holding of the relevant qualified shareholding must **18.141** nevertheless be communicated to the CMVM.

In addition, pursuant to Article 21-A of the PSC, the disclosure obligations set **18.142** out in Article 16 of the PSC do not arise in respect of issuers with a statutory office outside of the European Union if the information on qualified shareholdings is published under applicable law within a maximum of seven trading days of the triggering event.[76]

18.3.1.4 Attribution of voting rights

For purposes of calculating qualified shareholdings that require disclosure **18.143** Portuguese law (implementing relevant provisions of the Transparency Directive) treats similarly, the voting rights attached to securities held directly by the holder

---

[74] See section 18.3.4.1 below.
[75] See Section 18.3.1.5 below.
[76] See Section 18.3.1.6 below.

of the qualified shareholding (meaning securities of which such holder of the qualified shareholding has ownership or a right of use (*usufruct*)) and the following voting rights[77]:

(a) voting rights of securities held by third parties acting in their own name, but on behalf of the holder of the qualified shareholding;

(b) voting rights of securities held by an entity that is related to the holder of the qualified shareholding through control or group relationship;[78]

(c) voting rights of securities held by holders with whom the holder of the qualified shareholding has entered into an agreement for the exercise of such voting rights, except if, pursuant to such agreement, the holder of the qualified shareholding is bound to follow the third party's instructions;

(d) voting rights of securities held by the members of the management and supervisory bodies of the holder of the qualified shareholding;

(e) voting rights of securities that the holder of the qualified shareholding acquires pursuant to an agreement entered into with the holders of such voting rights;

(f) voting rights of shares granted as a security to the holder of the qualified shareholding or managed by or deposited with the holder of the qualified shareholding, if the corresponding voting rights have been attributed to such person or entity;

(g) voting rights the holders of which have granted to the holder of the qualified shareholding discretionary powers for exercising such voting rights;

(h) voting rights held by any party with whom the holder of the qualified shareholding has entered into any agreement to acquire control of or preventing the change of control of a company or constituting, by any other means, an instrument of exercise of concerted influence over a company; and

---

[77] PSC Article 20.

[78] Under PSC Article 21, an individual or entity is deemed to control a company where such individual or entity, irrespective of being domiciled or having its registered office in Portugal or abroad, can exercise, either directly or indirectly, a dominant influence over such company. In any event, control is deemed to exist where an individual or entity: (a) holds the majority of voting rights in a company; (b) may exercise the majority of voting rights, according to the terms of a shareholders' agreement; or (c) may appoint or dismiss the majority of the members of the board of directors or supervisory committee. For the purposes of the PSC, read together with the Portuguese Companies Code, two or more companies, as the case may be, irrespective of having their registered office in Portugal or abroad, are deemed to be a group in any of the following situations: (i) a public limited company is initially incorporated by one sole shareholder/company; (ii) a company takes control of another company by becoming, after the incorporation of such company, its sole shareholder; (iii) a company takes control of other company by means of a squeeze-out; (iv) two or more companies agree to submit to a common management by means of an agreement ('*contrato paritário*'); or (v) a company submits itself by means of an agreement to the management of other company ('*contrato de subordinação*').

(i) voting rights attributable to any individual or entity (other than the holder of the qualified shareholding) referred to in (a) to (h) above as a result of any of the criteria set out therein.

In short, pursuant to Article 20 of the PSC the same voting rights may be attrib- **18.144** uted to various individuals or entities. For example, voting rights attributed to an entity's directors may also be attributed to the entity itself. As a result, the sum of voting rights attributable to all parties exceeds in most cases 100% of the voting rights corresponding to the share capital of the relevant public company.

The underlying reason behind Article 20 is that the information regarding quali- **18.145** fied shareholdings should accurately reflect who bears the economic risk of an investment in an issuer's shares and who holds the actual power to acquire, dispose of, direct, control or influence the voting rights attached to such shares.

The assessment of whether or not specific circumstances or a given agreement **18.146** trigger notification duties pursuant to any of the provisions described above by attributing the relevant voting rights to a certain party must be made on a case-by-case basis.

18.3.1.5 *Form of notification and contents*

Form of notification. The notification by the holder of the qualified shareholding **18.147** must be made in writing to the issuer and the CMVM.

Since Portuguese law does not prescribe specific means to be used for the submis- **18.148** sion of the notification letter, the notification letter may be submitted by courier, fax and /or electronically to the issuer) and to the CMVM.

Contents. The disclosure report regarding the acquisition or disposal of qualified **18.149** shareholdings must disclose (i) the qualified shareholding expressed as a percent-age of the total share capital of the issuer; (ii) the voting rights attached to the qualified shareholding, expressed as a percentage of the total voting rights corresponding to the share capital of the issuer;[79] (iii) the corresponding number of shares; (iv) if applicable, the percentage of voting rights attributable to the participant by any reason other than the direct ownership, i.e. as an indirect shareholder; (v) the breakdown of the qualified shareholding per share category, if applicable; (vi) the date when the acquisition/disposal of the qualified

---

[79] For purposes of qualified shareholding disclosure obligations, voting rights are calculated on the basis of (a) the aggregate shareholding (shares held directly and through intermediary holdings) of the relevant individual or entity (numerator) over (b) the total number of shares with voting rights corresponding to the company's share capital, regardless of whether the exercise of such rights is suspended (denominator), such as treasury shares. Under Portuguese law, all rights attaching to treasury shares (in particular, the voting rights and rights to dividends) are suspended except for the right to receive shares free of charge in case of a share capital increase by means of incorporation of reserves.

shareholding occurred; (vii) the type of transaction giving rise to the acquisition/disposal of the qualified shareholding, including, if applicable, the number of shares acquired or disposed of; and (viii) the identification of the chain of entities to which the qualified shareholding is attributable pursuant to Article 20 of the PSC, irrespective of their governing law.

18.150 In case any of the factors for attribution of voting rights, as indicated in the disclosure notification, changes and thereby triggers a notifiable threshold,[80] a new notification is required.

18.151 The new notification must essentially contain the same information as the original notification but also disclose the circumstances of the change triggering the notification obligation.

18.152 Wherever a disclosure obligation is applicable to more than one person or entity, a single notification may be made, which would include disclosure regarding the chain of entities to which the qualified shareholding is attributable under Article 20 of the PSC. In this case, the communication made by such person or entity would exempt the others from their reporting duties, as the notification such other persons or entities would otherwise have to make would be deemed to have already been made.

18.3.1.6 *Notification and disclosure deadlines*

18.153 Notifications regarding qualified shareholdings must be made within four trading days from the date on which the event triggering the notification duty occurred or became known. A person or entity is presumed to have received knowledge of such event within two trading days after its occurrence.

18.154 The issuer must disclose to the market, through the CMVM's ISD (available at http://www.cmvm.pt), all information received by it concerning qualified shareholdings, as soon as possible and in any case within a maximum of three trading days after receiving the relevant notification. This obligation does not arise in respect of issuers with their statutory office outside of the European Union if, under applicable law, the information on qualified shareholdings is published within a maximum of seven trading days.

18.155 The disclosure duty may be complied with by a company controlling or otherwise in a group relationship with the issuer[81] and may be made in a language (other than Portuguese) commonly used in the international financial markets if that language was used in the original communication. As described above, in

---

[80] See Section 18.3.1.2 above.
[81] See note 78 above for the definition of control and group relationships.

practice the CMVM currently only accepts the use of English in addition to Portuguese.

Trading days are days when the regulated market on which the shares or other secu-   **18.156**
rities giving right to subscribe or acquire shares are admitted to trading is open for trading. The CMVM publishes the trading calendar of the regulated markets located or operating in Portugal through its IDS available at http://www.cmvm.pt.

18.3.1.7 Additional notification duties

Regulated industries: Under Portuguese law, acquisitions of holdings in companies   **18.157**
operating in certain business/industry sectors are subject to specific disclosure obligations. These include, among others, banking and investment services, insurance and pension funds, media (television, press and radio), telecommunications, energy and securities markets.

Company's by-laws: The statutory disclosure obligations described above may be   **18.158**
supplemented by additional notification duties set out in the by-laws of an issuer.

This type of provision is frequently found in the by-laws of Portuguese listed com-   **18.159**
panies, which provide an obligation for shareholders—in addition to any statutory notification duties—to notify the Board of Directors regarding the acquisition, disposition, increase or reduction of qualified shareholdings (according to the legally defined thresholds).

By-laws in this case typically provide that the disclosure is a condition precedent   **18.160**
for the exercise of shareholders rights. Failure to comply with such obligations thus prevents the shareholder from exercising its rights.

18.3.2 Shareholders' agreements

Shareholders' agreements aimed at acquiring, maintaining or reinforcing a   **18.161**
qualified shareholding in a public company (*sociedade aberta*), whether listed or not, or aimed at securing or frustrating the success of a takeover bid, must be communicated to the CMVM by any of the contracting parties within three days from the execution of the agreement.

18.3.3 Disclosure and control of inside information

18.3.3.1 Disclosure obligation and scope

Pursuant to Article 248 of the PSC, an issuer of securities admitted to trading   **18.162**
on a regulated market operating in Portugal or for which a request for admission to trading on such market has been made, must immediately disclose to the public any information of a precise nature that *directly* concerns such issuer or its securities,

which has not been made public and which, if it were made public, would be likely to have a significant effect on the price of those securities or the price of underlying or derivative instruments related to the listed securities.[82]

18.163 In this context, the inside information covers price-sensitive events that have occurred or may reasonably be expected to occur (regardless of the degree of formalization of such events) which, if they were made public, could be used by a reasonable investor as the rationale for an investment decision.[83]

18.164 The CMVM issued a set of opinions concerning the disclosure of inside information[84] including representative examples and conduct rules that constitute valuable guidance for the application of the regulatory provisions ('CMVM's Opinions on Disclosure of Inside Information').

18.3.3.2 *Disclosure exemption*

18.165 The CMVM may, at the issuer's request, exempt the issuer from disclosing inside information where such disclosure is against the public interest and might cause serious damages to the issuer, provided that such omission would not be likely to mislead the public in respect of key facts and circumstances for evaluating the issuer's securities. The exemption is considered granted if the CMVM does not communicate any decision up to 15 days after the receipt of the application for exemption.

18.3.3.3 *Delaying disclosure*

18.166 An issuer may delay the public disclosure of inside information provided that: (i) such disclosure would prejudice the issuer's legitimate interests;[85] (ii) the

---

[82] Portuguese Law has generally adopted the definition of inside information set out in the Market Abuse Directive (Directive 2003/6/EC of the European Parliament and of the Council, of 28 January 2003) pursuant to which inside information means all information of a precise nature which has not been made public, that *directly or indirectly* relates to one or more issuers or to one or more securities or financial instruments and which, if it were made public, would be likely to have a significant effect on the price of those securities or financial instruments. In contrast, the disclosure duty set out in Article 248 No 1 of the PSC covers only the information *directly* related to the issuer and its securities. However, under the PSC issuers must make an independent analysis of the potential consequences of non-public information that is only *indirectly* related to them or the respective securities. As soon as such indirectly related information *directly* affects the issuer's activity or its securities it is likely to constitute inside information for the purposes of the disclosure obligation set out in Article 248 No 1 of the PSC and must be promptly disclosed.

[83] For example, the CMVM generally regards information in respect of a potential acquisition/disposal of shareholdings in an issuer as inside information.

[84] At http://www.cmvm.pt/NR/exeres/7EA22282-8734-439D-AFEC-65450A36AF76.htm.

[85] Legitimate interests may, in particular, relate to (i) negotiations in course, or related information, where the outcome or normal course of those negotiations would likely be affected by public disclosure; or (ii) decisions taken or contracts executed by the management body of an issuer which require approval from another issuer's corporate body in order to become effective, where public

non-disclosure would not be likely to mislead the public; and (iii) the issuer shows that it is able to ensure the confidentiality of such information. The decision on delaying disclosure does not prevent the issuer from communicating inside information to the CMVM. The CMVM recommends that such communication be made in practice.

In the event that the financial viability of the issuer is in danger (provided that **18.167** the issuer is not in a situation that would fall within the scope of the applicable insolvency law) public disclosure of information may be delayed for a limited period of time where such public disclosure would seriously jeopardize the interests of existing and potential shareholders by undermining the conclusion of specific negotiations intended to ensure the financial recovery of the issuer.

If the issuer or a person acting on its behalf, while acting in the normal course of **18.168** their activity, profession or office, discloses any inside information to a third party who is not bound by a duty of confidentiality, the issuer must disclose that information to the public either simultaneously with (in the case of an intentional disclosure) or promptly after the disclosure (in the case of a non-intentional disclosure).

Ensuring the confidentiality and preventing misuse of delayed information disclosure: **18.169** In order to ensure the confidentiality and prevent the misuse of information, the disclosure of which is delayed, the issuer must take at least the following measures: (i) restricting access to such information only to persons who require such access for carrying out their duties within the issuer; (ii) ensuring that any person with access to such information acknowledges receipt of or access to such information and is made aware of the sanctions for misusing or improperly circulating such information; and (iii) having a mechanism in place which allows prompt public disclosure of the information in case of a breach of confidentiality due to disclosure to third parties who are not subject to a duty of confidentiality as described above.

18.3.3.4 Disclosure contents and deadlines

Contents: The disclosure notice on inside information must be easily understand- **18.170** able by investors. Information that is technically complete but does not provide insight does not comply with the duty to disclose, as it may encourage speculation regarding the meaning of the disclosed information itself.

The CMVM's 'Opinions on Disclosure of Inside Information' provides guidance **18.171** with respect to the contents of disclosure that should be considered by issuers when preparing the disclosure notice.

---

disclosure of information before such approval is granted, even if an announcement that approval is pending is made simultaneously, would jeopardize the correct assessment of the information by the public.

18.172 *Timing*: Inside information must be promptly disclosed by the issuer through the disclosure means set out in law.[86]

18.173 Issuers must ensure that the inside information is disclosed simultaneously to all investors and in all regulated markets in the EU on which they have securities admitted to trading or have requested admission.

18.3.3.5 Insider lists

18.174 Issuers must prepare and regularly update a list of persons who regularly or occasionally have access to inside information. Issuers must inform such persons that their names have been included in the insider list and of the legal consequences of misusing or improperly circulating such information.

18.175 The insider list must set forth the names of the persons, the reasons why they are on the list and the date on which the insider list was created and updated. The insider list must be kept by issuers for at least five years after being prepared or updated and must be promptly provided to the CMVM upon request.

18.3.3.6 Disclosure of transactions by persons discharging managerial responsibilities

18.176 *Notification duties*: Pursuant to Article 248-B of the PSC,[87] any person discharging managerial responsibilities within an issuer of securities admitted to trading on a regulated market in Portugal or a company controlling such issuer, as well as any persons closely associated with such person, must notify the CMVM and the issuer of any transactions that are either made for its own account, for the account of third parties or by third parties for such person's account in respect of the shares of the issuer or related financial instruments, the value of which taken either separately or together with other transactions made since the last disclosure date reaches or exceeds EUR 5,000.

18.177 If the transaction is with respect to shares (but not related financial instruments), information regarding such transaction provided to the issuer must be immediately disclosed by the issuer through the CMVM's information disclosure system available at CMVM's website.

18.178 In addition, any person discharging managerial responsibilities as described above must provide issuers, at the end of the month following the end of each semester, with a list of all transactions by such person in respect of the issuer's shares or related financial instruments made during the semester. The issuer must disclose

---

[86] See Section 18.3.6 below.
[87] The rules set out in Article 248-B of the PSC are further developed in the CMVM Regulation No 5/2008.

this information, together with its annual and semi-annual reports, under the terms prescribed by law.[88]

These notification obligations apply to persons discharging managerial duties **18.179** within issuers having their registered office in Portugal or which do not have their registered office in an EU member state but otherwise have an obligation to provide the CMVM with information regarding their annual accounts as described in Section 18.3.4.2.1. below.

18.3.3.6.1 Persons discharging managerial responsibilities

For the purposes of these reporting obligations: **18.180**

(a) a 'person discharging managerial responsibilities' means any person who is a member of the management or supervisory bodies of the issuer or a senior executive if not a member of such bodies, and who in each case has regular access to inside information and participates in decisions affecting the issuer's management and trading strategy; and

(b) a 'person closely associated with a person discharging managerial responsibilities' means: (i) the spouse of a person discharging managerial responsibilities, or any partner of that person considered by Portuguese law as equivalent to a spouse, dependent children and other relatives who have shared a household with such person for at least one year; (ii) any entity that is (directly or indirectly) controlled by such person, set up for the benefit of such person, or in which such person also discharges managerial duties.

Timing and contents of the notice: The notification must be made within five busi- **18.181** ness days of the transaction.

The disclosure report must contain the following information regarding the **18.182** transaction: (a) nature; (b) date; (c) place; (d) price; (e) amount; (f) identification of the issuer; (g) financial instrument in question; (h) the grounds for notification; and (i) the amount of shares in the issuer that the person discharging managerial responsibilities holds after the transaction.

List of persons discharging managerial responsibilities: Issuers of securities admitted **18.183** to trading on a regulated market in Portugal must prepare and regularly update a list of persons discharging managerial responsibilities. Issuers must inform such persons in writing that their names have been included in or excluded from the list and of the resulting legal duties, including the duty to identify any persons closely associated with them and to inform such closely related persons of the notification duties described above.

---

[88] See Sections 18.3.4.2.1 and 18.3.4.2.2 below.

18.184   The list must set forth the names of the persons, the reasons why they are on the list and the date on which the list was created and updated. The list must be kept by issuers for at least five years after being prepared or updated and must be promptly provided to the CMVM upon request.

18.3.4 Additional disclosure duties imposed on issuers of securities listed on a regulated market in Portugal

18.3.4.1 Competent authority

18.185   Pursuant to the applicable Portuguese law,[89] the CMVM is the competent authority with regards to disclosure obligations for the following issuers which must file with the CMVM the documents and information required by Articles 245 et seq of the PSC.

(a) issuers governed by Portuguese law of shares and debt securities with a nomi-nal value of less than EUR 1,000 admitted to trading on a regulated market located or operating in Portugal or in another EU member state;

(b) issuers with registered offices in another EU member state of shares and debt securities with a nominal value of less than EUR 1,000 exclusively admitted to trading on a regulated market located or operating in Portugal;

(c) issuers with registered offices in a non-EU country of shares and debt securities with a nominal value of less than EUR 1,000 exclusively admitted to trading on a regulated market located or operating in Portugal, or where the application for listing was first made in such regulated market in Portugal;

(d) issuers of debt securities with a nominal value of EUR 1,000 or more and other securities (other than shares) admitted to trading on a regulated market located or operating in Portugal or in another EU member state, where the issuer has chosen Portugal between the country where its registered office is located, and those countries where the regulated markets where the relevant securities are admitted to trading are located or operate. This choice belongs to the issuers and is valid for at least three years.

18.3.4.2 Periodic financial reporting

18.186   **18.3.4.2.1 Annual information**   *Annual financial reports*: The issuers listed in Section 18.3.4.1 above must, within four months from the close of their financial

---

[89] See Article 244 of the PSC. The scope of entities subject to the disclosure obligations imposed on issuers of securities admitted to trading under Portuguese law is determined by the legal concept of 'home member state' set out in Article 2, No 1, paragraph (i) of the Transparency Directive. This concept of home member state under the Transparency Directive is similar but not identical to the concept of home member state under the Prospectus Directive, as described above. See also Part 1.

year make the following items available to the public, and keep them available to the public for a period of five years:

(a) The management report, the annual accounts, the audit report and other accounting documents required by law or regulation, including where such documents have not yet been submitted for approval at the general meeting of shareholders.

    The documents that comprise the annual report and accounts must be submitted to the CMVM as soon as they are made available to the shareholders.

    If the annual report does not provide an exact picture of the net assets, financial position and results of the company, the CMVM may order the publication of supplementary information.

(b) The report of an auditor registered with the CMVM.[90]

(c) Responsibility statements from the persons responsible within the issuer, whose names and positions are to be clearly indicated, to the effect that, to the best of their knowledge, the information in the documents required to be disclosed pursuant to paragraph (a) was drawn up in accordance with applicable accounting standards, gives a true and fair view of the assets and liabilities, financial position and results of the issuer and the companies included in the consolidation as a whole, where applicable, and that the management report includes a fair review of the development and performance of the business and the position of the issuer and companies included in the consolidation as a whole, together with a description of the principal risks and uncertainties that they face.

Annual information on corporate governance. Issuers of shares must also publish as part of their annual management report specifically prepared for that purpose information on the structure and practices of their corporate governance provisions, including information on qualified shareholdings in the share capital of the company. **18.187**

In addition, the management body of an issuer of shares governed by Portuguese law must annually submit to the general shareholders' meeting of the company an explanatory report of the information disclosed in the corporate governance report. **18.188**

18.3.4.2.2 Half-yearly information The issuers listed in Section 18.3.4.1. above must also disclose, within two months from the end of the first six months of their financial year, the following documentation with regard to their activity **18.189**

---

[90] See note 53 above.

for such period, and keep such documents available to the public for a period of five years:

(a) A condensed set of financial statements. Where the issuer is not required to prepare consolidated accounts, the condensed set of financial statements must, at a minimum, contain a balance sheet, a condensed profit and loss account and explanatory notes on such accounts prepared in accordance with the same accounting principles used in the preparation of annual financial reports.

(b) An interim management report, including, at a minimum, an indication of significant events that have occurred during such period and their impact on the condensed set of financial statements, together with a description of the principal risks and uncertainties for the remaining six months of the financial year.

(c) Responsibility statements by the persons responsible within the issuer, whose names and functions are to be clearly indicated, to the effect that, to the best of their knowledge, the condensed set of financial statements which has been prepared in accordance with applicable accounting standards, gives a true and fair view of the assets and liabilities, financial position and results of the issuer and the companies included in the consolidation as a whole, where applicable, and that the interim management report includes a fair review of the information required in the management report described in (b) above.

18.190   **18.3.4.2.3 Quarterly and interim management information**   The obligation to report quarterly financial information only applies to large companies admitted to trading on a regulated market, while small and medium-sized companies are only required to disclose interim management information. In either case, the disclosure must be provided in consolidated form only unless the individual accounts include significant elements.

18.191   *Quarterly information*: Any issuer governed by Portuguese law of shares admitted to trading in a regulated market that exceeds, in two consecutive years, two of the following limits,[91] must publish quarterly financial information compliant with the minimum requirements set out in the IAS 34:

(a) a total balance sheet of at least EUR 100,000,000;
(b) total net sales and other revenues of at least EUR 150,000,000; and
(c) an average number of employees during the fiscal year of at least 150.

18.192   Quarterly financial information must be published within two months following the end of the first, third and, if applicable, fifth quarter of each fiscal year.

---

[91] For the purposes of the classification of issuers as small, medium and large companies, the CMVM has adopted the quantitative criteria used in the Portuguese Companies Code (Article 413, No 2) for the purposes of the definition of the supervisory corporate body of the company.

Interim information: Issuers of shares admitted to trading, which are not required **18.193** to publish quarterly financial information must publish interim management information according to the minimum content requirements set out in Annex I to the CMVM Regulation.

18.3.5 Transactions in own shares

Issuers governed by Portuguese law of shares (or other securities giving right to the **18.194** subscription, acquisition or sale of shares) admitted to trading on a regulated market in Portugal or exclusively admitted to trading in a regulated market located or operating in another EU member state, must, within three business days from the date of execution of the relevant transaction:

(a) disclose to the CMVM all acquisitions and sales of such securities by the issuer;
(b) publicly disclose:
   (i) the final position resulting from the relevant transaction reaching, exceeding or falling below 1% of the share capital or any multiples thereof; and
   (ii) all acquisitions and disposals, regardless of the respective net balance, executed on the same stock market session, reaching or exceeding 5% of the trade volume negotiated during such stock market session.

These disclosure obligations also arise for a parent company with respect to trans- **18.195** actions in its securities by a controlled company.[92]

However, the disclosure obligation described in (b) above does not apply to trans- **18.196** actions in an issuer's own securities that are made in execution of liquidity provider agreements entered into in accordance with the accepted market practice as stated by the CMVM.[93] Such transactions must nevertheless be disclosed to the CMVM by the end of each quarter.

The disclosure must include the following details regarding each transaction: **18.197**

(a) the company subject to the disclosure obligation and, if applicable, its controlled company;
(b) the securities acquired or disposed of;
(c) date of acquisition or disposal;
(d) market where the transaction took place;
(e) nature of the transaction;
(f) amount of securities negotiated;
(g) price per unit;

---

[92] For a discussion of the concept of 'control' under Portuguese law, see note 78 above.
[93] At http://www.cmvm.pt/NR/exeres/71DD7754-82AC-47D0-A136-BAC7F993AE66.htm.

(h) time of the transaction, if executed on market;

(i) amount of own securities held by the issuer.

18.3.6 Disclosure means

18.198 Pursuant to CMVM regulations,[94] information concerning issuers published in compliance with the disclosure duties set out in the PSC and in the CMVM regulations must be sent to the IDS available on the CMVM's website (http://www.cmvm.pt), no later than the time when such information is being disclosed through any other means.

18.199 In addition, all information submitted to the CMVM for disclosure by issuers of securities listed on a regulated market must be (i) disclosed in a manner ensuring that investors throughout the EU have prompt access (within the time periods specifically stipulated and without any specific costs to investors) to such information on a non-discriminatory basis and (ii) submitted simultaneously to the management entity of the relevant regulated market and published on the issuer's website.[95]

18.200 Any changes or amendments to published information must be disclosed using the same means used to distribute the original information.

18.3.7 Corporate Governance Code

18.201 The Portuguese Corporate Governance Code consists of a set of recommendations on corporate governance related matters approved by the CMVM and applicable to companies with shares listed on a regulated market.

18.202 As stated in its preamble, the Corporate Governance Code is not intended to impose rigid and uniform models. Rather, it is aimed at setting forth best practices intended to increase the efficiency of both listed companies and the securities markets generally. Although companies issuing shares admitted to trading on a regulated market and institutional investors are the primary addressees of the Corporate Governance Code, companies whose shares are not admitted to trading on a regulated market are also encouraged to follow the recommendations and best practices set forth in the Code.

18.203 Companies governed by Portuguese law with shares listed on a regulated market must use the Corporate Governance Code as a reference in the preparation of

---

[94] See Article 5 No 1 of CMVM Regulation No 5/2008.

[95] Pursuant to Article 244 No 7 of the PSC, the issuers of securities admitted to trading on a regulated market must disclose and maintain on its website, for one year (with the exception of any other time periods specifically prescribed in law) all the information that is required to be made public pursuant to the PSC and its supplementary regulations.

the annual corporate governance report pursuant to CMVM Regulation No 1/2007 on corporate governance. Under the 'comply or explain' principle, the corporate governance report must include an explanatory statement regarding the (non) compliance with each of the recommendations set out in the Corporate Governance Code.[96]

---

[96] The CMVM has recently submitted to public consultation a draft regulation on corporate governance that will replace Regulation No 1/2007 and make certain amendments to the existing Corporate Governance Code. According to the documents submitted to public consultation, the main change proposed in the draft regulation is the possibility for companies governed by Portuguese law having shares listed on a regulated market to adopt a corporate governance code different from the code published by the CMVM, subject to certain requirements. The date on which the new regulation and the amendments to the existing Corporate Governance Code will be enacted is at present uncertain.

19

SPAIN

19.1 Listing Securities in Spain

19.1.1 The Spanish securities markets

All Spanish securities markets are integrated in the company Bolsas y Mercados **19.01**
Españoles, Sociedad Holding de Mercados y Sistemas Financieros, SA (BME).
As part of an initiative to simplify the corporate structure governing the securities
markets and settlement systems in Spain, the individual corporations that formerly operated the Spanish stock exchanges, the Spanish clearing and settlement
system and certain other securities markets in Spain were reorganized in 2002
and are now owned and controlled by BME.

The Securities Market Law 24/1988 of 28 July 1988 (*Ley del Mercado de Valores* **19.02**
or the 'LMV') sets forth the definition of a regulated market and states that
Spanish regulated markets are referred to as 'official secondary markets' (*mercados
secundarios oficiales*).[1] For such purposes, the LMV designates the following
securities markets as regulated markets:

- the four Spanish stock exchanges;
- the public debt book-entry market;
- the futures and options markets, whether the underlying asset is financial
  or not;
- the AIAF fixed-income market; and
- any other market, of a national scope, which complies with the definition of
  regulated market and is authorized as such, and those markets of local scope
  which may be authorized by the competent autonomous regions within Spain.

BME, which is itself a company admitted to listing in the Spanish stock exchanges **19.03**
since June 2006, owns a 100% stake in each of the Spanish stock exchanges, the
Spanish private fixed income securities market (AIAF), the Spanish public debt
trading platform (SENAF), the Spanish derivatives markets (MEFF) and the
Spanish central securities depository and clearing and settlement system
(Iberclear). BME's operating model is based on the vertical integration of the
entire chain of the Spanish securities markets from admission to listing of
securities to trading in and clearing and settlement of such securities.

19.1.1.1 The four stock exchanges

Spain is home to four long-standing stock exchanges—Madrid, Barcelona, **19.04**
Valencia and Bilbao (which were officially founded in 1831, 1915, 1980 and
1890 respectively)—linked into a continuous trading system known as the

---

[1] See LMV Article 31. The definition of regulated market is further discussed in Section 19.2.2.1.

Spanish Stock Exchange Interlinking System (*Sistema de Interconexión Bursátil Español* or SIBE). Each of these four exchanges is governed and managed by a governing company in charge of its internal organization and functioning.

19.05 The four stock exchanges' governing companies are shareholders with an equal interest of Sociedad de Bolsas, the company which manages the Stock Exchange Interlinking System (SIBE).

19.06 At present, the only trading system in the Spanish securities market is the SIBE electronic trading platform (Stock Exchange Interlinking System).[2] The SIBE interconnects Spain's four stock exchanges in real time. Trading is continuous from Monday to Friday between 9:00 and 17:30, a session during which orders are entered, modified, cancelled and executed. The SIBE is an order-driven market, providing real-time information on the price of each security, where the orders received from individual terminals are collated in a mainframe computer.

19.1.1.2 Public debt book-entry market

19.07 The public debt book-entry market (*Mercado de deuda pública anotada*) specializes in the trading of debt securities represented exclusively by book entries and issued by the central government, regional governments, certain public agencies and other national or international institutions authorized by the Ministry of Economy. It is governed by the central Bank of Spain and currently integrated on the SENAF electronic platform (which, in turn, is integrated in BME).

19.08 Most of the securities traded on the public debt book-entry market are issued by the Spanish Treasury, which is responsible for deciding central government debt issuance, its characteristics and frequency, placement procedures and the volumes to be issued.

19.1.1.3 Futures and options markets

19.09 In Spain, financial futures and options are traded on the MEFF (*Mercado Español de Futuros Financieros*) derivatives market, and commodities derivatives are traded in the Futures Market on Olive Oil (MFAO).[3] Warrants and certificates are traded in a designated segment of the SIBE.

---

[2] The open outcry markets coexisted as trading platforms with the SIBE until July 2009 when they were closed.

[3] The Futures Market on Olive Oil (MFAO) began operations in January 2004. It is managed by a governing company whose members are the Andalusian Regional Government (Junta de Andalucía), financial entities and olive oil sector companies. Currently, it is the only commodities futures market in Spain after the closing of the Futures and Options Market on Citrus Fruits. Further information can be found on the market's website: www.mfao.es.

The MEFF was created in 1989 and is Spain's regulated futures and options **19.10** market. As a regulated market, the MEFF is regulated and supervised by the CNMV[4] and the Ministry of Economy.

The MEFF centralizes all trading, clearing and settlement and registration func- **19.11** tions in the derivative products traded on it. These functions are integrated within an advanced electronic system supporting real-time management of risk.

Any individual or legal entity, Spanish or foreign, can operate on the MEFF by **19.12** opening an account with a market-member intermediary.

19.1.1.4 AIAF fixed-income market

The AIAF market was set up by the Association of Securities Dealers (*Asociación* **19.13** *de Intermediarios en Activos Financieros*) as a platform for fixed-income trades. It is a regulated market offering fixed-income securities and specializing in large-volume transactions. As such, it is geared primarily to institutional investors. It is also part of BME Group.

The AIAF market covers all kinds of fixed-income instruments issued by private **19.14** companies and institutions (commercial paper, bank debentures, regional government paper public debt book-entry form market, corporate bonds in general and mortgage-backed securities). The exceptions are convertible bonds (which are traded on the stock exchanges) and central government debt (traded on the public debt book-entry market, under the supervision of the Bank of Spain, and on the stock exchanges).

The clearing and settlement of AIAF trades is handled exclusively by Iberclear. **19.15**

19.1.1.5 Other trading platforms: Latibex and MAB

Latibex, the trading market segment in euros for Latin American stocks, is the **19.16** only international market for Latin American securities. It was created in December 1999, approved by the Spanish government and is regulated by the LMV, Iberclear circulars and further self-regulation provisions. European investors can buy and sell shares and securities in leading Latin American companies through a single market, with a single operating system for trading and settlement and a single currency, the euro (EUR). The market is based on the trading and settlement platform of the Spanish stock market (SIBE), in a way that the Latin American securities listed on Latibex are traded and settled like any other Spanish security. It is not a new single market as such but rather a platform for the trading and

---

[4] The Spanish National Securities Market Commission, *Comisión Nacional del Mercado de Valores*. See Section 19.1.2.

settlement, in Europe, of the shares of Latin America's top listed companies. There are specific requirements for the admission to trading on Latibex.[5]

19.17 The Alternative Exchange Market (*Mercado Alternativo Bursátil* or 'MAB') was created in 2006 as an organized trading system authorized by the government and regulated by the LMV. This trading segment's primary aim is to offer an organized system of trading, settlement, clearing and registration of trades made in (i) shares and other securities of collective investment schemes; (ii) securities and instruments issued by or linked to small caps; and (iii) other securities or instruments that, by nature, require a special trading scheme.

19.18 The MAB includes a trading segment for open-ended investment funds (the so-called SICAVs), an alternative equity market for venture capital companies and is also expected to include stocks from small and medium-sized companies which also require specific treatment due to their special characteristics. These are small capitalization companies whose shares generally suffer from thin liquidity and scant visibility among the investing public and which have not considered trading on the stock exchange due to the costs and requirements involved.

19.19 The settlement and clearing of securities and cash from trades on the MAB are carried out via Iberclear in accordance with similar procedures and time periods which are currently followed for listed stocks.

19.20 As for Latibex, inclusion on the MAB requires specific prerequisites and must follow a formal admission procedure.[6]

19.1.1.6 Iberclear

19.21 Iberclear is the sole Spanish central securities depository that is part of the holding company BME. It is a private limited company with BME as sole shareholder.[7]

19.22 It handles the book-entry registration of securities traded on the Spanish stock exchanges, the public debt book-entry market, fixed-income market AIAF and the Latibex trading segment. There are also clearing and settlement services in Barcelona, Bilbao and Valencia for securities listed exclusively on the local stock exchanges.

19.23 Iberclear is supervised by the CNMV, although the supervision of the public debt book-entry market falls to the Bank of Spain.

19.24 Banks, brokers and foreign institutions are eligible to become participants of Iberclear.

---

[5] http://www.latibex.com.
[6] For further information on the admission procedure see http://www.bolsasymercados.es/mab.
[7] Iberclear regulation is electronically available at http://www.iberclear.es.

The settlement term is T+3, that is, three working days from the trade date (T). **19.25**
Money and securities change hands between the transacting parties on T+3.

19.1.2 The CNMV

The Spanish National Securities Market Commission, the *Comisión Nacional* **19.26**
del Mercado de Valores (or CNMV) is the main institution in the Spanish securities
markets. It was created in 1988 by the LMV,[8] which instituted in-depth reforms
in this area of the Spanish financial system. It is the regulator in charge of supervising and inspecting the Spanish securities markets and the activities of all
participants in those markets.

The main tasks of the CNMV are (i) to ensure transparency in the Spanish mar- **19.27**
kets and the correct determination of market prices and (ii) to protect investors.
The CNMV promotes the disclosure of any information to achieve these ends,
using the means at its disposal.

The main functions of the CNMV are as follows: **19.28**

- It verifies and registers any issue or public offering of securities in Spain.
- It is the competent authority regarding the admission to trading of securities
  on regulated markets in Spain.
- It supervises the secondary markets and the activity of any person or institution
  acting in them (except the public debt book entry market which is supervised
  by the Bank of Spain), including issuers of securities and investment services
  companies.
- It monitors issuers' compliance with continuing obligations once their securities are listed. In particular, the CNMV ensures that the material information
  regarding an issuer is made public to the market, including its main business,
  economic and financial information, and the changes in significant shareholdings of companies whose securities are admitted to trading.
- The CNMV also exercises prudential supervision over the following entities in
  order to ensure transaction security and the solvency of the system: (i) collective
  investment schemes, a category which includes: investment companies (securities and real estate), investment funds (securities and real estate) and their
  management companies; (ii) broker-dealers and dealers, which are entities
  engaging primarily in the purchase and sale of securities; and (iii) portfolio
  management companies, i.e. entities focusing primarily on managing individuals' assets (mainly securities).

---

[8] The Securities Market Law 24/1988 of 28 July 1988 (*Ley del Mercado de Valores* or 'LMV').
See Section 19.1.3.1.

- It has inspection and sanctioning powers, with the power to require provision of any information it deems necessary and to impose sanctions under Spanish law.
- It also has the power to issue certain rules (by means of circulars) in order to implement laws and regulations which expressly enable the CNMV to do so. It also advises the Government, the Ministry of Economy and, as the case may be, the regional governments in matters related to securities markets.
- Through the National Securities Numbering Agency, the CNMV assigns internationally valid ISIN and CFI codes to all securities issued in Spain.
- Also, the CNMV is empowered to detect and pursue illegal activities by unregistered intermediaries.

19.29 As a consequence of the above, in practice, the CNMV is likely to have frequent contact both with the issuer and with its legal counsel when conducting listings in Spain and also when complying with continuing obligations. For instance, the CNMV usually contacts the company to clarify certain material information made public or even rumours about the company which have been unofficially leaked into the markets.

19.30 The CNMV's general position is that the efficiency of regulations can be enhanced by simplifying bureaucratic procedures, and it has announced that it will proceed in this direction in the coming years. In this regard, there is a project to reform the Spanish financial supervision system which envisages replacing the current CNMV with a national commission of financial services, extending the current functions of the CNMV to include, among other things, supervision of insurance agents and companies.

19.31 The above follows the so-called 'twin peaks' model which consists of a double-regulator structure which in Spain would be closely linked to the Bank of Spain and the CNMV successor to be created. This new regulator to be created would focus on supervising the correct operating and transparency of the financial markets by controlling the conduct of intermediaries in their relationship with investors and, generally, consumers of financial services, while the Bank of Spain would supervise the solvency risks of all financial entities.

19.1.3 Legislative overview

19.1.3.1 The Securities Market Law (LMV)

19.32 The Securities Market Law 24/1988 of 28 July 1988 (*Ley del Mercado de Valores* or the 'LMV'), as amended, is the central piece of legislation regulating the Spanish securities markets.

19.33 Approved in 1988, the LMV represented a crucial development in the modernization of the capital and securities markets in Spain. Its main purpose was to improve and prepare the Spanish securities markets for the common European capital market that came into existence in 1992.

The contents of the LMV include rules governing (i) the CNMV; (ii) the primary **19.34** markets and the issuance of securities; (iii) the Spanish regulated markets; (including the stock exchanges, the public debt and the futures and options markets, the notification of transactions and the rules on takeover bids); (iv) the investment services companies; (v) the rules of conduct for the entities operating in the securities market; (vi) the inspection and sanctioning regime; (vii) the tax regime on securities transactions; (viii) listed companies and (ix) other trading systems (such as multilateral trading systems).

The LMV has been amended on many occasions and has been further imple- **19.35** mented by other Spanish laws and regulations, some of which are set forth below, in order to implement the European directives. In addition, the stock exchanges and other secondary markets and their operations are regulated in detail in several different legal provisions. As mentioned above, the CNMV has issued in turn various circulars to complete the provisions of these laws and regulations for their practical implementation, for instance to issue official forms or clarify accounting rules.

19.1.3.2 *The Royal Decree 1310/2005 on admission to trading and offers of securities and the Royal Decree Law 5/2005*

The Royal Decree Law 5/2005 of 11 March 2005, included measures to imple- **19.36** ment part of the Prospectus Directive[9] by restating Title III of the LMV. Although the Decree did not substantially deviate from the Directive, its full implementation in Spain required the enactment of additional secondary regulations. These regulations included the Royal Decree 1310/2005 of 4 November 2005 on admission to trading and offers of securities, which remains the central piece of Spanish legislation governing the requirements for admission to trading and offering of securities in Spanish secondary markets, and for the prospectus required for such offerings ('Royal Decree 1310/2005'). In addition, the Royal Decree 1310/ 2005 incorporated the provisions of Directive 2001/34/EC of the European Parliament and of the Council of 28 May 2001 on the admission of securities to official stock exchange listing and on information to be published on those securities.

Ministerial Order 3537/2005 of 10 November 2005 further develops these rules **19.37** by incorporating by reference the prospectus models set out in EU Regulation 809/2004.

---

[9] Directive 2003/71/EC of the European Parliament and of the Council of 4 November 2003.

19.1.3.3 *The Royal Decree 1333/2005 on market abuse*

19.38   On 11 November 2005, the Spanish government enacted Royal Decree 1333/2005 ('Royal Decree 1333/2005') to fully implement the four directives on market abuse.[10]

19.1.3.4 *The Royal Decree 1362/2007 on transparency requirements*

19.39   The Royal Decree 1362/2007, of 19 October 2007, on transparency requirements regarding information on issuers whose securities are admitted to trading on a Spanish regulated market ('Royal Decree 1362/2007'), amended the LMV in order to (i) partially implement the Transparency Directive[11] and (ii) implement Directive 2007/14/EC.[12]

19.40   The Royal Decree 1362/2007 covers the information regime for issuers focusing on what the directives define as 'regulated information'. This includes periodical information (mainly financial information) and information which should be disclosed and accessible on an ongoing basis.

19.1.3.5 *Law 6/2007 and the Royal Decree 1066/2007 on takeover bids*

19.41   On 13 August 2007, Law 6/2007, of 12 April 2007, amending the LMV, in order to modify the rules for takeover bids and the transparency of issuers ('Law 6/2007') entered into effect. Law 6/2007 was intended to partially transpose the Takeover[13] and the Transparency Directives into the Spanish legal system.

19.42   In addition to Law 6/2007, the Royal Decree 1066/2007 enacted on 27 July 2007 ('Royal Decree 1066/2007'), further implements the principles on takeovers set out in the LMV.

---

[10]   Directive 2003/6/EC of the European Parliament and of the Council of 28 January 2003, on insider dealing and market manipulation; Commission Directive 2003/124/EC of 22 December 2003 implementing Directive 2003/6/EC of the European Parliament and of the Council as regards the definition and public disclosure of inside information and the definition of market manipulation; Directive 2003/125/EC of 22 December 2003 implementing Directive 2003/6/EC of the European Parliament and of the Council as regards fair presentation of investment recommendations and the disclosure of conflicts of interest; and Directive 2004/72/EC of 29 April 2004 implementing Directive 2003/6/EC of the European Parliament and of the Council as regards accepted market practices, the definition of the inside information in relation to derivatives on commodities, the drawing up of lists of insiders, the notification of managers' transactions and the notification of suspicious transactions.

[11]   Directive 2004/109/EC of the European Parliament and of the Council of 15 December 2004 on the harmonisation of transparency requirements in relation to information about issuers whose securities are admitted to trading on a regulated market.

[12]   Commission Directive 2007/14/EC of 8 March 2007 laying down detailed rules for the implementation of certain provisions of Directive 2004/109/EC on the harmonisation of transparency requirements in relation to information about issuers whose securities are admitted to trading on a regulated market.

[13]   Directive 2004/25/EC of the European Parliament and of the Council of 21 April 2004 on takeover bids.

19.1.4 Eligibility listing requirements

19.1.4.1 General eligibility criteria

Spanish law[14] subjects the admission to trading of securities to two different sets of requirements: **19.43**

- suitability requirements regarding both the securities to be admitted and the issuer; and
- information requirements (see Section 19.1.5 below on documentation to be filed).

These requirements, which are subject to verification by the CNMV within 10 business days from the filing of the prospectus (if a prospectus is required) or within five business days (if no prospectus is required), are set forth in Title I of the Royal Decree 1310/2005. **19.44**

19.1.4.1.1 (a) Suitability requirements regarding the issuer The following conditions are to be met by any issuer seeking to admit securities to trading on a Spanish secondary market: **19.45**

Incorporation: the issuer must be (i) duly incorporated in accordance with the laws of the country where its corporate registered office is located and (ii) operating in conformity with its memorandum of incorporation, its articles of association or any equivalent organizational document. **19.46**

Equal treatment: the terms of issuers' shares admitted to trading may not contain disadvantages or different rights among shareholders in identical situations. In addition, an issuer of debt securities admitted to trading must assure equal rights and treatment to all holders of debt securities which are fungible or of a similar nature.[15] **19.47**

19.1.4.1.2 (b) Suitability requirements regarding the securities **19.48**

Validity: the securities to be admitted must conform to the legal regime which governs them.

Book-entry form: the relevant securities must be represented in book-entry form. **19.49**

Transferability: the securities must be freely transferable. Securities are considered freely transferable if neither the articles of association nor the resolution stating the terms and conditions of their issuing contain any restrictions to the right to transfer. However, securities do not need to be fully paid up. Partially paid-up securities will be deemed freely transferable if, in the view of the CNMV, their **19.50**

---

[14] In particular, the Royal Decree 1310/2005, of 4 November 2005.
[15] See Royal Decree 1310/2005 Article 8.

negotiability is not restricted and investors are provided with all necessary information to deal such securities in an open and transparent way.

19.51 *First listing before subscription*: where a public offer or issue precedes admission to trading, the first listing of securities may be made only after the end of the subscription period (save for certain exceptions).

19.52 *Market capitalization*: the total amount of securities to be listed must be at least (i) EUR 6 million of the expected aggregated market value[16] for equity securities, and (ii) EUR 200,000 of the issue's nominal value for debt securities.[17] These limits do not apply if securities of the same class are already listed. In addition, Spanish law allows the CNMV to admit to trading equity securities or debt securities which do not reach such limits, provided that the CNMV considers that there is enough liquidity in the market for such securities.

19.53 *Minimum public float*: shares to be admitted to trading must have sufficient distribution among the public by no later than admission to listing. Distribution is considered sufficient if, at least, 25% of the shares to be listed are in public hands or 'if the market can operate with a lower percentage in view of the large number of shares of the same class and the degree of their distribution to the public'.[18] There are no particular rules for the purposes of calculating whether the requirement is met. However, the CNMV may disregard this requirement where the shares are going to be distributed to the public through a stock exchange and the CNMV is satisfied that a sufficient number of shares will be distributed through the stock exchange within a short period of time. In practice, the CNMV has disregarded this requirement in a limited number of cases only.[19]

19.54 *Whole class to be listed*: the application for admission to trading must comprise the entire class of the securities to be listed; if securities of that class are already listed or proposed to be issued, then the application must relate to all further securities of that class.[20]

---

[16] According to Article 9 of the Royal Decree 1310/2005, in order to assess the expected market value and whether the requirement of minimum market capitalization is met for shares, the price paid by investors in the prior public offer (when such offer precedes the admission to trading) will be taken into consideration.

[17] In case of continuing issues of debt securities in the context of a debt programme, the capitalization is calculated with respect to the total amount of the programme.

[18] See Royal Decree 1310/2005 Article 9.7.

[19] In particular, the requirement of distribution of at least 25% of the shares to be listed was disregarded in the initial public offerings of Criteria Caixacorp, SA (September 2007) and of Iberdrola Renovables, SA (November 2007). Both cases were offerings of a large number of shares where the CNMV considered that there was sufficient distribution among the public.

[20] For debt securities, the application for admission to trading must also include all securities of the same issue, according to Royal Decree 1310/2005 Article 9.8.

19.1.4.2 *Additional eligibility requirements*

Admission to trading of securities on a Spanish secondary market also requires the **19.55** adoption of a formal approval by the governing body of the regulated market where admission of the securities is sought, according to the rules on admission to trading of such governing body. However, specific rules for admission to listing have not yet been issued by the governing bodies of the Spanish stock exchanges, so that, in practice, this additional requirement does not apply in the meantime.

19.1.4.3 *Additional eligibility criteria for convertible and exchangeable obligations, warrants*

Admission to trading of convertible and exchangeable obligations and warrants **19.56** requires that the underlying shares to which they refer have been previously or are expected to be simultaneously admitted to listing either on a Spanish stock exchange or on another regulated market in the European Union, or on similar OECD markets or any other markets that the CNMV considers equivalent.

However, this requirement will not apply if the CNMV considers that the holders **19.57** of the obligations have at their disposal all the necessary information to assess the value of the shares to which such obligations are linked.

19.1.5 Information requirements—documentation to be filed

In addition to meeting the suitability requirements, the following information **19.58** requirements must also be complied with prior to the admission to trading of securities.

19.1.5.1 *General information requirements*

The general information requirements are as follows:[21] **19.59**

- Filing and registration with the CNMV of any documents showing the submission of the issuer and its securities to a specific legal regime. The CNMV will specify on a case-by-case basis the documents to be provided by the issuer according to its nature and the securities to be admitted. In practice, the CNMV requires the incorporation deed or equivalent organizational document.
- Filing and registration with the CNMV of annual financial statements of the issuer for the last three years, both individual and consolidated (if applicable), prepared and audited in accordance with the law applicable to the issuer.[22]
- Filing, approval, registration and publication with the CNMV of a prospectus, if required.[23]

---

[21] According to Royal Decree 1310/2005 Article 11.

[22] Such accounts must have been prepared in accordance with the issuers' applicable law. For non-equity securities, the last two years' audited annual accounts are required.

[23] See Section 19.2 below on the prospectus.

19.60   In connection with the second requirement above, the CNMV may accept financial statements of an issuer covering a shorter period if (i) the issuer is a special purpose vehicle whose purpose is basically to issue securities and such securities that are securitization instruments or guaranteed securities, provided, in the latter case, that the guarantor has published audited financial accounts covering the last three years, or (ii) the CNMV so decides in the interest of the issuer or the investors, provided that it considers that investors have all necessary information to make an informed assessment of the issuer and the securities to be listed.

19.1.5.2 *Exceptions to the information requirements*

19.61   As set forth in the Prospectus Directive, the admission to trading of certain securities is not subject to any of the information requirements described above. This exception applies to non-equity securities issued by the following bodies: (a) the Spanish State, its autonomous regions or their local bodies; (b) any other EU member state; (c) international public bodies where at least one or more EU member state participates; (d) the European Central Bank; (e) central banks of EU member states; or (f) legal entities with their registered office in Spain and created by a special law, provided that the principal and the interest of such securities are subject to an irrevocable and unconditional guarantee of the Spanish State.

19.62   In addition, securities issued by the central bank of any EU member state, whether equity or non-equity, are not subject to information requirements.

19.1.5.3 *Annual information to be filed with the CNMV*

19.63   In addition to the above information requirements, pursuant to Article 10 of the Prospectus Directive, where Spain is the home member state, as determined under the Prospectus Directive, issuers of securities admitted to trading on a Spanish regulated market are required to file at least annually with the CNMV a document indicating where to obtain all the information that they have published or made available to the public over the preceding 12 months in one or more EU member states and in third countries in compliance with their obligations under EU rules and national laws, including rules governing the regulation of securities, issuers of securities and securities markets.[24] The document must be filed after the publication of the financial statements.

---

[24] Issuers must provide, at a minimum, the information required pursuant to company law directives, Directive 2001/34/EC and Regulation (EC) No 1606/2002 of the European Parliament and of the Council of 19 July 2002 on the application of international accounting standards (OJ L 243, 11.9.2002).

The obligation set out above does not apply to issuers of non-equity securities **19.64** with denominations of at least EUR 50,000, nor to issuers of non-equity securities who are exempt from the information requirements as stated in Section 19.1.5.2 above.

19.2 The Prospectus

19.2.1 Applicable law

Spanish rules implementing the prospectus requirements for admission to trading **19.65** of securities and public offers have remained very close to the Prospectus Directive. Accordingly, Spanish law in prospectus matters differs very little from the common framework for EU member states. Particularities arise mostly in practice, in connection with the approval procedure of the prospectus and the contacts with the CNMV.

The key sources of Spanish law in this area are (i) Title III and IV of the LMV (as **19.66** amended by the Royal Decree Law 5/ 2005) which sets out general provisions on the contents of the prospectus, the liability for prospectuses, cross border validity of the prospectus and definition of a public offer; (ii) the Royal Decree 1310/2005, which contains the detailed requirements of the prospectus: information to be included, format of the prospectus, approval and publication procedure, validity and liability of the prospectus, etc.; and (iii) Ministerial Order 3537/2005 of 10 November 2005, issued by the Economy and Finance Ministry, which develops Article 27.4 of the LMV by setting forth the contents and models of prospectus as set out in EU Regulation 809/2004.

In addition, recommendations issued by CESR also provide guidelines to inter- **19.67** pret Spanish law.

19.2.2 Requirements for a prospectus

19.2.2.1 *Triggering events*

Under Spanish law, as is the case throughout the EU, a prospectus must be **19.68** prepared, approved by the CNMV and published by a company to achieve any of the following: (i) the admission to trading on a Spanish regulated market of securities issued by the company; or (ii) a public offer (as defined by law) of securities issued or to be sold by the company.

The law defines certain terms in order to clarify the events which trigger the **19.69** obligation to publish a prospectus, which include the following, among others:

Issuer: the entity issuing or intending to issue any securities for which admission **19.70** to trading on a Spanish regulated market is requested. Individuals may not be considered as issuers.

19.71 *Transferable securities*: Transferable securities are any financial instrument conferring certain rights on its holder, which independently of their designation, are negotiable (i.e. capable of being traded in a widespread and impersonal manner) on a financial market. The Royal Decree 1310/ 2005 provides a list of transferable securities which includes among others, shares and securities equivalent to shares in companies or financial instruments giving right to acquire such shares; share quotas (*cuotas participativas*) of saving banks; debt obligations, including convertible or exchangeable; bonds and mortgage instruments, preferred quota-shares, securitization instruments; warrants; bond certificates; and deposit certificates. It also contains a list of securities which are not considered transferable securities.

19.72 *Regulated market*: regulated markets in Spain, which are referred to in applicable regulations as 'official secondary markets' (*mercados secundarios oficiales*) are defined in the LMV, following the definition set forth in MiFiD, as multilateral systems which bring together multiple third-party buying and selling interests in financial instruments that result in a contract, in respect of the financial instruments admitted to trading under their rules, and which are authorized and function regularly and in accordance with the provisions of law and subject to access conditions, admission to trading, operational procedures, information and publicity. The markets currently designated as regulated markets in Spain are described in Section 19.1.1 above. The CNMV keeps an updated list of the Spanish regulated markets which is sent to the European Commission and the EU member states.

19.73 *Public offer*: A public offer is any communication to any person in any form or by any means that presents sufficient information on the terms of the offer and on the securities offered to enable an investor to decide whether or not to purchase or subscribe for the securities.[25]

19.2.2.2 Other requirements

19.74 Offers of securities to the public (either initial public offerings or secondary offers) which are not exempt from the requirement to publish a prospectus, will also have to satisfy the following requirements:

- the *securities validity requirement* (also required for the admission to listing),[26] according to which the securities offered must conform with the legal regime to which they are subject; and
- the *issuer's suitability requirement* (also required for the admission to listing) according to which the issuer must be (i) duly incorporated in accordance with

---

[25] See LMV Article 30 *bis* 1 and Royal Decree 1310/2005 Article 38.1.
[26] See Section 19.1.4.1 b) above 'Eligibility listing requirements'.

the laws of the country of its registered office and (ii) operating in conformity with its memorandum of incorporation, its articles of association or any equivalent document.

The above requirements do not apply to public offers exempt from publishing a prospectus. **19.75**

19.2.2.3 Exemptions to the requirement to publish a prospectus

As in other EU member states that have transposed the Prospectus Directive, there are several exemptions and exceptions under Spanish rules to the requirement to publish a prospectus **19.76**

These exemptions include (i) situations that generally fall outside the scope of the Prospectus Directive, (ii) specific exceptions for certain types of offers that do not require publication of an offer prospectus (either because such offers are not considered offers to the public,[27] such as offers exclusively addressed to qualified investors,[28] or because they are otherwise exempted from the prospectus requirement [29]) and (iii) specific exemptions from the requirement to publish a listing prospectus for admission to trading on a regulated market.[30] **19.77**

With regard to these exemptions, Spanish rules have reproduced the provisions of the Prospectus Directive which are discussed in more detail in Part 1. **19.78**

19.2.3 Preparing a prospectus

19.2.3.1 Contact with the CNMV

The CNMV is the authority verifying compliance with all requirements for the admission to trading of securities, including the prospectus. **19.79**

The CNMV will only approve a prospectus if, as a result of its review of such prospectus, it concludes that the prospectus is complete, understandable and contains consistent information. **19.80**

As stated below,[31] the powers of the CNMV to request information include not only requests for additional information to complete the prospectus, but also any documents or information in connection with admissions to trading or public offerings. Such information may be requested from the issuer, its significant **19.81**

---

[27] See LMV Article 30 *bis* 1 and Royal Decree 1310/2005 Article 38 1310/2005.
[28] See Royal Decree 1310/2005 Article 39 defining qualified investors.
[29] See Royal Decree 1310/2005 Article 41.
[30] See Royal Decree 1310/2005 Article 26.
[31] See Section 19.2.7 below on 'Process and timing of prospectus approval and publication' and Section 19.2.10 on 'CNMV's powers in connection with the prospectus'.

shareholders, auditors or financial advisers involved in the offer or the listing to which the prospectus relates.

19.82 In practice, the applicant and its advisers meet with the CNMV at the outset to officially introduce the company and the main features of the offering or the application for admission to trading (as the case may be). This initial phase is particularly important in cases where a complex financial history of the issuer must be discussed.

19.83 When drafting the prospectus, the issuer and its advisers are likely to have a significant amount of contact with the CNMV both at high and medium levels of the company's structure. The approval process typically consists of several rounds of submissions of the draft prospectus to the relevant CNMV reader, who will request clarifications and further information and will provide comments on the draft, before a new submission or final approval of the prospectus by the CNMV board. Accordingly, the collaboration of both the issuer and its financial and legal advisers with the CNMV are key factors contributing to the success of a prospectus approval.

19.2.3.2 Prospectus format

19.84 In accordance with relevant provisions of the Prospectus Directive, Spanish law allows for different formats in which to present the prospectus:[32] (i) separate documents; (ii) single document; or (iii) base prospectus and final terms of the offer.

19.85 **19.2.3.2.1 Separate documents** If the issuer chooses to produce a prospectus consisting of separate documents, it will have to divide the necessary information into three different sections: registration document, securities note and summary:

1. *Registration document.* The registration document contains information relating to the issuer—basically, a description of the company and its business, together with its financial statements—and is valid for 12 months from the date of publication. The issuer might request the CNMV to accept its audited annual accounts as a valid registration document. In this case, the annual accounts must include all the information required by law for a registration document.[33] The registration document may be filed by the issuer to either register or deposit it.

   An issuer with a registration document already registered (and thus approved) by the CNMV, must only produce the short securities note

---

[32] Royal Decree 1310/2005 Articles 18 to 21.

[33] In such cases, the CNMV might request a summary chart comprising the information sections required by the registration document model and the equivalent sections of the annual accounts where such information may be found. See Royal Decree 1310/2005 Article 19.2.

(which will include any update on the issuer, if required) and the summary for each new issue and listing made during the year.

If the registration document is deposited with the CNMV (but not registered), the issuer must update the registration document and produce the short securities note and the summary prior to the admission of its securities. Where the registration document consists of the issuer's annual accounts, updates related to the issuer will be included in the securities note.

2. *Securities note.* The securities note contains information relating to the securities and must be produced when an issuance is made.
3. *Summary.* [34] The summary must be brief and use non-technical language and convey the essential characteristics and risks associated with the issuer, any guarantor and the securities. It must also contain a warning statement.

A prospectus approved for the admission to trading of non-equity securities with a denomination of at least EUR 50,000 does not require a summary.

19.2.3.2.2 Single document The single prospectus must contain all the ele- **19.86** ments of a three-part prospectus, including the summary. Such single prospectus may also be used as a registration document as described for separate documents. The single document prospectus is more likely to be used by issuers who are offering securities once during the year and do not intend to access the capital markets regularly in the following months.

19.2.3.2.3 Base prospectus and final terms of the offer The base prospectus **19.87** format is intended for issuers of non-equity securities or warrants issued under an offering programme.[35] Under Spanish rules, a programme means a plan which would allow for the issuance of non-equity securities, other than shares or transferable securities equivalent to company shares, in a continuous or repeated manner during a specified issuing period.

The base prospectus must contain all relevant information included in a prospec- **19.88** tus (i.e. concerning the issuer and the securities to be offered under the programme) other than the final terms of the offer. Such final terms are elements which are not known when the base prospectus is approved and can only be determined at the time of an individual issue, such as the principal amount issued, the issue price and the coupon. This additional information is supplied when each issue is made under the programme in a supplementary document, the final terms, which is not subject to the CNMV's approval. However, the final terms must be made available to investors and deposited with the CNMV for each issuance as

---

[34] See Royal Decree 1310/2005 Article 17. The summary must not exceed 2,500 words.
[35] Royal Decree 1310/2005 Article 21 states conditions required for securities whose issuer intends to use the base prospectus format.

soon as the applicant can provide them and, if possible, prior to the beginning of the offering.

19.89 Each prospectus structure responds to different profiles of issuers, depending essentially on the kind of securities to be offered and on the frequency with which issuers intend to access the capital markets. Issuers that wish to issue securities on several occasions over the course of a year will be likely to produce a separate document structure, while issuers planning a programme offering will likely opt for the base prospectus and final terms format. The single document option is more likely to be chosen by issuers of securities on a one-off basis, at least, within a one-year period.

19.2.4 Prospectus contents

19.2.4.1 *General contents*

19.90 The prospectus must generally provide all the information relating to the issuer and the securities to be admitted to trading on a regulated market which, according to the particular nature of the transferable securities and their issuer, is necessary to enable investors to make an informed assessment of the assets and liabilities, financial position, profits and losses, and prospects of the issuer of the transferable securities and any guarantor; and the rights attached to the transferable securities.[36]

19.91 This information must be presented in a form which is comprehensible and easy to analyse. Such information must be included unless certain exceptions apply as set forth in Ministerial Order 3537/2005 of 10 November 2005, issued by the Ministry of Economy and Finance, which develops Article 27.4 of the LMV.

19.2.4.2 *Exceptions to the content requirements of the prospectus—omission of information*

19.92 In certain cases, the CNMV has the power to authorize the omission of certain information from the prospectus. The CNMV may do so where: (a) disclosure of such information would be contrary to the public interest; (b) disclosure would be seriously detrimental to the issuer, provided non-disclosure would not be likely to mislead a person considering the acquisition of the securities as to any facts or circumstances, knowledge of which is essential for an informed assessment of the issuer, any guarantor, and the rights attaching to the securities to which the prospectus refers; and (c) the information is of minor importance only for the specific admission to trading on a regulated market and not such as to

---

[36] LMV Article 27.1 and Royal Decree 1310/2005 Article 16.

influence the assessment of the financial position or the prospects of the issuer or guarantor.[37]

In addition, under Spanish law the final offer price and the amount of securities **19.93** to be offered may not be included in the prospectus if: (a) the prospectus sets out the criteria or terms that will be used to determine the price and amount of securities or, in the case of the price, it sets out the maximum price; or (b) investors who have accepted offers to purchase or subscribe will have the right to withdraw their acceptances during a period of not less than two working days after the final price and amount of securities offered have been determined and filed with the CNMV. The final offer price and the amount of securities offered must be filed with the CNMV and published according to the prospectus publicity rules.

19.2.4.3 *Content of the prospectus*

Ministerial Order 3537/2005 of 10 November 2005, which develops Article 27.4 **19.94** of the LMV on the basic contents of the prospectus, states that the contents of the prospectus must be conformed to the prospectus models set forth by EU Commission Regulation 809/2004 of 29 April 2004 implementing the Prospectus Directive with respect to the information contained in prospectuses, as well as the format, incorporation by reference, publication of such prospectuses and the dissemination of advertisements.

In this regard, Spanish rules have not introduced particular variations or special **19.95** rules applicable to prospectuses in the context of an offer of securities to the public in Spain or an admission to trading on Spanish regulated markets. The structure, format and contents of the prospectus follow the requirements set forth in the EU Commission Regulation which is tailored depending on the issuer and the securities offered or to be admitted to trading. The CNMV may not require the inclusion of sections of information other than those set forth in the prospectus models of the Commission Regulation, although it is empowered to require additional information on a particular section of the model in order to complete the information required under such section.

19.2.4.4 *Incorporations by reference*

The prospectus may incorporate information by reference to one or more docu- **19.96** ments published before or simultaneously with the prospectus approval. Such documents must be either approved by or filed with the CNMV, pursuant to Article 15 of the Royal Decree 1310/ 2005 regulating the provision of annual

---

[37] See Fourth Provision of Ministerial Order 3537/2005 of 10 November, issued by the Ministry of Economy and Finance, which develops Article 27.4 of LMV.

information, or approved by or filed with the competent authority of the home member state. This information must be the latest available to the issuer.

19.97　Where information is incorporated by reference, a cross-reference list must be provided in order to enable investors to identify easily specific items of information. However, issuers may not incorporate any information by reference into the summary.

19.2.5 Use of languages in the prospectus

19.98　Prospectuses to be approved by the CNMV for an offer to the public or an admission to trading on a Spanish secondary official market may be drawn up either in Spanish or in a language customary in the sphere of international finance or in any other language accepted by the CNMV, at the choice of the issuer, offeror or person seeking admission.[38]

19.99　Prospectuses to be approved by the CNMV for an offer to the public or an admission to trading on a secondary official market in one or more member states other than Spain, might be drawn up either in a language accepted by the competent authorities of those member states or in a language customary in the sphere of international finance, at the choice of the issuer, offeror or person seeking admission, as the case may be. The competent authority of the host member state may only require that the summary, rather than the entire prospectus, be translated into its official language.

19.100　In particular, for admissions to trading on a secondary Spanish market, and independently from the competent authority approving the prospectus, the applicant must translate the summary into Spanish when the prospectus to which it relates is not drawn up in Spanish. This translation requirement shall not apply to non-equity securities with a nominal value of at least EUR 50,000 each.

19.2.6 Supplements to the prospectus[39]

19.101　A supplementary prospectus is required whenever a significant new factor, material mistake or inaccuracy relating to the information included in the prospectus and which is capable of affecting the assessment of the securities arises or is noted between the time when the prospectus is approved and the final closing of the offer to the public or the time when trading on a regulated market begins. In order to determine whether the factor is significant, or the mistake or inaccuracy actually affects the assessment of the securities, the type of securities to which the prospectus relates will be taken into consideration.

---

[38] See Royal Decree 1310/2005 Article 23.
[39] See Royal Decree 1310/2005 Article 22.

The supplementary prospectus must be approved in the same way as the original **19.102** prospectus within a maximum of five working days and published in accordance with the same requirements applicable to the original prospectus. The summary and any translations of it must also be supplemented, if necessary, to take into account the new information included in the supplement.

In the event of a public offer, investors who have already agreed to purchase **19.103** or subscribe for the securities before the supplement is published shall have the right, exercisable within two working days at least after the publication of the supplement, to withdraw their acceptances.

19.2.7 Process and timing of prospectus approval and publication

19.2.7.1 Prospectus approval

The official approval of the prospectus is an express act of the CNMV resulting **19.104** from the analysis of the document which leads the CNMV to conclude that the prospectus is complete, comprehensible and contains consistent information.

However, the approval of the prospectus does not imply an assessment of the **19.105** quality of the applicant issuer nor of the securities offered.

Approval by the CNMV is necessary prior to the publication of the prospectus. **19.106** The CNMV's decision on whether it approves the prospectus or not is communicated to the applicant issuer within ten working days (when an admission to listing is required) or 20 working days (when an offer of securities must be approved) from the day on which the draft prospectus has been submitted.

Such term may, however, be reduced (depending on the structuring of the **19.107** prospectus, the securities offered or the issuer itself) or interrupted by requests of additional information by the CNMV. The CNMV has the power to extend the time limits to provide supplementary information, considering the nature or complexity of such information.

Spanish law has also incorporated the 'negative silent rule' of the Prospectus **19.108** Directive, according to which if no decision has been notified by the CNMV in connection with the approval of the prospectus, silence of the competent authority should be construed as a denial of the approval.[40]

19.2.7.2 Prospectus registration and publication

Once approved, the prospectus must be filed with the CNMV and must be made **19.109** available to the public by the issuer, offeror or person requesting admission to trading as soon as practicable and in any case, with reasonable time in advance,

---

[40] See Royal Decree 1310/2005 Article 24.

and at the latest at the beginning of the offer to the public or the admission to trading of the securities.

19.110   In addition, in the case of an initial public offering of a class of shares not yet admitted to trading on a regulated market (i.e. admitted to trading for the first time), the prospectus must be available at least six working days before the end of the offer.

19.111   The text and the format of the prospectus, and/or the supplements to the prospectus, published or made available to the public, must be identical to the original version approved by the CNMV.

19.112   The prospectus is deemed to be available to the public when published either:[41]

- by insertion in one or more newspapers circulated throughout, or widely circulated in the member states in which the offer to the public is made or the admission to trading is sought;
- in printed form to be made available, free of charge, to the public at the offices of the market on which the securities are being admitted to trading, or at the registered office of the issuer and at the offices of the financial intermediaries placing or selling the securities, including paying agents;
- in electronic form on the issuer's website and, if applicable, on the website of the financial intermediaries placing or selling the securities, including paying agents;
- in electronic form on the website of the regulated market where the admission to trading is sought, at least during the validity term of the prospectus; or
- in electronic form on the website of the CNMV if it has decided to offer this service.

19.113   Where the prospectus is made available by publication in electronic form, a paper copy must nevertheless be delivered to the investor, upon request and free of charge, by the issuer, the offeror, the person asking for admission to trading, or the financial intermediaries placing or selling the securities.

19.2.7.3 Validity term

19.114   Generally, a time limit must be set for the validity of a prospectus in order to avoid outdated information. The validity of the prospectus is of particular importance when the structure or format of the prospectus is a three-part document. This allows updating of only certain parts of the prospectus and avoids redrafting the entire prospectus.

---

[41] See Royal Decree 1310/2005 Article 25.

As in the Prospectus Directive, Spanish law generally provides that a prospectus **19.115** is valid for 12 months after its publication for offers to the public in Spain or admissions to trading on a Spanish regulated market, provided that the prospectus is updated with any supplements as may be required.[42]

A base prospectus is valid for a period of 12 months from its publication. In the **19.116** case of non-equity securities issued in a continuous or repeated manner by credit institutions,[43] the prospectus is valid until no more of the securities concerned are issued in a continuous or repeated manner.

A registration document is valid for a period of up to 12 months from its publica- **19.117** tion provided that it has been updated. The registration document together with the securities note, updated if applicable, and the summary note are considered to constitute a valid prospectus.

19.2.7.4 Advertisements

Spanish rules regarding advertising closely resemble those in other EU member **19.118** states. This is not an area where Spain has introduced any innovative approach.

Spanish law gives freedom to publish any advertisements relating to the admission **19.119** to trading or the offer of securities to any interested party, including the applicant issuer or the financial intermediaries securing or participating in the placing of the offered securities.

Advertisements may be published through any media and at any moment, includ- **19.120** ing prior to the approval of the prospectus. However, such advertisements or any other types of publicity must be clearly recognizable as such. The information contained in an advertisement must not be inaccurate or misleading.

Where the issuer, the offeror or the person applying for admission to trading is **19.121** covered by the obligation to prepare a prospectus, the following rules apply:[44]

- Advertisements must state that a prospectus has been or will be published and indicate where investors are or will be able to obtain it.
- The information contained in an advertisement must be consistent with the information contained in the prospectus, if already published, or with the information required to be in the prospectus, if the prospectus is published afterwards.
- All information concerning the offer to the public or the admission to trading in oral or written form, even if not for advertising purposes, must be consistent with that contained in the prospectus.

---

[42] See Section 19.2.6 on 'Supplements to the prospectus'.
[43] In particular, non-equity securities described in Royal Decree 1310/2005 Article 21.1. b).
[44] See Royal Decree 1310/2005 Article 28.

19.122   Where no prospectus is required under Spanish law, material information provided by an issuer or an offeror and addressed to qualified investors or special categories of investors, including information disclosed in the context of meetings relating to offers of securities, must also be disclosed to all qualified investors or special categories of investors to whom the offer is exclusively addressed. Where a prospectus is required to be published, such information must be included in the prospectus or in a supplement to the prospectus.

19.123   Under Spanish law,[45] advertising is not subject to prior approval from the CNMV, although any party publishing any advertisement should maintain the advertising materials at the CNMV's disposal in order to confirm that the advertisements are clearly recognizable as such and that the information contained is accurate and not misleading. Where the CNMV must approve a prospectus, those materials should be at the CNMV's disposal for an undetermined term. The CNMV has authority to further develop these last provisions although no specific rules have been issued yet.

19.124   In practice, advertisements and other advertising materials in the context of offers or admission to trading in Spanish markets have historically been presented to the CNMV for informal approval. This practice continues to date.

19.2.8 Prospectus cross-border regime

19.125   Spanish law has implemented the provisions regarding the EU-wide validity of prospectuses set forth in the Prospectus Directive.[46]

19.2.8.1 Cross-border validity of a prospectus approved by the CNMV

19.126   A prospectus approved by the CNMV and any supplements are valid for public offers or admission to trading in any number of host EU member states[47] provided that the CNMV notifies its approval to the competent authority of each host member state as set forth below.

19.127   At the request of the issuer applying for admission to trading or the person responsible for preparing the prospectus and within three working days following that request or, if the request is submitted together with the draft prospectus, within one working day after the approval of the prospectus, the CNMV must provide the competent authority of the host member state with a certificate of approval attesting that the prospectus has been drawn up in accordance with the Prospectus

---

[45]   See Royal Decree 1310/2005 Article 28.5.
[46]   See Royal Decree 1310/2005 Articles 29, 30 and 31.
[47]   As stated in the Prospectus Directive, under Spanish law 'host member state' means the EU member state where an offer to the public is made or admission to trading is sought, when different from the home member state. The concept of 'home member state' is set forth in the Prospectus Directive and the Transparency Directive, and is discussed in Part 1.

Directive and with a copy of such prospectus. If applicable, this notification may be accompanied by a translation of the summary produced under the responsibility of the issuer or person responsible for drawing up the prospectus. The same procedure must be followed for any supplement to the prospectus.

If any omission of information has been authorized by the CNMV, this must be stated in the certificate, as well as its justification. **19.128**

19.2.8.2 *Validity in Spain of a prospectus approved in another EU member state*

A prospectus approved by the competent authority of another EU member state and any supplements thereto are valid for public offers in Spain or the admission to trading on a Spanish regulated market, provided that such competent authority notifies the CNMV and provides the CNMV with the documentation described above. In this case, the CNMV will not undertake any approval or administrative procedures relating to the prospectus. The CNMV may draw the attention of the competent authority of the home member state to the need for supplements to be published if any significant new factors, material mistakes or inaccuracies have arisen since the approval of the prospectus. **19.129**

19.2.8.3 *Validity in Spain of a prospectus approved in non-EU countries*

The CNMV, acting as home member state of issuers with their registered office in a non-EU country, may approve a prospectus prepared in accordance with the legislation of such non-EU country for an offer to the public in Spain or for admission to trading on a Spanish regulated market, provided that:[48] **19.130**

- the prospectus has been prepared in accordance with international standards set by international securities commission organizations, including the IOSCO disclosure standards; and
- the information requirements, including information of a financial nature, are equivalent to the requirements under Spanish law.

In addition to the above provisions reproduced almost literally from the Prospectus Directive, Spanish law clarifies that in the case of a prospectus approved in non-EU countries, the order of the various information sections to be included in the prospectus is at the choice of the issuer. Regarding the language of the prospectus, Spanish rules also state that the prospectus, at the choice of the issuer, offeror or person asking for admission, may be prepared either in Spanish, in a language customary in the sphere of international finance or in any other language accepted by the CNMV. **19.131**

---

[48] See Royal Decree 1310/2005 Article 31.

19.132 A prospectus prepared in accordance with the legislation of a non-EU country and approved according to the rules described above is valid for the admission to trading in any EU host member state. In this case the language provisions stated in Section 19.2.5 above and the cross-border regime in other EU countries described in this Section 19.2.8 will apply.

19.133 In turn, where an issuer has its registered office in a non-EU country, the prospectus approved by the competent authority of any EU member state is valid for the admission to trading in Spain, provided the requirements for the validity in Spain of a prospectus approved in other EU member states (as described above) are met.

19.134 In the absence of implementing measures adopted by the EU Commission declaring that specific non-EU countries ensure the equivalence of a prospectus prepared in such countries with the Prospectus Directive, the CNMV may declare that a specific non-EU country ensures such equivalence considering its national law and its practices or procedures based on international standards set by international organizations, including the IOSCO disclosure standards. In particular, Spanish law states that the following documents would be considered to comply with the information requirements described above:

- annual accounts prepared in accordance, among others, with international accounting standards or generally accepted international accounting principles;
- annual accounts audited in accordance, among others, with international auditing standards or generally accepted international auditing principles.

19.2.9 Liability for the prospectus

19.135 In accordance with the Prospectus Directive, specific regulation of civil liability for the contents of a prospectus was introduced into Spanish law for the first time after the implementation of the Directive. In this regard, persons liable for the information in a prospectus will be liable for any damages caused to the holders of the securities acquired as a result of any misleading information or omissions in the prospectus. In connection with the summary, no civil liability is incurred solely on the basis of the summary, including any translation thereof, unless it is misleading, inaccurate or inconsistent when read together with the other parts of the prospectus.

19.2.9.1 Persons liable for the contents of the prospectus

19.136 Under Spanish rules, the following persons are liable for the contents of the prospectus, including, as the case may be, any supplements to the prospectus:[49]

---

[49] See Royal Decree 1310/2005 Articles 32 and 33.

- the issuer, offeror or the person asking for the admission to trading of securities to which the prospectus refers. Where the offeror of the securities is not the issuer, the offeror is liable for the information given in the prospectus. However, if the issuer has prepared the prospectus, it can incur the liability in the place of the offeror;
- the directors of the entities included in the preceding paragraph above, according to the terms set forth in the applicable corporate law;
- persons accepting to assume liability for the prospectus if this is expressly stated in the prospectus;
- any persons or entities not included in the above paragraphs which have authorized part or all of the contents of the prospectus, if this is expressly stated in the prospectus.

Persons accepting liability according to the last two paragraphs above, may accept liability only for certain parts or certain information given in the prospectus. In such case, they will only be liable for such parts or information and only if these have been included in the context and format agreed. **19.137**

The issuer or offeror may not invoke vis-à-vis a bona fide investor any fact which is not expressly included in the prospectus. For such purposes, documents incorporated by reference to the prospectus are considered as included in the prospectus. **19.138**

Persons professionally advising on the contents of the prospectus are expressly exempt from liability, according to the Royal Decree 1310/2005.[50] **19.139**

19.2.9.2 *Liability of the guarantor*

All the provisions relating to the issuer in Section 19.2.9.1 above are applicable to the guarantor of the securities but only regarding the information such guarantor must prepare.[51] **19.140**

19.2.9.3 *Liability of the managing entity*

A managing entity is defined by Spanish law as an entity (or entities) to which the issuer or offeror has given a mandate to manage and conduct the transactions relating to and structure the financial, timing and commercial aspects of the offer or the admission to trading, as well as to coordinate the relationship with supervisory authorities, market operators, potential investors and placing and underwriting entities. Typically, underwriters, sponsors and similar intermediaries, depending on their exact role, would fall under the definition of managing entity. **19.141**

---

[50] See Royal Decree 1310/2005 Article 33.4.
[51] See Royal Decree 1310/2005 Article 34

19.142 Where an issuer or offeror has given a mandate to a managing entity, the managing entity has an obligation to carry out certain due diligence verifications prescribed under applicable rules to ensure that the prospectus does not contain any misleading statements or omit any required information.[52]

19.143 Accordingly, the managing entity incurs liability for information given in the prospectus whenever it does not diligently carry out the prescribed due diligence verifications. However, Spanish law has limited the managing entity's liability to information included in the part of the prospectus corresponding to the securities note, i.e. the information relating to the transaction or the securities. The managing entity would not, therefore, be liable for information regarding the issuer contained in the part of the prospectus corresponding to the registration document or the summary.

19.144 In practice, one of the essential documents to be included in the documentation of the offer or admission to trading required by the CNMV is a letter where each managing entity declares that it has carried out the required verifications.

19.2.9.4 *Seeking liability*

19.145 Persons responsible for the contents of the prospectus must indemnify a bona fide investor who acquires securities to which the prospectus refers during its validity term for any damages arising as a consequence of misleading information included in the prospectus or of the omission of any relevant information required by law provided such misleading information or omission has not been corrected by a supplement to the prospectus or has not been disclosed to the market prior to the acquisition of the relevant securities.

19.146 This liability is not incurred if the person responsible for the information given in a prospectus shows that at the time of publication of the prospectus, he or she acted with due diligence to ensure that:

- the information contained in the prospectus was accurate;
- the relevant facts the omission of which has caused the loss were appropriately omitted.

19.147 This exemption of liability does not apply if the person knew, after the publication of the prospectus, that the information was inaccurate or the omission was

---

[52] See Royal Decree 1310/2005 Article 35.3. The managing entity is required to make verifications 'which, reasonably and according to generally accepted market criteria, are necessary to verify that the information contained in the securities note relating to the transaction or the securities is not misleading and that no relevant facts required by applicable law are omitted. The above verifications may vary depending on the particular features of the transaction, of the issuer and its business, on the quality of the information available or provided by the issuer or on the previous knowledge that the managing entity might have of the issuer'.

incorrect and has not taken the necessary steps to diligently inform all affected investors during the validity of the prospectus.[53]

Claims for this type of liability must be brought within three years from the time the claimant could have been aware of the misleading information or omission in the prospectus.[54] This provision subjects issuers and offerors of securities to some uncertainty. Since the time frame is linked to a period after the claimant could have become aware of the errors in the prospectus, issuers and offerors of securities run the risk of being sued for damages many years after the offer was made or admission to listing was sought. **19.148**

19.2.10 CNMV's powers in connection with the prospectus

Spanish law expressly grants powers to the CNMV, as the Spanish competent authority in connection with the admission to trading and the offering of securities and the required prospectus, to require any information and carry out any inspection it deems appropriate. In particular, the CNMV may:[55] **19.149**

- require the person responsible for the contents of the prospectus to include additional information in order to comply with the requirements of the relevant section of the prospectus model;
- require issuers, offerors or persons asking for admission to trading on a Spanish regulated market, and the persons that control them or are controlled by them, to provide information and documents on matters described in the applicable regulations on admission to trading and offers of securities:[56]
- require auditors and managers of the issuer, offeror or person asking for admission to trading on a Spanish regulated market, as well as financial intermediaries commissioned to carry out the offer to the public or ask for admission to trading, to provide information on matters described in the applicable regulations on admission to trading and offers of securities;
- require the issuer to disclose all material information which may have an effect on the assessment of the securities admitted to trading on regulated markets in order to ensure investor protection or the smooth operation of the market; and
- suspend or order the correction of advertisements which may be contrary to the provisions of the Royal Decree 1310/2005.

---

[53] See Royal Decree 1310/2005 Articles 36 and 37.
[54] See LMV Article 28.
[55] See Royal Decree 1310/ 2005 Article 44.
[56] Basically matters described in the Royal Decree 1310/2005 and in Sections 19.1 and 19.2 above.

19.150 In addition, in the context of a sanctioning process for violations of legal provisions applicable to the admission to trading and public offers of securities, the CNMV is empowered to take the following precautionary measures:(i) suspend a public offer or admission to trading for a maximum of ten consecutive working days on any single occasion; (ii) prohibit or suspend advertisements for a maximum of ten consecutive working days on any single occasion; or (iii) prohibit a public offer.

19.151 In accordance with the powers expressly granted by the LMV, the CNMV is also empowered to (i) suspend or ask the governing bodies of the relevant markets to suspend trading in a security on a regulated market for a maximum period of ten consecutive working days on any single occasion if it has reasonable grounds to believe that the provisions of the Royal Decree 1310/2005 have been infringed or in order to protect investors; (ii) prohibit trading on a Spanish regulated market if it finds that the provisions of the Royal Decree 1310/2005 have been infringed. Such resolution would be adopted after hearing the interested party and without prejudice to any precautionary measures that may be also adopted.

19.152 The CNMV also ensures that issuers whose securities are traded on a Spanish regulated market comply with the obligations provided for in the EU legislation in connection with regulated information, that equivalent information is provided to investors and that equivalent treatment is granted by the issuer to all holders of its securities who are in the same position, in all EU member states where the offer to the public is made or the securities are admitted to trading.

19.3 Continuing Obligations

19.3.1 Applicable law

19.153 Spanish listed companies must comply with a number of obligations contained, generally, in the following rules:

- the Royal Decree 1333/2005 which implements the four directives on market abuse and deals with market manipulation, public disclosure of inside information by issuers, notification of managers' and directors' transactions and investment recommendations;
- the Royal Decree 1362/2007 on transparency requirements, regarding information on issuers whose securities are admitted to trading on a regulated market.

19.154 Whereas Directive 2003/6/EC of the European Parliament and of the Council of 28 January 2003 on insider dealing and market manipulation only contains the concept of inside information, Spanish regulations contain two different but closely related concepts:[57] '*inside information*'—which is information of a precise nature which has not been made public and that relates, directly or indirectly, to transferable securities or financial instruments which, if made public, would most likely have a significant effect on the prices of those securities in a regulated market—and '*relevant (price-sensitive) information*'— which is defined as information the knowledge of which may reasonably encourage an investor to acquire or transfer securities and, therefore, which may have a significant influence on the security's price on a secondary market. Both terms relate to a single concept of information at different stages: relevant (price-sensitive) information is likely to be inside information as long as it is not disclosed to the public.

Obligations applicable to those in possession of inside or relevant (price-sensitive) information are slightly different.   **19.155**

19.3.2 Disclosure of relevant (price-sensitive) information

The LMV sets forth an obligation for issuers to disclose all relevant (price-sensitive) information to the market immediately, by means of a communication to the CNMV, before the information is disclosed by any other means and, as the case may be, as soon as a fact becomes known, a decision has been adopted or an agreement or contract with third parties has been signed.[58]   **19.156**

Furthermore, when a significant change regarding the relevant information occurs, it is advisable to communicate the new information immediately to the CNMV and the market in the same way as the initial information was communicated.   **19.157**

The communication to the CNMV has to be truthful, clear, complete and, when the nature of the information so demands, quantified, in a manner that is not misleading. The Royal Decree 1333/2005[59] further provides that an issuer shall not combine, in a manner that is likely to be misleading, the provision of inside information to the public with the marketing of its activities.   **19.158**

Issuers of securities are also required to disseminate relevant information on their websites and to ensure that the disclosure of relevant information to the public is synchronized, as closely as possible, between all categories of investors in all EU member states in which an issuer's securities are listed.   **19.159**

The LMV[60] contains an exception to the rule of information disclosure, providing that disclosure of relevant information is not required during the study or   **19.160**

---

[57] See LMV Articles 81 and 82.
[58] See LMV Articles 82.2 and 82.3 and Royal Decree 1333/2005 Article 6.
[59] See Royal Decree 1333/2005 Article 6.3.
[60] See LMV Article 83 *bis* and Royal Decree 1333/2005 Article 7.1.

negotiation phases of any legal or financial operation if it may have a significant influence on the price of the financial instruments.

19.161 The Royal Decree 1333/2005 clarifies and develops that exception by providing that disclosure is not required in respect of:

- Negotiations that are under way, or any circumstances concerning the negotiations, where the outcome or development of the negotiations would likely be affected by public disclosure. In particular, in the event that the financial viability of the issuer is in serious and imminent danger, it is possible to delay the public disclosure of information where the disclosure could seriously jeopardize the negotiations to ensure the long-term financial recovery of the issuer; and

- Decisions adopted or contracts prepared by the management of an issuer which need the approval of another body of the issuer in order to become effective, provided that public disclosure indicating that such approval is still pending may be detrimental to the correct assessment of the information by the public.

19.162 According to the LMV, in order to guarantee the confidentiality of relevant information during the study or negotiation phases of any legal or financial operation, listed companies are obligated to:

- limit knowledge of the information strictly to essential persons;
- keep, for each transaction, a documentary record of the names of the persons, inside or outside the organization, who have access to the relevant information and expressly inform such individuals of the confidential nature of the information in their possession, the duty of confidentiality and the prohibition on using the information;
- establish security measures for the safekeeping, filing, access, reproduction and distribution of the information;
- supervise the market performance and price formation of their securities and the news issued by professional disseminators of economic information which may affect them; and
- in the event that the prices or the volumes traded are out of the ordinary and there are rational indications that this is due to a premature, partial or distorted disclosure of information, the listed company is obligated to communicate immediately to the market information which clearly indicates the status of the transaction.

19.163 According to the Royal Decree 1333/2005,[61] the lists of insiders will be kept for at least five years after being drawn up or updated.

---

[61] See Royal Decree 1333/2005 Article 8.5.

Issuers of securities are also obligated to subject the members of their management **19.164**
body, the executives and the personnel in the areas related to securities market
activities, to measures that prevent the use of relevant information relating to
securities and financial instruments issued by the company itself or by others in its
group.[62]

Moreover, the CNMV has recently published a 'Guide for Action on the **19.165**
Transmission of Inside Information to Third Parties' which contains a series of
non-binding measures and recommendations to ensure the confidentiality of
inside information held by issuers and disclosed to third parties in accordance
with the LMV. The purpose of the measures and recommendations contained in
the Guide is to safeguard the confidentiality of inside information and prevent
leaks and the ensuing risk of improper use of the information. The Guide describes
a number of organizational measures as well as recommendations regarding
employee training and information, safeguarding and controlling information
and commitments and contact with third parties.[63]

19.3.3 Disclosure and control of inside information

The Royal Decree 1333/2005[64] defines 'inside information' as information of **19.166**
a precise nature which has not been made public and that relates, directly or
indirectly, to transferable securities or financial instruments which, if made
public, would most likely have a significant effect on the prices of those securities
in a regulated market.

The Royal Decree 1333/2005 clarifies this definition by setting forth two ele- **19.167**
ments. First, 'information that is likely to have a significant effect on prices' is
defined as information a reasonable investor would be likely to use as part of the
basis of its investment decision. Second, 'information of a precise nature' is defined
as information that includes a set of facts, existing or reasonably expected to come
into existence, which are specific enough to draw a conclusion on their effect on
the prices of securities.

Pursuant to the LMV,[65] every person who has inside information must refrain **19.168**
from engaging in, directly or indirectly, on their own account or through third
parties, the following activities:

(a) preparing or carrying out any type of transaction on the securities or financial
instruments subject to the inside information; the preparation or execution

---

[62] See LMV Article 83.*bis* 3.
[63] Further information and the text of this Guide can be found on the CNMV's website: www.
cnmv.es.
[64] See Royal Decree 1333/2005 Article 1.
[65] See LMV Article 81.2.

of transactions the existence of which itself constitutes inside information and transactions conducted in the discharge of an obligation that has fallen due to acquire or dispose of financial instruments are not subject to this obligation;

(b) disclosing inside information to any other person unless such disclosure is made in the normal course of his/her employment, profession or duties; and

(c) recommending or inducing another person, on the basis of inside information, to acquire or dispose of instruments to which that information relates.

19.169 The prohibitions set out above apply to any person who is in possession of inside information as long as that person knows, or ought to have known, that it is inside information.

19.3.3.1 *Supervisory role of the CNMV*

19.170 One of the CNMV's tasks is to analyse information which is distributed about an issuer of securities in the absence of any communication or regulatory disclosure from the issuer to the CNMV on the subject. The CNMV has recently published an official document on the 'Criteria for Handling News and Rumours about Listed Securities' that has two specific goals: (i) the document sets out the main criteria normally applied by the CNMV when evaluating the impact on the market of news or rumours disseminated about an issuer and (ii) it sets out the actions that are expected of the issuers themselves and financial intermediaries in such circumstances, in pursuit of greater market integrity.[66]

19.3.4 Disclosure of transactions by persons discharging managerial responsibilities

19.171 Under the Royal Decree 1333/2005[67] directors, managers, and 'persons closely associated' with them are required to inform the CNMV of the acquisition and disposals of securities issued by the company in which they hold such positions.

19.172 The Royal Decree 1333/2005 also provides an indication of the concept of 'persons closely associated' with a manager or director in the general guidelines set out in Directive 2004/72/EC (among others, a spouse, dependent children, other relatives sharing the same household, and any legal person, trust or partnership, managed or controlled by the director or manager, or by any of the aforementioned persons, or in which any of these persons have an economic interest).

19.173 The notification regarding the transaction must be made to the CNMV within five working days from the date of the transaction and must include the

---

[66] Further information and the text of this document can be found on the CNMV's website: http://www.cnmv.es.
[67] See Royal Decree 1333/2005 Article 9.

information detailed in the Royal Decree 1333/2005, namely: (i) the name of the director, manager or person closely associated with them; (ii) the purpose of the notification; (iii) the name of the issuer of the securities; (iv) a description of the securities or financial instruments; (v) the nature of the transaction; (vi) the date and market in which the transaction is taking place; and (vii) the price and volume of the transaction.

According to the Royal Decree 1362/2007,[68] directors of listed companies, in **19.174** addition to notifying any transaction regarding the shares or other securities or financial instruments of the issuer which are linked to these shares will have to inform the CNMV of their shareholding upon appointment or resignation. The contents of the notification are set forth in the Royal Decree 1362/2007.[69] Notifications must be made within the first four trading days after the holder had known or should have known about the purchase or sale of stocks, or the possibility of exercising the voting rights. For the purposes of calculating the threshold, all transactions made on the same day are taken into account.[70]

19.3.5 Periodic financial reporting

The Royal Decree 1362/2007 has also introduced several amendments to the **19.175** financial reporting obligations of issuers of listed securities.

Regarding the annual report,[71] issuers of securities traded on regulated markets **19.176** must file their annual financial report (which must include the audited annual accounts, the audited management report and the declaration of liability regarding its contents), and the auditor's report within a maximum of four months after the closure of each financial year. In addition to this, issuers must ensure that the reports remain accessible to the public for at least five years.[72]

The Royal Decree 1362/2007[73] also sets forth an obligation for issuers of **19.177** securities admitted to trading on regulated markets to prepare and disclose a biannual financial report (comprising summarized financial statements, a midterm management report and declarations of liability regarding its contents) relating to the first six months of the financial year and the entire financial year (in the latter case, only if Spain is the home member state), during the two months following the end of the corresponding period. As for annual reports, issuers must ensure that the reports described above remain accessible to the public for at least five years.

---

[68] See Royal Decree 1362/2007 Article 31.
[69] See Royal Decree 1362/2007 Article 34.
[70] See Royal Decree 1362/2007 Article 36.
[71] See Royal Decree 1362/2007 Article 8.
[72] See LMV Article 35.1.
[73] See Royal Decree 1362/2007 Article 11.

19.178 Issuers of securities traded on regulated markets that publish their annual financial report within two months from the closure of the previous financial year are exempt from the requirement to draft and publish a complete biannual report relating to the second half of the previous year. Instead, such issuers must publish a summarized periodic report relating to the previous 12 months of the financial year.[74]

19.179 In addition, if Spain is the home member state, issuers of shares listed on a regulated market must publish on a quarterly basis,[75] during the first and second semester, an intermediate report (*declaración intermedia trimestral*) that must include (i) an explanation of the relevant facts and transactions which occurred during the corresponding period and its impact on the financial situation of the issuer; and (ii) an overall description of the general financial situation and results of the issuer and its group during this period. This intermediate report will not be mandatory for issuers who disclose quarterly financial reports.

19.180 The intermediate quarterly report for listed companies must be published as soon as possible after the closure of the corresponding period and, in any event, within 45 days from the closure of the first and third quarters of the year.[76]

19.181 These obligations regarding the disclosure of periodic financial information do not apply to investment funds and collective investment schemes with variable share capital regulated by the Collective Investment Law.[77]

19.3.6 Major shareholding notifications

19.182 Article 53 of the LMV provides that shareholders acquiring or transferring shares of a listed company which carry voting rights must notify the CNMV and the issuer when, owing to the acquisition or transfer of such shares, the proportion of voting rights owned by the shareholder in the listed company reaches, surpasses or falls below certain thresholds. These thresholds are currently 3%, 5%, 10%, 15%, 20%, 25%, 30%, 35%, 40%, 45%, 50%, 60%, 70%, 75%, 80% and 90% of the voting rights in the listed company.[78]

19.183 For purposes of this requirement, a shareholder is any person that holds, directly or indirectly through an affiliate or controlled entity, whether in its own name and on behalf of itself, or in its own name but on behalf of a third party, shares or certificates of deposit or similar depository receipts.

---

[74] See Royal Decree 1362/2007 Article 18.2.
[75] See Royal Decree 1362/2007 Article 20.
[76] See Royal Decree 1362/2007 Article 19.
[77] See LMV Article 35.8.
[78] See Royal Decree 1362/2007 Article 23.

Voting rights must be computed according to the last available information **19.184** published by the issuer on the CNMV website. If the total voting rights of the listed company change, the shareholders must report to the issuer and the CNMV that the proportion of the voting rights reaches, surpasses or falls below the thresholds.

These disclosure requirements[79] also apply to any person who, regardless of **19.185** who the legal owner of the shares is, acquires, transfers or has the possibility of exercising the voting rights attached to shares of the listed company, provided that the percentage of voting rights it holds reaches or exceeds the thresholds mentioned above.[80]

Lastly these disclosure obligations[81] further apply with respect to any person **19.186** who holds, acquires or transfers, directly or indirectly, any financial instruments which give the holder the right, exclusively at the initiative of the holder under a binding arrangement, to buy or be delivered issued shares at maturity.

The Royal Decree 1362/2007 also addresses the specific case of investment **19.187** management companies and collective investment schemes (which have voting rights that may only be exercised in the interest of a client or final investor) by providing two exemptions from the notification requirements, one for managers of collective investment schemes, and another one for discretionary portfolio asset managers.[82]

19.3.7 Treasury stock reporting

Under applicable rules[83] a listed company must inform the CNMV about the **19.188** transaction on its own shares when the relevant thresholds are reached, surpassed or reduced. In particular,[84] a listed company acquiring its own shares must inform the CNMV if, as a result, the proportion of voting rights held by the issuer in its own shares reaches or surpasses 1% of the total voting rights in the issuer.

When calculating this threshold, transfers or disposals of treasury shares are not **19.189** deducted, so that only acquisitions of own shares are taken into account.

---

[79] See Royal Decree 1362/2007 Article 24.
[80] Examples of these cases include agreements with third parties which expressly declare the intention to exercise the voting rights with the purpose of establishing a shared management policy; shareholder arrangements; entities performing custody or administration services where the custodian or administrator may exercise the voting rights in the absence of specific instructions from shareholders; proxy holders or other representatives in the absence of specific instructions from shareholders.
[81] See Royal Decree 1362/2007 Article 28.1.
[82] See Royal Decree 1362/2007 Article 26.
[83] See LMV Article 53.*bis*.
[84] See Royal Decree 1362/2007 Article 40.

19.190 For purposes of calculating the threshold, the total number of shares carrying voting rights must be considered, including where the voting rights cannot be exercised due to a suspension according to the last available information published by the issuer in the CNMV's website.

19.191 Notifications must be made within four business days after the acquisition. The Royal Decree 1362/2007 sets forth the contents of the notification to be filed with the CNMV, including the final position of own shares held by the issuer.[85]

19.3.8 Penalties in connection with ongoing reporting requirements

19.3.8.1 Penalties in connection with relevant (price-sensitive) and inside information

19.192 A breach of the obligations regarding the disclosure of relevant (price-sensitive) and inside information has several implications including both criminal and administrative liability which are covered respectively by the Criminal Code and the LMV.

19.193 **19.3.8.1.1 Criminal liability** Article 285 of the Criminal Code (Law 10/1995 of 23 November 1995) provides criminal sanctions for a person who directly or through another person uses any relevant (price-sensitive) information to alter the price of securities or negotiable instruments in any organized market to which he/she has had reserved access to exercise his/her professional or business activity, or provides such information and obtains for him or herself or for a third party, an economic profit in excess of EUR 600,000 or causes damages for an equivalent amount. These penalties are as follows:

(i) imprisonment from one to four years;

(ii) a fine ranging from one to three times the profits obtained; and

(iii) special disqualification from conducting a profession or activity for a term of two to five years.

19.194 A key element for determining whether criminal liability may arise is how to calculate the benefits obtained in order to assess whether the EUR 600,000 limit is exceeded or not.

19.195 In addition, the Spanish Criminal Code provides certain guidelines regarding the application of these sanctions. In particular, Article 285.2 states that these sanctions may be imposed if, in the conducts described above, any of the following circumstances occur:

(i) a person habitually engages in prohibited conducts; or

(ii) significant profits are obtained; or

(iii) serious damage is caused to the general public interest.

---

[85] See Royal Decree 1362/2007 Article 41.

19.3.8.1.2 Administrative liability The LMV sets forth different levels of **19.196** violations of the law by qualifying violations as 'very serious' (*infracciones muy graves*), 'serious' (*infracciones graves*) or 'minor' (*infracciones leves*). There are different sanctions imposed to each level of violation.

Article 99 ñ) of the LMV provides that failure to comply with the provisions **19.197** described in Section 19.3.2 above regarding the disclosure of relevant (price-sensitive) information, are considered a very serious violation if the violation results in 'serious harm' to the market or if the offender provides inexact or false data, misleading information or information which maliciously omits relevant aspects or data to the CNMV.

Article 99 o) of the LMV provides that failure to comply with the provisions **19.198** established in Section 19.3.3 (inside information) will be deemed a very serious violation if the volume of funds or financial instruments used in committing the violation is significant, or where the offender acquired the information through membership of the issuer's governing or management bodies or in the course of exercising his/her profession, work or duties. Otherwise, it will constitute a serious violation pursuant to Article 100 x) of the LMV.

Article 102 of the LMV provides a list of sanctions that may be imposed, either **19.199** alternatively or cumulatively, on the offender if found guilty of a very serious violation relating to the disclosure of relevant (price-sensitive) or inside information. These sanctions include:

- a fine of not less than, or more than five times the gross profit obtained as a result of the actions or omissions that constitute the violation; or, if this standard cannot be applied, of up to the greatest of 5% of the offender's own funds, 5% of the total amount of funds used in the violation, or EUR 600,000;
- the delisting of the offender's securities from any Spanish regulated markets or multilateral trading facilities; and
- the suspension or restriction of the type of activities that the offender may conduct in the Spanish market for up to five years.

The penalties for serious violations which are established in Article 103 of the **19.200** LMV, of which one or more may be imposed on the offender, are as follows:

- a fine of not less than, or more than two times the gross profit obtained as a result of the actions or omissions that constitute the violation; or, if this standard cannot be applied, of up to the greatest of 2% of the shareholders' equity of the bidder, 2% of the total amount of funds used in the violation, or EUR 300,000;
- the suspension or restriction of the type of activities that the offender may conduct in the Spanish market for up to one year;

- the suspension as a member of a regulated market or other market, for a period not exceeding one year; and
- the suspension for a period not exceeding one year from carrying out management duties at the entity which engaged in the misconduct.

19.201 Where the offender is a legal entity, in addition to the respective sanction imposed on the offender for the very serious or serious violations, each of the entity's directors may be subject to one or more of the additional sanctions set forth in Articles 105 and 106 of the LMV, respectively, including fines and suspension or removal from office.

19.3.8.2 *Penalties in connection with periodic financial reporting and major shareholding notifications*

19.202 Penalties in connection with periodic financial reporting and major shareholding notifications will vary depending on whether the disclosing person or entity commits (i) a very serious violation, which, according to Article 99 p) of the LMV, occurs in the event of non-compliance with the duty to disclose information, where there is an intentional concealment or a case of gross negligence, taking into account the importance of the undisclosed information and the delay in which it may have incurred; or (ii) a serious violation, which, according to Article 100 j) of the LMV, occurs in the event of a failure to disclose information to the CNMV, where such disclosure is compulsory, but it does not constitute a very serious violation under Article 99 p) of the LMV.

19.203 Sanctions for very serious violations are set forth in Article 102 of the LMV. Sanctions for serious violations are set out in Article 103 of the LMV, as mentioned above.

19.3.9 The Unified Code of Corporate Governance and the Annual Corporate Governance Report

19.204 Historically, two reports, the Olivencia[86] and Aldama[87] Reports, provided the main source for guidelines in Spain regarding corporate governance.

19.205 In July 2005 the Spanish Government agreed to set up a Special Working Group to advise the CNMV on the harmonization and update of the Olivencia and Aldama Reports' recommendations for the good governance of listed companies, and to make any supplementary recommendations that it considered appropriate. After several months of drafting work in 2005, a brief consultation round with

---

[86] The Olivencia Corporate Governance Code (1998), a code to review a code of ethics for board members of companies.

[87] The Aldama Report (2003) to foster transparency and security in the markets and listed companies.

market experts in early 2006 and a public consultation, the Unified Good Governance Code (the 'Unified Code') was approved on 19 May 2006.

The main characteristics of the Unified Code are as follows: **19.206**

- Voluntary nature, subject to the 'comply or explain' principle.

  Article 116 of the LMV requires listed Spanish companies to disclose their degree of compliance with corporate governance recommendations and to justify any non-compliance in their annual corporate governance reports. The Unified Code sets out the recommendations to be considered by listed companies when complying with their disclosure requirements under the LMV. In other words, it is left to the discretion of listed companies to decide whether or not to follow corporate governance recommendations, but they are required to give a reasoned explanation of any deviations, so that shareholders, investors and the markets in general can make an informed decision.

- Binding definitions

  Listed companies can freely decide to comply or not with the Code's good governance recommendations, but their disclosure on governance must comply with the underlying concepts used in the Unified Code. As an example, individual companies have discretion to follow Recommendation 13 on independent directors, but they may only refer to a director as 'independent' in their disclosure if that person meets the minimum independence conditions set forth in the Unified Code.

- Evaluation by the market

  Shareholders, investors and the markets in general will evaluate the explanations companies provide of their degree of compliance with Unified Code recommendations. However, under the CNMV's monitoring powers with regard to the annual corporate governance report of listed companies,[88] the CNMV may require companies to clarify any omission or false or misleading data in their annual corporate governance report. In practice, the CNMV is likely to contact the company after publication of the annual corporate governance report to clarify information contained in it or the explanations given by the company where recommendations are not followed, or not fully followed.

- Generality

  The Unified Code is directed at all listed companies, regardless of their size and market capitalization. Although some recommendations may be unsuitable or excessively burdensome for smaller-sized firms, all firms need to state their reasons for non-compliance and any alternatives chosen.

The Unified Code sets forth definitions for 'senior officer', 'significant shareholdings', 'executive directors', 'independent directors' and 'proprietary directors' for the purposes of the recommendations of the Unified Code. It includes 58 recommendations

---

[88] See LMV Article 116.

on (i) articles of association and general shareholders' meetings (in particular as to powers and voting); (ii) boards of directors (powers, duties, size, structure and type of directors, gender diversity, key figures, meetings, evaluation, etc.); (iii) directors (selection, appointment and renewal, disclosure of information related to directors, removal and resignation, remuneration and disclosure of such remuneration); and (iv) committees of the board of directors.

19.4 Takeover Bids in Spain

19.4.1 Applicable law

19.207 As described in Section 19.1.3.5. above, the main rules governing takeover bids for companies listed on a Spanish stock exchange are set forth in Law 6/2007 of 12 April, which has amended the LMV to implement the Takeover Directive in Spain, and the Royal Decree 1066/2007, which implements in detail the principles governing takeovers set out in the LMV.

19.208 In addition, takeover bids in Spain are also governed by the provisions of the LMV setting forth rules of conduct that apply generally to participants in the Spanish securities market.

19.209 The Criminal Code also contains provisions relating to insider dealing and market abuse which are relevant for takeovers; and certain provisions of the Corporations Law approved by the Royal Decree-Law 1564/1989 of 22 December (the 'Corporations Law') may be relevant in assessing the target board's response to a takeover bid and, in particular, whether takeover defences are permissible in any situation.

19.210 As the regulator of the Spanish securities markets, the CNMV also supervises takeover bids. The offer document and any announcements to be published in connection with a takeover bid by the offeror must be pre-approved by the CNMV before publication. The CNMV has the power to make comments, suggestions and amendments to such documentation. The CNMV also has the power to reduce or increase the equitable price, as described in Section 19.4.5 below, in certain circumstances.

19.4.2 Mandatory and voluntary takeover bids

19.211 The Spanish takeover bid system is a system of *ex-post* takeover bids for 100% of the share capital, once control of the voting rights in a listed company has been acquired, whether by acquisition of voting rights reaching the relevant threshold, appointment of majority of the board of directors, agreement or as a result of similar circumstances provided for in the regulations.

The law distinguishes between: **19.212**

(i) **Mandatory or compulsory bids** to be made by whoever obtains control of a listed company, as further described in Section 19.4.3. below, whether such control is obtained (1) by means of the acquisition of shares or other securities that directly or indirectly confer the right to subscribe or acquire voting shares in such company; (2) by means of shareholders' agreements (*pactos parasociales*) with other holders of securities; or (3) as a result of other instances of a similar nature, as provided in the regulations. Mandatory bids must be made in such cases:

- for all shares or other securities that might directly or indirectly confer the right of subscription or acquisition;
- to all holders thereof (100% of voting rights);
- at an equitable price;
- within one month from the moment control is reached; and
- not subject to any conditions.

(ii) **Voluntary bids,** which may be
- made at a price which is not equitable;
- subject to conditions (as set forth in the regulations); and
- subject to the same rules of procedure as those for mandatory bids.

Whenever control of a company has been acquired through a voluntary bid, the **19.213** launch of a mandatory bid will be required, except where the voluntary bid was already made for all the securities of the target company and (i) such bid is made at an equitable price or (ii) such bid has been accepted by holders of securities representing not less than 50% of the voting rights to which the bid was addressed, excluding from such calculation those already held by the offeror and those held by shareholders who have reached an agreement with the offeror in connection with the bid.[89]

19.4.3 Triggers for mandatory bids—acquisition of control

Under applicable rules,[90] a compulsory bid is required whenever a person obtains **19.214** 'control' of a listed company. This control may be acquired either by (i) directly or indirectly acquiring target securities with voting rights; or (ii) by entering into relevant shareholders' agreements or through the appointment of the majority of the members of a target's board of directors.

---

[89] See Royal Decree 1066/2007 Article 8 f).
[90] See Royal Decree 1066/2007 Article 3.1.

19.4.3.1 *Direct and indirect acquisition of control*

19.215 **19.4.3.1.1 Direct acquisition of control** Pursuant to the Royal Decree 1066/2007,[91] control of a target by a person or by a group of persons acting in concert is deemed to exist where: (a) they hold at least 30% of the voting rights of the listed company, directly or indirectly, or (b) they hold a stake of less than 30% of the voting rights but appoint (within the 24 months following the acquisition) a number of directors (together with any already appointed by them) representing a majority of the target's board of directors.

19.216 **19.4.3.1.2 Indirect acquisition of control** According to the Royal Decree 1066/2007,[92] control of a listed company may also be obtained by indirectly acquiring target securities with voting rights in certain situations where such acquisition was inadvertent, involuntary or otherwise the result of an unrelated event or actions by third parties. These situations include:

- a shareholder acquiring control, as defined above, as a result of a merger;
- a shareholder acquiring control as a result of a reduction of share capital in a listed company;
- a shareholder acquiring control over a listed company as a consequence of conversion or exchange of securities;
- a shareholder acquiring control over a listed company as a consequence of variations in the listed company's treasury shares; and
- a financial institution or any other person acquiring control as a result of the enforcement of an underwriting agreement.

19.217 A shareholder who indirectly acquires control as described above must launch a compulsory bid within three months following the acquisition of control. However, a mandatory bid is not required if the controlling holder sells its stake in excess of 30% within the three-month period and, in the meantime, does not exercise its voting rights.

19.218 In addition, the CNMV may authorize a holder acquiring (either directly or indirectly) more than 30% of a target's voting rights not to launch a compulsory offer[93] in the event that another shareholder, individually or together with persons with whom such shareholder is acting in concert, holds an equal or larger voting percentage in the target than that held by the party required to make the bid. The CNMV's waiver will be subject to two conditions: (i) the shareholder who has an equal or larger voting percentage in the target not reducing it below that held by

---

[91] See Royal Decree 1066/2007 Article 4.1.
[92] See Royal Decree 1066/2007 Article 7.
[93] As defined in Royal Decree 1066/2007 Articles 3 and 7.

the shareholder that is the beneficiary of the waiver; and (ii) the latter not appointing more than half of the members of the target's board of directors.[94]

If the waiver is not granted by the CNMV, or the above conditions are not satisfied, the interested party must launch an offer for the target, unless it transfers, within three months, the number of securities required to reduce the excess of voting rights over the above-mentioned 30% (or the agreement or action in concert by virtue of which the control was acquired ends) and provided that voting rights corresponding to the excess over such percentage are not exercised in the meantime.   **19.219**

The decision of the CNMV on the permission requested will be notified to the requesting shareholder and made public on the CNMV's website within ten business days from the request of the relevant shareholder or from the date where the documents requested by the CNMV, as the case may be, are registered.   **19.220**

19.4.3.2 *Shareholders' agreements and appointment of directors*

The takeover regulations set forth other events that trigger a mandatory bid including agreements between the target's shareholders and the appointment of the majority of the members of a target's board of directors. In addition, voting rights held by other third parties may be attributed to the target's shareholder in certain cases.   **19.221**

In particular,[95] two or more persons may be deemed to act in concert if they cooperate pursuant to an agreement (which may be express, implied, oral, or written) in order to obtain control of a listed company. Accordingly, two or more shareholders who are parties to an agreement of this kind will be deemed to act in concert and trigger the obligation to make a mandatory bid if they jointly obtain an interest carrying 30% or more of the voting rights.   **19.222**

The Royal Decree 1066/2007 presumes that persons are acting in concert if they are parties to a shareholders' agreement of the type described in Article 112 of the LMV, as long as such agreement is intended to establish a common policy for the management of the company or is aimed at exercising significant influence on it. Parties to an agreement that, while having the same purpose, governs voting rights on the board of directors or the executive committee of the company, are also presumed to be acting in concert. The entering into an arrangement of this nature will trigger an obligation to make a compulsory bid if the parties' aggregate shareholdings in the target exceed the relevant threshold.   **19.223**

---

[94] See Royal Decree 1066/2007 Article 4.2.
[95] See Royal Decree 1066/2007 Article 5.1 b).

19.224 In the cases of actions in concert, shareholders' agreements or other cases where the voting percentages corresponding to a shareholder are attributed to another person, the bid must be made by whoever holds the greatest percentage, directly or indirectly. When two or more shareholders hold the same percentage, they are required to make the bid jointly. Where a target holds its own shares in treasury, such shares are disregarded for the purposes of any of these threshold calculations.

19.4.3.3 Aggregation[96]

19.225 A number of indirect interests must be aggregated to determine the percentage a person holds. Among other provisions, the Royal Decree 1066/2007 states that a person has an indirect holding where (i) the shareholder has entered into an agreement with a third party holding voting rights that obligates them to adopt a common policy regarding the management of the issuer, by exercising the voting rights in concert; (ii) shares are held by a subsidiary of that person, in which case aggregation of the relevant holdings will be required for the purposes of determining the parent company's (but not the subsidiary's) obligations; (iii) that person has a proxy over shares, provided he or she can exercise the voting rights attaching to shares at his or her own discretion.

19.4.4 Preparation of the bid: break-up fees

19.226 The Royal Decree 1066/2007[97] expressly allows a target to grant a break-up fee to an initial bidder, but not to any subsequent offeror. Such a fee would be payable if the initial bid does not succeed as result of a competing bid that was subsequently launched.

19.227 A break-up fee is subject to four conditions: (i) the amount of the fee must not be greater than 1% of the total value of the bid; (ii) it must be approved by the board of directors of the target; (iii) the target company must obtain a favourable report from its financial adviser; and (iv) the break-up fee must be disclosed in the offer document.

19.4.5 Consideration

19.228 The offer price for a mandatory takeover bid has to be equitable. Specific rules apply depending on whether the bid is mandatory or voluntary. In any case, the consideration needs to be guaranteed only in case of a cash offer; a securities offer only requires that the bidder take the appropriate measures in order for the consideration to be available.

---

96 See Royal Decree 1066/2007 Article 5.
97 See Royal Decree 1066/2007 Article 42.4.

19.4.5.1 *Equitable price*

Compulsory bids must be made at an 'equitable price'.[98] The Royal Decree **19.229**
1066/2007 refers to the concept of 'equitable price' by stating that the price of mandatory bids must be no less than the highest price that the bidder, or those persons
acting in concert with it, as the case may be, has paid or agreed to pay for securities
of the same class over the 12 months prior to the announcement of the bid.

Specific rules apply where (i) the acquisition includes some compensation in **19.230**
addition to the price paid or agreed, (ii) a deferral in payment has been agreed, or
(iii) the purchase of the relevant securities results from the exercise of a prior
call or put option, the acquisition of derivative instruments or by means of an
exchange or conversion of other securities.

If the bidder has not acquired securities of the same class during the 12 months **19.231**
prior to the announcement of the bid, the equitable price must be no less than
the price calculated in accordance with the particular valuation rules regarding
delisting offers.

The CNMV may modify the equitable price resulting from the above provisions **19.232**
in certain specific circumstances.[99] In such cases, the CNMV may order the
offeror to submit a report on the valuation methods and criteria used to determine
the equitable price.

The target's directors must prepare a report supporting the proposed valuation **19.233**
and this report must be made available to the target's shareholders.[100] In addition,
particular valuation rules apply as regards the price of delisting offers.

---

[98] See Royal Decree 1066/2007 Article 9.
[99] In particular, according to Article 9.4 of the Royal Decree 1066/ 2007, the CNMV may
modify the equitable price resulting from these provisions in the following circumstances: (i) the
listing price of the target's securities during the reference period has been affected by the payment
of dividends, a corporate transaction or any extraordinary event that justifies an objective adjustment to the equitable price; (ii) the listing price of the target's securities during the reference period
shows signs of manipulation, as a result of which a sanctioning procedure has been initiated by the
CNMV, provided that notice of the statement of charges has been served upon the interested party;
(iii) the equitable price is lower than the trading range for the securities on the date of the acquisition
that sets the price, in which case, the bid price must not be less than the lower price in such range;
(iv) the equitable price is set by an acquisition of a volume of securities that is not significant in relative terms, provided that it was carried out at the listing price on the relevant day, in which case, the
equitable price will instead be the highest price paid or agreed upon under the other acquisitions
during the reference period; (v) the acquisitions during the reference period include some alternative
compensation in addition to the price paid or agreed upon, in which case the bid price must not
be less than the highest price that results after including the value of such compensation; or (vi) the
target is undergoing serious financial difficulties, in which case the consideration must be calculated
in accordance with the valuation rules regarding delisting offers.
[100] See Royal Decree 1066/2007 Article 24.

19.234 In the absence of rules specifying what price must be offered to holders of other classes of shares, of convertible securities or of options/warrants, the equality of treatment between holders of the same class of securities is the only applicable principle.

19.235 Subject to rules governing the acquisition of shares in a target during a bid, voluntary bids do not have to be made at an equitable price and therefore the price in such bids will not be reviewed by the CNMV.[101] However, acquiring control through a voluntary bid may lead to the obligation to make a compulsory bid, as described above, in which case the equitable price requirement will become applicable.[102]

19.236 In addition, where a bidder is making a competing offer, the offer price must be higher than the previous offer made[103] unless the offer is instead extended to more securities or is otherwise an improved offer, e.g. with fewer conditions.

19.4.5.2 Types of consideration[104]

19.237 The bidder may offer cash, securities issued or to be issued by the bidder or another company (such as a listed parent or subsidiary), or a combination thereof.

19.238 However, a bid must include as an alternative, a cash consideration equivalent at least to the exchange offer, in the following cases:

- where the offeror or the persons with whom it acts in concert, have acquired in cash, over the 12 months prior to the announcement of the bid, securities representing 5% or more of the voting rights in the target;
- in the case of a mandatory bid once the offeror has acquired control of the company; and
- in the event of an exchange or conversion of securities, unless the exchange offer consists of: (i) securities admitted to trading on a Spanish regulated market or on another regulated market in the European Union; or (ii) securities to be issued by the offeror company itself, provided that all or part of its shares are admitted to trading on any of such markets; and the offeror assumes the express commitment to request the admission to trading of the new securities within a maximum period of three months after the disclosure of the result of the bid.

19.239 Where the securities offered in exchange are not admitted to trading on any of the markets referred to above, a report prepared by an independent expert must be submitted with an assessment of the value of such securities.

---

[101] See Royal Decree 1066/2007 Article 13.5.
[102] See Royal Decree 1066/2007 Article 8.f).
[103] See Royal Decree 1066/2007 Article 42.1.c).
[104] See Royal Decree 1066/2007 Article 14.

The consideration offered to all holders of the same class of target securities in an **19.240** offer must be the same. Therefore, a bidder may not agree favourable conditions or inducements with one target shareholder but not the others.

19.4.5.3 *Guarantee of consideration*

The bidder is obligated to provide a guarantee for the fulfilment of its obligations **19.241** arising from the offer.[105] The terms of the guarantee must be provided to the CNMV when filing the application for the authorization of the offer or within seven business days of filing.

In the event that the consideration is in cash, the bidder must either deposit an **19.242** equivalent amount of cash with the CNMV, or provide a guarantee for the same amount issued by a credit institution. In the case of an exchange offer, the offeror must have adopted all reasonable measures to ensure that the consideration will be available.

If the offered consideration consists of securities already issued, evidence must be **19.243** provided that they are available and blocked in guarantee.

If the securities offered as all or part of the consideration are yet to be issued by **19.244** the offeror, the Royal Decree 1066/2007 requires compliance with certain obligations regarding the calling of a meeting of the bidder's shareholders.

19.4.6 Exceptions to the obligation to make a mandatory bid when acquiring control

Pursuant to Article 8 of the Royal Decree 1066/2007, the person acquiring con- **19.245** trol of a target's voting rights will not have an obligation to launch a mandatory bid where control is obtained in any of the following circumstances:

- where the shares are acquired by funds for the insurance of deposits in banking institutions and certain similar institutions, as well as acquisitions consisting of allotments approved by these bodies;
- acquisitions or other transactions made pursuant to the Compulsory Expropriation Law[106] or otherwise resulting from the exercise of public law powers;
- all of the target company's shareholders unanimously agree to a purchase or exchange of shares representing 100% of the company's capital, or unanimously waive the requirement to make a takeover bid;
- the significant shareholding is acquired as a consequence of the capitalization or conversion of debt into shares of listed companies, where that company is experiencing severe financial difficulty and the transaction in question is

---

[105] See Royal Decree 1066/2007 Article 15.
[106] Compulsory Expropriation Law of 16 December 1954.

intended to ensure the company's long-term financial recovery (the CNMV will decide whether this exception will apply on a case-by-case basis);

- control has been gained as a result of shares acquired through a donation or inheritance, provided that the recipient of such shares has not acquired target shares in the previous 12 months, and there is no agreement or concert with the transferor; and

- as a result of a merger, provided that the shareholder does not vote in favour of the merger at the relevant general meeting of shareholders of the target, and it can be shown that the primary purpose of the transaction is not the takeover but an industrial or corporate purpose.

19.4.7 Conditions of the bid

19.246 The general rule under Spanish legislation is the irrevocability of takeover bids.[107] However, one of the differences between voluntary bids and mandatory bids is that voluntary bids may be made subject to certain conditions, provided that satisfaction of such conditions can be verified at the end of the acceptance period of the bid. The following conditions are permitted in voluntary bids:[108]

- the approval of amendments to the articles of association of the target or the adoption of other structural resolutions by the target shareholders at a general meeting;
- the acceptance of the bid by the shareholders of a certain minimum percentage of target securities;
- the approval of the bid by the offeror shareholders at a general meeting; and
- any other condition that the CNMV considers admissible according to the law.

19.247 However, both voluntary and compulsory bids may be subject to obtaining relevant authorizations of the antitrust authorities. Once a compulsory or voluntary bid has been submitted, the bidder may withdraw (i) if, by the end of the acceptance period, antitrust authorization has not been obtained, or (ii) if, due to exceptional circumstances beyond the control of the offeror, the bid cannot be carried out or is manifestly not feasible, provided that the prior approval of the CNMV is obtained.[109]

19.248 The bidder is also allowed to withdraw a voluntary bid in the event that a competing offer is authorized by the CNMV; or if the target shareholders at a general meeting adopt a decision or resolution that, in the opinion of the offeror, prevents

---

[107] See Royal Decree 1066/2007 Article 30.
[108] See Royal Decree 1066/2007 Article 13.
[109] See Royal Decree 1066/2007 Article 26.

it from continuing with the bid (in this case, the prior approval of the CNMV is needed).[110]

In addition, pre-conditions are not standard practice in Spain. However, takeover **19.249** bids subject to regulatory authorizations other than antitrust clearance may be registered with the CNMV prior to obtaining the authorization. The CNMV will not authorize the offer until the regulatory approval has been obtained.[111]

19.4.8 Procedure for authorization of the bid: announcement, acceptance period and settlement

The decision to make a voluntary offer must be announced to the market as soon **19.250** as it is approved.[112]

The offer must be filed by the bidder with the CNMV within one month after it **19.251** has publicly announced its intention to launch the offer. The specific contents of such announcement have been regulated by the CNMV by issuing an official model announcement. According to this model, the bidder must set out, among other things, (i) whether the offer is mandatory, voluntary or a competing offer, (ii) an approximate timing for launching the offer and filing the offer document, (iii) its stake in the target company (including acquisitions during the 12 months prior to the announcement and appointments of directors, if any), (iv) the number of shares subject to the offer and the consideration (in euro per share if it is in cash, or if it consists of securities with the exchange ratio and an assessment of its value or cash equivalent, and an indication of any expected adjustments and whether such consideration is an equitable price or not), (v) the conditions of the offer, if any, (vi) whether the offer is subject to any antitrust or other administrative approval, (vii) whether agreements have been reached with shareholders or directors, (viii) the bidder's intention to maintain listed or delist the target company and (ix) the notification duties in the event of acquisition of shares by any significant shareholders during the offer.

The CNMV has also issued a model for the filing of the application for authoriza- **19.252** tion of the offer together with the prospectus which must include, among other items, the main terms and conditions of the offer, and whether the guarantee for the consideration is attached to the offer or will be evidenced subsequently.

In the case of a compulsory offer, the party that triggers the obligation to make an **19.253** offer must promptly make an announcement. In this case, the announcement must also specify if the party has the intention of applying for a waiver of the

---

[110] See Royal Decree 1066/2007 Article 33.
[111] See Royal Decree 1066/2007 Article 26.2.
[112] See Royal Decree 1066/2007 Article 16.1.

obligation and, in the case of an indirect acquisition of control, if it has the intention of reducing its interest in the target below the applicable threshold. If the request of a waiver is rejected, the bidder must then announce its obligation to make an offer.

19.254 The bidder has to publish the final offer document within five days from the date the CNMV notifies its authorization for the offer to the target and offeror. On the same date, terms of the offer must be published in the Trading Bulletin of the Spanish stock exchanges and in at least one national Spanish newspaper.[113]

19.255 The acceptance period of the offer, which may range from 15 to 70 days (to be specified in the offer document by the bidder) will commence on the day after the announcement.[114]

19.256 Within five business days from the end of the acceptance period, the Spanish stock exchanges will confirm and notify the number of shares accepting the offer to the CNMV. Within two days from such notification, the CNMV will in turn notify the result of the bid to the Spanish stock exchanges, the offeror and the target.[115] After the publication of the results by the Spanish stock exchanges, the regular payment of consideration to target shareholders will commence. Once the offer is settled, the CNMV will release the guarantee provided.[116]

19.4.9 Duty of non-interference of the board

19.257 The board of directors of a target company has a general duty to act in the interest of the target's shareholders. Under Spanish regulations,[117] once a takeover bid has been announced, directors are obligated to seek the prior approval of the shareholders before initiating activities or implementing decisions (even if such implementation is a consequence of resolutions previously adopted) that could interfere with the offer ('frustrating actions').

19.258 In this respect, the regulations specifically state that the board of directors of the target company must refrain from: (i) approving or implementing any issue of securities that may prevent the bid from being successful; (ii) carrying out or promoting, directly or indirectly, transactions involving securities subject to the bid (or any other securities) that may prevent the bid from being successful (e.g. purchasing shares in the open market in order to increase the share price above the offer price and reduce the number of shares available for the offeror); (iii) disposing of, encumbering or leasing real property or other corporate assets

---

[113] See Royal Decree 1066/2007 Article 22.1.
[114] See Royal Decree 1066/2007 Article 23.1.
[115] See Royal Decree 1066/2007 Article 36.
[116] See Royal Decree 1066/2007 Article 37.
[117] See Royal Decree 1066/2007 Article 28.

where such transactions may prevent the bid from being successful; (iv) paying extraordinary dividends or making any other distribution to shareholders that is not consistent with the policy for payment of dividends (unless the distributions were approved by the competent corporate decision-making body, and made public, before the offer was announced).

In this regard,[118] the target's governing bodies and management must obtain the **19.259** prior authorization (by qualified majority) of the general shareholders' meeting before taking any action that could frustrate the success of the offer with the exception of seeking other offers. As regards decisions previously adopted but not yet implemented, be it in whole or in part, the general shareholders' meeting must approve or confirm—again by qualified majority—any decision that does not fall within the ordinary course of business of the target, and that could frustrate the success of the offer.

Another characteristic of Spanish regulations is the principle of reciprocity, pursu- **19.260** ant to which shareholders acting at a general meeting of a listed company may choose to release the board of directors from its duty of non-interference if the company is the target of a takeover bid made by an entity that has its registered office outside Spain and that does not impose upon its board the same duty of non-interference as provided for in Spanish regulations, or an equivalent regime requiring the prior approval of frustrating actions. The principle of reciprocity only applies if the bidder does not have its registered office in Spain.

The decision to release the board of directors of the target company from its duty **19.261** of non-interference must be adopted by the shareholders at a general meeting in compliance with the requirements as to qualified quorum and majorities set forth in the Corporations Law for certain resolutions, within a maximum period of 18 months prior to the takeover bid being made public. For this purpose, the board of directors of the company is required to issue a report setting out the rationale for any frustrating actions that are submitted to the shareholders for approval at a general meeting. This report must include details about how each director intends to vote on such proposals and must be made available to the shareholders from the time the general meeting is convened.

19.4.10 Takeover defences and breakthrough rules

Spanish corporate law does not prevent listed companies from adopting certain **19.262** anti-takeover provisions in their articles of association. These include providing for a qualified quorum or voting majorities for the approval of certain resolutions (such as capital increases and mergers), setting forth special requirements for

---

[118] See Royal Decree 1066/2007 Article 28.

access to the board, or, generally, limitations to the exercise of voting rights held by a single shareholder or by shareholders belonging to the same group.

19.263 The Spanish legal system[119] does not contain any mandatory provisions that would neutralize these defensive measures. Instead, it has adopted the optional ('opt-in'/'opt-out') approach set out in the Takeover Directive. It is up to the target's shareholders to decide whether or not preventive defensive measures are to be neutralized, and their decision is revocable at any time.

19.264 Moreover, as with non-interference rules, targets whose shareholders have opted for the neutralization alternative, may choose not to apply it if they are subject to a tender offer by an entity or group that has not adopted equivalent neutralization measures. The decision to exclude the application of the neutralization measures must be approved with the same formal requirements as explained above for the exclusion of the duty of non-interference.

19.4.11 Competing offers

19.265 A takeover bid will be considered a 'competing offer'[120] if it affects securities for all or a part of which another takeover bid has previously been submitted to the CNMV.

19.266 Competing offers must comply with certain statutory restrictions:[121]

- they must be submitted at least five days before the acceptance period for the last preceding offer ends (whether it is the original offer or another competing offer);
- in the case of partial voluntary bids, they must cover a number of securities that must not be less than that of the immediately preceding offer; and
- they must improve the last preceding offer, either by raising the value of the consideration or by extending the offer to a larger number of securities (if securities are offered as consideration, a report from an independent expert certifying that the price is higher must be provided).

19.267 In a competitive offer situation where more than one competing offer is submitted, the acceptance periods of all offers will be consolidated into one single period.

19.268 The primary effect of a competing offer is the interruption of the acceptance period not only of the original bid but also of all competing offers previously submitted. The acceptance period of competing offers is 30 calendar days from the day following the date of publication of the first announcement of the offer that has already been authorized.

---

[119] See Royal Decree 1066/2007 Article 29.
[120] See Royal Decree 1066/2007 Article 40.
[121] See Royal Decree 1066/2007 Article 42.1.

The authorization of a competing offer may allow bidders to either withdraw their **19.269** offers or improve the terms of their own offers at any time after approval of the last competing offer up until the fifth day after the expiry of the deadline for filing new competing offers.

On the fifth day after the expiry of the deadline for filing new competing offers, **19.270** all competing bidders who have not withdrawn their offers must send a sealed envelope to the CNMV. The sealed envelope will include the bidders' last decision to improve the offers or not. The CNMV will open the sealed envelopes and announce the new offers on the next business day. Each bidder will have three business days to provide an additional guarantee for any increased consideration.

The Royal Decree 1066/2007 also grants an advantage to the first original bidder **19.271** who has not withdrawn its offer: the first offeror may improve the consideration of its offer for the last time, provided that (i) the consideration offered by such offeror in the sealed envelope is less than 2% lower than the highest consideration offered by any competing bidder; and (ii) the original offeror improves the price of the best offer made in an envelope by at least 1%, or extends the original bid to a number of securities that is at least 5% greater than that in the best competing offer submitted in a sealed envelope.

The CNMV will authorize any offer which has complied with the aforemen- **19.272** tioned requirements and bidders must issue the revised conditions of their offers within five business days of authorization. All the offers must be authorized and published on the same dates. The acceptance period for each offer will be extended automatically for 15 calendar days after publication. Target shareholders may submit multiple acceptances stating their order of preference of any of the offers.

19.4.12 Sell-out and squeeze-out levels: double level required

The Royal Decree 1066/2007 introduced the regulation of reciprocal squeeze-out **19.273** and sell-out rights for the bidder and the target's minority shareholders.

If, as a result of a takeover bid made for all the target's voting securities, the bidder **19.274** holds securities representing 90% or more of the voting rights of the target company; and if the offer has been accepted by holders of securities representing at least 90% of the securities to which the offer was addressed: (i) the bidder has the right to purchase the remaining securities at the offer price; and (ii) the minority holders of the remaining securities have the right to require the bidder to buy these securities at that price.[122]

---

[122] See Royal Decree 1066/2007 Article 47.1.

19.275   The consideration for the squeeze-out must be the same as the consideration offered in the prior takeover bid (e.g. cash, listed shares or a combination of both) and it is not subject to any fairness opinion or authorization.

19.276   If the squeeze-out procedure is available, the right must be exercised by the bidder in relation to all securities which were subject to the takeover bid within three months from the end of the acceptance period for the bid.

19.277   Following a squeeze-out (or sell-out) which leads to the offeror acquiring 100% of the share capital, the target will be automatically delisted.[123]

19.4.13 Delisting offers[124]

19.278   If a company approves the delisting of its shares from a Spanish stock exchange, an obligation to make a compulsory offer by the company or a third party (for example, a parent company) will be triggered. Corporate transactions pursuant to which the shareholders of a listed company may totally or partially become shareholders of another unlisted entity (e.g. the merger of a listed company with an unlisted company, or the total or partial spin-off of a listed company to one or more unlisted companies that are not going to request the admission of their shares to trading on the stock exchanges) also fall under the concept of delisting and the mandatory offer requirement.

19.279   Delisting offers must be addressed to (i) all holders of the target company's shares with voting rights, including holders without voting rights if their shares will have voting rights once the offer is launched; and (ii) all holders of the target company's convertible bonds or share subscription rights under a rights issue. In addition, resolutions on delisting and those relating to the takeover bid and the price offered, must be approved by the shareholders at a general shareholders' meeting.

19.280   Spanish regulations set forth the following exceptions to the takeover bid requirements in order to delist a company:[125]

- where, following a takeover bid, the bidder requires the minority shareholders of the target company to sell their shares under a squeeze-out, or such minority shareholders require the bidder to buy their shares under a sell-out and, in this latter case, the bidder becomes the holder of 100% of the company's share capital;
- where all shareholders waive their right to sell their securities in a public tender offer and the delisting is approved unanimously;

---

[123]   See Royal Decree 1066/2007 Article 48.10.
[124]   See Royal Decree 1066/2007 Article 10.
[125]   See Royal Decree 1066/2007 Article 11.

- if the company is dissolved through a corporate transaction, and as a result the dissolved company's shareholders become shareholders of another listed company;
- where a public takeover bid for 100% of the company's share capital has previously been launched and (i) the offer document included the intention of delisting the company; (ii) an independent report confirms that the price offered in the previous bid satisfied the requirements of a delisting bid; and (iii) the sale of the remaining shares is guaranteed by a permanent order from the offeror to buy all outstanding shares tendered to it at the price offered in the previous bid;
- lastly, in the event that the general shareholders' meeting (and if applicable the bondholders' meeting) of the target approves a procedure which the CNMV regards as being equivalent to a takeover bid in terms of shareholder protection.

19.4.14 Supervision and sanctions

The LMV and the Royal Decree 1066/2007 provide that a person or entity that breaches the obligation to make a takeover bid may not exercise the political rights (including voting rights) of any of the securities of a listed company to which he or she may be entitled, in addition to any further sanctions that may be imposed. This prohibition is also applicable to the securities held indirectly by the party required to make the takeover bid and to those securities belonging to parties acting in concert with the party making the bid. **19.281**

For these purposes, a party that does not submit a takeover bid at all, submits a bid after the term provided has elapsed, or submits a bid with material irregularities, will be deemed to have breached the obligation to make a takeover bid. This breach qualifies as a very serious violation of the LMV, as described in Section 19.3.8 above. **19.282**

The suspended political rights (including voting rights) of such securities may only be regained by the launch of a takeover bid on all the securities of the affected company at a price fixed according to the valuation methods and criteria established by the Royal Decree 1066/2007[126] or by the unanimous consent of the rest of the shareholders individually. **19.283**

In addition, resolutions adopted by the company's decision-making bodies will be invalid where, for the valid constitution of such bodies or the adoption of such resolutions, it is necessary to count securities the political rights of which are suspended pursuant to the provisions described above. The CNMV is authorized **19.284**

---

[126] See Article 27.2 in connection with Royal Decree 1066/2007 Article 10.

to bring the relevant challenges within a period of one year from becoming aware of such resolution, without prejudice to the standing that may be held by other persons. The CNMV may also challenge the resolutions of the board of directors of the target company within a period of one year from becoming aware of it.

19.285 Furthermore, the sanction rules are strengthened by classifying violations relating to the breach of obligations established in the takeover regulations, such as: (i) violation by directors of the duty of non-interference and violations relating to the rules on the adoption and neutralization of preventive measures, which are classified as very serious violations; (ii) breach of the obligations to provide information relating to the launching or the proceedings to complete takeover bids, which may constitute a very serious or a serious violation, (iii) the existence of omissions or inaccuracies that induce deception in the documentation related to the takeover bid, which may constitute a very serious or serious violation based on the relevance of the affected information or documentation on the amount of the takeover bid or the number of investors affected, whether or not significant.

19.286 Penalties for very serious violations, which are set forth in Article 102 of the LMV and may be imposed either alternatively or cumulatively, are described in Section 19.3.8. above.

20

SWEDEN*

20.1 Jurisdiction Overview

20.1.1 Swedish listings

Sweden offers a range of listing alternatives and venues. The largest and most **20.01**
frequently accessed market in Sweden is NASDAQ OMX Nordic,[1] which combines

---

  * The contribution of Emil Boström of Mannheimer Swartling to the drafting of this Chapter is acknowledged with thanks.
  [1] The NASDAQ OMX Nordic consists of four local stock exchanges in Copenhagen, Stockholm, Helsinki and Iceland. The four exchanges are separate legal entities in different jurisdictions, and therefore each exchange has its own regulations.

the benefits of a large global marketplace with a local presence, serving as a central gateway for international investors to the Nordic and Baltic financial markets.

20.02 Companies that achieve and maintain a listing on the main market of NASDAQ OMX Nordic (the 'Main Market') will have their shares quoted in the Main Market list.[2] Inclusion in the Main Market list, which is open to both Swedish and overseas companies, is dependent on applicants meeting a scheme of eligibility criteria, including a minimum market capitalization of at least EUR 1 million.

20.03 The Main Market of NASDAQ OMX Nordic is the most well-reputed marketplace in Sweden and a Main Market listing generally serves to enhance a company's public profile. A slot on the Main Market also ensures a level of liquidity in a company's securities as many institutional investors, such as pension funds, are bound to invest a portion of their funds into companies listed on the Main Market on the basis that investments in Main Market companies are deemed to be less risky than investments in unquoted companies.

20.04 A listing of shares on the Main Market is only one of several categories of listing in Sweden. Companies targeting the Swedish market can also list their securities on NASDAQ OMX First North, NGM Equity, Nordic MTF Stockholm and AktieTorget.[3] Being the largest of Sweden's listing venues, this Chapter will focus on NASDAQ OMX Nordic.

20.1.2 The Swedish Financial Supervisory Authority

20.05 The Swedish Financial Supervisory Authority (the 'SFSA') is Sweden's competent authority for the purposes of MiFID[4] and operates in four main areas: supervision, regulation, permits/licences and applications. One of the SFSA's key roles is to supervise and monitor companies operating in the Swedish financial markets. In doing so, its aims to contribute to the stability and efficiency of the financial sector and to promote investor protection. The SFSA is also authorized to issue regulations and guidelines relating to the Swedish financial markets. Companies offering financial services in Sweden require permits/licences issued by the SFSA.

---

[2] The Main Market list is divided into three principal segments: Large Cap, Mid Cap and Small Cap. Which segment a company's shares are placed in depends on the size of its market capitalization.

[3] See Sections 20.1.3, 20.1.4 and 20.1.5 below.

[4] Chapter 1, section 5(2) of the Securities Market Act (2007:528). The Swedish Companies Registration Office is regarded as the 'competent authority' in respect of registration of tied agents. Chapter 6, section 1 of the Securities Market Act.

All prospectuses prepared in conjunction with listings on a regulated market in   **20.06**
Sweden must be approved by the SFSA. In the prospectus vetting process, the
company's advisers are likely to have extensive contact with representatives of
the SFSA and, accordingly, maintaining a good working relationship can be an
important factor in the success of a securities offering.

20.1.3 NASDAQ OMX Stockholm

20.1.3.1 General

NASDAQ OMX was created by way of an acquisition by NASDAQ of OMX,   **20.07**
completed in early 2008. NASDAQ OMX Group Inc is listed on NASDAQ
Stock Market. NASDAQ OMX Stockholm AB ('NASDAQ OMX Stockholm')
is a subsidiary of NASDAQ OMX Group Inc.

NASDAQ OMX Stockholm's role includes admitting securities to trading,   **20.08**
publishing its Rulebook for Issuers and monitoring issuers' compliance with continuing disclosure obligations. NASDAQ OMX runs two principal markets for
shares in the Nordic region: NASDAQ OMX Nordic, which is the Main Market,
and NASDAQ OMX First North, which is the growth market ('First North'). In
addition, NASDAQ OMX Nordic offers listing and trading services for bonds,
warrants and fund products.

20.1.3.2 The Main Market

The Main Market of NASDAQ OMX Nordic is the flagship market in the Nordic   **20.09**
region and is intended principally for well-established companies. The Main
Market is an EU regulated market and, accordingly, its listing requirements are
based on the applicable European standards. The regulatory demands of a listing
on the Main Market are higher than on First North; hence there is a high stamp
of quality connected to such a listing.

A broad range of investors operate on the Main Market—from international to   **20.10**
local investors, as well as retail and professional investors—enjoying the enhanced
exposure that such a listing brings.

Generally, Swedish companies may only apply to the Main Market for a primary   **20.11**
listing,[5] in connection with which they must comply with the applicable listing
requirements and continuing obligations regime. For overseas companies, the
choices of Main Market listing are greater, extending beyond a primary listing of
shares to a secondary listing of shares or a listing of depositary receipts.[6]

---

[5] NASDAQ OMX Stockholm Rulebook for Issuers section 2.6.
[6] NASDAQ OMX Stockholm Rulebook for Issuers section 2.6.

20.12 All companies admitted to the Main Market must comply with the NASDAQ OMX Stockholm's listing requirements and disclosure rules, as set out in the NASDAQ OMX Stockholm Rulebook for Issuers (the 'Rulebook for Issuers').

20.13 As of August 2009, 673[7] companies were listed on the Main Market, representing an aggregate market cap of approximately EUR 553 billion (SEK 5,639 billion).[8] 259 companies were related to NASDAQ OMX Stockholm's part of the Main Market, representing a total market cap of approximately EUR 298 billion (SEK 3,042 billion).

20.1.3.3 *First North*

20.14 First North, a multilateral trading facility ('MTF') under EC legislation, is an alternative to the Main Market, with lighter requirements and rules. A company can join First North regardless of its country of origin or industry sector. First North normally suits small, young or growth companies and is often the first step towards the Main Market.[9]

20.15 First North is an exchange-regulated market supervised by the exchange and the certified advisers (see further below). The regulatory requirements that apply to companies listed on First North are lighter than those that apply to companies listed on a regulated market. Notable regulatory concessions in connection with a First North listing include the absence of requirements for (i) operating history; (ii) documented profitability or sufficient financial resources; (iii) minimum market value; and (iv) compliance with the Swedish Corporate Governance Code. Furthermore, provided the securities for which admission to First North is sought are not simultaneously the subject of a public offer, an applicant for a First North listing will not be required to publish a prospectus.[10]

20.16 First North listed companies are required to comply with the provisions in the First North Rulebook, which, *inter alia*, requires that the companies must at all times have a certified adviser. Before trading can commence, an application must be submitted for approval. The certified adviser is the representative that guides the company through the application process and ensures that the company thereafter fulfils the requirements of the First North Rulebook on a continuing basis.

---

[7] Including 11 multiple listings.

[8] The value includes the exchanges in Stockholm, Helsinki, Copenhagen and Iceland and also the exchanges in Tallinn, Riga and Vilnius.

[9] First North infrastructure is based on the same trading and settlement systems as the Main Market.

[10] As discussed at Section 20.2.2.1, the obligation to publish a prospectus applies to companies in two circumstances: (i) where a company offers its securities to the public and (ii) where a company makes an application for admission to trading on a regulated market. Since First North is not a regulated market, the obligation to publish a prospectus will not apply unless there is an offer to the public.

In discharging its duties, a certified adviser must, *inter alia*, (i) monitor that the relevant company complies with First North's admission requirements; (ii) monitor the First North listed company's compliance with First North's post-admission disclosure obligations; (iii) advise, support and update the First North listed company on its obligations on First North; and (iv) have at least one designated contact person available during normal trading hours to answer any queries from the exchange, the company or the market.[11]   **20.17**

A company whose shares are traded on First North may also apply for trading on First North in option rights or convertible debentures issued by the company. Other types of financial instruments may also be traded on First North.   **20.18**

As of August 2009, 130 companies were listed on First North, representing an aggregate market cap of approximately EUR 2.1 billion (SEK 21.6 billion).   **20.19**

20.1.4 NGM Stock Exchange

Alongside NASDAQ OMX Stockholm, NGM Stock Exchange ('NGM') is the only exchange in Sweden authorized by the SFSA. NGM is aimed primarily at small and medium-sized Nordic growth companies, but also has experience of listing larger companies and handling parallel listings on NGM and other exchanges.   **20.20**

NGM offers listing and trading in equities on its NGM Equity list, which is an EU regulated market. Companies listed on NGM Equity must navigate a listing process, which ensures that the company and its management meet the exchange's suitability criteria and have adequate systems for financial management and the disclosure of information. All companies admitted to the NGM Equity list must comply with listing requirements and disclosure rules set out in the listing agreement of NGM (the 'NGM Listing Agreement').   **20.21**

NGM also operates Nordic MTF Stockholm.[12] Being an MTF, it does not have the same legal status as a regulated market, and the requirements on its listed companies are accordingly less stringent than on the NGM Equity.   **20.22**

As of August 2009, 30 and 22 companies, respectively, were listed on NGM Equity and Nordic MTF Stockholm, representing an aggregate market cap of approximately EUR 500 million (SEK 5 billion) and EUR 58 million (SEK 580 million), respectively.   **20.23**

---

[11] First North Rulebook section 5.2.
[12] NGM also operates Nordic MTF Oslo and derivatives trading on the Nordic Derivatives Exchange (NDX).

20.1.5 AktieTorget

20.24 AktieTorget operates an MTF, and therefore is not an EU regulated market.

20.25 As of August 2009, 118 companies were listed on AktieTorget, representing an aggregate market cap of approximately EUR 500 million (SEK 5 billion).

20.1.6 Legislative overview

20.1.6.1 Admission to trading on a regulated market and offers of securities to the public

20.26 The principal pieces of legislation through which Sweden has implemented the EU directives relating to admission to trading on a regulated market and offers of securities to the public[13] are the Securities Market Act (the 'Market Act')[14] and the Financial Instruments Trading Act (the 'Trading Act').[15]

20.27 The Market Act stipulates that an exchange must adopt clear and openly reported rules for the admission of financial instruments to trading on a regulated market and that financial instruments may be admitted to trading only where the conditions exist for fair, orderly and efficient trading in the financial instruments and, in the case of transferable securities, provided they are freely negotiable.[16] The Rulebook for Issuers and the NGM Listing Agreement set out more detailed rules in this context.[17]

20.1.6.2 Disclosure and transparency[18]

20.28 The principle rules relating to the continuing obligations regime that applies to issuers in Sweden are set out in the Market Act, which provides, *inter alia*, that a listed company must make public all information regarding its operations and securities that is significant to the assessment of the price of the securities.[19] The Market Act also contains provisions requiring the publication of periodic financial information.[20] The Market Act operates in conjunction with two further sources of rules regarding the disclosure of pertinent information to the market: the Rulebook for Issuers and the NGM Listing Agreement;[21] as well as regulations laid down by the SFSA.[22] In addition, listed companies that are involved in

---

[13] For a detailed discussion of the Prospectus Directive and Prospectus Regulation, see Part 1.
[14] Sw: Lag (2007:528) om värdepappersmarknaden.
[15] Sw: Lag (1991:980) om handel med finansiella instrument.
[16] Market Act chapter 15 sections 1 and 2.
[17] See Section 20.1.6.4 below.
[18] Regarding disclosure and transparency rules, see Section 20.3 below.
[19] Market Act chapter 15 section 6.
[20] Market Act chapter 16.
[21] See Section 20.1.6.4 below.
[22] See Section 20.1.6.3 below.

takeovers are regulated by the Stock Market (Takeover Bids) Act (the 'Takeover Act')[23] and the NASDAQ OMX and NGM takeover rules (the 'Takeover Rules'), which include certain transaction disclosure requirements.[24]

Rules concerning the notification of major holdings of shares or voting rights are set out in the Trading Act, while rules regarding disclosure of transactions by persons discharging managerial responsibilities ('PDMRs') are set out in the Act on Notification of Certain Holdings of Financial Instruments (the 'Notification Act').[25]

20.29

20.1.6.3 *Regulations and guidance issued by the SFSA*

The SFSA is authorized to issue regulations and guidelines relating to the Swedish financial markets. In relation to disclosure requirements, the SFSA has issued regulations that set out detailed rules relating to the disclosure of price-sensitive information, the publication of periodic financial reports, issues of transferable securities and dividend payments. The regulations also prescribe the means for disclosing information.[26]

20.30

Occasionally, the SFSA produces memoranda in which it states its opinion on certain issues. In addition, it is open to anyone who has a question related to the SFSA's area of responsibility to submit questions by email or telephone. This enables companies' advisers and others to ascertain how the SFSA will apply specific rules on a case-by-case basis.

20.31

20.1.6.4 *The Rulebook for Issuers and the NGM Listing Agreement*

The Market Act stipulates that a securities exchange must adopt clear and openly reported rules for the admission of financial instruments to trading on a regulated market. This is achieved by the Rulebook for Issuers and the NGM Listing Agreement.

20.32

The Rulebook for Issuers is divided into three parts; the first deals with shares, the second with bonds and the third with exchange traded funds. The first part contains the following sections:

20.33

- Section 1: general requirements for the validity of and amendments to the rules;
- Section 2: the listing requirements;
- Section 3: the disclosure rules;

---

[23] Sw: Lag (2006:451) om offentliga uppköpserbjudanden på aktiemarknaden.
[24] See Section 20.1.6.5 below.
[25] Sw: Lag (2000:1087) om anmälningsskyldighet för vissa innehav av finansiella instrument.
[26] Regulations (2007:17) governing operations on trading venues chapter 10.

- Section 4: rules regarding transactions with closely related parties and repurchase and sales of a company's own shares;
- Section 5: rules about sanctions; and
- Section 6: the Takeover Rules.

20.34 As regards the NGM Listing Agreement, Exhibit 1 to the NGM Listing Agreement sets out the listing requirements while Exhibit 2 sets out the disclosure rules.

20.1.6.5 *Takeovers*

20.35 The main sources of Swedish takeover regulation are the Takeover Act and the Takeover Rules. The Swedish takeover regime is discussed further at Section 20.3.10 below.

20.1.6.6 *Market abuse*

20.36 Rules relating to prohibitions on insider dealing, unlawful disclosure of inside information and market manipulation are set out in the Financial Instruments Trading (Market Abuse Penalties) Act (the 'Market Abuse Act').[27] These rules are discussed at Section 20.3.11 below.

20.1.6.7 *The Swedish Securities Council*

20.37 The Swedish Securities Council (the 'Council') is a private body comprised of representatives of the business community. Through statements, advice and information, the Council's aim is to promote good practices in the Swedish securities market.

20.38 The Council is a self-regulatory body, meaning that its statements (with some exceptions) are not formally binding under statute. Nevertheless, it is common practice for market participants to comply with the Council's statements and those that do not put themselves at risk of severe reputational damage. In addition, under the Rulebook for Issuers and the NGM Listing Agreement, listed companies must comply with generally acceptable practices on the Swedish securities market, which may well be reflected in the Council's statements and, consequently, a listed company that does not comply with the Council's statements may be subject to sanctions by the exchange. Furthermore, in respect of takeover offers, the SFSA, NASDAQ OMX Stockholm and NGM have delegated certain of their powers to the Council.[28]

20.39 The scope of actions that may be evaluated by the Council is broad. Any Swedish company that has shares listed (or that has taken actions to list its shares) on NASDAQ OMX Stockholm or NGM Equity, or any shareholder of such a

---

[27] Sw: Lag (2005:377) om straff för marknadsmissbruk vid handel med finansiella instrument.
[28] See Section 20.3.10.2 below.

company, may be subject to the Council's evaluation. The same applies to foreign companies that have shares listed (or that have taken actions to list their shares) on NASDAQ OMX Stockholm or NGM Equity, to the extent that Swedish rules apply.

The Council can issue statements on its own initiative or in response to a petition. **20.40** Such statements are released publicly on the Council's website in order to contribute to the development of good practices in the securities market, unless confidentiality is required in a specific case.[29]

Since its operations began in 1986, the Council has issued approximately **20.41** 500 statements. During 2008 it issued 51 statements, the vast majority of which were related to takeover offers or changes in ownership that could give rise to mandatory offers.

20.1.7 Eligibility for listing on the Main Market

20.1.7.1 *Admission to trading*

To conduct a listing on the Main Market, securities must be admitted to trading **20.42** on the NASDAQ OMX Stockholm. In addition, the company must produce a prospectus, which must be approved and registered by the SFSA.

20.1.7.2 *The listing process in short*[30]

A company that considers applying for listing on the exchange begins the process **20.43** by contacting the exchange and asking it to initiate a listing process. Normally, the exchange arranges a meeting where the company is presented by its management and the listing process is discussed. If the company and the exchange agree to initiate a listing process, the exchange appoints an exchange auditor, who makes an assessment as to whether it would be appropriate to list and admit the shares of the company to trading on the exchange. The assessment will cover matters such as (i) whether there will be sufficient conditions for appropriate trading in the shares; (ii) the company's ability to comply with the listing requirements, in particular requirements pertaining to disclosure of financial and other price-sensitive information; (iii) whether the company's directors and management are fit and proper to direct the company's business and to enable the company to meet its responsibilities towards the exchange and the stock market; and (iv) the information provided in the prospectus.

The exchange auditor presents a report of his or her findings, which it submits to **20.44** the exchange together with a recommendation in respect of the listing decision to

---

[29] For further information regarding the Council and its operations, see the Council's website at http://www.aktiemarknadsnamnden.se.
[30] Rulebook for Issuers section 2.2.

be made by the exchange. A sub-committee of the board of directors of the exchange (the 'Listing Committee') is the body that ultimately makes listing decisions on behalf of the exchange.

20.45   The company must have prepared and published a prospectus prior to the listing and the relevant authority (normally the SFSA) must have approved the prospectus.[31] The exchange may require that the company posts supplementary information on its website, if the exchange considers such information to be important and in the interests of investors.

20.46   Prior to the listing, the company must obtain a legal opinion from an independent attorney. The legal opinion must at minimum include: (i) a statement that there is an adequate description of the legal risks relating to the company and its securities in the prospectus; (ii) a review of all material agreements entered into by the company; (iii) an assessment of the company's tax situation; and (iv) a confirmation that all relevant corporate formalities have been handled properly. The exchange auditor must receive a written summary of material observations arising out of the legal attorney's examination of the company and is authorized to obtain all information pertaining to the legal opinion that it requires for the purposes of the listing assessment.[32]

20.1.7.3 Listing requirements

20.47   NASDAQ OMX Stockholm will only grant admission to trading of an applicant's securities if it is satisfied that the applicant meets the listing requirements set out in section 2 of the Rulebook for Issuers (the 'Listing Requirements'). The Listing Requirements consist of general listing requirements (the 'General Listing Requirements'), as well as specific requirements regarding the administration of the company (the 'Administration Requirements'). All applications for admission to trading on the Main Market must be made in the manner required by the Listing Requirements and satisfy the General Listing Requirements as well as the Administration Requirements.

---

[31] If the company is domiciled in Sweden or a country outside the EEA, the exchange auditor will submit the prospectus to the exchange, which will give its opinion on the prospectus to the SFSA before the prospectus is formally approved. If the company is domiciled in a country other than Sweden but within the EEA, the company must submit the prospectus to the exchange together with a certificate of approval issued by a competent authority in the issuer's home country. The certificate of approval must, where appropriate, set out any exemption that has been granted from the requirements in the Prospectus Directive. In addition, the company must certify that the approved prospectus has been submitted to the SFSA.

[32] The exchange auditor may, in addition, require a separate or supplementary legal opinion in cases where there is a need to investigate any legal or regulatory issue that is deemed to be of material importance to the decision to list and admit the shares of the company to trading on the exchange.

The General Listing Requirements are as follows:[33]   **20.48**

- *Incorporation*: the company must be duly incorporated or otherwise validly established according to the relevant laws of its place of incorporation or establishment.
- *Validity*: the company's shares must: (i) conform to the laws of the company's place of incorporation and (ii) have the necessary statutory or other consents.
- *Negotiability*: the shares must be freely negotiable.
- *Entire class must be listed*: the application for listing must cover all issued shares of the same class.
- *Accounts and operating history*: the company must have published annual accounts for at least three years in accordance with the accounting laws applicable to the company in its home country. Where applicable, the accounts must also include consolidated figures for the company and all its subsidiaries. In addition, the company and its group's principal line(s) of business and field(s) of operation must be supported by a sufficient operating history.
- *Profitability and working capital*: the company must demonstrate that it possesses a documented earnings capacity on a business group level. Alternatively, a company that does not possess such documented earnings capacity must demonstrate that it has sufficient working capital available for its planned business for at least 12 months after the first day of listing.
- *Liquidity*: conditions for sufficient demand and supply of the company's securities must exist in order to facilitate a reliable price formation process. In particular, the company must have a sufficient number of shareholders and sufficient number of its shares in public hands, which for these purposes means that at least 25% of the shares within the same class being admitted to trading must be in public hands (the exchange may accept a percentage lower than 25% of the shares if it is satisfied that the market will operate properly with a lower percentage in view of the large number of shares that are distributed to the public).
- *Market value of shares*: the expected aggregate market value of the shares shall be at least EUR 1 million.
- *Suitability*: in cases where all Listing Requirements are fulfilled, the exchange may nevertheless refuse an application for listing if it considers that the listing would be detrimental to the securities market or investor interests.

---

[33] Rulebook for Issuers section 2.3.

20.49 The Administration Requirements are as follows:[34]

- *The management and the board of directors*: the requirements on the management and the board of directors are the following:
  - the company's management must collectively have sufficient competence and experience to manage a listed company and to comply with the obligations of such a company;
  - the company's board of directors must be composed in a way that sufficiently reflects the competence and experience required to control a listed company and to comply with the obligations of such a company;
  - not more than one member or deputy of the board elected by the shareholders may work as a senior executive in the company or its subsidiaries;
  - more than half of the members of the board elected by the shareholders must be independent of the company and its management; and
  - there must be at least two members of the board of directors elected by the shareholders who are independent of the company's principal shareholders (as well as independent of the company and its management), at least one of whom must be experienced in requirements for listed companies.
- *Capacity for providing information to the market*: well in advance of the listing, the company must establish and maintain adequate procedures, systems and controls, including for the purposes of financial reporting, to enable compliance with its obligation to provide the market with timely, reliable, accurate and up-to-date information as required by the exchange.

20.50 The exchange may approve an application for listing, even if the company does not fulfil all the Listing Requirements, provided it is satisfied that (i) the objectives behind the relevant Listing Requirements or any statutory requirements are not compromised, or (ii) the objectives behind certain Listing Requirements can be achieved by other means.

20.51 The Listing Requirements apply from the time at which the shares of the company are admitted to listing and trading, as well as continuously after listing has been granted, except for the requirements regarding profitability and working capital and market value of shares, which only apply at the time of the listing (as an eligibility pre-requisite to listing).

20.1.7.4 Specific listing requirements for special purpose acquisition companies

20.52 A special purpose acquisition company ('SPAC') is a company whose business plan is to complete one or more acquisitions within a certain time period. For such companies, the rules regarding the exchange auditor, financial statements and operating history and profitability (see Section 20.1.7.3 above) do not apply.

---

[34] Rulebook for Issuers section 2.4.

Instead, specific listing requirements (the 'SPAC Listing Requirements') apply.[35]   **20.53**
At least 90% of the gross proceeds from the initial public offering and any concurrent sale of equity securities by the company must be deposited in a blocked bank account for the purpose of conducting acquisitions. Further, within 36 months of the effectiveness of its prospectus, or such shorter period that the company specifies in its prospectus, the company must complete one or more acquisitions having an aggregate fair market value of at least 80% of the value of the deposit account (excluding any deferred underwriters' fees and taxes payable on the income earned on the deposit account) at the time of the agreement to enter into the initial acquisition (the '80% Requirement').

Before the company has satisfied the 80% Requirement, the SPAC Listing   **20.54**
Requirements provide that each acquisition must be approved by a majority of the board members who are independent of the company and its management and also by a majority of the shares voting at the shareholders' meeting at which the acquisition is being considered. Shareholders voting against an acquisition must have the right to convert their shares into a cash amount (a pro rata share of the aggregate amount then in the deposit account, net of taxes payable and amounts distributed to management for working capital purposes) if the acquisition is approved and completed.[36] When the company has satisfied the 80% Requirement and is no longer regarded as a SPAC, it must initiate a new listing process as soon as possible, in connection with which it must fulfil all listing requirements for listed companies.

20.1.7.5 Secondary listings

Subject to approval by NASDAQ OMX Stockholm, a company with a primary   **20.55**
listing on a foreign exchange may apply for secondary listing, and the exchange may under such circumstances waive one or more of the Listing Requirements.

Companies whose primary listing is on a regulated market, or equivalent, oper-   **20.56**
ated by NASDAQ, Deutsche Börse, London Stock Exchange, NYSE Euronext, Oslo Börs or Toronto Stock Exchange, may, for example, be granted a waiver from the requirements of an exchange auditor and a legal opinion from an independent attorney. Listing decisions regarding applications for secondary listings are made by the chief executive officer of the exchange.

---

[35] Rulebook for Issuers section 2.9.
[36] A company may establish a limit (set no lower than 10%) as to the maximum number of shares with respect to which any shareholder may exercise such conversion rights. The right of conversion excludes officers and directors of the company, the founding shareholders of the company and any related party of the foregoing persons.

20.57 When seeking a secondary listing on NASDAQ OMX Stockholm, the company must satisfy the exchange that there will be sufficient liquidity to facilitate orderly trading and an efficient price formation process.[37]

20.1.7.6 Depositary receipts

20.58 Overseas companies applying for a listing of depository receipts must comply with the requirements applicable to shares. Where the company has a primary listing elsewhere, which would normally be the case, the requirements for secondary listings become relevant. As stated at Section 20.1.7.5 above, NASDAQ OMX Stockholm may waive one or more of the Listing Requirements. Specific requirements apply in relation to the prospectus prepared for a listing of depository receipts.[38]

20.1.7.7 Debt and other specialist securities

20.59 Specific listing requirements apply for listings of bonds and exchange-traded funds.

20.60 In respect of bonds, there is a set of general listing requirements that apply to the issuer[39] and a set of general listing requirements for the instruments.[40] Further, there are additional specific listing requirements depending on which type of bond (structured bonds, retail bonds, tailor-made products, convertible bonds, corporate bonds or benchmark bonds) is subject to the listing.[41]

20.61 The listing requirements for exchange-traded funds are brief.[42] They provide for the possibility of a secondary listing of exchange-traded funds.[43]

20.62 Both in respect of bonds and exchange-traded funds, the Rulebook for Issuers includes disclosure requirements.[44] These requirements are less onerous than the equivalent requirements for listed shares.

20.1.8 Eligibility for listing on other Swedish listing venues

20.1.8.1 First North

20.63 First North is an MTF operated by NASDAQ OMX with less onerous requirements and rules than an EU regulated market. The admission criteria for companies

---

[37] Rulebook for Issuers section 2.6.
[38] Prospectus Regulation Annex X.
[39] Rulebook for Issuers section 2.2 (Bonds).
[40] Rulebook for Issuers section 2.3 (Bonds).
[41] Rulebook for Issuers sections 2.4 to 2.9 (Bonds).
[42] Rulebook for Issuers section 2.1 (Exchange Traded Funds).
[43] Rulebook for Issuers section 2.2 (Exchange Traded Funds).
[44] Rulebook for Issuers section 3 (Bonds and Exchange Traded Funds).

joining First North are laid out in detail in the First North Rulebook.[45] In summary, the key admission requirements include the following:

- *Requirements for shares*: sufficient number of shareholders; and at least 10% of the share capital must be in public hands; alternatively, the company can employ the services of a liquidity provider.
- *Company description/prospectus*: the company must publish a company description or a prospectus.
- *Certified adviser*: the company must at all times have an agreement with a certified adviser.
- *General terms and conditions for admission to trading*: the company must accept and sign the general terms and conditions for admission to trading on First North.
- *Organizational requirements*: the company must have the organization and staff required in order to comply with the relevant post-admission disclosure requirements.

20.1.8.2 NGM Equity

NGM Equity is an EU regulated market. In summary, the key admission require- **20.64**
ments include the following:

- *Requirements for shares*: at least 300 shareholders, each with at least one round lot, and at least 10% of shares and 10% of votes must be in public hands.
- *Listing prospectus*: the company must publish a prospectus, which must be approved and registered by the SFSA.
- *The company and its management*: the company must meet the exchange's suitability criteria; have adequate systems for financial management; have the capacity to meet applicable post-admission disclosure requirements; and meet certain independency requirements in relation to its board members.

20.1.8.3 Nordic MTF Stockholm

Nordic MTF Stockholm is an MTF for trading in companies not yet officially **20.65**
listed. In summary, the key admission requirements include the following:

- *Requirements for shares*: the company must have enough shareholders to ensure a basis for effective trading; and must have at least 10% of its shares in public hands.

---

[45] First North Rulebook section 2.

- *Information document/prospectus*: the company must publish either an information document (with basic information about the company) or a prospectus (which must be approved and registered by the SFSA).
- *The company and its management*: the company must meet the general requirement of sound finances; have at least three board members; and have its own website that provides certain corporate information.

20.1.8.4 AktieTorget

20.66 AktieTorget operates an MTF. In summary, the key admission requirements include the following:

- *Requirements for shares*: there must be at least 200 shareholders with one normal unit of trading each; the public must own a minimum of 10% of the equity and control 10% of the votes.
- *Listing memorandum/prospectus*: the company must present a listing memorandum (which must be approved by AktieTorget) or a prospectus (which must be approved and registered by the SFSA).
- *The company and its management*: AktieTorget's board of directors must consider the company to have good future prospects; preferably, but not necessarily, to have been in operation for several years; and report to its shareholders in accordance with AktieTorget's and the SFSA's regulations.

20.2 Listing Securities in Practice

20.2.1 Applicable law

20.67 The principal pieces of legislation through which Sweden has implemented the EU directives relating to admission to trading on a regulated market and offers of securities to the public are the Market Act and the Trading Act.

20.68 Since the Prospectus Directive is a maximum harmonization directive, and the Prospectus Regulation is directly applicable, the Swedish rules regarding prospectuses bear a close resemblance to those in other member states across the EU.

20.69 The key source of Swedish law for the purposes of the implementation of the Prospectus Directive is chapter 2 of the Trading Act, which contains provisions as to when a prospectus must be prepared and exemptions from such obligation; the responsibility for preparation of a prospectus; the content[46] and format requirements of a prospectus; provisions relating to the omission of information and reference to other documents; language provisions, the period of validity of a

---

[46] Detailed provisions regarding the contents of a prospectus are set out in the Prospectus Regulation.

prospectus; provisions relating to the approval and publication of a prospectus, advertisements and other information, supplements to a prospectus; passporting of prospectuses; and the definition of an issuer's home member state.

20.2.2 Requirement for a prospectus

20.2.2.1 *The requirement*

The circumstances in which a company will be required to prepare a prospectus **20.70** under Swedish law are essentially those set out under Article 3 of the Prospectus Directive: the so-called 'public offer' and 'admission to trading' triggers.[47] For further detail see the discussion of the Prospectus Directive requirement to publish a prospectus in Part 1.

20.2.2.2 *Exemptions to the requirement to publish a prospectus*

The circumstances in which a prospectus will be required are qualified by a series **20.71** of exemptions and exceptions.[48] The SFSA has no discretion under the Prospectus Directive in this area, and, accordingly, the exemptions under Swedish law to the requirement to publish a prospectus are essentially those laid down in the Prospectus Rules, which are discussed in Part 1.

20.2.3 Prospectus content

20.2.3.1 *The 'necessary information'*

As is the case in all jurisdictions in which the Prospectus Directive and Prospectus **20.72** Regulations apply, the overriding obligation of disclosure in a prospectus is to provide 'all information regarding the issuer and the transferable securities that is necessary to enable an investor to make an informed assessment of the assets and liabilities, financial position, results, and future prospects of the issuer and of any guarantor, as well as of the transferable securities'. Furthermore, the information must be written such that it is easy to understand and analyse.[49]

The 'necessary information' must be prepared having regard to the particular **20.73** nature of the transferable securities and their issuer. More detailed provisions regarding the information that must be included in a prospectus are set out in the Prospectus Regulation and are discussed in Part 1.

Although one might expect the final price or the number of transferable securities **20.74** to qualify as part of the 'necessary information', applicants are permitted to omit such details from a prospectus (for example, where the company intends to

---

[47] Trading Act chapter 2 section 1.
[48] Trading Act chapter 2 sections 2–7.
[49] Trading Act chapter 2 section 11, first paragraph.

approach retail investors to discover the level of interest in a particular issue before determining these elements). However, in such circumstances, the prospectus must instead contain information regarding the criteria or conditions which shall be applied to fix the price (or, if applicable, the ceiling price) and, the number of transferable securities to be offered. If it does not present such information, investors who have accepted offers to purchase or subscribe will be entitled to withdraw their acceptances within five business days of publication of the final fixed price and number of transferable securities.[50]

20.2.3.2 Derogations

20.75 In certain cases, the SFSA—like other financial regulators in Europe—has the power to grant derogations from the duty of disclosure. The SFSA may do this where it finds that: (i) publication of the information would be seriously detrimental to the issuer and the omission of the information would not mislead the public; or (ii) the information is of minor importance and would not influence the assessment of the financial position and prospects of the issuer, offeror or any guarantor. The SFSA may also permit issuers to omit information required pursuant to the Prospectus Regulation in cases where it determines that such information is not relevant to the issuer's line of business or legal form or to those transferable securities to which the prospectus relates (where possible, the prospectus shall contain comparable information).[51]

20.2.4 Draft prospectuses

20.76 When it is clear that a prospectus is required in connection with a proposed listing, the company and its advisers will begin the drafting process. One or more draft prospectuses are normally submitted to the SFSA for its continuing review during the course of the listing process. Unlike in certain other jurisdictions such as the United Kingdom, it is not common practice in Sweden for issuers to use their draft (or preliminary) prospectus as a marketing document to be distributed to potential investors.

20.2.5 The advertisement regime

20.77 The Trading Act includes provisions concerning advertisements for public offers and admissions to trading on a regulated market. In addition to the more straightforward rules that the information in advertisements must not be inaccurate or misleading and must conform to the information provided in the prospectus, advertisements must also state clearly that a prospectus has been published or will be published and where the prospectus is or will be available. Furthermore, the

---

[50] Trading Act chapter 2 section 18.
[51] Trading Act chapter 2 section 19.

advertisement must be formatted and presented so that it is clear that it is an advertisement.[52]

Notably, regardless of whether the obligation to prepare a prospectus arises in connection with an offering, all significant information in connection with the offering that is provided to any investor must be provided to all investors to whom the offer is directed.[53]

20.78

20.2.6 Supplementary prospectuses

20.2.6.1 *When a supplementary prospectus is required*

Following the SFSA's approval of the final prospectus but prior to the expiry of the acceptance period for the offer or the admission of the securities to trading on a regulated market, if a significant new circumstance occurs or if the issuer or its advisers spot a material factual error or omission in the prospectus that could influence an investor's assessment of the securities described in the prospectus, the issuer is required to publish a supplementary prospectus.[54]

20.79

20.2.6.2 *The 'five day put'*

Investors who subscribe to an offering prior to the publication of a supplementary prospectus are entitled to withdraw from the transaction. Under the so-called 'five day put', investors may withdraw their subscription or purchase within five business days of the publication of the supplementary prospectus,[55] which itself must explain to investors their right of withdrawal.[56]

20.80

20.2.6.3 *Supplementary prospectuses in practice*

The obligation to prepare a supplementary prospectus arises only where the new circumstance, factual error or omission could 'influence the assessment' of the securities described in the prospectus. In situations of doubt, it is prudent to adopt a cautious approach and prepare a supplementary prospectus, thereby avoiding a subsequent finding that a supplementary prospectus should have been prepared but was not.[57]

20.81

---

[52] Trading Act chapter 2 sections 32 and 33. Further provisions regarding advertising are to be found in Article 34 of the Prospectus Regulation.

[53] Trading Act chapter 2 section 33, second paragraph.

[54] Trading Act chapter 2 section 34, first and second paragraph.

[55] Trading Act chapter 2 section 34, second paragraph.

[56] Frequently asked questions regarding Prospectuses: Common positions agreed by CESR Members ('CESR FAQs'), Question 21.

[57] The SFSA guidance document regarding review of prospectuses (*Sw. Granskning av prospekt – en vägledning*), 17 April 2008 (the 'SFSA Guidance Document'), page 23.

20.2.7 The SFSA approval process

20.82   The SFSA must approve any prospectus before its publication if Sweden is the relevant home member state.[58] The SFSA will grant approval provided the prospectus is complete, internally consistent, comprehensible, and fulfils all requirements set out in the Trading Act and the Prospectus Regulation.[59]

20.83   The Trading Act provides that the SFSA will issue a decision on the approval of a prospectus within ten business days of its receipt of a complete application. However, if the offer to the public relates to transferable securities that are issued by an issuer which has not previously offered transferable securities to the public and which has not previously had transferable securities admitted for trading on a regulated market, the SFSA will have 20 business days from receipt of a complete application to give a decision.[60] In cases where the SFSA requires an applicant to amend and resubmit its prospectus in any way, the SFSA may argue that its 10- or 20-day review period is refreshed and begins again on the date it receives the amended prospectus. Where the SFSA has to approve a supplementary prospectus, it has seven business days to give a decision.[61]

20.84   In practice, one or more draft prospectuses are submitted to the SFSA for its continuing review during the course of the listing process. Although NASDAQ OMX Stockholm does not formally approve the prospectus, draft prospectuses are also handed in to the exchange. The prospectus and the exchange auditor's report constitute the supporting documents upon which NASDAQ OMX Stockholm is to make its decision whether to grant admission to trading on the exchange. If NASDAQ OMX Stockholm has any comments on a draft prospectus, it will usually forward them to the SFSA prior to the SFSA's decision on the approval of the prospectus.

20.85   The SFSA and NASDAQ OMX Stockholm have informally agreed on a schedule for listings on NASDAQ OMX Stockholm. In short, it is usually possible to submit the prospectus and the exchange auditor's report to NASDAQ OMX Stockholm and the prospectus to the SFSA on Day 1; obtain the Listing Committee's decision on Day 7; obtain the SFSA's approval of the prospectus on Day 13; and have the first trading day of the securities on Day 18.[62] However, neither the SFSA nor

---

[58] Trading Act chapter 2 section 25, first paragraph. Chapter 2, Sections 37 through 39 of the Trading Act contain provisions on when Sweden is regarded as the home member state.

[59] If the issuer's registered office is not located in an EEA state but Sweden is nonetheless its home member state, approval must also be given if the prospectus has been prepared pursuant to the rules of the state in which the issuer has its registered office, provided the information requirements pursuant to the rules in such state are comparable to the requirements of the Trading Act and the Prospectus Regulation. Trading Act chapter 2, section 25, third and fourth paragraph.

[60] Trading Act chapter 2 section 26.

[61] Trading Act chapter 2 section 34, second paragraph.

[62] 'Day' means for these purposes business day.

NASDAQ OMX Stockholm are under any statutory obligation to adhere to this schedule, so a specific schedule should always be agreed with the SFSA and NASDAQ OMX Stockholm on a case-by-case basis.

The fee payable by the issuer to the SFSA for the approval and registration of a prospectus in respect of shares is SEK 35,000.[63]   **20.86**

20.3 Continuing Obligations

20.3.1 Applicable law

The Transparency Directive states that 'the disclosure of accurate, comprehensive   **20.87** and timely information about security issuers builds sustained investor confidence and allows an informed assessment of their business performance and assets. This enhances both investor protection and market efficiency'. It goes on to say that 'security issuers should ensure appropriate transparency for investors through a regular flow of information. To the same end, shareholders, or natural persons or legal entities holding voting rights or financial instruments that result in an entitlement to acquire existing shares with voting rights, should also inform issuers of the acquisition of or other changes in major holdings in companies so that the latter are in a position to keep the public informed'.[64]

To achieve these aims, listed companies are subject to a number of continuing   **20.88** disclosure obligations, requiring listed companies to do the following:

- disclose price-sensitive information as soon as possible after it arises;
- prepare and disclose periodic financial reports in the prescribed manner;
- disclose certain other corporate actions; and
- comply with a variety of corporate governance rules.

In pursuit of the same aims, the following provisions also apply: **20.89**

- PDMRs within the listed company are required to notify their holdings and affiliated persons' holdings, as well as changes in such holdings, to the SFSA; and
- major shareholders are required to notify shareholding details at various specified thresholds.

The principal rules relating to the continuing obligations regime are set out in the   **20.90** Market Act, which, *inter alia*, states that a listed company must make public (i) such information regarding its operations and securities which is of significance for the

---

[63] Applicable amount as of August 2009.
[64] Transparency Directive Recitals (1) and (2).

assessment of the price of the securities;[65] and (ii) periodic financial reports.[66] Regulations issued by the SFSA, as well as the Rulebook for Issuers and the NGM Listing Agreement include more detailed rules in relation to continuing disclosure requirements and operate in conjunction with the relevant provisions under the Market Act. Rules in respect of the notification of major holdings of shares or voting rights are set out in the Trading Act,[67] while rules regarding disclosure of transactions by PDMRs are included in the Notification Act.

20.91 This Section 20.3 will also discuss the Swedish takeover regime, which includes certain transaction disclosure requirements, as well as the market abuse rules as applicable to companies listed in Sweden.

20.3.2 Disclosure and control of price-sensitive information

20.3.2.1 *Applicable provisions and extent of applicability*

20.92 The Market Act, the SFSA Regulations[68] governing operations on trading venues (the 'SFSA Regulations'), the Rulebook for Issuers and the NGM Listing Agreement each impose obligations on issuers in order to ensure the prompt and accurate disclosure of information equally to all market participants. The Rulebook for Issuers provides that 'the company must, as soon as possible, disclose information about decisions or other facts and circumstances that are *price sensitive*'. The Market Act, the SFSA Regulations and the NGM Listing Agreement include similarly worded provisions, which are ultimately based on the corresponding provisions under the Transparency Directive.[69]

20.93 To ensure that a listed company provides the market with timely, reliable, accurate and up-to-date information, the NASDAQ OMX Stockholm encourages the company to adopt an information policy. A company's information policy normally deals with a number of areas, such as who is to act as the company's spokesperson, which type of information is to be made public, how and when publication must

---

[65] A listed company must also continuously inform the exchange about its operations and otherwise provide the exchange with such information as it needs in order to fulfil its obligations. Market Act chapter 15 section 6.

[66] Market Act chapter 16.

[67] Trading Act chapter 4.

[68] FFFS 2007:17.

[69] Market Act chapter 15 section 6, first paragraph, item 3; SFSA Regulation chapter 10 section 3; Rulebook for Issuers section 3.1.1; and NGM Listing Agreement exhibit 2, section 28, respectively. The disclosure provisions under the Market Act and the SFSA Regulations only apply to companies whose shares are listed on a regulated market (for Swedish purposes this means the Main Market or NGM Equity list). Accordingly, they do not apply to companies whose securities are listed on First North, Nordic MTF Stockholm or AktieTorget.

take place, the handling of information in crises and the dealing with the stock market's demands for information.[70]

20.3.2.2 Identifying price-sensitive information

Since the obligation to disclose extends only to *price-sensitive* information, the key to satisfying this obligation is for listed companies to be able to properly identify such information as and when it arises.

20.94

Price-sensitive information means, for the purposes of the Rulebook for Issuers, information which is reasonably expected to affect the price of the company's securities. The Market Act states that an issuer must disclose such information regarding its operations and securities which is of significance for the assessment of the price of the securities. The SFSA Regulations and the NGM Listing Agreement supplement this obligation by requiring companies to make a disclosure promptly if a decision is made or if an event occurs that, in light of previously disclosed information or otherwise, to a non-negligible extent influences the market's perception of the issuer (or, if the issuer is a parent company, the issuer's group).[71]

20.95

The company's determination of what constitutes price-sensitive information must be based on the facts and circumstances in each case. If in doubt, the company may contact the exchange for advice. In determining whether a price movement is reasonably expected to occur, the Rulebook for Issuers guidance on the factors that should be considered:

20.96

- the expected extent or importance of the decision, fact or circumstance compared to the company's activities as whole;
- the relevance of the information as regards the main determinants of the price of the company's securities; and
- all other market variables that may affect the price of the securities.

Additional factors that might be relevant include:

20.97

- if the company has received the information from an external party, the reliability of the source; and
- whether similar information in the past had a price-sensitive effect or if the company itself has previously treated similar circumstances as price sensitive.

---

[70] The guidance text to section 2.4.6 of the Rulebook for Issuers. See also NASDAQ OMX advice 'Contact with analysts and information leaks', revised version 2008, section 7.

[71] Rulebook for Issuers section 3.1.1; Market Act chapter 15 section 6, first paragraph, item 3; SFSA Regulations chapter 10 section 3; and NGM Listing Agreement exhibit 2, section 28, respectively.

20.98 The obligation to disclose information arises where it is *reasonably expected* that the price of the securities will be affected and it is therefore not required that actual changes in the price of the securities occur. As the effect on the price of the securities is likely to vary depending on the company and its particular circumstances, the assessment should be made on a case-by-case basis, taking into account, among other things, trends in that particular company's share price, the relevant industry in question, and the actual market circumstances.

20.99 The obligation to disclose information may, for example, exist in the following situations:

- orders or investment decisions;
- cooperation agreements or other agreements of major importance;
- price or exchange rate changes;
- credit or customer losses;
- new joint ventures;
- research results;
- commencement or settlement of, or decisions rendered in, legal disputes;
- financial difficulties;
- decisions taken by authorities;
- shareholder agreements known to the company which pertain to the use of voting rights or transferability of the shares;
- market rumours;
- market making agreements; and
- information regarding subsidiaries and affiliated companies.[72]

20.3.2.3 Disclosure of price-sensitive information

20.100 **20.3.2.3.1 Timing and means of disclosure**   Once an issuer has concluded that it is in possession of price-sensitive information pertinent to itself, it must, as a general rule, disclose the information as soon as possible, unless the disclosure of price-sensitive information can be delayed in accordance with the Market Act (see Section 20.3.2.3.4 below).[73]

20.101 Disclosure must be made in a manner that ensures that the information is effectively disseminated to the public in Sweden and in other states within the EEA simultaneously and on a non-discriminatory basis. Information to be disclosed must also be submitted simultaneously to the exchange for monitoring purposes.[74]

---

[72] Guidance text to section 3.1.1 of the Rulebook for Issuers.
[73] Rulebook for Issuers section 3.1.3.
[74] Market Act chapter 17 section 2; SFSA Regulations chapter 10 section 10; and Rulebook for Issuers section 3.1.5.

20.3.2.3.2 Contents of disclosure The most important information in an **20.102**
announcement must be clearly presented at the beginning of the announcement
and the announcement's heading should clearly indicate the substance of the
information being disclosed. Furthermore, announcements must contain information stating the time and date of disclosure, the company's name, website
address, contact person and phone number.[75]

20.3.2.3.3 Simultaneous publication on website All price-sensitive informa- **20.103**
tion disclosed in accordance with the rules imposed on listed companies must, as
soon as possible after the information has been disclosed, be uploaded and be
made available to read on the issuer's website for a minimum of three years from
the date of disclosure. Financial reports must be available for a minimum of
five years from the date of disclosure.[76]

20.3.2.3.4 Delaying disclosure As described above, issuers in possession of **20.104**
price-sensitive information should as a general rule disclose the information as
soon as possible. Delaying disclosure is only permitted where special circumstances apply. Pursuant to the Market Act, an issuer may defer publication of
price-sensitive information where:

- it has legitimate reasons to delay disclosure;
- there is no risk that the public will be misled; and
- the issuer can ensure the confidentiality of the information (any recipient must
  be bound by professional secrecy pursuant to law or agreement).[77]

As to when *legitimate reasons* exist and the company may defer disclosure, examples **20.105**
include the following:

- negotiations are in progress and the outcome of the negotiation is likely to
  be affected by public disclosure: for example, if the issuer's financial viability
  is in grave and imminent danger, public disclosure of the negotiations
  (which would be likely to constitute *price-sensitive* information) could jeopardize shareholders' interests by undermining the negotiations and, thereby,
  jeopardizing the company's chances of financial recovery. Arguably, however,
  this provision does not allow an issuer to delay public disclosure of its financial
  difficulty but only of the substance of the negotiations in place to deal with such
  a situation; or

---

[75] Rulebook for Issuers section 3.1.5. SFSA Regulations chapter 10 section 11 stipulates that the
announcement must also include a clarification that the information is of the sort that must be made
public by the issuer (pursuant to the Market Act).
[76] Rulebook for Issuers section 3.1.6. See also SFSA Regulations chapter 10 section 12.
[77] Market Act chapter 15 section 7.

- a decision has been taken by the management which needs the approval of another body of the issuer in order to become effective and where public disclosure of the information before such approval would jeopardize the correct assessment of information by the public.

20.106 The requirement that there must be *no risk that the public will be misled* means that the scope to defer disclosure of information is very limited. For example where the company is in financial difficulties, particularly if its financial situation is not known to the market, it would be difficult to argue that delaying disclosure of the company's financial situation would not mislead investors.[78]

20.107 To ensure that information is not leaked, the issuer must:

- deny persons access to information they do not need;
- ensure that all persons who have access to price-sensitive information understand the attendant legal obligations and are aware of the sanctions associated with abuse and improper dissemination of the information; and
- immediately disclose such information in the event the issuer has not been able to guarantee that the involved information is kept confidential.

20.108 If an issuer defers disclosure in accordance with the Market Act, the issuer must immediately notify the exchange.[79]

20.109 20.3.2.3.5 **Selective disclosure of inside information**   In certain situations, unpublished information may be disclosed to persons who take an active role in a decision process or are involved in the information process, as a part of their professional role. For example, the company may selectively disclose information to:

- major shareholders or contemplated shareholders in conjunction with an analysis prior to a planned new share issue;
- advisers retained by the company, for example, to work on a prospectus prior to a planned share issue or other major transaction;
- contemplated bidders or target companies in conjunction with negotiations regarding takeover offers;
- rating institutions prior to credit ratings; or
- lenders prior to significant credit decisions.

20.110 The company must have a strong and legitimate reason to be permitted to release price-sensitive information selectively—the exceptions to the general disclosure obligation to disclose inside information to the market as soon as possible must be used very restrictively and subject to the continuous consideration of whether

---

[78] Government's Bill 2004/05:142 page 173.
[79] SFSA Regulations chapter 10 section 4.

the information requested is actually required for the intended purpose. Where information has been selectively disclosed, it should normally be possible to announce the information to the market at a later stage in order to neutralize the 'insider position' held by those persons receiving the information.

When making a selective disclosure, the company must make it clear to the recipient of the information that he or she must treat the information confidentially. Furthermore, the recipient must be informed that he or she has become an 'insider' by virtue of the receipt of the information and, consequently, is prohibited by law from exploiting the information for his or her own or another's profit. According to the rules in the Notification Act, the company must carefully maintain records of any selective disclosures, including the names of the recipients, the date of the disclosure and the substance of the information disclosed.[80]

20.111

Analysts and journalists: While it is important that analysts are able to obtain information from the company that supplements published information, and thereby obtain a better understanding of the company's operations, companies must take care to ensure that they do not disclose price-sensitive information selectively (which would be likely to constitute a breach of the exchange's rules and would also risk placing the analyst in a difficult situation in which he or she risks becoming liable for a violation of the Market Abuse Act[81]).

20.112

NASDAQ OMX Stockholm has issued guidelines regarding how to deal with contacts with analysts and information leaks (the 'Analyst and Information Leak Guide'). Although the Analyst and Information Leak Guide is not part of the exchange's rules, companies are nonetheless strongly recommended to follow the advice set out therein.

20.113

According to the Analyst and Information Leak Guide, companies are permitted to provide analysts with the following types of information:

20.114

- in-depth information regarding previously published information;
- reminders in respect of previously submitted information;
- correction of misunderstandings, calculation errors, and obvious misconceptions; and
- provision of industry statistics.

---

[80] The guidance text to section 3.1.1 of the Rulebook for Issuers. Regarding the obligation to maintain records in respect of recipients of the information, see Section 20.3.2.3.7. below.

[81] In short, the Market Abuse Act prohibits anyone who has received inside information from engaging in share transactions or advising anyone to engage in share transactions. See Section 20.3.11 below.

20.115   Further, the Analyst and Information Leak Guide provides that the company should keep the following considerations in mind when dealing with analysts and the media:

- where an analyst obtains certain information, the company cannot withhold the same information from another analyst or journalist;
- the company must not give analysts and journalists advance notice of upcoming news;
- there is no such thing as 'off the record';
- in order to decrease the risk that suspicion is cast on conferences with analysts, companies should consider inviting the media to such conferences;
- analysts must be treated properly and have access to the same information whether they represent a small or major owner, or firm of analysts; and
- when companies distribute analytical reports it can be interpreted that the company sanctions the content of the report, which could amount to a selective release of information. Accordingly, it is preferable to only make references to the relevant analyst firms, for example in the company's annual report and on the company's website, so that investors can obtain the analytical reports directly from the relevant analyst firms.[82]

20.116   **20.3.2.3.6 Handling of market rumours and information leaks**   The Analyst and Information Leak Guide includes the following guidelines on how a company should react to rumours and information leaks:

- the company should never lie;
- the company must follow the exchange rules regarding information leaks in the Rulebook for Issuers,[83] which state that a company must immediately publish price-sensitive information that has leaked prior to a planned publication;
- if the company applies a 'no comment' policy to rumours, it should be applied consistently: it is inappropriate, for example, to say in some cases that the information is untrue and in others 'no comment', as the latter response is then interpreted as a confirmation;
- it is inappropriate to maintain a 'no comment' position in all situations; where the rumour undermines the stock market's confidence in the company's provision of information or significantly affects the price of its securities, the company should provide a clarificatory press release; and
- where there is a risk of an information leak the company should be prepared to provide information, for example, by preparing a draft press release in

---

[82] NASDAQ OMX advice 'Contact with analysts and information leaks', revised version 2008, section 3.
[83] Rulebook for Issuers section 3.1.4.

conjunction with important decisions (in case information is leaked before the intended time for disclosure).[84]

20.3.2.3.7 Insider lists   Under the Notification Act, a Swedish company that **20.117** has its shares listed on a regulated market, or that has submitted an application for such listing, must continuously maintain a list of persons working for them (under a contract of employment or otherwise) who have access to inside information relating to the company, a so-called logbook. The logbook should state the following:

- reasons why the person is included in the logbook;
- the date when the person gained access to the relevant information; and
- when the list was last updated (it must be updated as soon as conditions change).

The logbook must be provided to the SFSA upon their request. Persons responsi- **20.118** ble for drawing up the logbook must ensure that all persons named therein are made aware (in writing) of their duties and the sanctions for non-compliance. The logbook should be updated and retained for at least five years from the date when it was created or last updated.

For the purposes of maintaining a logbook, a company should not differentiate **20.119** between persons working for the company and persons outside of the company: every person that receives the specific information should be included in the log-book. The managing director is usually responsible for maintaining the logbook, although he or she may delegate and appoint a trusted person, for example, the managing director's secretary, the company's in-house lawyer, or chief financial officer, as responsible in practice for maintaining the logbook.

Sometimes it may be practical for external advisers to maintain a separate 'shadow **20.120** logbook' of the persons in the organization who have been informed of the trans-action. In such cases, the company's logbook should include a note of the date on which the adviser was informed of the plans regarding the price-sensitive event and appointed as adviser, and that the adviser is maintaining his or her own logbook of the persons that he or she informs.[85]

If an issuer breaches its obligations to (i) continuously maintain a logbook; **20.121** (ii) ensure that all persons named in the logbook are made aware (in writing) of their duties and the sanctions for non-compliance; or (iii) submit the logbook to

---

[84] NASDAQ OMX advice 'Contact with analysts and information leaks', revised version 2008, section 6.

[85] Notification Act section 10a and the NASDAQ OMX advice 'Logbook', revised version 2008. Further, note that special rules apply to employees and contractors of securities companies and stock exchanges. Notification Act sections 12–14.

the SFSA upon its request, the SFSA may impose a fine of between SEK 15,000 and SEK 1,000,000.[86]

20.3.3 Certain other disclosure requirements

20.122 In addition to disclosure of price-sensitive information, the Rulebook for Issuers requires that the listed company make disclosures in relation to certain other corporate actions including:[87]

- financial reports;[88]
- forecasts and forward-looking statements;
- unexpected and significant deviation in financial result or financial position;
- general meetings of shareholders (notices to attend general meetings of shareholders and resolutions adopted by the general meeting of shareholders must be disclosed);[89]
- issues of securities;[90]
- changes in board of directors, management and auditors;
- share-based incentive programmes;
- closely-related party transactions (notable is that special rules apply for such transactions);[91]
- business acquisitions and divestitures;
- change in identity;
- decisions regarding listing; and
- information required by another trading venue.

20.123 The company is also required to publish a company calendar, listing the dates on which it expects to disclose financial statement releases, interim reports, and the date of its annual general meeting.[92]

---

[86] Notification Act section 21.

[87] Rulebook for Issuers sections 3.2 and 3.3. Similar provisions are set out in NGM Listing Agreement exhibit 2 sections 11–26.

[88] Notable in this respect is also chapter 10, section 3a of the SFSA Regulations: as soon as the board has approved the annual financial statements, the issuer must promptly publish a press release containing the financial results (the essential information of the coming annual report). If the annual accounts are subsequently altered such that they differ significantly from what was presented in the press release, the issuer must promptly publish amendments.

[89] SFSA Regulations chapter 10 section 5 states that an issuer shall disclose announcements about how dividends shall be distributed and paid.

[90] SFSA Regulations chapter 10 section 5 provides that when a decision is taken to issue transferable securities, it must immediately be disclosed and the exchange must be notified of the decision, the reason for the issue, the issue terms and to whom the issue is directed.

[91] Rulebook for Issuers section 4.1.

[92] Rulebook for Issuers section 3.3.12.

The Rulebook for Issuers states that in certain cases, companies must provide information to the exchange only. These include the following cases: **20.124**

- *takeover offers*: the company must notify the exchange if it has (i) made preparations to make a takeover offer for securities in another listed company (when there are reasonable grounds to assume that the preparations will result in a takeover offer); or (ii) been informed that a third party intends to make a takeover offer to the shareholders of the company, and such takeover offer has not been disclosed (when there are reasonable grounds to assume that the intention to make a takeover offer will be realized);[93] and
- *advance information*: if the company intends to disclose information that it expects to have a highly significant effect on the price of the securities, it must notify the exchange prior to disclosure.[94]

The Rulebook for Issuers contains special provisions regarding the purchase and sale of a company's own shares. It provides, *inter alia*, that the company must disclose as soon as possible (i) any resolution passed at a general shareholder meeting to purchase or sell its own shares; (ii) any resolution taken by the board of directors to exercise an authorization to purchase or sell the company's own shares; and (iii) any acquisitions or disposals in its own securities (which must be reported to the exchange not later than 30 minutes before the exchange opens on the trading day immediately following the acquisition or disposal).[95] **20.125**

20.3.4 Disclosure of transactions by PDMRs

Under the Notification Act, certain categories of persons are considered to have regular access to inside information relating to listed companies, and as such, are required to notify their holdings and affiliated persons' holdings, as well as changes to these holdings, to the SFSA. The Notification Act applies to information relating to the following categories of companies: **20.126**

- Swedish companies listed on a Swedish regulated market;
- Swedish companies listed on a regulated market within the EEA; and
- non-Swedish companies domiciled outside the EEA and listed on a Swedish regulated market.

The objective of the rules is to prevent abuse of inside information and to provide the market with information about relevant persons' securities transactions. For this purpose, the SFSA's register is public and accessible via the SFSA's website. **20.127**

---

[93] The obligation to notify the exchange in relation to takeover offers is also set out in SFSA Regulations chapter 10 sections 8 and 9 and NGM Listing Agreement exhibit 2 section 30.
[94] Rulebook for Issuers section 3.4. A corresponding obligation to notify the exchange is set out in the introduction to exhibit 2 of the NGM Listing Agreement.
[95] Rulebook for Issuers section 4.2. See also NGM Listing Agreement exhibit 2 sections 32–37.

20.128   The Notification Act applies to a number of categories of persons, such as board members, the managing director and the auditors of the listed company or a parent company of the listed company. It also applies to individuals who own, alone or together with an affiliated person, at least 10% of the issued share capital or the votes of the listed company.

20.129   Persons caught by the Notification Act must also notify the holdings and changes to the holdings of 'affiliated persons', including, *inter alia*, companies in which the relevant person (and/or his connected persons) own at least 10% of the issued share capital or voting rights and over which the person caught by the Notification Act has a significant influence.

20.130   The Notification Act applies to shares issued by the listed company. It also applies to other securities related to shares issued by the company, including subscription rights, warrants, convertible debt instruments, profit-sharing instruments, options forwards and futures.

20.131   Persons caught by the Notification Act must notify their holdings to the SFSA within five business days of the date on which the relevant position arose. Such persons must also notify any changes to their holdings within five business days of the transaction date.

20.132   Certain transactions are exempted from the notification requirement. These include changes to holdings that arise as a result of bonus issues and the division or consolidation of shares and changes resulting from the acquisition of subscription rights on a pre-emptive basis in a rights issue.

20.133   There is also an obligation on the listed company itself (and any parent company of the listed company) to notify the SFSA of the persons it considers to have regular access to inside information relating to the company. Such notification must be made within 14 days of the date on which the relevant position arose or changed.[96]

20.134   The SFSA may impose a fine (and, indeed, in several cases has done so) on anyone who does not comply with the notification obligations, the amount of which will be in the range of SEK 15,000 to SEK 350,000.[97]

20.3.5 Ban on transactions prior to the publishing of regular interim reports

20.135   Any board member, alternate board member, managing director, deputy managing director, auditor or deputy auditor in a listed company or its parent company, as well as related parties of these persons, is not permitted to trade in shares in the

---

[96] Notification Act sections 1–9.
[97] Notification Act section 21.

company 30 days prior to the publishing of regular interim reports (including the date of the announcement of the report) (the '30 Day Transaction Ban'). The same prohibition applies to any transactions conducted by a listed company in its own shares. The ban covers acquisitions both on and outside the securities market.

There are a number of exemptions from this prohibition, including the following: **20.136**

- disposals of shares in accordance with a takeover offer to purchase shares; and
- disposals of allocated issue rights, redemption rights, conversion rights and similar rights.

In exceptional circumstances, the SFSA may grant further exemptions to the prohibition.[98] **20.137**

Furthermore, in a particular case, the SFSA stated that the prohibition does not apply in respect of subscriptions to shares (i) in a rights issue or (ii) pursuant to an underwriting agreement, because it does not consider such subscriptions to constitute *trading in shares*. **20.138**

The SFSA may impose a fine on anyone who contravenes the 30 Day Transaction Ban of up to 10% of the price of the shares traded and in any event not less than SEK 15,000 and not more than SEK 350,000.[99] **20.139**

20.3.6 Periodic financial reporting and annual information update

20.3.6.1 *Applicable provisions and extent of applicability*

The Market Act imposes an obligation on listed companies to publish annual financial reports, half-yearly reports and interim management statements or quarterly reports. The scope of these obligations is limited to issuers whose transferable securities are admitted to trading on a regulated market and whose home state is Sweden. **20.140**

The following categories of issuers of securities and instruments are exempt from the periodic financial reporting requirement: **20.141**

- states, county councils or municipalities or comparable regional or local authorities in a state, international organizations of which one or several states in the EEA are members, the European Central Bank and central banks in a state within the EEA; and
- units in investment funds or certain UCIT management companies, money market instruments with a term to maturity of less than one year and bonds or other transferable debt instruments each with a nominal value equivalent to not

---

[98] Notification Act sections 15 and 16.
[99] Notification Act sections 20 and 21.

less than EUR 50,000 (and which are not convertible to shares or instruments comparable to shares).[100]

20.142　If a listed company fails to publish or publishes incomplete periodic financial information, the SFSA may order the company to make a correction and may impose a fine of between SEK 50,000 and SEK 10,000,000. If the listed company has not prepared financial periodic information in accordance with applicable provisions, the SFSA may issue a public reprimand, followed by a fine of between SEK 50,000 and SEK 10,000,000.[101]

20.3.6.2 *Annual reporting and group accounts*

20.143　Issuers must, as soon as possible and not later than four months after the close of each financial year, publish an annual report and, where applicable, group accounts. Annual reports and group accounts must be reviewed by the issuer's auditor and published alongside the auditor's statement.[102]

20.3.6.3 *Semi-annual financial reports*

20.144　Issuers of shares, bonds or transferable securities (which are not convertible to shares or instruments comparable to shares) must publish an interim report for the first six months of the financial year as soon as possible and not later than two months after the end of the reporting period.[103]

20.3.6.4 *Interim management statements or quarterly reports*

20.145　Issuers of shares must publish interim management reports during the first and second halves of the financial year. Reports must be published not earlier than ten weeks after the beginning, and not later than six weeks before the end, of the half year period.

20.146　An interim management statement must contain:

- information on the period between the beginning of the half-year and the day of the report's publication;
- information on material events and transactions that have taken place during the period; and
- a general description of the financial position and performance of the issuer and its subsidiaries during the period.[104]

100　Market Act chapter 16 sections 1–3.
101　Market Act chapter 25 sections 18–23.
102　Market Act chapter 16 section 4.
103　Market Act chapter 16 section 5.
104　Market Act chapter 16 section 6.

An interim management statement is not necessary where the issuer instead **20.147** publishes an interim report for the period from the beginning of the half-year and three months forward (quarterly report). The quarterly report must be published as soon as possible but not later than two months after the end of the reporting period.[105] In practice, companies invariably publish a quarterly report.

20.3.6.5 *Annual information update*

An issuer whose transferable securities have been admitted for trading on a regu- **20.148** lated market and whose home member state is Sweden must annually compile a document containing or referring to all information published by the issuer during the most recent twelve months pursuant to the continuing obligations regime. It must submit the document to the SFSA and make it available on its website no later than 20 business days following the publication of its annual financial statements.[106]

20.3.7 Major shareholding notifications

20.3.7.1 *Applicable provisions, extent of applicability and notification thresholds*

The Trading Act[107] imposes obligations on shareholders to make notifications **20.149** regarding changes in their holdings of shares and voting rights in the issuer beyond specified percentage thresholds. Under the Trading Act, a person or a company who, in terms of votes or shares, attains, exceeds or falls below 5%, 10%, 15%, 20%, 25%, 30%, 50%, 66.66% or 90% of all the votes or shares in a Swedish listed company (or a non-Swedish listed company with Sweden as its home member state) is required to notify the SFSA and the relevant issuer. Notification of ownership is based on voting rights and aggregated share capital (the two tests run separately).[108]

---

[105] Market Act chapter 16 section 7.

[106] Trading Act chapter 6 section 1b; the SFSA Regulation (2007:7) on issuers' obligations to submit annual information and Prospectus Regulation section 27. Some exemptions apply in relation to issuers of investment fund products, money market instruments, non-equity-related transferable securities (each with a nominal value equivalent to not less than EUR 50,000), as well as where securities have been issued or guaranteed by governmental bodies. Notably, the European Commission has proposed the abolition of the obligation in respect of the annual information update. See Consultation on a draft proposal for a Directive of the European Parliament and of the Council amending Directives 2003/71/EC on the prospectus to be published when securities are offered to the public or admitted to trading and 2004/109/EC on the harmonization of transparency requirements in relation to information about issuers whose securities are admitted to trading on a regulated market, item 9.

[107] Trading Act chapter 4.

[108] Note that treasury shares are included in the denominator of the threshold calculations, whereas warrants and convertible debt instruments that give a right to acquire newly issued shares are excluded.

20.3.7.2 *Notification triggers*

20.150 Notification requirements can be triggered by any acquisition (purchase, disposal, inheritance, gift or other) or transfer of shares where the result is that the holder attains, exceeds or falls below a relevant threshold. The notification obligation can also be triggered by an acquisition, transfer, exercise or expiry of financial instruments that confers a right to acquire shares that are already issued by the company.[109] The notification requirement is not triggered by an acquisition or transfer of a financial instrument that entitles the holder to acquire shares that are not yet issued by the company. It should be noted, however, that the exercise of a financial instrument of this kind, where the rights are exchanged for shares, would trigger the notification obligation if any of the relevant thresholds were attained or exceeded.

20.151 Corporate actions by the relevant issuer may also trigger a notification obligation if, as a result of the corporate action, the holding of shares attains, exceeds or falls below any of the relevant thresholds. Similarly, the borrowing of a financial instrument would generally trigger a notification obligation if any of the relevant thresholds were attained, exceeded or fallen below.

20.152 Issuers are under an obligation to announce changes in the total number of shares and/or voting rights on the last trading day in the calendar month during which the relevant change occurred. The notification of the change in shareholding must be made on the trading day following the relevant issuer's announcement of the change in the total number of shares and/or voting rights.

20.3.7.3 *Aggregation of holdings*

20.153 As a consequence of the aggregation rules described below, there are a number of situations where the access to, or transfer of, a right to vote will trigger the notification requirement even though the ownership of the shares has not changed.

---

[109] The requirement also catches holdings of depositary receipts that entitle the holder to vote for the underlying shares. The Market Act provides for a list of financial instruments, such as warrants, swaps, forwards, futures or options. This list, however, is not exhaustive. In general, any instrument that carries a right to acquire shares that are already issued by the company could trigger a notification obligation. Derivatives that only carry a right to cash settlement would not give rise to a notification obligation, as opposed to derivatives that entitle the holder to choose between a delivery of shares or cash. A notification obligation is triggered where the holding attains, exceeds or falls below 5%, 10%, etc. of the total number of shares or voting rights. The disclosure rules do not treat holdings of shares separately from holdings of other qualifying financial instruments. As a result, holdings of shares and other qualifying financial instruments are aggregated for the purposes of determining whether a person has a notification obligation in accordance with the relevant thresholds.

Aggregation of holdings of shares or votes is required where shares are held by a **20.154** subsidiary, in which case aggregation of the relevant holdings would be required for the purposes of determining the parent company's (but not the subsidiary's) notification obligation. However, it should be noted that the subsidiary will be subject to a separate notification obligation if the subsidiary's holding attains, exceeds or falls below any of the relevant thresholds, disregarding the parent company's holding.

A company is considered to be a parent company if it:[110] **20.155**

- holds more than 50% of the voting rights of all shares or interests in the relevant company;
- owns shares or interests in the company and, as a consequence of an agreement with other owners of such company, controls more than 50% of the voting rights of all shares or interests in the company;
- owns shares or interests in the company and is entitled to appoint or remove more than one-half of the members of the company's board of directors or equivalent management body; or
- owns shares or interests in the company and is entitled to exercise a sole controlling influence thereover as a consequence of an agreement with the legal person or as a consequence of provisions of the company's articles of association or comparable statutes.

The Swedish shareholding disclosure regime also provides for a number of other **20.156** situations where aggregation of shareholdings is required, including where:

- shareholders have entered into an agreement that obliges them to adopt, by the concerted exercise of the voting rights that they hold, a lasting common policy towards the management of the relevant issuer;
- shares are subject to a proxy where the proxy-holder can exercise the voting rights attaching to shares at his or her own discretion;
- shares are lodged as collateral, where the collateral-taker controls the voting rights attaching to the shares and declares his or her intention of exercising them; and
- shares are held under an agreement providing for the temporary transfer for consideration of the voting rights in question.

Any party whose holding of shares or votes attains, exceeds or falls below a relevant **20.157** threshold, either directly or as a consequence of the aggregation rules, is required to make a notification.

---

[110] Swedish Companies Act chapter 1 section 2, first paragraph.

20.3.7.4 Notification procedure

20.158 The notification is to be made by the shareholder to the SFSA and the relevant issuer and must reach both such recipients no later than on the trading day after the day on which the triggering event occurred. The SFSA will announce the information in the notification no later than at noon on the trading day following the trading day on which the notification was filed with the SFSA.

20.159 A subsidiary is not required to make a separate notification where the notification is made by the parent company. Joint notification is permitted where several parties become obliged to make a notification as a consequence of the same event.

20.160 The SFSA may impose a fine of between SEK 15,000 and SEK 5,000,000 for failure to comply with the notification obligations. The SFSA has in several cases imposed such fines. The SFSA may also order a party in default to make a notification.

20.161 Where the information regarding the change in a shareholding is likely to affect the share price, the issuer should consider whether it needs to make an announcement to the market immediately (i.e. before the SFSA announces the information).

20.3.8 Penalties

20.162 Penalties that may be imposed on listed companies that fail to comply with certain notification obligations have been addressed above, see Sections 20.3.2.3.7, 20.3.4, 20.3.5, 20.3.6.1 and 20.3.7.4 above.

20.163 In addition, the Rulebook for Issuers provides for sanctions, stipulating that in the event of a failure by the issuer to comply with law, other regulations, its agreement with the exchange, or generally acceptable behaviour in the securities market, the exchange may, in cases of serious violations, delist the company's securities or, in other cases, impose on the company a fine of up to 15 times the annual fee paid by the company to the exchange. Where the non-compliance is of a less serious nature or is excusable, the exchange may issue a warning to the company in lieu of a fine.[111]

---

[111] Rulebook for Issuers section 5. Similar sections are available pursuant to NGM Listing Agreement section 6.2.

20.3.9 The Swedish Code of Corporate Governance

20.3.9.1 An introduction to the Swedish Code of Corporate Governance

As of 1 July 2008, the Swedish Code of Corporate Governance (the 'Code') applies **20.164**
to all Swedish companies whose shares are listed on a regulated market in Sweden,
i.e. NASDAQ OMX Stockholm or NGM Equity.

The Code deals with the decision-making system through which shareholders **20.165**
directly or indirectly govern the company. The main emphasis is on company
boards in their role as central players in corporate governance. As regards shareholders, the line is drawn at shareholders' meetings: issues such as the interplay
between owners and the rules and workings of the stock market are not covered,
nor are issues regarding companies' relationships with other stakeholders. The Code
forms part of corporate Sweden's self-regulation. Additional corporate governance
rules are set out in the Swedish Companies Act (the 'Companies Act'),[112] stock
exchange listing requirements and statements issued by the Council.[113]

The Code is based on the 'comply or explain' principle, which means that a com- **20.166**
pany has the opportunity to deviate from a certain rule in the Code, if this
deviation in the specific case leads to better corporate governance. A company that
has deviated from the Code must, in its corporate governance report, describe
the deviation, the alternative action that the company has taken and the reason
for this action.

Under the Rulebook for Issuers and the NGM Listing Agreement, listed compa- **20.167**
nies must comply with generally acceptable practices on the Swedish securities
market. As generally accepted practices may be reflected in the Code, a listed
company that does not comply with the Code (and does not appropriately explain
its deviation), may be subject to sanctions by the exchange.

20.3.9.2 Shareholders' meetings

Section III.1 of the Code sets out corporate governance rules relating to share- **20.168**
holders' meetings, the underlying principle of which is that the planning and
running of the shareholders' meeting must create conditions in which shareholders
can exercise their ownership role in an active, well-informed manner.[114]

To this end, the Code lays down provisions relating to the following issues: **20.169**

• procedure relating to the publication of the time and venue of scheduled shareholders' meetings on the company's website;

---

[112] Sw: Aktiebolagslagen (2005:551).
[113] The Code section I.5.
[114] The Code section III.1, the introductory text.

- procedure relating to the availability of documents relevant to shareholders' meetings (including notices for meetings);
- attendance at meetings by the company chair, a quorum of the board and the chief executive officer; attendance at annual general meetings by least one member of the nomination committee, at least one of the company's auditors and, if possible, each member of the board;
- the nomination committee's obligation to propose a chair for the annual general meeting;
- the requirement to conduct meetings in Swedish and to ensure that material presented at such meetings is available in Swedish (translation may be necessary due to the ownership structure);
- the appointment of a person to verify the minutes of meetings; and
- the availability of the minutes of the latest annual general meeting and any subsequent extraordinary shareholders' meetings on the company's website (translation may be necessary due to the ownership structure).

20.3.9.3 *Appointment and remuneration of the board and auditors*

20.170 Section III.2 of the Code sets out rules relating to the appointment and remuneration of the board and auditors. The rules seek to provide conditions for well-informed decisions by the shareholders' meeting on these issues.[115] The relevant provisions relate to the following issues:

- the appointment of a nomination committee by the shareholders' meeting and the composition thereof;[116]
- the nomination committee's tasks, which include proposing candidates for the board of directors (including for the post of chair); dealing with fees and other forms of director remuneration; and making proposals on the election and remuneration of the company auditor;
- the announcement of the names of the nomination committee on the company's website;
- the inclusion of the nomination committee's proposals in the notice of the shareholders' meeting and on the company's website; and

---

[115] The Code section III.2, the introductory text.
[116] The nomination committee must consist of at least three members, one of whom is to be appointed committee chair. The majority of the members of the nomination committee are to be independent of the company and its executive management. Neither the chief executive officer nor other members of the executive management are to be members of the nomination committee. At least one member of the nomination committee is to be independent of the company's largest shareholder in terms of votes or any group of shareholders that act in concert in the governance of the company. Members of the board of directors may be members of the nomination committee but may not constitute a majority thereof. The chair of the company may not chair the nomination committee. If more than one member of the board is on the nomination committee, no more than one of these may be independent of a major shareholder in the company.

- the nomination committee's obligation to give an account of how it has conducted its work and to explain its proposals at a shareholders' meeting at which the election of board members or auditors will take place.

20.3.9.4 *The tasks of the board*

The Code provides in Section III.3 that the principle tasks of the board of directors include:　　**20.171**

- establishing the overall operational goals and strategy of the company;
- appointing, evaluating and, if necessary, dismissing the managing director;
- ensuring that there is an effective system for follow-up and control of the company's operations;
- ensuring that there is a satisfactory process for monitoring the company's compliance with laws and other regulations relevant to the company's operations;
- defining necessary guidelines to govern the company's ethical conduct; and
- ensuring that the company's external communications are characterized by openness, and that they are accurate, reliable and relevant.

The Code further states that the board is to approve any significant assignments undertaken by the chief executive officer outside the company.　　**20.172**

20.3.9.5 *The size and composition of the board*

Section III.4 of the Code is designed to ensure that the composition of the board shall be such as to enable it to manage the company's affairs efficiently and with integrity.[117] To that end, it prescribes the following:　　**20.173**

- the composition of the board must be suitable in light of the company's operations, its phase of development and other relevant circumstances; the board should exhibit diversity (including in terms of gender) and a breadth of qualifications, experience and background;
- deputies for directors elected by the shareholders' meeting are not to be appointed;
- no more than one member of the board may be a member of the executive management of the company or a subsidiary;
- the majority of the directors elected by the shareholders' meeting must be independent of the company and its executive management, and at least two of those directors must also be independent of the company's major shareholders; and
- members of the board should be appointed for a period that does not extend beyond the date of the next annual general meeting.

---

[117] The Code section III.4, the introductory text.

20.3.9.6 *The task of directors*

20.174   Section III.5 of the Code states that:

- each director is to form an independent opinion on each matter considered by the board and to request whatever information he or she believes necessary for the board to make well-founded decisions; and
- each director is obliged to acquire the knowledge of the company's operations, organization, markets etc. required for the assignment.

20.3.9.7 *The chair of the board*

20.175   Section III.6 of the Code addresses the particular responsibilities of the chair of the board. It prescribes the following:

- the chair of the board is to be elected by the shareholders' meeting;
- if the chair of the board is an employee of the company or has duties assigned by the company in addition to his or her responsibilities as chair, the division of work and responsibilities between the chair and the chief executive officer should be clearly stated in the formal work plan of the board and in its instructions to the chief executive officer; and
- the chair is to ensure that the work of the board is conducted efficiently and that the board fulfils its obligations.

20.3.9.8 *Board procedures*

20.176   Section III.7 deals with board procedures, including the following matters:

- the board is to review on an annual basis the relevance and suitability of its formal work plan, instructions to the chief executive officer and reporting instructions;
- if the board establishes special committees to prepare its decisions on specific issues, the board's formal work plan should specify the duties and decision-making powers that the board has delegated to such committees and how the committees are to report to the board; and
- the minutes of the board should provide a clear representation of the matters discussed, the material supporting each item and the substance of the decisions taken (the minutes are to be sent to each member of the board as soon as possible following the board meeting).

20.3.9.9 *Evaluation of the board and the chief executive officer*

20.177   The provisions in Section III.8 of the Code relating to the evaluation of the board and the chief executive officer provide that:

- the board of directors is to evaluate its work annually, using a systematic and structured process, with the aim of developing the board's working methods and efficiency; the results of this evaluation should be made available to the nomination committee;

- the board is to continuously evaluate the work of the chief executive officer; and
- the board is to examine this issue formally at least once a year, and no member of the executive management is to be present during this formal evaluation process.

20.3.9.10 *Executive management remuneration*[118]

Section III.9 of the Code lays down provisions relating to executive management remuneration, including the following:

20.178

- the board should establish a remuneration committee with the task of preparing proposals on remuneration and other terms of employment for the executive management;
- the shareholders' meeting should decide on all share- and share price-related incentive schemes for the executive management; members of the board should not participate in such schemes unless they are specifically designed for the board and have been approved by the shareholders' meeting;
- the content of the decision of the shareholders' meeting and all documentation relating to incentive schemes should be made available to shareholders in good time before the relevant shareholders' meeting; and
- certain requirements relating to the composition of the remuneration committee.[119]

20.3.9.11 *The audit committee, financial reporting and internal controls*

Section III.10 of the Code contains rules regarding the audit committee, financial reporting and internal controls. It includes provisions relating to the following:

20.179

- the requirement for the board to establish an audit committee;[120]
- the composition of the audit committee;
- the tasks of the audit committee;

---

[118] Companies Act chapter 7 section 61 provides that in a company whose shares are admitted to trading on a regulated market, the annual general meeting must adopt guidelines for remuneration of the senior management.

[119] The chair of the board may chair the remuneration committee. The other members of the committee are to be independent of the company and its executive management. If the board feels it is appropriate, the entire board may perform the remuneration committee's tasks, on condition that no director who is also a member of the executive management participates in this work.

[120] Companies Act chapter 8 section 49a provides that a company whose shares are admitted to trading on a regulated market must have an audit committee with a certain composition and experience, unless a shareholders' meeting resolves otherwise. Whilst the provision was effective as of 1 July 2009, concerned companies need to comply with these requirements only after the first annual general meeting held after 1 July 2009.

- the requirement that at least once a year, the board should meet the company's auditor without the chief executive officer or any other member of the executive management present;
- the requirement that the board should ensure that the company's six- or nine-month report is reviewed by the auditor;
- the requirement that the board should submit an annual report on the key aspects of the company's systems for internal controls and risk management regarding financial reports; and
- the requirement that, in relation to companies that do not have a separate internal audit function, the board is to evaluate on an annual basis the need for such a function and to justify its decision in its report on internal controls.

20.3.9.12 Information on corporate governance

20.180   The last section of the Code, Section III.11, contains provisions relating to the procedure the board should follow when making notifications to the company's shareholders and the market relating to corporate governance. The provisions include the following:

- the requirement that the company should produce a corporate governance report in conjunction with its annual accounts;
- requirements relating to the contents of the corporate governance report, including, *inter alia*, that the report should state clearly which rules of the Code the company has not complied with, together with a description of the alternative action taken and an explanation of the reasons for such action; and
- the requirement that a section of the company's website must be devoted to corporate governance matters (where the company's most recent corporate governance report, its current articles of association, information relating to its board, chief executive officer and auditors, information relating to any share incentive schemes and any other information required by the Code should be made available).

20.3.10 Takeover regulation

20.3.10.1 General

20.181   The main sources of Swedish takeover regulation are the Takeover Act and the Takeover Rules.[121] The Takeover Act requires a bidder to undertake to the relevant exchange to comply with the rules adopted by the exchange for takeover offers and

---

[121] The Market Act requires an exchange to adopt rules for takeovers. Market Act chapter 13 section 8.

to submit to the sanctions the exchange may impose for breach of such rules.[122] The Takeover Act also contains specific rules concerning, *inter alia*, mandatory offers, frustrating actions, information to trade unions, the supervision of takeover offers and sanctions, as well as the requirement to prepare an offer document.[123] More detailed provisions regarding the content of an offer document are set out in the Trading Act and in the Takeover Rules.

At the time of preparation of this publication, the Takeover Rules were in the process of revision. A proposal for revised Takeover Rules was published on 16 March 2009, which, in summary, proposed the following key changes:[124]

20.182

- more stringent requirements for 'pre announcements';
- new rules for price differences between Class A and Class B shares;
- more stringent rules for the withdrawal of offers;
- restrictions on the right to modify offers that have been launched;
- more stringent requirements for independence when issuing a fairness opinion;
- clearer rules for the role played by the target company board;
- rules for handling conflicts of interest in the target company board; and
- restrictions on the bidder's right to make a new offer.

The proposal for revised Takeover Rules was subsequently adopted and they entered into force on 1 October 2009.

20.183

20.3.10.2 *Market authority*

The SFSA supervises takeover offers and enforces compliance with the Takeover Act. It is also the competent authority for the purpose of vetting, approving and registering offer documents. The SFSA has delegated to the Council[125] certain of its duties referred to in the Takeover Act,[126] giving the Council the authority under statute to rule on, amongst other things, the application and/or exemption from mandatory offer and frustrating action provisions. In addition, NASDAQ OMX Stockholm and NGM have delegated to the Council the right to decide on exemptions from the provisions in the Takeover Rules and how these rules are interpreted.

20.184

---

[122] Takeover Act chapter 2 section 1.

[123] Takeover Act chapter 3, sections 1–4, chapter 5, chapter 4, chapter 7 and chapter 2 section 3; and Trading Act chapter 2a.

[124] Press release, 16 March 2009, by the Swedish Industry and Commerce Stock Exchange Committee (*Sw. Näringslivets Börskommitté*).

[125] See Section 20.1.6.7 above.

[126] Takeover Act chapter 7 section 10.

20.3.10.3 *Stakebuilding*

20.185   If a bidder wishes to build up a stake in the target through on-market or off-market purchases before or during the course of an offer, it must observe certain restrictions and disclosure requirements, as well as monitor the impact that stakebuilding might have on the offer price and the form of consideration offered (see below).

20.186   While the Market Abuse Act does not prevent the bidder from acquiring target shares where the only inside information such bidder has access to relates to its own intention to make an offer, the Takeover Rules provide that if the bidder carries out due diligence on the target and receives non-public price-sensitive information from the target, the bidder must not conduct any on-market or off-market dealings in the target shares until such information has been made public. In practice, this requirement often prevents the bidder from dealing in target shares once it has commenced a due diligence exercise. As a result, the bidder may sometimes seek an undertaking from the target that the target will warn the bidder before it receives any price-sensitive information during the course of a due diligence exercise.

20.187   The acquisition of target shares may trigger an obligation for the bidder to increase the offer price, as well as to offer a cash alternative (see Section 20.3.10.4 below). The bidder should also be aware of considerations relating to mandatory offers (see Section 20.3.10.7 below). The Swedish shareholding disclosure regime set out in the Trading Act must also be complied with in a stakebuilding process.[127] Specific shareholding disclosure obligations also apply during the course of an offer.[128]

20.3.10.4 *Consideration*

20.188   There are generally no restrictions on what sort of consideration may be offered in a Swedish voluntary offer. However, in practice, the consideration in voluntary offers invariably consists of cash, securities, or a combination of the two. A mandatory offer must always be accompanied by a cash alternative (see Section 20.3.10.7 below).

20.189   The bidder must generally offer all holders of shares of the same class identical consideration per share.[129] However, in special circumstances certain shareholders may be offered consideration in another form but with the same value.[130]

---

[127]   See Section 20.3.7 above.
[128]   See Section 20.3.10.8 below.
[129]   Takeover Act Rule II.8.
[130]   For example, where the target company has a very large number of shareholders, there may be practical reasons for offering cash for small blocks of shares, despite other shareholders being offered consideration in some other form. Takeover Rules commentary to Rule II.8.

Where a company has more than one class of shares, the bidder may offer consideration to the two classes of shareholders that differs both in form and value. However, shareholders of each class must always be treated fairly and any premium, calculated as a percentage of the value of the shares, must be the same for all classes of share, unless there are special reasons that justify different premiums.[131] Commercial and market reasons may justify different premiums, for instance where the different classes of share carry different voting rights.[132]

Under the Takeover Rules, the offer price must not be less than the highest price paid by the bidder for target shares during the six months prior to the announcement of the offer or during the course of an offer.[133] If the bidder has acquired more than 10% of all shares in the target for cash within six months prior to the announcement of the offer, the offer must be accompanied by a cash alternative.[134] This requirement also applies where the bidder acquires more than 10% of all shares in the target for cash during the course of an offer.[135] In this case, the terms of an offer would have to be revised to include the cash alternative if they did not already.

20.190

The Takeover Rules provide that a takeover offer must only be made if the bidder has made the preparations necessary to implement the offer and, in particular, only after ensuring that the bidder can meet any cash consideration in full.[136] While there is no requirement for any independent 'cash confirmation', the Takeover Rules provide that the offer must be made conditional (on objective grounds) on receipt by the bidder of any conditional debt financing on which the bidder is relying to pay the offer consideration.[137] The bidder can exclude the financing condition and assume the risk of the financing not becoming available if it has access to other alternative funds.

20.191

20.3.10.5 *Conditions to a takeover offer*

A bidder is not allowed simply to reserve a right to withdraw its offer once made. However, a voluntary takeover offer is usually made subject to the satisfaction of a number of conditions, which satisfaction must be objectively determinable.[138] The bidder is generally allowed to withdraw the offer only where the non-satisfaction

20.192

---

131 Takeover Rules Rule II.9.
132 Takeover Rules commentary to Rule II.9. A number of institutional shareholders have, however, taken the view that holders of different classes of shares with different voting rights should be offered identical consideration and the issue has been subject to a heated debate in Sweden. The issue has been addressed in the proposal for revised Takeover Rules.
133 Takeover Rules Rules II.10 and II.11.
134 Takeover Rules Rule II.10.
135 Takeover Rules Rule II.11.
136 Takeover Rules General Principle (e).
137 Takeover Rules Rule II.4.
138 Takeover Rules Rule II.4.

of a condition is of material importance to its acquisition of the target, and this is required to be stated (alongside the conditions) in both the offer announcement and the offer document.[139]

20.193 There is no requirement for an offer to be conditional on any particular level of acceptances. However, a voluntary offer usually contains a condition that the bidder is entitled to withdraw the offer unless a certain level of acceptances is received. Due to the threshold for squeeze-out rights, it is common practice to make voluntary offers conditional on the bidder becoming the owner of more than 90% of the target shares. The bidder generally reserves the right to waive the acceptance condition, as well as other conditions.

20.194 The exact conditions attached to a voluntary offer will vary depending on the circumstances in each case, but there is a set of conditions that form the basis for most offers. These include: (i) acceptances of the offer amounting to more than a certain percentage of the shares (and possibly also voting rights) in the target company being received by the bidder; (ii) the receipt of all necessary approvals and clearances; (iii) the offer not being rendered partially or wholly impossible or significantly impeded as a result of legislation, regulation, any decision of a court or public authority, or other measures beyond the bidder's control; (iv) no information regarding the target company which has been announced by the target company being materially inaccurate or misleading, and no information which should have been announced by the target having been omitted from public disclosure; (v) any resolutions necessary to implement the offer being passed by the shareholders of the bidder; (vi) the target company not taking any frustrating actions; (vii) the absence of any higher competing offer; and (viii) in some cases, a material adverse change condition. If the bidder is relying on conditional debt financing to pay the consideration in the offer, it would also typically make the offer conditional on receipt of the funds, unless the conditions of the debt financing are within the bidder's control.

20.3.10.6 *Frustrating actions*

20.195 The Takeover Act contains provisions regarding frustrating actions. In short, once the target board or the managing director of the target has good reason to assume that an offer is about to be made (or if an offer has already been made), the target must not take any action that would be liable to frustrate the making or the successful outcome of the offer, unless the action is approved by the general meeting

---

[139] Takeover Rules Rule II.4. This materiality requirement does not apply to acceptance conditions, conditions relating to the absence of higher competing offers or conditions regarding any necessary shareholder resolutions of the bidder or the target.

of the target. The Takeover Act contains a specific exception to this requirement for a target board seeking competing bidders.[140]

20.3.10.7 *Mandatory offers*

The Takeover Act requires a person who (alone or together with any concert party) acquires shares carrying 30% or more of the voting rights in the target company to make an offer for the remaining shares in the target company.[141] Under the Takeover Rules, the offer must also be extended to holders of other financial instruments issued by the target company, where the delisting of the target shares might materially affect the price of such instruments.[142] Any person attaining or exceeding the 30% mark must immediately announce its shareholding in the company.[143] If the shareholding is not reduced below the 30% mark within four weeks, the shareholder must announce a mandatory offer for the remaining shares.[144]   **20.196**

The rules requiring a mandatory offer do not apply to the mere holding of rights to acquire shares. Accordingly, the obtaining of irrevocable undertakings or the acquisition of call options, warrants or convertible debt instruments would not trigger the obligation to make a mandatory offer. Furthermore, the mandatory offer requirement is not triggered by corporate actions taken by the target company causing a shareholding which was below 30% of voting rights to rise above that threshold, for example, through the redemption of shares by the target company. However, any subsequent acquisition of shares will trigger the mandatory offer requirement.[145]   **20.197**

The Council may waive the requirement for a bidder to make a mandatory offer, for instance where: (i) the holding arises as a result of a 'rescue operation' for a company which is in serious financial difficulties; (ii) the holding arises as a result of the company issuing new shares as consideration for the acquisition of a company or a business; (iii) there has been no de facto change of control (for example where a corporate group is restructuring or where the company is controlled by the same family); or (iv) the holding arises as a result of the relevant shareholder exercising its pre-emptive rights in a rights issue. The Council may attach conditions to its waiver of the mandatory offer requirement.   **20.198**

---

[140] Takeover Act chapter 5 section 1.
[141] If a bidder held at least 30% on 1 July 2006 (without relying on a dispensation from the mandatory bid requirement), or acquires more than 30% as a result of acceptances of a bid, such bidder can acquire more shares without any restriction.
[142] Takeover Rules Rule II.9.
[143] Takeover Act chapter 3 section 1.
[144] Takeover Act chapter 3 section 1 and chapter 3 section 6.
[145] Takeover Act chapter 3 section 2, item 1.

20.199 For the purposes of the Takeover Act and the Takeover Rules, the following categories of persons are regarded as 'concert parties': (i) a company within the same corporate group as the bidder; (ii) any party with whom the bidder has agreed to adopt, by concerted exercise of the voting rights they hold, a lasting common policy to obtain a controlling influence over the management of the target (in practice, this rule often catches parties to shareholders' agreements that enable the parties to control the composition of the board of directors); or (iii) any party cooperating with the bidder with a view to obtaining control over the target.[146] The coming together of shareholders to act in concert under items (i) and (ii) would trigger the mandatory offer requirement where their aggregate shareholdings amount to or exceed the 30% mark.[147]

20.200 Also indirect acquisitions may trigger a mandatory offer under the Takeover Act.[148]

20.201 A mandatory offer must be accompanied by a cash alternative and must not be less than the highest price paid by the bidder or any person acting in concert with it for any shares in the target during the six months prior to the announcement of the offer.[149] In addition, in certain circumstances the price in a mandatory offer must not be less than the average (volume-weighted) stock market price of the target shares during a period of 20 trading days prior to the announcement that the 30% mark has been attained or exceeded.[150] This would be the case where the holding has arisen as a result of the exercise of warrants, the conversion of convertible debt instruments, the subscription of new shares or where there has been no relevant pre-offer acquisition. A mandatory offer may only be conditional on necessary regulatory approvals.[151]

20.3.10.8 Shareholding disclosure obligations during the course of an offer

20.202 The following specific shareholding disclosure obligations are imposed on a bidder attempting a takeover:[152]

- the bid announcement must state the number of target shares held by the bidder; and
- after the expiry of an acceptance period, the bidder must announce the number of target shares covered by acceptances, those that the bidder has acquired outside

---

[146] Takeover Act chapter 3 section 5; and Takeover Rules Rule I.3.

[147] Takeover Act chapter 3 section 2, item 2.

[148] Takeover Act chapter 3 section 2. (See also Council statement 2008:31 concerning Porsche's mandatory offer for the Swedish truck manufacturer Scania as a result of an indirect change of control over Volkswagen, the controlling shareholder in Scania.)

[149] Takeover Rules Rules II.10 and II.16.

[150] Takeover Rules Rule II.16.

[151] Takeover Rules Rule II.16.

[152] Takeover Rules Ruls II.3 and II.17.

the offer and any shares otherwise held directly or indirectly by the bidder (and in each case the percentage of share capital/voting rights they represent).

20.3.10.9 *Squeeze-out procedure*

The Companies Act allows the bidder to acquire minority shareholdings on a compulsory basis if (alone or together with any of its subsidiaries) it owns more than 90% of the target shares, whether or not these shares represent more than 90% of the voting rights in the target.[153] The squeeze-out right applies whether or not the bidder acquired the 90% through an offer or by some other means. The squeeze-out right also enables the bidder to buy out outstanding warrants and convertible debt instruments (unless the relevant warrants and/or convertible debt instruments were issued prior to 1 July 2007 and the terms and conditions of such securities disapply the squeeze-out right).[154] Where the 90% mark is exceeded, a minority shareholder also has a right to be bought out by the bidder.[155]

20.203

The squeeze-out procedure is settled by arbitration under the Swedish Arbitration Act.[156] The arbitration panel consists of three arbitrators: one appointed by the bidder and one appointed by a legal representative of the minority shareholders (or by the minority shareholders themselves), who together then agree on a third arbitrator to be the chairman of the arbitration panel.

20.204

The bidder typically requests the transfer of title to the minority shareholdings (referred to as 'advance title'). If the arbitration panel determines that the bidder is allowed to squeeze out the minority shareholdings and the bidder provides satisfactory security for the price of the shares, including interest, the bidder is granted advance title to the minority shareholders' shares.[157] Advance title is granted by a separate arbitration award, typically within eight to twelve months of the initiation of the squeeze-out procedure. However, obtaining advance title may sometimes take longer, particularly if the minority shareholders appeal against the separate arbitration award.

20.205

Once the bidder has been granted advance title to the minority shareholdings, the squeeze-out procedure concerns only the consideration for the shares. The consideration must be paid in cash, even if the consideration in the offer consisted, in whole or in part, of securities. The Companies Act provides that where an offer has been made to acquire all shares not already held by the bidder and the offer has been accepted by more than 90% of the target shareholders to whom the offer was made, the amount of the consideration for the remaining shares will be equivalent

20.206

---

[153] Companies Act chapter 22 section 1.
[154] Companies Act chapter 22 section 26.
[155] Companies Act chapter 22 section 1.
[156] Companies Act chapter 22 section 6.
[157] Companies Act chapter 22 section 12.

to the value of the offer consideration, unless there are any special reasons that justify a different amount; for example, where a long time has passed since the offer was completed, or where a material change affecting the value of the offer consideration has occurred.[158] If this rule does not apply, the consideration must reflect the market value of the shares at the time of the initiation of the squeeze-out procedure.[159] The Companies Act provides that where the shares are listed on a regulated market, the amount of the consideration must be the same as the quoted price of the shares at the time of the initiation of the squeeze-out procedure, unless there are any special reasons that justify a different amount.[160]

20.3.11 Market abuse

20.207 Rules relating to prohibitions on insider dealing, unlawful disclosure of inside information and market manipulation are set out in the Market Abuse Act.

20.208 The Market Abuse Act prohibits any person who has received inside information[161] from, on his own behalf or on behalf of any third party, acquiring or selling such financial instruments to which the information relates and advising or in any other manner causing any third party to acquire or sell financial instruments to which the information relates through trading on the securities market.[162] Furthermore, dealings that do not constitute or cause trading on the securities market are prohibited if such dealings relate to financial instruments (i) which are admitted (or for which an application for admission has been submitted) to trading on a regulated market; or (ii) whose value is dependent upon a financial instrument that is admitted (or for which an application for admission has been submitted) to trading on a regulated market.[163] The prohibition also extends to negligence and attempt.[164]

20.209 There are a number of exemptions to the rule, such as that financial instruments may be acquired where the inside information is expected to have a negative impact on the price of the instrument and vice versa.[165]

20.210 The Market Abuse Act also prohibits any person from intentionally disclosing information that he or she realizes, or should have realized, constitutes inside information, unless the disclosure occurs as a normal part of the performance of a

---

[158] Companies Act chapter 22 section 2.
[159] Ibid.
[160] Ibid.
[161] *Inside information* is defined as information regarding a circumstance which has not been made public or which is not generally known and is likely to materially affect the price of financial instruments. Market Abuse Act section 1 item 1.
[162] Market Abuse Act section 2.
[163] Market Abuse Act section 6.
[164] Market Abuse Act sections 3 and 4.
[165] Market Abuse Act section 5.

service, activities or obligations or where the information is placed into the public domain concurrently with disclosure thereof.[166]

Furthermore, the Market Abuse Act prohibits any person, either in conjunction with trading on the securities market or otherwise, from acting in a manner that he or she realizes, or should have realized, is likely to manipulate the market price or other terms and conditions in respect of trading in financial instruments or otherwise mislead purchasers or sellers of such instruments.[167]   **20.211**

Exemptions from the rules relating to insider dealing, unlawful disclosure of inside information and market manipulation are available for trading in own shares in buy-back programmes and stabilization of financial instruments, provided that trading is conducted in accordance with EC Regulation No 2273/2003.[168]   **20.212**

The rules in the Market Abuse Act can be difficult to apply in practice and often give rise to complex considerations. Non-compliance with the rules is a criminal offence with a term of imprisonment of up to four years.   **20.213**

---

[166] Market Abuse Act section 7.
[167] Market Abuse Act section 8.
[168] Market Abuse Act section 9.

21

UNITED KINGDOM

21.1 Listing Securities in London

21.1.1 The 'London Listing'

21.01 A Primary Listing on the London Stock Exchange (the 'LSE') has long been regarded as a badge of quality, connoting strict regulatory supervision and exacting standards of corporate governance. Companies that achieve and maintain a Primary Listing of securities (a listing of securities in relation to which the full regulatory requirements applicable to listing on the exchange apply) on the Main Market of the LSE must satisfy more stringent eligibility criteria, and more demanding continuing obligations, than the 'directive minimum' standards described in Part 1 require.

Much of what is unique about a London Primary Listing stems from the rigours **21.02** of such 'super-equivalent' standards.[1] Companies that choose to take on the challenge of a Primary Listing will hope to be rewarded by having their shares quoted in the FTSE UK Index Series.[2]

Inclusion in the FTSE UK Index Series, which is open to both UK and overseas **21.03** companies with Primary Listings,[3] is dependent on the size of a company's market capitalization and its ability to meet certain eligibility criteria.[4] A place on the FTSE UK Index Series, particularly the FTSE100, is coveted not only for the undeniable distinction of such a quotation, but, for the ready demand from institutional investors such as FTSE tracker funds that by their terms are bound to invest funds into FTSE companies.

The Primary Listing and the associated super-equivalent regulatory standards, **21.04** therefore, give substance to London's reputation as a premier listing venue. But it is important to bear in mind that the Primary Listing is but one of several categories of London listings. Other categories, such as secondary listings, listings of debt and listings of depositary receipts, together represent a substantial portion of London listings by value and do not involve super-equivalent regulatory standards; rather, they replicate directive minimum standards.

Driven in part by confusion arising from the multiple segments within the **21.05** UK regime (particularly between Primary Listings and other listings) the UK regulator, the United Kingdom Financial Services Authority (the 'FSA'), recently conducted a review of the UK listing regime. The FSA's recommendation is to retain and re-label the existing two-tier listing structure for equity, with 'Premium Listing' as the label for Primary Listings and 'Standard Listing' as the label for all other listings.[5]

---

[1] The super-equivalent provisions that apply in the United Kingdom are discussed below at Section 21.1.5.3. They are permissible as a matter of EU law because they pertain to areas covered by, *inter alia*, CARD, the Transparency Directive and the Market Abuse Directive, which impose *minimum* standards of harmonization. The Prospectus Directive and the Prospectus Regulation, on the other hand, impose maximum standards of harmonization and, accordingly, the relevant UK implementing legislation is not permitted to impose super-equivalent standards.

[2] The FTSE All Share Index consists of the three principal FTSE indexes: the FTSE100, the FTSE250 and the FTSE SmallCap.

[3] Overseas companies with controlling shareholders currently are not eligible for FTSE inclusion.

[4] FTSE All Share Index eligibility criteria include having a full listing on the LSE with a Sterling or Euro dominated price on SETS or SETSmm or a firm quotation on SEAQ or SEATS, passing screening for size and certain requirements as to liquidity.

[5] The FSA is considering a number of other issues as part of its listing review, in particular, whether UK companies should be able to obtain a secondary listing; whether super-equivalent standards should be retained and whether the FSA should be responsible for setting them; whether the FSA should adopt a more flexible approach as to the range of platforms that can operate a market

21.1.2 The United Kingdom Financial Services Authority

21.06   The FSA is the UK's 'competent authority' for the purposes of Part VI of the Financial Services and Markets Act 2000 ('FSMA') ('Part VI'). Its stated aim is to promote efficient, orderly and fair financial markets, while its statutory functions are (i) to make rules under Part VI; (ii) to give general guidance in relation to Part VI; and (iii) to determine the general policy and principles by reference to which it performs its functions under Part VI.[6]

21.07   The FSA discharges its role as the United Kingdom's competent authority regarding admission of securities to the Official List through one of its divisions, the UK Listing Authority (the 'UKLA'), whose specific role is to maintain the Official List.[7] In connection with this role, the UKLA is empowered to make listing rules for the purposes of Part VI, described in Section 21.1.4 below.[8]

21.08   The FSA also monitors issuers' compliance with rules passed under Part VI and other continuing obligations that apply to listed companies. If the FSA detects a breach of any of the relevant rules it is empowered to impose 'such penalty as it considers appropriate' on the offending listed company, including the discontinuation or suspension of its listing, an order to pay compensation, other financial penalties and/or the publication of a statement of public censure.[9] It also has the power to impose a penalty on a director of a listed company, typically in the form of a fine or a statement of public censure, if it considers that he or she was knowingly involved in a breach of relevant regulatory rules.[10]

21.09   In preparation for a London listing, a company's advisers are likely to have a significant amount of contact with the UKLA, particularly in connection with the document vetting process.[11] An applicant and its advisers' ability to maintain a good working relationship with the UKLA can be a crucial ingredient to a successful London listing. See Chapter 2, Section 3 (*Dealing with the Regulator*).

21.1.3 The London Stock Exchange

21.10   Until 2000, the LSE functioned not only as a stock exchange, but also as the United Kingdom's financial regulator, fulfilling many of the functions that now

---

for listed securities; and whether all Primary Listing equity issuers should be subject to the same requirements, whether they are UK or overseas entities.

   [6] FSMA section 73(2).
   [7] FSMA section 74(2).
   [8] FSMA section 74(4). The procedure the UKLA must follow when making such rules is set out in FSMA section 101.
   [9] FSMA section 91(1).
   [10] FSMA section 91(2).
   [11] This typically consists of about two rounds of submissions of the draft prospectus to the relevant UKLA readers, who will give comments on the draft, before final approval or 'stamp off'.

fall to the FSA. During 2001, the LSE conducted its own public offering and listing and became the 'London Stock Exchange plc'.

Today, the LSE's role is focused on the admission of securities to trading, publishing its Admission and Disclosure Standards and operating its Regulatory News Service ('RNS'). The LSE runs two principal markets, the Main Market and the Alternative Investment Market (the 'AIM'), as well as the Professional Securities Market (the 'PSM'),[12] which caters for specialist issuers and securities.

21.11

21.1.3.1 The Main Market

The Main Market is the LSE's flagship market. UK companies may apply to the Main Market for a Primary Listing of shares, in connection with which they must comply with the UK's super-equivalent eligibility criteria and continuing obligations regime. For overseas companies, the choices for Main Market listing are greater, extending beyond a Primary Listing of shares to a secondary listing of shares, a listing of depositary receipts or a listing of debt securities.[13]

21.12

Alongside the Main Market, the LSE operates another regulated market, the Specialist Fund Market, designed for more complex investment funds (see Section 21.3.4 below).[14]

21.13

All companies admitted to the Main Market must comply with the LSE's Admissions and Disclosure Standards. In practice, these standards overlap to a large extent with the eligibility and continuing obligations provisions to which applicants are already bound under the UKLA's Listing Rules (the 'LRs') and the Disclosure and Transparency Rules (the 'DTRs').

21.14

21.1.3.2 The Alternative Investment Market

As an alternative to the Main Market, both UK and overseas companies can apply for a quotation on AIM. AIM is designed for small and/or nascent businesses, offering a less prescriptive regulatory environment than the Main Market, which can help foster a company's development.[15] Notable regulatory concessions include the absence of requirements for (i) a minimum number of shares in public hands;[16] (ii) a minimum market capitalization; (iii) a trading history or financial track record; (iv) shareholder approval for transactions (except in the case of

21.15

---

[12] See chapter 4 of the UKLA's Listing Rules for provisions applicable to the PSM.
[13] The position regarding UK issuers is currently under consideration as part of the FSA's Listing Review. See Section 1.1 above.
[14] Neither AIM, nor the PSM is a 'regulated market' under the relevant directives.
[15] Applicants for an AIM listing and AIM-listed companies must comply with the AIM Rules but they are not bound by the Listing Rules or the DTRs.
[16] The NOMAD would, however, need to be comfortable that there will be a large enough public float to allow there to be an orderly market.

reverse takeovers); and (v) a document vetting procedure prior to the admission of securities to AIM (other than by the NOMAD, defined below). Furthermore, provided the securities for which admission to AIM is sought are not simultaneously the subject of a non-exempt public offer, an applicant for an AIM quotation will not be required to publish a UKLA-approved prospectus.[17]

21.16 However, AIM-quoted companies are required to comply with the AIM Rules, which, *inter alia*, require that the companies must at all times have a nominated adviser (a 'NOMAD'), who is responsible to the LSE for assessing the appropriateness of an applicant for admission to AIM and for advising and guiding a company on the admission process and its continuing obligations under the AIM Rules.[18]

21.17 For small and newly incorporated companies, the regulatory concessions that come with an AIM listing are attractive, notwithstanding the need to appoint a NOMAD. Some AIM listed companies eventually graduate to the Main Market, having benefited from the dual injections of capital and public exposure that follow from an AIM admission.

21.1.3.3 *The Professional Securities Market*

21.18 The PSM provides a platform for the listing of specialist securities such as GDRs, debt and convertible securities. Such securities, given their specialist nature, are generally not marketed to retail investors, but can be listed on the PSM and offered to professional or institutional investors.

21.19 A key attraction of a listing on the PSM is that applicants are not required to restate their financial information to IFRS or other GAAPs deemed equivalent to IFRS, a requirement that in practice can be a major barrier for some issuers in terms of time and cost to a Main Market listing. To be eligible for a PSM listing of GDRs, applicants must (i) produce audited accounts covering the latest three years (or such shorter period as the issuer has been in operation), together with a narrative description of the differences between IFRS and the local accounting principles used in their preparation; (ii) ensure that the securities to be listed achieve a minimum market capitalization of £700,000; and (iii) ensure that a minimum of 25% of the securities of the class to be admitted are in public hands. The requirements for debt are similar, except that two years' financial statements are adequate, minimum market capitalization is £200,000 and there is no minimum public float requirement.

---

[17] Since AIM is not an EU regulated market, the Prospectus Rules will not apply unless there is a non-exempt offer to the public.

[18] AIM Rules rule 1.

As with a Main Market listing, admission to the PSM involves a two-stage process: application to the UKLA for admission to the Official List and application to the LSE for admission to trading on the PSM. In connection with admission to trading on the PSM, applicants must comply with Chapter 4 of the Listing Rules and produce UKLA-approved 'listing particulars'.[19] Once admitted to the Official List, PSM-listed companies must comply with certain aspects of the continuing obligations regime that applies to issuers listed on the Main Market.[20]   **21.20**

21.1.3.4 The Specialist Funds Market

The Specialist Fund Market (the 'SFM') is the LSE's regulated market for specialist investment funds, targeting institutional, professional and highly knowledgeable investors. A key advantage to the SFM is that it is open to UK and non-UK domiciled investment funds and is specifically designed to admit a wide range of sophisticated fund vehicles, governance models and security types, including limited partnership interests and non-voting share structures.   **21.21**

Applicants to the SFM are required to gain admission to the Official List (by way of application to the UKLA) and admission to trading on the SFM (by way of application to the LSE), in connection with which it will be required to produce an approved Prospectus Directive compliant prospectus.   **21.22**

21.1.4 Legislative overview

21.1.4.1 The Financial Services and Markets Act 2000

FSMA remains the principal piece of legislation through which the UK implements the EU directives relating to listing, admission to trading on a regulated market, and offers of securities to the public. As discussed in Section 21.1.2 above, the UKLA is empowered under FSMA to create Part VI rules for purposes connected with the maintenance of the Official List, public offers and securities traded on regulated markets. Principally, these consist of the Listing Rules, the Prospectus Rules and the DTRs, which are published together in the FSA Handbook.   **21.23**

---

[19] Listing particulars are required in connection with an application for admission to the PSM and, indeed, in connection with any application for admission to the Official List in circumstances where a prospectus is not required. This includes certain issues of securities within Schedule 11A FSMA, most importantly open-ended collective investment schemes and non-equity securities issued by the government of a member state, a local or regional authority of a member state, or public international bodies of which a member state is a member.

[20] The general position is that most of the DTRs do not apply to companies with securities admitted to the PSM. The key exceptions to this are that companies admitted to the PSM are required to comply with DTR 2 as regards disclosure of price-sensitive information and UK companies with securities admitted to the PSM that also have shares admitted to a regulated market are required to comply with DTR 5 (notification of major shareholdings), DTR 6.3 and parts of DTR 4.

21.24 These rules occupy a vital place within the United Kingdom regulatory regime, sitting alongside a range of other provisions designed to safeguard the interests of investors and inspire confidence in the UK markets. These include the requirement that anyone who sells securities in the United Kingdom—unless an exemption applies— must be authorized by the FSA;[21] the rules[22] imposed by the FSA on FSA-authorized firms; as well as the rules that prohibit financial promotion, except where the relevant financial promotion is made by, or is approved by, a person authorized by the FSA.[23]

21.1.4.2 Listing Rules

21.25 The Listing Rules cover the processes and conditions for admission to the Official List, and certain of the continuing obligations that apply to issuers with listed securities.[24] Chapter 1 contains certain preliminary provisions (including the scope of application of the Listing Rules, the circumstances in which the FSA may dispense with or modify rules, and rules relating to the publication of information). Chapters 2 and 3 contain generally applicable provisions regarding the listing process; Chapter 4 applies to applicants to the PSM; and Chapter 5 deals with suspension and cancellation of listings. The remaining chapters contain additional listing requirements and/or continuing obligations that apply depending on the nature of the securities for which listing is sought, and which operate in conjunction with the DTRs. Chapters 6 to 16 generally apply to equity securities (including those of investment entities and venture capital trusts). Chapter 17 contains provisions applicable to debt securities, Chapter 18 deals with depositary receipts and Chapter 19 deals with securitized derivatives. The LRs are not entirely as straightforward as this due to a large number of cross-references within the rules, but the general picture is correct.[25]

21.1.4.3 Prospectus Rules

21.26 The Prospectus Rules, together with sections 84 to 87R FSMA, implement the Prospectus Directive, a maximum harmonization directive aimed at standardizing the requirements for prospectuses published in connection with (i) non-exempt offers to the public of transferable securities in the EU or (ii) the admission

---

[21] FSMA section 19.

[22] These rules include detailed requirements for those dealing with retail customers to ensure that they know the customer and his/her circumstances, and that they properly assess the suitability of the product in question for each such customer.

[23] See FSMA section 21 and the Financial Services and Markets Act 2000 (Financial Promotion) Order 2005 SI 2005/1529, discussed in Section 21.3.3 below.

[24] See FSMA sections 75, 77, 79, 88 and 96.

[25] By way of example, Listing Rule ('LR') 14 applies to overseas companies with secondary (or 'standard tier') listings of shares. But many rules within it also apply to GDRs as a result of a cross-reference in LR 18 to LR 14.

of such securities to trading on an EEA regulated market. The Prospectus Directive has been supplemented by the Prospectus Regulation, an EEA regulation with direct effect in the United Kingdom, which sets out detailed provisions about the contents of prospectuses. These requirements, which differ depending on the category of security, are detailed in the Annexes to the Prospectus Rules.

21.1.4.4 Disclosure and Transparency Rules

The DTRs, which implement segments of the Market Abuse Directive and the Transparency Directive,[26] constitute a significant part of the continuing obligations regime to which companies must adhere as long as they are admitted to listing or trading in London. Depending on the particular type of security listed or traded in London, the DTRs require immediate disclosure of inside information, the publication of periodic financial reports, the notification of major holdings of voting rights and contain obligations on the dissemination of regulated information and communications with shareholders.   **21.27**

The disclosure requirements in the DTRs operate in conjunction with the continuing obligations under the Listing Rules, as well as the Admission and Disclosure Standards of the LSE. In addition, broadly speaking, companies with securities admitted to trading on the LSE that are involved in takeovers are regulated by the City Code on Takeovers and Mergers (the 'Takeover Code')[27] and such companies must comply with the Takeover Code's rules in relation to secrecy and the content and timing of announcements to the market.   **21.28**

21.1.4.5 Other provisions

In addition to the Part VI Rules, listed issuers (and others, whether or not listed) must comply with a number of other regulatory regimes, including the criminal market abuse regime under the Criminal Justice Act 1993 (the 'CJA'), the civil market abuse regime under Part VIII FSMA discussed in Section 21.5 below and the financial promotion regime under section 21 FSMA discussed in Section 21.3 below.   **21.29**

---

[26] The scope of the DTRs is set out in FSMA sections 96A–96C.

[27] In summary, the Takeover Code applies on a primary basis to (i) UK companies with securities admitted to a regulated market in the United Kingdom or on a stock exchange in the Isle of Man or the Channel Islands; and (ii) UK, Isle of Man and Channel Island public companies whose central management and control is located in the United Kingdom, the Isle of Man or the Channel Islands (certain private companies may also fall within this limb if, *inter alia*, their securities have been admitted to the Oficial List within the previous 10 years). With respect to non-UK EEA-incorporated companies with securities admitted to a regulated market in the United Kingdom, sharing provisions apply, pursuant to which the Takeover Code applies on a secondary basis in conjunction with the law of the company's jurisdiction of incorporation.

21.1.4.6 FSA guidance and information

21.30   FSMA empowers the FSA to issue guidance on the application of Part VI Rules, which it does through multiple channels.[28] A key source of FSA guidance lies in the Listing Rules themselves: guidance paragraphs are set out adjacent to the rules to which they pertain (which are suffixed 'G'). The FSA also issues written guidance, including discussion papers and consultations papers, available on the FSA website.[29]

21.31   In addition, the UKLA operates a helpdesk that delivers guidance to questions submitted by fax or through the UKLA's electronic submissions system,[30] or over the telephone, on a case-by-case basis. This facility enables companies and their advisers to ascertain how the UKLA will apply specific rules in particular circumstances; however, in the interests of not over-burdening the helpdesk, it should only be used where published FSA or UKLA guidance does not yield an adequate answer.

21.32   Looking beyond formal guidance, two very useful sources of information are the newsletters 'List!', in which the UKLA discusses aspects of its interpretation or application of the Listing Rules, and 'Market Watch', in which the FSA discusses market conduct and transaction reporting issues.[31]

21.1.5 Eligibility for listing

21.1.5.1 Admission to the Official List and admission to trading

21.33   To conduct a London listing of any category, a company must apply to have its securities admitted (i) to the official list of the UKLA (the 'Official List') and

---

[28] FSA guidance procedures, which include a consultation process with market participants, are set out under FSMA section 157.

[29] FSA publications include (i) Communication Documents: Market Watch; press releases; statements; speeches; newsletters (Comparative tables bulletins, UKLA newsletters (List!)); enforcement notices and application refusals (final notices; supervisory notices; application refusals; approved persons refusals); Dear CEO letters; (ii) corporate documents: annual reports; business plan papers; financial risk outlook documents; international regulatory outlook documents; annual public meeting transcripts; FSA board meeting summary minutes; memorandums of understanding; detailed information on performance account.; and (iii) policy documents: consultation papers; discussion papers; policy statements; guidance notes; handbook related material (key rules; handbook notices; handbook development newsletters; handbook releases); occasional papers; pre-FSA regulatory material.

[30] The UKLA stated in issue 16 of List! (at para 2.6) that it will not accept written submissions by email since it is not a secure way to submit helpdesk queries. The UKLA's electronic submission system is an alternative method of submitting documents to the UKLA, which allows companies' advisers to send draft prospectuses, circulars, written queries and other connected draft documentation to the UKLA electronically. The system is free, works from a secure, web-based platform and can be accessed by sponsors and authorized advisers who have been issued with login details and passwords.

[31] The contents of List! and Market Watch does not constitute 'guidance' under FSMA, and is not binding on the FSA.

(ii) to trading on a recognized investment exchange.[32] The concepts of admission to the Official List and admission to trading are distinct, but clearly linked; admission of securities to the Official List is dependent on the securities gaining admission to trading on a recognized investment exchange, such as the LSE. [33]

21.1.5.2 *General eligibility criteria*

The UKLA will only admit securities to the Official List if it is satisfied that the applicant meets the requirements of the Listing Rules.[34] Accordingly, all applications for admission to the Official List must be made in the manner required by the Listing Rules.[35] All applicants must satisfy several general eligibility criteria, which can be found in Chapter 2 of the Listing Rules (the 'Chapter 2 Criteria').

21.34

The Chapter 2 Criteria are as follows:

21.35

- Incorporation: the applicant must be (i) duly incorporated or otherwise validly established in accordance with the laws of its place of incorporation or establishment; and (ii) operating in conformity with its constitution.
- Validity: the relevant securities must (i) conform with the law of the applicant's place of incorporation; (ii) be duly authorized according to the requirements of the applicant's constitution; and (iii) have any necessary statutory and other consents.
- Admission to trading: the securities must be admitted to trading on the market of a 'recognized investment exchange's' market— the LSE, among others, is a recognized investment exchange.
- Transferability: the relevant securities must be (i) freely transferable; and (ii) fully paid and free from all liens and from any restriction on the right to transfer (save for certain exceptions). Standard restrictions on transfer that go to restrictions imposed by securities laws do not constrain transferability within the meaning of this rule (or, indeed, under MiFID, whose definition of 'transferable securities' is that used in the Prospectus Directive).
- Market capitalization: the expected aggregate market value of all securities to be listed must be at least (i) £700,000 for shares and GDRs; and (ii) £200,000 for debt securities.
- Whole class to be listed: the application must relate to the entire class of those securities issued or proposed to be issued; if securities of that class are

---

[32] LR 2.2.3.

[33] LR 2.2.3. A full list of recognized investment exchanges can be found at http://www.fsa.gov.uk/register/exchanges.do.

[34] FSMA section 75(4). If an applicant is unable to meet certain requirements of the Listing Rules, it may nonetheless be possible to gain entry to the Official List if the applicant can reach an adequate compromise with the UKLA regarding the relevant requirement.

[35] FSMA section 75(1).

already issued then the application must relate to all further securities of that class.[36]

- Prospectus: a prospectus must have been approved by the FSA and published in relation to the securities, or if another EEA state is the Home member state, the relevant competent authority must have approved the prospectus to be 'passported' and supplied the FSA with (i) a certificate of approval; and (ii) a copy of the approved prospectus.[37]

21.1.5.3 *Primary Listings—additional eligibility criteria*

21.36   In addition to the Chapter 2 Criteria, further eligibility criteria apply depending on the type of security and the category of listing for which admission to the Official List is sought. In the context of a Primary Listing, such additional super-equivalent criteria can be found in Chapter 6 of the Listing Rules.

21.37   *Financial statements*: applicants[38] for a Primary Listing of shares must have three years' audited accounts covering the period ended not more than six months prior to the date of the prospectus the company will produce in connection with the application.[39] Such accounts must have been prepared in accordance with IFRS or an equivalent standard.[40] If the applicant's latest audited financial statements are more than six months old, it will have to produce interim audited financial statements for publication in the prospectus.[41]

21.38   *Nature and duration of business*: applicants for a Primary Listing of shares must fulfil three requirements relating to the nature and duration of its business: [42] (i) the three years' audited accounts produced in the applicant's prospectus must

---

[36] Companies should be careful to make block listings when available to avoid onerous prospectus obligations for further issuances of securities. This can be particularly problematic when issuance of those securities is not within the complete control of the company, for example in the context of GDRs.

[37] In addition, it might be necessary for the relevant issuer to prepare and submit to the FSA a translation of the summary of the prospectus. See Chapter 2.

[38] The requirements regarding financial statements and nature and duration of business differ for 'mineral companies' and 'scientific research based companies'. In particular, the requirement to produce three years' audited accounts does not apply. See LR 6.1.8 and LR 6.1.11.

[39] LR 6.1.3.

[40] See Regulation 1289/2008/EC, amending the Prospectus Regulation to reflect Commission decision 2008/961/EC, which determined, in accordance with the procedure set out for determining equivalence under the Equivalence Regulation, that the following third country GAAPs are equivalent to IFRS: Canada, China, India, Japan, South Korea and the United States.

[41] It is worth noting that this is more than would be required for SEC registration, which would allow interim accounts to be unaudited. Nevertheless, typical practice for SEC registered deals (and non-SEC registered deals with a 144A offering of securities to qualified institutional buyers in the United States) would be for those accounts to be reviewed so that the customary type of comfort letter could be issued to the underwriters.

[42] LR 6.1.4.

pertain to at least 75% of the applicant's business for the entire three-year period;[43] (ii) the company must control, and have controlled, the majority of its assets for the entire three-year period;[44] and (iii) the company must be carrying on an independent business as its main activity. The FSA states that these requirements are designed to enable prospective investors to make a reasonable assessment of the company's future prospects.[45] Where the company is unable to satisfy these requirements, it must discuss a compromise solution with the FSA. It is worthwhile to note that the three-year revenue-earning track record requirement needs to be considered in addition to, and alongside, the EEA-directive based consideration of 'complex financial histories'. See Chapter 2 in Part 2.

Working capital: applicants must provide a clean working capital statement: (a statement that it and its subsidiaries (if any) have sufficient working capital available for its requirements for at least the next 12 months beginning at the date of the prospectus prepared in connection with its admission to the Official List).[46] It is worth noting that the EEA-directive based requirement for a prospectus for shares requires a working capital statement that may be qualified (that is, it does not need to be 'clean'). A company that cannot give a clean working capital statement, therefore, can instead explain how it plans to make up the shortfall in working capital. Although this disclosure is unlikely to be attractive from a marketing standpoint, it is at least an option for directive minimum listings of shares. It is not, however, available for Primary Listings. The Primary Listing eligibility requirement for a clean working capital statement must not be, and is customarily not, taken lightly. It is the trigger for a substantial level of due diligence (with the aid of accountants) that culminates in the production of a working capital report addressed to the sponsor and the directors of the company. The report is expensive to produce and takes time, and needs to be built in to any timetable for a Primary Listing.   **21.39**

Shares in public hands: applicants must ensure that 25%[47] of the class of shares for which a Primary Listing is sought has been distributed to the public no later than   **21.40**

---

[43] LR 6.1.4. In determining what amounts to 75% of the company's business, the FSA will take into account factors such as the assets, profitability and market capitalization of the business.

[44] Although the words of this limb of the eligibility requirement suggest that a company that had made a lot of acquisitions recently would not be eligible for a primary listing, the actual purpose of this limb is essentially to make sure the business is not a fund in nature—that is, it is not a company that has minority stakes in a portfolio of assets. This type of company would instead have to be listed under Chapter 15 or 16, which deal with listings of closed-ended and open-ended funds.

[45] LR 6.1.6.

[46] LR 6.1.16. The FSA may dispose of this requirement in certain circumstances, for instance, if the applicant's business is substantially that of banking, insurance or similar financial services: LR 6.1.18.

[47] The UKLA may agree to a lower percentage if it considers that a sufficiently large number of shares will be in public hands to enable the market to operate properly: LR 6.1.20. Applicants who

the time of admission to the Official List.[48] For the purposes of calculating whether this requirement is met, the shareholdings of certain parties, including any of the applicant's directors and persons connected to them and any person who holds 5% or more of the shares in the relevant class, must be disregarded.[49] Treasury shares must also be disregarded.[50]

21.41 *Requirement for a sponsor*: In addition to the Chapter 6 eligibility criteria, one of the key super-equivalent areas of the UK Primary Listing regime is the sponsor regime. Chapter 8 of the Listing Rules lays down the circumstances in which a sponsor will be required and defines the sponsors' duties both to the FSA and to the issuers they advise. Broadly, a sponsor's role is to assess the suitability of an applicant for listing, advise on the structure and timetable of the offering, provide guidance to the applicant as to the application of the Listing Rules in connection with the relevant offering, and to act as the channel for communications between the applicant and the FSA. Accordingly, sponsors fulfil a dual role: (i) assisting applicants in their listing and (ii) providing the FSA with comfort that applicants are able to comply with the regulatory framework under Part VI.

21.42 The FSA is empowered to publicly censure sponsors for breach of any of their obligations under the Listing Rules,[51] although investors do not have a direct statutory right of action under FSMA against sponsors who breach the Listing Rules.[52]

21.1.5.4 Secondary listings—additional eligibility criteria

21.43 In addition to the eligibility criteria set out in Chapter 2 of the Listing Rules, overseas companies[53] applying for a secondary listing must comply with the requirements set out in Chapter 14 of the Listing Rules.[54] It used to be the case

---

want to modify the 25% requirement should consult with the UKLA at the earliest opportunity: LR 1.2.5.

[48] LR 6.1.19.

[49] See LR 6.1.19(4).

[50] See LR 6.1.19(5).

[51] FSMA section 89.

[52] FSMA section 150 provides that private persons who can show that they have suffered loss as a result of a breach of any FSA rules by an authorized person, may, unless the relevant rule expressly excludes that right, bring an action for damages against that authorized person for breach of statutory duty. However, the Listing Rules are excluded from this provision (under FSMA section 150(4)).

[53] UK companies are currently not eligible to obtain secondary Listings. But see FSA Consultation Paper 08/21, which discusses the consultation by the FSA that considers, among other things, whether UK companies should be permitted to obtain secondary listings.

[54] This includes the requirement that 25% of the class of shares for which application is sought is in public hands prior to admission to the Official List: LR 14.2.2. The same adjustments that apply in the context of a Primary Listing under LR 6.1.19 must be made to the calculation of shares in public hands: LR 14.2.2(4). The FSA is also likely to afford the same flexibility for a secondary listing as for a Primary Listing where a smaller percentage than 25% will be in public hands, if the size of the public float in absolute terms is large enough to allow an orderly market.

that a company seeking a secondary listing in London had to have its shares listed elsewhere, however this is no longer the case following changes to the rules made in 2005, when the rules were also revised to implement the Prospectus Directive.

21.1.5.5 *Depositary receipts—additional eligibility criteria*

Overseas companies[55] applying for a listing of depositary receipts must comply **21.44** with Chapter 18 of the Listing Rules, which, *inter alia*, requires applicants requesting admission of depositary receipts to the Official List to fulfil the Chapter 2 eligibility requirements.[56] In addition, such applicants must satisfy the requirement that 25% of the class of GDRs, for which application is sought, is in public hands prior to admission to the Official List.[57] Although the percentage is the same, this is a significant difference in practice to the public float requirement applicable to shares. 25% of GDRs might be a much smaller percentage of the equity share capital of a company if all of its shares are not held in the form of GDRs. In contrast, 25% of a company's shares is exactly that— 25% of all its shares of that class. This can make a big difference in deals where a large shareholder wants its company to go public, but without relinquishing a great degree of control. Whereas a share deal, whether primary listed or secondary listed, would generally require a 100% shareholder to relinquish 25% of its shareholding, the amount a GDR deal would require it to relinquish depends almost entirely on how large it wishes its GDR deal to be, since only 25% of the GDRs needs to be in public hands.

21.1.5.6 *Debt and other specialist securities—additional eligibility criteria*

Chapter 17 of the Listing Rules, the relevant chapter for applicants of a listing of **21.45** debt or other specialist securities,[58] imposes no further eligibility requirements beyond the generally applicable criteria set out in Chapter 2 of the Listing Rules.[59]

---

[55] UK companies are not permitted to obtain listings of GDRs unless they also obtain a primary listing of shares. If the UKLA consultation (see FSA Consultation Paper 08/21) results in secondary listings being open to UK companies, it will be interesting to see if GDR listings will also be opened up to UK companies. It would appear incongruous if they were not.

[56] LR18.2.11 requires applicants to comply with LR2.2.2 to 2.2.11, while LR18.2.2 and LR18.2.3 require applicants to comply with requirements regarding due incorporation and due authorization of the depositary receipts that mirror the corresponding requirements in LR2.2.1 and LR2.2.2, respectively.

[57] LR18.2.8. The same adjustments as those that apply in the context of a Primary Listing under LR6.1.19 must be made to the calculation of GDRs in public hands: LR18.2.8(4).

[58] Chapter 17 of the Listing Rules applies to debt securities, asset-backed securities, certificates representing debt securities, and securities that are convertible into either equity securities, debt securities or securities of another company: LR17.1.1.

[59] Note that the requirement for Primary Listings and listings of GDRs for 25% of the listed securities to be in public hands does not apply to listings of debt.

21.1.5.7 The Prospectus Regulation—impact on eligibility

21.46 While the Prospectus Rules themselves do not contain separate eligibility requirements for applicants to the Official List, in practice, the Prospectus Regulation contents requirements set out in the Annexes to the Prospectus Rules often prove to be a barrier to listing.

21.47 For example, applicants seeking to list depositary receipts are not required under the Listing Rules to produce financial statements for any particular period to gain admission to the Official List. However, under Article 20.1 of Annex X of the Prospectus Rules, such applicants must include audited historical financial information covering the latest three financial years (or such shorter period that the issuer has been in operation) in their prospectus and the latest two years of financial statements must be consistent with the GAAP under which the financial statements published after the anticipated listing will be prepared. These prospectus-related requirements may present unforeseen problems for applicants, particularly those that have a 'complex financial history',[60] or those in jurisdictions whose national accounting standards (in accordance with which their accounts have been prepared) are not deemed to be 'equivalent' to IFRS. Although listing on the PSM can be the solution to the second problem, the first requires delicate negotiation with the UKLA if the deal is to go forward.

21.1.5.8 Early contact with the UKLA: 'eligibility letters' and 'pre-eligibility letters'

21.48 A company planning to conduct a Primary Listing,[61] a secondary listing or a listing of depositary receipts[62] must submit a letter, setting out how it satisfies the applicable Listing Rules eligibility criteria, to the UKLA no later than the date that the first draft of the relevant prospectus is submitted to the UKLA. Such an 'eligibility letter' is designed not only to give the UKLA comfort as to the applicant's eligibility, but also to ensure that any issues that could impact on the listing are dispatched prior to the first submission of the draft prospectus. For Primary Listings, the sponsor typically submits the eligibility letter, while for secondary and GDR listings it is typically submitted by issuer's counsel or the issuer itself.

21.49 In practice, however, if issues are lurking regarding an applicant's eligibility that could impact on the listing, the applicant's advisers should raise the issue with the UKLA well before the submission of the required eligibility letter, by way of a voluntarily submitted 'pre-eligibility letter'. By submitting a pre-eligibility letter, an applicant gives itself the best chance of resolving its eligibility issues with

---

[60] See Chapter 2.
[61] LR8.4.3(4). Eligibility letters in the context of a Primary Listing must set out how the applicant meets the eligibility criteria in Chapters 2 and 6 of the Listing Rules.
[62] LR18.3.1A. Eligibility letters in the context of a listing of depositary receipts must set out how the applicant meets the eligibility criteria in the Listing Rules, Chapters 2 and 18.2.

the UKLA. It also ensures that it complies with its obligation under Chapter 1 of the Listing Rules to consult with the FSA at the earliest possible stage if in doubt about how the Listing Rules apply in a particular situation or if it may be necessary for the UKLA to dispense with or modify a Listing Rule.[63]

Pre-eligibility letters are not a feature in all London listings, but they are common in cases where an applicant may face a challenge to satisfy the three-year revenue-earning track record requirement or otherwise has a 'complex financial history' that could prevent it from fulfilling the Listing Rules or Prospectus Regulation requirements regarding audited financial statements.

21.50

21.1.5.9 *Drafting a pre-eligibility letter*

There is no definitive blueprint for a pre-eligibility letter. However, by way of example, for an adviser writing to the UKLA in connection with an applicant that may not satisfy either (i) the eligibility criteria relating to its financial track record; or (ii) the contents requirements for a prospectus relating to financial disclosure (either under the relevant Annex to the Prospectus Rules or under the wider disclosure obligation pursuant to Article 5.1 of the Prospectus Directive) due to its 'complex financial history', the following structure may be adopted:

21.51

- Introduction
  - Describe the structure of the transaction and the anticipated date of admission to the Official List.
  - Explain that an eligibility letter will be submitted in accordance with the Listing Rules in due course and that the purpose of the pre-eligibility letter is to reach an early agreement regarding the three-year revenue-earning track record (if applicable) the substantive elements of the financial information required for the purposes of satisfying the Prospectus Regulation and the related complex financial history regime.
- Description of business and historical development
  - Describe the applicant's current business: countries of operation, industry sector, market segments, services provided, trading name (if applicable).
  - Explain the applicant's historical development, beginning with details of incorporation and including all stages of development that are relevant to the applicant's three-year revenue-earning track record, if applicable, or its 'complex financial history', such as restructurings, acquisitions and other significant transactions. This description should consider covering the applicant's beneficial owners, as well as its subsidiary companies, if relevant to the analysis.
- Group structure
  - Prepare group structure charts that document the key stages of the applicant's historical development and, if relevant, shareholder ownership structure.

---

[63] LR1.2.5.

- Proposed historical financial information
  - Set out the financial information the applicant proposes to publish in the prospectus.
  - Explain how the proposed package of financial statements covers the relevant portions of the applicant's group (i.e. a 75% track record for the relevant period, a proxy for the coverage of materially all of the business).
- Disclosure obligations
  - Refer to the statutory provisions that contain the relevant disclosure obligations (for instance, for a listing of shares, the relevant obligations are LR 6, Article 20.1 of Annex I of the Prospectus Regulation,[64] Article 5.1 of the Prospectus Directive and Article 4 of the Prospectus Regulation).
  - Demonstrate how the proposed financial disclosure package satisfies each of these provisions.
- Request for confirmation
  - Request confirmation from the UKLA that the proposed financial disclosure package is acceptable.

21.52 Following submission of a pre-eligibility letter, the UKLA is likely to respond within one week or two weeks at the latest. By the time the actual eligibility letter[65] is submitted, therefore, the issues identified in the pre-eligibility letter are likely to have been resolved with the UKLA. Accordingly, the focus of the eligibility letter is on how the applicant complies with the relevant eligibility provisions under the Listing Rules, rather than on issues that could impact on the listing.

21.1.5.10 *Drafting an eligibility letter*

21.53 As noted above, if there are any expected sticking points with respect to an applicant's eligibility for listing, they should have been resolved well in advance of the submission of the required eligibility letter. As such, eligibility letters are generally easier to draft than pre-eligibility letters, although as with pre-eligibility letters, there is no set formula to follow. The following represents a structure that the UKLA is likely to find helpful as well as being in compliance with the relevant Listing Rule requirement:

- Introduction
  - Describe the structure of the transaction and the anticipated date of admission to the Official List.

---

[64] Under Article 20.1, the applicant is required to include in a prospectus audited historical financial information covering the latest three financial years (or such shorter period that the issuer has been in operation).

[65] Required under LR8.4.3(4) for applicants for a Primary Listing or LR18.3.1A for applicants for a listing of depositary receipts. Eligibility letters are not required in the context of secondary listings, listings of debt or other specialist securities. In practice, however, applicants for secondary listings or listings of debt or other specialist securities might decide to correspond with the UKLA in the form of a pre-eligibility letter if they face issues that could impact on the listing.

- Description of business
  - Describe the applicant's current business: countries of operation, industry sector, market segments, services provided and trading name (if applicable).
- Transaction timetable
  - Set out anticipated dates for key stages in the listing; for instance: (i) date of informal UKLA approval of the draft prospectus (i.e. 'comments cleared'); (ii) date of formal UKLA approval ('stamp off') and publication of prospectus; and (iii) date of admission to the Official List.
- Compliance with Listing Rules eligibility criteria
  - Set out the relevant eligibility requirements for the listing, commenting in each case on how the applicant will be in compliance at the time of admission to the Official List.

21.2 The Prospectus

21.2.1 Applicable law

Since the Prospectus Directive is a maximum harmonization directive, and the Prospectus Regulation is directly applicable as law in the United Kingdom, the UK's rules regarding prospectuses bear a close resemblance to those in other member states across the EU. **21.54**

Part VI, sections 72 to 103 of FSMA provides the framework for the UK implementation of the Prospectus Directive and empowers the FSA to make rules for that purpose. The key sources of English law in this area are (i) sections 84 to 87R FSMA, which contain provisions including the general standard of disclosure required in prospectuses, definitions of key terms, the nature of liability for prospectuses; and designating when a supplemental prospectus is required and the associated statutory right of withdrawal once a prospectus has been published; and (ii) the Prospectus Rules, published pursuant to Part VI of FSMA, which set out detailed requirements as to when a prospectus is required, what it should contain, and how it should be published. The Prospectus Rules also contain the detailed provisions regarding prospectus contents prescribed by the Prospectus Regulation. **21.55**

21.2.2 Requirement for a prospectus

The circumstances in which a company will be required to prepare a prospectus under English law are set out under Article 5(1) of the Prospectus Directive, the so-called 'public offer' and 'admission to trading' triggers.[66] The discussion in Part 1 of the triggers to the requirement to publish a prospectus, therefore, applies equally to the position under English law and very little further exposition is **21.56**

---

[66] FSMA sections 85 and 86.

required. One special provision in FSMA not found in the Prospectus Directive is worth pointing out, however, which the English legislature was very helpful in adding as a clarification. It is section 102B(5), which clarifies that a public offer does not include a communication in connection with trading on a regulated market or other specified trading facility. This was introduced to avoid the interpretation that prices quoted on stock exchanges were effectively public offers. It also opens the way to argue that fully marketed secondary offers of securities already admitted to trading on applicable stock exchanges, if the sales are made on-exchange, are not public offers.

21.2.3 Exemptions to the requirement to publish a prospectus

21.57 The circumstances in which a prospectus will be required are qualified by a series of exemptions and exceptions.[67] The FSA has no discretion under the Prospectus Directive in this area, and the exemptions laid down in the Prospectus Rules are therefore a direct lift from the Prospectus Directive. These are discussed in Part 1.

21.2.4 Preliminary prospectuses

21.58 When it is clear that a prospectus is required in connection with a proposed listing, the company and its advisers will begin the drafting process. In the first instance, the parties will typically work to produce a preliminary prospectus. A preliminary prospectus functions not only as a draft of the actual prospectus (which typically is submitted to the UKLA in connection with the document vetting process), but also functions, once published, as a marketing document that the company and its advisers will distribute to potential investors during the roadshow phase of the transaction.

21.59 The key difference between a preliminary prospectus and a final prospectus is that the preliminary prospectus will not contain the exact price of the relevant securities—in a typical offering, the exact price will only be determined once the offering has been marketed to potential investors (using the preliminary prospectus, as well as other marketing documents, such as a roadshow presentation) and the level of demand in the market has been gauged. Once the company and its advisers have determined a price, this final piece of information can be added to the preliminary prospectus. The preliminary prospectus, therefore, with the addition of details of price, becomes the final prospectus.

21.2.5 Supplementary prospectuses

21.60 There is typically a gap of several days between the UKLA approving a prospectus, and settlement and admission of the securities. If, at any point during this period,

---

[67] FSMA Schedule 11.

a significant new factor, material mistake or inaccuracy relating to the information provided in the prospectus arises or is identified, the company will be required to produce a supplement that rectifies any inaccuracy or omission. For these purposes, 'significant' means significant for the purposes of making an informed assessment of (i) the assets and liabilities, financial position, profits and losses, and prospects of the relevant transferable securities and any guarantor, and (ii) the rights attaching to the securities.[68]

Supplementary prospectuses must be approved and published in the same ways as the prospectus to which they relate.[69] **21.61**

The publication of a supplementary prospectus triggers a right among investors to reassess their investment decision and withdraw their acceptance of the company's offer within a period of two working days beginning the day after publication of the supplementary prospectus.[70] This so-called 'two day put' is discussed further in Section 1.3.1.9 of Chapter 1. **21.62**

21.3 Advertisements and Financial Promotions

21.3.1 Overview

As part of the listing process, companies preparing for admission to the LSE will frequently publish marketing materials such as roadshow presentations designed to promote the company and/or the offering. Indeed, as noted above, the preliminary prospectus will often function as a key marketing aid to attract potential subscribers to the company's securities. Investment institutions underwriting offerings will likewise look to publish promotional research with the purpose of increasing the success of the offer. Both the company and investment institutions involved in the offering must consider the regimes for both advertisements and for financial promotions in the United Kingdom when disseminating information to third parties, prior to and following the offering. **21.63**

21.3.2 Advertisements

21.3.2.1 Applicable law

Under the Prospectus Directive and the Prospectus Regulation, the FSA holds power to exercise authority over the content of ancillary marketing activities in the context of an admission of securities to trading on a regulated market or an offer to the public. These rules are set out in the Prospectus Rules chapter of the FSA Handbook at PR3.3. **21.64**

---

[68] FSMA section 87A(2).
[69] FSMA section 87G.
[70] FSMA section 87Q(4).

21.3.2.2 *What is an advertisement?*

21.65 An advertisement is defined in the Prospectus Rules and the FSA Handbook as an 'announcement relating to a specific offer to the public of securities or to an admission to trading on a regulated market [and which aims to] specifically promote the potential subscription or acquisition of securities'. Article 34 of the Prospectus Rules[71] sets out a non-exhaustive list of the typical methods by which advertisements are disseminated to the public by interested parties, including brochures, presentations, press releases, telephone conversations, emails and television. Guidance issued by the FSA[72] highlights the range of written and oral communications that might fall within the advertisement regime, including investor or roadshow presentations, unapproved preliminary prospectuses and discussions with potential investors or underwriters.

21.3.2.3 *Requirements for advertisements*

21.66 Once it has been ascertained that the information being disseminated to the public qualifies as an advertisement (noting that the definition is broad), a number of criteria must be satisfied before the information can be released:[73]

- the advertisement must state that a prospectus has been or will be published and indicate where potential investors are, or will be, able to obtain it;[74]
- the advertisement must clearly state that it is an advertisement;
- the issuer of the advertisement must ensure that the information contained therein is not inaccurate or misleading; and
- information contained in the advertisement must be consistent with information contained in the prospectus, if already published, or with the information required to be in the prospectus, if the prospectus has yet to be published.

21.67 In situations where advertisements fail to comply with the above provisions, the FSA has the authority to suspend or prevent their publication.

21.3.2.4 *Related considerations*

21.68 In addition to the requirements described above for advertisements, there is a broader obligation[75] to ensure that all information concerning an offer or an admission to trading disclosed in an oral or written form, even if not for advertising purposes, must be consistent with that contained in the prospectus.

---

[71] Included also in PR3.3.5.

[72] List! Issue 12(February 2006).

[73] Prospectus Rules 3.3.2.

[74] Prospectus Rules 3.3.3 states by way of guidance that 'to comply with PR3.3.2, a written advertisement should also contain a bold and prominent statement to the effect that it is not a prospectus but an advertisement and investors should not subscribe for any transferable securities referred to in the advertisement except on the basis of information in the prospectus'.

[75] Prospectus Rules 3.3.4.

Where the particular offering in question does not require a prospectus due to an **21.69** applicable Prospectus Directive exemption,[76] there is a requirement that potential investors in the offering are all furnished with the same material information relating to the offering so that, for example, no qualified investor or other special category of investor has material information that the remainder of the category does not.[77]

21.3.3 Financial promotions—applicable law

The key sources to consider, when evaluating whether a communication falls **21.70** within the financial promotion regime, are section 21 of FSMA, the Financial Services and Markets Act 2000 (Financial Promotion) Order 2005 (SI 2005/1529) (as amended) (the 'FPO'), chapter 4 of the FSA's New Conduct of Business Sourcebook ('COBS 4') and the FSA's guidance on financial promotion and related activities in its Perimeter Guidance Manual ('PERG').

21.3.3.1 *The legal prohibition on financial promotions*

Section 21 FSMA states that a person must not, in the course of business, com- **21.71** municate an invitation or inducement to engage in investment activity. Practitioners must therefore first consider whether the communication in question is an 'inducement to engage in investment activity'. It is the view of the FSA that an objective test should be applied—whether a reasonable observer, taking account of all the circumstances at the time the communication was made, would:

- consider that the communicator intended the communication to persuade or incite the recipient to engage in investment activity or that was its purpose; and
- regard the communication as seeking to persuade or incite the recipient to engage in investment activity.

Prior to or at the time of an offering or admission to the Official List, entities **21.72** making communications regarding the company should take a cautious approach in deciding whether the communication is a financial promotion or not. A communication that might otherwise be considered mere 'profile raising' in other circumstances could be more likely to be considered a financial promotion if an offering is imminent.[78]

The legal prohibition on financial promotion has a broad scope, both in terms of **21.73** geography and in terms of the type of communications it prohibits. The financial

---

[76] For example a secondary block trade to qualified investors or an application for an AIM quotation accompanied by an offering to qualified investors only.

[77] Prospectus Directive Article 15 and Prospectus Rules 5.6.1.

[78] The FSA has issued guidance on its interpretation of the financial promotion restriction and the principal exemptions from the regime, which can be found in PERG chapter 8. This guidance represents the FSA's views and although not binding on the courts, is likely to be persuasive. It is of general application and not only relevant to authorized persons.

promotion prohibition applies to (i) 'real time' communications (for example, personal visits, telephone conversations or other interactive dialogue); and (ii) 'non-real time' communications (for example, letters, faxes, emails, information posted on websites, teletext services and pre-recorded broadcasts). Geographically, the financial promotion prohibition applies to (i) communications which originate within the United Kingdom and are sent to or capable of being accessed by UK investors; (ii) communications which originate within the United Kingdom and are sent to or capable of being accessed by overseas persons; and (iii) communications which originate outside the United Kingdom but are capable of having an effect in the United Kingdom. It is irrelevant whether the communication actually has an effect in the United Kingdom. If it is 'capable' of doing so and accordingly when the communication is included on the Internet (without appropriate filters or screens) or in the press, it should be assumed that this criterion is met. In addition, it should not be assumed that the UK population speaks English only and that a communication in another language is not capable of having an effect in the United Kingdom.

21.74   As a result of the broad scope of the financial promotion restriction, there are a number of exemptions and caveats potentially available. The legal prohibition on financial promotions does not apply in the following situations:

- the person making the communication is authorized by the FSA;[79]
- the communication in question has been approved by a person authorized by the FSA;[80] or
- an exemption from the financial promotion restriction is available under the FPO.[81]

21.3.3.2 Authorized persons making or approving financial promotions

21.75   Persons authorized in the United Kingdom by the FSA may communicate or approve financial promotions provided the financial promotion meets the requirements of the FSA Handbook, in particular COBS 4. COBS 4 has a number of specific provisions governing the content of financial promotions, but the overarching rule is that all communications, including financial promotions, must be fair, clear and not misleading.[82]

21.76   COBS 4 applies to financial promotions made by financial institutions underwriting securities offerings, if the relevant financial institution is established or operating in the United Kingdom and authorized by the FSA. It used to be the case that if the relevant financial promotion was made only to certain professionals

---

[79] FSMA section 21(2)(a).
[80] FSMA section 21(2)(b) FSMA.
[81] FSMA section 21(4) FSMA and the FPO.
[82] COBS 4.2.1.

and/or high net worth companies, the equivalent of COBS 4 did not apply. However, following the United Kingdom's implementation of MiFID in November 2007, with respect to activities falling within the scope of MiFID (including underwriting securities offerings), such entities can no longer opt out of COBS 4 (or equivalent) rules by limiting communication to professionals and/or high net worth companies or otherwise relying on an FPO exemption. Even in circumstances where an FPO exemption would be available, FSA authorized entities must comply with COBS 4 when communicating with customers and ensure that such communications, including financial promotions, are fair, clear and not misleading, taking into account the means of communication and the information the communication is intended to convey.[83]

Financial institutions and others not authorized by the FSA can make financial promotions by either having that financial promotion approved by an authorized person or by applying an exemption for the financial promotion, if an exemption is available under the FPO. As explained above, if an authorized person agrees to approve the relevant financial promotion, it must comply with COBS 4.

21.77

21.3.3.3 Exemptions

The FPO sets out a number of exemptions from the general prohibition on financial promotions. Some relevant exemptions in the context of offerings of securities are as follows:

21.78

- *Investment professionals:*[84] the financial promotion restriction does not apply to any communication which is made only to recipients whom the person making the communication believes on reasonable grounds to be investment professionals, or may reasonably be regarded as directed only at such recipients. A financial promotion may reasonably be regarded as 'directed only at such recipients' if three criteria are satisfied: (i) the financial promotion is accompanied by language indicating to whom it is directed and stating that it is only directed at such persons; (ii) the financial promotion states that persons without professional experience in matters relating to investments should not rely on it; and (iii) there are proper systems and procedures in place to prevent recipients other than investment professionals engaging in activity to which the financial promotion relates. Satisfying these three criteria provides a clear and reliable safe harbour from the financial promotion prohibition. Even if all of these three criteria are not satisfied, a communication might still be

---

[83] COBS 4.2.2(1). A communication addressed to a professional client may not need to include the same information, or be presented in the same way, as a communication addressed to a retail client.

[84] FPO Article 19 (investment professionals).

regarded as directed to investment professionals, particularly if one or more of the conditions are met.

The definition of 'investment professionals' includes: (i) FSA-authorized persons; (ii) persons exempt from FSA authorization (provided the communication relates to those activities for which that person is exempt from FSA authorization); (iii) any other person (a) whose ordinary activities involve him carrying on the controlled activity to which the communication relates for the purpose of a business carried on by him; or (b) who it is reasonable to expect will carry on such activity for the purposes of a business carried on by him; (iv) a government, local authority (whether in the United Kingdom or elsewhere) or international organization; and (v) directors, officers and employees of any of the above, provided the financial promotion is made to them in their professional capacity and where the individual's responsibilities when acting in that capacity involve the carrying out of the employer's controlled activities.[85]

- *High net worth companies, unincorporated associations, etc*:[86] the financial promotion restriction does not apply to any communication which is made only to recipients whom the person making the communication believes on reasonable grounds to be persons falling within Article 49(2) of the FPO, or may reasonably be regarded as directed only at persons falling within Article 49(2) of the FPO. A financial promotion may reasonably be regarded as 'directed only at persons falling within Article 49(2) of the FPO' where three criteria are satisfied: (i) the financial promotion is accompanied by language indicating to whom it is directed and stating that it is only directed at such persons; (ii) the financial promotion states that persons other than those falling within Article 49(2) of the FPO should not rely on it; and (iii) there are in place proper systems and procedures to prevent recipients other than persons falling within Article 49(2) of the FPO engaging in activity to which the financial promotion relates. Satisfying these three criteria provide a clear and reliable safe harbour from the financial promotion prohibition. There is some leeway if not all of the conditions are satisfied, in the same way that there is for the investment professionals exemption above.

  Persons falling within Article 49(2) of the FPO include: (i) any body corporate, or an entity in the same group as a body corporate, which has a called-up share capital or net assets of not less than (a) £500,000, provided the body corporate has no more than 20 members or is a subsidiary undertaking of an undertaking with no more than 20 members; or (b) otherwise, £5 million; (ii) any unincorporated association or partnership which has net assets of not less than

---

[85] FPO Article 4 FPO: 'controlled activities' includes activities falling within paragraphs 1 to 11 of the FPO, including dealing in securities and contractually based investments, arranging deals in investments, managing investments and advising on investments.

[86] FPO Article 49 (high net worth companies, unincorporated associations, etc.).

£5 million; (iii) the trustee of a high value trust;[87] and (iv) directors, officers and employees of an entity falling within the above criteria, provided that when acting in that capacity, their responsibilities involve engaging in investment activity.

This exemption and the exemption for communications with high net worth entities, described below, are probably the most used exemptions for the typical underwritten securities offerings, including most IPOs.

- *Certified high net worth individuals and self-certified investors*:[88] provided certain requirements are met, the financial promotion restriction does not apply to a communication which: (i) is a non-real time communication or a solicited real time communication; (ii) is made to an individual whom the person making the communication believes on reasonable grounds to be a certified high net worth individual or a self-certified investor; and (iii) relates only to certain specified investments. The investments to which (iii) refers are financial instruments relating to unlisted companies. Accordingly, where the communication relates to listed securities, or instruments related to listed securities, this exemption is not available.

The requirements for this exemption are: (a) that the individual in question has signed, within the period of twelve months ending with the day on which the communication is made, a statement prescribed by the FPO;[89] (b) that the communication is accompanied by a risk warning and certain other specified language, the contents of which are prescribed by the FPO; and (c) the risk warning and other specified language is communicated at the beginning of the communication and must precede other written or pictorial matter.

- *Members and creditors of certain bodies corporate or open-ended investment companies*:[90] the financial promotion restriction does not apply to any non-real time communication or solicited real time communication relating to certain specified investments and which is communicated by or on behalf of a body corporate or open-ended investment company ('C') to persons whom C reasonably believes is (i) a creditor or member of C (including undertakings in the same group as the body corporate); (ii) a person who is entitled to a relevant investment[91] which is issued, or to be issued, by C; (iii) a person who is entitled,

---

[87] FPO Article 49(6) FPO: a 'high value trust' means a trust where the aggregate value of the cash and investments which form part of the trust's assets (before deducting the amount of its liabilities) (a) is £10 million or more; or (b) has been £10 million or more at any time during the year immediately preceding the date on which the communication in question was first made or directed.

[88] FPO Article 48 (certified high net worth individuals) and FPO Article 50A (self-certified sophisticated investors).

[89] FPO Schedule 5 contains template statements for certified high net worth individuals and self-certified sophisticated investors.

[90] FPO Article 43 (members and creditors of certain bodies corporate) and FPO Article 44 (members and creditors of open-ended investment companies).

[91] FPO Article 43: 'relevant investment' is defined with reference to Schedule 1 FPO and includes shares, debt instruments and instruments convertible into shares and debt instruments.

whether conditionally or unconditionally, to become a member of C but who has not yet done so; and (iv) a person who is entitled, whether conditionally or unconditionally, to have transferred to him title to a relevant investment which is issued by C but has not yet acquired title to the investment. This is an extremely useful exemption for communications with shareholders and bondholders.

- *Participation in employee share schemes*:[92] the financial promotion restriction does not apply to any communication by a person ('C'), a member of the same group as C or a relevant trustee, where the communication is (i) for the purposes of an employee share scheme; and (ii) relates to certain investments[93] issued, or to be issued, by C.

  An 'employee share scheme', in relation to investments issued by C as specified above, means arrangements made or to be made by C, or by a person in the same group as C, to enable or facilitate (i) transactions in such investments between or for the benefit of employees or former employees of C, or of another member of the same group as C, and their relatives; and (ii) the holding of those investments by, or for the benefit of, such persons.

  This is an extremely useful exemption for employee option schemes and similar incentive schemes for group employees.

- *Sale of body corporate*:[94] the financial promotion restriction does not apply to any communication by, or on behalf of, a body corporate, a partnership, a single individual or a group of connected individuals[95] where the communication relates to a transaction: (i) to acquire or dispose of shares in a body corporate (other than an open-ended investment company); or (ii) a transaction entered into for the purposes of such an acquisition or disposal.

  This exemption is further subject to the satisfaction of the following conditions: (i) either (a) the shares must consist of or include 50% or more of the voting shares[96] in the body corporate; or (b) the shares, together with any already held by the person acquiring them, consist of or include at least that

---

[92] FPO Article 60 (participation in employee share schemes).

[93] FPO Article 60(1) includes certain instruments with reference to Schedule 1 FPO: shares, debt instruments, and convertibles/options in relation to shares or debt instruments.

[94] FPO Article 62 (sale of body corporate).

[95] FPO Article 62: a 'group of connected individuals' means (a) in relation to a party disposing of shares in a body corporate, a single group of persons each of whom is (i) a director or manager of the body corporate (ii) a close relative of any such director or manager; or (iii) a person acting as trustee for, or nominee of, any person falling within paragraph (i) or (ii); and (b) in relation to a party acquiring shares in a body corporate, a single group of persons each of whom is (i) a person who is or is to be a director or manager of the body corporate (ii) a close relative of any such person or (iii) a person acting as trustee for or nominee of any person falling within paragraph (i) or (ii).

[96] FPO Article 62: 'voting shares', in relation to a body corporate, means shares carrying voting rights attributable to share capital which are exercisable in all circumstances at any general meeting of that body corporate.

percentage of shares; and (c) in either case, the acquisition or disposal must be, or is to be, between parties each of whom is a body corporate, a partnership, a single individual or a group of connected individuals (the 'hard-edged' test); or (ii) the object of the transaction may reasonably be regarded as being the acquisition of day-to-day control of the affairs of the body corporate (the 'purposive test').

The sale of body corporate exemption has caused notable practical difficulties. In particular, uncertainties have arisen in the application of certain aspects of the 'hard-edged' test, with the result that the less precise 'purposive test' is typically relied on instead. In addition, if read literally, the exemption could be seen to cover offer documents and related documentation in the context of public company takeover bids, to the extent that one might reasonably view the object of a takeover bid to be the acquisition of day-to-day control of the target public company. Conflicting views have emerged among legal practitioners, and some are reluctant to rely on such a literal reading of the provision, believing instead that an offer document constitutes a financial promotion that needs to be issued or approved by an authorized person. At one stage, proposals were being considered, *inter alia*, to narrow the exemption to apply to acquisitions of small companies only (companies owned by no more than 50 persons); however, there are no indications that these proposals will be implemented.

- *Promotions in connection with admission to certain EEA markets*:[97] the financial promotion restriction does not apply to any communication: (i) that is a non-real time communication or a solicited real time communication; (ii) that a relevant EEA market[98] requires to be communicated before an investment can be admitted to trading on that market; (iii) if it were included in a prospectus issued in accordance with prospectus rules under Part VI of the Act and would be required to be communicated by those rules; and (iv) is not accompanied by any information other than information which is required or permitted to be published by the rules of that market. This is a frequently used exemption that applies to prospectuses.

- *Promotions of securities already admitted to certain markets*:[99] The financial promotion restriction does not apply to any communication which (i) is a non-real time communication or a solicited real time communication; (ii) is communicated by a body corporate ('A'), other than an open-ended investment company; and (iii) relates only to relevant investments[100] issued, or to be issued,

---

[97] FPO Article 68 (promotions in connection with admission to certain EEA markets).

[98] FPO Article 68: 'relevant EEA market' means any market on which investments can be traded or dealt in and which (a) meets the criteria specified in Part 1 of Schedule 3 FPO; or (b) is specified in, or established under, the rules of an exchange specified in Part II of Schedule 3 FPO. This definition includes the major stock exchanges throughout Europe.

[99] FPO Article 69 (promotions of securities already admitted to certain markets).

[100] See footnote 20.

by A or by another body corporate in the same group, if relevant investments issued by A or by any such body corporate are permitted to be traded on a relevant EEA market.[101]

The above exemption further requires that the communication (i) is not, and is not accompanied by, an invitation to engage in investment activity; (ii) is not, and is not accompanied by, an inducement relating to an investment other than one issued, or to be issued, by A (or another body corporate in the same group); and (iii) is not, and is not accompanied by, an inducement relating to a relevant investment which refers to (a) the price at which relevant investments have been bought or sold in the past, or (b) the yield on such investments, unless the inducement also contains an indication that past performance cannot be relied on as a guide to future performance. This exemption is essentially designed to deal with the broad meaning of 'inducement'. The underlying rationale is that if the communication is a financial promotion because it is a clear invitation to engage in investment activity, then one had better find an exemption or have the communication approved by an authorized person. However, in broad terms, if it is only an inducement that relates to securities issued by its group of companies, because inducement is such a light trigger, then one can look to this exemption to avoid the full rigours of the financial promotion prohibition.

21.3.3.4 *Contravention of the financial promotion regime*

21.79 Contravention of the UK rules on financial promotion by an unauthorized person can lead to both criminal (a maximum of two years' imprisonment or a fine, or both) and civil sanctions.[102] The person who made the unlawful financial promotion or caused it to be made will be guilty of an offence and may be unable to enforce any agreement to which the communication related and which was entered into after the communication was made. The investor may be able to recover any money or other property paid or transferred by him under the resulting agreement, together with compensation for any loss sustained by him as a result of having parted with it. This rescission type remedy, however, is subject to the discretion of the court, which may allow the agreement to be enforced or consideration to be retained by the wrongdoer if it is just and equitable to do so. In exercising its discretion, the court is required to take into account whether the wrongdoer reasonably believed that he was not making such communication and, if he did not make the communication, whether he knew that the agreement was entered into as a consequence of the communication.

---

[101] See footnote 27.
[102] FSMA section 25(1).

In any event, it is a defence for the accused to show that: (i) he believed on reason- **21.80**
able grounds that the content of the communication was prepared, or approved,
by an authorized person; or (ii) that he took all reasonable precautions and
exercised all due diligence to avoid committing the offence.[103]

21.4 Continuing Obligations

21.4.1 Applicable law

Companies admitted to the LSE occupy a privileged position that allows them to **21.81**
benefit from access to public funds, as well as increased publicity and standing.
The key trade-off for such companies—and in certain cases, for their directors
and senior management—is that they must bear the burden of complying with a
substantial set of obligations for the duration of their listing.

The principal source for many of these obligations is the Transparency Directive, **21.82**
the key aim of which is to set out a scheme of obligations applicable to listed
entities that together 'enhance investor protection, attract investors to the European
market place and improve the efficiency, openness and integrity of European
capital markets'.[104]

To give effect to the provisions of the Transparency Directive in the United **21.83**
Kingdom, the FSA published the Transparency Obligations Directive (Disclosure
and Transparency Rules) Instrument 2006 (FSA 2006/70),[105] which created the
DTRs. The DTRs operate alongside the continuing obligations regime under the
FSA's Listing Rules, which impose various continuing obligations and notifica-
tion requirements on issuers whose equity securities are admitted to the Official
List. Also relevant are the LSE's Admission and Disclosure Standards, which apply
to issuers with securities admitted to trading on the LSE's Main Market.

Read together, the DTRs, Listing Rules and the LSE's Admission and Disclosure **21.84**
Standards lay down the continuing obligations regime to which UK-listed companies must adhere. In administering these rules, the FSA must maintain the
delicate balance between investor protection and ease of operation, both of
which are essential if the United Kingdom is to maintain its strong international
standing as a listing venue.

---

[103] FSMA section 25(2).
[104] European Commission press release IP/03/436 'Securities Markets: Commission proposes
Directive to increase investor protection and transparency' (26 March 2003).
[105] Available at http://www.fsa.gov.uk.

21.4.2 Disclosure and control of inside information

21.4.2.1 Disclosure of inside information

21.85   The DTRs impose obligations on issuers to ensure that there is equal and prompt disclosure of information to all market participants.[106] DTR 2 imposes the key obligation on all companies with securities listed (or who have applied to have their securities listed) on the Main Market of the LSE:[107] such companies must announce inside information to the market via a Regulatory Information Service ('RIS') as soon as possible after it arises.[108]

21.4.2.2 Identifying inside information

21.86   Inside information is defined as information that (i) is of a precise nature; (ii) is not generally available; (iii) relates (directly or indirectly) to the issuer or its securities; and (iv) if made generally available, would be likely to have a significant effect on the price of the issuer's securities.[109]

21.87   21.4.2.2.1 'Precise'   Information is precise if (i) it indicates circumstances that exist or may reasonably be expected to come into existence, or an event that has occurred or may reasonably be expected to occur; and (ii) it is specific enough to enable a conclusion to be drawn as to the possible effect of those circumstances or that event on the price of the securities or related investments.[110]

21.88   As an example, information that the issuer is in negotiations to acquire another issuer is precise in that the negotiations are already in existence, whether or not the acquisition may reasonably be expected to occur. Whether the existence of the negotiations satisfies the other requirements for it to constitute inside information, or whether or not it can be delayed, needs to be tested against the other conditions set out below (see in particular the circumstances in which announcements can be delayed, discussed in Section 21.4.2.4 below).

21.89   21.4.2.2.2 'Not generally available'   In its Code of Market Conduct, the FSA sets out a list of factors that issuers should take into account when determining whether or not information is generally available.[111] One such factor is the extent

---

[106] DTR 2.1.3G.

Note that relevant rules in relation to dealings in inside information are also contained in the market abuse provisions of FSMA sections 118 and 397, Part V of the Criminal Justice Act and the Takeover Code, and must be complied with in addition to DTR provisions. See DTR 2.1.1.G.

[107] The obligation under DTR2 does not apply to companies whose securities are listed on AIM or the PSM.

[108] DTR 2.2.1R.

Note also the Listing Principles under Chapter 7 of the Listing Rules. In particular, Listing Principle 4, which requires listed companies to communicate information in such a way as to avoid the creation or continuation of a false market in its securities.

[109] DTR 2.2.3G read with FSMA section 118C.

[110] FSMA section 118C(5).

[111] FSA Code of Market Conduct, MAR 1.2.12.

to which the information can be obtained by 'analysing or developing other information that is generally available', [112] which would include all published financial information relating to the issuer. Significantly, the Code of Market Conduct notes that 'it is not relevant that the observation or analysis is only achievable by a person with above average financial resources, expertise or competence'.[113] The FSA's guidance on this part of the definition of inside information, therefore, does not hinge on the notion of an ordinary retail investor. On the contrary, the guidance suggests that it may well be appropriate for an issuer to assume a level of sophistication among its investors for this purpose.

The fact that the information has become generally available because of a leak, or through another means of communication (other than an RIS announcement) does not, in itself, mean that the information is inside information. **21.90**

21.4.2.2.3 'Significant effect on price' The test for inside information that **21.91** tends to create the greatest uncertainty for issuers is that of price sensitivity. There is no numeric definition (percentage change or otherwise) of 'significant effect' on price.[114] The FSA has dismissed a view that emerged among some market participants that an anticipated 10% impact on price is the threshold for an announcement and has made it clear that a 'one size fits all' approach is not appropriate.[115]

What constitutes a 'significant effect' on price, therefore, will vary widely from **21.92** issuer to issuer and will depend on a variety of factors such as the issuer's size, recent developments and the market sentiment about the issuer and the sector in which it operates.[116] For instance, it is noted in EU guidance, that the volatility of 'blue chip' securities is typically less than that of smaller, less liquid stocks. [117] Similarly, issuers in sectors that have experienced recent turbulence may be required to announce information that in the past, during periods of greater stability, may not have triggered the disclosure obligation.

Issuers are required to assess the *likelihood* that the information in question will **21.93** have a significant effect on the price of the relevant securities. Therefore, the mere possibility that the information will have a significant price effect is not enough to render it inside information; equally, it is not necessary that there should be a degree of probability close to certainty. [118]

---

[112] FSA Code of Market Conduct, MAR 1.2.12 (5).
[113] FSA Code of Market Conduct, MAR 1.2.13 (2).
[114] DTR 2.2.4G (2).
[115] List! Issue 16, paragraph 7.2.
[116] DTR 2.2.5G (1).
[117] CESR Level 3 guidance, July 2007, paragraph 1.13.
[118] CESR Level 3 guidance, July 2007, paragraph 1.12.

21.94 In determining whether a significant effect on price is likely to occur, issuers are directed to consider (i) the anticipated magnitude of the matter or event in question in the context of the totality of the issuer's activity; (ii) the relevance of the information as regards the main determinants of the securities' price; (iii) the reliability of the source; and (iv) the market variables that affect the price of the securities in question (which could include prices, returns, volatility, liquidity, price relationships among financial instruments, volume, supply and demand).[119]

21.95 Useful indicators of whether information is likely to have a significant price effect are whether (i) the type of information is the same as information which has, in the past, had a significant effect on prices; (ii) the issuer itself has already treated similar events as inside information; and (iii) pre-existing analyst research reports and opinions indicate that the type of information in question is price sensitive.[120] Significantly, the fact that the issuer can point to a published body of opinion from analysts that information of the type in question, if made generally available, is not likely to have a significant effect on price is itself an indicator that the information is not price sensitive.

21.96 As noted above, issuers are guided to consider the price sensitivity question in the context of the totality of the issuer's activity. It follows from this that the larger the 'totality' of the issuer's activity, the more significant the information in question may need to be to qualify as inside information. For example, information that is material in the context of a peripheral or non-core division of the issuer's business may cease to be material when considered in the grand scheme of the issuer's operations.

21.97 Nevertheless, in assessing price sensitivity, issuers are not permitted to 'offset good news against bad'—the fact that the impact of the information in question on the price of the issuer's securities is likely to be balanced out by the impact of other factors— thus resulting in little or no movement in price – does not mean that the information in question is not inside information.[121] For example, the loss of a contract resulting in a significant loss of business cannot be ignored on the basis that the winning of another contract offsets it. But if the loss of the contract is not significant in the scheme of the group's business because of a fall in importance of the relevant segment, an issuer might well conclude that the loss of contract is not price sensitive.

21.98 21.4.2.2.4 **The 'reasonable investor' test** As an aid to assessing the criterion of price sensitivity, the guidance notes to the DTRs instruct issuers to consider whether the information in question 'would be likely to be used by a reasonable

---

[119] CESR Level 3 guidance, July 2007, paragraph 1.13.
[120] CESR Level 3 guidance, July 2007, paragraph 1.14.
[121] FSA Final Notice re Wolfson Microelectronics, 20 January 2009.

investor as part of the basis of his investment decisions and would therefore be likely to have a significant effect on the price'.[122]

It is important to note that the purpose of the so-called 'reasonable investor' test is merely to assist the issuer in its assessment of the primary question, which is that of price sensitivity (the rationale being that if the reasonable investor would be likely to use the information in question as part of his investment decision, it follows that such information is likely to have a significant effect on the price of the securities and therefore it should be disclosed to the market). **21.99**

When applying the reasonable investor test, the issuer should assume that a reasonable investor will make investment decisions relating to the relevant securities to maximize his economic self-interest.[123] However, according to the FSA, it is not possible to prescribe how the reasonable investor test will apply in all possible situations.[124] **21.100**

The guidance notes to the DTRs state that information which is likely to be considered relevant to a reasonable investor's investment decision includes information affecting the following (generally considered for the issuer's consolidated group as a whole, though sometimes information about the issuer on a stand-alone basis may well be price sensitive): (i) the assets and liabilities of the issuer; (ii) the performance, or the expected performance, of the issuer's business; (iii) the financial condition of the issuer; (iv) the course of the issuer's business; (v) major new developments in the business of the issuer; or (vi) information previously disclosed to the market.[125] **21.101**

Importantly, there is no specific guidance on the identity of the reasonable investor. However, given the nature of the factors set out in DTR 2.2.6, issuers appear to be steered to view the reasonable investor as someone who is capable of analysing and appreciating the significance of information relating to those factors, rather than an ordinary retail investor who may be reliant on expert advice from others to make his investment decision. **21.102**

21.4.2.3 *Timing of disclosure*

21.4.2.3.1 When does the obligation to disclose arise? The disclosure obligations applicable to the issuers under the DTRs are designed to ensure that there is prompt and fair disclosure of relevant information to the market. Generally, the issuer will be required to notify the RIS *as soon as possible* of any inside information that directly concerns itself, unless the issuer is permitted to delay disclosure in the limited range of circumstances discussed below.[126] **21.103**

---

[122] DTR 2.2.4 (1).
[123] DTR 2.2.5 (2).
[124] DTR 2.2.6.
[125] DTR 2.2.6.
[126] DTR 2.2.1.

21.104 If, however, the issuer is faced with an unexpected and significant event, a short delay may be acceptable if it is necessary to clarify the situation. If the issuer believes that there is a danger of inside information leaking before the facts and their impact can be confirmed, it should make a 'holding announcement' via the RIS. This announcement should detail as much of the subject matter as possible, contain the reasons why a fuller announcement could not be made and include an undertaking to announce further details as soon as possible. If the issuer is unable or unwilling to make a holding announcement, it may be appropriate to suspend the trading of its listed securities until the issuer is in a position to make an announcement.

21.105 In any event, the DTRs require a fast response and the issuer needs to have systems and procedures in place, including streamlined approval procedures, to release information, whether it is a holding announcement or a full announcement, in time to comply with the disclosure requirement. It will not be a defence from sanction by the FSA for the issuer to claim that approval for release could not be obtained readily from the relevant officers.[127]

21.4.2.4 *Delaying disclosure*[128]

21.106 In certain limited circumstances, the obligation to disclose inside information 'as soon as possible' is relaxed and an issuer may legitimately delay an announcement where such announcement would prejudice its legitimate interests.

21.107 The guidance notes to the DTRs acknowledge that delaying disclosure of inside information will not always mislead the public, although a developing situation should be monitored so that if circumstances change an immediate disclosure can be made.[129] The guidance notes also recognize that investors understand that some information must be kept confidential until developments are at a stage when an announcement can be made without prejudicing the legitimate interests of the issuer. This attributes a certain level of sophistication to investors. Issuers may rely on this attributed sophistication, provided they satisfy the requirements for delaying disclosure.

21.108 The issuer will be entitled to delay the public disclosure of inside information where such disclosure would prejudice its legitimate interests, provided that:

- such omission would not be likely to mislead the public;
- any person receiving the information from the issuer or its agents owes an actual duty of confidentiality to the issuer; and
- the issuer is able to ensure the confidentiality of that information.

---

[127] Note also the FSA's requirement, set out above, that the information be made by an alternative means if the RIS is closed for business.
[128] DTR 2.5.1–2.5.5.
[129] DTR 2.5.2.

For this purpose, the DTRs state that a legitimate interest to delay disclosure would relate to the following non-exhaustive circumstances:[130]

• negotiations in course, or related elements where the outcome or normal pattern of those negotiations would be likely to be affected by public disclosure;[131] in particular, where the financial viability of a listed issuer is in grave and imminent danger (although not within the scope of the applicable insolvency law), public disclosure of information may be delayed for a limited period, where such a public disclosure would seriously jeopardize the interest of existing and potential shareholders by undermining the conclusion of specific negotiations designed to ensure the long term financial recovery of such issuer;[132] or

• with regard to companies with a dual board structure only, decisions taken or contracts made by the management body which need to be approved by another body to become effective, provided that a public disclosure of the information before such approval, together with the simultaneous announcement that this approval is still pending, would jeopardize the correct assessment of the information by the public.

21.109 Whether or not a listed issuer has a legitimate interest that would be prejudiced by the disclosure of certain inside information is an assessment that must be made by the issuer in the first instance.[133]

21.110 The FSA has stated that companies should not delay an announcement to make preparations for the announcement of results, such as presentations to analysts or webcasts, but that such preparations can legitimately occur alongside the efforts to release results quickly.[134]

21.4.2.5 *Dealing with rumours*

21.111 The DTRs provide guidance on dealing with press speculation and rumours. Issuers are instructed to carefully assess whether the speculation or rumour has given rise to a situation where the issuer has inside information.[135]

21.112 If the rumour is largely accurate, the issuer should consider whether the information underlying the rumour constitutes inside information. If the issuer has been relying on the safe harbour for delaying disclosure, the existence of the rumour

---

[130] DTR 2.5.2.
[131] For example, a negotiation about a significant acquisition or disposal might satisfy this requirement.
[132] But note that in this case, the delay of disclosure relates to the fact or substance of such negotiations, and not to the issuer's financial condition.
[133] DTR 2.5.5.
[134] List! Issue 16, paragraph 7.3.
[135] DTR 2.7.

suggests that there has been a leak and that the issuer can no longer delay disclosure, as it is no longer able to ensure confidentiality. In such circumstances, an announcement should be made via the RIS as soon as possible.[136]

21.113   If, on the other hand, the rumour is false, FSA guidance states that it is unlikely that the issuer will be required to make an announcement—the issuer's knowledge that the rumour is false is not itself likely to amount to inside information. Even if it does amount to inside information, the FSA expects that in most of those cases the issuer would be able to delay disclosure (often indefinitely) in accordance with the requirements described in Section 21.3.2.[137]

21.4.2.6 Selective disclosure[138]

21.114   If an issuer delays public disclosure of inside information under the circumstances permitted by the DTRs, it may selectively disclose that information to persons bound by a duty of confidentiality (for example as a result of a contract or professional obligations).[139] Such persons would typically include:

- the issuer's advisers (including lawyers and auditors) and advisers of any other persons involved in the matter in question;
- persons with whom the issuer is negotiating, or intends to negotiate, any commercial, financial or investment transaction (including prospective underwriters or placees of the issuer's financial instruments);
- employee representatives or trade unions acting on their behalf;
- any government department, or any other statutory or regulatory body or authority;
- major shareholders of the issuer;
- the issuer's lenders; and
- credit-rating agencies.

21.115   Analysts are not automatically included in the category of persons to whom selective disclosure is permitted; however, disclosure to analysts may be justified if the analyst is acting in an advisory capacity to the issuer. The FSA has provided informal advice on what constitutes good practice when dealing with analysts.[140]

21.116   If inside information is released to a third party in the normal exercise of an issuer's employment, profession or duties, then such issuer must make complete and effective public disclosure of that information via an RIS, simultaneously if it was an intentional disclosure or as soon as possible if it was non-intentional.

---

[136] DTR 2.7.2.
[137] DTR 2.7.3.
[138] DTR 2.5.6.
[139] DTR 2.5.7.
[140] List! Issue 9, June 2005.

Issuers should have a clear communications policy in place that clearly identifies **21.117**
the process for communication and the employees responsible for communication,
thereby reducing the risk of inadvertent disclosure.[141]

21.4.2.7 *Making an announcement in practice*

21.4.2.7.1 Publication via an RIS The responsibility to ensure that inside **21.118**
information is disclosed properly lies with the company's directors (although the
directors may delegate such responsibility).[142] The principal means by which this
responsibility may be discharged is by way of announcement to an RIS, such as
the LSE's Regulatory News Service.[143] The RIS will then disseminate the full text
of the announcement to newsvendors.

RIS announcements must be drafted such that the key content of the message **21.119**
is prominently noted and easily understood by a reasonable investor. The
announcement should clearly identify the name of the issuer and the time and
date of the communication of the information,[144] and the headline should reflect
the information that has the greatest significance.[145]

The company must take all reasonable care to ensure that any information it **21.120**
releases to an RIS is not misleading, false or deceptive and does not omit anything
likely to affect the import of the information.[146] Upon request by the FSA, the
company must provide to the FSA the name of the person that communicated the
information to the RIS, the security validation details, the time and date of the
communication of the information to the RIS, the medium in which the information was communicated to the RIS and details of any embargo placed by the issuer
on the relevant information.[147]

There is a further requirement that the company must not combine an RIS **21.121**
announcement with the marketing of its activities in a manner likely to be
misleading.[148] The issuer must have regard to the wider context of its marketing
activities against which any announcement will be interpreted.

---

[141] List! Issue 9, June 2005, paragraph 2.3.

[142] It is pertinent to note the following Listing Principles which re-affirm directors' responsibility
to disclose:

Listing Principle 1: A listed company must take reasonable steps to enable its directors to
understand their responsibilities as directors.

Listing Principle 2: A listed company must take reasonable steps to establish and maintain
adequate procedures, systems and controls to enable it to comply with its obligations.

[143] The rules make it clear that an issuer will be deemed to have complied with the obligation
to disclose where, upon the coming into existence of a set of circumstances or the occurrence of an
event, albeit not yet formalized, the issuer notifies an RIS as soon as possible.

[144] DTR 6.3.7.

[145] 'List!' Issue 9 (June 2005) paragraph 2.6.

[146] LR1.3.3.

[147] DTR 6.3.8.

[148] DTR 1.3.5.

21.122 The company must not charge investors any specific cost for information required to be disclosed under the FSA Rules.[149]

21.123 **21.4.2.7.2 Publication of information on the company's Internet site**[150] Inside information about the company that is announced via the RIS must be made available on the company's website by the close of business of the day following the RIS announcement.[151] The company may wish to create a special section on its website relating to such required regulatory announcements. The company must not publish inside information on its website before such inside information is notified to an RIS.[152] The issuer must, for a period of one year following publication, post on its website all inside information that it is required to disclose via the RIS.[153]

21.124 **21.4.2.7.3 Equivalent information**[154] The issuer must take reasonable care to ensure that the disclosure of inside information to the public is synchronized as closely as possible in all jurisdictions in which it has securities admitted to trading, or for which the issuer requested admission to trading on a regulated market in the United Kingdom or overseas. Information that may be of importance to the public in the EEA but is disclosed in a non-EEA state must be announced through an RIS.

21.4.2.8 Insider lists

21.125 **21.4.2.8.1 The requirement for an insider list** DTR 2 requires issuers to compile lists of persons working for them (under a contract of employment or otherwise) who have regular or occasional access to inside information relating, directly or indirectly, to the issuer.[155] Issuers must also ensure that persons acting on their behalf (lawyers, financial advisers, etc.) compile such lists with respect to persons working for them.[156] Such insider lists must be provided to the FSA as soon as possible upon request.[157] Issuers should consider supplementing insider lists with notes, timetables of discussion, actions and decisions surrounding the price-sensitive event, and insert details of instances where individuals had access to inside information because the FSA, when conducting market abuse investigations, may request

---

[149] DTR 6.3.9.
[150] DTR 2.3.1.
[151] Note that all RIS announcements must be made in English.
[152] DTR 2.3.3.
[153] DTR 2.3.5.
[154] DTR 2.4.1.
[155] DTR 2.8.1R.
    The list should include the issuer's own employees who have access to inside information and the issuer's principal contacts at any other firm or company acting on its behalf who also have access to inside information concerning the issuer: DTR 2.8.7G.
[156] DTR 2.8.1R.
[157] DTR 2.8.2R.

specific details regarding who had access to inside information and at what time to determine whether there has been inappropriate use of inside information.[158]

In preparing insider lists, the issuer's primary consideration is to ensure that the insider list is comprehensive and extends to both senior managers and support staff.[159] The less care a company takes regarding the disclosure of inside information in internally circulated documents, the larger the group of people the FSA could regard as having access to inside information (even those further down in the chain of hierarchy such as secretarial and administrative staff) and should therefore be included on the relevant insider list. Companies must adopt strict procedures (including, *inter alia*, passwords, closed access systems, etc.) to identify confidential documents and to regulate access to such confidential documents. Issuers must also ensure (through training sessions or distribution of explanatory notes) that employees with access to inside information acknowledge the legal duties imposed on them vis-à-vis access to such information and the penalties for violation of such duties.[160] Issuers can rely on contractual confidentiality provisions to ensure compliance with the DTR.[161] **21.126**

21.4.2.8.2 Drafting an insider list   An insider list must clearly identify the person with access to inside information, the reason for including such person on the list (this need not be a detailed description—it can be limited to mentioning the categories of information to which the insider has access) and the date on which the insider list was created and updated.[162] In addition, the FSA has suggested that it is good practice to go beyond the strict requirements of the DTRs and include information such as the insider's home address, telephone numbers, and date and time he became aware of the event giving rise to inside information.[163] **21.127**

Insider lists can be maintained in electronic form and must be kept for five years from the date on which they are drawn up or updated.[164] Further, they must be updated promptly to reflect pertinent changes, including the addition of new insiders and changes to the reason why a person is on the list.[165] **21.128**

21.4.2.9 *Disclosure of transactions by persons discharging managerial responsibilities*

The rationale that underpins DTR 2—investor protection, by means of the publication of all information that might be pertinent to their investment **21.129**

---

[158] Market Watch Issue 24 (October 2007).
[159] Ibid.
[160] DTR 2.8.9R and DTR 2.8.10R.
[161] FSA Policy Statement 05/3, Implementation of the Market Abuse Directive, page 15.
[162] DTR 2.8.3R.
[163] Market Watch Issue 24 (October 2007).
[164] DTR 2.8.5R.
[165] DTR 2.8.4R.

decisions—applies equally to DTR 3, which sets out the obligation for issuers[166] to disclose to the market all dealings in the issuer's securities by their own directors and senior management (or, as they are referred to in the DTRs, persons discharging managerial responsibilities ('PDMRs')) and their connected persons.

21.130   DTR 3 sets up a two-step mechanism to enable issuers to meet this disclosure obligation. Firstly, PDMRs are required to notify the issuer of all transactions conducted by them or their connected persons on their own account[167] in the issuer's securities, within four business days from the day on which the relevant transaction occurred.[168]

21.131   Secondly, once in receipt of a PDMR disclosure, issuers must disclose the relevant information to the market via an RIS as soon as possible and in any event, by no later than the end of the business day following receipt of the information.[169]

21.132   DTR 3 also requires issuers to disclose any information they receive pursuant to the Companies Act 2006[170] regarding the shareholdings of directors and their connected persons.[171]

21.133   **21.4.2.9.1 Identifying PDMRs**   Although the requirement under DTR 3 is fairly straightforward, difficulties have arisen in interpreting the terms 'PDMR' and 'connected persons'.

21.134   PDMRs include directors and senior executives of the issuer who have regular access to inside information and the power to make managerial decisions affecting the future prospects of the issuer. The FSA has indicated that the term is likely

---

[166] DTR 3 applies to both UK and overseas issuers with shares admitted to trading on a regulated market where the United Kingdom is the designated home member state. In practice, certain other categories of issuers (such as an EEA incorporated issuer with shares admitted to trading in its home country and in the UK or a non-EEA issuer with shared admitted on its domestic market, the United Kingdom and another EEA jurisdiction where the other EEA jurisdiction has been chosen as the home state) are required to disclose information of the type listed in DTR 3 as soon as possible after they become aware of it. This is to ensure that information disclosed by the issuer in its home state or country of listing is also made available in the United Kingdom and not to impose an obligation to disclose more information than they are required to disclose in their home state or country of listing. See UKLA newsletter List! Issue 11 (September 2005). However, DTR 3 does not apply to issuers of GDRs admitted to trading on a regulated market, provided the issuer's shares are not also admitted to trading on a regulated market.

[167] The UKLA notes that 'transactions conducted on their own account' includes transactions which are the result of an action taken by the person concerned or undertaken with such person's consent, transactions whose beneficiaries are mainly persons discharging managerial responsibilities and transactions having a material impact on such a person's interest in an issuer. See UKLA newsletter List! Issue No. 11, September 2005, paragraph 8.2.

[168] DTR 3.1.2R. DTR 3.1.3R sets out the information the relevant disclosure must contain.

[169] DTR 3.1.4R(2).

[170] Under s 793 of the Companies Act, an issuer may ask anyone it reasonably believes to be one of its current or former shareholders to provide details of such shareholding.

[171] DTR 3.1.4R.

to include (i) senior employees who are executive committee members; and (ii) directors/senior executives at subsidiaries within the group if they regularly access inside information and make decisions affecting the business and development of the issuer.[172]

On the other hand, employees who merely provide information or analysis that enables others to make decisions, such as company secretaries or general counsel, are excluded.   **21.135**

The meaning of 'connected persons' is drawn largely from section 345 of the Companies Act 1985, which includes the following: **21.136**

- the spouse, civil partner, minor child or step-child of a person discharging managerial responsibilities;
- an associated body corporate, i.e. a body corporate where the manager and persons connected with him together control, or can exercise, more than 20% of the voting power in general meeting or are interested in at least 20% of the equity shares;
- the trustees of a trust of which the beneficiaries include the manager, his spouse, children or step-children aged under 18 years or a body corporate with which he is associated;
- any partner of the manager or of any person connected with the manager.

In addition, the following two categories of person are brought within the definition of 'connected persons' for the purposes of DTR 3:   **21.137**

- a relative of a person discharging managerial responsibilities within an issuer, who, on the date of the transaction in question has shared the same household as that person for at least 12 months; and
- a body corporate in which a person discharging managerial responsibilities within an issuer, or any person connected with him as above is a director/senior executive who has the power to make management decisions affecting the business prospects of that body corporate.[173]

21.4.3 Periodic financial reporting

To enable investors to assess the performance of a listed company on an ongoing basis, the Listing Rules and the DTRs require the periodic publication of certain financial information and management commentary to the market. Although an issuer's auditors will assist the board with the preparation and publication of   **21.138**

---

[172] Market Watch Issue 12 (June 2005) pages 8–9.

[173] The FSA has clarified that the last category of connected persons does not extend to include all companies that share a common director but rather only such companies that the manager or connected person can control, i.e. the level of control must extend beyond merely the ability to exert influence. List! Issue 9 (June 2005) paragraph 13.4.

ongoing financial information, directors must now in many instances take public responsibility for financial information. It is therefore important that companies and their officers understand their obligations and work with the auditors on an ongoing basis.

21.139 The UK periodic financial reporting regime was updated in 2007 to reflect the implementation of the Transparency Directive. This was aimed at ensuring comparability of financial information for listed companies throughout the EU.

21.4.3.1 *Scope and sources of requirements*

21.140 The basic financial reporting requirements for all issuers with securities admitted to trading on a regulated market are set out in DTR 4. Subject to the exemptions set out in DTR 4.4 and the individual rules, these apply to all issuers for whom the United Kingdom is their home state. All issuers must publish an annual financial report, with the exception of supra-national public sector issuers.[174] Whilst issuers of shares must publish semi-annual reports and either interim management statements or quarterly reports, companies with GDRs and convertibles admitted to trading on a regulated market are excused from these requirements, and ordinary debt and preference share issuers are excused from the latter.[175] There is an equivalence regime for EEA issuers whose relevant laws are considered equivalent by the FSA, which maintains a list for this purpose.[176] Certain US and Swiss provisions have been deemed currently equivalent for this purpose.[177]

21.141 The DTRs set out the basic content requirements derived from the Transparency Directive for annual financial reports, semi-annual reports and interim management statements. However, companies with a primary listing of shares must also comply with the parallel regime in Chapter 9 of the Listing Rules, which requires the disclosure of significant additional information. The requirements imposed on issuers by the Listing Rules and DTRs are in addition to the underlying accounting requirements that apply in the relevant jurisdiction to the entity in question (e.g. the requirements in the Companies Act 2006 that apply to a UK public limited company).

21.4.3.2 *Annual financial reports*

21.142 **21.4.3.2.1 DTR requirements** Issuers required to publish annual financial reports must do so as soon as possible after they have been approved and at the

---

[174] DTR 4.1, DTR 4.4.1–2. Although the Transparency Directive and DTR requirements exempt wholesale high-denomination debt issuers, the requirement to produce an annual report is maintained by the Listing Rules.

[175] DTR 4.2–3, DTR 4.4.5 et seq.

[176] DTR 4.4.8.

[177] See: http://www.fsa.gov.uk/Pages/Doing/UKLA/company/non_eea/index.shtml.

latest within four months after the end of the financial year to which they relate.[178] A delay in publication may result in the suspension of the issuer's listing. All listed companies must ensure that their annual financial reports remain publicly available for at least five years.[179]

21.143 An annual financial report must include: (i) audited financial statements; (ii) a management report; and (iii) a responsibility statement.[180] The financial statements must generally comprise consolidated accounts prepared in accordance with IFRS, as well as accounts for the parent company prepared in accordance with the national law of the EEA state in which it is incorporated.[181] There are separate rules for companies not required to prepare consolidated accounts. In addition, the relevant audit opinions must be included, and non-EEA companies traded in the United Kingdom must ensure that the auditor fulfils one of the requirements set out in DTR 4.1.7(4).

21.144 The management report should contain a 'fair review' of the issuer's business and a description of the principal risks and uncertainties facing the issuer.[182] To constitute a fair review, the report should include a balanced and comprehensive analysis of the development and performance of the issuer's business and of the position of its subsidiaries included in the consolidation taken as a whole, consistent with the size and complexity of the business. In addition, to the extent necessary for an understanding of the issuer's development, performance or position, the analysis should include both financial and, where appropriate, non-financial key performance indicators.[183] Additional information requirements for the annual management report set out in DTR 4.1.11 include disclosure on events subsequent to the balance sheet date, likely future developments, research and development 'R&D' activity and information surrounding the issuer's use of financial instruments.

21.145 While an issuer is responsible for all information made public pursuant to the DTRs, the FSA has recently introduced a requirement for issuers to include responsibility statements on certain financial information (akin to a prospectus) to be made by the relevant persons 'responsible within the issuer'.[184] This statement, included in the annual financial report and the semi-annual report (discussed below), must confirm to the best of the knowledge of the person making the statement (whose name and function must be clearly indicated in the

---

[178] DTR 4.1.3.
[179] DTR 4.1.4.
[180] DTR 4.1.5.
[181] See, generally, DTR 4.1.6–7.
[182] DTR 4.1.8.
[183] DTR 4.1.9.
[184] DTR 4.1.12. This requirement is derived from the Transparency Directive.

responsibility statement), that (i) the financial statements, prepared in accordance with the applicable set of accounting standards, give a true and fair view of the assets, liabilities, financial position and profit or loss of the company and the undertakings included in the consolidation as a whole; and (ii) the management report includes a fair review of the development and performance of the business and the position of the issuer and the undertakings included in the consolidation taken as a whole, together with a description of the principal risks and uncertainties that they face. The FSA has stated that an issuer has the discretion to decide who will issue the responsibility statement, but has indicated that it would usually envisage the directors performing this function.[185]

21.146   The Transparency Directive classifies annual reports and accounts as regulated information. As such, annual reports must be published to an RIS in full, if possible, and the RIS must indicate on which website the full document is available.

21.147   **21.4.3.2.2 Super-equivalent requirements for issuers with a Primary Listing** The Listing Rules contain a number of super-equivalent requirements over and above the Transparency Directive minimums, aimed at ensuring best practice disclosure of financial and related information for issuers with a Primary Listing of shares.[186]

21.148   All primary listed issuers must include the information contained in Listing Rule 9.8.4, which includes, *inter alia*: (i) additional financial disclosure concerning previous disclosures of unaudited financial information and amounts of interest capitalized by the group; (ii) details of certain related-party transactions and incentive schemes; (iii) information on directors' emoluments; and (iv) disclosure of certain significant and connected contracts between the company or its subsidiaries and directors or controlling shareholders. In addition, companies incorporated in the United Kingdom are required by Listing Rule 9.8.6 to include further details on notifiable interests, an audited going concern statement, details of market purchases and authorities and statements as to the issuer's compliance throughout the period with the Combined Code on Corporate Governance (certain of which must be reviewed by the issuer's auditors). This latter requirement reflects the 'comply or explain principle' discussed below and aims (where relevant) to explain to shareholders how and why the company has not complied with perceived corporate governance best practice.

21.149   In contrast to the above, for overseas issuers with a Primary Listing, Listing Rule 9.8.7 requires disclosure only of whether or not the issuer complies with the corporate governance regime of its country of incorporation, the significant ways in

---

[185] See List! Issue 14.
[186] See, generally, LR 9.8.

which such corporate governance regime differs from that set out in the Combined Code and the unexpired term of the service contract of any director proposed for election or re-election at the forthcoming annual general meeting. This divergence in practice between UK and overseas issuers with a Primary Listing has been increasingly controversial in recent years, as more and more international companies have sought the liquidity and caché of a London primary listing, leading to criticism from certain investor protection bodies and other market participants. As seen below, where an applicant seeks admission to the prestigious FTSE All Share Index, additional requirements apply to attempt to correct any perceived best practice shortfalls in this and related areas.

Finally, the Listing Rules require a UK issuer with a Primary Listing to publish a report to shareholders containing detailed information on executive directors' remuneration, benefits and service contracts, including certain audited information.[187] **21.150**

21.4.3.2.3 Preliminary statement of annual results For issuers with a Primary Listing, should a preliminary statement of annual results be prepared, it must be published via an RIS as soon as possible after the board has approved it. Following the Transparency Directive, such a statement is optional for issuers, but if it is prepared, it must comply with the rules on preliminary statements. Any statement must have been agreed with the issuer's auditors and comply with the disclosure requirement set out in the Listing Rules. The statement must show the figures in the form of a table, including the items (discussed below) required for a semi-annual report, and it must be consistent with the presentation to be adopted in the annual accounts for that financial year.[188] **21.151**

Any statement of annual results must give details of the nature of any likely modification that may be contained in the auditor's report and include any additional information necessary for the purpose of assessing the results announced. **21.152**

Although these 'prelims' are now optional, issuers are still required to comply with the general obligation to disclose inside information as soon as possible, which may require earlier disclosure of information than might traditionally have been announced in a prelim. **21.153**

21.4.3.3 Semi-annual financial reports

As above, certain issuers will also be required to publish a semi-annual financial report covering the first six months of their financial year. These reports must be published as soon as possible, and no later than two months after the end of the **21.154**

---

[187] See, generally, LR 9.8.8 as referred to in LR 9.8.6(7).
[188] LR 9.7A.1.

period to which they relate. As with annual financial reports, these must remain available for five years.[189]

21.155 A half-yearly report must include a condensed set of financial statements (including certain comparative information from previous periods),[190] an interim management report, which must include an indication of important events that have occurred during the first six months of the financial year and their impact on the condensed financial statements, a description of the principal risks and uncertain ties for the remaining six months of the financial year and details of related-party transactions.[191]

21.156 There are a number of rules aimed at ensuring the comparability of the half-yearly report with the annual financial report.

As with the annual financial report, responsibility statements must be made by the persons responsible within the issuer,[192] although the company will also remain responsible for all information drawn up and made public under the rules. Finally, if the half-yearly financial report has been audited or reviewed, the audit report or review report must be reproduced in full.[193]

21.4.3.4 Interim management statements

21.157 Issuers with a primary or secondary listing of shares that do not prepare quarterly financial reports are required to publish a public statement of the management during the first six-month period and the second six-month period, of the financial year. The concept of an interim management statement was introduced by the Transparency Directive as an alternative to quarterly reporting, and there was

---

[189] DTR 4.2.2.

[190] If an issuer is required to prepare consolidated accounts, the condensed set of financial statements must be prepared in accordance with IAS 34. If not, the statements must contain, as a minimum, a condensed balance sheet, a condensed profit and loss account, and explanatory notes (DTR 4.2.4) and comply with the requirements of DTR 4.2.5.

[191] DTR 4.2.3, 4.2.7–8.

[192] For the half-yearly report, the statement made by such person must confirm that to the best of his or her knowledge, the condensed set of financial statements, which has been prepared in accordance with the applicable set of accounting standards, gives a true and fair view of the assets, liabilities, financial position and profit or loss of the issuer, or the undertakings included in the consolidation as a whole and that the interim management report includes a fair review of the information required. A person making a responsibility statement will satisfy the requirement to confirm that the condensed set of financial statements gives a true and fair view of the assets, liabilities, financial position and profit or loss of the issuer (or the undertakings included in the consolidation as a whole) by including a statement that the condensed set of financial statements have been prepared in accordance with IAS 34, or, for UK issuers not using IFRS, pronouncements on interim reporting issued by the Accounting Standards Board, provided always that a person making such a statement has reasonable grounds to be satisfied that the condensed set of financial statements prepared in accordance with such a standard is not misleading (DTR 4.2.10).

[193] DTR 4.2.9.

significant discussion between practitioners and the regulator on the content of such a statement.

Each statement must be made between ten weeks after the beginning, and six weeks before the end, of the relevant period.[194] It must contain information that covers the period between the beginning of the relevant six-month period and the date of publication of the statement, including an explanation of material events and transactions that have taken place during the relevant period and their impact on the financial position of the issuer and its controlled undertakings, and a general description of the financial position and performance of the issuer and its controlled undertakings during the relevant period.[195]   **21.158**

The FSA has given guidance on the content of interim management statements,[196] noting that it does not expect issuers to apply the conventions currently required for annual and interim reporting, and that the content of performance reports, trading statements or other similar reports may satisfy the requirements for interim management statements, provided the information required by DTR 4.3.5 is also included, i.e. details of the material events and transactions that have taken place and their impact on the financial position of the issuer. The FSA goes as far as saying that an interim management statement may not require financial data in certain circumstances, such as where the nature of the issuer enables a narrative description of events during the period. The guidance is not exhaustive, and above all the content of an interim management statement must be appropriate for the issuer and stakeholders in question.   **21.159**

21.4.3.5 *Notification of dividends*

Any decision by an issuer with a Primary Listing to pay or make any dividend or other distribution or to withhold any dividend or interest payment must be disclosed as soon as possible to an RIS and must give details of the exact net amount payable per share, the payment date, and certain other information required by the Listing Rules.[197] This requirement is super-equivalent to the Transparency Directive.   **21.160**

21.4.3.6 *Liability for misstatements and omissions in periodic reports*

Issuers may be liable for certain statements made in their periodic financial disclosure if their securities are admitted to trading on a regulated market in the United Kingdom, or if they are admitted to trading on an EEA regulated market and the   **21.161**

---

[194] DTR 4.2.3–3.
[195] DTR 4.3.4–5.
[196] See List! Issue 14, paragraphs 22 et seq.
[197] LR 9.7A.2.

United Kingdom is their home member state.[198] If such an issuer's accounts or reports contain untrue or misleading statements or omit material facts, and a person acquires securities in reliance on the information and suffers loss, the issuer may incur statutory liability to investors.[199] The relevant provisions ensure that investors have the right to take action against companies in respect of financial statements that were made fraudulently.

21.162   Issuers may be liable under FSMA to pay compensation to a person who has acquired securities and suffered loss as a result of any untrue or misleading statement in, or omission of, any matter required to be published in (i) an annual report; (ii) a half-yearly report; (iii) an interim management statement; or (iv) any voluntary preliminary statement published in advance of a report or statement.[200] FSMA does not impose liability for delay in making announcements.

21.163   An issuer is only liable if a PDMR in relation to the publication[201] knew that the statement was untrue or misleading, was reckless as to whether it was, or knew the omission was a dishonest concealment of a material fact, and the investor acquired securities in reliance on the information at a time when, and in circumstances in which, it was reasonable for him to rely on that information.[202] There is a safe harbour from liability if the directors are merely negligent,[203] but there is no requirement that the maker of the statement intends the recipient to rely on it and the provision merely requires that the recipient's reliance should be reasonable in the circumstances. As such, the claimant may not succeed under the relevant provision if he has available means of checking the publication but chooses not to do so.

21.164   The issuer is only liable to an acquirer of securities who has suffered a loss. FSMA also excludes any liability of the issuer or any other person (including directors) to any investor or person in respect of reliance on the same errors, other than as contemplated under FSMA section 90A(4)–(5). FSMA also limits the liability of persons other than the issuer (including directors) to being liable only to the issuer and not to third parties.[204] These limitations are subject to certain specific criminal and civil penalties.

---

198   FSMA section 90A.
199   FSMA section 90A(3).
200   FSMA section 90A(1).
201   In this context, PDMRs in relation to a publication are defined specifically as any director of the issuer (or person occupying the position of director and called by another name) (i) where an issuer's affairs are managed by its members, any of the issuer's members; and (ii) where an issuer has no persons in the above two categories, any of the issuer's senior executives who has responsibilities in relation to the publication (FSMA section 90A(9)).
202   FSMA section 90A(4)–(5).
203   FSMA section 90A(6)(a).
204   FSMA section 90A(6)(b)–(8).

Although directors are not liable to investors under these provisions, a new **21.165**
provision in the Companies Act 2006 gives UK listed companies a right of action
on a back-to-back basis against directors in certain circumstances.[205] Under this
provision, a director can be liable to compensate a UK issuer for any loss that the
company suffers as a result of any untrue or misleading statement in, or omission
from, the directors' report (including the business review section), the directors'
remuneration report, or the summary financial statement (so far as it is derived
from either of the above reports). However, a director is only liable to compensate
the issuer for reimbursing an investor who suffered loss, if the director knew, or
was reckless as to whether, the relevant statement was untrue or misleading, or
knew the omission to be dishonest concealment of a material fact.

21.4.3.7 *Disclosure of interests in an issuer's securities*

The DTRs impose various obligations on a UK issuer of shares to inform the **21.166**
market of transactions in its shares (and certain related financial instruments.
To facilitate such market announcements, the DTRs also impose back-to-back
obligations on relevant securityholders to inform issuers of their holdings. These
disclosure obligations consist of (i) the general voteholder and issuer notification
regime for the acquisition or disposal of major shareholdings in DTR 5 (discussed
in this Section); and (ii) the specific disclosure regime for transactions in company
securities by PDMRs within an issuer in DTR 3 (discussed above).

The regime in DTR 5 was introduced by the Transparency Directive in 2007 and **21.167**
focuses on the disclosure of control over voting rights attached to shares. This
represents a significant shift from the historic UK regime, as set out in the
Companies Act 1985, which required the disclosure of 'interests in shares'.
Alongside this change, responsibility for overseeing the regime passed from the
(then) Department of Trade and Industry to the FSA.

21.4.3.7.1 **Applicable provisions and scope of rules** The UK regime on dis- **21.168**
closure of significant interests in shares centres on the acquisition and disposal,
whether directly or indirectly, of voting rights in shares listed on a regulated
market or prescribed market (such as AIM).[206] Holders must notify both the issuer
and the FSA of changes to their interest, and the issuer must notify the market.
The new regime catches not only direct interests in shares, but also the direct or
indirect holding of certain qualifying 'financial instruments' (and, in the case of

---

[205] Companies Act 2006 section 463.

[206] DTR 5.1.2. The regime is drafted broadly, such that an acquisition or disposal of shares
is to be regarded as effective for this purpose when the relevant transaction is executed unless the
transaction provides for settlement to be subject to conditions which are beyond the control of the
parties. Similarly, a stock-lending agreement which provides for the outright transfer of securities
and provides the lender with a right to call for re-delivery is not (as respects the lender) to be taken
as involving a disposal of any shares the subject of the stock loan (DTR 5.1.1).

UK issuers, certain instruments having similar economic effect).[207] The FSA has published extensive guidance, including helpful examples, on the notification regime.[208]

21.169   Various super-equivalent provisions have been retained to ensure that best practice disclosure requirements continue for UK issuers. As a result, it is acknowledged among practitioners that the provisions of DTR 5 are often difficult for issuers to interpret. In short, UK issuers on regulated markets (such as the Main Market of the LSE) are subject to the existing Companies Act 1985 disclosure thresholds, discussed below. Non-EEA issuers with a listing of shares on a regulated market, and for whom the United Kingdom is their home member state, and their share-holders, must comply with Directive-minimum standards, as set out in Part 1, unless the relevant home regime is deemed equivalent to UK requirements. UK issuers on prescribed markets (such as AIM) must comply with DTR 5, whereas overseas issuers on such markets need not. Finally, EEA issuers incorporated in another member state will be required only to comply with the corresponding requirements in their home member state.

21.170   The FSA has declared that the relevant laws in the United States, Japan, Israel and Switzerland are equivalent to the provisions of DTR 5 for the purposes of Article 23 of the Transparency Directive; accordingly, non-EEA issuers with shares admitted to trading on a regulated market in the United Kingdom that are incorporated in these countries are exempt from the disclosure requirements.[209] However, they will continue to be required to comply with DTR 6, which sets out requirements relating to the filing of information with the FSA, language, and the dissemination of information.

21.171   21.4.3.7.2 **Notification thresholds and notifiable interests**   The general rule is that a person must simultaneously notify an issuer and the FSA of the percentage of the voting rights he holds as shareholder—indirectly, or through his direct or

---

[207] These comprise transferable securities, options, futures, swaps, forward rate agreements and other derivative contracts specified in Section C of Annex 1 of MiFID (DTR 5.3.1–2, being so-called 'qualifying financial instruments') and, save in respect of non-UK issuers and holdings through certain client-serving intermediaries, instruments which have similar economic effects to such qualifying financial instruments (DTR 5.3.1(2) et seq). Only long positions must be disclosed, and cannot be set off against short positions. To be a qualifying financial instrument, the instrument must result in an entitlement to acquire, on the holder's own initiative alone, under a formal binding agreement, shares to which voting rights are attached, already issued of an issuer whose shares are admitted to trading on a regulated market or a UK prescribed market. As part of this, the holder must enjoy, on maturity, either the unconditional right to acquire the underlying shares or the discretion as to his right to acquire such shares or not (DTR 5.3.2). The FSA includes guidance in DTR 5.3.3 as to its reasoning behind imposing a super-equivalent regime in respect of UK issuers. Where a financial instrument relates to more than one underlying share, a separate notification should be made to each issuer of the underlying shares.
[208] See List! Issue 14, section 3.
[209] DTR 5.11.4.

indirect holding of certain financial instruments (or a combination of such holdings)[210]—if the percentage of those voting rights reaches, exceeds or falls below certain thresholds. For a UK issuer, these thresholds are set at 3%, and each 1% threshold thereafter up to 100% as a result of an acquisition or disposal of shares or financial instruments. A notification is also required where a holding reaches, exceeds or falls below an applicable threshold as a result of events changing the breakdown of voting rights.[211] In respect of non-UK issuers, the applicable thresholds reflect the Transparency Directive and are set at 5%, 10%, 15%, 20%, 25%, 30%, 50% and 75%. An issuer must, in turn, disclose such information to the market.[212]

There are detailed rules as to interests that may be discounted when calculating whether a notification obligation exists,[213] and DTR 5.4 gives guidance in respect of the aggregation of managed holdings, such as those held by management companies or investment firms.   **21.172**

As above, in determining whether a threshold has been crossed, both direct and indirect holdings in shares or relevant financial instruments that carry voting rights are relevant.[214] DTR 5.2.1 sets out the circumstances in which the FSA considers a person indirectly able to control the manner of the exercise of voting rights (or to be an indirect holder of financial instruments).[215] Further guidance on these categories is given by the FSA in DTRs 5.2.2–3.   **21.173**

---

[210] A person making a notification must do so by reference to (i) the aggregate of all voting rights which the person holds as shareholder and as the direct or indirect holder of qualifying financial instruments and financial instruments with similar economic effects; (ii) the aggregate of all voting rights held as direct or indirect shareholder (disregarding for this purpose holdings of financial instruments); (iii) the aggregate of all direct and indirect holdings of qualifying financial instruments; and (iv) the aggregate of all direct and indirect holdings of financial instruments with similar economic effects (DTR 5.7). The effect is that a person may have to make a notification if the overall percentage level of his voting rights remains the same but there is a notifiable change in the percentage level of one or more of the categories of voting rights held.

[211] DTR 5.1.2.

[212] DTR 5.8.12.

[213] Certain voting rights are to be disregarded for the purposes of determining whether a person has a notification obligation, (subject in each case to certain conditions), including shares (i) acquired for the sole purpose of clearing and settlement within a limited settlement cycle; (ii) held by a custodian (or nominee) in its custodian (or nominee) capacity; (iii) held by a market maker acting in that capacity; (iv) held by a credit institution or investment firm; (v) held by a collateral taker under a collateral transaction which involves the outright transfer of securities; and (vi) acquired by a borrower under a stock lending agreement (DTR 5.1.3). In addition, certain further voting rights are to be disregarded except in respect of thresholds of 5%, 10% and above, including shares forming part of property belonging to another which that person lawfully manages, voting rights attaching to shares exercisable by a person as the operator of certain schemes and voting rights which may be exercisable by an ICVC (an investment company with variable capital) or a category of investment entity which for this purpose is prescribed by the FSA (DTR 5.1.5).

[214] DTR 5.2.3.

[215] For this purpose, a person is an indirect holder of shares if he is entitled to acquire, dispose of, or exercise voting rights: (i) held by a third party obliged to adopt a lasting common policy towards

21.174   **21.4.3.7.3 Notification contents and deadlines**   A person who is required to make a notification may appoint another person to make the notification on his behalf and two persons may together make a single notification.[216] The overall number of voting rights should be calculated on the basis of all shares to which voting rights attach, even if suspended,[217] and be based on the issuer's most recent month-end disclosure.[218] It should not include treasury shares held by the issuer, as an issuer is not permitted to vote in respect of such shares.[219]

21.175   Notifications to the FSA must be made electronically, and notifications must specify (i) the resulting situation in terms of voting rights; (ii) the chain of undertakings through which the voting rights are held, if any; (iii) the date of which the threshold was triggered; and (iv) the identity of the shareholder and of the person entitled to exercise voting rights on behalf of the shareholder.[220]

21.176   Notification to issuers must be made as soon as possible, and in any event within four trading days (in respect of a non-UK issuer) and two trading days (in respect of a UK issuer) after the date on which the person concerned is informed of, or learns of, the acquisition, disposal or of the possibility of exercising voting rights or should have learnt of it.[221] Notably, if the person concerned is party to the transaction or has 'instructed the transaction', he is deemed to have knowledge of it no later than two trading days following the transaction.[222] Further, if the transaction is conditional upon approval by a regulator or on a future uncertain

---

the management of the issuer in question; (ii) held by a third party under an agreement providing for the temporary transfer for consideration of the voting rights in question; (iii) attached to shares which are lodged as collateral with the relevant person where he controls the voting rights and declares the intention of exercising them; (iv) attached to shares in which that person has the life interest; (v) held or which may be exercised by an undertaking controlled by that person; (vi) held by a third party in his own name on behalf of that person; (vii) attached to shares deposited with that person which the person can exercise at its discretion in the absence of specific instructions from the shareholder; and (viii) which that person may exercise as proxy where that person can exercise the voting rights at his discretion in the absence of specific instructions from the shareholders.

[216] DTR 5.2.5.
[217] DTR 5.8.7; although, for disclosure in respect of financial instruments having a similar effect to qualifying financial instruments, notification must be made on a delta-adjusted basis (DTR 5.8.2(4)).
[218] Monthly disclosure by the issuer is required DTR 5.6.1.
[219] DTR 5.8.8.
[220] DTR 5.8.1. See also DTR 5.8.2 for certain additional categories of information that must be provided in relation to financial instruments. In the case of shares admitted to trading on a regulated market, the notification must be made in form TR1, which is available on the FSA's website: DTR 5.8.10.
[221] DTR 5.8.3. Note that an undertaking is not required to make a notification if it is instead made by its parent undertaking or, where the parent undertaking is controlled by another entity, by such other controlling entity: DTR 5.8.6.
[222] DTR 5.8.3.

event, parties are deemed to have notice of the transaction only when the relevant approvals are obtained or the event occurs.[223]

If a notification relates to shares admitted to trading on a regulated market, then the person making the notification must also file a copy of the notification with the FSA at the same time as it notifies the issuer.[224]

21.177

21.4.3.7.4 Notification obligations of the issuer   When a UK issuer receives a notification from an interest-holder under the above provisions, it must make the relevant information public as soon as possible (and in any event no later than the end of the trading day following the receipt of the notification).[225] Non-EEA issuers are treated as meeting equivalent requirements provided that they make the requisite notification within seven trading days.[226] In the case of non-UK issuers (and UK issuers of shares traded on a prescribed market), the information must be made public as soon as possible and in any event no later than the end of the third trading day following receipt of the notification. [227]

21.178

In addition, issuers must themselves make public notifications if they acquire or dispose of their own shares—either directly or through a party acting in its own name but on behalf of the issuer—where the percentage of voting rights attributable to the shares it holds as a result of the acquisition or disposal reaches, exceeds or falls below the thresholds of 5% or 10% of the voting rights.[228]

21.179

Notification by an issuer in respect of acquisitions or disposals by the issuer must be made as soon as possible and not later than four trading days following such acquisition or disposal.[229] However, under the provisions of the Listing Rules, if a company, a member of the group or any person acting on their behalf acquires shares in a listed company, then an RIS must be notified no later than 7.30 am on the following business day.[230] At the end of each calendar month during which an increase or decrease has occurred, the issuer must disclose to the public the total number of voting rights and capital in respect of each class of

21.180

---

[223] Ibid.
[224] DTR 5.9.1.
[225] DTR 5.8.12(1).
[226] DTR 5.11.1.
[227] DTR 5.8.12(2).
[228] DTR 5.5.1.
[229] DTR 5.5.1.
[230] LR 12.4.6. The notification to the RIS must detail (i) the date of purchase, (ii) the number of equity shares purchased, (iii) the purchase price for each of the highest and lowest price paid, (iv) the number of equity shares purchased for cancellation and the number that will be held as equity shares, and (v) where the purchased shares will be held as treasury shares, a statement of the total number of treasury shares of each class held by the company following the purchase and the number of equity shares of each class that the company has in issue less the total number of treasury shares following the purchase.

shares which it issues, and the total number of voting rights attaching to shares of the issuer which are held by it in treasury.[231]

21.4.3.8 Dissemination of regulated information

21.181 **21.4.3.8.1 Applicable provisions** DTR 6 lays out various rules on the dissemination of regulated information. It applies to issuers whose home state is the United Kingdom.[232]

21.182 **21.4.3.8.2 Regulated information** The concept of 'regulated information' is critical to an issuer's disclosure obligations under the DTRs, and refers to all information that an issuer (or any person who has applied for the admission of financial instruments to trading on a regulated market without the issuer's consent) is required to disclose under the Transparency Directive, Article 6 of the Market Abuse Directive, the Listing Rules and the DTRs.

21.183 DTR 6 itself makes provision for certain information in respect of key issuer actions to be disclosed to the market as regulated information. This includes constitutional amendments,[233] changes in rights attached to various classes of shares[234] and other securities,[235] new issues,[236] details of shareholders' meetings,[237] information concerning the allocation and payment of dividends,[238] and board approval of a decision to make or pay a dividend or withhold any dividend or interest payment on listed securities.[239] Such regulated information must also be filed with the FSA.[240]

21.184 **21.4.3.8.3 Disclosing regulated information** A number of rules govern the dissemination of any information that an issuer is required to disclose. The information must be capable of reaching as wide a public as possible, and as close as possible to simultaneous disclosure must occur in the home member state and other member states.[241] Information must be communicated in full text, except that this condition does not apply to annual financial reports that are

---

[231] DTR 5.6.1.
[232] Note DTR 6.1.16–19, which lay out certain exemptions from the requirements of DTR 6. The FSA has declared that the law governing information requirements for issuers of shares in Switzerland is equivalent to certain provisions of DTR 6; therefore, issuers of shares admitted to trading on a regulated market in the United Kingdom that are incorporated in Switzerland will be exempt from these requirements.
[233] DTR 6.1.2.
[234] DTR 6.1.9.
[235] DTR 6.1.10. This disclosure obligation is imposed on issuers of securities other than shares admitted to trading on a regulated market.
[236] DTR 6.1.11.
[237] DTR 6.1.12 and DTR 6.1.14.
[238] DTR 6.1.13.
[239] LR 9.7A.2 read with DTR 6.1.13.
[240] DTR 6.2.2 and DTR 6.2.3.
[241] DTR 6.3.4.

required to be made public, unless the information is of a type that would be required to be disseminated in a semi-annual financial report.[242] Issuers must ensure that the mode of communication ensures the security of the communication, minimizes the risk of data corruption and unauthorized access and provides certainty as to the source of the regulated information.[243] The communication must clearly state that the information is of a type required to be disclosed and must identify the issuer, the subject matter of the information and the time and date of the communication.[244] Finally, investors must not be charged by the issuer or the person concerned to access the information.[245]

These rules are important because, if required, the issuer or other person concerned must be able to communicate to the FSA the name of the person making the communication, the security validation details, the time and date on which the information was communicated, the medium in which the information was communicated and details of any embargo placed by the issuer on the information.[246]

21.185

21.4.3.8.4 Electronic communications with security holders The DTRs implement the Transparency Directive provisions enabling issuers to use electronic means to convey information to shareholders or debt securities holders.[247] The FSA also makes it clear that the DTR regime should be read, where applicable, in light of the similar provisions under the UK Companies Acts.[248]

21.186

To utilize the electronic communications regime, an issuer's securityholders must pass a resolution in a general meeting to use electronic means to convey information to shareholders or debt security holders, and the use of electronic means must not depend on the location of the holder. Identification arrangements must be put in place so that the shareholders, debt securityholders or other persons entitled to exercise voting rights, are effectively informed. Such persons must be contacted in writing to request their consent for the use of electronic means for conveying information. If they do not object within a reasonable period of time, their consent can be presumed.[249] Such persons must also have the right to request at any time in the future that information be conveyed in writing.

21.187

21.4.3.8.5 Penalties If an issuer breaches its obligations under the various provisions described above relating to inside information, disclosure of transactions

21.188

---

[242] DTR 6.3.5.
[243] DTR 6.3.6.
[244] DTR 6.3.7.
[245] DTR 6.3.9.
[246] DTR 6.3.8.
[247] DTR 7.1.7.
[248] See List! Issue 14, section 4.
[249] See, generally, DTR 6.1.8.

by PDMRs, periodic financial reporting, major shareholding notifications and dissemination of regulated information, then the FSA can publicly censure or fine the issuer or any director knowingly involved in the breach.[250] In less serious cases, the FSA can resort to private censure.[251] If the breach in question involves a company with securities listed on the Main Market, the FSA can also suspend the issuer's listing[252] or delist the securities.

21.4.4 The Combined Code on Corporate Governance

21.4.4.1 Background

21.189   UK companies with a Primary Listing are subject to market leading corporate governance requirements. The most significant is the requirement to comply with the Combined Code on Corporate Governance, last published by the Financial Reporting Council in June 2008 (the 'Combined Code') and to explain to shareholders any non-compliance. A UK company with a primary listing of shares is required by the Listing Rules to disclose in its annual report how the main principles of the Combined Code have been complied with during the relevant period and the reasons for any non-compliance.[253] In addition to the Listing Rules provisions, the Combined Code is enforced through the expectation of shareholders. Alongside the Combined Code, a number of institutional shareholder bodies publish corporate governance guidance for listed companies, both separate from and in addition to the provisions of the Combined Code— notably the Association of British Insurers ('ABI') and the Institute of Chartered Secretaries and Administrators ('ICSA').

21.190   Overseas companies with a Primary Listing are not required to comply in full with the Combined Code. However, following the results of a recent FTSE consultation on nationality requirements,[254] where an overseas company wishes to qualify for the coveted FTSE UK Index Series (including the FTSE100), it will be required to publicly adhere to the principles of the Combined Code, as well as to market-standard pre-emption right commitments and to the key principles of the City Code on Takeovers and Mergers. This is likely to result in greater consistency in corporate governance practice among UK and overseas issuers.

21.191   The aim of the Combined Code is to achieve better company performance by helping the board to discharge its duties in the best interests of shareholders. Rather than being a rigid set of rules, the Combined Code is a compilation of best practice standards distilled from industry experience and consultation. Published alongside the Combined Code are the Turnbull Guidance on internal controls

---

[250]   DTR 1.5.3.
[251]   Note that private censure can be taken into account in any future enforcement proceedings.
[252]   DTR 1.4.1.
[253]   LR 9.8.6(6).
[254]   See FTSE Nationality Practice Note.

and the Smith Guidance on the establishment and role of audit committees. As above, the Combined Code operates on a 'comply or explain' basis. Although substantial compliance is expected to be the norm, it is envisaged that deviations from normal practice can be acceptable in many circumstances, provided that the reasons for this are explained to shareholders. There are also relaxations from many of the rules for smaller companies below the FTSE 350.

Recently, the Financial Reporting Council has consulted on possible changes to the Combined Code in light of the financial crisis. A number of FTSE100 companies have suggested that a more appropriate test is for issuers to 'apply or explain', reflecting the fact that corporate governance should not be a box-ticking exercise and that,with an appropriate explanation, non-compliance should not be seen as a breach.　　**21.192**

The Combined Code is drafted around a series of main principles, fleshed out with supporting guidance and detailed provisions. These principles relate to the role of directors, accountability and audit, relations with shareholders and institutional investors. The key recommendations of the Combined Code are discussed below.　　**21.193**

21.4.4.2 *Directors*

21.4.4.2.1 The board, chairman and chief executive Section A of the Combined Code deals with directors. Central to the Combined Code is the principle that an effective board should head every company and should be collectively responsible for the success of the company.[255] The company's board is required to meet regularly and to publish a schedule of matters reserved for its decision. The annual report must specify how the board operates and detail the types of decisions that the board takes and the types that are delegated to management.[256] The board is expected to provide entrepreneurial leadership while ensuring that prudent controls exist. It must set out the aims of the company, ensure availability of resources and review performance.　　**21.194**

In particular, non-executive directors are expected to play a key role within listed companies, to scrutinize management performance and ensure the integrity of financial controls and risk management systems.[257] The Combined Code also　　**21.195**

---

[255] Main Principle, Section 1, A.1 of the Combined Code.

[256] Combined Code A.1.1. There is overlap between this provision and the requirements of DTR 7.2.7 under which an issuer must provide a corporate governance statement in its directors' report (or in a separate report published with its annual report or on its website) which sets out a description of the composition and operation of the issuer's administrative management and supervisory bodies and their committees. DTR 7.2.8 provides that compliance with the Code provision will satisfy the requirements of DTR 7.2.7.

[257] Combined Code Supporting Principles, Section 1, A.1

requires non-executive directors to be responsible for determining the appropriate levels of remuneration for executive directors, and to have a key role in appointing (and removing) executive directors.

21.196 It is a key principle of the Combined Code that no one individual should have unfettered powers of decision.[258] As such, it requires the roles of chairman and chief executive officer ('CEO') to be exercised by different people.[259] The chairman should be responsible for the leadership of the board, act as a link between the executive and non-executive directors, and the non-executive directors should appraise his performance at least annually. To this end, the chairman is responsible for ensuring that directors are adequately informed, shareholders are able to communicate effectively and non-executive directors are capable of participating constructively in company affairs.[260] Conversely, the CEO's responsibility is to run the business of the company, with the division of his and the chairman's responsibilities clearly established in writing. On his appointment, the chairman should meet the criteria for 'independence' from the company as defined in the Combined Code and, discussed below, with the result that a CEO should not progress to become chairman of the same company.[261] If (in an exceptional situation) the board decides to allow this, it should first consult all major shareholders and explain the reasons for its decision at the time of appointment and in the annual report.[262]

21.197 21.4.4.2.2 **Board balance and independence** It is important to ensure that no individual or small group can monopolize decision-making at the board level. As such, the Combined Code recommends that boards include a balance of skills and experience and a balance of both executive and non-executive directors.[263] While there is no legal distinction under English law between executive and non-executive directors—meaning that each owes the same responsibilities to the company and its stakeholders—executive directors are generally entrusted with the day-to-day management of the company, while non-executive directors are generally expected to constructively challenge policy and develop proposals on strategy. The Higgs Guidance provides further best practice suggestions on the role of non-executives directors, as well as providing a sample letter of appointment and pre-appointment due diligence checklist. Committee membership should be periodically refreshed so as to avoid concentration of power.[264]

---

[258] Combined Code Main Principle, Section 1, A.2.
[259] Combined Code A.2.1.
[260] Combined Code Supporting Principles, Section 1, A.2.
[261] Combined Code A.2.2. See 'Board Balance and Independence' for criteria to determine independence.
[262] Combined Code A.2.2.
[263] Combined Code Main Principle, Section 1, A.3.
[264] Combined Code Supporting Principles, Section 1, A.3.

The Combined Code places particular emphasis on the corporate governance role   **21.198**
of independent non-executives, recommending that they comprise at least half of
the board, excluding the chairman, except in the case of smaller companies.[265]
It is ultimately for the board to decide whether a director is independent in character and judgment, or whether there are relationships or circumstances that
render him non-independent. Although there is no exhaustive list of criteria for
the board to consider, the Combined Code specifically highlights factors such as
past employment within the group, material business relationships, additional
remuneration, family ties, cross directorships, significant shareholdings and long
board service as constituting situations where the board would need to justify a
finding of independence to shareholders.[266] One of the independent directors
should be appointed as the senior independent director, whom shareholders can
contact should they have unresolved concerns.[267]

21.4.4.2.3 Board appointments and re-election   It is a key principle of the   **21.199**
Combined Code that there should be a formal, rigorous and transparent procedure for the appointment of new directors to the board.[268] Objective criteria
should be set to ensure in particular that appointees have sufficient time to
dedicate to the role, and plans should be in place to maintain planned and progressive refreshing of the board over time.[269] New directors should receive a formal
tailored introduction on joining the board, and major shareholders should be
offered the opportunity to meet new non-executive directors.

The Combined Code requires listed companies to establish a 'nominations com-   **21.200**
mittee', composed primarily of independent non-executive directors to lead the
appointment process.[270] Like all board committees, its terms of reference should
be made available, and model terms have been published for this purpose by
shareholder bodies such as the ICSA. In addition, directors should be submitted
for re-election at regular intervals, conditional on satisfactory performance.[271]
The board should not agree to a full-time executive director taking more than one
non-executive directorship in a FTSE100 company, nor the chairmanship of such
a company.[272]

---

[265] A smaller company is a company that is below the FTSE 350 throughout the year immediately prior to the reporting year.
[266] Combined Code A.3.1.
[267] Combined Code A.3.3.
[268] Combined Code Main Principle, Section 1, A.4.
[269] Combined Code Supporting Principles, Section 1, A.4.
[270] Combined Code A.4.1.
[271] Combined Code Main Principle, Section 1, A.7.
[272] Combined Code A.4.5.

21.201 New directors must be submitted for election by shareholders at the first AGM after their appointment and thereafter re-elected at least every three years.[273] For non-executives any term beyond six years should be subject to particularly rigorous review and take into account the need to refresh the board. Non-executive directors may serve a term of more than nine years subject only to annual re-election.[274]

21.202 The committee's work must be described in the annual report and an explanation provided if the committee has not relied on an external search consultancy or utilized open advertising in recommending appointments.[275]

21.203 **21.4.4.2.4 Information, professional development and evaluation** The chairman is responsible for ensuring that the directors receive accurate, timely and clear information, and that directors continually update their skills, knowledge and familiarity with the company.[276] In practice it is the company secretary, under the chairman's direction, who is generally responsible for ensuring information flow between the board, committees and senior management, and the secretary is ultimately responsible for advising the board on all governance matters and ensuring that board procedures are complied with. The appointment and removal of the company secretary is a matter for the board as a whole.[277] To ensure they are able to discharge their responsibilities, directors should have access to advice from, and the services of, the company secretary and to independent professional advice at the company's expense.[278]

21.204 To ensure the continued functioning of the board, it should undertake a formal and rigorous annual evaluation of its own performance, and that of its committees and members.[279] The results may lead the chairman to propose that new members be added, or that existing members resign. The non-executive directors must evaluate the chairman, taking into account the views of executive directors. The board must state in the annual report how such performance evaluation has been conducted.[280]

21.4.4.3 Directors' remuneration

21.205 The remuneration of listed company directors continues to be a controversial topic. Section B of the Combined Code deals in detail with issues of directors'

---

[273] Combined Code A.7.1.
[274] Combined Code A.7.2.
[275] Combined Code A.4.6.
[276] Combined Code Main Principle, Section 1, A.5.
[277] Combined Code A.5.3.
[278] Combined Code A.5.2.
[279] Combined Code Main Principle, Section 1, A.6.
[280] Combined Code A.6.1.

remuneration, including the level and composition of the remuneration and the procedure for determining compensation. The Code provides that remuneration should be sufficient to attract, retain and motivate directors of the quality required to run the company successfully,[281] but that the company should avoid paying more than is necessary. Crucially, a significant proportion of executive directors' remuneration should be structured to link rewards to corporate and individual performance, so as to align their interests with those of the shareholders.[282] Non-executive directors' remuneration should reflect the time, commitment and responsibilities of the role and should not ordinarily include share options.[283] The company must disclose the extent of compliance with these and the more detailed provisions and the reasons for non-compliance, if any.

The procedure for determining the compensation policy and for fixing individual compensation packages should be formal and transparent, and no director should be involved in deciding his own remuneration.[284] The committee should consult with the chairman or chief executive in determining compensation (though taking care to avoid conflicts of interest), and the chairman should ensure that the company maintains contact with its principal shareholders about remuneration.[285]   **21.206**

The Combined Code recommends that the company forms a 'remuneration committee' of independent non-executive directors,[286] which should design remuneration packages for the executive directors and the chairman, recommend the level and structure of remuneration for senior management and compare the company's remuneration policies against those of comparative firms.[287] It should act with regard to the provisions of Schedule A of the Combined Code on performance related elements, and be mindful of the pay and employment conditions elsewhere in the group. The committee should also scrutinize service contract commitments on termination to ensure there is no perception of rewarding poor performance. Service contracts, notice and contract periods should generally be set at one year or less. The board itself generally sets the remuneration of non-executive directors. Shareholders should be asked to approve all new long-term incentive schemes and significant changes to existing schemes, except where such matters are permitted by the Listing Rules.[288]   **21.207**

---

[281] Combined Code Main Principle, Section 1, B.1.
[282] Combined Code B.1.1.
[283] Combined Code B.1.3.
[284] Combined Code Main Principle, Section 1, B.2.
[285] Combined Code Supporting Principles, Section 1, B.2.
[286] Combined Code B.2.1.
[287] Combined Code B.2.2.
[288] Combined Code B.2.4.

21.4.4.4 Accountability and audit

21.208 Section C of the Combined Code contains various provisions dealing with financial reporting, internal controls, and audit, and is seen by many as the most critical element of the Combined Code regime, from which deviations occur least often.

21.209 **21.4.4.4.1 Financial reporting** In terms of financial reporting, the board should present a balanced and understandable assessment of the company's position and prospects,[289] which extends to interim and other price-sensitive public reports, reports to regulators and information required to be presented by statutory requirements.[290] Accordingly, the directors should explain in the annual report their responsibility for preparing the accounts, and there should be a statement by the auditors about their reporting responsibilities.[291] In addition, the directors must report that the business is a going concern, with supporting assumptions or qualifications as necessary.[292]

21.210 **21.4.4.4.2 Internal controls** The board should maintain internal control systems so as to protect shareholders' investments and the company's assets.[293] The effectiveness of the internal controls should be reviewed at least annually and such review reported to the shareholders. The review should detail all material controls, including financial, operational and compliance controls and risk management systems.[294] Formal arrangements should be put in place to consider the application of financial reporting and internal control principles and to maintain an appropriate relationship with the company's auditors.[295]

21.211 **21.4.4.4.3 The Audit Committee** An issuer should establish an audit committee consisting of at least three independent non-executive directors. At least one member of the audit committee must have recent and relevant financial experience.[296]

21.212 The role and responsibilities of the audit committee should be set out in writing and include:[297] (i) monitoring the integrity of the company's financial statements and any formal announcements relating to the company's financial performance and reviewing significant financial reporting judgments contained in them; (ii) reviewing the company's internal financial controls and, unless expressly

---

[289] Combined Code Main Principle, Section 1, C.1.
[290] Combined Code Supporting Principles, Section 1, C.1.
[291] Combined Code C.1.1.
[292] Combined Code C.1.2.
[293] Combined Code Main Principle, Section 1, C.2.
[294] Combined Code C.2.1.
[295] Combined Code Main Principle, Section 1, C.3.
[296] Combined Code C.3.1. See also DTR 1B.1.1.
[297] Combined Code C.3.2.

addressed by a separate board risk committee composed of independent directors, or by the board itself, reviewing the company's internal control and risk management systems; (iii) monitoring and reviewing the effectiveness of the company's internal audit function; (iv) making recommendations to the board, for it to put to the shareholders for their approval in general meeting, in relation to the appointment, re-appointment and removal of the external auditor and approving the remuneration and terms of engagement of the external auditor; (v) reviewing and monitoring the external auditor's independence and objectivity and the effectiveness of the audit process, taking into consideration relevant UK professional and regulatory requirements; and (vi) developing and implementing policy on the engagement of the external auditor to supply non-audit services, taking into account relevant ethical guidance regarding the provision of non-audit services by the external audit firm and reporting to the board, identifying any matters in respect of which it considers that action or improvement is needed and making recommendations as to the steps to be taken.

The terms of reference of the audit committee should be made available and the **21.213** annual report should contain a description of the work of the committee.[298] The audit committee should review the mechanism whereby company staff can raise concerns about possible improprieties and the procedure for independent investigation and follow-up action.[299] The audit committee should be primarily responsible for making recommendations on the appointment and removal of external auditors. If the board disagrees with the committee's recommendation it must explain in the annual report the reasons for its differing view.[300] Finally, if the auditor provides non-audit services then the annual report must explain how auditor objectivity and independence is safeguarded.[301]

In addition to the provisions of the Combined Code, DTRs 7.1 and 7.2 lay down **21.214** provisions concerning audit committees and corporate governance statements, respectively, and implement part of the EU audit directive. The provisions apply to all UK companies with transferable securities admitted to trading on a regulated market, and the requirements under DTR 7.1 as to audit committees also apply to any other issuer required to appoint a statutory auditor under the Companies Act 2006. The relevant rules provide that an issuer must constitute a committee that comprises at least one independent member and at least one member with competence in accounting and/or auditing. This committee must monitor the financial reporting process, the statutory audit and the independence of the statutory auditor and also monitor the effectiveness of the company's

---

[298] Combined Code C.3.3.
[299] Combined Code C.3.4.
[300] Combined Code C.3.6.
[301] Combined Code C.3.7.

internal controls, internal audit and risk management systems. The composition of this committee must be disclosed as part of the corporate governance statement that must be included either in the directors' report or in a separate report published with the annual report or published on the issuer's website, as required by DTR 7.2. The 'comply or explain' formulation of the Combined Code is adopted by the DTRs. Guidance in DTRs 7.1 and 7.2 makes it clear that issuers that comply with the relevant provisions of the Combined Code will be deemed to have satisfied the requirements.

21.4.4.5 *Relations with shareholders*

21.215   Section D of the Combined Code provides for effective dialogue with institutional shareholders, and sets out how companies ought to make constructive use of their annual general meeting.

21.216   **21.4.4.5.1 Dialogue with institutional shareholders**   The Combined Code provides that the board should ensure a healthy dialogue with shareholders to mutually understand the objectives of the company.[302] To achieve this goal, the chairman must ensure that the shareholders' views are communicated to the board and should discuss governance and strategy issues with major shareholders.[303] Non-executive directors should be offered the opportunity to attend meetings with major shareholders and the senior independent director, in particular, should meet with major shareholders to understand their concerns.[304] The board should also state in the annual report the steps taken to ensure that board members understand the views of major shareholders.[305]

21.217   **21.4.4.5.2 Constructive use of the AGM**   The aim of the Combined Code is that the AGM should function as a tool to communicate with investors and encourage them to participate in the affairs of the company.[306] To facilitate this, each separate issue should be dealt with by way of a separate resolution. For each resolution, shareholders should be provided with clear proxy forms.[307] All valid proxy appointments received by the company should be recorded and counted, and after a vote (except where taken on a poll) the company's website should disclose (i) the number of shares in respect of which proxy appointments have been validly made; (ii) the number of votes for the resolution; (iii) the number of votes against the resolution; and (iv) the number of shares in respect of which the vote was directed to be withheld.[308]

---

[302]   Combined Code Main Principle, Section 1, D.1.
[303]   Combined Code D.1.1.
[304]   Combined Code D.1.1.
[305]   Combined Code D.1.2.
[306]   Combined Code Main Principle, Section 1, D.2.
[307]   Combined Code D.2.1.
[308]   Combined Code D.2.2.

The Combined Code requires all directors to attend the AGM, and the chairmen **21.218** of the audit, remuneration and nomination committees should be present to answer questions.[309] Notice of the AGM and related papers must be sent to shareholders at least 20 working days before the meeting.[310]

21.4.4.6 *Institutional investors*

Section E, the final section of the Combined Code, provides for dialogue between **21.219** institutional shareholders and issuers. The provisions state that institutional shareholders must apply the principles laid down in the statement of principles issued by the Institutional Shareholders' Committee.[311] Further, when evaluating a company's corporate governance regime, the institutional shareholders should carefully consider the company's explanations for departures from the Combined Code and be prepared to enter into a dialogue with the company if they disagree with the company's view.[312] Institutional shareholders should attend AGMs and make considered use of their votes.[313] Given the increase in shareholder activism over recent years, these best practice provisions are likely to be increasingly important.

21.5 Market Abuse

21.5.1 Background to the UK market abuse regime

Two of the four statutory objectives of the FSA set out in FSMA[314] are to maintain **21.220** the confidence in the financial markets of the United Kingdom and to reduce financial crime. The market abuse regime in the United Kingdom is one of the primary initiatives that enables the FSA to prevent certain types of behaviour by market participants and gives the FSA powers to meet and maintain those objectives. The market abuse regime is designed to give market participants a clear set of guidelines indicating what is and is not acceptable behaviour, and also provides the FSA with certain remedies and enforcement provisions by which they can punish behaviour constituting market abuse, and deter market participants from committing such offences.

The current market abuse regime in the United Kingdom can be divided into **21.221** two parts: (i) the civil regime contained in FSMA, for which the FSA provides

---

[309] Combined Code D.2.3.
[310] Combined Code D.2.4.
[311] Combined Code E.1. This statement of principles is available at http://www.institutional shareholderscommittee.co.uk.
[312] Combined Code E.2.
[313] Combined Code E.3.
[314] FSMA section 2.

additional guidance in the FSA's Code of Market Conduct ('MAR'), established under FSMA;[315] and (ii) the criminal regime set out in the CJA[316] and in section 397 FSMA. There is overlap between the regimes with respect to the types of behaviour that may constitute market abuse, although the remedies and powers available to the FSA differ in each case.

21.5.2 The civil market abuse regime

21.5.2.1 Background and scope

21.222   The civil market abuse regime is based around the UK implementation of the Market Abuse Directive[317] ('MAD') on 1 July 2005. MAD sought to establish a common regulatory framework across the EEA and to harmonize the various market abuse regimes in operation at the time across Europe. However, MAD permitted member states to maintain their national regimes to the extent those regimes went beyond the minimum standards in MAD (commonly referred to as a 'minimum harmonisation directive') and, accordingly, the United Kingdom retained certain aspects of its pre-MAD civil market abuse regime (often referred to as the 'super-equivalent' rules or 'sunset provisions') in addition to the new elements the implementation of MAD introduced to the market abuse regime.

21.223   Section 118 of FSMA contains the basis for the civil market abuse regime that applies to all companies and individuals that act in a manner falling within one of the seven types of behaviour listed below (without an applicable defence), whether or not such behaviour is carried out in, or from, the United Kingdom. The scope of the civil market abuse regime is, however, limited by section 118 of FSMA to behaviour that occurs in relation to any of the following:

- 'qualifying investments' admitted to trading on a 'prescribed market';
- qualifying investments in respect of which a request for admission to trading on such a market has been made; and
- with respect to insider dealing and improper disclosure (see Section 21.5.2.2 below), related investments.[318]

21.224   'Qualifying investments' refers to all financial instruments within the meaning given in Article 1 MAD, which includes shares, bonds or other debt instruments, GDRs, units in collective investment undertakings, futures, swaps and other forms of derivative instrument.

---

[315]   FSMA section 119.
[316]   As defined in Section 21.1.4.5 above.
[317]   2003/6/EC.
[318]   FSMA section 130A: 'related investment', in relation to a qualifying instrument, means an investment whose price or value depends on the price or value of the qualifying instrument.

'Prescribed markets' means all markets that are established under the rules of a **21.225** recognized investment exchange and all other markets that are categorized as regulated markets.[319]

21.5.2.2 *Types of behaviour*

According to section 118 FSMA, the following seven types of behaviour may **21.226** constitute market abuse if there is no applicable defence in MAR:

1. behaviour where an insider deals, or attempts to deal, in a qualifying investment or related investment on the basis of inside information relating to the investment in question (referred to in MAR as 'insider dealing');
2. behaviour where an insider discloses inside information to another person otherwise than in the proper course of the exercise of his employment, profession or duties (referred to in MAR as 'improper disclosure');
3. behaviour (not falling within (1) or (2) above) that is based on information that is not generally available to those using the market but which, if available to a regular user of the market, would be or would be likely to be regarded by him as relevant when deciding the terms on which transactions in investments of the kind in question should be effected, and is likely to be regarded by a regular user of the market as a failure on the part of the person concerned to observe the standard of behaviour reasonably expected of a person in the position of the person in question in relation to the market (referred to in MAR as 'misuse of information');
4. behaviour that consists of effecting transactions or orders to trade (other than for legitimate reasons and in conformity with accepted market practices on the relevant market) that:
   (a) give, or are likely to give a false or misleading impression as to supply of, or demand for, or as to the price of, a qualifying investment; or
   (b) secure the price of a qualifying investment at an abnormal or artificial level (referred to in MAR as 'manipulation transactions');
5. behaviour that consists of effecting transactions or orders to trade that employ fictitious devices or any other form of deception or contrivance (referred to in MAR as 'manipulating devices');
6. behaviour that consists of the dissemination of information by any means which gives, or is likely to give, a false or misleading impression as to a qualifying investment by a person who knew or could reasonably be expected to have known that the information was false or misleading (referred to in MAR as 'dissemination'); and

---

[319] Qualifying investments and prescribed markets are defined by the Financial Services and Markets Act 2000 (Prescribed Markets and Qualifying Investments) Order 2001.

7. behaviour (not falling within (4), (5) and (6)):

    (a) likely to give a regular user of the market a false or misleading impression as to the supply of, demand for or price or value of, qualifying investments; or

    (b) that would be, or would be likely to be, regarded by a regular user of the market as behaviour that would distort, or would be likely to distort, the market in such an investment,

and the behaviour in each case is likely to be regarded by a 'regular user' of the market as a failure on the part of the person concerned to observe the standard of behaviour reasonably expected of a person in his position in relation to the market (referred to in MAR as 'misleading behaviour and distortion').

21.5.2.3 *Insider*[320]

21.227   For the purposes of (1) 'insider dealing' and (2) 'improper disclosure' above, an 'insider' is any person who has 'inside information': (i) as a result of his membership of an administrative, management or supervisory body of an issuer or qualifying investments; (ii) as a result of his holding in the capital of an issuer of qualifying investments; (iii) as a result of having access to the information through the exercise of his employment, profession or duties; (iv) as a result of his criminal activities; or (v) which he has obtained by other means and which he knows, or could reasonably be expected to know, is inside information.

21.5.2.4 *Inside information*[321]

21.228   Inside information in the context of insider dealing is defined in the same way as in the context of post-admission continuing obligations, pursuant to which listed companies are required under DTR 2 to disclose inside information to the market as soon as possible. In summary, inside information is information that (i) is of a precise nature; (ii) is not generally available; (iii) relates (directly or indirectly) to the issuer or its securities; and (iv) if made generally available, would be likely to have a significant effect on the price of the issuer's securities. See Section 21.5.2.2 above.

21.5.2.5 *Regular user*[322]

21.229   For the purposes of (3) 'misuse of information' and (7) 'misleading behaviour and distortion' above, 'regular user', in relation to a particular market, means a reasonable person who regularly deals on that market in investments of the kind in question. According to the Code of Market Conduct, the 'regular user' test imports an objective element into the elements listed for the relevant types

---

of behaviour while retaining some subjective features of the markets for the investments in question.[323] Given that the regular user is someone who regularly deals on the market in the particular types of investments, it appears fair to attribute a level of sophistication to that user. This could be helpful in market abuse analyses, which often involve a complex set of facts that an unsophisticated user may have difficulty getting comfortable with. However, the absence of a reference to the regular user elsewhere in the market abuse regime can lead to somewhat difficult considerations. These complexities might be exacerbated if and when the concept of the regular user disappears altogether as it is one of the 'sunset' provisions in the current market abuse regime (see Section 21.5.2.8 below).

21.5.2.6 Examples of market abuse

MAR 1 of the FSA's Code of Market Conduct includes a number of examples of types of behaviour that would, in the FSA's opinion, fall within the seven categories of abusive behaviour listed in Section 21.5.2.2 above.

21.230

- *insider dealing*: if a person were to (i) front run or pre-position a transaction for his own benefit ahead of an order which he is to carry out with or for another, that takes advantage of the anticipated impact of the order on the market price; or (ii) in the context of acting for the offeror or potential offeror in the context of a takeover, deal for his own benefit on the basis of inside information concerning the proposed bid;
- *improper disclosure*: if a person were to (i) disclose inside information to another in a social context; or (ii) selectively brief analysts or others who are PDMRs;
- *misuse of information*: (i) if a person were to deal or arrange deals in investments based on relevant information (which is not generally available and relates to matters which a regular user would reasonably expect to be disclosed to users of the particular prescribed market), but which does not constitute insider dealing; or (ii) if a director were to give relevant information (which is not generally available and relates to matters which a regular user would reasonably expect to be disclosed to users of the particular prescribed market) to another otherwise than in the proper course of the exercise of his employment or duties, but which does not constitute improper disclosure;
- *manipulating transactions*: if a person were to (i) buy or sell qualifying investments at the close of the market with the effect of misleading investors who act on the basis of closing prices, other than for legitimate reasons; (ii) sell or purchase of a qualifying instrument where there is no change in beneficial interest or market risk, or where the transfer of beneficial interest or market risk is only between parties acting in concert or collusion, other than for legitimate reasons ('wash trade'); (iii) enter into a series of transactions that are shown on a public

---

[323] MAR 1.2.21.

display for the purposes of giving the impression of activity or price movement in a qualifying investment ('painting the tape'); (iv) enter orders into an electronic trading system, at prices that are higher than the previous bid or lower than the previous offer, and withdraw them before they are executed to give a misleading impression as to the demand or supply of the qualifying investment at that particular price; or (v) take delivery or defer delivery to satisfy their obligations in relation to a qualifying investment (the purpose need not be the sole purpose of entering into the transaction or transactions, but must be an actuating purpose), where said person has (a) a significant influence over the supply of, or demand for, or delivery mechanisms for a qualifying investment, related investment or the underlying product of a derivative contract, and (b) a position (directly or indirectly) in an investment under which quantities of the qualifying investment, related investment or the underlying product of a derivative contract, engages in behaviour with the purpose of positioning at a distorted level the price at which others have to deliver ('abusive squeeze');

- *manipulating devices*: if a person were to (i) voice an opinion on a qualifying instrument in which that person has taken a position and profit from the impact the opinion has had on the qualifying instrument, without first disclosing the conflict of interest; (ii) conduct a transaction or series of transactions designed to conceal the ownership of a qualifying instrument such that disclosure requirements are circumvented and are misleading as to the true underlying holder; (iii) take a long position in a qualifying instrument and then disseminate misleading positive information about the qualifying instrument with a view to increasing its price ('pump and dump'); and (iv) take a short position in a qualifying instrument and then disseminate misleading negative information about the qualifying investment, with a view to driving down its price ('trash and cash');
- *dissemination*: if a person were to (i) knowingly or recklessly spread false or misleading information about a qualifying investment through the media, including in particular through an RIS or similar information channel; or (ii) undertake a course of conduct to give a false or misleading impression about a qualifying investment; and
- *misleading behaviour and distortion* (if they give, or are likely to give, a regular user of the market a false or misleading impression): if a person were to (i) cause the movement of physical commodity stocks or an empty cargo ship, which might create a misleading impression as to the supply of, or demand for, or price or value of, a commodity or the deliverable into a commodity futures contracts; or (ii) fail to give adequate disclosure that he has reached or exceeded a disclosable short position where (a) that position relates, directly or indirectly, to securities which are the subject of a rights issue, and (b) the disclosable short position is reached or exceeded during a rights issue period.

The Code of Market Conduct does not provide an exhaustive list of the various **21.231** types of behaviour that will constitute market abuse, but in addition to the above, it provides some hypothetical examples that *may* constitute market abuse.

21.5.2.7 *Safe harbours and behaviour not amounting to market abuse*

MAD provided exemptions for several types of behaviour that would otherwise **21.232** constitute market abuse. These provisions are implemented in FSMA[324] and are commonly referred to as 'safe harbours'.

The two safe harbours provided for in MAD are share buy-backs and price **21.233** stabilization activities. The share buy-back safe harbour provides that in certain circumstances, an issuer can reduce its share capital by buying back its own securities in the open market provided certain conditions are satisfied, including making public all such transactions and imposing constrictions on the price at which the buy-back can be conducted. Price stabilization for shares involves the selective purchases of shares in the aftermarket to promote the orderly operation of the market. The effect of stabilization should be to reduce the volatility in share prices by smoothing the spikes and the troughs. Section 118A(5)(b) FSMA imposes certain conditions on managers when entering into price stabilization activities, including the following: (i) the stabilization activity may only be carried on for a limited time period, generally 30 days; (ii) there must be adequate public disclosure before and after the stabilization activity; (iii) all stabilization trades must be reported to the FSA within seven days; (iv) restrictions on the price at which stabilization trades can occur; and (v) restrictions on ancillary stabilization activities such as over-allotments and 'greenshoe' options.

In addition, the Code of Market Conduct sets out a number of examples of **21.234** behaviour that, in the FSA's opinion, does not constitute market abuse. For example, in the context of a public takeover, seeking irrevocable undertakings or expressions of support to accept a proposed takeover bid, does not constitute market abuse. The Code of Market Conduct also permits market participants to disclose information to the Bank of England, the Competition Commission, the Takeover Panel and other regulatory authorities when required to do so by law.

21.5.2.8 *Super-equivalent provisions*

MAD is a minimum harmonization directive that sets the floor for market abuse **21.235** regulation across the EEA, while allowing for super-equivalent provisions at a national level. As such, the FSA, in an effort to prevent the narrowing of the pre-existing UK market abuse regime, retained certain provisions that were in place in

---

[324] FSMA Section 118A.

the United Kingdom prior to the implementation of MAD.[325] These pre-existing regulations are considered super-equivalent to the EEA regime to the extent that they provide for a wider definition of market abuse.

21.236 These super-equivalent categories of behaviour are misuse of information and misleading behaviour and distortion. These, and the related concept of the regular user, are to remain in force until 31 December 2011.[326]

21.237 To illustrate the super-equivalent status of the UK regime, the FSA has stated that the following behaviour would constitute misleading behaviour and distortion, but would not constitute market abuse in the pure MAD portion of the regime:

1. the non-disclosure of major shareholdings that could result in the market being misled as to the true composition of the shareholder base of a company and may conceal the intention of a shareholder to accumulate a significant stake;[327]
2. a company director who is approaching retirement instructing his broker to begin looking for a buyer for his sizeable holding in the company's shares, then upon hearing that the company has received a takeover approach from another company, instructing his broker that he has changed his mind and will be holding on to his shares for the time being;[328] and
3. '[t]he movement of an empty cargo ship that is used to transport a particular commodity' as this activity could create a false impression of the supply or demand of the commodity, thus artificially changing the price of the commodity or related futures contracts.[329]

21.238 While the foregoing super-equivalent provisions in the FSA's market abuse regime are undoubtedly significant, it is worth noting that the FSA has not brought any new cases under the super-equivalent provisions since July 2005, when the MAD was implemented in the United Kingdom.[330] A likely explanation for this is that the FSA has agreed to only bring charges under one of its super-equivalent provisions if it cannot establish a case under the MAD provisions.[331] Accordingly, if the

---

[325] FSA, 'FSA publishes rules implementing Market Abuse Directive' (2005), available at http://www.fsa.gov.uk/Pages/Library/Communication/PR/2005/029.shtml.

[326] The Financial Services and Markets Act 2000 (Market Abuse) Regulations 2009 (SI 2009/3128).

[327] HM Treasury, 'FSMA market abuse regime: a review of the sunset clauses: A consultation' 11 (2008), available at http://www.hm-treasury.gov.uk/d/consult_fsmamarket_abuse070208.pdf.

[328] HM Treasury, 'FSMA market abuse regime: a review of the sunset clauses: A consultation' 12 (2008), available at http://www.hm-treasury.gov.uk/d/consult_fsmamarket_abuse070208.pdf.

[329] FSA, 'Why market abuse could cost you money – The revised Code of Market Conduct is here to help protect you' 2 (2008), available at http://www.fsa.gov.uk/pubs/public/market_abuse.pdf.

[330] HM Treasury, 'FSMA market abuse regime: a review of the sunset clauses: A consultation' 15 (2008), available at http://www.hm-treasury.gov.uk/d/consult_fsmamarket_abuse070208.pdf.

[331] HM Treasury, 'FSMA market abuse regime: a review of the sunset clauses: A consultation' 15 (2008), available at http://www.hm-treasury.gov.uk/d/consult_fsmamarket_abuse070208.pdf.

MAD provisions are deemed to cover the suspected case of market abuse, then the FSA will seek to use the MAD regime, rather than the super-equivalent types of behaviour. However, the FSA has also stated that the lack of cases brought under the super-equivalent provisions should be balanced against the fact that 'there are current investigations that rely on the super-equivalent provisions' and that 'there might be an increased use of the super-equivalent provisions in [the] future'.[332]

21.5.2.9 *Penalties*

The penalties for an offence committed under the UK civil market abuse regime are included in Part VIII of FSMA. These penalties range from public censure by the FSA in accordance with section 123(3) FSMA, levying a fine 'of such amount as [the FSA] consider appropriate' under section 123(1) FSMA and in extreme cases, the FSA revisiting the offender's permission to conduct regulated activities under Part IV of FSMA.

21.239

If the FSA has determined that any of the above are applicable, it must publish a 'statement of policy' as per section 124 FSMA, setting out the offence and the punishment. Each published statement of policy is included on the FSA's website.[333]

21.240

21.5.3 Criminal regime

21.5.3.1 *Introduction*

The UK criminal market abuse regime is contained in two principal pieces of legislation: (i) section 52 of the CJA (insider dealing); and (ii) section 397 of FSMA (misleading statements and practices). Although there is overlap between the civil regime described in Section 21.5.2 above, and the criminal regime, there are also some important distinctions.

21.241

21.5.3.2 *Insider dealing under the CJA*

The criminal offence of insider dealing, as opposed to the civil offence set out in Section 21.5.2, is established under section 52 of the CJA. In certain 'relevant circumstances', there are three categories of offence:

21.242

1. an individual who has information as an 'insider' is guilty of insider dealing if he 'deals' in 'securities' that are 'price-affected securities' in relation to the information (the 'dealing' offence);
2. an individual who has information as an 'insider' is also guilty of insider dealing if he encourages another person to 'deal' in 'securities' that are (whether or

---

[332] HM Treasury, 'FSMA market abuse regime: a review of the sunset clauses: A consultation' 15–16 (2008), available at http://www.hm-treasury.gov.uk/d/consult_fsmamarket_abuse070208.pdf.
[333] http://www.fsa.gov.uk.

not that person knows it) 'price-affected securities' in relation to the information, knowing or having reasonable cause to believe that the 'dealing' would take place in the circumstances mentioned in the third offence below (the 'encouraging' offence); and

3. an individual who has information as an 'insider' is also guilty of insider dealing if he discloses the information, otherwise than in the proper performance of the functions of his employment, office or profession, to another person (the 'disclosure' offence).

21.243 The 'relevant circumstances' for the above offences are that the 'acquisition or disposal' in question occurs on a 'relevant market', or that the person dealing relies on a 'professional intermediary' or is himself a 'professional intermediary'.

21.244 These offences, broadly referred to in the CJA as 'insider dealing', contain a number of concepts specifically defined in the CJA:

- 'insider' means a person who has information and (i) that information is, and he knows that it is, inside information; and (ii) he knows that the information comes from an inside source. An inside source is a director, employee or shareholder of an issuer of securities, or a person having access to the information by virtue of his employment, office or profession;[334]

- 'inside information' is defined under the CJA as information that (i) relates to particular securities or to a particular issuer of securities, rather than to issuers or securities generally; (ii) is specific or precise; (iii) has not been made public; and (iv) if it were made public would be likely to have a significant effect on the price of any securities. Inside information in this context, therefore, is essentially the same as inside information in the context of post-admission continuing obligations and in the context of the civil offence of insider dealing;[335]

- information 'made public' means information that: (i) is published in accordance with the rules of a regulated market; (ii) is contained in records which by virtue of an enactment are open to inspection by the public; (iii) can readily be acquired by those likely to deal in any securities to which the information relates, or of an issuer to which the information relates; or (iv) can be derived from information which has been made public. Information may be treated as made public even though: (a) it can be acquired only by persons exercising diligence or expertise; (b) it is communicated to a section of the public and not to the public at large; (c) it can be acquired only by observation; (d) it is communicated only on payment of a fee; or (e) it is published only outside the United Kingdom;[336]

---

[334] CJA section 57.
[335] CJA section 56(1).
[336] CJA section 58.

- securities are 'price-affected securities' in relation to inside information, and inside information is 'price-sensitive information' in relation to securities, if and only if the information would, if made public, be likely to have a significant effect on the price of the securities;[337]
- 'dealing' in securities occurs when a person (i) acquires or disposes (or agrees to acquire or dispose) of securities (whether as principal or agent); or (ii) procures, directly or indirectly (including through a person's nominee, agent, or another person acting at his direction), an acquisition or disposal (or an agreement for an acquisition or disposal) of the securities by any other person;[338]
- 'securities' includes shares, debt securities, warrants, depositary receipts, options, futures and contracts for difference;
- 'professional intermediary' means a person who, by way of business, acquires or disposes of securities or acts as an intermediary between such persons. However, a person does not carry on such activities by way of business if the activity in question is (a) merely incidental to some other activity, or (b) only conducted occasionally;[339] and
- 'relevant market' includes any market that is established under the rules of the LSE and other major EEA investment exchanges. [340]

Section 53 CJA sets out a number of specific defences to the offences included **21.245** above. The concepts and definitions used above are also applicable to the following defences:

- A person is not guilty of dealing or encouraging if he shows that (i) he did not expect the dealing to result in a profit attributable to the fact that the relevant information was price-sensitive information; (ii) that at the time he believed on reasonable grounds that the information had been disclosed widely enough to ensure that no one dealing in the securities would be prejudiced by not having the information; or (iii) he would have done what he did even if he had not had the information.
- A person is not guilty of disclosure if he shows that (i) he did not at the time expect any person, because of the disclosure, to deal in securities in the circumstances mentioned in the description of disclosure above; or (ii) that, although he had such an expectation at the time, he did not expect the dealing to result in a profit attributable to the fact that the information was price-sensitive information in relation to the securities.

---

[337] CJA section 56(2).
[338] CJA section 55.
[339] CJA Section 59.
[340] 'Relevant market' is defined using the term 'regulated market' by the Insider Dealing (Securities and Regulated Markets) Order 1994, as amended. Note that the term 'relevant market' has been used in this Chapter to draw a distinction between 'regulated market' in the context of insider dealing (as defined under the aforementioned Order) and the concept of a regulated market under MiFID. These concepts are not equivalent.

21.246 In addition to these specific defences set out in section 53 CJA, there are also a number of 'special defences' included in Schedule 1 CJA, which mirror some of the 'safe harbours' included in the FSA Handbook in relation to the civil market abuse regime. The special defences essentially provide defences for entities in the business of day-to-day dealing, and as such are at a higher risk of encountering market abuse related issues. Accordingly there is a special defence for a market maker acting in good faith in the course of his business, or a person acting in accordance with the price stabilization rules.[341]

21.5.3.3 *Territorial scope*

21.247 Section 62 CJA establishes the territorial scope of the relevant offences set out in dealing, encouraging and disclosure above.

21.248 Section 62(1) CJA provides that an individual is not guilty of the dealing offence unless (i) he was within the United Kingdom at the time he was alleged to have committed the dealing offence; (ii) the regulated markets on which the dealing is alleged to have occurred is regulated in the United Kingdom; or (iii) the professional intermediary was within the United Kingdom at the time when he is alleged to have done anything by means of which the offence is alleged to have been committed.

21.249 Section 62(2) CJA provides that an individual is not guilty of the encouraging or disclosure offences unless (i) he was within the United Kingdom at the time he was alleged to have encouraged the dealing or disclosed the information; or (ii) the alleged recipient of the encouragement or the information was within the UK at the time when he is alleged to have received the encouragement or information.

21.5.3.4 *Penalties*

21.250 Under section 61 CJA, an individual guilty of insider dealing shall be liable (i) on summary conviction, to a fine not exceeding the statutory maximum or imprisonment for a term not exceeding six months or to both; or (ii) on indictment, to a fine or imprisonment for a term not exceeding seven years, or to both.

21.5.3.5 *Misleading statements and practices*

21.251 Section 397 FSMA contains several criminal offences that are broadly categorized as making 'misleading statements' and 'market manipulation'. The former is set out at section 397(1) and (2) of FSMA as follows: a person who (i) makes a statement, promise or forecast which he knows to be misleading, false or deceptive in a material particular; (ii) dishonestly conceals any material facts whether in

---

[341] The 'price stabilization rules' means the rules made under FSMA section 144(1) and set out in MAR 2.

connection with a statement, promise or forecast made by him or otherwise; or (iii) recklessly makes (dishonestly or otherwise) a statement, promise or forecast which is misleading, false or deceptive in a material particular, is guilty of an offence if he does (i), (ii) or (iii) for the purpose of inducing, or is reckless as to whether it may induce, another person (whether or not that person is the person to whom the statement, promise or forecast is made):

- to enter or offer to enter into, or refrain from entering or offering to enter into, a relevant agreement; or
- to exercise, or refrain from exercising, any rights conferred by a relevant investment.

Section 397(4) FSMA provides the person with a defence if he can demonstrate that the statement, promise or forecast was made, among other things, in conformity with the price stabilizing rules.[342] **21.252**

'Market manipulation' is set out in section 397(3) FSMA; it occurs when a person does any act or engages in any course of conduct that creates a false or misleading impression as to the market in or the price or value of, any relevant investments, if he does so for the purpose of creating that impression and of inducing another person to acquire, dispose of, subscribe for or underwrite those investments or to refrain from doing so or to exercise, or refrain from exercising, any rights conferred by those investments. **21.253**

Section 397(5) provides a defence to a section 397(3) FSMA offence if that person can demonstrate that (i) he reasonably believed that his act or conduct would not create a misleading impression; or (ii) his act was in conformity with, among other things, the price stabilizing rules.[343] **21.254**

21.5.3.6 *Territorial scope*

The scope of the section 397(1) and (2) FSMA offence of 'misleading statements', is limited by section 397(6) FSMA which states that the 'misleading statements' offence does not apply unless (i) the statement, promise or forecast is made in or from, or the facts are concealed in or from, the United Kingdom or arrangements are made in or from the United Kingdom for the statement, promise or forecast to be made or the facts to be concealed; (ii) the person on whom the inducement is intended to or may have effect on is in the United Kingdom; or (iii) the agreement is or would be entered into or the rights are or would be exercised in the United Kingdom. **21.255**

---

[342] The 'price stabilization rules' means the rules made under FSMA section 144(1) and set out in MAR 2.

[343] The 'price stabilization rules' means the rules made under FSMA section 144(1) and set out in MAR 2.

21.256   The section 397(3) FSMA 'market manipulation' offence is limited in scope by section 397(7) FSMA which states that the offence does not occur unless (i) the act is done, or the course of conduct is engaged in, in the UK; or (ii) the false or misleading impression is created there.

21.5.3.7 *Penalties*

21.257   Section 397(8) FSMA states that if a person is guilty of either misleading statements or market manipulation under section 397 FSMA, then he will be liable for either (i) on summary conviction, to imprisonment for a term not exceeding six months or a fine not exceeding the statutory maximum; or (ii) on indictment, to imprisonment for a term not exceeding seven years or a fine, or both. This should be considered in addition to any measures the FSA may take, for example removing the individual's ability to conduct approved person activities for any length of time by deeming that person not 'fit and proper' in accordance with the FSA Handbook.

21.5.4 Civil or criminal regime?

21.258   As will be noted above, the civil market abuse regime and the criminal market abuse regime share broadly the same elements. There are, however, some important differences in the regimes that can dictate whether the FSA will elect to use one regime over the other in a particular case.

- *Companies and individuals*: the civil regime applies to both companies and individuals and therefore the seven types of behaviour listed in Section 21.5.2 above will apply, regardless of the legal form of the alleged offender. The criminal regime contained in the CJA applies only to individuals; however, the criminal offences included in section 397 FSMA, like the civil market abuse regime, apply to both individuals and companies. Accordingly, section 400 of FSMA states that if an offence under FSMA (including but not limited to 'misleading statements' or 'market manipulation' under section 397 of FSMA) committed by a body corporate is shown (i) to have been committed with the 'consent' or 'connivance' of an 'officer';[344] or (ii) to be attributable to any 'neglect' on such officer's part, the officer, as well as the body corporate, is guilty of the offence and is liable to be proceeded against and punished. Equivalent provision is made in relation to partnerships. For these purposes, 'consent' requires knowledge of the principal crime. 'Connivance' includes wilfully ignoring the offence. 'Neglect' is an objective test, although it implies a breach of duty to check. Liability under section 400 of FSMA for 'neglect' is secondary and can

---

[344] 'Officer' includes, *inter alia*, directors, members of committees, company secretaries, managers and 'controllers'. 'Controllers' include individuals who, together with their associates, directly or indirectly control 10% or more of the relevant body corporate.

only arise for officers where (a) the necessary *mens rea* for the principal offence can be attributed to the body corporate; and (b) the body corporate is in fact found guilty of the principal offence.

- *Territorial scope*: the application of the civil regime is limited to behaviour occurring in the United Kingdom, or behaviour relating to instruments that are trading on a prescribed market in the United Kingdom (regardless of the location of the alleged offender). The criminal regimes are more complicated in this respect and each offence is subject to a different territorial application (see Sections 21.5.3.6 and 5.3.3 above). However, the basic principle in both regimes is that either the alleged behaviour, or the effect of the alleged behaviour, must be manifest in the United Kingdom for the FSA to have jurisdiction.

- *Burden of proof*: the civil regime requires it to be demonstrated that, on the balance of probabilities, the accused committed the offence. The criminal burden of proof requires the prosecutor to prove guilt beyond any reasonable doubt. Once achieved, the defendant must then prove that a relevant defence applies. The Financial Services and Markets Tribunal has stated, however, that in cases where the charge is a grave one, 'it is difficult to draw meaningful distinctions [between the civil and criminal standards]'.[345]

- *Penalties*: as noted above in Sections 21.5.2.7, 21.5.3.4 and 21.5.3.7, the various offences under the civil and criminal regimes carry different potential penalties, and in practice it is likely to be these differences (rather than differences in the burden of proof) that determine whether the FSA pursues an individual for insider dealing (in particular) under the civil or criminal regime, rather than issues over the burden of proof.

21.259 The FSA stated in April 2008[346] that to increase the 'credible deterrence' to prevent market users from committing offences falling within the UK civil or criminal market abuse regimes, the 'effective use of both routes is critical to achieving [its] aims'. The FSA specifically noted that it was its intention, 'in recognition of the significant deterrent effect of custodial sentences', to make more use of criminal sanctions in appropriate circumstances. In reflection of this statement of policy, the FSA initiated its first criminal prosecution proceedings for insider dealing under the CJA in January 2008, and since then there have been a number of similar cases. In March 2009, the FSA announced that it had arrested several individuals, including a corporate finance adviser, on suspicion of criminal insider dealing. Whereas prior to 2007 the focus had been on the civil regime and breaches of the FSA Principles as outlined in the FSA Handbook, recently the criminal regime has been used where appropriate, typically in the more serious cases.

---

[345] *Parker v FSA* [2006].
[346] Market Watch Issue 26 29 April 2008.

21.5.5 Resources for guidance

21.5.5.1 The Code of Market Conduct

21.260 As mentioned in Section 21.5.1 above, the FSA has produced the regulations, additional guidance and examples as to what constitutes market abuse in MAR, which is included in the FSA Handbook. As well as providing guidance on the civil market abuse regime in MAR chapter 1, MAR chapter 2 contains guidance on the stabilization rules which can also provide a relevant defence to certain offences in the criminal market abuse regime, as noted in sections 21.5.3.2 and 21.5.3.5 above.

21.5.5.2 Market Watch

21.261 Beginning in September 2001, the FSA began publishing Market Watch, a news-letter on market conduct issues. The approach taken by the FSA in Market Watch differs greatly from the regulation-based guidance found in MAR. Market Watch has sought to be a channel of dialogue through which the FSA provides updates on relevant market conduct issues as they arise, and then in subsequent issues, it responds to and follows up on the feedback generated from those updates. As part of those updates, the FSA reports on recently concluded enforcement activity, publishes both good practices and areas of weakness identified during visits to firms subject to FSMA and conducts thematic reviews of areas of particular concern, such as controls over inside information relating to public takeovers and market rumours. Market Watch is made available on the website of the FSA.[347]

---

[347] http://www.fsa.gov.uk.

INDEX